NEW ENGLAND

28th Edition

Where to Stay and Eat for All Budgets

Must-See Sights and Local Secrets

Ratings You Can Trust

Fodor's Travel Publications   New York, Toronto, London, Sydney, Auckland

www.fodors.com

FODOR'S NEW ENGLAND

Editor: Debbie Harmsen

Writers: Neva Allen, Stephen Allen, Diane Bair, John Blodgett, Elisabeth Coen, Lelah Cole, Andrew Collins, Sherry Hanson, Jo Kadlecek, Susan MacCallum-Whitcomb, Sandy MacDonald, Erin Byers Murray, Lisa Oppenheimer, Sarah Pascerella, Andrew Rimas, Mary Ruoff, Laura V. Scheel, George Semler, Pamela Wright, and Michael de Zayas
Editorial Contributors: Bethany Beckerlegge, Shannon Kelly, Christina Knight, Amanda Theunissen, Eric B. Wechter

Editorial Production: Evangelos Vasilakis
Maps & Illustrations: David Lindroth, *cartographer*; Bob Blake, Rebecca Baer, and William Wu, *map editors*
Design: Fabrizio LaRocca, *creative director*; Guido Caroti, Siobhan O'Hare, *art directors*; Tina Malaney, Chie Ushio, Ann McBride, *designers*; Melanie Marin, *senior picture editor*; Moon Sun Kim, *cover designer*
Cover Photo (Vermont): Russell Burden/Index Stock
Production/Manufacturing: Angela McLean

28th Edition

ISBN 978-1-4000-0721-9

ISSN 0192-3412

SPECIAL SALES

This book is available at special discounts for bulk purchases for sales promotions or premiums. Special editions, including personalized covers, excerpts of existing books, and corporate imprints, can be created in large quantities for special needs. For more information, write to Special Markets/Premium Sales, 1745 Broadway, MD 6-2, New York, New York 10019, or e-mail specialmarkets@randomhouse.com.

AN IMPORTANT TIP & AN INVITATION

Although all prices, opening times, and other details in this book are based on information supplied to us at press time, changes occur all the time in the travel world, and Fodor's cannot accept responsibility for facts that become outdated or for inadvertent errors or omissions. So **always confirm information when it matters**, especially if you're making a detour to visit a specific place. Your experiences—positive and negative— matter to us. If we have missed or misstated something, **please write to us**. We follow up on all suggestions. Contact the New England editor at editors@fodors.com or c/o Fodor's at 1745 Broadway, New York, NY 10019.

PRINTED IN THE UNITED STATES OF AMERICA

10 9 8 7 6 5 4 3 2 1

Be a Fodor's Correspondent

Your opinion matters. It matters to us. It matters to your fellow Fodor's travelers, too. And we'd like to hear it. In fact, we need to hear it.

When you share your experiences and opinions, you become an active member of the Fodor's community. That means we'll not only use your feedback to make our books better, but we'll publish your names and comments whenever possible. Throughout our guides, look for "Word of Mouth," excerpts of your unvarnished feedback.

Here's how you can help improve Fodor's for all of us.

Tell us when we're right. We rely on local writers to give you an insider's perspective. But our writers and staff editors—who are the best in the business—depend on you. Your positive feedback is a vote to renew our recommendations for the next edition.

Tell us when we're wrong. We're proud that we update most of our guides every year. But we're not perfect. Things change. Hotels cut services. Museums change hours. Charming cafés lose charm. If our writer didn't quite capture the essence of a place, tell us how you'd do it differently. If any of our descriptions are inaccurate or inadequate, we'll incorporate your changes in the next edition and will correct factual errors at fodors.com immediately.

Tell us what to include. You probably have had fantastic travel experiences that aren't yet in Fodor's. Why not share them with a community of like-minded travelers? Maybe you chanced upon a beach or bistro or B&B that you don't want to keep to yourself. Tell us why we should include it. And share your discoveries and experiences with everyone directly at fodors.com. Your input may lead us to add a new listing or highlight a place we cover with a "Highly Recommended" star or with our highest rating, "Fodor's Choice."

Give us your opinion instantly at our feedback center at www.fodors.com/feedback. You may also e-mail editors@fodors.com with the subject line "New England Editor." Or send your nominations, comments, and complaints by mail to New England Editor, Fodor's, 1745 Broadway, New York, NY 10019.

You and travelers like you are the heart of the Fodor's community. Make our community richer by sharing your experiences. Be a Fodor's correspondent.

Happy traveling in beautiful New England!

Tim Jarrell, Publisher

CONTENTS

MAPS

ABOUT THIS BOOK

Our Ratings

Sometimes you find terrific travel experiences and sometimes they just find you. But usually the burden is on you to select the right combination of experiences. That's where our ratings come in.

As travelers we've all discovered places whose worthiness is obvious. And sometimes a place is so wonderful that superlatives don't do it justice: you just have to see for yourself. These sights, properties, and experiences get our highest rating, **Fodor's Choice,** indicated by orange stars throughout this book.

Black stars highlight sights and properties we deem **Highly Recommended,** places that our writers, editors, and readers praise again and again for consistency and excellence.

By default, there's another category: any place we include in this book is by definition worth your time, unless we say otherwise. And we will.

Disagree with any of our choices? Care to nominate a place or suggest that we rate one more highly? Visit our feedback center at www.fodors.com/feedback.

Budget Well

Hotel and restaurant price categories from ¢ to $$$$ are defined in the opening pages of each chapter. For attractions, we always give standard adult admission fees; reductions are usually available for children, students, and senior citizens. Want to pay with plastic? **AE, D, DC, MC, V** following restaurant and hotel listings indicate if American Express, Discover, Diners Club, MasterCard, and Visa are accepted.

Restaurants

Unless we state otherwise, restaurants are open for lunch and dinner daily. We mention dress only when there's a specific requirement and reservations only when they're essential or not accepted—it's always best to book ahead.

Hotels

Hotels have private bath, phone, TV, and air-conditioning and operate on the European Plan (a.k.a. EP, meaning without meals), unless we specify that they use the Continental Plan (CP, with a continental breakfast), Breakfast Plan (BP, with a full breakfast), or Modified American Plan (MAP, with breakfast and dinner), Full American Plan (FAP, with all meals), or are all-inclusive (AI, with all meals and most activities). We always list facilities but not whether you'll be charged an extra fee to use them, so when pricing accommodations, find out what's included.

Many Listings

★ Fodor's Choice
★ Highly recommended
✉ Physical address
✛ Directions
🕮 Mailing address
☎ Telephone
🖷 Fax
🌐 On the Web
✍ E-mail
🗏 Admission fee
🕑 Open/closed times
Ⓣ Subway stations
▭ Credit cards

Hotels & Restaurants

🏨 Hotel
🛏 Number of rooms
⟁ Facilities
🍴 Meal plans
✕ Restaurant
⟁ Reservations
✂ Smoking
🍶 BYOB
✕🏨 Hotel with restaurant that warrants a visit

Outdoors

🏌 Golf
⛺ Camping

Other

☕ Family-friendly
⇨ See also
✉ Branch address
☞ Take note

WHAT'S NEW IN NEW ENGLAND

Boston's Harbor Nears Completion

Big Dig, Boston Harbor's massive face-lift, is almost finished. The massive public works projects begun in 1982 to ease traffic congestion through the heart of the city and beneath the harbor in the Ted Williams Tunnel. On the ambulatory side of the coin, almost 40 mi of the 47-mi HarborWalk are now complete. Connecting existing trails with new walkways, the HarborWalk meanders about the city's waterfront, passing through East Boston, the North End, Downtown, Dorchester, and other parts of Boston. The quarter-of-a-century affair went way over budget, coming in at a price tag of $14.6 billion.

Celtics Celebrate

Boston fans went wild in June 2008, as the Celtics won the NBA Championship, beating the L.A. Lakers 4–2 in the series. The Celtics ended a 22-year championship-less era, gaining themselves a 17th championship banner to hang in the Garden.

Covering up the Past in Style

In Newport, Rhode Island, a city known for its stunning mansions, Chateau-sur-Mer stands out as one of the greatest Victorian houses ever built in the United States. Constructed in the Italianate style in 1852, it transformed into a Second Empire French chateau over the years in one remodel after another. At press time the multiyear, multimillion-dollar roof restoration was expected to be completed in 2008. It may sound like a lot to spend on a roof, but what a roof it is, with towers, gables, and the like. The repairs will ensure that leaks caused by rain and snow will no longer threaten the grand rooms within this stone house considered a "time capsule of the Victorian age."

Trio at the Top

At Dartmouth's commencement ceremonies in June 2008, the university had a recorded first: three students all tied for valedictorian. They each earned a perfect 4.0 GPA at the Ivy League school in Hanover, New Hampshire. The salutatorian had a 3.99 GPA. The dean of faculty praised the graduates as having achieved not only academically but also in extracurricular affairs, including volunteer projects to improve the community.

Flurry of Activity in the Hills

New England's top two ski resorts keep getting better. Skiers and snowboarders hitting the seven-mountain slopes of Vermont's Killington Resort do so on the heels of more than $5 million in improvements, including the addition of low-energy snow guns, part of an environmental initiative. Sugarloaf Resort, in Carrabassett Valley, Maine, has introduced the Stomping Grounds, one of the East's best and biggest terrain parks.

Presidential Pick

While the world watched the political primaries in speculation about whether a woman would gain entrance to (or at least be a nominee for) the hallowed walls of 1300 Pennsylvania Avenue, the powers that be at Harvard University began 2008 after its own female first that fall. In 2007, Drew G. Foust, a historian, author, and founding dean at Radcliffe Institute for Advanced Study, became Harvard's 28th president, the first woman to hold the prestigious position.

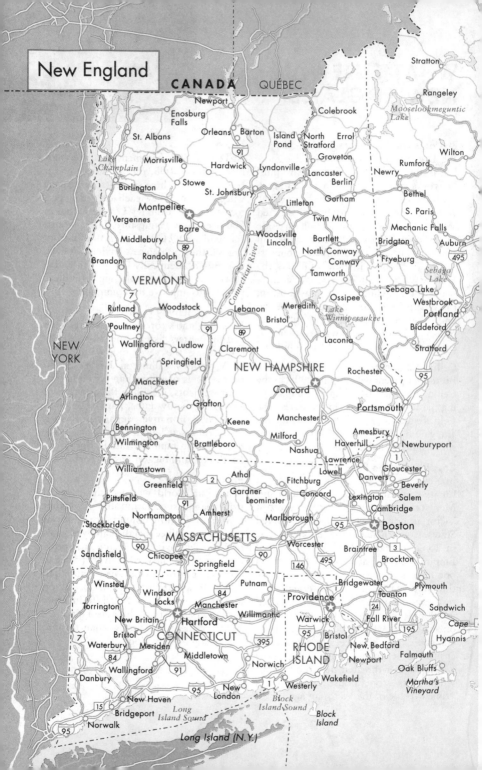

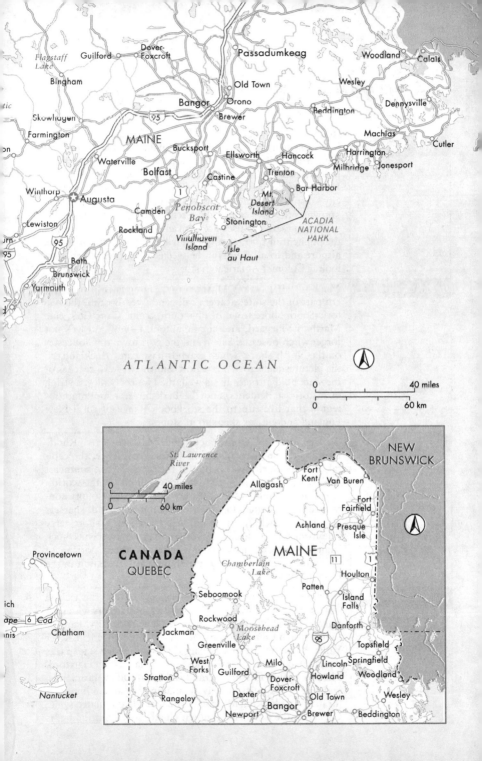

WHAT'S WHERE

BOSTON	If any one place can be called New England's hub, it's Boston. Numerous colleges and universities help make it a cosmopolitan town, but the blue-collar roots are easily found in the Irish South End and the Italian North End, just two of the city's distinct neighborhoods. An extensive light-rail network, known as the "T," can render a rental car moot and help preserve your sanity. Buses are convenient, too, and altogether the public transportation system will get you to and from the airport and to all points in between. Most everywhere you look is Colonial American history.
MASSACHUSETTS	Much of what makes Massachusetts famous is in the eastern part of the state: academically endowed Boston, the historic South Shore town of Plymouth, scenic Cape Cod, chic Martha's Vineyard, and cozy Nantucket—oh, and let's not forget witch-obsessed Salem and the port town of Gloucester on the North Shore, which extends past grimy docklands to the picturesque Cape Ann region. But the western reaches of the state hold attractions as well: the Pioneer Valley, a string of historic settlements, and the Berkshires, a mountainous region that lives up to the storybook image of rural New England and entices skiers to its slopes.
RHODE ISLAND	Wedged between Connecticut and Massachusetts, Rhode Island is the smallest of the 50 states. Providence, the capital, is in the northeast portion of the state. To the southeast is Newport, home to glitzy mansions and one of the world's great sailing capitals. The area known as South County contains coastal towns along U.S. 1, rolling farmland, sparsely populated beaches, and wilderness; it's just a short ferry ride from the South County town of Galilee to scenic Block Island. The Blackstone Valley, in the northern portion of the state, was the cradle of the Industrial Revolution in the United States.
CONNECTICUT	Southwestern Connecticut, the richest part of the richest state, is home to commuters, celebrities, and others who seek privacy, rusticity, and proximity to New York City. Far less touristy than other parts of the state, the Connecticut River Valley is a stretch of small villages and uncrowded state parks punctuated by a few small cities and one large one: Hartford. The Litchfield Hills have grand old inns, rolling farmlands, and plenty of forests and rivers, making the area a big draw for urbanites looking to retreat. The sparsely populated Quiet Corner in the northeast, known chiefly for its antiquing, is

emerging as another weekend escape spot for New Yorkers. In south-central Connecticut, New Haven is home to Yale and several fine museums. Along the southeastern coast lie quiet shoreline villages and casinos.

VERMONT

Southern Vermont has farms, freshly starched New England towns, quiet back roads, bustling ski resorts, and strip-mall sprawl. Central Vermont's trademarks include famed marble quarries, just north of Rutland, and large dairy herds and pastures that create the quilted patchwork of the Champlain Valley. The heart of the area is the Green Mountains, and the surrounding wilderness of the Green Mountain National Forest. Both the state's largest city (Burlington) and the nation's smallest state capital (Montpelier) are in northern Vermont, as are some of the most rural and remote areas of New England. Much of the state's logging, dairy farming, and skiing takes place here. With Montréal only an hour from the border, the Canadian influence is strong.

NEW HAMPSHIRE

Portsmouth, the star of New Hampshire's 18-mi coastline, boasts great shopping, restaurants, music, and theater, as well as one of the best historic districts in the nation. Exeter is New Hampshire's enclave of Revolutionary War history. The Lakes Region, rich in historic landmarks, also has good restaurants, golf courses, hiking trails, and antiques shops. People come to the White Mountains to hike and climb, to photograph the dramatic vistas and vibrant foliage, and to ski. Luring visitors to western and central New Hampshire are Lake Sunapee, the charming college town of Hanover, and Mt. Monadnock, the second-most-climbed mountain in the world.

MAINE

Maine is by far the largest state in New England. At its extremes it measures 300 mi by 200 mi; all other New England states could fit within its perimeter. Maine's southernmost coastal towns are too overdeveloped to give you the rugged, Down East experience, but the Kennebunks will: classic townscapes, rocky shorelines punctuated by sandy beaches and picturesque downtown districts. Purists hold that the Maine Coast begins at Penobscot Bay, where the vistas over the water are wider and bluer, the shore a jumble of granite boulders. East of the bay is Acadia National Park, Maine's principal tourist attraction, with waterfront Bar Harbor being the park's main gateway town. The vast North Woods region attracts outdoors enthusiasts.

NEW ENGLAND TODAY

The People

The idea of the self-reliant, thrifty, and often stoic New England Yankee has taken on almost mythic proportions in American folklore, but in some parts of New England—especially in Maine, New Hampshire, and Vermont—there still is some truth to that belief. Locals initially may be wary of newcomers and visitors, but they still wave at passing vehicles while ambling along country roadsides. The relative isolation and poverty of rural New England are probably primary causes of the evolution of self-reliance and thriftiness, yet undeniably there is a cultural divide between these plain and proud residents and the urbanites of larger cities such as Boston, Stamford, and Hartford.

New Englanders tend to be well educated—according to 2006 U.S. Census figures, only Maine's population falls (though not far) below the national average of residents 25 and older who have completed a bachelor's degree; Massachusetts ranks second and the rest of New England (except Rhode Island at #14) falls within the top ten.

In terms of ethnicity, Vermont, Maine, and New Hampshire are the nation's whitest states; the remaining three are above average. African American and Asian populations are increasing, especially in Massachusetts and Connecticut. In Northern Maine, there is a heavy French influence from nearby Quebec.

The Politics

New England predominantly has gone from one end of the political spectrum to the other, from right to left, since its founding by those with Puritanical roots. Representation in both the United States Senate and the United States House of Representatives is heavily Democratic, even in those states that elect a Republican governor. Voters in New Hampshire, which hosts the nation's first primary each presidential election season, tend to lean conservative but with a distinctly libertarian slant. During the civil rights era in the 1960s, racial tension in Boston was high, with people clashing in the streets over public school segregation. In 2006, however, Massachusetts residents elected Deval Patrick as governor, the second black governor ever to be elected in the United States. Today, New England legislators are pressing for healthcare reform and overturning capital punishment.

The Economy

Long gone are the days since New England's shoe and textile industries sailed overseas, when many a mill town suffered blows to employment and self-image. In recent years, the unemployment rate has fallen below the national average. Exports are a major part of the modern New England economy, consisting heavily of computer and other electronics, chemicals, and specialized machinery.

The service industries are also strong, especially in the insurance and financial sectors. Some towns are known for a particular export: Groton, Connecticut, and Bath, Maine, both have naval shipyards supplying the military with high-technology fighting ships; Springfield, Massachusetts, is a gun-manufacturing center; and Barre, Vermont, quarries granite. Assorted foods produced include maple syrup, blueberries, cranberries, lobster, and other seafood. (Maine potatoes, though still exported, have fallen far behind the spuds produced in Idaho.)

Sports

Professional sports are a huge draw in New England. Though Massachusetts is home to the region's major-league teams—Boston Red Sox baseball, Boston Bruins hockey, New England Patriots football, and Boston Celtics basketball—fans from the other five states follow them as if they were the home team. Red Sox fans in particular are as long-suffering as they are fanatical. It is said that the "curse of the Bambino," caused when Babe Ruth was traded to the New York Yankees in 1920, was behind the team's inability to win a World Series after 1918. Fans were rewarded for their patience, however, when the BoSox became World Champions in 2004 and 2007.

In a similar fashion, the Patriots, perennial lackluster performers, have won an unprecedented three Super Bowls since the start of the 21st century. The team's 2007 regular season was "perfect," in that they won all 16 games; going into the Super Bowl their record was 18–0—but in one of the greatest upsets of all time, the New York Giants beat them with a touchdown in the final moments of the game. The Bruins and Celtics both have successful and storied pasts, with the Celtics enjoying a championship season in '07–'08.

The Language

As people move around, the local accents have begun to blend, creating more of a general New England accent, if an accent at all. However linguistic differences are still evident in some areas, especially the closer you get to the coast.

Boston's distinct accent is similar in tone to that of New York City's Bronx and is noted by the dropping of the "r" in certain places, as in the pronunciation of the famous sports arena "the Gahden." Bostonians also lengthen their vowels, so chowder sounds like "chowdah." Town names in Massachusetts are often spoken very differently than they are spelled; Gloucester, for example, becomes "Glawstuh" and Holyoke becomes "Hoy–yoke." Bostonians also rush their speech, so "Hi, how are you?" is "hihawaya?" and "Did You Eat?" sounds like "Jeet?"

Connecticut, Maine, and Rhode Island also have a Boston-like accent with nuanced differences. Rhode Islanders drop their r's at the end of words and use an "aw" sound for the "o" or "a" in words like coffee or talk but an "ah" sound for the short o's in words like Providence and mom. In Connecticut and New Hampshire the accent is not nearly as strong, but it comes out in certain words, like how locals pronounce their capital "Cahn–cuhd."

Meanwhile, true Mainers drop or soften their r's—making their favorite dish "lobstah"; they also often accentuate the vowel so a one-word syllable can be pronounced like two, meaning "here" may become "hee-yuh." To hear the classic Coastal Maine accent in lively fashion, listen to the lobstermen talk to one another as they unload their traps.

A few New England words and phrases:

- **The Cape**—short for Cape Cod
- **Gravy**—tomato sauce
- **Grinda (grinder)**—a submarine sandwich
- **Jimmies**—ice-cream sprinkles
- **Regular Coffee**—not black, but with cream and sugar

QUINTESSENTIAL NEW ENGLAND

Fall Foliage

It's impossible to discuss New England without mentioning that time of year when the region's deciduous trees—maples, oaks, birches, and beeches—explode in reds, yellows, oranges, and other rich hues. Autumn is the most colorful season in New England but it can be finicky, defined as much by the weather as it is by the species of trees—a single rainstorm can strip trees of their grandeur. But what happens in one section of the region doesn't necessarily happen in another, and if you have the time you can follow the colors from one area to the next. You'll be competing with thousands of other like-minded leaf peepers, so be sure to book lodging early. Your preparedness will pay off the first time you drive down a winding country road aflame in the bright sun of a New England autumn day.

The Coast

The coast of New England is both workplace and playground. Starting in the 17th century onward, boat-builders sprung up in one town after another to support the shipping and fishing trades. Today, the boatyards are far fewer than in historical times, but shipping and especially fishing remain important to the economy on the coast and beyond. But it's not all work and no play—some of the classic wooden sailboats now serve cruise-goers, and some fisherman have traded in their lobster boats for whale-watching vessels. The coast's lighthouses and beaches are also New England staples, especially in Maine and Cape Cod, respectively. More than 60 of these beacons of light line Maine's jagged coast like sentinels along the shore. Cape Cod is a beachcombers paradise, and the relatively chilly waters of the North Atlantic don't scare away swimmers come summertime.

New Englanders are a varied group joined together by a shared past and a singular pride of their roots. It's therefore no surprise that New England spans a spectrum of activities and locales, yet offers visitors and residents alike distinct experiences that still can perfectly define the region.

Food, Glorious Food

Maine lobster. Vermont Grade A maple syrup. Portuguese sausage from Cape Cod. Blueberries from Maine. Fine food prepared under the influence of every region of Italy in Boston's North End and plenty of Italian to go around Atwells Avenue in Providence's Federal Hill, too. This is just a sampling to whet your appetite. New England dining is truly a feast for the gastronomist to behold, and it runs the gamut from the simply prepared to the most artistic of presentations; from blueberry pie just like grandma used to make to slow-cooked Long Island duck with kumquat, stuffed profiterole, glazed carrots, and long pepper. Chefs who grew up here leave to learn their trade, only to return and enrich the dining scene, but the region is known for attracting newcomers as well.

Artisans

New England's independent artisans have built a thriving cottage industry. Some of the finest potters spin their wheels on the coast, and one-off, often whimsical jewelry is wrought in silver, pewter, and other metals. Modern furniture makers take classic simple New England designs, including those of the Shakers and Quakers, and refine them for buyers the world over who are willing to pay thousands for craftsmanship that has withstood the test of time. The varied landscapes of Vermont and New Hampshire, with its Green and White Mountains; Massachusetts, with its Berkshire Mountains, Pioneer Valley and historic coast; Connecticut, with its southern shore; and Rhode Island with its oceanfront cliffs have patiently sat for thousands of painters, whose canvases are sold in small shops and local museums.

NEW ENGLAND'S TOP EXPERIENCES

Peep a Leaf

Tourist season in most of New England is concentrated in the late spring and summer, but especially in the northern states a resurgence happens in September and October when leaf peepers from all corners descend by the car- and bus-load upon deciduous woodlands to see the leaves turn red, yellow, orange, and all shades in between. Foliage season can be fragile—temperature, winds, latitude, and rain all influence when the leaves turn and how long they remain on the trees—but it makes the season even more precious. Don't discount the beauty of fallen leaves; watch them glisten in fall rains or float in the winds of approaching winter.

Comb a Beach

Whether sandy or rocky, New England beaches can be a veritable treasure trove of flotsam and jetsam—so long as you set your sights below, finding lost watches, jewelry, and the like. Anything from crab traps unmoored by heavy waves to colored glass worn smooth by the water can appear at your feet. Also common are shells of sea urchins, clams, and other bivalves that gulls have dropped from on high to crack open to eat the tender insides. During certain times of the year sand dollars of all sizes and colors are plentiful. You may even find one still whole.

Take Yourself out to a Ballgame

Boston Red Sox fans are best known for being two things: unwaveringly fanatical, and vehemently opposed to all things New York Yankees (pity the family with members in both camps). Fenway Park is among the oldest in the nation, and one of the few left to use a hand-operated scoreboard. Though the cheapest seats and farthest from the field, the bleach-ers are quite popular with the faithful, who gather to drink beer in plastic cups and watch as batters attempt to clear the 37-foot-tall left-field wall, known as the Green Monster. Seat 21 of Section 42, Row 37 in the right bleachers is painted red in honor of the longest measurable home run ever to be hit at Fenway, when the legendary Ted Williams blasted the ball 502 feet on June 9, 1946.

Hit the Slopes

Though the mountain snow in New England is not as legendary as it is out West, and in fact can be downright unpleasant when packed powder turns into the scrape of crusty ice, skiing remains popular. Vermont has several ski areas, and its Killington is the largest resort in the Northeast, with 200 trails spanning seven mountains. New Hampshire and Massachusetts's Berkshires also cater to snow sport lovers, and Sunday River and Sugarloaf in Maine are perennial favorites with advanced intermediate and expert skiers. Beginners (and lift-ticket bargain hunters) can choose from a number of small but still fun hills throughout Northern New England.

Eat a Maine Lobster

Maine lobsters are world-renowned, and lobstermen and fish markets all along the coast will pack a live lobster in seaweed for overnight shipment to most anywhere. These delectable crustaceans are available throughout New England, but without a doubt, the best place to eat them is near the waters of origin. Lobster meat is sweet, especially the claws, and most agree that simple preparation is the best way to go: steamed and eaten with drawn butter, or pulled into chunks and placed in a hot dog roll with a leaf of lettuce and

the barest amount of mayonnaise. Any of these ways it's absolutely delicious.

Rise and Shine at a B&B

New England's distinct architecture, much of it originating in the 18th and 19th centuries, has resulted in beautiful buildings of all shapes and sizes, many of which have been restored as bed-and-breakfasts. These inns typify the cozy, down-home, and historic feel of New England, and as such are an ideal lodging choice, though prices are often more expensive than a hotel or motel.

Watch a Whale

The deep, cold waters of the North Atlantic serve both as feeding ground and migration routes for a variety of whales, including the fin, humpback, the occasional blue, and the endangered right whales. Cape Cod and Maine's Southern Coast and Mid-Coast regions are the best places to hop aboard a whale-watching boat to motor 10 mi or more off the coast. Some boat captains go so far as to guarantee at least a single sighting.

Breathe in the Ocean Air and Fragrance of the Forests

New England might be known for its flashy foliage in the fall and spectacular slopes in the winter, but the outdoors in the spring and summer delights all the senses as well. Three nurturing nature experiences to try are 1) a carriage ride at Acadia National Park, 2) an amble on the Cliff Walk along the ocean behind the mansions of Newport, and 3) a hike along a portion of the Applachian Trail.

On the 45 mi of old carriage roads that John D. Rockefeller had created throughout Acadia National Park, you'll be treated to front-and-center views of waterfalls, the ocean, and many patches of green, and you might just catch the scent of the blueberries and ferns growing along the sides of the stone path.

In Newport on the 3½-mi Cliff Walk you can walk along the water's edge, balancing the mammoth mansions on one side and an inlet of the Atlantic Ocean on your other. It's not as scary as it sounds, though, and it's a scenic way to burn off some calories from any vacation indulges.

The 2,160-mi Appalachian Trail, running from Springer Mountain, Georgia, to Katahdin, Maine, cuts through five of New England's six states: Connecticut, Massachusetts, New Hampshire, Vermont, and Maine.

Fair Thee Well

New Englanders love their fairs and festivals. Maine-iacs celebrate the moose, clam, lobster, and blueberry, and a fair highlights organic farmers and their products. Maple sugar and maple syrup are fested in Vermont, while "live free or die" New Hampshire honors American independence. Newport, Rhode Island, hosts two highly regarded music festivals, one folk and one jazz. Many rural communities throughout New England hold agricultural fairs in late August and September.

Get the First Sight of First Light

Cadillac Mountain, in Maine's Acadia National Park, is the highest mountain on the New England Coast. As such, the summit, which is reachable by car except when the Loop Road is closed in the winter, is an excellent vantage point, where you can, quite possibly, be the first person in the United States to witness the sunrise.

IF YOU LIKE

The Beach

Long, wide beaches edge the New England coast from southern Maine to southern Connecticut, with dozens dotting the shores of Cape Cod, Martha's Vineyard, and Nantucket. Though most hit these sandy getaways in summer, beaches can even be enjoyable in winter—for a stroll, not swim—since you'll likely have the shore to yourself or share it with only a few people. Many of the beaches have lifeguards on duty; some have picnic facilities, restrooms, changing facilities, and concession stands. Depending on the locale, you may need a parking sticker to use the lot. The waters are at their warmest in August, though they're cold even at the height of summer along much of Maine. Inland, small lake beaches abound, most notably in New Hampshire and Vermont.

■ **Block Island, Rhode Island.** Some liken the rolling green hills of this 11-square-mi island to Ireland. Located 12 mi off the coast, this tiny island has 12 mi of shoreline, 365 fresh water ponds, and plenty of hiking trails. Preserved homes and inns lend it a Victorian charm. Most arrive via ferry from Port Judith, a one-hour trip, but if you're strapped for time and not for cash hop a plane at the airport in Westerly for a 20-min flight.

■ **Cape Cod National Seashore, Massachusetts.** Cape Cod has more than 150 beaches—roughly 40 mi worth—enough to keep any beachcomber happy and sandy year-round. Favorite activities include swimming, bicycling, and even off-road, called "oversand," travel (permit required).

■ **Gloucester Beaches, Massachusetts.** Along the North Shore, a trio of beaches cools those coming north of Boston for some sun and sand. You'll find dunes at all three—Good Harbor Beach, Long Beach, and Wingaersheek Beach—and a lighthouse at Wingaersheek. Gloucester is the oldest seaport in the nation.

■ **Hampton Beach State Park, New Hampshire.** New Hampshire's ocean shore is short, but this state park along historic Route 1 takes full advantage of the space it has. In addition to swimming and fishing, there are campsites with full hookups for RVs and an amphitheater with a band shell for fair-weather concerts.

■ **Old Orchard Beach, Maine.** Think Coney Island on a smaller scale. A ghost town in the off season, the main drag fills with cruising cars and amblers of all ages come summer. There's a white sand beach to be sure (lapped by cold North Atlantic waters), but many come to ride the Pirate Ship at Palace Playland, drop quarters at the arcade, and browse the multitude of trinket-and-t-shirts shops. Grab a slice of pizza and french fries doused with white vinegar.

■ **Reid State Park, Maine.** Located just east of Sheepscot Bay, right along the ocean, Reid State Park is a beach bum's wonderland. The water is cold much of the year, and the waves roil during a storm (much to wet-suited surfers' delight), but it's a beautiful and quiet place to spend some solitary time looking for sand dollars or climbing amongst the rocks at low tide, exploring tidal pools.

Bicycling

Biking on a road through New England's countryside is an idyllic way to spend a day. Every state in the region has its share of good choices for bicyclists, and many ski resorts allow mountain bikes in summer.

■ **Acadia National Park, Maine.** At the heart of this popular park is the 45-mi network of historic carriage roads covered in crushed rock that bicyclists share only with equestrians and hikers. Sturdier riders can ascend the road to the top of Cadillac mountain, but take caution: heavy traffic in the high season can make this a dangerous proposition. Biking in Maine is also scenic in and around Kennebunkport, Camden, Deer Isle, and the Schoodic Peninsula.

■ **Cape Cod, Massachusetts.** Cape Cod has miles of bike trails, some paralleling the national seashore, most on level terrain. On either side of the Cape Cod Canal is an easy 7-mi straight trail with views of the canal traffic. Extending 28 mi from South Dennis to Wellfleet, a converted railbed that is paved and mostly flat passes through a handful of the Cape's scenic towns, offering plenty of incentive to take side trips.

■ **Killington Resort, Vermont.** Following the lead of many ski resorts in the Western United States, Killington allows fat-tire riders on many of its ski trails long after the snow has melted. Stunt riders can enjoy the jumps and bumps of the mountain bike park. Rent a bike on-site or bring your own.

Boating

Along many of New England's larger lakes, sailboats, rowboats, canoes, and outboards are available for rent at local marinas. Sailboats are available for rent at a number of seacoast locations; however, you may be required to prove your seaworthiness. Lessons are also frequently available.

■ **Newport & Block Island, Rhode Island.** Many consider Newport Harbor, Narragansett Bay, and Block Island Sound the premier sailing areas anywhere. The local opinion may be biased, but the boast has a basis in fact. Numerous outfitters provide sailing tours (public and private), sailing lessons, and boat rentals.

■ **Allagash Wilderness Waterway, Maine.** This scenic and remote waterway—92 mi of lakes, ponds, rivers, and streams—is part of the 740-mi Northern Forest Canoe Trail, which floats through New York, Vermont, Quebec, and New Hampshire as well as Maine.

■ **Lake Champlain, Vermont.** Called by some the Sixth Great Lake, 435-square-mi Lake Champlain is bordered by Vermont's Green Mountains to the east and the Adirondack's of New York to the west. Burlington, Vermont is the largest lakeside city, and a good bet for renting a boat—be it canoe, kayak, row boat, skiff, or motorboat. Attractions include numerous islands and deep-blue water that's often brushed by pleasant New England breezes beneath sunny skies punctuated by clouds.

IF YOU LIKE

Eating Out

Seafood is king throughout New England. Clams are a favorite, fried, steamed, or in New England chowder, which is made with milk or cream (unlike the tomato-based Manhattan version) and big, meaty quahogs. Lobster classics include plain boiled lobster—a staple at "in the rough" picnic-bench-and-paper-plate spots along the Maine Coast—and lobster rolls, a lobster meat and mayo (or just melted butter) preparation served in a hot dog bun. The leading fin fish is scrod—young cod or haddock—best sampled baked or broiled. Inland specialties run to the familiar dishes of old-fashioned Sunday-dinner America—pot roast, roast turkey, baked ham, hefty stacks of pancakes (with local maple syrup, of course), and apple pie. One regional favorite is Indian pudding, a long-boiled cornmeal-and-molasses concoction that's delicious with vanilla ice cream. And speaking of ice cream, New England has its home-grown varieties, from Ben & Jerry's in Vermont to Emack & Bolio's out of Boston.

- **Boston's North End.** Ethnic Italians put this corner of Boston on the map, and the area is known for its Italian restaurants and bakeries. Know as "Little Italy," the North End contains almost 90 restaurants ranging from the elegant to the pizza shop down the street. Find a café for a dessert of gelato or an after-dinner espresso.

- **Federal Hill & the Waterfront, Providence, Rhode Island.** The Ocean State may be a small one, but its capital's food reputation is big, thanks to its status as the home of Johnson & Wales, an upper echelon culinary academy. Some of its graduates open restaurants in town, drawing discriminating diners near and far. Savor Italian food in along Atwells Avenue in the Federal Hill neighborhood, or nosh with posh at upscale establisments with river views in downtown Providence.

- **Gilbert's Chowderhouse & Becky's Diner, Maine.** Portland, Maine's waterfront Commercial Street is book ended by these two typical Maine diners. The former has one of the state's finest lobster rolls and homemade clam cakes; the latter opens for breakfast at 4 AM to feed the fisherman before they head out to sea. Order a slice of fresh pie or buy one whole to take with you.

Fishing

Anglers will find sport aplenty throughout the region—surf casting along the shore; deep-sea fishing in the Atlantic on party and charter boats; fishing for trout in streams; and angling for bass and landlocked salmon in freshwater lakes. Sporting-goods stores and bait-and-tackle shops are reliable resources for licenses—necessary in freshwater—and leads to the nearest hot spots.

- **Lake Winnipesaukee, New Hampshire.** As fun to fish as it is to pronounce, the largest lake in New Hampshire is home to three species of trout, small and largemouth bass, bluegill, and more. Visitors 16 years old and older must purchase a one-, three-, or seven-day temporary fishing license.

- **Rangeley Lakes Region, Maine/New Hampshire border.** This collection of ponds, lakes, and rivers offers some of New England's finest fishing (including fly-fishing Big Kennebago Lake). Brook trout and landlocked salmon are the big attractions.

Golf

Golf caught on early in New England. The region has an ample supply of public and semiprivate courses, many of which are part of distinctive resorts or even ski areas. One dilemma facing golfers is keeping their eyes on the ball instead of the scenery. The views are marvelous at Balsams Wilderness grand resort in Dixville Notch, New Hampshire, and the nearby course at the splendid old Mount Washington Hotel in Bretton Woods. During prime season, make sure you reserve ahead for tee times, particularly near urban areas and at resorts.

- **The Gleneagles Golf Course At the Equinox, Vermont.** One of the most stately lodging resorts in all of New England, The Equinox opened in 1769 and has hosted the likes of Teddy Roosevelt and Mary Todd Lincoln. The golf course is par-71 and 6,423 yards, and is especially alluring in the fall when the deciduous trees that line the fairways explode in color. After golf, go to the 13,000-square-foot spa for some pampering. The resort is ringed by mountain splendor.

- **Newton Commonwealth Golf Course, Massachusetts.** Located minutes from downtown Boston, this municipal golf course is open to the public 7 days a week. Even with 18 holes it isn't a long course, but it can't be beat for a quick break from sightseeing Beantown.

- **Samoset Resort on the Ocean, Maine.** Few things match playing 18 holes on a championship course that's bordered by the North Atlantic Ocean. Located in Rockport, Maine along Penobscot Bay, this is a golf cart path only facility that's open from May through October. Book a room at the luxurious Samoset Resort Hotel to make it a complete golf vacation.

Hiking

Probably the most famous trails are the 255-mi Long Trail, which runs north–south through the center of Vermont, and the Maine-to-Georgia Appalachian Trail, which runs through New England on both private and public land. The Appalachian Mountain Club (AMC) maintains a system of staffed huts in New Hampshire's Presidential Range, with bunk space and meals available by reservation. State parks throughout the region afford good hiking.

- **Mt. Washington**, New Hampshire. The cog railroad and the auto road to the summit are popular routes up New England's highest mountain, but for those with stamina and legs of steel it's one heckava hike. Actually, there are a handful of trails to the top, the most popular beginning at Pinkham Notch Visitor's Center. Be sure to dress in layers and have some warm clothing for the frequent winds toward the peak.

- **The Long Trail, Vermont.** Following the main ridge of the Green Mountains from one end of Vermont to the other, this is the nation's oldest long-distance trail. In fact, some say it was the inspiration for the Appalachian Trail. Hardy hikers make a go of its 270 mi length, but by no means should this scare away day hikers who can drop in and out at many places along the way.

GREAT ITINERARIES

ESSENTIAL NEW ENGLAND

In a nation where distances can often be daunting, New England packs its highlights into a remarkably compact area. Understanding Yankeedom might take a lifetime—but it's possible to get a good appreciation for the six-state region in a two- to two-and-a-half-week drive. The following itinerary assumes you're beginning your trip in Hartford, Connecticut (or you're adding it onto a trip to New York City, about three hours southwest of Hartford).

Hartford

1 day. The Mark Twain House resembles a Mississippi steamboat beached in a Victorian neighborhood (adjacent to it is the Harriet Beecher Stowe House museum). Downtown, visit Connecticut's ornate State Capitol and the Wadsworth Atheneum, which houses fine Impressionist and Hudson River School paintings. *(⇨ Hartford & the Connecticut River Valley in Chapter 4.)*

Lower Connecticut River Valley & Block Island Sound

1 or 2 days. Here centuries-old towns such as Essex and Chester coexist with a well-preserved natural environment. In Rhode Island, sandy beaches dot the coast in Watch Hill, Charlestown, and Narragansett. *(⇨ Hartford & the Connecticut River Valley in Chapter 4, South County in Chapter 3.)*

Newport

1 day. Despite its Colonial downtown and seaside parks, to most people Newport means mansions—the most opulent, cost-be-damned enclave of private homes ever built in the United States. Turn-of-the-20th-century "cottages" such as the Breakers and Marble House are beyond duplication today. *(⇨ Newport County in Chapter 3.)*

Providence

1 day. Rhode Island's capital holds treasures in places such as Benefit Street, with its Federal-era homes, and the Museum of Art at the Rhode Island School of Design. Savor a knockout Italian meal on Federal Hill and visit Waterplace Park. *(⇨ Providence in Chapter 3.)*

Cape Cod

2 or 3 days. Meander along Massachusetts' arm-shaped peninsula and explore Cape Cod National Seashore. Provincetown, at the Cape's tip, is Bohemian, gay, and touristy, a Portuguese fishing village on a Colonial foundation. In season, you can whale-watch here. *(⇨ Cape Cod in Chapter 2.)*

Plymouth

1 day. "America's hometown" is where 102 weary settlers landed in 1620. You can climb aboard the replica *Mayflower II*, then spend time at Plimoth Plantation, staffed by costumed "Pilgrims." *(⇨ North & South of Boston in Chapter 2.)*

Boston

2 or 3 days. In Boston, famous buildings such as Faneuil Hall are not merely civic landmarks but national icons. From the Boston Common, the Freedom Trail extends to encompass foundation stones of American liberty such as Old North Church. Walk the gaslit streets of Beacon Hill, too. On your second day, explore the Museum of Fine Arts and the grand boulevards and shops of Back Bay. Another day, visit the Cambridge campus of Harvard University and its museums. *(⇨ Boston, Chapter 1.)*

Salem & Newburyport

1 or 2 days. In Salem, many sites, including the Peabody Essex Museum, recall the dark days of the 1690s witch hysteria, and the fortunes amassed in the China trade. Newburyport's Colonial and Federal-style homes testify to Yankee enterprise on the seas. (⇨ *The North Shore in Chapter 2.*)

Manchester & Concord

1 day. Manchester, New Hampshire's largest city, holds the Amoskeag Mills, a reminder of New England's industrial past. Smaller Concord is the state capital. Near the State House is the fine Museum of New Hampshire History, housing one of the locally built stagecoaches that carried Concord's name throughout the West. (⇨ *The Monadnocks & Merrimack Valley in Chapter 6.*)

Green Mountains & Montpelier

1 or 2 days. Route 100 travels through the heart of the Green Mountains, whose rounded peaks assert a modest grandeur. Vermont's vest-pocket capital, Montpelier, has the gold-dome Vermont State House and the quirky Vermont Museum. (⇨ *Central Vermont & Northern Vermont in Chapter 5.*)

White Mountains

1 day. U.S. 302 threads through New Hampshire's White Mountains, passing beneath brooding Mt. Washington and through Crawford Notch. In Bretton Woods, the Mt. Washington Cog Railway still chugs to the summit, and the Mount Washington Hotel recalls the glory days of White Mountain resorts. (⇨ *The White Mountains in Chapter 6.*)

Portland

1 day. Maine's maritime capital shows off its restored waterfront at the Old Port. Nearby, two lighthouses on Cape Elizabeth, Two Lights and Portland Head, stand vigil. (⇨ *Portland to Waldoboro in Chapter 7.*)

GREAT ITINERARIES

FALL FOLIAGE

In fall, New England's dense forests explode into reds, oranges, yellows, and purples. Like autumn itself, this itinerary works its way south from northern Vermont into Connecticut. Nature's schedule varies from year to year; as a rule, it's best to begin this trip around the third week of September. Book accommodations well in advance.

Northwestern Vermont

1 or 2 days. In Burlington, the elms will be turning color on the University of Vermont campus. A ferry ride across Lake Champlain affords great views of Vermont's Green Mountains and New York's Adirondacks. After visiting the resort town of Stowe, continue beneath the cliffs of Smugglers' Notch. The north country's palette unfolds in Newport, where the blue waters of Lake Memphremagog reflect the foliage. (⇨ *Northern Vermont in Chapter 5.*)

Northeast Kingdom

1 day. After a side trip along Lake Willoughby, explore St. Johnsbury, where the St. Johnsbury Athenaeum and Fairbanks Museum reveal Victorian tastes in art and natural-history collecting. In Peacham, stock up for a picnic at the Peacham Store. (⇨ *Northern Vermont in Chapter 5.*)

White Mountains & Lakes Region

1 or 2 days. In New Hampshire, Interstate 93 narrows as it winds through craggy Franconia Notch. The sinuous Kancamagus Highway passes through the mountains to Conway. In Center Harbor, in the Lakes Region, you can ride the MS *Mount Washington* for views of the Lake Winnipesaukee shoreline, or ascend to Moultonborough's Castle in the Clouds for a falcon's-eye look at the colors. (⇨ *The White Mountains & Lakes Region in Chapter 6.*)

Mt. Monadnock

1 or 2 days. In Concord, stop at the Museum of New Hampshire History and the State House. Several trails climb Mt. Monadnock, near Jaffrey Center, and colorful vistas extend as far as Boston. (⇨ *The Monadnocks & Merrimack Valley in Chapter 6.*)

The Mohawk Trail

1 day. In Shelburne Falls, Massachusetts, the Bridge of Flowers displays the last of autumn's blossoms. Follow the Mohawk Trail as it ascends into the Berkshire Hills—and stop to take in the view at the hairpin turn just east of North Adams. In Williamstown, the Sterling and Francine Clark Art Institute houses a collection of impressionist works. (⇨ *The Pioneer Valley & the Berkshires in Chapter 2.*)

The Berkshires

1 or 2 days. The scenery around Lenox, Stockbridge, and Great Barrington has long attracted the talented and the wealthy. You can visit the homes of novelist Edith Wharton (the Mount, in Lenox), sculptor Daniel Chester French (Chesterwood, in Stockbridge), and diplomat Joseph Choate (Naumkeag, in Stockbridge). (⇨ *The Berkshires in Chapter 2.*)

The Litchfield Hills

1 or 2 days. This area of Connecticut combines the feel of up-country New England with exclusive urban polish. The wooded shores of Lake Waramaug are home to country inns and wineries in New Preston and other pretty towns. Litchfield has a village green that could be the template for anyone's idealized New England town center. (⇨ *The Litchfield Hills in Chapter 4.*)

GREAT ITINERARIES

THE SEACOAST

Every New England state except Vermont borders on saltwater. For history buffs, vivid links to the days when the sea was the region's lifeblood abound; for watersports enthusiasts, the sea guarantees fun on beaches from the sandy shores of Long Island Sound to the bracing waters of Down East Maine. A journey along the coast also brings the promise of fresh seafood, incomparable sunrises, and a quality of light that has entranced artists from Winslow Homer to Edward Hopper.

Southeastern Connecticut & Newport

1 to 3 days. Begin in New London, home of the U.S. Coast Guard Academy, and stop at Groton to tour the *Nautilus* at the Submarine Force Museum. In Mystic, the days of wooden ships and whaling adventures live on at Mystic Seaport. In Rhode Island, savor the Victorian resort of Watch Hill and the Block Island Sound beaches. See the extravagant summer mansions in Newport. *(⇨ New Haven & the Southeastern Coast in Chapter 4; South County, Block Island & Newport County in Chapter 3.)*

Massachusetts' South Shore & Cape Cod

2 to 4 days. New Bedford was once a major whaling center; exhibits at the New Bedford Whaling Museum capture this vanished world. Cape Cod can be nearly all things to all visitors, with quiet Colonial villages and lively resorts, gentle bayside wavelets, and crashing surf. In Plymouth, visit the *Mayflower II* and Plimoth Plantation, the re-created Pilgrim village. *(⇨ Boston & Cape Cod in Chapters 1 and 2.)*

Boston & the North Shore

2 days. To savor Boston's centuries-old ties to the sea, take a half-day stroll by Faneuil Hall and Quincy Market or a boat tour of the harbor. In Salem, the Peabody Essex Museum and the Salem Maritime National Historic Site chronicle America's early shipping fortunes. Spend a day exploring more of the North Shore, including the old fishing port of Gloucester and Rockport, one possible place to buy that seascape painted in oils. Newburyport, with its Federal-style shipowners' homes, is home to the Parker River National Wildlife Refuge, beloved by birders and beach walkers. *(⇨ Boston & the North Shore in Chapters 1 & 2.)*

New Hampshire & Southern Maine

1 or 2 days. New Hampshire fronts the Atlantic for a scant 18 mi, but its coastal landmarks range from honky-tonk Hampton Beach to quiet Odiorne Point State Park in Rye and pretty Portsmouth, where the cream of pre-Revolutionary society built Georgian- and Federal-style mansions—visit a few at Strawbery Banke Museum and elsewhere. Between here and Portland, Maine's largest city and the site of a waterfront revival, lie ocean-side resorts such as Kennebunkport. Near Portland is Cape Elizabeth, with its Portland Head and Two Lights lighthouses. *(⇨ The Coast in Chapter 6; York County Coast & Portland to Waldoboro in Chapter 7.)*

Down East

2 or 3 days. Beyond Portland ranges the ragged, island-strewn coast that Mainers call Down East. On your first day, travel to Camden or Castine. Some highlights are the retail outlets of Freeport, home of L. L. Bean; Brunswick, with the museums of Bowdoin College; and Bath, with the Maine Maritime Museum. Perhaps you'll think about cruising on one of the schooners that sail out of Rockland. In Camden and Castine, exquisite inns occupy homes built from inland Maine's gold, timber. On your second day, visit the spectacular rocky coast of Acadia National Park, near the resort town of Bar Harbor. If you have another day, drive the desolately beautiful stretch of Maine's granite coast to the New Brunswick border, where President Franklin Roosevelt's "beloved island,"

Campobello, and Roosevelt Campobello International Park lie across an international bridge. (⇨ *Portland to Waldoboro, Penobscot Bay, Mount Desert Island & Way Down East in Chapter 7.*)

WHEN TO GO

All six New England states are year-round destinations, with winter popular with skiers, summer a draw for families and beach lovers, and fall a delight to those who love the bursts of autumnal color. Spring can also be a great time, with sugar shacks transforming maple sap into all sorts of tasty things. But, take note that you'll probably want to avoid rural areas during mud season (April) and black-fly season (mid-May to mid-June).

Memorial Day signals the migration to the beaches and the mountains; summer begins in earnest on July 4. Those who want to drive to Cape Cod in July or August beware: on Friday and Sunday weekenders clog the overburdened U.S. 6. The same applies to the Maine Coast and its feeder roads, Interstate 95 and U.S. 1.

In the fall, as the green is stripped away from the leaves of New England's dense hardwoods a rainbow of reds, oranges, yellows, purples, and other vibrant hues emerges. The first scarlet and gold colors appear in mid-September in northern areas; "peak" color occurs at different times from year to year. Generally, it's best to visit the northern reaches in late September and early October and move southward as October progresses.

Climate

In winter, coastal New England is cold and damp; inland temperatures may be lower, but generally drier conditions make them easier to bear. Snowfall is heaviest in the interior mountains and can range up to several hundred inches per year in northern Maine, New Hampshire, and Vermont. Spring is often windy and rainy; in many years winter appears to segue almost immediately into summer. Coastal areas can be quite humid in summer, while inland, particularly at higher elevations, there's a prevalence of cool summer nights. Autumn temperatures can be mild even into October. The charts below show the average daily maximum and minimum temperatures.

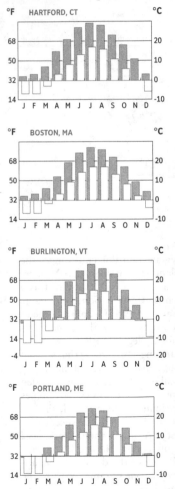

Boston

WORD OF MOUTH

"Bring your walking shoes!!! [Boston] is a perfect-sized city to walk to everything. You can walk over the Mass Ave. Bridge to explore Cambridge and Harvard Square; you can walk the Charles, Comm. Ave., the Public Garden to the Commons to Gov. Center, the Waterfront, and the North End. And if the weather turns, then you can walk to a cab or train! Have a blast. Explore!"

-gyppielou

"Why not explore Boston? It's on the water, [has] great restaurants, music, photo ops, museums . . . and sightseeing galore. For the small-town experience include a trip out to nearby Lexington and Concord."

-Barblab

NEW ENGLAND'S LARGEST AND MOST important city, Boston was the cradle of American independence. The city's most famous buildings are not merely civic landmarks, but national icons, and its local heroes are known to the nation: John and Samuel Adams, Paul Revere, John Hancock, and many more who live at the crossroads of history and myth.

At the same time, Boston is a contemporary center of high finance and high technology, a place of granite and glass towers rising along what once were rutted village lanes. Its many students, artists, academics, and young professionals have made the town a haven for the arts, international cinema, late-night bookstores, ethnic food, alternative music, and unconventional politics.

Best of all, Boston is meant for walking. Most of its historical and architectural attractions are in neighborhoods that are easy to explore on foot. Its varied and distinctive enclaves reveal their character to visitors who take the time to stroll through them. Should you need to make short or long hops between neighborhoods, the safe, easy-to-ride trains of the "T"—the metropolitan train system of the Massachusetts Bay Transportation Authority—cover the city.

EXPLORING BOSTON

By Andrew Rimas

There's history and culture at every turn in Boston, but a down-to-earth attitude can always be found on the edges of its New England pride. The city defies stereotype because it consists of different layers. The deepest layer is the historical base, the place where musket-bearing revolutionaries vowed to hang together or hang separately. The next tier, a dense spread of Brahmin fortune and fortitude, might be labeled the Hub. The Hub saw only journalistic accuracy in the label "the Athens of America" and felt only pride in the slogan "Banned in Boston." Over that layer lies Beantown, home to the Red Sox faithful and the raucous Bruins fans who crowded the old Boston "*Gah*-den"; this is the city whose ethnic loyalties account for its many distinct neighborhoods. Crowning these layers are the students who throng the area's universities and colleges every fall, infuriating some but pleasing many with their infusion of high spirits and money from home.

BEACON HILL & BOSTON COMMON

Past and present home of the old-money elite, contender for the "Most Beautiful" award among the city's neighborhoods, and hallowed address for many literary lights, Beacon Hill is Boston at its most Bostonian. The redbrick elegance of its narrow streets sends you back to the 19th century just as surely as if you had stumbled into a time machine. But Beacon Hill residents would never make the social faux pas of being out of date. The neighborhood is home to hip boutiques and trendy restaurants, frequented by young, affluent professionals rather than D.A.R. matrons. Beacon Hill is bounded by Cambridge Street on the north, Beacon Street on the south, the Charles River Esplanade on the west, and Bowdoin Street on the east.

BOSTON TOP 5

1

■ **Freedom's Ring.** Walk through time as you stand before sites related to America's early history on the 2½-mi Freedom Trail that snakes through town.

■ **Ivy-Draped Campus.** Feel collegiate sitting in Harvard Square and then hit the university's museum circuit: the Sackler for ancient art; the Botanical Museum for unique glass flowers; and the Peabody and the Natural History Museum for artifacts and culture.

■ **Posh Purchases.** Strap on some stilettos and join the quest for fashionable finds among the moneyed crowd on Newbury Street, Boston's answer to Manhattan's 5th Avenue.

■ **Sacred Ground.** Root for the Boston Red Sox at baseball's most hallowed shrine, Fenway Park.

■ **Painted Glory.** Gaze at paintings, listen to concerts, and stare down statuary at the beautiful Isabella Stewart Gardner Museum. But wait; you haven't even begun to see all the canvases in this town. While away hours upon hours at the Museum of Fine Arts, contemplating the works of great artists like French masters Edouard Manet, Camille Passarro, and Pierre-Auguste Renoir, and American painters Mary Cassatt, Childe Hassam, John Singer Sargent, and Edward Hopper.

Boston Common. Nothing is more central to Boston than the Common, the oldest public park in the United States. Boston Common started as 50 acres where the freemen of Boston could graze their cattle. (Cows were banned in 1830.) Dating from 1634, it's as old as the city around it. The Common is home to such landmarks as the **Boston Massacre Memorial**, the **Frog Pond**, and the **Robert Gould Shaw 54th Regiment Memorial**. The **Central Burying Ground** (⊠*Boylston St., near Tremont St., Beacon Hill* Ⓣ*Park St.*) is the final resting place of Tories and Patriots alike, as well as many British casualties of the Battle of Bunker Hill. The Burying Ground is open daily 9-5. ⊠*Bounded by Beacon, Charles, Tremont, and Park Sts., Beacon Hill* Ⓣ*Park St.*

Granary Burying Ground. If you found a resting place here at the Old Granary, as it's called, chances are your headstone would have been impressively ornamented with skeletons and winged skulls. Your neighbors would have been impressive, too: buried here are Samuel Adams, John Hancock, Benjamin Franklin's parents, and Paul Revere. ⊠*Entrance on Tremont St., Beacon Hill* ☉*Daily 9-5* Ⓣ*Park St.*

Louisburg Square. One of the most charming corners in a neighborhood that epitomizes charm, Louisburg Square was an 1840s model for town-house development that was never repeated on the Hill because of space restrictions. Today, the grassy square—enclosed by a wrought-iron fence and considered the very heart of Beacon Hill—belongs collectively to the owners of the houses facing it. The statue at the north end of the green is of Columbus, while the one at the south end is of Aristides the Just; both were donated in 1850 by a Greek merchant who lived on the square. The houses, most of which are now divided into apartments and condominiums, have seen their share of famous

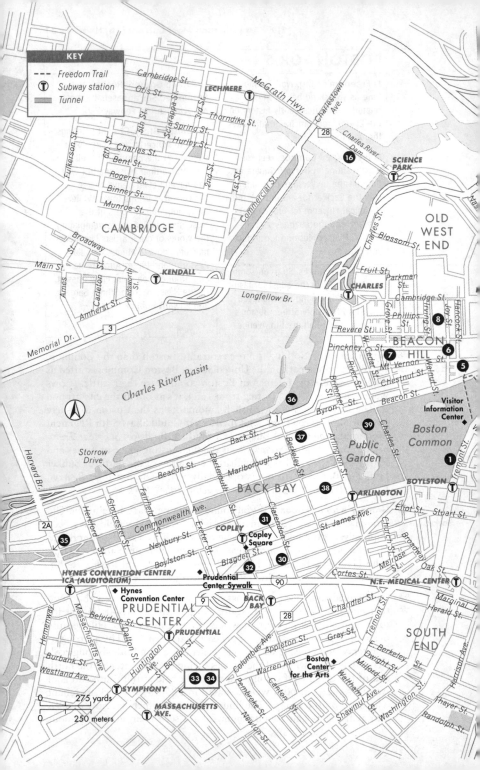

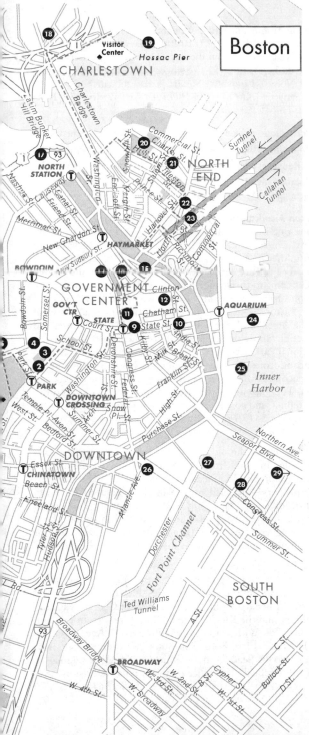

Boston

tenants, including author and critic William Dean Howells at Nos. 4 and 16, and the Alcotts at No. 10 (*Little Women* author Louisa May Alcott not only lived here, but, on the day of her father's funeral of all days, she also died here). In 1852 the singer Jenny Lind was married in the parlor of No. 20. Louisburg Square is also the current home of Massachusetts Senator John Kerry. ⊠*Between Mt. Vernon and Pickney Sts., Beacon Hill* Ⓣ*Park St.*

DID YOU KNOW?

Beacon Hill's north slope played a key part in African-American history. A community of free blacks lived here in the 1800s; many worshipped at the African Meeting House, established in 1805 and still standing. It came to be known as the "Black Faneuil Hall" for the fervent antislavery activism that started within its walls.

Ⓒ ➑ **Museum of African American History.** Ever since runaway slave Crispus
Fodor'sChoice Attucks became one of the famous victims of the Boston Massacre
★ of 1770, the African-American community of Boston has played an important part in the city's history. Throughout the 19th century, abolition was the cause célèbre for Boston's intellectual elite, and during that time, blacks came to thrive in neighborhoods throughout the city. The Museum of African American History was established in 1964 to promote this history. The umbrella organization includes a trio of historic sites: the Abiel Smith School; the African Meeting House; and the African Meeting House on the island of Nantucket, off the coast of Cape Cod. National Park Service personnel lead tours of the Black Heritage Trail, starting from the Robert Gould Shaw and 54th Regiment Memorial at Beacon and Park streets (to reserve a spot on a tour, call *617/742-5414*). The museum is the site of such activities as lectures, children's storytelling, and concerts focusing on black composers. ⊠*46 Joy St., Beacon Hill* ☎*617/725-0022* ⊕*www.afroammuseum.org* ✉ *$5 suggested donation* ⊙*Mon.-Sat. 10-4* Ⓣ*Charles/MGH.*

➍ **Boston Athenaeum.** One of the oldest libraries in the country, the Athenaeun was founded in 1807 from the seeds sown by the Anthology Club (headed by Ralph Waldo Emerson's father). It moved to its present imposing quarters—modeled after Palladio's Palazzo da Porta Festa in Vicenza, Italy—in 1849. Only 1,049 proprietary shares exist for membership in this cathedral of scholarship, and most have been passed down for generations; the Athenaeum is, however, open for use by qualified scholars, and yearly memberships are open to all by application.

The first floor is open to the public and houses an art gallery with rotating exhibits, marble busts, porcelain vases, lush oil paintings, and books. Among the Athenaeum's holdings are most of George Washington's private library and the King's Chapel Library, sent from England by William III in 1698. With a nod to the Information Age, an online catalog contains records for more than 600,000 volumes. The Athenaeum extends into 14 Beacon Street, which you might recognize as the exterior of Ally McBeal's law office on the popular television series that ended in 2002. ⊠*10½ Beacon St., Beacon Hill* ☎*617/227-0270*

PLANNING YOUR TRIP

BUDGETING YOUR TIME

If you have a couple of days, hit Boston's highlights—Beacon Hill, the Freedom Trail and the Public Garden—the first day, and then check out the Museum of Fine Arts or the Isabella Stewart Gardner Museum the morning of the second day. Reserve day two's afternoon for an excursion to Harvard or shopping on Newbury Street. To get an overview of town, try one of the fun yet informative duck tours or a walking tour.

WHEN TO GO

Bostonians often find their city to be too hot and humid in July and August, but if you're visiting from points south, the cool evening coastal breezes might strike you as downright refreshing. The perfect season to visit is fall, when the humidity has passed and the leaves are turning.

GETTING THERE & AROUND

Shuttle buses and water ferries run from Boston's Logan International Airport to downtown, about 2 mi away. You can also fly into New Hampshire's Manchester Boston Regional Airport, about 50 mi northwest of Boston; there's a free shuttle bus service from here to Boston.

Driving the clogged, hard-to-figure streets of Boston (former cow paths) is a nightmare. The MBTA (dubbed "the T" by locals), Boston's public subway system, is the best and cheapest way to get around the city and will get you within a block or two of most places you want to go.

⊕ *www.bostonathenaeum.org* ⊠ *Free* ☼ *Mon. 9-8, Tues.-Fri. 9-5:30, Sat. 9-4. Tours Tues. and Thurs. at 3* Ⓣ *Park St.*

⑥ Nichols House. The only Mt. Vernon Street home open to the public, the Nichols House was built in 1804 and attributed to Charles Bulfinch. It became the lifelong home of Rose Standish Nichols (1872-1960), Beacon Hill eccentric, philanthropist, peace advocate, and one of the first female landscape designers. Nichols made arrangements in her will for the house to become a museum, and knowledgeable volunteers from the neighborhood have been playing host since then. ⊠ *55 Mt. Vernon St., Beacon Hill* ☎ *617/227-6993* ⊕ *www.nicholshousemuseum.org* ⊠ *$7* ☼ *Apr.-Oct., Tues.-Sat. noon-4; Nov.-Mar., Thurs.-Sat. noon-4. Tours on the ½ hr; last tour starts at 4* Ⓣ *Park St.*

② Park Street Church. If this Congregationalist church at the corner of Tremont and Park streets could sing, what a joyful song it would be. Inside the church, which was designed by Peter Banner and erected in 1809-10, Samuel Smith's hymn "America" was first sung on July 4, 1831. The country's oldest musical organization, the Handel & Haydn Society, was founded here in 1815; in 1829 William Lloyd Garrison began his long public campaign for the abolition of slavery here. The distinguished steeple is considered by many critics to be the most beautiful in New England. ⊠ *1 Park St., Beacon Hill* ☎ *617/523-3383* ⊕ *www. parkstreet.org* ☼ *Tours mid-June through Aug., Tues.-Sat. 9:30-3. Sun. services at 8:30, 11, 4, and 6* Ⓣ *Park St.*

Following the Freedom Trail

More than a route of historic sites, the Freedom Trail is a 2½-mi walk into history, bringing to life the events that exploded on the world during the Revolution. Its 16 way stations allow you to reach out and touch the very wellsprings of U.S. civilization. Follow this famous route marked on most city maps, and keep an eye on the sidewalk for the red stripe that marks the trail. A few sites charge admission.

Follow the red-brick road in Boston to 16 historic sites with national significance.

It takes a full day to complete the entire route comfortably. Begin at Boston Common. Get your bearings at the Visitor Information Center on Tremont Street, then head for the **State House,** Boston's finest piece of Federalist architecture. Several blocks away is the **Park Street Church,** whose 217-foot steeple is considered by many to be the most beautiful in all of New England.

Reposing in the church's shadows is the **Granary Burying Ground,** final resting place of Samuel Adams, John Hancock, and Paul Revere. A short stroll to Downtown brings you to **King's Chapel,** built in 1754 and a hotbed of Anglicanism during the colonial period. Follow the trail past the statue of Benjamin Franklin to the **Old Corner Bookstore** site, where Hawthorne, Emerson, and Longfellow were published. Nearby is the **Old South Meeting House,** where pretempest arguments, heard in 1773, led to the Boston Tea Party. Overlooking the site of the Boston Massacre is the city's earliest-known public building, the **Old State House,** a Georgian beauty.

Cross the plaza to **Faneuil Hall** and explore its upstairs Assembly Room, where Samuel Adams fired the indignation of Bostonians during those times that tried men's souls. Find your way back to the red stripe and follow it into the North End.

The **Paul Revere House** takes you back 200 years—here are the hero's own saddlebags, a toddy warmer, and a pine cradle made from a molasses cask. Next to the Paul Revere House is one of the city's oldest brick buildings, the **Pierce-Hichborn House.**

Next, tackle a place guaranteed to trigger a wave of patriotism: the **Old North Church** of "One if by land, two if by sea" fame—sorry, the 154 creaking stairs leading to the belfry are out-of-bounds for visitors. Then head toward **Copp's Hill Burying Ground,** cross the bridge over the Charles, and check out that revered icon the **USS Constitution,** "Old Ironsides."

The photo finish? A climb to the top of the **Bunker Hill Monument** for the incomparable vistas. Finally, head for the nearby Charlestown water shuttle, which goes directly to the downtown area, and congratulate yourself: you've just completed a unique crash course in American history.

NEED A BREAK? There arc two Starbucks on the 3/10-mi-long Charles Street—but hold out for Panificio Bakery (⊠*144 Charles St., Beacon Hill* ☎*617/227-4340*), a cozy neighborhood hangout and old-fashioned Italian café. For quick fortification, go for one of the Mediterranean sandwiches, or apply your sweet tooth to a raspberry turnover with a cappuccino.

❺ State House. On July 4, 1795, the surviving fathers of the Revolution were on hand to enshrine the ideals of their new Commonwealth in a graceful seat of government designed by Charles Bulfinch. Governor Samuel Adams and Paul Revere laid the cornerstone; Revere would later roll the copper sheathing for the dome.

Bullfinch's neoclassical design is poised between Georgian and Federal; its finest features are the delicate Corinthian columns of the portico, the graceful pediment and window arches, and the vast yet visually weightless golden dome (gilded in 1874 and again in 1997). During World War II, the dome was painted gray so that it would not reflect moonlight during blackouts and thereby offer a target to anticipated Axis bombers. It's capped with a pinecone, a symbol of the importance of pine wood, which was integral to the construction of Boston's early houses and churches—as well as the State House itself.

Inside the building are Doric Hall, with its statuary and portraits; the Hall of Flags, where an exhibit shows the battle flags from all the wars in which Massachusetts regiments have participated; the Great Hall, an open space used for state functions that houses 351 flags from the cities and towns of Massachusetts; the governor's office; and the chambers of the House and Senate. ⊠*Beacon St., between Hancock and Bowdoin Sts., Beacon Hill* ☎*617/727-3676* ⊕*www.state.ma.us/sec/trs/trsidx.htm* ⊠*Free* ⊙ *Weekdays 9-5. Tours 10-4; call ahead to schedule* Ⓣ*Park St.*

GOVERNMENT CENTER

This is a section of town Bostonians love to hate. Not only does Government Center house what they can't fight—City Hall—but it also contains some of the bleakest architecture since the advent of poured concrete. But though the stark, treeless plain surrounding City Hall has been roundly jeered for its user-unfriendly aura, the expanse is enlivened by feisty political rallies, free summer concerts, and the occasional festival.

⓫ ★ Faneuil Hall. The single building facing Congress Street is the real Faneuil Hall, though locals often give that name to all five buildings in this shopping complex. Bostonians pronounce it *Fan*-yoo'uhl or *Fan*-yuhl. Like other Boston landmarks, Faneuil Hall has evolved over many years. It was erected in 1742, the gift of wealthy merchant Peter Faneuil, who wanted the hall to serve as both a place for town meetings and a public market. It burned in 1761 and was immediately reconstructed according to the original plan of its designer, the Scottish portrait painter John Smibert (who lies in the Granary Burying Ground). In 1763 the political leader James Otis helped inaugurate the era that cul-

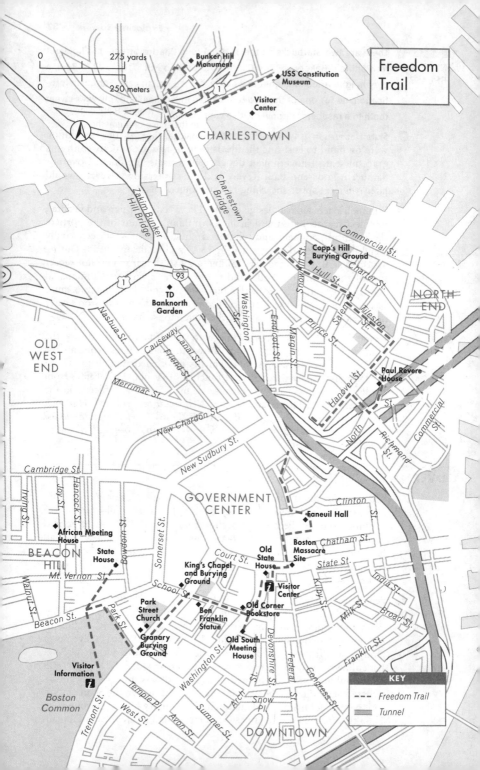

minated in American independence when he dedicated the rebuilt hall to the cause of liberty.

In 1772 Samuel Adams stood here and first suggested that Massachusetts and the other colonies organize a Committee of Correspondence to maintain semiclandestine lines of communication in the face of hardening British repression. In later years the hall again lived up to Otis's dedication when the abolitionists Wendell Phillips and Charles Sumner pleaded for support from its podium. The tradition continues to this day: in presidential-election years, the hall is the site of debates between contenders in the Massachusetts primary.

Inside Faneuil Hall are dozens of paintings of famous Americans, including the mural *Webster's Reply to Hayne,* Gilbert Stuart's portrait of Washington at Dorchester Heights. Park rangers give informational talks about the history and importance of Faneuil Hall on the hour and half hour. The rangers are a good resource, as interpretive plaques are few. Faneuil Hall has always sat in the middle of Boston's main marketplace: when such men as Andrew Jackson and Daniel Webster debated the future of the Republic here, the fragrances of bacon and snuff—sold by merchants in **Quincy Market** across the road—greeted their noses. Today, the aroma of coffee wafts through the hall from a snack bar. The shops at ground level sell New England bric-a-brac. ⊠ *Faneuil Hall Sq., Government Center* ☎ *617/242-5690* ⊕ *www.cityofboston.gov/freedomtrail/faneuilhall. asp* ⊠ *Free* ⊙ *Great Hall daily 9-5; informational talks every ½ hr. Shops Mon.-Sat. 10-9 and Sun. noon-6* Ⓣ *Government Center, Aquarium, State.*

THE STORY BEHIND THE GRASSHOPPER

Why is the gold-plated weather vane atop Faneuil Hall's cupola in the shape of a grasshopper? One apocryphal story has it that Sir Thomas Gresham—founder of London's Royal Exchange—was discovered in a field in 1519 as a babe by children chasing grasshoppers. He later placed a gilded metal version of the insect over the Exchange to commemorate his salvation. Years later Peter Faneuil admired the critter (a symbol of good luck) and had a model of it mounted over Faneuil Hall. The 8-pound, 52-inch-long grasshopper is the only unmodified part of the original structure.

Ⓑ **Holocaust Memorial.** At night, its six 50-foot-high glass-and-steel towers

Fodor's Choice

★ glow like ghosts. During the day the monument seems at odds with the 18th-century streetscape of Blackstone Square behind it. Shoehorned into the north end of Union Park, the Holocaust Memorial is the work of Stanley Saitowitz, whose design was selected through an international competition; the finished memorial was dedicated in 1995. Recollections by Holocaust survivors are set into the glass-and-granite walls; the upper levels of the towers are etched with 6 million numbers in random sequence, symbolizing the Jewish victims of the Nazi horror. Manufactured steam from grates in the granite base makes for a particularly haunting scene after dark. ⊠ *Union St., near Hanover St., Government Center.*

12 **Quincy Market.** Not everyone likes Quincy Market, also known as Faneuil Hall Marketplace; some people prefer grit to polish, and disdain the shiny cafés and boutiques. But there's no denying that this pioneer effort at urban recycling set the tone for many similar projects throughout the country, and that it has brought tremendous vitality to a once-tired corner of Boston.

The market consists of three block-long annexes: **Quincy Market, North Market,** and **South Market,** each 535 feet long and across a plaza from Faneuil Hall. The structures were designed in 1826 by Alexander Parris as part of a public-works project instituted by Boston's second mayor, Josiah Quincy, to alleviate the cramped conditions of Faneuil Hall and clean up the refuse that collected in Town Dock, the pond behind it. The central structure, made of granite, with a Doric colonnade at either end and topped by a classical dome and rotunda, has kept its traditional market-stall layout, but the stalls now purvey international and specialty foods: sushi, frozen yogurt, bagels, calzones, sausage-on-a-stick, Chinese noodles, barbecue, and baklava, plus all the boutique chocolate-chip cookies your heart desires. This is perhaps Boston's best locale for grazing; the hardest part is choosing what to sample.

Along the arcades on either side of the Central Market are vendors selling sweatshirts, photographs of Boston, and arts and crafts—some schlocky, some not—along with a couple of patioed bars and restaurants. The North and South markets house a mixture of chain stores and specialty boutiques. Quintessential Boston remains here only in Durgin Park, opened in 1826 and known for its plain interior, brassy waitresses, and large portions of traditional New England fare.

A greenhouse flower market on the north side of Faneuil Hall provides a splash of color; at Christmastime, trees along the cobblestone walks are strung with thousands of sparkling lights. In summer, up to 50,000 people a day descend on the market; the outdoor cafés are an excellent spot to watch the hordes if you can find a seat. Year-round the pedestrian walkways draw street performers, and rings of strollers form around magicians and musicians. *⊠ Bordered by Clinton, Commercial, and Chatham Sts., Government Center ☎ 617/523-1300 ⊕ www.faneuilhallmarketplace.com ☉ Mon.-Sat. 10-9, Sun. noon-6. Restaurants and bars generally open daily 11 AM-2 AM; food stalls open earlier ⊺ Government Center, Aquarium, State.*

14 **Union Oyster House.** Billed as the oldest restaurant in continuous service in the United States, the Union Oyster House first opened its doors as the Atwood & Bacon Oyster House in 1826. With its scallop, clam, and lobster dishes—as well as the de rigueur oyster—the menu hasn't changed much from the restaurant's early days (though the prices have). *⊠ 41 Union St., Government Center ☎ 617/227-2750 ⊕ www. unionoysterhouse.com ☉ Sun.-Thurs. 11-9:30, Fri. and Sat. 11-10; bar open until midnight ⊺ Haymarket.*

15 **The Haymarket.** Loud, self-promoting vendors pack this exuberant maze of a marketplace at Marshall and Blackstone streets on Friday and Sat-

BOSTON FOR KIDS

■ Children's Museum. Founded in 1913, this was among the first children's museums to focus on hands-on learning. It hasn't let up since. Kids take the lead here, where learning about science and cultural diversity is one big game in which exhibits come out of their cases and into the hands of young ones. The exhibits are fun for adult chaperones, too. (⇨*Downtown.*)

■ Museum of Science. Your youngsters can be shocked in the Theater of Electricity (housed in a two-story, 2.5 million-volt Van de Graaf generator), step back in time with a life-size Tyrannosaurus rex, and learn Newton's laws of physics while swinging or playing on a seesaw. Science is made fun here, where other attractions include a 3-D and Omni cinema (the latter with a five-story screen), planetarium and laser shows, and live presentations that might feature animals, optical illusions, or lightning. (⇨*Old West End.*)

■ New England Aquarium. The little ones will find more than Nemo with exhibits on all kinds of sea life, sea lion shows, and a 24-foot deep, 200,000-gallon ocean reef tank that supports more than 3,000 chorals and sponges, as well as sharks, sea turtles, and the scary moray eel. The see-through tank permits a view not unlike that enjoyed by divers. An activity center provides a quieter place for storytelling, puppet shows, and hands-on projects. Here, too, is a library that adds to the educational experience. (⇨*Downtown.*)

urday from 7 AM until mid-afternoon (all vendors will likely be gone by 5 at the latest). Pushcart vendors hawk fruits and vegetables against a backdrop of fish, meat, and cheese shops. The accumulation of debris left every evening has been celebrated in a whimsical 1976 public-arts project—Mags Harries's *Asaroton,* a Greek word meaning "unswept floors"—consisting of bronze fruit peels and other detritus smashed into pavement. Another Harries piece, a bronze depiction of a gathering of stray gloves, tumbles down between the escalators in the Porter Square T station in Cambridge.

At Creek Square, near the Haymarket, is the **Boston Stone.** Set into the brick wall of the gift shop of the same name, this was a marker long used as milepost zero in measuring distances from Boston. ⊠*Marshall and Blackstone Sts., Government Center* ☉*Fri. and Sat. 7 AM-mid-afternoon.*

THE OLD WEST END

Just a few decades ago, this district—separated from Beacon Hill by Cambridge Street—resembled a typical medieval city: thoroughfares that twisted and turned, maddening one-way lanes, and streets that were a veritable hive of people. Today, little remains of the *old* Old West End except for a few brick tenements and a handful of monuments, including the first house built for Harrison Gray Otis. The biggest surviving structures in the Old West End with any real history are two public institutions, Massachusetts General Hospital and the former

Suffolk County Jail, which dates from 1849 and was designed by Gridley Bryant. The onetime prison is now part of the luxurious, and wryly named, Liberty Hotel. Here you'll also find TD Banknorth Garden, the home away from home for loyal Bruins and Celtics fans. In addition, the innovative Museum of Science is one of the neighborhood's more modern attractions. The newest addition to the skyline here is the Leonard P. Zakim Bunker Hill Bridge, which spans the Charles River just across from the TD Banknorth Garden.

Ⓒ ⑯ **Museum of Science.** With 15-foot lightning bolts in the Theater of Electricity and a 20-foot-long *Tyrannosaurus rex* model, this is just the place to ignite any child's scientific curiosity. More than 550 exhibits cover astronomy, astrophysics, anthropology, progress in medicine, computers, the organic and inorganic earth sciences, and much more. The museum is also home to the **Charles Hayden Planetarium** (☎617/723-2500), which produces exciting programs on astronomical discoveries, and the **Mugar Omni Theater** (☎617/723-2500), a five-story dome screen. ✉*Science Park at the Charles River Dam, Old West End* ☎*617/723-2500* ⊕*www.mos.org* 💵*$17* 🕐*July 5–Labor Day, Sat.–Thurs. 9–7, Fri. 9–9; early Sept.–July 4, Sat.–Thurs. 9–5, Fri. 9–9* Ⓣ*Science Park.*

FodorsChoice
★

Ⓒ ⑰ **TD Banknorth Garden.** Diehards still moan about the loss of the old Boston Garden, a much more intimate venue than this mammoth facility, which opened in 1995. Well, now they've got the next best thing. A decade after it opened as the FleetCenter, the home of the Celtics (basketball) and Bruins (hockey) is once again known as the Garden. The original—which opened in 1928 and was famously the only indoor court in the National Basketball Association where games could be called on account of rain—is fondly remembered as the playing grounds for the likes of Larry Bird and Bobby Orr. The fifth and sixth levels of the TD Banknorth Garden house the **Sports Museum of New England** (✉*Use the west premium seating entrance* ☎*617/624-1234* ⊕*www. sportsmuseum.org*), where displays of memorabilia and photographs showcase the history and the legends behind Boston's obsession with sports. ✉*Causeway St. at Canal St., Old West End* ☎*617/624-1000* ⊕*www.tdbanknorthgarden.com* Ⓣ*North Station.*

CHARLESTOWN

Boston started here. Charlestown was a thriving settlement a year before colonials headed across the Charles River at William Blaxton's invitation to found the city proper. Today the district's attractions include two of the most visible—and vertical—monuments in Boston: the Bunker Hill Monument, which commemorates the grisly battle that became a symbol of patriotic resistance against the British, and the USS *Constitution,* whose masts continue to tower over the waterfront where she was built more than 200 years ago.

⑱ **Bunker Hill Monument.** Three misunderstandings surround this famous monument. First, the Battle of Bunker Hill was actually fought on Breed's Hill, which is where the monument sits today. (The real Bun-

FodorsChoice
★

ker Hill is about ½ mi to the north of the monument; it's slightly taller than Breed's Hill.) Bunker was the original planned locale for the battle, and for that reason its name stuck. Second, although the battle is generally considered a colonial success, the Americans lost. It was a Pyrrhic victory for the British Redcoats, who sacrificed nearly half of their 2,200 men; American casualties numbered 400-600. And third: the famous war cry "Don't fire until you see the whites of their eyes" may never have been uttered by American Colonel William Prescott or General Israel Putnam, but if either one did shout it, he was quoting an old Prussian command made necessary by the notorious inaccuracy of the musket. No

RIDE THE DUCKS!

Boston Duck Tours is something of an overnight success story. Founded in 1994, the company and its colorful "ducks" quickly became Boston fixtures. The amphibious World War II vehicles take more than half a million people a year on 80-minute trips through the city. Tours depart from the Prudential Center and the Museum of Science, and run daily, rain or shine, from late March to late November (all ducks are heated). Tickets are $29 for adults and $19 for ages 3-11. Reserve early. ☎617/267-3825 ⊕www.bostonducktours.com.

matter. The Americans did employ a deadly delayed-action strategy on June 17, 1775, and conclusively proved themselves worthy fighters, capable of defeating the forces of the British Empire.

In 1823 the committee formed to construct a monument on the site of the battle chose the form of an Egyptian obelisk. Architect Solomon Willard designed a 221-foot-tall granite obelisk, a tremendous feat of engineering for its day. The Marquis de Lafayette laid the cornerstone of the monument in 1825, but because of a nagging lack of funds, it wasn't dedicated until 1843. Daniel Webster's stirring words at the ceremony commemorating the laying of its cornerstone have gone down in history: "Let it rise! Let it rise, till it meets the sun in his coming. Let the earliest light of the morning gild it, and parting day linger and play upon its summit."

The monument's zenith is reached by a flight of 294 steps. There's no elevator, but the views from the observatory are worth the effort of the arduous climb. A statue of Colonel Prescott stands guard at the base. In the Bunker Hill Museum across the street, artifacts and exhibits tell the story of the battle, while a detailed diorama shows the action in miniature. ☎617/242-5641 ⊕*www.cityofboston.gov/FreedomTrail/bunkerhill.asp* ▨ *Free* ⊙*Museum daily 9-5, monument daily 9-4:30* Ⓣ*Community College.*

ⓒ ⑲   **USS Constitution.** Better known as "Old Ironsides," the USS *Constitution*
Fodor'sChoice   rides proudly at anchor in her berth at the Charlestown Navy Yard.
   ★   The oldest commissioned ship in the U.S. fleet is a battlewagon of the old school, of the days of "wooden ships and iron men"—when she and her crew of 200 succeeded at the perilous task of asserting the sovereignty of an improbable new nation. Every July 4 and on certain

other occasions she's towed out for a turnabout in Boston Harbor, the very place her keel was laid in 1797.

The nickname "Old Ironsides" was acquired during the War of 1812, when shots from the British warship *Guerrière* appeared to bounce off her tough oaken hull. Talk of scrapping the ship began as early as 1830, but she was saved by a public campaign sparked by Oliver Wendell Holmes's poem "Old Ironsides." She underwent a major restoration in the early 1990s, and only about 8%-10% of her original wood remains in place. The keel, the heart of the ship, is original. Today she continues, the oldest commissioned warship afloat in the world, to be a part of the U.S. Navy. ✉*Charlestown Navy Yard, 55 Constitution Rd., Charlestown* ☎*617/242-5670* ⊕*www.ussconstitution.navy.mil* ✉*Free* ⊙*Apr. 1-Oct., Tues.-Sun. 10-5:50; Nov.-Mar. 31, Thurs.-Sun. 10-3:50; last tour at 3:30* Ⓣ*North Station.*

THE NORTH END

The warren of small streets on the northeast side of Government Center is the North End, Boston's Little Italy. In the 17th century the North End *was* Boston, as much of the rest of the peninsula was still under water or had yet to be cleared. Here the town bustled and grew rich for a century and a half before the birth of American independence. Now visitors can get a glimpse into Revolutionary times while filling up on some of the most scrumptious pastries and pastas to be found in modern Boston.

Gentrification diluted the quarter's ethnic character some, but linger for a moment along Salem or Hanover Street, and you can still hear people speaking with Abruzzese accents. If you wish to study up on this fascinating district, head for the North End branch of the Boston Public Library on Parmenter Street, where a bust of Dante acknowledges local cultural pride.

㉑ Copp's Hill Burying Ground. An ancient and melancholy air hovers like a fine mist over this colonial-era burial ground. The North End graveyard incorporates four cemeteries established between 1660 and 1819. Near the Charter Street gate is the tomb of the Mather family, the dynasty of church divines (Cotton and Increase were the most famous sons) who held sway in Boston during the heyday of the old theocracy. Also buried here is Robert Newman, who crept into the steeple of the Old North Church to hang the lanterns warning of the British attack the night of Paul Revere's ride. Look for the tombstone of Captain Daniel Malcolm; it's pockmarked with musket-ball fire from British soldiers, who used the stones for target practice. Across the street at 44 Hull is the **narrowest house in Boston**—it's a mere 10 feet across. ✉*Intersection of Hull and Snow Hill Sts., North End* ⊙*Daily 9-5* Ⓣ*North Station.*

Hanover Street. This is the North End's main thoroughfare, along with the smaller and narrower Salem Street. Hanover's business center is thick with restaurants, pastry shops, and Italian cafés; on week-

1

ends, Italian immigrants who have moved to the suburbs return to share an espresso with old friends and maybe catch a soccer game broadcast via satellite.

Old North Church. Standing at one

Fodor's Choice end of the **Paul Revere Mall** is a
★ church famous not only for being the oldest one in Boston (built in 1723) but for housing the two lanterns that glimmered from its steeple on the night of April 18, 1775. This is Christ Church, or the Old North, where Paul Revere and the young sexton Robert Newman managed that night to signal the departure by water of the British regulars to Lexington and Concord. Try to visit when changes are rung on the bells, after the 11 AM Sunday service; they bear the inscription, WE ARE THE FIRST RING OF BELLS CAST FOR THE BRITISH EMPIRE IN NORTH AMERICA. On the Sunday closest to April 18, descendants of the patriots reenact the raising of the lanterns in the church belfry during a special evening service. ✉ *193 Salem St., North End* ☎ *617/523-6676* ⊕ *www.oldnorth.com* ⊙ *Daily 9-5. Sun. services at 9 and 11 AM* Ⓣ *Haymarket, North Station.*

> ## A STICKY SUBJECT
>
> Boston has had its share of grim historic events, from massacres to stranglers, but on the sheer weirdness scale, nothing beats the Great Molasses Flood. In 1919, a steel container of molasses exploded on the Boston Harbor waterfront, killing 21 people and 20 horses. More than 2.3 million gallons of goo oozed onto unsuspecting citizenry, a veritable tsunami of sweet stuff. Some say you can still smell molasses on the waterfront during steamy weather; smells to us like urban myth!

 Paul Revere House. It's an interesting coincidence that the oldest house standing in downtown Boston should also have been the home of Paul Revere, patriot activist and silversmith, as many homes of famous Bostonians have burned or been demolished over the years. The Revere house could easily have become one of them back when it was just another makeshift tenement in the heyday of European immigration. It was saved from oblivion in 1902 and restored to an approximation of its original 17th-century appearance. Revere owned it from 1770 until 1800, although he lived there for only 10 years and rented it out for the next two decades. Pre-1900 photographs show it as a shabby warren of storefronts and apartments. The clapboard sheathing is a replacement, but 90% of the framework is original; note the Elizabethan-style overhang and leaded windowpanes. A few Revere furnishings are on display here, and just gazing at his silverwork—much more of which is displayed at the Museum of Fine Arts—brings the man alive. ✉ *19 North Sq., North End* ☎ *617/523-2338* ⊕ *www.paulreverehouse.org* 🎟 *$3, $4.50 with Pierce-Hichborn House* ⊙ *Jan.-Mar., Tues.-Sun. 9:30-4:15; Nov. and Dec., and 1st 2 wks of Apr., daily 9:30-4:15; mid-Apr.-Oct., daily 9:30-5:15* Ⓣ *Haymarket, Aquarium, Government Center.*

Pierce-Hichborn House. One of the city's oldest brick buildings, this structure just to the left of the Paul Revere House, was once owned by Nathaniel Hichborn, a boatbuilder and Revere's cousin on his mother's side. Built about 1711 for a window maker named Moses Pierce, the Pierce-Hichborn House is an excellent example of early Georgian architecture. The home's symmetrical style was a radical change from the wood-frame Tudor buildings, such as the Revere House, then common. Its four rooms are furnished with modest 18th-century furniture, providing a peek into typical middle-class life. ☒*29 North Sq., North End* ☎*617/523-2338* ☜*$3, $4.50 with Paul Revere House* ☉*Guided tours only; call to schedule* ⒯*Haymarket, Aquarium, Government Center.*

DOWNTOWN

Boston's commercial and Financial districts—the area commonly called Downtown—are concentrated in a maze of streets that seem to have been laid out with little logic; they are, after all, only village lanes that happen to be lined with modern 40-story office towers. Just as the Great Fire of 1872 swept the old Financial District clear, the Downtown construction in more-recent times has obliterated many of the buildings where 19th-century Boston businessmen sat in front of their rolltop desks. Yet many historic sites remain tucked among the skyscrapers; a number of them have been linked together to make up a fascinating section of the Freedom Trail.

The area is bordered by State Street on the north and by South Station and Chinatown on the south. Tremont Street and the Common form the west boundary, and the harbor wharves the eastern edge. Locals may be able to navigate the tangle of thoroughfares in between (Downtown Crossing, the pedestrian shopper's haven lies within), but very few of them manage to give intelligible directions when consulted, so you're better off carrying a map.

☺ ㉘ **Children's Museum.** Most children have so much fun here that they don't
Fodor'sChoice realize they're actually learning something. Creative hands-on exhibits
★ demonstrate scientific laws, cultural diversity, and problem solving. After completing a massive 23,000-square-foot expansion in 2007, the museum has updated a lot of its old exhibitions and added new ones, like the aptly named "Adventure Zone." Some of the most popular stops are also the simplest: bubble-making machinery, the two-story climbing maze, and "Boats Afloat," where children can float wooden objects down a 28-foot-long model of the Fort Point Channel. There's also a full schedule of special exhibits, festivals, and performances. ☒*300 Congress St., Downtown* ☎*617/426-6500, 617/426-8855 recorded information* ⊕*www.bostonkids.org* ☜*$10, Fri. 5-9 $1* ☉*Sat.-Thurs. 10-5, Fri. 10-9* ⒯*South Station.*

㉙ **Institute of Contemporary Art.** Housed in a breathtaking cantilevered edifice
Fodor'sChoice that juts out over the Boston waterfront, the ICA moved to this site in
★ 2006 as part of a massive reinvention that's seeing the museum grow into one of Boston's most exciting attractions. Since its foundation in 1936, the institute has cultivated its cutting-edge status: it's played host to works by Edvard Munch, Egon Schiele, and Oskar Kokoschka. Andy Warhol, Robert Rauschenberg, and Roy Lichtenstein each mounted pivotal exhibitions here early in their careers. Now the ICA is building a

1

major permanent collection for the first time in its history while continu
ing to showcase innovative paintings, videos, installations, and multimedia shows. The performing arts get their due in the museum's new
theater, and the Water Café features cuisine from Wolfgang Puck. ⊠*100
Northern Ave., South Boston* ☎*617/478-3100* ⊕*www.icaboston.org*
☎*$12, Thurs. 5-9 free, last Sat. of month free for families* ☉*Tues. and
Wed. 10-5, Thurs. and Fri. 10-9, weekends 10-5. Tours on select weekends at 2 and select Thurs. at 6* Ⓣ*Courthouse.*

⊕ ㉔   **New England Aquarium.** This aquarium challenges you to really imagine
Fodor's Choice   life under and around the sea. Seals bark outside the West Wing, its
★   glass-and-steel exterior constructed to mimic fish scales. This facility
has a café, a gift shop, and changing exhibits; one exhibit, "Amazing
Jellies," features thousands of jellyfish, many of which were grown in
the museum's labs. Inside the main facility, you can see penguins, sea
otters, sharks, and other exotic sea creatures—more than 2,000 species
in all. Some make their home in the aquarium's four-story, 200,000-
gallon ocean reef tank, one of the largest of its kind in the world.
Ramps winding around the tank lead to the top level and allow you to
view the inhabitants from many vantage points. Don't miss the five-
times-a-day feedings; each lasts nearly an hour and takes divers 24
feet into the tank. The 6½-story-high IMAX theater takes you on virtual journeys from the bottom of the sea to the depths of outer space
with its 3-D films. The gift shop seems to have every stuffed aquatic
animal ever made. ⊠*Central Wharf, between Central and Milk Sts.,
Downtown* ☎*617/973-5200* ⊕*www.neaq.org* ☎*Aquarium $18.95,
IMAX $9.95, aquarium plus IMAX $23.95* ☉*July-early Sept., weekdays 9-6, weekends 9-7; early Sept.-June, weekdays 9-5, weekends 9-6*
Ⓣ*Aquarium, State.*

⊕ ㉗   **Boston Tea Party Ships & Museum.** After a lengthy renovation, the museum
is, as of this writing, scheduled to reopen in the summer of 2009 (though
the opening date has been extended more than once). The *Beaver II,*
a reproduction of one of the ships forcibly boarded and unloaded the
night Boston Harbor became a teapot, is supposed to return to the Fort
Point Channel at the Congress Street Bridge and be joined by two tall
ships, the *Dartmouth* and the *Eleanor.* Visitors are promised a chance
to explore the ships and museum exhibits, meet reenactors, or drink a
cup of tea in a new Tea Room. ⊠*Fort Point Channel at Congress St.
Bridge, Downtown* ☎ ⊕*www.bostonteapartyship.com* ☉*Check the
Web site for updated information* Ⓣ*South Station.*

㉕   **Rowes Wharf.** Take a Beacon Hill redbrick town house, blow it up to
the *n*th power, and you get this 15-story Skidmore, Owings & Mer-
rill extravaganza from 1987, one of the more-welcome additions to
the Boston Harbor skyline. From under the complex's gateway six-
story arch, you can get great views of Boston Harbor and the yachts
docked at the marina. Water shuttles pull up here from Logan Airport—the most intriguing way to enter the city. A windswept stroll
along the HarborWalk waterfront promenade at dusk makes for an
unforgettable sunset on clear days. ⊠*Atlantic Ave., south of India
Wharf* Ⓣ*Aquarium.*

㉖ South Station. The colonnaded granite structure is the terminal for all Amtrak trains in and out of Boston. Next door on Atlantic Avenue is the terminal for Greyhound, Peter Pan, and other bus lines. Behind the station's grand 1900s facade, a major renovation project has created an airy, modern transit center. Thanks to its eateries, coffee bars, newsstand, flower stand, and other shops, waiting for a train here can actually be a pleasant experience. ⊠*Atlantic Ave. and Summer St., Downtown* Ⓣ*South Station.*

❾ State Street. During the 19th century, State Street was headquarters for banks, brokerages, and insurance firms; although these businesses have spread throughout the Downtown District, "State Street" still connotes much the same thing as "Wall Street" does in New York. The early commercial hegemony of State Street was symbolized by Long Wharf, built in 1710 and extending some 1,700 feet into the harbor. If today's Long Wharf doesn't appear to be that long, it's not because it has been shortened but because the land has crept out toward its end. State Street once met the water at the base of the Custom House; landfill operations were pursued relentlessly through the years, and the old coastline is now as much a memory as such colonial State Street landmarks as Governor Winthrop's 1630 house and the Revolutionary-era Bunch of Grapes Tavern, where Bostonians met to drink and wax indignant at their treatment by King George.

❿ U.S. Custom House. This 1847 structure resembles a Greek Revival temple that appears to have sprouted a tower. It's just that. This is the work of architects Ammi Young and Isaiah Rogers—at least, the bottom part is. The tower was added in 1915, at which time the Custom House became Boston's tallest building. It remains one of the most visible and best loved in the city's skyline. To appreciate the grafting job, go inside and look at the domed rotunda. The outer surface of that dome was once the roof of the building, but now the dome is embedded in the base of the tower.

The federal government moved out of the Custom House in 1987 and sold it to the city of Boston, which, in turn, sold it to the Marriott Corporation, which has converted the building into hotel space and luxury time-share units, a move that disturbed some historical purists. You can now sip a cocktail in the hotel's Counting Room Lounge, or visit the 26th-floor observation deck. The magnificent Rotunda Room sports maritime prints and antique artifacts, courtesy of the Peabody Essex Museum in Salem. ⊠*3 McKinley Sq., Downtown* ☏*617/310-6300* Ⓣ*State, Aquarium.*

THE BACK BAY

In the folklore of American neighborhoods, the Back Bay stands with New York's Park Avenue and San Francisco's Nob Hill as a symbol of propriety and high social standing. Before the 1850s it really was a bay, a tidal flat that formed the south bank of a distended Charles River. By the late 1800s, Bostonians had filled in the shallows to as far as the marshland known as the Fenway, and the original 783-acre peninsula

TAKE A TOUR

■ Don't look now, but it's **Codzilla**—a speedboat that seats 135 people, blasts rock 'n' roll music, and can reach speeds of up to 40 mph during a 40-minute harbor tour. This is one boat you can't miss—just watch for the garish red paint job and the menacing eyes and teeth of a cartoon cod at the bow. ⊠ *Long Wharf, one block from Faneuil Hall, Government Center ⊕ www bostonharborcruises.com/codzilla* ☎ *617/227-4321* ⊠ *$19* ☉ *Daily, hours vary* Ⓣ *Government Center, Aquarium, State.*

■ **Boston Movie Tours** takes you to Boston's film and movie hot spots like the South Boston of *The Departed*, the *Ally McBeal* building, the tavern from *Good Will Hunting*, the *Cheers* bar, and Fenway Park, home of the Red Sox and location for movies like *Field of Dreams* and *Fever Pitch*. Guides share filming secrets and trivia from movies like *Legally Blonde* and *Mystic River* along with the best celeb spots in town. Choose between a 90-minute walking tour ($19) or a two- to three-hour theater-on-wheels experience ($34). ⊠ *Boston Common Visitors Center, 148 Tremont St.* ☎ *866/668-4345* ⊕ *www.bostonmovietours.net* ⊠ *$35* ☉ *Weekends Apr.-Sept., also Thurs.-Fri. July and Aug.* Ⓣ *Park St.*

■ **The Literary Trail of Greater Boston** offers walking tours of Boston, Cambridge, and Concord, answering questions such as "What inspired Hawthorne to write *The Scarlet Letter?*" and "Where did Charles Dickens hang out when in Beantown?" ☎ *617/621-4020* ⊕ *www.literarytrailofgreaterboston.org* ⊠ *Prices vary* ☉ *Mid-June-mid-Oct.; call for times and locations.*

had been expanded by about 450 acres. Thus the waters of Back Bay became the neighborhood of Back Bay.

Heavily influenced by the then-recent rebuilding of Paris according to the plans of Baron Georges-Eugène Haussmann, the Back Bay planners created thoroughfares that resemble Parisian boulevards. Almost immediately, fashionable families began to decamp from Beacon Hill and the recently developed South End and establish themselves in the Back Bay's brick and brownstone row houses. By 1900 the streets between the Public Garden and Massachusetts Avenue had become the smartest, most desirable neighborhood in all of Boston. Today the area retains its posh spirit, but now locals and tourists alike flock to the commercial streets of Boylston and Newbury to shop at boutiques, galleries, and the usual mall stores. The Boston Public Library, Symphony Hall, and numerous churches ensure that high culture is not lost amid the frenzy of consumerism.

🖐 ㉟
Fodor'sChoice
★
Boston Public Garden. Although the Boston Public Garden is often lumped together with Boston Common, the two are separate entities with different histories and purposes and a distinct boundary between them at Charles Street. The Common has been public land since Boston was founded in 1630, whereas the Public Garden belongs to a newer Boston, occupying what had been salt marshes on the edge of the Com-

mon. By 1837 the tract was covered with an abundance of ornamental plantings donated by a group of private citizens. The area was defined in 1856 by the building of Arlington Street, and in 1860 the architect George Meacham was commissioned to plan the park.

The central feature of the Public Garden is its irregularly shaped pond, intended to appear, from any vantage point along its banks, much larger than its nearly 4 acres. The pond has been famous since 1877 for its foot-pedal-powered (by a captain) **Swan Boats** (⊕ *www.swan boats.com* ✉ *$2.75* ⊗ *mid-Apr.-June 20, daily 10-4; June 21-Labor Day, daily 10-5; day after Labor Day-mid-Sept., weekdays noon-4, weekends 10-4*), which make leisurely cruises during warm months. Near the Swan Boat dock is what has been described as the world's smallest suspension bridge, designed in 1867 to cross the pond at its narrowest point.

The Public Garden is America's oldest botanical garden and has the finest formal plantings in central Boston. The beds along the main walkways are replanted for spring and summer. The tulips during the first two weeks of May are especially colorful, and there's a sampling of native and European tree species. The park contains a special delight for the young at heart; follow the children quack-quacking along the pathway between the pond and the park entrance at Charles and Beacon streets to the *Make Way for Ducklings* bronzes sculpted by Nancy Schön, a tribute to the 1941 classic children's story by Robert McCloskey. ⊠ *Bounded by Arlington, Boylston, Charles, and Beacon Sts., Back Bay* ☎ *617/522-1966* Ⓣ *Arlington.*

❸❷ Boston Public Library. This venerable institution is a handsome temple
★ to literature and a valuable research library. When the building was opened in 1895, it confirmed the status of architects McKim, Mead & White as apostles of the Renaissance Revival style while reinforcing Boston's commitment to an enlightened citizenry that goes back 350 years, to the founding of the Public Latin School. Philip Johnson's 1972 addition emulates the mass and proportion of the original, though not its extraordinary detail; this skylighted annex houses the library's circulating collections. The corridor leading from the annex opens onto the Renaissance-style **courtyard**—an exact copy of the one in Rome's Palazzo della Cancelleria—around which the original library is built. A covered arcade furnished with chairs rings a fountain; you can bring books or lunch into the courtyard, which is open all the hours the library is open, and escape the bustle of the city. Beyond the courtyard is the main entrance hall of the 1895 building, with its immense stone lions, vaulted ceiling, and marble staircase. The corridor at the top of the stairs leads to **Bates Hall,** one of Boston's most sumptuous interior spaces. This is the main reference reading room, 218 feet long with a barrel-arch ceiling 50 feet high. ⊠ *700 Boylston St., at Copley Sq., Back Bay* ☎ *617/536-5400* ⊕ *www.bpl.org* ⊗ *Mon.-Thurs. 9-9, Fri. and Sat. 9-5; Oct.-May, also Sun. 1-5. Free guided art and architecture tours Mon. at 2:30, Tues. and Thurs. at 6, Fri. and Sat. at 11, Sun. (Oct.-May) at 2* Ⓣ *Copley.*

NEED A BREAK? You can take a lunch break at Sebastians Map Room Café or Novel (⊠ 700 Boylston St., at Copley Sq., Back Bay ☎ 617/385-5660), adjoining restaurants in the Boston Public Library. The café serves breakfast and lunch in the map room, while the main restaurant, overlooking the courtyard, is open for lunch and afternoon tea. Enter through the Dartmouth entrance and turn right; the restaurants are at the end of the corridor. Sebastians Map Room Café is open Monday-Saturday 9-5, and Novel is open weekdays 11:30-4:30.

③① ★ Trinity Church. In his 1877 masterpiece, architect Henry Hobson Richardson brought his Romanesque Revival style to maturity; all the aesthetic elements for which he was famous come together magnificently—bold polychromatic masonry, careful arrangement of masses, sumptuously carved interior woodwork. The Episcopal church remains the crowning centerpiece of Copley Square. A full appreciation of its architecture requires an understanding of the logistical problems of building it here. The Back Bay is a reclaimed wetland with a high water table. Bedrock, or at least stable glacial till, lies far beneath wet clay. Like all older Back Bay buildings, Trinity Church sits on submerged wooden pilings. But its central tower weighs 9,500 tons, and most of the 4,500 pilings beneath the building are under that tremendous central mass. The pilings are checked regularly for sinkage by means of a hatch in the basement.

Richardson engaged some of the best artists of his day—John LaFarge, William Morris, and Edward Burne-Jones among them—to execute the paintings and stained glass that make this a monument to everything that was right about the pre-Raphaelite spirit and the nascent aesthetic of Morris's Arts and Crafts movement. LaFarge's brilliant paintings, including the intricate ornamentation of the vaulted ceilings, received a much-needed overhaul during the extensive renovations that have recently wrapped up. It was a mammoth job, but the brilliant LaFarge murals have now been returned to their colorful glory, while his spectacular stained-glass windows (restored to full sparkle) are justly considered among the finest in the country. Along the north side of the church, note the Augustus Saint-Gaudens statue of Phillips Brooks—the most charismatic rector in New England, who almost single-handedly got Trinity built and furnished. Shining light of Harvard's religious community and lyricist of "O Little Town of Bethlehem," Brooks is shown here with Christ touching his shoulder in approval. For a nice respite, try to catch one of the Friday organ concerts beginning at 12:15. ■ TIP→ **The 11:15 Sunday service is followed by a free guided tour.** ⊠ 206 Clarendon St., Back Bay ☎ 617/536-0944 ⊕ www.trinityboston.org ⌦ Church free, guided and self-guided tours $6 ☉ Mon.-Sat. 9-5, Sun. 1-5; services Sun. at 7:45, 9, and 11:15 AM, and 6 PM; Tues. and Thurs. at 6 PM; Wed. at 12:10. Tours take place several times daily; call to confirm times Ⓣ Copley.

③⑥ Esplanade. Near the corner of Beacon and Arlington streets, the Arthur Fiedler Footbridge crosses Storrow Drive to the Esplanade and the **Hatch Memorial Shell.** The free concerts here in summer include the Boston Pops' immensely popular televised Fourth of July performance.

③⑦ Gibson House. Through the foresight of an eccentric bon vivant, this house provides an authentic glimpse into daily life in Boston's Victorian era. One of the first Back Bay residences (1859), the Gibson House is relatively modest in comparison with some of the grand mansions built during the decades that followed; yet its furnishings, from its circa-1790 Willard clock to the raised and gilded wallpaper to the multipiece faux-bamboo bedroom set, seem sumptuous to modern eyes. Unlike other Back Bay houses, the Gibson family home has been preserved with all its Victorian fixtures and furniture intact. That's the legacy of Charles Gibson Jr., a poet, travel writer, and horticulturist who continued to appear in formal attire—morning coat, spats, and a walking stick— well into the 1940s when he dined daily at the Ritz nearby. As early as 1936, Gibson was roping off furniture and envisioning a museum for the house his grandmother built. His dream was realized in 1957, three years after he died. You can see a full-course setting with a China-trade dinner service in the ornate dining room and discover the elaborate system of servants' bells in the 19th-century basement kitchen. The house serves as the meeting place for the New England chapter of the Victorian Society in America; it was also used as an interior for the 1984 Merchant-Ivory film *The Bostonians.* ■**TIP→Though the sign out front instructs visitors not to ring the bell until the stroke of the hour, you will have better luck catching the beginning of the tour if you arrive a few minutes early and ring forcefully.** ✉*137 Beacon St., Back Bay* ☎*617/267-6338* ⊕*www.thegibsonhouse.org* ⌨*$7* ☉*Tours Wed.-Sun. at 1, 2, and 3 and by appointment* Ⓣ*Arlington.*

> **FRUGAL FUN**
>
> Take a cue from locals and sign up for one of the Boston Park Rangers' programs. Top picks include a visit to the city stables to meet the Mounties and their horses, regularly scheduled readings of Robert McCloskey's *Make Way for Ducklings* in Boston's Public Garden, and city scavenger hunts geared for families. Contact Boston Parks and Recreation ☎617/635-7487 ⊕*www.cityof boston.gov/parks.*

③⓪ John Hancock Tower. In the early 1970s, the tallest building in New England became notorious as the monolith that rained glass from time to time. Windows were improperly seated in the sills of the stark and graceful reflective blue rhomboid tower, designed by I. M. Pei. Once the building's 13 acres of glass were replaced and the central core stiffened, the problem was corrected. Bostonians originally feared the Hancock's stark modernism would overwhelm nearby Trinity Church, but its shimmering sides reflect the older structure's image, actually enlarging its presence. The Tower is closed to the public. ✉*200 Clarendon St., Back Bay* Ⓣ*Copley.*

③⑧ Newbury Street. Eight-block-long Newbury Street has been compared to New York's 5th Avenue, and certainly this is the city's poshest shopping area, with branches of Chanel, Brooks Brothers, Armani, Burberry, and other top names in fashion. But here the pricey boutiques are more intimate than grand, and people live above the trendy restaurants and hair salons, giving the place a neighborhood feel. Toward the Mass Avenue end, cafés proliferate and the stores get funkier, ending with Newbury Comics, Urban Outfitters, and now, in a nod to the times, Best Buy.

THE FENWAY & KENMORE SQUARE

The marshland known as the Back Bay Fens gave this section of Boston its name, but two quirky institutions give it its character: Fenway Park, which in 2004 saw the triumphant reversal of an 86-year dry spell for Boston's beloved Red Sox, and the Isabella Stewart Gardner Museum, the legacy of a high-living Brahmin who attended a concert at Symphony Hall in 1912 wearing a headband that read, OH, YOU RED SOX. Not far from the Gardner is another major cultural magnet: the Museum of Fine Arts. Kenmore Square, a favorite haunt for Boston University students, adds a bit of funky flavor to the mix.

35 Fenway Park. For 86 years, the Boston Red Sox were unable to claim a
Fodor'sChoice World Series championship, a streak of bad luck that fans attributed
★ to the "Curse of the Bambino," which, stories have it, struck the team in 1920 when they sold Babe Ruth (the "Bambino") to the New York Yankees. All that changed in 2004, when a maverick squad—including local heroes Manny Ramirez, Curt Schilling, and particular favorite David Ortiz—broke the curse in a thrilling seven-game series against the team's nemesis in the Series semifinals. This win against the Yankees was followed by a four-game sweep of St. Louis in the finals. Boston, and its citizens' ingrained sense of pessimism, hasn't been the same since. The repeat World Series win in 2007 has just cemented Bostonians' sense that the universe is finally working correctly. There's a palpable sense of justice being served, and more than a little pride in the way Red Sox caps have become residents' semiofficial uniform.

Fenway may be one of the smallest parks in the major leagues (capacity almost 39,000), but it's one of the most beloved, despite its oddball dimensions and the looming left-field wall, otherwise known as the Green Monster. Parking is expensive and the seats are a bit cramped, but the air is thick with legend. Ruth pitched here when the stadium was new; Ted Williams and Carl Yastrzemski slugged out their entire careers here. ⊠4 *Yawkey Way, between Van Ness and Lansdowne Sts., The Fenway* ☎*617/267-1700 box office, 617/226-6666 tours* ⊕*http:// boston.redsox.mlb.com* ⊠*Tours $12* ☉*Tours Mon.-Sat. 9-4, Sun. 9-3; on game days, last tour is 3½ hrs before game time.*

33 Isabella Stewart Gardner Museum. A spirited young society woman, Isa-
Fodor'sChoice bella Stewart had come in 1860 from New York—where ladies were
★ more commonly seen *and* heard than in Boston—to marry John Lowell Gardner, one of Boston's leading citizens. Through her flamboyance and energetic acquisition of art, "Mrs. Jack" promptly set about becoming the most un-Bostonian of the Proper Bostonians. When it came time finally to settle down with the old master paintings and Medici treasures she and her husband had acquired in Europe, she decided to build the Venetian palazzo of her dreams in an isolated cor-

ner of Boston's newest neighborhood. Today, it's probably America's most idiosyncratic treasure house.

In a city where expensive simplicity was the norm, Gardner's palazzo was amazing: a trove of paintings—including such masterpieces as Titian's *Rape of Europa,* Giorgione's *Christ Bearing the Cross,* Piero della Francesca's *Hercules,* and John Singer Sargent's *El Jaleo*—overflows rooms bought outright from great European houses. Spanish leather panels, Renaissance hooded fireplaces, and Gothic tapestries accent salons; eight balconies adorn the majestic Venetian courtyard. There's a Raphael Room, a Spanish Cloister, a Gothic Room, a Chinese Loggia, and a magnificent Tapestry Room for concerts, where Gardner entertained Henry James and Edith Wharton. Throughout the two decades of her residence, Mrs. Jack continued to build her collection under the tutelage of the young Bernard Berenson, who became one of the most respected art connoisseurs and critics of the 20th century.

At one time Gardner lived on the fourth floor of Fenway Court. When she died, the terms of her will stipulated that the building remain exactly as she left it—paintings, furniture, everything, down to the smallest object in a hall cabinet. Mrs. Jack never believed in insurance, putting her faith in her mansion's entry portal, which carries Renaissance-period figures of both St. George and St. Florian, the patron saints protecting believers from theft and fire. Today, the collection has more than 2,500 works. ■TIP→If you've visited the MFA in the past two days, there's a $2 discount to the admission fee. Also note that a charming quirk of the museum's admission policy waives entrance fees to anyone named Isabella, forever. ⊠*280 The Fenway The Fenway* ☎*617/566-1401, 617/566-1088 café* ⊕*www.gardnermuseum.org* ⊠*$12* ⊗*Museum Tues.-Sun. 11-5, open some holidays; café Tues.-Fri. 11:30-4, weekends 11-4. Weekend concerts at 1:30* Ⓣ*Museum.*

(📷 ㉞ **Museum of Fine Arts.** Count on staying a while if you have any hope of Fodor'sChoice even beginning to see what's here. Eclecticism and thoroughness, often
★ an incompatible pair, have coexisted agreeably at the MFA since its earliest days. From Renaissance and baroque masters to impressionist marvels to African masks to sublime samples of Native American pottery and contemporary crafts, the collections are happily shorn of both cultural snobbe ry and shortsighted trendiness.The museum's holdings of American art—supplemented by intensive acquisitions in the early 1990s—surpass those of all but two or three U.S. museums. The MFA has more than 60 works by John Singleton Copley; major paintings by Winslow Homer, John Singer Sargent, Fitz Hugh Lane, and Edward Hopper; and a wealth of American works ranging from native New England folk art and colonial portraiture to New York abstract expressionism of the 1950s and 1960s. Also of particular note are the John Singer Sargent paintings adorning the Rotunda. They were specially commissioned for the museum in 1921 and make for a dazzling first impression on visitors coming through the Huntington Street entrance.

The museum also owns one of the world's most extensive collections of Asian art under one roof. Its Japanese art collection is the finest out-

1

side Japan, and Chinese porcelains of the Tang Dynasty are especially well represented. The Egyptian rooms display statuary, furniture, and exquisite gold jewelry; a special funerary-arts gallery exhibits coffins, mummies, and burial treasures. French impressionists abound and are perhaps more comprehensively displayed here than at any other new-world museum outside the Art Institute of Chicago; many of the 38 Monets (the largest collection of his work outside France) vibrate with color. There are canvases by Renoir, Pissarro, Manet, and the American painters Mary Cassatt and Childe Hassam.

In 2005, the museum broke ground on a massive construction project that the trustees hope will keep it in America's cultural vanguard for the next 100 years. The first phase of the project is expected to finish in 2009; the museum will remain open during construction. ⊠465 Huntington Ave., The Fenway ☎617/267-9300 ⊕www.mfa.org ☎$17, by donation Wed. 4-9:45 ⊙Sat.-Tues. 10-4:45, Wed.-Fri. 10-9:45. West Wing open Thurs. and Fri. until 9:45. 1-hr tours daily; call for individual times. ⓣMuseum

EXPLORING CAMBRIDGE

Updated by Lisa Oppenheimer

The city of Cambridge takes a lot of hits—most of them thrown across the Charles River by jealous Bostonians. Cambridge is Boston's Left Bank—an überliberal academic enclave where the city council spends more energy arguing about the regulation of nanotechnologies than on fixing potholes and funding preschools.

The city is punctuated at one end by the funky tech-noids of MIT, and at the other by the soaring—and occasionally seething—rhetoric of the Harvard University community. Civic life connects the two camps into an urban stew of 100,000 residents who represent nearly every nationality in the world, work at every kind of job from tenured professor to taxi driver, and are passionate about living on this side of the river.

The Charles River is Cantabrigians' backyard, running track, and festival ground, and there's virtually no place in Cambridge more than a 10-minute walk from its banks. No visit to Cambridge would be complete without an afternoon (at least) in Harvard Square. It's a hub, a hot spot, and home to every variation of the human condition. Ten minutes away is MIT, with its eclectic architecture, from postwar pedestrian to Frank Gehry's futuristic fantasyland. Cambridge dates from 1630, when the Puritan leader John Winthrop chose this meadowland as the site of a carefully planned village he named Newtowne. The Massachusetts Bay Colony chose Newtowne as the site for the country's first college in 1636. Two years later, John Harvard bequeathed half his estate and his private library to the fledgling school, and the college was named in his honor. The town elders changed the name to Cambridge, emulating the university in England where most of the Puritan leaders had been educated.

When Cambridge was incorporated as a city in 1846, the boundaries were drawn to include the university area (today's Harvard Square and Tory Row), and the more-industrial communities of Cambridge-port and East Cambridge. Today's city is much more a multiethnic urban community than an academic village. Visitors in search of any kind of ethnic food or music will find it in Cambridge—the local high school educates students who speak more than 40 different languages at home. When MIT, originally Boston Tech, moved to Cambridge in 1916, it was the first educational institution that aimed to be more than a trade school, training engineers but also grounding them in humanities and liberal arts. Many of MIT's postwar graduates remained in the area, and went on to form hundreds of technology-based firms engaged in camera manufacturing, electronics, and space research. By the 1990s, manufacturing had moved to the burbs and software developers, venture capitalists, and robotics and biotech companies claimed the former industrial spaces. This area around Kendall Square is now nicknamed "Intelligence Alley."

⑤ Arthur M. Sackler Museum. The artistic treasures of the ancient Greeks, Egyptians, and Romans are a major draw here. Make a beeline for the Ancient and Asian art galleries, the permanent installations on the fourth floor, which include Chinese bronzes, Buddhist sculptures, Greek friezes, and Roman marbles. Currently, the Sackler is the only of the University's art museums open to the public. As of June 2008, the Busch-Reisinger and Fogg museums are closed, in the throes of major renovations spanning about five years. At present, visitors to the Sackler will enjoy a sampling of works culled from its art-museum siblings. Eventually, the combined collections of all three museums will be represented under one roof under the umbrella name, Harvard Art Museum. Works include Picasso, Klee, Toulouse-Lautrec, or Manet. ✉ *485 Broadway* ☎ *617/495-9400* ⊕ *www.artmuseums.harvard.edu/sackler* 🎫 *$9, but free Sat. 10-noon and daily after 4:30* ⊙ *Mon.-Sat. 10-5, Sun. 1-5* Ⓣ *Harvard.*

④ Harvard Museum of Natural History. The vast Harvard Museum complex actually delivers what many a museum promises: something for everyone. Swiss naturalist Louis Agassiz, who founded the zoology museum, envisioned a museum that would bring under one roof the study of all kinds of life: plants, animals, and humankind. The result is three distinct museums, all accessible for one admission fee.

Ardent explorers and naturalists combed the world for the treasures found in the **Museum of Comparative Zoology.** You can't miss—lliterally—the 42-foot-long skeleton of the underwater *Kronosaurus*. Dinosaur fossils and a zoo of stuffed exotic animals can occupy young minds for hours. It's also the right size and pace for kids—not jazzy and busy, but a good place to ask and answer questions.

Perhaps the most famous exhibits of the museum complex are the glass flowers in the **Botanical Museum,** created as teaching tools that would never wither and die. This unique collection holds 3,000 models of 847 plant species. Each one is a masterpiece, meticulously created in glass by a father and son in Dresden, Germany, who worked continuously from 1887 to 1936. Even more amazing than the colorful flower petals are the delicate roots of some plants; numerous signs assure the viewer that everything is, indeed, of glass.

Meanwhile, at the **Mineralogical and Geological Museum,** founded in 1784, oversize garnets and crystals sparkle. Also here is an extensive collection of meteorites. ⊠*26 Oxford St.* ☎*617/495-3045* ⍟*www. hmnh.harvard.edu* ✉*$9, includes admission to Peabody Museum of Archaeology & Ethnology, accessible through the museum; free for Massachusetts residents Sun. 9-noon, year-round, and Wed. 3-5 Sept.- May* ⊘*Daily 9-5* Ⓣ *Harvard.*

Harvard Square. Tides of students, tourists, political-cause proponents, and bizarre street creatures are all part of the nonstop pedestrian flow at this most celebrated of Cambridge crossroads.

Harvard Square is where Mass Avenue, coming from Boston, turns and widens into a triangle broad enough to accommodate a brick peninsula (above the T station). The restored 1928 kiosk in the center of the square once served as the entrance to the MBTA station (it's now a newsstand). Harvard Yard, with its lecture halls, residential houses, libraries, and museums, is one long border of the square; the other three are composed of clusters of banks and a wide variety of restaurants and shops.

On an average afternoon, you'll hear earnest conversations in dozens of foreign languages; see every kind of youthful uniform from Goth to impeccable prep; wander by street musicians playing Andean flutes, singing opera, and doing excellent Stevie Wonder or Edith Piaf imitations; and lean in on a tense outdoor game of pickup chess between a street-tough kid and an older gent wearing a beard and a beret, while you slurp a cappuccino or an ice-cream cone (the two major food groups here). An afternoon in the square is people-watching raised to a high art; the parade of quirkiness never quits.

As entertaining as the locals are, Harvard Square has fine inanimate attractions, too. The historic buildings are worth noting and, even if you're only a visitor (as opposed to a prospective student genius), it's still a thrill to walk though the big brick-and-wrought-iron gates to Harvard Yard, past the residence halls and statues, on up to Widener Library.

Across Garden Street, through an ornamental arch, is **Cambridge Common,** decreed a public pasture in 1631. It's said that under a large tree that once stood in this meadow George Washington took command of the Continental Army on July 3, 1775. A stone memorial now marks the site of the "Washington Elm." Also on the Common is the Irish Famine Memorial by Derry artist Maurice Herron, unveiled in 1997 to coincide with the 150th anniversary of "Black '47," the deadliest year of the potato famine. It depicts a desperate Irish mother sending her child off to America. At the center of the Common, a large memorial commemorates the Union soldiers and sailors who lost their lives in the Civil War. ⊕*www.harvardsquare.com* Ⓣ *Harvard.*

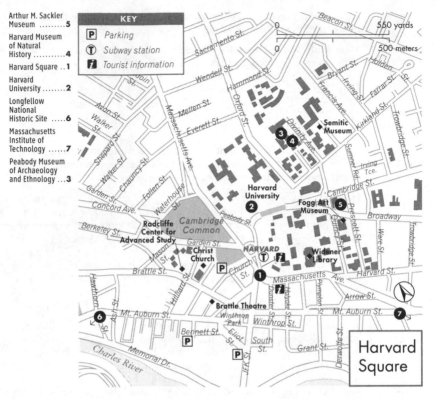

Harvard Square

Herrell's Ice Cream (⊠ *15 Dunster St., Harvard Sq.* ☎ *617/497-2179*) is a Harvard Square institution. Mix-ins (those yummy bits of candy and cookie that make ice cream a full-fledged decadence) were born here. Add the hand-rolled cones and nine flavors of chocolate, and you've got a don't-miss delicacy. The friendly scoopers are young, punk Cambridge-ites—their tattoos and body piercings make odd counterpoints to the sweet sundaes.

★ ❷ **Harvard University.** The tree-studded, shady, and redbrick expanse of **Harvard Yard**—the very center of Harvard University—has weathered the footsteps of Harvard students for more than 300 years. In 1636 the Great and General Court of the Massachusetts Bay Colony voted funds to establish the colony's first college and a year later chose Cambridge as the site. Named in 1639 for John Harvard, a young Charlestown clergyman who died in 1638 and left the college his entire library and half his estate, Harvard remained the only college in the New World until 1693, by which time it was firmly established as a respected center of learning. Local wags refer to Harvard as WGU—World's Greatest University—and it is certainly the oldest and most famous American university. It boasts numerous schools or "faculties," including the Faculty of Arts and Sciences, the Medical School, the Law School, the Business School, and the John F. Kennedy School of Government.

Although the college dates from the 17th century, the oldest build-ings in Harvard Yard are of the 18th century; together the buildings chronicle American architecture from the colonial era to the present. **Holden Chapel,** completed in 1744, is a Georgian gem. The graceful **University Hall** was designed in 1815 by Charles Bulfinch. An 1884 statue of John Harvard by Daniel Chester French stands outside; ironi-cally for a school with the motto of "Veritas" ("Truth"), the model for the statue was a member of the class of 1882, as there is no known con-temporary likeness of Harvard himself. **Sever Hall,** completed in 1880 and designed by Henry Hobson Richardson, represents the Roman-esque revival that was followed by the neoclassical (note the pillared facade of Widener Library) and the neo-Georgian, represented by the sumptuous brick houses along the Charles River, many of which are now undergraduate residences. **Memorial Church,** a graceful steepled edifice of modified Colonial revival design, was dedicated in 1932. Just north of the Yard is **Memorial Hall,** completed in 1878 as a memorial to Harvard men who died in the Union cause; it's High Victorian both inside and out. It also contains the 1,166-seat Sanders Theatre, site of year-round concerts—student and professional—and the venue for the festive Christmas Revels.

Many of Harvard's cultural and scholarly facilities are important sights in themselves, including the **Harvard Museum of Natural History** and the **Peabody Museum of Archaeology & Ethnology** (⇨*separate list-ings*). Of the three much-loved art museums (the Fogg, the Busch Reis-inger and the Arthur M. Sackler) only the latter is currently open (the former two are closed for extensive renovations). Collections of all three will eventually open under one roof with the singular umbrella title of Harvard Art Museum. Be aware that most campus buildings other than museums and concert halls are off-limits to the general public.

Harvard University Events & Information Center (⊠*Holyoke Center, 1350 Massachusetts Ave.* ☎*617/495-1573* ⊕*www.harvard.edu*), run by students, includes a small library, a video-viewing area, computer ter-minals, and an exhibit space. It also distributes maps of the univer-sity area and has free student-led tours of Harvard Yard. The tour doesn't include visits to museums, and it doesn't take you into campus buildings, but it provides a fine orientation. The information center is open year round (except for during spring recess and other semester breaks), Monday through Saturday 9-5. Tours are offered September-June, weekdays at 10 am and 2 pm and Saturdays at 2 pm. In July and August, guides offer four tours: Monday-Saturday at 10 am, 11:15 am, 2 pm, and 3:15 pm. Groups of 20 or more can schedule their tours ahead. ⊠*Bounded by Massachusetts Ave., Mt. Auburn St., Holyoke St., and Dunster St.* ☎*617/495-1573 for Harvard directory assistance* ⊕*www.harvard.edu* Ⓣ *Harvard.*

❸ **Peabody Museum of Archaeology & Ethnology.** With one of the world's outstanding anthropological collections, the Peabody focuses on Native American and Central and South American cultures; there are also inter-esting displays on Africa. The Hall of the North American Indian is particularly outstanding, with art, textiles, and models of traditional dwellings from across the continent. The Mesoamerican room juxtaposes ancient relief carvings and weavings with contemporary works from the Maya and other peoples. ⊠*11 Divinity Ave.* ☎*617/496-1027* ⊕*www.peabody. harvard.edu* ☁*$9, includes admission to Harvard Museum of Natural History, accessible through the museum; Massachusetts residents free Sun. 9-noon year-round and Wed. 3-5, Sept.-May* ⊙*Daily 9-5* Ⓣ *Harvard.*

★ ❻ **Longfellow National Historic Site.** Henry Wadsworth Longfellow, the poet whose stirring tales of the Village Blacksmith, Evangeline, Hiawatha, and Paul Revere's midnight ride thrilled 19th-century America, once lived in this elegant mansion. If there's one historic house to visit in Cambridge, this is it. The house was built in 1759 by John Vassall Jr., and is one of several original Tory Row homes on Brattle Street; George Washington lived here during the Siege of Boston from July 1775 to April 1776. Longfellow first boarded here in 1837, and later received the house as a gift from his father-in-law on his marriage to Frances Appleton, who burned to death here in an accident in 1861. For 45 years Longfellow wrote his famous verses here and filled the house with the exuberant spirit of his own work and that of his literary circle, which included Ralph Waldo Emerson, Nathaniel Hawthorne, and Charles Sumner, an abolitionist senator. Longfellow died in 1882; but the splendor of the house remains—from the Longfellow family furniture to the wallpaper to the books on the shelves (many the poet's own)—all preserved for future generations by the National Park Service that currently runs it. ■TIP➔**Longfellow Park, across the street, is the place to stand to take photos of the house.** The park was created to preserve the view immortalized in the poet's "To the River Charles." ⊠*105 Brattle St.* ☎*617/876-4491* ⊕*www.nps.gov/long* ☁*$3* ⊙*Ranger-led tours May-June 3, Thurs.-Sat. 10:30-4; June 4-Sept., Wed.-Sun. 10:30-4. Call for occasional extended hours.* Ⓣ *Harvard.*

❼ **Massachusetts Institute of Technology.** MIT, at Kendall Square, occupies 135 acres 1½ mi southeast of Harvard, bordering the Charles River. The campus, divided into east and west by Massachusetts Avenue, is studded with a public art collection including works by Henry Moore, Jacques Lipchitz, Louise Nevelson, Alexander Calder, and Frank Stella. It also has some extraordinary buildings. The **Kresge Auditorium,** designed by Eero Saarinen, with a curving roof and unusual thrust, rests on three, instead of four, points. It was dedicated in 1955 along with the nondenominational **MIT Chapel,** a circular Saarinen design. Alvar Aalto's **Baker House,** now a dormitory, from 1947, is another post-war modernist landmark on the West Campus. On the East Campus, besides the **List Visual Arts Center** in a building designed by MIT grad I.M. Pei, is the recently completed **Stata Center** for computer, artificial intelligence, and information systems laboratories, designed by Frank Gehry. An information center in the Rogers Building offers free tours of the campus weekdays at 11 am and 3 pm. ⊠ *77 Massachusetts Ave.* ☎ *617/253-4795* @*web.mit.edu* Ⓣ *Kendall/MIT.*

NIGHTLIFE AND THE ARTS

Updated
by Sarah
Pascarella

Boston's classic cultural attractions include the Museum of Fine Arts, the Boston Symphony Orchestra and Pops, and the Isabella Stewart Gardner Museum. Newcomers such as the Institute for Contemporary Art and the revitalized Children's Museum are also a big draw. For those enjoying live shows, the compact Theater District offers traveling Broadway shows, national comedy and music acts, and previews of new plays soon headed to New York.

For those preferring a more casual, less expensive night out, Boston provides plenty of alternatives. Indie rock and jazz clubs abound, dance clubs and lounges cater to all types of night owls, and countless bars blaring that night's game can be found in any neighborhood.

NIGHTLIFE

BARS

★ **The Black Rose** is decorated with family crests, pictures of Ireland, and portraits of the likes of Samuel Beckett, Lady Gregory, and James Joyce—just like a Dublin pub. Its Faneuil Hall location draws as many tourists as locals, but nightly performances by traditional Irish and contemporary performers make it worth braving the crowds. ⊠ *160 State St., Faneuil Hall* ☎ *617/742-2286* @*www.irishconnection.com* Ⓣ *Government Center, Haymarket, State.*

Boston Beer Works is a "naked brewery," with all the works exposed— the tanks, pipes, and gleaming stainless-steel and copper kettles used in producing beer. Seasonal brews, in addition to a regular selection, are the draw for students, young adults, and tourists. It's too crowded and noisy for intimate chats, and good luck trying to get in when there's a home game. ⊠ *61 Brookline Ave., Fens* ☎ *617/536-2337* Ⓣ *Kenmore.*

Cheers, formerly known as the Bull & Finch Pub, was dismantled in England, shipped to Boston, and reassembled here. Though it was the inspiration for the TV series *Cheers,* it doesn't look anything like the bar in the show. Addressing that complaint, however, a branch in Faneuil Hall that opened in 2001 is an exact reproduction of the TV set. ⊠ *Hampshire House, 84 Beacon St., Beacon Hill* ☎ *617/227-9605* @*www.cheersboston.com* Ⓣ *Park St., Arlington, Charles/MGH.*

Fodor'sChoice **Saint,** despite its name, draws patrons who are anything but. The spa-
★   cious underground lounge consists of two rooms: an airy main space is decorated in blue and silver, with long couches to lounge on over appe-

tizers while making eyes across the room. A more-devilish Bordello room is all plush red velvet and tasseled light fixtures, and has private alcoves for more-intimate conversation. ✉ *90 Exeter St., Back Bay* ☎ *617/236-1134*   ⊕ *www.saint nitery.com* Ⓣ *Copley.*

Sonsie keeps the stereo volume at a manageable level. The bar crowd, which spills through the French doors onto a sidewalk café in warm weather, is full of young, trendy, cosmopolitan types and professionals. ✉ *327 Newbury St., Back Bay* ☎ *617/351-2500* ⊕ *www.son-sieboston.com* Ⓣ *Hynes/ICA.*

> ### WHERE EVERYBODY KNOWS YOUR NAME
>
> TV's *Cheers* may have ended in 1993, but that doesn't stop die-hard fans from paying their respects at the "real" Cheers bar on Beacon Street (or its new second location in Faneuil Hall). So what if there's no Norm or Cliff around, or the place doesn't look quite the same as the TV version? You can find your own kind of notoriety here, by devouring the double-decker "Norm burger" and adding your name to the Hall of Fame.

Top of the Hub is a lounge with a wonderful view over the city; that and the hip jazz help to ease the sting of pricey drinks. ✉ *Prudential Tower, 800 Boylston St., 52nd fl., Back Bay* ☎ *617/536-1775* ⊕ *www.selectrestaurants.com/tophub/* Ⓣ *Prudential Center, Hynes/ICA.*

COMEDY CLUBS

Comedy Connection, which has been voted the best comedy club in the country by USA Today, has a mix of local and nationally known acts seven nights a week, with two shows Friday and Saturday. The cover is $15-$29. ✉ *245 Faneuil Hall Marketplace, Quincy Market Bldg., 2nd fl., Faneuil Hall* ☎ *617/248-9700* ⊕ *www.comedyconnectionboston. com* Ⓣ *Government Center, Haymarket, State.*

★ **ImprovAsylum** features comedians who weave audience suggestions into seven weekly shows blending topical sketches with improv in shows such as "Lost in Boston" and "New Kids on the Blog." Tickets are $20; students can get a two-for-one deal for $10 apiece. ✉ *216 Hanover St., North End* ☎ *617/263-6887* ⊕ *www.improvasylum.com* Ⓣ *Haymarket, North Station.*

DANCE CLUBS

Gypsy Bar half calls to mind the decadence of a dark European castle, with rich red velvet and crystal chandeliers. Its rows of video screens broadcasting the Fashion Network, however, add a sexier, more-modern touch. Thirtysomething revelers and European students snack on lime-and-ginger-marinated tiger shrimp and sip "See You in Church" martinis (vodka with fresh marmalade) while the trendy dance floor throbs to Top 40 and house music. ✉ *116 Boylston St., Theater District* ☎ *617/482-7799* ⊕ *www.gypsybarboston.com* Ⓣ *Boylston.*

★ **The Roxy** has a spacious interior that resembles an early-20th-century ballroom, but this club is hardly sedate. It throws theme nights such as "Sexy Fridays," as well as Chippendales male reviews and Latin dance parties. Watch for occasional rock concerts with bands such as The Killers. ✉ *279 Tremont St., Theater District* 🏠*617/338-7699* ⊕*www. roxyboston.com* Ⓣ*Boylston.*

Venu brings Miami's South Beach to Boston. A warm energy distinguishes this club from the city's other dark, techno-industrial spots. The crowd is diverse—stylish international students mix with young downtown suits cutting loose on their off-hours. Local DJs spin Top 40 and international tunes. Friday offers house, Latin, and hip-hop DJs, and Saturday features Top 40, rock, and mash-ups. ✉ *100 Warrenton St., Theater District* 🕿*617/338-8061* ⊕*www.venuboston.com* Ⓣ*Boylston, Arlington.*

BLUES & R&B CLUBS

★ **The Cantab Lounge/Third Rail** hums every night with live Motown, rhythm and blues, folk, or bluegrass. The Third Rail bar, downstairs, holds poetry slams, open-mike readings, bohemia nights, and improv comedy. It's friendly and informal, with a diverse under-40 crowd. ✉ *738 Massachusetts Ave., Cambridge* 🕿*617/354-2685* ⊕*www.cantab-lounge.com* ▢*No credit cards* Ⓣ*Central.*

JAZZ CLUBS

Regattabar is host to some of the top names in jazz, including Sonny Rollins and Herbie Hancock. Tickets for shows are $15-$35. Even when there's no entertainment, the large, low-ceiling club is a pleasant (if expensive) place for a drink. ✉ *Charles Hotel, 1 Bennett St., Cambridge* 🕿*617/661-5000 or 617/395-7757* ⊕*www.regattabarjazz.com* Ⓣ*Harvard.*

★ **Ryles Jazz Club** uses soft lights, mirrors, and greenery to set the mood for first-rate jazz. The first-floor stage is one of the best places for new music and musicians. Upstairs is a dance hall staging regular tango, salsa, and merengue nights, often with lessons before the dancing starts. Ryles also holds occasional open-mike poetry slams and a Sunday jazz brunch (call for reservations). It's open nightly, with a cover charge. ✉ *212 Hampshire St., Cambridge* 🕿*617/876-9330* ⊕*www. ryles.com* Ⓣ*Bus 69, 83, or 91.*

ROCK CLUBS

★ **The Middle East Restaurant & Nightclub** manages to be both a Middle Eastern restaurant and one of the area's most eclectic rock clubs, with three rooms showcasing live local and national acts. Local phenoms the Mighty Mighty Bosstones got their start here. Music-world celebs often drop in when they're in town. There's also belly dancing, folk, jazz, and even the occasional country-tinged rock band. ✉ *472-480 Massachusetts Ave., Cambridge* 🕿*617/497-0576 or 617/864-3278* ⊕*www. mideastclub.com* Ⓣ*Central.*

Fodor'sChoice **Paradise Rock Club** is a small place known for hosting big-name talent
★ like U2, Coldplay, and local stars such as the Dresden Dolls. Two tiers of booths provide good sight lines anywhere in the club, as well as some intimate and out-of-the-way corners, and four bars quench the crowd's thirst. The 18-plus crowd varies with the shows. The newer Paradise

Lounge, next door, is a more-intimate space to experience local, often acoustic songsters, as well as literary readings and other artistic events. It serves dinner. ⊠967-969 Commonwealth Ave., Allston, Near Boston University ☎617/562-8800 or 617/562-8814 ⊕www.thedise.com Ⓣ Pleasant St.

THE ARTS

BALLET

★ **Boston Ballet,** the city's premier dance company, performs at the **Citi Performing Arts Center** (⊠ 270 Tremont St.) from October through May. In addition to a world-class repertory of classical and high-spirited modern works, it presents an elaborate signature Nutcracker during the holidays at the restored downtown Boston Opera House. ⊠19 Clarendon St., South End ☎617/695-6950 ⊕www.bostonballet.org.

José Mateo's Ballet Theatre is a troupe building an exciting, contemporary repertory under Cuban-born José Mateo, the resident artistic director-choreographer. The troupe's performances include an original Nutcracker, and take place October through April at the **Sanctuary Theatre,** a beautifully converted former church at Massachusetts Avenue and Harvard Street in Harvard Square. ⊠400 Harvard St., Cambridge ☎617/354-7467 ⊕www.ballettheatre.org.

FILM

Brattle Theatre shows classic movies, new foreign and independent films, themed series, and directors' cuts. Tickets sell out every year for its acclaimed Bogart festival, scheduled around Harvard's exam period; the Bugs Bunny Film Festival in February; and Trailer Treats, an annual fund-raiser featuring an hour or two of classic and modern movie previews in July. It also has holiday screenings such as It's a Wonderful Life at Christmas. ⊠40 Brattle St., Harvard Sq., Cambridge ☎617/876-6837 ⊕www.brattlefilm.org Ⓣ Harvard.

Harvard Film Archive screens works from its vast collection of classics and foreign films that are not usually shown at commercial cinemas. Actors and directors frequently appear to introduce newer work. The theater was created for student and faculty use, but the general public may attend regular screenings for $8 per person. ⊠Carpenter Center for the Visual Arts, 24 Quincy St., Cambridge ☎617/495-4700 ⊕www.harvardfilmarchive.org Ⓣ Harvard.

MUSIC

CONCERT   **Bank of America Pavilion** gathers up to 5,000 people on the city's water-
HALLS   front for summertime concerts. National pop, folk, and country acts
★   play the tentlike pavilion from about mid-June to mid-September. ⊠290 Northern Ave., South Boston ☎617/728-1600 ⊕www.bankof americapavilion.com Ⓣ South Station.

Berklee Performance Center, associated with Berklee College of Music, is best known for its jazz programs, but it also is host to folk performers such as Joan Baez and pop and rock stars such as Andrew Bird, Aimee Mann, and Henry Rollins. ⊠136 Massachusetts Ave., Back

Bay ☎617/747-2261 box office, 617/747-8890 recorded info ⊕www. berkleebpc.com Ⓣ Hynes/ICA.

The Boston Opera House hosts plays, musicals, and traveling Broadway shows, but also has booked diverse performers such as David Copperfield, BB King, and Pat Metheny. The occasional children's production may schedule a run here as well. ⊠ 539 Washington St., Downtown ☎617/259-3400 Ⓣ Boylston, Chinatown, Downtown Crossing, Park Street.

CONCERTS

Ⓒ ★ **Hatch Memorial Shell.** The Boston Pops perform its famous free summer concerts (including the traditional Fourth of July show, broadcast live nationwide on TV) at this wonderful acoustic shell. April through October, local radio stations also put on music shows and festivals here. The shell is on the Esplanade on the bank of the Charles River. ⊠ Off Storrow Dr., at the embankment, Beacon Hill ☎617/626-1470 or 617/626-1250 ⊕www.mass.gov/dcr/hatch_events.htm Ⓣ Charles/ MGH, Arlington.

Fodor'sChoice

★ **New England Conservatory's Jordan Hall** is one of the world's acoustic treasures, and is ideal for chamber music yet large enough to accommodate a full orchestra. The Boston Philharmonic and the Boston Baroque ensemble often perform at the relatively intimate 1,000-seat hall. ⊠ 30 Gainsborough St., Back Bay ☎617/585-1260 box office ⊕www.newenglandconservatory.edu/concerts Ⓣ Symphony.

Fodor'sChoice
★ **Symphony Hall,** one of the world's best acoustical settings—if not *the* best—is home to the Boston Symphony Orchestra (BSO) and the Boston Pops. The BSO is led by the incomparable James Levine, who's known for commissioning special works by contemporary composers, as well as for presenting innovative programs such as his two-year Beethoven/Schoenberg series. The Pops concerts, led by conductor Keith Lockhart, take place in May and June and around the winter holidays. The hall is also used by visiting orchestras, chamber groups, soloists, and many local performers. Rehearsals are sometimes open to the public, with tickets sold at a discount. ⊠ 301 Massachusetts Ave., Back Bay ☎617/266-1492, 617/266-2378 recorded info ⊕www. bostonsymphonyhall.org Ⓣ Symphony.

OPERA

Boston Lyric Opera stages four full productions each season at **Citi Performing Arts Center** (⊠ 270 Tremont St.), which usually include one 20th-century work. Recent highlights have included Puccini's *La Boheme* and Englebert Humperdinck's *Hansel and Gretel.* ☎617/542-4912, 617/542-6772 audience services office ⊕www.blo.org.

THEATER

The Huntington Theatre Company, Boston's largest resident theater company, consistently performs a high-quality mix of 20th-century plays, new works, and classics under the leadership of dynamic artistic director Nicholas Martin, and commissions artists to produce original dramas. ⊠ Boston University Theatre, 264 Huntington Ave., Back Bay

☎617/266-0800 *box office* ⊕*www.huntingtontheatre.org* ⊤*Symphony* ✉*Calderwood Theatre Pavilion, Boston Center for the Arts, 527 Tremont St., South End* ☎617/426-5000 ⊕*www.bcaonline.org* ⊤*Back Bay/South End, Copley.*

★ **American Repertory** stages experimental, classic, and contemporary plays, often with unusual lighting, stage design, or multimedia effects. Its home at the Loeb Drama Center has two theaters; the smaller also holds productions by the Harvard-Radcliffe Drama Club. A modern theater space down the street, called the Zero Arrow Theatre, has a more-flexible stage design for electrifying contemporary productions. ✉*64 Brattle St., Harvard Sq., Cambridge* ☎617/547-8300 ⊕*www.amrep.org* ⊤*Harvard.*

★ **Boston Center for the Arts** houses more than a dozen quirky, low-budget troupes in six performance areas, including the 300-seat Stanford Calderwood Pavilion, two black box theaters, and the massive Cyclorama, built to hold a 360-degree mural of the Battle of Gettysburg (the painting is now in a building at the battlefield). The experimental Pilgrim Theater, multiracial Company One, gay/lesbian Theatre Offensive, Irish-American Súgan Theatre troupe, and contemporary SpeakEasy Stage Company put on shows here year-round. ✉*539 Tremont St., South End* ☎617/426-5000 ⊕*www.bcaonline.org* ⊤*Back Bay/South End, Copley.*

Harvard's Hasty Pudding Theatricals at Harvard University calls itself the "oldest collegiate theatrical company in the United States." It produces one show annually, which plays in Boston in February and March and then goes on tour. The troupe also honors a famous actor and actress each year with an awards ceremony and a parade (in drag) through Cambridge. Recent honorees include Charlize Theron and Christopher Walken. *Harvard Square Cambridge* ☎617/495-5205 ⊕*www.hastypudding.org* ⊤*Harvard.*

SPORTS & THE OUTDOORS

Updated by Sarah Pascarella

Boston's known for its spectator sports, from rooting for home teams like the Red Sox, the New England Patriots, and the Celtics to cheering on athletes from all over the world as they run the Boston Marathon. But with its waterfront location, Beantown also has some great beaches and parks, with opportunities to bike, boat, jog, skate, and more.

NATURAL PARKS & BEACHES

Ⓒ
Fodor'sChoice
★

Comprising 34 islands, the **Boston Harbor Islands National Park Area** is somewhat of a hidden gem for nature lovers and history buffs, with miles of lightly traveled trails and shoreline and several little-visited historic sites to explore. The focal point of the national park is 39-acre Georges Island, where you'll find the partially restored pre-Civil War Fort Warren that once held Confederate prisoners. Other islands worth visiting include Peddocks Island, which holds the remains of Fort Andrews, and Lovells Island, a popular destination for campers. Lovells, Peddocks, Grape, and Bumpkin islands allow camping with a permit from late June through Labor Day. There are swimming areas at the four camping-friendly islands as well, but only Lovells has lifeguards. Pets and alcohol are not allowed on the Harbor Islands. The **National Park Service** (☎ 617/223-8666 ⊕ *www.bostonislands.com*) is a good source for information about camping, transportation, and the like. To reach the islands, take the **Harbor Express** (☎ 617/222-6999 ⊕ *www.harborexpress.com*) from Long Wharf (Downtown) or the Hingham Shipyard to Georges Island or Spectacle Island. High-speed catamarans run daily from May through mid-October and cost $14. Other islands can be reached by the free interisland water shuttles that depart from Georges Island.

As soon as the snow begins to recede, Bostonians emerge from hibernation. Runners, bikers, and in-line skaters crowd the **Charles River Reservation** (⊕ *www.mass.gov/dcr*) at the Esplanade along Storrow Drive, the Memorial Drive Embankment in Cambridge, or any of the smaller and less-busy parks farther upriver. Here you can cheer a crew race, rent a canoe or a kayak, or simply sit on the grass, sharing the shore with packs of hard jogging university athletes, in-line skaters, moms with strollers, dreamily entwined couples, and intense academics, often talking to themselves as they sort out their intellectual—or perhaps personal—dilemmas.

PARTICIPANT SPORTS

BICYCLING It's common to see suited-up doctors, lawyers, and businessmen commuting on two wheels through Downtown; unfortunately, bike lanes are few and far between. Boston's dedicated bike paths are well used, as much by joggers and in-line skaters as by bicyclists.

★ The **Dr. Paul Dudley White Bike Path,** about 17 mi long, follows both banks of the Charles River as it winds from Watertown Square to the Museum of Science. The **Pierre Lallement Bike Path** winds 5 mi through the South End and Roxbury, from Copley Place to Franklin Park. The tranquil **Minuteman Bikeway** courses 11 mi from the Alewife Red Line T station in Cambridge through Arlington, Lexington, and Bedford. The trail, in the bed of an old rail line, cuts through a few busy intersections—be particularly careful in Arlington Center. For other path locations, consult the **Department of Conservation & Recreation** (*DCR* ⊕ *www.mass.gov/dcr*) Web site.

The **Massachusetts Bicycle Coalition** (*MassBike* ✉ *171 Milk St., Suite 33, Downtown* ☎ 617/542-2453 ⊕ *www.massbike.org*), an advocacy group working to improve conditions for area cyclists, has information on organized rides and sells good bike maps of Boston and the state. Thanks to MassBike's lobbying efforts, the MBTA now allows bicycles on subway and commuter-rail trains during nonpeak hours.

Community Bicycle Supply (✉ *496 Tremont St., at E. Berkeley St., South End* ☎ 617/542-8623 ⊕ *www.communitybicycle.com*) rents cycles from April through October, at rates of $25 for 24 hours. **Back Bay Bicycles** (✉ *362 Commonwealth Ave., Back Bay* ☎ 617/247-2336 ⊕ *www.backbaybicycles.com*) has mountain bike rentals for $25 per day and

The Boston Marathon

Though it missed being the first U.S. marathon by one year (the first, in 1896, went from Stamford, Connecticut, to New York City), the Boston Marathon is arguably the nation's most prestigious. Why? It's the only marathon in the world for which runners have to qualify; it's the world's oldest continuously run marathon; it's been run on the same course since it began. Only the New York Marathon compares with it for community involvement. Spectators have returned to the same spot for generations, bringing their lawn chairs and barbecues.

Runners compete in the world's oldest, and most prestigious, marathon.

Held every Patriots' Day (the third Monday in April), the marathon passes through Hopkinton, Ashland, Framingham, Natick, Wellesley, Newton, Brookline, and Boston; only the last few miles are run in the city proper. The first marathon was organized by members of the Boston Athletic Association (BAA), who in 1896 had attended the first modern Olympic games in Athens. When they saw that the Olympics ended with a marathon, they decided the same would be a fitting end to their own Spring Sports Festival, begun in the late 1880s.

The first race was run on April 19, 1897, when Olympian Tom Burke drew a line in the dirt in Ashland and began a 24.5-mi dash to Boston with 15 men. For most of its history, the race concluded on Exeter Street outside the BAA's clubhouse. In 1965 the finish was moved to the front of the Prudential Center, and in 1986 it was moved to its current location, Copley Square. The race's guardian spirit is the indefatigable John A. Kelley, who ran his first marathon shortly after Warren G. Harding was sworn in as president. Kelley won twice—in 1935 and 1945—took the second-place spot seven times, and continued to run well into his eighties, finishing 58 Boston Marathons in all. Until his retirement in 1992, his arrival at the finish signaled the official end of the race. A double statue of an older Kelley greeting his younger self stands at the route's most strenuous incline—dubbed "Heartbreak Hill"—on Commonwealth Avenue in Newton.

Women weren't allowed to race until 1972, but in 1966 Roberta Gibb slipped into the throngs under a hooded sweatshirt; she was the first known female participant. In 1967 cameras captured BAA organizer Jock Semple screaming, "Get out of my race," as he tried to rip off the number of Kathrine Switzer, who had registered as K. Switzer. But the marathon's most infamous moment was when 26-year-old Rosie Ruiz came out of nowhere to be the first woman to cross the finish line in the 1980 race. Ruiz apparently started running less than 1 mi from the end of the course, and her title was stripped eight days later. Bostonians still quip about her taking the T to the finish.

road bikes for $35 per day. Staff members also lead group mountain bike rides on nearby trails.

BOATING Except when frozen over, the waterways coursing through the city serve as a playground for boaters of all stripes. All types of pleasure craft, with the exception of inflatables, are allowed from the Charles River and Inner Harbor to North Washington Street on the waters of Boston Harbor, Dorchester inner and outer bays, and the Neponset River from the Granite Avenue Bridge to Dorchester Bay.

Sailboats can be rented from one of the many boathouses or docks along the Charles. Downtown, public landings and float docks are available at the **Christopher Columbus Waterfront Park** (⊠ *Commercial St., Boston Harbor, North End* ☎ *617/635-4505*) with a permit from the Boston harbormaster. Along the Charles, **boat drop sites** are at **Clarendon Street** (⊠ *Back Bay*); the **Hatch Shell** (⊠ *Embankment Rd., Back Bay*); **Pinckney Street Landing** (⊠ *Back Bay*); **Brooks Street** (⊠ *Nonantum Rd., Brighton*); **Richard T. Artesani Playground** (⊠ *Off Soldiers Field Rd., Brighton*); **Charles River Dam, Museum of Science** (⊠ *Cambridge*); and **Watertown Square** (⊠ *Charles River Road, Watertown*).

The **Charles River Watershed Association** (☎ *781/788-0007* ⊕ *www. charlesriver.org*) publishes a 32-page canoe and kayaking guide with detailed boating information.

SPECTATOR SPORTS

Fodor'sChoice Hide your Yankees cap and practice pronouncing "Fenway Pahk."
★ Boston is a baseball town, where the crucible of media scrutiny burns hot, fans regard myth and superstition as seriously as player statistics, and grudges are never forgotten. The **Boston Red Sox** (⊠ *Fenway Park, The Fenway* ☎ *617/482-4769* ⊕ *www.bostonredsox.com*) made history in 2004, crushing the Yankees in the American League Championship after a three-game deficit and then sweeping the Cardinals in the World Series for their first title since 1918. More than 3 million fans from "Red Sox Nation" celebrated the championship team and the reversal of the "Curse of the Bambino" with a victory parade through the streets of Boston and down the Charles River. And as icing on the cake, they did it again in 2007, this time defeating the Colorado Rockies in another historic sweep. The Red Sox ownership has committed to staying in the once-threatened Fenway Park for the long term, so you can still watch a game in the country's oldest active ballpark and see (or, for a premium price, get a seat on top of) the fabled "Green Monster" (the park's 37-foot-high left-field wall) and one of the last hand-operated scoreboards in the major leagues. Baseball season runs from early April to early October. The play-offs continue several more weeks, and postseason buzz about contracts, trades, and injuries lasts all winter long.

DID YOU KNOW? **The longest measurable home run hit inside Fenway Park—502 feet—was batted by legendary Red Sox slugger Ted Williams on June 9, 1946. A lone red seat in the right-field bleachers marks the spot where the ball landed.**

★ The **Boston Celtics** (✉ *TD Banknorth Garden, Old West End* ☎ *617/624-1000, 617/931-2222 Ticketmaster* ⊕ *www.celtics.com*) have won the National Basketball Association (NBA) championship 17 times since 1957, more than any other franchise in the NBA. Until its 4–2 series victory over the L.A. Lakers in June 2008, the team hadn't won the championship since 1986. With the addition of Kevin Garnett to the team, the city's excitement toward basketball has gotten a much-needed jolt. Basketball season runs from October to April, and play-offs last until mid-June.

FOOTBALL   Since 2002, Boston has been building a football dynasty, starting with the **New England Patriots** (✉ *Gillette Stadium, Rte. 1, off I-95 Exit 9, Foxborough* ☎ *617/931-2222 Ticketmaster* ⊕ *www.patriots.com*) come-from-behind Super Bowl victory against the favored St. Louis Rams. Coach Bill Belichick and heartthrob quarterback Tom Brady then brought the team two more Super Bowl rings, in 2004 and 2005, and have made Patriots fans as zealous as their baseball counterparts. The team's heartbreaking Super Bowl loss in 2008 has only increased fan fervor for coming seasons. Exhibition football games begin in August, and the season runs through the play-offs in January. The state-of-the-art Gillette Stadium is in Foxborough, 30 mi southwest of Boston.

HOCKEY   The **Boston Bruins** (✉ *TD Banknorth Garden, 100 Legends Way, Old West End* ☎ *617/624-1000, 617/931-2222 Ticketmaster* ⊕ *www.bostonbruins.com*) are on the ice from September until April, frequently on Thursday and Saturday evenings. Play-offs last through early June.

Boston College, Boston University, Harvard, and Northeastern teams face off every February in the **Beanpot Hockey Tournament** (☎ *617/624-1000*) at the TD Banknorth Garden. The colleges in this fiercely contested tournament traditionally yield some of the finest squads in the country.

RUNNING   Every Patriots' Day (the third Monday in April), fans gather along the
Fodor's Choice   Hopkinton-to-Boston route of the **Boston Marathon** (⇨ box) to cheer on
★   more than 20,000 runners from all over the world. The race ends near Copley Square in the Back Bay. For information, call the **Boston Athletic Association** (☎ *617/236-1652* ⊕ *www.bostonmarathon.org*).

SHOPPING

By Erin Byers Murray   Boston's shops are generally open Monday through Saturday from 10 or 11 until 6 or 7 and Sunday noon to 5. Many stay open until 8 PM one night a week, usually Thursday. Malls are open Monday through Saturday from 9 or 10 until 8 or 9 and Sunday noon to 6. Most stores accept major credit cards and traveler's checks. There's no state sales tax on clothing. However, there's a 5% luxury tax on clothes priced higher than $175 per item; the tax is levied on the amount in excess of $175.

MAJOR SHOPPING DISTRICTS

1

Boston's shops and department stores are concentrated in the area bounded by Quincy Market, the Back Bay, and Downtown. There are plenty of bargains in the Downtown Crossing area. The South End's gentrification creates its own kind of consumerist milieus, from housewares shops to avant-garde art galleries. In Cambridge you can find lots of shopping around Harvard and Central squares, with independent boutiques migrating west along Massachusetts Avenue (or Mass Ave., as the locals and almost everyone else calls it) toward Porter Square and beyond.

BOSTON

Pretty **Charles Street** is crammed beginning to end with top-notch antiques stores such as Judith Dowling Asian Art, Eugene Galleries, and Devonia as well as a handful of independently owned fashion boutiques whose prices reflect their high Beacon Hill rents. River Street, parallel to Charles Street, is also an excellent source for antiques. Both are easy walks from the Charles Street T stop on the Red Line.

Copley Place (⊠ *100 Huntington Ave., Back Bay* ☎ *617/369-5000* T *Copley*), an indoor shopping mall in the Back Bay, includes such high-end shops as Christian Dior, Louis Vuitton, and Gucci, anchored by the pricey but dependable Neiman Marcus and the flashy, over-priced Barneys. A skywalk connects Copley Place to the **Prudential Center** (⊠ *800 Boylston St., Back Bay* ☎ *800/746-7778* T *Copley, Prudential Center*). The Pru, as it's often called, contains moderately priced chain stores such as Ann Taylor and the Body Shop.

Downtown Crossing (⊠ *Washington St. from Amory St. to about Milk St., Downtown* T *Downtown Crossing, Park St.*) is a pedestrian mall with a Macy's, the famous Filene's Basement in a new, temporary location until 2009, and a handful of decent outlets. Millennium Place, a 1.8-million-square-foot complex with a Ritz-Carlton Hotel, condos, a massive sports club, a 19-screen Loews Cineplex, and a few upscale retail stores, seems to be transforming the area, as promised, from a slightly seedy hangout to the newest happening spot.

Faneuil Hall Marketplace (⊠ *Bounded by Congress St., Atlantic Ave., the Waterfront, and Government Center, Downtown* ☎ *617/338-2323* T *Government Center*) is a huge complex that's also hugely popular, even though most of its independent shops have given way to Banana Republic, the Disney Store, and other chains. The place has plenty of history, one of the area's great à la carte casual dining experiences (Quincy Market), and carnival-like trappings: pushcarts sell everything from silver jewelry to Peruvian sweaters, and buskers carry out crowd-pleasing feats such as balancing wheelbarrows on their heads.

★ **Newbury Street** (T *Arlington, Copley, Hynes/ICA*) is Boston's version of New York's 5th Avenue. The entire street is a shoppers' paradise, from high-end names such as Brooks Brothers to tiny specialty boutiques such as Diptyque. Upscale clothing stores, up-to-the-minute art galleries, and dazzling jewelers line the street near the Public Garden.

As you head toward Mass Ave., Newbury gets funkier and the cacophony builds, with skateboarders zipping through traffic and garbage-pail drummers burning licks outside the hip boutiques. The best stores run from Arlington Street to the Prudential Center. Parallel to Newbury Street is **Boylston Street,** where a few standouts, such as Shreve, Crump & Low, are tucked among the other chains and restaurants.

South End (Ⓣ *Back Bay/South End*) merchants are benefiting from the ongoing gentrification that has brought high real-estate prices and trendy restaurants to the area. Explore the chic home-furnishings and gift shops that line Tremont Street, starting at Berkeley Street. The MBTA's Silver Line bus runs through the South End.

CAMBRIDGE

CambridgeSide Galleria (✉*100 CambridgeSide Pl., Kendall Sq.* ☎*617/ 621-8666* Ⓣ *Lechmere, Kendall/MIT via shuttle*) is a basic three-story mall with a food court. Macy's makes it a good stop for appliances and other basics; it's a big draw for local high-school kids.

Central Square (✉*East of Harvard Sq.* Ⓣ *Central*) has an eclectic mix of furniture stores, used-record shops, ethnic restaurants, and small, hip performance venues.

Harvard Square (Ⓣ *Harvard*) takes up just a few blocks but holds more than 150 stores selling clothes, books, records, furnishings, and specialty items.

The Galleria (✉*57 JFK St.* Ⓣ *Harvard*) has various boutiques and a few decent, independently owned restaurants. A handful of chains and independent boutiques are clustered in **Brattle Square** (✉*Behind Harvard Sq.* Ⓣ *Harvard*).

Porter Square (✉*West on Mass Ave. from Harvard Sq.* Ⓣ *Porter*) has distinctive clothing stores, as well as crafts shops, coffee shops, natural-food stores, restaurants, and bars with live music.

DEPARTMENT STORES

★ The hoopla generated by the arrival of **Barneys New York** (✉*100 Huntington Ave., Back Bay* ☎*617/385-3300* Ⓣ *Copley*) was surprising in a city where everything new is viewed with trepidation. But clearly Boston's denizens have embraced the lofty, two-story space because it's filled with cutting-edge lines like Comme des Garçons and Nina Ricci, as well as a few bargains in the second-level Co-op section. **Lord & Taylor** (✉*760 Boylston St., Back Bay* ☎*617/262-6000* Ⓣ *Prudential Center*) is a reliable, if somewhat overstuffed with merchandise, stop for classic clothing by such designers as Anne Klein and Ralph Lauren, along with accessories, cosmetics, and jewelry. At **Macy's** (✉*450 Washington St., Downtown* ☎*617/357-3000* Ⓣ *Downtown Crossing*) three floors offer men's and women's clothing and shoes, housewares, and cosmetics. Although top designers and a fur salon are part of the mix, Macy's doesn't feel exclusive; instead, it's a popular source for family basics.

1

Neiman Marcus (✉ *5 Copley Pl., Back Bay* ☎ *617/536-3660* Ⓣ *Back Bay/South End*), the flashy Texas-based retailer known to many as "Needless Markup," has three levels of swank designers such as Gaultier, Gucci, Ferragamo, and Calvin Klein, as well as cosmetics and housewares. The clothing and accessories at **Saks Fifth Avenue** (✉ *Prudential Center, 1 Ring Rd., Back Bay* ☎ *617/262-8500* Ⓣ *Prudential Center*) runs from the traditional to the flamboyant. It's a little pricey, but an excellent place to find high-quality merchandise, including shoes and cosmetics.

SPECIALTY STORES

ANTIQUES

Newbury Street and the South End have some excellent (and expensive) antiques stores, but Charles Street—coincidentally, one of the city's oldest streets—is the place to go for a concentrated selection.

★ Come to **Autrefois Antiques** (✉ *130 Harvard St., Brookline* ☎ *617/566-0113* Ⓣ *Coolidge Corner*) to find French country and Italian 18th-, 19th-, and 20th-century furniture, mirrors, and lighting. A flea market–style collection of dealers occupies two floors at **Boston Antique Co-op** (✉ *119 Charles St., Beacon Hill* ☎ *617/227-9810 or 617/227-9811* Ⓣ *Charles/MGH*), containing everything from vintage photos and paintings to porcelain, silver, bronzes, and furniture. **Cambridge Antique Market** (✉ *201 Monsignor O'Brien Hwy., Cambridge* ☎ *617/868-9655* Ⓣ *Lechmere*) may be off the beaten track, but it has a selection bordering on overwhelming: five floors of goods ranging from 19th-century furniture to vintage clothing, much of it reasonably priced. There are two parking lots next to the building.

BOOKS

If Boston and Cambridge have bragging rights to anything, it's their independent bookstores, many of which stay open late and sponsor author readings and literary programs.

The rare and wonderful books on display at **Ars Libri Ltd.** (✉ *500 Harrison Ave., South End* ☎ *617/357-5212* Ⓣ *New England Medical Center*) make it easy to be drawn in. The airy space is filled with books on photography and architecture, out-of-print art books, monographs, and exhibition catalogs.

☺ Don't come looking for the same old kids' books at **Barefoot Books**

Fodor's Choice (✉ *1771 Massachusetts Ave., Cambridge* ☎ *617/349-1610* Ⓣ *Porter*);

★ Barefoot is full of beautifully illustrated, creatively told reading for kids of all ages—these are the kind of books that kids remember and keep as adults. The late George Gloss built **Brattle Bookshop** (✉ *9 West St., Downtown* ☎ *617/542-0210 or 800/447-9595* Ⓣ *Downtown Crossing*) into Boston's best used- and rare-book shop. Today, his son Kenneth fields queries from passionate book lovers. If the book you want is out of print, Brattle has it or can probably find it.

★ The intellectual community is well served at **Harvard Book Store** (✉ *1256 Massachusetts Ave., Cambridge* ☎ *617/661-1515* Ⓣ *Harvard*), with a slew of new titles upstairs, and used and remaindered books downstairs. The collection's diversity has made the store a frequent destination for academics. At **Trident Booksellers & Café** (✉ *338 Newbury St., Back Bay* ☎ *617/267-8688* Ⓣ *Hynes/ICA*) browse through an eclectic collection of books, tapes, and magazines; then settle in with a snack. It's open until midnight daily, making it a favorite with students.

CLOTHING & SHOES

The terminally chic shop on Newbury Street, the hip hang in Harvard Square, and everyone goes Downtown for the real bargains.

★ Satisfying the Euro crowd, **Alan Bilzerian** (✉ *34 Newbury St., Back Bay* ☎ *617/536-1001* Ⓣ *Arlington*) sells luxe men's and women's clothing by such fashion darlings as Yohji Yamamoto and Ann Demeulemeester. The simple, sophisticated designs at **Anne Fontaine** (✉ *318 Boylston St., Back Bay* ☎ *617/423-0366* Ⓣ *Arlington, Boylston*) are mostly executed in cotton and priced around $160. You can never have too many white shirts—especially if they're designed by this Parisienne.

Ms. Jenney herself is likely to wait on you in the small, personal **Betsy Jenney** (✉ *114 Newbury St., Back Bay* ☎ *617/536-2610* Ⓣ *Copley*) store, where the well-made, comfortable lines are for women who cannot walk into a fitted size-4 suit—in other words, most of the female population. The designers found here, such as Philippe Adec, Teenflo, and Nicole Miller, are fashionable yet forgiving. The women's and children's clothing at **Calypso** (✉ *115 Newbury St., Back Bay* ☎ *617/421-1887* Ⓣ *Copley*) bursts with bright colors, beautiful fabrics, and styles so fresh you might need a fashion editor to help you choose.

Fodor's Choice

★ Local designer **Daniela Corte** (✉ *91 Newbury St., Back Bay* ☎ *617/262-2100* Ⓣ *Copley*) cuts women's clothes that flatter from her sunny Back Bay studio. Look for gorgeous suiting, flirty halter dresses, and sophisticated formal frocks that can be bought off the rack or custom tailored. Drop by Copley's sassy little boutique **Grettaluxe** (✉ *Copley Place, 100 Huntington Ave., Back Bay* ☎ *617/266-6166* Ⓣ *Copley*) and pick up the latest "it" pieces—from velour hoodies by Juicy Couture to the must-have Stella McCartney design du moment. There's also jewelry, handbags, and other accessories.

Fodor's Choice

★ Impeccably tailored designs, subtly updated classics, and the latest Italian styles highlight a wide selection of imported clothing and accessories at **Louis Boston** (✉ *234 Berkeley St., Back Bay* ☎ *617/262-6100* Ⓣ *Arlington*). Visiting celebrities might be trolling the racks along with you as jazz spills out into the street from the adjoining Restaurant L.

GIFTS

It's Howdy Doody time at **Buckaroo's Mercantile** (✉ *5 Brookline St., Cambridge* ☎ *617/492-4792* Ⓣ *Central*)—a great destination for the kitsch inclined. Find pink poodle skirts, lunch-box clocks, Barbie lamps, *Front Page Detective* posters, and everything Elvis.

★ The venerable Paris house **Diptyque** (✉ *123 Newbury St., Back Bay* ☎ *617/351-2430* Ⓣ *Copley*) has its flagship U.S. store right here on Newbury Street. The hand-poured candles, room sprays, and gender-neutral eau de toilettes are expensive, but each is like a little work of art—and just entering the calmly inviting store is like having a mini aromatherapy session. At **The Flat of the Hill** (✉ *60 Charles St., Beacon Hill* ☎*617/619-9977* Ⓣ *Charles/MGH*) There's nothing flat about this fun collection of seasonal items, toiletries, toys, pillows, and whatever else catches the fancy of the shop's young owner. Her passion for pets is evident—pick up a Fetch & Glow ball and your dog will never again have to wait until daytime to play in the park.

★ While browsing at **Fresh** (✉ *121 Newbury St., Back Bay* ☎*617/421-1212* Ⓣ*Copley*) you won't know whether to wash with these soaps or nibble on them. The shea-butter-rich bars come in such scents as clove hazelnut and orange-cranberry. They cost $6 to $7 each, but they carry the scent to the end.

WHERE TO EAT

Updated by
Erin Murray

When it comes to food, in Boston the Revolution never ended. While Bostonians have proudly clung to their traditional eats (chowders, baked beans, and cream pies can still be found), most diners now choose innovative food without excessive formality. There are still palaces of grand cuisine, but Boston and Cambridge now favor the kind of restaurant overseen by a creative mastermind, often locally born, concocting inspired food served in human surroundings.

Bostonians have caught the passion for artisanal breads, cafés with homemade pastries, and all manner of exquisite and unique specialties. As an example, many high-end restaurants have added uncommon flavors of ice cream—central to Boston living for more than 150 years—to their menus. A young generation of highly trained and well-traveled chefs is reclaiming the regional cuisine. It turns out that the area's wild mushrooms work in a ragout, the cheddar makes a fine quiche, the clambake can be miniaturized, and rabbit fits into a savory ravioli.

A rule of thumb is to seek out what the locals most enjoy—the fish and shellfish abundant from the nearby shores. Although the city has many notable seafood restaurants, almost anyplace you eat will likely have two or three offerings from the sea. Treatments used to be limited to lobsters boiled or baked and fish broiled or fried, but nowadays chefs are more inventive. You may be offered a wood-roasted lobster with vanilla sauce or, in a Chinese restaurant, lobster stir-fried with ginger and scallion. Others are pushing scallops sliced thin and served raw under a dab of olive oil and chickpea puree.

Anything spicy and different has long been popular in the university culture of Cambridge, and the high rate of immigration in recent decades has fueled Bostonians' appetite for foreign cuisines. Variety abounds, evoking the bygone aristocracies of Russia, Persia, Thailand, Ethiopia, or Cambodia, or serving large immigrant communities from Latin America, Asia, Europe, and Africa. In the last few years, an influx of Italian restaurants, both traditional and contemporary, has landed on city corners outside the North End.

The dominant trend today, however, is homegrown—both on the plate and in the kitchen. Because most of Boston's talented chefs have worked their way up the ranks in local kitchens, they prefer to sponsor and cultivate their sous-chefs rather than hire anonymous talent. And while a handful of local chefs have garnered celebrity status, the city has yet to draw (some might say invite) big-name, nationally known chefs into its tight-knit circle.

To find the best around Boston—gustatorily speaking—follow the roads that radiate out from Downtown like the spokes of a giant wheel. Smack inside the hub are the huge, and hugely famous, waterfront seafood restaurants—but go north, west, or south and you're suddenly in the neighborhoods, home to numerous smaller restaurants on the way up.

WHAT IT COSTS				
¢	$	$$	$$$	$$$$
RESTAU-RANTS	under $8	$8–$14	$15–$24	$25–$32	over $32
HOTELS	under $75	$75–$150	$151–$225	$226–$325	over $325

For restaurants, prices are per person, for a main course at dinner. For hotels, prices are for two people in a standard double room in high season, excluding 12.45% tax and service charges.

BEST BEST FOR BOSTON & CAMBRIDGE DINING

With thousands of restaurants to choose from, how will you decide where to eat? Fodor's writers and editors have selected their favorite restaurants by price, cuisine, and experience in the Best Bets lists below. In the first column, Fodor's Choice designations represent the "best of the best" in every price category. You can also search by neighborhood for excellent eats—just peruse the following pages. Or find specific details about a restaurant in the full reviews, listed alphabetically later in the chapter.

Fodor's Choice ★

Chez Henri, Cambridge $$-$$$

Clio $$$$

East Coast Grill and Raw Bar, Cambridge $$

Eastern Standard, Back Bay (Kenmore Sq.) $$

Excelsior, Back Bay $$$$

L'Espalier, Back Bay $$$$

No. 9 Park, Beacon Hill $$$$

Oleana, Cambridge $$-$$$

Pigalle, Back Bay $$$$

Radius, Downtown $$$-$$$$

Toro, Bay Back/South End $$-$$$

By Price

¢

Barking Crab Restaurant, Downtown (Waterfront)

Wagamama, Government Center (Faneuil Hall), Harvard Square

$

Ginza, Downtown (Chinatown)

Pomodoro, North End

$$

Bricco, North End

Lala Rokh, Beacon Hill

$$$

Les Zygomates, Downtown

Neptune Oyster, North End

Olives, Charlestown

Sel de la Terre, Downtown

$$$$

Aujourd'hui, Back Bay

Grill 23 & Bar, Back Bay

By Cuisine

ASIAN

Ginza, Downtown (Chinatown) $-$$

Wagamama, Government Center (Faneuil Hall), Harvard Square ¢-$

MEDITERRANEAN

Oleana, Cambridge $$-$$$

Olives, Charlestown $$-$$$

SEAFOOD

Legal Sea Foods, Back Bay $$-$$$

STEAKHOUSE

Grill 23 and Bar, Back Bay/South End $$$$

By Experience

BREAKFAST

Aujourd'hui, Back Bay $$$$

Clio, Back Bay $$$$

CHILD-FRIENDLY

Full Moon, Cambridge, $-$$

Legal Sea Foods, Back Bay $$-$$$

HISTORIC INTEREST

Durgin Park Market Dining Room $

Union Oyster House, Government Center $$-$$$

HOTEL DINING

Meritage $$$

Nine Zero, Downtown $$$$

BACK BAY & SOUTH END

$$$$
FRENCH

✕**Aujourd'hui.** This culinary landmark is elaborate and formal—one of a few remaining palaces of elegance in town. There are New England touches but the entire space sports a Continental (and specifically French) vibe. Discreetly located on the second floor of the Four Seasons hotel, Aujourd'hui is a magnet for the city's power brokers and well-heeled travelers who cozy up to the renovated bar and lounge, which serves tasty martinis year-round. The food reflects an inventive approach to regional ingredients and New American cuisine. Some entrées, such as beef strip loin with foie gras or roasted striped bass over crispy veal sweetbreads can be extremely rich, but the menu also offers several solid vegetarian options. Window tables overlook the Public Garden. ⊠ *Four Seasons, 200 Boylston St., Back Bay* ☎ *617/351-2071* ⚞ *Reservations essential* ☰ *AE, D, DC, MC, V* Ⓣ *Arlington.*

$$$$
Fodor's Choice
★
FRENCH

✕**Clio.** Years ago when Ken Oringer opened his snazzy leopard skin-lined hot spot in the tasteful boutique Eliot Hotel, the hordes were fighting over reservations. Things have quieted down since then, but the food hasn't. Luxury ingredients pack the menu, from foie gras and tiny eels called elvers to the octopus sashimi and Kobe beef Oringer serves at Uni, the small but adventurous sushi bar set up in a side room off the main dining room. A magnet for romantics and foodies alike, the place continues to serve some of the city's most decadent and well-crafted meals. ⊠ *Eliot Hotel, 370 Commonwealth Ave., Back Bay* ☎ *617/536-7200* ⚞ *Reservations essential* ☰ *AE, D, MC, V* Ⓣ *Hynes/ICA.*

$$
Fodor's Choice
★
AMERICAN

✕**Eastern Standard Kitchen and Drinks.** A vivid red awning beckons those entering this spacious brasserie-style restaurant. The bar area and red banquettes are filled most nights with Boston's power players (members of the Red Sox management are known to stop in), thirty-somethings, and students from the nearby universities all noshing on raw-bar specialties and comfort dishes such as veal schnitzel, rib eye, and burgers. The cocktail list is one of the best in town, filled with old classics and new concoctions. ⊠ *528 Commonwealth Ave., Kenmore Sq.* ☎ *617/532-9100* ☰ *AE, D, DC, MC, V* Ⓣ *Kenmore.*

$$$$
Fodor's Choice
★
AMERICAN

✕**Excelsior.** Here, at the cream of Boston's culinary crop, Chef Eric Brennan uses his gift for creating exquisite handcrafted American cuisine. His innovative use of fresh local seafood and luxury ingredients serves him well here, especially with his selection of raw-bar items and entrées like black-cumin-rubbed duck breast and Maine lobster-tail "schnitzel." Try to finagle a seat near the windows on the second floor for a terrific view of the Public Garden or snag a seat at the bar for one of the incomparable lobster pizzas and a hand-muddled *bajito* (made with rum, sugar, and basil). ⊠ *272 Boylston St., Back Bay* ☎ *617/426-7878* ⚞ *Reservations essential* ☰ *AE, D, DC, MC, V* Ⓣ *Arlington.*

★ **$$$$**
STEAK

✕**Grill 23 & Bar.** Dark paneling, Persian rugs, waiters in white jackets, and patrons in power suits, give this steak house a posh demeanor. The food is anything but predictable, with dishes such as prime steak tartar with a shallot marmalade and weekly cuts of beef like the flat-iron steak or the Berkeley, a 16-ounce ribeye. Seafood specialties such as spice-crusted salmon give beef sales a run for their money. Chef Jay

Murray gets his beef supply from organic and all-natural farms. Desserts, such as the wonderful apple-blackberry potpie and the sticky toffee pudding, are far above those of the average steak house. ⊠*161 Berkeley St., Back Bay* ☎*617/542-2255* ⚲*Reservations essential* ⊟*AE, D, DC, MC, V* ⊗*No lunch* Ⓣ *Back Bay/South End.*

$$-$$$ ✗**Legal Sea Foods.** What began as a tiny restaurant upstairs over a Cambridge fish market has grown to important regional status, with more than 20 East Coast locations (including several in Boston and two in Cambridge), plus a handful of national ones. The hallmark is the freshest possible seafood, whether you have it wood grilled, in New England chowder, or doused with an Asia-inspired sauce. The smoked-bluefish pâté is delectable, and the clam chowder is so good it has become a menu staple at presidential inaugurations. View the chain's Web site (⊕*www.legalseafoods.com*) for various venues and to make online reservations. The Theater District location (just south of the Public Garden) has private dining inside its beautiful, bottle-lined wine cellar. ⊠*26 Park Sq., Back Bay* ☎*617/426-4444* ⊟*AE, D, DC, MC, V* Ⓣ *Arlington.*

SEAFOOD

$$$$ ✗**L'Espalier.** From sole with black truffles to foie gras with quince, chef-owner Frank McClelland's masterpieces are every bit as impeccable and elegant as the dining room in which they are served. You can skip the opulent menu by choosing a prix-fixe tasting, such as the innovative and flat-out fabulous vegetarian degustation, or try the Saturday-afternoon tea, one of the city's hidden treasures, for bite-size sandwiches with flair. With two fireplaces and subtle decor in earthy colors, this is known as one of Boston's most romantic places, with consistently reliable service and cuisine. ⊠*30 Gloucester St, Back Bay* ☎*617/262-3023* ⚲*Reservations essential* ⊟*AE, D, DC, MC, V* ⊗*Closed Sun. No lunch* Ⓣ *Hynes/ICA.*

Fodor'sChoice
★
FRENCH

$$$ ✗**Pigalle.** A quaint, 20-table spot, Pigalle is a romantic destination to hit before taking in a show in the neighboring Theater District. Chef Marc Orfaly spices up basic French fare (steak frites, cassoulet) by throwing in the occasional Asian-inspired special. He plays around with global flavors so don't be alarmed to find spicy Szechuan pork on the nightly specials. For a delicious, cozy meal, this spot consistently has some of the best service in town. ⊠*75 Charles St. S, Back Bay* ☎*617/423-4944* ⚲*Reservations essential* ⊟*AE, D, DC, MC, V* ⊗*No lunch* Ⓣ *Arlington.*

Fodor'sChoice
★
FRENCH

$$-$$$ ✗**Toro.** The buzz from chef Ken Oringer's tapas joint still hasn't quieted down—for good reason. Small plates of saffron-and-garlic shrimp and crusty bread smothered in tomato paste are hefty enough to make a meal out of many, or share the regular or vegetarian paella with a group. An all-Spanish wine list complements the plates. Crowds have been known to wait it out for more than an hour. ⊠*1704 Washington St., Bay Back/South End* ☎*617/536-4300* ⚲*Reservations not accepted* ⊟*AE, D, MC, V* Ⓣ *Massachusetts Ave.*

Fodor'sChoice
★
SPANISH

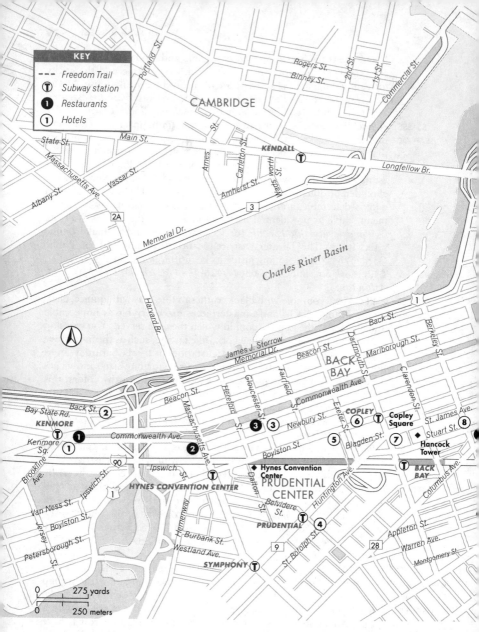

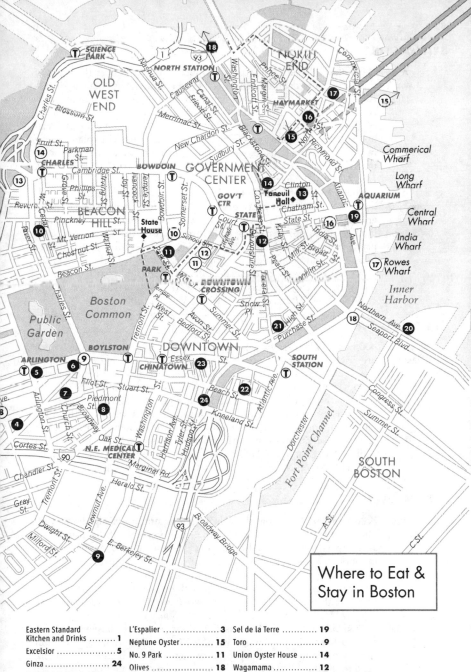

Where to Eat & Stay in Boston

BEACON HILL

★ $$ ✕ **Lala Rokh.** Persian miniatures and medieval maps cover the walls of
MIDDLE   this beautifully detailed fantasy of food and art. The focus is on the
EASTERN   Azerbaijanian corner of what is now northwest Iran, including exoti-
cally flavored specialties and dishes such as familiar (and superb here)
eggplant puree, pilaf, kebabs, *fesanjoon* (the classic pomegranate-wal-
nut sauce), and lamb stews. The staff obviously enjoys explaining the
menu, and the wine list is well selected for foods that often defy wine
matches. ✉*97 Mt. Vernon St., Beacon Hill* ☎*617/720-5511* ▤*AE,
DC, MC, V* Ⓣ *Charles/MGH.*

$$$$ ✕ **No. 9 Park.** Chef Barbara Lynch's stellar cuisine draws plenty of well-
Fodor'sChoice   deserved attention from its place in the shadow of the State House's
★   golden dome. Settle into the plush but unpretentious dining room and
CONTINENTAL   indulge in pumpkin risotto with rare lamb or the memorably rich
prune-stuffed gnocchi drizzled with bits of foie gras. The wine list
bobs and weaves into new territory but is always well chosen and the
savvy bartenders are of the classic ilk, so you'll find plenty of classics
and very few cloying, dessertlike sips here. ✉*9 Park St., Beacon Hill*
☎*617/742-9991* ▤*AE, D, DC, MC, V* Ⓣ *Park St.*

CHARLESTOWN

★ $$-$$$ ✕ **Olives.** No longer will you see chef Todd English tending the wood-
MEDITERRANEAN   fire brick oven here—these days he's too busy watching over his many
restaurants in New York and elsewhere. But don't worry, English's
recipes are in good hands. Witness smart signature offerings such as
the signature Olives tart with caramelized onions and goat cheese, or
a number of wood-grilled fish and meat dishes. A view into the open
kitchen and noisy dining room only add to the excitement. If you can't
secure a reservation, come early or late or be prepared for an extended
wait. ✉*10 City Sq., Charlestown* ☎*617/242-1999* ▤*AE, D, DC,
MC, V* ✪*No lunch* Ⓣ *Community College.*

DOWNTOWN

¢-$$ ✕ **Barking Crab Restaurant.** It is, believe it or not, a seaside clam shack
SEAFOOD   plunk in the middle of Boston, with a stunning view of the downtown
skyscrapers. An outdoor lobster tent in summer, in winter it retreats
indoors to a warmhearted version of a waterfront dive, with chest-
nuts roasting on a cozy woodstove. Look for the classic New England
clambake—chowder, lobster, steamed clams, corn on the cob—or the
spicier crab boil. ✉*88 Sleeper St., Northern Ave. Bridge, Waterfront*
☎*617/426-2722* ▤*AE, DC, MC, V* Ⓣ *South Station.*

$$-$$$ ✕ **Chau Chow City.** Spread across three floors, this is the largest, glitziest,
CHINESE   and most versatile production yet of the Chau Chow dynasty, with dim
sum by day and live-tank seafood by night. Overwhelmed? At lunch,
head to the third floor for dim sum. Or sit on the main floor and order
the clams in black-bean sauce, the sautéed pea-pod stems with garlic,
or the honey-glazed shrimp with walnuts. ✉*83 Essex St., Chinatown*
☎*617/338-8158* ▤*AE, D, MC, V* Ⓣ *Chinatown.*

★ $-$$
JAPANESE
✕**Ginza.** One of Chinatown's best restaurants—and one of Boston's best sushi spots—turns out a remarkably fresh and creative raw-fish menu. The *kmeeks* maki is a roll of crab-stick tempura, grilled eel, cucumber, avocado, and roe. For something equally fresh but much simpler, opt for the sashimi appetizer—small, gleaming slabs of maguro (bluefin) tuna, salmon, and yellowtail. Cooked foods are also available, but sushi is the real star. Late night, the room feels even more like Tokyo: waitresses in kimonos flit from the sushi bar

> **GREET THE CHEF**
>
> Eating out is considered an event in Boston, and—true to their natures—Bostonians have strong opinions on the subject, which they like to share with their restaurateurs. Everything from menus to mood lighting is open to debate. So if you've had a particularly satisfying gastronomic experience, ask to meet the chef. Chances are that he or she will gladly visit your table.

to tables at top speed, and Japanese-American club kids table-hop and flirt. There's another location in Brookline (⇨*below*). ✉16 Hudson St., Chinatown ☎617/338-2261 ☐AE, DC, MC, V Ⓣ Chinatown.

★ $$-$$$
FRENCH
✕**Les Zygomates.** *Les zygomates* is the French expression for the muscles on the human face that make you smile—and this combination wine bar-bistro inarguably lives up to its name, with quintessential French bistro fare that is both simple (made with a number of New England sourced ingredients) and simply delicious. The menu beautifully matches the ever-changing wine list, with all wines served by the 2-ounce taste, 6-ounce glass, or bottle. Prix-fixe menus are available at lunch and dinner, and could include oysters by the half dozen or seared duck breast with pomegranate jus and wild rice. There's live jazz several nights a week. ✉*129 South St., Downtown* ☎*617/542-5108* ⚠*Reservations essential* ☐*AE, D, DC, MC, V* ◷*Closed Sun. No lunch Sat.* Ⓣ *South Station.*

$$$-$$$$
FRENCH
Fodor's Choice
★
✕**Radius.** Acclaimed chef Michael Schlow's notable contemporary French cooking lures scores of designer-and-suit clad diners to the Financial District. The decor and menu are minimalist at first glance, but closer inspection reveals equal shares of luxury, complexity, and whimsy. Peruse the menu in the dining room for such choices as roasted beet salad, a selection of ceviches, buttery Scottish salmon, or coconut panna cotta (cooked cream) for dessert. At the bar they serve a phenomenal (and award-winning) burger. Either way, it's a meal made for special occasions and business dinners alike. ✉8 *High St., Downtown* ☎*617/426-1234* ⚠*Reservations essential* ☐*AE, DC, MC, V* Ⓣ *South Station.*

★ $$$
FRENCH
✕**Sel de la Terre.** Sitting between the waterfront and what used to be the Central Artery, this is a hot spot to hit before the theater, after sightseeing, or for a simple lunch Downtown. The rustic, country-French menu is brilliantly priced so that all entrées cost the same. Dinner mates can choose between braised beef short ribs with rosemary-infused mashed potatoes or a hazelnut-crusted rack of lamb. Stop by the *boulangerie* (bread shop) to take home fresh, homemade loaves, which are some

of the best in the city. ⊠*255 State St., Downtown* ☎*617/227-1579* ⌖*Reservations essential* ▤*AE, D, DC, MC, V* Ⓣ *Aquarium.*

GOVERNMENT CENTER/FANEUIL HALL

$
AMERICAN
✗ **Durgin Park Market Dining Room.** You should be hungry enough to cope with enormous portions, yet not so hungry you can't tolerate a long wait (or sharing a table with others). Durgin Park was serving its same hearty New England fare (Indian pudding, baked beans, corned beef and cabbage, and a prime rib that hangs over the edge of the plate) back when Faneuil Hall was a working market instead of a tourist attraction. The service is as brusque as it was when fishmongers and boat captains dined here. ⊠*340 Faneuil Hall Marketplace, North Market Bldg., Government Center* ☎*617/227-2038* ▤*AE, D, DC, MC, V* Ⓣ *Government Center.*

$$-$$$
SEAFOOD
✗ **Union Oyster House.** Established in 1826, this is Boston's oldest continuing restaurant, and almost every tourist considers it a must-see. If you like, you can have what Daniel Webster had—oysters on the half shell at the ground-floor raw bar, which is the oldest part of the restaurant and still the best. The rooms at the top of the narrow staircase are dark and have low ceilings—very Ye Olde New England—and plenty of nonrestaurant history. The small tables and chairs (as well as the endless lines and kitschy nostalgia) are as much a part of the charm as the simple and decent (albeit pricey) food. One cautionary note: locals hardly ever eat here. There is valet parking after 5:30 PM. ⊠*41 Union St., Government Center* ☎*617/227-2750* ▤*AE, D, DC, MC, V* Ⓣ *Haymarket.*

¢-$
JAPANESE
✗ **Wagamama.** Students and young families give this popular London-based noodle chain high marks for its cheap bowls of noodles and broth. Customers rotate quickly through this airy, communal-style dining room in the Faneuil Hall area as spiky-haired servers take orders on handheld electronic devices. The easy-to-read menu includes a glossary of terms and dish names. Vegetarian curry arrives with hearty fried slices of sweet potato, eggplant, and squash while the teriyaki steak soba is a flavorful combo of beef, panfried soba noodles, and bok choi. A short list of domestic wines and Japanese and American beers rounds out the list. There's also a location at Harvard Square in Cambridge. ⊠*1 Faneuil Hall Sq., Government Center* ☎*617/742-9242* ▤*AE, D, DC, MC, V* Ⓣ *Government Center.*

NORTH END

★ **$$-$$$**
ITALIAN
✗ **Bricco.** A sophisticated but unpretentious enclave of nouveau Italian, Bricco has carved out quite a following. And no wonder: the handmade pastas alone are argument for a reservation. Simple but well-balanced main courses such as roast chicken marinated in seven spices and a brimming brodetto (fish soup) with half a lobster and a pile of seafood may linger in your memory. You're likely to want to linger in the warm room, too, gazing through the floor-to-ceiling windows while sipping a glass of Sangiovese from the all-Italian wine list. ⊠*241 Hanover St., North End* ☎*617/248-6800* ⌖*Reservations essential* ▤*AE, D, MC, V* Ⓣ *Haymarket.*

★ **$$-$$$** ✕**Neptune Oyster.** This tiny oyster bar, the first of its kind in the neighbor-
SEAFOOD hood, has only six tables, but the long marble bar has extra seating for
a dozen more and mirrors hang over the bar with handwritten menus.
From there, watch the oyster shuckers as they deftly undo handfuls of
bivalves. The *plateau di frutti di mare* is a gleaming tower of oysters
and other raw-bar items piled over ice that you can order from the slip
of paper they pass out listing each day's crustacean options. And the
lobster roll, hot or cold, overflows with meat. Service is prompt even
when it gets busy (as it is most of the time). Go early to avoid a long
wait. ✉*63 Salem St., North End* ☎*617/742-3474* ☜*Reservations not
accepted* ▭*AE, DC, MC, V* Ⓣ *Haymarket.*

$-$$ ✕**Pomodoro.** This teeny trattoria—just eight tables—is worth the wait,
ITALIAN with excellent country Italian favorites such as rigatoni with white
beans and arugula, and a sweet veal scaloppini with balsamic glaze.
light-but-filling zuppa di pesce. The best choice could well be the clam-
and-tomato stew with herbed flat bread, accompanied by a bottle of
Vernaccia. Pomodoro doesn't serve dessert, but it's easy to find great
espresso and pastries in the cafés on Hanover Street. ✉*319 Hanover
St., North End* ☎*617/367-4348* ☜*Reservations essential* ▭*No credit
cards* Ⓣ*Haymarket.*

CAMBRIDGE

$$-$$$ ✕**Blue Room.** Totally hip, funky, and Cambridge, the Blue Room blends
AMERICAN a host of cuisines from Southwestern to Mediterranean with fresh, local
ingredients. Brightly colored furnishings, counters where you can meet
others while you eat, and a friendly staff add up to a good-time place
that's serious about food. Try the seared scallops grilled over French
green lentils, or perhaps a cassoulet brimming with braised pork and
wild-boar sausage. An extraordinary buffet brunch with grilled meats
and vegetables, as well as regular breakfast fare and a gorgeous array of
desserts, is served on Sunday. ✉*1 Kendall Sq., Cambridge* ☎*617/494-
9034* ▭*AE, D, DC, MC, V* ☺*No lunch* Ⓣ*Kendall/MIT.*

$$-$$$ ✕**Chez Henri.** French with a Cuban twist—odd bedfellows, but it
ECLECTIC works for this sexy, confident restaurant. The dinner menu gets seri-
Fodor'sChoice ous with cassoulet with braised lamb and white beans, tuna au poivre,
★ and sinfully sweet double-decker chocolate cake. At the cozy bar you
can sample spiced fries, clam fritters, and the best grilled three-pork
Cuban sandwich in Boston. The place fills quickly with Cantabrigian
locals—an interesting mix of students, professors, and sundry intel-
ligentsia. ✉*1 Shepard St., Cambridge* ☎*617/354-8980* ▭*AE, DC,
MC, V* ☺*No lunch* Ⓣ *Harvard.*

$$ ✕**East Coast Grill and Raw Bar.** Owner-chef-author Chris Schlesinger built
AMERICAN his national reputation on grilled foods and red-hot condiments. The
Fodor'sChoice Jamaican jerk, North Carolina pulled pork, and habañero-laced "pasta
★ from Hell" are still here, but this restaurant has made an extraordi-
nary play to establish itself in the front ranks of fish restaurants. Spices
and condiments are more restrained, and Schlesinger has compiled a
wine list bold and flavorful enough to match the highly spiced food.
The dining space is completely informal. A killer brunch (complete
with a do-it-yourself Bloody Mary bar) is served on Sunday. ✉*1271*

Where to Eat & Stay in Cambridge

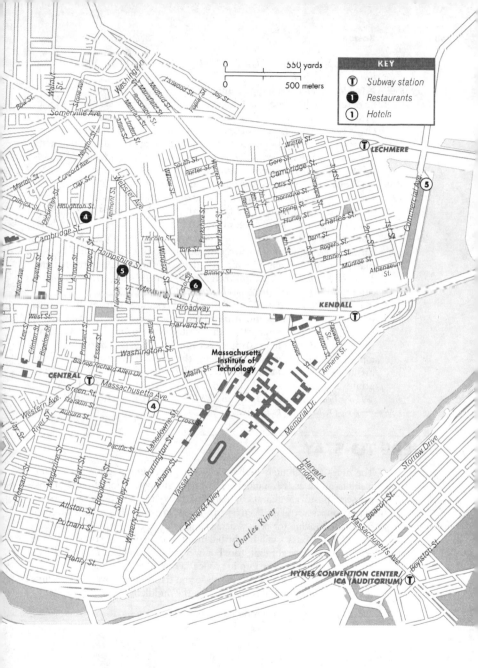

Cambridge St., Cambridge ☎*617/491-6568* ▤*AE, D, MC, V* ⊘*No lunch* ⊤ *Central.*

☾ $-$$
AMERICAN

✕**Full Moon.** Here's a happy reminder that dinner with children doesn't have to mean hamburgers. Choices include child pleasers such as pasta as well as grown-up entrées that include herb grilled pork chops with citrus salsa. Youngsters can spread out with plenty of designated play space and juice-filled sippy cups while adults weigh the substantial menu and a well-paired wine list. ✉*344 Huron Ave., Cambridge* ☎*617/354-6699* ♿*Reservations not accepted* ▤*MC, V* ⊤ *Harvard.*

$$-$$$
MEDITERRANEAN

✕**Oleana.** Chef and owner Ana Sortun is one of the city's culinary treasures—and so is Oleana. Here, flavors from all over the Middle Eastern Mediterranean sing loud and clear, in the hot, crispy fried mussels starter, and in the smoky eggplant puree beside tamarind-glazed beef. Fish gets jacked up with Turkish spices, then grilled until it just barely caramelizes. In warm weather, the back patio is a hidden piece of utopia—a homey garden that hits the perfect note of casual refinement. ✉*134 Hampshire St., Cambridge* ☎*617/661-0505* ♿*Reservations essential* ▤*AE, MC, V* ⊘*No lunch* ⊤ *Central.*

★ $
INDIAN

✕**Tanjore.** The menu at this fully regional restaurant, from the owners of Rangoli in Allston and Rani in Brookline, reaches from Sindh to Bengal, with some strength in the western provincial foods (Gujarat, Bombay) and their interesting sweet-hot flavors. The *Baigan Bhurta* is a platter of grilled, mashed eggplant; the rice dishes, chais, and breads are all excellent and the lunchtime buffet is usually a quick in-and-out affair. The spicing starts mild, so don't be afraid to order "medium." ✉*18 Eliot St., Cambridge* ☎*617/868-1900* ♿*Reservations essential* ▤*AE, D, MC, V* ⊤ *Harvard.*

WHERE TO STAY

Updated by
Diane Bair
and Pamela
Wright

The times are definitely a-changing. The gilt ceilings, Colonial-style furnishings and massive chandeliers that have always bespoke luxury in Boston seem positively quaint compared to the stylish newcomers all done up in fiber optics, art-glass, even (egad!) Texas limestone. For those who come to Boston looking for period details and white-glove pampering, the old-style glamour-pusses will fill the bill nicely, but if your taste runs to cutting edge design, we've got that, too. For every gilded old historic hotel, there's a brash newcomer, tarted up in red leather and black lacquer. There's the place you'd send you mother, the place you'd meet your lover, and a whole bunch of places that fall somewhere in the middle.

Please see price categories on page 76.

BEST BETS FOR BOSTON & CAMBRIDGE LODGING

Fodor's offers a selective listing of quality lodging experiences in every price range, from the city's best budget beds to its most sophisticated luxury hotels. Here, we've compiled our top recommendations by price and experience. The very best properties—in other words, those that provide a particularly remarkable experience in their price range—are designated in the listings with the Fodor's Choice logo.

Fodor's Choice ★

Boston Harbor Hotel at Rowes Wharf, Downtown $$$$

Charles Hotel, Cambridge $$$$

Charlesmark Hotel, Back Bay $$

Fairmont Copley Plaza, Back Bay $$$$

Fifteen Beacon, Beacon Hill $$$-$$$$

Four Seasons, Back Bay $$$$

InterContinental Hotel Boston, Downtown (Waterfront) $$$$

Jurys, Back Bay $$$-$$$$

Lenox Hotel, Back Bay $$$-$$$$

Nine Zero, Downtown $$$$

Royal Sonesta Hotel, Cambridge $$$$

By Price

¢

Hostelling International Boston

$

463 Beacon Street Guest House

John Jeffries House, Beacon Hill

$$

Charlesmark Hotel, Back Bay

Harvard Square Hotel, Cambridge

$$$

Colonnade Hotel, Back Bay

Gryphon House, Kenmore Sq.

$$$$

Hotel Commonwealth, Kenmore Sq.

Liberty Hotel, Beacon Hill

By Experience

BEST POOL

Colonnade Hotel, Back Bay $$$-$$$$

InterContinental Hotel Boston, Downtown (Waterfront) $$$$

BEST HOTEL BAR

Hotel Commonwealth, Kenmore Sq. $$$$

Jurys, Back Bay $$$-$$$$

Liberty Hotel, Beacon Hill $$$$

BEST GYM

Four Seasons, Back Bay $$$$

InterContinental Hotel Boston, Downtown (Waterfront) $$$$

BEST FOR KIDS

Fairmont Copley Plaza, Back Bay $$$$

Royal Sonesta, Cambridge $$$$

BEST FOR ROMANCE

Boston Harbor Hotel at Rowes Wharf, Downtown, $$$$

Fairmont Copley Plaza, Back Bay $$$$

InterContinental Hotel Boston, Downtown (Waterfront) $$$$

BEST SERVICE

Boston Harbor Hotel at Rowes Wharf, Downtown $$$$

Charles Hotel, Cambridge $$$$

Jurys Boston, Back Bay $$$-$$$$

BEST VIEWS

Four Seasons, Back Bay $$$$

HIPSTER HOTELS

Charlesmark, Back Bay $$

BEST LOCATION

Four Seasons, Back Bay $$$$

Lenox, Back Bay $$$-$$$$

BEST KEPT SECRET

Gryphon House, Kenmore Sq. $$$

John Jeffries House, Beacon Hill $-$$

BACK BAY

$$ **Charlesmark Hotel.** Hipsters and romantics who'd rather spend their
Fodor's Choice cash on a great meal than a hotel bill have put this skinny little bou-
★ tique hotel on the map. You can typically grab a room for around $139
($119 in winter), an amazing value considering the Copley Square loca-
tion: the shops and restaurants of Boylston and Newbury streets are
at the doorstep. An outdoor patio is a great place to watch the passing
parade (or the Boston Marathon—this hotel is right on the finish line).
Smallish guest rooms have contemporary custom-made oak furnish-
ings (yacht-like, with lots of nooks and crannies to stash belongings)
plus surround-sound stereo and wireless throughout. Free continental
breakfast and Wi-Fi are examples of how the hotel provides cost-saving
incidentals. You can get order Thai food in the cocktail lounge, but if
that doesn't suit you, walk to one of 40-some restaurants in the 'hood.
The Charlesmark doubles as a gallery, with the work of local artists
lining the winding brick corridors. **Pros:** great price point for what you
get; great location near T, shopping, and dining; free Wi-Fi and water
bottles. **Cons:** hot-air heating system is noisy, not much storage space,
rooms at the front of the house can be noisy due to lounge and traf-
fic. ✉*655 Boylston St. Back Bay* ☎*617/247-1212* ⊕*www.thecharles
markhotel.com* ⇒*33 rooms* ☆*In-room: VCR, Wi-Fi. In-hotel: bar,
laundry service, public Wi-Fi, some pets allowed* ▤*AE, D, DC, MC,
V* ⑩*CP* Ⓣ*Copley.*

★ **$$$-$$$$** **Colonnade Hotel.** Whoa. Did the stylists at Saks Fifth Avenue, across
the street at the Pru, sneak in and give the Colonnade an extreme make-
over? The hotel has gone from so-*over* '80s brass-and-mahogany to
a clean, modern look with tones of espresso, khaki, chocolate, and
chrome. All this would be mere window dressing if it weren't for new,
guest-friendly touches like flat-panel TVs, DVD players, and alarm
clock/MP3 players, plus extendable reading lights and fab high-tech
coffeemakers. Even the minibar goodies got an upgrade, with fresh
shortbread cookies and the like. The look is slightly masculine but quite
comfy, with pillow-top mattresses, high-thread-count sheets, and a
round worktable (replacing the typical desk) so guests can eat or work
comfortably. Floor-to-ceiling windows (these actually open) have been
triple glazed to keep out the traffic noise of Huntington Avenue. Alas,
the downside of all this is that rates have gone up a bit. In summer, the
roof deck pool is a huge draw. Open to hotel guests only, the pool area
has great views of the neighborhood, and live music. For your gusta-
tory needs, Brasserie Jo is an authentic French brasserie. **Pros:** roof deck
pool, T stop a few steps away, across the street from Prudential Center
for shopping and restaurants. **Con:** prices have gone up since hotel
was renovated. ✉*120 Huntington Ave., Back Bay,* ☎*617/424-7000
or 800/962-3030* ⊕*www.colonnadehotel.com* ⇒*276 rooms, 9 suites*
☆*In-room: safe, Wi-Fi. In-hotel: restaurant, room service, bar, pool,
gym, laundry service, concierge, public Wi-Fi, parking (fee), some pets
allowed* ▤*AE, D, DC, MC, V* Ⓣ*Prudential Center.*

$$$$ **Fairmont Copley Plaza.** Back in the day, Judy Garland slept here, and
Fodor's Choice made rowdy guest appearances at the piano bar, according to a waiter
★ at the Fairmont's Oak Room. For those who, like Judy, believe that

too much of a good thing is just about right, the deliciously decadent, unabashedly romantic Fairmont lures. Richly decorated, and very
ornate—we're talking clouds on the ceiling here—this 1912 landmark
favors romance and tradition over sleek and modern. Really love pampering? Stay on the Fairmont Gold floor, an ultra-deluxe club level
offering a dedicated staff, free breakfast and tea-time snacks (mini crab
cakes and other delectables), and library. Shopping fanatics adore the
close proximity to Newbury Street, the Prudential Center, and Copley
Place. Although updated with modern conveniences like high-speed
Internet access, the real appeal here lies in how the Fairmont's Oak
Room restaurant matches its mahogany-paneled twin in New York's
Plaza Hotel; the equally stately—and tryst-worthy—Oak Bar has live
music and one of the longest martini menus in town. If you're missing
Fido, take Catie Copley, the in-house Labrador retriever, for a walk
around the 'hood. (Paul Newman does when he stays here.) **Pros:** very
elegant, great Copley Square location, cozy bar. **Cons:** tiny bathrooms
with scratchy towels, charge for Internet access (no charge on Fairmont
Gold level), not much shelving or storage. ⊠ *138 St. James Ave., Back
Bay* ☎ *617/267-5300 or 800/441-1414* 📠 *617/375-9648* ⊕ *www.fair
mont.com/copleyplaza* ⇆ *366 rooms, 17 suites* ⟳ *In-room: safe, refrigerator, Ethernet. In-hotel: restaurant, room service, bar, gym, laundry
service, concierge, executive floor, public Wi-Fi, parking (fee), some
pets allowed* ⊟ *AE, D, DC, MC, V* Ⓣ *Copley, Back Bay/South End.*

★ $$$$ ⸬ **Four Seasons.** Jeans-clad billionaires and assorted business types cluster in the glossy lobby of the Four Seasons, while TV anchorfolk diss
the competition over 'tinis and Bristol Burgers in the Bristol Lounge.
(Visiting celebs are whisked to the 3,000-square-foot, $6,600-per-night
Presidential Suite—no waiting in the lobby for them!) Thanks to a
recent face-lift, the Four Seasons retains its perch as Boston's go-to
hotel for luxury with a *soupçon* of hip. Designers resisted the trend of
soothing taupe for bright shots of citron and apricot in public spaces;
guest rooms sport black-and-cream toile with gold and lemon accents,
large bay windows, and oversize work areas. Luxury amenities include
DVD players, 42-inch plasma TVs, and L'Occitane toiletries. (Celebrities stash the full-size soaps in their luggage, we're told.) Even if you
spring for the basic city-view room (Tip: Check the web for awesome
winter-weekend deals), you can enjoy fab views of the Public Garden
from the pool and whirlpool on the eighth floor, or from Aujourd'hui,
the hotel's top-rated contemporary French restaurant, or the Bristol
Lounge. **Pros:** great location overlooking the Public Garden and a short
walk to Newbury Street shops and the Theater District, Mercedes courtesy car makes drop-offs (within a 2-mi radius) around town, excellent gym. **Cons:** front entrance can get busy (you might have to wait
for your valet-parked car), restaurants are pricey. ⊠ *200 Boylston St.,
Back Bay* ☎ *617/338-4400 or 800/819-5053* ⊕ *www.fourseasons.
com/boston* ⇆ *197 rooms, 76 suites* ⟳ *In-room: safe, refrigerator, Ethernet, Wi-Fi. In-hotel: 2 restaurants, room service, bar, pool, gym, laundry service, concierge, public Wi-Fi, parking (fee), some pets allowed*
⊟ *AE, D, DC, MC, V* Ⓣ *Arlington.*

$$$-$$$$
Fodor'sChoice
★
⊞ **Jurys Boston Hotel.** "Great staff." "Great bar." "Great vibe." Sense a theme here? Readers rave about this hotel, one of the few in the city where you can nip into the bar for a beverage and actually chat with a friendly local or two. There's something about this place that thaws even the frostiest Bostonian—and it's not just the Irish coffee talking. Part of a Dublin-based hotel chain, Jurys may remind you more of Iceland than Ireland, design-wise. There's a fire-and-ice thing going on, from the bed of icy glass shards in the igloolike gas fireplace on the lower level to the puffs of steam coming from the staircase waterfall. Eye-catching blown-glass chandeliers add to the cool appeal. Rooms are decorated with warm taupes and golds, and Ireland-themed artwork adorns the walls. The hotel gets the small touches right, such as the Aveda products in the sleek, modern bathrooms; free bottled water in the fridge; toasty down comforters; and heated towel racks. **Pros:** lively, friendly bar; great amenities, like large-screen TVs, at a good price point; friendly staff. **Cons:** not the prettiest location in the city, but close to the T (subway). ⊠ *350 Stuart St., Back Bay* ☎ *617/266-7200* ≞ *617/266-7203* ⊕ *www.jurysdoyle.com* ⋑ *220 rooms, 3 suites* ⚘ *In-room: refrigerator, DVD, Wi-Fi. In-hotel: restaurant, room service, bar, laundry service, concierge, public Wi-Fi, parking (fee)* ⊟ *AE, D, DC, MC, V* Ⓣ *Back Bay/South End.*

$$$-$$$$
Fodor'sChoice
★
⊞ **Lenox Hotel.** Family-owned and graced with period (circa 1901) details, this boutique-ish Back Bay property is a pleasing alternative to the nearby big-box hotels. It's also a dandy option if you need more services--like room service, a business center, and a fitness room—than the more-basic Charlesmark Hotel (across the street) can deliver. The Copley Square location means you're steps away from a slew of restaurants and shops, and a T stop is right across the street. No car needed—a good thing, since overnight parking costs a bundle. (Skip the hotel's garage and use a city parking facility to save some cash.) This longtime Back Bay landmark won several awards for restoration work on its grand brick-and-granite facade. The smallish size of this hotel lends a feeling of personalized service, although some say the staff can be chilly. Recently-updated guest rooms have custom-made furnishings, marble baths, and flat-screen TVs (suites have mirror TVs in bathrooms). Of the 24 airily spacious corner rooms, 12 have working wood-burning fireplaces. The sophisticated City Bar is a popular evening destination for its infused vodka martinis. The Sólás pub is a more-casual option. **Book your reservation from the hotel's Web site; they guarantee the best price. Pros:** fantastic Copley Square location, historic/architectural charm. **Cons:** bathrooms are small; no minibar/mini-fridge, safe, or coffeemaker (though available upon request). ⊠ *61 Exeter St., Back Bay* ☎ *617/536-5300 or 800/225-7676* ≞ *617/267-1237* ⊕ *www.lenoxhotel.com* ⋑ *187 rooms, 27 suites* ⚘ *In-room: Wi-Fi. In-hotel: 3 restaurants, room service, bars, gym, laundry service, concierge, public Wi-Fi, parking (fee)* ⊟ *AE, D, DC, MC, V* Ⓣ *Copley.*

$$
⊞ **Newbury Guest House.** "Stay here—it's the center of the universe!" a reader raves about this elegant redbrick-and-brownstone 1882 row house. On Boston's most fashionable shopping street, the inn looks the part, with natural pine flooring, elegant reproduction Victorian

furnishings, and prints from the Museum of Fine Arts. These days, it looks even better—a recent re-do has expanded and prettied-up the lobby. Also, guests can now order room service from the tiny French bistro, La Voile, located downstairs. Alas, this added gloss comes at a price—room rates have gone up about $20 a night. Some rooms have bay windows; others have decorative fireplaces. Room 209 is the prettiest, with its lovely but nonworking fireplace. Limited parking is available at $20 for 24 hours—a good deal for the area. Pros: cozy, homey, great location. Cons: some say that rooms don't look as nice as the Web site indicates; small bathrooms, small TVs. ⊠ *261 Newbury St., Back Bay* ☎ *617/670-6100 or 800/437-7668* 📠 *617/262-4243* ⊕ *www. newburyguesthouse.com* ⊷ *32 rooms* ⬙ *In-room: Wi-Fi. In-hotel: no elevator, concierge, public Wi-Fi, parking (fee)* ▤ *AE, D, DC, MC, V* ⭕ *BP* Ⓣ *Hynes/ICA, Copley.*

BEACON HILL

$$$-$$$$ 🏨 **Fifteen Beacon.** Although it's housed in an old (1903) beaux arts
Fodor's Choice building, this boutique hotel is anything but stodgy. The tiny lobby is
★ all black mahogany with bold splashes of red, brightened with recessed lighting and abstract art. Even the cage elevator is paneled in red leather. Just when you're thinking, "Hmm, bordello chic?" you enter a guest room and go, "Ahh!" Rooms are done up in soothing-but-gender-neutral shades of espresso, taupe, and cream, and each has a flat-screen TV, a gas fireplace, and surround-sound stereo. Fab little touches abound, like bath amenities from Newbury Street's Fresh, and baby TVs in the bathroom, plus huge mirrors and heated towel bars. A nearby health club is available to hotel guests, and the hotel's restaurant, the Federalist, is a favorite for fine dining. Tip: This is *the* place to be for Boston's Harborfest (July 4th) celebration, when guests can watch fireworks from the roof deck (open from Memorial Day to Labor Day). Pros: courtesy car service, friendly concierge, you can charge your laptop in your in-room safe. Cons: mattresses are just average. ⊠ *15 Beacon St., Beacon Hill* ☎ *617/670-1500 or 877/982-3226* ⊕ *www.xvbeacon. com* ⊷ *58 rooms, 2 suites* ⬙ *In-room: safe, refrigerator, Ethernet. In-hotel: restaurant, room service, bar, gym, laundry service, concierge, parking (fee), some pets allowed* ▤ *AE, D, DC, MC, V* Ⓣ *Government Center, Park St.*

★ $-$$ 🏨 **John Jeffries House.** It's devilishly tricky to locate, especially if you're driving, but once you do, you'll discover the JJH is a real find. This turn-of-the-20th-century building, across from Massachusetts General Hospital, was once a housing facility for nurses. Now it's a sedate four-story inn, and one of the best values in town. Recently redecorated, the Federal-style double parlor has a cluster of floral-pattern chairs and sofas where you can relax with afternoon tea or coffee. Guest rooms are furnished with handsome upholstered pieces, and nearly all have kitchenettes. Triple-glazed windows block much noise from busy Charles Circle; many rooms have views of the Charles River. The inn is adjacent to Charles Street, home to lovely cafés, specialty boutiques, and antiques shops. Guests are a well-mannered mix of business travelers, Europeans, and hospital visitors. (The party people landed at the Liberty Hotel, a former jail across the street.) **Pros:** close to Beacon Hill, free Wi-Fi, good value. **Cons:** located near a hospital so you might hear ambulance sirens. ⌧*14 David G. Mugar Way, Beacon Hill* ☎*617/367-1866* ⊕*www.johnjeffrieshouse.com* ⤙*23 rooms, 23 suites* ♿ *In-room: kitchen, DVD (some), Wi-Fi. In-hotel: public Wi-Fi, parking (fee)* ▤*AE, D, DC, MC, V* ⦿*CP* Ⓣ*Charles/MGH.*

$$$$ 🖼 **Liberty Hotel Boston.** Boston's most buzz-worthy hotel, bar none, is the new Liberty Hotel, set in the old circa 1851 Charles Street Jail. The jail puns eventually wear thin—the bar is called Alibi, a restaurant is Clink, and so on—but you can't escape the cool factor of this unique luxury hotel. Jailhouse rock meets modern style here, where they've incorporated some of the jail's features into the $150 million re-do, including the trademark windows, catwalks, and even jail cells. A soaring lobby of exposed brick leads to 18 guest rooms in the main building, while an adjacent 16-story tower houses 280 more rooms with expansive views of the city. Guest rooms don't have a smidgen of "prison" about them (other than the solitary sign you hang from your door when you wish to be alone); they're small but freshly modern, with luxe linens, flat-panel TVs, and Wi-Fi. Don't expect a quiet getaway here—the Alibi bar (the former drunk tank) draws lines to get in—so just go with it, and join the party. (Check out the DUI mug shot of Lindsay Lohan in the bar, and don't miss the fried mac-and-cheese balls at Clink.) **Pros:** great lobby, lively nightlife, Beacon Hill location. **Cons:** some say HVAC system is noisy, lively nightlife, service has a few bugs to work out. ⌧*215 Charles St.Beacon Hill, 02114* ☎ *617/224-4000 or 860/507-5245* ⊕ *www.libertyhotel.com* ⤙ *298 rooms* ♿ *In-room: safe, DVD, Ethernet, Wi-Fi. In-hotel: 2 restaurants, room service, bar, gym, laundry service, concierge, public Wi-Fi, parking (fee), some pets allowed (fee)* ▤ *AE, D, DC, MC, V.*

DOWNTOWN

$$$$
Fodor's Choice
★

🖼 **Boston Harbor Hotel at Rowes Wharf.** Red Sox owner John Henry parks his yacht here in summertime, but the rest of us can arrive by boat in a less-grand fashion—the water shuttle runs from Logan Airport to the back door of this deluxe waterfront hotel. The hotel's dramatic entryway is an 80-foot archway topped by a rotunda, so eye-catching that it qualifies as a local landmark. The lobby, too, is stunningly elegant, with marble arches, antique maps, and a huge tumble of fresh flowers. Guest rooms—recently refreshed to the tune of $12 million—sport marble bathrooms, custom-made desks, Frette linens, high-end radio/CD players, flat-panel TVs and laptop-size safes—in short, every conceivable amenity, even complimentary daily shoe shines. The older, well-heeled clientele appreciates these niceties, along with the fabviews of the city and Boston harbor. Meritage restaurant has a unique, wine-inspired menu that pairs small plates with appropriate vintages, under light fixtures that mimic a starry sky. Want to work out in the hotel's health club, but forgot your exercise duds? Not to worry—they provide them for their guests. Now if only they would exercise for you. Ask, and they probably would; that's the level of service they offer here. **Pros:** readers praise the impeccable service, beautiful rooms and views, easy walk to Faneuil Hall. Cons: gym equipment somewhat outdated; spa gets booked, so may not have availability. ✉ *70 Rowes Wharf, Downtown/Waterfront,* ☎ *617/439-7000 or 800/752-7077* ⊕ *www.bhh.com* ↘ *206 rooms, 24 suites* ♿ *In-room: refrigerator, Wi-Fi. In-hotel: 2 restaurants, room service, bar, pool, gym, spa, laundry service, concierge, public Wi-Fi, airport shuttle, parking (fee), some pets allowed* ▭ *AE, D, DC, MC, V* ⓣ *Aquarium, South Station.*

★ **$$-$$$** 🖵**Harborside Inn.** "We're not a pampering hotel like the Four Seasons," owner Mark Hagopian warns. Then again, the Harborside Inn won't charge you for incidentals, and room rates are commonly 20 percent less than those of neighboring properties. The independent-minded travelers who discover this place, a mix of youngish business travelers and weekenders, don't feel that they're missing out. A recent renovation has slicked up this former 19th-century mercantile warehouse. It's easier to get a room here now, too, since they've knocked out a wall and doubled its size. The look is sort of marine-modern-minimalist, with shipwreck prints and scenes of Boston Harbor, exposed brick walls, hardwood floors, Federal-style furnishings and teak accents. Amenities include new flat-screen TVs and complimentary Wi-Fi. Walk to lively Faneuil Hall, Quincy Market, and the North End, and then return to the homey vibe of the inn. Many of the snug, variously shaped rooms (no two are alike) have windows overlooking the small, open lobby, which extends eight stories up to the roof. If an outdoor view is important to you, request a room overlooking the city, but if you value quiet even more, book a room that faces the interior atrium. **Pros:** good value for the area; close to Quincy Market, North End, New England Aquarium, water taxi; good reading lights. **Cons:** nearby nightclubs can be noisy; rooms differ in terms of size and configuration; atrium-view rooms feel closed-in, some say. ✉ *185 State St., Downtown/Waterfront* ☎ *617/723-7500 or 888/723-7565* ⊕ *www.harborsideinnboston.com* ↘ *98 rooms, 2 suites* ♿ *In-room: safe (some), refrigerator (some), DVD, VCR, Wi-Fi. In-hotel: laundry service, concierge, public Wi-Fi, parking (fee)* ▭ *AE, D, DC, MC, V* ⓣ *Aquarium.*

$$$$
Fodor'sChoice
★ 🖵**InterContinental Hotel Boston.** Call it the anti-boutique hotel. Boston's 424-room InterContinental Hotel, facing the harbor and the grassy strip known as the Rose Kennedy Greenway—is housed in two opulent, 22-story towers wrapped in blue glass. In a nod to the city's history, the towers equal the height of the masts of the old tall ships, and the pewter bar in RumBa, the hotel's rum bar, would surely delight metalsmith Paul Revere. (It also harks back to Boston's connection with the rum trade.) Miel, the hotel's organic Provencal brasserie, is open 24/7. Hallways are lined with Texan limestone, and lobbies are gleaming with Italian marble and leather—there's not a red brick in the place. Guest rooms are oversize, wired with the latest technology, and have flat-screen TVs, and readers rave about the spalike bathrooms ("the best bathroom I have ever seen"), done in mosaic tile and granite, with separate tubs and showers. Another drawing card here is the 6,600-square-foot spa and health club, and a pool that overlooks Atlantic Avenue and the Rose Kennedy Greenway. Sushi-Teq, the hotel's sushi-tequila restaurant, draws crowds, while mov-

ers and shakers from local financial, real estate, and law firms of the Financial District make merry after workin the bars. Pros: rooms have great views and great bathrooms, close to Financial District and South Station, brasserie open 24 hours. Cons: huge function rooms mean lots of conventioneers, far from Newbury Street and museums, guests say that sound-proofing could be better. ✉ *510 Atlantic Ave., Downtown/Waterfront* ☎ *617/747-1000* ⊕ *www.intercontinentalboston. com* ⌘ *424 rooms, 38 suites* ♿ *In-room: safe, refrigerator, DVD, Wi-Fi. In-hotel: 2 restaurants, room service, bar, pool, gym, spa, laundry service, concierge, executive floor, public Wi-Fi, parking (fee)* ▭ *AE, D, DC, MC, V.*

$$$$
Fodor'sChoice
★

☷ **Nine Zero.** The little doggie dish outside the entrance is a tip-off—this isn't an ordinary hotel. Owned by Kimpton Hotels, this property is stylish and swank. The lobby is a knockout, with copper metallic draperies and high-backed leather chairs. Giant suspended glass globes stand in for chandeliers. It all adds up to a spare feel, the better to compliment the cool threads of the youngish, style-conscious crowd. Guest rooms sport bold patterns, curvy black armoires, and full martini bars; some have floor-to-ceiling windows. Unexpected features include in-room yoga (turn on their yoga channel, and ask them to bring you a yoga basket) and "guppy love" (they'll lend you a goldfish bowl if you get lonely). Corner rooms (ending in 05) have awesome views of the Longfellow Bridge and the gold dome of the State House, but you'll pay a premium for them. The gym is really small, so ask for a free pass to a local fitness club. Pros: great style; lobby wine-tasting every evening (from 5 to 6); Mario Russo (Newbury Street) bath products; KO Prime, a popular steak house run by überchef Ken Oringer. Cons: smallish rooms, overlooks a cemetery. ✉ *90 Tremont St., Downtown* ☎ *617/772-5800 or 866/646-3937* ⊕ *www.ninezero.com* ⌘ *185 rooms, 5 suites* ♿ *In-room: safe, refrigerator, Ethernet, Wi-Fi. In-hotel: restaurant, room service, bar, gym, laundry service, concierge, public Wi-Fi, parking (fee), some pets allowed* ▭ *AE, D, DC, MC, V* Ⓣ *Park St., Government Center.*

★ $$$

☷ **Omni Parker House.** America's oldest continuously-operating hotel just got a $30 million facelift, so you can seep yourself in Boston history but still watch a flat-screen TV, work out with the latest equipment, and stash your stuff in a laptop-sized safe. And, happily, you can still get Boston cream pie for breakfast, since they invented it here. If any hotel really says "Boston," it's this one, where JFK proposed to Jackie, and Charles Dickens gave his first reading of *A Christmas Carol*. In fact, you may well see a Dickens impersonator in the lobby, since history tours put the Parker House on their hit list. The downside: guests rooms are small (furnishings were custom-built to fit). At least they're nicely turned out, with red-and-gold Roman shades, ivory wall coverings and cushy mattress covers. Another plus: rooms are extremely quiet—a claim that can't be made by some of the Parker House's newer neighbors. The hotel stands opposite old City Hall, on the Freedom Trail. Pros: historic, quiet, located near Downtown Crossing on Freedom Trail. Cons: small rooms, some say that staff could be friendlier. ✉ *60 School St., Downtown* ☎ *617/227-8600 or 800/843-6664*

⊕ *www.omniparkerhouse.com* ⮐ *551 rooms, 21 suites* ⊘ *In room: Wi-Fi. In-hotel: 2 restaurants, room service, bars, gym, laundry service, concierge, public Wi-Fi, parking (fee), some pets allowed* ☰ *AE, D, DC, MC, V* Ⓣ *Government Center, Park St.*

KENMORE SQUARE

$$$

Fodor'sChoice

★

⌕ **Gryphon House.** Many of the suites in this four-story, 19th-century brownstone are thematically decorated; one evokes rustic Italy, another is inspired by neo-Gothic art. Among the many amenities—including gas fireplaces, wet bars, VCRs, CD players, and private voice mail—the enormous bathrooms with oversize tubs and separate showers are the most appealing. Even the staircase (there is no elevator) is extraordinary: a 19th-century wallpaper mural, *El Dorado*, wraps along the walls. Trompe-l'oeil paintings and murals by local artist Michael Ernest Kirk decorate the common spaces. Another nice touch: free passes to the Museum of Fine Arts and Isabella Stewart Gardner Museum. Pros: elegant suites are lush and spacious; gas fireplaces are in all the rooms; helpful, friendly staff. Cons: may be too fussy for some; there's no elevator or handicapped access. ✉ *9 Bay State Rd., Kenmore Sq.* ☎ *617/375-9003 or 877/375-9003* ⊕ *www.gryphonhouseboston.com* ⮐ *8 suites* ⊘ *In-room: refrigerator, VCR, Ethernet, Wi-Fi. In-hotel: no elevator, public Internet, public Wi-Fi, parking (fee)* ☰ *AE, D, MC, V* ⦿ *CP* Ⓣ *Kenmore.*

★ **$$$$**

⌕ **Hotel Commonwealth.** Luxury and service without pretention makes this hip hotel anything but common, blending old-world charm with modern conveniences for a sophisticated, boutiquey feel. Rich color schemes enhance the elegant rooms, and king- or queen-size beds are piled with down pillows and Italian linens. Choose rooms with views of bustling Commonwealth Avenue or Fenway Park. All rooms have marble baths and floor-to-ceiling windows, separate work areas (divided by a curtain), and flat-screen TVs. The bend-over-backwards staff and car and driver available to guests are added bonuses. The much-acclaimed seafood restaurant Great Bay (be sure to make reservations upon arrival) and the Eastern Standard bar and restaurant are also on-site. Pros: luscious bedding and bath products, great service, Red Sox fans will love the views of Fenway Park from some of the rooms (request these when booking), on-site restaurant is one of the best in the city for fresh fish. Cons: hotel and surroundings can be mobbed during a Red Sox game, small gym. ✉ *500 Commonwealth Ave., Kenmore Sq.* ☎ *617/933-5000 or 866/784-4000* ⊕ *www.hotel commonwealth.com* ⮐ *149 rooms, 1 suite* ⊘ *In-room: safe, refrigerator, DVD, Ethernet, Wi-Fi. In-hotel: 2 restaurants, room service, bar, gym, laundry service, concierge, public Wi-Fi, parking (fee)* ☰ *AE, D, DC, MC, V* Ⓣ *Kenmore.*

LOGAN AIRPORT (EAST BOSTON)

$$-$$$

⌕ **Hilton Boston Logan Airport.** Quiet rooms, competitive prices and an airport location makes this modern Hilton a popular choice with in-and-out visitors to Boston. There's a skywalk to terminals A and E and a free shuttle bus to the airport. Rooms have been recently updated with granite countertops in the baths and desks with ergonomic chairs. There's an unremarkable restaurant and an Irish pub on the premises, and a health club with a steam room. **Pros:** easy access to Logan Airport, competitive prices. **Cons:** extras like Internet access and parking can add up. ⊠*1 Hotel Dr., East Boston* ☎*617/568-6700* ⊕*www. hilton.com* ⇆*595 rooms, 4 suites* ⚭*In-room: refrigerator, Ethernet, Wi-Fi. In-hotel: restaurant, room service, bar, pool, gym, executive floor, public Internet, public Wi-Fi, parking (fee)* ⊟*AE, D, DC, MC, V* ⓣ*Silver Line.*

CAMBRIDGE

$$-$$$ 🏠**A Cambridge House Bed & Breakfast.** A gracious 1892 Greek Revival home listed on the National Register of Historic Places, A Cambridge House has richly carved cherry paneling, a grand fireplace, elegant Victorian antiques, and polished wood floors overlaid with Oriental rugs. One of the antiques-filled guest rooms has fabric-covered walls, and many have four-poster canopy beds. Rooms in the adjacent carriage house are smaller, but all have fireplaces. Harvard Square isn't terribly close, but public transportation is available nearby. The owner also has a town house with hotel-style, plain-Jane rooms next door; be sure you know what you're getting when you book the room. **Pros:** pretty public sitting areas with fireplaces are cozy places to relax; free parking; complimentary coffee, tea, and hot chocolate served all day. **Cons:** not a lot happening in the area, the removed-from-it-all setting is not for everyone. ⊠*2218 Massachusetts Ave., Cambridge* ☎*617/491-6300 or 800/232-9989* ⊕*www.acambridgehouse.com* ⇆*15 rooms* ⚭*In-room: Ethernet, Wi-Fi. In-hotel: no elevator, public Internet, public Wi-Fi, parking (no fee), some pets allowed* ⊟*AE, D, MC, V* �🍽*CP* ⓣ*Davis.*

$$$$ 🏠**Charles Hotel.** Gracious service, top-notch amenities, and a great
Fodor'sChoice   location on Harvard Square keeps this first-class hotel in high demand.
★   The New England Shaker interior is contemporary yet homey; antique quilts and art by nationally recognized artists hang throughout. Relax in the lobby library, chock-full of titles, some autographed by authors who frequent the hotel; also sign up for a guided art tour of the hotel or pick up a self-guided map. Guest rooms come with lots of nice touches, like terry robes, quilted down comforters, flat-screen TVs (plus LCD mirror TVs in the bathroom), and Bose radios. If you're looking for a river or skyline view, ask for something above the seventh floor. Both of the hotel's restaurants—Rialto and Henrietta's Table—are excellent. **Pros:** your wish is their command; on-site spa, health club, premier jazz club, and two of the area's top restaurants; Harvard Square is out the door; outdoor skating rink is a fun gathering spot for families during the winter months. **Cons:** luxury comes with a price, great for visiting Cambridge sites, less convenient to downtown Boston (though Red Line T is two blocks away). ⊠*1 Bennett St., Cambridge* ☎*617/864-1200 or 800/882-1818* ⊕*www.charleshotel.com* ⇆*249 rooms, 45 suites* ⚭*In-room: safe, refrigerator, Ethernet, Wi-Fi. In-hotel: 2 restaurants, room service, bars, pool, gym, spa, laundry service, concierge,*

public Internet, public Wi-Fi, parking (fee), some pets allowed ⊟AE, *DC, MC, V* ⊤*Harvard.*

$$-$$$ ⊡**Harvard Square Hotel.** Want to be in Harvard Square and not pay the big bucks? If you'll settle for basic lodgings in a great location, you won't go wrong at this nondescript property that feels more dormitory than hotel. Just steps from the neighborhood's many restaurants, shops, and lively street corners, the hotel has simple but clean rooms, with refrigerators and Internet access. The desk clerks are particularly helpful, assisting with everything from sending faxes to securing dinner reservations. **Pros:** location can't be beat, some windows open for fresh air. **Cons:** rooms need updating and baths are small (many with exposed pipes); Wi-Fi, in-lobby computer use, and parking cost extra. ⊠*110 Mt. Auburn St., Cambridge* ☎*617/864-5200 or 800/458-5886* ⊕*www.harvardsquarehotel.com* ⟳*73 rooms* ♿*In-room: safe, refrigerator, Ethernet, Wi-Fi. In-hotel: laundry service, concierge, public Internet, public Wi-Fi, parking (fee)* ⊟AE, D, DC, MC, V ⊤*Harvard.*

★ **$$$-$$$$** ⊡ **Le Meridien Cambridge.** Witty and stylish, without going overboard, this modern hotel (formerly the Hotel at MIT, now a Starwood property) plays off its high-tech Cambridge location. Art on loan from the MIT collection playfully introduces guests to the world of artificial intelligence; early robotic specimens act as sculptures. Rooms are simple and sleek with maple armoires, inlaid with computer circuit boards. Whimsical touches abound, such as the pattern of the elevator's carpeting that uses stylized molecules and bed coverings with scientific-equation fabric. Rooms have floor-to-ceiling windows behind wood shutters, ergonomically designed furniture, and luxurious bedding. In the lobby and the large, open-kitchen restaurant, cool metal highlights are mixed with burnished maple, redwood, and oak. It's a hub for techie business travelers and a real bargain for weekend vacationers. **Pros:** unique, tech-savvy rooms and surroundings; fitness center is open 24 hours, great off-season, Internet rates. **Cons:** a bit out of the way, with a 10-minute or so walk to the T; may be too sleek for some tastes; time for a freshening-up of furnishings, linens ⊠*20 Sidney St., Cambridge* ☎*617/577-0200 or 800/222-8733* ⊕*www.starwoodhotels.com* ⟳*196 rooms, 14 suites* ♿*In-room: safe, Ethernet, Wi-Fi. In-hotel: restaurant, room service, bar, gym, laundry service, concierge, public Internet, public Wi-Fi, parking (fee)* ⊟AE, D, DC, MC, V ⊤*Central, Kendall/MIT.*

★ **$$$$** ⊡**Royal Sonesta Hotel.** An impressive collection of modern art, dis-
Fodor's Choice played throughout the hotel, sleek, updated rooms, and a friendly,
★ professional staff make this Cambridge riverfront property a bit of a surprise. Its location next to the Museum of Science and Galleria shopping center and an attractive indoor/outdoor pool add to its appeal. Some rooms have superb views of Beacon Hill and the Boston skyline. Guest rooms are done in neutral earth tones, with modern amenities such as flat-screen TVs, Sony PlayStation consoles, high-speed Internet, and CD clock radios. The hotel has family suites and great excursion packages. **Pros:** kids feel welcome here; easy to drive to and parking is on-site (fee), nice pool. **Cons:** a bit sterile. ⊠*40 Edwin Land Blvd., off*

Memorial Dr., Cambridge ☎*617/806-4200 or 800/766-3782* ⊕*www.
sonesta.com/boston/* ➡*379 rooms, 21 suites* &*In-room: safe, refrigerator, Ethernet, Wi-Fi. In-hotel: 2 restaurants, room service, bars, pool,
gym, bicycles, laundry service, concierge, public Internet, public Wi-Fi,
parking (fee)* ▤*AE, D, DC, MC, V* Ⓣ*Lechmere.*

BOSTON ESSENTIALS

TRANSPORTATION

BY AIR

Boston's major airport, Logan International (BOS), is across the harbor
from Downtown, about 2 mi outside the city center, and can be easily
reached by taxi, water taxi, or subway (called the "T") via the Silver
or Blue Line. Logan has five terminals, identified by letters A through
E. A free airport shuttle runs between the terminals and airport hotels.
Some airlines use different terminals for international and domestic
flights. Most international flights arrive at Terminal E. Most charter
flights arrive at Terminal D. A visitor center in Terminal C offers tourist information. Green Airport, in Providence, Rhode Island, and the
Manchester Airport in Manchester, New Hampshire, are both about
an hour from Boston.

Airport Information Green Airport (✉*Off I-95, Exit 13, Providence, RI*
☎*888/268-7222 or 401/737-8222* ⊕*www.pvdairport.com*). **Logan International**
(✉*I-90 east to Ted Williams Tunnel* ☎*800/235-6426* ⊕*www.massport.com*
Ⓣ*Airport*). **Manchester Airport** (✉*Off I-293/Rte. 101, Exit 2, Manchester, NH*
☎*603/624-6556* ⊕*www.flymanchester.com*).

GROUND TRANSPORTATION

BY TAXI Taxis can be hired outside each terminal. Fares to and from Downtown
should be about $15-$18, including tip. Taxis must pay an extra toll of
$4.50 and a $2 airport fee when leaving the airport (but not going in) that
will be tacked onto your bill at the end of the trip. (Major traffic jams or
taking a longer route to avoid traffic will add to the fare.) (⇨ *By Taxi for
cab companies.*)

BY SUBWAY The Blue and Silver lines on the subway, commonly called "the T" (and
operated by the MBTA), run from the airport to downtown Boston
in about 20 minutes. The Blue Line is best if you're heading to North
Station, Faneuil Hall, North End/Waterfront, or Back Bay (Hynes Convention Center, Prudential Center area). Take the Silver Line to South
Station, Boston Convention and Exhibition Center, Seaport World
Trade Center, Chinatown Theater, and South End areas. From North
and South stations, you can reach the Red, Green, or Orange lines, or
commuter rail. The T costs $2 for in-town travel if you're paying in
cash or $1.70 if you purchase a CharlieCard (a prepaid stored-value
card). *See By Subway, Train, and Trolley, below for more information.*
Free 24-hour shuttle buses connect the subway station with all airline
terminals. Shuttle Bus 22 runs between the subway and Terminals A

and B, and Shuttle Bus 33 runs between the subway and Terminals C, D, and E.

Contact MBTA (☎ 800/392-6100, 617/222-3200 ⊕ www.mbta.com).

BY BUS OR SHUTTLE   Several companies offer shared-van service to many Boston-area destinations. J. C. Transportation, Logan/Boston Hotel Shuttle, and Ace American provide door-to-door service to several major Back Bay and Downtown hotels. (Check their Web sites for a listing of hotels.) Reservations are not required, because vans swing by all terminals every 20 minutes to half hour. One-way fares are $14 per person. Easy Transportation is also a shared-van service which runs from the airport to the Back Bay Hilton, Radisson, and Lenox hotels from 7 AM to 10 PM. Star Shuttle operates shared vans from the airport to the Marriott Copley Place and Sheraton Copley, every hour on the half hour, from 5:30 AM to 11:30 PM. Logan Express buses travel from the airport to the suburbs of Braintree, Framingham, Peabody, and Woburn. One-way fares are $11.

Contacts Ace American (☎ 800/517-2281) **Easy Transportation** (☎ 617/069-7760 ⊕ www.easytransportationinc.com). **J. C. Transportation** (☎ 800/517-2281 ⊕ www.jctransportationshuttle.com). **Logan/Boston Hotel Shuttle** (☎ 617/331-8388). **Logan Express** (☎ 800/235-6426 ⊕ www.massport.com). **Star Shuttle** (☎ 617/230-6005 ⊕ www.starshuttleboston.com).

BY CAR

Driving isn't easy in Boston. It's important to plan out a route in advance if you are unfamiliar with the city. There is a profusion of one way streets, so always keep a detailed map handy. It's also a good idea to pay extra attention to other drivers. Boston drivers have a bad reputation, and you should watch out for those using the emergency breakdown lanes (illegal unless posted otherwise), passing on the right, or turning from the wrong lane.

PARKING   Major public lots are at Government Center and Quincy Market, beneath Boston Common (entrance on Charles Street), beneath Post Office Square, at the Prudential Center, at Copley Place, and off Clarendon Street near the John Hancock Tower. Smaller lots and garages are scattered throughout Downtown, especially around the Theater District and off Atlantic Avenue in the North End. Most are expensive; expect to pay up to $8 an hour or $24 to park all day. The few city garages are a bargain at about $7-$11 per day.

BY SUBWAY

The Massachusetts Bay Transportation Authority (MBTA)—or "T" when referring to the subway line—operates subways, elevated trains, and trolleys along five connecting lines. A 24-hour hotline and the MBTA Web site offer information on routes, schedules, fares, wheelchair access, and other matters. Free maps are available at the MBTA's Park Street Station information stand, open daily from 7 AM to 10 PM. They're also available online at ⊕ www.mbta.com.

"Inbound" trains head into the city center and "outbound" trains head away from downtown Boston. If you get on the Red Line at South Sta-

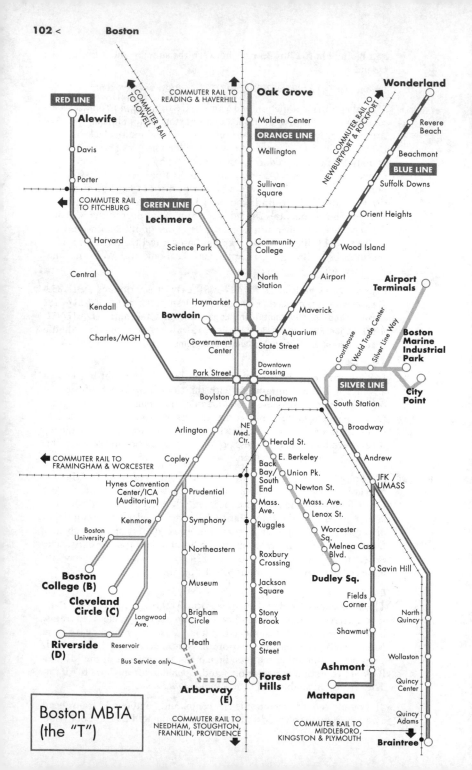

Boston MBTA
(the "T")

tion, the train heading toward Cambridge is inbound. But once you pass the Park Street station, the train becomes an outbound train. The best way to figure out which way to go is to know the last stop on the train, which is usually listed on the front of the train. So, from Downtown, the Red Line to Cambridge would be the Alewife train and the Green Line to Fenway would be the Boston College or Cleveland Circle train.

Trains operate from about 5:30 AM to about 12:30 AM. T fares are $2 for adults paying in cash or $1.70 with a prepurchased CharlieCard. There are CharlieCard dispensing machines at almost every subway stop. Children under age 11 ride free and senior citizens pay 60¢. An extra fare is required outbound on the most distant Red Line stops (for example, the fare each way from Braintree is $2.50). Fares on the commuter rail—the Purple Line—vary widely; check with the MBTA.

One-day ($9) and seven-day ($15) passes are available for unlimited travel on subways, city buses, and inner-harbor ferries. You must pay a double fare if you're headed to some suburban stations such as Braintree; pay the second fare as you exit the station. Buy passes at any full-service MBTA stations. Passes are also sold at the Boston Common Visitor Information Center (⇨ *Visitor Information)* and at some hotels.

Contact **MBTA** (☎ *800/392-6100, 617/222-3200* ⊕ *www.mbta.com).*

BY TAXI
Cabs are available around the clock. You can also call for a cab or find them outside most hotels and at designated cab stands around the city which are marked by signs. Taxis generally line up in Harvard Square, around South Station, near Faneuil Hall Marketplace, at Long Wharf, near Massachusetts General Hospital, and in the Theater District. A taxi ride within the city of Boston starts at $1.75, and costs 30¢ for each 1/8 mi thereafter. Licensed cabs have meters and provide receipts. An illuminated rooftop sign indicates an available cab. If you're going to or from the airport or to the suburbs, ask about flat rates. Cabdrivers sometimes charge extra for multiple stops. One-way streets often make circuitous routes necessary and increase your cost.

Taxi Companies **Boston Cab Association** (☎ *617/536-3200).* **Checker Cab** (☎ *617/536-7000).* **Green Cab Association** (☎ *617/625-5000).* **Independent Taxi Operators Association (ITOA)** (☎ *617/825-4000).* **Town Taxi** (☎ *617/536-5000).*

BY TRAIN
Boston is served by Amtrak at North Station, South Station, and Back Bay Station, which accommodate frequent departures to and arrivals from New York, Philadelphia, and Washington, DC. Amtrak's pricey high-speed Acela train cuts the travel time between Boston and New York from 4½ hours to 3½ hours. South Station is also the eastern terminus of Amtrak's *Lake Shore Limited,* which travels daily between Boston and Chicago by way of Albany, Rochester, Buffalo, and Cleveland. An additional Amtrak station with ample parking is just off Route 128 in suburban Westwood, southwest of Boston.

The MBTA runs commuter trains to points south, west, and north. Those bound for Worcester, Needham, Forge Park, Providence (RI), and Stoughton leave from South Station and Back Bay Station; those to Fitchburg, Lowell, Haverhill, Newburyport, and Rockport operate out of North Station.

Amtrak tickets and reservations are available at Amtrak stations, by telephone, through travel agents, or online. Amtrak schedule and fare information can be found at South Station, Back Bay Station, or the Route 128 station in suburban Westwood, as well as online. The 24-hour hotline is another good source for route, schedule, fare, and other information. Free maps are available at the MBTA's Park Street Station information stand.

Amtrak ticket offices accept all major credit cards, cash, traveler's checks, and personal checks when accompanied by a valid photo ID and a major credit card. You may pay on board with cash or a major credit card, but a surcharge may apply. MBTA commuter-rail stations generally accept only cash. You may also pay in cash on board commuter trains, but there may be a $1-$2 surcharge.

Amtrak has both reserved and unreserved trains. During peak times, such as a Friday night, get a reservation and a ticket in advance. Trains at nonpeak times are unreserved, with seats assigned on a first-come, first-served basis.

Train Information **Back Bay Station** (⊠ *145 Dartmouth St., Back Bay*). **North Station** (⊠ *Causeway and Friend Sts., North End*). **South Station** (⊠ *Atlantic Ave. and Summer St., Downtown*).

CONTACTS & RESOURCES

VISITOR INFORMATION
Contacts **Greater Boston Convention and Visitors Bureau** (⊠ *2 Copley Pl., Suite 105, Back Bay* ☏ *888/733-2678 or 617/536-4100* ⊟ *617/424-7664* ⊕ *www. bostonusa.com*).

Massachusetts

WORD OF MOUTH

"I love the Berkshires, especially in the summer. Tanglewood, antiquing, Jacob's Pillow, Mass MoCA, all set in gorgeous greenery."

–HHoward

"We were in Concord overnight Friday to Saturday . . . the foliage was spectacular. There were no other tourists when we arrived at the Old North Bridge Saturday morning and it was beautiful and peaceful."

–Vttraveler

THE MASSACHUSETTS TOWN MEETING SET the tone for politics in the 13 original colonies. A century later, Boston was a hotbed of rebellion—Samuel Adams and James Otis, the "Sons of Liberty," started a war with words, inciting action against British Colonial policies with patriotic pamphlets and fiery speeches at Faneuil Hall. Twentieth-century heirs to Adams include Boston's flashy mid-century mayor James Michael Curley; Thomas "Tip" O'Neill, the late Speaker of the House; and, of course, the Kennedys. In 1961 the young senator from the Boston suburb of Brookline, John Fitzgerald Kennedy, became president of the United States. JFK's service to Massachusetts was family tradition: in the years before World War I, Kennedy's grandfather John "Honey Fitz" Fitzgerald served in Congress and as mayor of Boston. But political families are nothing new here—Massachusetts has sent both a father and a son (John Adams and John Quincy Adams) to the White House.

The seaside towns of Massachusetts—from Newburyport to Provincetown—were built before the Revolution, during the heyday of American shipping. Their grand old houses and bustling waterfronts evoke a bygone world of clipper ships, robust fishermen, and sturdy sailors bound for distant points. In our own time, the high-tech firms of the greater Boston area helped launch the information age, and the Massachusetts Institute of Technology and Harvard supplied intellectual heft to deliver it to the wider world.

Massachusetts has an extensive system of parks, protected forests, beaches, and nature preserves. Like medieval pilgrims, readers of *Walden* come to Concord to visit the place where Henry David Thoreau wrote his prophetic essay. Thoreau's disciples can be found hiking to the top of the state's highest peak, Mt. Greylock; shopping for organic produce in an unpretentious college burg like Williamstown; or strolling the beaches of Cape Cod. For those who prefer the hills to the ocean, the rolling Berkshire terrain defines the landscape from North Adams to Great Barrington in the western part of the state.

The list of Bay State writers, artists, and musicians who have shaped American culture is long indeed. The state has produced great poets in every generation: Anne Bradstreet, Phillis Wheatley, Emily Dickinson, Henry Wadsworth Longfellow, William Cullen Bryant, e. e. cummings, Robert Lowell, Elizabeth Bishop, Sylvia Plath, and Anne Sexton. Massachusetts writers include Louisa May Alcott, author of the enduring classic *Little Women*; Nathaniel Hawthorne, who re-created the Salem of his Puritan ancestors in *The Scarlet Letter*; Herman Melville, who wrote *Moby-Dick* in a house at the foot of Mt. Greylock; Eugene O'Neill, whose early plays were produced at a makeshift theater in Provincetown on Cape Cod; Lowell native Jack Kerouac, author of *On the Road*; and John Cheever, chronicler of suburban angst. Painters Winslow Homer and James McNeill Whistler both hailed from the Commonwealth. Norman Rockwell lived and worked in Stockbridge. Joan Baez got her start singing in Harvard Square, and contemporary Boston singer-songwriter Tracy Chapman picked up the beat with folk songs for the new age.

MASSACHUSETTS TOP 5

■ **Early American History.** From Plimoth Plantation to Salem, Deerfield, Sturbridge Village, and Hancock Shaker Village, you can visit re-enactment museums, preserved villages, homes, and inns where memories of Colonial history and personalities are kept alive.

■ **Summer Festivals.** Watch renown dance companies perform against the Berkshire mountains backdrop at Jacob's Pillow, celebrate cranberries on the Cape, or have the Boston Symphony Orchestra accompany your lawn picnic at Tanglewood in Lenox.

■ **Sea-faring Communities.** Set off on a whale watch from Gloucester, warm yourself after a windy coastal walk in Rockport with clam chowder, and admire the dedicated routine of fishermen along the North Shore.

■ **Unwinding in Cape Cod.** Once you've braved the traffic over the one bridge to the long-armed peninsula, catch up on your wave-watching, cliff-walking, and cranberry-picking. For some excitement, head to Provincetown for some nightlife or a whale-watching trip.

■ **Revist your Reading.** Nathaniel Hawthorne's *House of Seven Gables* still stands in Salem, the town that also served as the setting for *The Scarlett Letter.* Liberate yourself with a swim in Thoreau's Walden Pond. In Concord, see where both Louisa May Alcott and Ralph Waldo Emerson penned their thoughts.

EXPLORING MASSACHUSETTS

History lies thick on the ground in the towns surrounding Boston—from Pilgrims to pirates, witches to whalers, the American Revolution to the Industrial Revolution. The sights outside the city are at least as interesting as those on the Boston's Freedom Trail. Visit Concord and Lexington, to the northwest of Boston, and that history class from high school may suddenly come rushing back to you. The state's coast from Boston to Cape Ann is called the North Shore, visited for its beautiful beaches, quintessential New England seaside communities, and the bewitching Salem. South of Boston lies more history in Quincy and Plymouth, and more seaside scenery at Cape Cod, Martha's Vineyard, and Nantucket. To the west is Pioneer Valley and the Berkshires, home to centuries-old towns, antiques shops, and rolling green hills.

ABOUT THE RESTAURANTS

Massachusetts invented the fried clam, and it's served in many North Shore and Cape Cod restaurants. Creamy clam chowder is another specialty. Eating seafood "in the rough"—from paper plates in seaside shacks—is a revered local custom. On the Cape, specialties from the Portuguese community like kale soup and linguiça sausage appear on some menus. At country inns in the Berkshires and the Pioneer Valley you'll find creative contemporary fare as well as traditional New England "dinners" strongly reminiscent of old England: double-cut pork chops, rack of lamb, game, Boston baked beans, Indian pudding, and the dubiously glorified "New England boiled dinner."

PLANNING YOUR TRIP

BUDGETING YOUR TIME

Though Massachusetts is small compared to some states in the country, you could easily spend several weeks exploring it. If you have a few days, head to Boston and then a town or two north and south of it, such as Concord, Plymouth, and Salem. Those who have a week may want to add on the Berkshires or spend the entire time relaxing at Cape Cod or Martha's Vineyard.

WHEN TO GO

The dazzling foliage and cool temperatures make fall the best time to visit western Massachusetts. Summer, especially late in the season when the water is a bit warmer, is ideal for visits to the beaches. Many towns save their best for winter—inns open their doors to carolers, shops serve eggnog, and lobster boats parade around Gloucester harbor adorned with lights. The off-season is the perfect time to try cross-country skiing, take a walk on a stormy beach, or spend a night by the fire, tucked under a quilt, catching up on books by Hawthorne or Thoreau.

GETTING THERE & AROUND

Boston's Logan International Airport is the state's major airline hub. Flights also come into Manchester Boston Regional Airport in New Hampshire, 50 mi northwest of Boston, and TF Green International Airport in Providence, Rhode Island, 59 mi south of Boston.

ABOUT THE HOTELS

The signature accommodation outside Boston is the country inn; in the Berkshires, where magnificent mansions have been converted into lodgings, the inns reach a very grand scale indeed. Less extravagant and less expensive are B&B establishments, many of them in private homes. On Cape Cod, inns are plentiful, and rental homes and condominiums are available for long-term stays. You'll want to make reservations for inns well in advance during peak periods: summer on the Cape and islands, and summer through winter in the Berkshires. Smoking has been banned in all Massachusetts hotels.

WHAT IT COSTS					
	¢	$	$$	$$$	$$$$
RESTAU-RANTS	under $8	$8–$14	$15–$24	$25–$32	over $32
HOTELS	under $75	$75–$150	$151–$225	$226–$325	over $325

For restaurants, prices are per person, for a main course at dinner. For hotels, prices are for two people in a standard double room in high season, excluding 12.45% tax and service charges.

Updated by
Diane Bair &
Pamela Wright

Northwest of the city, Lexington and Concord embody the spirit of the American Revolution. These two quintessential New England towns enclose several historic homes and small museums dedicated to some of the country's first substantial writers—Ralph Waldo Emerson,

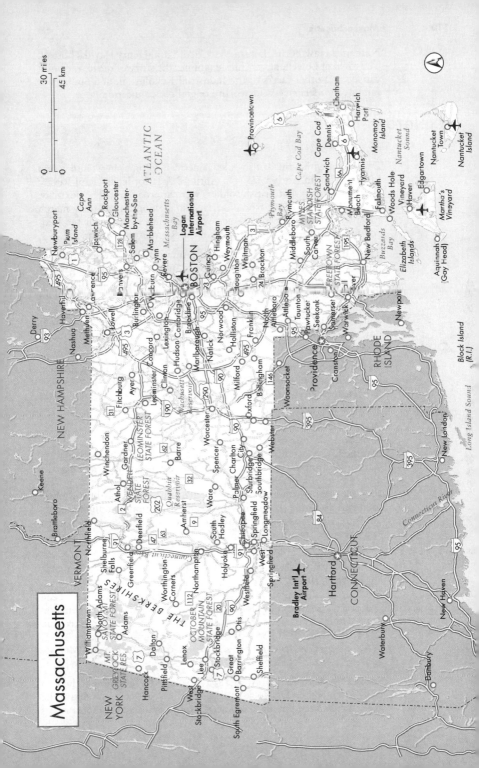

Massachusetts

30 miles
45 km

ATLANTIC OCEAN

NEW HAMPSHIRE

VERMONT

NEW YORK

RHODE ISLAND

CONNECTICUT

THE BERKSHIRES

Cape Cod

Cape Cod Bay

Massachusetts Bay

Nantucket Sound

Buzzards Bay

Long Island Sound

Connecticut River

Block Island (R.I.)

Provincetown
Chatham
Harwich Port
Monomoy Island
Harwich
Dennis
Sandwich
6A
Hyannis
Monument Beach
Falmouth
Woods Hole
Nantucket Town
Nantucket Island
Edgartown
Martha's Vineyard
Aquinnah (Gay Head)
Elizabeth Islands
New Bedford
195
Somerset
Seekonk
Swansea
Fall River
Ayer
Taunton
Middleboro
South Carver
Plymouth
Weymouth
Hingham
Whitman
Brockton
Stoughton
Newport
Warwick
Cranston
Providence
Pawtucket
Woonsocket
Webster
Milford
Bellingham
Franklin
North Attleboro
Attleboro
Norwood
Holliston
Natick
Marlborough
Hudson
Clinton
Leominster
Fitchburg
Oxford
Charlton City
Spencer
Worcester
Barre
Gardner
Winchendon
Athol
Deerfield
Amherst
South Hadley
Ware
Palmer
Sturbridge
Southbridge
Longmeadow
West Springfield
Springfield
Holyoke
Northampton
Westfield
Worthington Corners
Shelburne Falls
Northfield
Greenfield
Williamstown
North Adams
Adams
Dalton
Pittsfield
Hancock
West Stockbridge
South Egremont
Great Barrington
Stockbridge
Lee
Lenox
Sheffield
Otis
Danbury
Waterbury
New Haven
New London
Hartford
Bradley Int'l Airport
Keene
Brattleboro
Derry
Nashua
Haverhill
Methuen
Lawrence
Lowell
Burlington
Lexington
Concord
Cambridge
Brookline
BOSTON
Logan International Airport
Revere
Lynn
Saugus
Marblehead
Salem
Manchester-by-the-Sea
Gloucester
Rockport
Cape Ann
Ipswich
Newburyport
Plum Island
Quincy

LEOMINSTER STATE FOREST
WENDELL STATE FOREST
Quabbin Reservoir
Wachusett Reservoir
OCTOBER MOUNTAIN STATE FOREST
MT GREYLOCK STATE RES.
SAVOY MT STATE FOREST
MYLES STANDISH STATE FOREST
FREETOWN STATE FOREST

95
93
495
128
1
3
2
202
9
63
112
7
8
20
90
290
146
395
84
24
23

Connecticut River

Nathaniel Hawthorne, Louisa May Alcott, and Henry David Thoreau. The town of Lowell, meanwhile, examines the story of the textile mills, canals, and other facets of the Industrial Revolution, and Sudbury is famous for its Henry Wadsworth Longfellow connection.

LEXINGTON

16 mi northwest of Boston.

Discontent within the British-ruled American colonies burst into action in Lexington in April 1775. On April 18, patriot leader Paul Revere alerted the town that British soldiers were approaching. The next day, as the British advance troops arrived in Lexington on their march toward Concord, the minutemen were waiting to confront the Redcoats in what became the skirmish of the Revolutionary War.

These first military encounters of the American Revolution are very much a part of present-day Lexington, a modern suburban town that sprawls out from the historic sites near its center. Although the downtown area is generally lively, with ice-cream and coffee shops, boutiques, and a great little movie theater, the town becomes especially animated each Patriots' Day (April 19 but celebrated on the third Monday in April), when costume-clad groups re-create the minutemen's battle maneuvers and Paul Revere rides again.

To learn more about the city and the 1775 clash, stop by the **Lexington Visitor Center** (⊠ *1875 Massachusetts Ave.* ☎ *781/862–2480* ⊕ *www.lexingtonchamber.org* ⊘ *Apr.–Nov., daily 9–5; Dec.–Mar., daily 10–4*).

WHAT TO SEE

Battle Green. It was on this two-acre triangle of land, on April 19, 1775, that the first confrontation between British soldiers, who were marching from Boston toward Concord, and the colonial militia known as the minutemen took place. The minutemen—so called because they were able to prepare themselves at a moment's notice—were led by Captain John Parker, whose role in the American Revolution is commemorated in Henry Hudson Kitson's renowned 1900 *Minuteman* statue. Facing downtown Lexington at the tip of Battle Green, the statue's in a traffic island and therefore makes for a difficult photo op.

Buckman Tavern. While waiting for the arrival of the British on the morning of April 19, 1775, the minutemen gathered at this 1690 tavern. A half-hour tour takes in the tavern's seven rooms, which have been restored to the way they looked in the 1770s. Among the items on display is an old front door with a hole made by a British musket ball. ⊠ *1 Bedford St.* ☎ *781/862–1703* ⊕ *www.lexingtonhistory.org* ✎ *$5; $10 combination ticket includes Hancock-Clarke House and Munroe Tavern* ⊘ *Apr.–Oct., daily 10–4.*

Hancock-Clarke House. On April 18, 1775, Paul Revere came to here to warn patriots John Hancock and Sam Adams, who were staying at the house while attending the Provincial Congress in nearby Concord, of

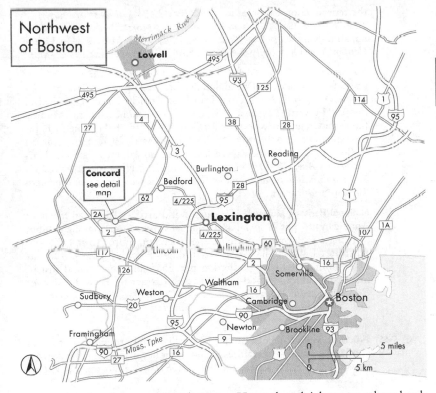

Northwest
of Boston

the advance of British troops. Hancock and Adams, on whose heads
the British king had put a price, fled to avoid capture. The house, a
parsonage built in 1698, is a 10-minute walk from Lexington Common. Inside are the pistols of the British major John Pitcairn as well as
period furnishings and portraits. ⊠*36 Hancock St.* ☎*781/862–1703*
⊕*www.lexingtonhistory.org* ✉*$5; $10 combination ticket includes
Buckman Tavern and Munroe Tavern* ◷*Apr.–mid-June weekends,
mid-June–Oct., daily 11–2.*

★ **Minute Man National Historical Park.** West of Lexington's center stretches
this 1,000-acre, three-parcel park that also extends into nearby Lincoln and Concord (⇨Concord, What to See). Begin your park visit
at Lexington's **Minute Man Visitor Center** to see its free multimedia
presentation, "The Road to Revolution," a captivating introduction to
the events of April 1775. Then, continuing along Highway 2A toward
Concord, you pass the point where Revere's midnight ride ended with
his capture by the British; it's marked with a boulder and plaque, as
well as an enclosure where rangers sometimes give educational presentations. You can also visit the 1732 **Hartwell Tavern** (open late May
through October, daily 9–5), a restored drover's (driver's) tavern staffed
by park employees in period costume; they frequently demonstrate
musket firing or open-hearth cooking, and children are likely to enjoy

the reproduction Colonial toys. ⊠*Hwy. 2A, ¼ mi west of Hwy. 128* ☎*978/369–6993* ⊕*www.nps.gov/mima* ⊙*North Bridge Visitor Center, Apr.–Nov., daily 9–4; Dec.–Mar., daily 11–3. Minute Man Visitor Center, Apr.–Oct., daily 9–5; Oct.–Nov., daily 9–4; closed Dec.–Mar.*

Munroe Tavern. As April 19, 1775, dragged on, British forces met fierce resistance in Concord. Dazed and demoralized after the battle at Concord's Old North Bridge, the British backtracked and regrouped at this 1695 tavern, 1 mi east of Lexington Common, while the Munroe family hid in nearby woods. The troops then retreated through what is now the town of Arlington. After a bloody battle there, they returned to Boston. Tours of the tavern last about 30 minutes. ⊠*1332 Massachusetts Ave.* ☎*781/862–1703* ⊕*www.lexingtonhistory.org* ⊠*$5; $10 combination ticket includes Hancock-Clarke House and Buckman Tavern* ⊙*June–Oct., 11–3* PM.

National Heritage Museum. View items and artifacts from all facets of American life, put in social and political context. An ongoing exhibit, "Lexington Alarm'd," outlines events leading up to April 1775 and illustrates Revolutionary-era life through everyday objects such as blacksmithing tools, bloodletting paraphernalia, and dental instruments, including a "tooth key" used to extract teeth. ⊠*33 Marrett Rd., Hwy. 2A at Massachusetts Ave.* ☎*781/861–6559* ⊕*www.monh. org* ⊠*Donations accepted* ⊙*Mon.–Sat. 10–5, Sun. noon–5.*

WHERE TO EAT

C $-$$ ✕**Bertucci's.** Part of a popular chain, this family-friendly spot offers
ITALIAN   good Italian food—specialities include ravioli, calzones, and brick-oven pizzas. ⊠*1777 Massachusetts Ave.* ☎*781/860–9000* ▭*AE, D, DC, MC, V.*

CONCORD

About 10 mi west of Lexington, 21 mi northwest of Boston.

The Concord of today is a modern suburb with a busy center filled with arty shops, places to eat, and (recalling the literary history made here) old bookstores. Autumn lovers, take note: Concord is a great place to start a fall foliage tour. From Boston, head west along Highway 2 to Concord, and then continue on to find harvest stands and do-it-yourself apple-picking around Harvard and Stow.

WHAT TO SEE

C ❼ **Concord Museum.** The original contents of Emerson's private study, as well as the world's largest collection of Thoreau artifacts, reside in this 1930 Colonial-revival building just east of the town center. The museum provides a good overview of the town's history, from its original American Indian settlement to the present. Highlights include American Indian Indian artifacts, furnishings from Thoreau's Walden Pond cabin, and one of the two lanterns hung at Boston's Old North Church to signal that the British were coming by sea. If you've brought the children, ask for a free family activity pack. ⊠*200 Lexington Rd., entrance on Cambridge Tpke.* ☎*978/369–9763* ⊕*www.concordmu-*

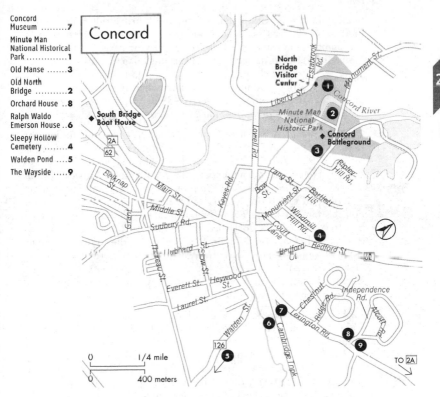

seum.org ✉*$10* ⏱*Jan.–Mar., Mon.–Sat. 11–4, Sun. 1–4; Apr.–Dec,*
Mon.–Sat. 9–5, Sun. noon–5; June–Aug., daily 9–5.

🌣 ❶ **Minute Man National Historical Park.** Along Highway 2A is a three-parcel
★ park with 1,000 acres. The park contains many of the sites important to Concord's role in the Revolution, including Old North Bridge,
as well as two visitor centers, one each in Concord and Lexington
(⇨ Lexington, What to See). Although the initial Revolutionary War
sorties were in Lexington, word of the American losses spread rapidly to surrounding towns: when the British marched into Concord,
more than 400 minutemen were waiting. A marker set in the stone
wall along Liberty Street, behind the North Bridge Visitors Center,
announces: ON THIS FIELD THE MINUTEMEN AND MILITIA FORMED BEFORE
MARCHING DOWN TO THE FIGHT AT THE BRIDGE. The park's **North Bridge
Visitor Center** (✉*174 Liberty St.* ☎*978/369–6993*) is open from
April through November, daily 9–4 and December through March,
daily 11–3. ✉*Bounded by Monument St., Liberty St., and Lowell
Rd.* ⊕*www.nps.gov/mima* ⏱*Grounds daily dawn–dusk.* ✉*Bounded
by Monument St., Liberty St., and Lowell Rd.* ⊕*www.nps.gov/mima*
⏱*Grounds daily dawn–dusk.*

❸ **Old Manse.** The Reverend William Emerson, grandfather of Ralph
Waldo Emerson, watched rebels and redcoats battle from behind his

home, which was within sight of the Old North Bridge. The house, built in 1770, was occupied continuously by the Emerson family for almost two centuries, except for a 3½-year period during which Nathaniel Hawthorne rented it. Furnishings date from the late 18th century. Tours run throughout the day and last 45 minutes, with a new tour starting within 15 minutes of when the first person signs up. ⊠*269 Monument St.* ☎*978/369–3909* ⛹*$8* ⊘*Mid-Apr.–Oct., Mon.–Sat. 10–5, Sun. noon–5; last tour departs 4:30.*

❷ **Old North Bridge.** A half-mile from Concord center, at this bridge, the Concord minutemen turned the tables on the British on the morning of April 19, 1775. The Americans didn't fire first, but when two of their own fell dead from a redcoat volley, Major John Buttrick of Concord roared, "Fire, fellow soldiers, for God's sake, fire." The minutemen released volley after volley, and the redcoats fled. Daniel Chester French's famous statue *The Minuteman* (1875) honors the country's first freedom fighters. Inscribed at the foot of the statue are words Ralph Waldo Emerson wrote in 1837 describing the confrontation: BY THE RUDE BRIDGE THAT ARCHED THE FLOOD / THEIR FLAG TO APRIL'S BREEZE UNFURLED / HERE ONCE THE EMBATTLED FARMERS STOOD / AND FIRED THE SHOT HEARD ROUND THE WORLD. The lovely wooded surroundings give a sense of what the landscape was like in more rural times.

❻ **Ralph Waldo Emerson House.** The 19th-century essayist and poet Ralph Waldo Emerson lived briefly in the Old Manse in 1834–35, then moved to this home, where he lived until his death in 1882. Here he wrote the *Essays*. Except for items from Emerson's study, now at the nearby Concord Museum, the Emerson House furnishings have been preserved as the writer left them, down to his hat resting on the newel post. You must join one of the half-hour-long tours to see the interior. ⊠*28 Cambridge Tpke., at Lexington Rd.* ☎*978/369–2236* ⊕*www.rwe. org/emersonhouse* ⛹*$7* ⊘*Mid-Apr.–mid-Oct., Thurs.–Sat. 10–4:30, Sun. 1–4:30; call for tour schedule.*

❽ **Orchard House.** The dark brown exterior of Louisa May Alcott's family home sharply contrasts with the light, wit, and energy so much in evidence inside. Named for the apple orchard that once surrounded it, Orchard House was the Alcott family home from 1857 to 1877. Here, Louisa wrote *Little Women,* based on her life with her three sisters; and her father, Bronson, founded his school of philosophy—the building remains behind the house. Because Orchard House had just one owner after the Alcotts left and because it became a museum in 1911, many of the original furnishings remain, including the semicircular shelf-desk where Louisa wrote *Little Women.* ⊠*399 Lexington Rd.* ☎*978/369–4118* ⊕*www.louisamayalcott.org* ⛹*$9, tours free* ⊘*Apr.–Oct., Mon.–Sat. 10–4:30, Sun. 1–4:30; Nov.–Dec. and Jan. 16–Mar., weekdays 11–3, Sat. 10–4:30, Sun. 1–4:30. Half-hr tours begin every 30 mins Apr.–Oct.; call for off-season schedule.*

❹ **Sleepy Hollow Cemetery.** In the Author's Ridge section of this cemetery are the graves of American literary greats Louisa May Alcott, Ralph Waldo Emerson, Henry David Thoreau, and Nathaniel Hawthorne.

Literary Concord

The first wholly American literary movement was born in Concord, the tiny town west of Boston that, quite coincidentally, also witnessed the beginning of the American Revolution.

Under the influence of essayist and poet Ralph Waldo Emerson, a group eventually known as the Transcendental Club (but called the Hedges Club at the time) assembled regularly in Emerson's Concord home. Henry David Thoreau, a fellow townsman and famous proponent of self-reliance, was an integral club member, along with such others as pioneering feminist Margaret Fuller and poet Ellery Channing, both drawn to Concord simply because of Emerson's presence.

These are the names that have become indelible bylines in high school anthologies and college syllabi, but Concord also produced beloved authors outside the Transcendental movement. These writers include Louisa May Alcott of *Little Women* fame and children's book author Harriet Lothrop, pseudonymously known as Margaret Sydney. Even Nathaniel Hawthorne, whose various places of temporary residence around Massachusetts constitute a literary trail all their own, abided in Concord during the early and late portions of his career.

The cumulative inkwells of these authors have bestowed upon Concord a literary legacy unique in the United States, both for its influence on literature in general and for the quantity of related sights packed within such a small radius. From Alcott's Orchard House to Hawthorne's Old Manse, nearly all their houses remain standing, well preserved and open for tours.

Louisa May Alcott wrote *Little Women* while living at Orchard House in Concord.

The Thoreau Institute, within walking distance of a reconstruction of Thoreau's famous cabin in the woods at Walden Pond, is a repository of his papers and original editions. Emerson's study sits in the Concord Museum, across the street from his house. Even their final resting places are here, on Authors Ridge in Sleepy Hollow Cemetery, a few short blocks from the town common.

Various tours make the rounds of all of Concord's literary landmarks. The **Literary Trail of Greater Boston** (☎ *617/621–4020* ⊕ *www. literarytrailofgreaterboston.org*) offers trolley tours mid-June through mid-October, while **Concord Bike Tours** (☎ *978/697–1897* ⊕ www.concord-biketours.com) guide you through the sites via two wheels, usually early April through November (weather permitting).

Each Memorial Day, Alcott's grave is decorated in commemoration of her death. ⊠*Bedford St. (Hwy. 62)* ☎*978/318-3233* ⊘*Daily dawn–dusk.*

★ ❺ **Walden Pond.** For lovers of early American literature, a trip to Concord isn't complete without a pilgrimage to Henry David Thoreau's most famous residence. Here, in 1845, at age 28, Thoreau moved into a one-room cabin—built for $28.12—on the shore of this 100-foot-deep kettle hole formed by the retreat of an ancient glacier. Living alone for the next two years, Thoreau discovered the benefits of solitude and the beauties of nature. The essays in *Walden*, published in 1854, are a mixture of philosophy, nature writing, and proto-ecology. The site of the first cabin is staked out in stone. A full-size, authentically furnished replica of the cabin stands about ½ mi from the original site, near the Walden Pond State Reservation parking lot. Even when it's closed, you can peek through its windows. Now, as in Thoreau's time, the pond is a delightful summertime spot for swimming, fishing, and rowing, and there's hiking in the nearby woods. To get to Walden Pond State Reservation from the center of Concord—a trip of only 1½ mi—take Concord's Main Street a block west from Monument Square, turn left onto Walden Street, and head for the intersection of Highways 2 and 126. Cross over Highway 2 onto Highway 126, heading south for ½ mi. ⊠*915 Walden St. (Hwy. 126)* ☎*978/369-3254* ⊕*www.mass.gov/dcr/parks/walden* 🔄*Free, parking $5* ⊘*Daily from 8* AM *until about ½ hr before sunset, weather permitting.*

❾ **The Wayside.** Nathaniel Hawthorne lived at the Old Manse in 1842–45, working on stories and sketches; he then moved to Salem (where he wrote *The Scarlet Letter*) and later to Lenox (*The House of the Seven Gables*). In 1852 he returned to Concord, bought this rambling structure called The Wayside, and lived here until his death in 1864. The subsequent owner, Margaret Sidney, wrote the children's book *Five Little Peppers and How They Grew* (1881). Before Hawthorne moved in, the Alcotts lived here, from 1845 to 1848. An exhibit center, in the former barn, provides information about the Wayside authors and links them to major events in American history. Hawthorne's tower-study, with his stand-up writing desk, is substantially as he left it. ⊠*455 Lexington Rd.* ☎*978/369-6993* ⊘*Open by guided tour only, May–Oct., Fri.–Sun., at 11, 1, 3, and 4:30.*

WHERE TO EAT

$ ✕ **La Provence.** This little taste of France, a casual café and take-out shop
FRENCH opposite the Concord train station, makes a good stop for a light meal. In the morning you can start off with a croissant or a brioche, and at midday you can pick up sandwiches (perhaps pâté and cheese or French ham), quiches, or salads. Leave room for an éclair or a petite fruit tart. Just don't plan a late night here; the café closes at 7 PM during the week and at 5:30 on Saturday. ⊠*105 Thoreau St.* ☎*978/371-7428* ⊕*www.laprovence.us* 🔄*D, MC, V* ⊘*Closed Sun.*

$$-$$$ ✕ **Walden Grille.** Chowders, salads and sandwiches are typical fare at
AMERICAN this old brick firehouse-turned-dining room, but in a town with limited dining options, this isn't a bad choice. Start with the Philly spring rolls

or crispy fried oysters. Sandwiches include run-of-the-mill burgers and BLTs, plus more creative options like the chicken curry roll-up. Entrées run the gamut from the Asian veggie noodle roll to the crab mac and cheese. ⊠*24 Walden St.* ☎*978/371–2233* ⊕*www.waldengrille.com* ▬*AE, D, MC, V.*

LOWELL

30 mi northwest of Boston.

Everyone knows that the American Revolution began in Massachusetts. But the Commonwealth, and in particular the Merrimack Valley, also nurtured the Industrial Revolution. Lowell's first mill opened in 1823; by the 1850s, 40 factories employed thousands of workers and produced 2 million yards of cloth every week.

WHAT TO SEE

Boott Cotton Mills Museum. About a 10-minute walk northeast from the National Park Visitor Center is this museum devoted to industrialization. The textile worker's grueling life is shown with all its grit, noise, and dust. You know you're in for an unusual experience when you're handed earplugs—they're for the re-created 1920s weave room, authentic down to the deafening roar of 88 working power looms. Other exhibits at the complex include weaving artifacts, cloth samples, video interviews with workers, and a large, meticulous scale model of 19th-century production. ⊠*Foot of John St.* ☎*978/970–5000* ⊕*www.nps.gov/lowe* ▣*$6* ☯*Apr.–Nov., daily 9:30–5; Dec.–Mar., weekdays 10–2, Sat. 9:30-4, Sun. 1–4.*

Lowell National Historical Park. This park tracks the history of a gritty era when the power loom was the symbol of economic progress. It encompasses several blocks in the downtown area, including former-mills-turned-museums, a network of canals, and a helpful visitor center. Begin at the National Park Visitor Center where you can watch a multimedia presentation on the Industrial Age in Lowell. Several tours, including canal boat trips and guided walking and trolley tours, depart from here. ⊠*246 Market St.* ☎*978/970–5000* ⊕*www.nps.gov/lowe* ▣*Free* ☯*Mid-Mar.–Nov., daily 9–5; Dec.–mid-Mar., Mon.–Sat. 9–4:30, Sun. 10–4:30.*

THE NORTH SHORE

Updated by Elisabeth Coen & Jo Kadlecek

The slice of Massachusetts's Atlantic Coast known as the North Shore extends past Boston to the picturesque Cape Ann region just shy of the New Hampshire border. In addition to miles of woods and beaches, the North Shore's highlights include Marblehead, a stunningly classic New England sea town; Salem, which thrives on a history of witches, writers, and maritime trades; Gloucester, the oldest seaport in America; Rockport, rich with crafts shops and artists' studios; and Newburyport, with its redbrick center and clapboard mansions, and a handful of typical New England towns in between. Bustling during the short summer season and breathtaking during the autumn foliage, the North Shore is calmer (and colder) between November and June. Since many restaurants, inns, and attractions operating during reduced hours, it's worth calling ahead off-season.

MARBLEHEAD

17 mi north of Boston.

Marblehead, with its narrow and winding streets, beautifully preserved clapboard homes, sea captains' mansions, and harbor, looks much the way the village must have when it was founded in 1629 by fishermen from Cornwall and the Channel Islands. One of New New England's premier sailing capitals, Marblehead's Race Week—first held in 1889—continues to attract boats each July from along the eastern seaboard. Parking in town can be difficult; lots at the end of Front Street or on State Street by the Landing restaurant are the best options.

WHAT TO SEE

The 1768 Jeremiah Lee Mansion. Marblehead's 18th-century high society is exemplified in this mansion run by the town's museum and historical society. Colonel Lee was the wealthiest merchant and ship owner in Massachusetts in 1768, and although few original furnishings remain, the unique hand-painted wallpaper and fine collection of traditional North Shore furniture provide clues into the life of an American gentleman. ⊠*161 Washington St.* ☎*781/631–1768* ⊕*www.marbleheadmuseum.org/LeeMansion.htm* ⊠*$5* ☉*June–Oct., Tues.–Sat. 10–4.*

Abbott Hall. The town's Victorian-era municipal building, built in 1876, displays Archibald Willard's painting *The Spirit of '76.* Many visitors, familiar since childhood with this image of the three Revolutionary veterans with fife, drum, and flag, are surprised to find the original in an otherwise unassuming town hall. Also on site is a small naval museum exploring Marblehead's maritime past. ⊠*188 Washington St.* ☎*781/631–0000* ⊠*Free* ☉*Mon., Tues., and Thurs. 8–5; Wed. 7:30–7:30; Fri. 8–1; Sat.–Sun. 10–5.*

Fort Sewall. Marblehead's magnificent views of the harbor, the Misery islands, and the Atlantic are best seen from this fort that was built in 1644 atop the rocky cliffs of the harbor. Used as a defense against the French in 1742 as well as during the War of 1812, Fort Sewall today is open to the public as community parkland. Barracks and underground quarters can still seen, and Revolutionary War re-enactments by members of the modern-day Glover's Marblehead Regiment occur at the fort annually. ⊠*End of Front St.* ⊕*www.essexheritage.org/sites/fort_sewall.shtml* ⊠*Free* ☉*Daily, sunrise to sunset.*

WHERE TO EAT & STAY

$-$$
SEAFOOD
✕**The Landing.** Decorated in nautical blues and whites, this pleasant restaurant sits right on Marblehead harbor, with a deck that's nearly in the water. The menu mixes classic New England fare (clam chowder, lobster, broiled scrod) with more contemporary dishes like boneless roast duck on a bed of wild rice. Brunch is served on Sunday. The pub

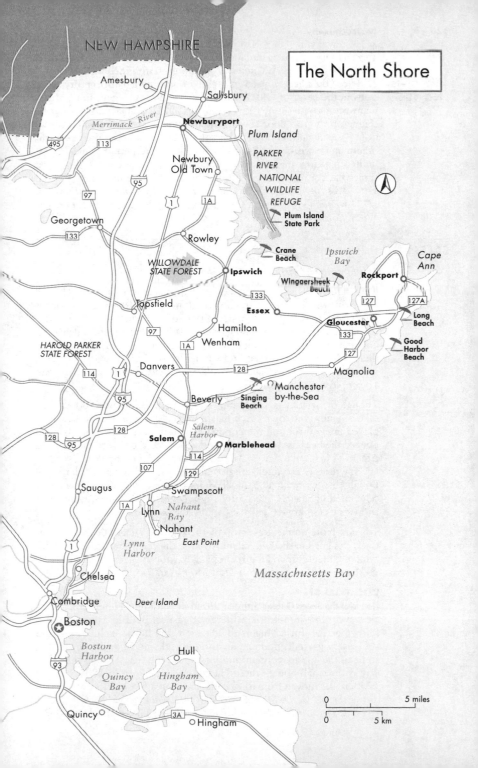

area has a lighter menu and local feel. ⊠*81 Front St.* ☎*781/639–1266* ☰*AE, D, DC, MC, V* ⊕*www.thelandingrestaurant.com.*

$$–$$$
Fodor's Choice
★

Harbor Light Inn. Housed in a pair of adjoining 18th-century mansions in the heart of Old Town Marblehead, this elegant inn features many rooms with canopy beds, brick fireplaces, and jacuzzis. A soaring ceiling on the top floor reveals the original post-and-beam construction. Rates include continental breakfast buffet, and require two-night minimum on weekends. **Pros:** nice location amid period homes. **Cons:** limited parking; many one-way and narrow streets make this town somewhat confusing to get around by car, and the inn tricky to find. ⊠*58 Washington St.* ☎*781/631–2186* ⊕*www.harborlightinn.com* ⇤*21 rooms* ⚷*In-room: VCR, Wi-Fi. In-hotel: pool, no kids under 8, Wi-Fi, no-smoking rooms* ☰*AE, MC, V* ⑩*CP.*

SALEM

16 mi northeast of Boston, 4 mi west of Marblehead.

Known for years as the "Witch City," Salem is redefining itself. Though numerous witch-related attractions and shops still draw tourists, there's much more to the city. But first, a bit on its bewitched past. The witchcraft hysteria emerged from the trials of 1692, when several Salem-area girls fell ill and accused some of the townspeople of casting spells on them. More than 150 men and women were charged with practicing witchcraft, a crime punishable by death. After the trials later that year, 19 people were hanged.

Though the witch trials might have built Salem's infamy, it'd be a mistake to ignore the town's rich maritime and creative traditions, which played integral roles in the country's evolution. Frigates out of Salem opened the Far East trade routes and generated the wealth that created America's first millionaires. Among its native talents are writer Nathaniel Hawthorne, the intellectual Peabody Sisters, navigator Nathaniel Bowditch, and architect Samuel McIntire. This creative spirit is today celebrated in Salem's internationally-recognized museums, waterfront shops and restaurants, galleries, and wide common.

To learn more on the area, stop by the **Regional Visitor's Center.** Innovatively designed in the Old Salem Armory, the center has exhibits, a 27-minute film, maps, and a gift shop. (⊠*2 Liberty St.* ☎*978/740–1650* ⊙*Memorial Day–Columbus Day, Mon.–Sat. 9–5, Sun. noon–5*).

WHAT TO SEE

★ **House of the Seven Gables.** Immortalized in Nathaniel Hawthorne's classic novel, this site itself is a literary treasure. Built in 1668 and also known as the Turner-Ingersoll Mansion, the house includes a secret staircase, a garret containing an antique scale model of the house, and some of the finest Georgian interiors in the country. Also on the property is the small house where Hawthorne was born in 1804; built in 1750, it was moved from its original location a few blocks away. ⊠*54 Turner St. off Derby St.* ☎*978/744–0991* ⊕*www.7gables.org* 🎫*$11* ⊙*Nov., Dec., and mid-Jan.–June, daily 10–5; July–Oct., daily 10–7.*

Fodor'sChoice **Peabody Essex Museum.** Salem's world-class museum celebrates maritime
★ art, history, and the spoils of the Asian export trade. Its 30 galleries,
housed in a contemplative blend of modern design, represent a diverse
range of styles; ranging from American decorative and oceanic art to
idea studios and photography. ⊠*East India Sq.* ☎*978/745–9500 or
866/745–1876* ⊕*www.pem.org* ☜*$15* ⊙*Daily 10–5.*

Salem Maritime National Historic Site. Near Derby Wharf, this 9¼-acre
site focuses on Salem's heritage as a major seaport with a thriving overseas trade. It includes an orientation center with an 18-minute film;
the 1762 home of Elias Derby, America's first millionaire; the 1819
Customs House, made famous in Nathaniel Hawthorne's *The Scarlet
Letter;* and a replica of the *Friendship,* a 171-foot, three-masted 1797
merchant vessel. There's also an active lighthouse dating from 1871, as
well as the nation's last surviving 18th-century wharves. The West India
Goods Store, across the street, is still a working 19th-century store with
glass jars of spices, teas, and coffees. ⊠*193 Derby St.* ☎*978/740–
1660* ⊕*www.nps.gov/sama* ☜*Site free, tours $5* ⊙*Daily 9–5.*

Salem Witch Museum. An informative, if somewhat hokey, introduction
to the 1692 witchcraft hysteria, this museum has a short walk-through
exhibit, "Witches: Evolving Perceptions," that describes witch hunts
through the years. ⊠*Washington Sq. N* ☎*978/744–1692* ⊕*www.
salemwitchmuseum.com* ☜*$8* ⊙*Sept.–June, daily 10–5; July–Aug.,
daily 10–7.*

Salem Witch Trials Memorial. Dedicated by Nobel Laureate Elie Wiesel in
1992, this melancholy space—an antidote to the relentless marketing of
the merry-witches motif—honors those who died because they refused
to confess that they were witches. A stone wall is studded with 20 stone
benches, each inscribed with a victim's name, and sits next to Salem's
oldest burying ground. ⊠*Off Liberty St. near Charter St.*

ARTS & ENTERTAINMENT
THEATER **Cry Innocent: the People Versus Bridget Bishop.** This show, the longest con-
tinuously-running play north of Boston, transports audience members
to Bridget Bishop's trial of 1692. After hearing historical testimonies,
the audience cross-examines the witnesses and must then decide the
verdict. Actors respond in character revealing much about the Puritan frame of mind. Each show is different and allows audience members to play their "part" in history. ⊠*Old Town Hall, 32 Derby Sq.*
☎*978/867–4767* ⊕*www.gordon.edu/historyalive* ☜*$9* ⊙*Jun.-Oct.,
showtimes vary.*

WHERE TO EAT & STAY
$$-$$$ ✕**The Lyceum Bar & Grill.** Always a hit for classy fare, the restaurant
Fodor'sChoice takes advantage of its historic building where Alexander Graham Bell
★ made the first long-distance phone call. The "local ingredients, global
SEAFOOD flavors" philosophy is seen best in the panko crusted fish 'n chips, oys-
ters, and lobster crepe. Jazz is played most weekends. ⊠*43 Church
Street St.* ☎*978/745–7665* ⊕*www.lyceumsalem.com* ▭*AE, D, MC,
V* ⊙*No dinner Sun. (brunch only).*

$-$$ ☷ **Amelia Payson House.** Built in 1845, this Greek-revival house is a comfortable bed-and-breakfast near all the historic attractions. With high ceilings, floral-print wallpaper, and marble fireplaces, the four guest rooms are delicate and feminine. **Pros:** spotless, cozy and decorated in period furniture. **Cons:** no children under 14, telephones and Internet connection are not available in guest rooms (though easily accessed in a common room). ✉ *16 Winter St.* ☎ *978/744–8304* ⊕ *www.ameliapaysonhouse.com* ⇥ *4 rooms* ⚇ *In-hotel: parking (no fee), Wi-Fi, no-smoking rooms* ⊟ *AE, D, MC, V* ⊘ *Closed Nov.–Mar.* ⊙ *CP.*

$-$$$ ☷ **The Hawthorne Hotel.** Elegantly restored, this full-service landmark hotel celebrates its town's most famous writer. The historic hotel and tavern is within walking distance from the town common, all museums, and the waterfront. Across the street is Nathaniel's statue and a fine gifts shop named after his wife, Sophia (Peabody), located in the couple's former home. **Pros:** lobby is historic and lovely, parking available behind hotel; easy walking access to all the town's features. **Cons:** many rooms are small, management sometimes too busy to give personal attention. ✉ *18 Washington Sq. W* ☎ *978/744–4080* ⊕ *www. hawthornehotel.com* ⇥ *93 rooms* ⚇ *In-room: Wi-Fi. In-hotel: public Wi-Fi, no-smoking rooms.*

GLOUCESTER

37 mi northeast from Boston, 8 mi northeast from Manchester.

On Gloucester's fine seaside promenade is a famous statue of a man steering a ship's wheel, his eyes searching the horizon. The statue, which honors those "who go down to the sea in ships" was commissioned by the town citizens in celebration of Gloucester's 300th anniversary in 1923. The oldest seaport in the nation (with some of the North Shore's best beaches), this is still a major fishing port. Sebastian Junger's 1997 book, *A Perfect Storm,* was an account of the fate of the *Andrea Gail,* a Gloucester fishing boat caught in "the storm of the century" in October 1991. In 2000 the book was made into a movie, filmed on location in Gloucester.

WHAT TO SEE

Hammond Castle Museum. Inventor John Hays Hammond Jr. built this structure in 1926 to resemble a "medieval" stone castle. Hammond is credited with more than 500 patents, including ones associated with the organ that bears his name. The museum contains medieval-style furnishings and paintings, and the Great Hall houses an impressive 8,200-pipe organ. From the castle you can see "Norman's Woe Rock," made famous by Longfellow in his poem "The Wreck of the Hesperus." ✉ *80 Hesperus Ave., south side of Gloucester off Rte. 127* ☎ *978/283–2080 or 978/283–7673* ⊕ *www.hammondcastle.org* ▣ *$9* ⊙ *Apr.–early Sept., daily 10–4; early Sept.–Mar., Sat.–Sun. 10–3.*

Rocky Neck. The town's creative side thrives in this neighborhood, the first-settled artists' colony in the United States. Its alumni include Winslow Homer, Maurice Prendergast, Jane Peter, and Cecilia Beaux.

✉ *Rocky Neck Ave. at L. Main St.* ⊕ *www.rockyneckartcolony.org* ⊙ *Galleries 10–10 in summer.*

The Cape Ann Historical Association. Downtown in Captain Elias Davis 1804 house, this is Gloucester's surprise museum and gallery. It reflects the town's commitment to artists and has the world's largest collection of by maritime luminist Fitz Henry (Hugh) Lane. There's also an excellent exhibit on Gloucester's maritime history. ✉ *27 Pleasant St.* ☎ *978/283–0455* ⊕ *www.capeannmuseum.org* ☞ *$6–$8* ⊙ *Closed Feb.*

SPORTS & THE OUTDOORS

BEACHES Gloucester has the best beaches on the North Shore. From Memorial Day through mid-September, parking costs $15 to $20 on weekdays and $20 to $25 on weekends, when the lots often fill by 10 AM. **Good Harbor Beach** (✉ *easily signposted from Rte. 127A*) is a huge, sandy, dune-backed beach, with showers and snack bar, and a rocky islet just offshore. For excellent sunbathing, visit **Long Beach** (✉ *Off Rte. 127A on Gloucester-Rockport town line*). **Wingaersheek Beach** (✉ *Exit 13 off Rte. 128*) is a well-protected cove of white sand and dunes, with the white Annisquam lighthouse in the bay.

WHERE TO EAT & STAY

$$ ✕ **Franklin Cape Ann.** This contemporary nightspot offers bistro-style
AMERICAN chicken, roast cod, and upscale meat loaf, perfect for the late-night crowd (it's open until midnight). Live jazz is on tap most Tuesday evenings. Look for the signature martini glass over the door. ✉ *118 Main St.* ☎ *978/283–7888* ▬ *AE, D, MC, V* ⊙ *No lunch.*

$ ⊡ **Cape Ann's Marina Resort.** This year-round hostelry and spa less than a mile from Gloucester comes alive in summer. Two restaurants, a whale-watch boat, and deep-sea fishing excursions are available from the premises. The rooms all have balconies and water views. The Gull restaurant is closed November to mid-April. **Pros:** guests get a free river cruise during summer stays. **Cons:** "resort" is a bit of a misnomer, as the hotel is surrounded by parking lots, with no walking path to or from town. ✉ *75 Essex Ave.* ☎ *978/283–2116 or 800/626–7660* ⊕ *www.capeannmarina.com* ↵ *31 rooms* ⊙ *In-room: kitchen (some). In-hotel: restaurant, pool, no elevator, no-smoking rooms* ▬ *AE, D, DC, MC, V.*

ROCKPORT

41 mi northeast of Boston, 4 mi northeast of Gloucester on Rte. 127.

Rockport, at the very tip of Cape Ann, derives its name from the local granite formations. Many Boston-area structures are made of stone cut from its long-gone quarries. Today, the town is a tourist center with a well-marked, centralized downtown that is easy to navigate and access on foot. Unlike typical tourist-trap landmarks, Rockport's shops sell quality arts, clothing, and gifts, and its restaurants serve seafood, or home-baked cookies rather than fast food. Walk past shops and colorful clapboard houses to the end of Bearskin Neck for an impressive view of the Atlantic Ocean and the old, weather-beaten lobster shack known as "Motif No. 1" because of its popularity as a subject for amateur painters and photographers.

WHERE TO EAT & STAY

$-$$
SEAFOOD

✗ **Brackett's Ocean View.** A big bay window in this quiet, homey restaurant gives an excellent view across Sandy Bay. The menu includes chowders, fish cakes, and other seafood dishes. ✉ *25 Main St.* ☎ *978/546–2797* ▭ *AE, D, DC, MC, V* ⊘ *Closed Nov.–mid-Apr. Closed Mon.–Tues.*

$-$$
★

⊡ **Addison Choate Inn.** Just a minute's walk from both the center of Rockport and the train station, this 1851 inn sits in prime location. The sizable and beautifully decorated rooms have their share of antiques and local seascape paintings, as well as pine floors and large bathrooms; the captain's room contains a canopy bed, handmade quilts, and Oriental rugs. In the third-floor suite, huge windows look out over the rooftops to the sea. Two spacious stable-house apartments have skylights, cathedral ceilings, and exposed wood beams. Rates include afternoon tea. Pros: Proximity to the ocean, shopping and train station. Cons: Only one bedroom on the first floor. ✉ *49 Broadway* ☎ *978/546–7543 or 800/245–7543* ⊕ *www.addisonchoateinn.com* ⇜ *5 rooms, 1 suite, 2 apartments* ⌂ *In-room: no TV. In-hotel: restaurant, Wi-Fi, no elevator, no-smoking rooms* ▭ *MC, V* ⊘ *Closed Jan.–Mar.* ⑩ *CP.*

$
Fodor'sChoice
★

⊡ **Sally Webster Inn.** This inn was named for a member of Hannah Jumper's "hatchet gang," teetotalers who smashed up the town's liquor stores in 1856 and turned Rockport into the dry town it remains today. Sally lived in this house for much of her life, and the poshly decorated guest rooms are named for members of her family. Caleb's room is a romantic retreat with a canopy bed and floral quilts, and William's room has a crisply nautical theme. Other rooms have pine wide-board floors, nonworking brick fireplaces, rocking chairs, and four-poster, brass, or canopy beds. Pros: Homey atmosphere in an excellent location with attentive staff. ✉ *34 Mt. Pleasant St.* ☎ *978/546–9251 or 877/546–9251* ⊕ *www.sallywebster.com* ⇜ *8 rooms* ⌂ *In-room: no TV, Internet access in main room. In-hotel: no elevator, no-smoking rooms* ▭ *MC, V* ⊘ *Closed Jan.* ⑩ *CP.*

ESSEX

30 mi northeast of Boston, 12 mi west of Rockport. Head west out of Cape Ann on Rte. 128, turning north on Rte. 133.

The small, seafaring town of Essex, once an important shipbuilding center, is surrounded by salt marshes and is filled with antiques stores and seafood restaurants.

WHAT TO SEE

☯ **Essex Shipbuilding Museum.** Still an active shipyard, this museum traces the evolution of the American schooner, which was first created in Essex. The museum sometimes offers shipbuilding demonstrations. One-hour tours take in the museum's many buildings and boats, especially the *Evelina M. Goulart*—one of only seven remaining Essex-built schooners. ✉ *66 Main St. (Rte. 133)* ☎ *978/768–7541* ⊕ *www.essex-*

shipbuildingmuseum.org ≤≞*$7* ☉ *Summer and Fall (June Oct.),* Wed.–
Sun. 10–5; Winter and Spring (Nov.–May), Sat. and Sun., 10–5.

SHOPPING

Chebacco Antiques (✉ *38 Main St.* ☎978/768–7371), open every weekend, concentrates on lighting and country furniture, as well as Staf-
fordshire plates and sterling silver. Open only on weekends, **Howard's
Flying Dragon Antiques** (✉ *136 Main St.* ☎978/768–7282) is a general
antiques shop that carries statuary and glass.

WHERE TO EAT

$-$$$ ✕**Woodman's of Essex.** According to local legend, this is where Law-
Fodor'sChoice   rence "Chubby" Woodman invented the first fried clam back in 1916.
★   Today this sprawling wooden shack with indoor booths and outdoor
SEAFOOD   picnic tables is *the* place for seafood in the rough. Besides fried clams,
you can tuck into clam chowder, lobster rolls, or the popular "down-
river" lobster combo. ✉ *121 Main St. (Rte. 133)* ☎*978/768–6451 or
800/649–1773* ⊕*www.woodmans.com* ▭*AE, MC, V.*

IPSWICH

36 mi north of Boston, 6 mi northwest of Essex.

Quiet little Ipswich, settled in 1633 and famous for its clams, is said
to have more 17th-century houses standing and occupied than any
other place in America; more than 40 were built before 1725. Infor-
mation and a booklet with a suggested walking tour are available at
the **Visitor Information Center** (✉ *Hall Haskell House, 36 S. Main St.*
☎*978/356–8540* ☉*Memorial Day–Columbus Day, Mon.–Sat. 9–5,
Sun. noon–5*).

SPORTS & THE OUTDOORS

BEACHES   **Crane Beach,** one of New England's most beautiful beaches, is a sandy,
★   4-mi-long stretch backed by dunes and a nature trail. Public parking is
available, but on a nice summer weekend, it's usually full before lunch.
There are lifeguards and changing rooms. Check ahead before visiting
mid-July to early-August, when greenhead flies terrorize sunbathers.
✉*Argilla Rd.* ☎*978/356–4354* ⊕*www.thetrustees.org* ≤≞*Beach free.
Parking $10 Weekdays, $20 Sat.–Sun. mid-May–early Sept., $5 early
Sept.–mid-May* ☉*Daily 8–sunset.*

HIKING   The Massachusetts Audubon Society's **Ipswich River Wildlife Sanctuary**
has trails through marshland hills, where there are remains of early
Colonial settlements as well as abundant wildlife. Make sure to grab
some birdseed and get a trail map from the office. Enjoy bridges,
man-made rock structures, and other surprises on the Rockery Trail.
✉*87 Perkins Row, southwest of Ipswich, 1 mi off Rte. 97, Topsfield*
☎*978/887–9264* ⊕*www.massaudubon.org* ≤≞*$4* ☉*Office May–
Oct., Tues.–Sun. 9–5; Nov.–Apr., Tues.–Fri. 9–4, Sat.–Sun. 10–4. Trails
Tues.–Sun. dawn–dusk.*

WHERE TO EAT

¢-$ ✕**Clam Box.** Shaped like a giant fried clam box, this small roadside stand
Fodor's Choice is the best place to sample Ipswich's famous bivalves. Since 1938, locals
★ and tourists have been lining up for clams, oysters, scallops, and onion
SEAFOOD rings. ⊠*246 High St. (Rte. 1A) Ipswich, MA 01938* ☎*978/356–9707*
⊕*www.ipswichma.com/clambox* ⋨*Reservations not accepted* ▭*No
credit cards* ⊘*Closed mid-Dec.–Feb.*

$$-$$$ ✕**Stone Soup Café.** It may look like nothing more than a simple store-
SEAFOOD front, but this cheery café in the center of town is booked days in
advance for dinner. There are two seatings of eight tables a night for
lobster bisque, porcini ravioli, or whatever contemporary fare the chef
is inspired to cook from the day's farm-stand finds. If you can't book
ahead, stop in for breakfast or lunch. ⊠*0 Central St., off Rte. 1A*
☎*978/356–4222* ⋨*Reservations essential* ▭*No credit cards* ⊘*No
dinner Sun.–Wed., breakfast but no lunch Sun.*

NEWBURYPORT

38 mi north of Boston, 12 mi north of Ipswich on Rte. 1A.

Newburyport's High Street is lined with some of the finest examples of
Federal-period (roughly, 1790–1810) mansions in New England. The
city was once a leading port and shipbuilding center; the houses were
built for prosperous sea captains. Although Newburyport's maritime
significance ended with the decline of the clipper ships, the town was
revived in the 1970s. Today, the town bustles with shops, restaurants,
galleries and a waterfront park and boardwalk. The civic improvements have been matched by private restorations of the town's housing
stock, much of which dates from the 18th century, with a scattering of
17th-century homes in some neighborhoods.

Newburyport is walker-friendly, with well-marked restrooms and free
parking all day down by the water.

A stroll through the **Waterfront Park & Promenade** offers a view of the
harbor as well as the fishing and pleasure boats that moor here. A
causeway leads from Newburyport to a narrow piece of land known
as Plum Island, which harbors a summer colony (rapidly becoming
year-round) at one end.

SPORTS & THE OUTDOORS

Parker River National Wildlife Refuge. On Plum Island, this 4,662-acre
refuge of salt marsh, freshwater marsh, beaches, and dunes is one of
the few natural barrier beach–dune–salt marsh complexes left on the
Northeast coast. Here you can bird-watch, fish, swim, and pick plums
and cranberries. The refuge is a popular place in summer, especially
on weekends; cars begin to line up at the gate before 7 AM. There's
no restriction on the number of people using the beach, but only a
limited number of cars are let in; no pets are allowed in the refuge.
⊠*Plum Island 6 Plum Island Turnpike Newburyport, Massachusetts*
☎*978/465–5753* ⊕*www.parkerriver.org* ▣*$5 per car, bicycles and*

walk-ins $2 ☉ *Daily dawn–dusk. Beach usually closed during nesting season in spring and early summer.*

BEACH **Salisbury Beach State Reservation.** Relax at the long sandy beach, or play
🕐 ★ at the amusement area and nearby arcades. From Newburyport center, follow Bridge Road north, take a right on Beach Road, and follow it until you reach State Reservation Road. ✉ *Rte. 1A, 5 mi northeast of Newburyport, Salisbury* ☎ *978/462–4481* 🎫 *Beach free, parking $7.*

NIGHTLIFE & THE ARTS
The **Grog** (✉ *13 Middle St.* ☎ *978/465–8008* ⊕ *www.thegrog.com*) hosts blues, rock bands, and salsa lessons several nights weekly.

SHOPPING
Todd Farm Flea Market. A New England tradition since 1971, the Todd Farm Flea Market features up to 240 vendors from all over New England and New York. It's open every Sunday from mid-April through late November, though its busiest months are May, September, and October. Merchandise varies from antique furniture, clocks, jewelry, recordings, and tools to fishing rods, golf accessories, honey products, cedar fencing, vintage toys, and seasonal plants and flowers. Antique hunters often arrive before the sun comes up for the best deals. ✉ *303 Main St. Rowley, off of Route 1A* ☎ *978/948–3300* ⊕ *www.toddfarm. com* ☉ *Apr.–Nov., Sun. 5 AM–3 PM.*

WHERE TO EAT
$$-$$$ ✗ **Glenn's.** A block from the waterfront parking lot, Glenn's offers cre-
SEAFOOD ative combinations from around the world, with the occasional New England twist. The ever-changing menu might include sesame-crusted yellowfin tuna or house-smoked baby-back ribs. There's live jazz or blues on Sunday. ✉ *44 Merrimac St.* ☎ *978/465–3811* ▭ *AE, D, DC, MC, V* ☉ *Closed Mon. No lunch.*

SOUTH OF BOSTON

Updated by
Diane Bair &
Pamela Wright

People all over the world travel south of Boston to visit Plymouth for a glimpse into the country's earliest beginnings. The two main stops are the Plimoth Plantation, which re-creates the everyday life of the Pilgrims; and the Mayflower II, which gives you an idea of how frightening the journey across the Atlantic must have been. Farther south, New Bedford reveals the world of whaling.

EN
ROUTE

While driving from Boston to Plymouth, you can easily make a stop at **Quincy,** where sites pay tribute to the nation's second and sixth presidents. The **Adams National Historic Park** (✉ *Carriage house 135 Adams St., visitor center & bookstore 1250 Hancock St.* ☎ *617/770–1175* ⊕ *www.nps.gov/adam* 🎫 *$5* ☉ *Tours 9:15–3:15 daily mid-Apr.–mid-Nov.*) contains the birthplace, home, and grave of both John Adams and his son John Quincy Adams.

PLYMOUTH

40 mi south of Boston.

On December 26, 1620, 102 weary men, women, and children disembarked from the *Mayflower* to found the first permanent European settlement north of Virginia. Today, Plymouth is characterized by narrow streets, clapboard mansions, shops, antiques stores, and a scenic waterfront. To mark Thanksgiving, the town holds a parade, historic-house tours, and other activities. Historic statues dot the town, including depictions of William Bradford, Pilgrim leader and governor of Plymouth Colony for more than 30 years, on Water Street; a Pilgrim maiden in Brewster Gardens; and Massasoit, the Wampanoag chief who helped the Pilgrims survive, on Carver Street.

WHAT TO SEE

★ **Mayflower II.** This seaworthy replica of the 1620 *Mayflower* was built in England through research and a bit of guesswork, then sailed across the Atlantic in 1957. As you explore the interior and exterior of the ship, sailors in modern dress answer your questions about both the reproduction and the original ship, while costumed guides provide a 17th-century perspective. Plymouth Rock is nearby. ⊠*State Pier* ☎*508/746–1622* ⊕*www.plimoth.org* ☜*$10, $28 with admission to Plimoth Plantation* ☉*Late Mar.–Nov., daily 9–5.*

National Monument to the Forefathers. The largest freestanding granite statue in the United States, this allegorical monument stands high on a grassy hill. Designed by Hammet Billings of Boston in 1854 and dedicated in 1889, it depicts Faith, surrounded by Liberty, Morality, Justice, Law, and Education and includes scenes from the Pilgrims' early days in Plymouth. ⊠*Allerton St.*

Pilgrim Hall Museum. From the waterfront sights it's a short walk to one of the country's oldest public museums. Established in 1824, Pilgrim Hall Museum transports you back to the time of the Pilgrims' landing with objects carried by those weary travelers to the New World. Included are a carved chest, a remarkably well-preserved wicker cradle, Myles Standish's sword, John Alden's Bible, American Indian artifacts, and the remains of the *Sparrow Hawk*, a sailing ship that was wrecked in 1626. ⊠*75 Court St. (Hwy. 3A)* ☎*508/746–1620* ⊕*www.pilgrim hall.org* ☜*$7* ☉*May–Dec., daily 9:30–4:30.*)

♻
Fodor'sChoice
★
Plimoth Plantation. Over the entrance of this popular attraction is the caution: YOU ARE NOW ENTERING 1627. Believe it. Against the backdrop of the Atlantic Ocean, and just 3 mi south of downtown Plymouth, this Pilgrim village has been carefully re-created, from the thatch roofs, cramped quarters, and open fireplaces to the long-horned livestock. Throw away your preconception of white collars and funny hats; through ongoing research, the Plimoth staff has developed a portrait of the Pilgrims that's more complex than the dour folk in school textbooks. Listen to the accents of the "residents," who never break out of character. You might see them plucking ducks, cooking rabbit stew, or tending garden. Feel free to engage them in conversation about their

life, but expect only curious looks if you ask about anything that happened after 1627. "Thanksgiving: Memory, Myth & Meaning," an exhibit in the visitor center, offers a fresh perspective on the 1621 harvest celebration that is now known as "the first Thanksgiving." Note that there's not a lot of shade here in the summer. ✉ *137 Warren Ave. (Hwy. 3A)* ☎ *508/746–1622* ⊕ *www.plimoth.org* ✉ *$24, $28 with Mayflower II* ⊙ *Late Mar.–Nov., daily 9–5.*

★ **Plymouth Rock.** This landmark rock, just a few dozen yards from the *Mayflower II*, is popularly believed to have been the Pilgrims' stepping-stone when they left the ship. Given the stone's unimpressive appearance—it's little more than a boulder—and dubious authenticity (as explained on a nearby plaque), the grand canopy overhead seems a trifle ostentatious.

Sparrow House. Built in 1640, this is Plymouth's oldest structure. It is among several historic houses in town that are open for visits. You can peek into a pair of rooms furnished in the spartan style of the Pilgrims' era. The contemporary crafts gallery also on the premises seems somewhat incongruous, but the works on view are high quality. ✉ *42 Summer St.* ☎ *508/747–1240* ⊕ *www.sparrowhouse.com* ✉ *House $2, gallery free* ⊙ *Thurs.–Tues. 10–5.*

WHERE TO EAT & STAY

$$ ✕ **Blue-eyed Crab Grille & Raw Bar.** Grab a seat on the outside deck
SEAFOOD overlooking the water at this friendly, somewhat funky (plastic fish dangling from the ceiling), fresh fish shack. If the local Island Creek raw oysters are on the menu, go for them! Otherwise start with thick crab bisque full of hunks of floating crabmeat or the steamed mussels. Dinner entrées include seafood stew with chorizo and sweet potatoes and the creamy lobster mac and cheese. Locals come for the brunch specials, too, like grilled shrimp and poached eggs over red-pepper grits, the lobster omelet, and banana-ginger pancakes. ✉ *170 Water St.* ☎ *508/747–6776* ⊕ *www.blueeyedcrab.com* ▤ *D, MC, V* ⊙ *No lunch Tues.–Thurs.*

$$ 🏨 **John Carver Inn & Spa.** This three-story, Colonial-style redbrick building is steps from Plymouth's main attractions. The public rooms are lavish, with period furnishings and stylish drapes. The guest rooms include six "environmentally sensitive" options with filtered air and water and four-poster beds; others are a bit dark and drab (time for refurbishing!). The suites have fireplaces and whirlpool baths. There's also an indoor pool with a *Mayflower* ship model and a waterslide. **Pros:** waterfront setting; on-site amenities include theme pool, restaurant, spa. **Cons:** pool is noisy and often overcrowded, some rooms need updating. ✉ *25 Summer St.* ☎ *508/746–7100 or 800/274–1620* ⊕ *www.johncarverinn.com* ⇨ *79 rooms, 6 suites* ⚲ *In-room: Wi-Fi. In-hotel: restaurant, bar, pool, gym, spa, laundry facilities, public Wi-Fi, parking (no fee), no-smoking rooms* ▤ *AE, D, DC, MC, V.*

NEW BEDFORD

45 mi southwest of Plymouth, 50 mi south of Boston.

In 1652 colonists from Plymouth settled in the area that now includes the city of New Bedford. The city has a long maritime tradition, beginning as a shipbuilding center and small whaling port in the late 1700s. By the mid-1800s, it had developed into a center of North American whaling. Today, New Bedford has the largest fishing fleet on the East Coast. Although much of the town is industrial, the restored historic district near the water is a delight. It was here that Herman Melville set his masterpiece, *Moby-Dick,* a novel about whaling.

WHAT TO SEE

☺ **New Bedford Whaling Museum.** Established in 1903, this is the world's largest museum of its kind. A highlight is the skeleton of a 66-foot blue whale, one of only three on view anywhere. An interactive exhibit lets you listen to the underwater sounds of whales, dolphins, and other sea life—plus the sounds of a thunderstorm and a whale-watching boat—as a whale might hear them. You can also peruse the collection of scrimshaw, visit exhibits on regional history, and climb aboard an 89-foot, half-scale model of the 1826 whaling ship *Lagoda*—the world's largest ship model. A small chapel across the street from the museum is the one described in *Moby-Dick.* ⊠*18 Johnny Cake Hill* ☎*508/997–0046* ⊕*www.whalingmuseum.org* ⊠*$10* ⊙*Daily 9–5.*

New Bedford Whaling National Historical Park. The city's whaling tradition is commemorated at this park that takes up 13 blocks of the waterfront historic district. The park visitor center, housed in an 1853 Greek-revival building that was once a bank, provides maps and information about whaling-related sites. Free walking tours of the park leave from the visitor center at 10 AM and noon in July and August. ⊠*33 William St.* ☎*508/996–4095* ⊕*www.nps.gov/nebe* ⊠*Free* ⊙*Daily 9–5.*

Rotch-Jones-Duff House & Garden Museum. For a glimpse of upper-class life during New Bedford's whaling heyday, head one-half mile south of downtown to this 1834 Greek Revival mansion. Amid a full city block of gardens, it housed three prominent families in the 1800s and is filled with elegant furnishings from the era including a mahogany piano, a massive marble-top sideboard, and portraits of the house's occupants. A free self-guided audio tour is available. ⊠*396 County St.* ☎*508/997–1401* ⊕*www.rjdmuseum.org* ⊠*$5* ⊙*Mon.–Sat. 10–4, Sun. noon–4.*

WHERE TO EAT

$-$$ ✗**Antonio's.** Expect the wait to be long and the dining room to be loud
PORTUGUESE   but it's worth the hassle to sample the traditional fare of New Bedford's large Portuguese population at this friendly, unadorned restaurant. Dishes include hearty portions of pork and shellfish stew, *bacalau* (salt cod), and grilled sardines, often on plates piled high with crispy fried potatoes and rice. ⊠*267 Coggeshall St., near intersection of I–195 and Hwy. 18* ☎*508/990–3636* ▭*No credit cards.*

$-$$$
SEAFOOD ✗ **Davy's Locker.** A huge seafood menu is the main draw at this spot overlooking Buzzards Bay. Choose from more than a dozen shrimp preparations, or a choice of healthful entrées—dishes prepared with olive oil, vegetables, garlic, and herbs. For landlubbers, chicken, steak, ribs, and the like are also available. ✉ *1480 E. Rodney French Blvd.* ☎ *508/992-7359* ▭ *AE, D, DC, MC, V.*

2

CAPE COD

Updated by Laura V. Scheel and Andrew Collins

A Patti Page song from the 1950s promises that "If you're fond of sand dunes and salty air, quaint little villages here and there, you're sure to fall in love with old Cape Cod." The tourism boom since the '50s has certainly proved her right. Continually shaped by ocean currents, this windswept land of sandy beaches and dunes has compelling natural beauty. Everyone comes for the seaside, yet the crimson cranberry bogs, forests of birch and beech, freshwater ponds, and marshlands that grace the interior are just as splendid. Local history is equally fascinating; whale-watching provides an exhilarating experience of the natural world; cycling trails lace the landscape; shops purvey everything from antiques to pure kitsch; and you can dine on simple fresh seafood, creative contemporary cuisine, or most anything in between.

Separated from the Massachusetts mainland by the 17.5-mi Cape Cod canal—at 480 feet the world's widest sea-level canal—and linked to it by two heavily trafficked bridges, the Cape is always likened in shape to an outstretched arm bent at the elbow, its Provincetown fist turned back toward the mainland. A bodybuilder "showing off his bulging bicep" is how one writer aptly described it.

Each of the Cape's 15 towns is broken up in to villages, which is where things can get complicated. The town of Barnstable, for example, consists of Barnstable, West Barnstable, Cotuit, Marston Mills, Osterville, Centerville, and Hyannis. The terms Upper Cape and Lower Cape can also be confusing. Upper Cape—think upper arm, as in the shape of the Cape—refers to the towns of Bourne, Falmouth, Mashpee, and Sandwich. Mid Cape includes Barnstable, Yarmouth, and Dennis. Brewster, Harwich, Chatham, Orleans, Eastham, Wellfleet, Truro, and Provincetown make up the Lower Cape.

Three major roads traverse the Cape. U.S. 6 is the fastest way to get from the mainland to Orleans. Route 6A winds along the North Shore through scenic towns; Route 28 dips south through some of the overdeveloped parts of the Cape. If you want to avoid malls, heavy traffic, and tacky motels, avoid Route 28 from Falmouth to Chatham. Past Orleans on the way out to Provincetown, the roadside clutter of much of U.S. 6 masks the beauty of what surrounds it.

SANDWICH

★ *3 mi east of Sagamore Bridge, 11 mi west of Barnstable.*

The oldest town on Cape Cod, Sandwich was established in 1637 by some of the Plymouth Pilgrims and incorporated on March 6, 1638. Today, it is a well-preserved, quintessential New England village with a white-columned town hall and streets lined with 18th- and 19th-century houses.

WHAT TO SEE

Sandwich Glass Museum. From 1825 to 1888, the main industry in Sandwich was the production of vividly colored glass made in the Boston and Sandwich Glass Company's factory. This museum contains relics of the town's early history and displays of shimmering blown and pressed glass. The extensive, ornate gift shop sells some handsome reproductions, including some made by local and national artisans. The museum also sponsors several walking tours of the town in July and August. ✉ *129 Main St., Sandwich Center* ☎ *508/888–0251* ⊕ *www. sandwichglassmuseum.org* ✉ *$4.75* ☉ *Apr.–Dec., daily 9:30–5; Feb. and Mar., Wed.–Sun. 9:30–4.*

Fodor's Choice   **Heritage Museums and Gardens.** On 100 beautifully landscaped acres
★   overlooking the upper end of Shawme Pond, this complex includes
Ⓒ   gardens and a café as well as an impressive array of museum buildings with specialty collections ranging from cars to toys. A highlight is the Shaker Round Barn, which showcases classic and historic cars as well as art exhibitions. The art museum has an extensive Currier & Ives collection, antique toys, and a working 1912 Coney Island–style carousel that both adults and little ones can ride as often as they like. Paths crisscross the grounds, which include gardens planted with daylilies, hostas, heather, herbs, and fruit trees. ✉ *67 Grove St.* ☎ *508/888–3300* ⊕ *www.heritagemuseumsandgardens.org* ✉ *$12* ☉ *Apr.–Nov., daily 10–5; Nov.–Mar., call for very limited hrs.*

SHOPPING

Fodor's Choice   **Titcomb's Bookshop** (✉ *432 Rte. 6A, East Sandwich* ☎ *508/888–2331*
★   ⊕ *www.titcombsbookshop.com*) stocks used, rare, and new books, including a large collection of Cape and nautical titles and Americana, as well as an extensive selection of children's books.

NIGHTLIFE & THE ARTS

NIGHTLIFE   **Bobby Byrne's Pub** (✉ *65 Rte. 6A* ☎ *508/888–6088*), with other locations in Hyannis and Mashpee, is a comfortable pub with a jukebox and good light and full menus.

WHERE TO EAT & STAY

$-$$ ✗ **Aqua Grille.** At this smart-casual and reasonably priced bistro by the
★   marina, offerings range from Cape basics (clam chowder, fried sea-
ECLECTIC   food, boiled lobsters) to more creative contemporary fare, such as nut-crusted halibut with an orange beurre blanc. The excellent lobster salad comprises a hearty serving of greens, tomatoes, avocados, baby green beans, and big, meaty lobster chunks. ✉ *14 Gallo Rd.* ☎ *508/888–8889* ⊕ *www.aquagrille.com* ▭ *AE, DC, MC, V* ☉ *Closed Nov.–mid-Apr.*

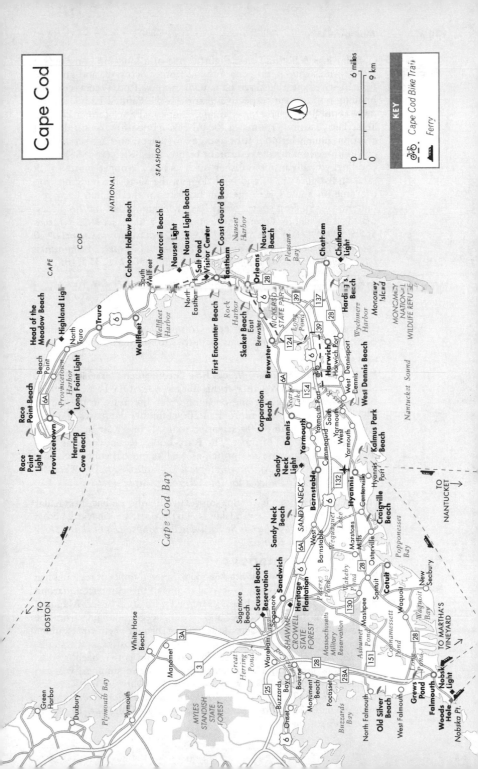

Cape Cod

SEASHORE

CAPE COD NATIONAL

CAPE

Race Point Light
Race Point Beach
Provincetown
Beach Point
Provincetown Harbor
Herring Cove Beach
Long Point Light

Head of the Meadow Beach
Highland Light
North Truro
Truro
6
Wellfleet Harbor
Wellfleet

Cahoon Hollow Beach
South Wellfleet
Marconi Beach
Nauset Light
North Eastham
Salt Pond Visitor Center
Eastham
Nauset Light Beach
Coast Guard Beach
Nauset Harbor

First Encounter Beach
Rock Harbor
6
Orleans
28
Nauset Beach
Pleasant Bay

Skaket Beach
East Brewster
NICKERSON STATE PARK
Chatham
Chatham Light
Monomoy Island

Brewster
6A
124
Long Pond
39
137
Harding's Beach
Wychmere Harbor
MONOMOY NATIONAL WILDLIFE REFUGE

Corporation Beach
6
28
Harwich
Howich Port
28

Dennis
Yarmouth
Scargo Lake
154
Yarmouth Port
South Yarmouth
West Dennis
Dennis
West Yarmouth
West Dennis Beach

Cummaquid
6
6A
Barnstable
Wequaquet Lake
132
Hyannis Port
Hyannis
Kalmus Park Beach

Nantucket Sound

Sandy Neck Light
SANDY NECK
Sandy Neck Beach
West Barnstable
Barnstable
Marstons Mills
Osterville
Centerville
Craigville Beach
Poponnesset Bay
TO NANTUCKET

Cape Cod Bay

TO BOSTON

Scusset Beach Reservation
Sagamore Beach
Sagamore
Cape Cod Canal
SHAWME CROWELL STATE FOREST
Sandwich
6A
6
Heritage Plantation
Massachusetts Military Reservation
130
Mashpee
Santuit
Cotuit
New Seabury
Waquoit
28
Waquoit Bay

White Horse Beach
Manomet
3A
3
Wareham
Great Herring Pond
MYLES STANDISH STATE FOREST
25
28
Buzzards Bay
Bourne
151
Cohasset
Ashumet Pond
Coonamessett Pond
TO MARTHA'S VINEYARD

Green Harbor
Duxbury
Plymouth
Plymouth Bay

Monument Beach
Pocasset
23A
28
North Falmouth
West Falmouth
Old Silver Beach
Buzzards Bay
Peters Pond
Mashpee Pond
Johns Pond
Long Pond
Grews Pond
Falmouth
Woods Hole
Nobska Light
Nobska Pt.

$$-$$$ ⌂**Belfry Inne & Bistro.** This delightful one-of-a-kind inn comprises a
Fodor's Choice   1902 former church, an ornate wood-frame Victorian, and an 1830
★   Federal-style house clustered on a main campus. Room themes in each
building nod to their respective histories—the Painted Lady's charm-
ingly appointed rooms, for example, are named after former inhabitants. The luxurious rooms in the Abbey, named for the six days of
creation, have whirlpool tubs and gas fireplaces, and are set along a
corridor overlooking the restaurant below. The Bistro ($$–$$$) serves
dazzling, globally inspired dishes, such as black grouper roasted with
tamarind-yogurt sauce, and next door in the Victorian building, you
can dine on home-style American favorites at the Painted Lady restaurant ($–$$). **Pros:** some rooms have whirlpool tubs and fireplaces;
massages available. **Cons:** some rooms don't have TVs. ⌂*8 Jarves
St.* ☎*508/888–8550 or 800/844–4542* ⊕*www.belfryinn.com* ✍*20
rooms* ⚴*In-room: no TV (some), Wi-Fi (some). In-hotel: 2 restaurants,
bar, no elevator no-smoking rooms* ⊟*AE, D, DC, MC, V* ⍾*BP.*

WOODS HOLE

15 mi south of Bourne Bridge.

The village of Woods Hole is home to several major scientific institutions, and it's a departure point for ferries to Martha's Vineyard.

WHAT TO SEE

Marine Biological Laboratory–Woods Hole Oceanographic Institution Library.
Scientific forces join together at this library, one of the best collections
of biological, ecological, and oceanographic literature in the world.
The library has access to more than 200 computer databases and sub-
scribes to more than 5,000 scientific journals in 40 languages, with
complete collections of most. The Rare Books Room contains photographs, monographs, and prints, as well as journal collections that
date from 1665. ⌂*7 Marine Biological Laboratory St., off Water St.*
☎*508/289–7002* ⊕*www.mbl.edu* ✍*Free* ☾ *Mon.–Fri. 8–5*

Nobska Light. From its base, this impressive lighthouse has spectacular
views of the nearby Elizabeth Islands and of Martha's Vineyard, across
Vineyard Sound. ⌂*Church St.* ⊕*www.lighthouse.cc/nobska* ✍*Free*
☾*See Web site for tour times*

SPORTS & THE OUTDOORS

ↅ   **National Marine Fisheries Service Aquarium.** Sixteen tanks of regional fish
Fodor's Choice   and shellfish are on display in several rooms of this compact aquarium
★   that is cramped but nonetheless crammed with stuff to see. Magnifying glasses, a dissecting scope, and mini-squeegees hanging from the
frosty tanks (a favorite tool for kids passing through) help you examine
marine life. Several hands-on pools hold banded lobsters, crabs, snails,
starfish, and other creatures. The top attraction is two harbor seals,
on view in the outdoor pool near the entrance in summer; you can
watch their feedings weekdays at 11 and 4. ⌂*Albatross and Water Sts.*
☎*508/495–2267, 508/495–2001 recorded information* ⊕*www.nefsc.
nmfs.gov/nefsc/aquarium* ✍*Free* ☾*June–Aug., Tues.–Sat. 11–4; call
for hrs off-season.*

☼ **Waquoit Bay National Estuarine Research Reserve.** Encompassing 2,500 acres of estuary and barrier beach around the bay, this reserve it a good birding site. **South Cape Beach** is part of the reserve; you can lie out on the sand or join one of the interpretive walks. **Flat Pond Trail** runs through several different habitats, including fresh- and saltwater marshes. ✉*149 Rte. 28, 3 mi west of Mashpee rotary, Waquoit* ☎*508/457-0495* ⊕*www.waquoitbayreserve.org* ✍*Free* ☉*Exhibit center late June–early Sept., Mon.–Sat. 10–4; late May–late June, Mon.–Fri. 10–4*

BEACHES **Old Silver Beach** (✉*Off Quaker Rd., North Falmouth*) is a long, beauti
★ ful crescent of soft white sand bordered by the Sea Crest Resort at one end. It's especially good for small children because a sandbar keeps it shallow at the southern end and creates tidal pools full of crabs and minnows. The beach has lifeguards, restrooms, showers, and a snack bar. There's a $20 fee for parking in summer.

FISHING Freshwater ponds are good for perch, pickerel, trout, and more; you can obtain the required license (along with rental gear) at tackle shops, such as **Eastman's Sport & Tackle** (✉*150 Rte. 28, Falmouth* ☎*508/548-6900* ⊕*www.eastmanstackle.com*).

SHOPPING
★ **Bean & Cod** (✉*140 Rte. 28, Falmouth Center* ☎*508/548-8840 or 800/558-8840* ⊕*www.beanandcod.com*), a specialty food shop, sells cheeses, breads, and picnic fixings, along with pastas, coffees, and teas, and unusual condiments. The store also packs and ships gift baskets.

NIGHTLIFE & THE ARTS
Nimrod Inn (✉*100 Dillingham Ave., Falmouth Center* ☎*508/540-4132*) presents jazz and contemporary music at least six nights a week year-round. The Nimrod is also a great spot for late-night dining.

WHERE TO EAT & STAY
$$-$$$ ✗**La Cucina Sul Mare.** Northern Italian and Mediterranean cooking is
Fodor'sChoice the specialty at this classy, popular place. The staff is friendly and the
★ setting is both intimate and festive, if a bit crowded. Calamari, warm green salad with goat cheese and cranberries, a classic lemon chicken sautéed with shallots and capers, and a variety of specials—including plenty of local fresh fish—adorn the menu. The *zuppa de pesce*, a medley of seafood sautéed in olive oil and garlic and finished in a white wine herb-and-tomato broth, is a specialty. ✉*237 Main St. (Rte. 28)* ☎*508/548-5600* ⚘*No reservations* ▭*AE, D, MC, V.*

$$-$$$ ▦**Mostly Hall B&B.** With its deep, landscaped yard and wrought-iron
★ fence, this elegant inn with a wraparound porch resembles a private estate. The imposing 1849 Italianate house has an upscale European style with painted wall murals in several bedrooms; the Tuscany Room's walls suggest an intimate Tuscan garden. Three of the rooms are more traditionally decorated, with colonial antiques; all have canopy beds. **Pros:** walk to town center, ample, parklike grounds, grand home in the Victorian tradition. **Cons:** rooms accessed via steep stairs, bathrooms are a bit small, the bathroom for one room (discounted) is down a set of stairs. ✉*27 Main St. (Rte. 28)* ☎*508/548-3786* ⊕*www.mostly hall.com* ▦*6 rooms* ⚹*In-room: DVD, Wi-Fi. In-hotel: no kids under*

18, *no-smoking rooms, no elevator, no kids under 18* ▤*AE, D, MC, V* ⦿*BP.*

HYANNIS

23 mi east of the Bourne Bridge.

Perhaps best known for its association with the Kennedy clan, the Hyannis area was also a vacation site for President Ulysses S. Grant in 1874 and later for President Grover Cleveland. A bustling year-round hub of activity, Hyannis has the Cape's largest concentration of businesses, shops, malls, hotels and motels, restaurants and entertainment venues.

WHAT TO SEE

John F. Kennedy Hyannis Museum. In Main Street's Old Town Hall, this museum explores JFK's Cape years (1934–63). ⊠*397 Main St.* ☎*508/790–3077* ⊕*www.jfkhyannismuseum.org* ⌖*$5* ⊙*Memorial Day–Oct., Mon.–Sat. 9–5, Sun. noon–5; Nov.–early Dec. and mid-Feb.–mid-Apr., Thurs.–Sat. 10–4, Sun. noon–4.*

▐ OFF THE BEATEN PATH

Cape Cod Potato Chips Factory. There's a standing invitation on the back of the bag: come for a free tour of the factory and get free samples of the crunchy all-natural chips hand-cooked in kettles in small batches. ⊠*Independence Dr. (opposite Cape Cod Mall) to Breed's Hill Rd., off Rte. 132* ☎*508/775–3358* ⊕*www.capecodchips.com* ⊙*Mon.–Fri. 9–5.*

SPORTS & THE OUTDOORS

BEACHES **Kalmus Park Beach,** at the south end of Ocean Street, is a wide sandy beach with an area set aside for windsurfers and a sheltered area that's good for kids. It has a snack bar, restrooms, showers, and lifeguards.

NIGHTLIFE & THE ARTS

In 1950 actress Gertrude Lawrence and her husband, producer-manager Richard Aldrich, opened the **Cape Cod Melody Tent** (⊠*21 W. Main St., at West End rotary, Hyannis* ☎*508/775–5630, 800/347–0808 for tickets* ⊕*www.melodytent.com*) to showcase Broadway musicals. Today it's the Cape's top venue for pop concerts and comedy shows.

★ **Harry's Blues Bar** (⊠*700 Main St., Hyannis* ☎*508/778–4188* ⊕*www. harrysbluesbar.com*) is hopping nearly every night year-round, drawing blues lovers of all ages.

WHERE TO EAT & STAY

$$-$$$ ✕**Naked Oyster.** The big draw at
Fodor's Choice this dapper restaurant with dark-
★ wood-paneled walls and soft light-
SEAFOOD ing is the extensive list of weekly changing specials, which truly show off the kitchen's estimable talents. You'll always find several raw and "dressed" oyster dishes (such as barbecue oysters on the

> **TAKE A TOUR**
>
> The Cape Cod Central Railroad offers two-hour, 42-mi narrated rail tours from Hyannis to the Cape Cod Canal (⌖*$18*) from late May through October; trains generally run daily, but call for a schedule. (⊠*Hyannis Train Depot, 252 Main St., Hyannis* ☎*508/771–3800 or 888/797–7245* ⊕*www.capetrain.com*).

2

half shell with blue cheese, caramelized onions, and bacon) plus a nice range of salads and appetizers. Among the main dishes, consider the superb sliced duck breast with a port-wine and Rainier cherry sauce, or the out-of- this-world oyster stew. ✉ *20 Independence Dr., off Rte. 132* ☎ *508/778–6500* ☐ *AE, D, DC, MC, V* ⊘ *No lunch weekends.*

$-$$ ✗ **Baxter's Fish 'n' Chips.** Since fried seafood is a Cape staple, you may
BRAZILIAN want to pay homage to one of the best Fry-o-lators around. Right on Hyannis Harbor, it's been a favorite of boaters and bathers alike since 1955. Generous portions of fried clams are delicious and cooked hot to order. The picnic tables outside, some set up on an old floating ferry, allow you to catch some rays while enjoying lobster, fish-and-chips, or something from the raw bar. If the weather's not on your side, there's indoor seating overlooking the harbor. ✉ *Pleasant St., Hyannis Harbor* ☎ *508/775–4490* ⌖ *Reservations not accepted* ☐ *AE, DC, MC, V* ⊘ *Closed mid-Oct.–Apr. and weekdays early Sept.–mid-Oct.*

$$ ▦ **Breakwaters.** These privately owned, weathered gray-shingle cottages rent by the week in summer (or nightly in spring and fall). Cottages are divided into one-, two-, and three-bedroom units and offer all the comforts of home. Each unit has one or two full baths; a kitchen with microwave, coffeemaker, refrigerator, toaster, and stove; TV and phone (local calls are free); and a deck or patio with a grill and picnic table. An in-ground heated pool is less than 200 feet from the lifeguarded town beach on Nantucket Sound. **Pros:** excellent waterfront location, ideal for families and groups traveling together. **Cons:** hard to reserve unless you're staying for a week; not the place for a quiet, private getaway (unless it's spring or fall). ✉ *432 Sea St., Box 118* ☎🖶 *508/775–6831* ⊕ *www.thebreakwaters.com* ⇥ *19 cottages* ⌖ *In-room: no a/c, kitchen. In-hotel: pool, beachfront, no elevator, no-smoking rooms* ☐ *No credit cards* ⊘ *Closed mid-Oct.–Apr.*

BARNSTABLE

4 mi north of Hyannis, 11 mi east of Sandwich.

With nearly 50,000 year-round residents, Barnstable is the largest town on the Cape. It's also the second oldest (it was founded in 1639). You can get a feeling for its age in Barnstable Village, on and near Main Street (Route 6A), a lovely area of large old homes.

SPORTS & THE OUTDOORS

BEACHES Hovering above Barnstable Harbor and the 4,000-acre **Great Salt Marsh, Sandy Neck Beach** stretches some 6 mi across a peninsula that ends at **Sandy Neck Light.** The beach is one of the Cape's most beautiful—dunes, sand, and sea spread endlessly east, west, and north. The lighthouse, standing a few feet from the eroding shoreline at the tip of the neck, has been out of commission since 1952. The main beach at Sandy Neck has lifeguards, a snack bar, restrooms, and showers. ✉ *Sandy Neck Rd., West Barnstable* ⊘ *Daily 8* AM*–9* PM*, but staffed only until 5* PM.

WHERE TO STAY

$$ ⊞ **Beechwood Inn.** Debbie and Ken Traugot's yellow-and-pale-green
★ 1853 Queen Anne house has gingerbread trim and is wrapped by a wide
porch with wicker furniture and a glider swing. Although the parlor is
pure mahogany-and-red-velvet Victorian, guest rooms have antiques in
lighter Victorian styles; several have fireplaces, and one has a bay view.
Bathrooms have pedestal sinks and antique lighting fixtures. Breakfast
is served in the dining room, which has a pressed-tin ceiling, a fireplace,
and lace-covered tables. **Pros:** exquisite lodging in historic Victorian, spa-
cious rooms, choose from seven different beaches within a 5-mi radius.
Cons: most rooms accessed via narrow, curved stairs. ⊠ *2839 Main St.
(Rte. 6A)* ☎ *508/362–6618 or 800/609–6618* ⊕ *www.beechwoodinn.
com* ⊅ *6 rooms* ⌂ *In-room: no phone, refrigerator. In-hotel: bicycles,
no elevator, no kids under 12* ⊟ *AE, D, MC, V* ⌀ *BP.*

$$-$$$ ⊞ **Honeysuckle Hill.** Innkeepers Freddy and Ruth Riley provide plenty
Fodor's Choice of little touches here: a guest fridge stocked with beverages (includ-
★ ing wine and beer), beach chairs with umbrellas, and an always-full
cookie jar. The airy, country-style guest rooms in this 1810 Queen
Anne–style cottage have lots of white wicker, featherbeds, checked
curtains, and pastel-painted floors. **Pros:** gracious and generous inn-
keepers, lush gardens on the grounds, tasteful, large rooms, very short
drive to Sandy Neck Beach. **Cons:** most rooms are accessed via steep
stairs. ⊠ *591 Main St. (Rte. 6A), West Barnstable* ☎ *508/362–8418 or
866/444–5522* ⊕ *www.honeysucklehill.com* ⊅ *4 rooms, 1 suite* ⌂ *In-
room: no phone, VCR (some). In-hotel: bicycles, no kids under 12, no
elevator, no-smoking rooms* ⊟ *AE, MC, V* ⌀ *BP.*

YARMOUTH

*Yarmouth Port is 3 mi east of Barnstable Village, West Yarmouth is 2
mi east of Hyannis.*

Once known as Mattacheese, or "the planting lands," Yarmouth was
settled in 1639 by farmers from the Plymouth Bay Colony. The town's
northernmost village of **Yarmouth Port** wasn't established as a distinct
village until 1829. By then the Cape had begun a thriving maritime
industry, and men turned to the sea to make their fortunes. Many
impressive sea captains' houses—some now B&Bs and museums—still
line enchanting Route 6A and nearby side streets, and Yarmouth Port
has some real old-time stores in town.

WHAT TO SEE

↻ **Bass Hole Boardwalk.** One of Yarmouth Port's most beautiful areas is
★ Bass Hole, which stretches from Homer's Dock Road to the salt marsh.
The boardwalk extends over a marshy creek; amid the salt marshes,
vegetated wetlands, and upland woods meander the 2½-mi **Callery-
Darling nature trails.** Gray's Beach is a little crescent of sand with calm
waters. ⊠ *Trail entrance on Center St. near Gray's Beach parking lot.*

**NEED A
BREAK?**
Jerry's Seafood and Dairy Freeze (⊠ *654 Main St. [Rte. 28], West Yarmouth*
☎ *508/775–9752*), open year-round, serves fried clams and onion rings,

along with thick frappes (milk shakes), frozen yogurt, and soft-serve ice cream at good prices.

SHOPPING

Peach Tree Designs (⊠ *173 Rte. 6A, Yarmouth Port* ☎ *508/362–8317*) carries home furnishings and decorative accessories; some are from local craftspeople, all are beautifully made.

WHERE TO EAT & STAY

$-$$$

Fodor's Choice

★

JAPANESE

✕**Inaho.** Yuji Watanabe, chef-owner of the Cape's best Japanese restaurant, makes early-morning journeys to Boston's fish markets to shop for the freshest local catch. His selection of sushi and sashimi is vast and artful, and vegetable and seafood tempura come out of the kitchen fluffy and light. If you're a teriyaki lover, you can't do any better than the chicken's beautiful blend of sweet and sour. ⊠ *157 Main St. (Rte. 6A)* ☎ *508/362–5522* ☐*MC, V.*

$-$$$

★

⌨**Bayside Resort.** A bit more upscale than most of the properties along Route 28, the Bayside overlooks pristine salt marshes and Lewis Bay. Although it's not right on the water, there is a small beach and a large outdoor pool with a café (there's also an indoor pool). Rooms have contemporary light-wood furnishings, and several have whirlpool tubs. **Pros:** ideal for families with children (organized kids' programs available), close to attractions of busy Route 28, reasonable rates, some water views, lots of specialized package deals. **Cons:** beach is more like a sandy tanning area; no swimming, not for those seeking quiet and intimate surroundings. ⊠ *225 Main St. (Rte. 28)* ☎ *508/775–5669 or 800/243–1114* ⊕*www.baysideresort.com* ↵*128 rooms* ⌂*In-room: refrigerator, Wi-Fi. In-hotel: bar, pools, gym, beachfront, no elevator* ☐*AE, D, MC, V* ⊨⊙*CP.*

$$-$$$

Fodor's Choice

★

⌨**Liberty Hill Inn.** Smartly but traditionally furnished common areas are a major draw to this dignified 1825 Greek-revival house. Guest rooms are filled with a mix of old-world romantic charm and modern amenities; each is uniquely decorated, and some have whirlpool tubs and fireplaces for those chilly evenings. Those traveling with children under five should make advance arrangements with the innkeepers. **Pros:** elegant, historic, and tasteful surroundings, beautiful grounds, romantic and intimate setting. **Cons:** some rooms accessed only via some steep stairs, some bathrooms have only small shower stalls, not a waterfront location. ⊠ *77 Main St. (Rte. 6A)* ☎ *508/362–3976 or 800/821–3977* ⊕*www.libertyhillinn.com* ↵*8 rooms, 1 suite* ⌂*In-room: Wi-Fi. In-hotel: no elevator, no-smoking rooms, public Wi-Fi* ☐*AE, D, MC, V* ⊨⊙*BP.*

DENNIS

Dennis Village is 4 mi east of Yarmouth Port, West Dennis is 1 mi east of South Yarmouth.

The backstreets of Dennis Village still retain the colonial charm of its seafaring days. The town, which was incorporated in 1793, was named for the Reverend Josiah Dennis. There were 379 sea captains living here when fishing, salt making, and shipbuilding were the main industries, and the elegant houses they constructed—now museums and B&Bs—still line the streets.

WHAT TO SEE

Cape Cod Museum of Art. The permanent collection of more than 850 works by Cape-associated artists includes important pieces such as a portrait of a fisherman's wife by Charles Hawthorne, the father of the Provincetown art colony. ✉ *60 Hope La., on grounds of Cape Playhouse, off Rte. 6A, Dennis Village* ☎ *508/385-4477* ⊕ *www.ccmoa. org* ☎ *$8* ⊙ *Late May–mid-Oct. Mon.–Sat. 10–5, Sun. noon–5; mid-Oct–late May Tues.–Sat. 10–5, Sun. noon–5.*

SPORTS & THE OUTDOORS

BEACHES Parking at all Dennis beaches is $15 a day in season for nonresidents. **Corporation Beach** (✉ *Corporation Rd., Dennis Village*) has lifeguards, showers, restrooms, and a food stand. Once a packet landing owned by a corporation of the townsfolk, the beautiful crescent of white sand backed by low dunes now serves a decidedly noncorporate purpose as a public beach.

NIGHTLIFE & THE ARTS

The **Cape Playhouse** (✉ *820 Main St. (Rte. 6A), Dennis Village* ☎ *508/385-3911 or 877/385-3911* ⊕ *www.capeplayhouse.com*), an 1838 former Unitarian meetinghouse, is the oldest professional summer theater in the country.

WHERE TO EAT & STAY

$-$$ ✕**Cap'n Frosty's.** A great stop after the beach, this is where locals go
Fodor'sChoice to get their fried seafood. This modest joint has a regular menu that
★ includes ice cream, a small specials board, and a counter where you
SEAFOOD order and take a number written on a french-fries box. There's seating inside as well as outside on a shady brick patio. ✉ *219 Main St. (Rte. 6A)* ☎ *508/385-8548* ⚁*Reservations not accepted* ▤*MC, V* ⊙ *Closed early Sept.–Mar.*

$$-$$$ ✕**Red Pheasant.** In Dennis Village, this is one of the Cape's best cozy
Fodor'sChoice country restaurants, with a consistently good kitchen where creative
★ American food is prepared with elaborate sauces and herb combi-
SEAFOOD nations. For instance, organic chicken is served with an intense pre-served-lemon-and-fresh-thyme sauce, and exquisitely grilled veal chops come with a dense red-wine-and-portobello-mushroom sauce. ✉ *905 Main St. (Rte. 6A)* ⌖*Box 486, Dennis, MA 02638* ☎ *508/385-2133* ⊕*www.redpheasantinn.com* ⚁*Reservations essential* ▤*AE, D, MC, V* ⊙*No lunch.*

$-$$ ▦ **Isaiah Hall B&B Inn.** Lilacs and pink roses trail along the white-picket
Fodor'sChoice fence outside this 1857 Greek-revival farmhouse on a quiet residential
★ road near the bay. Innkeepers Jerry and Judy Neal set the scene for a romantic getaway with guest rooms that have country antiques and floral-print wallpapers. In the attached carriage house, some rooms have small balconies overlooking a wooded lawn with gardens, grape arbors, and berry bushes. **Pros:** beautiful grounds in very quiet, historic setting, not far from area beaches and attractions. **Cons:** many rooms accessed via very steep steps, some rooms are on the small side. ✉ *152*

Whig St. ☎*508/385–9928 or 800/736–0160* ⊕*www.isaiahhallinn. com* ⇆*10 rooms, 2 suites* &*In-room: VCR, Wi-Fi (some). In-hotel: no elevator, no-smoking rooms* ☰*AE, D, MC, V* ⦿*CP.*

BREWSTER

2

7 mi northeast of Dennis, 20 mi east of Sandwich.

Brewster's location on Cape Cod Bay makes it a perfect place to learn about the region's ecology. The Cape Cod Museum of Natural History is here, and the area is rich in conservation lands, state parks, forests, freshwater ponds, and brackish marshes. When the tide is low in Cape Cod Bay, you can stroll the beaches and explore tidal pools up to 2 mi from the shore on the Brewster flats.

WHAT TO SEE

☼ **Cape Cod Museum of Natural History.** For nature enthusiasts, a visit to this

Fodor'sChoice ★ museum is a must; it's just a short drive west from the heart of Brewster along Route 6A. The spacious museum and pristine grounds include guided field walks, a shop, a natural-history library, lectures, classes, nature and marine exhibits such as a sea-life room with live specimens. Walking trails wind through 80 acres of forest, marshland, and ponds, all rich in birds and other wildlife. ⊠*869 Main St. (Rte. 6A), West Brewster* ☎*508/896–3867, 800/479–3867 in Massachusetts* ⊕*www. ccmnh.org* ⌸*$8* ⊙*Oct.–early Apr., Wed.–Sun. 11–3; late Apr.–May, Wed.–Sun. 10–4; June–Sept., daily 10–4.*

SPORTS & THE OUTDOORS

☼ **Nickerson State Park.** The 1,961 acres of this park were once part of a vast estate belonging to Roland C. Nickerson, son of Samuel Nickerson, a Chatham native who became a multimillionaire and founded of the First National Bank of Chicago. Today the land is open to the public for recreation. The park consists of acres of oak, pitch pine, hemlock, and spruce forest speckled with seven freshwater ponds. ⊠*3488 Rte. 6A, East Brewster* ☎*508/896– 3491* ⊕*www.mass.gov/dcr* ⌸*Free* ⊙*Daily dawn–dusk.*

WATER SPORTS **Jack's Boat Rentals** (⊠*Flax Pond, Nickerson State Park, Rte. 6A, East Brewster* ☎*508/896–8556*) rents canoes, kayaks, Seacycles, Sunfish, pedal boats, and sailboards; guided kayak tours are also offered.

SHOPPING

★ Built in 1852 as a church, **Brewster Store** (⊠*1935 Main St. (Rte. 6A), at Rte. 124* ☎*508/896–3744* ⊕*www.brewsterstore.com*), a local landmark, is a typical New England general store with such essentials as

---

BIKE THE RAIL TRAIL

The Cape's premier bike path, the Cape Cod Rail Trail, follows the paved right-of-way of the old Penn Central Railroad. About 25 mi long, the easy-to-moderate trail passes salt marshes, cranberry bogs, and ponds.

The trail starts at the parking lot off Route 134 south of U.S. 6, near Theophilus Smith Road in South Dennis, and it ends at the post office in South Wellfleet. Access points in Brewster are Long Pond Road, Underpass Road, and Nickerson State Park.

the daily papers, penny candy, and benches out front for conversation. Open April through October, the **Satucket Farm Stand** (✉ *76 Harwich Rd. [Rte. 124], off Rte. 6A* ☎ *508/896–5540*) is a real old-fashioned farm stand and bakery. Most produce is grown on the premises, and you can fill your basket with home-baked scones and breads, fruit pies, produce, herbs, and flowers.

WHERE TO EAT & STAY

$$$$
Fodor's Choice
★
SEAFOOD

✕**Chillingsworth.** One of the crown jewels of Cape restaurants, Chillingsworth combines formal presentation with an excellent French menu and a diverse wine cellar to create a memorable dining experience. Super-rich risotto, roast lobster, and grilled Angus sirloin are favorites. Dinner in the main dining rooms is prix fixe and includes seven courses—appetizer, soup, salad, sorbet, entrée, "amusements," and dessert, plus coffee or tea. ✉ *2449 Main St. (Rte. 6A), East Brewster* ☎ *508/896–3640* ▤ *AE, DC, MC, V* ⊘ *Closed Thanksgiving –mid-May.*

$-$$
Fodor's Choice
★

▨**Old Sea Pines Inn.** With its white-column portico and wraparound veranda overlooking a broad lawn, Old Sea Pines, which housed a young ladies' boarding school in the early 1900s, resembles a vintage summer estate. Climb the sweeping staircase to guest rooms decorated with reproduction wallpaper, antiques, and framed old photographs. Children under eight years are allowed only in the family suites. **Pros:** not far from town center, beautiful grounds, reasonable rates in historic setting. **Cons:** some rooms have shared baths, many rooms accessed steep stairway on upper floors. ✉ *2553 Main St. (Rte. 6A), Box 1070,* ☎ *508/896–6114* ⊕ *www.oldseapinesinn.com* ⇘ *24 rooms, 19 with bath, 5 suites* ⚹ *In-room: no phone, no TV (some), Wi-Fi. In-hotel: restaurant, no elevator, no-smoking rooms* ▤ *AE, D, MC, V* ⊘ *Closed Jan.–Mar.* �"⃝| *BP.*

HARWICH

6 mi south of Brewster, 5 mi east of Dennis.

The Cape's famous cranberry industry took off in Harwich in 1844, when Alvin Cahoon was its principal grower. Today you'll still find cranberry bogs throughout Harwich, and each September the town holds a **Cranberry Festival** to celebrate the importance of this indigenous berry; the festival is usually scheduled during the week after Labor Day.

WHERE TO STAY

$$$$
Fodor's Choice
★

▨**Wequassett Inn Resort & Golf Club.** Twenty Cape-style cottages and an attractive hotel make up this traditionally elegant resort by the sea. An attentive staff, evening entertainment, fun in the sun, and golf at the exclusive Cape Cod National Golf Club are just a few of the benefits you can count on at Wequassett. Chef Bill Brodsky's creative globally inspired cuisine graces the menus of the three restaurants—the star being the sophisticated 28 Atlantic ($$$–$$$$), which is one of the top destination restaurants on the Cape, serving such stellar creations as yellowfin and salmon tartare, and caramelized skate wing with beet-daikon-horseradish salad and watercress jus. After a day at the beach or on the links, retire to your spacious room and relax amid fresh pine furniture, floral bedcovers or handmade quilts, and overflowing window boxes. **Pros:** full-service resort in idyllic, waterfront setting, activities and programs for all ages, babysitting services on-site, elegant surroundings. **Cons:** rates are very steep, not an in-town location. ⊠ *2173 Orleans Rd. (Rte. 28)* ☎ *508/432–5400 or 800/225–7125* ⊕ *www.wequassett.com* ⇆ *102 rooms, 2 suites* ♿ *In-hotel: 3 restaurants, room service, bar, tennis courts, pool, gym, water sports, no smoking rooms, no elevator, children's programs* ☰ *AE, D, DC, MC, V* ⦾ *Closed Nov.–Mar.* ⎰ *FAP.*

CHATHAM

5 mi east of Harwich, 8 mi south of Orleans.

At the bent elbow of the Cape, with water nearly surrounding it, Chatham has all the charm of a quietly posh seaside resort, with plenty of shops but none of the crass commercialism that plagues some other towns on the Cape. And it's charming: the town has gray-shingle houses with tidy awnings and cheerful flower gardens, an attractive Main Street with crafts and antiques stores alongside dapper cafés, and a five-and-dime. Although it can get crowded in high season—and even on weekends during shoulder seasons—Chatham remains a true New England village.

WHAT TO SEE

★ **Atwood House Museum.** Built by sea captain Joseph C. Atwood in 1752 and occupied by his descendants until it was sold to the Chatham Historical Society in 1926, the Atwood House Museum has a gambrel roof, variable-width floor planks, fireplaces, an old kitchen with a wide hearth and a beehive oven, and some antique dolls and toys. ⊠ *347 Stage Harbor Rd., West Chatham* ☎ *508/945–2493* ⊕ *www.chathamhistoricalsociety.org* ⛁ *$5* ⦾ *Mid–late June and Sept.–mid-Oct., Tues.–Sat. 1–4 (opens at 10 AM on rainy days); July and Aug., Tues.–Sat. 10–4.*

★ **Chatham Light.** The famous view of the harbor, the offshore sandbars, and the ocean beyond from this lighthouse justifies the crowds that gather to share it. ⊠ *Main St. near Bridge St., West Chatham*

SPORTS & THE OUTDOORS

Fodor's Choice **Monomoy National Wildlife Refuge.** This 2,500-acre preserve includes the Monomoy Islands, a fragile 9-mi-long barrier-beach area south of Chatham. A haven for bird-watchers, the island is an important stop along the North Atlantic Flyway for migratory waterfowl and shorebirds—peak migration times are May and late July. The only structure on the islands is the **South Monomoy Lighthouse**, built in 1849.

SHOPPING

★ **Chatham Jam and Jelly Shop** (⊠ *10 Vineyard Ave., at Rte. 28, West Chatham* ☎ *508/945–3052 or 877/526–7467*) sells delicious concoctions like rose-petal jelly, apple-lavender chutney, and beach-plum jam, as well as all the old standbys. **Clambake Celebrations** (⊠ *1223C Main St.* ☎ *508/945–7771 or 877/792–7771*) prepares full clambakes, including lobsters, clams, mussels, corn, potatoes, onions, and sausage, for you to take out. They'll even lend you a charcoal grill.

NIGHTLIFE & THE ARTS

Chatham Squire (⊠*487 Main St.* ☎*508/945–0945*), with four bars—including a raw bar—is a rollicking hangout, drawing a young crowd to the bar side and a mixed crowd of locals to the restaurant.

WHERE TO EAT & STAY

$-$$$
★
SEAFOOD

✕**Impudent Oyster.** A cozy, festive locals' tavern with an unfailingly cheerful staff and superb but reasonably priced seafood, this always-packed restaurant sits inside a dapper house just off Main Street. It's a great place for a romantic meal or dinner with friends or kids, and the menu offers light burgers and sandwiches as well as more substantial fare. Mussels with white-wine sauce is a consistent favorite. ⊠*15 Chatham Bars Ave.* ☎*508/945-3545* ⊟*AE, MC, V.*

$$$-$$$$
★

🏨**Queen Anne Inn.** Built in 1840 as a wedding present for the daughter of a famous clipper-ship captain, the Queen Anne first opened as an inn in 1874. Some of the large guest rooms have working fireplaces, balconies, and hot tubs. Run by locally renowned chef Toby Hill, the Eldredge Room ($$$–$$$$; closed Jan.–Apr., no lunch) turns out sublime regional American fare, including an updated fish-and-chips consisting of truffle-crusted flounder, frites, truffle tartar sauce, and a malt vinaigrette. **Pros:** spacious and thoughtfully decorated rooms in historic setting, well-suited for relaxing with hot tubs and fireplaces. **Cons:** it's a generous walk to the town center, rooms accessed via steep stairs. ⊠*70 Queen Anne Rd.* ☎*508/945-0394 or 800/545-4667* ⊕*www.queen anneinn.com* ⊷*33 rooms* ♿*In-room: Wi-Fi. In-hotel: restaurant, bar, tennis courts, pool, no-smoking rooms, no elevator* ⊟*AE, D, MC, V* ⊘*Closed Jan. and Mar. (open Feb.).*

ORLEANS

8 mi north of Chatham, 35 mi east of Sagamore Bridge.

Orleans has a long heritage in fishing and seafaring, and many beautifully preserved homes remain from the colonial era. Many are found in the small village of East Orleans, home of the town's Historical Society and Museum. In other areas of town, such as down by Rock Harbor, more modestly grand homes stand near the water's edge.

WHAT TO SEE

Rock Harbor. A walk along Rock Harbor Road, a winding street lined with gray-shingle Cape houses, white-picket fences, and neat gardens, leads to this bay-side harbor, site of a War of 1812 skirmish in which the Orleans militia kept a British warship from docking.

SPORTS & THE OUTDOORS

BEACHES The town-managed **Nauset Beach** (⊠*Beach Rd., Nauset Heights* ☎*508/240–3780*)—not to be confused with Nauset Light Beach on the National Seashore—is a 10-mi sweep of sandy ocean beach with low dunes and large waves good for bodysurfing or board surfing. The beach has lifeguards, restrooms, showers, and a food concession. **Skaket Beach** (⊠*Skaket Beach Rd., Namskaket* ☎*508/240–3775*) on Cape Cod Bay is a sandy stretch with calm, warm water good for children. There are restrooms, lifeguards, and a snack bar.

BOATING & **Arey's Pond Boat Yard** (⊠*43 Arey's La., off Rte. 28, South Orleans*
FISHING ☎*508/255–0994*) has a sailing school with individual and group lessons. Many of Orleans's freshwater ponds offer good fishing for perch, pickerel, trout, and more. The required fishing license, along with rental gear, is available at the **Goose Hummock Shop** (⊠*15 Rte. 6A* ☎*508/255–0455*).

WHERE TO STAY

$$-$$$$ ⊡**Orleans Inn.** This 1875 sea captain's mansion nearly met with the
Fodor'sChoice wrecking ball in the late '90s; now this bustling inn and restaurant is
★ run with warmth and enthusiasm. Rooms here are simply but charmingly appointed with classic wood furniture and floral quilts on the beds; the larger waterfront suites have sitting areas and great views of the harbor. The restaurant ($–$$$), which uses creative ingredients and serves up large portions of fish-and-chips, grilled sirloin, and grilled salmon with orange-honey glaze. **Pros:** great waterfront location, outdoor dining overlooking the cove (about the only place in town), gracious hosts, many amenities. **Cons:** some rooms face busy intersection rather than the water, rooms accessed via steep stairs. ⊠*3 Old County Rd.* ☎*508/255–2222 or 800/863–3039* ⊕*www.orleansinn.com* ⌖*8 rooms, 3 suites* ☖*In-room: DVD, VCR, Wi-Fi. In-hotel: restaurant, bar, no-smoking rooms, no elevator* ☴*AE, MC, V* ⦿|*BP.*

EASTHAM

3 mi north of Orleans, 6 mi south of Wellfleet.

Often overlooked on the speedy drive up toward Provincetown on U.S. 6, Eastham is a town full of hidden treasures. Unlike other towns on the Cape, it has no official town center or Main Street; the highway bisects Eastham, and the town is spread out on both Cape Cod Bay and the Atlantic. Amid the gas stations, convenience stores, restaurants, and large motel complexes, Eastham's wealth of natural beauty takes a little exploring to find.

WHAT TO SEE

♺ **Cape Cod National Seashore.** The Cape's most expansive national treasure
Fodor'sChoice was established in 1961 under the administration of President John F.
★ Kennedy, for whom Cape Cod was home and haven. The 27,000-acre seashore, extending from Chatham to Provincetown, encompasses and protects 30 mi of superb ocean beaches; great rolling dunes; swamps, marshes, and wetlands; pitch-pine and scrub-oak forest; all kinds of wildlife; and a number of historic structures. Self-guided nature trails,

as well as biking and horse trails, lace through these landscapes. The seashore's main information center, the Salt Pond Visitor Center, offers guided walks, tours, boat trips, demonstrations, and lectures from mid-April through Thanksgiving, as well as evening beach walks, campfire talks, and other programs in summer. ⊠*Doane Rd. off U.S. 6* ☏*508/255–3421* ⊕*www.nps.gov/caco* ⊠*Free* ☉*Daily 9–4:30 (hrs extended slightly in summer).*

SPORTS & THE OUTDOORS

Fodor'sChoice
★ **Nauset Light Beach** (⊠*Off Ocean View Dr.*), adjacent to Coast Guard Beach, continues the National Seashore landscape of long, sandy beach backed by tall dunes and grass. It has showers and lifeguards in summer, but as with other National Seashore beaches, there's no food concession. Nauset charges $15 daily per car; a $45 season pass admits you here and to the other five National Seashore swimming beaches.

WHERE TO EAT & STAY

¢-$
SEAFOOD
✕ **The Friendly Fisherman.** Not just another roadside lobster shack with buoys and nets for decoration, this place is serious about its fresh seafood. It's both a great place to pick up ingredients to cook at home— there's a fish and produce market on-site—and a good bet for dining out on such favorites as fish-and-chips, fried scallops, and lobster. The market also sells homemade pies, breads, soups, stews, and pasta. ⊠*U. S. 6, North Eastham* ☏*508/255–6770 or 508/255–3009* ⊟*AE, MC, V* ☉*Closed Nov.–Apr.*

$$$-$$$$
Fodor'sChoice
★ 🏨 **Whalewalk Inn & Spa.** This 1830 whaling master's home is on three landscaped acres. Rooms in the main inn have four-poster twin, double, or queen-size beds; floral fabrics; and antique or reproduction furniture. Suites with fully equipped kitchens are in the converted barn and guesthouse. **Pros:** beautiful grounds, elegantly appointed rooms with added benefit of decadent spa treatments. **Cons:** no water views or beachfront, not an in-town location. ⊠*220 Bridge Rd.* ☏*508/255– 0617 or 800/440–1281* ⊕*www.whalewalkinn.com* ⏏*11 rooms, 5 suites* ⌂*In-room: kitchen (some), refrigerator (some), DVD (some) VCR (some), Wi-Fi. In-hotel: pool, gym, spa, no-smoking rooms, no elevator* ⊟*AE, D, MC, V* ⃝|*BP.*

WELLFLEET & SOUTH WELLFLEET

6 mi north of Eastham, 13 mi southeast of Provincetown.

Still famous for its world-renowned and succulent namesake oysters, Wellfleet is today a tranquil community; many artists and writers call it home. Less than 2 mi wide, it's one of the most attractively developed Cape resort towns, with a number of fine restaurants, historic houses, art galleries, and a good old Main Street in the village proper.

WHAT TO SEE

★ **Marconi Station.** On the Atlantic side of the Cape's forearm, Marconi Station is the site of the first transatlantic wireless station erected on the U.S. mainland. Italian radio and wireless-telegraphy pioneer Guglielmo Marconi sent the first American wireless message from here to Europe—"most cordial greetings and good wishes" from President

Theodore Roosevelt to King Edward VII of England—on January 18, 1903. Off the parking lot, a 1½-mi trail and boardwalk lead through the **Atlantic White Cedar Swamp,** one of the most beautiful trails on the seashore. ⊠ *Marconi Site Rd., South Wellfleet* ☎ *508/349–3785* ⊕ *www.nps.gov/caco* ⊠ *Free* ⊘ *Daily 8–4:30.*

SPORTS & THE OUTDOORS

Massachusetts Audubon Wellfleet Bay Wildlife Sanctuary. A trip to the Outer Cape isn't complete without a visit to this 1,100-acre haven for more than 250 species of birds attracted by the varied habitats found here. The jewel of the Massachusetts Audubon Society, the sanctuary is a superb place for walking, birding, and watching the sun set over the salt marsh and bay. The **Esther Underwood Johnson Nature Center** contains two 700-gallon aquariums that offer an up-close look at marine life common to the Cape's tidal flats and marshlands. Other rotating exhibits illustrate different facets of the area's ecology and natural history. ⊠ *291 U.S. 6* ☎ *508/349–2615* ⊕ *www.wellfleetbay. org* ⊠ *$5* ⊘ *Trails daily 8 AM–dusk; nature center late May–mid-Oct., daily 8:30–5; mid-Oct.–late May, Tues.–Sun. 8:30–5.*

BEACHES **Cahoon Hollow Beach** (⊠ *Ocean View Dr.*) has lifeguards, restrooms, and a restaurant and music club on the sand. This beach tends to attract younger and slightly rowdier crowds; it's a big Sunday-afternoon party place. **White Crest Beach** (⊠ *Ocean View Dr.*) is a prime surfer hangout where the dudes often spend more time waiting for waves than actually riding them.

BOATING **Jack's Boat Rental** (⊠ *Gull Pond, south of U.S. 6* ☎ *508/349–9808 or 508/221–8226* ⊕ *www.jacksboatrental.com*) has canoes, kayaks, Sunfish, pedal boats, surfboards, Boogie boards, and sailboards. Guided kayak tours are also available.

NIGHTLIFE & THE ARTS

The drive-in movie is alive and well on Cape Cod at the **Wellfleet Drive-In Theater** (⊠ *51 U.S. 6, South Wellfleet* ☎ *508/349–7176* ⊕ *www.wellfleetcinemas.com*), which is right by the Eastham town line. Films start at dusk nightly in season.

WHERE TO EAT & STAY

$-$$$ ✕ **Finely JP's.** Chef John Pontius consistently turns out wonderful, affordable food full of the best Mediterranean and local influences and ingredients at his beloved restaurant along U.S. 6. The unassuming roadhouse restaurant was redesigned and enlarged in 2006—it's now a handsome, Arts and Crafts–inspired structure. Appetizers are especially good, and the Wellfleet paella draws rave reviews. ⊠ *554 U.S. 6, South Wellfleet* ☎ *508/349–7500* ⊠ *Reservations not accepted* ▤ *D, MC, V* ⊘ *Closed some nights during off-season. No lunch.*

$$ ⊞ **Stone Lion Inn.** The Stone Lion Inn, a gracious mansard-roof Victorian, sits just outside the town center and is a short walk away from both the harbor and the village. Rooms have queen beds, ceiling fans to encourage the breezes, hardwood floors, and a mix of antiques and contemporary pieces that balance the house's 19th-century heritage with today's decorating sensibilities. Pros: short walk from harbor and shopping,

stylish yet unpretentious décor, friendly and helpful owners. Cons: no phone or TV in most rooms, need a car to get to ocean, not appropriate for younger kids. ☒*130 Commercial St.* ☎*508/349–9565* ⊕*www. stonelioncapecod.com* ⌁*3 rooms, 1 apartment, 1 cottage* ♿*In-room: no phone (some), kitchen (some), refrigerator, no TV (some), Wi-Fi. In-hotel: no elevator, no kids under 10* ▭*MC, V* ⏀*BP.*

▌ **EN**
ROUTE

Edward Hopper summered in **Truro** from 1930 to 1967, finding the Cape light ideal for his austere brand of realism. One of the largest towns on the Cape in terms of land area—almost 43 square mi—it's also the smallest in population, with about 1,400 year-round residents. Truro is also the Cape's narrowest town, and from a high perch you can see the Atlantic Ocean on one side and Cape Cod Bay on the other. Its Highland Light (also called Cape Cod Light) is the Cape's oldest lighthouse and truly a breathtaking sight. Tours (▤*$4)* of the lighthouse are given daily in summer.

PROVINCETOWN

★ *9 mi northwest of Wellfleet, 62 mi from Sagamore Bridge.*

Many people know that the Pilgrims stopped here at the curved tip of Cape Cod before proceeding to Plymouth. Historical records suggest that an earlier visitor was Thorvald, brother of Viking Leif Erikson, who came ashore here in AD 1004 to repair the keel of his boat and consequently named the area Kjalarness, or Cape of the Keel. Bartholomew Gosnold came to Provincetown in 1602 and named the area Cape Cod after the abundant codfish he found in the local waters.

Incorporated as a town in 1727, Provincetown was for many decades a bustling seaport, with fishing and whaling as its major industries. In the late 19th century, groups of Portuguese fishermen and whalers began to settle here, lending their expertise and culture to an already cosmopolitan town. Fishing is still an important source of income for many Provincetown locals, but now the town ranks among the world's leading whale-watching—rather than whale-hunting—outposts.

Artists began coming here in the late 1890s to take advantage of the unusual Cape Cod light—in fact, Provincetown is the nation's oldest continuous art colony. By 1916, with five art schools flourishing here, painters' easels were nearly as common as shells on the beach. This bohemian community, along with the availability of inexpensive summer lodgings, attracted young rebels and writers as well, including John Reed (*Ten Days That Shook the World*) and Mary Heaton Vorse (*Footnote to Folly*), who in 1915 began the Cape's first significant theater group, the Provincetown Players. The young, then unknown Eugene O'Neill joined them in 1916, when his *Bound East for Cardiff* premiered in a tiny wharf-side East End fish house.

WHAT TO SEE

★ **Commercial Street.** Driving the 3 mi of Provincetown's main downtown thoroughfare, Commercial Street, in season could take forever, so opt for a walk instead. Take a casual stroll by the many architectural styles

(Greek revival, Victorian, Second Empire, and Gothic, to name a few) used in the design of the impressive houses for wealthy sea captains and merchants. The Provincetown Historical Society puts out a series of walking-tour pamphlets available for about $1 each at many shops in town. The center of town is where the crowds and most of the touristy shops are. The quiet East End is mostly residential, with an increasing number of nationally renowned galleries; the similarly quiet West End has a number of small inns with neat lawns and elaborate gardens.

★ **Pilgrim Monument.** The first thing you'll see in Provincetown is this grandiose edifice, which seems somewhat out of proportion to the rest of the low-rise town. The monument commemorates the Pilgrims' first landing in the New World and their signing of the Mayflower Compact (the first colonial-American rules of self-governance) before they set off from Provincetown Harbor to explore the mainland. Climb the 116 steps and 60 short ramps of the 252-foot-high tower for a panoramic view—dunes on one side, harbor on the other, and the entire bay side of Cape Cod beyond. At the tower's base is a museum of Lower Cape and Provincetown history, with exhibits on whaling, shipwrecks, and scrimshaw. ⊠*High Pole Hill Rd.* ☎*508/487-1310* ⊕*www.pilgrim-monument.org* ☞*$7* ⊙*Early Apr.–June and Sept. and Oct., daily 9–4:15; July and Aug., daily 9–6:15; Nov., weekends 9–4:15.*

SPORTS & THE OUTDOORS

BEACHES
FodorsChoice
★ **Race Point Beach** (⊠*Race Point Rd., east of U.S. 6*), one of the Cape Cod National Seashore beaches in Provincetown, has a wide swath of sand stretching far off into the distance around the point and Coast Guard station. Because of its position on a point facing north, the beach gets sun all day long. Parking costs $15 per day.

WHALE-
WATCHING **Dolphin Fleet.** Tours are accompanied by scientists from the Center for Coastal Studies in Provincetown, who provide commentary while collecting data on the whales they've been monitoring for years. They know many of them by name and will tell you about their habits and histories. ⊠*Ticket office: Chamber of Commerce building at MacMillan Wharf, Downtown Center* ☎*508/240-3636 or 800/826-9300* ⊕*www.whalewatch.com* ☞*$33* ⊙*Tours mid-Apr.–Oct.*

▮ **DUNES TOUR** **Fodors**Choice ★ Art's Dune Tours (⊠ *Commercial and Standish Sts., Downtown Center* ☎ 508/487-1950 ⊕ www.artsdunetours.com) has been taking eager passengers into the dunes of Province Lands since 1946. Bumpy but controlled rides transport you through sometimes surreal sandy vistas peppered with beach grass and along shoreline patrolled by seagulls and sandpipers.

NIGHTLIFE

NIGHTLIFE **Atlantic House** (⊠*4 Masonic Pl., Downtown Center* ☎*508/487-3821*) is the grandfather of the gay nightlife scene.

WHERE TO EAT

¢-$$
Fodor's Choice
★
SEAFOOD

✗**Clem & Ursie's.** It's worth the short drive or long walk from downtown to sample the tantalizing seafood prepared at this colorful café, grocery market, cocktail bar, and bakery. The mammoth menu touches on just about every kind of food from the ocean: tuna steaks, crab claws, squid stew, Japanese baby octopus salad, hot lobster rolls, lobster scampi. The Buffalo shrimp are addictive, and be sure to try the Portuguese clam pie. ⌂*85 Shank Painter Rd.* ☎*508/487–2333* ▭*MC, V* ⊙ *Closed mid-Nov.–mid-Apr.*

$$-$$$
Fodor's Choice
★
AMERICAN

✗**Devon's.** This unassuming, tiny white cottage—with a dining room that seats just 42 lucky patrons—serves up some of the best food in town. Specialties from the oft-changing menu include pan-seared halibut with caramelized orange glaze, black rice, and sautéed beet greens; and free-range seared duck with a Syrah reduction, red-onion marmalade, and couscous primavera. Be sure to save some room for knockout dessert selections like blackberry mousse over ginger-lemon polenta cake with wild-berry coulis. ⌂*401½ Commercial St.* ☎*508/487–4773* ⚘*Reservations essential* ▭*MC, V* ⊙ *Closed Wed. and Nov.–Apr.*

$-$$$
SEAFOOD

✗**Lobster Pot.** Provincetown's Lobster Pot is fit to do battle with all the lobster shanties anywhere (and everywhere) else on the Cape—it's often jammed with tourists, but that's truly a reflection of the generally high quality. The hardworking kitchen turns out classic New England cooking: lobsters, generous and filling seafood platters (try the seafood Pico with a half lobster, shrimp, littlenecks, mussels, calamari, and fish over pasta with tomatoes, rose wine, onions, and garlic), and some of the best chowder around. ⌂*321 Commercial St.* ☎*508/487–0842* ⚘*Reservations not accepted* ▭*AE, D, DC, MC, V* ⊙ *Closed Jan.*

¢
PIZZA

✗**Spiritus.** The local bars close at 1 AM, at which point this pizza joint–coffee stand becomes the town's epicenter. It's the ultimate place to see and be seen, pizza slice in hand and witty banter at the ready. In the morning, the same counter serves restorative coffee and croissants as well as Häagen-Dazs ice cream. ⌂*190 Commercial St.* ☎*508/487–2808* ▭*No credit cards* ⊙ *Closed Nov.–Apr.*

WHERE TO STAY

$$$-$$$$
Fodor's Choice
★

☷ **Brass Key.** One of the Cape's most luxurious small resorts, this meticulously kept year-round getaway comprises a beautifully restored main house—originally an 1828 sea captain's home—and several other carefully groomed buildings and cottages. Rooms mix antiques with such modern amenities as Bose stereos and TV–VCRs (loaner laptops and iPod docks are also available). Deluxe rooms come with gas fireplaces and whirlpool baths or French doors opening onto wrought-iron balconies. A widow's-walk sundeck has a panoramic view of Cape Cod Bay. **Pros:** ultra-posh rooms; beautiful and secluded grounds; pool on-site.

Cons: among the highest rates in town, rooms close to Bradford Street can get a bit of noise, significant minimum-stay requirements in summer. ⌂*67 Bradford St.* ☎*508/487–9005 or 800/842–9858* ⊕*www. brasskey.com* ⇆*42 rooms* ♿*In-room: safe, VCR, Wi-Fi. In-hotel: pool, no elevator, no kids under 16* ▭*AE, D, MC, V* ⋈*CP.*

MARTHA'S VINEYARD

By Andrew
Collins

Far less developed than Cape Cod—thanks to a few local conservation organizations—yet more cosmopolitan than neighboring Nantucket, Martha's Vineyard is an island with a double life. From Memorial Day through Labor Day the quieter, some might say real, Vineyard quickens into a vibrant, star-studded place.

The busy main port, Vineyard Haven, welcomes day-trippers fresh off ferries and private yachts to browse in its own array of shops. Oak Bluffs, where pizza and ice-cream emporiums reign supreme, has the air of a Victorian boardwalk. Edgartown is flooded with seekers of chic who wander tine streets that hold boutiques, stately whaling captains' homes, and charming inns.

Summer regulars have included a host of celebrities over the years, among them Walter Cronkite, Spike Lee, and Diane Sawyer. If you're planning to stay overnight on a summer weekend, be sure to make reservations well in advance; spring is not too early. Things stay busy on September and October weekends, a favorite time for weddings, but begin to slow down soon after. In may ways the Vineyard's off-season persona is even more appealing that its summer self. There's more time to linger over pastoral and ocean vistas, free from the throngs of cars, bicycles, and mopeds.

The Vineyard, except for Oak Bluffs and Edgartown, is "dry." Many restaurants allow you to bring your own beer or wine, however.

VINEYARD HAVEN (TISBURY)

7 mi southeast of Woods Hole, 3½ mi west of Oak Bluffs, 8 mi northwest of Edgartown.

Most people call this town Vineyard Haven because of the name of the port where ferries arrive, but its official name is Tisbury. Not as high-toned as Edgartown or as honky-tonk as Oak Bluffs, Vineyard Haven blends the past and the present with a touch of the bohemian. Visitors arriving here step off the ferry right into the bustle of the harbor, a block from the shops and restaurants of Main Street.

SPORTS & THE OUTDOORS

BEACHES **Lake Tashmoo Town Beach** (⊠ *End of Herring Creek Rd.*) provides swimmers with access to the warm, relatively shallow, brackish lake—or cooler, gentler Vineyard Sound. **Owen Park Beach** (⊠ *Off Main St.*), a small, sandy harbor beach, is just steps away from the ferry terminal in Vineyard Haven, making it a great spot to catch some last rays before heading home. **Tisbury Town Beach** (⊠ *End of Owen Little Way, off Main St.*) is a public beach next to the Vineyard Haven Yacht Club.

SHOPPING

Fodor'sChoice
★
Rainy Day (⊠ *66 Main St.* ☎ *508/693–1830*) carries gifts and amusements that are perfect for one of the island's gloomy rainy days. You'll find toys, crafts, cards, soaps, and more.

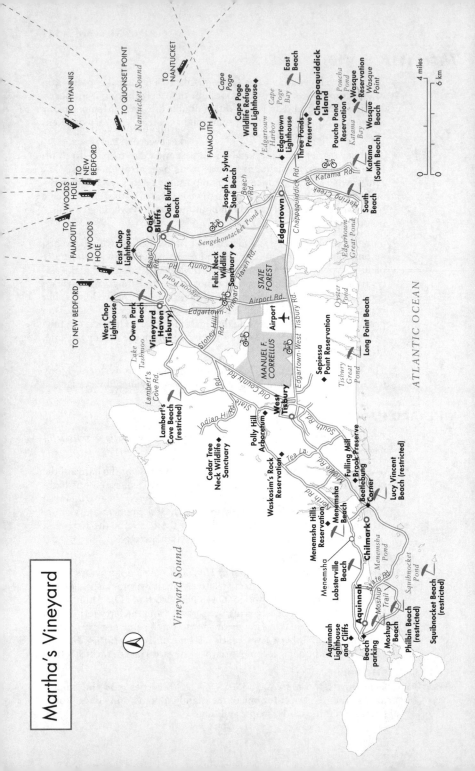

Martha's Vineyard

TO HYANNIS

TO QUONSET POINT

Nantucket Sound

TO NANTUCKET

TO FALMOUTH

Cape Poge

Cape Poge Wildlife Refuge and Lighthouse

Cape Poge Bay

East Beach

Three Ponds Preserve

Chappaquiddick Island

Poucha Pond

Wasque Reservation

Wasque Point

Poucha Pond Reservation

Katama Bay

Wasque Beach

TO NEW BEDFORD

TO NEW BEDFORD

TO WOODS HOLE

TO FALMOUTH

TO WOODS HOLE

Oak Bluffs

Oak Bluffs Beach

Joseph A. Sylvia State Beach

Beach Rd.

Edgartown Harbor

Edgartown Lighthouse

Chappaquiddick Rd.

Katama Rd.

Katama (South Beach)

South Beach

East Chop Lighthouse

Sengekontacket Pond

County Rd.

Felix Neck Wildlife Sanctuary

Vineyard Haven Rd.

Edgartown

Herring Creek

Edgartown Great Pond

West Chop Lighthouse

Owen Park Beach

Beach Rd.

Vineyard Haven (Tisbury)

Lagoon Pond

Edgartown–Vineyard Haven Rd.

Airport Rd.

STATE FOREST

Airport

Oyster Pond

Long Point Beach

Lake Tashmoo

Stoney Hill Rd.

MANUEL F. CORRELLUS

Edgartown–West Tisbury Rd.

Sepiessa Point Reservation

Tisbury Great Pond

ATLANTIC OCEAN

Lambert's Cove Rd.

Lambert's Cove Beach (restricted)

Old County Rd.

State Rd.

West Tisbury

Polly Hill Arboretum

South Rd.

Cedar Tree Neck Wildlife Sanctuary

Indian Hill Rd.

Tea La.

Fulling Mill Brook Preserve

Waskosim's Rock Reservation

Middle Rd.

North Rd.

Menemsha Beach

Beetlebung Corner

Lucy Vincent Beach (restricted)

Menemsha Hills Reservation

Chilmark

Menemsha Pond

Menemsha Lobsterville Beach

State Rd.

Squibnocket Pond

Squibnocket Beach (restricted)

Aquinnah

Moshup Trail

Aquinnah Lighthouse and Cliffs

Beach parking

Moshup Beach

Philbin Beach (restricted)

Vineyard Sound

4 miles

6 km

WHERE TO EAT & STAY

$$$-$$$$ ✕**Black Dog Tavern.** This island landmark—which is more popular with
AMERICAN tourists than locals—lies just steps from the ferry terminal in Vineyard
Haven. In July and August, the wait for breakfast (with an expansive
omelet assortment) can be as much as an hour from 8 AM on. Why?
Partly because the ambience inside—roaring fireplace, dark-wood
walls, and a grand view of the water—makes everyone feel so at home.
The menu is heavy on local fish, chowders, and chops. ⊠ *20 Beach St.
Ext.* ☎*508/693–9223* ⚲*Reservations not accepted* ▤*AE, D, MC,
V* ⚑*BYOB.*

$$$-$$$$ 🏠**Crocker House Inn.** This 1924 farmhouse-style inn is tucked into a
★   quiet lane off Main Street, minutes from the ferries and Owen Park
Beach. The rooms are decorated casually with understated flair—pas-
tel-painted walls, softly upholstered wing-back chairs, and white-
wicker nightstands. No. 6, with a small porch and a private entrance,
has the best view of the harbor. **Pros:** great owners, short walk from
town, easygoing vibe. **Cons:** you pay a premium for this location, decor
is more casual than posh, books up quickly in summer. ⊠*12 Crocker
Ave.* ☎*508/693–1151 or 800/772–0206* ⊕*www.crockerhouseinn.com*
⌂*8 rooms* ⚐*In-room: Wi-Fi. In-hotel: no elevator, no kids under 12*
▤*MC, V* ⦿*CP.*

OAK BLUFFS

3½ mi east of Vineyard Haven.

Circuit Avenue is the bustling center of the Oak Bluffs action, with
most of the town's shops, bars, and restaurants. Colorful gingerbread-
trimmed guesthouses and food and souvenir joints enliven Oak Bluffs
Harbor, once the setting for several grand hotels (the 1879 Wesley
Hotel on Lake Avenue is the last remaining one). This small town is
more high spirited than haute, more fun than refined.

WHAT TO SEE

East Chop Lighthouse. In 1876 this lighthouse was built out of cast iron
to replace an 1828 tower (used as part of a semaphore system of visual
signaling between the island and Boston) that burned down. The 40-
foot structure stands high atop a 79-foot bluff with spectacular views
of Nantucket Sound. ⊠*E. Chop Dr.* ☎*508/627–4441* ▦*$3* ⊙*Late
June–mid-Sept., Sun. 1 hr before sunset–1 hr after sunset.*

☺   **Flying Horses Carousel.** This is the nation's oldest continuously operat-
ing carousel and a National Historic Landmark. Handcrafted in 1876
(the horses have real horse hair and glass eyes), the ride gives chil-
dren a taste of entertainment from a TV-free era. ⊠*Oak Bluffs Ave.*
☎*508/693–9481* ▦*Rides $1.50 each, book of 8 tickets $10* ⊙ *Eas-
ter–late May, Sat. –Sun. 10–5; Late May–early Sept., daily 10–10; early
Sept.–mid-Oct., weekdays 11–4:30, Sat. –Sun. 10–5.*

SPORTS & THE OUTDOORS

BEACH **Joseph A. Sylvia State Beach** (⊠*Between Oak Bluffs and Edgartown, off Beach Rd.*) is a 6-mi-long sandy beach with a view of Cape Cod across Nantucket Sound. Food vendors and calm, warm waters make this a popular spot for families.

FISHING **Dick's Bait & Tackle** (⊠*New York Ave.* ☎*508/693–7669*) rents gear, sells accessories and bait, and keeps a current copy of the fishing regulations.

GOLF **Farm Neck Golf Club** (⊠*County Rd.* ☎*508/693–3057*), a semiprivate club on marsh-rimmed Sengekontacket Pond, has a driving range and 18 holes in a championship layout. Reservations are required 48 hours in advance.

NIGHTLIFE & THE ARTS

The island's only family brewpub, **Offshore Ale** (⊠*Kennebec Ave.* ☎*508/693–2626*) hosts live Latin, folk, and blues year-round and serves its own beer and ales and a terrific pub menu. Cozy up to the fireplace with a pint on cool nights.

WHERE TO EAT & STAY

$$$$ ✕**Sweet Life Café.** Housed in a charming Victorian house, this island
Fodor'sChoice favorite's warm tones, low lighting, and handsome antique furniture
★ will make you feel like you've entered someone's home—but the cook-
SEAFOOD ing is more sophisticated than home-style. Dishes on the menu are prepared in inventive ways; duck breast is roasted with a lavender-rosemary-honey glaze, and the gazpacho is a white version with steamed clams, sliced red grapes, and smoked-paprika oil. ⊠*Upper Circuit Ave. at far end of town* ☎*508/696–0200* ⚖*Reservations essential* ▭*AE, D, MC, V* ⊘*Closed Jan.–Mar.*

$–$$ ✕**Sharky's Cantina.** This small storefront restaurant serves tasty Mexi-
★ can and Southwestern fare and great drinks, and you may wait awhile
MEXICAN to get a table. But once you're in, savor spicy tortilla soup, lobster quesadillas, steak burritos, chicken mole, and skirt steak with chimichurri sauce. There's an extensive margarita list (they're strong here), and for dessert try apple-pie empanadas drizzled with caramel sauce. ⊠*31 Circuit Ave.* ☎*508/693–7501* ⊕*www.sharkyscantina.com* ⚖*Reservations not accepted* ▭*AE, MC, V.*

$$$ ⌸**Oak House.** The wraparound veranda of this courtly pastel-painted
★ 1872 Victorian looks across a busy street to the beach and out across Nantucket Sound. Several rooms have private terraces or balconies. Ceilings, wall paneling, wainscoting, and furnishings are all in richly painted or polished oak, complementing the antique furniture and nautical-theme accessories. **Pros:** stunning decor, romantic and adult-oriented, some rooms have water views. **Cons:** some rooms get street noise, old-fashioned vibe might turn off minimalists, busy location. ⊠*79 Seaview Ave., Box 299* ☎*508/693–4187 or 866/693–5805* ⊕*www. vineyardinns.com* ⤳*8 rooms, 2 suites* ⚐*In-hotel: no elevator, no kids under 10* ▭*AE, D, MC, V* ⊘*Closed mid-Oct.–mid-May* ⍟*CP.*

EDGARTOWN

6 mi southeast of Oak Bluffs.

Once a well-to-do whaling center, Edgartown remains the Vineyard's toniest town and has preserved parts of its elegant past. Sea captains' houses from the 18th and 19th centuries, ensconced in well-manicured gardens and lawns, line the streets.

SPORTS & THE OUTDOORS

C **Felix Neck Wildlife Sanctuary.** This
★ 350 acre Massachusetts Audubon Society preserve 3 mi outside Edgartown toward Oak Bluffs and Vineyard Haven has 2 mi of hiking trails traversing marshland, fields, woods, seashore, and waterfowl and reptile ponds. ⊠ *Off Edgartown–Vineyard Haven Rd.* ☎ *508/627–4850* ☎ *$4* ☺ *Center June–Aug., Mon.–Sat. 8–4, Sun. 10–3; Sept.–May, Tues.–Sat. 8–4, Sun. noon–4. Trails daily sunrise–7 PM.*

FISHING **Big Eye Charters** (☎ *508/627–3649*) leads fishing charters from Edgartown Harbor. **Coop's Bait and Tackle** (⊠ *147 W. Tisbury Rd.* ☎ *508/627–3909*) sells accessories and bait, rents fishing gear, and books fishing charters.

▌ OFF THE BEATEN PATH

A sparsely populated area with many nature preserves, where you can fish, **Chappaquiddick Island,** 1 mi southeast of Edgartown, makes for a pleasant day trip or bike ride on a sunny day. The "island" is actually connected to the Vineyard by a long sand spit that begins in South Beach in Katama. It's a spectacular 2¾-mi walk, or you can take the ferry, which departs about every five minutes. On the island's Mytoi preserve, a boardwalk runs through part of the grounds, where you're apt to see box turtles and hear the sounds of songbirds. Elsewhere you can fish, sunbathe, or even dip into the surf—use caution, as the currents are strong.

SHOPPING

David Le Breton, the owner of **Edgartown Books** (⊠ *44 Main St.* ☎ *508/627–8463*), is a true bibliophile. He carries a large selection of current and island-related titles and will be happy to make a summer reading recommendation. The **Old Sculpin Gallery** (⊠ *58 Dock St.* ☎ *508/627–4881*) is the Martha's Vineyard Art Association's headquarters.

NIGHTLIFE & THE ARTS

NIGHTLIFE The **Atria Bar** (⊠ *137 Main St.* ☎ *508/627–5850*) is off the beaten path, but it's a quiet, comfortable place to escape the summer crowds. **Outerland** (⊠ *Martha's Vineyard Airport, Edgartown–W. Tisbury Rd.* ☎ *508/693–1137*) books big-name acts such as Medeski, Martin and Wood, Ben Lee, Kate Taylor, and the Derek Trucks Band play.

TAKE A TOUR

Liz Villard's **Vineyard History Tours** (☎ *508/627–8619*) leads walking tours of Edgartown's "history, architecture, ghosts, and gossip," including a stop at the Vincent House. Tours are run from April through December; call for times. Liz and her guides also lead similar tours of Oak Bluffs and Vineyard Haven. Walks last a little more than an hour.

2

NEED A BREAK?
If you need a pick-me-up, pop into Espresso Love (⊠*3 S. Water St.* ☎*508/627–9211*) for a cappuccino and a homemade raspberry scone or blueberry muffin. If you prefer something cold, the staff also makes fruit smoothies. Light lunch fare is served: bagel sandwiches, soups, and delicious pastries and cookies—all homemade, of course. It's by the Edgartown bus station.

WHERE TO EAT & STAY

¢-$
★
AMERICAN

✗**Morning Glory Farm.** Fresh farm greens in the salads and vegetables in the soups; homemade pies, cookies, and cakes; and a picnic table and grass to enjoy them on make this an ideal place for a simple country lunch. ⊠ *W. Tisbury Rd.* ☎*508/627–9003* ▤*No credit cards.*

$$$$
Fodor'sChoice
★

▦**Charlotte Inn.** From the moment you walk up to the dark-wood Scottish barrister's check-in desk at this regal 1864 inn, you'll be surrounded by the trappings and customs of a bygone era. The elegant atmosphere that pervades the property extends to the inn's swank restaurant, the Catch. **Pros:** over-the-top lavish, quiet yet convenient location, beautifully landscaped. **Cons:** restaurant has changed over a lot lately, can feel overly formal, intimidating if you don't adore museum-quality antiques. ⊠*27 S. Summer St.,* ☎*508/627–4751 or 800/735–2478* ⊕*www.relaischateaux.com* ⬧*21 rooms, 2 suites* ♿*In-room: Ethernet. In-hotel: restaurant, no elevator, no kids under 14* ▤*AE, MC, V* ▯*CP.*

WEST TISBURY

8 mi west of Edgartown, 6½ mi south of Vineyard Haven.

West Tisbury retains its rural appeal and maintains its agricultural tradition at several active horse and produce farms. The town center looks very much like a small New England village, complete with a white-steepled church.

SHOPPING

Step back in time with a visit to **Alley's General Store** (⊠*State Rd.* ☎*508/693–0088*), the heart of town since 1858. Alley's sells a truly general variety of goods: everything from hammers to housewares and dill pickles to sweet muffins as well as great things you find only in a country store. There's even a post office inside. Behind the parking lot, Garcia's at Back Alley's serves tasty sandwiches and pastries to go year-round.

SPORTS & THE OUTDOORS

Sepiessa Point Reservation. A paradise for bird-watchers, this reservation consists of 164 acres on splendid Tisbury Great Pond, with expansive pond and ocean views, walking trails around coves and saltwater marshes, bird-watching, horse trails, swimming, and a boat launch. ⊠*New La., which becomes Tiah's Cove Rd., off W. Tisbury Rd.* ☎*508/627–7141* ▨*Free* ☉*Daily sunrise–sunset.*

CHILMARK

5½ mi southwest of West Tisbury.

Chilmark is a rural village where ocean-view roads, rustic woodlands, and lack of crowds have drawn chic summer visitors and resulted in stratospheric real-estate prices. Laced with rough roads and winding stone fences that once separated fields and pastures, Chilmark reminds people of what the Vineyard was like in an earlier time, before the developers came.

SHOPPING

★ **Chilmark Chocolates** (⊠*State Rd.* ☎*508/645–3013*) sells superior chocolates and what might just be the world's finest butter crunch, which you can sometimes watch being made in the back room.

WHERE TO STAY

$$$ **Inn at Blueberry Hill.** Exclusive and secluded, this cedar-shingle retreat on 56 acres of former farmland puts you in the heart of the rural Vineyard. The restaurant, Theo's ($$$–$$$$), is relaxed and elegant, with fresh, health-conscious food that is thoughtfully prepared. You might dine on maple-spiced duck breast with sweet-potato gnocchi, or seared sea scallops with a basil-grapefruit-tarragon beurre blanc. Rooms are sparsely but tastefully decorated with simple island-made furniture. **Pros:** lots of privacy, many rooms have terraces with views, terrific restaurant. **Cons:** not a great choice for children, a long drive from town centers. ⊠*74 North Rd.* ☎*508/645–3322 or 800/356–3322* ⊕*www. blueberryinn.com* ⌁*25 rooms* ⚑*In-hotel: restaurant, tennis court, pool, gym, no elevator, airport shuttle, public Wi-Fi, no kids under 12* ▤*AE, MC, V* ⊗*Closed Nov.–Apr.* ⊙*CP.*

AQUINNAH

6½ mi west of Menemsha, 10 mi southwest of West Tisbury, 17 mi southwest of Vineyard Haven.

Aquinnah, called Gay Head until the town voted to change its name in 1997, is an official American Indian township. The Wampanoag tribe is the guardian of the 420 acres that constitute the Aquinnah Native American Reservation. Aquinnah (pronounced a-*kwih*-nah) is Wampanoag for "land under the hill." You can get a good view of Menemsha and Nashaquitsa ponds, the woods, and the ocean beyond from Quitsa Pond Lookout on State Road. The town is best known, though, for the red-hued Aquinnah Cliffs.

WHAT TO SEE

Fodor's Choice **Aquinnah Cliffs.** These spectacular cliffs, a National Historic Landmark,
★ are part of the Wampanoag reservation land. The dramatically striated walls of red clay are the island's major attraction, as evidenced by the tour bus–filled parking lot. American Indian crafts and food shops line the short approach to the overlook, from which you can see the Elizabeth Islands to the northeast across Vineyard Sound and Noman's Land Island—part wildlife preserve, part military bombing-practice site—

3 mi off the Vineyard's southern coast. The brick **Aquinnah Lighthouse** (⊠*Lighthouse Rd.* ☎*508/645–2211* ⊠*$2* ⊙*Summer, weekends at sunset, weather permitting)* is stationed precariously atop the rapidly eroding cliffs. ⊠*State Rd.*

NANTUCKET

By Sandy
MacDonald

At the height of its prosperity in the early 19th century, the little island of Nantucket was the foremost whaling port in the world. Its harbor bustled with whaling ships and merchant vessels; chandleries, cooperages, and other shops crowded the wharves. Burly ship hand loaded barrels of whale oil onto wagons, which they wheeled along cobblestone streets to refineries and candle factories. Sea breezes carried the smoke and smells of booming industry through town as its inhabitants eagerly took care of business. Shipowners and sea captains built elegant mansions, which today remain remarkably unchanged, thanks to a very strict building code initiated in the 1950s. The entire town of Nantucket is now an official National Historic District encompassing more than 800 pre-1850 structures within 1 square mile.

Day-trippers usually take in the architecture and historical sites, dine at one of the many delightful restaurants, and browse in the pricey boutiques, most of which stay open from mid-April through December. Signature items include Nantucket lightship baskets, originally crafted by sailors whiling away a long watch; artisans who continue the tradition now command prices of $700 and up, and the antiques are exponentially more expensive.

NANTUCKET TOWN

30 mi southeast of Hyannis, 107 mi southeast of Boston.

Nantucket Town has one of the country's finest historical districts, with beautiful 18th- and 19th-century architecture and a museum of whaling history.

WHAT TO SEE

Fodor's Choice
★

Nantucket Historical Association (NHA). An assortment of venerable properties in town, including the gloriously expanded Whaling Museum, are maintained by the NHA. An $18 pass gets you into all of the association's sites. ☎*508/228–1894* ⊕*www.nha.org.*

African Meeting House. When the island abolished slavery in 1773, Nantucket became a destination for free blacks and escaping slaves. The African Meeting House was built in the 1820s as a schoolhouse, and it functioned as such until 1846, when the island's schools were inte-

> **TAKE A TOUR**
>
> Sixth-generation Nantucketer Gail Johnson of **Gail's Tours** (☎*508/257–6557* ⊕*www. nantucket.net/tours/gails*) narrates a lively 1½-hour van tour of the island's highlights: the moors, the cranberry bogs, and the lighthouses, in addition to Nantucket Town.

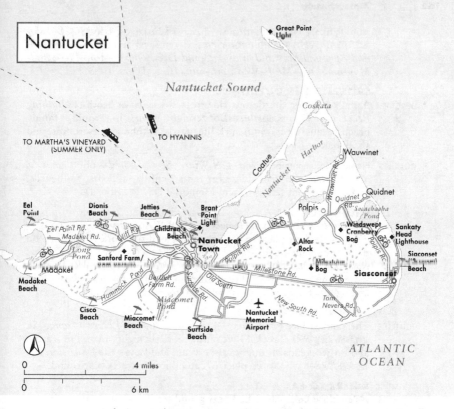

Nantucket

Nantucket Sound

Coskata

TO MARTHA'S VINEYARD
(SUMMER ONLY)

TO HYANNIS

Great Point
Light

Wauwinet

Harbor

Coatue

Nantucket

Eel
Point

Dionis
Beach

Jetties
Beach

Brant
Point
Light

Children's
Beach

Nantucket
Town

Polpis

Quidnet
Rd.

Quidnet

Sesachacha
Pond

Windswept
Cranberry
Bog

Sankaty
Head
Lighthouse

Eel Point Rd.
Madaket Rd.

Cliff Rd.

Sanford Farm/

Altar
Rock

Siasconset
Beach

Long
Pond

Polpis Rd.

Polpis Rd.

Madaket

Bartlett
Farm Rd.

Hummock Pond

Milestone Rd.

Milestone
Bog

Siasconset

Madaket
Beach

Cisco
Beach

Miacomet
Beach

Miacomet
Pond

Surfside
Beach

Surfside Rd.

Old South Rd.

Nantucket
Memorial
Airport

New South Rd.

Tom
Nevers Rd.

ATLANTIC
OCEAN

0 ____ 4 miles
0 ____ 6 km

grated. A complete restoration has returned the site to its authentic 1880s appearance. ⊠29 York St. ☎508/228–9833 ⊕www.afroam-museum.org ☞Free ☉July and Aug., Tues.–Sat. 11–3, Sun. 1–3.

Brant Point Light. This 26-foot-tall, white-painted beauty has views of the harbor and town. The point was once the site of the second-oldest lighthouse in the country (1746); the present, much-photographed light was built in 1902. ⊠End of Easton St., across footbridge.

★ **First Congregational Church.** The tower of this church provides the best view of Nantucket—for those willing to climb its 92 steps. Rising 120 feet, the tower is capped by a weather vane depicting a whale catch. ⊠62 Centre St. ☎508/228–0950 ⊕www.nantucketfcc.org ☞Tower tour $2.50 ☉Mid-June–mid-Oct., Mon.–Sat. 10–4; Daffodil and Memorial Day weekends, Fri. and Sat.; services Sun. 10 AM.

☺ **Whaling Museum.** Immersing you in Nantucket's whaling past with
Fodor'sChoice exhibits that include a fully rigged whaleboat and a skeleton of a 46-
★ foot sperm whale, the Whaling Museum—a complex that includes a restored 1846 spermaceti candle factory—is a must-see. Items on view in the handsome galleries include harpoons and other whale-hunting implements, portraits of whaling captains and their wives, a large collection of sailors' crafts, and the original 16-foot-high 1850 lens

from Sankaty Head Lighthouse. ⊠*13–15 Broad St.* ☏*508/228–1894*
🖃*$15 or NHA Combination Pass* ⊙*Jan.–mid-Apr., Fri.–Sun. 11–4;
mid-Apr.–mid-May and mid-Oct.–mid-Dec., Thurs.–Mon. 11–4; mid-
May–mid-Oct., Mon.–Wed., Fri.–Sun. 10–5, Thurs. 10–8.*

SPORTS & THE OUTDOORS

BEACHES
★ � A short bike- or shuttle-bus ride from town, **Jetties Beach** (⊠*Bathing
Beach Rd., 1½ mi northwest of Straight Wharf*) is a popular family
beach because of its calm surf, lifeguards, bathhouse, restrooms, and
snack bar.

BOATING **Nantucket Community Sailing** (⊠*4 Winter St.* ☏*508/228–6600* ⊕*www.
nantucketcommunitysailing.org*) rents Sunfish sailboats, sailboards,
and kayaks from Jetties Beach, Memorial Day to Labor Day.

SHOPPING

ARTWORK The **Artists' Association of Nantucket** (⊠*19 Washington St.* ☏*508/228–
0772*) is the best place to get an overview of the work being done on
the island; many members have galleries of their own.

★ **Nantucket Looms** (⊠*16 Federal St.* ☏*508/228–1908*) stocks luscious
woven-on-the-premises textiles and chunky Susan Lister Locke jewelry,
among other adornments for self and home.

NIGHTLIFE & THE ARTS

NIGHTLIFE The **Chicken Box** (*The Box* ⊠*14 Dave St., off Lower Orange St.*
☏*508/228–9717*) rocks! Live music plays six nights a week in season,
and on weekends throughout the year. The **Muse** (⊠*44 Surfside Rd.*
☏*508/228–6873*) is *the* place to catch big-name acts year-round.

WHERE TO EAT & STAY

� $-$$ ✗**Fog Island Café.** Cherished year-round for its exceptional breakfasts,
AMERICAN Fog Island is just as fine a spot for lunch—or, in season, a charitably
priced dinner. The chef-owners Mark and Anne Dawson—both Culinary Institute of America grads—seem determined to provide the best
possible value to transients and natives alike. Consider starting the day
with pesto scrambled eggs and ending it with sesame-crusted tuna with
Thai noodles. ⊠*7 S. Water St.* ☏*508/228–1818* ⊕*www.fogisland.
com* 🖃*MC, V.*

$$$$ 🏨**Nantucket Whaler.** Let's not mince words: the suites carved out of
★ this 1850 Greek-revival house are gorgeous. Each suite has a private
entrance and a kitchen. The spacious bedrooms are lavished with flowers, well-chosen antiques, and fine linens, including plush robes. **Pros:**
pretty rooms, well-kitted out, romantic. **Cons:** no real reception area,
lacks a common room, the usual in-town noise. ⊠*8 N. Water St.02554*
☏*508/228–6597 or 888/808–6597* ⊕*www.nantucketwhaler.com*
🛏*12 suites* ⌂*In-room: DVD, Wi-Fi. In-hotel: no kids under 11, no-
smoking rooms* 🖃*AE, MC, V* ⊙*Closed Jan. and Feb.*

$$$–$$$$ 🏨**Union Street Inn.** Ken Withrow worked in the hotel business, Debo-
Fodor'sChoice rah Withrow in high-end retail display, and guests get the best of both
★ worlds. This 1770 house, a stone's throw from the bustle of Main
Street, has been respectfully yet lavishly restored. Guests are treated
to Frette linens, plump duvets, and lush robes (the better to lounge
around in, my dear), as well as a full gourmet breakfast served on

the tree-shaded garden patio. **Pros:** conducive to romance. **Cons:** no nearby beach, some small rooms. ⊠7 *Union St.* ☎*508/228–9222 or 800/225–5116* ⊕*www.unioninn.com* ⇆*12 rooms* ⚇*In-room: Wi-Fi. In-hotel: no kids under 12, no-smoking rooms* ⊟*AE, MC, V* ⯄*BP.*

SIASCONSET

★ *7 mi east of Nantucket Town.*

First a fishing outpost and then an artist's colony (Broadway actors favored it in the late 19th century), Siasconset—or 'Sconset, in the local vernacular—is a charming cluster of rose-covered cottages linked by driveways of crushed clamshells; at the edges of town, the former fishing shacks give way to magnificent sea-view mansions. The small town center consists of a market, post office, café, lunchroom, and liquor store–cum–lending library.

WHAT TO SEE

Altar Rock. The view from the island's highest point is spectacular. The hill overlooks open moor and bog land—technically called lowland heath—which is very rare in the United States. The entire area is laced with paths leading in every direction. ⚘*Altar Rock Road, a dirt track about 3 mi west of the Milestone Road Rotary on Polpis Road, leads to Altar Rock.*

WHERE TO EAT & STAY

$$$$ ★ ECLECTIC
✕**Topper's.** The Wauwinet—a lavishly restored 19th-century inn on Nantucket's northeastern shore—is where islanders and visitors alike go to experience utmost luxury. David Daniel's cuisine delivers on the fantasy with a menu of intentional "simplicity"—if that's how you would describe, for example, a "surf and turf" of butter-basted lobster in a carrot-yuzu (a Japanese citrus fruit) broth with foie-gras-and-Kobe-beef dim sum. ⊠*120 Wauwinet Rd., Wauwinet* ☎*508/228–8768* ⚘*Reservations essential* ⊟*AE, D, DC, MC, V* ⊘*Closed Nov.–Apr.*

$$$$ Fodor'sChoice ★
⛺**Wauwinet.** This resplendently updated 1850 resort straddles a "haulover" poised between ocean and bay—which means beaches on both sides. Head out by complimentary van or launch to partake of utmost pampering. Of course, it's tempting just to stay put, what with the cushy country-chic rooms (lavished with Pratesi linens) and a splendid restaurant, Topper's. **Pros:** solicitous staff, dual beaches, peaceful setting, town shuttle. **Cons:** distance from town, tiny rooms on the 3rd floor. ⊠*120 Wauwinet Rd., Wauwinet* ⌂*Box 2580, Nantucket 02584* ☎*508/228–0145 or 800/426–8718* ⊕*www.wauwinet.com* ⇆*25 rooms, 5 cottages* ⚇*In-room: safe, DVD, Wi-Fi. In-hotel: restaurant, room service, bar, tennis courts, spa, beachfront, bicycles, no elevator, concierge, town shuttle, no kids under 12, no-smoking rooms* ⊟*AE, DC, MC, V* ⊘*Closed Nov.–Apr.* ⯄*BP.*

STURBRIDGE AND THE PIONEER VALLEY

Updated by
Diane Bair &
Pamela Wright

A string of historic settlements lines the majestic Connecticut River, the wide and winding waterway that runs through the heart of western Massachusetts. The bustling city of Springfield, known for its family-friendly attractions and museums, along with a cluster of college towns and quaint, rural villages are part of the Pioneer Valley, which formed the western frontier of New England from the early 1600s until the late 1900s. The river and its fertile banks first attracted farmers and traders, and later became a source of power and transport for the earliest industrial cities in America.

Educational pioneers came to this region as well and created a wealth of major colleges including Mt. Holyoke, America's first college for women; Amherst; Smith; Hampshire; and the University of Massachusetts. Northampton and Amherst, two hubs of higher learning, serve as the valley's cultural hubs; with the rise of the telecommunications era, both have become increasingly desirable places to live, drawing former city dwellers who relish the ample natural scenery, sophisticated cultural venues, and lively dining and shopping.

SPRINGFIELD

90 mi west of Boston; 30 mi north of Hartford, Connecticut.

Springfield, easily accessed from interstates 90 and 91, is the busy hub of the Pioneer Valley. Known as the birthplace of basketball (the game was devised by local gym instructor James Naismith in 1891 as a last-minute attempt to keep a group of unruly teenagers occupied in winter), the city is home to a cluster of fine museums, family fun attractions, and a thriving restaurant and nightlife scene.

You can glimpse Springfield's prosperous industrial past by exploring either of the city's most noted neighborhoods: the Maple Hill Historic District, which preserves several lavish mansions from the 1840s through the 1920s; and the McKnight Historic District, a Victorian neighborhood developed between 1870 and 1900, where you'll see a bounty of ornate Queen Anne, Tudor revival, and Italianate Victorian houses. Self-guided tour brochures of both neighborhoods are available at the Greater Springfield Convention & Visitors Bureau, along with discount coupons to Springfield's major attractions.

WHAT TO SEE

☾ **Forest Park.** This leafy, 735-acre retreat is ideal for families. Hiking paths wind through the trees, paddleboats navigate Porter Lake, and hungry ducks float on a small pond. The zoo, where Theodore Geisel—better known as Dr. Seuss—found inspiration for his children's books, is home to nearly 200 animals, from black bears and bobcats to emus, lemurs, and wallabies. ⊠ *Off Sumner Ave.* ☎ *413/787–6461 or 413/733–2251* ⊕ *www.forestparkzoo.org* ⊠ *Zoo $6* ☉ *Zoo Apr.–mid-Oct., daily 10–4:30; mid-Oct.–Nov., weekends 10–3:30.*

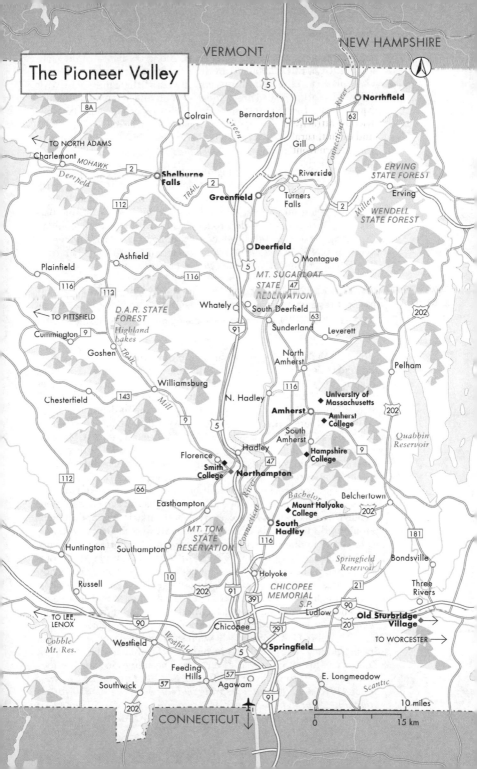

Ⓒ **Naismith Memorial Basketball Hall of Fame.** Along the banks of the Con-
Fodor'sChoice   necticut River, this 80,000-square-foot facility is dedicated to Spring-
★   field's own Dr. James Naismith, who invented the game in 1891. It
includes a soaring domed arena, dozens of high-tech interactive exhibits, and video footage and interviews with former players. The Honors Rings pay tribute to the hall's nearly 250 enshrinees. ⊠*1150 W.
Columbus Ave.* ☎*413/781–6500 or 877/446–6752* ⊕*www.hoophall.
com* ⊠*$17* ⊙ *Weekdays 10–4, weekends 10–5.*

Ⓒ **Six Flags New England.** Containing more than 160 rides and shows, this
mega attraction, 4 mi southwest of Springfield, is the region's largest theme park and water park. Rides include the Superman Ride of
Steel, the tallest and fastest steel coaster on the East Coast; the Batman–The Dark Knight floorless roller coaster; Mr. Six's Pandemonium,
a spinning coaster; and the Typhoon water coaster. ⊠*1623 Main St.,
Agawam* ☎*413/786–9300* ⊕*www.sixflags.com* ⊠*$50* ⊙ *Hrs vary.
Check Web site or call for more information.*

**NEED A
BREAK?**   Springfield's South End is the home of a lively Little Italy that supports some
excellent restaurants, as well as La Fiorentina Pastry Shop (⊠ *883 Main
St.* ☎ *413/732-3151*), which has been doling out heavenly pastries, butter
cookies, and coffees since the 1940s.

Ⓒ **Springfield Museums.** One of the most ambitious cultural venues in New
Fodor'sChoice   England, this complex includes four impressive facilities. The most
★   modest, the **Connecticut Valley Historical Museum** presents changing exhibits drawn from its collections of furniture, silver, industrial
objects, autos, and firearms; its main draw is the in-depth genealogi-
cal library, where folks from all over the world come to research their
family trees. The must-see **George Walter Vincent Smith Art Museum**
houses a fascinating private art collection that includes 19th-century
American paintings by Frederic Church and Albert Bierstadt. A Japanese antiquities room is filled with armor, textiles, and porcelain, as well
as carved jade and rock-crystal snuff bottles. The **Museum of Fine Arts**
has paintings by Gauguin, Monet, Renoir, Degas, Winslow Homer, and
J. Alden Weir, as well as 18th-century American paintings and contemporary works by Georgia O'Keeffe, Frank Stella, and George Bellows.
Rotating exhibits are open throughout the year. The **Springfield Science
Museum** has an Exploration Center of touchable displays, the oldest operating planetarium in the United States, an extensive collection
of stuffed and mounted animals, dinosaur exhibits, and the African
Hall, through which you can take an interactive tour of that continent's
flora and fauna. On the grounds is the **Dr. Seuss National Memorial
Sculpture Garden,** an installation of five bronze statues depicting scenes
from Theodore Geisel's famously whimsical children's books. Born in
Springfield in 1904, Geisel was inspired by the animals at Forest Park
Zoo, where his father served as director. The statues include a 4-foot
Lorax and a 10-foot Yertle the Turtle. ⊠*220 State St., at Chestnut
St.* ☎*413/263–6800* ⊕*www.springfieldmuseums.org* ⊠*$10 for all
museums* ⊙*Springfield Science Museum Tues.–Sat. 10–5, Sun 11–5.
Museum of Fine Arts, George Walter Vincent Art Museum, and Con-*

necticut Valley Historical Museum Tues.–Sun. 11–4, outdoor Dr. Seuss Sculpture Garden daily dawn–dusk.

OFF THE BEATEN PATH

FodorsChoice ★ A strip of hotels, restaurants, fast-food outlets, and shops line the main street of Sturbridge (Route 20), 34 mi east of Springfield, to accommodate visitors who come to tour the 200-acre living history museum, **Old Sturbridge Village** (⊠*1 Old Sturbridge Village Rd.* ☎*508/347–3362 or 800/733–1830* ⊕*www.osv.org* ⊠*$20* ⊙*Mid-Apr.–late Oct., daily 9:30-4; late Oct.–mid-Apr., Tue.–Sun. 9:30–4*). Modeled on an early-19th-century New England town, this re-creation of a Colonial-era village has more than 40 historic buildings that were moved here from other towns. Some of the homes are filled with canopy beds and elaborate furnishings; in the simpler, single-story cottages, interpreters wearing period costumes demonstrate home based crafts like spinning, weaving, and shoe making. The village store contains an amazing variety of goods necessary for everyday life in the 19th century. There are several industrial buildings, including a working sawmill. On the informative boat ride along the Quinebaug River, you can learn about river life in 19th-century New England and catch a glimpse of ducks, geese, turtles, and other local wildlife. Nearby is the tiny town of Brimfield, home to one of the country's largest antique fairs, held several times a year.

SHOPPING

Wild Bird Crossing (⊠*4 Cedar St., Sturbridge* ☎*508/347–2473* ⊕*www. wildbirdxing.com*) carries every imaginable accoutrement for bird-watching, including birdbaths, binoculars, and books.

NIGHTLIFE & THE ARTS

Worthington Street, the city's nightlife center, is lined with bars, clubs, and cafés. **Theodore's** (⊠*201 Worthington St.* ☎*413/736–6000*) is known for its "booze, blues, and BBQ." The decor is yard-sale chic, the music loud, and the crowd often rowdy. **The Hippodrome** (⊠*1700 Main St.* ☎*413/787–0600* ⊕*www.hdrome.com*) brings top traveling acts to town.

WHERE TO EAT

$-$$
CREOLE

✕**Big Mamou.** If you're cravin' Creole, you can't miss this casual joint, with seriously good, uncomplicated Louisiana cuisine. Owner/chef Wayne Booker stands behind the kitchen counter and his hometown recipes, like the sausage and chicken ya-ya (chicken breast wrapped around andouille sausage with Creole spices), shrimp-and-sausage jambalaya, BBQ pulled pork, and Bayou meatloaf. Added bonus: You can bring your own bottle. ⊠*63 Liberty St.* ☎*413/732–1011* ⊕*www. chefwaynes-bigmamou.com* ⊟*MC, V* ⊙*Closed Sun.*

$$-$$$
FodorsChoice
★
ECLECTIC

✕**Cedar Street.** Arguably the finest, most creative place to dine in Sturbridge and beyond, this intimate eatery, housed in a modest but charming Victorian house, is a showcase for culinary creations. The menu changes frequently but you can expect starters like crab Napoleon topped with cucumber ceviche, or sweet-potato ravioli. Entrées include signature dishes like the cedar plank salmon and the rich bouillabaisse brimming with shrimp, scallops, tuna, clams, and more. ⊠*12 Cedar*

St., Sturbridge 🕿*508/347–5800* ⊕*www.cedarstreeetrestaurant.com* ⊟*AE, MC, V* ⊗*No lunch.*

¢-$ ✕**Pho Saigon.** It's small, tastefully understated, and a little out of
★ the way, but this ethnic eatery serves up some of the best, authentic
VIETNAMESE Vietnamese cuisine in the city, at wallet-pleasing prices. You can't go wrong, but don't miss the full-of-flavor, made-from-scratch soups, the shrimp cakes with shredded yam, and the vermicelli dishes. There are lots of rice dishes and vegetarian options, as well as house specialties like the sizzling catfish filets and the Vietnamese Happy Pancake, a rice batter crepe stuffed with shrimp and chicken. ⊠*400 Dickinson St.* 🕿*413/781–4488* ⊟*MC, V* ⊗*Closed Wed.*

$$-$$$ ✕**Student Prince.** Housed in an old fort, home to one of the largest beer
GERMAN stein collections in the country, and host to a slew of celebrities since it opened more than seven decades ago, the casual, dark wood paneled Student Prince (or the Fort, as the locals call it) is nearly an institution in Springfield. The menu is huge, with several selections of beef, chicken, seafood, veal, lamb, pork, and sausage dishes. The specialties of the house are the German dishes; try the sampler of goulash, pork loin, *weisswurst* (sausage made with veal and fresh pork bacon), and sauerkraut. There's also *hoppel poppel* (farmer's omelet), *zwiebelfleisch* (onion roast), *jaeger schnitzel* (veal steak), sauerbraten served with potato dumplings and cabbage, *eisbein* (pigs knuckle), and more. ⊠*8 Fort St.* 🕿*413/788–6628* ⊕*www.studentprince.com* ⊟*AE, MC, V.*

WHERE TO STAY

$ 🏠**Naomi's Inn.** "I'm taking the shower home with me," gushed one
★ guest. "This is the nicest, friendliest, and classiest place in town," said another. We couldn't agree more. This elegantly restored house in a residential neighborhood has six individually decorated suites, all with lush comfort and artistic flair. The Louis XIV suite has two large rooms, 19th-century armoires, a down-filled sofa, and custom-tiled bath. The French Provincial suite has a custom-made iron king-sized bed, tiled bath, and an adjoining room with two twin beds that is perfect for families. The bright and airy kitchen is a pleasant place to gather, and a group of area restaurants will deliver food, which the owner is happy to serve on china plates. **Pros:** elegantly designed, deluxe linens and baths, warm and knowledgeable hosts. **Cons:** near the hospital, so you may hear sirens in the night. ⊠*20 Springfield St.* 🕿*413/732–3924 or 888/762–6647* ⊕*www.naomisinn.net* ⌖*6 suites* ⚷*In-room: refrigerator (some), Wi-Fi. In-hotel: no elevator, laundry facilities, public Wi-Fi, parking (no fee)* ⊟*AE, D, DC, MC, V* ⊗⦿*BP.*

$-$$ 🏠**Publick House Historic Inn.** Step back in time when you stay at this
Fodor'sChoice rambling 1771 inn that oozes colonial character and charm. Rooms are
★ Colonial in design, with wide plank floors, period antiques and reproductions, and canopy beds. The public areas, including several dining rooms and a tavern, have original woodwork and fireplaces. The inn, with 60 surrounding acres, sits on the picturesque Town Green. It also owns and maintains the neighboring Chamberlain House, consisting of six larger suites (all need serious updating!), and the Country Motor Lodge with spacious, no-frills motel-style rooms. **Pros:** colonial ambiance and architecture, historical significance, log fires and candlelight

throughout. Cons: rattling pipes; thin walls; small, basic bathrooms ⊠*Hwy. 131, Sturbridge* ☎*508/347–3313 or 800/782–5425* ⊕*www. publickhouse.com* ⇆*14 rooms, 3 suites in main inn* &*In-room: Wi-Fi. In-hotel: 4 restaurants, bar, no elevator, concierge, public Internet, parking (no fee)* ☰*AE, D, DC, MC, V.*

SOUTH HADLEY

12 north of Springfield.

Nestled in the heart of Pioneer Valley, this small, quiet college town, with a cluster of Main Street cafés and stores, is surrounded by rolling hills and farmlands. It's best known for the top-notch Mount Holyoke College Art Museum, one of the finest in the region.

WHAT TO SEE

Mount Holyoke College. Founded in 1837, Mount Holyoke was the first women's college in the United States. Among its alumnae are poet Emily Dickinson and playwright Wendy Wasserstein. The handsome wooded campus, encompassing two lakes and lovely walking or riding trails, was landscaped by Frederick Law Olmsted. ⊠*Hwy. 116* ☎*413/538–2000* ⊕*www.mtholyoke.edu.*

Mount Holyoke College Art Museum. This museum contains some 11,000 works including Asian, European, and American paintings and sculpture. ⊠*Lower Lake Rd.* ☎*413/538–2245* ⊕*www.mtholyoke.edu* 🎟*Free* ⊙*Tues.–Fri. 11–5, weekends 1–5.*

SHOPPING & THE ARTS

In addition to stocking more than 50,000 new and used titles, the **Odyssey Bookshop** (⊠*9 College St.* ☎*413/534–7307* ⊕*www.odysseybks. com*) has a packed schedule of readings and book signings by locally and nationally known authors.

WHERE TO EAT

$$-$$$
Fodor'sChoice
★
ECLECTIC

✕**Food 101 Bar and Bistro.** There's nothing basic about this popular, oh-so-calm, candlelit eatery across from the Mount Holyoke campus. Dishes are complicated but mostly successful, like the best-selling risotto with sautéed green squash and basil oil; the upscale pommes frites with spicy ketchup and wasabi mayonnaise; and the pan-seared sea scallops with cauliflower risotto, crab-mâche salad, and warm curry oil. This spot is a magnet for foodies, yuppies, and college students on their parents' tab. ⊠*19 College St.* ☎*413/535–3101* ☰*AE, DC, MC, V* ⊙*Closed Mon., no lunch.*

¢
FAST FOOD

✕**Tailgate Picnic.** Pop into this friendly deli for fresh-made soups and sandwiches, along with warmed dishes like lasagna, turkey roast, and mac and cheese. The upscale grocery-deli has a handful of tables inside and out, or order to go and picnic on the lovely Mount Holyoke grounds. ⊠*7 College St.* ☎*413/532–7597* ☰*MC, V.*

NORTHAMPTON

10 mi northeast of South Hadley.

The cultural center of western Massachusetts is without a doubt the city of Northampton, whose vibrant downtown scene reminds many people of lower Manhattan (hence its nickname "Noho"). No wonder John Villani ranked Northampton at the top in his book *The 100 Best Small Art Towns in America.* Packed with interesting eateries, lively clubs, and offbeat boutiques, the city attracts artsy types, academics, activists, lesbians and gays, and just about anyone else seeking the culture and sophistication of a big metropolis but the friendliness and easy pace of a small town.

WHAT TO SEE

Forbes Library. The Coolidge Room at this library contains a collection of President Calvin Coolidge's papers and memorabilia. Northampton was the 30th president's Massachusetts home. He practiced law here and served as mayor from 1910 to 1911. ⊠*20 West St.* ☎*413/587–1011* ⊕*www.forbeslibrary.org.*

■ NEED A BREAK? On the lower level of Thorne's Marketplace, Herrell's Ice Cream (⊠ *8 Old South St.* ☎ *413/586–9700* ⊕ *www.herrells.com*) is famous for its chocolate pudding, vanilla malt, and cinnamon flavors of ice cream, as well as delicious homemade hot fudge.

Historic Northampton Museum and Education Center. Three houses here are open for tours: Parsons House (1730), Shepherd House (1798), and Damon House (1813). Together, they hold some 50,000 historical artifacts, including photographs, manuscripts dating back to the 17th century, fine furniture, ceramics, glass, and costumes. Exhibits in the main building chronicle the history of Northampton with some 50,000 documents, photos, and collectibles. ⊠*46 Bridge St.* ☎*413/584–6011* ⊕*www.historic-northampton.org* ⊇*$3* ⊘*Mon.–Sat. 10–5, Sun. noon–5.*

Smith College. The nation's largest liberal arts college for women opened its doors in 1875 (thanks to heiress Sophia Smith, who bequeathed her estate to the college's foundation). World renowned for its esteemed School of Social Work, Smith has a long list of distinguished alumnae, among them activist Gloria Steinem, chef Julia Child, and writer Margaret Mitchell. One of the most serene campuses in all of New England, the college is also a leading center of political and cultural activity. Two sites on Smith's campus, the Lyman Plant House and the Botanic Garden of Smith College are worth visiting. The **Lyman Plant House** (☎*413/585–2740* ⊕*www.smith.edu*).The flourishing **Botanic Garden of Smith College** covers the entirety of Smith's 150-acre campus.

The **Smith College Museum of Art** (⊠*Brown Fine Arts Center, Elm St.* ☎*413/585–2760* ⊕*www.smith.edu/artmuseum* ⊇*$5* ⊘*Tues.–Sat. 10–4, Sun. noon–4*) includes a floor of skylighted galleries, an enclosed courtyard for performances and receptions, and a high-tech art history library. Highlights of the comprehensive permanent collection include

European masterworks by Cézanne, Degas, Rodin, and Seurat, and works by women artists like Mary Cassatt and Alice Neel.

William Cullen Bryant Homestead. About 20 mi northwest of Northampton, in the scenic hills west of the Pioneer Valley, is the country estate of the 19th-century poet and author, William Cullen Bryant. Inside the Dutch Colonial 1783 mansion are furnishings and collectibles from Bryant's life, work, and travels. Outside, the wild 465-acre grounds overlooking the Westfield River valley are a great venue for bird-watching, cross-country skiing, snowshoeing, fishing, hiking, and picnics. ⊠*207 Bryant Rd., Cummington* ☎*413/634–2244* ⊕*www.thetrustees.org* ✉*Grounds free, house open by guide tours only, $5* ⊙*House late June–Columbus Day, Sat.–Mon. and holidays 1–5; Grounds daily sunrise–sunset.*

SPORTS & THE OUTDOORS

⟳ The **Norwottuck Rail Trail**, part of the Connecticut River Greenway State Park, is a paved 10-mi path that links Northampton with Belchertown by way of Amherst. Great for biking, rollerblading, jogging, and cross-country skiing, it runs along the old Boston & Maine Railroad route. ⊠*Entry points include Highway 9 in Northampton at the junction of Damon Road (near Coolidge Bridge) and Highway 9 in Hadley at the junction of River Drive (Highway 47 north).*

SHOPPING

An eclectic mix of books, art, pottery, jewelry, clothing, and more can be found at **AG The Artisan Gallery** (⊠*162 Main St.* ☎*413/586–1942* ⊕*www.theartisangallery.com*). The **Williamsburg General Store** (⊠*12 Main St., Williamsburg* ☎*413/268–3036* ⊕*www.wgstore.com*), a Pioneer Valley landmark, sells breads, penny candy, and gifts galore.

NIGHTLIFE & THE ARTS

The stately **Calvin Theater** (⊠*19 King St.* ☎*413/586–8686* ⊕*www.iheg.com*), a onetime classic old-time movie house, hosts a variety of nationally recognized performing artists throughout the year. The spacious **Diva's** (⊠*492 Pleasant St.* ☎*413/586–8161* ⊕*www.divasofnoho.com*) serves the region's sizable lesbian and gay community with great music that draws people to the cavernous dance floor. The reliable **Fitzwilly's** (⊠*23 Main St.* ☎*413/584–8666* ⊕*www.fitzwillys.com*) draws a friendly mix of locals and tourists for drinks and tasty pub fare. The dimly lighted and somewhat dive-y **Hugo's** (⊠*315 Pleasant St.* ☎*413/534–9800*) has cheap beer, affordable pool, a rocking jukebox, and all the local color you'll ever want to see.

WHERE TO EAT

$-$$ ✕**Mulino's Trattoria.** In sleek quarters (which also contain the upstairs
ITALIAN Bishop's Lounge), this modern trattoria carefully prepares Sicilian-inspired, home-style Italian food with authentic ingredients. You'll rarely taste a better carbonara sauce this side of the Atlantic, but don't overlook the smoked salmon in a lemon-caper-shallot sauce tossed with fettuccine, or the melt-in-your-mouth grilled veal porterhouse. Portions are huge, and the wine list is extensive. This is the place parents take

their college kids for a special night out. ✉ *41 Strong Ave.* ☎*413/586–8900* ⊕*www.mulinos.com* ▤*AE, D, DC, MC, V* ⊘*No lunch.*

$-$$
AMERICAN

✕**Northampton Brewery.** In a rambling building in Brewster Court, this noisy and often-packed pub and microbrewery has extensive outdoor seating on an airy deck. The kitchen serves an array of sandwiches and tasty comfort food, including black-bean dip, chicken-and-shrimp jambalaya, and the blackened bleu burger (with blue cheese and caramelized onions). ✉*13 Old South St.* ☎*413/584–9903* ⊕*www.northamptonbrewery.com* ▤*AE, D, DC, MC, V.*

$$
Fodor'sChoice
★
ITALIAN

✕**Spoleto.** A Noho mainstay since the 1980s, busy Spoleto, in the heart of Northampton's downtown, offers a something-for-everyone menu: basic beef, chicken, seafood, and pasta dishes served with a dash of creative flair and flavor. The beef carpaccio and angel-hair crab cakes are first-rate. You'll find typical spaghetti and meatball and chicken Parmesan dishes alongside the more adventurous pork saltimbocca. The Gorgonzola bread makes a nice side dish. Join the locals and stop by for the excellent Sunday brunch (11–2:30). ✉*50 Main St.* ☎*413/586–6313* ⊕*www.spoletorestaurants.com* ▤*AE, DC, MC, V* ⊘*No lunch.*

AMHERST

★ *8 mi northeast of Northhampton.*

One of the most visited spots in all of New England, Amherst is known for its scores of world-renowned authors, poets, and artists. The above-average intelligence quotient of its population is no accident, as Amherst is home to a trio of colleges—Amherst, Hampshire, and the University of Massachusetts. The high concentration of college-age humanity bolsters Amherst's downtown area, which includes a wide range of art galleries, music stores, and clothing boutiques.

WHAT TO SEE

Emily Dickinson Museum. The famed Amherst poet lived here her entire life (1830–86), and many of her belongings are contained within (though her manuscripts are housed elsewhere). The museum is outfitted with period accoutrements including original wall hangings and lace curtains. Next door is **The Evergreens** (✉*214 Main St.* ☎*413/253–5272*), an imposing Italianate Victorian mansion in which Emily's brother Austin and his family resided for more than 50 years. ✉*280 Main St.* ☎*413/542–8161* ⊕*www.emilydickinsonmuseum.org* ▨*Guided tours $3–$8* ⊘*Mar.–mid-Dec., Wed.–Sun. 11–5.*

NEED A BREAK?
Newspapers and books are strewn about the tables at the Black Sheep (✉ 79 Main St. ☎413/253-3442 ⊕ www.blacksheepdeli.com), a funky downtown café specializing in flavorful coffees, satays, sushi, and creative sandwiches such as the truffle mousse pâté. It's also a great place to pick up on the college vibe; free Wi-Fi, too.

☾ **Eric Carle Museum of Picture Book Art.** This museum celebrates and preserves not only the works of renowned children's book author Eric Carle (who penned *The Very Hungry Caterpillar*) but also such luminaries as Maurice Sendak, Lucy Cousins, Petra Mathers, and Leo and Diane Dillon. Puppet shows, lectures, and storytelling are all part of the museum's ongoing calendar of events. ✉*125 W. Bay Rd.* ☎*413/658–1100* ⊕*www.picturebookart.org* ✑*$7* ⊙*Tues.–Fri. 10–4, Sat. 10–5, Sun. noon–5.*

★ **National Yiddish Book Center.** Founded in 1980 by a student on a mission to rescue Yiddish books from basements and dumpsters, this nonprofit organization has become a major force in the effort to preserve the Yiddish language and Jewish culture. On the campus of Hampshire College, the center is housed in a thatch-roof building that resembles a cluster of houses in a traditional Eastern European *shtetl,* or village. Inside, a contemporary space contains more than 1½ million books, a fireside reading area, a kosher dining room, and a visitor center with changing exhibits. The work here is performed out in the open: hundreds of books pour in daily, everything from family keepsakes to rare manuscripts among them. ✉*Hwy. 116* ☎*413/256–4900* ⊕*www.yiddishbookcenter.org* ✑*Free* ⊙*Weekdays 10–4, Sun. 11–4.*

SHOPPING & ENTERTAINMENT

An institution in the Pioneer Valley, the **Atkins Farms Country Market** (✉*Hwy. 116, South Amherst* ☎*413/253–9528 or 800/594–9537* ⊕*www.atkinsfarms.com*) is surrounded by apple orchards and gorgeous views of the Holyoke Ridge. Hayrides are offered in fall, and children's events are hosted throughout the year.

WHERE TO EAT

$-$$
★
✕ **Bub's Bar-B-Q.** Practically an institution, this rib joint, open for more than three decades, is arguably one of the best in the state. Maybe it's the tangy, homemade sauce; maybe it's the sides, like wilted collard greens, orange-glazed sweet potatoes, black-eyed corn, and spicy ranch beans; likely, it's the heaping platters of fall-off-the-bone ribs and pulled pork. ✉*Hwy. 116 north of Amherst town line, Sunderland* ☎*413/548–9630* ⊕*www.bubsbbq.com* ▭*MC, V* ⊙*Closed Mon. No lunch on weekdays.*

¢-$$
Fodor'sChoice
★
✕ **Judie's.** Since 1977, academic types have crowded around small tables on the glassed-in porch, ordering traditional dishes like grilled chicken topped with lobster ravioli, steak and potatoes, seafood gumbo, and probably the best bowl of French onion soup the town has to offer. Your best bet? Try the more creative popover specials (not just for breakfast anymore!), including the chicken, chorizo sausage, and shrimp popover platter. The atmosphere is hip and artsy; a painting covers each tabletop. ✉*51 N. Pleasant St.* ☎*413/253–3491* ⊕*www.judiesrestaurant.com* ▭*AE, D, MC, V.*

WHERE TO STAY

$$
▦ **Allen House Victorian & Amherst Inns.** A rare find, these late-19th-century inns a block apart from each other have been gloriously restored in accordance with the aesthetic of the Victorian era. Busy, colorful wall coverings reach to the high ceilings. Antiques include a burled-walnut headboard and dresser set, carved golden-oak beds, and wicker steamship chairs. Lace curtains and hand-stenciling grace the rooms, which

have supremely comfortable beds with goose-down comforters. **Pros:** classy design elements, with lots of charm and elegance; great linens; free parking. **Cons:** rooms chock-full of ornate furnishings may be a bit much for some, tiny baths with (tiled) shower stalls. ⊠ *599 Main St. and 257 Main St., 01002* ☎*413/253–5000* ⊕*www.allenhouse.com* ↩*14 rooms* ♿*In-room: no TV, Wi-Fi. In-hotel: no elevator, public Wi-Fi, parking (no fee)* ☐*AE, MC, V* ⦿*BP.*

$ 🖫**Lord Jeffrey Inn.** Smack dab on the town common of downtown Amherst, this rambling 1926 inn, owned by Amherst College, is a bit like one of your favorite, old professors: a bit tattered around the edges, somewhat old-fashioned, but endearing nonetheless. It's a favorite among visiting parents and professors who choose from a variety of rooms, from smallish doubles to larger suites, all with a mismatch of antique furniture (garnered from Amherst College) and reproductions. Avoid the garden-facing wing rooms when a wedding is going on! **Pros:** great location on the town common, good value. **Cons:** some baths are closet size; hallways in the wing section are dark and dreary; lots of wedding, school, and graduation celebrations are held here. ⊠ *30 Boltwood Ave., 01002* ☎*413/253–2576* ⊕*www.lordjefferyinn.com* ↩*40 rooms, 8 suites* ♿*In-room: refrigerator (some), Ethernet. In-hotel: 2 restaurants, room service, bar, public Internet, parking (fee), some pets allowed* ☐*AE, D, MC, V* ⦿*BP.*

DEERFIELD

10 mi northwest of Amherst.

In Deerfield, a horse pulling a carriage clip-clops past perfectly maintained 18th-century homes, neighbors leave their doors unlocked and tip their hats to strangers, kids play ball in fields by the river, and the bell of the impossibly beautiful brick church peals from a white steeple. This is the perfect New England village, though not without a past darkened by tragedy. Its original American Indian inhabitants, the Pocumtucks, were all but wiped out by deadly epidemics and a war with the Mohawks. English pioneers eagerly settled into this frontier outpost in the 1660s and 1670s, but two bloody massacres at the hands of the American Indians and the French caused the village to be abandoned until 1707, when construction began on the buildings that remain today.

WHAT TO SEE

Fodor'sChoice   **Historic Deerfield.** Although it has a turbulent past, this village now basks
★   in a genteel aura. With 52 buildings on 93 acres, Historic Deerfield provides a vivid glimpse into 18th- and 19th-century America. Along the tree-lined main street are 13 museum houses, built between 1720 and 1850; two are open to the public on self-guided tours and the remainder can be seen by guided tours that begin on the hour. At the **Wells-Thorn House,** various rooms depict life as it changed from 1725 to 1850. The adjacent **Frary House** has arts and crafts from the 1700s on display; the attached Barnard Tavern was the main meeting place for Deerfield's villagers. Also of note is the **Hinsdale and Anna Williams**

2

House, the stately home for this affluent early New England couple. A ticket that lets you visit all the houses can be purchased at the **Flynt Center of Early New England Life** (⊠ *37-D Old Main St.*), which contains two galleries full of silver and pewter as well as needlework and clothing dating back to the 1600s. Plan to spend at least one full day at Historic Deerfield. ⊠ *Old Main St.* ☎ *413/775-7214* ⊕ *www.historic-deerfield. org* ☞ *$14* ⊙ *Apr.–Dec., daily 9:30–4:30; Jan.–Mar., house museums open by appointment only, Flynt Center open weekends 9:30–4:30.*

NEED A BREAK? A short drive from Historic Deerfield, **Richardson's Candy Kitchen** (⊠ 500 Greenfield Rd. ☎ 413/772-0443 ⊕ www.richardsonscandy.com) makes and sells luscious cream-filled truffles as well as other handmade chocolates and confections.

○
Fodor's Choice
★

Magic Wings Butterfly Conservatory & Gardens. This warm and lush place has a glass conservatory filled with more than 4,000 fluttering butterflies, as well as an extensive three-season outdoor garden filled with plants that attract local species. You can also observe the butterfly nursery, where newborns first take flight. An extensive garden shop sells butterfly-friendly plants; there's also Sunday afternoon children's programs and events, a snack bar, and gift shop. ⊠ *281 Greenfield Rd., South Deerfield* ☎ *413/665-2805* ⊕ *www.magicwings.net* ☞ *$10* ⊙ *Daily 9–5.*

SHOPPING

Sure, it's one big retail outlet, designed to display and sell its astonishing array of candle products—more than 160 scents including outlandish aromas such as cantaloupe and banana-nut bread—but **Yankee Candle Company** (⊠ *U.S. 5 and Hwy. 10, near junction of Hwy. 116, South Deerfield* ☎ *877/636-7707* ⊕ *www.yankeecandle.com* ⊙ *Daily 9:30–8*) is also a fun, free place to visit. Check out the small candle-making museum off the main showroom where you can watch costumed docents practicing the art of candle dipping, using historically accurate implements. Highlights for younger kids include the Bavarian Christmas Village and Santa's Toy Factory, where electric trains chug by overhead and faux snow falls lightly. You can have lunch at either the pleasant café or Chandler's, the full-service restaurant.

NIGHTLIFE & THE ARTS

Every weekend at the hotel-turned-roadhouse called **Hot-L-Warren** (⊠ *13 Elm St., South Deerfield* ☎ *413/665-2301*) you can hear some of the best rock and country bands in the region.

WHERE TO STAY

$$$
Fodor's Choice
★

Deerfield Inn. Period wallpaper, wide pine flooring, and original fireplaces decorate this historic 1884 inn and tavern. Rooms are snug and handsomely appointed with both period antiques and reproductions; some rooms have four-poster or canopy beds. Check out the cozy, colonial tavern, with leather booths and candlelight. **Pros:** authentic Colonial details and architecture; tiny on-site tavern oozes atmosphere; set in historic Deerfield Village, surrounded by museum houses. **Cons:** linens need upgrading, bathrooms are basic and tiny. ⊠ *81 Old Main*

St. ☎*413/774–5587 or 800/926–3865* ⊕*www.deerfieldinn.com* ⟲*23 rooms* ⅋*In room: DVD, Wi-Fi. In-hotel: 2 restaurants, bar, no elevator, public Wi-Fi, parking (no fee)* ▭*AE, MC, V* ⦿|*BP.*

$ 🖭**Sunnyside Farm Bed & Breakfast.** Homey atmosphere, reasonable prices, and a quiet, out-of-the-way location make this countryside B&B a favorite with older couples and outdoor lovers. Maple antiques and family heirlooms decorate this circa-1800 Victorian farmhouse's country-style rooms, all of which are hung with fine-art reproductions and have views across the fields. A full country breakfast is served family-style in the dining room. The 50-acre farm is about 8 mi south of Deerfield, convenient to cross-country skiing, mountain biking, and hiking. **Pros:** quiet and serene, wallet-pleasing prices. **Cons:** looking for action? Forget about it, you're miles from anywhere; shared baths. ✉*21 River Rd., Whately* ☎*413/665–3113* ⟲*5 rooms without bath* ⅋*In-hotel: restaurant, pool, no elevator, parking (no fee), no kids under 10* ▭*No credit cards* ⦿|*BP.*

GREENFIELD

4 mi north of Deerfield.

If you like convenience and amenities close at hand, Greenfield makes a pleasant base for exploring the northern region of Pioneer Valley. Sprawl has hit the area, and you'll find fast food joints and chain stores lining the main drags in and out of the city; but downtown Main Street has been left largely untouched, as evidenced by mainstays such as Wilson's Department Store or the old-style Garden Cinemas.

SPORTS & THE OUTDOORS

High on a ridge between downtown Greenfield and the Connecticut River, **Poet's Seat Tower** (✉*Rocky Mountain, follow signs from Maple St.*) makes for one of the valley's most rewarding short jaunts. It's a 1-mi hike from the parking area, and there are inspiring 360-degree views of the countryside from the summit.

WHERE TO EAT & STAY

¢ ✗**Bart's Cafe.** Committed to supporting local farmers, fair trade, and

CAFE eco-friendly producers, this soda shop-style café is a longtime local favorite. Year-round, people crowd the counter for Bart's homemade, ultrarich ice-cream cones and soda creations. There's also a light lunch and dinner menu of fresh-made sandwiches and soups, and the signature vegetarian chili. ✉*286 Main St.* ☎*413/641–0030* ⊕*www. bartshomemade.com* ▭*No credit cards* ⊘*Closed Sun.*

$$ 🖭**Brandt House Country Inn.** This turn-of-the-20th-century Colonial-

★ revival mansion is set on 3½ manicured acres. The sunlit, spacious common rooms are filled with plants, plump easy chairs, and handsome contemporary furnishings; the elegantly appointed guest rooms have featherbeds, fine linens, and lively, original artwork. The stunning penthouse, with a full kitchen and sleeping loft, sleeps up to five. **Pros:** classy, elegant furnishings; nice common areas inside and out. **Cons:** not especially kid-friendly. ✉*29 Highland Ave.* ☎*413/774–3329 or 800/235–3329* ⊕*www.brandthouse.com* ⟲*9 rooms, 6 with bath; 1* suite ♿ *In-room: refrigerator, VCR (some), DVD (some), Wi-Fi. In-hotel: no elevator, public Wi-Fi, parking (no fee), some pets allowed* ▭ *AE, D, MC, V* ◉ *IBP*.

SHELBURNE FALLS

14 mi west of Greenfield.

A tour of New England's fall foliage wouldn't be complete without a trek across the famed Mohawk Trail, a 63-mi section of Highway 2 that runs past picturesque Shelburne Falls. The community, separated from neighboring Buckland by the Deerfield River, is filled with little art galleries and surrounded by orchards, farm stands, and sugar houses.

WHAT TO SEE

★ **Bridge of Flowers.** From May to October, an arched, 400-foot trolley bridge is transformed into this promenade bursting with color. ✉ *Water St.* ☎ *413/625–2544.*

Shelburne Falls Trolley Museum. Take a ride on this real working tribute to the old Colrain Street Railway Combine No. 10, the trolley car that served businesses in and around Shelburne during the early part of the 20th century. ✉ *14 Depot St.* ☎ *413/625–9443* ⊕ *www.sftm.org* ✉ *$2.50* ☉ *May–Nov., weekends and holidays 11–5.*

SPORTS & THE OUTDOORS

RAFTING White-water rafting in the Class II–III rapids of the Deerfield River is a popular summer activity. From April to October, **Zoar Outdoor** (✉ *7 Main St., off Hwy. 2, Charlemont* ☎ *800/532–7483* ⊕ *www.zoaroutdoor.com*) conducts daylong rafting trips along 10 mi of challenging rapids, as well as floats along gentler sections of the river.

SHOPPING

The **Salmon Falls Artisans Showroom** (✉ *1 Ashfield St.* ☎ *413/625–9833* ⊕ *www.penguin-works.com/sfas*) carries sculpture, pottery, glass (including handblown pieces by Josh Simpson), and furniture by more than 175 artisans. The **Young & Constantin Gallery** (✉ *4 Deerfield St.* ☎ *413/625–6866* ⊕ *www.yandcglass.com*) carries top-notch, handmade glass vases, platters, ornaments, and more.

NORTHFIELD

24 mi north of Greenfield; 88 mi northwest of Boston; 20 mi south of Brattleboro, Vermont.

Just south of the Vermont and New Hampshire borders, this country town is known mainly as a center for hikers, campers, and other lovers of the outdoors.

SPORTS & THE OUTDOORS

Northfield Mountain Recreation & Environmental Center. The 26 mi of trails here are suited for biking, hiking, and horseback riding. You can rent canoes, kayaks, and rowboats at the campground at Barton Cove; from here you can paddle to the Munn's Ferry campground, accessible only by canoe. The center also runs 1½-hour riverboat tours of the Pioneer Valley along a 12-mi stretch of the Connecticut River between North-field and Gill, where you'll pass through a dramatically narrow gorge and get a close look at a nesting ground for bald eagles. The tours, offered between mid-June and mid-October, are Friday to Sunday at 11, 1:15, and 3. The cost is $10. In winter, the center rents cross-country skis and snowshoes and offers lessons. ⊠ *99 Miller's Falls Rd.* ☎ *413/659–3714 or 800/859–2960* ⊕ *www.neenergyinc.com/north-field* ⊠ *Free* ⊘ *Daily 9–5.*

WHERE TO EAT

¢-$ ✗**Roosters Bistro.** Cheap, clean, and friendly, this tiny diner on Main
AMERICAN   Street is a great place to stop for a quick bite to eat. Grab a seat at the counter or at one of the handful of tables, and order breakfast all day. There's a decent selection of burgers, sandwiches (try the hefty Monte Cristo dusted with powdered sugar and drizzled with local maple syrup), quesadillas, and paninis, too. ⊠ *72 Main St., Northfield* ☎ *413/498–0006* ⊟ *No credit cards.*

THE BERKSHIRES

Updated by
Diane Bair &
Pamela Wright

More than a century ago, wealthy families from New York, Philadel-phia, and Boston built "summer cottages" in the Berkshire Hills in western Massachusetts—great country estates that earned Berkshire County the nickname "Inland Newport." Many of those grand houses have been razed, and still others are now occupied by schools or hotels. But the region's legacy as a desirable vacation getaway and cultural hub continues unabated.

Occupying the far western end of the state, the Berkshires lie about two-and-a-half hours by car from Boston and New York City, yet the region lives up to the storybook image of rural New England, with wooded hills, narrow winding roads, and compact historic villages. Many cultural events take place in summer, among them the renowned Tanglewood classical music festival in Lenox. The foliage blazes bril-liantly in fall, skiing is popular in winter, and spring is the time for maple sugaring. The scenic Mohawk Trail runs east to west across the northern section of the Berkshires.

NORTH ADAMS

130 mi northwest of Boston; 73 mi northwest of Springfield; 20 mi south of Bennington, Vermont.

If you're looking for a Berkshires getaway that combines culture with outdoor fun (and a cool place to stay as a bonus), put North Adams on your short list.

Established as the military outpost Fort Massachusetts in the mid-18th century, North Adams started out as a part of East Hoosac, and then became part of Adams, before incorporating as its own city in the late

19th century. By then its economy had become dependent upon its textile industry. After North Adams became a strong producer of electrical and radio parts, its fortunes waned just like those of most other industrial New England cities following World War II.

In the recent past, however, the city has staged an impressive comeback as a center of contemporary art. In addition to the famous Mass MoCA arts space, North Adams has a bounty of mills and factory buildings that have been converted to artists' studios and residences. The Porches Inn, a row of eye-catching multihued Victorians, has added an additional helping of hip to downtown. Preservation efforts continue to spruce things up, and new shops and eateries seem to open every few months. In addition, the 11-mi Ashuwillticook Rail Trail is easily accessible in nearby Adams, as is Mount Greylock State Reservation, if you explore it by foot via one of the local trailheads.

WHAT TO SEE

★ **North Adams Museum of History & Science.** North Adams' best kept secret, this museum has more than 25 permanent exhibits on three floors of a building that was once part of a railroad yard. A store sells local historical society publications. ⊠ *Western Gateway Heritage State Park, Bldg. 5A, State St.* ☎413/664–4700 ☒*Free* ⊙*Jan.–Apr., Sat. 10–4, Sun. 1–4; May–Dec., Thurs.–Sat. 10–4, Sun. 1–4.*

★ **Western Gateway Heritage State Park.** This park occupies the old Boston & Maine railroad yard. The visitor center houses exhibits that trace the impact of train travel on the region. A 30-minute documentary provides a look at the intense labor that went into the construction of the nearby Hoosac Tunnel. ⊠*115 State St.* ☎413/663–6312 ☒*Free* ⊙ *Visitor center daily 10–5.*

SPORTS & THE OUTDOORS

★ A hidden gem in the city is **Natural Bridge State Park** (⊠*Hwy. 8* ☎413/663–6392), named for the 30-foot span that crosses Hudson Brook. The marble arch at the center of this 48-acre park sits in what was a marble quarry from the early 1880s to the mid-1900s. There are picnic sites, hiking trails, and well-maintained restrooms. In winter the park is popular for cross-country skiing.

KAYAKING   If you're itching to explore the Cheshire (Hoosic) lakes by kayak, Ashuwillticook Rail Trail by bike, or Mt. Greylock's summit on snowshoes, visit **Berkshire Outfitters** (⊠*Hwy. 8, Adams* ☎413/743–5900 ⊕*www.berkshireoutfitters.com*). Located just 300 yards from the Rail Trail, this shop rents bicycles, kayaks, canoes, Nordic skis, and snowshoes, and the knowledgeable staff will get you on the right track for outdoor fun.

SHOPPING

Housed in the former J. J. Newberry storefront, **Moulton's General Store** (⊠*75 Main St.* ☎413/664–7770) sells country knickknacks, candles, handcrafted soaps, Berkshire Ice Cream, Green Mountain Coffee, and all the penny candy you can eat.

NIGHTLIFE & THE ARTS

At 13 acres, the **Massachusetts Museum of Contemporary Arts** (⊠ *87 Mar-*
Fodor's Choice *shall St.* ☎*413/664–4111* ⊕*www.massmoca.org* ≈*$12.50* ⊙*July–*
★ *Aug., daily 10–6; Sept.–June, Wed.–Mon. 11–5*) is nation's largest
center for contemporary performing and visual arts. The 19th-century
complex of 27 buildings once housed the now-defunct Sprague Electric Co. Six of the factory buildings have been transformed into more
than 250,000 square feet of galleries, studios, performance venues,
cafés, and shops. Its size enables the museum to display monumentally
scaled works such as Robert Rauschenberg's ¼ *Mile or 2 Furlong Piece.*
Exhibits and performances include everything from art shows and concerts to dance and film presentations.

WHERE TO EAT

$$-$$$ ✗**Gramercy Bistro.** Occupying what was once a downtown diner, this
★ casual, upbeat eatery has developed a loyal following. The intimate
AMERICAN space, with a wood-beam ceiling and walls lined with black-and-white
photos of the town, serves an eclectic menu, ranging from sautéed
sweetbreads to an irresistible paella. Chef/owner Alexander Smith
relies on organic meats and locally-grown produce when possible, adding serious zip with sauces made from wasabi and fire-roasted poblano
peppers. Come by on weekends for the memorable brunch. ⊠*26 Mar-*
shall St. ☎*413/663–5300* ⊟*AE, MC, V* ⊙*Closed Tues. No lunch.*

¢- ✗**Jack's Hot Dog Stand.** A North Adams institution since 1917, this hole-
AMERICAN in-the-wall is where locals go for a frank. It also serves burgers and fries
any way you like them. There is minimal seating, so be prepared to eat
on the run. ⊠*12 Eagle St.* ☎*413/664–9006* ⊟*No credit cards.*

WHERE TO STAY

$$-$$$ ⊡**Porches Inn.** These once-dilapidated mill-workers' houses dating
Fodor's Choice from the 1890s were refurbished to become one of New England's
★ quirkiest hotels. They now strike a perfect balance between high-tech
and historic—rooms have a mix of retro 1940s and '50s lamps and
bungalow-style furnishings along with such contemporary touches as
stunning bathrooms with slate floors, hot tubs, and mirrors fashioned
out of old window frames. Some two-room suites have loft sleeping
areas reached by spiral staircases. Suites have pull-out sofas and can
sleep up to six. **Pros:** outdoor heated pool and hot tub (hot tub is open
all year), large guest rooms, walk to town. **Cons:** small breakfast room.
⊠*231 River St.* ☎*413/664–0400* ⊕*www.porches.com* ⇨*47 rooms,*
12 suites ⌂*In-room: kitchen (some), Wi-Fi.* *In-hotel: bar, pool, laun-*
dry service, concierge ⊟*AE, DC, MC, V* ⊙*CP.*

$-$$ ⊡**Topia Inn.** Park your shoes, and your toiletries, at the door. This
★ Adams property, which opened in 2007 just off the Ashuwillticook Rail
Trail, is the greenest inn in the Berkshires. Innkeepers Nana Simopou-
lous and Caryn Heilman transformed a derelict downtown Colonial
into an LEED-rated marvel, with a solar hot water system, soybean
oil heating, and natural clay walls. Beds and linens are organic cotton,
and the innkeepers provide non-toxic toiletries, so the inn is friendly to
guests with chemical sensitivities. Rooms are decorated by the innkeepers' artsy pals; themes include Morocco and Retro '60s. A fun quirk:

Some rooms have spa tubs with colored lights (chromatherapy, it's called), so you can have a little light show as you bathe. **Pros:** organic toiletries in guest rooms include deodorant, hairspray, and toothpaste; organic breakfast; steam showers and spa tubs. **Cons:** located next door to a bar, some of the room designs aren't that well-executed, neighborhood is dreary. ✉ *10 Pleasant St., Adams* ⊕ *www.topiainn. com* ☎ *413/743–9605* ⇆ *10 rooms* ⚬ *In-room: DVD, Wi-Fi. In-hotel: no elevator* ⊟ *AE, MC, V, D* ⍩ *BP.*

WILLIAMSTOWN

5 mi west of North Adams.

When Colonel Ephraim Williams left money to found a free school in what was then known as West Hoosac, he stipulated that the town's name be changed to Williamstown. Williams College opened in 1793 and even today, life in this placid town revolves around it. Graceful campus buildings like the Gothic cathedral, built in 1904, line wide Main Street. Along Spring Street, you'll find a handful of upscale shops and lively eateries.

WHAT TO SEE

Fodor'sChoice ★ **Clark Art Institute.** One of the nation's notable small art museums, the Clark Art Institute has more than 30 paintings by Renoir (among them *Mademoiselle Fleury in Algerian Costume*) as well as canvases by Monet and Pissarro. *The Little Dancer,* an important sculpture by Degas, is another exceptional work. Other items include priceless English silver, European and American photography from the 1840s through the 1910s, and Flemish and Dutch masterworks from the 17th and 18th centuries. ✉ *225 South St.* ☎ *413/458–2303* ⊕ *www. clarkart.edu* ⌚ *July–Oct. $12.50, Nov.–May free* ⊙ *Sept.–June, Tues.– Sun. 10–5; July and Aug., daily 10–5.*

Fodor'sChoice ★ **Williams College Museum of Art.** The collection and exhibits at this fine museum focus on American and 20th-century art. Considered to be one of the best college art museums in the country, the WCMA houses 12,000 works spanning a broad range of eras and cultures, with an emphasis on modern and contemporary American works. The original octagonal structure facing Main Street was built as a library in 1846. ✉ *15 Lawrence Hall Dr.* ☎ *413/597–2429* ⊕ *www.wcma.org* ⌚ *Free* ⊙ *Tues.–Sat. 10–5, Sun. 1–5.*

SPORTS & THE OUTDOORS

The centerpiece of the 10,327-acre **Mt. Greylock State Reservation** (✉ *Rockwell Rd., Lanesboro* ☎ *413/499–4262 or 413/499–4263*) is 3,491-foot-high Mt. Greylock, the highest point in Massachusetts. The reservation, south of Williamstown, has facilities for cycling, fishing, horseback riding, camping, and snowmobiling. Many treks—including a portion of the Appalachian Trail—start from the parking lot at the summit, an 8-mi drive from the base of the mountain. At press time, the road to the summit was closed for renovation, but due to re-open

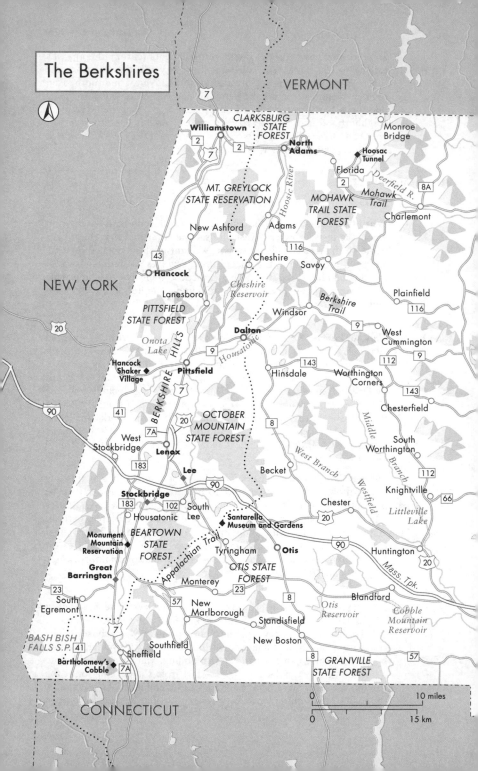

sometime in 2009. In the meantime, the Appalachian Trail is the only available route to the summit.

SHOPPING

ⓒ Spring Street is downtown Williamstown's main drag, lined with upscale shops and cafés. At **Library Antiques** (⊠*70 Spring St.* ☎*413/458-3436* ⊕*www.libraryantiques.com*), you'll find an array of prints, folk art, jewelry, antiquarian books, and distinctive gifts. Some people consider tiny **Toonerville Trolley** (⊠*131 Water St.* ☎*413/458-5229*) the best music store in the world. One thing they appreciate is the vast musical knowledge of proprietor Hal March. Toonerville carries hard-to-find jazz, rock, and classical recordings. Jam-packed with every imaginable toy and game, **Where'd You Get That?** (⊠*100 Spring St.* ☎*413/458-2206* ⊕*www.wygt.com*) also benefits from the warmth and enthusiasm generated by owners Ken and Michele Gietz.

NIGHTLIFE & THE ARTS

Fodor'sChoice
★
At the Adams Memorial Theatre, the **Williamstown Theatre Festival** (⊠*1000 Main St.* ☎*413/597-3400* or *413/597-3399* ⊕*www.wtfestival.org*) is summer's hottest ticket. From June through August, the long-running production presents well-known theatrical works with famous performers on the Main Stage and contemporary works on the Nikos Stage.

WHERE TO EAT

$-$$
Fodor'sChoice
★
AMERICAN
✕**'6 House Pub.** Set in an old cow barn at the 1896 House Inn, this dark, wood-paneled pub has loads of character—and a mounted mascot, Harold the Hereford, who doesn't seem to mind that at least half the patrons are downing burgers. Not a meat eater? Not a problem. Chef Matt Schilling's extensive menu includes several "supper salads" (including a grilled plum salad with Granny Smith apples, Gorgonzola crumbles, and glazed walnuts over mixed greens), veggie three-bean chili, and sweet-potato fries. They also sell a bazillion lobster rolls, as well they should; this toothsome roll is all lobster meat, sans fillers, on a buttery grilled roll. ⊠*U.S. 7* ☎*413/458-1896* ☰*AE, D, MC,V.*

$$-$$$
Fodor'sChoice
★
ECLECTIC
✕**Mezze Bistro & Bar.** This is, without a doubt, Williamstown's hot spot. On summer evenings it's not uncommon to find yourself rubbing elbows with stars from the Williamstown Theatre Festival. The interior mixes urban chic and rustic charm with hardwood floors and exposed-brick walls. The spectacular menu is always in flux, but don't be surprised to encounter sashimi with watercress alongside filet mignon with roasted root vegetables. ⊠*16 Water St.* ☎*413/458-0123* ⊕*www.mezzeinc.com* ⌂*Reservations essential* ☰*AE, D, MC, V* ⊙*No lunch.*

WHERE TO STAY

$$-$$$
★
🛏 **Guest House at Field Farm.** Built in 1948, this guesthouse contains a fine collection of art on loan from Williams College. The former owners, who gave part of their own art collection to the college, donated the 296-acre property to the Trustees of Reservations, which runs it as a B&B. The large windows in the guest rooms have expansive views of the grounds. Three rooms have private decks; two rooms have working tile fireplaces. The East Room has the best views of Mt. Greylock, while

the Gallery Room has the best art. You can prepare your own simple meals in the pantry. The grounds, open to the public, have 4 mi of hiking trails. **Pros:** great views of the Berkshires, luxury (Frette) robes and towels and high thread-count linens, free coffee and soft drinks. **Cons:** no TV in rooms. ⊠*554 Sloan Rd.* ☎*413/458–3135* ⊕*www.guest houseatfieldfarm.org* ☞*5 rooms* ⚿*In-room: Wi-Fi. In-hotel: pool, no elevator, no kids under 12* ⊟*D, MC, V* ⊙⎮*BP.*

$ ⊡**River Bend Farm.** On the National Register of Historic Places, this

★ authentic 1770 Georgian Colonial was once the home and tavern of Colonel Benjamin Simonds. It's not located on a river, nor is it a farm, but this rustic inn is a great place to discover simpler times, before TV and Internet and (alas) private bathrooms! The guest rooms are sprinkled with antique pieces—chamber pots, washstands, wing chairs, and spinning wheels. Some bedrooms have wide-plank walls, curtains of unbleached muslin, and four-poster beds or rope beds. A gracious library awaits you downstairs. The kitchen contains an open-range stove and an oven hung with dried herbs. **Pros:** good breakfast, friendly innkeepers. **Cons:** set on a busy road with train sounds at night, guests share one shower. ⊠*643 Simonds Rd.* ☎*413/458–3121* ⊕*www.riverbendfarmbb.com* ☞*4 rooms without bath* ⚿*In-room: no a/c, no phone, no TV. In-hotel: no elevator* ⊟*No credit cards* ⊙*Closed Nov.– Mar.* ⊙⎮*CP.*

HANCOCK

15 mi south of Williamstown.

Tiny Hancock, the village closest to the Jiminy Peak ski resort, comes into its own in winter. It's also a great base for outdoors enthusiasts year-round, with biking, hiking, and other options in summer.

WHAT TO SEE

☺ **Ioka Valley Farm.** Established in the 1930s, this 600-acre farm is one of the best-known pick-your-own farms in the Berkshires. You can pick berries all summer, then apples and pumpkins in fall. In winter you can cut your own Christmas tree. Other activities include hay rides, pedal tractors for kids, and a petting zoo with pigs, sheep, goats, and calves. ⊠*Hwy. 43* ☎*413/738–5915.*

SKI AREA   ## SPORTS & THE OUTDOORS

The only full-service ski and snowboard resort in the Berkshires, and the largest in southern New England, **Jiminy Peak** (⊠*Corey Rd.* ☎*413/738–5500, 888/454–6469* ⊕*www.jiminypeak.com*) is also a splendid destination during fall foliage season and in summer. A new mountain coaster operates daily in summer and fall, and on weekends and holidays in winter. This two-person cart shoots down the mountain at speeds of up to 25 mph. The resort has also gone green in a big way: Jiminy Peak now operates a wind turbine, making it the only ski resort in the U.S. that's generating its own power.

The resort has a 3,000-foot alpine super-slide with tunnels and dips, a four-in-one Euro-bungee trampoline, a two-story rock-climbing wall,

2

mountain biking, and a swimming pool. You can ride up the mountain on a high-speed chairlift, or take a wilder ride on the mountain coaster. Children ages 4–12 can take ski lessons; those 6–15 can take a series of eight weekends of instruction with the same teacher. The kids' ski area has its own lift.

With a vertical of 1,150 feet and 44 trails and 9 lifts, Jiminy has near-big-time status in terms of downhill skiing. It is mostly a cruising mountain—trails are groomed daily, and only on some are small moguls left to build up along the side of the slope. The steepest black-diamond runs are on the upper head walls; longer, outer runs make for good intermediate terrain. There's skiing nightly, and snowmaking covers 93% of the skiable terrain. Jiminy also has three terrain parks and a mountain coaster (weekends and holidays only).

WHERE TO STAY

$$-$$$ 🎏 **Country Inn at Jiminy Peak.** Massive stone fireplaces in its lobby and lounge lend this hotel a ski-lodge atmosphere. The condo-style suites—privately owned but put into a rental pool—accommodate up to four people and have kitchenettes separated from living areas by bars with high stools. The roomiest units are on the second and third floors; the suites at the rear of the building overlook the slopes. Ski packages are available. **Pros:** John Harvard's Restaurant is on site, bathrooms are nice, eat-in kitchenettes. **Cons:** hallways are a bit dark, burgundy and green color scheme is dated. ⊠ *Corey Rd.* ☎ *413/738–5500 or 800/882–8859* ⊕ *www.jiminypeak.com* 🛏 *105 suites* ⅙ *In-room: kitchen, VCR. In-hotel: 2 restaurants, bar, tennis courts, pool, gym, public Wi-Fi* ▤ *AE, D, DC, MC, V.*

PITTSFIELD

21 mi south of Williamstown, 11 mi southeast of Hancock.

A mere agricultural backwater at the time of the American Revolution, the seat of Berkshire County grew steadily throughout the 19th century into an industrial powerhouse of textile, paper, and electrical machinery manufacturing. In the 1930s, the WPA guidebook on Massachusetts described Pittsfield as possessing a "prosperous, tranquil look of general comfort and cultivation which makes it one of the most attractive industrial cities in the state." The city's economy took a nosedive following World War II, and much of that apparent prosperity diminished.

Modern Pittsfield has reversed the downward slide of the past several decades and reclaimed a number of intriguing industrial buildings, actively courting artists with inexpensive work/living space downtown. Still, this is a workaday city without the monied urbanity of Great Barrington or the quaint, rural demeanor of the comparatively small Colonial towns that surround it. There's a positive buzz in Pittsfield these days, though. Symbols of the Pittsfield's resurgence include the gorgeous Colonial Theatre, which was restored in 2007. It hosts 250 nights of performances per year, and a spate of new shops and eateries along North Street, including Spice, one of the hottest restaurant/bars in the Berkshires. City-sponsored art walks and a major renovation of the venerable Berkshire Museum are more evidence of Pittsfield's comeback.

WHAT TO SEE

☺ **Berkshire Museum.** Opened in 1903, this museum houses three floors of exhibits, which display a varied and sometimes curious collection of objects relating to history, the natural world, and art. A highlight of the latter is a collection of Hudson River School paintings, including works by Frederic Church and Albert Bierstadt. In 2008, the museum unveiled its first new gallery in more than 100 years: the Feigenbaum Hall of Innovation. This multimedia, interactive exhibit includes historical artifacts, works of art, and video about Berkshire innovators such as Crane & Co., the paper company that prints U.S. currency, and Douglas Trumbull, who created special effects for films including *2001: A Space Odyssey* and *Star Wars*. An aquarium contains 26 tanks of sea creatures, including a touch tank. At 10 feet high and 26 feet long, "Wally" the Stegosaurus highlights the Dinosaurs and Paleontology gallery. At the Dino Dig, kids and adults can dig together for replicas of dinosaur bones. An ancient civilization gallery displays Roman and Greek jewelry and an ancient Egyptian mummy. Check out the expanded museum shop, now located down the street. ⊠*39 South St.* ☏*413/443–7171* ⊕*www.berkshiremuseum.org* ⊠*$10* ☉*Mon.–Sat. 10–5, Sun. noon–5.*

Fodor'sChoice **Hancock Shaker Village.** The third Shaker community in America, Han-
★ cock was founded in the 1790s. At its peak in the 1840s, the village had almost 300 inhabitants, who made their living farming, selling seeds and herbs, making medicines, and producing crafts. The religious community officially closed in 1960, its 170-year life span a small miracle considering its population's vows of celibacy (they took in orphans to maintain their constituency). Many examples of Shaker ingenuity are visible at Hancock today: the **Round Stone Barn** and the **Laundry and Machine Shop** are two of the most interesting buildings. Also on site are a farm, some period gardens, a museum shop with reproduction Shaker furniture, a picnic area, and a café. ⊠*U.S. 20, 6 mi west of Pittsfield* ☏*413/443–0188 or 800/817–1137* ⊕*www.hancockshaker-village.org* ⊠*$15, $12.50 in winter* ☉*Late May–late Oct., daily 10–5 for self-guided tours; late Oct.–late May, daily 10–3 for guided tours.*

SPORTS & THE OUTDOORS

SKI AREA Some ski areas have entered an era of glamour and high prices, but the **Bousquet Ski Area** (⊠*101 Dan Fox Dr., off U.S. 7 near Pittsfield Airport* ☏*413/442–8316, 413/442–2436 snow conditions* ⊕*www.bousquets. com*) remains an economical, no-nonsense place to ski. The inexpensive lift tickets are the same price every day, and there's night skiing every night except Sunday. You can go snow tubing for just $18 for the day when conditions allow.

Play Bousquet uses three drop funnels to pour kids out into a large activity pool and enough twists and turns and chute-to-chutes to scare

HOLISTIC HIDEAWAYS

A place to stay can be as simple as a clean room and cable TV. Or, it can completely transform your life. The Berkshires area has become known for holistic retreats, places that send you home with the ultimate souvenir: a new-and-improved you, with a refreshed spirit, revitalized body, and healthier habits that can last a lifetime. Here are two places you might like to try.

The Berkshires' outpost of **Canyon Ranch** (☎ *800/742-9000* ⊕ *www. canyonranch.com*) in Lenox couldn't be more elegantly old-fashioned; the famous spa is set in Bellefontaine mansion, a 1897 replica of Le Petit Trianon in Versailles. Looks can be deceiving, though. This holistic spa is home to a state-of-the-art, 100,000-square-foot fitness center, with the latest classes and the best equipment—perfect for gym-junkies. Choose from among more than 40 fitness classes per day, plus lifestyle management workshops and private consultations with wellness experts in the field of medicine, nutrition, behavior, and physiology. You can change your life in three days (truly),

while trying new fitness techniques, eating great food (even chocolate sauce, craftily made from white grape juice and cocoa), and enjoying the Berkshires countryside on hikes and paddling excursions.

Who cares what your body looks like if your personal life is a shambles? **The Option Institute** (☎ *www. option.org* ⊕ *800/714-2779*) in Sheffield, is all about learning to make emotional choices that enhance your life experience. Founded in 1983 by author Barry Neil Kaufman (*Happiness is a Choice*) and Samahria Lyte Kaufman, the Option Institute is based on the premise that emotions like misery, fear, anger, and distress are optional, not inevitable. Personal growth workshops are designed to help participants develop tools that will improve the quality of their relationships, which leads to a happier life. "Energizing" and "empowering" are words used by happy fans to describe their experience with the Option Institute. Participants stay in rustic guesthouses, and eat veggie meals served family-style.

the pants off many parents. A miniature-golf course, 32-foot climbing wall, go-karts, alpine carts, and a scenic chairlift make Bousquet a suitable reward for children who have stoically accompanied their parents to the assortment of galleries, concerts, and plays that are the area's major tourism resource.

With a 750-foot vertical drop, Bousquet has 21 trails, but only if you count every change in steepness and every merging slope. Though this is a generous figure, you will find some good beginner and intermediate runs, with a few steeper pitches. There are two double chairlifts, three surface lifts, and a small snowboard park. Ski instruction classes are given twice daily on weekends and holidays for children age five and up.

NIGHTLIFE & THE ARTS

For the serious music lover, **South Mountain Concerts** (⊠ *U.S. 7 and 20 2 mi south of Pittsfield center* ☎*413/442–2106*) is one of the most distinguished centers for chamber music events in the country. Set on the wooded slope of South Mountain, the 500-seat auditorium presents concerts every Sunday in September at 3. The newly-restored **Colonial Theatre** (⊠*11 South St.* ☎*413/997–4444*) looks like the inside of a jewel box, with modern seats built to look like vintage. First opened in 1903, the theater hosted stars like Helen Hayes and Al Jolson; now guests fill the 775 seats to see artists like Audra McDonald and James Taylor, off-Broadway musical tryouts, comedy, and children's theater.

WHERE TO EAT

$–$$
STEAKHOUSE

✕**Dakota.** Moose and elk heads watch over diners, and the motto is "Steak, seafood, and smiles" at this large and popular chain restaurant, decorated like a rustic hunting lodge. Meals cooked on the mesquite grill include steaks and salmon, shrimp, and trout; the 32-item salad bar has many organic foods. A hearty Sunday brunch buffet includes Belgian pancakes, omelets, ham, lox and bagels, fruit, salads, and rich desserts. ⊠*1035 South St.* ☎*413/499–7900* ▭*AE, D, DC, MC, V* ⊙*No lunch Mon.–Sat.*

$$–$$$$
Fodor'sChoice
★
ECLECTIC

✕**Spice.** Set in the old Besse-Clark Department Store on revitalized North Street, Spice is agleam with hipness. Jeans-and-tees types and glammed-up theatergoers bound for a show at the Colonial seem equally merry here. Exposed beams and light fixtures wrapped with white sheets (for acoustics, and "to make women look beautiful," according to co-owner Joyce Bernstein) give diners something to admire while they wait for Chef Douglas Luf's food. Then, the real admiration begins, thanks to Luf's winning ways with everything from wild-mushroom Toad in a Hole (a poached egg cooked in brioche with wild mushrooms) to maple-smoked duck breast with sweet-potato-apple hash. Even the ubiquitous hanger steak is better than average, and boosted by terrific hand-cut fries. Desserts go retro: think chocolate-cashew caramel corn and root-beer floats. ⊠*297 North St.* ☎*413/443–1234* ▭*AE, D, MC, V* ⊙*Closed Sun. and Mon.*

LENOX

10 mi south of Pittsfield, 130 mi west of Boston.

The famed Tanglewood music festival has been a fixture in upscale Lenox for decades, and it's a part of the reason the town remains fiercely popular in summer. Booking a room here or in any of the nearby communities can set you back dearly when music or theatrical events are in town. Many of the town's most impressive homes are downtown; others you can only see by setting off on the curving, tortuous back roads that traverse the region. In the center of the village, a few blocks of shabby-chic Colonial buildings contain shops and eateries.

WHAT TO SEE

Berkshires Scenic Railway Museum. In a restored 1903 railroad station in central Lenox, this museum displays antique rail equipment, vintage exhibits, and a large working model railway. It's the starting point for the diesel-hauled **Berkshire Scenic Railway**, a one-and-a-half-hour narrated round-trip train ride between Lenox and Stockbridge. There's also a 45-minute trip to Lee. ⊠ *Willow Creek Rd.* ☎*413/637–2210* ⊕*www. berkshirescenicrailroad.org* ⊠*Museum free, Lenox–Stockbridge train $15, Lenox–Lee train $9* ⊙*May–Oct., Sat.–Sun. 10–4 (see Web site for current schedule).*

Frelinghuysen Morris House & Studio. This sleek, modernist property occupies a verdant 46-acre site and exhibits the works of American abstract artists Suzy Frelinghuysen and George L. K. Morris as well as those of contemporaries including Picasso, Braque, and Gris. A 57-minute documentary on the lives and work of Frelinghuysen and Morris plays on a continuous loop in the classroom. ⊠*92 Hawthorne St.* ☎*413/637–0166* ⊕*www.frelinghuysen.org* ⊠*$10* ⊙*Late June–early Sept., Thurs.–Sun. 10–4, early Sept.–mid-Oct., Thurs.–Sat. 10–4.*

Fodor$Choice
★

The Mount. This mansion built in 1902 with myriad classical influences was the summer home of novelist Edith Wharton. The 42-room house and 3 acres of formal gardens were designed by Wharton, who is considered by many to have set the standard for 20th-century interior decoration. In designing the Mount, she followed the principles set forth in her book *The Decoration of Houses* (1897), creating a calm and well-ordered home. Nearly $15 million has been spent to date on an extensive, ongoing restoration project. ⊠*2 Plunkett St.* ☎*413/551–5104 or 888/637–1902* ⊕*www.edithwharton.org* ⊠*$10* ⊙*May–Dec., daily 10–4.*

Museum of the Gilded Age. Built in 1893, Ventfort Hall was the summer "cottage" of Sarah Morgan, the sister of financier J. P. Morgan. Inside is the hall is this museum, which explores the role of Lenox and the Berkshires as the definitive mountain retreat during that fabled era. Since the late '90s a top restoration team has been hard at work repairing the elegant exterior brickwork and roofing, the ornate interior paneling and grand staircase, and the gabled carriage house. Lively, information-packed tours offer a peek into the lifestyles of Lenox's super-rich "cottage class." ⊠*104 Walker St.* ☎*413/637–3206* ⊕*www.gilded age.org* ⊠*$12* ⊙*May–Oct., Mon.–Sat. tours on the hr 11:30–2:30; Nov.–Apr., Sat. tours at 10 and 11.*

SPORTS & THE OUTDOORS

HIKING Part of the Massachusetts Audubon Society's system, the **Pleasant Valley Wildlife Sanctuary** (⊠*472 W. Mountain Rd.* ☎*413/637–0320* ⊕*www. massaudubon.org*) abounds with beaver ponds, meadows, hardwood forests, and woodlands. Its 1,400 acres and 7 mi of trails offer excellent bird- and beaver-watching. Open daily July to Columbus Day; open the rest of the year from Tuesday through Sunday and on Monday holidays. Hiking trails are open for cross-country skiing and snowshoeing in winter. Town-owned **Kennedy Park** (⊠*Main St.*) offers hiking and cross-country skiing on old carriage roads, plus nearly 15 mi of trails within a hardwood forest.

HORSEBACK Travel along the beautiful shaded trails of Kennedy Park and Lenox
RIDING Mountain and enjoy breathtaking views of Berkshire County when you book an hour, half-day, or overnight ride at **Berkshire Horseback Adventures** (⊠*293 Main St.* ☎*413/637–9090*).

SHOPPING

One of the foremost crafts centers in New England, **Hoadley Gallery** (⊠*21 Church St.* ☎*413/637–2814* ⊕*www.hoadleygallery.com*) shows American arts and crafts with a strong focus on pottery, jewelry, and textiles. **R. W. Wise** (⊠*81 Church St.* ☎*413/637–1589* ⊕*www.rwwise.com*) produces high-quality creative jewelry and also sells estate and antique pieces.

NIGHTLIFE & THE ARTS

Fodor'sChoice **Tanglewood** (⊠*West St. off Hwy. 183* ☎*617/266–1492 or 888/266–*
★ *1492* ⊕*www.tanglewood.org*), the 200-acre summer home of the Boston Symphony Orchestra, attracts thousands every year to concerts by world-famous performers from mid-June to Labor Day. The 5,000-seat main shed hosts larger concerts; the Seiji Ozawa Hall (named for the former BSO conductor—James Levine took the helm in 2003) seats around 1,200 and is used for recitals, chamber music, and more intimate performances by summer program students and soloists. One of the most rewarding ways to experience Tanglewood is to purchase lawn tickets, arrive early with blankets or lawn chairs, and have a picnic. Except for the occasional celebrity concert, lawn tickets remain below $20, and concerts can be clearly heard from just about any spot on the lawn. Inside the shed, tickets vary in price, with most of the good seats costing between $38 and $100.

Shakespeare & Company (⊠*70 Kemble St.* ☎*413/637–1199, 413/637–3353 tickets*) performs the works of Shakespeare and Edith Wharton from late May through October at the 466-seat Founders' Theatre and the 99-seat Spring Lawn Theatre. Also under way is the authentic reconstruction of an Elizabethan theater, the Rose Playhouse, the original of which stood on the south bank of London's Thames River in the 16th century.

WHERE TO EAT

$$–$$$ ✕**Bistro Zinc.** Crisp lemon-yellow walls, warm tile floors, and tall win-
FRENCH dows are bright and inviting in this stellar French bistro, which feels like a country house in Provence. The kitchen turns out expertly prepared and refreshingly simple classics like steak frites, grilled lamb chops, and mussels marinieres. Zinc's long, zinc-topped wood bar, always full and determinedly sophisticated, is the best Lenox can offer for nightlife. If you can overlook the occasionally self-important attitudes of the staff, Zinc is top-notch. ⊠*56 Church St.* ☎*413/637–8800* ⊟*AE, MC, V.*

$$–$$$ ✕**Café Lucia.** *Bistecca alla fiorentina* (porterhouse steak grilled with
ITALIAN olive oil, garlic, and rosemary) and ravioli *basilico e pomodoro* (with fresh tomatoes, garlic, and basil) are among the dishes that change seasonally at this northern Italian restaurant. The sleek café has track

lighting and photographs of the owners' Italian ancestors. Weekend reservations are essential during the Tanglewood music festival. ✉️*80 Church St.* ☎️*413/637-2640* ▭*AE, D MC, V* ⊘*Closed Mon. July–Oct., Sun. and Mon. Nov.–June. No lunch.*

¢ ✕**Chocolate Springs Cafe.** Escape into chocolate bliss here, where even the aroma is intoxicating. This award-winning chocolatier offers wedges of decadent cakes, store-made ice cream and sorbets, and a dazzling array of chocolates, including green-tea bonbons, chocolate-covered pretzels, even chocolate-dipped prunes. You can eat at one of a handful of tables, but don't expect so much as a salad or a wrap—it's all chocolate, all the time. ✉️*Aspinwell Shops 55 Pittsfield/Lenox Rd.* ☎️*413/637-9820* ▭*AE, D, MC, V.*

Fodor's Choice

★

BAKERY

$$-$$$ ✕**Church Street Café.** A little more laid-back than its nearby competitors, Church Street Café presents a no-less-ambitious and -intriguing menu of globally inspired dishes. From the baked onion-and-Saint-André-cheese tart to the vegetarian moussaka and the New Mexican home-style tortilla stuffed with barbecued brisket, the dishes served here are an international culinary treat that change with the seasons. In warm weather you can dine on a shaded outdoor deck. ✉️*65 Church St.* ☎️*413/637-2745* ▭*MC, V* ⊘*Closed Sun. and Mon. mid-Oct.–May.*

CAFE

WHERE TO STAY

$$-$$$ 🖼️**Brook Farm Inn.** This 1870s Victorian and its gardens are tucked away in a beautiful wooded glen a short distance from Tanglewood. The inn-keepers are music and literature aficionados and often have light opera, jazz, or Broadway tunes playing in the fireplace-lighted library, whose shelves contain copious volumes of verse. On some Saturdays, mostly in winter, poetry readings enhance afternoon tea. Rooms have antiques, light-pastel color schemes, and in many cases four-poster beds. Even the smallest units, with their eaved ceilings and cozy configurations, are very romantic. **Pros:** attentive innkeepers, delicious breakfast, afternoon tea with scones. **Cons:** thin towels, no TV. ✉️*15 Hawthorne St.* ☎️*413/637-3013 or 800/285-7638* 🌐*www.brookfarm.com* 🛏️*12 rooms, 1 suite* ♿*In-room: no TV, Wi-Fi. In-hotel: pool, no elevator, no kids under 15* ▭*MC, V* 🍴*BP.*

$$$-$$$$ 🖼️**Cranwell Resort, Spa and Golf Club.** The best rooms in this 380-acre, five-building complex are in the century-old Tudor mansion; they're furnished with antiques and have marble bathrooms. Two smaller buildings have 20 rooms each, and there are several small cottages, each of which has a kitchen. Somewhat marring the property is an abundance of tightly spaced condos behind the hotel buildings. Most of the facilities are open to the public, as are the resort's restaurants, where you can dine formally or informally. There's also a full golf school. The 35,000-square-foot spa has a full complement of women's and men's treatments, plus several types of massage. This is a good option for families, since there's so much to do on-property (and since so many inns in the Berkshires aren't child-friendly.) **Pros:** good golf course, lots of activities, nice swimming pool. **Cons:** extra cost for amenities like tennis and bike rentals, some complaints of housekeeping issues. ✉️*55 Lee Rd.* ☎️*413/637-1364 or 800/272-6935* 🌐*www.cranwell.*

com ⌕*113 rooms* &*In-hotel: 4 restaurants, golf course, tennis courts, pool, gym, spa, bicycles, concierge* ☰*AE, D, DC, MC, V* ⌾❘*CP.*

$$$-$$$$ ⚏**Devonfield Inn.** This grand, yellow-and-cream Federal house sits atop
Fodor'sChoice a birch-shaded hillside, dotted with a few quaint outbuildings and 32
★ acres of rolling meadows. The nine guest rooms have Colonial-style furnishings—many have Oriental rugs, lace-canopy four-poster beds, and working fireplaces. An immense penthouse suite is a favorite for special occasions, and a separate, contemporary cottage with a pitched cathedral ceiling has its own kitchen and private deck. A gracious pool and cottage unit sit behind the house. Expect such toothsome fare as vanilla-cinnamon crème brûlée or orange yogurt pancakes at breakfast, and details such as chocolates and spring water in each room. There is a video library and a butler's pantry with cookies, popcorn, and beverages. **Pros:** charming innkeepers, good breakfasts, nice pool and lawn. **Cons:** not great for families with young kids. ⊠*85 Stockbridge Rd., Lee* ☎*413/243-3298 or 800/664-0880* ⊕*www.devonfield.com* ⌕*6 rooms, 3 suites, 1 cottage* &*In-room: DVD, Wi-Fi. In-hotel: tennis court, pool, bicycles, no elevator, public Wi-Fi, no kids under 12 in summer* ☰*AE, MC, V, D* ⌾❘*BP.*

$$-$$$$ ⚏**Gateways Inn.** The 1912 summer cottage of Harley Proctor (as in
Fodor'sChoice Proctor and Gamble) has experienced some ups and downs during its
★ tenure as a country inn. But under the skillful direction of innkeepers Fabrizio and Rosemary Chiariello, it looks better than ever. Rooms come in a variety of configurations and styles, most with working fireplaces, detailed moldings, and plush carpeting. Some guest rooms and bathrooms have been recently upgraded; ask if one of these are available when you make your reservation. The on-site restaurant, La Terrazza, offers late night dining in summertime. **Pro:** great location in the heart of Lenox; concierge service can arrange activities for you, including in-room massage. **Cons:** public areas have a faded glory feel, lots of stairs. ⊠*51 Walker St.* ☎*413/637-2532* ⊕*www.gatewaysinn. com* ⌕*11 rooms, 1 suite* &*In-room: DVD (some), Internet. In-hotel: restaurant, bar, no elevator, concierge service* ☰*AE, MC, V* ⌾❘*BP.*

$$-$$$ ⚏**Whistler's Inn.** The antiques decorating the parlor of this eccentric
★ 1820s English Tudor mansion are ornate, with a touch of the exotic thanks to items gleaned from the innkeepers' world travels. The 4,000-volume library, formal parlor, music room (with a Steinway grand piano and Louis XVI original furniture), and gracious dining room all impress. Designer drapes and bedspreads adorn the guest rooms, three of which have working fireplaces. The carriage house is only open May through October; one room in it is decorated to reflect an African style, and another has a Southwestern style. The inn is nestled amid 7 acres of gardens and woods across from Kennedy Park. **Pros:** interesting innkeepers, lavish public areas. **Cons:** rooms could use updating, bathrooms are old and small. ⊠*5 Greenwood St.* ☎*413/637-0975 or 866/637-0975* ⊕*www.whistlersinnlenox.com* ⌕*14 rooms* &*In-hotel: no elevator, no kids under 10* ☰*AE, D, MC, V* ⌾❘*BP.*

$-$$ ⚏**Yankee Inn.** Custom-crafted Amish canopy beds, gas fireplaces, and
★ high-end fabrics decorate the top rooms at this immaculately kept, two-story motor inn, one of several modern hotels and motels along U.S. 7.

2

The more economical units contain attractive, if nondescript, country-style furnishings and such useful amenities as coffeemakers and irons with ironing boards. If you can, avoid the wings of the motel and stay in the main building for a nicer, less motel-y experience. **Pros:** convenient location to attractions, good value, clean. **Cons:** closer to Pittsfield than Lenox; some rooms smell musty, dreary pool area. ⊠*461 Pittsfield-Lenox Rd. off U.S. 7 and 20* ☎*413/499–3700 or 800/835–2364* ⊕*www.yankeeinn.com* ↝*96 rooms* ⌂*In-room: refrigerator, dial-up. In-hotel: pool, gym, public Wi-Fi, no-smoking rooms* ▤*AE, D, MC, V* ¶*CP.*

EN ROUTE

Founded after the Revolutionary War, **Lee,** 5 mi south of Lenox, began as a farming community. Though the land was fertile, it was burdened with many large stones, which luckily turned out to be marble. In fact, Lee marble turned out to be one of the hardest marbles available, making it perfect for buildings. Soon, quarries sprang up to produce the marble for 19th-century buildings such as the cottages of the Vanderbilts and Westinghouses. Today the bustling downtown contains a mix of touristy and workaday shops, and an outlet shopping center sits just off the Mass Pike highway exit. At Lee's **Highlawn Farm** (⊠*535 Summer St.* ☎*413/243–0672*) you can visit the cows and buy fresh milk, cream, butter, and blue cheese.

OTIS

20 mi southeast of Lenox.

A more rustic alternative to the polish of Stockbridge and Lenox, Otis, with a ski area and 20 lakes and ponds, supplies plenty of what made the Berkshires desirable in the first place—the great outdoors. The dining and lodgings options here are slim; your best bet is to stay in Lee or Great Barrington and choose from among their tempting array of restaurants. Or head southwest to Old Marlborough and stay at the Old Inn on the Green (a circa-1760 B&B that began life as a stagecoach stop), where you can sample chef Peter Platt's swoon-worthy cuisine. Nearby Becket hosts the outstanding Jacob's Pillow Dance Festival in summer.

WHAT TO SEE

Deer Run Maples. This is one of several sugarhouses where you can spend the morning tasting freshly tapped maple syrup that's been drizzled onto a dish of snow. Sugaring season varies with the weather; it can be anytime between late February and early April. Call before coming to confirm opening hours. ⊠*135 Ed Jones Rd.* ☎*413/269–7588* ⊡*Free* ⊗*Late Feb.–early Apr., hrs vary.*

SPORTS & THE OUTDOORS

SKI AREA The least-expensive ski area in New England, **Otis Ridge** has long been a haven for beginners and families, but experts will find slopes here, too. The remote location is quite stunning, the buildings historic. There are six downhill trails serviced by a pair of lifts, with 100 percent snowmaking coverage and night skiing Tuesday through Sunday. ⊠*Hwy. 23* ☎*413/269–4444* ⊕*www.otisridge.com.*

NIGHTLIFE & THE ARTS

For nine weeks each summer, the tiny town of Becket, 8 mi north of Otis, becomes a hub of the dance world during the **Jacob's Pillow Dance Festival** (⊠*358 George Carter Rd., at U.S. 20* ☎*413/327–1234* ⊕*www.jacobspillow.org*), which showcases world-renowned performers of ballet, modern, and ethnic dance. Before the main events, works-in-progress and even some of the final productions are staged outdoors, often free of charge.

STOCKBRIDGE

20 mi northwest of Otis, 7 mi south of Lenox.

Stockbridge is the quintessence of small-town New England charm, untainted by industry or large-scale development. It is also the blueprint for small-town America as represented picture perfectly on the covers of the *Saturday Evening Post* by painter Norman Rockwell. From 1953 until his death in 1978, Rockwell lived in Stockbridge and painted its buildings and its residents, inspired by their simple charm. James Taylor sang about the town in his hit "Sweet Baby James," as did balladeer Arlo Guthrie in his famous Thanksgiving anthem "Alice's Restaurant," in which he tells what ensued when he tossed some garbage out the back of his Volkswagen bus down a Stockbridge hillside.

Indeed, Stockbridge is the stuff of story and legend. Travelers have been checking into the Red Lion Inn on Main Street since the 18th century, and Stockbridge remains only slightly altered in appearance since that time. In 18th- and 19th-century buildings surrounding the inn, you'll find a handful of engaging shops and eateries. The rest of Stockbridge is best appreciated via a country drive or bike ride over its hilly, narrow lanes.

WHAT TO SEE

Berkshire Botanical Gardens. This 15-acre garden contains perennial, rose, day lily, and herb gardens of both exotic and native plantings—some 2,500 varieties in all—plus greenhouses, ponds, and nature trails. ⊠*Hwys. 102 and 183, 2 mi east of downtown* ☎*413/298–3926* ⊕*www.berkshirebotanical.org* ☞*$7* ⊙*May–mid-Oct., daily 10–5.*

FodorŚChoice **Chesterwood.** For 33 years, this was the summer home of the sculptor
★ Daniel Chester French (1850–1931), who created *The Minuteman* in Concord and the Lincoln Memorial in Washington, D.C. Tours are given of the house, which is maintained in the style of the 1920s, and of the studio, where you can view the casts and models French used to create the Lincoln Memorial. The beautifully landscaped 122-acre grounds also make for an enchanting stroll. ⊠*4 Williamsville Rd. off Hwy. 183* ☎*413/298–3579* ⊕*www.chesterwood.org* ☞*$12* ⊙*Late May–mid-Oct., daily 10–5.*

★ **Naumkeag.** This Berkshire cottage once owned by Joseph Choate, a successful New York lawyer and an ambassador to Great Britain during the administration of President William McKinley, provides a glimpse into the gracious living of the gilded era of the Berkshires. The 26-room gabled mansion, designed by Stanford White in 1886, sits atop Prospect Hill. It is decorated with many original furnishings and art that spans three centuries; the collection of Chinese porcelain is also noteworthy. The meticulously kept 8 acres of formal gardens designed by Fletcher Steele are themselves worth a visit. ⊠ *5 Prospect Hill Rd.* ☎*413/298–3239* ⊕*www.thetrustees.org* ⊠*$10* ⊙*Memorial Day–Columbus Day, daily 10–5.*

Norman Rockwell Museum. This charming museum traces the career of one of America's most beloved illustrators, beginning with his first *Saturday Evening Post* cover in 1916. In addition to housing its collection of 570 Rockwell illustrations, the museum also mounts exhibits by other artists. Rockwell's studio was moved to the museum grounds and is complete in every detail. Stroll the 36-acre site, picnic on the grounds, or relax at the outdoor café (open from Memorial Day to Columbus Day.) A child's version of the audio tour ($5 adults/$4 children) with a scavenger-hunt theme makes this museum more fun for kids. There's also a kid's creativity room with storybooks and art materials. ⊠*Hwy. 183, 2 mi from Stockbridge* ☎*413/298–4100* ⊕*www.nrm. org* ⊠*$12.50* ⊙ *Weekdays 10–4, weekends 10–5.*

SHOPPING
The dynamic **Holsten Galleries** (⊠*3 Elm St.* ☎*413/298–3044*) shows the wares of top contemporary glass sculptors, including Dale Chihuly and Lino Tagliapietra. **Origins Gallery** (⊠*36 Main St.* ☎*413/298–0002*) is filled with colorful carved animals, baskets, stone sculpture from Zimbabwe, and other works from Africa.

WHERE TO EAT
$$-$$$
ECLECTIC

✕ **Once Upon a Table.** The atmosphere is casual yet vaguely romantic at this little restaurant-in-the-mews off Stockbridge's Main Street. The Continental and contemporary American cuisine includes seasonal dishes, with appetizers such as potpie of escargots, and entrées that include seared crab cakes with horseradish-cream sauce as well as rack of lamb with garlic-mashed potatoes. At lunch try the Caesar salad or the Reuben sandwich. ⊠*36 Main St.* ☎*413/298–3870* ♨*Reservations essential* ▤*AE, MC, V.*

$$-$$$
Fodor'sChoice
★
FRENCH

✕ **Rouge.** In West Stockbridge, 5 mi northwest of Stockbridge, this little house with its gray-green shingles, illuminated small red sign, and simple and comfortable interior, is reminiscent of a restaurant in the French countryside. Owner-chef William Merelle is indeed from Provence, where he met his American wife (and co-owner) Maggie, formerly a wine merchant. They ensure that the food, wine, and surroundings give pleasure. Try the steak au poivre with watercress, pommes frites, and cognac sauce or the lemon-crusted free-range chicken. ⊠*3 Center St., West Stockbridge* ☎*413/232–4111* ▤*AE, D, MC, V* ⊙*Closed Mon. and Tues. No lunch.*

CLOSE UP

Norman Rockwell: Illustrating America

I was showing the America I knew and observed to others who might not have noticed. My fundamental purpose is to interpret the typical American. I am a story teller.

—Norman Rockwell

If you've ever seen old copies of the *Saturday Evening Post*, no doubt you're familiar with American artist Norman Rockwell. He created 321 covers for the well-regarded magazine, and the *Post* always sold more copies when one of Rockwell's drawings was on the front page. The accomplished artist also illustrated Boy Scouts of America calendars, Christmas cards, children's books, and even a few stamps for the U.S. Postal Service—and in 1994, a stamp bearing his image came out in his honor. His illustrations tended to fit the theme of Americana, family, or patriotism.

Born in New York City in 1894, the talented designer had a knack for art early on, but strengthened his talent with instruction at the National Academy of Design and later Art Students League. He was only 22 when he sold his first cover to the *Post*. He was married three times and had three sons by his second wife. He died in

The Norman Rockwell Museum showcases more than 700 of the artist's works.

1978 in Stockbridge, Massachusetts, where he had lived since 1953.

Famous works include his *Triple Self Portrait* and the *Four Freedoms* illustrations done during World War II. They represent the freedom of speech, freedom to worship, freedom from want, and freedom from fear. In a poetic twist, decades later, in 1977, President Gerald R. Ford bestowed on Rockwell the Presidential Medal of Freedom, the highest civilian honor a U.S. citizen can be given. Ford praised Rockwell for his "vivid and affectionate portraits of our country."

—Debbie Harmsen

WHERE TO STAY

$$–$$$

Fodor's Choice
★

🏨 **Inn at Stockbridge.** Antiques and feather comforters are among the accents in the rooms of this 1906 Georgian-revival inn run by the attentive Alice and Len Schiller. The two serve breakfast in their elegant dining room, and every evening they provide wine and cheese. Each of the rooms in the adjacent "cottage" building has a decorative theme such as Kashmir, St. Andrews, or Provence; the junior suites in the barn building have Berkshire themes. The airy and posh rooms have CD players, and in some cases gas fireplaces, flat panel TVs, and whirlpool tubs. **Pros:** beautiful grounds; good breakfast; butler's pantry stocked with coffee, cookies, and pretzels. **Cons:** noise from MA turnpike (most noticeable in suites), not within walking distance to town. ⊠*30 East St.* ☎*413/298–3337 or 888/466–7865* ⊕*www.stockbridgeinn.com* ⇄*8 rooms, 8 suites* ⅙*In-room: DVD (some). In-hotel: pool, gym,* *no elevator, public Internet, no kids under age 12* ⊟*AE, D, MC, V* ‖◎‖*BP.*

$$-$$$$

Fodor'sChoice

★

☑**Red Lion Inn.** An inn since 1773, the bustling Red Lion has hosted presidents, near-presidents (Al Gore), senators, and celebrities. It consists of a large main building and eight annexes, each of which is different (one is a converted fire station). If you like historic buildings filled with antiques, request a room in the main building: many of these units are small, and the furnishings are a tad worn in places, but this is the authentic inn. If you want more space and more modern furnishings, request a room in one of the annex buildings. **Pros:** inviting lobby with fireplace, free Internet in library, quaintly romantic. **Cons:** overpriced dining room, fitness center is hard to reach and puny. ☒*30 Main St.* ☎*413/298-5545 or 413/298-1690* ⊕*www.redlioninn.com* ⇆*82 rooms, 71 with bath; 26 suites* ⟨√⟩*In-room: DVD (some). In-hotel: 3 restaurants, 2 bars, pool, hot tub, gym, public Internet* ⊟*AE, D, DC, MC, V* ‖◎‖*CP.*

GREAT BARRINGTON

7 mi southwest of Stockbridge; 13 mi north of Canaan, Connecticut.

The largest town in South County became, in 1781, the first place in the United States to free a slave under due process of law and was also the birthplace, in 1868, of W. E. B. DuBois, the civil rights leader, author, and educator. The many ex–New Yorkers who live in Great Barrington expect great food and service, and the restaurants here deliver complex, delicious fare. The town is also a favorite of antiques hunters, as are the nearby villages of South Egremont and Sheffield.

SPORTS & THE OUTDOORS

Bartholomew's Cobble. This natural rock garden beside the Housatonic River (the American Indian name means "river beyond the mountains") is filled with trees, ferns, wildflowers, and 5 mi of hiking trails. The 277-acre site has a visitor center and museum. ☒*Weatogue Rd., U.S. 7A* ☎*413/229-8600* ☒*$5* ⊙*Daily dawn–dusk.*

HIKING

A 90-mi swath of the Appalachian Trail cuts through the Berkshires. You'll also find hundreds of miles of trails elsewhere throughout the area's forests and parks. On Highway 23, about 4 mi east of where U.S. 7 and Highway 23 intersect, is a sign for the **Appalachian Trail** (⊕*www. nps.gov/appa*) and a parking lot. Enter the trail for a moderately strenuous 45-minute hike. A little way in, you will cross a stream. At the top of the trail is Ice Gulch, a gorge so deep and cold that there is often ice in it even in summer. Follow the Ice Gulch ridge to the shelter and a large flat rock from which you can see a wide panorama of the valley.

For great views with minimal effort, hike **Monument Mountain** (☎*413/298-3239* ⊕*www.thetrustees.org*), famous as a spot for literary inspiration. Nathaniel Hawthorne and Herman Melville trekked it on August 5, 1850, and sought shelter in a cave when a thunderstorm hit. In the cave, they discussed ideas that would become part of a novel called "Moby-Dick." While poet William Cullen Bryant stayed in the area, he penned a lyrical poem, "Monument Mountain," about a lovesick Mohican maiden who jumped to her death from the cliffs. Three miles of hiking trails, including an easy 2.5-mi loop, are reachable via a parking lot off U.S. 7, 4 mi north of Great Barrington.

SKI AREAS   With a 1,000-foot vertical drop, 100% snowmaking capacity, and slow and even grades, **Catamount Ski Area** (⊠*Hwy. 23, South Egremont* ☎*413/528–1262, 800/342–1840 snow conditions* ⊕*www. catamountski.com*) is ideal for family skiing. Nevertheless, the most varied terrain in the Berkshires is here, meaning that skiers of all abilities and tastes can find something to keep them happy. There are 28 trails, served by seven lifts, plus a snowboard area called Megaplex Terrain Park, which is separated from the downhill area and has its own lift and a 400-foot half pipe. The Sidewinder, an intermediate cruising trail, is more than 1 mi from top to bottom. There's also lighted nighttime boarding and skiing.

Ski Butternut (⊠*Hwy. 23* ☎*413/528–2000 Ext. 112, 413/528–4433 ski school, 800/438–7669 snow conditions* ⊕*www.skibutternut.com*) has good base facilities, pleasant skiing, 100% snowmaking capabilities, and the longest quad lift in the Berkshires. Two top-to-bottom terrain parks are for snowboarders, and Butternut Basin has 8 km (6 mi) of groomed cross-country trails. There are also five lanes of snow tubing. For downhill skiing, only a steep chute or two interrupt the mellow terrain on 22 trails, most of them intermediate. Eight lifts keep skier traffic spread out. Ski and snowboard lessons are available. In summer Butternut usually hosts a crafts show and children's activities. Call for details.

SHOPPING

ANTIQUES   The Great Barrington area, including the small towns of Sheffield and South Egremont, has the greatest concentration of antiques stores in the Berkshires. Some shops are open sporadically, and many are closed on Tuesday. At the **Great Barrington Antiques Center** (⊠*964 S. Main St., U.S. 7* ☎*413/644–8848*) 50 dealers crowd onto one floor, selling Oriental rugs, furniture, and smaller decorative pieces. At the **Country Dining Room** (⊠*178 Main St., U.S. 7* ☎*413/528–5050*) you can find elegant antique furniture, glass, and china. **Elise Abrams Antiques** (⊠*11 Stockbridge Rd., U.S. 7* ☎*413/528–3201*) sells fine antique china, glassware, and furniture. **Emporium Antique Center** (⊠*319 Main St., U.S. 7* ☎*413/528–1660*) specializes in art glass, sterling, and fine decorative arts.

FOOD &   Satisfy your sophisticated palate at **Bizalion** (⊠*684 Main St.*
COOKWARE   ☎*413/644–9988*), a French specialty food shop and café, where you can find imported cheeses, 10 different olive oils, cured meats, and brick-oven-baked baguettes and pastries. The **Chef Shop** (⊠*31 Railroad St.* ☎*413/528–0135*) is the place for cookware, bakeware, and much more.

NIGHTLIFE & THE ARTS

Club Helsinki (⊠*284 Main St.* ☎*413/528–3394*) draws some of the region's top jazz, blues, soul, and folk acts; it's open mike on Sunday. Catch a classic movie, or a performance by, perhaps, Suzanne Vega or the Berkshire Bach Society at **The Mahaiwe Performing Arts Center** (⊠ *14 Castle St.* ☎ *413/528–0100*). This stunning 1905 theater—one of the oldest in the country—offers a year-round schedule of live music, dance, and film.

WHERE TO EAT & STAY

$–$$
PIZZA

✕ **Baba Louie's Sourdough Pizza Co.** How good is the pizza at Baba Louie's? So good that, even in a restaurant-rich town like Great Barrington, crowds spill into the sidewalk waiting for a table. At 2 PM. In the off season. Could be the wonderful chewy crunchy crusts made of organically-grown wheat and spelt berries (just in case you need to feel virtuous about eating pizza). Could be the inspired toppings, like wilted spinach, figs, prosciutto, and Parmesan (on the Dolce Vita) and roasted sweet potatoes and parsnips, shaved fennel, caramelized onions, and fresh mozzarella with a hint of balsamic vinegar (on the Isabella Pizzarella). Whatever. The wait for the table is so worth it. ⊠ *286 Main St.* ☎ *413/528–8100* ▭ *AE, MC, V.*

$$–$$$
★
CAFE

✕ **Castle Steet Café.** Chef-owner Michael Ballon wins raves for his simple but elegant cuisine and masterful hand with fresh local produce. Local artwork, hardwood floors and sleek furnishings create an understated interior—a perfect backdrop for sautéed sea scallops with wild ramps and garlic sauce, local shad roe with bacon and onion, and warm duck salad with cashews and Asian slaw. Other things to love about Castle Street Café: The fabulous wine list, the bread basket (featuring a warm potato-onion loaf from Berkshire Mountain Bakery), and nightly jazz at the Celestial Bar (no cover charge). ⊠ *10 Castle St.* ☎ *413/528–5244* ▭ *AE, MC, V* ☉ *Closed Tues.*

$$$–$$$$
STEAKHOUSE

✕ **Pearl's.** Run by the same owners as Lenox's trendy Bistro Zinc, Pearl's adds a dash of big-city atmosphere to the Berkshires with its pressed-tin ceilings, tall booths, exposed-brick walls, and well-coiffed crowd. The menu updates the old bigger-is-better steak-house tradition by serving thick-and-tender chops, prime rib, wild game, raw oysters, and fresh lobsters with innovative ingredients. Call ahead for a table on weekends, or simply hobnob and sip well-chosen wines and creative drinks at the elegant bar. ⊠ *47 Railroad St.* ☎ *413/528–7767* ▭ *AE, MC, V* ☉ *No lunch.*

WHERE TO STAY

$–$$$

🏠 **Egremont Inn.** The public rooms in this 1780 stagecoach inn are enormous and each has a fireplace. Bedrooms are on the small side but have four-poster beds (some have claw-foot baths) and, like the rest of the inn, unpretentious furnishings. On weekends in July and August you can book only two-night packages, which include breakfast daily and one dinner during your stay. **Pro:** good food in on-site restaurant. **Cons:** small, rustic bathrooms; some signs of age throughout. ⊠ *10 Old Sheffield Rd., South Egremont,* ☎ *413/528–2111 or 800/859–1780* ⊕ *www.egremontinn.com* ⇆ *22 rooms, 1 suite* ♿ *In-room: no phone, no TV. In-hotel: restaurant, bar, tennis court, pool, no elevator* ▭ *AE, D, MC, V* ◎ *CP, MAP.*

MASSACHUSETTS ESSENTIALS

Research prices, get travel advice, and book your trip at fodors.com.

TRANSPORTATION

BY AIR

Boston's Logan International Airport (BOS) is also the gateway to Cape Cod. Smaller Cape Cod airports include the Barnstable (HYA), in Hyannis, and Provincetown (PVC) municipal airports. Bradley International Airport in Windsor Locks, Connecticut, 18 mi south of Springfield on Interstate 91, serves the Pioneer Valley.

Airport Information Barnstable Municipal Airport (☎ *508/775-2020* ⊕ *www.town.barnstable.ma.us*). **Bradley International Airport** (☎ *860/292-2000* ⊕ *www.bradleyairport.com*). **Logan International** (☎ *617/561-1800, 800/235-6426 24-hr information* ⊕ *www.massport.com* Ⓜ *Airport*). **Martha's Vineyard Airport** (☎ *508/693-7022*). **Nantucket Memorial Airport** (☎ *508/325-5300*). **Provincetown Airport** (☎ *508/487-0241*).

BY BOAT & FERRY

Bay State Cruise Company offers both standard and high-speed ferry service between Commonwealth Pier in Boston and MacMillan Wharf in Provincetown on Cape Cod. High-speed service runs a few times daily from mid-May through September (with a few additional weekend runs through mid-October) and costs $69 round trip; the ride takes 90 minutes. Standard service runs weekends from late June through early September and costs $33 round trip; the ride takes three hours.

The Steamship Authority runs the only car ferries to Martha's Vineyard, which make the 45-minute trip from Woods Hole on Cape Cod to Vineyard Haven year-round and to Oak Bluffs from late May through mid-October. In summer and on autumn weekends, you must have a reservation if you want to bring your car (passenger reservations are never necessary). One-way passenger fare year-round is $7; bicycles are $3. The cost for a car traveling one-way in season (April–October) is $65 (not including passengers), $40 off-season.

The Island Queen makes the 35-minute trip from Falmouth Harbor to Oak Bluffs from late May through early October. The round-trip fare is $15. Only cash and traveler's checks are accepted for payment.

The Vineyard Fast Ferry offers high-speed passenger service from North Kingstown, Rhode Island (a half-hour south of Providence and a half-hour northwest of Newport) to Martha's Vineyard. The ride takes 90 minutes, making this a great option for those flying in to T.F. Green Airport, just south of Providence. Service is from late May through early October and costs $46 each way.

Ferries run from Falmouth Harbor to Oak Bluffs from late May through early October. Round-trip fare is $15. Only cash and traveler's checks are accepted for payment.

Hy-Line offers both high-speed and conventional ferry service to Martha's Vineyard from Hyannis. The conventional ferries offer a 95-minute run from Hyannis to Oak Bluffs early May to late October. One-way fare is $18.50. The high-speed runs from from late May through late November, takes 55 minutes, and costs $31.50. ■TIP→ The parking lot fills up in summer, so call to reserve a parking space in high season. From June to mid-September, Hy-Line's Around the Sound cruise makes a one-day round-trip from Hyannis with stops at Nantucket and Martha's Vineyard ($73.50).

The New England Fast Ferry Company makes the hour-long trip by high-speed catamaran from New Bedford to Oak Bluffs and Vineyard Haven from mid-May to mid-October, several times daily. One-way is $29.

The Steamship Authority runs car-and-passenger ferries to Nantucket from Hyannis year-round, a 2¼-hour trip. There's also high-speed passenger ferry service, which takes only an hour, from late March through late December. Note that there are no standby car reservations on ferries to Nantucket. One-way passenger fare is $15. Cost for a car traveling one-way April through October is $180 November through April, $120. One-way high-speed passenger ferry fare is $29.50.

Hy-Line's high-end, high-speed Grey Lady ferries run between Hyannis and Nantucket year-round in an hour. One-way fare is $38. Hy-Line's slower ferry makes the roughly two-hour trip from Hyannis between early May and late October. The MV Great Point offers a first-class section ($24.50 one-way) with a private lounge and a bar. Standard one-way fare is $18.50.

From Harwich Port, the Freedom Cruise Line runs express high-speed 75-minute ferries to Nantucket between late May and early October. Round-trip fare is $57 ($38 one-way).

Cape Cod Boat & Ferry Lines **Bay State Cruise Company** (☎617/748–1428 ⊕ www.baystatecruisecompany.com).

Martha's Vineyard & Nantucket Boat & Ferry Lines **Freedom Cruise Line** (✉ Saquatucket Harbor, Harwich Port ☎508/432–8999 ⊕ www.nantucketislandferry.com). **Hy-Line** (✉ Ocean St. dock ☎508/778–2600 or 800/492–8082 ⊕ www.hy-linecruises.com). **Island Queen** (✉ Falmouth Harbor ☎508/548–4800 ⊕ www.islandqueen.com). **New England Fast Ferry** (✉ State Pier Ferry Terminal ☎866/683–3779 ⊕ www.nefastferry.com). **Steamship Authority** (☎508/477–8600, 508/693–9130 on the Vineyard, 508/495–3278 on Nantucket ⊕ www.steamshipauthority.com). **Vineyard Fast Ferry** (✉ Quonset Point, North Kingstown, RI ☎401/295–4040 ⊕ www.vineyardfastferry.com).

BY BUS

Besides various regional bus companies, Massachusetts is served by national carriers Greyhound and Peter Pan, which links most major Northeast cities with Pioneer Valley and Berkshire towns and provides transportation to Bradley and Logan airports. Pioneer Valley Transit Authority provides service in 24 communities. The Massachusetts Bay Transportation Authority, or MBTA, operates bus service in the greater

Boston area (such as to Plymouth, Lowell, Concord, New Bedford, Marblehead, Salem).

The Cape Ann Transportation Authority, or CATA, provides local bus service in the Gloucester, Rockport, and Essex regions (North Shore). The Coach Company bus line runs a commuter bus between Newburyport and Boston on weekdays. The Cape Cod Regional Transit Authority operates several bus services. All buses are wheelchair accessible and equipped with bike racks.

Martha's Vineyard Transit Authority (VTA) provide regular bus service to all six towns on the island, with frequent stops in peak season and very limited service in winter.

The Nantucket Regional Transit Authority (NRTA) runs shuttle buses in town and to Madaket, mid-island areas (including the airport and Surfside Beach), and 'Sconset. Service is available May to late September.

Bus Information Berkshire Regional Transit Authority (☎ *413/499-2782 or 800/292-2782* ⊕ *www.berkshirerta.com*). **Cape Ann Transportation Authority** (☎ *978/283-7278* ⊕ *www.canntran.com*). **Cape Cod Regional Transit Authority** (☎ *508/790-2613 or 800/352-7155* ⊕ *www.capecodtransit.org*). **Coach Company** (☎ *800/874-3377* ⊕ *www.coachco.com*). **Greyhound** (☎ *800/231-2222* ⊕ *www. greyhound.com*). **MBTA** (☎ *617/222-3200 or 800/392-6100* ⊕ *www.mbta.com*). **Martha's Vineyard Transit Authority VTA** (☎ *508/693-9940* ⊕ *www.vineyard transit.com*). **Nantucket Regional Transit Authority (NRTA)** (✉ *22 Federal St.* ☎ *508/228-7025* ⊕ *www.shuttlenantucket.com*). **Peter Pan** (☎ *413/781-2900 or 800/237-8747* ⊕ *www.peterpanbus.com*). **Pioneer Valley Transit Authority** (☎ *413/781-7882* ⊕ *www.pvta.com*). **Plymouth & Brockton** (☎ *508/746-0378* ⊕ *www.p-b.com*).

BY CAR

Boston is the traffic hub of New England, with interstate highways approaching it from every direction. New England's chief coastal highway, Interstate 95, skirts Boston; Interstate 90 (the Massachusetts Turnpike) leads west to the Berkshires. The main north–south road within the Berkshires is U.S. 7. Highway 2 runs from the northern Berkshires to Greenfield at the head of the Pioneer Valley and continues across Massachusetts into Boston. The scenic section of Highway 2 known as the Mohawk Trail runs from Williamstown to Orange. Interstate 91 runs north–south in the Pioneer Valley in western Massachusetts.

The primary link between Boston and the North Shore is Route 128, which splits off from Interstate 95 and follows the coast northeast to Gloucester. To pick up Route 128 from Boston, take Interstate 93 north to Interstate 95 north to Route 128.

From Boston to Salem or Marblehead, follow Route 128 to Route 114 into Salem and on to Marblehead. This route is confusing and poorly marked, particularly returning to Route 128. An alternative route to Marblehead: follow Route 1A north, and then pick up Route 129 north along the shore through Swampscott and into Marblehead.

To reach Cape Cod from Boston (60 mi), take Route Interstate 93 south, then Route 3 south, and cross the Sagamore Bridge, which puts you onto U.S. 6, the Cape's main artery. From western Massachusetts, northern Connecticut, and upstate New York, take Interstate 84 east to the Massachusetts Turnpike (Interstate 90) and take Interstate 495 south to the Bourne Bridge. From New York City and southern Connecticut and Rhode Island, take Interstate 95 north toward Providence, where you pick up Interstate 195 east (toward Fall River–New Bedford) to Route 25 east to the Bourne Bridge. From the Bourne Bridge you can take Route 28 south to Falmouth and Woods Hole (about 15 mi), or—as you approach the Bourne Bridge—follow signs to U.S. 6 if you're headed elsewhere on the Cape. ■TIP➔ On summer weekends, when more than 100,000 cars a day cross each bridge, make every effort to avoid arriving in late afternoon, especially on holidays.

Ferrying a car to Martha's Vineyard in summer requires reservations far in advance, costs almost double what it does in the off-season, and necessitates standing in long lines—it's sometimes easier and more economical to rent a car once you're on the island, and then only for the days when you plan to explore.

The Steamship Authority runs car-and-passenger ferries from Hyannis to Nantucket year-round. There are no standby car reservations on ferries. The cost for a car traveling one-way April through October is $180; November through April, $120.

BY TRAIN & TRANSIT
The Northeast Corridor and high-speed Acela services of Amtrak link Boston with the principal cities between it and Washington, D.C. Amtrak's Lake Shore Limited, which stops at Springfield and Pittsfield in the Berkshires, carries passengers from Chicago to Boston.

For destinations north and west of Boston, trains depart from Boston's North Station, while trains to Plymouth depart from South Station. Concord is a 40-minute ride on the Fitchburg Line. Lowell is a 45-minute ride on the Lowell Line—catch a Lowell Regional Transit Authority bus from the station.

You can take MBTA's Newburyport/Rockport commuter rail line from Boston's North Station to Salem (25–30 minutes), Gloucester (55–60 minutes), Rockport (70–75 minutes), Ipswich (50–55 minutes), and Newburyport (60–65 minutes). The stations at Salem, Gloucester, Rockport, and Ipswich are within about one-half mile of the towns' historic sights. From the Newburyport station to downtown (about 1 mi), take the Merrimack Valley Regional Transit Authority Bus 51, but note that there's no Sunday service.

Train Information Amtrak (☎800/872-7245 ⊕www.amtrak.com). **Lowell Regional Transit Authority** (✉145 Thorndike St., Lowell ☎978/452-6161 ⊕www.lrta.com). **MBTA** (☎617/222-3200 or 800/392-6100, 617/222-5146 TTY ⊕www.mbta.com).

CONTACTS & RESOURCES

BOATING With numerous lakes, rivers, and ponds throughout western Massachusetts, the region is rife with opportunities for sailing, canoeing, kayaking, rafting, and boating. For more information, contact **Mass Outdoors** (☎*617/626–1600* ⊕*www. sport.state.ma.us*).

FISHING For information about fishing and licenses, call the **Massachusetts Division of Fisheries & Wildlife** (☎*617/626–1600* ⊕*www.mass.gov*).

VISITOR INFORMATION

State Information Massachusetts Office of Travel & Tourism (✉*10 Park Plaza, Suite 4510, Boston* ☎*617/973–8500, 800/447–6277* brochures ⊕*www. massvacation.com*).

Cape Cod, Martha's Vineyard, & Nantucket Contacts Cape Cod Chamber of Commerce (✉*Junction of Rtes. 6 and 132, Hyannis* ☎*508/862–0700 or 888/332–2732* ⊕*www.capecodchamber.org*). **Martha's Vineyard Chamber of Commerce** (✉*Beach Rd., Vineyard Haven* ☎*508/693–4486 or 800/505–4815* ⊕*www.mvy.com*). **Nantucket Visitor Services and Information Bureau** (✉*25 Federal St.* ☎*508/228–0925*).

Northwest & South of Boston Contacts Concord Visitor Center (✉*58 Main St., Concord* ☎*978/369–3120*). **Lexington Visitor Center** (✉*1875 Massachusetts Ave., Lexington* ☎*781/862–1450* ⊕*www.lexingtonchamber.org*). **Plymouth Visitor Information Center** (✉*170 Water St., at Hwy. 44, Plymouth* ☎*508/747–7533 or 800/872–1620* ⊕*www.visit-plymouth.com*).

North Shore Contacts Cape Ann Chamber of Commerce (✉*33 Commercial St., Gloucester* ☎*978/283–1601* ⊕*www.capeannvacations.com*). **Destination Salem** (✉*54 Turner St., Salem* ☎*978/741–3252 or 877/725–3662* ⊕*www. salem.org*). **Marblehead Chamber of Commerce Information Booth** (✉*Corner of Pleasant and Spring Sts., Box 76, Marblehead* ☎*781/639–8469* ⊕*www.visit-marblehead.com*). **Rockport Chamber of Commerce** (✉*22 Broadway, Rockport* ☎*978/546–6575* ⊕*www.rockportusa.com*).

Pioneer Valley & Berkshires Contacts Amherst Area Chamber of Commerce (✉*409 Main St., Amherst* ☎*413/253–0700* ⊕*www.amherstarea.com*). **Berkshires Visitors Bureau** (✉*3 Hoosac St., Adams* ☎*413/743–4500 or 800/237–5747* ⊕*www.berkshires.org*). **Greater Springfield Convention & Visitors Bureau** (✉*1441 Main St., Springfield* ☎*413/787–1548 or 800/723–1548* ⊕*www. valleyvisitor.com*). **Stockbridge Chamber of Commerce** (✉*Elm St., Stockbridge* ☎*413/298–5200 or 866/626–5327* ⊕*www.stockbridgechamber.org*). **Sturbridge Area Tourist Association** (✉*380 Main St., Sturbridge* ☎*888/788–7274 or 800/628–8379* ⊕*www.sturbridge.org*).

Rhode Island

WORD OF MOUTH

"Rhode Island is tiny and there is a reason they call it the Ocean State. Practically every town is "coastal" or within very easy reach of the coast, with the exception of industrialized Woonsocket, and even that isn't very far away."

—cherylli

By Andrew
Collins

RHODE ISLAND, THE SMALLEST STATE in the nation—just 1,500 square mi (500 of that being water)—can be an enthralling destination. A Rhode Island getaway can encompass historic tours, visits to galleries, and fine dining in Providence; apple picking and canal boat rides in the Blackstone Valley; boating and beaching in South County or Block Island; biking in East Bay; and sunset sails and gilded-age mansions in Newport. Packed with American history, the state holds 20% of the country's National Historic Landmarks and has more restored Colonial and Victorian buildings than anywhere else in the United States.

In May 1776, before the Declaration of Independence was issued, Rhode Island and Providence Plantations—the state's official name to this day—passed an act removing the king's name from all state documents. This action was typical of the independent-thinking colony, which had been founded on principles of religious tolerance and attracted Baptists, Jews, Quakers, and others seeking refuge throughout the 17th and 18th centuries. The first public school was established in forward-thinking Newport in 1664. (Rhode Island continues to be a force in education, with 70,000 students at the state's 10 colleges and universities.) In the 19th century, the state flourished as its entrepreneurial leaders constructed some of the nation's earliest textile mills, silver foundries, and jewelry companies. Industry attracted workers from French Canada, Italy, Ireland, England, Portugal, and Eastern Europe, descendants of whom have retained much of their heritage in numerous ethnic enclaves across the state.

Rhode Island does have some less-attractive elements: crowded state highways, especially around Providence, and, in certain areas, sprawling commercial development. But as tourism has become one of the state's biggest moneymakers, a more thoughtful approach to development seems to be the norm. Neighborhoods, remote villages, and even rough-hewn cities like Pawtucket and Woonsocket are now constructing bike paths, historic walkways, and visitor centers. The capital, Providence, is being aggressively reshaped by its leaders.

Rhode Island's 39 towns and cities—none more than 50 mi apart—all hold architectural gems and historic sights. Natural attractions, inspired culinary artistry, and fine accommodations complement the mix. With so much to see in such a compact space, it's easy to explore the Rhode Island that fits your interests.

EXPLORING RHODE ISLAND

The Blackstone Valley region and the capital city of Providence compose the northern portion of Rhode Island. South County to the west and Newport County to the east make up the southern portion of the state. The museums and country roads of the Blackstone Valley make it a good family destination; Providence has history, great food, and intellectual and cultural vitality. Both southerly regions have beaches, boating, and historical sights, with Newport being more historically significant, more upscale, and more crowded.

RHODE ISLAND TOP 5

■ **Famous Mansions:** It may be a slight cliché, but you simply can't gain a sense of Newport's Gilded Age mansion without taking a tour of the singularly immense and ornate Breakers mansion, built for Cornelius Vanderbilt and containing some 70 rooms.

■ **Most Historic Street:** On Providence's East Side, in the shadows of Brown University, ornate Colonial homes built by the leading merchants of the day line Benefit Street.

■ **Communing with Nature:** Block Island is one of the most tranquil, serene spots on the Eastern Seaboard, and you can truly unwind and enjoy the flora and fauna with a hike into Rodman's Hollow, a glacial outwash basin laced with winding paths that lead to the sea.

■ **A Spectacular Stretch of Sand:** South County is rife with sugary, white beaches, with Scarborough State Beach offering the best stretch to spread a blanket, soak up the rays, and admire the ocean.

■ **Excellent Food Enclave:** You could eat lunch and dinner at a different restaurant in the Little Italy area of Providence's Federal Hill neighborhood and never run out of memorable dining options—it's better than Boston's or New York City's.

WHAT IT COSTS					
	¢	$	$$	$$$	$$$$
RESTAURANTS	under $8	$8–$15	$15–$22	$22–$30	over $30
HOTELS	under $80	$80–$120	$121–$170	$171–$220	over $220

For restaurants, prices are per person, for a main course at dinner. For hotels, prices are for two people in a standard double room in high season, excluding tax and service charges.

ABOUT THE RESTAURANTS

Rhode Island has been winning national accolades for its restaurants, which serve cuisine from every part of the world. You can still find regional fare such as johnnycakes, a corn cake–like affair cooked on a griddle, and the native clam, the quahog (pronounced "*ko*-hog"), which is served stuffed, fried, and in chowder. "Shore dinners" consist of clam chowder, steamed soft-shell clams, clam cakes, sausage, corn-on-the-cob, lobster, watermelon, and Indian pudding (a steamed pudding made with cornmeal and molasses). Providence's Federal Hill neighborhood holds superlative Italian restaurants, and dozens of other restaurants in the city rival many of Boston's finest eateries.

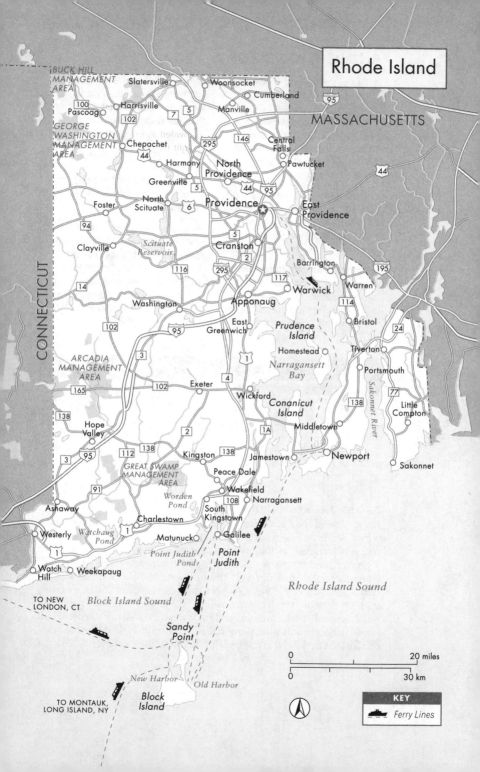

PLANNING YOUR TRIP

BUDGETING YOUR TIME

By car it's less than an hour from any one place in Rhode Island to another. Though the distances are short, the state is densely populated, and getting around its cities and towns can be confusing; it's best to map out your route in advance. In five days, you can visit all four regions of the state, as well as Block Island. On a shorter visit of several days, you can still take in two regions, such as Providence and Newport. Most of the sights in Providence can be seen in one day. The Blackstone Valley will also occupy one day, though you'll want to spend longer in fall foliage season. Newport has many facets and will require two busy days. South County, with its superb beaches, is generally a relaxing two-day destination.

WHEN TO GO

The best time to visit Rhode Island is between May and October. Newport hosts several high-profile music festivals in summer; Providence is at its prettiest; and Block Island and the beach towns of South County are in full swing (though not nearly as crowded as Newport). Because of the light traffic and the often gorgeous weather, October is a great time to come to Rhode Island. The colorful fall foliage of the Blackstone Valley is as bright and varied as any in New England.

GETTING THERE & AROUND

Rhode Island is best reached by car via Interstate 95, coastal New England's main interstate, which connects to both Boston and New York, or by air via T. F. Green Airport, which is served by the majority of the nation's air carriers. Boston's Logan Airport is only an hour away, too. Once you're here, a car is your best way to get around the state, although it's quite practical to explore Providence and Newport on foot and using public transportation.

ABOUT THE HOTELS

The major chain hotels are represented in Rhode Island, but the state's many smaller bed-and-breakfasts and other inns provide a more down-home experience. Rates are very much seasonal; in Newport, for example, winter rates are often half those of summer. Many inns in coastal towns are closed in winter.

PROVIDENCE

New England's second-largest city (with a population of 175,000, behind Boston) comes into the 21st century as a renaissance city. Once regarded, even by its own residents, as an awkward stepchild of greater Boston (50 mi to the north), Providence has metamorphosed from an area that empties out at the end of a workday to a clean, modern, cultural and gastronomical hub. In the past decade, stretches of river downtown that had been paved over in the mid-1900s were uncovered and rerouted, and parks were built along the banks. Railroad tracks moved underground, and money was spent on transportation improvements. Dilapidated neighborhoods began to perk up, and luxury apartments and artists' lofts started sprouting downtown.

The focal point of this new Providence is Waterplace Park, a series of footbridges, walkways, and green spaces running along both sides of the Providence River, which flows through the heart of downtown. Within walking distance of the park are a convention center and several hotels, a large outdoor ice skating rink, and a glittering, upscale shopping center called Providence Place.

Providence's renaissance isn't all looks. Besides the glitzy new apartment buildings, the shopping center, and hotels and parks, the city has cultivated a more worldly, sophisticated spirit. As a result, it has, in recent years, hosted the National Governors Conference, the annual meeting of the International Association of Culinary Professionals, and the NCAA hockey finals. Time spent courting Hollywood deal makers has resulted in a string of movies filmed in the city, including *Federal Hill* and *Outside Providence,* as well as NBC's show *Providence.* With dozens of outstanding restaurants, Providence—home to the Johnson & Wales University Culinary Institute—legitimately lays claim to being one of the nation's best places to eat.

Roger Williams founded Providence in 1636 as a refuge for freethinkers and religious dissenters escaping the dictates of the Puritans of Massachusetts Bay Colony. The city still embraces independent thinking in business, the arts, and academia. Brown University, the Rhode Island School of Design (RISD), and Tony award–winning Trinity Repertory Company are major forces in New England's intellectual and cultural life. Playing to that strength, Providence is striving to populate its once-abandoned downtown (now called Downcity, to erase the connotations of the old downtown) with artists and their studios.

The narrow Providence River cuts through the city north to south. West of the river lies the compact business district. An Italian neighborhood, Federal Hill, pushes west from here along Atwells Avenue. To the north you'll see the white-marble capitol. South Main and Benefit streets run parallel to the river, on the East Side. College Hill constitutes the western half of the East Side. At the top of College Hill, the area's primary thoroughfare, Thayer Street, runs north to south. Don't confuse East Providence, a city unto itself, with Providence's East Side.

WHAT TO SEE

❸ **Benefit Street.** The centerpiece of any visit to Providence is the "mile
FodorsChoice of History," where a cobblestone sidewalk passes a row of 18th- and
★ early-19th-century candy-color houses crammed shoulder-to-shoulder on a steep hill overlooking downtown. Romantic Benefit Street, with one of the nation's highest concentrations of Colonial architecture, is a reminder of the wealth brought to Rhode Island through the triangular trade of slaves, rum, and molasses. The **Providence Preservation Society** (⌧*21 Meeting St., at Benefit St., East Side* ☎*401/831–7440* ⊕*www. ppsri.org*) distributes maps and pamphlets with self-guided tours. The **Rhode Island Historical Society** (☎*401/438–0463* ⊕*www.rihs.org*) conducts summer (mid-June–mid-Oct.) walks on Benefit Street. The 90-

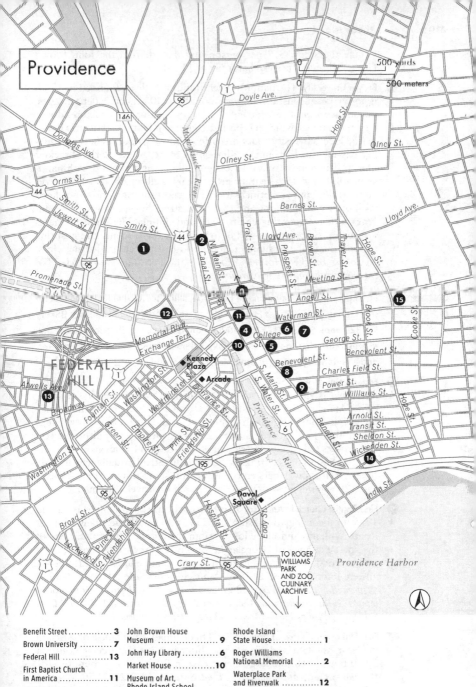

Providence

minute tours cost $12 per person and depart from the John Brown House Museum Tuesday–Saturday at 11 AM.

❼ Brown University. The nation's seventh-oldest college, founded in 1764, is an Ivy League institution with more than 40 academic departments, including a school of medicine. Gothic and beaux arts structures dominate the campus, which has been designated a National Historic Landmark. Free university tours are offered most weekdays several times per day and leave from the admissions office, in the Corliss-Brackett House. The university is on College Hill, a neighborhood with handsome 18th- and 19th-century architecture well worth a stroll. Thayer Street is the campus's principal commercial thoroughfare—once lined with offbeat indie shops and cafés, the street has given way in recent years to less interesting chain retail and dining. The imposing gates are opened twice a year—in fall to welcome the students and in spring to bid adieu for the summer and good-bye to the graduating class. ✉ *Corliss-Brackett House, 45 Prospect St., East Side* ☎ *401/863–2378 tour information* ⊕ *www.brown.edu.*

> ▌**NEED A BREAK?**
>
> For memorable snacking on the East Side, skip the ho-hum fast-food restaurants along Thayer Street and venture up Hope Street to Seven Stars Bakery (✉ *820 Hope St.* ☎ *401/521–2200*), a convivial spot for first-rate coffee and espresso drinks, sandwiches on flaky kalamata-olive bread and baguettes, and a tantalizing variety of brownies, cookies, and sweets.

⓭ Federal Hill. ★ You're as likely to hear Italian as English in this neighborhood that is vital to Providence's culture and sense of self. The stripe down Atwells Avenue is painted in red, white, and green, and a huge *pigna* (pinecone), an Italian symbol of abundance and quality, hangs on an arch soaring over the street. Hardware shops sell boccie sets and grocers sell pastas, pastries, and hard-to-find Italian groceries. The neighborhood shines during the Federal Hill Stroll (usually held in early June) when festivalgoers enjoy music and sample signature cuisine at some 20 eateries all within a ¾-mi stretch of Atwells Avenue.

⓫ First Baptist Church in America. ★ This historic house of worship was built in 1775 for a congregation established in 1638 by Rhode Island founder Roger Williams and his fellow Puritan dissenters. The church, one of the finest examples of Georgian architecture in the United States, has a carved wood interior, a Waterford crystal chandelier, and graceful but austere Ionic columns. ✉ *75 N. Main St., East Side* ☎ *401/454–3418* ⊕ *www.fbcia.org* ✉ *Free, $2 guided tours, $1 self-guided tour booklets* ⊙ *Guided tours June–Oct., weekdays 10–noon and 1–3, Sat. 10–1. Self-guided tours Nov.–May, weekdays 10–noon and 1–3.*

❽ First Unitarian Church of Providence. This Romanesque house of worship made of Rhode Island granite was built in 1816. Its steeple houses a 2,500-pound bell, the largest ever cast in Paul Revere's foundry. ✉ *1 Benevolent St., at Benefit St., East Side* ☎ *401/421–7970* ⊕ *www. firstunitarianprov.org* ✉ *Free* ⊙ *Guided tours by appointment.*

⑮ Governor Henry Lippit House Museum. The two-term Rhode Island governor made his fortune selling textiles to both armies during the Civil War, and he spared no expense in building his home, an immaculate Renaissance Revival mansion, in 1863. The floor of the billiard room uses nine types of inlaid wood; the ceilings are intricately hand-painted (some look convincingly like tiger maple), and the neoclassical chandeliers are cast in bronze. The home was fitted with central heating and electricity, quite an extravagance at the time. ⊠ *199 Hope St., East Side* ☏ *401/453–0688* ⊕ *www.preserveri.org* ⊡ *$5* ⊗ *By appointment.*

③

⑨ John Brown House Museum. The four Brown brothers—John, Joseph,
★ Moses, and Nicholas—were prominent Providence merchants who made a fortune trading with the West Indies, Europe, and, later, China. This three-story Georgian mansion, designed for John by his brother Joseph in 1786, has elaborate woodwork and is filled with furniture, decorative art, silver, and items from the China trade. John Brown was a patriot, famous for his role in the burning of the British customs ship *Gaspee* in 1772. He was also a slave trader: in fact, his abolitionist brother Moses brought charges against him for illegally engaging in the buying and selling of human lives. Despite his fame, it is not John who is remembered in Brown University, but his nephew, Nicholas Jr., whose gift to Rhode Island College in 1804 prompted it to change its name. Across the street and open Friday 1–4 is Nightingale House, built by a Brown business rival. ⊠ *52 Power St., East Side* ☏ *401/331–8575 or 401/273–7507* ⊕ *www.rihs.org* ⊡ *$8* ⊗ *Apr.–Dec., Tues.–Sat. 10–5; Jan.–Mar., Fri and Sat. 10–4.*

⑥ John Hay Library. Built in 1910 and named for Abraham Lincoln's secretary, the "Hay" houses 11,000 items related to the 16th president. The noncirculating research library, part of ⇨ **Brown University,** also stores American drama and poetry collections, 500,000 pieces of American sheet music, the Webster Knight Stamp Collection, the letters of horror and science-fiction writer H. P. Lovecraft, military prints, and a world-class collection of toy soldiers. ⊠ *20 Prospect St., East Side* ☏ *401/863–2146* ⊡ *Free* ⊗ *Sept.–May, weekdays 9–6, Sun. 1–5; June–Aug., limited hours (call first).*

⑩ Market House. Though this building is not open to the public, it is a historically significant site. Designed by Joseph Brown, this brick structure was central to Colonial Providence's trading economy. Tea was burned here in March 1775, and the upper floors were used as barracks for French soldiers during the Revolutionary War. From 1832 to 1878, Market House served as the seat of city government. A plaque shows the height reached by floodwaters during the Great Hurricane of 1938. ⊠ *Market Sq. and S. Main St., Downtown.*

⟲ **④ Museum of Art, Rhode Island School of Design.** This superb museum is
Fodor'sChoice a multilevel complex housing paintings, sculptures, prints, drawings,
★ photographs, textiles, and decorative arts—80,000 works are in frequent rotation. A 43,000-square-foot expansion is slated for completion in September 2008—the five-story Chace Center, which will be connected to the original 1926 museum building via a glass bridge,

will add exhibit space, a new auditorium, and additional studios and classrooms. The museum's permanent holdings include the Aldrich collection of Japanese prints, Gorham silver, American furniture, Latin American art, and French Impressionist paintings including works by Monet, Manet, Degas, and Renoir. Also here are galleries filled with Greco-Roman, Egyptian, Asian, and Islamic art, as well as European and American art from the Middle Ages through the 20th century. Keep an eye out for purposeful juxtapositioning: a 19th-century bronze bust of an African woman is displayed in a gallery dominated by a formal family portrait of the Napoleonic era; a machine-age painting of flowers flanks a window to the museum's garden courtyard; an early Gauguin landscape hangs beside a Pissarro painted at the same site. Since this is a university museum, exhibits may include demonstration videos, or unfinished works by masters such as Cassatt and Cézanne. The Egyptian mummy, which dates from 300 BC, is popular with children. The latest addition to the permanent collection is a new exhibit on RISD alum and famed glassblower Dale Chihuly. Admission includes the adjoining **Pendleton House,** a replica of an early-19th-century Providence house. ⊠ *224 Benefit St., East Side* ☎ *401/454–6500* ⊕ *www.risdmuseum.org* ▨ *$8, free Sun. 10–1 and Fri. noon–1:30* ⊙ *Tues.–Sun. 10–5.*

> **PROVIDENCE TOURS**
>
> ■ The **Providence Preservation Society** (☎ *401/831–7440* ⊕ *www.ppsri.org*) publishes the *PPS/AIAri Guide to Providence Architecture,* which describes a dozen walking tours of the city.
>
> ■ From May through October, **Conway Tours/Grayline Rhode Island** (☎ *401/658–3400* ⊕ *www.conwaytours.com*) runs a hop-on, hop-off 90-minute Historic Providence bus tour. Its a great way to learn the lay of the land.

⑤ ★ Providence Athenaeum. Established in 1753 and housed in a Greek-revival structure of 1838, this is among the oldest lending libraries in the world. The Athenaeum was the center of the intellectual life of old Providence. Here Edgar Allan Poe, visiting Providence to lecture at Brown, met and courted Sarah Helen Whitman, who was said to be the inspiration for his poem "Annabel Lee." The library holds Rhode Island art and artifacts, an original set of *Birds of America* prints by John J. Audubon, and one of the world's best collections of travel literature. Changing exhibits showcase parts of the collection. ⊠ *251 Benefit St., East Side* ☎ *401/421–6970* ⊕ *www.providenceathenaeum.org* ▨ *Free* ⊙ *June–Aug., Mon.–Thurs. 9–7, Fri. 9–5, Sat. 9–1; Sept.–May, Mon.–Thurs. 9–7, Fri. and Sat. 9–5, Sun. 1–5.*

❶ Rhode Island State House. Designed by the noted firm of McKim, Mead & White and erected in 1900, Rhode Island's capitol has an ornate white Georgia marble exterior and the fourth largest self-supporting dome in the world. The gilded statue that tops the dome, representing the Independent Man, is said to have been struck by lightning more than 25 times. Engraved on the south portico is a passage from the Royal Charter of 1663: "To hold forth a lively experiment that a most flourishing civil state may stand and best be maintained with full liberty in religious concernments." In the state room you'll see a full-length portrait of George Washington by Rhode Islander Gilbert Stuart. You'll also see the original parchment charter granted by King Charles to the colony of Rhode Island in 1663 and military accoutrements of Nathaniel Greene, Washington's second-in-command during the Revolutionary War. Although booklets are available for self-guided tours, guided tours are recommended. A gift shop is on the basement level. ⊠ *82 Smith St., Downtown* ☎ *401/222–2357* ⊙ *Weekdays 8:30–4:30; tours weekdays by appointment.*

② **Roger Williams National Memorial.** Roger Williams contributed so significantly to the development of the concepts that underpin the Declaration of Independence and the Constitution that the National Park Service dedicated a 4½-acre park to his memory. Displays provide a quick glimpse into the life and times of Rhode Island's founder, who wrote the first book on the languages of the American Indian native people. ⊠ *282 N. Main St., Downtown* ☎ *401/521–7266* ⊕ *www.nps.gov/rowi* ☎ *Free* ⊙ *Daily 9–4:30.*

OFF THE
BEATEN
PATH

Roger Williams Park and Zoo. This regal 430-acre Victorian park is immensely popular. You can picnic, feed the ducks in the lakes, rent a paddleboat or miniature speedboat, or ride a pony. At Carousel Village, kids can ride the vintage carousel or a miniature train. The Museum of Natural History and Cormack Planetarium are also here; the Tennis Center has Rhode Island's only public clay courts. More than 950 animals of 160 different species live at the zoo, which opened in 1872. Among the attractions are the Tropical America, Plains of Africa, Australasia exhibits, and polar bears. From downtown, take Interstate 95 south to U.S. 1 south (Elmwood Avenue); the park entrance is the first left turn. ⊠ *1000 Elmwood Ave., South Providence* ☎ *401/785–9457 museum, 401/785–3510 zoo* ⊕ *www.rogerwilliamsparkzoo.org* ☎ *Museum $3, planetarium $3 (includes museum), zoo $12* ⊙ *Museum daily 10–5 (planetarium shows weekends 2); zoo May–Sept., daily 9–5; Oct.–Apr., daily 9–4.*

⑫ **Waterplace Park and Riverwalk.** Romantic Venetian-style footbridges, cobblestone walkways, and an amphitheater encircling a tidal pond set the tone at this four-acre tract, which has won national and international design awards. The Riverwalk passes the junction of three rivers—the Woonasquatucket, Providence, and Moshassuck—a nexus of the shipping trade during the city's early years, but an area that had been covered over with highways and parking lots by the middle of the 20th century. The focus of an urban-renewal project that uncovered the buried rivers, rerouted them, and surrounded them with amenities for pedestrians rather than cars, Waterplace Park is now a gathering place for the city. It's also the site of the popular **Waterfire** (⊕ *www.waterfire.org*), a multimedia installation featuring music and nearly 100 burning braziers that rise from the water and are tended from boats; the dusk-to-midnight Waterfire happens approximately 18 times a year and attracts more than 500,000 visitors annually. The Rosa Parks Amphitheater is the site of free concerts in summer. ⊠ *1 Financial Way, Downtown.*

Roger Williams: Pushing the Providential Envelope

Banished by the Puritans of Massachusetts for his then-seditious advocacy of separation of church and state and criticisms of New World leadership, Roger Williams headed south with a vision of a colony of religious tolerance. He paid American Indians for land at the confluence of the Woonasquatucket and Moshassuck rivers in Narragansett Bay, establishing the town of Providence in 1636.

William's radical experiment proved quickly successful, and over roughly the next half century, the controversial theologian set up America's first (some say second) Baptist church (though he separated himself from the church shortly after founding it) and saw his backwater village grow into a prosperous colonial shipping port—though the town did have its challenges; for one, it had to be rebuilt after American Indians fighting the King of England in 1675 set off a fire that burned the majority of Providence's buildings.

OFF THE BEATEN PATH

Culinary Arts Museum. An offbeat, fascinating museum in an otherwise nondescript building on the Harborside campus of Johnson & Wales University, this archive of food and restaurant memorabilia delights foodies with its exhibits of vintage menus, reconstruction of an ancient diner car, enormous cookbook collection, displays of kitchen gadgets through the years, and other assorted kitchen minutiae. Check out the original letters by assorted past presidents to friends and food providers who supplied gourmet gifts on various occasions. ⊠ *315 Harborside Blvd., South Providence* ☎ *401/598–2805* ⊕ *www.culinary.org* ⌦$7 ⊙ *Tues.–Sun. 10–5.*

 Wickenden Street. The main artery in the Fox Point district, a formerly working-class Portuguese neighborhood that's seen a steady gentrification, Wickenden Street has antiques stores, galleries, and trendy cafés. Professors, artists, and students are among the newer residents here. Many of the houses along Wickenden, Transit, Gano, and nearby streets are still painted the pastel colors of Portuguese homes.

SPORTS & THE OUTDOORS

BIKING

The best biking in the Providence area is along the 14½-mi **East Bay Bicycle Path** (⊕ www.riparks.com/eastbay.htm), which hugs the Narragansett Bay shore from India Point Park through four towns before it ends in Independence Park in Bristol.

BOATING

Prime boating areas include the Providence River, the Seekonk River, and Narragansett Bay. The **Narragansett Boat Club** (⊠ *River Rd., East Side* ☎ *401/272–1838* ⊕ *www.rownbc.org*) has advice on the best places for boating and also offers rowing and sculling classes.

HOCKEY

The **Providence Bruins** (☎*401/273–5000* ⊕*www.providencebruins. com*), a farm team of the Boston Bruins, play at the **Dunkin' Donuts Center Providence** (⊠*1 LaSalle Sq., Downtown* ☎*401/331–6700 events information* ⊕*www.dunkindonutscenter.com*).

ICE-SKATING

The outdoor rink **Bank of America City Center** (⊠*Kennedy Plaza, Downtown* ☎*401/331–5544* ⊕*www.providenceskating.com* ◻*Skating $6, rentals $4*) is open 10 AM to 8 PM daily mid-November through April.

SHOPPING

Providence has a handful of small but engaging shopping areas. In Fox Point, Wickenden Street contains many antiques stores and several art galleries. Near Brown University, Thayer Street has a number of boutiques, but the high rents here have led to an influx of chain stores. On the other hand, downtown's Westminster Street has morphed from a dull row of workaday stores to a strip of independently owned clothiers, galleries, and design stores.

ANTIQUES AND HOME FURNISHINGS

CAV (⊠*14 Imperial Pl., Jewelry District* ☎*401/751–9164* ⊕*www. cavrestaurant.com*) is a large restaurant, bar, and coffeehouse (with music Friday and Saturday nights) in a revamped factory space. It sells fine rugs, tapestries, prints, portraits, and antiques, many with African or Asian provenance. Along increasingly gentrified Westminster Street, drop by **HomeStyle** (⊠*229 Westminster St., Downtown* ☎*401/277–1159* ⊕*www.homestyleri.com*) for eye-catching objets d'art, stylish housewares, and other decorative items. **Tilden-Thurber** (⊠*292 Westminster St., Downtown* ☎*401/272–3200* ⊕*www.stanleyweiss.com*) carries high-end Colonial- and Victorian-era furniture, antiques, and estate jewelry.

ART GALLERIES

The **Bert Gallery** (⊠*540 S. Water St., Old Harbor/India Point* ☎*401/751–2628* ⊕*www.bertgallery.com*) displays late-19th- and early-20th-century paintings by regional artists. **JRS Fine Art** (⊠*218 Wickenden St., Fox Point* ☎*401/331–4380*) sells works by national and Rhode Island artists, plus carvings and crafts by artisans from Panama's Darien rain forest. The **Peaceable Kingdom** (⊠*116 Ives St., East Side* ☎*401/351–3472*) stocks folk art from around the world, including tribal weavings and rugs, ethnic clothing and jewelry, masks, musical instruments, and paintings.

Risdworks (⊠*10 Westminster St.* ☎*401/277–4949* ⊕*www.risdworks. com*) hosts changing exhibitions that showcase the work of Rhode Island School of Design alumni and faculty; works range from $1 greeting cards to $50 flatware patterns to $1,000 fine art.

FOOD

★ On the East Side, **Garrison Chocolates** (⊠*815 Hope St., East Side* ☎*401/ 490–2740* ⊕*www.tonyscolonial.com*) carries the stunningly artful confections of former New York pastry chef Andrew Shotts—think minted-mango ganache or Moroccan spice bonbons, dark-chocolate coconut patties, and white chocolate–lime bars.

Tony's Colonial (✉*311 Atwells Ave., Federal Hill* ☎*401/621–8675* ⊕*www.tonyscolonial.com*), a superb Italian grocery and deli, stocks freshly prepared foods.

★ **Venda Ravioli** (✉*275 Atwells Ave., Federal Hill* ☎*401/421–9105* ⊕*www.vendaravioli.com*) carries an amazing selection of imported and homemade Italian foods.

MALLS

★ The **Arcade** (✉*65 Weybosset St., Downtown* ☎*401/598–1199*), built in 1828, was America's first shopping mall. A National Historic Landmark, this graceful Greek-revival building has three tiers of shops and restaurants. Expect the unusual at **Copacetic Rudely Elegant Jewelry** (✉*The Arcade, 65 Weybosset St., Downtown* ☎*401/273–0470* ⊕*www.copaceticjewelry.com*), which sells the work of more than 120 artists. Upscale **Providence Place** (✉*1 Providence Pl., at Francis and Hayes Sts., Downtown* ☎*401/270–1000*) has 170 shops, anchored by JCPenney, Macy's, and Nordstrom, and a 16-screen cinema.

MAPS

The **Map Center** (✉*671 N. Main St., East Side* ☎*401/421–2184* ⊕*www.mapcenter.com*) carries maps of all types and nautical charts.

NIGHTLIFE & THE ARTS

For events listings, consult the daily *Providence Journal* and the weekly *Providence Phoenix* (free in restaurants and bookstores).

NIGHTLIFE

BARS   Fashionable with professionals, **Hot Club** (✉*575 S. Water St., Fox Point* ☎*401/861–9007*) is where the waterside scenes in the movie *There's Something About Mary* were shot. **Snookers** (✉*145 Clifford St., Jewelry District* ☎*401/351–7665*) is a stylish billiard hall in the Jewelry District that hosts live bands almost every night of the week. Through a double doorway at the rear of the billiard room is a '50s-style lounge where food is served. Swank hipsters flock to **Bevo** (✉*566 S. Main St., Fox Point* ☎*401/751–2386*), an always packed singles hangout with a long martini list. Long-running **Mirabar** (✉*35 Richmond St., Jewelry District* ☎*401/331–6761*) is one of the most popular gay bars in Providence (which has an openly gay mayor).

MUSIC CLUBS   Hear musical styles from techno-pop and hip-hop to folk and jazz at
★   the gallery/performance space **AS220** (✉*115 Empire St., Downtown* ☎*401/831–9327* ⊕*www.as220.org*). Talent shows, poetry readings, and comedy nights are also scheduled. The **Century Lounge** (✉*150 Chestnut St., Jewelry District* ☎*401/751–2255* ⊕*www.centurylounge.com*) hosts touring rock bands. The **Living Room** (✉*23 Rathbone St., Downtown* ☎*401/521–5200*) presents live entertainment nightly, often by prominent local blues musicians. **Lupo's at the Strand** (✉*79 Washington St., Downtown* ☎*401/331–5876, 401/272–5876 concert line* ⊕*www.lupos.com*),

housed in a historic, five-story theater, hosts national alternative, rock, blues, and punk bands.

THE ARTS

FILM The **Cable Car Cinema & Café** (✉201 S. Main St., Downtown ☎401/272–3970 ⊕www.cablecarcinema.com) showcases a fine slate of alternative and foreign flicks. You sit on couches and comfy chairs, and singers entertain prior to most evening shows. An espresso café substitutes for the traditional soda-and-popcorn concession.

GALLERY TOURS During **Gallery Night Providence** (☎401/751-2628 ⊕www.gallery night.info), held the third Thursday evening of every month, March–November, free art buses circulate along downtown, East Side, West Side, and Wickenden Street routes connecting some 40 participating art galleries and museums that hold open houses and mount special exhibitions.

> **TWO HURRICANES HIT NEW ENGLAND**
>
> Winds blew 100 mph during the Great New England Hurricane of 1938, wreaking utter havoc up and down the coast. Nearly 700 people died (compared with about 1,840 during Katrina) and damages totaled $308 million (estimated to be about $5 billion in today's economy). Just 16 years later, Hurricane Carol roared into Rhode Island, with water some eight feet deep in Providence. Across the region, Carol's death toll was 60 and damages were $416 million (about $41 million in Providence alone).

LECTURES Both the **Rhode Island School of Design** (✉224 Benefit St., East Side ☎401/454–6500 ⊕www.risd.edu) and **Brown University** (✉71 George St., East Side ☎401/863-2474 ⊕www.brown.edu) present lectures throughout the year, often with free admission.

MUSIC Rock bands and country acts occasionally perform at the 14,500-seat **Dunkin' Donuts Center Providence** (✉1 LaSalle Sq., Downtown ☎401/331-6700 ⊕www.dunkindonutscenter.com). The **Providence Performing Arts Center** (✉220 Weybosset St., Downtown ☎401/421-2787 ⊕www.ppacri.org), a 3,200-seat theater and concert hall that opened in 1928, hosts touring Broadway shows, concerts, and other large-scale happenings. Its lavish interior is painted with frescoes and contains art-deco chandeliers. The **Rhode Island Philharmonic** (☎401/248-7000 ⊕www.ri-philharmonic.org) presents concerts at Veterans Memorial Auditorium and Providence Performing Arts Center between October and May. The Philharmonic is also home to the Music School, a learning center for young musicians, which has its own children's orchestra. **Veterans Memorial Auditorium** (✉1 Ave. of the Arts St., Downtown ☎401/272-4862) hosts concerts, plays, children's theater, and ballet.

THEATER **Brown University** (✉Catherine Bryan Dill Center for the Performing Arts, 77 Waterman St., East Side ☎401/863-2838 ⊕www.brown. edu/tickets) mounts productions of contemporary, sometimes avant-garde, works as well as classics.

★ The **Trinity Repertory Company** (✉ *201 Washington St., Downtown* ☎ *401/351-4242* ⊕ *www.trinityrep.com*), one of New England's most esteemed theater companies, presents plays in the renovated Majestic movie house. The varied season generally includes classics, foreign plays, new works by groundbreaking young playwrights, and an annual version of *A Christmas Carol*.

WHERE TO EAT

Providence is small enough that you can easily reach every neighborhood from any other, making restaurant locations less of a factor than in larger cities. That being said, there are certain areas that discriminating diners shouldn't miss, such as Federal Hill's Little Italy area along Atwells Avenue, the hip ethnic restaurants of Fox Point along Wickenden Street and South Water Street, and the swanky dining spots clustered along the riverfront downtown, near Providence Place Mall. This is a city that has long taken food seriously, in part because it's home to one of the most prestigious culinary academies in the country, Johnson & Wales—more than a few graduates from the school have opened acclaimed restaurants in Providence.

AMERICAN

$$
Fodor's Choice
★
✕ **Nick's on Broadway.** What might pass as a no-frills luncheonette from the street actually turns out some of the best breakfast food in Rhode Island, plus extraordinary wonderful lunches and dinners. Young chef Derek Wagner delights morning patrons with such memorable fare as vanilla-battered French toast with warm fruit compote and rosemary ham; later in the day, he prepares a knockout barbecue pulled-pork sandwich with cheddar and caramelized onion, as well as rare-seared tuna with mashed parsnip-potatoes and sage jus. Service is low-key, and the dining room basic, with a polished wood counter and a row of tightly spaced tables—food is the star here. ✉ *500 Broadway, West Side* ☎ *401/421-0286* ▤ *AE, D, MC, V* ⊘ *Closed Mon. and Tues.*

$-$$
✕ **Oak.** The quintessential down-home yet up-market neighborhood bar in an attractive residential neighborhood on the northern fringes of the East Side, Oak is a perfect getaway when you're seeking first-rate food but a relaxed vibe away from big-city crowds. Reasonably priced, innovative takes on traditional American dishes are served: spice-rub tuna steak with tomato-rosemary risotto and lemon pan sauce, meat loaf with mashed potatoes and a delicious Maker's Mark bourbon gravy. You can also order terrific burger, and the lobster cakes Benedict hit the spot for weekend brunch. ✉ *959 Hope St., East Side* ☎ *401/273-7275* ▤ *AE, D, MC, V* ⊘ *No lunch Mon.*

$$-$$$
✕ **Temple.** A boisterous bar and restaurant that evolves—or devolves—into a full-fledged nightclub on weekends, Temple occupies the dark and sexy basement of the Renaissance Providence. If it's quite conversation you're after, book a seat toward the back—ideally in one of the curvaceous red booths. The menu mixed little and larger plates. You might start with a platter of miniature lobster roll (or three), or perhaps a selection of imported meats and cheeses from the cheese-and-butcher bar. Among the more substantial offerings, the skirt steak with crispy

oysters, rock shrimp, and horseradish-barbecue sauce deserves praise. Service can be a tad haughty, but this is still a fun place to spend a night on the town. ⊠ *106 Francis St., Downtown* ☎ *401/919–5050* ⊟ *AE, D, MC, V.*

ECLECTIC

$-$$ ✕ **DownCity.** Youthful, arty, and energetic, this contemporary take on a city tavern pulls in plenty of students from nearby Johnson & Wales, as well as revelers heading out to the neighborhood's clubs later in the evening (you can also socialize here till well after midnight). The menu pulls from around the globe: Korean-barbecue steak skewers, country French veal stew, classic California Caesar salad. During the day, it's a fab brunch/lunch option—try the crab cakes with eggs and toast. ⊠ *311 Westminster St., Downtown* ☎ *401/861–8000* ⊟ *AE, D, MC, V.*

$$-$$$ ✕ **Mills Tavern.** Tile mosaics and paintings by the former head of the Rhode Island School of Design illustration department enhance this postmodern take on the classic colonial tavern concept. The menu is divvied up into several categories: raw bar, wood-burning oven, wood rotisseries, and so on. Don't miss the crispy salmon with French lentils and tomato-citrus jam, or the addictive side dish of grilled sweet onions topped with Roquefort. Take advantage of the $29 three-course fixed price menu on weeknights. ⊠ *101 N. Main St., Downtown* ☎ *401/272–3331* ⊟ *AE, D, DC, MC, V* ✵ *No lunch.*

$$-$$$ ✕ **Rue de l'Espoir.** At this homey, longtime Providence favorite, dishes are designed to be fun, and the menu offers an even mix of wallet- and waistline-friendly lighter dishes and richer, more serious fare. Worthy bets include creamy risotto with asparagus, shiitake mushrooms, sweet peas, and a mascarpone-ricotta salad; and duck-leg confit with fresh herbs and crispy fries. Wide-plank pine floors, an ornate tin ceiling, and upholstered booths set the mood in the dining room. The spacious barroom, where many locals prefer to dine, has a large mural of a French village street scene and jazz tunes humming in the background. Weekday breakfast and weekend brunch are popular. ⊠ *99 Hope St., East Side* ☎ *401/751–8890* ⊟ *AE, D, DC, MC, V.*

FRENCH

$$-$$$ ✕ **Pot au Feu.** As night falls, business-driven downtown Providence clears
★ out, and this bastion of French country cuisine lights up. Here the chefs work to perfect such dishes as pâté de foie gras, beef Bourguignon, bouillabaisse Marseilles, and *pot de crème au chocolat*. The dining experience is more casual at the downstairs Bistro than at the pricier upstairs Salon. ⊠ *44 Custom House St., Downtown* ☎ *401/273–8953* ⊟ *AE, DC, MC, V* ✵ *Bistro closed Sun. Salon closed Sun. and Mon.*

ITALIAN

$$$ ✕ **Al Forno.** When it opened in 1980, Al Forno, which means "from
Fodor's Choice the oven" in Italian, put Providence on the national dining map, and it
★ continues to garner ebullient praise from critics and patrons. From the oven come a number of stellar dishes, among them thin-crust pizzas, roasted duck with prune-stuffed gnocchi, spicy clam roasts, and bacon-wrapped wild boar loin. Also consider the extraordinary pastas, such

as house-made *cavatelli pasta* with prosciutto and butternut squash. For dessert, look to the pear-and-walnut tart. Meals are served both upstairs, in the rustic dining room, and downstairs, in a room with white marble floors. ⊠*577 S. Main St., Fox Point* ☎*401/273–9760* ⚲*Reservations not accepted* ▭*AE, DC, MC, V* ⊘*Closed Sun. and Mon. No lunch.*

¢–$ ✕**Angelo's Civita Farnese.** In the heart of Federal Hill, boisterous Angelo's has been dispensing first-rate home-style red-sauce fare and Old-World charm since the 1920s. Locals come here for good-size portions of fresh, simply prepared pasta and traditional Italian specialties (fried peppers, veal parmigiana) at bargain prices. ⊠*141 Atwells Ave., Federal Hill* ☎*401/621–8171* ▭*No credit cards* ⊘*Closed Sun. late May–early Sept.*

$$–$$$ ✕**Bacaro.** Chef Brian Kingsford and partner Jennifer Matta, both for-
★ merly of Al Forno, opened this handsome, bilevel restaurant in 2007. On the informal ground floor you can sip wine and nosh on olives, *soppressata sausage,* and fresh buffalo mozzarella from the *salumeria* (cured-meat shop) and *enoteca* (wine cellar). Upstairs, you'll find a more traditional dining room, where you can sample such dazzling fare as fettuccine with mascarpone, smoked prosciutto, green lentils, and butternut squash and grilled pork tenderloin with a pomegranate glaze and roasted-chestnut stuffing. There are also terrific grilled pizzas. Bacaro makes fantastic chocolates in house—consider the grappa-scented bittersweet truffles. ⊠*262 S. Water St., Downtown* ☎*401/751–3700* ▭*AE, D, MC, V.*

JAPANESE

$ ✕**Tokyo Restaurant.** The Japanese cuisine served here is some of the best in town. Choose regular or traditional Japanese seating—or take a stool at the sushi bar, where local fish such as tuna, mackerel, and eel are prepared alongside red snapper and fish from points beyond. The designer rolls include beef, squid, duck, and seaweed. Service can be brusque. ⊠*388 Wickenden St., Fox Point* ☎*401/331–5330* ▭*AE, D, MC, V* ⚱*BYOB.*

SEAFOOD

$$–$$$ ✕**Providence Oyster Bar.** In a neighborhood where Italian food dominates, this spirited seafood restaurant offers a refreshing alternative. The handsomely turned out dining room sparkles with polished wood floors, brick walls, and a tin ceiling, the raw bar serves more than a dozen varieties of fresh oysters. Favorite appetizers include blackened ahi tuna and steamed Prince Edward Island mussels with a Pernod-fennel broth. For entrées, try grilled swordfish steak truffle french fries and a balsamic reduction—the sirloin with bacon and blue cheese pleases carnivores. ⊠*283 Atwells Ave., Federal Hill* ☎*401/272–8866* ▭*AE, DC, MC, V* ⊘*Closed Sun. No lunch Mon.–Thurs.*

WHERE TO STAY

$$-$$$ 🖭 **Courtyard by Marriott Providence.** One of downtown's few mid-priced hotels is housed in a seven-story redbrick building carefully designed to match the other buildings in its historic Union Station Plaza location. Nearly all of the large rooms, in tones of tans and greens with mauve accents, have views of either the State House, Waterplace Park, or the Financial District. The hotel is steps away from the Providence Place mall. **Pros:** many rooms overlook riverfront, price is reasonable, central location. **Cons:** rooms are a bit nondescript. ⊠ *32 Exchange Terr., Downtown* ☎ *401/272–1191 or 888/887–7955* ⊕ *www.marriott.com* ➟ *210 rooms, 6 suites* ⚷ *In-room: refrigerator, Ethernet. In-hotel: restaurant, pool, gym, no-smoking rooms* ☱ *AE, D, DC, MC, V.*

$ 🖭 **C.C. Ledbetter's.** Innkeeper C.C. Ledbetter's mansard-roof 1770 home is in a great location on College Hill, the city's historic East Side. With its lively art, quilts, contemporary and antique furnishings, loads of books and magazines, plus a dog, you feel more like you're staying in someone's home than an inn. With reasonably priced rooms and a location across from the John Brown House Museum, this inn is a favorite of the parents of Brown University students. **Pros:** affordable rates, a short walk from Brown and RISD, knowledgeable hosts. **Cons:** least expensive rooms share bath. ⊠ *326 Benefit St., East Side* ☎ *401/351–4699* ⊕ *www.ccledbetter.com* ➟ *5 rooms, 2 with bath* ⚷ *In-room: no phone. In-hotel: no-smoking rooms* ☱ *MC, V* ⫶◯⫶ *CP.*

$$$ 🖭 **Hotel Dolce Villa.** This small, upscale, well-managed inn opened in
★ 2005 and is the only accommodation in Federal Hill—it actually overlooks DePasquale Square and its vibrant cafés, gelato stands, and gourmet markets. The striking Mediterranean-inspired building contains 14 one- and two-bedroom suites, all with gleaming contemporary decor, white-marble floors, fully stocked kitchens, and such luxe amenities as flat-screen TVs and whirlpool tubs; larger suites have gas fireplaces. It's ideal for longer stays, and also makes for a perfect weekend retreat for those planning to eat their way through Federal Hill. **Pros:** great value, fun location, huge suites. **Cons:** the modern decor may not please traditionalists, no gym. ⊠ *63 DePasquale Plaza, Federal Hill* ☎ *401/383–7031* ⊕ *www.dolcevillari.com* ➟ *14 suites* ⚷ *In-room: DVD, Ethernet. In-hotel: no-smoking rooms* ☱ *AE, D, MC, V.*

$$$-$$$$ 🖭 **Hotel Providence.** Intimate, urbane, and set along downtown's best
★ shopping street, this lavishly decorated boutique property is set inside a restored late-19th-century building. Each of the 80 oversized rooms and suites contain artwork by local talent Nancy Friese (chairman of RISD), along with such perks as terry robes, free Wi-Fi, CD players, and bathrooms with rain showerheads and Bulgari bath amenities. The hotel relaunched and renamed its restaurant in May 2008; Aspire serves creative Mediterranean food. **Pros:** in the heart of the Arts and Entertainment District, relatively small size encourages personal staff attention, a good value for such plush rooms. **Cons:** on a busy street, not much greenery around. ⊠ *311 Westminster St., Downtown* ☎ *401/861–8000 or 800/861–8990* ⊕ *www.thehotelprovidence.com* ➟ *64 rooms, 16 suites* ⚷ *In-room: safe, Wi-Fi. In-hotel: restaurant, room service, gym, parking (fee), no-smoking rooms* ☱ *AE, D, DC, MC, V.*

$$-$$$ ⊡**Old Court Bed & Breakfast.** This three-story Italianate inn on historic Benefit Street was built in 1863 as a rectory. Antique furniture, richly colored wallpaper, and memorabilia throughout the house reflect the best of 19th-century style. The comfortable, spacious rooms have high ceilings and chandeliers; most have nonworking marble fireplaces, and some have views of the State House and downtown. **Pros:** on a regal residential street, elegant furnishings, friendly service. **Cons:** lacks the anonymity of a larger hotel. ⊠*144 Benefit St., East Side* ☎*401/751–2002* ⊕*www.oldcourt.com* ⋫*10 rooms* ⚭*In-room: Wi-Fi. In-hotel: no elevator, no-smoking rooms* ⊟*AE, D, MC, V* ⦿|*BP.*

$$$$ ⊡**Providence Biltmore.** Built in 1922, the Biltmore has a sleek art-deco
★ exterior, an external glass elevator with delightful views of Providence, a grand ballroom, an Elizabeth Arden Red Door Spa, and an in-house Starbucks. The personal attentiveness of its staff, downtown location, and modern amenities make this hotel one of the city's best. Plus, with its skyscraping neon sign, it couldn't be easier to find. **Pros:** truly the grande dame of Providence, suites are huge, an impressive spa. **Cons:** very pricey, not as modern and hip as some. ⊠*Kennedy Plaza, Dorrance and Washington Sts., Downtown* ☎*401/421–0700 or 800/294–7709* ⊕*www.providencebiltmore.com* ⋫*117 rooms, 162 suites* ⚭*In-room: some kitchenettes, Wi-Fi. In-hotel: restaurant, room service, gym, parking (fee), no-smoking rooms* ⊟*AE, D, DC, MC, V.*

$$$-$$$$ ⊡**Renaissance Providence Hotel.** The city's hippest hotel opened in 2007
Fodor's Choice inside one of its most mysterious buildings, a stately nine-story neoclas-
★ sical 1929 building constructed as a Masonic temple but never occupied, as it was completed just after the Stock Market Crash. Developers have restored the building and even incorporated vintage graffiti found within its empty corridors into the arty, whimsical room design. Try to get a room overlooking the statehouse, across the street, and be sure to dine in the swank on-site restaurant, Temple Downtown. **Pros:** terrific location by mall and capitol grounds, super-cushy linens and bedding, you can custom-design your own in-room honor bar. **Cons:** some rooms have smallish windows. ⊠*5 Ave. of the Arts, Downtown* ☎*401/919–5000 or 800/468–3571* ⊕*www.renaissanceprovidence.com* ⋫*269 rooms, 3 suites* ⚭*In-room: safe, Ethernet. In-hotel: restaurant, room service, gym, parking (fee), no-smoking rooms* ⊟*AE, D, DC, MC, V.*

$$$-$$$$ ⊡**Westin Providence.** A recent massive expansion added about 200
★ rooms to this multi-turreted 25-story hotel towers over Providence's compact downtown, connected by skywalks to the city's gleaming convention center and the Providence Place mall. Its rooms have reproduction period furniture, and half have king-size beds; many have views of the city. Restaurants include a very good steak house and a more casual American bistro. **Pros:** rooms have incredibly comfy heavenly beds, convenient location, wonderful views from upper floors. **Cons:** it can feel like a zoo when there's a convention going on. ⊠*1 W. Exchange St., Downtown* ☎*401/598–8000 or 800/937–8461* ⊕*www.westin.com* ⋫*542 rooms, 22 suites* ⚭*In-room: refrigerator, Ethernet. In-hotel: 2 restaurants, room service, bar, pool, gym, parking (fee), no-smoking rooms* ⊟*AE, D, DC, MC, V.*

THE BLACKSTONE VALLEY

America's Industrial Revolution began in this region north of Providence in 1790, when the power of the Blackstone River, which runs south from Worcester, Massachusetts, was first harnessed at Pawtucket. The advent of water-powered factory mills along the 45-mi river catapulted a young agricultural United States into the Industrial Age. In the 1800s, Pawtucket and Woonsocket became large cities as a steady flow of French, Irish, and Eastern European immigrants came to work the mills, a system of canals, and later railroads came into being as distribution channels, and the local industry grew. Much of that industry is gone now, and the old mills are slowly but surely being renovated into condominiums, offices, and gallery space, but its heritage remains to be explored. The Blackstone River Valley National Heritage Corridor provides a backdrop to museums, historic villages, and country drives. Most of the Blackstone Valley experience is about taking in the history of the area, understanding its importance in the country's growths, and enjoying the slices of Americana it has to offer.

The Blackstone River and its valley are named after William Blackstone, who in 1628 became the first European to settle in Boston. In 1635, having grown weary of the ways of the Puritan settlers who had become his neighbors, this Anglican clergyman built a new home in what was wilderness and is now called Rhode Island.

PAWTUCKET

5 mi north of Providence.

Providence's neighbor to the immediate north is a slightly gruff, blue-collar factory town that's gradually gentrified of late, as real-estate prices have risen a bit in the capital. In Algonquian, "petuket" (similar to standard Rhode Island pronunciation of the city's name today, accent on the second syllable) means "waterfalls." A small village was established at the falls in 1670 by Joseph Jenks Jr., who considered the area a prime spot for an iron forge. When Samuel Slater arrived 120 years later, he was delighted to find a corps of skilled mechanics ready to assist him in his dream of building a textile mill and bringing America's first factory system into being. Although many of Pawtucket's older buildings were torn down as part of urban renewal projects in the 1970s, significant portions of the city's history have been preserved, and Slater Mill is a must for history buffs.

WHAT TO SEE

Fodor'sChoice ★

Slater Mill Historic Site. In 1793, Samuel Slater and two Providence merchants built the first factory in America to produce cotton yarn from water-powered machines. The Slater Mill Historic Site celebrates America's Industrial Revolution, comprising the old yellow clapboard mill, since restored, and housing machinery illustrating the conversion of raw cotton to finished cloth, and the stone Wilkinson Mill, built in 1810, where a 9-ton reproduction of an 1826 waterwheel powers a 19th-century machine shop using a system of leather belts and pulleys to drive the machines. Interpreters demonstrate activities of daily family life in the 1758 Sylvanus Brown House and garden, and guides in period clothing conduct living history tours. ⊠*67 Roosevelt Ave.* ☎*401/725–8638* ⊕*www.slatermill.org* ☒*$9* ⊙*Mar.–June, Oct., and Nov., Tues.–Sat. 11–3; July–Sept., Tues.–Sat. 10–5.*

The **Blackstone Valley Visitor Center** (⊠*175 Main St.* ☎*401/724–2200 or 800/454–2882* ⊕*www.tourblackstone.com* ☒*Free* ⊙*Daily 9–5*), across the street from Slater Mill, has information kiosks, maps, hospitable tourism consultants, a café, and a gallery. Ask to see the 18-minute documentary on the region.

ⓒ **Slater Memorial Park.** Within the stately grounds of this park along Ten Mile River are picnic tables, tennis courts, playgrounds, and a river walk. The park's **Looff Carousel,** built by Charles I. D. Looff in 1894, comprises 42 horses, three dogs, and a lion, camel, and giraffe that are the earliest examples of the Danish immigrant's work. The carousel animals don't go up and down, but they sure move fast. Bargains don't get much better than this: rides are 25¢. ⊠*Newport Ave. (Rte. 1A)* ☎*401/728–0500 Ext. 252 park information* ☒*Free* ⊙*Park daily dawn–dusk. Carousel July–early Sept., daily 10–4; late Apr.–June and early Sept.–mid-Oct., weekends 10–5.*

SPORTS & THE OUTDOORS
From April through September, the **Pawtucket Red Sox** (⊠*1 Ben Mondor Way* ☎*401/724–7300* ⊕*www.pawsox.com* ☒*Tickets $4–$10*), the Triple-A international league affiliate of the Boston Red Sox, play around 70 home games at **McCoy Stadium.**

NIGHTLIFE & THE ARTS
Known for its Shakespearian productions, the **Sandra Feinstein Gamm Theatre** (⊠*172 Exchange St.* ☎*401/723–4266* ⊕*www.gammtheatre. org*) produces works of classic and contemporary theater from fall through spring in an intimate setting of 130 seats.

WHERE TO EAT
¢–$ ✕**Modern Diner.** This 1941 Sterling Streamliner eatery—a classic from
AMERICAN   the heyday of the stainless-steel diner painted in dashing burgundy and white—was the first diner listed on the National Register of Historic Places. The family-run Modern serves standard diner fare and some specialty items, including lobster Benedict, French toast with custard sauce and berries, and pancakes packed with cranberries and almonds. ⊠*364 East Ave.* ☎*401/726–8390* ▭*No credit cards* ⊙*No dinner.*

WOONSOCKET

10 mi north of Pawtucket, 15 mi north of Providence.

Gritty Woonsocket, population 43,000, sees very few tourists and offers little in the way of sightseeing. However, it is home to one of the best museums about immigrant factory life and textile milling in the country, and this compact city on the Blackstone River also has a prolific French Canadian community. A steep hill on the city's northern edge looks down on the Blackstone River, which makes a dozen turns in its 5-mi course through town. The river's flow spawned textile mills that made the town a thriving community in the 19th and early 20th centuries.

WHAT TO SEE

Museum of Work and Culture. Set up in a former textile mill, this attraction examines the lives of American factory workers and owners during the Industrial Revolution. Focusing on French Canadian immigrants to Woonsocket's mills, the museum's cleverly laid-out walk-through

Fodor'sChoice
★

exhibits begin with a 19th-century Quebecois farmhouse, then continue with displays of life in a 20th-century tenement, in a parochial school, in church, and on the shop floor. The genesis of the textile workers' union is described, as are the events that led to the National Textile Strike of 1934. Kids should check out the engaging presentations about child labor. ⊠ *42 S. Main St.* ☎ *401/769–9675* ⊕ *www. rihs.org* ⊠ *$7* ◷ *Weekdays 9:30–4, Sat. 10–5, Sun. 1–4.*

NIGHTLIFE & THE ARTS

The impressive entertainment lineup at **Chan's Fine Oriental Dining** (⊠ *267 Main St.* ☎ *401/765–1900* ⊕ *www.chanseggrollsandjazz.com*) includes blues, jazz, and folk performers. Reservations are advisable; tickets generally run from about $10 to $20.

WHERE TO EAT & STAY

$ ✕ **Wright's Farm Restaurant.** Chicken served family-style and with all-
AMERICAN you-can-eat bread, salad, roast chicken, pasta, and potatoes, a northern Rhode Island tradition, was born of a Woonsocket social club's need to feed many people efficiently. More than a dozen restaurants in the Blackstone Valley serve this food combo; Wright's Farm, the largest (with 75 ovens), has become a certifiable tourist attraction (complete with gift shop), dishing up 1 million pounds of chicken each year. The mammoth banquet-hall setting lacks charm, but this is still a must for fans of local food lore. ⊠ *84 Inman Rd., 2 mi west of Slatersville off Rte. 102, Harrisville* ☎ *401/769–2856* ⌔ *Reservations not accepted* ⊟ *No credit cards* ◷ *Closed Mon.–Wed. No lunch Thurs. and Fri.*

¢-$ ✕ **Ye Olde English Fish & Chips.** Fresh fried fish and potatoes have been
AMERICAN served at this Woonsocket institution for generations. The interior is unassuming (wood paneling and booths) so it must be the inexpensive and consistently excellent food that has kept folks coming back since 1922—not just fish-and-chips but first-rate clam chowder and fish cakes. In warm weather dine outside in Market Square, admiring the rush of the Blackstone River and waterfalls. ⊠ *Market Sq. and S. Main St.* ☎ *401/762–3637* ⊟ *MC, V* ◷ *Closed Sun. and Mon.*

$-$$ ⚏**Pillsbury House.** Stately Prospect Street stretches along the crest of the ridge north of the Blackstone River; its mansions, like the mansard-roof Pillsbury House, were built by mill owners in the late 1800s. The common room has a fireplace with a maple hearth. The three guest rooms on the second floor are furnished in Victorian style, with antiques, plants, high beds, and fringed lamp shades; the third-floor suite favors a more rustic-country aesthetic. Complimentary refreshments are served throughout the day, and there's a guest kitchenette on second floor. **Pros:** one of the only non-chain accommodations in the region, stunning architecture, great rates. **Cons:** old-fashioned decor and vibe isn't for everyone. ⊠*341 Prospect St.* ☎*800/205–4112* ☎☎*401/766–7983* ⊕*www.pillsburyhouse.com* ⇆*3 rooms, 1 suite* ⊟*AE, D, DC, MC, V* ₠*In-room: no TV. In-hotel: public Internet, no-smoking rooms* ⧖*BP.*

SOUTH COUNTY

When the principal interstate traffic through Rhode Island shifted from U.S. 1 to Interstate 95 in the 1960s, the coastal part of the state—known locally as South County, although its true name is Washington County—was given a reprieve from the inevitabilities of development. In the past four decades, strong local zoning laws have been instituted and a park system established. In some communities, land trusts were set up to buy open space.

Always a summertime destination, South County is now growing into a region of year-round residents. It is, indeed, the fastest-growing region in the state, but the changes are being well managed by the respective communities, and the area's appeal as a summer playground has not diminished. South County is a wonderfully slower-paced alternative to Newport and Providence, a place where you can savor more than 100 mi of beautiful beaches, numerous public golf courses, and countless farm stands and historic sites, and participate in outdoor sports, camping, and family amusements. The area's also popular for shopping, with cute village boutiques, arts and crafts stores, and an assortment of antiques shops.

WESTERLY

50 mi southwest of Providence, 100 mi southwest of Boston, 140 mi northeast of New York City.

Westerly is a busy little railroad town that grew up in the late 19th century around a major station on what is now the New York–Boston Amtrak corridor. Victorian and Greek Revival mansions line many streets off the town center, which is divided by Connecticut from the Pawcatuck River. During the Industrial Revolution and into the 1950s, Westerly was distinguished for its flawless red granite, from which monuments throughout the country were made. It has since sprawled out along U.S. 1 and grown to include seven villages—Westerly itself, or downtown Westerly, plus Watch Hill, Dunn's Corners, Misquamicut, Bradford, Shelter Harbor, and Weekapaug—encompassing a 33-square mi-area.

Watch Hill and Misquamicut are summer communities recognized without mention of the township to which they belong, Westerly. Casinos in Uncasville and Ledyard, Connecticut (less than an hour away), have steadily changed Westerly's economic climate. Many residents work in the Mohegan Sun and Foxwoods casinos, and Westerly's B&Bs have become popular alternatives to casino hotels.

SPORTS & THE OUTDOORS
Wilcox Park Designed and created in 1898 by Warren Manning (an associate of Fredrick Law Olmsted), this 14.5-acre Victorian strolling park in the heart of downtown Westerly boasts a pond, meadow, arboretum, perennial garden, sculptures, fountains, and monuments. Concerts, plays, and arts festivals are held periodically. ⊠71½ *High St.* ☎401/596-8590 ⊕*www.westerlylibrary.org.*

WHERE TO STAY
✦ ✦✦ 📺 **Grandview Bed and Breakfast.** Relaxed, homey, and affordable, this B&B on a rise above Route 1A has comfortable rooms with pastel and white hues and a slightly frilly sensibility. Those at the front have ocean views. The common room has a TV with VCR. Breakfast is served on the porch year-round. **Pros:** affordable, great views of Block Island Sound. **Cons:** no TV in rooms, some rooms share a bath. ⊠*212 Shore Rd., between Misquamicut and Weekapaug, Dunn's Corners* ☎401/596-6384 *or* 800/447-6384 ⊕*www.grandviewbandb.com* ➿*8 rooms, 4 with bath* &*In-room: Wi-Fi, no TV. In-hotel: no elevator, no-smoking rooms* ⊟*AE, MC, V* ❢⊙*CP.*

WATCH HILL

★ *6 mi south of downtown Westerly.*

Watch Hill, a Victorian-era resort village, contains almost 2 mi of beautiful beaches. Many of its well-kept summerhouses are owned by wealthy families who have passed ownership down through generations. Sailing and socializing are the top activities for Watch Hill residents. Bay Street is also a good place to shop for jewelry, summer clothing, and antiques.

WHAT TO SEE
☾ **Flying Horse Carousel.** At the beach end of Bay Street, this is the oldest merry-go-round in America, built in 1867. It was part of a traveling carnival that stopped traveling in Watch Hill. The horses, suspended from above rather than fastened to the floor, swing out when in motion; the faster the ride, the more they seem to "fly." Each is hand-carved from a single piece of wood and has glass eyes and a real horsehair mane and tail. Only kids may ride the carousel. ⊠*Bay St.* ☎*$1* ⊙*Memorial Day–Columbus Day, weekdays 11–9, weekends 10–9.*

Watch Hill Lighthouse. An active U.S. Coast Guard station, this lighthouse has great views of the ocean and of Fishers Island, New York. A tiny

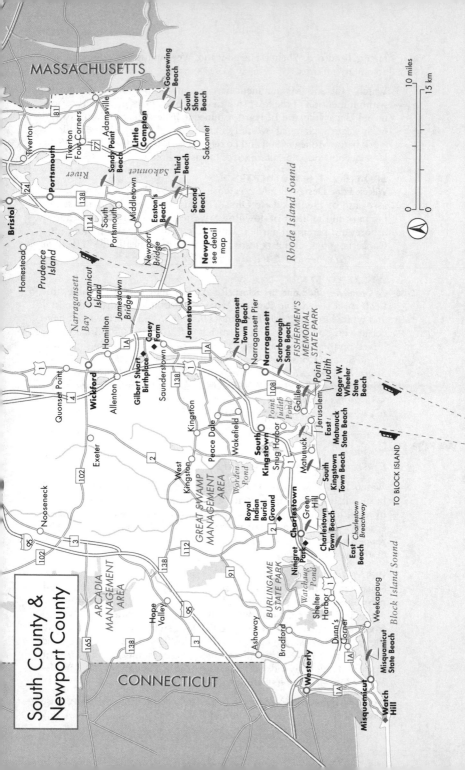

South County & Newport County

MASSACHUSETTS

Goosewing Beach

81

Adamsville

Tiverton Four Corners

Tiverton

77

Sandy Point Beach

Little Compton

South Shore Beach

Portsmouth

24

138

South Portsmouth

Sakonnet

Third Beach

River

Sakonnet

114

Middletown

Easton's Beach

Second Beach

Bristol

Newport Bridge

Newport see detail map

Homestead

Prudence Island

Narragansett Bay *Conanicut Island*

Hamilton

Jamestown Bridge

Jamestown

Rhode Island Sound

1

Wickford

Gilbert Stuart Birthplace

Casey Farm

1A

Saunderstown

Narragansett Town Beach

Narragansett Pier

Narragansett

FISHERMEN'S MEMORIAL STATE PARK

Quonset Point

4

Allenton

138

1A

Scarborough State Beach

Point Judith

Exeter

102

Kingston

Peace Dale

Wakefield

108

Galilee

Jerusalem

Roger W. Wheeler State Beach

Point Judith Pond

2

West Kingston

South Kingston

Snug Harbor

East Matunuck State Beach

Matunuck

Nooseneck

GREAT SWAMP MANAGEMENT AREA

Worden Pond

South Kingstown Town Beach

95

102

3

Royal Indian Burial Ground

Green Hill

Charlestown

Charlestown Breachway

Block Island Sound

112

2

Charlestown Town Beach

East Beach

ARCADIA MANAGEMENT AREA

138

91

Ninigret Park

BURLINGAME STATE PARK

Watchaug Pond

TO BLOCK ISLAND

165

Hope Valley

Shelter Harbor

Weekapaug

Dunn's Corner

Ashaway

Bradford

1

Westerly

1A

Misquamicut State Beach

1A

Watch Hill

Misquamicut

CONNECTICUT

10 miles

15 km

museum contains exhibits. Parking is for the elderly only; everyone else must walk from lots at the beach. The grounds here are worth a stroll, whether the museum is open or not. ⊠ *14 Lighthouse Rd.* ☎ *401/596-7761* ☜ *Free* ⊙ *Grounds daily 8–8. Museum July and Aug., Tues. and Thurs. 1–3.*

WHERE TO EAT

$$-$$$ ✕ **Olympia Tea Room.** Opened in 1916 as a ice cream parlor, the Olympia
AMERICAN has become one of South County's most celebrated dining options. Var-
★ nished wood booths and a soda fountain behind a long marble counter echo the restaurant's rich history—it overlooks the water, too. The kitchen prepares a nice mix of contemporary and traditional dishes, such as lamb shanks, cod with capers, and lobster salad. Try to save room for the "world-famous Avondale swan" dessert—a fantasy of ice cream, whipped cream, chocolate sauce, and puff pastry. ⊠ *74 Bay St.* ☎ *401/348-8211* ⊕ *www.olympiatearoom.com* ♿ *Reservations not accepted* ⊟ *AE, MC, V* ⊙ *Closed Nov.–mid-Apr.*

MISQUAMICUT

2½ mi northeast of Watch Hill.

Motels with beach towels hanging over porch railings jostle for attention in Misquamicut, where a giant waterslide, a 1915-vintage carousel, miniature golf, a game arcade, children's rides, batting cages, and fast-food stands attract visitors by the thousands. The 7-mi-long beach, Rhode Island's longest state beach, is accessible year-round, but this is primarily a summertime destinations, with the amusements and most businesses open between Memorial Day and Labor Day.

SPORTS & THE OUTDOORS

☺ **Atlantic Beach Park** (⊠ *337 Atlantic Ave.* ☎ *401/322–0504*) has more games and rides for kids than any other Misquamicut facility. Sevenmile-long **Misquamicut State Beach** (⊠ *Atlantic Ave.* ☎ *401/596–9097*) has parking, showers, and a snack bar at the state-run beach pavilion.

NIGHTLIFE & THE ARTS

Dance to rock bands at the **Windjammer** (⊠ *323 Atlantic Ave.* ☎ *401/322–9283*), open Memorial Day to Labor Day; the room holds more than 1,000.

WHERE TO EAT & STAY

$$-$$$ ✕ **Maria's Seaside Cafe.** Although casual, this breezy and upbeat dinner
MEDITERRANEAN spot serves such complex dishes as sea scallops over Italian couscous with lobster meat and black-truffle essence, and tagliatelle pasta with fresh tomatoes, spinach, pine nuts, and goat cheese. Maria's has the best wine list in the area. You'll find a kids' menu, but Maria's is more oriented toward adults than others along the beachfront. ⊠ *132 Atlantic Ave.* ☎ *401/596–6886* ⊕ *www.mariasseasidecafe.com* ⊟ *AE, MC, V* ⊙ *Closed early Oct.–May. No lunch.*

$$-$$$ ✕ **Paddy's Seafood Restaurant.** This tropical, turquoise hangout is directly
SEAFOOD on the sand in plain view of beach volleyball and the ocean. By day, the place is geared toward families; by night, live music and the bar are the

focus. Seafood plates, many with Asian twists, rule the menu, which is surprisingly innovative for such a casual place, but you'll also find a nice range of pastas, salads, and grills. Start with the Thai-roasted mussels, before tucking into a bowl of lobster risotto with fresh peas and Parmesan. ⌧*159 Atlantic Ave.* ☎*401/596–2610* ⊕*www.paddys-beach.com* ▤*MC, V* ☾*Closed Nov.–mid-June.*

$$-$$$ ★ 🏨 **Breezeway Resort.** The Bellone family takes great pride in its accommodations: summery rooms, suites, villas with fireplaces, and hot tubs. The grounds hold a pool, shuffleboard, and fountains. **Pros:** spotless rooms, friendly vibe for families, nice range of room configurations. **Cons:** a bit noisy with so many kids, closed in winter. ⌧*70 Winnapaug Rd., Box 1368,* ☎*401/348–8953 or 800/462–8872* ⊕*www.breezewayresort.com* 🛏*52 rooms, 14 suites, 2 villas* ⚒*In-room: some kitchens, refrigerator, Wi-Fi. In-hotel: pool, laundry service, no-smoking rooms* ▤*AE, D, DC, MC, V* ☾*Closed Nov.–Mar.* ⎁*CP.*

CHARLESTOWN

12 mi northeast of Misquamicut.

Charlestown stretches along the Old Post Road (Route 1A). The 37-square-mi town, which is suburban in character, has parks, the largest saltwater marsh in the state, 7 mi of pristine beaches, and many oceanfront motels, summer chalets, and cabins.

SPORTS & THE OUTDOORS

Burlingame State Park. This 2,100-acre park has nature trails, picnic and swimming areas, and campgrounds, as well as boating and fishing on Watchaug Pond. ⌧*75 Burlingame Park Rd.* ☎*401/322–7337.*

Ninigret National Wildlife Refuge. Here, 9 mi of trails cross 400 acres of diverse upland and wetland habitats—including grasslands, shrublands, wooded swamps, and freshwater ponds. It's a great spot for bird-watchers, consists of two stretches of beach lands and marshes, plus the abandoned naval air station on Ninigret Pond. ⌧*Rte. 1A* ☎*401/364–9124* ⊒*Free* ☾*Daily dawn–dusk.*

Ninigret Park. This 72-acre park features picnic grounds, ball fields, a bike path, tennis and basketball courts, nature trails, and a three-acre spring-fed swimming pond. Also here is the **Frosty Drew Observatory and Nature Center** (☎*401/364–9508* ⊕*www.frostydrew.org*), which presents free nature and Friday night astronomy programs. ⌧*Park La., off Rte. 1A* ☎*401/364–1222.*

BEACHES The ½-mi **Charlestown Town Beach** (⌧*Charlestown Beach Rd.*) ends at a breachway that is part of Ninigret National Wildlife Refuge. Glorious **East Beach** (⌧*E. Beach Rd.*), composed of 3½ mi of dunes backed by the crystal-clear waters of Ninigret Pond, is a 2-mi hike from the breachway at Charlestown Town Beach. You'll find a snack bar and restrooms; parking is at the end of East Beach Road.

BOATING **Ocean House Marina** (✉ *60 Town Dock Rd., at Cross Mills exit off U.S. 1* ☎ *401/364–6040* ⊕ *www.oceanhousemarina.com*) is a full-service marina with fuel, fishing supplies, and boat rentals.

SHOPPING

☞ Follow the myriad pathways at the **Fantastic Umbrella Factory** (✉ *4820 Old Post Rd., off U.S. 1* ☎ *401/364–6616*) to discover four rustic shops and a barn built around a wild garden. For sale are hardy perennials and unusual daylilies, jewelry, pottery, blown glass, penny candy, greeting cards, crafts, and incense. There is also an art gallery, greenhouse, and café that serves organic foods. For 50¢ you can scoop a cone full of seeds to feed the fenced-in ostrich, guinea hens, peacocks, and sheep.

SOUTH KINGSTOWN

10 mi northeast of Charlestown.

In summer, the 55-square-mi town of South Kingstown—encompassing Wakefield, Snug Harbor, Matunuck, Green Hill, Kingston, and nine other villages—unfolds a wealth of history, outdoor recreation, beaches, and entertainment. The town's seat of government is in Wakefield.

SPORTS & THE OUTDOORS

BEACHES **East Matunuck State Beach** (✉ *Succotash Rd.*) is popular with the college crowd for its white sand, picnic areas, pavilion with showers, and concessions. Crabs, mussels, and starfish populate the rock reef that extends to the right of **Matunuck Beach** (✉ *Succotash Rd.*). Southward, the reef gives way to a sandy bottom. When the ocean is calm, you can walk on the reef and explore its tidal pools. **South Kingstown Town Beach** (✉ *Matunuck Beach Rd.*), with a playground, picnic tables, grills, and showers, draws many families.

FISHING On the docks at Snug Harbor it is not uncommon to see giant tuna and sharks weighing more than 300 pounds. **Snug Harbor Marina** (✉ *410 Gooseberry Rd., Wakefield* ☎ *401/783–7766 or 866/543–1897* ⊕ *www.snugharbormarina.com*) sells bait and arranges fishing charters.

SHOPPING

Dove and Distaff Antiques (✉ *365 Main St., Wakefield* ☎ *401/783–5714*) carries home goods such as window treatments, slipcovers, and lamp shades. A women's art cooperative, **Hera Gallery** (✉ *327 Main St., Wakefield* ☎ *401/789–1488* ⊕ *www.heragallery.org*) exhibits works by emerging local artists, including children and young adults.

NIGHTLIFE & THE ARTS

Ocean Mist (✉ *895 Matunuck Beach Rd., Matunuck* ☎ *401/782–3740* ⊕ *www.oceanmist.net*) is a distinctive beachfront barroom with music nightly in summer and on weekends off-season. The hard-drinking crowd at this hangout of South County's younger generation can be as rough-hewn as the building.

WHERE TO EAT & STAY

$-$$ ✕**Mews Tavern.** The food at this cheery tavern is tasty if unimagina-
AMERICAN tive, but when you're in the mood for a burger (there are many variet-
ies—the one topped with bourbon sauce, sautéed onions, and Swiss
cheese is a favorite), this place hits the spot. You'll also find plenty of
Mexican dishes, chicken wings, pizzas, and other comfort foods. Beer
is also popular here; more than 70 microbrews are on draft. ⊠*465
Main St., Wakefield* ☎*401/783–9370* ⚓*Reservations not accepted*
▤*AE, D, MC, V.*

$-$$ ▥**Admiral Dewey Inn.** Victorian antiques furnish the rooms of this inn,
which was built in 1898 as a seaside boardinghouse—it's across the
road from Matunuck Beach—and is now on the National Register of
Historic Places. Some rooms, which have polished wood floors and
elegant period-style wallpapering, have views of the ocean; others are
tucked cozily under the eaves. You can soak up the gentle afternoon
breezes on the wraparound veranda, which is filled with old-fashioned
rocking chairs. **Pros:** right by the water, affordable. **Cons:** some rooms
share a bath, no TV or phone in rooms. ⊠*668 Matunuck Beach Rd.,
Wakefield* ☎*401/783–2090 or 800/457–2090* ⊕*www.admiraldewey-
inn.com* ⚲*10 rooms, 8 with bath* ⚐*In-room: no TV. In hotel: public
Internet, no-smoking rooms* ▤*MC, V* ⦾*CP.*

NARRAGANSETT

5 mi east of Wakefield.

The popular beach town of Narragansett draws people for a scenic drive
along the ocean (Route 1A) or for a stroll along its beach or its seawall.
Set on the peninsula east of Point Judith Pond and the Pettaquamscutt
River, the town has many grand old shingle houses that overlook the
ocean and a handful of restaurants and shops directly across the street
from the beach.

WHAT TO SEE

Galilee. The third-largest fishing port in New England, the village is a
busy, workaday fishing port from which whale-watching excursions,
fishing trips, and the **Block Island Ferry** (⊠*Galilee State Pier* ☎*401/783–
4613*) depart. The occasionally pungent smell of seafood and bait will
lead you to the area's "in-the-rough" restaurants and markets.

Narragansett Pier. Often called simply the Pier, this beach community
was named for an amusement wharf that no longer exists. The Pier—
now populated by summertime "cottagers," college students, and commuting professionals—was a posh resort in the late 1800s linked by
rail to New York and Boston. Many summer visitors headed for the
Narragansett Pier Casino, which had a bowling alley, billiard tables,
tennis courts, a rifle gallery, a theater, and a ballroom. The grand edifice
burned to the ground in 1900. Only the **Towers** (⊠*Rte. 1A* ☎*401/783–
7121*), the grand stone entrance to the former casino, remains. Most of
the mansions built during Narragansett's golden age are along Ocean
Road, from Point Judith to Narragansett Pier.

Point Judith Lighthouse. From the port of Galilee it's a short drive to the this lighthouse and a beautiful ocean view. The lighthouse is open daily from dawn to dusk. ⊠*1460 Ocean Rd.* ☎*401/789–0444* 🖾*Free* ⊙*Daily dawn–dusk.*

🌣 **South County Museum.** Set on the former estate (now a town park) of an early-19th-century Rhode Island governor, William Sprague, this museum holds 20,000 artifacts dating from 1800 to 1933. The campus consists of six exhibit buildings, including a print shop, blacksmith and carpentry shops, transportation barn, and textile arts center. ⊠*Strathmore St., off Rte 1A* ☎*401/783–5400* ⊕*www.southcountymuseum. org* 🖾*$5* ⊙*May–June and Sept.–Oct. Fri. and Sat. 10–4, Sun. noon–4; July and Aug. Wed.–Sat. 10–4, Sun. noon–4.*

SPORTS & THE OUTDOORS

BEACHES
Fodor'sChoice
★

Popular mile-long **Narragansett Town Beach** (⊠*Rte. 1A*) is regarded as a great surfing beach due to its smooth, curling waves. The beach is within walking distance of many hotels and guesthouses. Its pavilion has changing rooms, showers, and concessions.

Roger W. Wheeler State Beach (⊠*Sand Hill Cove Rd., Galilee*) has fine white sand, calm water, and a slight drop-off. There is a playground area, picnic tables, a bathhouse, and parking. **Scarborough State Beach** (⊠*Ocean Rd.*), considered by many the jewel of the Ocean State's beaches, has a pavilion with showers and concessions, observation tower, and sitting areas along the boardwalk. On weekends, teenagers and college students blanket the sands.

FISHING
The **Frances Fleet** (⊠*33 State St., Point Judith* ☎*401/783–4988* ⊕*www. francesfleet.com*), with four vessels, operates day and overnight fishing trips. **Persuader** (☎*401/783–5644*) leads sportfishing charters. Excursions on the **Prowler** (☎*401/783–8487* ⊕*www.prowlerchartersri.com*) include tuna and striped bass fishing. The **Seven B's V** (☎*401/789–9250* ⊕*www.sevenbs.com*) is an 80-foot boat that holds up to 120 passengers.

WHALE-
WATCHING
During July and August, whale-watching excursions aboard the **Lady Frances** (⊠*33 State St., Point Judith* ☎*401/783–4988* ⊕*www.frances fleet.com* 🖾*$35*) daily depart at 1 PM and return at 5:30 PM.

SURFING
Gansett Juice (⊠*74 Narragansett Ave.* ☎*401/789–7890* ⊕*www. gansettjuice.com*) rents surfboards, body boards, and wet suits. Call 401/789–1954 for the daily surf report.

WHERE TO EAT

$–$$
SEAFOOD
★

✕**Aunt Carrie's.** You'd hard-pressed to find a better short-order seafood joint than this family-owned restaurant that's been serving up Rhode Island shore dinners, clam cakes and chowder, and fried seafood since 1920. At the height of the season the lines can be long; one alternative is to order from the take-out window and picnic on the grounds of the nearby lighthouse. ⊠*1240 Ocean Rd., Point Judith* ☎*401/783–7930* 🍴*Reservations not accepted* ▭*MC, V* ⊙*Closed Oct.–Mar. and Mon.–Thurs. Apr., May, and Sept.*

$-$$ ✕**George's of Galilee.** This restaurant at the mouth of the Point Judith
SEAFOOD Harbor has been a must for tourists since 1948. The "stuffies" (baked
stuffed quahogs) are some of the best in the state, but you can also
sample fried and broiled seafood, chicken, steak, and pasta, all at reasonable prices, plus an extensive selection of sushi. Its proximity to
the beach and its large outside bar on the second floor keep George's
a busy place all summer. The building has been undergoing a massive
renovation, slated for completion in 2012, but remains open during the
process. ⊠*250 Sand Hill Cove Rd.* ☎*401/783–2306* ⌨*Reservations
not accepted* ▭*D, MC, V* ⊙*Closed Dec. and weekdays Nov. and
Jan.–Mar.*

$$-$$$ ✕**Spain of Narragansett.** This swank Spanish restaurant earns high
Fodor'sChoice marks for superbly prepared food and deft service. Worthy appetiz-
★ ers include shrimp in garlic and olive oil, mushroom caps stuffed with
SPANISH seafood, and grilled smoked chorizo. Prized entrées range from traditional paella to hefty *jefe* steak for two (sautéed tenderloin with artichoke hearts, mushrooms, and a Rioja-mustard-garlic sauce). There are
few more impressive wine lists in the state. Arched entryways and tall
plants help create a Mediterranean mood, and in summer you can dine
on a festive patio anchored by three-tier fountain. ⊠*1144 Ocean Rd.*
☎*401/783–9770* ▭*AE, D, DC, MC, V* ⊙*Closed Mon. No lunch.*

$$-$$$ ✕**Turtle Soup.** Be prepared to wait for a table at this locally revered
AMERICAN restaurant inside a restored Victorian house overlooking Narragansett
★ Bay. The dining room oozes simplicity and comfort, with its gleaming
wood paneling and wood floors; a sitting room provides a fireplace and
overstuffed chairs. The menu focuses on contemporary American cuisine with Mediterranean influences. You might try the pan-seared crab
cakes with a smoked-jalapeño remoulade, followed by roast duck with
a marsala-fig glaze and topped with a black-cherry emulsion. There's
also a light menu of pizzas, burgers, and small plates. ⊠*113 Ocean
Rd.* ☎*401/792–8683* ⌨*Reservations not accepted* ▭*AE, D, MC, V*
⊙*No lunch weekdays. Closed Mon. Oct.–Mar.*

WHERE TO STAY

$$ ⊡**The Richards.** Imposing and magnificent, this 8,500-square-foot, Eng-
★ lish-style stone mansion anchoring a 200-acre estate has a Gothic mys-
tique that is quite different from the spirit of the typical summerhouse.
French windows in the wood-paneled common rooms downstairs open
up to views of a lush landscape, and a fishpond is the centerpiece of
the gardens. A fire crackles in the library fireplace on chilly afternoons.
Some rooms have 19th-century English antiques, floral-upholstered
furniture, and fireplaces, and in each a decanter of sherry awaits guests.
Pros: a singularly remarkable architectural example, breakfast is first-
rate, reasonable rates. **Cons:** a bit of a walk from the beach, no TV in
rooms. ⊠*144 Gibson Ave.,* ☎*401/789–7746* ⊕*www.therichardsbnb.
com* ⇆*3 rooms, 1 suites* ⌂*In-room: no TV. In-hotel: no elevator, no-
smoking rooms* ▭*No credit cards* ⏐⊙⏐*BP.*

WICKFORD

★ *12 mi north of Narragansett Pier, 15 mi south of Providence.*

The Colonial village of Wickford has a little harbor, dozens of 18th-
and 19th-century homes, several antiques shops, and boutiques selling
locally made jewelry and crafts, home accents and gifts, and clothing.
This bayside spot is the kind of almost-too-perfect salty New England
period piece that is usually conjured up only in books and movies. It is
rumored that Wickford was John Updike's model for the New England
of his novel *The Witches of Eastwick.*

WHAT TO SEE

Casey Farm. The historic farm, whose mid-18th-century homestead
overlooks Narragansett Bay off Route 1A south of Wickford, still functions much as it has since its earliest days. During the 19th century the
summer residence of the Casey family, who leased the land to tenant
farmers, it is today a community-supported farm operated by resident
managers who raise organically grown vegetables. Nearly 30 mi of
stone walls surround the 300 acre farmstead. ⊠2325 Boston Neck
Rd., Saunderstown ☎*401/295–1030* ⊕*www.historicnewengland.org*
⊠*$4* ⊙*June–mid-Oct., Sat. 11–5.*

Old Narragansett Church. Now called St. Paul's, this church was built
in 1707 and is one of the oldest Episcopal churches in America. ⊠*55
Main St.* ☎*401/294–4357* ⊕*www.episcopalri.org/org_onc.cfm* ⊙*July
and Aug., Thurs.–Mon. 11–4; Sun. services at 8, 9:30, and 10:30.*

★ **Smith's Castle.** Built in 1678 by Richard Smith Jr. and nearly demolished
in the 1940s, this castle is a beautifully preserved saltbox plantation
house on the quiet shore of an arm of Narragansett Bay. It was the site
of many orations by Roger Williams, from whom Smith bought the
surrounding property. The grounds have one of the first military burial
grounds (open during daylight hours) in the country: a marked mass
grave holding 40 colonists killed in the Great Swamp battle of 1676,
during which the Narragansetts were nearly annihilated, ending King
Philip's War in Rhode Island. ⊠*55 Richard Smith Dr., 1 mi north of
Wickford* ☎*401/294–3521* ⊕*www.smithscastle.org* ⊠*$5* ⊙*Guided
tours at noon, 1, 2, and 3 June–Aug., Thurs.–Sun.; May, Sept.–Oct.,
Fri.–Sun.*

**EN
ROUTE**

Built in 1751, the **Gilbert Stuart Birthplace** was the childhood home of
America's foremost portraitist of George Washington—reproductions
of Stuart's famed works hang in different rooms of the house, which
also contains early furniture, tools, and original architectural details.
It lies on a pretty country road along little Mattatuxet River. The adjacent 18th-century snuff mill was the first in America. The site includes
a gristmill and herring reserve, where river herring migrate up a fish
ladder. You can hike the trail along the river. ⊠*815 Gilbert Stuart
Rd., Saunderstown* ☎*401/294–3001* ⊕*www.gilbertstuartmuseum.
com* ⊠*$6* ⊙*May–Oct., Thurs.–Mon. 11–4.*

SPORTS & THE OUTDOORS

BOATING   In Wickford Harbor, the **Kayak Centre** (✉ *9 Phillip St.* ☎*401/295–4400* ⊕*www.kayakcentre.com*) rents kayaks and provides lessons.

SHOPPING

ANTIQUES   The **Hour Glass** (✉ *15 W. Main St.* ☎*401/295–8724* ⊕*www.the-hourglass. com*) carries antique barometers, clocks, tide clocks, thermometers, and the like. The **Wickford Art Association** (✉ *36 Beach St.* ☎*401/294–6840*) sells the wares of numerous local talents and has juried art shows.

CRAFTS   Needlepoint pillows, leather journals, lamps, and woven throws are a few of the gifts and home furnishings at **Askham & Telham Inc.** (✉ *12 Main St.* ☎*401/295–0891*).

BLOCK ISLAND

Block Island, 12 mi off Rhode Island's southern coast, is 7 mi long and 3 mi wide. With its 17 mi of beaches, Block Island has been a popular travel destination since the 19th century. Despite the number of visitors who come here each summer and thanks to the efforts of local conservationists, the island's beauty remains intact (40% of the land is preserved); its 365 freshwater ponds support more than 150 species of migrating birds.

The original inhabitants of the island were American Indians who called it Manisses, or "isle of the little god." Following a visit in 1614 by the Dutch explorer Adrian Block, the island was given the name Adrian's Eyelant, and later Block Island. In 1661 the island was settled by farmers and fishermen from Massachusetts Bay Colony. They gave Block Island what remains its second official name, the Town of New Shoreham, when it became part of Rhode Island in 1672.

Block Island, with 800 year-round residents, is a laid-back community. People exchange phone numbers by the last four digits (466 is the prefix) alone, and you can dine at any of the island's establishments in shorts and a T-shirt. The busiest season is between May and Columbus Day—at other times, most restaurants, inns, stores, and visitor services close down. If you plan to stay overnight in summer, make reservations well in advance; for weekends in July and August, March is not too early.

Block Island has two harbors, Old Harbor and New Harbor. Approaching the island by sea from New London (Connecticut), Newport, or Point Judith, you'll see Old Harbor, the island's only village, and its group of Victorian hotels. Most of the smaller inns, shops, and restaurants are also here, and it's a short walk from the ferry landing to most of the interesting sights.

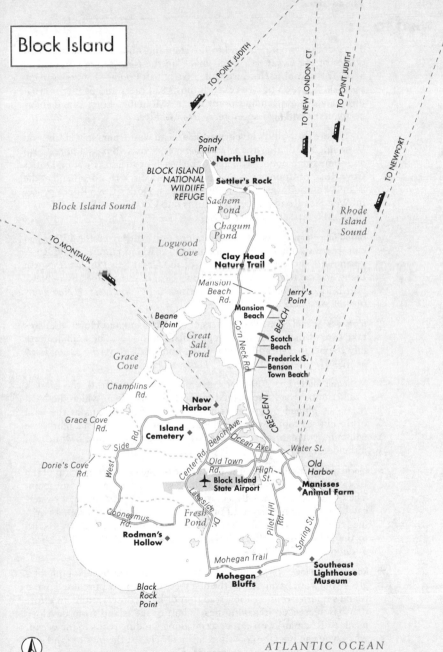

Block Island

TO POINT JUDITH

TO NEW LONDON, CT

TO POINT JUDITH

TO NEWPORT

Sandy
Point

North Light

BLOCK ISLAND
NATIONAL
WILDLIFE
REFUGE

Settler's Rock

Block Island Sound

Sachem
Pond

Chagum
Pond

Rhode
Island
Sound

Logwood
Cove

**Clay Head
Nature Trail**

TO MONTAUK

Mansion
Beach
Rd.

Jerry's
Point

Beane
Point

**Mansion
Beach**

BEACH

Grace
Cove

Great
Salt
Pond

Corn Neck Rd.

**Scotch
Beach**

**Frederick S.
Benson
Town Beach**

Champlins
Rd.

**New
Harbor**

Grace Cove
Rd.

**Island
Cemetery**

Beach Ave.

Ocean Ave.

CRESCENT

Side Rd.

West Rd.

Center Rd.

Water St.

Dorie's Cove
Rd.

Old Town
Rd.

Old
Harbor

High
St.

✈ **Block Island
State Airport**

**Manisses
Animal Farm**

Cooneymus
Rd.

Lakeside Dr.

Fresh
Pond

Pilot Hill Rd.

Spring St.

**Rodman's
Hollow**

Mohegan Trail

**Mohegan
Bluffs**

**Southeast
Lighthouse
Museum**

Black
Rock
Point

ATLANTIC OCEAN

N

0   900 yards

0   900 meters

WHAT TO SEE

Three docks, two hotels, and four restaurants huddled in the southeast corner of the Great Salt Pond make up the **New Harbor** commercial area. The harbor itself—also called Great Salt Pond—shelters as many as 1,700 boats on busy weekends, hosts sail races and fishing tournaments, and is the landing point for the Montauk, Long Island (New York), ferry and high-speed ferry from Galilee.

To explore the island's lovely **west side,** head west from New Harbor on West Side Road; after the Island Cemetery, you will pass a horse farm and some small ponds. You get to the beach by turning right on Dories Cove Road or Cooneymus Beach Road; both dirt roads dead-end at the island's tranquil west shore. One mile past Dories Cove Road, peaceful West Side Road jogs left and turns into Cooneymus Road. On your right ½ mi farther is a deep ravine.

Island Cemetery. At this well-maintained graveyard from the 1700s you can spot the names of long-standing Block Island families (Ball, Rose, Champlin) and take in fine views of the Great Salt Pond, the North Light, and the Rhode Island coast; on a clear day, the Jamestown–Newport Bridge will be visible to the northeast. ⊠ ½ mi west of New Harbor on West Side Rd.

Ↄ **Manisses Animal Farm.** The owners of the 1661 Inn and Hotel Manisses take care of llamas, emus, sheep, goats, and ducks. The animals happily coexist in a meadow next to the hotel. ⊠ Off Spring St. or High St. ☎ 401/466–2063 ☞ Free ☉ Daily dawn–dusk.

Fodor'sChoice **Mohegan Bluff.** The 200-foot cliffs along Mohegan Trail, the island's
★ southernmost road, are named for an Indian battle in which the local Manisses pinned down an attacking band of Mohegans at the base of the cliffs. From Payne Overlook, west of the Southeast Lighthouse Museum, you can see to Montauk Point, New York, and beyond. An intimidating set of stairs leads down to the beach.

★ **North Light.** This 1867 granite lighthouse on the northernmost tip of the Block Island National Wildlife Refuge serves as a maritime museum. The protected area nearby is a temporary home to American oystercatchers, piping plovers, and other rare migrating birds. From a parking lot at the end of Corn Neck Road, it's a ¾-mi-long hike over sand to the lighthouse. ⊠ Corn Neck Rd. ☎ 401/466–3200 ☞ $2 ☉ July 5–Labor Day, daily 10–4.

★ **Rodman's Hollow.** Off Cooneymus Road, this spot is a fine example of a glacial outwash basin. It was the first piece of property purchased in the island's quarter-century-long tradition of land conservation, an effort that has succeeded in saving nearly half of the island from development. At Rodman's you can descend along winding paths to the ocean, where you can hike the coastline, lie on beaches at the foot of sand and clay cliffs, or swim if the waters are calm.

Settler's Rock. On the spit of land between Sachem Pond and Cow Beach, this monument lists the names of the original settlers and marks the spot where they landed in 1661 (with their cows swimming to shore). Hiking a mile over sandy terrain will get you to the North Light.

Southeast Lighthouse Museum. The small repository is inside a "rescued" 1873 redbrick beacon with gingerbread detail that was moved back from the eroded 150-foot cliff. The lighthouse is a National Historic Landmark. ⊠*Mohegan Trail* ☎*401/466–5009* ☚*$5* ☉*Memorial Day–Labor Day, daily 10–4.*

SPORTS & THE OUTDOORS

BEACHES
The east side of the island has a number of beaches.

★ The 2½-mi **Crescent Beach** runs from Old Harbor to Jerry's Point. **Frederick J. Benson Town Beach,** a family beach less than 1 mi down Corn Neck Road from Old Harbor, has a beach pavilion, parking, showers, and lifeguards. **Mansion Beach,** off Mansion Beach Road south of Jerry's Point, has deep white sand and is easily one of New England's most beautiful beaches. In the morning, you may spot deer on the dunes. Young summer workers congregate ½ mi north of Town Beach at **Scotch Beach** to play volleyball, surf, and sun themselves.

BIKING
The best way to explore Block Island is by bicycle (about $15 to $20 a day to rent) or moped (about $45). Most rental places are open spring through fall and have child seats for bikes, and all rent bicycles in a variety of styles and sizes, including mountain bikes, hybrids, tandems, and children's bikes.

Near Harborside Inn, **Island Bike & Moped** (⊠ *Weldon's Way)* ☎*401/466–2700*) has bikes of all kinds. **Moped Man** (⊠ *Weldon's Way and Water St.* ☎*401/466–5444*) has motorized bikes on hand. Descend from the Block Island Ferry and get right on a bike at **Old Harbor Bike Shop** (⊠*South of ferry dock* ☎*401/466–2029* ⊕*www.oldharborbikeshop. com*), which also rents mopeds, Jeeps, and other vehicles.

BOATING
Block Island Boat Basin (⊠ *West Side Rd., New Harbor* ☎*401/466–2631*) is the island's best-stocked ship's store. **New Harbor Kayak** (⊠*Ocean Ave., New Harbor* ☎*401/466–2890*) rents kayaks, paddleboats, and motorboats. **Oceans & Ponds** (⊠*Ocean and Connecticut Aves.* ☎*401/466–5131*) rents kayaks, charters fishing boats and trimaran sail cruises, sells and rents fishing tackle, offers fishing guides, and sells outdoor clothing.

FISHING
Most of Rhode Island's record fish have been caught on Block Island. In fact, Block Island has held the striped bass fishing record since 1984. From almost any beach, skilled anglers can land tautog and bass. Bonito and fluke are often hooked in the New Harbor channel. Shellfishing licenses may be obtained at the town hall, on Old Town Road.

Oceans & Ponds (⊠*Ocean and Connecticut Aves.* ☏*401/466–5131*) sells tackle and fishing gear, operates charter trips, and provides guide services. **Twin Maples** (⊠*Beach Ave.* ☏*401/466–5547*) sells bait.

HIKING

★ The outstanding **Clay Head Nature Trail** (⊹*Begins at the end of a dirt road that begins at Corn Neck Rd., just past Mansion Beach Rd., about 2 mi from town*) meanders past Clay Head Swamp and along 150-foot-high ocean-side cliffs. Songbirds chirp and flowers bloom along the paths that lead to the beach or into the interior—an area called the Maze. The trailhead is recognizable by a simple white post marker. Trail maps are available at the **Nature Conservancy** (⊠*352 High St.* ☏*401/466–2129*). The **Greenway,** a well-maintained trail system, meanders across the island, but some of the best hikes are along the beaches. You can hike around the entire island in about eight hours. Trail maps for the Greenway are available at the **Chamber of Commerce** (⊠*Water St.* ☏*401/466–2982*) and at the **Nature Conservancy** (⊠*352 High St.* ☏*401/466–2129*). The Nature Conservancy conducts nature walks; call for times or check the *Block Island Times.*

WATER SPORTS

Island Outfitters (⊠*Ocean Ave.* ☏*401/466–5502*) rents wet suits, spearguns, and scuba gear. PADI-certification diving courses are available, and beach gear and bathing suits are for sale. **Parasailing on Block Island** (⊠*Old Harbor Basin* ☏*401/864–2474*) will take you parasailing and also rents five-person jet boats and 10-person banana boats.

SHOPPING

Scarlet Begonia (⊠*Dodge St.* ☏*401/466–5024*) carries jewelry and crafts like handmade quilts. **Spring Street Gallery** (⊠*Spring St.* ☏*401/466–5374* ⊕*www.springstreetgallery.org*) shows and sells work like paintings, photographs, stained glass, and serigraphs by island artists and artisans. **Jessie Edwards Studios** (⊠*Post Office Square* ☏*401/466–5314* ⊕*www.jessieedwardsgallery.com*) showcases contemporary photographs, sculptures, and paintings, often with nautical themes.

NIGHTLIFE

Nightlife, at least in season, is one of Block Island's highlights, and you have approximately two dozen places to grab a drink. Check the *Block Island Times* for band listings. **Ballard's** (⊠*On docks at Old Harbor* ☏*401/466–2231*), a popular tourist destination, is a family restaurant with a beach and an outdoor bar by day. By night it becomes a dance club with live entertainment. **Captain Nick's Rock and Roll Bar** (⊠*34 Ocean Ave.* ☏*401/466–5670*), a fortress of summertime debauchery and the host of June's Block Island Music Festival, has four bars and two decks on two floors. In season, bands play nightly. In one of the few year-round spots, **Club Soda** (⊠*35 Connecticut Ave.* ☏*401/466–5397*) has a 360-degree mural depicting Block Island in the 1940s.

McGovern's Yellow Kittens Tavern (⊠ *Corn Neck Rd.* 🕾 *401/466–5855*) has darts, Ping-Pong, pool, and bands on summer weekend nights.

WHERE TO EAT

$$$$
AMERICAN
✕ **Atlantic Inn.** The romantic restaurant at this venerable inn serves imaginative contemporary American fare in its airy dining room, which is arguably the swankiest on the island. Meals are served from a four-course, prix-fixe dinner that's available with wine pairings, and the menus change often. Typical, however, is the starter of charred-tuna poke with Asian greens and a sesame-honey sauce, and the main dish of roasted halibut with mussels, leeks, and a beer buerre blanc. ⊠ *High St.* 🕾 *401/466–5883* 🖃 *D, MC, V* ⊘ *Closed late Oct.–mid-Apr. No lunch.*

$$–$$$
AMERICAN
✕ **The BeacHead.** The food—especially the Rhode Island clam chowder—is very good, the price is right, and you won't feel like a tourist at this locals' hangout. Play pool, catch up on town gossip, or sit at the bar and stare out at the sea. The menu and service are unpretentious; you can stop in for a burger at lunch, or try somewhat more ambitious fare, such as Thai shrimp pasta or steak au poivre, at dinner. ⊠ *Corn Neck Rd.* 🕾 *401/466–2249* ⚭ *Reservations not accepted* 🖃 *MC* ⊘ *Closed Mon.–Wed. Dec.–Mar.*

$$$
AMERICAN
Fodor's Choice
★
✕ **Eli's.** A spaghetti eatery turned bistro, Eli's is Block Island's preferred restaurant. Pastas are the menu's mainstays, but the kitchen makes extensive excursions into local seafood, and steaks like the Carpetbagger, a 12-ounce filet mignon filled with lobster, mozzarella, and sundried tomatoes, topped with a béarnaise sauce. The food keeps people coming back. ⊠ *457 Chapel St.* 🕾 *401/466–5230* ⚭ *Reservations not accepted* 🖃 *AE, D, MC, V* ⊘ *Closed Jan.–Apr.*

$–$$
SEAFOOD
✕ **Finn's.** A Block Island institution, Finn's serves reliable fried and broiled seafood and prepares a wonderful smoked bluefish pâté. For lunch try the Workman's Special platter—a burger, coleslaw, and french fries. You can eat inside or out on the deck, or get food to go. Finn's raw bar is on an upstairs deck that overlooks Old Harbor. ⊠ *Ferry Landing* 🕾 *401/466–2473* ⚭ *Reservations not accepted* 🖃 *MC, V* ⊘ *Closed mid-Oct.–May.*

$$$–$$$$
AMERICAN
★
✕ **Hotel Manisses.** The chef at the island's premier restaurant for American cuisine uses herbs and vegetables from the hotel's garden and locally caught seafood to prepare superb dishes such as littleneck clams Dijonnaise, baked lobster mac-and-cheese, and seared halibut with *brandade* potatoes, bay scallops, and a leek confit. Be sure to try a side of the lobster mashed potatoes. ⊠ *1 Spring St.* 🕾 *401/466–2421* 🖃 *MC, V* ⊘ *Closed Nov.–Apr.*

WHERE TO STAY

Lodgings on Block Island is booked well in advance for weekends in July and August. Many visitors rent homes for stays of a week or more. Many houses, however, are booked solid by April, so book early. Reliable agents include **Ballard Hall Real Estate** (⊠ *Ocean Ave.* 🕾 *401/466–*

8883 ⊕*www.blockislandproperty.com*), and **Sullivan Real Estate** (⊠ *Water St.* ☎*401/466–5521* ⊕*www.blockislandhouses.com*).

$$$-$$$$
Fodor'sChoice
★
🖺 **Atlantic Inn.** Perched on a hill of floral gardens and undulating lawns, away from the hubbub of the Old Harbor area, this long, white, classic 1879 Victorian resort has big windows, high ceilings, a sweeping staircase, and lovely views. Most of the oak and maple furnishings in the rooms are original to the building. Each morning the inn's pastry chef prepares a buffet breakfast with fresh baked goods. The on-site restaurant is a favorite for a special occasion. Pros: Spectacular hilltop location; beautiful veranda for whiling away the afternoon; grand decor. Cons: no TVs in rooms. ⊠*High St., Box 1788* ☎*401/466–5883 or 800/224–7422* ⊕*www.atlanticinn.com* ➷*20 rooms, 1 suite* �& *In-room: no TV. In-hotel: restaurant, tennis courts, no elevator, no-smoking rooms* ☰*D, MC, V* ☉*Closed late Oct.–mid-Apr.* ⦿*CP.*

$$-$$$
🖺 **Barrington Inn.** This 1886 inn is quiet and bright with views of Trims Pond, Great Salt Pond, and Crescent Beach. Three rooms have private decks; there's also a large common deck. A hearty continental breakfast is served in the dining room and outside on the deck. Two apartments (rented by the week in season) in a separate building are good options for families. The inn has a pair of sister properties run by the same owners, the Inn at Block Island and the Jane Marie Cottage. Pros: open year-round, reasonably priced. Cons: furnishings are quite simple. ⊠*Beach Ave., Box 397* ☎*401/466–5510 or 888/279–9400* ⊕*www. thebarringtoninn.com* ➷*6 rooms, 2 apartments* �& *In-room: VCR. In-hotel: no kids under 12, no-smoking rooms* ☰*D, MC, V* ⦿*CP.*

$$$-$$$$
★
🖺 **Blue Dory Inn.** This Old Harbor district inn has been a guesthouse since its construction in 1898. Thanks to Ann Law, the dynamic owner-manager, its main building and three small shingle-and-clapboard outbuildings run efficiently. Though not large, the rooms are tastefully appointed with Victorian antiques, some have Jacuzzi tubs, and each has either an ocean or a harbor view. Couples looking for a romantic hideaway often enjoy the Tea House, which has a porch overlooking Crescent Beach. Pros: great in-town location; relatively affordable; open in winter. Cons: some units are quite small. ⊠*61 Dodge St., Box 488* ☎*401/466–2254 or 800/992–7290* ⊕*www.thebluedoryinn.com* ➷*12 rooms, 4 cottages, 3 suites* �& *In-room: VCR. In-hotel: no elevator, no-smoking rooms* ☰*AE, MC, V* ⦿*BP.*

$$-$$$
🖺 **1661 Inn and Hotel Manisses.** Comprising two main hotel buildings also offering accommodations in a few other nearby cottages and houses, this rambling compound has something for every traveler, from luxurious rooms with water views to relatively simple units with shared bathrooms. In Hotel Manisses, an 1872 mansion, there are period furnishings, floral wallpaper, white wicker, wrought iron, and heavily carved furniture. The extras here include picnic baskets, an animal farm, island tours, afternoon wine and hors d'oeuvres in the parlor, and many rooms with whirlpool baths. If your island vacation fantasy includes lounging in bed while gazing at swans in marshes that overlook the blue Atlantic, consider the 1661 Inn. Loll on the inn's expansive deck or curl up in a chair on the lawn; you'll enjoy the panorama of the water below. Rooms have a combination of ocean views, decks,

canopy beds, whirlpool tubs, and gas fireplaces. Pros: lots of room configurations, pastoral grounds, a very good restaurant. Cons: no TVs or other modern amenities in rooms. ⊠*1 Spring St.* ☎*401/466–2421 or 800/626–4773* ⊕*www.blockislandresorts.com* ⇌*40 rooms, 36 with bath* ⚫*In-room: no a/c, no TV. In-hotel: restaurant, no elevator, no kids under 12, no-smoking rooms* ▬*MC, V* ⍥*BP.*

NEWPORT COUNTY

Perched gloriously on the southern tip of Aquidneck Island and bounded on three sides by water, Newport is one of the great sailing cities of the world and the host to world-class jazz, blues, folk, classical music, and film festivals. Colonial houses and gilded-age mansions grace the city. Besides Newport itself, Newport County also encompasses the two other communities of Aquidneck Island—Middletown and Portsmouth—plus Conanicut Island, also known as Jamestown, to the west, and Tiverton and Little Compton, abutting Massachusetts to the east. Little Compton is a remote, idyllic town that presents a strong contrast to Newport's quick pace.

JAMESTOWN

25 mi south of Providence, 3 mi west of Newport.

The 9-mi-long, 1-mi-wide landmass that goes by the names Jamestown and Conanicut Island is encompassed by the east and west passages of Narragansett Bay. Valuable as a military outpost in days gone by, the island was once considered an impediment to commercial cross-bay shipping. In 1940 the Jamestown Bridge linked it to western Rhode Island, and in 1969 the Newport Bridge completed the cross-bay route, connecting Newport to the entire South County area. Summer residents have come to Jamestown since the 1880s, but never to the same extent as to Watch Hill, Narragansett, or Newport. The locals' "We're not a T-shirt town" attitude has resulted in a relatively low number of visitors, even in July and August, making this a peaceful alternative to the bustle of nearby Newport and South County.

Handy if you're staying in Newport but want to hop over to Jamestown to explore or enjoy a meal, the **Jamestown and Newport Ferry** stops in Newport at Bowen's Landing, Fort Adams, and Goat Island (and will stop at Rose Island upon request). The 35-foot passenger ferry departs on its half-hour voyage from Ferry Wharf about every 1½ hours, from 9:50 AM to 8 PM (until 9 PM on weekends). The last run leaves from Newport at 8:30 PM (9:45 on weekends). ⊠*Ferry Wharf* ☎*401/423–9900* ▦*$15 all-day pass* ⊙*Memorial Day–Labor Day.*

WHAT TO SEE

☾ **Jamestown Fire Department Memorial Museum.** A working 1859 hand tub and a horse-drawn steam pump are among the holdings at this informal display of firefighting equipment in a garage that once housed the fire company. ✉*50 Narragansett Ave.* ☎*401/423–1820* 🖱*Free* ☉*Daily 7–3; inquire next door at fire department if door is locked.*

Jamestown Windmill. Once common in Rhode Island, the English-designed windmill, built in 1789, ground corn for more than 100 years—and it still works. ✉*North Rd. southeast of Watson Farm* ☎*401/423–1798* 🖱*Free* ☉*Mid-June–Aug., weekends 1–4.*

Watson Farm. Come here for the view and a bit of history. The 285-acre spread, dedicated to educating the public about agrarian culture, has 2 mi of trails along Jamestown's southwestern shore with amazing views of Narragansett Bay and North Kingstown. Thomas Carr Watson's family had worked this farm for 190 years before he bequeathed it to the Society for the Preservation of New England Antiquities when he died in 1979. ✉*455 North Rd.* ☎*401/423–0005* 🖱*$3* ☉*June–mid-Oct., Tues., Thurs., and Sun. 1–5.*

SPORTS & THE OUTDOORS

Beavertail State Park. The water conditions range from tranquil to harrowing at this park straddling the southern tip of Conanicut Island. The currents and surf here are famously deadly during rough seas and high winds; but on a clear, calm day, the park's craggy shoreline seems intended for sunning, hiking, and climbing. The **Beavertail Lighthouse Museum,** in what was the lighthouse keeper's quarters, has displays about Rhode Island's lighthouses. ✉*Beavertail Rd.* ☎*401/423–3270* 🖱*Free* ☉*Museum June–Labor Day, daily 10–4; park daily dawn–dusk.*

Fort Wetherill State Park. An outcropping of stone cliffs at the tip of the southeastern peninsula, this green space has been a picnic destination since the 1800s. There's great swimming at the small cove here, and it's a favorite spot for local snorkelers and scuba divers. ✉*Ocean St.* ☎*401/423–1771* 🖱*Free* ☉*Daily dawn–dusk.*

BEACHES Sandy **Mackerel Cove Beach** (✉*Beavertail Rd.*) is sheltered from the currents of Narragansett Bay, making it a great spot for families.

DIVING & **Ocean State Scuba** (✉*79 N. Main Rd.* ☎*401/423–1662 or 800/933–*
KAYAKING *3483*) rents kayaks and diving equipment.

GOLF **Jamestown Country Club** (✉*245 Conanicus Ave.* ☎*401/423–9930*) has a crisp 9-hole course for a mere $10.

WHERE TO EAT

$–$$ ✕**Jamestown Oyster Bar.** An easygoing neighborhood hangout in New-
SEAFOOD port's laid-back neighbor across the water, this is actually a full restaurant with a substantial—and quite traditional—seafood menu. Freshly shucked oysters are kept on ice behind the bar, where tenders pour fine microbrews and wines. Among main dishes, consider the scampi with shrimp and littleneck clams, and also check out the chalkboard of more creative nightly specials. The burgers are locally renowned. ✉*22 Narragansett Ave.* ☎*401/423–3380* 🖱*Reservations not accepted* 🖃*AE, MC, V.*

$$-$$$ ✕**Trattoria Simpatico.** A jazz trio plays on weekday evenings and sunny
ITALIAN Sunday afternoons at Jamestown's signature restaurant, while patrons
★ dine alfresco under copper beech tree that dates to the 18th century.
An herb garden, fieldstone walls, and white linen complete the picture. You can munch on splendid salads, Northern Italian pasta dishes, meats prepared with a Continental flair, and a handful of Asian-fusion dishes. Memorable are the tamarind-glazed ribs and braised-beef cassoulet appetizers and the maple-soy glazed tuna pad thai as an entrée. Reservations are essential on summer weekends. ⊠*13 Narragansett Ave.* ☎*401/423-3731* ⊟*AE, D, MC, V* ⊘*No lunch Mon.–Thurs.*

3

WHERE TO STAY

$$$$ ⊡**Bay Voyage.** In 1889 this Victorian inn was shipped from Newport
to its current location and named in honor of its trip. The one-bedroom suites, furnished in floral prints and pastels, have been sold as time-shares, which makes availability tight in summer. The facilities are plentiful, the view memorable. The restaurant is known for its Sunday brunch, but dinner, where you might find juniper-rubbed venison in an espresso demiglace, is first-rate, too. Prout kitchens in rooms, overlooks water, easy walk to village restaurants. **Cons:** feels a bit like a timeshare. ⊠*150 Conanicus Ave.* ☎*401/423-2100* ⊕*www.bayvoyageinn.com* ⌂*32 suites* ⌂*In-room: kitchen. In-hotel: restaurant, bar, pool, gym, public Internet, no-smoking rooms* ⊟*AE, D, DC, MC, V.*

$-$$ ⊡**East Bay B&B.** This 1896 Victorian is peaceful day and night, even
though it's only a block from Jamestown's two main streets and bustling wharf. Rooms are generous in size; the common room has a fireplace. The owner, a trained pastry chef, prepares a copious homemade breakfast. **Pros:** much more affordable than Newport accommodations, large rooms, close to restaurants. **Cons:** some rooms share a bath. ⊠*14 Union St.* ☎*401/423-0330 or 800/243-1107* ⊕*www.eastbaybnb.com* ⌂*4 rooms, 2 with bath* ⌂*No-smoking rooms* ⊟*AE, MC, V* ⊺◎*BP.*

NEWPORT

30 mi south of Providence, 80 mi south of Boston.

The island city of Newport preserves Colonial industry and gilded-age splendor like no other place in the country. Settled in 1639 by a small band of religious dissenters from Massachusetts, Newport earned a reputation for tolerance, and its prime location at the mouth of Narragansett Bay ensured its success. The golden age of Colonial Newport ran from roughly 1720 to the 1770s. Making the city a leader in New World maritime commerce were its shipbuilders, the best in North America; its products, such as cheese, candles, clocks, furniture, and livestock; and its profitable slave trade (although in 1774 progressive Rhode Island became the first colony to outlaw trading in slaves).

In the 19th century, Newport became a summer playground for the wealthy, those titans of the gilded age who built their fabulous "cottages" overlooking the Atlantic. These mansions served as proving grounds for the country's best young architects, who designed estates

NEWPORT TOURS

TOURS BY BOAT

More than a dozen yacht companies operate tours of Newport Harbor and Narragansett Bay. Outings usually run two hours and about $25 per person.

■ **Conway Tours/Grayline Rhode Island** (☎ 401/658–3400 ⊕ www. conwaytours.com) cruises the bay and also visits Belcourt Castle.

■ **Madeleine** (☎ 401/847–0298 ⊕ www.cruisenewport.com), a 72-foot schooner, departs from Bannister's Wharf.

■ **RumRunner II** (☎ 401/847–0298 ⊕ www.cruisenewport.com), a vintage 1929 motor yacht, once carried "hooch"; it leaves from Bannister's Wharf.

■ A schooner and two sailboats with **Sightsailing of Newport** (☎ 401/849–3333 or 800/709–7245 ⊕ www.sightsailing.com) depart from Bowen's Wharf for 75-minute tours of Newport Harbor and Narragansett Bay.

TRAIN RIDES

■ **Old Colony & Newport Railway** (☎ 401/849–0546 ⊕ www.ocnrr. com) follows an 8-mi route along Narragansett Bay. The vintage diesel train and coaches make 80-minute round-trips to Middletown on Sunday at 11:45 and 1:45.

TROLLEY TOURS

■ **Viking Tours of Newport** (☎ 401/847–6921 ⊕ www.viking-toursnewport.com) conducts trolley tours of Newport daily from May through October and on Saturdays the rest of the year; it also operates one-hour boat tours from mid-May to Columbus Day weekend.

WALKING TOURS

■ The **Newport Historical Society** (☎ 401/846–0813 ⊕ www.new-porthistorical.org) sponsors walking tours focusing on varying themes from April through December.

for the Vanderbilts, Berwinds, Astors, and Belmonts. Many of the mansions are now open to the public for tours.

Recreational sailing, a huge industry in Newport today, convincingly melds the attributes of two eras: the nautical expertise of the Colonial era and the conspicuous consumption of the late 19th century. Tanned young sailors often fill Newport's bars and restaurants. For those not arriving by water, a boat tour of the harbor is a great way to get your feet wet.

Newport has much to offer in a relatively small geographical area—mansions, beaches, seafood restaurants, art galleries, shopping, and, some say, more B&Bs per capita than anywhere else in the country. In summer, it can be crowded (3.5 million people visit each year). Yet the quality of its sights and its arts festivals persuade many people to brave the crowds. In fall and spring, you can explore the city without having to stand in line.

Away from downtown, the gilded-age mansions of Bellevue Avenue are what many people associate most with Newport. These late-19th-century homes are almost obscenely grand, laden with ornate rococo detail and designed with a determined one-upmanship (⇨ *Greater Newport* under *What to See*).

WHAT TO SEE

DOWNTOWN NEWPORT

More than 200 pre-Revolutionary buildings (mostly private residences) remain in Newport, more than in any other city in the country. Most of these treasures are in the neighborhood known as the Point.

With the exception of Ocean Drive, Newport is a walker's city. In summer, traffic is thick, and the narrow one-way streets can be mazelike. It's worth parking in a pay lot and leaving your car behind while you visit in-town sights; one lot is at the Newport Visitors' Information Center on America's Cup Avenue.

❻ **Colony House.** This 1739 redbrick structure above downtown's Washington Square was the center of activity in Colonial Newport and Rhode Island. On July 20, 1776, the Declaration of Independence was read here to Newporters. In 1781, George Washington met here with French commander Count Rochambeau, cementing the alliance that led to the American victory at Yorktown. ⊠ *Washington Sq.* ☎ *401/846–0813* ⊕ *www.newporthistorical.org* ⊟ *$5* ☉ *Tours by appointment.*

❷ **Common Burial Ground.** Located on Farewell Street, which is lined with historic cemeteries, this 17th-century graveyard holds many a tombstone done by John Stevens, who opened his stone-carving shop in 1705 (the business still thrives today). The tombstones are fine examples of Colonial stone carving.

❹ **Great Friends Meeting House.** Built in 1699, this is the oldest house of worship in Rhode Island. With its wide-plank floors, simple benches, balcony, and beam ceiling (considered lofty by Colonial standards), the two-story shingle structure reflects the quiet reserve and steadfast faith of Colonial Quakers. ⊠ *29 Farewell St.* ☎ *401/846–0813* ⊟ *$5* ☉ *Tours by appointment.*

❶ **Hunter House.** The French admiral Charles Louis d'Arsac de Ternay used
★ this lovely 1748 home as his Revolutionary War headquarters. The carved pineapple over the doorway was a symbol of welcome throughout Colonial America; a fresh pineapple placed out front signaled an invitation to neighbors to visit a returned seaman or to look over a shop's new stock. The elliptical arch in the central hall is a typical Newport detail. Pieces made by Newport artisans Townsend and Goddard furnish much of the house, which also contains the first commissioned painting by a young Gilbert Stuart, best known for his portraits of George Washington. ⊠ *54 Washington St.* ☎ *401/847–1000* ⊕ *www. newportmansions.org* ⊟ *$25* ☉ *Late June–early Sept., daily 10–5.*

❼ **Museum of Newport History.** This restored brick market building houses a museum that explores Newport's social and economic influences. Antiques such as the printing press of James Franklin (Ben's brother) inspire the imagination. Built in 1762 and designed by Peter Harrison, who was also responsible for the Touro Synagogue and the Redwood Library, the building also served as a theater and a town hall. The

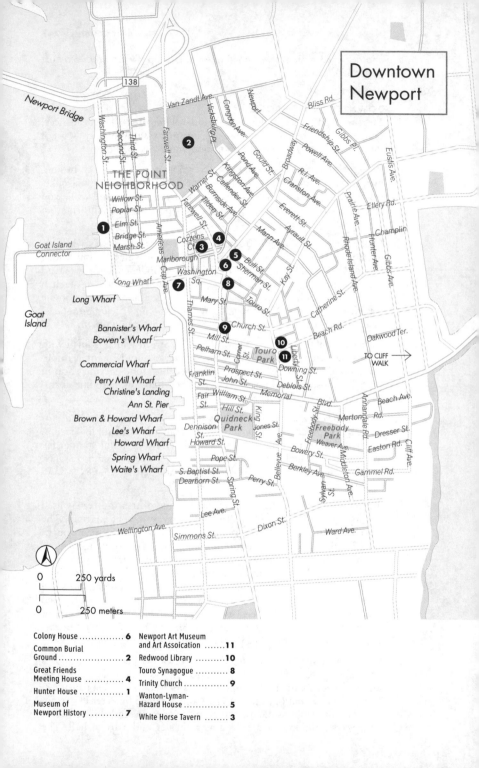

Downtown Newport

THE POINT NEIGHBORHOOD

Newport Bridge

Goat Island Connector

Goat Island

Long Wharf
Bannister's Wharf
Bowen's Wharf
Commercial Wharf
Perry Mill Wharf
Christine's Landing
Ann St. Pier
Brown & Howard Wharf
Lee's Wharf
Howard Wharf
Spring Wharf
Waite's Wharf

Quidneck Park

Touro Park

Freebody Park

TO CLIFF WALK

0 250 yards

0 250 meters

museum and the Newport Visitors' Information Center are departure points for walking tours of Newport; call for times. ✉127 Thames St. ☎401/841–8770 ⊕www.newporthistorical.org ✉$4 ☉May–Sept., daily 10:30–6:30; Oct.–Apr., Sun.–Wed. 10–5, Thurs. and Fri. 10–6.

⑪ Newport Art Museum and Art Association. Richard Morris Hunt designed the Stick-style Victorian building that houses this community-supported center for the arts. The galleries exhibit contemporary New England works, as well as paintings by such esteemed regional luminaries as John La Farge, George Inness, Fitz Henry Lane, Gilbert Stuart, and many others. ✉76 Bellevue Ave. ☎401/848–8200 ⊕www.newport artmuseum.com ✉$6 ☉Late May–early Sept., Mon.–Sat. 10–5, Sun. noon–5; early Sept.–late May, Mon.–Sat. 10–4, Sun. noon–4.

⑩ Redwood Library. This Roman templelike building, complete with Doric
★ columns, was built in 1747 and has been in use for that purpose ever since, making it America's oldest lending library. Although it may look like a Roman temple, it is actually made of wood; the exterior paint is mixed with sand to make it resemble cut stone. The library's paintings include works by Gilbert Stuart and Rembrandt Peale. Free guided tours are given on weekday mornings at 10:30 AM. ✉50 Bellevue Ave. ☎401/847–0292 ⊕www.redwoodlibrary.org ✉Free ☉Mon., Fri., and Sat. 9:30–5:30, Tues.–Thurs. 9:30–8, Sun. 1–5.

⑧ Touro Synagogue. Jews, like Quakers and Baptists, were attracted by
★ Rhode Island's religious tolerance; they arrived in Newport as early as 1658, possibly from Holland or the West Indies. At first they worshipped in homes, but by 1758 they were numerous enough to begin building a synagogue. Dedicated in 1763, the Touro Synagogue is the oldest surviving synagogue in the United States. Although simple on the outside, the Georgian building, designed by Peter Harrison, has an elaborate interior. Its classical style influenced Thomas Jefferson in the building of Monticello and the University of Virginia. ✉85 Touro St. ☎401/847–4794 ⊕www.tourosynagogue.org ✉Free ☉Guided tours on the ½ hr: early July–early Sept., Sun.–Fri. 10–5; late May–early July and early Sept.–Oct., weekdays 1–3, Sun. 1–3; Nov.–late May, Fri. 1 PM tour only, Sun. 11–3. Services: 1 in morning and 1 in evening, call for times.

NEED A BREAK? Ideal for a quick and affordable bite, Ocean Coffee Roasters (✉22 Washington Sq. ☎401/846–6060) serves fresh-roasted coffee and enticing baked goods, plus a nice range of egg dishes, soups, salads, and sandwiches.

⑨ Trinity Church. This Colonial beauty was built in 1724 and modeled after London churches designed by Sir Christopher Wren. A special feature of the interior is the three-tier wineglass pulpit, the only one of its kind in America. The lighting, woodwork, and palpable feeling of history make attending Episcopal services here an unforgettable experience. ✉Queen Anne Sq. ☎401/846–0660 ⊕www.trinitynewport.org ✉Free ☉May and June, weekdays 10–1; July and Aug., Mon.–Sat., 10–4; Sept.–mid-Oct., weekdays 10–1. Sun. services at 8 and 10.

⑤ Wanton-Lyman-Hazard House. This late-17th-century residence presents a window on the fascinating Colonial and Revolutionary history of Newport. The dark-red building was the site of the city's Stamp Act riot of 1765. After the British Parliament levied a tax on most printed material, the Sons of Liberty stormed the house, which was occupied by a prominent and outspoken Loyalist. ✉ *17 Broadway* ☎ *401/846–0813* ⊕ *www.newporthistorical.org* 🎫 *$5* ☽ *Tours by appointment.*

❸ White Horse Tavern. William Mayes, the father of a successful and notorious pirate, received a tavern license in 1687, which makes this building, built in 1673, the oldest still-operating tavern in America. Its gambrel roof, low dark-beam ceilings, cavernous fireplace, and uneven plank floors epitomize Newport's Colonial charm. ✉ *26 Marlborough St.* ☎ *401/849–3600* ⊕ *www.whitehorsetavern.com.*

GREATER NEWPORT

Greater Newport is where the elaborate, stunning mansions are located. Along the waterfront, these "summer cottages" were built by wealthy families in the late 1800s and early 1900s as seasonal residences. Eleven historic properties are maintained by the **Preservation Society of Newport County** (☎ *401/847–1000* ⊕ *www.newportmansions.org*). Both guided tours and audio tours are available; you can purchase a combination ticket to see multiple properties for a substantial discount. (Astors' Beechwood, Belcourt Castle, and Rough Point, not operated by the preservation society, are not included in the combination ticket.) The hours and days the houses are open in fall and winter do change, so it's wise to call ahead. The Breakers, the Elms, and Marble House are decorated for Christmas and open for tours daily from mid-November to New Year's Day.

⇨ "Which Mansion Should I Visit?" chart for help on deciding which mansions to include in your visit to Newport.

Fodor's Choice   The spectacular 3½-mi **Cliff Walk** runs south along Newport's cliffs from ★   Easton's Beach (also called First Beach) to Bailey's Beach. The promenade has views of sumptuous mansions on one side and the rocky coastline on the other; walking any section of it is worth the effort. The Cliff Walk can be accessed from any road running east off Bellevue Avenue. The unpaved sections can be difficult for small children, strollers, or people with mobility problems.

For a scenic drive along the waterfront, you can follow **Ocean Drive,** an 11-mi route. Allow at least an hour to drive it without stops, and up to three or four hours if you stop at Brenton State Park to walk along the beach, or explore Fort Adams and the Museum of Yachting. As you drive along, take in the views of the ocean, rocky coast, and spectacular homes. Consider stopping at Brenton State Park for a picnic or to take in the sunset.

❾ Astors' Beechwood. The original mistress of this oceanfront mansion, Caroline Schermerhorn Astor, was the queen of American society in the late 19th century; her list of the "Four Hundred" was the first social register. Her husband, William Backhouse Astor, was a member of one

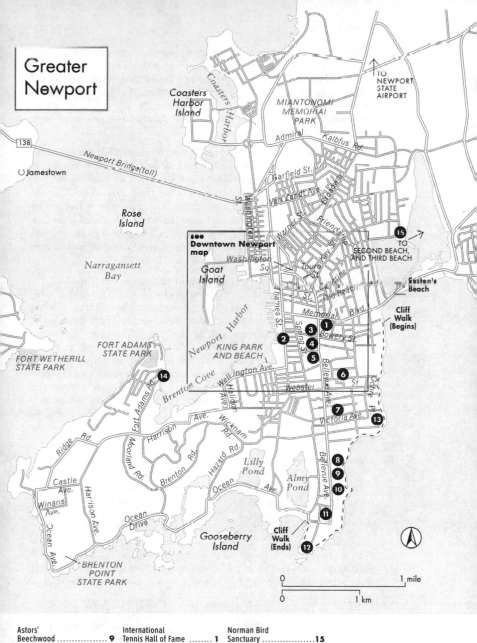

Greater Newport

138 ⊙ Jamestown

Newport Bridge (toll)

Coasters Harbor Island

Coasters Harbor

MIANTONOMI MEMORIAL PARK

Admiral

Kalbfus Rd.

TO NEWPORT STATE AIRPORT

Garfield St.

Van Zandt Ave.

Warner St.

Broadway

Friendship

Rose Island

Narragansett Bay

see **Downtown Newport map**

Washington Sq.

Goat Island

Touro St.

Mary St.

Spring St.

15

TO SECOND BEACH, AND THIRD BEACH

Easton's Beach

Cliff Walk (Begins)

Mill St.

Pell Beach

Memorial Blvd.

FORT ADAMS STATE PARK

FORT WETHERILL STATE PARK

Newport Harbor

KING PARK AND BEACH

Brenton Cove

1
2
3
4
5
6

Bowery St.

Spring St.

Bellevue Ave.

Webster

Wellington Ave.

Halidon Ave.

14

Fort Adams Rd.

Harrison Ave.

Wickham Rd.

Brenton Rd.

Hazard Rd.

Ridge Rd.

Moorland Rd.

Castle Ave.

Harrison Ave.

Winans Ave.

Ocean Ave.

Ocean Drive

Ocean Ave.

Lilly Pond

Almy Pond

Webster

Victoria Ave.

7
13
8
9
10
11
12

Bellevue Ave.

Ochre Pt.

Cliff Walk (Ends)

Gooseberry Island

BRENTON POINT STATE PARK

0 ———— 1 mile
0 ———— 1 km

of the wealthiest families in the nation. As you're guided through the 1857 mansion, actors in period costume play the family, servants, and household guests. Murder mysteries and musical events are performed July through October; Victorian holiday events are held in November and December. ⊠ *580 Bellevue Ave.* ☎ *401/846–3772* ⊕ *www.astors beechwood.com* ✉ *$20* ⊙ *Mid-May–Dec., daily 10–4; Feb.–mid-May, Thurs.–Sun. 10–4.*

⓫ **Belcourt Castle.** Richard Morris Hunt based his design for this 60-room mansion, built in 1894 for wealthy bachelor Oliver H. P. Belmont, on the hunting lodge of Louis XIII. The home, privately owned by the Tinney family since 1956, is filled with treasures from more than 30 countries. Admire the stained glass and carved wood throughout. Don't miss the Golden Coronation Coach and inquire about the haunted chair and suit of armor. The mansion's 5 PM Thursday and Saturday ghost tours are great fun. ⊠ *657 Bellevue Ave.* ☎ *401/846–0669* ⊕ *www.belcourt castle.com* ✉ *$12* ⊙ *Guided tours Wed.–Sun. noon–5.*

⓭ **The Breakers.** The largest of the Newport mansions was built in 1895
FodorśChoice for Cornelius Vanderbilt II, president of the New York Central Rail-
★ road. Architect Richard Morris Hunt modeled the four-story, 70-room residence after the palaces of the Italian Renaissance. From the outside, beginning with your walk through the Ivy League-like gate, you can see that this mansion is not only big but grand—be sure to spy out the sculptured figures tucked above the pillars. The Breakers' interior includes rich marbles and gilded rooms, with open-air terraces revealing magnificent ocean views. A few of the marvels within are a blue marble fireplace, rose alabaster pillars in the dining room, and a porch with a mosaic ceiling that took Italian artisans six months, lying on their backs, to install. ⊠ *Ochre Point Ave.* ☎ *401/847–1000* ⊕ *www.newportmansions.org* ✉ *$16* ⊙ *Jan.–Mar., daily 10–4; Apr.–Dec., daily 9–5.*

➐ **Chateau-sur-Mer.** Bellevue Avenue's first stone mansion was built in the Victorian Gothic style in 1852 for William S. Wetmore, a tycoon involved in the China trade, and enlarged in the 1870s by Richard Morris Hunt. The Gold Room by Leon Marcotte and the Renaissance Revival–style dining room and library by the Florentine sculptor Luigi Frullini are sterling examples of the work of leading 19th-century designers. Upstairs, the bedrooms are decorated in the English Aesthetic style with wallpaper by Arts and Crafts designers William Morris and William Burges. ⊠ *Bellevue and Shepard Aves.* ☎ *401/847–1000* ⊕ *www. newportmansions.org* ✉ *$11* ⊙ *Mid-Apr.–mid-Nov., daily 10–5.*

➏ **Chepstow.** This Italianate-style villa with a mansard roof is not as grand as other Newport mansions, but it houses a remarkable collection of art and furniture gathered by the Morris family of New York City. Built in 1861, the home was designed by Newport architect George Champlin Mason. ⊠ *120 Narragansett Ave.* ☎ *401/847–1000* ⊕ *www. newportmansions.org* ✉ *$11* ⊙ *Mid-June–mid-Sept., daily 10–5; tours offered on the hr by reservation.*

⑤ The Elms. Architect Horace Trumbauer modeled this graceful 48
Fodor's Choice room French neoclassical mansion and its grounds after the Château
★ d'Asnières near Paris. The Elms was built for Edward Julius Berwind,
a bituminous-coal baron, in 1901 and was one of the first in Newport
to be fully electrified. At the foot of the 10-acre estate is a spectacular
sunken garden. The Behind the Scenes tours, which offer a glimpse into
the life of staff and the operations (such as the boiler room and kitchen)
of the mansion, is one of the best of any mansion tour. ⊠ *Bellevue Ave.*
🕾 *401/847–1000* ⊕ *www.newportmansions.org* 🖭 *$11, guided tour*
$15 ⊙ *Mid-Apr.–Dec., daily 10–5; Jan.–Mar., weekends 10–4.*

3

★ ❶ **International Tennis Hall of Fame.** The photographs, memorabilia, and
multimedia exhibits at the Hall of Fame chronicle the entire history
of the game dating back to the 12th century and portray the sport's
greatest champions and most memorable moments. The magnificent,
shingle-style Newport Casino housing the collection was designed by
Stanford White and built in 1880. Now a National Historic Landmark, it was commissioned by publisher James Gordon Bennett Jr.,
who had quit the nearby club, the Newport Reading Room, after a
polo player—at Bennett's behest—rode a horse into the building and
was subsequently banned. Built in retaliation, Bennett's casino quickly
became the social and recreational hot spot of the gilded age. Today, the
six-acre venue has thirteen grass courts, one clay court, a court-tennis
facility, and three indoor courts—all available for public play. In mid-
July, the facility hosts the prestigious Campbell's Hall of Fame Tennis
Championships, the only men's professional tournament in the nation
held on grass courts. ⊠ *194 Bellevue Ave.* 🕾 *401/849–3990* ⊕ *www.*
tennisfame.com 🖭 *$9* ⊙ *Daily 9:30–5.*

❷ **International Yacht Restoration School.** This school, off Thames Street
in a former power plant, lets you watch shipwrights and students as
they overhaul historically significant sailboats and powerboats. Plac-
ards recount each boat's past. The 1885 racing schooner *Coronet* and
the original "cigarette boat" are two standouts. ⊠ *449 Thames St.*
🕾 *401/848–5777* ⊕ *www.iyrs.org* 🖭 *Free* ⊙ *Apr.–Nov., daily 9–5;*
Dec.–Mar., Mon.–Sat. 10–5.

❹ **Isaac Bell House.** Designed by McKim, Mead & White, this 1883 home
for wealthy cotton broker Isaac Bell is considered one of the finest
examples of American shingle-style architecture. The home is currently
being restored, but it is open to the public as a work in progress. ⊠ *Bel-*
levue Ave. and Perry St. 🕾 *401/847–1000* ⊕ *www.newportmansions.*
org 🖭 *$11* ⊙ *Mid-June–mid-Sept., daily 10–5.*

❸ **Kingscote.** This Gothic Revival mansion, completed in 1841, was one of
Newport's first summer cottages. Richard Upjohn designed Kingscote
for George Noble Jones, a plantation owner from Savannah, Georgia.
Decorated with antique furniture, glass, and Asian art, it contains one
of the first installations of Tiffany glass windows in its dining room.
⊠ *Bowery St., off Bellevue Ave.* 🕾 *401/847–1000* ⊕ *www.newport-*
mansions.org 🖭 *$11* ⊙ *Mid-June–mid-Sept., daily 10–5.*

★ **Marble House.** One of the most opulent of the Newport mansions, Mar-
⑩ ble House is known for its extravagant gold ballroom. The house was
built between 1888 and 1892 by William Vanderbilt, who gave it as a
gift to his wife, Alva, in 1892. Alva divorced William in 1895 and married Oliver Perry Belmont, becoming the lady of Belcourt Castle. When
Oliver died in 1908, she returned to Marble House and spent much of
her time campaigning for women's rights. She hosted many suffragette
rallies in the intriguing Chinese teahouse that she had built behind the
estate in 1914. It was designed by the sons of Richard Morris Hunt,
who designed Marble House itself. ⊠*Bellevue Ave., near Ruggles St.*
☎*401/847–1000* ⊕*www.newportmansions.org* ⊠*$11* ☽*Mid-Apr.–
Dec., daily 10–5; Jan.–Mar., weekends 10–4.*

⑭ **Museum of Yachting.** The museum has four displays: the Single-Handed
Sailors Hall of Fame, the World of Model Yachts, the Classic Wooden
Boat Collection, and Seasonal Marine Art exhibits. You can also see
the legendary two-time America's Cup winner and Rhode Island State
Yacht *Courageous,* which are highlights in the America's Cup Gallery.
In 2007, the museum joined with the International Yacht Restoration
School to form one organization. ⊠*Ft. Adams State Park, Ocean Dr.*
☎*401/847–1018* ⊕*www.museumofyachting.org* ⊠*$5* ☽*Mid-May–
Oct., daily 10–5.*

⑮ **Norman Bird Sanctuary.** Seven miles of trails, from ¼-mi to 1-1/5-mi
★ long, loop through this 300-acre sanctuary, which in summer provides
refuge from downtown Newport's hustle and bustle. More than 300
species of birds, plus deer, fox, mink, dragonflies, turtles, and rabbits
live in the fields and woodlands. From higher elevations you can see the
ocean, some ponds, and the marshy lowlands. Exhibits at the visitor
center explain the sanctuary's history and animal and plant life. ⊠*583
Third Beach Rd., Middletown* ☎*401/846–2577* ⊕*www.normanbird
sanctuary.org* ⊠*$4* ☽*Daily 9–5.*

⑧ **Rosecliff.** Newport's most romantic mansion was built in 1902, commissioned by Tessie Hermann Oelrichs, who inherited a Nevada silver fortune from her father. Stanford White modeled the palace after
the Grand Trianon at Versailles. Rosecliff has a heart-shaped staircase
and Newport's largest private ballroom. Some scenes from *The Great
Gatsby* and *True Lies* were filmed here. ⊠*Bellevue Ave.* ☎*401/847–
1000* ⊕*www.newportmansions.org* ⊠*$11* ☽*Mid-Apr.–mid-Nov.,
daily 10–5.*

⑫ **Rough Point.** The late tobacco heiress and preservationist Doris Duke
Fodor's Choice hosted such celebs as Elizabeth Taylor at her Newport mansion perched
★ on Cliff Walk. The 105-room home (with 49 principal rooms) was
built in the English-manor style in 1889. An avid collector of art and
antiques, Miss Duke filled Rough Point with works by such masters
as Renoir and Reynolds (of all the Newport mansions, Duke's has the
best art collection). Furnishings range from the elaborate to the pecu-
liar (count the mother-of-pearl bedroom suite among the latter) and
reflect the look of the mansion during Duke's final days here. Tours
include an annual changing exhibit. To tour the mansion, take the

Rough Point shuttle from the Newport Visitors' Information Center. If you prefer to drive, you must make an online reservation. ✉*Bellevue Ave. and Ocean Dr.* ☎*401/845–9130* ⊕*www.newportrestoration.org* ✉*$25 (first come, first-served basis)* ⊙*Mid-Apr.–mid-May, Thurs.– Sat. 9:45–1:45; mid-May–early Nov., Tues.–Sat. 9:45–3:45, tours leave from Newport Visitors' Information Center (23 America's Cup Ave.) and run every 30 mins.*

SPORTS & THE OUTDOORS

BEACHES **Easton's Beach** (✉*Memorial Blvd.*), also known as First Beach, is popular for its 50¢ carousel rides, aquarium, and playground. **Fort Adams State Park** (✉*Ocean Dr.*), a small beach with a picnic area and lifeguards in summer, has views of Newport Harbor and is fully sheltered from ocean swells. **Sachuest Beach,** or Second Beach, east of First Beach in the Sachuest Point area of Middletown, is a beautiful, long, sandy beach adjacent to the Norman Bird Sanctuary. Dunes and a campground make it popular with young travelers and families. **Third Beach,** in the Sachuest Point area of Middletown, is on the Sakonnet River. It has a boat ramp and is a favorite of windsurfers.

BIKING The 12-mi swing down Bellevue Avenue, along Ocean Drive and back, is a great route to ride your wheels. **Ten Speed Spokes** (✉*18 Elm St.* ☎*401/847–5609* ⊕*www.tenspeedspokes.com*) rents specialized comfort bikes for $25 per day and $75 per week.

BOATING Take lessons or rent sailboats by the hour at **Sail Newport** (✉*60 Ft.* & DIVING *Adams Rd., Ft. Adams State Park* ☎*401/846–1983* ⊕*www.sailnewport.org*). **Newport Diving Center** (✉*550 Thames St.* ☎*401/847–9293* ⊕*www.newportdivingcenter.com*) operates charter dive trips, refills Nitrox, and conducts PADI training and certification, as well as rents, sells, and does service.

FISHING **Fishin' Off** (☎*401/683–5557* ⊕*www.fishinoff.com*) runs charter-fishing trips on a 36-foot Trojan. The **Saltwater Edge** (✉*561 Thames St.* ☎*401/842–0062* ⊕*www.saltwateredge.com*) conducts guided trips, give lessons, and sells tackle for both fly-fishing and surf-casting. **Sam's Bait & Tackle** (✉*936 Aquidneck Ave.* ☎*401/849–5909*) stocks gear and bait.

SHOPPING

Many of Newport's shops and art and crafts galleries are on Thames Street, Spring Street, and at Bowen's and Bannister's wharves. The Brick Market area—between Thames Street and America's Cup Avenue—has more than 40 shops. Bellevue Avenue just south of Memorial Boulevard (near the International Tennis Hall of Fame) contains a strip of pricey shops with high-quality merchandise.

ANTIQUES **Aardvark Antiques** (✉*9 Connell Hwy.* ☎*401/849–7233*) carries archi-★ tectural pieces such as mantels, doors, and stained glass, plus fountains and garden statuary. The 125 dealers at the **Armory** (✉*365 Thames St.* ☎*401/848–2398*), a vast 19th-century structure, carry antiques, china, and estate jewelry. **Harbor Antiques** (✉*134 Spring St.* ☎*401/848–9711*) stocks unusual furniture, prints, and glassware. Inside **Antiques at the**

WHICH MANSION SHOULD I VISIT?

Mansion	Built for	Why Go	Why Skip It
Astors' Beechwood	Built in 1857 for William and Caroline Astor, the queen of American society in the late 1800s.	Tour guides are actors in period-costume posing as family, guests, and staff; less stuffy and more fun than most mansion-museums.	Fairly pricey; some find the costumed tours a bit hokey.
Belcourt Castle	Built by Richard Morris Hunt in 1894 for Oliver H.P. Belmont; based on French 18th-century hunting lodge.	Incredible collection of furnishings and art from more than 30 countries; "ghost tours" are given Thursdays and Saturdays.	The somewhat quirky and kooky interior isn't to everybody's taste.
The Breakers	Built by Richard Morris Hunt in 1895 for New York railroad mogul Cornelius Vanderbilt II; style is Italian Renaissance	Over-the-top grand—it's the most opulent of Newport's mansions; huge Preservation Society retail store in basement.	Tours are often big and very crowded; it's an enormous house that can feel a bit overwhelming.
Chateau-sur-Mer	Built in 1852 by local contractor for China Trade merchant William Wetmore; significantly modified in 1870s by Richard Morris Hunt; style is Second Empire	A must if you're a fan of High Victorian style; the elaborate grand staircase is one of Hunt's seminal creations; among the prettiest gardens and grounds in Newport.	Open for just half the year.
Chepstow	Built by George Champlin Mason in 1861; style is Italianate villa.	Fine collection of landscape paintings by Hudson River School artists.	Has a bit less wow factor than other Newport mansions; open for just three months of year.
The Elms	Built by Horace Trumbauer in 1901 for Philadelphia coal magnate Edward Berwind; style is French chateau.	Offers a fascinating "behind-the-scenes" tour; you can explore the house at your own pace with digital audio tour; 10 acres of stunningly restored grounds.	If you'd prefer a tour given by a person rather than an audio-headset, this isn't the mansion for you.
Hunter House	Built by Jonathan Nichols in 1748 for local sea merchant.	Fantastic collection of colonial furniture by renowned Newport artisans; in the city's historic Point District.	In different part of town from the Bellevue Avenue mansions; pricey admission; has a much smaller scale than other mansions in town; open just three months of the year.

Mansion	Built for	Why Go	Why Skip It
Isaac Bell House	Built in 1883 by the firm of McKim, Mead, and White for Isaac Bell, a cotton merchant; style is shingle Victorian.	Offers an interesting look at a mansion currently undergoing restoration; unusual mix of Continental European, Early English, and Asian influences; less visited than others, and thus less crowded.	Less dramatic in sheer size and grandeur than some others in Newport; open for just three months of the year.
Kingscote	Built in 1841 by Richard Upjohn for a plantation owner from Georgia; style is Gothic Revival	One of the earliest summer cottages built in Newport; contains one of the first installations of Tiffany glass.	Open for just three months of the year.
Marble House	Built in 1892 by Richard Morris Hunt for William K. Vanderbilt.	Outrageously opulent, arguably more so than The Breakers; you can tour house at your own pace with digital audio tour; be sure to check out teahouse overlooking ocean.	One of the most-visited mansions in town, so tours can be crowded.
Rosecliff	Built in 1902 by Stanford White for Nevada silver heiress Theresa Fair Oelrichs; modeled after Grand Trianon in Versailles.	It's been featured in many movies, from The Great Gatsby to Amistad.	Somewhat crowded; open for just half the year.
Rough Point	Built in 1889 in the English manor style; home of tobacco heiress Doris Duke until her death.	Most recently lived-in Newport mansion gives a more contemporary perspective on the city's Gilded Age.	Limited availability and high cost of tours; you can only come to the mansion via a shuttle from Newport Visitors' Information Center downtown; open for just half the year.

CLOSE UP

Newport's Social Scene in the Gilded Age

To truly appreciate a visit to Newport's mansions, you need to understand the players—those who built and lived in these opulent homes—and the times.

Newport at the turn of the 19th century was where the socialites of Boston, New York, and Philadelphia came for the summer. They were among the richest people in America at the time—from railroad tycoons and coal barons to plantation owners.

The era during which they lived here, the late 1800s up through the 1920s, is often referred to as the Gilded Age, a term coined by Mark Twain and co-author Charles Dudley Warner in a book by the same name. It was a time when whom you knew was everything. Three übersocialites were Alva Vanderbilt Belmont, Mary Ann (Mamie) Fish, and Tessie Oelrichs. These ladies who seriously lunched threw most of *the* parties in town. The social register—capped at 400 names—was created by Caroline Astor. While the women gossiped, planned soirees, and dressed and redressed thoughout the day, the men were usually off yachting.

In terms of the deepest pockets, the two heavy-weight families in Newport were the Vanderbilts and the Astors. Cornelius Vanderbilt I, called Commodor Cornelius Vanderbilt, built his empire on steamships and railroads. Cornelius had amassed almost $100 million before he died in 1877. He gave most of it to his son William Henry, who, also shrewd in the railroading business, nearly doubled the family fortune over the next decade. William Henry Vanderbilt willed $70 million to his son Cornelius Vanderbilt II, who became the chairman and president of New York Central

The Vanderbilts' grand lifestyle is easily seen at their Breakers mansion.

Railroad; and $55 million to son William K. Vanderbilt, who also managed railroads for awhile and saw his yacht, *The Defender*, win the America's Cup in 1895. One of Cornelius Vanderbilt II's sons, Alfred Gwynne Vanderbilt, died on the *Lusitania*, which sank three years after the *Titanic*.

Meanwhile in the Astor camp, John Jacob Astor IV, who perished on the *Titanic*, had the riches his great-grand-dad had made in the fur trade as well as his own millions earned from successful real estate ventures, including New York City hotels such as the St. Regis and the Astoria (later the Waldorf–Astoria, originally at the site of what is now the Empire State Building). His mother was Caroline Astor.

Homes in Newport related to the Vanderbilts are The Breakers, built for Cornelius II; and Marble House, built by William K. Vanderbilt for his wife, Alva, who later divorced him to marry tycoon Oliver H. P. Belmont. Astors' Beechwood Mansion is Newport's only Astor home. Actors in the mansion relive the year 1891, so the Mrs. Astor herself might just say hello to you.

—Debbie Harmsen

Drawing Room (✉*152 Spring St.* ☎*401/841–5060* ⊕*www.drawrm. com*) you'll find an exemplary collection of museum-quality estate pieces, including antique glass, fine porcelain, and marble statuary.

ART & CRAFTS GALLERIES **Arnold Art Store and Gallery** (✉*210 Thames St.* ☎*401/847–2273* ⊕*www. arnoldart.com*) collects marine-inspired paintings and prints. **DeBlois Gallery** (✉*138 Bellevue Ave.* ☎*401/847–9977* ⊕*www.debloisgallery.com*) exhibits the works of Newport's emerging artists. **Cadeaux du Monde** (✉*26 Mary St.* ☎*401/848–0550* ⊕*www.cadeauxdumonde.com*) focuses on folk art and tapestries from Africa, Asia, and Latin America. **Spring Bull Gallery** (✉*55 Bellevue Ave.* ☎*401/849–9166* ⊕*www.spring-bullgallery.com*), an artists' cooperative, displays diverse local art.

★ The delicate, dramatic blown-glass gifts at **Thames Glass** (✉*688 Thames St,* ☎*401/846–0576* ⊕*www.thamesglass.com*) are designed by Matthew Buechner and created in the adjacent studio. **William Vareika Fine Arts** (✉*212 Bellevue Ave.* ☎*401/849–6149* ⊕*www.vareikafinearts. com*) exhibits and sells American paintings and prints from the 18th to the 20th century.

BEACH GEAR **Water Brothers** (✉*38 Broadway* ☎*401/849–4990*) is the place to go for surf supplies, including bathing suits, wet suits, sunscreen, sunglasses, and surfboards.

BOOKS The **Armchair Sailor** (✉*543 Thames St.* ☎*401/847–4252*) stocks marine and travel books, charts, and maps.

CLOTHING Look to **Angela Moore** (✉*119 Bellevue Ave.* ☎*401/848–9695* ⊕*www. angelamoore.com*) for stylish, mod resort threads and hand-painted beaded jewelry. **Cathers & Coyne** (✉*18 Bowen's Wharf* ☎*401/849–5757*) carries hot shoes for cool people.

Karol Richardson (✉*24 Washington Sq.* ☎*401/849–6612* ⊕*www.karol-richardson.com*) sells upscale, hip contemporary women's clothing and accessories. **Michael Hayes** (✉*202 and 204 Bellevue Ave.* ☎*401/846–3090*) sells fine clothing for men, women, and children.

JEWELRY Talented artist Meg Reagan produces distinctive jewelry and housewares from colorful, contemporary art glass at **9 Manning Square** (✉*24 Waites Wharf* ☎*401/633–4088* ⊕*www.9manningsquare.com*). **Three Golden Apples** (✉*140 Bellevue Ave* ☎*401/846–9930* ⊕*www.three-goldenapples.com*) sells high-end jewelry.

NIGHTLIFE & THE ARTS

Detailed events calendars can be found in *Newport This Week* and the *Newport Daily News*. For a sampling of Newport's lively nightlife, you need only stroll down Thames Street after dark. Also, Broadway has developed an increasingly hip bar and lounge scene in recent years.

BARS **Fastnet Pub** (✉*1 Broadway* ☎*401/845–9311*) occasionally hosts live Irish music. The **Candy Store** (✉*Bannister's Wharf* ☎*401/849–2900*) in the Clarke Cooke House is a snazzy place for a drink. If you're up for dancing, head downstairs to the Boom Boom Room. **Newport Blues Café** (✉*286 Thames St.* ☎*401/841–5510*), housed in a former bank, hosts great blues performers. **One Pelham East** (⊠*270 Thames St.* ☎*401/847–9460*) draws a young crowd for live rock bands.

POP (⊠*162 Broadway* ☎*401/846–8456*) is a martini and tapas bar, where a DJ spins on weekends. **Salvation Café** (⊠*140 Broadway* ☎*401/847–2620*), a funky, kitchy, eclectically decorated, happening spot, is popular with the local thirtysomethings. The tiki bar out back is open in summer.

FESTIVAL
In mid-August the **JVC Newport Jazz Festival** (☎*401/847–3700*) takes place at Fort Adams State Park. Performers have included Ray Charles, Dave Brubeck, Cassandra Wilson, Natalie Cole, Wynton Marsalis, Harry Connick Jr., and Ornette Coleman.

FILM
The **Newport International Film Festival** (☎*401/846–9100* ⊕*www.new portfilmfestival.com*), an impressive six-day event, takes place at the beginning of June at the Jane Pickens Theater and other venues.

THEATER
Murder-mystery plays are performed on Thursday evenings at 8 PM from July to late October at **Astors' Beechwood** (⊠*580 Bellevue Ave.* ☎*401/846–3772*); on Tuesday at 7, July through September, members of the Beechwood Theatre Company sing and dance in a mock 1920s-style speakeasy. **Newport Playhouse & Cabaret** (⊠*102 Connell Hwy.* ☎*401/848–7529* ⊕*www.newportplayhouse.com*) stages comedies and musicals; dinner packages are available.

WHERE TO EAT

$$–$$$
AMERICAN
Fodor'sChoice
★
✕**Asterisk.** Urbane dining draws big crowds to this snazzy, cleverly renovated auto-repair garage. Asian twists (a lobster-ginger-cream sauce with the four-cheese ravioli) enliven the mostly French-bistro fare, accompanied by a carefully selected menu of wines, brandies, and aperitifs. Escargots in garlic butter, chicken-liver-and-foie-gras mousse, and streak frites are all terrific. High ceilings and an open floor lend to a lively metro vibe, and on Sunday, there's live jazz. ⊠*599 Thames St.* ☎*401/841–8833* ⊟*AE, D, DC, MC, V.*

$$$–$$$$
AMERICAN
✕**Black Pearl.** At this converted dock shanty, popular with yachters, clam chowder is sold by the quart. Dining is in the casual tavern ($$, reservations not accepted) or the formal Commodore's Room ($$$–$$$$ jacket required, reservations essential), with its vintage nautical paintings and silver flatware. The latter serves an appetizer of black-and-blue tuna with red-pepper sauce. The French and American entrées include duck breast with raspberry-Burgundy sauce and swordfish with tomato-basil beurre blanc. The outdoor patio is packed in summer. ⊠*Bannister's Wharf* ☎*401/846–5264* ⊟*AE, MC, V* ⊘*Closed Jan.–mid-Feb.*

$$–$$$
AMERICAN
✕**Clarke Cooke House.** Formal dining is on the upper level, on the Porch, a dining room with a timber-beam ceiling, green latticework, richly patterned cushions, and water views; there's open-air dining in warm weather. The refined menu incorporates local seafood and utilizes a mix of American and Mediterranean recipes; game dishes often appear as specials. On the middle levels are the Candy Store and the Grill Room, plus the Midway Bar serving sushi; in summer, the large windows are opened so diners can view Bannister's Wharf. Late at night, the dark,

downstairs Boom Boom Room comes alive with a DJ. A dance-floor cam provides a simulcast viewing of your dance moves at the TV across the bar. ⊠ *Bannister's Wharf* ☎ *401/849–2900* ⚑ *Reservations essential* ☰ *AE, D, DC, MC, V.*

¢–$
SEAFOOD
✕ **Flo's Clam Shack.** With an old boat in front, peeling paint, and a bamboo-lined walkway leading to the order windows, this local favorite across from Easton's Beach is as casual as it gets. Fried seafood, steamed clams, clam cakes, cold beer, and a great raw bar keep the lines long here in summer. An upstairs bar serves baked, chilled lobster, and outside seating is available. ⊠ *4 Wave Ave.* ☎ *401/847–8141* ⚑ *Reservations not accepted* ☰ *No credit cards* ☉ *Closed Jan. and Feb. and Mon.–Wed. Mar.–late May.*

$$–$$$
AMERICAN
✕ **Fluke Wine Bar.** Whether to snack on tapas and sip well-chosen wines by the glass or partake of a more substantial meal, this Bowen's Wharf newcomer with a sleek, airy dining room serves any mood. The cheese-and-charcuterie plate and citrus-lobster-roll sliders (miniature lobster rolls) stand out among the small-plate options, while broiled striped bass in a simple lemon–white wine reduction stars among the entrées. Finish off with a almond tart accompanied by mango ice cream and fresh berries. It's open till 1 AM nightly. ⊠ *41 Bowen's Wharf,* ☎ *401/849–7778* ☰ *AE, MC, V* ☉ *No lunch.*

$$
AMERICAN
✕ **Puerini's.** This humble and reasonably priced family-run eatery has been turning out soul-warming Italian classics since the 1980s inside a cheery dining room midway between the Bellevue Avenue and Thames Street sections of town. There's always a house-made polenta starter on the menu, its preparation varying daily. Follow this with fresh eggplant *melanzane* baked with mozzarella and homemade tomato sauce, or veal sautéed with rosemary, shallots, mushrooms, and a light cream sauce. ⊠ *24 Memorial Blvd. W* ☎ *401/847–5506* ☰ *AE, MC, V.*

$$$–$$$$
FRENCH
✕ **Restaurant Bouchard.** Regional takes on French cuisine fill the menu at this upscale yet homey establishment inside a stately gambrel-roof 1785 Colonial on Thames Street. There are always nightly specials based on the fresh catch from Rhode Island waters (scallops, swordfish, clams), plus such Gallic classics as Dover sole with sorrel sauce, and pork tenderloin with goat cheese and vegetables in a puff pastry. The wine list offers a nice range of new and old-world varietals. ⊠ *505 Thames St.* ☎ *401/846–0123* ☰ *AE, D, MC, V* ☉ *No lunch.*

$$–$$$
SEAFOOD
✕ **Scales & Shells.** Busy, sometime noisy, but always excellent, this restaurant serves as many as 15 kinds of superbly fresh wood-grilled fish, including grilled lobster and plenty of local species: monkfish, bluefish, halibut, tautog. Similar dishes are available in the more formal dining room upstairs at UpScales, open late May through early September. ⊠ *527 Thames St.* ☎ *401/846–3474* ⚑ *Reservations not accepted* ☰ *No credit cards* ☉ *No lunch.*

$$
ECLECTIC
✕ **Spark.** Part of the culinary renaissance that's overtaken the formerly workaday lower Broadway section of town, this colorful little storefront café with orange walls, funky wall sconces, and affordable yet memorable chow pulls in a mix of local hipsters and adventuresome tourists. The menu mixed small plates, dishes for sharing, and judiciously portioned entrées. Highlights in this mix include Roquefort

cheesecake with port syrup, Thai shrimp tacos with crispy wontons, and fennel-dusted pork chops with apple compote and chicken-liver-sausage stuffing. ⊠*12 Broadway* ☎*401/842–0023* ⊟*AE, MC, V* ⊘*Closed Sun. and Mon.*

$$$$
AMERICAN
Fodors Choice
★
✕**Spiced Pear.** Anytime of year, but especially from May through mid-October, when there's seating on the sprawling terrace with its million-dollar cliff-top ocean views, this refined restaurant at the Chanler Inn ranks among Rhode Island's very finest dining experiences. Typically complex fare from the regional American dinner menu includes Southern-style foie gras with toasted pistachio flapjacks and brandy-cherry foam, followed by seared diver scallops with kobe-beef oxtail and a Madeira-truffle jus. For an all-out feast, opt for the eight-course tasting menu with pairings from the extensive wine list. ⊠*117 Memorial Blvd.* ☎*401/847–2244* ⊟*AE, D, DC, MC, V.*

$$$–$$$$
AMERICAN
★
✕**Tucker's Bistro.** The red lacquered walls crowded with artwork, shelves lined with books, and gilded mirrors creates a vibe that is part library, part art gallery, and part bordello. Contemporary creations include braised pork shank with cheddar-mashed potatoes, and pan-seared sea scallops with creamy Parmesan risotto. Regulars will never allow Tucker's to take favorite appetizers Thai shrimp nachos or pear-Gorgonzola salad off the menu. ⊠*150 Broadway* ☎*401/846–3449* ⊟*D, MC, V* ⊘*No lunch.*

$$$–$$$$
STEAKHOUSE
✕**22 Bowen's Wine Bar & Grille.** Newport's most respected prime beef steak house also serves seafood, along with a 600-plus-label wine list. You can't go wrong with the bacon-wrapped scallops as a starter. Steak lovers swear by the 24-ounce porterhouse. Distressed brick floors on the first floor, stained red oak wood on the second floor, white linens, leather chairs, and a mahogany bar lend a sumptuous air to the eatery. There's a festive Sunday brunch. ⊠*Bowen's Wharf* ☎*401/841–8884* ⊟*AE, D, DC, MC, V.*

$$$–$$$$
AMERICAN
★
✕**West Deck.** Among the several breezy dining options set in waterfront wharves along Newport Harbor, West Deck excels for its creatively prepared, artful regional American food. The space comprises a bustling bar, an open-deck dining area, and a simple yet sophisticated indoor space with tall windows taking in the water. Memorable openers include baked oysters au gratin with a leeks-fennel sauce, and tuna tartar with black-truffle vinaigrette. Mussels Catalan with white wine, green olives, and artichokes draws raves among the entrées. ⊠*1 Waites Wharf* ☎*401/847–3610* ⊟*AE, D, DC, MC, V.*

$$$$
AMERICAN
★
✕**White Horse Tavern.** The first license to operate a tavern here was obtained in 1673, and almost uninterruptedly since then the premises have served as a tavern, boardinghouse, or restaurant. Once a meetinghouse for Colonial Rhode Island's General Assembly, the tavern provides intimate dining with its low dark-beam ceilings, cavernous fireplace, and uneven plank floors. The service is black tie, the wine list top notch, and the American cuisine—including pan-seared blue cod with roasted-tomato coulis and lemon-thyme oil, and a stellar beef Wellington—consistently excellent. ⊠*Marlborough and Farewell Sts.* ☎*401/849–3600* ⚛*Reservations essential* ⊟*AE, D, DC, MC, V.*

3

WHERE TO STAY

$$-$$$ ⌷**Admiral Fitzroy Inn.** This tidy 1854 Victorian provides a restful retreat in the heart of Newport's bustling waterfront district. Period antiques decorate the rooms, each of which has either an antique brass or hand-carved wood bed. All rooms have access to the rooftop deck with a view of the harbor. Two rooms have semiprivate decks and hot tubs. The inn's namesake, Admiral Fitzroy, commanded the *Beagle*, whose most famous passenger was Charles Darwin. **Pros:** relatively affordable for the area. **Cons:** lots of crowds and some noise on Thames Street in summer. ✉*398 Thames St.* ☎*401/848–8000 or 866/848–8780* ⊕*www.admiralfitzroy.com* ⬑*17 rooms* ⬙*In-room: refrigerator. In-hotel: parking (no fee), no-smoking rooms* ⊟*AE, D, MC, V* ⏿*BP.*

$$-$$$ ⌷**Architect's Inn.** Built by noted Newport architect George Champlin Mason (Chepstow, Fort Adams Commandant House), this distinctive Swiss chalet–inspired house just off of Bellevue Avenue contains five romantic rooms done in classic Victorian style, but with plenty of modern creature comforts (DVD players or VCRs, fireplaces, CD players, individual climate control). Rooms are done with bold period-style wallpapering and fabrics and are accented with Oriental rugs. The cozy Woodbine Cottage suite takes up the third floor has a sitting room and can accommodate up to four guests. **Pros:** reasonably priced by Newport standards, central location, fireplaces in every room. **Cons:** pure Victorian decor won't suit every taste. ✉*2 Sunnyside Pl.* ☎*401/847–7081 or 877/466–2547* ⊕*www.architectsinn.com* ⬑*3 rooms, 2 suites* ⬙*In room: some DVD, some VCR, Wi-Fi. In-hotel: parking (free), no-smoking rooms* ⊟*AE, MC, V* ⏿*BP.*

$$$$ ⌷**Castle Hill Inn and Resort.** The 1874 main house and its 40 acres of
Fodor'sChoice lawns and woodland have views of Narragansett Bay, the Newport
★ Bridge, and the Atlantic Ocean. Amenities abound: Adirondack chairs to take in the view, patio dining, private beach, and trails to the Castle Hill Lighthouse. The tastefully appointed rooms, varied in style, are in the main house, harbor houses, and beach houses. The inn, 3 mi from the center of Newport, is also a perfect spot for a special meal. The restaurant serves stellar food and is known for its elaborate Sunday brunches with live jazz music, and prix-fixe tasting menus with wine pairings. **Pros:** to-die-for views, superb restaurant, a wide variety of room configurations. **Cons:** you need a car to get into town, among the highest rates in Newport. ✉*590 Ocean Dr.* ☎*401/849–3800 or 888/466–1355* ⊕*www.castlehillinn.com* ⬑*7 rooms, 18 suites* ⬙*In-room: some kitchens, DVD, Ethernet. In-hotel: restaurant, beachfront, no-smoking rooms* ⊟*AE, D, DC, MC, V* ⏿*BP.*

$$$$ ⌷**Chanler at Cliff Walk.** Nearly all of the enormous rooms and suites at
★ this stunning small hotel perched atop a bluff at the foot of Cliff Walk afford dramatic ocean views, and about half have outdoor balconies or deck. This is one of the swankiest accommodations in a city rife with them—consider the regal room appointments, such as swagged damask bedding or an antique fireplace with Tudor mantel. Rooms have two or three TVs, and sprawling marble bathrooms with Jacuzzi tubs and separate showers. A fantastic à la carte full breakfast is included, and the staff graciously attends to guests' every possible whim. **Pros:** panoramic

water views from many rooms, museum-quality antiques, one of the best on-site restaurants in the state. Cons: rooms have a rather formal air, ultra-pricey. ⊠*117 Memorial Blvd.* ☎*401/847–1300 or 866/793–5664* ⊕*www.thechanler.com* ⬧*7 rooms, 13 suites* ♿*In room: DVD, Ethernet. In-hotel: restaurant, parking (free), no-smoking rooms* ⊟*AE, D, DC, MC, V* ⦿|*BP.*

$$$$
Fodor's Choice
★

Cliffside Inn. Grandeur and comfort come in equal supply at this swank Victorian home on a tree-lined street near Cliff Walk. On the walls are more than 100 paintings by artist Beatrice Turner, who lived in the house for many years and painted hundreds of self portraits. All rooms have one to three fireplaces and are furnished with Victorian antiques. The Governor's Suite (named for Governor Thomas Swann, of Maryland, who built the home in 1876) has a two-sided fireplace, a whirlpool bath, a four-poster king-size bed, and a brass birdcage shower. Afternoon tea is an experience here, complete with scones with Devonshire cream; finger sandwiches of salmon mousse, caviar, or cucumber; and a bevy of sweets. Breakfast may include poached eggs nestled on crab cakes or crepes lavish with berries. This inn is sister to the Adele Turner and Abigail Stoneman inns. **Pros:** one of the best breakfasts in town, museum-quality artwork throughout, highly solicitous service. **Cons:** quite pricey. ⊠*2 Seaview Ave.* ☎*401/847–1811 or 800/845–1811* ⊕*www.cliffsideinn.com* ⬧*8 rooms, 8 suites* ♿*In-room: DVD, Wi-Fi. In-hotel: parking (free), no-smoking rooms* ⊟*AE, D, DC, MC, V* ⦿|*BP.*

$$$$
★

Francis Malbone House. The design of this stately painted-brick house is attributed to the architect responsible for the Touro Synagogue and the Redwood Library. A lavish inn with period reproduction furnishings, the 1760 structure was tastefully doubled in size in the mid-1990s. The rooms in the main house overlook the courtyard, which has a fountain, or across the street to the harbor; all rooms have working fireplaces, iPod-docking stations, and bathrooms with Jacuzzis. Breakfast is served in a domed ceiling dining room. The owners also run the lovely Hilltop Inn, at the foot of Bellevue Avenue, a handsome Arts and Crafts house with similarly elegant rooms. **Pros:** steps from many restaurants and shops, highly professional service, working fireplaces in each room. **Cons:** Thames Street abounds with tourists in summer. ⊠*392 Thames St.* ☎*401/846–0392 or 800/846–0392* ⊕*www.malbone.com* ⬧*17 rooms, 3 suites* ♿*In-room: DVD, Wi-Fi. In-hotel: parking (no fee), no-smoking rooms* ⊟*AE, MC, V* ⦿|*BP.*

$$$$

Hotel Viking. The elegant redbrick Hotel Viking, built in 1926, stands at the north end of Bellevue Avenue. The wood paneling and chandeliers evoke the hotel's sophisticated history. The stately rooms, adorned with reproduction Colonial furniture and appointments, resemble the homes of Colonial merchant seamen. Bathrooms are done in marble and have "rain" showerheads. One Bellevue Restaurant serves fresh seafood and afternoon tea service; Top of the Viking, a rooftop bar, is open in summer; the outstanding Spa Terre provides Thai and Indonesian massage and body treatments. **Pros:** lovely location on hilltop, exceptional spa facilities. **Cons:** despite many renovations it still feels a bit dark and somber. ⊠*1 Bellevue Ave.* ☎*401/847–3300 or 800/556–*

7126 ⊕*www.hotelviking.com* ⟐197 *rooms, 12 suites* ⟐*In-room: refrigerator, VCR, Ethernet. In-hotel: restaurant, bar, pool, spa, no-smoking rooms* ⊟*AE, D, DC, MC, V.*

$$$$ ⊡**Hyatt Regency Newport.** On Goat Island across from the Colonial Point district, the Hyatt, which completed a massive $30 million renovation in 2007, affords panoramic views of the harbor and the Newport Bridge. Most rooms have water views. Although the hotel is a 10-minute walk to the center of Newport, bike and moped rentals are nearby. All rooms are decorated with light-wood and dark-granite-top furniture, cushy bedding with pillowtop mattresses, and modern nautical color schemes. The outdoor restaurant, Pineapples, is a little-known spot to watch the sunset in summer. **Pros:** most recently renovated major Newport hotel, spectacular water views from many rooms, relatively secluded location. **Cons:** a bit of a walk to shopping and dining. ⊠*1 Goat Island* ☎*401/851–1234 or 800/233–1234* ⊕*www.newport.hyatt.com* ⟐*264 rooms* ⟐*In-room: Wi-Fi. In-hotel: 2 restaurants, tennis court, pools, gym, spa, no-smoking rooms* ⊟*AE, D, DC, MC, V.*

$$$$ ⊡**Hydrangea House Inn.** This mid 19th century inn near the foot of Bellevue Avenue exudes romance, with its decadent suites and rooms, each a work of interior design. The dark and masculine Chesterfield Suite is a favorite, with its massive four-poster dark and opulent bed and cheetah-print bathrobes. The owners have thought of every detail, including flat-screen TVs that revert to tasteful, gilt-frame mirrors when not in use. Some rooms have fireplaces, whirlpool tubs, and steam showers. In the evening, guests are treated to a reception of wine and cheese, and rates also include a bountiful full breakfast, served family-style beneath a stunning crystal chandelier. Complimentary Wi-Fi and free long-distance and local calls are among the pluses. **Pros:** central location, huge rooms, highly personal service. **Cons:** slightly over-the-top decor may not please minimalists. ⊠*16 Bellevue Ave.* ☎*401/846–6602 or 800/945–4667* ⊕*www.hydrangeahouse.com* ⟐*3 rooms, 6 suites* ⟐*In room: Wi-Fi. In-hotel: parking (free), no-smoking rooms* ⊟*AE, D, DC, MC, V* ⟐*BP.*

$$$$ ⊡**Newport Marriott.** A light-filled atrium lobby with marble floors and a nautical theme unfolds as you enter this luxury hotel on the harbor at Long Wharf. Rooms overlook the atrium, city, or waterfront. Fifth-floor rooms facing the harbor have sliding French windows that open onto large decks. A major overhaul in 2007 added granite-and-wood detailing to the bathrooms, and plasma-screen TVs and iPod docks to the guest rooms. Rates vary greatly according to season and location; concierge and harbor-view rooms cost more. **Pros:** central location, water views from many rooms. **Cons:** although snazzy, the rooms feel as though they could be anywhere; pricey for a Marriott. ⊠*25 America's Cup Ave.* ☎*401/849–1000 or 800/228–9290* ⊕*www.newportmarriott.com* ⟐*310 rooms, 7 suites* ⟐*In room: safe. In-hotel: restaurant, bar, pool, gym, spa, laundry facilities, public Internet, parking (fee), no-smoking rooms* ⊟*AE, D, DC, MC, V.*

$$$$ ⊡**Vanderbilt Hall.** Built in 1909 as the Newport Men's Social Club, a
★ Vanderbilt family gift to the Newport townspeople, this was turned into a YMCA during the Great Depression. It became a sophisticated inn

with European flair in the 1990s and has undergone a major renovation over the past two years, resulting in fewer but much larger rooms, the opening of a full-service spa and indoor pool, and all sorts of cushy new perks added to the rooms, from DVD players and iPod docking stations to high-definition plasma-screen TVs and lavish new bedding. Room design now balances a contemporary, minimalist aesthetic with antique accents. In the Club Restaurant, extremely good contemporary American is served. **Pros:** rich history, ultraposh spa and facilities, highly personal service. **Cons:** pricey, on a narrow street that's very busy in summer. ⊠*41 Mary St.* ☎*401/846–6200* ⊕*www.vanderbilthall.com* ↶*33 suites* ⚒*In-room: refrigerator, DVD, Wi-Fi. In-hotel: restaurant, bar, pool, spa, no-smoking rooms* ⊟*AE, D, MC, V.*

PORTSMOUTH

11 mi north of Newport.

Portsmouth is now mainly a bedroom community for professionals who work in other parts of Rhode Island and Massachusetts. Its founder was Anne Hutchinson, a religious dissident and one of the country's first feminists, who led a group of settlers to the area in 1638 after being banished from the Massachusetts Bay Colony.

WHAT TO SEE

☼ **Green Animals Topiary Garden.** This large topiary garden on a Victorian estate contains more than 80 shrubs sculpted in a variety of shapes including animals and geometric designs; among the oldest, begun before 1920, are an elephant, a camel, and a giraffe. Also here are flower gardens, winding pathways, a variety of trees, and the 1872 estate house, which displays original family furnishings and an antique toy collection. ⊠*Cory's La. off Rte. 114* ☎*401/847–1000* ⊕*www.newportmansions.org* ⊠*$11* ⊙*Mid-May–Oct., daily 10–5.*

SPORTS & THE OUTDOORS

Sandy Point Beach (⊠*Sandy Point Ave.*) is a choice spot for families and beginning windsurfers because of the calm surf along the Sakonnet River.

EN ROUTE Route 77, the main thoroughfare to Little Compton, passes through **Tiverton Four Corners,** a great place to stretch your legs and catch your first breath of East Bay air.

BRISTOL

5 mi north of Portsmouth, 20 mi southeast of Providence.

The largest town in Rhode Island's somewhat overlooked but quite enticing East Bay region, Bristol lies about midway between Newport and Providence. Once a center of boat-building, this dapper town that hugs the eastern shores of Narragansett Bay is home to a handful of prominent attractions as well as a beguiling downtown with a smattering of noteworthy places to stay and eat. The main drag, Hope Street, is painted with a red-white-and-blue center stripe—this patriotic community has been celebrating the Fourth of July with a downtown parade longer than any other town in America. It's also the terminus of the 14½-mi East Bay Bike Path, which begins in Providence and follows an abandoned railroad right-of-way.

★ On the grounds of the prestigious Herreshoff boat manufacturing company, which produced some of the world's sleekest racing yachts during its operations from 1863 to 1945, the **Herreshoff Marine Museum** traces the company's illustrious history. The museum contains some 60 vintage Herreshoff boats, some dating to the mid-19th century, including several that defended the prestigious America's Cup yacht races. Old ship engines, photographs, and memorabilia sheds further light on the museum heyday, often referred to as the "Golden Age of Yachting." On the grounds, the **America's Cup Hall of Fame** celebrates the careers of the many great yachting enthusiasts who have excelled during this seminal international sailing regatta. ⊠ *1 Burnside St.* ☎ *401/253–5000* ⊕ *www.herreshoff.org* 🖃 *$8* ☉ *Late Apr.–early Nov, daily 10–5.*

The **Blithewold Mansion and Arboretum** is somewhat overlooked compared with the many lavish compounds in Newport, but this 33-acre estate merits a visit. You can tour the 45-room mansion, which dates to 1908 and is pattered after a 17th-century English manor—its contents include a mix of period antiques and reproduction pieces. But the real prize here are the gardens, trees, and dramatic 10-acre lawn fringing Narragansett Bay. There are more than 3,000 shrubs and trees, including the largest giant sequoia on the East Coast (it's nearly 100 feet tall). ⊠ *101 Ferry Rd.* ☎ *401/253–2707* ⊕ *www.blithewold.org* 🖃 *$10* ☉ *Grounds daily 10–5, mansion mid-Apr.–mid-Oct. and Dec., Wed.–Sat. 10–4, Sun. 10–3.*

Operated by Brown University, the **Haffenreffer Museum of Anthropology** abound with some 80,000 objects and artifacts that relate to the studies of indigenous people from all over the world. Highlights include Taoist paintings from 17th-century China, canoes and kayaks used by native peoples from Alaska and northern Canada, and katsina dolls from the Hopi tribal lands of Arizona. ⊠ *300 Tower St.* ☎ *401/423–8388* 🖃 *$3* ☉ *June–Aug., Tues.–Sun. 11–5; Sept.–May, weekends 11–5.*

WHERE TO EAT

$$-$$$
ECLECTIC
Fodor'sChoice
★

✕ **DeWolf Tavern.** A cleverly conceived menu of fusion Indian, Mediterranean, and regional American cuisine has earned this cozy, warmly lit space inside the Bristol Harbor Inn serious praise from foodies. Timber ceilings and fieldstone walls—along with wonderful bay views—create a romantic mood. Dishes of note include veal–and–pine nut samosas with mango chutney, naan pizzas topped with truffle oil and Parmesan, and seared local sea scallops with chestnut spaetzle and a thyme–garam masala sauce. Save room for the homemade cardamom or fig-port ice cream. ⊠ *267 Thames St., Bristol* ☎ *401/254–2005* 🖃 *AE, D, MC, V* ☉ *No lunch.*

$$-$$$
AMERICAN
★

✕ **Persimmon.** A smartly simple bistro with space for no more than 40 patrons, Persimmon is run by young chef-owner Champe Speidel and his wife Lisa. It's a genial neighborhood spot, a short walk from the bay and just off Bristol's main street—the sort of place where half the patrons know one another, and the rest are out-of-town gourmands who have caught wind of Speidel's considerable talents. The seasonal menu has featured white wine–braised rabbit with gnocchi and sage, and a tasting of Texas wild boar that comprises roasted saddle, seared chop, braised shoulder, and smoked sausage. ✉*31 State St.* ☎*401/254–7474* ▭*AE, MC, V* ◷*Closed Mon. Closed Sun. Jan.–June.*

WHERE TO STAY

$$$$
★
⌂ **Point Pleasant Inn.** A regal East Bay estate set on a peninsula near Colt State Park, this rambling 1940 mansion anchors a gloriously situated 33-acre compound of well-tended lawns and manicured gardens. The seven rooms and suites have Bose CD stereos and DVD players; some have immense sitting rooms, and many afford expansive views of Narragansett Bay. Bathrooms have deep tubs and stand-alone showers. A well-trained, multilingual staff tends to guests' every needs, and the park-like grounds include an in-ground pool with a slate lanai, a tennis court, and fishing on the bay. **Pros:** magnificent waterfront setting, huge rooms, gracious staff. **Cons:** pricey, not within walking distance of shopping and dining, site of many weddings and functions. ✉*333 Poppasquash Rd.* ☎*401/253–0627* ⊕*www.pointpleasantinn. com* ⇌*4 rooms, 3 suites* ⚒*In-room: DVD, Wi-Fi. In-hotel: pool, tennis court, no-smokine rooms* ▭*AE, MC, V* ❘◯❘*BP.*

$$-$$$
⌂ **Bristol Harbor Inn.** Part of the Thames Street Landing redevelopment along Bristol's dapper bay front, this contemporary 40-room hotel has been constructed with timber and architectural detailing from a pair of early-1800s buildings that stood here previously. The sunny rooms contain Colonial reproduction furniture, writing desks, and armoires, and many of them overlook Narragansett Bay. The on-site restaurant, DeWolf Tavern, is one of the best in the state, and the hotel is also steps from several shops and other restaurants. Thames Landing also has a marina and bike-rental shop. **Pros:** reasonably priced for a waterfront hotel, stellar restaurant, convenient location. **Cons:** other than shops and marina, there are no exterior grounds. ✉*259 Thames St.* ☎*401/254–1444 or 866/254–1444* ⊕*www.bristolharborinn.com* ⇌*36 rooms, 4 suites* ⚒*In-room: Ethernet. In-hotel: restaurant, bar, no-smoking rooms* ▭*AE, D, MC, V* ❘◯❘*BP.*

SPORTS & THE OUTDOORS

BIKING   Flat and affording majestic views of Narragansett Bay, the 14½-mi **East Bay Bike Path** (⊕*www.riparks.com/eastbay.htm*) passes from Providence into Bristol's charming downtown.

In Bristol, **Northwind Sports** (✉*267 Thames St.* ☎*401/254–4295* ⊕*www.northwindsports.com*) has bikes for rent as well as kayaks for exploring the town's placid harbor.

LITTLE COMPTON

15 mi south of Bristol, 19 mi southeast of Portsmouth.

The rolling estates, lovely homes, farmlands, woods, and gentle western shoreline make Little Compton one of the Ocean State's prettiest areas, although the community lacks for restaurants and accommodations and is thus best approached as an afternoon excursion from Portsmouth, Newport, or Bristol. Little Compton and Tiverton were part of Massachusetts until 1747—to this day, residents here often have more roots in Massachusetts than in Rhode Island. "Keep Little Compton little" is a popular sentiment, but considering the town's remoteness and its steep land prices, there may not be all that much to worry about.

Little Compton Commons (⊠ *Meetinghouse La.*) is the epitome of a New England town square. As white as the clouds above, the spire of the Georgian-style United Congregational Church rises over the tops of adjacent oak trees. Within the triangular lawn is a cemetery with Colonial headstones, among them that of Elizabeth Pudubie, said to be the first white girl born in New England. Surrounding the green is a rock wall and all the elements of a small community: town hall, community center, police station, and school.

Sakonnet Point, a surreal spit of land, reaches out toward three tiny islands. The point begins where Route 77 ends. The ½-mi hike to the tip of the spit passes tide pools, a beach composed of tiny stones, and outcroppings that recall the surface of the moon. Parking is sometimes available in the lot adjacent to Sakonnet Harbor.

WHAT TO SEE

★ **Sakonnet Vineyard.** Tours and tastings are free at New England's largest winery. Varietals include chardonnay, pinot noir, cabernet franc, and vidal blanc. ⊠ *162 W. Main Rd.* ☎ *401/635–8486* ⊕ *www.sakonnet wine.com* ⊠ *Free* ☉ *Memorial Day–Oct., daily 10–6; Nov.–Memorial Day, daily 11–5.*

SPORTS & THE OUTDOORS

HIKING **Wilbur Woods** (⊠ *Swamp Rd.*), a 30-acre hollow with picnic tables and a waterfall, is a good place for a casual hike. A trail winds along and over Dundery Brook.

RHODE ISLAND ESSENTIALS

Research prices, get travel advice, and book your trip at fodors.com.

TRANSPORTATION

BY AIR

T. F. Green Airport, 10 mi south of Providence, has scheduled daily flights by most major airlines, including Air Canada, American, Continental, Delta, Northwest, Southwest, United, and US Airways, with additional service by regional carriers. Westerly, Newport (charters only), and Block Island airports are the main regional airports in Rhode Island. New England Airlines operates scheduled flights from Westerly to Block Island and also provides charter service.

By cab, the ride from T.F. Green Airport to downtown Providence takes about 15 minutes and costs about $25 to $30. The Airport Taxi & Limousine Service shuttle costs $11 per person each way. Cozy Cab runs a shuttle service ($20) between T.F. Green Airport and the Newport Visitors' Information Center, as well as major hotels.

Airport Information **Block Island Airport** (⊠ *Center Rd.* ☏ *401/466–5511*). **T.F. Green Airport** (⊠ *U.S. 1 (Exit 13 off I–95), Warwick* ☏ *401/737–8222 or 888/268–7222* ⊕ *www.pvdairport.com*). **Westerly Airport** (⊠ *Airport Rd., 2 mi south of Westerly off U.S. 1* ☏ *401/596–2357*).

Airport Transfers **Airport Taxi & Limousine Service** (☏ *401/737–2868* ⊕ *www. airporttaxiri.com*). **Cozy Cab** (☏ *401/846–2500 or 800/846–1502* ⊕ *www.cozy trans.com*).

BY BOAT & FERRY

Block Island Ferry operates both conventional car-passenger service and high-speed passenger service between Block Island's Old Harbor and Galilee, in South County. By conventional ferry, the one-hour trip is $10.60 one-way, and the frequency varies from two to three times a day in winter to nine times a day in peak season. Make auto reservations well ahead. Foot passengers cannot make reservations; arrive 45 minutes ahead in high season—boats do fill up. From early June to mid-October Block Island Hi-Speed Ferry makes a half dozen daily trips from Galilee to Old Harbor; the 30-minute trip is $16 one-way. There is no auto service on the Hi-Speed; passenger reservations are accepted.

Block Island Ferry also operates a seasonal service from Newport's Fort Adams State Park to Old Harbor. The passengers-only ferry leaves Newport for Block Island once a day from July through Labor Day at 9:15 AM and leaves Block Island at 4:45 PM. Same-day round-trip rates are $15. Approximate sailing time is two hours.

From late May to mid-October, a high-speed passenger-only ferry operated by Block Island Express runs between New London, Connecticut, and Old Harbor. The ferry departs New London every three hours, four or five times a day, and takes a little more than an hour. Tickets are $21 one-way. Reservations are recommended.

Viking Fleet runs passenger service from Montauk, Long Island, to Block Island from late May to mid-October. The boat departs Montauk at 10 AM and leaves Block Island at 4:30. Fare is $30 one-way. There's also a "dinner special" offered on Saturdays in July and August, leaving Montauk at 3:30 and returning at 8:30 (allowing you just enough time for dinner on Block Island) and costing $40 round-trip. Travel time is one hour; the ferry docks at New Harbor.

All the above lines take bicycles; rates range from $3 to $10 one-way.

Rhode Island Public Transit Authority (RIPTA) runs seasonal high-speed passenger-only ferry service between Providence and Newport several times per day from mid-May through mid-October. One-way fare is $8, and reservations are advised. The Jamestown and Newport Ferry Co. runs a passenger ferry about every one-and-a-half hours from Newport's Bowen's Landing and Long Wharf (and, on request, Fort Adams, Rose Island, and Goat Island) to Jamestown's Ferry Wharf. The ferry operates from Memorial Day to mid-October, and the cost is $15 for an all-day pass. Oldport Marine Company operates a water-taxi service ($3 per ride) for boaters in Newport Harbor.

Boat & Ferry Information **Block Island Express** (⊠ *2 Ferry St., New London* ☎ *401/466-2212 or 860/444-4624* ⊕ *www.goblockisland.com*). **Block Island Ferry** (⊠ *Galilee State Pier, Narragansett* ☎ *866/783-7996* ⊕ *www.block islandferry.com*). **Jamestown and Newport Ferry Co.** (☎ *401/423-9900* ⊕ *www. conanicutmarina.com/ferry.html*). **Oldport Marine Services** (☎ *401/847-9109* ⊕ *www.oldportmarine.com*). **Rhode Island Public Transit Authority** (*RIPTA* ☎ *401/453-6800 ferry reservations* ⊕ *www.ripta.com*). **Viking Fleet** (☎ *631/668-5700* ⊕ *www.vikingfleet.com*).

BY BUS

Greyhound and Peter Pan/Bonanza Bus Lines operate out of the Providence Bus Terminal. A shuttle service connects the terminal with Kennedy Plaza in downtown Providence, where you can board the local Rhode Island Public Transit Authority (RIPTA) buses, or the RIPTA Link trolley, whose two routes around downtown, the green and the gold lines, meet here.

These two routes serve most points of interest. RIPTA fares range from $1.50 to $3. RIPTA buses also service T. F. Green Airport.

Bus Information **Greyhound** (☎ *800/231-2222* ⊕ *www.greyhound.com*). **Peter Pan/Bonanza Bus Lines** (☎ *888/331-7500* ⊕ *www.peterpanbus.com*). **Providence Bus Terminal** (⊠ *Bonanza Way off Exit 25 from I-95, Providence* ☎ *888/751-8800* ⊠ *Kennedy Plaza, Washington and Dorrance Sts., Providence*). **Rhode Island Public Transit Authority** (*RIPTA* ⊠ *Kennedy Plaza, Washington and Dorrance Sts., Downtown* ☎ *401/781-9400* ⊕ *www.ripta.com*).

BY CAR

Interstate 95, which cuts diagonally across the state, is the fastest route to Providence from Boston, coastal Connecticut, and New York City. Interstate 195 southeast from Providence leads to New Bedford, Massachusetts, and Cape Cod. Route 146 northwest from Providence leads to Worcester and Interstate 90, passing through the northeastern portion of the Blackstone Valley. U.S. 1 follows much of the Rhode Island coast east from Connecticut before turning north to Providence. Route 138 heads east from Route 1 to Jamestown, Newport, and Portsmouth, in easternmost Rhode Island.

Parking is easy to find outside of cities, but it can be challenging and expensive in downtown Providence and Newport. Overnight parking is not allowed on Providence streets, and during the day it can be difficult to find curbside parking, especially downtown and on Federal and College hills. There's a large parking garage at Providence Place mall. In Newport, a number of lots around town offer pay parking (the largest and most economical is the garage right behind the Newport Visitors' Information Center), but street parking is near impossible in summer.

All of the major car-rental agencies have branches at T. F. Green airport. On Block Island, your only option for renting a car is **Block Island Car Rental** (⊠ *Ocean Ave.* ☎ *401/466–2297*).

BY TRAIN

Amtrak service between New York City and Boston makes stops at Westerly, Kingston, and Providence. Providence Station is the city's main station. The Massachusetts Bay Transportation Authority (MBTA) commuter rail service connects Boston and Providence during weekday morning and evening rush hours for about half the cost of an Amtrak ride.

Train Information Amtrak (☎ *800/872–7245* ⊕ *www.amtrak.com*). **MBTA** (☎ *617/722–3200* ⊕ *www.mbta.com*). **Providence Station** (⊠ *100 Gaspee St., Providence* ☎ *401/727–7379*).

CONTACTS & RESOURCES

SPORTS & THE OUTDOORS

For information on pricing and where to buy licenses for freshwater fishing, contact the Department of Environmental Management's Division of Licensing. No license is needed for saltwater fishing.

One of the best trail guides for the region is the *AMC Massachusetts and Rhode Island Trail Guide,* available at local outdoors shops or from the Appalachian Mountain Club. The Rhode Island Audubon Society leads interesting hikes and field expeditions around the state.

Contacts Appalachian Mountain Club (*AMC* ⊠ *5 Joy St., Boston, MA* ☎ *617/523–0636* ⊕ *www.amcnarragansett.org*). **Department of Environmental Management's Division of Licensing** (☎ *401/222–3576* ⊕ *www.dem.ri.gov*). **Rhode Island Audubon Society** (⊠ *12 Sanderson Rd., Smithfield* ☎ *401/949–5454* ⊕ *www.asri.org*).

VISITOR INFORMATION

Blackstone Valley Tourism Council (⊠ *175 Main St., Pawtucket* ☎ *401/724–2200 or 800/454–2882* ⊕ *www.tourblackstone.com*). **Block Island Chamber of Commerce** (⊠ *Drawer D, 1 Water St., Block Island* ☎ *401/466–2982 or 800/383–2474* ⊕ *www.blockislandchamber.com*). **Newport County Convention and Visitors Bureau** (⊠ *Newport Visitors' Information Center, 23 America's Cup Ave., Newport* ☎ *401/845–9123 or 800/976–5122* ⊕ *www.gonewport.com*). **Providence Warwick Convention and Visitors Bureau** (⊠ *144 Westminster St., Providence* ☎ *401/274–1636 or 800/233–1636* ⊕ *www.pwcvb.com*). **Rhode Island Department of Economic Development, Tourism Division** (☎ *800/556–2484* ⊕ *www.visitrhodeisland.com*). **South County Tourism Council** (⊠ *4808 Tower Hill Rd., Wakefield* ☎ *401/789–4422 or 800/548–4662* ⊕ *www.southcountyri.com*).

Connecticut

4

WORD OF MOUTH

"Old Wethersfield is amazingly cute. There's a cove at one end and a big town green—a great little area to walk around or rollerblade in, or just hang out and get great ice cream."

—emcash

"We loved the drive down the 169 from Woodstock to Lisbon in Connecticut. This is as nice as many drives in Vermont, but less travelled, and underrated IMO . . . another lovely drive was the coastal route along I—95 from Mystic . . . the little towns along this route Guilford/Clinton/Madison all the way from Mystic to the outskirts of New Haven were lovely."

—AnnRiley

By Andrew
Collins

CONNECTICUT MAY BE THE THIRD-SMALLEST state in the nation, but it is among the hardest to define. Indeed, you can travel from any point in the Nutmeg State, as it is known, to any other in less than two hours, yet the land you traverse—fewer than 60 mi top to bottom and 100 mi across—is as varied as a drive across the country. Connecticut's 253 mi of shoreline blows salty sea air over such beach communities as Old Lyme and Stonington. Patchwork hills and peaked mountains fill the state's northwestern corner, and once-upon-a-time mill towns line rivers such as the Housatonic. Connecticut has seemingly endless farmland in the northeast, where cows just might outnumber people, as well as chic New York City bedroom communities such as Greenwich and New Canaan, where boutique shopping bags seem to be the dominant species. Unique as each section is, each defines Connecticut.

Just as diverse as the landscape are the state's residents, who numbered close to 3.5 million at last count. There really is no such thing as the definitive Connecticut Yankee, however. Yes, families can trace their roots back to the 1600s, when Connecticut was founded as one of the 13 original colonies, but the state motto is also "He who transplanted still sustains." And so the face of the Nutmegger is that of the family from Naples now making pizza in New Haven and the farmer in Norfolk whose land dates back five generations, the grandmother in New Britain who makes the state's best pierogi and the ladies who lunch in Westport, not to mention the celebrity nestled in the Litchfield Hills and the Bridgeport entrepreneur working to close the gap between Connecticut's struggling cities and its affluent suburbs.

A unifying characteristic of the Connecticut Yankee, however, is a propensity for inventiveness. Nutmeggers are historically known for both their intellectual abilities and their desire to have a little fun. As evidence of the former, consider that the nation's first public library was opened in New Haven in 1656 and its first statehouse built in Hartford in 1776; Tapping Reeve opened the first law school in Litchfield in 1784; and West Hartford's Noah Webster published the first dictionary in 1806. As proof of the latter, note that Lake Compounce in Bristol was the country's first amusement park; Bethel's P. T. Barnum staged the first three-ring circus; and the hamburger, the lollipop, the Frisbee, and the Erector set were all invented within the state's 5,009 square mi.

Not surprisingly, Nutmeggers have a healthy respect for their history. For decades, Mystic Seaport, which traces the state's rich maritime past, has been the premier tourist attraction. Today, however, slot machines in casinos in the southeastern woods are giving the sailing ships a run for their money. Foxwoods Casino near Ledyard, run by the Mashantucket Pequots, is the world's largest casino, drawing more than 40,000 visitors per day. Thanks in large part to these lures, not to mention rich cultural attractions, cutting-edge restaurants, shopping outlets, first-rate lodgings, and abundant natural beauty (including 92 state parks and 30 state forests), tourism is now the state's second leading industry. Anyone who has explored even part of Connecticut will discover that a small state can be big in its appeal.

CONNECTICUT TOP 5

■ **Most Scenic Country Driving:**
Follow the rolling, twisting roads
of Litchfield County, such as U.S. 7,
US 44, and Route 63, through the
charmed villages of Kent, Salisbury,
Litchfield, and others, stopping in
antiques shops, upscale cafés, and
verdant state parks.

■ **Maritime History:** The diminu-
tive village of Mystic is packed with
engaging attractions and activities
that relate to Connecticut's rich
seafaring history, from the Mysic
Seaport living history museum to the
state-of-the-art Mystic Aquarium.

■ **Best Urban Exploring:** Anchored
by Yale University, downtown New
Haven has enjoyed a stunning reju-

venation in recent years and now
buzzes with hip restaurants, smart
boutiques, and acclaimed theaters.

■ **Literary Giants:** In the same historic Hartford neighborhood, you can
explore the homes—and legacies—of
two of the New England's greatest
literary figures, Mark Twain and Har-
riett Beecher Stowe.

■ **Hunting for Antiques:** Connecticut is arguably New England's
leading source of antiques shopping, and you'll find numerous fine
shops, galleries, and auction houses
specializing in vintage decor all over
the state, but two towns stand out in
particular for this activity: Woodbury
and Putnam.

4

EXPLORING CONNECTICUT

Southwestern Connecticut contains the wealthy coastal communities.
Moving east of them along the coast (in most states when you travel
along the coast you go north or south, but in Connecticut you actually travel east or west), you come to New Haven and the southeastern
coast, which is broken by many small bays and inlets. Northeast Connecticut's Quiet Corner provides a tranquil countryside with rolling
hills. West of it are the fertile farmlands of the Connecticut River valley
and the state's capital, Hartford. In the northwest is the Litchfield Hills
area, covered with miles of forests, lakes, and rivers.

ABOUT THE RESTAURANTS

Call it the fennel factor or the arugula influx: southern New England
has witnessed a gastronomic revolution. Preparation and ingredients
reflect the culinary trends of nearby Manhattan and Boston; indeed,
the quality and diversity of Connecticut restaurants now rival those of
such sophisticated metropolitan areas. Although traditional favorites
remain—such as New England clam chowder, buttery lobster rolls,
Yankee pot roast, and fish-and-chips—Grand Marnier is now favored
on ice cream over hot fudge sauce; sliced duck is wrapped in phyllo and
served with a ginger-plum sauce (the orange glaze decidedly absent); and
everything from lavender to fresh figs is used to season and complement
dishes. Dining is increasingly international: you'll find Indian, Vietnamese, Thai, Malaysian, South American, and Japanese restaurants—even
Spanish tapas bars—in cities and suburbs. Designer martinis are quite
the rage, brewpubs have popped up around the state—even caviar is
making a comeback. The one drawback of this turn toward sophistication is that finding an under-$10 dinner entrée is difficult.

PLANNING YOUR TIME

BUDGETING YOUR TIME

The Nutmeg State is a confluence of different worlds, where farm country meets country homes, and fans of the New York Yankees meet Down-Easter Yankees. To get the best sense of this variety, start in the scenic Litchfield Hills, where you can see historic town greens and trendy cafés. If you have a bit more time, head south to the wealthy southwestern corner of the state and then over to New Haven, with its cultural pleasures. If you have five days or a week, take in the capital city of Hartford and the surrounding towns of the Connecticut River valley and head down to the southeastern shoreline.

WHEN TO GO

Connecticut is lovely year-round, but fall and spring are particularly appealing times to visit. A fall drive along the state's back roads or the Merritt Parkway (a National Scenic Byway) is a memorable experience. Leaves of yellow, orange, and red color the fall landscape, but the state blooms in springtime, too—town greens are painted with daffodils and tulips, and blooming trees punctuate the rich green countryside. Summer, of course, is prime time for most attractions; travelers have the most options then but also plenty of company, especially along the shore.

GETTING THERE & AROUND

Regionally, it's best to reach Connecticut by car via its main highways (Interstate 95, Interstate 91, Interstate 84, and the Merritt Parkway). It you're coming from farther away, you can fly into Bradley International Airport, just north of Hartford. Additionally, there's bus and train service to Connecticut from New York City *(See Transportation in Connecticut Essentials).* Once you arrive, it's most practical to explore the state by car.

ABOUT THE HOTELS

Connecticut has plenty of business-oriented chain hotels and low-budget motels, along with many of the more unusual and atmospheric inns, resorts, bed-and-breakfasts, and country hotels that are typical of New England. You'll pay dearly for rooms in summer on the coast and in autumn in the hills, where thousands of visitors peek at the changing foliage. Rates are lowest in winter, but so are the temperatures, making spring the best time for bargain seekers to visit.

WHAT IT COSTS

	¢	$	$$	$$$	$$$$
RESTAU-RANTS	under $8	$8–$12	$13–$20	$21–$28	over $28
HOTELS	under $80	$80–$120	$121–$170	$171–$220	over $220

Prices are per person, for a main course at dinner. For lodging, prices are for a standard double room during peak season and not including tax or gratuities. Some inns add a 15% service charge.

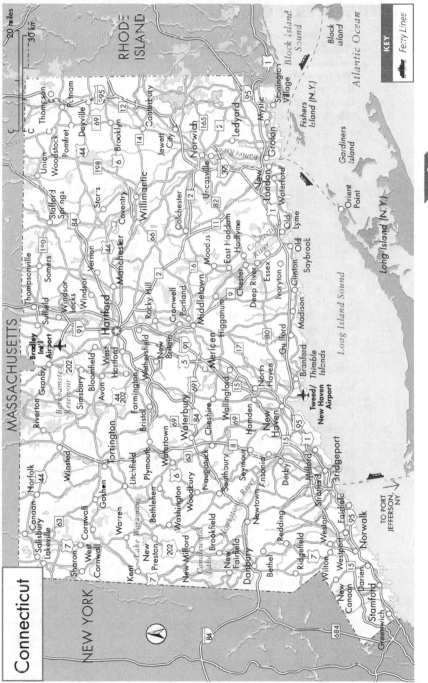

Connecticut

MASSACHUSETTS

NEW YORK

RHODE ISLAND

20 miles

30 km

Thompson
Putnam
295
Woodstock
Pomfret
Dayville
69
12
Union
198
Brooklyn
Somers
6
14
Canterbury
Thompsonville
190
Stafford
Springs
44
Jewett
City
84
Coventry
Willimantic
Norwich
165
Stafford
Springs
Starr's
66
2
Ledyard
2
Suffield
Vernon
44
Colchester
Uncasville
395
Windsor
Locks
Manchester
Mystic
95
Windsor
Rocky Hill
2
Mood Js.
11
New
London
Groton
Hartford
91
16
East Haddam
Haddyme
82
Waterford
Bradley
Int'l
Airport
Cromwell
Portland
Chester
Old
Lyme
Riverton
Granby
West
Hartford
Wethersfield
New
Britain
Middletown
Higganum
9
Deep River
Essex
Ivoryton
Old
Saybrook
Barkhamsted
Reservoir
202
Bloomfield
Simsbury
Avon
5
91
Meriden
17
Clinton
Madison
Norfolk
44
Farmington
44
202
Wallingford
15
North
Haven
Guilford
80
Branford
Thimble
Islands
Winsted
Torrington
Bristol
691
Cheshire
69
Hamden
Canaan
Salisbury
Lakeville
63
Goshen
Litchfield
Plymouth
Waterbury
84
63
Naugatuck
8
Seymour
Ansonia
Derby
New
Haven
Tweed/
New Haven
Airport
95
1
Sharon
7
West
Cornwall
Cornwall
Warren
Bethlehem
6
Woodbury
Southbury
Milford
Stratford
Kent
New
Preston
202
Washington
Brookfield
Newtown
Bridgeport
Fairfield
Westport
New
Milford
New
Fairfield
Danbury
Redding
Behel
Westport
Norwalk
15
Ridgefield
7
Wilton
New
Canaan
Darien
Stamford
684
Greenwich

Lake Waramaug

Lake Candlewood

Housatonic River

Naugatuck River

Connecticut River

Thames River

Long Island Sound

Block Island Sound

Atlantic Ocean

Block
Island

Stonington
Village

Fishers
Island (N.Y.)

Gardiners
Island

Orient
Point

Long Island (N.Y.)

TO PORT
JEFFERSON,
NY →

KEY

Ferry Lines

4

SOUTHWESTERN CONNECTICUT

Southwestern Connecticut is a rich swirl of old New England and new New York. This region consistently reports the highest cost of living and most expensive homes of any area in the country. Its bedroom towns are home primarily to white-collar executives; some still make the hour-plus dash to and from New York, but most enjoy a more civilized morning drive to Stamford, which is reputed to have more corporate headquarters per square mile than any other U.S. city.

Venture away from the wealthy communities, and you'll discover cities struggling in different stages of urban renewal: Stamford, Norwalk, Bridgeport, and Danbury. These four have some of the region's best cultural and shopping opportunities, but the economic disparity between Connecticut's troubled cities and its upscale towns is perhaps nowhere more visible than in Fairfield County.

GREENWICH

28 mi northeast of New York City, 64 mi southwest of Hartford.

You'll have no trouble believing that Greenwich is one of the wealthiest towns in the United States when you drive along U.S. 1 (called Route 1 by the locals, as well as West Putnam Avenue, East Putnam Avenue, and the Post Road, among other monikers), where the streets are lined with ritzy car dealers, posh boutiques, oh-so-chic restaurants, and well-heeled, well-to-do residents clearly pleased to be able to call Greenwich "home." The median home price in Greenwich hovers around $2 million these days. In other words, bring your charge cards.

WHAT TO SEE

Audubon Center. Established in 1942 as the National Audubon Society's first nature-education facility, this center in northern Greenwich is a prime hawk-watching site. It's directly on the East Coast flyway and more than a dozen species have been spotted migrating during the Fall Hawkwatch Festival. Other annual events are the Spring into Audubon Festival and the summer and Christmas bird counts. Not only is the center filled with "real-life" interactive exhibits, galleries, and classrooms, but also observation decks that offer sweeping views of wildlife activity, a wildlife observation room with solar-powered video technology, and a 144-person capacity lecture hall. Outside, the sanctuary includes protected wildlife habitats and 7 mi of hiking trails on 285 acres of woodland, wetland, and meadow. ⊠*613 Riversville Rd.* ☎*203/869–5272* ⊕*www.greenwich.center.audubon.org* ⊠*$3* ⊙*Daily 9–5.*

Bruce Museum of Arts and Science. In 1908, the owner of this then-private ★ home (built in 1853), wealthy textile merchant Robert Moffat Bruce, bequeathed it to the town of Greenwich with the stipulation that it be used "as a natural history, historical and art museum, for the use and benefit of the public." Today this diversity remains reflected in the museum's collection of some 15,000 objects in fine and decorative arts, natural history, and anthropology—including paintings by Childe Hassam, sculptures by Auguste Rodin and George Segal, and stained glass

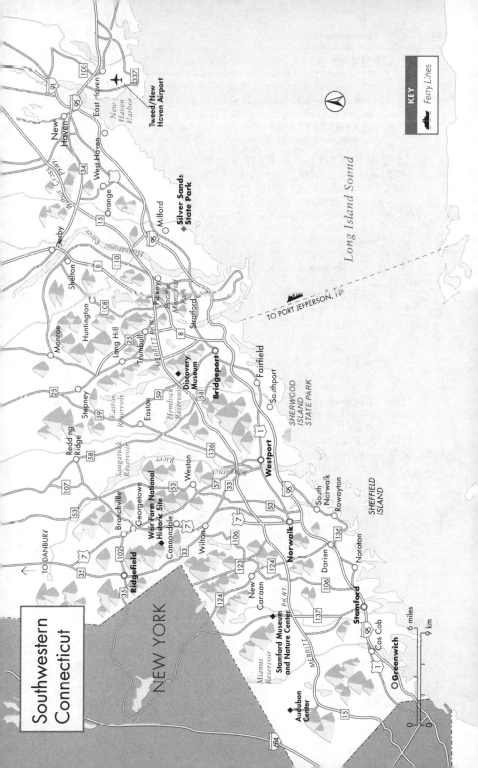

Southwestern Connecticut

NEW YORK

TO DANBURY

Long Island Sound

TO PORT JEFFERSON, NY

KEY
Ferry Lines

New Haven

New Haven Harbor

Tweed/New Haven Airport 337

East Haven

West Haven 34

Orange

Milford

Silver Sands State Park

15

Derby

Shelton 8

110

Huntington 108

Monroe

Long Hill

Trumbull 25

MERRITT PKWY

Putney

Stratford

Milford

8

Discovery Museum

Bridgeport

Fairfield

Southport

SHERWOOD ISLAND STATE PARK

Hemlock Reservoir 59

58

Stepney

Easton Reservoir 59

Easton

136

Weston 57

33

1

Westport

95

Redding Ridge 58

Saugatuck Reservoir

Saugatuck River

107

Branchville

Georgetown 53

Weir Farm National Historic Site

Cannondale 7

Wilton 7

106

53

Norwalk

South Norwalk

Rowayton

SHEFFIELD ISLAND

136

53

102

Ridgefield

35

7

35

123

New Canaan 124

33

Darien

Noroton

106

137

Stamford

Miamus Reservoir

Stamford Museum and Nature Center

MERRITT PKWY

95

Cos Cob

Greenwich

1

15

Audubon Center

684

0   6 miles
0   9 km

by Louis Comfort Tiffany and Dale Chihuly—from which the museum selects items for changing exhibitions. Permanently on display, however, is the spectacular mineral collection. Kids enjoy viewing the wiggly creatures in the Bruce's marine touch tank and listening to stories from long ago and far away in the full-size reconstruction of a Woodland Indian wigwam. ⊠*1 Museum Dr. off I–95 (Exit 3)* ☎*203/869–0376* ⊕*www. brucemuseum.org* ⊠*$7, free Tues.* ☉*Tues.–Sat. 10–5, Sun. 1–5.*

WHERE TO EAT & STAY

$$–$$$

ECLECTIC

✕**Nuage.** Stellar French-Asian cuisine and a sleek dining room with mod, indirect lighting have earned this see-and-be-seen restaurant a loyal following. The food is complex and creative without devolving into gimmickry. You might start with monkfish pâté with sesame miso and caviar, before tucking into big-eye tuna with sunflower-seed crust, puree of artichoke, and a balsamic-tamarind glaze. ⊠*203 E. Putnam Ave.* ☎*203/869–2339* ⊟*AE, D, DC, MC, V* ☉*No lunch weekends.*

$$$$

Fodor'sChoice

★

FRENCH

✕**Restaurant Jean-Louis.** Chef Jean-Louis Gerin specializes in what he calls "la nouvelle classique" French cuisine, a style based on complex stocks and reductions—and his own dedication to excellence. A choice way to sample it is via the five-course degustation menu that explores the day's special offerings, which might include sea salt–encrusted foie gras with aged sherry vinegar and a duck *à l'orange* reduction, or pan-seared lamb with a shallot-tomato *concassé* (coarsely chopped mixture). Heady roses, signature fine china, custom glassware, and touches of lace create a romantic, sophisticated atmosphere. ⊠*61 Lewis St.* ☎*203/622–8450* ⊟*AE, D, DC, MC, V* ☉*Closed Sun. No lunch Sat.*

$$$$

▣**Delamar Greenwich Harbor Hotel.** This three-story luxury hotel with yellow stucco exterior and terra-cotta tile roof resembles a private villa on the Italian Riviera. Handcrafted furnishings from all over the world enrich all rooms; many have working fireplaces and wrought-iron balconies overlooking Greenwich Harbor. Bathrooms have coral marble vanities, hand-painted framed mirrors, and deep cast-iron tubs. The hotel has its own 600-foot private dock on the harbor for boat owners to tie up; it's just a few blocks from downtown Greenwich and one block from the train station. A luxe spa offers a full range of treatments. L'Escale restaurant and bar shares the hotel's superb water views and focuses on classic Provençal dishes. **Pros:** waterfront location, posh spa, easy walk to downtown restaurants. **Cons:** super-pricey. ⊠*500 Steamboat Rd.* ☎*203/661–9800 or 866/335–2627* ⊕*www.thedelamar.com* ⬸*74 rooms, 8 suites* ♿*In-room: DVD, Ethernet. In-hotel: restaurant, gym, spa, no-smoking rooms* ⊟*AE, D, DC, MC, V.*

STAMFORD

6 mi northeast of Greenwich, 38 mi southwest of New Haven.

Glitzy office buildings, chain hotels, and major department stores are among the landmarks in Stamford, the most dynamic city on the southwestern shore. Restaurants, nightclubs, and shops line Atlantic and lower Summer streets, poised to harness the region's affluence and satisty the desire of suburbanites to spend an exciting night on the town without having to travel to New York City.

WHAT TO SEE

Bartlett Arboretum. This 91-acre arboretum is home to more than 2,000 varieties of annuals, perennials, wildflowers, and woody plants; an art gallery, research library; greenhouse; marked ecology trails; 2-acre pond; and boardwalk through a red maple swamp. Brilliant purples, sunny yellows, and bold oranges make the wildflower garden stunning in spring. Sunday afternoons are the time to visit for guided walks. ⊠ *151 Brookdale Rd., off High Ridge Rd. (Merritt Pkwy. Exit 35)* ☎ *203/322–6971* ⊕ *www.bartlettarboretum.org* ☺ *$5 suggested donation* ⊙ *Grounds daily 8:30–dusk, visitor center weekdays 8:30–4:30, greenhouse daily 10–noon.*

☺ **Stamford Museum and Nature Center.** Oxen, sheep, pigs, and other animals roam this 118-acre New England farmstead with many nature trails to explore. Once the estate of Henri Bendel, the property includes a Tudor revival stone mansion, which houses exhibits surveying natural history, art, and Americana. Also here is a planetarium and observatory with a 22-inch research telescope—perfect for stargazing. ⊠ *39 Scofieldtown Rd. (Rte. 137)* ☎ *203/322–1646* ⊕ *www.stamfordmuseum.org* ☺ *Grounds $8, planetarium an additional $3, observatory an additional $3* ⊙ *Grounds daily 9–5; buildings and galleries Jan.–Mar. Tues.–Sun. 11–5, Apr.–Dec. daily 11–5; observatory May–Labor Day 8:30 PM–10:30 PM, Sept.–Apr. Fri. 8 PM–10 PM; planetarium shows 2nd Sun. each month at 3 PM.*

NIGHTLIFE & THE ARTS

NIGHTLIFE At the **Palms Nightclub** (⊠ *78 W. Park Pl.* ☎ *203/961–9770* ⊕ *www.palmsnightclub.com*) you can dance to everything from ballroom and country western to hip-hop and Latin. The **Thirsty Turtle** (⊠ *84 W. Park Pl.* ☎ *203/973–0300* ⊕ *www.thethirstyturtle.net*) is a combination of a pub, dance club, and shaken-not-stirred martini lounge. The Irish **Tigín Pub** (⊠ *175 Bedford St.* ☎ *203/353–8444* ⊕ *www.fadoirishpub.com*) hosts live music on Friday and Saturday nights.

THE ARTS The **Connecticut Grand Opera and Orchestra** (☎ *203/327–2867* ⊕ *www.ctgrandopera.org*) perform at the **Palace Theatre** (⊠ *61 Atlantic St.*). Opera season runs from October to May. The **Stamford Center for the Arts** (☎ *203/325–4466* ⊕ *www.stamfordcenterforthearts.org*) presents everything from one-act plays and comedy shows to musicals and film festivals. The **Stamford Symphony Orchestra** (☎ *203/325–1407* ⊕ *www.stamfordsymphony.org*) stages performances from October to April, including a family concert series.

WHERE TO EAT

$-$$ ✗**City Limits Diner.** This art-deco, deluxe diner, alive with bright colors and
AMERICAN shiny chrome, likes to describe its food as running the gamut from "haute to homespun." Roughly translated, this is the place for everything from New York egg creams to French martinis to hot pastrami on New York rye to pan-roasted Atlantic salmon with Israeli couscous and shiitake mushrooms. ⊠ *135 Harvard Ave.* ☎ *203/348–7000* ▤ *AE, D, DC, MC, V.*

NORWALK

14 mi northeast of Stamford, 47 mi northeast of New York City.

In the 19th century, Norwalk became a major New England port and also manufactured pottery, clocks, watches, shingle nails, and paper. It later fell into a state of neglect, in which it remained for much of the 20th century. In the early 1990s, however, Norwalk's coastal business district was the focus of a major redevelopment project, which has turned it into a hot spot for trendy shopping, culture, and dining, much of it along the main drag, Washington Street. The stretch is known as SoNo (short for South Norwalk), and in the evening especially it is without a doubt the place to be seen if you're young, single, and living it up in Fairfield County.

Norwalk is the home of Yankee Doodle Dandies: in 1756, Colonel Thomas Fitch threw together a motley crew of Norwalk soldiers and led them off to fight at Ft. Crailo, near Albany, New York. Supposedly, Norwalk's women gathered feathers for the men to wear as plumes in their caps in an effort to give them some appearance of military decorum. Upon the arrival of these foppish warriors, one of the British officers sarcastically dubbed them "macaronis"—slang for dandies. The name caught on, and so did the song.

WHAT TO SEE

Lockwood-Mathews Mansion Museum. This ornate tribute to Victorian decorating was built in 1864 as the summer home of LeGrand Lockwood. It remains one the oldest (and finest) surviving Second Empire–style country homes in the United States; it's hard not to be impressed by its octagonal skylighted rotunda and more than 50 rooms of gilt, frescoes, marble, intricate woodwork, and etched glass. ⊠ *295 West Ave.* ☎ *203/838–9799* ✉ *$8* ⊘ *June.–Dec., Wed.–Sun. noon–4, or by appointment.*

☾ **Maritime Aquarium at Norwalk.** This 5-acre waterfront center, the cor-
★ nerstone of the SoNo district, explores the marine life and maritime culture of Long Island Sound. The aquarium's more than 20 habitats include some 1,000 creatures indigenous to the sound. You can see toothy bluefish and sand tiger sharks in the 110,000-gallon Open Ocean Tank, dozens of jellyfish performing their ghostly ballet in "Jellyfish Encounter," stately loggerhead sea turtles, winsome river otters, and happy harbor seals. The center also operates an Environmental Education Center and marine-mammal cruises aboard the *Oceanic,* and has a towering IMAX theater. ⊠ *10 N. Water St.* ☎ *203/852–0700* ⊕ *www.maritimeaquarium.org* ✉ *Aquarium $11, IMAX theater $9, combined $16.50* ⊘ *Labor Day–June, daily 10–5; July–Labor Day, daily 10–6.*

Sheffield Island Lighthouse. The 3-acre park here is a prime spot for a picnic. The 1868 lighthouse has four levels, 10 rooms to explore, and is adjacent to the Stewart B. McKinney U.S. Fish and Wildlife Refuge. Clambakes with all the fixings are held Thursday evenings from June through September. ⊠ *Ferry service from Hope Dock, at corner of*

Washington and North Water Sts. ☎*203/838 9111 ferry and light-house* ⊕*www.seaport.org* ✉*Round-trip ferry service and lighthouse tour $20* ⊗*Ferry May–late June, weekends at 11, 2, and 3:30; late June–Aug., weekdays at 11 and 3, weekends at 11, 2, and 3:30.*

☺ **Stepping Stones Museum for Children.** Except for the ColorCoaster, a 27-foot-high mechanical toy in constant motion, the exhibits at this museum are not permanent, but they are always educational and encourage hands-on exploration. Popular exhibits are Rainforest Adventure, where kids under 10 can climb a kapok tree or explore a gorilla's nest, and Waterscape, where they can learn about weather and even role-play as weather reporters. For kids 3 and under, there's Toddler Terrain. ✉*Mathews Park, 303 West Ave.* ☎*203/899–0606* ⊕*www.steppingstonesmuseum.org* ✉*$9* ⊗*Sept.–June, Tues. 1–5, Wed.–Sun. 10–5; July and Aug., daily 10–5.*

WHERE TO EAT & STAY

$$$-$$$$
CARIBBEAN

✕**Habana.** Ceiling fans, banana trees, and a high energy level characterize Habana, which serves contemporary Cuban cuisine with some Argentinean, Peruvian, Mexican, Puerto Rican, and Brazilian dishes thrown in for spice. Try the roasted sea bass with a crispy plantain crust or the baby back ribs with a spicy guava sauce, and top it off with a mojito. Grab a seat on the street-side patio in warm weather. ✉*70 N. Main St.* ☎*203/852–9790* ▭*AE, D, MC, V* ⊗*No lunch.*

$$-$$$

🛏️**Silvermine Tavern.** The simple rooms at this venerable, late-18th-century inn on a quiet road near the New Canaan and Wilton border are furnished with hooked rugs, canopy beds, and antiques—the look is vintage New England. There's a rather grand restaurant with large, low-ceiling dining rooms overlooking a millpond. Traditional New England favorites receive modern accents, and Sunday brunch is popular. **Pros:** historic charm makes this a nice alternative to the area's many chain hotels, reasonable rates, tranquil setting. **Cons:** rooms lack phones and TVs, old-fashioned vibe isn't everybody's cup of tea, you need a car to reach South Norwalk's shopping and dining. ✉*194 Perry Ave.* ☎*203/847–4558 or 888/693–9967* ⊕*www.silverminetavern.com* 🛏*10 rooms, 1 suite* ⚘*In-room: no phone, no TV. In-hotel: restaurant, no-smoking rooms* ▭*AE, MC, V* ⊙❘*CP.*

RIDGEFIELD

11 mi north of New Canaan, 43 mi west of New Haven.

In Ridgefield you'll find a rustic Connecticut atmosphere within an hour of Manhattan. The inviting town center is a largely residential sweep of lawns and majestic homes, with a feel more reminiscent of the peaceful Litchfield Hills, even though the town is in the northern reaches of Fairfield County.

WHAT TO SEE

★ **Aldrich Contemporary Art Museum.** Cutting-edge art is not exactly what you'd expect to find in a stately 18th-century Main Street structure that was once a general store, Ridgefield's first post office, a private home, and, for 35 years, a church. But inside the Aldrich Contemporary Art Museum are 12 galleries, a screening room, a sound gallery, a 22-foot-high project space for large installations, a 100-seat performance space, and an education center. Outside is a 2-acre sculpture garden. ⊠*258 Main St.* ☎*203/438–4519* ⊕*www.aldrichart.org* ⊠*$7, free Tues.* ⊘*Tues.–Sun. noon–5.*

Keeler Tavern Museum. A British cannonball is lodged in a corner of this 1713 former inn, tavern, and stagecoach stop that was also the home of the noted architect Cass Gilbert (1859–1934). Period furniture and Revolutionary War memorabilia fill the museum, where guides dressed in Colonial costumes conduct tours. The circa-1910 Charleston garden was designed by Gilbert and contains a reflecting pool. ⊠*132 Main St.* ☎*203/438–5485* ⊕*www.keelertavernmuseum.org* ⊠*$5* ⊘*Feb.–Dec., Wed. and weekends 1–4.*

Weir Farm National Historic Site. Connecticut's lone national park service property encompasses 153 wooded acres on the Ridgefield-Wilton border where the noted American impressionist painter J. Alden Weir (1852–1919) lived and worked from the early 1880s onward. Rangers give tours of the Weir home, studio, outbuildings, gardens, and grounds where the artist set many of his paintings, and also congregated with such notable fellow painters as Childe Hassam and John Singer Sargent. ⊠*735 Nod Hill Rd.* ☎*203/834–1896* ⊕*www.nps.gov/wefa* ⊠*Free* ⊘*Grounds year-round, visitor center May–Oct., Wed.–Sun. 9–5; Nov.–Apr., Thurs.–Sun. 10–4.*

WHERE TO EAT & STAY

$$-$$$ ✗**Luc's Cafe and Restaurant.** A cozy bistro set inside a stone building with
FRENCH   low ceilings, closely spaced tables, and a handy location in the Ridgefield's quaint downtown, Luc's charms patrons with carefully prepared food and low-key, friendly service. You can opt for a simple salade niçoise or croque monsieur sandwich, or enjoy a classic steak au poivre with a velvety Roquefort sauce and crispy frites. There's an extensive wine list, plus a range of aperitifs and single-malt whiskies. Enjoy live jazz on some evenings. ⊠*Stonehenge Rd., off U.S. 7* ☎*203/438–6511* ⊟*AE, MC, V* ⊘*Closed Sun. No lunch.*

$$-$$$ ▦**Stonehenge Inn.** The manicured lawns and bright white-clapboard buildings of Stonehenge are visible just off U.S. 7. The rooms are tasteful, but not overly fancy, and it's a good base for enjoying the excellent on-site restaurant and exploring the area's antiques shops and handful of noteworthy attractions. **Pros:** verdant and neatly kept grounds, polished service, terrific restaurant. **Cons:** not within walking distance of downtown Ridgefield, room décor is pleasant but not especially memorable. ⊠*Stonehenge Rd. off U.S. 7* ☎*203/438–6511* ⊕*www.stonehengeinn-ct.com* ⊲*12 rooms, 4 suites* ⊗*In-hotel: restaurant, no-smoking rooms* ⊟*AE, MC, V* ▯*CP.*

WESTPORT

15 mi southeast of Ridgefield, 47 mi northeast of New York City.

Westport, an artists' community since the turn of the 20th century, continues to attract creative types. Despite commuters and corporations, the town remains more artsy and cultured than its neighbors: if the rest of Fairfield County is stylistically five years behind Manhattan, Westport lags by just five months. Paul Newman and Joanne Woodward have their main residence here.

NIGHTLIFE & THE ARTS

The **Levitt Pavilion for the Performing Arts** (⊠*Jesup Rd.* ☎*203/221–4422* ⊕*www.levittpavilion.com*) sponsors an excellent series of mostly free summer concerts that range from jazz to classical, folk rock to blues. Long associated with ardent benefactors Paul Newman and Joanne Woodward, the venerable and intimate **Westport Country Playhouse** (⊠*25 Powers Ct.* ☎*203/227–4177* ⊕*www.westportplayhouse.org*) presents high-quality plays throughout the year.

WHERE TO EAT & STAY

$$$
Fodor's Choice
★
AMERICAN

✕**Dressing Room.** Opened beside the esteemed Westport Playhouse by Paul Newman and renowned cookbook author Michel Nischan, this favorite pretheater venue celebrates regional American, farm-to-table cuisine— many key ingredients on the menu are sourced locally, and others from prominent ranches and farms around the country. Highlights include dry-barbecue baby back ribs from California's Niman Ranch, served with an apple-cabbage slaw; pancetta-wrapped "day-boat" (caught that day) monkfish served alongside braised red cabbage and a parsnip-sage puree. A huge fieldstone fireplace warms the rustic-chic dining room, with its sturdy ceiling beams and barn-board walls. ⊠*27 Powers Ct.* ☎*203/226–1114* ⊟*AE, MC, V* ⊘*Closed Mon. No lunch Tues.*

$$$$
★

☵**Inn at National Hall.** Each whimsically exotic room at this towering Italianate redbrick inn in the heart of downtown Westport is a study in innovative restoration, wall stenciling, and decorative painting— including magnificent trompe l'oeil designs. The furniture collection is exceptional. Some rooms and suites have sleeping lofts and floor-to-ceiling windows overlooking the Saugatuck River. The Turkistan Suite—with its two-story-high bookcase, striped swag drapes, curving balcony, and king-size bed with Egyptian print canopy and painted valance—is one glorious example. **Pros:** fabulously artful and cushy rooms, enchanted setting overlooking Saugatuck River, walking distance from downtown shopping and dining. **Cons:** ultrapricey, service can be a little stiff. ⊠*2 Post Rd. W* ☎*203/221–1351 or 800/628–4255* ⊕*www.innatnationalhall.com* ➫*8 rooms, 8 suites* ♿*In-room: refrigerator, VCR, Ethernet. In-hotel: no kids under 12, no-smoking rooms* ⊟*AE, DC, MC, V* ¹⊚¹*CP.*

4

BRIDGEPORT

10 mi east of Westport, 63 mi west of New London.

Bridgeport, a city that has endured some economic hard times, is working hard to revitalize itself and overcome its negative image with improvements such as the Ballpark at Harbor Yard and the Arena at Harbor Yard sports and entertainment complex. A handful of noteworthy, family-friendly attractions make it worthwhile for a day visit, but it's not a particularly appealing destination for an overnight.

WHAT TO SEE

Barnum Museum. This Romanesque red sandstone-and-brick building stands out in downtown Bridgeport, much like P.T. Barnum, the "Greatest Showman on Earth" and former mayor of Bridgeport, did in his day. The museum depicts the life and times of Barnum, who founded his circus in 1871 and presented performers such as General Tom Thumb and Jenny Lind, the Swedish Nightingale. Among the exhibits is a scaled-down model of Barnum's legendary five-ring circus containing more than 3,000 pieces. ⊠ *820 Main St.* ☎ *203/331–1104* ⊕ *www.barnum-museum.org* ☜ *$5* ☉ *Tues.–Sat. 10–4:30, Sun. noon–4:30.*

Connecticut's Beardsley Zoo. The indoor walk-through South American rain forest alone justifies a visit to this zoo. It's alive with dozens of species, some rare and endangered, such as keel-billed toucans, broad-snouted caimans, and black-and-gold howler monkeys living in a lush environment of waterfalls, ponds, greenery, and bamboo. The zoo itself has 36 acres of exhibits including bison, Amur (Siberian) tigers, timber wolves, and proud peacocks who freely roam the property right along with you. Also here is a working carousel and a New England farmyard. ⊠ *1875 Noble Ave.* ☎ *203/394–6565* ⊕ *www.beardsleyzoo.org* ☜ *$9* ☉ *Park daily 9–4, rain forest daily 10:30–3:30.*

Discovery Museum and Planetarium. Visitors, young and old alike, learn about science and technology through hands-on exhibits that explore electricity, computers, sound, light, magnetism, and energy. Other draws include the *Challenger* learning center, which provides computer-simulated space missions, and the preschooler-friendly DiscoveryTown, with puppets and a life-size school bus. ⊠ *4450 Park Ave.* ☎ *203/372–3521* ⊕ *www.discoverymuseum.org* ☜ *$8.50* ☉ *Sept.–June, Tues.–Sat. 10–5, Sun. noon–5; July and Aug., Mon.–Sat. 10–5, Sun. noon–5.*

HARTFORD & THE CONNECTICUT RIVER VALLEY

Westward expansion in the New World began along the meandering Connecticut River. Dutch explorer Adrian Block first explored the area in 1614, and in 1633 a trading post was set up in what is now Hartford. Within five years, throngs of restive Massachusetts Bay colonists had settled in this fertile valley. What followed was more than three centuries of shipbuilding, shad hauling, and river trading with ports as far away as the West Indies and the Mediterranean.

Less touristy than the coast and northwest hills, the Connecticut River valley is a swath of small villages and uncrowded state parks punctuated by a few small cities and a large one: the capital city of Hartford. South of Hartford, with the exception of industrial Middletown, genuinely quaint hamlets vie for attention with antiques shops, scenic drives, and romantic French restaurants and country inns.

ESSEX

29 mi east of New Haven.

4

Essex, consistently named one of the best small towns in America, looks much as it did in the mid-19th century, at the height of its shipbuilding prosperity. So important to a young America was Essex's boat manufacturing that the British burned more than 40 ships here during the War of 1812. Gone are the days of steady trade with the West Indies, when the aroma of imported rum, molasses, and spices hung in the air. Whitewashed houses—many the former roosts of sea captains—line Main Street, which has shops that sell clothing, antiques, paintings and prints, and sweets.

WHAT TO SEE

★ **Connecticut River Museum.** In an 1878 steamboat warehouse at the foot of Main Street, this museum tells the story of the Connecticut River through paintings, maritime artifacts, interactive displays, and ship models. The riverfront museum even has a full-size working reproduction of the world's first submarine, the *American Turtle*; the original was built by David Bushnell in 1775 as a "secret weapon" to win the Revolutionary War. ⊠ *At dock, 67 Main St.* ☎*860/767–8269* ⊕*www. ctrivermuseum.org* ✉*$7* ☾*Tues.–Sun. 10–5.*

SCENIC TRIP

Essex Steam Train and Riverboat. This ride offers some of the best views of the Connecticut River valley from the vantage point of a restored train (1920s coaches pulled by a vintage steam locomotive) and an old-fashioned Mississippi-style riverboat. The train, traveling along the Connecticut River through the lower valley, makes a 12-mi roundtrip from Essex Station to Deep River Station; from there, if you wish to continue, you board the riverboat for a ride up the river to East Haddam (the open promenade deck on the third level has the best views). Special trains, including a dinner train and a wine train, as well as a Santa Special and hugely popular visits by Thomas the Tank Engine, occur periodically. ⊠ *Valley Railroad Company, 1 Railroad Ave. (Rte. 9 Exit 3)* ☎*860/767–0103* ⊕ *www.essexsteamtrain.com* ✉*Train fare $17, train-boat fare $26* ☾ *May–Dec.; call for schedule.*

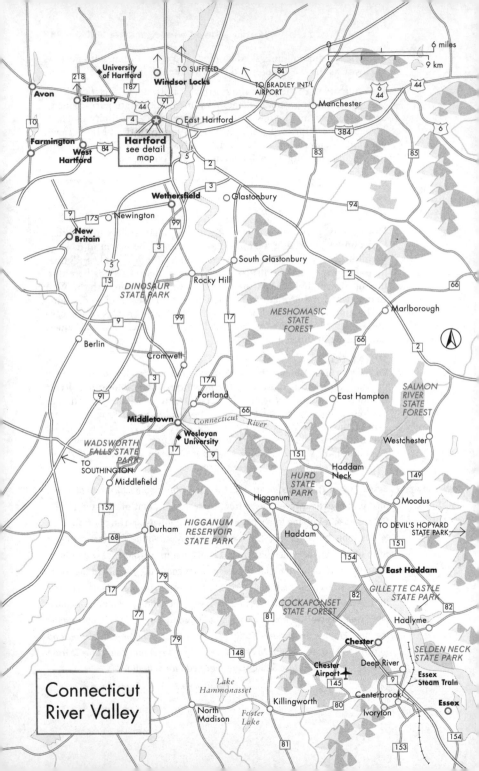

Connecticut River Valley

WHERE TO EAT

$$ ✗ **Brasserie Pip.** As wonderful as the Copper Beech Inn's formal res-
Fodor'sChoice taurant is, the hipper and more relaxed brasserie—which opened in
★ 2006—may just be the true gem, given its fantastic value, superbly
FRENCH authentic fare, and delightful outdoor seating in warm weather (on a
porch overlooking the inn's extensive gardens). You could make a night
of the cheese and charcuterie plates, plus a selection of fresh oysters
on the half shell. Or opt for more substantial fare, such as prosciutto-
wrapped cod over polenta, or classic steak frites. Pip's chic cocktail
bar makes its own flavored vodkas—such as blood-orange-and-cori-
ander—to prepare memorable martinis. ⊠*46 Main St., 4 mi west of
Essex, Ivoryton* ☎*860/767-0330* ⊟*AE, D, DC, MC, V* ⊘*Closed
Mon. No lunch.*

$$$$ ✗ **Copper Beech Inn Restaurant.** Crystal sparkles, silver shines, and can-
★ dles glow in the formal dining room of this grand country inn, lauded
FRENCH for its excellent French country cuisine. A four prix-fixe menu is pre-
sented each evening, by a competent and knowledgeable staff. Notable
recent dishes have included a starter of Catalan-style grilled vegetables
drizzled with smoked olive oil and imported sea salt, and an entree of
venison au poivre over a potato-and-celery-root puree with crisp green
beans. The 4,000-bottle wine cellar is one of the best in the state. ⊠*46
Main St., 4 mi west of Essex, Ivoryton* ☎*860/767-0330* ⚯*Reserva-
tions essential* ⊟*AE, D, DC, MC, V* ⊘*Closed Mon. No lunch.*

CHESTER

5 mi north of Ivoryton, 24 mi northwest of New London.

Upscale boutiques and artisans' studios fill the chiefly 19th-century
buildings along Chester's quaint and well-preserved Main Street. Ches-
ter sits on a portion of the Connecticut River that has been named "one
of the last great places on earth" by the Nature Conservancy and is the
starting point of the Chester–Hadlyme Ferry, which crosses the river in
a grand total of five minutes.

AERIAL **At tiny Chester Airport, Chester Charter** (⊠*Off Rte. 9* ☎*860/526-4321 or*
TOUR *800/752-6371* ⊕*www.chester-charter.com* ⊠*Call for rates* ⊘*By appoint-
ment*) offers scenic flights over the lower Connecticut River Valley either in
a single-passenger, open-cockpit, 1941 biplane or multi-passenger, modern
Cessnas. Bring your own bomber jacket and you're set.

SHOPPING

Ceramica (⊠*36 Main St.* ☎*800/782–1238* ⊕*www.ceramicadirect.
com*) carries hand-painted Italian tableware and decorative accessories.
Connecticut River Artisans (⊠*5 W. Main St.* ☎*860/526–5575* ⊕*www.
ctartisans.com*), a cooperative of local artists, sells traditional and
contemporary handcrafts, from stained-glass kaleidoscopes to original
watercolors. Peruse handcrafted gifts, music boxes, linens, and Kosta
Boda and Orrefors crystal at **Chez Manon** (⊠*21 Main St.* ☎*860/526–
2554* ⊕*www.chezmanon.net*), an elegant storefront gallery.

WHERE TO EAT

$$$–$$$$
FRENCH

✕ **Restaurant du Village.** A black wrought-iron gate beckons you away from the boutiques of Chester's Main Street, and an off-white awning draws you through the door of this classic little Colonial storefront, painted in historic Newport blue and blooming with flower boxes. Here you can sample exquisite French country cuisine—escargots broiled in garlic and parsley sauce in the traditional Alsatian manner, crispy roast duckling with olives, raisins, and sundried tomatoes in port wine sauce—while recapping the day's shopping coups. ⊠ *59 Main St.* ☎ *860/526–5301* ⚲ *Reservations essential* ⊟ *AE, MC, V* ⊗ *Closed Mon. and Tues. No lunch.*

$$–$$$
★
ECLECTIC

✕ **River Tavern and Wine Bar.** This sleek and sophisticated tavern in the heart of Chester functions both as a cheery neighborhood restaurant and a bona fide destination for fans of first-rate contemporary international food. The emphasis here is on freshness, and the menu changes frequently. Favorites have included mussels with lemongrass and coconut milk, and crispy duck confit served in Hunan-style pork broth with duck-liver-mousse wontons. The adjacent wine bar serves simpler victuals and numerous vintages by the glass. ⊠ *23 Main St.* ☎ *860/526–9417* ⊟ *AE, MC, V.*

EAST HADDAM

7 mi north of Chester, 28 mi southeast of Hartford.

Fishing, shipping, and musket making were the chief enterprises at East Haddam, the only town in the state that occupies both banks of the Connecticut River. This lovely community retains much of its old-fashioned charm, most of it centered around its historic downtown.

WHAT TO SEE

★ **Gillette Castle State Park.** The outrageous 24-room oak-and-fieldstone hilltop castle, modeled after medieval castles of the Rhineland and built between 1914 and 1919 by the eccentric actor and dramatist William Gillette, is the park's main attraction. You can tour the castle and hike on trails near the remains of the 3-mi private railroad that chugged about the property until the owner's death in 1937. Gillette, who was born in Hartford, wrote two famous plays about the Civil War and was beloved for his play *Sherlock Holmes* (he performed the title role). ⊠ *67 River Rd., off Rte. 82* ☎ *860/526–2336* ⊕ *www.friendsofgillettecastle.org* ⚲ *Park free, castle $5* ⊗ *Park daily 8–sunset; castle Memorial Day–Columbus Day, daily 10–4:30.*

★ **Goodspeed Opera House.** This magnificent 1876 Victorian-gingerbread "wedding cake" theater on the Connecticut River—so called for all its turrets, mansard roof, and grand filigree—is widely recognized for its role in the preservation and development of American musical theater. More than 16 Goodspeed productions have gone on to Broadway, including *Annie*. Performances take place from April to early December. ⊠ *6 Main St. (Rte. 82)* ☎ *860/873–8668* ⊕ *www.goodspeed.org* ⚲ *Tour $5* ⊗ *Tours June–Oct; call for times.*

OFF THE
BEATEN
PATH **Devil's Hopyard State Park.** Sixty-foot cascades flow down Chapman Falls at this 860-acre park, an idyllic spot for bird-watching, picnicking, fishing, camping, and hiking. ✉ *366 Hopyard Rd., 3 mi north of junction of Rtes. 82 and 156* ☎ *860/873–8566* ✆ *Free* ☉ *Daily 8* AM–*dusk.*

MIDDLETOWN

15 mi northwest of East Haddam, 24 mi northeast of New Haven.

With its Connecticut River setting, easy access to major highways, and historic architecture, Middletown is a popular destination for recreational boaters and tourists alike. The town's High Street is an architecturally eclectic thoroughfare. Charles Dickens once called it "the loveliest Main Street in America," though Middletown's actual Main Street runs parallel to it a few blocks east.

4

WHAT TO SEE

Wesleyan University. Originally named for its location halfway between Hartford and Long Island, Middletown is highlighted by the imposing campus of Wesleyan University, founded in 1831 and one of the oldest Methodist institutions of higher education in the United States. The campus has roughly 2,700 undergrads, 150 graduate students, and a vibrant science-and-arts scene, which gives Middletown a contemporary college-town feel. On campus, note the massive, fluted Corinthian columns of the Greek-revival Russell House (circa 1828) at the corner of Washington Street, across from the pink Mediterranean-style Davison Art Center, built just 15 years later; farther on are gingerbreads, towering brownstones, Tudors, and Queen Annes. A few hundred yards up on Church Street, which intersects High Street, is the Olin Library. The 1928 structure, Wesleyan University's library, was designed by Henry Bacon, the architect of the Lincoln Memorial. The school bookstore is at 45 Broad St. ✉ *High St.*

OFF THE
BEATEN
PATH **Lyman Orchards.** If you are looking for a quintessential New England outing, these orchards, just south of Middletown, are not to be missed. Here you can pick your own fruits and vegetables–berries, peaches, pears, apples, and even pumpkins from June to October. ✉ *Rtes. 147 and 157, Middlefield* ☎ *860/349–1763* ✆ *www.lymanorchards.com* ☉ *Nov.–Aug., daily 9–6; Sept.–Oct., daily 9–7.*

SPORTS & THE OUTDOORS

✿ **Dinosaur State Park.** See some 500 tracks left by the dinosaurs that once roamed the area around this park north of Middletown. The tracks are preserved under a giant geodesic dome. You can even make plaster casts of tracks on a special area of the property; call ahead to learn what materials you need to bring. ✉ *400 West St., east of I-91 Exit 23, Rocky Hill* ☎ *860/529–8423* ✆ *www.dinosaurstatepark.org* ✆ *$5* ☉ *Exhibits Tues.–Sun. 9–4:30, trails daily 9–4:30.*

SHOPPING

Wesleyan Potters (✉ *350 S. Main St.* ☎ *860/347–5925* ✆ *www.wesley anpotters.com*) sells jewelry, clothing, baskets, pottery, weavings, and more. The shop also runs classes and workshops.

NIGHTLIFE & THE ARTS

★ At Wesleyan University's **Center for the Arts** (⊠*283 Washington Terr.* ☎*860/685–3355* ⊕*www.wesleyan.edu/cfa*) see modern dance or a provocative new play, hear top playwrights and actors discuss their craft, and take in an art exhibit or concert. At last count, **Eli Cannon's** (⊠*695 Main St.* ☎*860/347–3547*) had more than 35 beers on draft and an extensive bottled selection, making it a hot late-night hangout.

WHERE TO EAT

¢-$ ✕**O'Rourke's Diner.** A devastating fire closed this beloved steel, glass, and
★ brick diner in summer 2007, but the owners—partly through donations
AMERICAN from the community—have rebuilt it better than ever. It continues to be the place to go for top-notch diner fare, including a number of creative specialties, such as the omelet stuffed with roasted Portobello mushrooms, Brie, and asparagus. The steamed cheeseburgers are another favorite. Arrive early: lines are often out the door and it closes at 3 PM. ⊠*728 Main St.* ☎*860/346–6101* ▤*AE, DC, MC, V* ⊗*No dinner.*

WETHERSFIELD

7 mi northeast of New Britain, 32 mi northeast of New Haven.

Wethersfield, a vast Hartford suburb, dates from 1634 and has the state's largest—and, some say, most picturesque—historic district, with more than 100 pre-1849 buildings. Old Wethersfield has the oldest firehouse in the state, the oldest historic district in the state, and the oldest continuously operating seed company. Today, this "old" community is making improvements with new parks and new shops. But history is still Wethersfield's main draw.

WHAT TO SEE

Webb-Deane-Stevens Museum. For a true sample of Wethersfield's historic past, stop by the Joseph Webb House, the Silas Deane House, and the Isaac Stevens House—all next door to each other along Main Street and all built in the mid- to late 1700s. These well-preserved examples of Georgian architecture reflect their owners' lifestyles as, respectively, a merchant, a diplomat, and a tradesman. The Webb House, a registered National Historic Landmark, was the site of the strategy conference between George Washington and the French general Jean-Baptiste Rochambeau that led to the British defeat at Yorktown. ⊠*211 Main St., off I–91 (Exit 26)* ☎*860/529–0612* ⊕*www.webb-deane-stevens. org* ▧*$8* ⊗*May–Oct., Mon. and Wed.–Sat. 10–4, Sun. 1–4; Apr. and Nov., Sat. 10–4, Sun. 1–4; other times by appointment.*

★ **New Britain Museum of American Art.** An important stop for art lovers in a small industrial city 8 mi west of Wethersfield, this museum more than doubled its exhibit space with the opening of a new building in 2006. The inauguration came not a moment too soon—the 100-year-old museum's collection of more than 5,000 works from 1740 to the present had seriously outgrown the turn-of-the-20th-century house that held it. Among the treasures are paintings by artists of the Hudson River and Ash Can schools; by John Singer Sargent, Winslow Homer,

CLOSE UP

Garden Party

Nine extraordinary Connecticut gardens form Connecticut's Historic Gardens, a "trail" of natural beauties across the state.

The re-created Colonial-revival garden at the **Webb-Deane-Stevens Museum** (✉ *211 Main St., Wethersfield* ☎ *860/529–0612*) is a presentation of old-fashioned flowers such as peonies, pinks, phlox, hollyhocks, larkspur, and antique roses.

Statuary decorates the Bellamy-Ferriday House & Garden in Bethlehem.

A high-Victorian texture garden, a wildflower meadow, Connecticut's largest magnolia tree, an antique rose garden, a 100-year-old pink dogwood, and a blue cottage garden are the highlights of the grounds at the **Harriet Beecher Stowe Center** (✉ *77 Forest St., Hartford* ☎ *860/522–9258*). At the **Butler-McCook House & Garden** (✉ *396 Main St., Hartford* ☎ *860/522–1806*), landscape architect Jacob Weidenmann created a Victorian garden oasis amid downtown city life.

The centerpiece of the **Hill-Stead Museum** (✉ *35 Mountain Rd., Farmington* ☎ *860/677–4787* ⊕ *www.hillstead.org*) is a circa-1920 sunken garden by Beatrix Farrand. It is enclosed in a yew hedge and surrounded by a wall of rough stone; at the center of the octagonal design is a summerhouse with 36 flowerbeds and brick walkways radiating outward. Farrand also designed the garden at **Promisek Beatrix Farrand Garden** (✉ *694 Skyline Ridge Rd., Bridgewater* ☎ *860/354–1788*), which overflows with beds of annuals and perennials such as hollyhocks, peonies, and always-dashing delphiniums.

Legendary British garden writer and designer Gertrude Jekyll designed only three gardens in the United States, and the one at the **Glebe House Museum** (✉ *Hollow Rd., Woodbury* ☎ *203/263–2855*) is the only one still in existence. The garden is a classic example of Jekyll's ideas of color harmonies and plant combinations; a hedge of mixed shrubs encloses a mix of perennials.

An apple orchard and a circa-1915 formal parterre garden that blossoms with peonies, historic roses, and lilacs highlight the **Bellamy-Ferriday House & Garden** (✉ *9 Main St. N., Bethlehem* ☎ *203/266–7596*). At **Roseland Cottage** (✉ *556 Route 169, Woodstock* ☎ *860/928–4074*), the boxwood parterre garden includes 21 flowerbeds surrounded by boxwood hedge.

The gardens at the historic **Florence Griswold Museum** (✉ *96 Lyme St., Old Lyme* ☎ *860/434–5542*), once the home of a prominent Old Lyme family and then a haven for artists, have been restored to their 1910 appearance and feature hollyhocks and black-eyed Susans.

4

Georgia O'Keeffe, and others on up through op-art works and sculpture by Isamu Noguchi. Deserving of special note is the selection of impressionist artists, including Mary Cassatt, William Merritt Chase, Childe Hassam, and John Henry Twachtman, as well as Thomas Hart Benton's five-panel mural *The Arts of Life in America*. The museum also has a café, a large shop, and a library of art books. ⊠ *56 Lexington St.* ☎ *860/229–0257* ⊕ *www.nbmaa.org* 🎫 *$9, free Sat. 10–noon* ◷ *Tues., Wed., and Fri. 11–5; Thurs. 11–8; Sat. 10–5; Sun. noon–5.*

HARTFORD

4 mi north of Wethersfield, 45 mi northwest of New London, 81 mi northeast of Stamford.

Midway between New York City and Boston, Hartford is Connecticut's capital city. Founded in 1635 on the banks of the Connecticut River, Hartford was at various times home to authors Mark Twain and Harriet Beecher Stowe, inventors Samuel and Elizabeth Colt, landscape architect Frederick Law Olmsted, and Ella Grasso, the first woman to be elected a state governor. Today, Hartford, where America's insurance industry was born in the early 19th century, is poised for change, with a new convention center and new hotels (the Hilton Hartford and the Hartford Marriott Downtown) opened in 2005 and ground broken for the Connecticut Center for Science and Exploration (scheduled to open in 2008). Hartford, which already ranks in the top 6% of metropolitan areas in North America for its arts and culture, is a destination on the verge of discovery.

WHAT TO SEE

❸ **Butler-McCook Homestead.** Hartford's oldest house was built in 1782 and continuously occupied by the same family until 1971. Inside are furnishings, family possessions, antiques, and Victorian-era toys that show the evolution of American taste over time. The beautifully restored Victorian garden, originally designed by Jacob Weidenmann, is a must-see. ⊠ *396 Main St.* ☎ *860/522–1806 or 860/247–8996* ⊕ *www.ctlandmarks.org* 🎫 *$7* ◷ *May–Dec., Wed.–Sat. 10–4 (1st Thurs. of most months until 8), Sun. 1–4; Jan.–Apr., Sat. 10–4, Sun. 1–4.*

NEED A BREAK? | **Mozzicato–De Pasquale's Bakery, Pastry Shop & Caffe** (⊠ *329 Franklin Ave.* ☎ *860/296–0426* ⊕ *www.mozzicatobakery.com*), in the heart of the city's Little Italy neighborhood along Franklin Avenue, serves delectable Italian pastries in the bakery, and espresso, cappuccino, and gelato in the café.

❶ **Old State House.** This Federal-style house with an elaborate cupola and roof balustrade was designed in the early 1700s by Charles Bulfinch, architect of the U.S. Capitol. It served as Connecticut's state capitol until a new building opened in 1879, then became Hartford's city hall until 1915. In the 1820 Senate Chamber, where everyone from Abraham Lincoln to George Bush has spoken, you can view a portrait of George Washington by Gilbert Stuart, and in the Courtroom you can find out about the trial of the *Amistad* Africans in the very place where it was first held. In summer, enjoy the concerts and farmers' market.

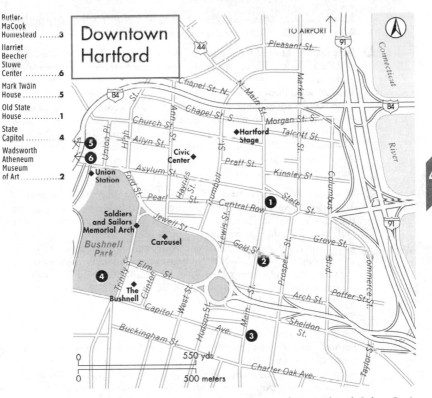

Downtown
Hartford

And don't forget to stop by the Museum of Natural and Other Curiosities. ⊠ *800 Main St.* ☎*860/522–6766* ⊕*www.ctosh.org* ⊠*Free* ☉*Tues.–Fri. 10–4, Sat. 10–4.*

⑤ **Mark Twain House & Museum.** Built in 1874, this building was the home
Fodor's Choice of Samuel Langhorne Clemens, better known as Mark Twain, until
★ 1891. While he and his family lived in this 19-room Victorian mansion, Twain published seven major novels, including *Tom Sawyer, Huckleberry Finn,* and *The Prince and the Pauper.* The home is one of only two Louis Comfort Tiffany–designed domestic interiors open to the public. A contemporary museum on the grounds presents an up-close look at the author, and also shows an outstanding Ken Burns documentary on his life. ⊠*351 Farmington Ave., at Woodland St.* ☎*860/247–0998* ⊕*www.marktwainhouse.org* ⊠*$14* ☉*Apr.–Dec., Mon.–Sat. 9:30–5:30, Sun. noon–5:30; Jan.–Mar., Mon. and Wed.–Sat. 9:30–5:30, Sun. noon–5:30.*

⑥ **Harriet Beecher Stowe Center.** Stowe (1811–96) spent her final years at
★ this Victorian Gothic cottage, on the Connecticut Freedom Trail. The center was built around the cottage, created as a tribute to the author of the influential antislavery novel, *Uncle Tom's Cabin.* Stowe's personal writing table and effects are inside the home. ⊠*77 Forest St.* ☎*860/522–9258* ⊕*www.harrietbeecherstowecenter.org* ⊠*$8* ☉*Late*

*May–mid-Oct., Mon.–Sat. 9:30–4:30, Sun. noon–4:30; mid-Oct.–late
May, Tues.–Sat. 9:30–4:30, Sun. noon–4:30.*

❹ State Capitol. The gold-leaf dome of the State Capitol rises above Bushnell Park. Built in 1878, the building houses the state's executive offices
and legislative chamber, as well as historical memorabilia. On a tour,
you can walk through the Hall of Flags, gape at a statue of Connecticut
state hero Nathan Hale, and observe the proceedings of the General
Assembly from the public galleries, when in session. ⊠ *210 Capitol Ave.*
☎ *860/240–0222* ⊕ *www.cga.ct.gov/capitoltours* ⊠ *Free* ⊙ *Building
weekdays 9–3. Tours given hourly, Nov.–Mar. weekdays 9:15–1:15;
Apr.–June and Sept. and Oct. weekdays 9:15–1:15, Sat. 10:15–2:15;
July and Aug., weekdays 9:15–2:15, Sat. 10:15–2:15.*

❷ Wadsworth Atheneum Museum of Art. With more than 50,000 artworks
Fodor'sChoice and artifacts spanning 5,000 years, this is the oldest art museum in
★ the nation. The first American museum to acquire works by Salvador
Dalí and the Italian artist Caravaggio, the large museum also houses
7,000 items documenting African-American history and culture in
partnership with the Amistad Foundation. Particularly impressive are
the museum's collections of baroque, impressionist, and Hudson River
School artists. ⊠ *600 Main St.* ☎ *860/278–2670* ⊕ *www.wadsworth
atheneum.org* ⊠ *$10* ⊙ *Wed.–Fri. 11–5 (1st Thurs. of most months
until 8), weekends 10–5.*

SPORTS & THE OUTDOORS

⟳ **Bushnell Park.** Fanning out from the State Capitol building, this city
park, created in 1850, was the first public space in the country with
natural landscaping. The original designer, a Swiss-born landscape
architect and botanist named Jacob Weidenmann, planted 157 varieties of trees and shrubs to create an urban arboretum. Added later
were the Soldiers and Sailors Memorial Arch, dedicated to Civil War
soldiers; the Corning Fountain; the Bushnell Park Carousel (open May
through September), intricately hand-carved in 1914 by the Artistic
Carousel Company of Brooklyn, New York; the Pumphouse Gallery;
and a performance venue. An oasis of green, the park has a pond and
about 750 trees, including four state champion trees. ⊠ *Asylum and
Trinity Sts.* ☎ *860/232–6710* ⊕ *www.bushnellpark.org.*

SKI AREA A 20-minute drive southwest of Hartford, **Mt. Southington** (⊠ *396
Mount Vernon Rd., Plantsville* ☎ *860/628–0954* ⊕ *www.mountsouth
ington.com*) is a relatively simple dayhill with mostly a local following;
it's ideal for a casual and affordable day of skiing and boarding.

NIGHTLIFE & THE ARTS

NIGHTLIFE For barbecue and blues head to **Black-Eyed Sally's** (⊠ *350 Asylum St.*
☎ *860/278–7427* ⊕ *www.blackeyedsallys.com*). **Coach's** (⊠ *187 Allyn
St.* ☎ *860/524–8888*) is one of the area's best sports bars.

THE ARTS The **Bushnell** (⊠ *166 Capitol Ave.* ☎ *860/987–6000 or 888/824–
2874* ⊕ *www.bushnell.org*) hosts the **Hartford Symphony Orchestra**
(☎ *860/244–2999* ⊕ *www.hartfordsymphony.org*) and tours of major
musicals. The **Hartford Conservatory** (⊠ *834 Asylum Ave.* ☎ *860/246–*

2588 ⊕*www.hartfordconserva tory.org*) presents musical theater, concerts, and dance performances, with an emphasis on traditional works. The Tony Award–winning **Hartford Stage Company** (✉*50 Church St.* ☎*860/527–5151* ⊕*www.hartfordstage.org*) puts on classic and new plays from around the world and premieres a fair number of productions that go on to become Broadway hits. **Real Art Ways** (✉*56 Arbor St.* ☎*860/232– 1006* ⊕*www.realartways.org*) presents modern and experimental musical compositions in addition to avant-garde and foreign films. **TheatreWorks** (✉*233 Pearl St.* ☎*860/527–7838* ⊕*www.theaterworkshartford.org*), the Hartford equivalent of off Broadway, presents experimental new dramas.

> ### TAKE A TOUR
>
> The **Connecticut Freedom Trail** (⊕*www.ctfreedomtrail. com*) has more than 50 historic sights associated with the state's African-American heritage. The **Connecticut Impressionist Art Trail** (⊕*www.arttrail.org*) is a self-guided tour of 14 museums and sites important to the 19th-century American Impressionist movement. The **Connecticut Wine Trail** (☎*860/267-1399* ⊕*www. ctwine.com*) travels among 15 member vineyards.

4

WHERE TO EAT

$-$$
★
PIZZA

✕**First and Last Tavern.** What looks to be a simple neighborhood joint south of downtown is actually one of the state's most hallowed pizza parlors, serving superb thin-crust pies (locals love the Puttanesca) since 1936. The old-fashioned wooden bar in one room is jammed most evenings with suburbia-bound daily-grinders shaking off their suits. The main dining room, which is just as noisy, has a brick outer wall covered with celebrity photos. This is the original, but other branches have opened around the state. ✉*939 Maple Ave.* ☎*860/956–6000* ⌂*Reservations not accepted* ☐*AE, D, DC, MC, V.*

$$$-$$$$
Fodor'sChoice
★
AMERICAN

✕**Max Downtown.** With its contemporary design, extensive array of martinis and wines, and sophisticated cuisine, Max Downtown is a favorite with the city's well-heeled and a popular after-work spot. Creative entrées include lemon-scented black cod with roasted fennel and cherry-tomatoes confit; and a wide range of perfectly prepared steaks, with such toppings as foie-gras butter and cognac-peppercorn cream. Desserts such as the chocolate-chip ice cream cake and banana praline crepe are not to be missed. The restaurant is part of a small empire of excellent Hartford-area restaurants that includes Max's Oyster in West Hartford, Max a Mia in Avon, and several others. ✉*185 Asylum St.* ☎*860/522–2530* ⌂*Reservations essential* ☐*AE, DC, MC, V* ⊙*No lunch weekends.*

$$-$$$
ITALIAN

✕**Peppercorn's Grill.** This mainstay of Hartford's restaurant scene presents contemporary Italian cuisine in both a lively (colorful murals adorn the walls) and formal (tables are topped with white linen) setting. Look for house-made potato gnocchi, ravioli, and top-quality steaks, but save room for the warm chocolate bread pudding and the Valrohna chocolate cake. ✉*357 Main St.* ☎*860/547–1714* ☐*AE, DC, MC, V* ⊙*Closed Sun. No lunch Sat.*

$$-$$$
ECLECTIC

✕**Trumbull Kitchen.** Upbeat, hip, and casual, Trumbull Kitchen (part of the popular Max restaurant group) is the place to see and be seen—a top pick of local politicos. The menu is divided into categories including dim sum, tapas, and noshes; soups, noodles, and bowls; fondues; and stone pizzas and sandwiches. Expect to find everything from cutting-edge to home-style favorites, including sushi rolls, chili crab with crispy noodles, organic cheddar-bacon fondue, pear-and-Gorgonzola pizzas, and pan-seared sea scallops with butternet-squash gnocchi. You decide in what order you'd like them served. ⊠*150 Trumbull St.* ☎*860/493–7412* ☐*AE, D, DC, MC, V* ⊘*No lunch Sun.*

WHERE TO STAY

$$$-$$$$

⊞**Goodwin Hotel.** Built in 1881, the Goodwin is an ornate, dark-red structure across the street from the civic center in the heart of the city. Rooms are tastefully appointed with rich wood furnishings, sleigh beds, and marble baths. The hotel is undergoing a massive $12 million renovation through 2009. Its Pierpont's Restaurant is a popular breakfast spot. **Pros:** central location, historic building, polished staff. **Cons:** major renovations ongoing through 2009. ⊠*1 Haynes St.* ☎*860/246–7500 or 800/922–5006* ⊕*www.goodwinhotel.com* ⊅*113 rooms, 11 suites* ☐*In-room: Ethernet, Wi-Fi. In-hotel: restaurant, bar, gym, parking (fee), no-smoking rooms* ☐*AE, D, DC, MC, V.*

$-$$

⊞**Residence Inn Hartford-Downtown Marriott.** Part of the rehabilitation project at the historic Richardson building, the all-suites Residence Inn is convenient to Pratt Street, Hartford Stage, and the Old State House. Rooms come with a kitchen, microwave, refrigerator, and coffeemaker, and there's an on-site 24-hour convenience store. A full breakfast is included daily, as is a light dinner buffet Monday–Thursday. The onsite City Steam microbrewery is a fun spot for a drink or a hearty meal. **Pros:** spacious rooms, great value, right in middle of downtown. **Cons:** right in the middle of downtown, cookie-cutter furnishings. ⊠*942 Main St.* ☎*860/524–5550 or 800/960–5045* ⊕*www.marriott.com* ⊅*120 suites* ☐*In-room: kitchen, Ethernet. In-hotel: restaurant, gym, no-smoking rooms* ☐*AE, D, DC, MC, V* ⦿*BP.*

WEST HARTFORD

5 mi west of Hartford.

More metropolitan than many of its suburban neighbors, West Hartford is alive with a sense of community. Gourmet-food and ethnic grocery stores abound, as do unusual boutiques and oh-so-chic shops. A stroll around West Hartford Center (Interstate 84 Exit 42) reveals well-groomed streets busy with pedestrians and lined with coffee shops and restaurants with outdoor seating.

WHAT TO SEE

Noah Webster House/Museum of West Hartford History. This 18th century farmhouse is the birthplace of the famed author (1758–1843) of the *American Dictionary.* Inside is Webster memorabilia and period furnishings; outside there is a garden planted with herbs, vegetables, and flowers that would have been available to the Websters when they lived here. ✉227 S. Main St. ☎860/521–5362 ⊕www.noahwebsterhouse. org ⊠$6 ⊙Thurs.–Mon. 1–4.

☾ **Children's Museum.** A life-size walk-through replica of a 60-foot sperm
★ whale greets patrons at this museum, formerly known as the Science Center of Connecticut. The museum also includes a giant walk-in kaleidoscope, a wildlife sanctuary, and real-life images "beamed" in from NASA, plus exhibits on earthquakes and special software in the center's computer lab that will let even the youngest visitors feel like experienced Web surfers. ✉950 Trout Brook Dr. ☎860/231–2824 ⊕www.thechildrensmuseumct.org ⊠Museum $8, laser and planetarium shows an additional $3 each ⊙Tues.–Sat. 10–5, Sun. noon–5.

FARMINGTON

5 mi southwest of West Hartford.

Busy Farmington, incorporated in 1645, is a classic river town with lovely estates, a perfectly preserved main street, and the prestigious **Miss Porter's School** (✉60 Main St.), the late Jacqueline Kennedy Onassis's alma mater. Antiques shops can be found near the intersection of Routes 4 and 10, along with some excellent house museums.

WHAT TO SEE
★ **Hill-Stead Museum.** Converted from a private home into a museum by its talented owner, Theodate Pope, a turn-of-the-20th-century architect, the house has a superb collection of French impressionist art displayed in situ, including Monet's haystacks and Manet's *Guitar Player* hanging in the drawing room. Poetry readings by nationally known writers take place in the elaborate Beatrix Farrand–designed sunken garden every other week in summer. ✉35 Mountain Rd. ☎860/677–4787 ⊕www.hillstead.org ⊠$9 ⊙May–Oct., Tues.–Sun. 10–5 (last tour at 4); Nov.–Apr., Tues.–Sun. 11–4 (last tour at 3).

WHERE TO EAT & STAY
$$$–$$$$ ✕**Apricots Restaurant and Pub.** A white Colonial with dozens of windows
AMERICAN overlooking gardens and the Farmington River is a long-term staple of the Hartford dining scene. American classics such as scrumptious oven-roasted, cashew-crusted rack of lamb and seared jumbo sea scallops over white-truffle risotto are presented in a formal dining room; less-expensive fare is served in the downstairs pub. ✉1591 Farmington Ave. ☎860/673–5405 ⊟AE, DC, MC, V.

$$–$$$ ⊡**Avon Old Farms Hotel.** A country hotel at the base of Avon Mountain, this 20-acre compound of Colonial-style buildings with manicured grounds is midway between Farmington and Simsbury. The rooms, some with four-poster beds, are appointed with elegant furnishings and brass chandeliers. The inn's Seasons Restaurant & Pub serves a very good Sunday brunch. **Pros:** attractive pool area, central location, well-kept rooms. **Cons:** rooms need a little upgrading. ✉279 Avon Mountain Rd., Avon ☎860/677–1651 ⊕www.avonoldfarmshotel.com ⇌160 rooms ♿In-room: Wi-Fi. In-hotel: restaurant, room service, bar, pool, gym, no-smoking rooms ⊟AE, D, DC, MC, V ⊗CP.

$$ **Farmington Inn.** Large guest rooms with four-poster canopied beds and European linens, antiques, and reproductions, highlight this stately inn. Fresh flowers and paintings by local artists add homey touches, and bathrooms are done in Carrera marble. In the center of Farmington's historic district, the hotel is within walking distance of several excellent restaurants, including the adjacent Piccolo Arancio, serving contemporary Italian food. **Pros:** good value, walking distance of downtown shopping and dining, fluffy linens and featherbeds. **Cons:** continental breakfast is unremarkable; lacks a pool or other recreational facilities. ⊠ *827 Farmington Ave.* ☎ *860/677–2821 or 800/648–9804* ⊕ *www. farmingtoninn.com* ↩ *59 rooms, 13 suites* ⚬ *In-room: VCR, Ethernet, no-smoking rooms* ☰ *AE, D, DC, MC, V* ¶⚬*CP.*

SIMSBURY

12 mi north of Farmington via Rte. 10.

Colonial-style shopping centers, a smattering of antiques shops, and a proliferation of insurance-industry executives define this chic bedroom community near Hartford. Once the home of many Revolutionary War soldiers, the community offers great shopping.

WHAT TO SEE

Phelps Tavern Museum. Headquarters of the Simsbury Historical Society, this museum is in a Colonial house built in 1771 for Captain Elijah Phelps and his family. Period-furnished rooms constitute the permanent exhibit, which highlights the home's use as a tavern from 1786 to 1849, when it was a stop on the Farmington Canal. You can learn about Simsbury's history, and view a period garden on the 2-acre grounds. ⊠ *800 Hopmeadow St.* ☎ *860/658–2500* ⊕ *www.simsburyhistory.org* ⚬ *$6* ⊙ *Tues.–Sat. noon–4.*

SPORTS & THE OUTDOORS

ICE-SKATING   The **International Skating Center of Connecticut** (⊠ *1375 Hopmeadow St.* ☎ *860/651–5400* ⊕ *www.isccskate.com* ⚬ *$7 skating, $3 rentals*) is a world-class twin-rink facility used for practice by up-and-coming skating stars and national, international, and Olympic champions. Lessons and public skating sessions are offered mid-November through mid-March; ice shows are held periodically year-round.

SHOPPING

Arts Exclusive Gallery (⊠ *690 Hopmeadow St.* ☎ *860/651–5824* ⊕ *www. arts-exclusive.com*) represents around 30 contemporary artists and has an inventory of more than 700 original works of art in the gallery at all times. The **Farmington Valley Arts Center** (⊠ *25 Arts Center La., Avon* ☎ *860/678–1867*) provides studio space for more than 20 resident artists and shows and sells their works along with the works of other nationally known artists in its two galleries.

WHERE TO EAT & STAY

$$ ✕ **Metro Bis.** A casual bistro in the center of downtown Simsbury has
AMERICAN   become a hallmark for creative, farm-fresh (often organic) mod American food. The oft-changing menu might feature house-smoked salmon

with roasted golden beets and Osetra caviar, slow-roasted Niman Ranch pork with steamed baby bok choy and braised fennel, and maple–white chocolate bread pudding with crème anglaise. Prices are remarkably reasonable for such high-quality food. ⊠ *928 Hopmeadow St.* ☎ *860/651–1908* ☐ *AE, D, DC, MC, V* ☉ *Closed Sun.*

$$-$$$ ⊞ **Simsbury 1820 House.** The rooms at this large restored New England country manor on a hill overlooking Simsbury contain a judicious mix of antiques and modern furnishings. The main house was built in 1820 and has an 1890 addition on its west side. Rooms are decorated with period fabrics and antiques, and most have four-poster, mahogany canopy beds. **Pros:** centrally located, the personal service of a romantic inn but anonymity of a larger property, attractive hilltop setting. **Cons:** on a busy road, no recreational facilities on site (although guests have free access at nearby health club). ⊠ *731 Hopmeadow St.* ☎ *860/658–7658 or 800/879–1820* ⊕ *www.simsbury1820house.com* ↰ *29 rooms, 3 suites* ⚒ *In-room: VCR, Ethernet. In-hotel: restaurant, some pets (fee), no-smoking rooms* ☐ *AE, D, DC, MC, V* ⊚ *CP.*

WINDSOR LOCKS

13 mi northeast of Simsbury, 94 mi northeast of Greenwich, 48 mi northeast of New Haven, 56 mi northwest of New London.

Incorporated in 1854, Windsor Locks is halfway between Hartford and Springfield, Massachusetts. Named for the locks of a canal built to bypass falls in the Connecticut River in 1833, this small suburban town is home to Bradley International Airport.

WHAT TO SEE

☾ **New England Air Museum.** The more than 70 aircraft at this museum ★ include gliders and helicopters, a World War II–era P-47 Thunderbolt, and a B-29 Superfortress, along with other vintage fighters and bombers. There's even a jet fighter simulator. The museum also frequently holds open-cockpit days, allowing young and old to play pilot. Call to find out when the next day will be held. ⊠ *Next to Bradley International Airport, off Rte. 75* ☎ *860/623-3305* ⊕ *www.neam.org* ⊞ *$9.50* ☉ *Daily 10–5.*

THE LITCHFIELD HILLS

★ Here in the foothills of the Berkshires is some of the most spectacular and unspoiled scenery in Connecticut. Two highways, Interstate 84 and Route 8, form the southern and eastern boundaries of the region. New York, to the west, and Massachusetts, to the north, complete the rectangle. Grand old inns are plentiful, as are sophisticated eateries. Rolling farmlands abut thick forests, and trails—including a section of the Appalachian Trail—traverse the state parks and forests. Two rivers, the Housatonic and the Farmington, attract anglers and canoeing enthusiasts, and the state's three largest natural lakes, Waramaug, Bantam, and Twin, are here. Sweeping town greens and stately homes anchor Litchfield and New Milford. Kent, New Preston, and Woodbury draw avid antiquers, and Washington and Norfolk provide a glimpse into New England village life as it might have existed two centuries ago.

Favorite roads for admiring fall foliage are U.S. 7, from New Milford through Kent and West Cornwall to Canaan; Route 41 to Route 4 from Salisbury through Lakeville, Sharon, Cornwall Bridge, and Goshen to Torrington; and Route 47 to U.S. 202 to Route 341 from Woodbury through Washington, New Preston, and Warren to Kent.

NEW MILFORD

28 mi west of Waterbury, 46 mi northeast of Greenwich.

If you're approaching the Litchfield Hills from the south, New Milford is a practical starting point to begin a visit. It was also a starting point for a young cobbler named Roger Sherman, who, in 1743, opened his shop where Main and Church streets meet. A Declaration of Independence signatory, Sherman also helped draft the Articles of Confederation and the Constitution. You'll find old shops, galleries, and eateries all within a short stroll of New Milford green—one of the longest in New England.

WHAT TO SEE

Silo at Hunt Hill Farm Trust. The former property of the late Skitch Henderson, onetime music director of NBC and the New York Pops, consists of several attractions in the old buildings of two farms dating back to the 1700s. Inside a barn is the Silo Store, packed with objets de cookery, crafts, and assorted goodies and sauces; the Silo gallery presents art shows and literary readings; and the Silo cooking school draws culinary superstars to teach cooking classes between March and December. The latest addition, the Skitch Henderson Living Museum, focuses on Henderson's collections of musical memorabilia, including rare recordings and scores, as well as other items as diverse as the Steinway he used at NBC and an antique marble soda fountain. ⊠*44 Upland Rd., 4 mi north of the New Milford town green on U.S. 202* ☎*860/355–0300* ⊕*www.thesilo.com* ✉*Donation suggested* ☉ *Wed.–Mon. 10–5.*

WHERE TO EAT & STAY

$$$ ╳**Adrienne.** Set in an 18th-century farmhouse with terraced gardens,
AMERICAN Adrienne serves New American cuisine from a seasonal menu. You may be lucky enough to encounter Maine diver scallops with a roasted-tomato cream sauce, or grilled American lamb chops with sweet-potato latkes and a balsamic reduction. Sunday brunch (think eggs Florentine, seafood crepe, and vegetable scampi) on the outdoor terrace is also popular. ⊠*218 Kent Rd.* ☎*860/354–6001* ⊟*AE, D, DC, MC, V* ☉*Closed Mon. No dinner Sun.*

$$ 🏨**Homestead Inn.** The Homestead, high on a hill overlooking New Milford's town green, was built in 1853 and opened as an inn in 1928. Breakfast is served in a cheery living room, where you can sit by the fire. Rooms are decorated in a well-chosen mix of country antiques, reproductions, and an abundance of floral accents. The eight rooms in the main house have more personality than those in the motel-style structure next door. **Pros:** reasonably priced, close to shops and restaurants, friendly owners. **Cons:** on a busy street and right by (relatively small) hospital. ⊠5 *Elm St.* ☎860/354–4080 ⊕*www.homesteadct. com* ⥱*14 rooms* ♿*In-room: Wi-Fi. In-hotel: some pets (fee), no-smoking rooms* ⊟*AE, D, DC, MC, V* †◎I*CP.*

NEW PRESTON

4 mi north of New Milford.

The crossroads village of New Preston, perched above a 40-foot water-fall on the Aspetuck River, has a little town center that's packed with antiques shops specializing in everything from 18th-century furnishings to contemporary art.

Lake Waramaug, north of New Preston on Route 45, is an area that reminds many of Austria and Switzerland. The lake is named for Chief Waramaug, one of the most revered figures in Connecticut's American Indian history. A drive around the 8-mi perimeter of the lake takes you past beautiful inns—many of which serve delicious food—and homes.

WHAT TO SEE

Hopkins Vineyard. If you like your wine served with a water view try this 35-acre vineyard overlooking Lake Waramaug, which produces more than 11 varieties of wine, from sparkling to dessert. A weathered red barn houses a gift shop and a tasting room, and there's a picnic area. A wine bar in the hayloft serves a fine cheese-and-pâté board and has views of the lake. ⊠*25 Hopkins Rd.* ☎*860/868–7954* ⊕*www. hopkinsvineyard.com* ⬛*Free* ⊘*Jan. and Feb., Fri. and Sat. 10–5, Sun. 11–5; Mar. and Apr., Wed.–Sat. 10–5, Sun. 11–5; May–Dec., Mon.– Sat. 10–5, Sun. 11–5.*

SPORTS & THE OUTDOORS

Lake Waramaug State Park. At the northwest tip of the lake, this idyllic 75-acre spread is great for picnicking and lakeside camping. ⊠*30 Lake Waramaug Rd.* ☎*860/868–0220 or 860/868–2592* ⬛*Free. Parking $7–$10 weekends.*

SHOPPING

Dawn Hill Antiques (⊠*11 Main St.* ☎*860/868–0066* ⊕*dawnhillantiques. com*) specializes in 18th- and 19th-century Swedish and French fur-niture. **J. Seitz & Co.** (⊠*9 E. Shore Rd. [Rte. 45]* ☎*860/868–0119* ⊕*www.jseitz.com*) fills 5,000 square feet with stylish home furnish-ings, fashions, and gifts.

WHERE TO EAT & STAY

$$$
★
AMERICAN
✕**Boulders Inn.** The exquisite menu at the window-lined, stone-wall din-ing room of this swanky country inn changes seasonally. You might start with pan-seared foie gras with pumpkin-herb French toast and a tart-cherry reduction. Notable entrées have included braised lamb with garlic sausage and green-lentil stew, and crispy pan-roasted duck breast with a carmelized quince–thyme bread pudding and a natural port reduction. Although there's no lunch available here, a terrific brunch is served on Sundays. ⊠*218 Kent Rd.* ☎*860/354–6001* ⊟*AE, D, DC, MC, V* ⊘*Closed Mon. and Tues. No lunch.*

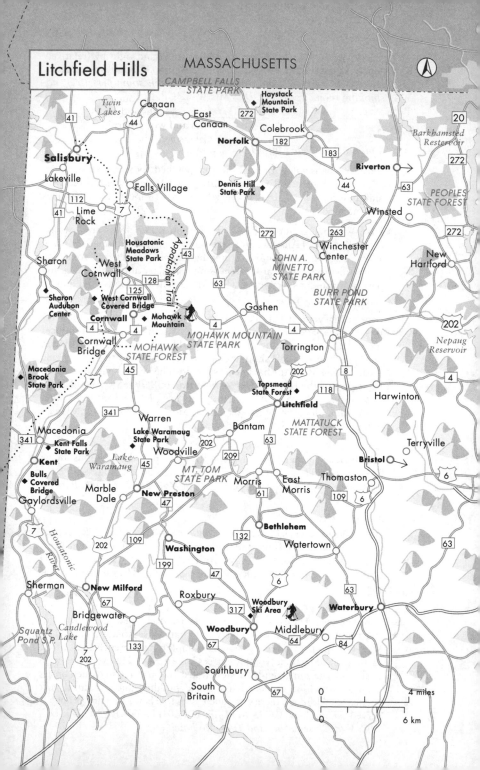

$$$$
Fodor'sChoice
★ **Boulders Inn.** The most idyllic and prestigious of the inns along Lake Waramaug opened in 1940 but still looks like the private home it was a century ago. Apart from the main house, a carriage house and several hillside cottages command panoramic views of the countryside and the lake. The rooms, four with double whirlpool baths and most with deep soaking tubs, contain Victorian antiques and wood-burning fireplaces. You can book a facial or massage in the small but well-outfitted spa. **Pros:** spectacular setting, gorgeous furnishings, terrific restaurant on-site. **Cons:** very expensive. ⊠*E. Shore Rd. (Rte. 45)* ☎*860/868–0541 or 800/455–1565* ⊕*www.bouldersinn.com* ⊄*15 rooms, 5 suites* ⚬*In-room: DVD, Ethernet. In-hotel: restaurant, gym, spa, beachfront, no elevator, no kids under 12, no-smoking rooms* ⊟*AE, MC, V* ⊚|*BP.*

$-$$
★ **Hopkins Inn.** A grand 1847 Victorian atop a hill overlooking Lake Waramaug, the Hopkins is one of the best bargains in the Hills. Most rooms have plain white bedspreads, simple antiques, and floral wallpaper—it's nothing fancy, but considering the setting and views, it's quite nice. In winter, the inn smells of burning firewood; year-round, it is redolent with aromas from the rambling dining rooms, which serve tasty Austrian dishes—sweetbreads Viennese is a favorite. When the weather is kind, you can dine on the flagstone terrace underneath the grand old horse chestnut tree and view the lake. **Pros:** very affordable for this part of the state, magnificent views, good restaurant. **Cons:** decor is simple and a bit dated, service can be a little uneven, minimal in-room amenities. ⊠*22 Hopkins Rd. (1 mi off Rte. 45)* ☎*860/868–7295* ⊕*www. thehopkinsinn.com* ⊄*11 rooms (2 share a bath), 2 suites* ⚬*In-room: no TV (some). In-hotel: restaurant, beachfront, no elevator, no-smoking rooms* ⊟*AE, D, MC, V.*

KENT

12 mi northwest of New Preston.

Kent has the area's greatest concentration of art galleries, some nationally renowned. Home to a prep school of the same name, Kent once held many ironworks. The Schaghticoke Indian Reservation is also here. During the Revolutionary War, 100 Schaghticokes helped defend the Colonies by transmitting messages of army intelligence from the Litchfield Hills to Long Island Sound, along the hilltops, by way of shouts and drumbeats.

WHAT TO SEE

Sloane-Stanley Museum. Hardware-store buffs and vintage-tool aficionados will feel right at home at this museum. Artist and author Eric Sloane (1905–85) was fascinated by Early American woodworking tools, and his collection showcases examples of American craftsmanship from the 17th to the 19th centuries. The museum contains a re-creation of Sloane's last studio and also encompasses the ruins of a 19th-century iron furnace. Sloane's books and prints, which celebrate vanishing aspects of Americana such as barns and covered bridges, are on sale here. ⊠*U.S. 7* ☎*860/927–3849* ▦*$4* ⊙*Late May–late Oct., Wed.–Sun. 10–4.*

SPORTS & THE OUTDOORS

The **Appalachian Trail**'s longest river walk, off Route 341, is the almost-8-mi hike from Kent to Cornwall Bridge along the Housatonic River. The early-season trout fishing is superb at 2,300-acre **Macedonia Brook State Park** (⊠ *Macedonia Brook Rd. off Rte. 341* ☎ *860/927–3238*), where you can also hike and cross-country ski.

SHOPPING

★ The **Bachelier-Cardonsky Gallery** (⊠ *10 N. Main St.* ☎ *860/927–3129* ⊕ *www.bacheliercardonsky.com*), one of the foremost galleries in New England, exhibits works by local artists and contemporary masters such as Alexander Calder, Carol Anthony, and Jackson Pollock. **Belgique** (⊠ *1 Bridge St.* ☎ *860/927–3681*) sells sublime handmade chocolates, plus gelato and sorbet and—perfect on a winter day—pure and decadently rich Belgian hot chocolate. **Pauline's Place** (⊠ *79 N. Main St.* ☎ *860/927–4475*) specializes in Victorian, Georgian, art deco, Edwardian, and contemporary jewelry.

EN ROUTE   Heading north from Kent toward Cornwall, you'll pass the entrance to 295-acre **Kent Falls State Park** (⊠ *U.S. 7* ☎ *860/927–3238*), where you can hike a short way to one of the most impressive waterfalls in the state and picnic in the green meadows at the base of the falls.

CORNWALL

12 mi northeast of Kent.

Connecticut's Cornwalls can get confusing. There's Cornwall, Cornwall Bridge, West Cornwall, Cornwall Hollow, East Cornwall, and North Cornwall. What this quiet corner of the Litchfield Hills is known for is its fantastic vistas of woods and mountains and its covered bridge, which spans the Housatonic and is easily one of the most photographed spots in the state.

WHAT TO SEE

West Cornwall Covered Bridge. A romantic reminder of the past, the wooden, barn-red, one-lane bridge, not to be confused with the town of Cornwall Bridge (which was named for an earlier covered bridge that stood originally on that site), is several miles up U.S. 7 on Route 128 in West Cornwall. The bridge was built in 1841 and incorporates strut techniques that were copied by bridge builders around the country.

SPORTS & THE OUTDOORS

Housatonic Meadows State Park. The park is marked by its tall pine trees near the Housatonic River, and has terrific riverside campsites. Fly-fishers consider this 2-mi stretch of the river among the best places in New England to test their skills against trout and bass. ⊠ *U.S. 7, Cornwall Bridge* ☎ *860/672–6772*.

⟳ **Sharon Audubon Center.** With 11 mi of hiking trails, this 860-acre property—a mixture of forests, meadows, wetlands, ponds, and streams—provides myriad hiking opportunities. It's also home to Princess, an American crow, who shares the visitor center with small hawks, an owl, and other animals in a live-animal display. Also here is a natural history museum and children's adventure center. An aviary provides permanent housing for a bald eagle, a red-tailed hawk, and two turkey vultures. ⊠*325 Cornwall Bridge Rd., Sharon* ☎*860/364–0520* ⊕*www.sharon.audubon.org* ⤬*$3* ⊙*Tues.–Sat. 9–5, Sun. 1–5; trails daily dawn–dusk.*

CANOEING & KAYAKING **Clarke Outdoors** (⊠*U.S. 7, West Cornwall* ☎*860/672–6365* ⊕*www. clarkeoutdoors.com*) rents canoes, kayaks, and rafts and operates 10-mi trips from Falls Village to Housatonic Meadows State Park.

FISHING **Housatonic Anglers** (⊠*26 Bolton Hill Rd.* ☎*860/672–4457* ⊕*www. housatonicanglers.com*) operates half- and full-day tours, as well as some evening outings, and provides fly-fishing instruction for trout and bass on the Housatonic and its tributaries. **Housatonic River Outfitters** (⊠*24 Kent Rd., Cornwall Bridge* ☎*860/672–1010* ⊕*www.dryflies. com*) operates a full-service fly shop; leads guided trips of the region; runs classes in fly-fishing, fly-tying, and casting; and stocks a good selection of vintage and antique gear.

SKI AREA The 24 trails at **Mohawk Mountain** (⊠*46 Great Hollow Rd., off Rte. 4* ☎*860/672–6100 or 800/895–5222*), ranging down 650 vertical feet, include plenty of intermediate terrain, with a few trails for beginners and a few steeper sections toward the top of the mountain. A small section is devoted to snowboarders. Trails are serviced by one triple lift and four doubles; 14 trails are lighted for night skiing. The base lodge has munchies and a retail shop, and halfway up the slope the Pine Lodge Restaurant has an outdoor patio. There are facilities for ice-skating and a kids ski program for those ages 5–12.

SHOPPING

Cornwall Bridge Pottery Store (⊠*Rte. 128, West Cornwall* ☎*860/672–6545 or 800/501–6545* ⊕*www.cbpots.com*) sells its own pottery, from dinnerware to garden pots, lamps, and vases. **Ian Ingersoll Cabinetmakers** (⊠*Main St., by the covered bridge, West Cornwall* ☎*860/672–6334* ⊕*www.ianingersoll.com*) stocks handsome Shaker-style furniture.

WHERE TO STAY

$$–$$$ ⟦⟧**Cornwall Inn.** This 19th-century inn on scenic U.S. 7 combines country charm with contemporary elegance; eight rooms in the adjacent "lodge" are slightly more private and rustic in tone and have white cedar-post beds. The restaurant, which overlooks the pool and colorful gardens, serves a seasonally changing American menu. The Housatonic River is a short walk from the inn. **Pros:** tranquil setting, lovely grounds, very welcoming toward kids and pets. **Cons:** quiet location is a bit far from antiquing and restaurants of neighboring towns, country-house decor might not suit every taste. ⊠*270 Kent Rd. (U.S. 7)* ☎*860/672–6884 or 800/786–6884* ⊕*www.cornwallinn.com* ⤬*13 rooms* ⚷*In-room: no a/c (some), Wi-Fi. In-hotel: restaurant, bar, pool, no elevator, some pets allowed (fee), no-smoking rooms* ⊟*AE, D, MC, V* ⎇*CP.*

SALISBURY

15 mi northwest of Cornwall Bridge.

The town of Salisbury, which comprises the smaller villages of Lakeville and Lime Rock and is home to a pair of noted prep schools (Hotchkiss and Salisbury), occupies the very northwestern corner of the state, and although it's short on formal attractions, it is home to few excellent restaurants, plus a picture-perfect downtown with a smattering of antiques shops and galleries. Country roads traverse the wooded, rolling terrain and are perfect for leisurely bike or car rides. The Appalachian Trails passes through town, crossing Connecticut's highest peak (at 2,316 feet), and Lime Rock Park is home to the prestigious Skip Barber Racing and Driving School, where the likes of Paul Newman and Jerry Seinfeld have been known to zoom around the track.

NIGHTLIFE & THE ARTS

★ A few miles southeast of Salisbury, Falls Village is home to **Music Mountain** (☎860/824-7126 ⊕*www.musicmountain*.org), the nation's longest-running continuous summer chamber music festival, dating back to 1930. Throughout the season (mid-June–Aug.), 16 chamber concerts take place, plus several Jazz and Chorale performances.

WHERE TO EAT & STAY

$$-$$$
FRENCH
✕ **Pastorale.** In an unimposing house in Lakeville, this relaxed yet sophisticated bistro turns out exceptionally tasty French food, with a few northern Italian dishes thrown in for good measure. Start with poached pear–and–frisée salad with bacon and blue cheese, before graduating to grilled leg of lamb with Parmesan polenta and roast-garlic sauce, or a simple penne pasta with homemade fennel sausage, roasted tomatoes, and crème fraîche. An excellent brunch is served Sunday—try the French toast with caramelized strawberries and chantilly cream. ⊠*223 Main St., Lakeville* ☎*860/435–1011* ⊘*Closed Mon. No lunch* ⊟*AE, MC, V.*

$$-$$$
★
☷ **Wake Robin Inn.** Down a long driveway and surrounded by towering pine trees and neatly manicured grounds, the Wake Robin consists of a grand 1914 mansion that once housed a private girls school and now contains 23 spacious, antiques-appointed rooms, and a newer motel-style lodge (open only May–October) containing 15 pleasant but less fancy units. An eager-to-please staff tends to guests' every need, and in summer, the on-site Michael Bryan's Irish Pub serves a fine selection of ales. **Pros:** pastoral setting, rooms to fit a wide range of budgets and tastes, top-notch staff. **Cons:** more affordable motel units aren't open in winter, pub is only seasonal. ⊠*106 Sharon Rd. (Rte. 41)* ☎*860/435–2000* ⊕*www.wakerobininn.com* ⤳*38 rooms* ☖*In-room: Wi-Fi. In-hotel: bar, no elevator, no-smoking rooms* ⊟*AE, D, MC, V* ⊣☉*CP.*

NORFOLK

14 mi east of Salisbury, 59 mi north of New Haven.

Norfolk, thanks to its severe climate and terrain, is one of the best-preserved villages in the Northeast. Notable industrialists have been summering here for two centuries, and many enormous homesteads still exist. The striking town green, at the junction of Route 272 and U.S. 44, has a fountain designed by Augustus Saint-Gaudens and executed by Stanford White at its southern corner. It stands as a memorial to Joseph Battell, who turned Norfolk into a major trading center.

SPORTS & THE OUTDOORS

Dennis Hill State Park. Dr. Frederick Shepard Dennis, former owner of the 240 acres now making up the park, lavishly entertained guests, among them President Howard Taft and several Connecticut governors, in the stone pavilion at the summit of the estate. From its 1,627-foot height, you can see Haystack Mountain, New Hampshire, and, on a clear day, New Haven harbor, all the way across the state. Picnic on the park's grounds or hike one of its many trails. ⊠*Rte. 272* ☎*860/482–1817* ☜*Free* ⊗*Daily 8 AM–dusk* .

Haystack Mountain State Park. One of the most spectacular views in the state can be seen from this park via its challenging trail to the top or a road halfway up. ⊠*Rte. 272* ☎*860/482–1817*

HORSEBACK RIDING **Loon Meadow Farm** (☎*860/542–6085* ⊕*www.loonmeadowfarm.com*) runs horse-drawn carriage, hay, and sleigh rides by appointment.

NIGHTLIFE & THE ARTS

★ The **Norfolk Chamber Music Festival** (☎*860/542–3000 or 203/432–1966* ⊕*www.yale.edu/norfolk*), at the Music Shed on the 70-acre Ellen Battell Stoeckel Estate at the northwest corner of the Norfolk green, presents world-renowned artists and ensembles on Friday and Saturday summer evenings. Students from the Yale School of Music perform on Thursday evening and Saturday morning. Early arrivals can stroll or picnic on the 70-acre grounds or visit the art gallery.

WHERE TO EAT & STAY

¢-$ ★ AMERICAN ✕ **Speckled Hen Pub.** Bottles of trendy beers line the shelves of this down-to-earth restaurant on the ground floor of a redbrick Victorian near the town green. Burgers and other pub fare are on the menu alongside more eclectic choices. This place is a real melting pot. ⊠*U.S. 44* ☎*860/542–5716* ⊟*AE, MC, V* ⊗*Closed Mon. No dinner Tues.*

$$$-$$$$ Fodor'sChoice ★ ⊡ **Manor House.** Among this 1898 Bavarian Tudor's remarkable appointments are its bibelots, mirrors, carpets, antique beds, and prints—not to mention the 20 stained-glass windows designed by Louis Comfort Tiffany. The vast Spofford Room has windows on three sides, a king-size canopy bed with a cheery fireplace opposite, and a balcony, and many rooms have Jacuzzi tubs. **Pros:** sumptuous decor, lavish breakfasts, secluded and peaceful setting. **Cons:** no phones or TVs in the rooms (and cell phone reception is iffy in these parts), no Internet use. ⊠*69 Maple Ave.* ☎*860/542–5690 or 866/542–5690* ⊕*www.manorhouse-norfolk. com* ⊸*8 rooms, 1 suite* ⚖*In-room: no phone, no TV. In-hotel: no children under 10, no-smoking rooms* ⊟*AE, MC, V* ⊚*BP.*

RIVERTON

6 mi north of Winsted.

Almost every New Englander has sat in a Hitchcock chair. Riverton, formerly Hitchcockville, is where Lambert Hitchcock made the first one, in 1826. The Farmington and Still rivers meet in this tiny hamlet. It's in one of the more unspoiled regions in the hills, and great for hiking and driving.

SPORTS & THE OUTDOORS

SKI AREA   **Ski Sundown** (⊠*126 Ratlum Rd., New Hartford* ☎*860/379–7669 snow conditions* ⊕*www.skisundown.com*) has the state's most challenging trails as well as excellent facilities and equipment, plus night skiing. The vertical drop is 625 feet. Of the 15 trails, nine are for beginners, three for intermediates, and three for advanced skiers. They are serviced by three triple chairs and one double. Ski lessons are available for ages four and up.

TUBING   **Farmington River Tubing** (⊠*U.S. 44, New Hartford* ☎*860/693–6465* ⊕*www.farmingtonrivertubing.com*) rents tubes and flotation devices for exhilarating rides down the scenic Farmington River.

WHERE TO STAY

$-$$ **☶Old Riverton Inn.** This historic inn, built in 1796 and overlooking the west branch of the Farmington River, is a peaceful weekend retreat. Rooms are small—except for the fireplace suite—and the decorating, which includes Hitchcock furnishings, is for the most part ordinary, but the inn always delivers warm hospitality, and the rates are fair. The inviting dining room serves traditional, if predictable, New England fare. **Pros:** right along the river, friendly staff, good value. **Cons:** basic and old-fashioned decor, remote location. ⊠*436 E. River Rd.* ☎*860/379–8678 or 800/378–1796* ⊕*www.rivertoninn.com* ⦑*11 rooms, 1 suite* ⅋*In-room: refrigerator (some), Wi-Fi. In-hotel: restaurant, bar, no elevator, no-smoking rooms* ⊟*AE, D, DC, MC, V* ⦿|*BP.*

LITCHFIELD

19 mi southwest of Riverton, 34 mi west of Hartford.

Everything in Litchfield, the wealthiest and most noteworthy town in the Litchfield Hills, seems to exist on a larger scale than in neighboring burgs, especially the impressive Litchfield Green and the white Colonial and Greek-revival homes that line the broad elm-shaded streets. Harriet Beecher Stowe, author of *Uncle Tom's Cabin,* and her brother, abolitionist preacher Henry Ward Beecher, were born and raised in Litchfield, and many famous Americans earned their law degrees at the Litchfield Law School. Today, lovely but exceptionally expensive boutiques and hot-spot restaurants line the downtown, attracting celebrities and the town's monied citizens.

WHAT TO SEE

Haight Vineyard. The state's oldest winery planted its first wine grapes in Connecticut in 1975. You can stop in for complimentary tastings and winery tours. Seasonal events include barrel tastings in April and a harvest festival in September. ✉ *29 Chestnut Hill Rd., off Rte. 118 (1 mi east of Litchfield)* ☎ *860/567–4045* ⊕ *www.haightvineyards.com* ⌨ *Free* ⊙ *Mon.–Sat. 10:30–5, Sun. noon–5.*

★ **Tapping Reeve House and Litchfield Law School.** In 1773, Judge Tapping Reeve enrolled his first student, Aaron Burr, in what was to become the first law school in the country. (Before Judge Reeve, students studied the law as apprentices, not in formal classes.) This school is dedicated to Reeve's remarkable achievement and to the notable students who passed through its halls: Oliver Wolcott Jr., John C. Calhoun, Horace Mann, three U.S. Supreme Court justices, and 15 governors, not to mention senators, congressmen, and ambassadors. This museum is one of the state's most worthy attractions, with interactive multimedia exhibits, an excellent introductory film, and beautifully restored facilities. ✉ *82 South St.* ☎ *860/567–4501* ⊕ *www.litchfieldhistoricalsociety. org* ⌨ *$5 (includes Litchfield History Museum)* ⊙ *Mid-Apr.–late Nov., Tues.–Sat. 11–5, Sun. 1–5.*

SPORTS & THE OUTDOORS

Topsmead State Forest. The chief attractions in this 511-acre forest are an English Tudor–style cottage built by architect Richard Henry Dana Jr. (and seemingly straight out of the English countryside) and a 40-acre wildflower preserve. The forest holds picnic grounds, hiking trails, and cross-country ski areas. ✉ *Buell Rd. off E. Litchfield Rd.* ☎ *860/567– 5694* ⌨ *Free* ⊙ *Forest daily 8 AM–dusk; cottage tours June–Oct., 2nd and 4th weekends of month.*

Fodor's Choice ★ **White Memorial Conservation Center.** At the heart of the White Memorial Foundation, this 4,000-acre nature preserve houses top-notch natural-history exhibits and a gift shop. The foundation, one of the state's prime birding areas, contains some 30 bird-watching platforms; two self-guided nature trails; several boardwalks; campgrounds; boating facilities; fishing areas; and 35 mi of hiking, cross-country skiing, and horseback-riding trails. ✉ *Off U.S. 202 (2 mi west of village green)* ☎ *860/567–0857* ⊕ *www.whitememorialcc.org* ⌨ *Conservation center $5, grounds free* ⊙ *Conservation center Mon.–Sat. 9–5, Sun. noon–5; grounds daily dawn to dusk.*

HORSEBACK RIDING **Lee's Riding Stables** (✉ *57 E. Litchfield Rd.* ☎ *860/567–0785*) conducts trail and pony rides. At **Mt. Tom State Park** (✉ *U.S. 202* ☎ *860/868– 2592*) you can boat, hike, swim, and fish in summer.

SHOPPING

Jeffrey Tillou Antiques (✉ *39 West St.* ☎ *860/567–9693*) specializes in 18th- and 19th-century American furniture and paintings.

WHERE TO EAT

$$-$$$
AMERICAN

✕**Village Restaurant.** The folks who run this storefront eatery in a red-brick town house serve tasty, unfussy food—inexpensive pub grub in one room, updated contemporary American cuisine in the other. Whether you order a burger or herb-crusted pork chops, you're bound to be pleased. ✉*25 West St.* ☎*860/567–8307* ▭*AE, D, MC, V.*

$$$-$$$$
★
AMERICAN

✕**West Street Grill.** This sophisticated dining room on the town green is *the* place to see and be seen, both for patrons and for the state's up-and-coming chefs, many of whom got their start here. Imaginative grilled fish, steak, poultry, and lamb dishes are served with fresh vegetables and pasta or risotto. The ice cream and sorbets, made by the restaurant, are worth every calorie. ✉*43 West St.* ☎*860/567–3885* ▭*AE, MC, V.*

WHERE TO STAY

$$$-$$$$

🏨**The Litchfield Inn.** This reproduction Colonial-style inn lies little more than a mile west of the center of Litchfield. Period accents adorn its modern rooms, including themed "designer" rooms such as an "Irish" room (which has a four-poster bed draped in green floral chintz) and a "Southwestern" room (which employs a rustic picket fence as a headboard). **Pros:** well-kept property, efficient staff, the central location is a good base for exploring entire region. **Cons:** on busy road with not much curb appeal, standard rooms have pleasant but prosaic furnishings, not within walking distance of downtown shopping and dining. ✉*Rte. 202* ☎*860/567–4503 or 800/499–3444* ⊕*www.litchfieldinnct. com* ⇱*32 rooms* ⚫*In-room: dial-up. In-hotel: restaurant, room service, bar, laundry service, no-smoking rooms* ▭*AE, DC, MC, V.*

$$$$
Fodor'sChoice
★

🏨**Winvian.** Opened in 2007 by the owners of Vermont's swanky Pitcher Inn, this ultra-posh, 113-acre hideaway adjacent to the grounds of the White Memorial Foundation consists of 19 of the most imaginatively themed and luxuriously outfitted cottages you'll ever lay eyes on. Each of the huge one-bedroom cottages has a distinctive, often amusing, theme: the Stone Cottages is made with massive boulders and has a wavy-slate roof and and enormous fireplace, and the Helicopter Cottage contains—you guessed it—a genuine 17,000-pound U.S. Coast Guard helicopter (the fuselage has been refitted with a wetbar). Bathrooms are consistently big, with deep whirlpool tubs and top-of-the-line amenities. Rates, which begin at an eye-popping $1,450 per night, include all meals and snacks (including wet-bar goodies) and unlimited use of all facilities. On-site are a full-service spa and elegant restaurant. **Pros:** whimsical and super-plush accommodations, outstanding cuisine, stunning setting. **Cons:** super-pricey, all-inclusive meal plan discourages guests from exploring the region's other fantastic restaurants. ✉*155 Alain White Rd., Morris* ☎*860/567–9600* ⊕*www.winvian.com* ⇱*19 cottages, 1 suite* ⚫*In-room: DVD, Wi-Fi. In-hotel: restaurant, bar, gym, spa, no elevator, no-smoking rooms* ▭*AE, MC, V* ⏛*AI.*

BRISTOL

17 mi southeast of Litchfield.

There were some 275 clock makers in and around Bristol during the late 1800s—it is said that by the end of the 19th century just about every household in America told time by a Connecticut clock. Eli Terry (for whom nearby Terryville is named) first mass-produced clocks in the mid-19th century. Seth Thomas (for whom nearby Thomaston is named) learned under Terry and carried on the tradition.

WHAT TO SEE

American Clock & Watch Museum. One of the few museums in the country devoted entirely to clocks and watches, this museum in an 1801 house has more than 1,400 timepieces on display. Though the majority of them are American timepieces from 1800 to 1940, the museum does have clocks dating from 1680 and watches dating from 1595. Many of the clocks are kept running and chiming, making the museum a prime place to be when the big hand strikes 12. ☒*100 Maple St.* ☎*860/583–6070* ⊕*www.clockmuseum.org* ☐*$5* ☉*Apr.–Nov., daily 10–5.*

☼ **Lake Compounce.** The oldest amusement park in the country, opened in ★ 1846, is known simply as "the Lake." Today's attractions at the 325-acre facility include a lakefront beach; an ever-expanding water park with a wave pool, waterslides (high speed and otherwise), spray fountains, and a clipper ship with a 300-gallon bucket of water that gives unsuspecting guests a good dousing; and such hair-raising rides as the Sky Coaster, the Twister, and the Zoomerang. ☒*Rte. 229 N (I–84 Exit 31)* ☎*860/583–3631* ⊕*www.lakecompounce.com* ☐*$33.95* ☉*Memorial Day–Oct.; call for hrs.*

★ **New England Carousel Museum.** One of the largest collections of antique carousel pieces in the country is housed here. Full-size pieces in the Coney Island, Country Fair, and Philadelphia styles are on display, as are miniature carousels. The museum is also home to the **Bristol Center for Arts and Culture,** which hosts changing art exhibitions, and the **Museum of Fire History,** which displays firefighting photos, antique equipment, and memorabilia. The museum also oversees the Bushnell Park Carousel in Hartford (in operation May–October). ☒*95 Riverside Ave.* ☎*860/585–5411* ⊕*www.thecarouselmuseum.org* ☐*$5* ☉*Apr.–Nov., Mon.–Sat. 10–5, Sun. noon–5; Dec.–Mar., Thurs.–Sat. 10–5, Sun. noon–5.*

WHERE TO STAY

$$ ☐**Chimney Crest Manor.** All the rooms in this impressive 1930 Tudor mansion have spectacular views of the Farmington Valley. The 40-foot-long Garden Suite, in what was the mansion's ballroom, has gleaming hardwood floors, a fireplace, a queen-size canopy bed, its own kitchen, and tile walls with a dazzling sunflower motif. Breakfast, which might include yogurt pancakes, is served on fine china in the formal dining room or, more casually, on the grand fieldstone patio. Among the handsome public spaces are a sunroom and salon. **Pros:** Jacuzzi tubs in rooms, elegant breakfast. **Cons:** in a rather suburban town. ☒*5*

Founders Dr. ☎*860/582–4219* ⊕*www.chimneycrest.com* ➳*2 rooms, 3 suites* ♿*In-room: refrigerator, VCR (some). In-hotel: no elevator, no kids under 10, no-smoking rooms* ☰*AE, MC, V* ⏀|*BP.*

BETHLEHEM

16 mi west of Bristol.

Come Christmas, Bethlehem is the most popular town in Connecticut. Cynics say that towns such as Canaan, Goshen, and Bethlehem were named primarily with the hope of attracting prospective residents and not truly out of religious deference. In any case, the local post office has its hands full postmarking the 220,000 pieces of holiday greetings mailed from Bethlehem every December. Also, the **Bethlehem Christmas Town Festival** (☎*203/266–5557*), which takes place in early December, draws quite a crowd.

WHAT TO SEE
Abbey of Regina Laudis. The Benedictine nuns at the abbey, who were made famous by their best-selling CD *Women in Chant,* sell their own pottery, candles, honey, cheese, herbs, beauty products, wool from abbey sheep, and more in an art shop near the main entrance to the abbey. The abbey's 18th-century Neapolitan crèche has more than 100 hand-carved baroque figures. ✉*273 Flanders Rd.* ☎*203/266–7637* ⊕*www.abbeyofreginalaudis.com* ⊗*Mon., Tues., and Thurs.–Sun. 10–noon and 1:30–4.*

WHERE TO EAT
$$–$$$ ✗**Woodward House.** Set inside an imposing 1740 house on Bethlehem's
★ quaint town green, this chef-owned restaurant has garnered plenty of
AMERICAN kudos since it opened in 2005, serving the inventive regional American fare of Jerry Reveron. Favorites among the appetizers include lobster-pineapple spring rolls and Maryland crab–corn fritters with rémoulade. Among the main dishes, you can't go wrong with the lamb duet, consisting of rack of lamb and roast lamb loin, with a cabernet-Dijon reduction. Sunday brunch is great. ✉*4 The Green* ☎*203/266–6902* ☰*AE, MC, V* ⊗*Closed Mon. and Tues. No lunch Wed.–Sat.*

WASHINGTON

11 mi west of Bethlehem.

The beautiful buildings of The Gunnery prep school mingle with stately Colonials and churches in Washington, one of the best-preserved Colonial towns in Connecticut. The Mayflower Inn, south of The Gunnery on Route 47, attracts an exclusive clientele. Washington, which was settled in 1734, in 1779 became the first town in the United States to be named for the first president.

WHAT TO SEE
Institute for American Indian Studies. The exhibits in this small but excellent and thoughtfully arranged collection detail the history and continuing presence of more than 10,000 years of American Indian life in

New England. Highlights include nature trails, a simulated archaeological site, and an authentically constructed Algonquian Village with wigwams, a longhouse, a rock shelter, and more. The Collections and Research Center has a research library, a large exhibit hall, and a gift shop that presents the work of some of the country's best American Indian artists. The institute is at the end of a forested residential road (just follow the signs from Route 199 South). ✉*38 Curtis Rd., off Rte. 199* ☎*860/868–0518* ⊕*www.birdstone.org* ✉*$5* ☉*Mon.–Sat. 10–5, Sun. noon–5.*

WHERE TO STAY

$$$
Fodor'sChoice
★

🏨 **Mayflower Inn & Spa.** Though the most-expensive suites at this inn cost a whopping $1,400 a night, the Mayflower is often booked months in advance. Running streams, rambling stone walls, and rare specimen trees fill the country manor–style inn's 28 manicured acres. Fine antiques, 18th- and 19th-century art, and four-poster canopy beds define each of the rooms. The colossal baths have mahogany wainscoting, marble, and Limoges and brass fittings. The Mayflower's 20,000-square-foot spa has earned a reputation as one of New England's finest such facilities—treatments like antioxidant-rich violet facials and Moor mud wraps are highly popular. Be sure to dine in the superb restaurant ($$$–$$$$), where the changing menu might list Block Island swordfish with rosemary-white-bean stew and tangerine-glazed pancetta, or Kobe-beef carpaccio with Parmesan aioli. **Pros:** idyllic and perfected landscaped grounds, soliticious but relaxed service, outstanding spa. **Cons:** some rooms starting to show a little age, very pricey. ✉*118 Woodbury Rd. (Rte. 47)* ☎*860/868–9466* ⊕*www.mayflowerinn.com* ⇌*19 rooms, 11 suites* ⚴*In-room: Wi-Fi. In-hotel: restaurant, bar, tennis court, pool, gym, spa, no kids under 12, no-smoking rooms* ☐*AE, MC, V.*

WOODBURY

10 mi southeast of Washington.

There may very well be more antiques shops in the quickly growing town of Woodbury than in all the towns in the rest of the Litchfield Hills combined. Five magnificent churches and the Greek-revival King Solomon's Temple, formerly a Masonic lodge, line U.S. 6; they represent some of the best-preserved examples of Colonial religious architecture in New England.

WHAT TO SEE

Glebe House Museum and Gertrude Jekyll Garden. This property consists of the large, antique-filled, gambrel-roof Colonial in which Dr. Samuel Seabury was elected America's first Episcopal bishop, in 1783, and its historic garden. The latter was designed in the 1920s by renowned British horticulturist Gertrude Jekyll. Though small, it is a classic, old-fashioned English-style garden, and the only one of the three gardens Jekyll designed in the United States still in existence. ✉*Hollow Rd.* ☎*203/263–2855* ⊕*www.theglebehouse.org* ✉*$5* ☉*May.–Oct., Wed.–Sun. 1–4; Nov., weekends 1–4.*

SPORTS & THE OUTDOORS

SKI AREA **Woodbury Ski Area.** This small, laid-back ski area with a 300-foot vertical drop has 22 downhill trails of varying difficulty. There's a snowboard and alpine park, a skateboard and in-line skating park, and a special area for sledding and tubing serviced by two lifts and three tows. Snowbiking and snowshoeing are other options. ⊠*Rte. 47* ☎*203/263–2203* ⊕*www.woodburyskiarea.com.*

SHOPPING

Country Loft Antiques (⊠*557 Main St. S* ☎*203/266–4500* ⊕*www. countryloftantiques.com*) specializes in 18th- and 19th-century country French antiques. **David Dunton** (⊠*Rte. 132 off Rte. 47* ☎*203/263– 5355* ⊕*www.daviddunton.com*) is a respected dealer of formal American Federal–style furniture. **Mill House Antiques** (⊠*1068 Main St. N* ☎*203/263–3446* ⊕*www.millhouseantiques-ct.com*) carries formal and country English and French furniture and has the state's largest collection of Welsh dressers. **Monique Shay Antiques & Design** (⊠*920 Main St. S* ☎*203/263–3186* ⊕*www.moniqueshayantiques.com*) favors Canadian country antiques. The **Woodbury Pewter Factory Outlet Store** (⊠*860 Main St. S* ☎*203/263–2668 or 800/648–2014* ⊕*www. woodburypewter.com*) has discounts on fine reproductions of Early American tankards, Revere bowls, candlesticks, and more.

WHERE TO EAT & STAY

$$–$$$
Fodor'sChoice
★
AMERICAN
✕**Good News Café.** Carole Peck is a well-known name throughout New England, and since the café opened in 1992, foodies have been flocking to Woodbury to sample her superb cuisine. The emphasis is on healthful, innovative, and surprisingly well-priced fare: wok-seared Gulf shrimp with new potatoes, grilled green beans, and a garlic aioli, or Cuban-style black-bean cassoulet with duck confit, pork, chorizo, and wild boar are good choices. In the simpler room next to the bar, you can order from a less expensive café menu. ⊠*694 Main St. S* ☎*203/266–4663* ▤*AE, D, MC, V* ⊙*Closed Tues.*

$$–$$$
★
🏨**Cornucopia at Oldfield.** A regal Federal Colonial house in northern Southbury, a short drive from Woodbury antiques shops and restaurants, Cornucopia contains a bounty of pleasing comforts: from high-quality antiques and soft Kingdown-brand bedding to CD-clock radios and DVD players in the rooms, to a floral gardens and a pool surrounded by a private hedge. A substantial full breakfast is served beneath a chandelier in the formal dining room, in which you can also arrange—with advance notice—for a romantic dinner. **Pros:** filled with fine antiques, beautifully kept grounds, lots of modern in-room amenities. **Cons:** on somewhat busy road, pool open seasonally. ⊠*782 N. Main St., Southbury* ☎*203/267–6772* ⊕*www.cornucopiabnb.com* 🛏*3 rooms, 2 suites* &*In-room: DVD, Wi-Fi. In-hotel: pool, no elevator, no-smoking rooms* ▤*AE, MC, V* ⊚❘*BP.*

WATERBURY

15 mi east of Woodbury, 28 mi southwest of Hartford.

Waterbury, in the Naugatuck River valley, was once known as Brass City for its role as the country's top producer of brass products in the 19th and early-20th centuries. Evidence of the prosperity of the city's brass barons can still be seen in the hillside district northwest of downtown, where grand old Queen Anne, Greek and Georgian-revival, and English Tudor homes remain, a few of which have been turned into bed-and-breakfasts. Today Waterbury and its shops and restaurants serve as an urban center for people in the nearby Litchfield Hills.

WHAT TO SEE

Clock Tower. The dramatic 240-foot clock tower downtown was modeled after the city-hall tower in Siena, Italy. ⊠ *389 Meadow St.*

Mattatuck Museum. The pieces in this fine collection of 19th- and 20th-century paintings and sculptures by artists who have lived or worked in Connecticut range from the 19th-century folk paintings of Erastus Salisbury Field and one of the celebrated "iceberg" paintings of Frederic Church to works by modern masters such as Josef Albers and Alexander Calder. The museum's Brass Roots exhibit looks back at the lives of the leaders and workers who transformed Waterbury into one of the nation's leading industrial centers. Within the Mattatuck, the Waterbury Button Museum exhibits approximately 10,000 of these miniature works of art from Waterbury and around the world. Also here is a 300-seat performing arts center and charming museum café. ⊠ *144 W. Main St.* ☏ *203/753–0381* ⊕ *www.mattatuckmuseum.org* ⊠ *$4* ☉ *Sept.–June, Tues.–Sat. 10–5, Sun. noon–5.*

Timexpo Museum. Housed in a renovated brass mill, this museum curiously combines the history of Timex, which came into being as Waterbury Clock in the 1850s, with archaeological exhibits tracing the travels of Norwegian explorer Thor Heyerdahl. Additional components include a timepiece collection, interactive exhibits, and crafts activities. A museum store sells Timex watches, clocks, and related merchandise. ⊠ *175 Union St., Brass Mill Commons* ☏ *203/755–8463* ⊕ *www.timexpo.com* ⊠ *$6* ☉ *Tues.–Sat. 10–5.*

NIGHTLIFE & THE ARTS

Seven Angels Theatre (⊠ *Hamilton Park Pavilion, Plank Rd.* ☏ *203/757–4676* ⊕ *www.sevenangelstheatre.org*) presents first-rate plays, musicals, children's theater, cabaret concerts, and youth programs.

SHOPPING

Inside the historic Howland-Hughes building, the **Connecticut Store** (⊠ *120 Bank St.* ☏ *203/753–4121*) is stocked with made-in-Connecticut items, from Wiffle balls and Pez candies to pottery and glassware.

WHERE TO EAT & STAY

$$$–$$$$
STEAKHOUSE

✕**Carmen Anthony Steakhouse.** A worthy re-creation of the steak houses of old, Carmen Anthony has rich wood paneling, handsome oil paintings on the walls, and white linen on the tables. You can order Delmonico, filet mignon, porterhouse, and other steaks served in all their charbroiled glory or go for something like filet mignon Milanese. Seafood is also available; try the fresh Maine lobsters. ⊠ *496 Chase Ave.* ☎ *203/757–3040* ☐ *AE, D, DC, MC, V* ⊘ *No lunch weekends.*

$$–$$$ ✕ **Diorio Restaurant and Bar.** The dining room at Diorio, a Waterbury
★ tradition for more than a half century, retains its original mahogany
ITALIAN bankers' booth, marble brass bar, high tin ceilings, exposed brick, and white-tile floors. The dishes here are expertly prepared, from the fresh lobster ravioli with blue crab sauce to the dozens of pasta, chicken, veal, steak, and seafood plates. ⊠ *231 Bank St.* ☎ *203/754–5111* ☐ *AE, D, DC, MC, V* ⊘ *Closed Sun. No lunch Sat.*

$$$–$$$$ ▦ **House on the Hill.** Owner-innkeeper Marianne Vandenburgh's fanciful B&B is surrounded by lush gardens in a historic hillside neighborhood. The three-story 1888 Victorian, former home of a brass baron, has a glorious exterior color scheme of teal, sage green, red, and ivory. The rich original woodwork and details remain, and guest rooms—four suites—are furnished in a welcoming blend of antiques and nostalgia. One suite has two bedrooms and another has a kitchenette. **Pros:** meticulously restored house, highly professional innkeeper, fantastic breakfasts. **Cons:** historic but urban location in a slightly rough-around-the-edges-city. ⊠ *92 Woodlawn Terr.* ☎ *203/757–9901* ⊕ *www.house onthehillbedandbreakfast.com* ↵ *4 suites* ⅍ *In-room: kitchen (some), Wi-Fi. In-hotel: no elevator, parking (no fee), no-smoking rooms* ☐ *AE, D, DC, MC, V* ⊘ *Closed mid-Dec.–mid-Jan.* ⊨⊙⊨ *BP.*

NEW HAVEN TO MYSTIC

As you drive northeast along Interstate 95, culturally rich New Haven is the final urban obstacle between southwestern Connecticut's overdeveloped coast and southeastern Connecticut's quieter shoreline. The remainder of the jagged coast, which stretches all the way to the Rhode Island border, consists of small coastal villages, quiet hamlets, and relatively undisturbed beaches. The only interruptions along this mostly undeveloped seashore are the industry and piers of New London and Groton. Mystic, Stonington, Old Saybrook, Clinton, and Guilford are havens for fans of antiques and boutiques. North of Groton, near the town of Ledyard, the Mashantucket Pequot Reservation owns and operates Foxwoods Casino and the Mashantucket Pequot Museum & Research Center. The Mohegan Indians run the Mohegan Sun casino in Uncasville. These two properties have added noteworthy hotels and marquee restaurants in recent years and now rank among the East's swankiest casino resorts.

MILFORD

6 mi northeast of Stratford.

Milford, established in 1639, is Connecticut's sixth-oldest municipality, and it retains the feel of a small coastal town despite its more than 48,000 residents and the commercial stretch of the Boston Post Road

Southeastern
Connecticut:
New Haven
to Mystic

KEY
Ferry Lines

THE QUIET CORNER

Jewett City
Norwich
Foxwoods Casino and Mashantucket
Pequot Museum
N. Stonington
Stonington
BLOCK ISLAND
Mystic
Old Mystic
Ledyard
Gales Ferry
U.S.S. Nautilus Memorial
Mohegan Sun
Uncasville
Quaker Hill
Ft. Griswold Battlefield State Park
Groton
Eastpoint
Fishers Island Sound
Fishers Island (N.Y.)
Thames River
Groton/New London Airport
Montville
Fort Trumbull State Park
New London
Waterford
Ocean Beach Park
Colchester
Salem
Hamburg
NEHANTIC STATE FOREST
Rogers Lake
Niantic
ROCKY NECK STATE PARK
HARKNESS MEMORIAL STATE PARK
Plum Island (N.Y.)
Mcheganct
Hadlyme
East Haddam
Deep River
Essex
Connecticut River
Old Lyme
Orient Point
Long Island (N.Y.)
Moodus
Higganum
COCKAPONSET STATE FOREST
Centerbrook
Ivoryton
Old Saybrook
Knollwood
Long Island Sound
Portland
Middletown
Cromwell
Durham
Killingworth
Westbrook
Clinton
Hammonasset Beach State Park
Madison
Wallingford
North Haven
Northford
North Branford
Guilford
Stony Creek
Thimble Islands
New Haven
see detail map
East Haven
Branford
Milford
Tweed/New Haven Airport

10 miles
15 km

that runs through its center. The large town green is at the heart of this community, and it sparkles in winter with thousands of tiny white lights strung in its trees. The duck pond and waterfall behind city hall is a pleasant place to while away a spring afternoon, and Milford's many beaches, open to the public for the price of parking, are inviting in summer.

SPORTS & THE OUTDOORS

Connecticut Audubon Coastal Center. On a barrier beach next door to an 840-acre reserve where the Housatonic River meets Long Island Sound, this center has educational exhibits, lectures, and classes indoors; outdoors are a 70-foot observation tower that provides a view of all the reserve has to offer, a boardwalk and observation platform at the water's edge, and an amazing assortment of birds year-round. ⊠ *1 Milford Point Rd.* ☎ *203/878–7440* ⊕ *www.ctaudubon.org/visit/milford. htm* ⊠ *Donation suggested at center, grounds free* ⊙ *Center Tues.–Sat. 10–4, Sun. noon–4; grounds daily dawn–dusk.*

BEACHES   **Silver Sands State Park,** with its signature beach and old-fashioned wooden boardwalk, is an inviting spot to while away an afternoon—whatever the season. You can walk out to Charles Island (where Captain Kidd is rumored to have buried his treasure) at low tide. ⊠ *600 E. Broadway* ☎ *203/735–4311* ⊠ *Free* ⊙ *Daily 8* AM*–dusk.*

WHERE TO EAT

$$$ ✕ **Jeffrey's.** This popular restaurant serves up-to-the-minute innova-
AMERICAN   tive American cuisine in a refined yet welcoming setting that includes an antique Dutch armoire and a grand piano. Changing specials have included rib-eye pork chop stuffed with pancetta, mozzarella, and spinach, and pan-seared duck with a foie gras–port wine–sour cherry sauce and Creole-spiced sweet potatoes. ⊠ *501 New Haven Ave.* ☎ *203/878–1910* ▤ *AE, D, DC, MC, V* ⊙ *No dinner Sun.*

¢   ✕ **Paul's Famous Hamburgers.** "Not serving numbers, but generations" is
FAST FOOD   the motto of this drive-in established in 1946. It's the place to go for extraordinarily fresh and juicy burgers, hot dogs on toasted buns, fries, Reubens, and milk shakes thick enough to stand a spoon in. ⊠ *829 Boston Post Rd.* ☎ *203/874–7586* ▤ *No credit cards* ⊙ *Closed Sun.*

NEW HAVEN

9 mi east of Milford, 46 mi northeast of Greenwich.

New Haven's history goes back to the 17th century, when its squares, including a lovely central green for the public, were laid out. The city, a cultural center, is home to Yale University. The historic district surrounding Yale and the distinctive shops, prestigious museums, and highly respected theaters downtown are a major draw—New Haven has developed an acclaimed restaurant scene in recent years.

WHAT TO SEE

❶ **New Haven Green.** Bordered on the west side by the Yale campus, the green is a fine example of early urban planning. As early as 1638, village elders set aside the 16-acre plot as a town common. Three early-

On a Roll

Behold the lobster roll. Sweet, succulent, and sinfully rich, it's the ultimate buttery icon of a Connecticut summer Other New England states may prefer to chill out with lobster rolls created from a cool mix of lobster meat, mayonnaise, and chopped celery, but Nutmeggers like their one-of-a-kind rolls served hot, hot, hot.

The traditional Connecticut lobster roll, said to have been invented in the early 1930s at Perry's, a now-defunct seafood shack on the Boston Post Road in Milford, consists of nothing more than plump chunks of hot lobster meat and melted butter served on a butter-toasted roll. In other words: heaven on a bun. From seafood shanties along the shore to more gourmet getaways farther inland, Connecticut is fairly swimming with eateries that offer these revered rolls. Three favorites: A roll at **Abbott's Lobster in the Rough** (⊠ *117 Pearl St., Noank* ☎ *860/536-7719* ⊕ *www. abbotts-lobster.com* ⊙ *Closed mid-Oct.–May)* is best enjoyed seated at a picnic table at the edge of Noank Harbor watching the boats bob by. At **Lenny and Joe's Fish Tale Drive-in** (⊠ *1301 Boston Post Rd., Madison* ☎ *203/245-7289* ⊕ *www.ljfishtale. com*), kids of all ages love to eat outdoors by a hand-carved Dentzel carousel with flying horses (and a whale, frog, lion, seal, and more), which the restaurant runs from early May through early October. **Marnick's** (⊠ *10 Washington Pkwy., Stratford* ☎ *203/377-6288* ⊕ *www.marnicks. nv.switchboard.com*), on a small beach on the Long Island Sound, is a place where you can kick off your shoes for a picnic on the sand or leave them on and enjoy a leisurely after-dinner stroll along a sea wall.

19th-century churches—the Gothic-style **Trinity Episcopal Church,** the Georgian-style **Center Congregational Church,** and the predominantly Federal-style **United Church**—contribute to its present appeal. ⊠ *Between Church and College Sts..*

★ **Yale University.** New Haven as a manufacturing center dates from the 19th century, but the city owes its fame to merchant Elihu Yale. In 1718 Yale's contributions enabled the Collegiate School, founded in 1701 at Saybrook, to settle in New Haven, where it changed its name to Yale University. This is one of the nation's great universities, and its campus holds some handsome neo-Gothic buildings and a number of noteworthy museums. The university's knowledgeable guides conduct one-hour walking tours that include Connecticut Hall in the Old Campus, which has had a number of illustrious past residents. ⊠ *Yale Visitor Center, 149 Elm St.* ☎ *203/432-2300* ⊕ *www.yale.edu/visitor* ⊠ *Free* ⊙ *Tours weekdays at 10:30 and 2, weekends at 1:30* ⊂ *Tours start from 149 Elm St. on north side of New Haven Green.*

DID YOU KNOW?

Yale University—including both undergraduate and graduate schools—has matriculated countless notables, from world leaders to darlings of the literary and entertainment worlds. Five U.S. presidents (William Howard Taft, Gerald Ford, Bill Clinton, and both George Bushes) have Yale degrees. Other standouts have included commentator William F. Buckley and writers James

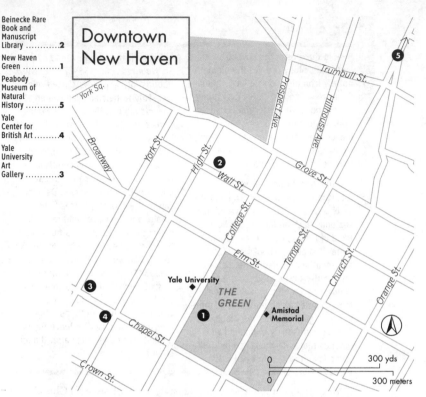

Fenimore Cooper and Tom Wolfe; artist Mark Rothko, composer Cole Porter, cartoonist Gary Trudeau, lexicographer Noah Webster, architect Eero Saarinen, and actors Jodie Foster, Edward Norton, Meryl Streep, Sam Waterston, and Sigourney Weaver.

② Beinecke Rare Book and Manuscript Library. The collections here include a Gutenberg Bible, illuminated manuscripts, and original Audubon bird prints, but the building is almost as much of an attraction—the walls are made of marble cut so thin that the light shines through, making the interior a breathtaking sight on sunny days. ✉ *121 Wall St.* ☎*203/432–2977* ⊕*www.library.yale.edu/beinecke* ✉*Free* ☉*Mon.– Thurs. 8:30–8, Fri. 8:30–5, Sat. 10–5.*

⑤ Peabody Museum of Natural History. Opened in 1876, the Peabody, with more than 11 million specimens, is one of the largest natural history museums in the nation. In addition to exhibits on Andean, Mesoamerican, and Pacific cultures, the venerable museum has an excellent collection of birds, including a stuffed dodo and passenger pigeon. But the main attractions for children and amateur paleontologists alike are some of the world's earliest reconstructions of dinosaur skeletons. ✉*170 Whitney Ave.* ☎*203/432–5050* ⊕*www.peabody.yale.edu* ✉*$7* ☉*Mon.–Sat. 10–5, Sun. noon–5.*

④ **Yale Center for British Art.** With the most comprehensive collection of
Fodor's Choice   British art outside Britain, the center surveys the development of Eng-
★   lish art, life, and thought from the Elizabethan period to the present.
The skylighted galleries, architect Louis I. Kahn's final work (completed after his death), contain works by Constable, Hogarth, Gainsborough, Reynolds, and Turner, to name but a few. You'll also find
rare books and paintings documenting English history. ✉ *1080 Chapel
St.* ☎ *203/432–2800* ⊕ *www.yale.edu/ycba* ✇ *Free* ☉ *Tues.–Sat. 10–5,
Sun. noon–5.*

❸ **Yale University Art Gallery.** Since its founding in 1832, this art gallery
has amassed more than 85,000 objects from around the world, dat-
ing from ancient Egypt to the present day. Highlights include works
by van Gogh, Manet, Monet, Picasso, Winslow Homer, and Thomas
Eakins, as well as Etruscan and Greek vases, Chinese ceramics and
bronzes, early Italian paintings, and a collection of American decorative arts that is considered one of the world's finest. The gallery's
landmark main building is also of note. Opened in 1953, it was Louis
I. Kahn's first major commission and the first modernist building on
the neo-Gothic Yale campus. Over the years, its extensive open spaces
were subdivided into galleries, classrooms, and offices, but a major
renovation, completed in 2006, restored it to Kahn's original concep-
tion. ✉ *1111 Chapel St.* ☎ *203/432–0600* ⊕ *www.yale.edu/artgallery*
✇ *Free* ☉ *Tues.–Sat. 10–5, Sun. 1–6.*

4

NIGHTLIFE & THE ARTS

NIGHTLIFE   **Anna Liffey's** (✉ *17 Whitney Ave.* ☎ *203/773–1776* ⊕ *www.annaliffeys.
com*) is one of the city's liveliest Irish pubs. **BAR** (✉ *254 Crown St.*
☎ *203/495–1111*) is a cross between a nightclub, a brick-oven pizzeria, and a brewpub. **Richter's** (✉ *990 Chapel St.* ☎ *203/777–0400*) is
famous for its half-yard glasses of beer. Alternative and traditional rock
bands play at **Toad's Place** (✉ *300 York St.* ☎ *203/624–8623* ⊕ *www.
toadsplace.com*).

THE ARTS   The **New Haven Symphony Orchestra** (☎ *203/865–0831* ⊕ *www.newhaven
symphony.com*) plays at Yale University's **Woolsey Hall** (✉ *College and
Grove Sts.*). The well-regarded **Long Wharf Theatre** (✉ *222 Sargent Dr.*
☎ *203/787–4282* ⊕ *www.longwharf.org*) presents works by contemporary writers and imaginative revivals of neglected classics. The **Shu-
bert Performing Arts Center** (✉ *247 College St.* ☎ *203/624–1825* ⊕ *www.
capa.com/newhaven*) hosts Broadway musicals and dramas, usually
following their run in the Big Apple, plus dance and classical-music
performances.

The highly professional **Yale Repertory Theatre** (✉ *Chapel and York
Sts.* ☎ *203/432–1234* ⊕ *www.yale.edu/yalerep*) premieres new plays
and mounts fresh interpretations of the classics. **Yale School of Music**
(☎ *203/432–4157* ⊕ *www.yale.edu/music*) presents an impressive roster of performers, from classical to jazz; most events take place in the
Morse Recital Hall in **Sprague Hall** (✉ *College and Wall Sts.*).

SHOPPING

Chapel Street, near the town green, has a pleasing assortment of shops and eateries. **Atticus Bookstore & Café** (⊠*1082 Chapel St.* ☎*203/776–4040*), in the heart of Yale University, was one of the first stores to combine books and food; it's been a favorite among museum groupies and theatergoers for years.

WHERE TO EAT

$$-$$$ ✕**Bentara.** With so many wonderful Asian restaurants in New Haven,
★ it's hard to single out one stellar selection, but Bentara has plenty going
MALAYSIAN for it—a cuisine (Malaysian) somewhat uncommon in America, a charismatic and talented chef with a penchant for innovative preparations, and a charmed setting inside a vintage redbrick building on an up-and-coming downtown street. Apart from traditional noodle stir-fries and soups, watch for such tempting dishes as filet mignon with a fire-roasted red-pepper curry sauce, or grilled salmon with a coconut-turmeric-lime sauce. ⊠*76 Orange St.* ☎*203/562–2511* ☐*AE, DC, MC, V.*

$$$-$$$$ ✕**Bespoke.** New Haven's latest, hottest upscale dining option, Bespoke
ECLECTIC opened in 2007 to plenty of buzz and mostly wonderful reviews—a few have complained of uneven service, but time should iron this out. Vaunted local restaurateurs Arturo and Suzette Franco-Camacho have opened this sleek three-level eatery with a big-city feel and pricey but artfully executed contemporary international fare. Kick things off with a Thai-style confit of duck with tamarind glaze and fiery chilies, before sampling a boldly seasoned fennel-garlic-crusted pork tenderloin with quince-apple ragout. The wine list is impressive. ⊠*266 College St.* ☎*203/562–4644* ☐*AE, DC, MC, V* ⊘*Closed Sun.*

$-$$ ✕**Frank Pepe's.** Does this place serve the best pizza in the world, as so
★ many reviewers claim? If it doesn't, it comes close. Pizza is the only
PIZZA thing prepared here—try the justifiably famous white-clam pie (it's especially good with bacon on top). Expect to wait an hour or more for a table—or, on weekend evenings, come after 10. ⊠*157 Wooster St.* ☎*203/865–5762* ⚑*Reservations not accepted* ☐*No credit cards.*

$$$ ✕**Ibiza.** Owner Ignacio Blanco and chef Luis Bollo are *the* names in
Fodor'sChoice Spanish cuisine in the state. Tall ceilings, multipaned windows, exposed
★ brick, and vibrant murals create a backdrop for such extraordinary
SPANISH dishes as Catalan noodle paella with codfish, salmon, shrimp, bay scallops, and cockles, and raviolis stuffed with braised oxtail and wild mushrooms, with sweet potatoe puree and scallion vinaigrette. A tasting menu is available Monday–Thursday. Ibiza has a sister restaurant, Meigas, in Norwalk. ⊠*39 High St.* ☎*203/865–1933* ☐*AE, MC, V* ⊘*Closed Sun. No lunch Fri.–Wed.*

¢ ✕**Louis' Lunch.** This all-American luncheonette on the National Register
AMERICAN of Historic Places claims to be the birthplace of the hamburger in America. Its first-rate burgers are cooked in an old-fashioned, upright broiler and served with either a slice of tomato or cheese on two slices of toast. And, as most customers who come from far and wide for these tasty morsels agree, it doesn't get much better than that. Louis' is open till 2 AM Thursday–Saturday. ⊠*263 Crown St.* ☎*203/562–5507* ☐*No credit cards* ⊘*Closed Sun. and Mon. No dinner Tues. and Wed.*

WHERE TO STAY

$$$-$$$$ 🏨**Omni New Haven Hotel at Yale.** This 19-floor Omni is the only large hotel in the city. With modern amenities, it's comfortable and convenient to the heart of New Haven. John Davenport's at the Top of the Park, the upscale rooftop restaurant, serves traditional American fare along with views of the Yale campus, New Haven Green, and Long Island Sound; many upper-level rooms enjoy the same great views. **Pros:** upscale furnishings, nice gym and spa, walking distance from many shops and restaurants. **Cons:** somewhat steep rates, in busy part of downtown. ✉155 Temple St. 🖀203/772–6664 ⊕*www.omni hotels.com* ⇄299 rooms, 7 suites ♿In-room: Wi-Fi. In-hotel: restaurant, bar, gym, spa, some pets allowed, no-smoking rooms ⊟AE, D, DC, MC, V.

4

EN ROUTE The village of Stony Creek, roughly 9 mi east of New Haven, with a few tackle shops, antiques shops, a general store, and a marina, is the departure point for cruises around the **Thimble Islands.** This group of more than 90 tiny islands was named for its abundance of thimbleberries, which are similar to gooseberries. Legend has it that Captain Kidd buried pirate gold on one island. Three sightseeing vessels vie for your patronage: the *Islander* (🖀203/397–3921 ⊕*www.thimbleislander. com*); the *Sea Mist* (🖀203/488–8905 ⊕*www.thimbleislandcruise. com*); and the *Volsunga IV* (🖀203/481–3345 ⊕*www.thimbleislands. com*). All three depart from Stony Creek Dock, at the end of Thimble Island Road, from May to Columbus Day.

GUILFORD

5 mi northeast of Branford, 37 mi west of New London.

The Guilford town green, crisscrossed by pathways, dotted with benches, and lined with historic homes and specialty shops, is considered by many to be the prettiest green in the state and is actually the third largest in the Northeast.

WHAT TO SEE

Henry Whitfield State Museum. Built in 1639, this is the oldest house in the state and the oldest stone house in New England. The furnishings in the post-medieval-style building were made between the 17th and 19th centuries. View exhibitions at the visitor center. ✉248 Old Whitfield St. 🖀203/453–2457 ⊕*www.whitfieldmuseum.org* 💲$4 ⊙Apr.–mid-Dec., Wed.–Sun. 10–4:30.

WHERE TO EAT

$$-$$$ ✕**Whitfield's.** A beautifully restored Victorian building with a wall of
AMERICAN windows overlooking Guilford Green is the backdrop for this lively café's mix of traditional and contemporary American cuisine. You might find New York prosciutto-wrapped grilled shrimp or peach-barbecue-glazed salmon with mango-chipotle salsa coloring your plate. ✉25 Whitfield St. 🖀203/458–1300 ⊟AE, MC, V.

MADISON

5 mi east of Guilford, 62 mi northeast of Greenwich.

Coastal Madison has an understated charm. Ice cream parlors, antiques stores, and quirky gift boutiques prosper along U.S. 1, the town's main street. Stately Colonial homes line the town green, site of many a summer antiques fair and arts-and-crafts festival. The Madison shoreline, particularly the white stretch of sand known as Hammonasset Beach and its parallel boardwalk, draws visitors year-round.

SPORTS & THE OUTDOORS

★ **Hammonasset Beach State Park,** the largest of the state's shoreline sanctuaries, has 2 mi of white-sand beaches, a top-notch nature center, excellent birding, and a hugely popular campground with about 550 sites. ⊠*I–95 Exit 62* ☎*203/245–2785 park, 203/245–1817 campground* ☞*Park $7–$15 mid-Apr.–mid-Oct., free off-season* ☉*Park daily 8* AM*–dusk.*

SHOPPING

The **Harp & Hearth** (⊠*45 Wall St.* ☎*203/245–1414* ⊕*www.harpand hearth.com*) occupies one of Connecticut's oldest houses, a 1690s colonial packed with all things British, from jewelry, pottery, and crystal to English and Irish teas and sweets. Lunch and afternoon tea are served in a shop's charming dining room.

WHERE TO STAY

$$-$$$ ⬚ **Inn at Lafayette.** Skylights, painted murals, and handcrafted woodwork are among the design accents at this airy hostelry in a converted 1830s church. The rooms may be small, but they are decorated with beautiful fabrics and reproduction 17th- and 18th-century antique furniture. The modern marble baths come equipped with telephones. Fresh food and flawless service are highlights at Café Allegre ($$; closed Monday), the inn's popular restaurant. The menu is largely southern Italian, with French accents. **Pros:** steps from shopping and restaurants, excellent restaurant, distinctive architecture. **Cons:** on a busy street. ⊠*725 Boston Post Rd.* ☎*203/245–7773 or 866/623–7498* ⊕*www.innat lafayette.com* ➫*5 rooms* ₺*In-room: Ethernet. In-hotel: restaurant, bar, no elevator, no-smoking rooms* ☰*AE, D, DC, MC, V* ⦿*CP.*

OLD SAYBROOK

9 mi east of Madison, 29 mi east of New Haven.

Old Saybrook, once a lively shipbuilding and fishing town, bustles with summer vacationers and antiques shoppers. Its downtown is an especially pleasing place for a window-shopping stroll. At the end of the afternoon, stop at the old-fashioned soda fountain, where you can share a sundae with your sweetie.

SHOPPING

More than 125 dealers operate out of the **Old Saybrook Antiques Center** (⊠*756 Middlesex Tpke.* ☎*860/388–1600* ⊕*www.oldsaybrook antiques.com*). **Beautiful Impressions** (⊠*30 Westbrook Pl., Westbrook*

☎*860/399–8855* ⊕*www.beautiful impressions.com*) sells both water-colors and ice-cream sodas in a historic former general store and phar-macy. **North Cove Outfitters** (✉*75 Main St.* ☎*860/388–6585* ⊕*www.northcove.com*) is Connecticut's version of L. L. Bean. **Saybrook Country Barn** (✉*2 Main St.* ☎*860/388–0891*) sells everything country, from tiger-maple dining-room tables to hand-painted pottery.

WHERE TO EAT & STAY

$$-$$$ ✕**Café Routier.** Grilled trout with lyonnaise potatoes and a whole-grain
★ mustard sauce, fried oysters with a chipotle rémoulade, and a duck-
FRENCH and-wild-mushroom ragout are among the favorites at this classy
Yankee bistro. ✉*1353 Boston Post Rd., 5 mi west of Old Saybrook, Westbrook* ☎*860/399–8700* ▤*AE, D, DC, MC, V* ☉*No lunch.*

$$$$ ▦**Saybrook Point Inn & Spa.** Rooms at the cushy Saybrook are furnished
★ mainly in 18th-century style, with reproductions of British furniture
and impressionist art—many have fireplaces. The pools overlook the
inn's marina and the Connecticut River, and a full-service spa offers
Swedish-style aromatherapy, sea-clay facial masques, and a nice range
of salon treatments. The Terra Mar Grille, which sits on the river, serves
stylish Continental cuisine. **Pros:** swanky rooms, top-notch service,
superb restaurant. **Cons:** pricey, a car is needed to get to downtown
shops and dining. ✉*2 Bridge St.* ☎*860/395–2000 or 800/243–0212*
⊕*www.saybrook.com* ⬖*56 rooms, 12 suites* ♿*In-room: refrigerator, DVD (some), Wi-Fi. In-hotel: restaurant, pools, gym, spa, some pets allowed, no-smoking rooms* ▤*AE, D, DC, MC, V.*

$$$$ ▦**Water's Edge Inn & Resort.** With its spectacular setting on Long Island
Sound, this traditional weathered gray-shingle compound in Westbrook has one of the Connecticut shore's premier resort settings. The
main building has warm, bright public rooms furnished with antiques
and reproductions, and its upstairs bedrooms, with wall-to-wall carpeting and clean, modern bathrooms, afford priceless views of the sound.
✉*1525 Boston Post Rd., 5 mi west of Old Saybrook, Westbrook*
☎*860/399–5901 or 800/222–5901* ⊕*www.watersedgeresortandspa.com* ⬖*162 rooms* ♿*In-room: VCR, Ethernet. In-hotel: restaurant, bar, tennis courts, pools, gym, spa, beachfront, no-smoking rooms* ▤*AE, D, DC, MC, V.*

OLD LYME

4 mi east of Old Saybrook, 40 mi south of Hartford.

Old Lyme, on the other side of the Connecticut River from Old Saybrook, is renowned among art lovers for its past as the home of the
Lyme Art Colony, the most famous gathering of impressionist painters
in America. Artists continue to be attracted to the area for its lovely
countryside and shoreline. The town also has handsome old houses,
many built for sea captains.

WHAT TO SEE

Fodor'sChoice **Florence Griswold Museum.** Central to Old Lyme's artistic reputation is
★ this grand late-Georgian-style mansion owned by Miss Florence Griswold that served as a boardinghouse for members of the Lyme Art

Colony in the first decades of the 20th century. When artists such as Willard Metcalf, Clark Voorhees, Childe Hassam, and Henry Ward Ranger flocked to the area to paint its varied landscape, Miss Florence offered housing as well as artistic encouragement. The house was turned into a museum in 1947 and underwent a major restoration completed in 2006, which restored it to its appearance in 1910, when the colony was in full flower (clues to the house's layout and decor in that era were provided by many of the members' paintings). The museum's 10,000-square-foot Krieble Gallery, on the riverfront, hosts changing exhibitions of American art. ⊠*96 Lyme St.* ☎*860/434–5542* ⊕*www. florencegriswoldmuseum.org* ⊠*$8* ⊙*Tues.–Sat. 10–5, Sun. 1–5.*

WHERE TO STAY

$$$–$$$$ 🅣**Bee & Thistle Inn.** Behind a weathered stone wall in the Old Lyme
Fodor'sChoice historic district is a three-story 1756 Colonial house with 5.5 acres
★ of broad lawns, formal gardens, and herbaceous borders. The scale of rooms throughout is small and inviting, with fireplaces in the parlors and dining rooms and light and airy curtains in the multipaned guest-room windows. Most rooms have canopy or four-poster beds. Fireplaces and candlelight exude romance in the restaurant ($$$–$$$$; closed Monday and Tuesday), where innovative American cuisine— with entrées such as herb-grilled filet mignon with lobster-mashed potatoes—is served with style. **Pros:** a short walk from Griswold Museum, lovely old home, fantastic restaurant. **Cons:** can hear noise from I–95, historic rooms don't have many modern amenities. ⊠*100 Lyme St.* ☎*860/434–1667 or 800/622–4946* ⊕*www.beeandthistleinn.com* ⮑*11 rooms* ⌕*In-room: dial-up. In-hotel: restaurant, no elevator, no kids under 12, no-smoking rooms* ▤*AE, DC, MC, V* ⦿*BP.*

NEW LONDON

3 mi northeast of Waterford, 46 mi east of New Haven.

New London, a small and slightly gritty city on the banks of the Thames River, has long had ties to the sea. In the mid-1800s it was the second-largest whaling port in the world. Today the U.S. Coast Guard Academy uses its campus on the Thames to educate and train its cadets. Ocean Beach Park, an old-fashioned beach resort with a wooden boardwalk, provides an up-close-and-personal view of New London's connection to the deep blue sea.

WHAT TO SEE

Lyman Allyn Art Museum. Housed in a neoclassical building that overlooks both the U. S. Coast Guard Academy and Long Island Sound, this museum was founded in 1932 by Harriet Upson Allyn in memory of her whaling merchant father, Lyman Allyn. Inside is an impressive collection of more than 10,000 objects covering a span of 5,000 years. Works include contemporary, modern, and Early American fine arts; American impressionist paintings; and Connecticut decorative arts. European works from the 16th through the 19th centuries round out the permanent collection. ⊠*625 Williams St.* ☎*860/443–2545* ⊕*www.lymanallyn.org* ⊠*$8* ⊙*Tues.–Sat. 10–5, Sun. 1–5.*

U.S. Coast Guard Academy. The 100-acre cluster of redbrick buildings you see overlooking the Thames River makes up one of the country's four military academies. A museum on the property explores the Coast Guard's 200 years of maritime service and includes some 200 ship models, as well as figureheads, paintings, uniforms, and cannon. The three-mast training bark, the USCGC *Eagle,* may be boarded Friday–Sunday 1–5, when in port. ⊠*15 Mohegan Ave.* ☏*860/444–8270* ⊕*www.cga. edu* ⌨*Free* ⊙ *Weekdays 9–5, Sat. 10–5, Sun. noon–5.*

SPORTS & THE OUTDOORS

At **Fort Trumbull State Park** (⊠*90 Walbach St.* ☏*860/444–7591*) on the Thames River, former location of the Naval Undersea Warfare Center, you'll find a 19th-century stonework-and-masonry fort, an extensive visitor center focusing on military history, a top-rate fishing pier, a boardwalk with fantastic views, and a picnic area for when you want to relax. **Ocean Beach Park** (⊠*1225 Ocean Ave.* ☏*860/447–3031*) has a ½-mi-long beach, an Olympic-size outdoor pool (with a waterslide), a miniature golf course, a video arcade, a boardwalk, and a picnic area.

NIGHTLIFE & THE ARTS

The **Garde Arts Center** (⊠*325 State St.* ☏*860/444–7373* ⊕*www. gardearts.org*) hosts touring Broadway shows, national and international opera and dance companies, and children's events. Connecticut College's **Palmer Auditorium** (⊠*270 Mohegan Ave.* ☏*860/439–2787*) plans a full schedule of dance and theater programs.

WHERE TO STAY

$$$–$$$$ 🖫 **Lighthouse Inn Resort and Conference Center.** This Mediterranean-style mansion-turned-inn was built in 1902 as the summer home of a steel magnate. When it opened as an inn in 1927 it was a retreat for film stars such as Bette Davis and Joan Crawford. The hotel retains its original grandeur, including the grounds designed by renowned landscape architect Frederick Law Olmsted, designer of New York's Central Park. Rooms in the semicircular mansion are appointed with a mix of antiques and period pieces; some face Long Island Sound. Treatments are offered in the Looking Glass Salon and Spa. **Pros:** great water views, lavish decor. **Cons:** service can be a little uneven, rather expensive. ⊠*6 Guthrie Pl.* ☏*860/443–8411 or 888/443–8411* ⊕*www.lighthouseinn-ct.com* ⇌*16 rooms, 11 suites* ⌕*In-room: Ethernet. In-hotel: restaurant, bar, spa, beachfront, no-smoking rooms* ▤*AE, MC, V* ⅋*CP.*

NORWICH

15 mi north of New London, 37 mi southeast of Hartford.

Outstanding Georgian and Victorian structures surround the triangular town green in Norwich, and more can be found downtown by the Thames River. The former mill town is hard at work at restoration and rehabilitation efforts. So eye-catching are these brightly colored structures that the Paint Quality Institute has designated the town one of the "Prettiest Painted Places in New England."

WHAT TO SEE

The **Slater Memorial Museum & Converse Art Gallery,** on the grounds of the Norwich Free Academy, houses one of the country's largest collections of Greek, Roman, and Renaissance plaster casts of some of the world's greatest sculptures, including the *Winged Victory, Venus de Milo,* and Michelangelo's *Pietà.* The Converse Art Gallery adjacent to the museum hosts six to eight shows a year, many of which focus on Connecticut artists and craftsmen as well as student work. ✉ *108 Crescent St.* ☎ *860/887–2506* 🌐 *www.norwichfreeacademy.com/museum* 🎟 *$5* ⏲ *Tues.–Fri. 9–4, weekends 1–4.*

WHERE TO STAY

$$$–$$$$ **Spa at Norwich Inn.** This posh Georgian-style inn is on 42 rolling acres right by the Thames River. The spa, the state's finest, provides an entire spectrum of skin care, massages, body treatments, and fitness classes. You'll find four-poster beds, wood-burning fireplaces, CD players, and a complete galley kitchen in the luxe villas as well as comfy country furnishings in the guest rooms. The inn's elegant restaurant serves tasty, yet health-conscious, fare. The top-notch seafood scampi with fresh Maine lobster, sea scallops, and Gulf shrimp over linguine has just 425 calories—and you'd never know it. **Pros:** one of the best spas in the state, short drive from casinos, beautiful grounds. **Cons:** oriented toward spa guests, so less appealing if that's not your interest. ✉ *607 W. Thames St. (Rte. 32)* ☎ *860/886–2401 or 800/275–4772* 🌐 *www.thespaatnorwichinn.com* *49 rooms, 54 villas* *In-room: Wi-Fi. In-hotel: 2 restaurants, golf course, tennis courts, pool, spa, no-smoking rooms* 💳 *AE, D, DC, MC, V.*

LEDYARD

10 mi south of Norwich, 37 mi southeast of Hartford.

There's no doubt that Ledyard, in the woods of southeastern Connecticut between Norwich and the coastline, is known first and foremost for the vast Mashantucket Pequot Tribal Nation's Foxwoods Resort Casino. With the opening of the excellent Mashantucket Pequot Museum & Research Center, however, the tribe has moved beyond gaming to educating the public about its history, as well as that of other Northeast Woodland tribes.

WHAT TO SEE

Fodor's Choice ★ **Mashantucket Pequot Museum & Research Center.** A large complex a mile from the Foxwoods Resort Casino, this museum brings the history and culture of Northeastern Woodland tribes in general and the Pequots in particular to life in exquisite detail. Some highlights include re-creations of an 18,000-year-old glacial crevasse that you can travel right into, a caribou hunt from 11,000 years ago, and a 17th-century fort. Perhaps most remarkable is a sprawling "immersion environment"—a 16th-century village with more than 50 life-size figures and real smells and sounds—in which you use audio devices to obtain detailed information about the sights. The research center, open to scholars and schoolchildren free of charge, holds some 150,000 volumes. Also on-site is a full-service restaurant that serves both Native and traditional American

cuisine. ⊠*110 Pequot Trail, Mashantucket* ☎*800/411–9671* ⊕*www.
pequotmuseum.org* ⚄*$15* ⊙*Daily 10–4.*

CASINOS

Foxwoods Resort Casino. On the Mashantucket Pequot Indian Reservation near Ledyard, Foxwoods is the world's largest resort casino.
The skylighted compound draws more than 50,000 visitors daily to its
more than 7,200 slot machines, 380 gaming tables, 3,200-seat high-
stakes bingo parlor, poker rooms, Keno station, theater, and Race Book
room. This 4.7-million-square-foot complex includes the Grand Pequot
Tower, the Great Cedar Hotel, and the Two Trees Inn, which have
more than 1,400 rooms combined, as well as a full-service spa, retail
concourse, food court, and numerous restaurants. In spring 2008 Fox-
wood unveiled the MGM Grand at Foxwoods, an ultraluxury branch
of the Las Vegas gaming resort; it added another 825 posh rooms and
suites, plus several notable restaurants. ⊠*39 Norwich Westerly Rd.,
Ledyard* ☎*860/312–3000 or 800/752–9244* ⊕*www.foxwoods.com*
⊙*Daily 24 hrs.*

Mohegan Sun. The Mohegan Indians, known as the Wolf People, operate this casino west of Ledyard and just south of Norwich, which has
more than 300,000 square feet of gaming space, including 6,000 slot
machines and more than 250 gaming tables. Also part of the complex: the Kids Quest family entertainment center; a 130,000-square-
foot shopping mall; more than 30 restaurants and food-and-beverage
suppliers; and a 34-story, 1,200-room luxury hotel with a full-service
spa. Free entertainment, including nationally known acts, is presented
nightly in the Wolf Den; a 10,000-seat arena hosts major national acts
and is home to the WNBA's Connecticut Sun; and a swanky 300-seat
cabaret hosts intimate shows and comedy acts. Mohegan After Dark is
a 22,000-square-foot complex with three nightclubs. ⊠*Mohegan Sun
Blvd., off I–395, Uncasville* ☎*888/226–7711* ⊕*www.mohegansun.
com* ⊙*24 hours.*

WHERE TO EAT & STAY

$$$
★
AMERICAN

✕**Stonecroft.** The sunny dining room at the this peaceful, elegant 1807
inn serves some of the finest and most creative food in the region.
Favorites from the seasonally changing menu have included curried
sweet-corn-and-lump-crab bisque, and Stonington sea scallops seared
in pumpkin-seed oil with mulled-cider-roasted acorn squash. ⊠*515
Pumpkin Hill Rd.* ☎*860/572–0771 or 800/772–0774* ▭*AE, D, MC,
V* ⊙*Closed Mon. No lunch.*

$$$–$$$$

⊞**Grand Pequot Tower.** Mere steps from the gaming floors, this expan-
sive 17-story showpiece contains deluxe rooms and suites in pleas-
antly neutral tones. However, since its opening in spring 2008, the
new MGM Grand at Foxwoods hotel is now the top accommodation
at Foxwoods Resort Casino. **Pros:** elegant rooms, easy access to the
casino, nice views from upper floors. **Cons:** not much to entice if you're
not planning on gambling. ⊠*Rte. 2, Box 3777, Mashantucket 06339*
☎*800/369–9663* ⊕*www.foxwoods.com* ⮑*824 rooms* ⌂*In-room:
refrigerator, Ethernet. In-hotel: 4 restaurants, bars, golf course, pool,
gym, spa, no-smoking rooms* ▭*AE, D, DC, MC, V.*

$$$-$$$$ ⚅ **Mohegan Sun Hotel.** The emphasis of this 34-story hotel is on luxury.
★   As you enter, towering red cedar trees (simulated, but realistic) form
a canopy above you, gleaming glass and birch-lined walls surround
you, and a stream and pool of water lead to the impressive Taughan-
nick Falls across the lobby in the connecting Shops at Mohegan Sun.
Guest rooms are large—a minimum of 450 square feet—and all have
king or queen beds and marble baths. The 22,300-square-foot Elemis
Spa is one of the finest in the state. **Pros:** numerous fine restaurants
and gaming areas are steps from lobby, incredible views from upper
floors, excellent spa and fitness center. **Cons:** not much reason to stay
here if you're not a fan of casinos. ✉ *1 Mohegan Sun Blvd., Uncas-
ville* ☎ *888/777–7922* ⊕ *www.mohegansun.com* ✎ *1,020 rooms, 180
suites* ♿ *In-room: kitchen (some), Ethernet. In-hotel: restaurants, bars,
pool, gym, spa, no-smoking rooms* ⊟ *AE, D, MC, V.*

$$-$$$ ⚅ **Stonecroft.** A sunny 1807 Georgian Colonial on 6½ acres of green
★   meadows, woodlands, and rambling stone walls is the center of Stone-
croft. Although individually thematic, the rooms here and in the historic
barn are united in their refined but welcoming country atmosphere; all
have fireplaces and most have two-person whirlpool tubs. The restau-
rant is excellent. **Pros:** scenic and verdant grounds, cheerful service,
great restaurant. **Cons:** in secluded location that requires a car to get
around. ✉ *515 Pumpkin Hill Rd.* ☎ *860/572–0771 or 800/772–0774*
⊕ *www.stonecroft.com* ✎ *10 rooms* ♿ *In-room: Ethernet. In-hotel:
restaurant, no-smoking rooms* ⊟ *AE, D, MC, V* ⊚ *BP.*

GROTON

10 mi south of Ledyard.

Home to the U. S. Navy's first submarine base, the Naval Submarine
Base New London, and the Electric Boat Division of General Dynam-
ics, designer and manufacturer of nuclear submarines, Groton is often
referred to as the "submarine capital of the world." The submarine
Nautilus, a National Historic Landmark, is a major draw, as is the
Submarine Force Museum.

WHAT TO SEE

Ft. Griswold Battlefield State Park. At this site are the remnants of a Revolution-
ary War fort whose American defenders were massacred in 1781 by Brit-
ish troops under the command of the American traitor Benedict Arnold.
The 134-foot-tall Groton Battle Monument is a memorial to those who
lost their lives; you can climb it for a sweeping view of the shoreline. The
adjacent Monument House Museum has historic displays. ✉ *Monument
St. and Park Ave.* ☎ *860/445–1729* ⊟ *Free* ⊙ *Park daily 8–dusk; museum
and monument Memorial Day–Labor Day, daily 10–5.*

♻ **Submarine Force Museum.** The world's first nuclear-powered submarine,
the *Historic Ship Nautilus,* was launched and commissioned in Groton
in 1954 and spent her 25-year active career as a show horse of U.S.
technological know-how. She is permanently berthed at the Submarine
Force Museum, where you're welcome to climb aboard and explore.
The museum, outside the entrance to the submarine base, is a reposi-

tory of artifacts, documents, and photographs detailing the history of the U.S. Submarine Force component of the U.S. Navy, and has educational and interactive exhibits. ⊠*Crystal Lake Rd.* 📞*860/694–3174* ⊕*www.ussnautilus.org* 🎫*Free* ☉*May–Oct., Wed.–Mon. 9–5, Tues. 1–5; Nov.–Apr., Wed.–Mon. 9–4.*

MYSTIC

8 mi east of Groton.

Mystic has devoted itself to recapturing the seafaring spirit of the 18th and 19th centuries. Some of the nation's fastest clipper ships were built here in the mid-19th century; today's Mystic Seaport is the state's most popular museum. Downtown Mystic has an interesting collection of boutiques and galleries.

WHAT TO SEE

Fodor's Choice
★
Mystic Aquarium and Institute for Exploration. The animals here go through 1,000 pounds of herring, capelin, and squid each day. Inuk, a male beluga whale, is responsible for consuming 85 pounds of that himself. He calls the aquarium's Arctic Coast exhibit home. This exhibit, which holds 800,000 gallons of water, measures 165 feet at its longest point by 85 feet at its widest point, and ranges from just inches to 16½ feet deep, is just a small part of this revered establishment. You can also check out world-renowned ocean explorer Dr. Robert Ballard's Institute for Exploration and its Challenge of the Deep exhibition center (dedicated to revealing what lies on the world's deep ocean floors), as well as see African penguins, harbor seals, graceful sea horses, Pacific octopuses, and sand tiger sharks. ⊠*55 Coogan Blvd.* 📞*860/572–5955* ⊕*www.mysticaquarium.org* 🎫*$22* ☉*Mar.–Nov., daily 9–6; Dec.–Feb., weekdays 10–5, weekends 9–6.*

Fodor's Choice
★
Mystic Seaport. The world's largest maritime museum, Mystic Seaport encompasses 37 acres of indoor and outdoor exhibits, with more than 1 million artifacts, that provide a fascinating look at the area's rich shipbuilding and seafaring heritage. In the narrow streets and historic homes and buildings (some moved here from other sites), craftspeople give demonstrations of open-hearth cooking, weaving, and other skills of yesteryear. The museum's more than 480 vessels include the *Charles W. Morgan*, the last remaining wooden whaling ship afloat, and the 1882 training ship *Joseph Conrad*. You can climb aboard for a look or for sail-setting demonstrations and reenactments of whale hunts. Special events are held throughout the year. Children younger than 5 are admitted free. ⊠*75 Greenmanville Ave., 1 mi south of Exit 90, off I–95* 📞*860/572–0711* ⊕*www.mysticseaport.org* 🎫*$19* ☉*Apr.–Oct., daily 9–5; Nov.–Mar., daily 10–4.*

SHOPPING

The **Finer Line Gallery** (⊠*48 W. Main St.* 📞*860/536–8339* ⊕*www.finerlinegallery.com*) exhibits nautical and other prints, including some local scenes. **Olde Mistick Village** (⊠*Coogan Blvd., off I–95 Exit 90* 📞*860/536–4941* ⊕*www.oldmysticvillage.com*), a re-creation of what an American village might have looked like in the early 1700s, has more than 50 shops

4

that sell everything from crafts and clothing to souvenirs and munchies. The duck pond and gazebo are favorite gathering spots for pint-size shoppers. **Whyevernot** (⊠*17 W. Main St.* ☎*860/536–6209*) is a colorful spot for clothing, jewelry, pottery, linens, handmade papers, and much more.

WHERE TO EAT

$$-$$$
Fodor's Choice
★
SEAFOOD

✕**Abbott's Lobster in the Rough.** If you want some of the state's best lobsters, mussels, crabs, or clams on the half shell, head down to this unassuming seaside lobster shack in sleepy Noank, a few miles southwest of Mystic. Most seating is outdoors or on the dock, where the views of Noank Harbor are magnificent. ⊠*117 Pearl St., Noank* ☎*860/536–7719* ▤*AE, MC, V* ☞*BYOB* ⊘*Closed Columbus Day–1st Fri. in May and weekdays Labor Day–Columbus Day.*

$$-$$$
★
SEAFOOD

✕**Go Fish.** In this town by the sea, one hungers for seafood, and this sophisticated restaurant captures all the tastes—and colors—of the ocean. There's a raw bar, wine bar, coffee bar, and a black granite sushi bar, which, with its myriad tiny, briny morsels, is worth the trip in itself. The glossy blue tables in the two large dining rooms perfectly complement the signature saffron-scented shellfish bouillabaisse. The menu lists options for vegetarians and carnivores as well, but the lobster ravioli in a light cream sauce is a must-try. ⊠*Olde Mistick Village, Coogan Blvd., off I–95 (Exit 90)* ☎*860/536–2662* ▤*AE, D, MC, V.*

WHERE TO STAY

$$-$$$

⊡**Old Mystic Inn.** This cozy inn, built in 1784, was once a bookshop specializing in antique books and maps. Today, all its rooms, in the main house and a carriage house, are named after New England authors. Some have working fireplaces and whirlpools, and each is a welcoming and comfortable mix of antiques and owner-innkeeper Michael Cardillo Jr.'s personal touches. You can enjoy a game of checkers by the oversize Colonial hearth in the keeping room; a full country breakfast is served. **Pros:** beautifully kept historic house, quiet neighborhood, friendly host. **Cons:** need a car to get into downtown. ⊠*52 Main St.* ☎*860/572–9422* ⊕*www.oldmysticinn.com* ☞*8 rooms* ⊘*In-room: no phone, no TV, Ethernet (some), Wi-Fi (some). In-hotel: no elevators, no-smoking rooms* ▤*AE, MC, V* ⦿*BP.*

$$-$$$

⊡**Whaler's Inn.** A perfect compromise between a chain motel and a country inn, this complex with public rooms furnished with lovely antiques is one block from the Mystic River and downtown. The motel-style guest rooms feel Victorian, with quilts and reproduction

---

SETTING SAIL AT MYSTIC SEAPORT

Kids can learn the ropes—literally—of what it takes to be a sailor during Mystic Seaport's many sailing classes and camps. Younger children and those who just wish to stay onshore can sign up for courses on building boats (including how to varnish them), blacksmithing, carving, as well as, you guessed it, roping (from knotting to splicing). The Seaport's planetarium also offers instruction on navigating a ship by the stars. Prices for classes vary. Call Mystic Seaport (☎860/572-0711) or see its Web site (⊕ *www.mystic seaport.org*) for details.

four-poster beds—the best rooms have deep whirlpool baths. The restaurant, Bravo Bravo, serves well prepared Italian food, such as lobster ravioli bathed with a chive sauce. Pros: within walking distance of downtown shopping, excellent restaurant. Cons: rooms in motel-style building have less character, on a busy street. ⊠*20 E. Main St.* ☎*860/536–1506 or 800/243–2588* ⊕*www.whalersinnmystic.com* ⟳*49 rooms* ⚭*In-room: Wi-Fi. In-hotel: 2 restaurants, no-smoking rooms* ⊟*AE, DC, MC, V.*

STONINGTON

7 mi southeast of Mystic, 57 mi east of New Haven.

The pretty village of Stonington pokes into Fishers Island Sound. A quiet fishing community clustered around white-spired churches, Stonington is far less commercial than Mystic. In the 19th century, though, this was a bustling whaling, sealing, and transportation center. Historic buildings line the town green and border both sides of Water Street up to the imposing Old Lighthouse Museum.

WHAT TO SEE

Old Lighthouse Museum. This museum occupies a lighthouse that was built in 1823 and moved to higher ground 17 years later. Climb to the top of the tower for a spectacular view of Long Island Sound and three states. Six rooms of exhibits depict the varied history of the small coastal town. ⊠*7 Water St.* ☎*860/535–1440* ⊕*www.stonington history.org/light.htm* ⊠*$5* ⊗*May–Oct., daily 10–5; Nov.–Apr., by appointment.*

Stonington Vineyards. At this small coastal winery, you can browse through the works of local artists in the small gallery or enjoy a picnic lunch on the grounds. The vineyard's Seaport White, a vidal-chardonnay blend, is a nice accompaniment. ⊠*523 Taugwonk Rd.* ☎*860/535–1222 or 800/421–9463* ⊕*www.stoningtonvineyards.com* ⊠*Free* ⊗*Daily 11–5, tours at 2.*

WHERE TO STAY

$$$–$$$$ ★ ▓**Inn at Stonington.** The views of Stonington Harbor and Fishers Island Sound are spectacular from this waterfront inn in the heart of Stonington Village. Each room is individually decorated; all have fireplaces, and most have whirlpool baths. Kayaks and bicycles are available for use. Those coming by boat can use the inn's 400-foot deepwater pier. Pros: smartly furnished rooms, walking distance from village shops and dining, great water views. Cons: no restaurant on site, this is a new building that looks but isn't actually historic. ⊠*60 Water St.* ☎*860/535–2000* ⊕*www.innatstonington.com* ⟳*18 rooms* ⚭*In-room: Ethernet. In-hotel: gym, bicycles, no kids under 14, no-smoking rooms* ⊟*AE, MC, V* ⟊*CP.*

$$$–$$$$ ▓**Randall's Ordinary.** The inn's very simple accommodations are across the way in the early 19th-century barn; all have authentic early Colonial appointments, along with modern baths with whirlpool tubs and showers; some have fireplaces. There is also a cabin and a circular-

shaped suite in the silo. At the on-site restaurant the waiters dress in Colonial garb and choices, which change daily, might include Nantucket scallops or smoked turkey. **Pros:** romantic and historic rooms, peaceful setting, convenient to the coast and casinos. **Cons:** restaurant somewhat overrated. ✉ *Rte. 2, 7 mi north of Stonington North Stonington* 🕾 *860/599–4540 or 877/599–4540* ⊕ *www.randallsordinary. com* ⤳ *11 rooms, 1 suite, 1 cabin* ᴸ *In-room: dial-up. In-hotel: restaurant, no elevator, no-smoking rooms* ⊟ *AE, MC, V.*

THE QUIET CORNER

Few visitors to Connecticut experience the old-fashioned ways of the state's "Quiet Corner," a vast patch of sparsely populated towns that seem a world away from the rest of the state. The Quiet Corner has a reclusive allure: people used to leave New York City for the Litchfield Hills; now many are leaving for northeastern Connecticut, where the stretch of Route 169 from Brooklyn past Woodstock has been named a National Scenic Byway.

The cultural capital of the Quiet Corner is Putnam, a small mill city on the Quinebaug River whose formerly industrial town center has been transformed into a year-round antiques mart. Smaller jewels are Pomfret and Woodstock—two towns where authentic Colonial homesteads still seem to outnumber the contemporary, charmless clones that are springing up all too rapidly across the state.

POMFRET

6 mi north of Brooklyn.

Pomfret, one of the grandest towns in the region, was once known as the inland Newport because it attracted the wealthy, who summered here in large "cottages." Today it is a quiet stopping-off point along Route 169, designated one of the most scenic byways in the country by the National Scenic Byway Program.

WHAT TO SEE

Sharpe Hill Vineyard. Centered around an 18th-century-style barn in the hills of Pomfret, this vineyard gives tastings and serves lunch and dinner in a European-style wine garden and Fireside Tavern, Friday through Sunday, depending on the season (advance reservations are essential). Its Ballet of Angels, a heavenly semidry white, just may be New England's top-selling wine. ✉ *108 Wade Rd.* 🕾 *860/974–3549* ⊕ *www.sharpehill.com* 🎫 *Free* ⊙ *Fri.–Sun. 11–5.*

SPORTS & THE OUTDOORS

Connecticut Audubon Center at Pomfret. Adjacent to the Connecticut Audubon Bafflin Sanctuary's more than 700 acres of rolling meadows, grassland habitats, forests, and streams, this nature center presents environmental-education programs for all ages, seasonal lectures and workshops, and changing natural-history exhibits. Miles of self-guided trails provide excellent birding. ✉ *189 Pomfret St. (Rte. 169)*

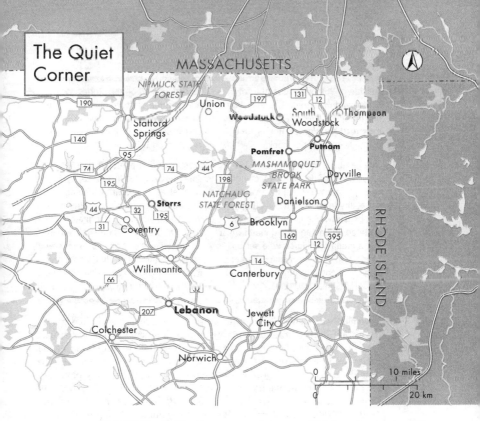

☎ 860/928-4948 ⊕ www.ctaudubon.org/visit/pomfret.htm ✉ Free ☉ Sanctuary daily dawn–dusk, center Wed.–Sun. noon–4.

WHERE TO EAT

$$$$
Fodor's Choice
★
CONTINENTAL

✕ **Golden Lamb Buttery.** Connecticut's most unusual dining experience has achieved almost legendary status. Eating here—in a converted barn on a 1,000-acre farm—is far more than a chance to enjoy good continental food: it's a social and gastronomical event. There is one seating each for lunch and dinner; choose from one of four entrées, which might include roast duck or chateaubriand. Owners Bob and Virginia "Jimmie" Booth have a hay wagon that you can ride before dinner (a musician accompanies you). ⊠ *499 Bush Hill Rd., off Rte. 169, Brooklyn* ☎ *860/774-4423* ⚞ *Reservations essential* ▭ *AE, D, MC, V* ☉ *Closed Sun. and Mon. No dinner Tues.–Thurs.*

$$–$$$
AMERICAN

✕ **The Harvest.** This romantic country restaurant is alive with fresh flowers, glimmering candles, antiques, and touches of chintz. The menu focuses heavily on steaks with a wide range of cuts and sauces, as well as such contemporary American grills as pistachio-crusted salmon with a mango sauce, and blue-crab cakes with pineapple salsa. There's an excellent Sunday brunch. ⊠ *37 Putnam Rd.* ☎ *860/928-0008* ▭ *AE, MC, V* ☉ *Closed Mon. No lunch Sat.*

CLOSE UP

Gertrude Chandler Warner: Teacher Turned Writer

Outside of Putnam, you might not have heard of Getrude Chandler Warner, but many kids across the country have read her beloved Boxcar Children adventure series books.

Though never having finished high school, Warner became a teacher during World War I and discovered her ability to connect with youngsters. She began writing children's books centered around an abandoned boxcar and a group of children who set up house in it. She was inspired by her own childhood adventures at the railroad tracks near her home.

As she worked on the stories, Warner read the drafts to her first-grade classes. There are 10 books in the classic series as well as several special spin-off titles.

Warner died at age 89 in 1979. A small museum/bookstore set up in—what else?—a boxcar at the edge of town pays tribute to the author who was a Putnam native and lifelong resident. The museum is generally open on the weekends from 11 AM to 3 PM early May through early October, but it's best to call ahead before visiting. Try the city office at 860/963–6800.

$$ ✕**Vanilla Bean Café.** Homemade soups, sandwiches, and baked goods ★ have long been a tradition at this comfortable café inside a restored AMERICAN 19th-century barn. Dinner entrées such as smoked mozzarella-and-basil ravioli and pan-seared sea scallops served over baby spinach are also becoming increasingly popular. Belgian waffles and blueberry pancakes are breakfast highlights. Enjoy all this, along with an art gallery and folk entertainment, too. ✉*450 Deerfield Rd. (off U.S. 44, Rte. 97, and Rte. 169)* ☎*860/928–1562* ▭*AE, MC, V* ☉*No dinner Mon. and Tues.*

PUTNAM

5 mi northeast of Pomfret.

Ambitious antiques dealers have reinvented Putnam, a mill town 30 mi west of Providence, Rhode Island, that became neglected after the Depression. Putnam's downtown, with more than 400 antiques dealers, is the heart of the Quiet Corner's antiques trade.

SHOPPING
The four-level **Antiques Marketplace** (✉*109 Main St.* ☎*860/928–0442*) houses the wares of nearly 300 dealers, from fine furniture to tchotchkes and collectibles. **Arts & Framing** (✉*112 Main St.* ☎*860/963–0105* ⊕*www.artsandframingputnam.com*) sells antique art and also provides art restoration and framing services. **Antiques Unlimited** (✉*91 Main St.* ☎*860/963–2599*) specializes in 19th- and 20th-century sofas, desks, light fixtures, and decorative accents.

WHERE TO EAT & STAY
$$-$$$ ✕**85 Main.** This stylish trattoria-bistro is *the* place to go for a break AMERICAN from antiquing. If you go for lunch, your choice could be a curried chicken salad, a veal meatloaf sandwich, or a burger and fries; at din-

ner anything from a lobster risotto to the orange-and-coriander chicken with chipotle-mashed sweet potatoes, or Asian beef skewers with a citrus-soy sauce. There is also a raw bar serving clams, oysters, shrimp, and ceviche. ✉85 Main St. ☎860/928–1660 ☲AE, MC, V.

¢-$ 🔠**Country Hearth Inn & Suites.** Less than 2 mi from downtown Putnam, the Country Heart Inn is a good base for antiquers. Half the rooms, which are decorated with cream-color walls or print wallpaper and run-of-the-mill furnishings typical of a budget property, overlook a pond. **Pros:** close to downtown Putnam, affordable rates. **Cons:** fairly bland decor. ✉5 Heritage Rd. ☎860/928–7961 or 800/511–7304 ⊕www.kingsinnputnam.com ⤳40 rooms, 1 suite ₰In-room: refrigerator (some), dial-up. In-hotel: restaurant, bar, pool ☲AE, D, DC, MC, V ❑CP.

WOODSTOCK

5 mi northwest of Putnam.

The landscape of this enchanting town is splendid in every season—the rolling hills seem to stretch for miles. Scenic roads take you past antiques shops, a country inn in the grand tradition, orchards, grassy fields and grazing livestock, and the fairgrounds of one of the state's oldest—and most popular—agricultural fairs held each Labor Day weekend.

WHAT TO SEE

★ **Roseland Cottage.** This pink board-and-batten Gothic-revival house was built in 1846 as a summer home for New York silk merchant, publisher, and abolitionist Henry C. Bowen. The house and outbuildings (including a carriage house with a private bowling alley) hold a prominent place in history, having hosted four U.S. presidents (Grant, Hayes, Harrison, and McKinley). The parterre garden includes 21 flower beds surrounded by 600 yards of boxwood hedge. ✉556 Rte. 169 ☎860/928–4074 ⊕www.spnea.org/visit/homes/roseland.htm ☑$8 ☉June–mid-Oct., Fri.–Sun. 11–4.

SHOPPING

The **Christmas Barn** (✉835 Rte. 169 ☎860/928–7652 ⊕www.thechrist masbarnonline.com) has 12 rooms of country and Christmas goods. **Scranton's Shops** (✉300 Rte. 169 ☎860/928–3738) sells antiques and the wares of 60 regional artisans. **Whispering Hill Farm** (✉Rte. 169 ☎860/928–0162) sells supplies for rug hooking and braiding, quilting, and needlework, mixed with an assortment of antiques.

WHERE TO STAY

$$-$$$ 🔠**Inn at Woodstock Hill.** This inn on a hill overlooking the countryside has sumptuous rooms with antiques, four-poster beds, fireplaces, pitched ceilings, and timber beams. The attractive chintz-and-prints restaurant ($$$) serves creative interpretations of Continental and American fare, such as seared tuna steak with sesame seeds, and New Zealand venison chops with a red-wine reduction. **Pros:** beautiful grounds, many rooms have fireplaces, very good restaurant. **Cons:** Traditional decor is very old-fashioned, somewhat remote location requires a car. ✉94 Plaine

Hill Rd., South Woodstock ☎860/928–0528 ⊕*www.woodstockhill. com* ⇆*19 rooms, 3 suites* ⚷*In-room: Ethernet (some), Wi-Fi (some). In-hotel: restaurant, no-smoking rooms* ☰*AE, D, MC, V* ⍟*CP.*

STORRS

25 mi southwest of Woodstock.

The majority of Storrs's hillside and farmland is occupied by the 4,400 acres and some 18,000 students of the main campus of the University of Connecticut (UConn). Many cultural programs, sporting events, and other happenings take place here.

WHAT TO SEE

⟳ **Ballard Institute and Museum of Puppetry.** Hand puppets, rod puppets, body puppets, shadow puppets, marionettes—this museum has more than 2,000 puppets in its extraordinary collection. Half were created under the direction of Frank Ballard, a master of puppetry who established the country's first complete undergraduate and graduate degree program in puppetry at UConn more than three decades ago. Exhibits change seasonally. If you're lucky you might even catch Oscar the Grouch from *Sesame Street* on display. ⊠*University of Connecticut Depot Campus, Weaver Rd. off U.S. 44* ☎*860/486–4605* ⊕*www. bimp.uconn.edu* ⊠*Donation suggested* ⊙*Late Apr.–early Nov., Fri.– Sun. noon–5.*

William Benton Museum of Art. The permanent collection of this museum includes European and American paintings, drawings, prints, photographs, and sculptures from the 16th century to the present. Its galleries host changing exhibitions, lectures, recitals, and readings. The museum also has a café and museum shop. ⊠*University of Connecticut, 245 Glenbrook Rd.* ☎*860/486–4520* ⊕*www.benton.uconn.edu* ⊠*Free* ⊙*Tues.–Fri. 10–4:30, weekends 1–4:30; café and shop weekdays 10– 4:30, weekends 1–4:30.*

NIGHTLIFE & THE ARTS

From spring through fall, the **Mansfield Drive-In** (⊠*Rtes. 31 and 32, Mansfield* ☎*860/423–4441*), with three big screens, is one of the state's few remaining drive-in theaters—there's a huge flea market held on the grounds each Sunday.

LEBANON

20 mi southeast of Coventry.

Lebanon is a quiet town known for its expansive town green stretching 1 mi head to toe and for the Trumbulls: Revolutionary resident Jonathan Trumbull was royal governor of the colony of Connecticut. He was the only Colonial governor to side with the Continentals and provided highly valuable food supplies to the starving soldiers in the winter of 1780. President George Washington is said to have written in his diary, "No other man than Trumbull would have procured them and no other state could have furnished them."

WHAT TO SEE

Governor Jonathan Trumbull House Museum. This circa-1735 home, furnished in period decor, belonged to the only Connecticut governor (1769–84) to turn against the Crown and support the Colonies' War for Independence. Also on the property is the Wadsworth Stable, where George Washington's horse slept. ⊠ *West Town St,* ☎ *860/642-7558* ⊕ *www.lebanontownhall.org/historic-sites.htm* ⊠ *$3* ⊘ *Mid-May–mid-Oct., Wed.–Sun. noon–4.*

CONNECTICUT ESSENTIALS

Research prices, get travel advice, and book your trip at fodors.com.

4

TRANSPORTATION

BY AIR

Most people visiting Connecticut from afar fly into **Bradley International Airport** (⊠ *11 Schoephoester Rd., Windsor Locks* ☎ *860/292-2000* ⊕ *www.bradleyairport.com*), north of Hartford, which is served by most major airlines, including discount carrier Southwest, and has direct flights from most major cities. But depending on where you're headed in Connecticut, it can also make sense to fly into New York City, Boston, or Providence. Additionally, **Tweed/New Haven Airport** (⊠ *155 Burr St., New Haven* ☎ *203/466-8833* ⊕ *www.flytweed.com*) has several flights per day on US Airways to Philadelphia.

AIRPORT TRANSFERS **Connecticut Limo** (☎ *800/472-5466* ⊕ *www.ctlimo.com*) operates bus and van service from Bradley International Airport and both New York City airports to many towns throughout Connecticut. **Prime Time Shuttle** (☎ *800/377-8701* ⊕ *www.2theairport.com*) serves mainly New Haven and Fairfield counties with service to and from both New York airports.

BY BOAT & FERRY

From New London, **Cross Sound Ferry** (☎ *860/443-5281* ⊕ *www.longislandferry.com*) operates year-round passenger and car service to and from Orient Point, Long Island, New York. Its high-speed passenger ferry can make the trip in 40 minutes. **Interstate Navigation Co.** (☎ *860/442-9553* ⊕ *www.blockislandferry.com*) operates passenger and car service from New London to and from Block Island, Rhode Island, from June to early September. From Bridgeport, the **Bridgeport-Port Jefferson Steamboat Co.** (☎ *203/335-2040* ⊕ *www.bpjferry.com*) operates year-round.

BY BUS

Peter Pan Bus Lines (☎ *800/343-9999* ⊕ *www.peterpanbus.com*) and **Greyhound Lines Inc.** (☎ *800/231-2222* ⊕ *www.greyhound.com*) connect a number of towns throughout Connecticut with Boston, New York, and other cities in the Northeast.

BY CAR

The interstates are the quickest routes between many points in Connecticut, but they can be busy and ugly. From New York City head north on Interstate 95, which hugs the Connecticut shoreline into Rhode Island, or, to reach the Litchfield Hills and Hartford, head north on Interstate 684, then east on Interstate 84. From center New England, go south on Interstate 91, which bisects Interstate 84 in Hartford and Interstate 95 in New Haven. From Boston take Interstate 95 south through Providence or take the Massachusetts Turnpike west to Interstate 84. Interstate 395 runs north–south from southeastern Connecticut to Massachusetts.

If time allows, skip the interstates in favor of the historic Merritt Parkway (Route 15), which winds between Greenwich and Middletown; U.S. 7 and Route 8, extending between Interstate 95 and the Litchfield Hills; Route 9, which heads south from Hartford through the Connecticut River valley to Old Saybrook; and scenic Route 169, which meanders through the Quiet Corner. Maps are available free from the Connecticut Office of Tourism.

BY TRAIN

Amtrak (☎ *800/872–7245* ⊕ *www.amtrak.com*) runs from New York to Boston, stopping in Stamford, Bridgeport, and New Haven before heading either north through Hartford and several other towns or east to Old Saybrook and Mystic. **Metro-North Railroad** (☎ *212/532–4900 or 800/638–7646* ⊕ *www.mta.info*) trains from New York stop locally between Greenwich and New Haven, and a few trains head inland to New Canaan, Danbury, and Waterbury. **Shoreline East** (☎ *203/777–7433, 800/255–7433 toll-free in CT* ⊕ *www.shorelineeast.com*) commuter rail service provides weekday service between New Haven and New London.

CONTACTS & RESOURCES

VISITOR INFORMATION

State Tourism Contacts **Connecticut Commission on Culture & Tourism** (✉ *1 Financial Plaza, 755 Main St., Hartford* ☎ *888/288-4748* ⊕ *www.ctvisit.com*).

Local & Regional Tourism Contacts **Connecticut's Heritage River Valley–Central Regional Tourism District** (✉ *31 Pratt St., 4th fl., Hartford* ☎ *860/244-8181 or 800/793-4480* ⊕ *www.visitctriver.com*). **Coastal Fairfield County Convention and Visitors Bureau** (✉ *Mathews Park, 297 West Ave., Norwalk* ☎ *203/853-7770 or 800/866-7925* ⊕ *www.coastalct.com*). **Greater New Haven Convention and Visitors Bureau** (✉ *59 Elm St., New Haven* ☎ *203/777-8550 or 800/332-7829* ⊕ *www.newhavencvb.org*). **Litchfield Hills–Northwest Connecticut Convention and Visitors Bureau** (☏ *Box 968, Litchfield 06759* ☎ *888/588-7880* ⊕ *www. northwestct.com*). **Mystic Country–Eastern Regional Tourism District** (✉ *32 Huntington St., New London* ☎ *800/863-6569* ⊕ *www.mysticmore.com*).

Vermont

WORD OF MOUTH

"Vermont is probably the most bucolic and relaxing state in the Northeast. Towns like Woodstock, Chester, Stowe and Waitsfield make good choices. The Round Barn Inn in Waitsfield is very idyllic, as is Marshland Farm in Quechee. . . ."

—zootsi

By Michael de
Zayas

VERMONT IS AN ENTIRE STATE of hidden treasures. Sprawl has no place here. The pristine countryside is dotted with farms and tiny towns with church steeples, village greens, and clapboard colonial-era houses. Highways are devoid of billboards by law, and on some roads, cows still stop traffic twice a day, en route to and from the pasture. In spring, sap boils in sugarhouses, some built generations ago, and up the road, a chef trained at the New England Culinary Institute in Montpelier might use the maple syrup to glaze a pork tenderloin.

It's the landscape, for the most part, that attracts people to Vermont. The rolling hills belie the rugged terrain underneath the green canopy of forest growth. In summer, clear lakes and streams provide ample opportunities for swimming, boating, and fishing; the hills attract hikers and mountain bikers. The more than 14,000 mi of roads, many of them only intermittently traveled by cars, are great for road biking. In fall, the leaves have their last hurrah, painting the mountainsides a stunning array of yellow, gold, red, and orange. In winter, Vermont's ski resorts are the prime enticement. Here you'll find the best ski resorts in the eastern U.S., centered along the spine of the Green Mountains north to south. The traditional heart of skiing is the town of Stowe.

Vermont may, in many ways, seem locked in time, but technological sophistication appears where you least expect it: wireless Internet access in a 19th-century farmhouse-turned-inn and cell phone coverage from the state's highest peaks. Luckily, these 21st-century perks have been able to infiltrate without many visual cues. Like an old farmhouse under renovation, Vermont's historic exterior is still the main attraction.

EXPLORING VERMONT

Vermont can be divided into three regions. The southern part of the state, flanked by Bennington on the west and Brattleboro on the east, played an important role in Vermont's Revolutionary War–era drive to independence (yes, there was once a Republic of Vermont) and its eventual statehood. The central part is characterized by rugged mountains and the gently rolling dairy lands near Lake Champlain. Northern Vermont is home to the state's capital, Montpelier, and its largest city, Burlington, as well as its most rural area, the Northeast Kingdom.

ABOUT THE RESTAURANTS
Home to the New England Culinary Institute, Vermont tends to keep the chefs who train here. The result: cuisine in Vermont is often exceptional. Seasonal menus use local fresh herbs and vegetables, along with native game. Look for imaginative approaches to native New England foods such as maple syrup (Vermont is the largest U.S. producer), dairy products (especially cheese), native fruits and berries, "new Vermont" products such as salsa and salad dressings, and venison, quail, pheasant, and other game.

Many of the state's restaurants belong to the Vermont Fresh Network (⊕www.vermontfresh.net), a partnership that encourages chefs to cre-

VERMONT TOP 5

■ **Small-town charm.** Vermont rolls out a seemingly never-ending supply of tiny, picturesque towns made of steeples, general stores, village squares, red barns, and B&Bs.

■ **Skiing.** The East's best skiing takes place in uncrowded, modern facilities, with great views and lots and lots of fresh snow.

■ **Fall foliage.** Perhaps the most vivid colors in North America wave from the trees in September and October, when the whole state is ablaze.

■ **Gorgeous landscapes.** A sparsely populated, heavily forested state, this is an ideal place to find peace and quiet amid the mountains and valleys.

■ **Tasty and healthy eats.** The state's great soil and focus on local farming and ingredients yields great cheeses, dairies, orchards, local food resources, and restaurants.

5

ate menus from local produce. A participating chef might have picked the mesclun greens on your salad plate that morning, or the butternut squash in your soup might have been harvested by the restaurant's neighboring farmer. The food is delicious and the chefs are helping to keep Vermont's farmers in business. Your chances of finding a table for dinner vary with the season: lengthy waits are common at peak times (a reservation is always advisable); the slow months are April and November. Some of the best dining is found at country inns.

ABOUT THE HOTELS

Vermont's only large chain hotels are in Burlington and in Rutland. Elsewhere you'll find just quaint inns, bed-and-breakfasts, and small motels. The many lovely and sometimes quite luxurious inns and B&Bs provide what many people consider the quintessential Vermont lodging experience. Most areas have traditional base ski condos; at these you'll sacrifice charm for ski and stay deals and proximity to the lifts. Rates are highest during foliage season, from late September to mid-October, and lowest in late spring (April is typically the heart of "mud season") and November, although many properties close during these times. Winter, of course, is high season at Vermont's ski resorts.

WHAT IT COSTS					
	¢	$	$$	$$$	$$$$
RESTAU-RANTS	under $10	$10–$16	$17–$24	$25–$35	over $35
HOTELS	under $100	$100–$149	$150–$199	$200–$250	over $250

Prices are per person, for a main course at dinner. Prices are for a standard double room during peak season and not including tax or gratuities. Some inns add a 15%–18% service charge.

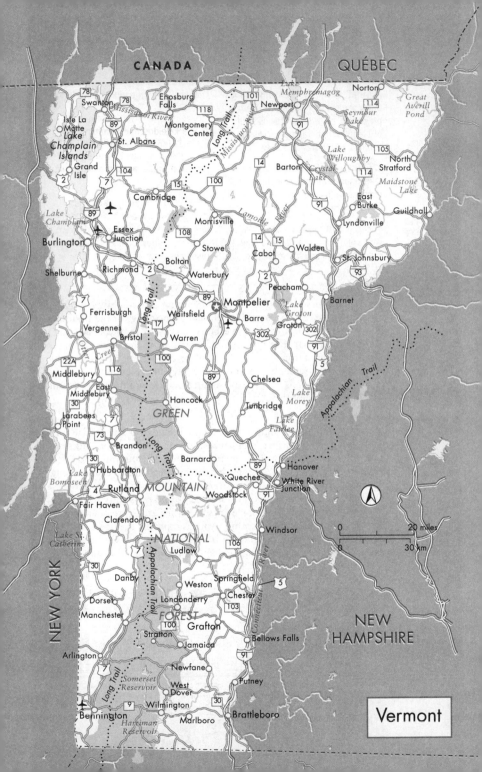

PLANNING YOUR TRIP

BUDGETING YOUR TIME

There are many ways to take advantage of Vermont's beauty—skiing or hiking its mountains, biking or driving its back roads, fishing or sailing its waters, shopping for local products, visiting its museums and sights, or simply finding the perfect inn and never leaving the front porch.

Distances are relatively short, yet the mountains and many back roads will slow a traveler's pace. You can see a representative north–south section of Vermont in a few days; if you have up to a week you can hit the highlights. Note that many inns have two-night minimum stays on weekends and holidays.

WHEN TO GO

In summer, the state is lush and green, while in winter, the hills and towns are blanketed with snow and skiers travel from around the East Coast to challenge Vermont's peaks. Fall is one of the most amazing times to come. If you have never seen a kaleidoscope of autumn colors, a trip to Vermont is worth braving the slow-moving traffic and paying the extra money for fall lodging. The only time things really slow down is during "mud" season—otherwise known as late fall and spring. Even innkeepers have told guests to come another time.

GETTING THERE & AROUND

Vermont is bifurcated by a mountainous north–south middle; on either side are two main highways: scenic Route 7 on the western side, and I-91 on the east (I-91 begins in New Haven, and runs through Hartford, central Massachussets, and along the Connecticut River in Vermont to the Canadian border). Flights from Boston connect to Rutland; otherwise the only major airport is Burlington.

SOUTHERN VERMONT

Cross into the Green Mountain State from Massachusetts on Interstate 91, and you might feel as if you've entered a new country. There isn't a town in sight. What you see are forested hills punctuated by rolling pastures. When you reach Brattleboro, no fast-food joints or strip malls line the exits to signal your arrival at southeastern Vermont's gateway city. En route to downtown, you pass by Victorian-era homes on tree-lined streets. From Brattleboro, you can cross over the spine of the Green Mountains toward Bennington and Manchester.

The state's southwest corner is the southern terminus of the Green Mountain National Forest, dotted with lakes, threaded with trails and old forest roads, and home to four big ski resorts: Bromley, Stratton, Mt. Snow, and Haystack Mountain.

The towns are listed in counterclockwise order in this chapter, beginning in the east in Brattleboro, then traveling west along Route 9 toward Bennington, then north to Manchester and Weston and south along scenic Routes 100 and 30 back to Townshend and Newfane.

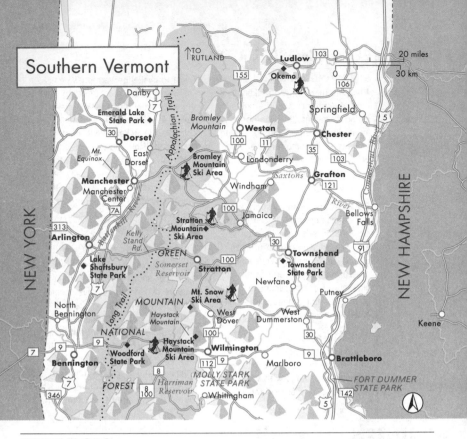

BRATTLEBORO

60 mi south of White River Junction.

Brattleboro has drawn political activists and earnest counterculturists since the 1960s. Today, the city of 12,000 is still politically and culturally active, making it Vermont's hippest city outside of Burlington.

WHAT TO SEE

Brattleboro Museum and Art Center. Downtown is the hub of Brattleboro's art scene, with this museum in historic Union Station at the forefront. It presents changing exhibits created by locally, nationally, and internationally renowned artists. ⊠*10 Vernon St.* ☎*802/257–0124* ⊕*www.brattleboromuseum.org* ⊠*$4, free 1st Fri. each month 5–8:30* ⊙ *Wed.–Mon. 11–5, 1st Fri. each month 11–8:30.*

SPORTS & THE OUTDOORS

CANOEING **Vermont Canoe Touring Center** (⊠*451 Putney Rd.* ☎*802/257–5008*) conducts guided and self-guided tours, rents canoes and kayaks, and provides a shuttle service.

SHOPPING

ARTWORKS **Gallery in the Woods** (✉ *143 Main St.* ☎ *802/257–4777* ⊕ *www.galleryin thewoods.com*) sells art, jewelry, and glassware from around the world. To get a sense of the vibrant works being produced by young local artists, head to the back of Brattleboro's **Turn it Up** record shop to find **Through the Music** (✉ *2 Elliot St.* ☎ *802/779–3188*), an otherwise easy-to-miss gallery. The excellent contemporary art spans genres from painting to pottery. **Vermont Artisan Designs** (✉ *106 Main St.* ☎ *802/257–7044* ⊕ *www.vtartisans.com*) displays ceramics, glass, wood, clothing, jewelry, and furniture from over 300 artists.

OFF THE
BEATEN
PATH

Putney. Nine miles upriver, this small town, with a population of just over 2,000, is the country cousin of bustling Brattleboro and is a haven for writers, artists, and craftspeople. There are dozens of pottery studios to visit and a few orchards. The town also has a great general store. Watch wool being spun into yarn at the **Green Mountain Spinnery** (✉ *7 Brickyard La., off I–91 Exit 4* ☎ *802/387–4528 or 800/321–9665* ⊕ *www.spinnery.com*). The factory shop sells yarn, knitting accessories, and patterns. Tours are conducted at 1:30 on the first and third Tuesday of the month. **Harlow's Sugar House** (✉ *563 Bellows Falls Rd., Putney* ☎ *802/387–5852* ⊕ *www.vermontsugar.com*), 2 mi north of Putney, has a working cider mill and sugarhouse, as well as seasonal apple and berry picking. You can buy cider, maple syrup, and other items in the gift shop.

NIGHTLIFE & THE ARTS

NIGHTLIFE **Molo's Eye Cafe** (✉ *4 High St.* ☎ *802/257–0771*) hosts an open-mike night every Thursday, and live bands Friday and Saturday. **Tinderbox** (✉ *17 Elliot St., 3rd floor* ☎ *no phone*) hosts indie rock shows. **Lathis Theater** (✉ *50 Main St.* ☎ *802/254–6300*) hosts art exhibits when movies aren't playing.

ARTS Brattleboro has a gallery walk on the first Friday of each month from 5:30 to 8:30 PM.

NEED A
BREAK?

The authentic gathering spot in town for coffee and conversation is Mocha Joe's (✉ *82 Main St.* ☎ *802/257-7794*), which takes great care in sourcing beans from places like Kenya, Ethiopia, and Guatemala. This is ground zero for Brattleboro's contemporary bohemian spirit.

WHERE TO EAT

¢-$
AMERICAN

✕**Brattleboro Food Co-op.** Pick up a pre-made sandwich or order a plate of curry chicken at the deli counter, then eat it in a small sitting area in this busy market. The focus is on the natural and organic, with everything from tofu sandwiches to beef satay. The delicatessen is connected to a natural-food market, and serves breakfast. ✉ *2 Main St.* ☎ *802/257–0236* ▭ *MC, V.*

$$-$$$
ITALIAN

✕**Max's.** Pasta creations at this trendy place include artichoke-mascarpone ravioli or Tuscan style cauliflower with linguine. Complementing this *nuovo* Italian menu are eclectic entrées such as mahimahi in parchment, and lavender tea–smoked salmon. Sunday brunch is both traditional and adventurous, with everything from eggs to curry rice kedgeree. ✉ *889 Putney Rd.* ☎ *802/254–7747* ▣ *MC, V* ⊘ *No dinner Mon. Closed Tues.*

$$-$$$ × **Peter Havens.** In a town better known for tofu than toniness, this chic
★ little bistro knows just what to do with a filet mignon: serve it with
STEAKHOUSE Roquefort walnut butter. One room is painted a warm red, another
in sage; both are punctuated by copies of Botero paintings creating a
look that is one of the most sophisticated in the state. Try the house-
cured gravlax made with lemon vodka or the fresh seasonal seafood,
which even includes a spring fling with soft-shell crabs. The wine list
is superb. ✉ *32 Elliot St.* ☎ *802/257–3333* ▣ *AE, MC, V* ⊘ *Closed
Sun. and Mon. No lunch.*

$$$$ × **T.J. Buckley's.** It's easy to miss this tiny restaurant, but those who
FodorśChoice know about it consider it one of the most romantic little restaurants
★ in southern Vermont. Open the doors to the sleek black 1920s diner,
ECLECTIC and you'll enter what amounts to an intimate—a very intimate—theater. There are 18 seats for the show. The stage is an open kitchen, the
kitchen flames a few feet away. And working under the whisper of
vocal jazz and candlelight is the star of the show: Michael Fuller, the
dashing owner and sole chef who has been at the helm for 25 years.
The three tactful waitresses are delightful supporting players. The contemporary menu is conveyed verbally each day and is based on locally
available ingredients. It's pre-theater dinner and theater all in one, a
romantic triumph. ✉ *132 Elliot St.* ☎ *802/257–4922* ⫣ *Reservations
essential* ▣ *No credit cards* ⊘ *No lunch. Closed Mon. and Tues.*

¢-$ × **Top of the Hill Grill.** Hickory-smoked ribs, beef brisket, apple-smoked
SOUTHERN turkey, and pulled pork are a few of the favorites at this barbecue
just outside town. Larger parties can opt for "family-style" dinners.
Homemade pecan pie is the dessert of choice. You can sit indoors in
the informal dining room with big windows, but the best seats are outdoors at picnic tables overlooking the West River. ✉ *632 Putney Rd.*
☎ *802/258–9178* ▣ *No credit cards* ⊘ *Closed Nov.–mid-Apr.*

WHERE TO STAY

$$ ▦ **Forty Putney Road.** Tim and Amy Brady, the young and engaging
couple who took over the property in 2007, have breathed new life into
this French-style manse, restoring some of its more interesting original
features, like nickel plated bathroom fixtures, and adding new ones
like flat screen TVs. They've also made sure that it's full of thoughtful
and comforting details, like a mini-fridge stocked with complimentary
soda, water, granola bars, and chips. Other treats include a hot tub,
a billiard table, and the neighboring Retreat Meadows, a bird sanctu-
ary at the junction of the West and Connecticut rivers that offers good
hiking trails. There's no restaurant, but a decent pub menu and wine
are offered. Stay here if you want a good B&B within walking distance
of downtown. **Pros:** caring hosts; clean, remodeled rooms. **Cons:** short
walk into town. ✉ *192 Putney Rd.* ☎ *802/254–6268 or 800/941–2413*
⊕ *www.fortyputneyroad.com* ↩ *5 rooms, 1 suite* ♿ *In-room: DVD,
Wi-Fi. In-hotel: room service, bar, no elevator, laundry service, public
Internet, public Wi-Fi, no kids under 12, no-smoking rooms* ▣ *AE,
D, MC, V* ⏹*BP.*

$$-$$$
Fodor's Choice
★

⊞ Hickory Ridge House. If you're looking for a relaxing country getaway in southeast Vermont, this historic, redbrick, 1808 Federal-style mansion, a former sheep farm set on a wide meadow, is a sure bet. The house has a sturdy comfort that distinguishes it from daintier inns. Owners Gillian and Dennis, along with their dog Jack, bring an English touch to it all. Most rooms have Rumford fireplaces and canopy beds; they all have fine linens. A separate two-bedroom cottage has a full kitchen. Thousands of acres of nature preserve surround

> **BILLBOARDS NO MORE**
>
> Did you know that there are no billboards in Vermont? The state banned them in 1967 (similar laws exist in Maine, Alaska and Hawaii). The last one came down in 1975. The motive, of course, was so that when you look out your window, you see trees and other scenic sights, not advertisements. (It may, however, make playing the Alphabet Game with your child a bit difficult.)

the property's eight acres of meadow, making it great for hiking and cross-country skiing. Pros: peaceful, scenic property; terrific house, quintessential B&B experience. Cons: can be expensive. ⊠ *53 Hickory Ridge Rd., 11 mi north of Brattleboro, Putney* ☎ *802/387–5709 or 800/380–9218* ⊕ *www.hickoryridgehouse.com* ⇆ *6 rooms, 1 cottage* ⚷ *In-room: DVD, VCR (some), Wi-Fi. In-hotel: no elevator, public Internet, public Wi-Fi, some pets allowed, no-smoking rooms* ⊟ *MC, V* ⎮⊚⎮*BP.*

¢-$$

⊞ Latchis Hotel. To stay in the heart of town at a low rate, you can do no better than the Latchis. The three-story art deco landmark is run by a non-profit group dedicated to preserving and restoring the 1938 building. Rooms are not lavish, but they are clean and functional, and have original sinks and tiling in the bathrooms. Most overlook Main Street, with New Hampshire's mountains in the background. The lobby has original and notably colorful terrazzo floors. Downstairs you can catch a movie under the impressive zodiac ceiling of the Latchis Theater or eat at the Flat St. Brew Pub. **Pros:** heart-of-town location; inexpensive. **Cons:** clean but dull furnishings. ⊠ *50 Main St.* ☎ *802/254–6300 or 800/798–6301* ⊕ *www.latchis.com* ⇆ *30 rooms, 3 suites* ⚷ *In-room: refrigerator, Wi-Fi. In-hotel: public Wi Fi, no smoking rooms* ⊟ *AE, MC, V* ⎮⊚⎮*CP.*

WILMINGTON

18 mi west of Brattleboro.

The village of Wilmington, with its classic Main Street lined with 18th- and 19th-century buildings, anchors the Mt. Snow Valley. Most of the valley's lodging and dining establishments, however, line Route 100, which travels 5 mi north to West Dover and Mt. Snow, where skiers flock on winter weekends. The area abounds with cultural activity year-round, from concerts to art exhibits.

5

WHAT TO SEE

☺ ★ **Adams Farm.** At this working farm you can collect fresh eggs from the chicken coop, feed a rabbit, milk a goat, ride a tractor or a pony, and jump in the hay—and run through the corn maze in summer and take sleigh rides in winter. The indoor livestock barn is open Wednesday through Sunday, November to mid-June; an outdoor version is open daily the rest of the year. The farm store sells more than 200 handmade quilts and sweaters. Open all year Wednesday–Sunday 10–5. ⊠ *15 Higley Hill Rd., 3 mi north of Wilmington, off Rte. 100* ☎ *802/464–3762* ⊕ *www.adamsfamilyfarm.com.*

☺ **Southern Vermont Natural History Museum.** This museum, 5 mi east of Wilmington on Route 9, houses one of New England's largest collections of mounted birds, including three extinct birds and a complete collection of mammals native to the Northeast. The museum also has live hawk and owl exhibits. ⊠ *Rte. 9* ☎ *802/464–0048* ⊠ *$3* ⊗ *Memorial Day–late Oct., daily 10–5; late Oct.–Memorial Day, most weekends 10–4, call ahead.*

SPORTS & THE OUTDOORS

BOATING **Green Mountain Flagship Company** (⊠ *Rte. 9, 2 mi west of Wilmington* ☎ *802/464–2975* ⊕ *www.greenmountainflagship.com*) runs Mt. Mills, a 55-passenger cruise boat on Lake Whitingham. The 90-minute cruise takes you by New England's largest nudist beach. You can also rent canoes, kayaks, and sailboats from May to late October.

SKI AREA The closest major ski area to all of the Northeast's big cities, **Mount Snow Resort** (⊠ *400 Mountain Rd., Mount Snow* ☎ *802/464–3333, 802/464–2151 snow conditions, 800/245–7669 lodging* ⊕ *www. mountsnow.com*), is also one of the state's premier family resorts and has a full roster of year-round activities. The almost 800-acre facility encompasses a hotel, 10 condo developments, an 18-hole golf course, a health club and spa, 45 mi of mountain-biking trails, and an extensive network of hiking trails.

Mount Snow prides itself on its 101 fan guns, which has given it the earliest open time of any ski area in the state. More than half of the 107 trails down its 1,700-foot vertical summit are intermediate, wide, and sunny. There are four major downhill areas. The main mountain is where you'll find most of the beginner slopes, especially toward the bottom. The North Face is where you'll find the majority of expert terrain. Corinthia used to be a separate ski mountain, but is now connected with a mix of trail levels. The south face, Sunbrook, has wide, sunny trails. The trails are served by 19 lifts, including 3 high-speed quads. Snowmaking covers 85% of the terrain. There are 98 acres of glades. The ski school's instruction program is designed to help skiers of all ages and abilities. Mount Snow also has five terrain parks of different skill levels, and a 400-foot halfpipe with 18-foot walls. Skiing programs start with the Cub Camp, designed for kids age 3. Snow Camp teaches kids 4 to 6, and Mountain Camp and Mountain Riders is for kids 7 to 14.

Two cross-country ski centers near Mount Snow provide more than 68 mi of varied terrain. **Timber Creek** (⊠*Rte. 100, north of Mount Snow* ☎*802/464–0999* ⊕*www.timbercreekxc.com*) is appealingly small with 9 mi of groomed loops. The groomed trails at the **White House of Wilmington** (⊠*178 Rte. 9* ☎*802/464–2135* ⊕*www.whitehouseinn. com*) cover 30 mi. Both areas have Nordic equipment and snowshoes for rent.

SNOWMOBILE TOURS

High Country Tours (⊠*Rte. 100, West Dover* ☎*802/464–2108*) runs one-hour, two-hour, and ½-day snowmobile tours from two locations: one near Mount Snow, the other west of Wilmington in Searsburg.

SHOPPING

Downtown Wilmington is lined with unique shops and galleries. **Quaigh Design Centre** (⊠*11 W. Main St. [Rte. 9]* ☎*802/464–2780*) sells artwork from Britain and New England—including works by Vermont woodcut artists Sabra Field and Mary Azarian—and Scottish woolens and tartans. **Young and Constantin Gallery** (⊠*10 S. Main St.* ☎*802/464–2515*) sells handblown glassware, ceramics, and art from local and nationally known artisans.

THE ARTS

ARTS

A year-round roster of music, theater, film, and fine art is presented at the **Memorial Hall Center for the Arts** (⊠*14 W. Main St.* ☎*802/464–8411*). In addition to steak and Mexican specialties, the standard fare on weekends at **Poncho's Wreck** (⊠*S. Main St.* ☎*802/464–9320*) is acoustic jazz or mellow rock.

WHERE TO EAT

¢-$

DINER

✕ **Dot's Restaurant.** Look for the classic red neon sign (one of only a handful still permitted in Vermont) at the main corner of Wilmington: Dot's is a local landmark. A photo inside depicts the interior in the early 1940s—except for the soda fountain, all else is identical, from the long counter with swivel chairs to the fireplace in the back. This friendly place is packed with locals and skiers; the menu ranges from chicken cordon bleu to homemade rost beef. Berry berry pancakes are de rigeur for breakfast, and a bowl of turkey chili for lunch. A second location is in a strip mall in West Dover. ⊠*3 West Main St.* ☎*802/464–7284* ⊟*MC, V.*

$$$-$$$$

Fodor'sChoice

★

CONTINENTAL

✕ **Inn at Sawmill Farm.** No other restaurant in Vermont aims as high with its haute Continental food, wine, and service as the restaurant at Sawmill. Order a beer and the bottle is served chilled in a small ice bucket, as if it were champagne. This reverent service, and deference to potables, comes from the top: chef and owner Brill Williams passionately cares for his 17,000-bottle cellar, the biggest restaurant collection in the state. It's also Vermont's only Wine Spectator Grand Award winner. The aim is haute Continental. Try the potato-crusted fish of the day served in beurre blanc sauce, or grilled loin of venison. Gourmands of Mount Snow, this is your place, if only because nobody is trying harder. ⊠*7 Crosstown Rd., at Rte. 100, West Dover* ☎*802/464–8131* or *800/493–1133* ⊕*www.theinnatsawmillfarm.com* ⊟*AE, D, MC, V* ⊗*Closed Easter–late May.*

WHERE TO STAY

$$-$$$ **Deerhill Inn.** The exterior of this inn leaves something to be desired, but the interior makes up for it. The common living room features a large stone fireplace and works by local artists hang on the walls. Guest rooms are cozy and adorned with English floral linens; balcony rooms are more spacious. The wonderful dining room headed by chef and owner Michael Allen is one of the best in town. **Pros:** great restaurant, nicely renovated rooms. **Cons:** building exterior is unimpressive. ⊠ *Valley View Rd., West Dover* ✆ *Box 136, West Dover 05356* ☎ *802/464–3100 or 800/993–3379* ⊕ *www.deerhill.com* ➲ *12 rooms, 2 suites* ⊘ *Closed weekdays in Apr. and Nov.* ♿ *In-room: no a/c, no phone, DVD (some), no TV (some), Wi-Fi. In-hotel: restaurant, bar, pool, no elevator, public Internet, public Wi-Fi, no kids under 12, no-smoking rooms* ▤ *AE, MC, V* ᵀᴼ⎮ *BP, MAP.*

$$$$ **Grand Summit Hotel.** The 200-room base lodge at Mount Snow will be an easy choice for skiers who don't care about anything but getting on the slopes as quickly as possible. Ski-in ski-out ease is the main sell and package deals can make the lodging cheap. The lobby has the look of a traditional ski lodge, with a big center fireplace, but the overall feel is that of an efficient, new hotel. Rooms are clean and fairly basic. A big outdoor heated pool sits beside two hot tubs at the base of the slopes. In summer guests enjoy the property golf and tennis courts. **Pros:** easy ski access; clean, modern property. **Cons:** somewhat bland decor in rooms. ⊠ *Mount Snow Rd., West Dover 05356* ☎ *800/451–4211* ⊕ *www.mountsnow.com/grandsummit.html* ➲ *104 rooms, 96 suites* ♿ *In room: kitchen (some), refrigerator (some), DVD (some), VCR (some), Wi-Fi. In-hotel: 2 restaurants, bar, golf course, tennis courts, pool, gym, spa, children's programs (ages 4–14), laundry service, public Internet, public Wi-Fi, no-smoking rooms* ▤ *AE, D, MC, V.*

$$$$ **Inn at Sawmill Farm.** Full of character and charm, this inn in a converted barn has common rooms elegantly accented with English chintzes, antiques, and Oriental rugs. Each of the guest rooms—in the main inn or in cottages scattered on the property's 22 acres—is individually decorated, and many have sitting areas and fireplaces. Dinner in the formal dining room, as well as a full breakfast, is included in the price of a stay. **Pros:** spacious grounds, attentive service. **Cons:** overload of floral prints in some rooms. ⊠ *7 Crosstown Rd., at Rte 100, West Dover* ☎ *802/464–8131 or 800/493–1133* ⊕ *www.theinnatsaw millfarm.com* ➲ *21 rooms* ♿ *In-room: no phone, no TV. In-hotel: restaurant, tennis court, pool, no kids under 8, no-smoking rooms* ▤ *AE, D, MC, V* ⊘ *Closed Easter–late May* ᵀᴼ⎮ *BP, MAP.*

$$ **White House of Wilmington.** It's hard to miss this 1915 Federal-style ♨ mansion standing imposingly atop a high hill off Route 9 east of Wilmington. Indeed if the President took up residence in Vermont, he (or she) would surely feel at home here. Grand balconies and the main balustraded terrace overlook the hill. If you have kids, you can trust they'll create memories tubing down the hill in winter (tubes are provided). The grand staircase leads to rooms with antique bathrooms and brass wall sconces; some rooms have fireplaces and lofts. There is a cross-country ski touring and snowshoeing center on-site along with 7 mi of

groomed trails. The restaurant has an extensive wine list and undeniably romantic dining in the Mahogany Room, which has its original fireplace and wood paneling. And for anyone who thinks they've seen it all: take a dunk in the small indoor pool, which is formed from an old coal bin and surrounded by hand-painted murals of Roman bath scenes. Pros: great for kids and families; intriguing, big, old-fashioned property; intimate dining. Cons: removed from town activity. ⊠*178 Rte. 9, Wilmington,* ☎*802/464–2135 or 800/541–2135* ⊕*www. whitehouseinn.com* ⤺*24 rooms, 1 cottage* ⚷*In-room: no a/c (some), no phone, no TV, Wi-Fi (some). In-hotel: restaurant, bar, pools, no elevator, laundry service, public Internet, public Wi-Fi, no-smoking rooms* ⊟*AE, D, MC, V* ⓘⓄⓘ*BP.*

BENNINGTON

21 mi west of Wilmington.

Bennington is the commercial focus of Vermont's southwest corner. It's really three towns in one: Downtown Bennington, Old Bennington, and North Bennington. Downtown Bennington, where U.S. 7 and U.S. 9 intersect, has retained much of the industrial character it developed in the 19th century, when paper mills, gristmills, and potteries formed the city's economic base.

West of downtown, Old Bennington is a National Register Historic District centered along the axis of Monument Avenue and well endowed with stately Colonial and Victorian mansions. Here, at the Catamount Tavern (now a private home just north of Church Street), Ethan Allen organized the Green Mountain Boys, who helped capture Fort Ticonderoga in 1775.

WHAT TO SEE

Fodor'sChoice
★ **Old First Church.** In the graveyard of this church, the tombstone of the poet Robert Frost proclaims, "I had a lover's quarrel with the world." ⊠*Church St. and Monument Ave.*

☾ **Bennington Battle Monument.** This 306-foot stone obelisk (with an elevator to the top) commemorates General Stark's victory over the British, who attempted to capture Bennington's stockpile of supplies. Inside the monument you can learn all about the battle, which took place near Walloomsac Heights in New York State on August 16, 1777, and helped bring about the surrender of the British commander "Gentleman Johnny" Burgoyne two months later. The summit provides commanding views of the Massachusetts Berkshires, the New York Adirondacks, and the Vermont Green Mountains. ⊠*15 Monument Cir., Old Bennington* ☎*802/447–0550* ⤳*$2* ⊙*Mid-Apr.–Oct., daily 9–5.*

Bennington Museum. The rich collections at this museum include military artifacts, early tools, dolls, toys, and the Bennington Flag, one of the oldest Stars and Stripes in existence. One room is devoted to early Bennington pottery, and two rooms cover the history of American glass (fine Tiffany specimens are on display). The museum displays the world's largest public collection of the work of Grandma Moses (1860–

1961), the popular self-taught folk artist who lived and painted in the area. ⊠*75 Main St. (Rte. 9)* ☎*802/447–1571* ⊕*www.bennington museum.com* ⊠*$8* ☉*Thurs.–Tues. 10–5.*

North Bennington. Just north of Old Bennington is this village, home to Bennington College, lovely mansions, Lake Paran, three covered bridges, and a wonderful old train depot. Contemporary stone sculpture and white-frame neo-Colonial dorms surrounded by acres of cornfields punctuate the green meadows of **Bennington College's** placid campus (⊠*Rte. 67A off U.S. 7 (look for stone entrance gate)* ☎*802/442–5401*). The architecturally significant **Park-McCullough House** (⊠*Corner of Park and West Sts.* ☎*802/442–5441* ⊕*www. parkmccullough.org* ⊠*$8* ☉*Mid-May–mid-Oct., daily 10–4; last tour at 3*) is a 35-room classic French Empire–style mansion, built in 1865 and furnished with period pieces. Several restored flower gardens grace the landscaped grounds, and a stable houses a collection of antique carriages. Call for details on the summer concert series.

Robert Frost Stone House Museum. A few miles north along Route 7A is the town of Shaftsbury. It was here that Robert Frost came in 1920 "to plant a new Garden of Eden with a thousand apple trees of some unforbidden variety." The museum tells the story of the nine years (1920–29) Frost spent living in the house with his wife and four children. (Frost spent the 1930s in a house up the road in Shaftsbury, now owned by a Hollywood movie producer.) It was here that he penned "Stopping by Woods on a Snowy Evening" and published two books of poems. Seven of the Frost family's original 80 acres can be wandered. Among the apple boughs you just might strike inspiration of your own. ⊠*75 Main St. (Rte. 9)* ☎*802/447–1571* ⊕*www.frostfriends.org* ⊠*$5* ☉*May–Christmas daily 10–5.*

SPORTS & THE OUTDOORS

Lake Shaftsbury State Park (⊠*Rte. 7A, 10½ mi north of Bennington* ☎*802/375–9978*) has a swimming beach, nature trails, boat and canoe rentals, and a snack bar. **Woodford State Park** (⊠*Rte. 9, 10 mi east of Bennington* ☎*802/447–7169*) has an activities center on Adams Reservoir, playground, boat and canoe rentals, and nature trails.

SHOPPING

The **Apple Barn and Country Bake Shop** (⊠*U.S. 7 S* ☎*802/447–7780*) sells home-baked goodies, fresh cider, Vermont cheeses, and maple syrup and has a cornfield maze. The shop is open from September to mid-October. The showroom at the **Bennington Potters Yard** (⊠*324 County St.* ☎*802/447–7531 or 800/205–8033*) stocks first-quality pottery and seconds from the famed Bennington Potters. Take a free tour on weekdays from 10 to 3 when the potters are working, or follow a self-guided tour around the yard.

THE ARTS

The **Bennington Center for the Arts** (⊠*Rte. 9 at Gypsy La.* ☎*802/442–7158*) hosts cultural events, including exhibitions by local and national artists. The on-site **Oldcastle Theatre Co.** (☎*802/447–0564*) hosts fine regional theater from May through October. The **Basement Music Series**

(⌂29 Sage St.North Bennington ☎802/442–5549), run by the non-profit Vermont Arts Exchange, is a funky basement cabaret venue in an old factory buiding. It hosts the best contemporary music performances in town.

WHERE TO EAT

¢ ✗**Blue Benn Diner.** Breakfast is served all day in this authentic diner,
AMERICAN where the eats include turkey hash and breakfast burritos with scrambled eggs, sausage, and chilies, plus pancakes of all imaginable varieties. The menu lists many vegetarian selections. Lines may be long, especially on weekends: locals and tourists alike can't stay away. ⌂*314 North St.* ☎*802/442–5140* ⚘*Reservations not accepted* ▭*No credit cards* ⊘*No dinner Sat. Tues.*

$$-$$$ ✗**Four Chimneys Inn.** It's a treat just to walk up the long path to this
CONTINENTAL classic Old Bennington mansion, the most refined setting around. The dining room is a discrete, quiet room lit by candlelight and a gas fireplace. Thom Simonetti creates a sophisticated seasonal menu. If you're lucky you might find a wonderful hand-crafted agnolotti pasta with angus beef—braised in port with a shallot confit and cherry ragout and topped with a local blue cheese. The poached salmon comes in a lemon-dill beurre blanc sauce. Desserts are hit or miss. ⌂*21 West Rd. (Rte. 9), Old Bennington* ☎*802/447–3500* ⊕*www.fourchimneys.com* ⚘*Reservations essential* ▭*AE, D, MC, V* ⊘*No lunch. Nov.–Aug. closed Mon. and Tues.; Sept.–Oct. closed Mon.*

$-$$ ✗**Pangaea Lounge.** Don't let the dusty old storefront fool you, Benning-
★ ton's in-the-know crowd comes here before anywhere else for afford-
ECLECTIC able comfort food and an excellent bar. Directly next door is Pangaea, the fancier twin restaurant, where the menu is somewhat overpriced. We prefer the Lounge, which is handsome and irresistible, with its scuffed-up floor, intimate proportions, and fine approach to simple food and service. At the helm at the corner bar is Jason, an impressive mixologist. The eclectic pub fare includes such dishes as pot roast chimichangas, Cobb salad with Danish blue cheese, salmon burgers, and seared pork loin with a potato croquette. On weekends in warmer months, follow the crowd out the back stairs to the deck. ⌂*3 Prospect St., 3 mi north of Bennington, North Bennington* ☎*802/442–7171* ▭*AE, MC, V* ⊘*No lunch.*

WHERE TO STAY

¢-$ ⌨**Eddington House.** You can thank Patti Eddington for maintaining this
★ three-bedroom house, probably the best value in all of Vermont. You get a spotless and updated room in a house you can't help but feel is all your own. Patti lives in an attached barn, giving you all the privacy you need. Homemade desserts and wine are always out on the counter. The house is in the heart of North Bennington, across the street from a market and two restaurants. The most expensive room, the Village Suite, is $109, a fantastic value. Another at $89 has a four-poster bed with a lovely old tub, separate shower, and great light. Ask about the excellent dinner package. **Pros:** spotlessly clean home and rooms; privacy and gentle service. **Cons:** slightly off usual tourist track. ⌂*21 Main St., North Bennington,* ☎*802/442–1551* ⊕*www.eddingtonhouseinn.com*

⚘3 rooms ⚘ *In room: no phone, no TV (some), Wi-Fi. In-hotel: no elevator, public Wi-Fi, some pets allowed, no children under 12, no-smoking rooms ☰AE, MC, V ⎮◎⎮BP.*

$$-$$$
Fodor'sChoice
★

☒ **Four Chimneys Inn.** This is the quintessential Old Bennington mansion, and one of the best inns in Vermont. The three-story 1915 neo-Georgian looks out over a substantial lawn and a wonderful old stone wall. On the second floor, rooms 1, 3, and 11 have great bay windows and fireplaces. One has a chandelier hung over a hot tub, reproduction antique washstands, and a flat screen TV cleverly concealed by a painting. All rooms are light and bright. This property has long been an inn but only recently did it spring back to life in high style, under the careful attention of new owner and innkeeper Lynn Green. Luster was returned to the original hardwood floors in 2008. Two cottages in back (a two-story brick former ice house, and a former carriage house) overlook a pond. **Pros:** stately mansion that's extremely well kept; formal dining; very clean, spacious, renovated rooms. **Cons:** common room/bar closes early. ☒*21 West Rd. (Rte. 9), Old Bennington,* ☏*802/447–3500* ⊕*www.fourchimneys.com* ⚘*9 rooms, 2 suites* ⚘*In-room: DVD, Ethernet, Wi-Fi. In-hotel: restaurant, bar, bicycles, no elevator, laundry service, public Wi-Fi, no kids under 5, no-smoking rooms ☰AE, D, MC, V ⎮◎⎮BP.*

ARLINGTON

15 mi north of Bennington.

Smaller than Bennington and more down to earth than upper-crust Manchester to the north, Arlington exudes a certain Rockwellian folksiness. And it should. Illustrator Norman Rockwell lived here from 1939 to 1953, and many of the models for his portraits of small-town life were his neighbors.

WHAT TO SEE

Norman Rockwell Exhibition. Although no original paintings are displayed at this gallery, the rooms are crammed with reproductions of the illustrator's works, arranged in every way conceivable: chronologically, by subject matter, and juxtaposed with photos of the models, several of whom work here. ☒*Main St. (Rte. 7A)* ☏*802/375–6423* ☒*$3* ☽*May–Oct., daily 9–5; Nov.–Apr., Fri.–Mon. 9–5.*

OFF THE BEATEN PATH

The endearing town of **East Arlington** (☒*1 mi east of Arlington on East Arlington Rd.*) sits on the shore of Roaring Brook just east of Arlington. An 18th-century gristmill is now home to a fine antiques shop, one of a few in town, and other fun shops, including a fudge and teddy bear store (⇨Shopping).

A covered bridge leads to the quaint town green of **West Arlington** ☒*West of Arlington on Rte. 313 West)*, where Norman Rockwell once lived. River Road follows along the south side of the Battenkill River, a scenic drive. If you continue west along Route 313, you'll come to the Wayside General Store, a real charmer where you can pick up sandwiches and chat with locals. The store is frequently mentioned (anonymously) in the Vermont columns written by Christopher Kimball, editor of *Cooks Illustrated.*

★ **SPORTS & THE OUTDOORS**

BattenKill Canoe (✉6328 *Rte. 7A, Sunderland* ☎802/362–2800 *or 800/421–5268* ⊕*www.battenkill.com*) rents canoes for trips along the Battenkill River, which runs directly behind the shop. If you're hooked, they also run bigger white-water trips as well as inn-to-inn tours.

SHOPPING

ANTIQUES   More than 70 dealers display their wares at **East Arlington Antiques Center** (✉*East Arlington Rd., East Arlington* ☎802/375–6144), which is in a converted 1930s movie theater.

Fodor'sChoice   **Gristmill Antiques** (✉*316 Old Mill Rd.,East Arlington* ☎802/375–
★   2500) is a beautiful two-floor shop in a historic mill that looks out over Roaring Brook.

GIFTS   **The Bearatorium** (✉*Old Mill Rd., East Arlington* ☎802/375–6037) has
🐾   a chocolate museum where you can learn all about chocolate. It does wine and chocolate pairings, sells fudge and other candies, and has a large collection of teddy bears for sale. In the winter, it's closed on Tuesdays and Wednesdays.

NIGHTLIFE & THE ARTS

The **Friday Night Fireside Music Series** in the cozy tavern at the West Mountain Inn (✉*River Rd., West Arlington* ☎802/375–6516) features great live music acts every other Friday evening from November through May. There's a $10 cover.

WHERE TO STAY

$$-$$$ 🏨**Arlington Inn.** Greek-revival columns at this 1848 home lend it an imposing presence in the middle of town, but the atmosphere is friendly and old-fashioned. Rooms are dainty and Victorian, dressed heavily in florals, and are spread among the main inn, parsonage, and carriage house. Landscaping includes a garden, gazebo, pond, and waterfall. The inn runs one of the most respected restaurants in town, and its bar is one of the most colonial in the state. **Pros:** heart-of-town location, friendly atmosphere. **Cons:** rooms are dated. ✉*Rte. 7A* ☎802/375–6532 *or 800/443–9442* ⊕*www.arlingtoninn.com* ⇆*13 rooms, 5 suites* &*In-room: Wi-Fi. In-hotel: restaurant, bar, no elevator, public Wi-Fi, no-smoking rooms* ▤*AE, D, MC, V* ❘○❘*BP, MAP.*

$$$-$$$$ 🏨**West Mountain Inn.** This 1810 farmhouse sits on 150 acres on the
🐾   side of a mountain, offering plenty of hiking trails and easy access
Fodor'sChoice   to the Battenkill River where you can canoe or go tubing. In winter
★   you can sled down a former ski slope, or borrow the inn's snow shoes or cross-country skis. It's a beautiful place made more so by blithe innkeeper Amie Emmons, who lines the front yard in summer with Adirondack chairs that overlook the mountains. Families will love the alpacas, and there's a kids room painted with Disney characters and filled with games and videos. (Amie's young son Owen and Siriu, the inn's golden retriever, are the resident play pals.) Since the house is a patchwork of additions and gables, rooms have eccentric configura-

tions. Though they are not luxurious or flawless, they are comfortable and have great views and interesting sitting areas. The onsite restaurant is well-respected; dishes have a strong focus on organic and locally grown vegetables and meats. **Pros:** mountainside location, great for families, lots of outdoor activities. **Cons:** slightly outdated bedding and carpets. ⊠*River Rd., Arlington* ☎*802/375-6516* ⊕*www.west mountaininn.com* ⬡*16 rooms, 6 suites* ⚬*In-room: no phone, no TV. In-hotel: restaurant, bar, water sports, bicycles, no elevator, laundry service, no- smoking rooms* ⊟*AE, D, MC, V* ⦿*BP, MAP.*

MANCHESTER

★ *9 mi northeast of Arlington.*

Well-to-do Manchester has been a popular summer retreat since the mid-19th century when city dwellers traveled north to take in the cool clean air at the foot of 3,816-foot Mt. Equinox. Manchester Village's tree-shaded marble sidewalks and stately old homes—Main Street here could hardly be more picture perfect—reflect the luxurious resort life-style of more than a century ago. A mile north on 7A, Manchester Cen-ter is the commercial twin to colonial Manchester Village. This is where you'll find the town's famed upscale factory outlets doing business in attractive faux-colonial shops. If you're coming here from Arlington, take scenic Route 7A.

WHAT TO SEE

Manchester Village is home to the world headqurters of Orvis, the outdoors goods brand that began here in the 19th century. Its complex includes a fly-fishing school with lessons in its casting ponds and the Battenkill River (⇨ Sports & the Outdoors).

American Museum of Fly Fishing. This museum houses the world's largest collection of angling art and angling-related objects. Displays include more than 1,500 rods, 800 reels, 30,000 flies, and the tackle of famous people like Winslow Homer, Bing Crosby, and Jimmy Carter. ⊠*4070 Main St. (Rte. 7A)* ☎*802/362-3300* ⊕*www.amff.com* ⬡*$5* ⊘*Daily 10–4.*

Fodor'sChoice **Hildene.** The "Lincoln Family Home" is a twofold treat, providing his-
★ torical insight into the life of the Lincolns while escorting you into the lavish Manchester life of the 1900s. Abraham had only one son who survived to adulthood, Robert Todd Lincoln, who served as secretary of war and head of the Pullman Company. Robert bought the beauti-fully preserved 412-acre estate and built a 24-room mansion where he and his descendants lived from 1903–75. The entire grounds are open for exploration—you can hike, picnic, and ski; use the astronomical observatory; loll across beautiful gardens; and walk through the sturdy Georgian-revival house, which holds the family's original furniture, books, and possessions. One of three surviving stovepipe hats owned by Abraham Lincoln and Robert's Harvard yearbook are among the treasures you'll find. When the 1,000-pipe aeolian organ is played, the music reverberates as though from the mansion's very bones. The high-

light, though, may be the elaborate formal gardens: in June a thousand peonies bloom. When snow conditions permit, you can cross-country ski and snowshoe on the property. Robert's carriage house now houses the attractive gift shop and visitor center that showcases his daughter's 1928 vintage Franklin. ✉ *Rte. 7A* ☎ *802/362–1788* ⊕ *www.hildene. org* ☞ *Tour $12.50, grounds pass $5* ⊙ *Daily 9:30–4:30.*

Southern Vermont Arts Center. Rotating exhibits and a permanent collection of more than 700 pieces of 19th- and 20th-century American art are showcased at this 12,500-square-foot museum. The arts center's original building, a graceful Georgian mansion set on 407 acres, is the frequent site of concerts, performances, and film screenings. In summer and fall, a pleasant restaurant with magnificent views serves lunch. ✉ *West Rd.* ☎ *802/362–1405* ⊕ *www.svac.org* ✉ *$8* ⊙ *Tues.–Sat. 10–5, Sun. noon–5.*

SPORTS & THE OUTDOORS

FISHING **Battenkill Anglers** (✉ *6204 Main St., Manchester* ☎ *802/379–1444*) teaches the art and science of fly-fishing in both private and group lessons. **Orvis Co.** (✉ *Rte. 7A, Manchester Center* ☎ *800/235–9763*) hosts a nationally known fly-fishing school on the Battenkill, the state's most famous trout stream, with 2- and 2½-day courses offered weekly between June and October.

HIKING One of the most popular segments of Vermont's **Long Trail** starts from a parking lot on Route 11/30 and goes to the top of Bromley Mountain. The 6-mi round-trip trek takes about four hours. The **Mountain Goat** (✉ *4886 Main St.* ☎ *802/362–5159*) sells hiking and backpacking equipment and rents snowshoes and cross-country and telemark skis.

SHOPPING

ART & In Manchester Village, **Frog Hollow at Equinox** (✉ *3566 Main St. [Rte.*
ANTIQUES *7A]* ☎ *802/362–3321*) is a nonprofit collective that sells such contemporary works as jewelry, glassware, and home furnishings from a huge
★ range of Vermont artisans.

Long Ago and Far Away (✉ *Green Mountain Village Shops, 4963 Main St.* ☎ *802/362–3435* ⊕ *www.longagoandfaraway.com*) specializes in fine indigenous artwork, including Canadian Inuit stone sculpture. The large **Tilting at Windmills Gallery** (✉ *24 Highland Ave.* ☎ *802/362–3022* ⊕ *www.tilting.com*) displays and sells the paintings and sculpture of nationally known artists.

BOOKS **Northshire Bookstore** (✉ *4869 Main St.* ☎ *802/362–2200 or 800/437–*
Fodor'sChoice *3700*) is the heart of Manchester Center, and no wonder—it's a huge
★ independently owned bookseller with a massive children's section and is considered one of the finest bookstores in the country. Connected to the bookstore is the Spiral Press Café, where you can sit for a grilled pesto-chicken sandwich on focaccia bread or a latte and scone.

CLOTHING The two-story, lodge-like **Orvis Flagship Store** (✉ *4200 Rte. 7A* ☎ *802/*
★ *362–3750*) has a trout pond as well as the company's latest clothing and accessories.

Fodor'sChoice
★
Spread out across Manchester Center, **Manchester Designer Outlets** (⊠ *U.S. 7 and Rte. 11/30* ☎ *802/362–3736 or 800/955–7467* ⊕ *www. manchesterdesigneroutlets.com*) is the most upscale collection of stores in northern New England—and every store is a discount outlet! Adding to the allure, town ordinances decree the look of the shops be in tune in with the surrounding historic homes, making these the most attractive and decidedly colonial-looking outlets you'll ever see. In 2008, three new outlets opened: Michael Kors, Betsey Johnson, and Ann Taylor. These add to such esteemed lines as Tumi, Escada, Armani, Coach, Polo Ralph Lauren, Brooks Brothers, and Theory. There's also a few less expensive brands like Gap and Banana Republic.

NIGHTLIFE & THE ARTS

Near Bromley Mountain, **Johnny Seesaw's** (⊠ *3574 Rte. 11* ☎ *802/824–5533*) is a classic rustic ski lodge, with live music on weekends and an excellent "comfort food" menu. It's closed April through Memorial Day. The **Marsh Tavern** (⊠ *3567 Main St. [Rte. 7A]* ☎ *802/362–4700*) at the Equinox resort hosts folk music and jazz from Thursday to Sunday in summer and on weekends in winter. The **Perfect Wife** (⊠ *2594 Depot St. [Rte. 11/30]* ☎ *802/362–2817*) hosts live music on Friday.

WHERE TO EAT

$$$
FRENCH
✕ **Bistro Henry.** The active presence of chef and owner Henry Bronson accounts for the continual popularity of this friendly place that's about $5 per dish cheaper than the other good restaurants in town. The menu works off a bistro foundation, with a peppery steak au poivre and a medium rare duck breast served with a crispy leg, and mixes things up with eclectic dishes like seared tuna with wasabi and soy; crab cakes in a Cajun rémoulade; and a delicious scallop dish with Thai coconut curry and purple sticky rice. The wine list is extensive. Dina Bronson's desserts are memorable—indulge in the "gooey chocolate cake," a great molten treat paired with a homemade malt ice cream. ⊠ *1942 Rte. 11/30, 3 mi east of Manchester Center* ☎ *802/362–4982* ▭ *AE, D, DC, MC, V* ⊘ *Closed Mon. No lunch.*

$$$-$$$$
CONTINENTAL
✕ **Chantecleer.** There is something wonderful about eating by candlelight in an old barn. Chantecleer's dining rooms (in winter ask to sit by the great fieldstone fireplace) are wonderfully romantic, even with a collection of roosters atop the wooden beams. The menu leans toward the Continental with starters like a fine escargot glazed with Pernod in a hazlenut and parsely butter. Crowd pleasers include Colorado rack of lamb, and whole Dover sole filleted table-side. A recipe from the chef's Swiss hometown makes a winning dessert: Basel Rathaus Torte, a delicious hazlenut layer cake. ⊠ *Rte. 7A, 3½ mi north of Manchester, East Dorset* ☎ *802/362–1616* ⚞ *Reservations essential* ▭ *AE, DC, MC, V* ⊘ *Closed Mon. and Tues. No lunch.*

$
PIZZA
✕ **Depot 62 Cafe.** The best pizzas in town are topped with terrific fresh ingredients and served in the middle of a high-end antiques showroom, making it a local's secret worth knowing about. The wood-fired yields masterful results—like the arugula pizza, a beehive of fresh greens atop a thin crust base. This a great place for lunch or an inexpensive but sat-

isfying dinner. Sit on your own or at the long communal table. ⊠*505 Depot St.* ☎*802/366–8181* ⊟*MC, V.*

$$$–$$$$ ✕**Mistral's.** This classic French restaurant is tucked in a grotto off Route
FRENCH 11/30 on the climb to Bromley Mountain. The two dining rooms are perched over the Bromley Brook, and at night, lights magically illuminate a small waterfall. Ask for a window table. Specialties include chateaubriand béarnaise and rack of lamb with rosemary for two. Chef Dana Markey's crispy sweetbreads with porcini mushrooms are a favorite. ⊠*10 Toll Gate Rd.* ☎*802/362–1779* ⊟*AE, DC, MC, V* ⊘*Closed Wed. No lunch.*

$–$$ ✕**Perfect Wife.** Owner-chef Amy Chamberlain, the self-proclaimed
ECLECTIC aspiring flawless spouse, creates freestyle cuisine like turkey schnitzel and grilled venison with a caramelized shallot and dried cranberry demi-glace. The upstairs tavern serves burgers and potpies, plus Vermont microbrews on tap. ⊠*2594 Depot St. (Rte. 11/30), 2½ mi east of Manchester Center* ☎*802/362–2817* ⊟*AE, D, MC, V* ⊘*Closed Sun. No lunch.*

WHERE TO STAY

$$$$ 🏨**The Equinox.** Though this multi-building property is the geographic
Fodor's Choice center and historic heart of Manchester Village, and though it has
★ been *the* fancy hotel in town—in the state—since the 18th century, the Equinox had lost its luster in the past decade. That all changed in 2008, however, thanks to a complete renovation that's elevated the property, finally, to the lofty tier befitting its white columns. Rooms now have huge flat-screen TVs, leather chairs, contemporary carpets, and two-tone cream wallpaper, new plush-top mattresses, and marble bathrooms with granite sinks and Molton Brown toiletries. If you crave colonial, the Equinox bought the pink 1811 House across the street, which had been an independent B&B and is one of New England's most heart-grabbing properties. If you've got big bucks, ask for a room in the Charles Orvis Inn, which has a billiard room, hot tubs, and private porches. The spa is the best in southern Vermont, you can take falconry lessons, the resort's golf course is across the street, and there's a new wine bar in addition to the good restaurant. **Pros:** heart-of-town location, full-service hotel, great golf and spa. **Cons:** big-hotel feeling, overrun by New Yorkers on weekends. ⊠*3567 Main St. (Rte. 7A)* ☎*802/362–4700 or 888/367–7625* ⊕*www.equinoxresort. com* ⇆*154 rooms, 29 suites* ♿*In-room: kitchen (some), refrigerator (some), Wi-Fi. In-hotel: 2 restaurants, bar, golf course, tennis courts, pool, spa, laundry service, concierge, public Wi-Fi, no-smoking rooms* ⊟*AE, D, DC, MC, V.*

$$$–$$$$ 🏨**Wilburton Inn.** A few miles south of Manchester and overlooking the Battenkill Valley from a hilltop all its own, this turn-of-the-20th-century complex is centered around a Tudor mansion with 11 bedrooms and suites, and richly paneled common rooms containing part of the owners' vast art collection. Besides the main inn, five guest buildings are spread over the grounds, dotted with more owner-created sculpture. Rooms at the Wilburton vary greatly in condition, so choose carefully. The dining room is an elegant affair, with a menu to match the wood-paneled interiors and the bucolic surroundings. Entrées might include poached Maine lobster with gnocchi or a roasted antelope chop with bordelaise sauce. One note: weddings take place here most summer weekends. **Pros:** beautiful setting with easy access to Manchester; fine dining. **Cons:** rooms in main inn, especially, need updating. ⊠*River Rd.* ☎*802/362–2500 or 800/648–4944* ⊕*www.wilburton.com* ⇗*30 rooms, 4 suites* ⸹*In-hotel: restaurant, tennis courts, pool, no-smoking rooms* ⊟*AE, MC, V* ⏏*BP.*

DORSET

★ *7 mi north of Manchester.*

Lying at the foot of many mountains and blessed with a village green surrounded by white clapboard homes and inns, Dorset has a solid claim on the title of Vermont's most picture-perfect town. It also has two of the state's best and oldest general stores (⇨Shopping). The town has just 2,000 residents.

The country's first commercial marble quarry was opened here in 1785. Dozens followed suit. They provided the marble for the main research branch of the New York City Public Library and many Fifth Avenue mansions, among other notable landmarks, as well as the sidewalks that border the streets here and in Manchester. A remarkable private home made entirely of marble can be seen on Dorset West Road, a beautiful residential road just west of the town green. The marble Dorset Church on the green features two Tiffany stained-glass windows.

WHAT TO SEE

Fodor'sChoice **Dorset Quarry.** On hot summer days the sight of dozens of families jump-
★ ing, swimming, and basking in the sun around this massive swimming hole makes it one of the most wholesome and picturesque recreational spots in all America. Mined in 1785, this is the oldest marble quarry in the United States. The popular area visible from Route 30 is actually just the lower quarry. Footpaths lead to the quiet upper quarry. ⊠*Rte. 30, 1 mi south of Dorset green* ☎*No phone* ⸹*Free.*

⟳ **Merck Forest and Farmland Center.** This 3,100-acre farm and forest is a
★ nonprofit educational center with 30 mi of nature trails for hiking, cross-country skiing, snowshoeing, and horseback riding. You can visit the farm, which grows organic fruits and vegetables (and purchase them at the farm stand), and check out the pasture-raised horses, cows, sheep, pigs, and chickens. There are also remote cabins and tent sites. ⊠*3270 Rte. 315, Rupert* ☎*802/394–7836* ⊕*www.merckforest.org* ⸹*Free* ⟳*Daily, dawn–dusk.*

SPORTS & THE OUTDOORS

Emerald Lake State Park (⊠*U.S. 7, East Dorset* ☎*802/362–1655*) has a small beach, marked nature trail, an on-site naturalist, boat rentals, and a snack bar.

SHOPPING

The **H.N. Williams General Store** (⊠2732 Rte. 30 ☏802/824-3184 ⊕www.hnwilliams.com) is quite possibly the most authentic and comprehensive general store in the state. It was started in 1840 by William Williams and has been run by the same family for six generations. This is one of those unique places where you can buy maple syrup and a rifle, and catch up on posted town announcements. A farmer's market (⊕www.dorsetfarmersmarket.com) is held outside on Sundays in summer. The **Dorset Union Store** (⊠Dorset Green ☏802/867-4400 ⊕www.dorsetunionstore.com) first opened in 1816 as a village co-op. Today this privately owned general store makes good prepared dinners, has a big wine selection, rents DVDs, and sells food and gifts.

THE ARTS

Dorset is home to a prestigious summer theater troupe that presents the annual Dorset Theater Festival. Plays are held in a wonderful converted pre-Revolutionary barn, the **Dorset Playhouse** (⊠104 Cheney Rd., off town green ☏802/867-2223 or 802/867-5777). The playhouse also hosts a community group in winter.

WHERE TO EAT

$-$$
AMERICAN
✕**Dorset Inn.** The inn that houses this restaurant has been continuously operating since 1796, and even today you can count on three meals a day, every day of the year. The comfortable tavern, which serves the same menu as the more formal dining room, is popular with locals, and Patrick, the amiable veteran bartender, will make you feel at home. The menu features ingredients from local farms. Popular choices include fried yam fritters served in maple syrup, and a lightly breaded chicken breast saltimbocca, stuffed with prosciutto and mozzarella. ⊠Dorset Green at Rte. 30, Dorset ☏802/867-5500 ⊕www.dorsetinn.com ⊟AE, MC, V.

$$$
★
ECLECTIC
✕**West View Farm.** Chef-owner Raymond Chen was the lead line cook at New York City's The Mercer Kitchen under Jean-Georges Vongerichten before opening this local-ingredient-friendly restaurant. Like Dorset's other eateries, you'll find traditional floral wallpaper and soft classical music; but that's where the similarities end. Chen's dishes are skillful and practiced, starting with an amuse-bouche like brandade (salt cod) over pesto. French influences are evident in the sautéed mushrooms and mascarpone ravioli in white truffle oil. Asian notes are evident, too, as in the lemongrass ginger soup with shiitake mushrooms that's ladled over grilled shrimp. A tavern serves enticing, inexpensive small dishes. ⊠2928 Rte. 30, Dorset ☏802/867-5715 or 800/769-4903 ⊕www.westviewfarm.com ⊟AE, MC, V ☯Closed Tues. and Wed.

WHERE TO STAY

$$-$$$
⊞**Squire House.** This 10-acre estate sits on a wonderfully quiet road. The house has an excellent mix of modern comforts and antique fixtures. And there's enough space and quiet, with three big common rooms (and only three guest rooms), that it can feel like home. The house was built in 1918 and was designed with 9-foot ceilings and great light throughout. Rooms are newly carpeted, and clean freaks will breathe easy here. Owners Gay and Roger Squire are rightly proud

of their breakfasts served in a richly paneled dining room. Roger is a flute player and enjoys the company of other musicians, who get a 10% discount. **Pros:** big estate feels your own, spotless. **Cons:** bathrooms less exciting than rooms, no credit cards. ⊠*3395 Dorset West Rd.* ☎*802/867–0281* ⊕*www.squirehouse.com* ⤴*2 rooms, 1 suite* &*In-room: no phone, refrigerator (some), DVD (some), no TV (some), Wi-Fi. In-hotel: no elevator, laundry service, public Wi-Fi, no kids under 14, no-smoking rooms* ⊟*No credit cards* ⵙ*BP.*

\$-\$\$ ⛽**Inn at West View Farm.** While these aren't the best rooms in town, they're not bad and they offer an inexpensive way to stay in an old farmhouse with comfortable common rooms—along with easy access to perhaps the best dining room in southwestern Vermont (⇨West View Farm *under* Where to Eat). The white clapboard farmhouse is part of a former 1870 dairy farm. A deck in back looks out at the smaller farm buildings that dot the 5-acre yard. Rooms display imperfections, like an occasional stain or crack, and the carpeting could use an update, but they are very clean, and the furniture and wallpaper satisfy the colonial farmhouse urge. **Pros:** great restaurant. **Cons:** rooms aren't perfectly maintained. ⊠*2928 Rte. 30* ☎*802/867–5715* ⊕*www.innatwestviewfarm.com* ⤴*9 rooms, 1 suite* &*In-room: Wi-Fi. In-hotel: restaurant, bar, no elevator, laundry service, public Wi-Fi, no kids under 10, no-smoking rooms* ⊟*AE, MC, V* ⵙ*BP.*

STRATTON

26 mi southeast of Dorset.

Stratton is really Stratton Mountain Resort—a mountaintop ski resort with a self-contained "town center" of shops, restaurants, and lodgings clustered at the base of the slopes. When the snow melts, golf, tennis, and a host of other summer activities are big attractions, but the ski village remains quiet. For those arriving from the north along Route 30, Bondville is the town at the base of the mountain. At the juncture of Rtes. 30 and 100 is the tiny Vermont village of Jamaica, with its own cluster of inns and restaurants on the east side of the mountain.

SPORTS & THE OUTDOORS

SKI AREA   About 30 minutes from Manchester, sophisticated, exclusive **Stratton Moun-**
★   **tain** (⊠*5 Village Rd., Bondville. Turn off Rte 30 and go 4 mi up access road* ☎*802/297–2200, 802/297–4211 snow conditions, 800/787–2886 lodging* ⊕*www.stratton.com*) draws affluent families and young professionals from the New York–southern Connecticut corridor. An entire village, with a covered parking structure for 700 cars, is at the base of the mountain. Activities are afoot year-round. Stratton has 15 outdoor tennis courts, 27 holes of golf, a climbing wall, horseback riding, hiking accessed by a gondola to the summit, and instructional programs in tennis and golf. The sports center, open year-round, has two indoor tennis courts, three racquetball courts, a 25-meter indoor swimming pool, a hot tub, a steam room, a fitness facility with Nautilus equipment, and a restaurant. Adjacent to the base lodge are a condo-hotel, restaurants, and about 25 shops lining a pedestrian mall.

In terms of downhill skiing, Stratton prides itself on its immaculate grooming, making it excellent for cruising. The lower part of the mountain is beginner to low intermediate, served by several chairlifts. The upper mountain is served by several high-speed quads and a 12-passenger gondola. Down the face are the expert trails, and on either side are intermediate cruising runs with a smattering of wide beginner slopes The third sector, the Sun Bowl, is off to one side with two high-speed, six-passenger lifts and two expert trails, a full base lodge, and plenty of intermediate terrain. Snowmaking covers 95% of the slopes. Every March, Stratton hosts the U.S. Open Snowboarding championships; its snowboard park has a 380-foot half-pipe. A Ski Learning Park provides its own Park Packages for novice skiers. In all, Stratton has 15 lifts that service 92 trails and 90 acres of glades. There is a ski school for children ages 4–12. The resort also has more than 18 mi of cross-country skiing and the Sun Bowl Nordic center.

NIGHTLIFE & THE ARTS

Popular **Mulligan's** (⊠ *Mountain Rd.* ☎ *802/297-9293*) hosts bands or DJs in the late afternoon and on weekends in winter. Year round, the **Red Fox Inn** (⊠ *Winhall Hollow Rd., Bondville* ☎ *802/297-2488*) is probably the best nightlife spot in southern Vermont. It hosts Irish music Wednesday night; an open mike Thursday night; and rock and roll at other times.

WHERE TO EAT

$$$-$$$$ ✕ **Red Fox Inn.** This two-level converted barn has the best nightlife in
AMERICAN   southern Vermont, and a fun dining room to boot. The restaurant has been here for 30 years, but you'd believe 100. The upper level is the dining room—the big A-frame has wagon wheels and a carriage suspended from the ceiling. Settle in near the huge fireplace for rack of lamb, free-range chicken, or penne à la vodka. Downstairs is the tavern where there's Irish music, half-price Guinness, and fish-and-chips on Wednesday. Other nights there might be live music, karaoke, or video bowling. The bar operates daily year-round. ⊠ *Winhall Hollow Rd., Bondville* ☎ *802/297-2488* ▭ *AE, MC, V* ⊗ *No lunch. Closed Mon.–Wed. June–Oct.*

$$$$ ✕ **Three Mountain Inn.** If you're in the Stratton area and can splurge on
FodorsChoice   an expensive meal, don't miss dinner at this charming inn. The prix fixe
★   meal include amuse bouche, starter, salad, entrée, and dessert for $55.
CONTEMPORARY   (It also includes the best restaurant bread in Vermont, a homemade herb focaccia). A starter might be baked Malpec oysters with a chorizo and fennel jam; entrées include grilled swordfish with toasted couscous, with a mint cucumber sauce. Fireplaces in each dining room and common areas have terrific original wall and ceiling beams. A romantic winner. ⊠ *3732 Rte. 30/100, Jamaica* ☎ *802/874-4140* ▭ *AE, D, MC, V* ⊗ *No dinner Mon., Tues.*

WHERE TO STAY

$$ ⛺ **Long Trail House.** Directly across the street from Stratton's ski village, this fairly new condo complex is one of the best choices close to the slopes. Units have fully equipped kitchens with ovens and dishwashers. The studios are an excellent value; they come with Murphy beds

that fold into the living room area for additional sleepers. **Pros:** across from skiing, good rates available, outdoor heated pool. **Cons:** individualistic rooms, two-night stay required on weekends. ✉ *Middle Ridge Rd.* ☎ *802/297–2200 or 800/787–2886* ⊕ *www.stratton.com* ➷ *100 units* ♿ *In-room: safe (some), kitchen, refrigerator, DVD (some), VCR (some). In-hotel: pool, laundry facilities, no-smoking rooms* ▤ *AE, D, DC, MC, V.*

$$–$$$　　🏨 **Red Fox Inn.** Stay here for great mid-week rates (50% off Sunday through Thursday) and relaxed, no-frills accommodations off the noisy mountain. Tom and Cindy Logan's "white house," an early 1800s farmhouse, is set in an open meadow 4 mi from Stratton and 8 mi from Bromley. The feeling here is warm and cozy, with original wood floors and simple furnishings. Downstairs rooms have bay windows; upstairs rooms are smaller. **Pros:** great nightlife and food next door, real local hosts, secluded. **Cons:** a drive to ski, weekends overpriced. ✉ *Winhall Hollow Rd., Bondville* ☎ *802/297–2488* ⊕ *www.redfox inn.com* ➷ *8 rooms, 1 suite* ♿ *In-room: no a/c, no phone, no TV, Wi-Fi. In-hotel: restaurant, bar, no elevator, public Wi-Fi, no-smoking rooms* ▤ *AE, MC, V.*

$$$–$$$$　　🏨 **Three Mountain Inn.** A 1780s tavern, this romantic inn in downtown
Fodor'sChoice　Jamaica (10 mi northeast of Stratton) feels authentically Colonial, from
★　　the wide paneling to the low ceilings. It's one of the coziest inns in Vermont. Rooms are appointed with a blend of historic and modern furnishings, including featherbeds. Most rooms have fireplaces and mountain views, and three have private decks. Owners Ed and Jennifer Dorta-Duque attend to your stay, and oversee truly romantic dinners. **Pros:** charming, authentic, romantic, small town B&B; well-kept and clean rooms; great dinners. **Cons:** can be expensive. ✉ *3732 Rte. 30/100* ☎ *802/874–4140* ⊕ *www.threemountaininn.com* ➷ *14 rooms, 1 suite* ♿ *In-room: DVD (some), no TV (some), Wi-Fi. In-hotel: restaurant, bar, pool, bicycles, no elevator, laundry service, public Internet, public Wi-Fi, some pets allowed, no kids under 12, no-smoking rooms* ▤ *AE, D, MC, V* ❢*BP.*

WESTON

17 mi north of Stratton.

Best known for the Vermont Country Store, Weston was one of the first Vermont towns to discover its own intrinsic loveliness—and marketability. With its summer theater, pretty town green with a Victorian bandstand, and an assortment of shops, the little village really lives up to its vaunted image.

SHOPPING

For paintings, prints, and sculptures by Vermont artists and craftspeople, go to the **Todd Gallery** (✉ *614 Main St.* ☎ *802/824–5606* ⊕ *www. toddgallery.com*). It's open Thursday–Monday, 10–5.

★　The **Vermont Country Store** (✉ *Rte. 100* ☎ *802/824–3184* ⊕ *www. vermontcountrystore.com*) sets aside one room of its old-fashioned emporium for Vermont Common Crackers and bins of fudge and other candy. The retail store and its mail-order catalog carry nearly forgotten items such as Lilac Vegetol aftershave and horehound drops, and practical items such as sturdy outdoor clothing and even typewriters. Nostalgia-evoking implements dangle from the store's walls and ceiling. (There's another store on Route 103 in Rockingham.)

THE ARTS

The members of the **Weston Playhouse** (⊠ *703 Main St., Village Green, off Rte. 100* ☎ *802/824–5288* ⊕ *www.westonplayhouse.org*), the oldest professional theater in Vermont, produce Broadway plays, musicals, and other works. Their season runs from late June to early September. Throughout the summer, the **Kinhaven Music School** (⊠ *354 Lawrence Hill Rd.* ☎ *802/824–4332*) stages free student concerts on Friday at 4 and Sunday at 2:30. Faculty concerts are Saturday at 8 PM.

WHERE TO STAY

¢–$ 🏨**Colonial House Inn & Motel.** You'll find warmth and charm at this family-friendly complex just 2 mi south of the village. Relax on comfortable furniture in the large living room or enjoy the sun in the solarium. Homey, country furnishings adorn the inn rooms and the motel units. Breakfast includes fresh goodies from the family-owned bakery; a family-style dinner is served Thursday–Saturday nights. **Pros:** inexpensive. **Cons:** located outside of town. ⊠ *287 Rte. 100* ☎ *802/824–6286 or 800/639–5033* ⊕ *www.cohoinn.com* ⌨ *9 motel units, 6 inn rooms without bath* �*In-room: no a/c, no TV (some). In-hotel: restaurant, no-smoking rooms* ▤ *D, MC, V* ⫯⊙*BP, MAP.*

$$–$$$ 🏨**Inn at Weston.** Highlighting the country elegance of this 1848 inn, a short walk from the Vermont Country Store and Weston Playhouse, is innkeeper Bob Aldrich's collection of 500 orchid species—rare and beautiful specimens surround the dining table in the gazebo and others enrich the indoors. Rooms in the inn, carriage house, and Coleman House (across the street) are comfortably appointed, and some have fireplaces. The restaurant ($$$; closed Monday) serves contemporary regional cuisine amid candlelight. Vermont cheddar cheese and Granny Smith–apple omelets are popular choices for breakfast. **Pros:** great rooms; terrific town location. **Cons:** top end rooms are expensive. ⊠*Rte. 100* ☎ *802/824–6789* ⊕ *www.innweston.com* ⌨ *13 rooms* ⚠*In-room: no TV (some). In-hotel: restaurant, bar, no kids under 12, no-smoking rooms* ▤ *AE, DC, MC, V* ⫯⊙*BP.*

LUDLOW

9 mi northeast of Weston.

Ludlow was once a nondescript factory town that just happened to have a small ski area—Okemo. Today, that ski area is one of Vermont's largest and most popular resorts, and downtown Ludlow is a collection of restored buildings with shops and restaurants.

SPORTS & THE OUTDOORS

HORSEBACK
RIDING

Cavendish Trail Horse Rides (⊠ *20 Mile Stream Rd., Proctorsville*
☏ *802/226–7821*) operates horse-drawn sleigh rides in snowy weather,
wagon rides at other times, and guided trail rides from mid-May to
mid-October.

SKI AREA

Family-owned since 1982 and still run by Tim and Diane Mueller,
Okemo Mountain Resort (⊠ *77 Okemo Ridge Rd.* ☏ *802/228–4041, 802/
228–5222 snow conditions, 800/786–5366 lodging* ⊕ *www.okemo.
com*) has evolved into a major year-round resort, now with two base
areas. Known for its wide, well-groomed trails, it's a favorite among
intermediates. The Jackson Gore expansion, a new base village north
of Ludlow off Route 103, has an inn, restaurants, a child-care center,
and shops. The resort offers numerous ski and snowboarding packages. There's also ice skating at the Ice House, a covered, open-air ice
skating rink open 10–9 daily in the winter. The Spring House next to
the entrance of Jackson Gore Inn has a great kids pool with slides, a
racquetball court, fitness center, and sauna. The yoga and Pilates studio
has classes a few times a week. A day pass is $12.

At 2,200 feet, Okemo has the highest vertical drop of any resort in
southern Vermont. The beginner trails extend above both base areas,
with more challenging terrain higher on the mountains. Intermediate
trails are the theme here, but experts will find steep trails and glades
at Jackson Gore and on the South Face. Of the 113 trails, 42% have
an intermediate rating, 33% are rated novice, and 25% are rated for
experts. They are served by an efficient system of 18 lifts, including nine
quads, three triple chairlifts, and six surface lifts; 95% are covered by
snowmaking. Okemo has four terrain parks for skiers and snowboarders, including one for beginners; two 400-foot-long Superpipes, and a
mini half-pipe.

For cross-country skiing, the **Okemo Valley Nordic Center** (⊠ *Fox La.*
☏ *802/228–1396*) has 16 mi of groomed cross-country trails and 6 mi
of dedicated snowshoe trails, and rents equipment.

If you're looking for non-snow-related activities, you can play basketball and tennis at the Ice House next to Jackson Gore Inn, or perfect
your swing at the 18-hole, par-70, 6,400-yard, Heathland-style course
at the Okemo Valley Golf Club. Seven target greens, four putting
greens, a golf academy, an indoor putting green, swing stations, and a
simulator provide plenty of ways to improve your game year-round.
The newer, off-site 9-hole **Tater Hill Golf Course** (⊠ *6802 Popple Dun-
geon Rd., Windham, 22 mi south of Ludlow* ☏ *802/875–2517*) has a
pro shop, putting green, and a driving range.

WHERE TO EAT

$-$$
ITALIAN

✕ **Cappuccino's.** This local's place in town serves mostly Italian fare.
Pasta dishes include Pasta Pink, which is loaded with crabmeat and
shrimp in a sherry cream tomato sauce, and Pasta Balsamic, with
chicken and tomatoes. ⊠ *41 Depot St.* ☏ *802/228–7566* ⊟ *MC, V*
☉ *No lunch. Closed Mon.*

$$-$$$
AMERICAN
✕**Coleman Brook Tavern.** Slopeside at the Jackson Gore Inn, Colebrook is the fanciest and most expensive of Okemo's 19 places to eat, but it's not formal—you'll find ski-boot-wearing diners crowding the tables at lunch. Big wing chairs and large banquettes line window bays. If possible, ask to sit in the Wine Room, a separate seating section where tables are surrounded by the noteworthy collection of wines. Start with a pound of steamed clams steamed in butter, garlic, white wine, and fresh herbs. Then move on to the sesame seed-crusted ahi tuna served over green-tea soba noodles in a ginger-miso broth. If you're with kids, they'll love the s'mores dessert, cooked with a tabletop "campfire." ⊠*Jackson Gore, Okemo* ☎*802/228–1435* ⊟*AE, D, DC, MC, V.*

¢-$
☼
PIZZA
✕**Goodman's American Pie.** This pizzeria has the best wood-fired oven pizza in town, maybe even in the state. It also has character to spare— sit in chairs that are old ski lifts, and order from a counter that's an old purple VW bus. Though it's on Main Street, it's set back and kind of hidden—you may consider it your Ludlow secret. Locals and Okemo regulars already in the know stop by to design their own pizza from 25 ingredients; there is also a section of six specials. The Rip Curl has mozzarella, Asiago, ricotta, chicken, fresh garlic, and fresh tomatoes. Slices are available. Arcade games are in the back. ⊠*106 Main St.* ☎*802/228–4271* ⊟*No credit cards* ☽*Closed Wed.*

$-$$
ECLECTIC
✕**Harry's.** The local favorite when you want to eat a little out of town, this casual roadside restaurant 5 mi northwest of Ludlow is an oasis of eclectic food. The menu ranges from such traditional contemporary entrées as pork tenderloin to Mexican dishes. The large and tasty burrito, made with fresh cilantro and black beans, is one of the best bargains around. Chef-owner Trip Pearce also owns the equally popular Little Harry's in Rutland. ⊠*Rte. 103, Mount Holly* ☎*802/259–2996* ⊟*AE, MC, V* ☽*Closed Mon. and Tues. No lunch.*

$$$
Fodor'sChoice
★
ECLECTIC
✕**Inn at Weathersfield.** Just 15 mi east of Ludlow is this culinary gem, one of Vermont's best restaurants, located in a rural 1792 inn. A chalkboard in the foyer lists the area farms that grow the food you'll eat here, and it's no gimmick: chef Jason Tostrup (a former sous chef at David Keller's Bouchon in Napa, and a veteran of New York's Vong, Daniel, and Jean George) is passionate about local ingredients. Get converted to "farm-to-table" via a daily five-course "VerTerra" prix-fixe menu ($65) that might feature stuffed local quail in a cider-soy glaze or local "humanely-rasied" veal served two ways—veal breast braised over heirloom polenta and sautéed liver over mashed potatoes, topped with a single onion ring—each is masterful. Service is excellent and the wine list is large and reasonably priced. ⊠*1342 Rte. 106, Perkinsville* ☎*802/263–9217* ⊟*AE, D, MC, V* ☽*No lunch. Closed Mon. and Tues. and Apr. and beginning of Nov.*

WHERE TO STAY

$$-$$$
▦**Inn at Water's Edge.** Want to ski but resent the busy Ludlow and Okemo scene? You'll find a happy middle ground at this inn 10 mi north of town. Former Long Islanders Bruce and Tina Verdrager converted their old ski house and barns into this comfortably refined haven. The centerpiece of the relaxed common areas is a huge 1850 English bar, with comfortable banquettes, a big double sided fireplace, and a

5

billiards table. Rooms are standard Victorian B&B affairs, clean and nice, but uninspiring compared to the grounds and setting. While most guests come for skiing, golf and spa packages are also available, and in summer the inn's dock has two canoes and a small sailboat on charming Echo Lake. **Pros:** bucolic setting on a lakefront; interesting, big house. **Cons:** ordinary rooms. ⊠*45 Kingdom Rd.* ☎*802/228–8134 or 888/706–9736* ⊕*www.innatwatersedge.com* ➦*9 rooms, 2 suites* ᴧ*In-room: no phone, no TV, Wi-Fi. In-hotel: restaurant, room service, bar, water sports, laundry service, public Internet, public Wi-Fi, no kids under 12, no-smoking rooms* ⊟*AE, MC, V* ⑩*BP, MAP.*

$$$$ ⚇ **Jackson Gore Inn.** This slope-side base lodge is the place to stay if your aim is convenience to Okemo's slopes. The resort includes three restaurants and a martini bar ($12 a pop, but they're served in generous portions), plus an arcade. You can use the Spring House health center, which includes a fitness center, a raquetball court, hot tubs, a sauna, and great kid pools with slides. Right next to the original Jackson Gore structure are the newest annexes, Adams House (which opened in 2007) and Bixby House (2008), which feature whirlpool tubs and slightly more contemporary furnishings. Most units have full kitchen facilities. Besides Jackson Gore, Okemo offers 145 other condo units all across the mountain. **Pros:** ski-in, ski-out at base of mountain; good for families. **Cons:** chaotic and noisy on weekends. ⊠*Okemo Ridge Rd. off Rte. 103* ☎*802/228–1400 or 800/786–5366* ⊕*www.okemo. com* ➦*263 rooms* ᴧ*In-room: kitchen (some), refrigeraor, DVD, VCR, Wi-Fi. In-hotel: 3 restaurants, bar, golf courses, tennis courts, pools, gym, spa, children's programs (ages 2–12), laundry facilities, concierge, public Internet, public Wi-Fi, some pets allowed, no-smoking rooms* ⊟*AE, MC, V.*

CHESTER

13 mi southeast of Ludlow.

At the junction of Routes 11 and 103, Chester is the town that time forgot. Gingerbread Victorians line the town green, the pharmacy on Main Street has been in continuous operation since the 1860s, and the hardware store across from the train station opened in 1858.

TRAIN RIDE

From the Chester Depot, dating from 1852, you can board the historic Green Mountain Flyer (⊠*Rte. 103* ☎*802/463–3069 or 800/707–3530* ⊕*www. rails-vt.com* 🎟*$14* ☉ *Late June–mid-Sept., Tues.–Sun.; mid-Sept.–late-Oct., daily. Call for schedule*) for a two-hour round-trip journey to Bellows Falls. The route passes covered bridges and goes through the Brockway Mills gorge. Fall foliage trips are spectacular.

SHOPPING

More than 125 dealers sell antiques and country crafts at **Stone House Antique and Craft Center** (⊠*Rte. 103 S* ☎*802/875–4477*).

WHERE TO EAT & STAY

$-$$
AMERICAN

✕**Raspberries and Thyme.** Breakfast specials, homemade soups, a large selection of salads, homemade desserts, and a menu listing more than 40 sandwiches make this one of the area's most popular spots for casual dining. ⊠*On the green* ☏*802/875–4486* ⊟*AE, D, MC, V* ⊗*No dinner Tues.*

$-$$

⌂**Chester House Inn.** All of the rooms in this handsomely restored 1780 historic inn on the green have private baths. Five have gas fireplaces, and three have hot tubs or steam showers. Breakfast is served in the elegant Keeping Room, which has a fireplace. Pros: quaint and friendly B&B. Cons: not luxurious. ⊠*266 Main St.* ☏*802/875–2205 or 888/875–2205* ⊕*www.chesterhouseinn.com* ⇆*7 rooms* ᵫ*In-room: no TV. In-hotel: bar, no-smoking rooms* ⊟*DC, MC, V* ⦿❘*BP.*

GRAFTON

★ *8 mi south of Chester.*

Out-of-the-way Grafton is as much a historical museum as a town. During its heyday, citizens grazed some 10,000 sheep and spun their wool into sturdy yarn for locally woven fabric. When the market for wool declined, so did Grafton. Then in 1963, the Windham Foundation—Vermont's second-largest private foundation—commenced the town's rehabilitation. Not only was the Old Tavern preserved, but many other commercial and residential structures in the village center were as well. The **Historical Society** (⊠*Main St. [Rte. 121]* ☏*802/843–1010* 🖽*$3* ⊗*Memorial Day–Columbus Day, weekends and holidays 10–noon and 2–4*) documents the town's renewal.

SHOPPING

Gallery North Star (⊠*151 Townshend Rd.* ☏*802/843–2465*) exhibits the oils, watercolors, lithographs, and sculptures of Vermont-based artists. Sample the best of Vermont cheddar at the **Grafton Village Cheese Company** (⊠*533 Townshend Rd.* ☏*802/843–2221*).

WHERE TO STAY

$$$-$$$$
★

⌂**Old Tavern at Grafton.** Two-story white-column porches wrap around this commanding 1801 inn, one of Vermont's greatest lodging assets. While the rooms don't show the marks of a designer's touch (and they could use it, without forgoing a link to the past), languid pleasures are to be had lingering with a book by the fire in the library, on the porches, and the authentically Colonial common rooms. In the main building are 11 guest rooms; the rest are dispersed among six other close-by buildings. Two dining rooms ($$$), one with formal Georgian furniture, the other with rustic paneling and low beams, serve American fare. The bar at the Phelps Barn is available only to guests, and offers much character. The inn runs the nearby Grafton Ponds Cross-Country Ski Center. Pros: classic Vermont inn and tavern; professionally run; appealing common areas. Cons: rooms are attractive but not stellar. ⊠*Rte. 121* ☏*802/843–2231 or 800/843–1801* ⊕*www.old-tavern. com* ⇆*39 rooms, 7 suites* ᵫ*In-room: no a/c (some), no TV, Wi-Fi.*

In-hotel: 2 restaurants, bar, tennis court, bicycles, public Internet, public Wi-Fi, no-smoking rooms ☰*AE, MC, V* ⊘*Closed Apr.* ⦶*BP.*

TOWNSHEND

9 mi south of Grafton.

One of a string of pretty villages along the banks of the West River, Townshend embodies the Vermont ideal of a lovely town green presided over by a gracefully proportioned church spire. The spire belongs to the 1790 Congregational Meeting House, one of the state's oldest houses of worship. Just north on Route 30 is the Scott Bridge (closed to traffic), the state's longest single-span covered bridge.

OFF THE BEATEN PATH With a village green surrounded by pristine white buildings, **Newfane**, 6 mi southeast of Townshend, is sometimes described as the quintessential New England small town. The 1839 First Congregational Church and the Windham County Court House, with 17 green-shuttered windows and a rounded cupola, are often open. The building with the four-pointed spire is Union Hall, built in 1832.

SPORTS & THE OUTDOORS

At **Townshend State Park** (⊠*Rte. 30 N* ☎*802/365–7500*) you'll find a sandy beach on the West River and a trail that parallels the river for 2½ mi, topping out on Bald Mountain Dam. Up the dam, the trail follows switchbacks literally carved into the stone apron.

SHOPPING

The **Big Black Bear Shop** (⊠*Rte. 30* ☎*802/365-4160 or 888/758–2327* ⊕*www.bigblackbear.com*) at Mary Meyer Stuffed Toys Factory, the state's oldest stuffed toy company, offers discounts of up to 70% on stuffed animals of all sizes. The **Newfane Country Store** (⊠*Rte. 30, Newfane* ☎*802/365–7916* ⊕*www.newfanecountrystore.com*) carries many quilts (which can also be custom ordered), homemade fudge, and other Vermont foods, gifts, and crafts.

WHERE TO EAT

¢

AMERICAN

✕**Townshend Dam Diner.** Folks come from miles around to enjoy traditional fare such as Mom's meat loaf, chili, and roast beef croquettes, as well as Townshend-raised bison burgers, and creative daily specials. Breakfast, served all day every day, includes such tasty treats as raspberry chocolate-chip walnut pancakes and homemade French toast. You can sit at any of the collection of 1930s enamel-top tables or at the big swivel-chairs at the big U-shaped counter. The diner is a few miles northwest of the village on Route 30. ⊠*5929 Rte. 30 West Townshend* ☎*802/874–4107* ☰*No credit cards* ⊘*Closed Tues.*

$$$

CONTINENTAL

✕**Windham Hill Inn.** This remote inn is a fine choice for a romantic dinner. Chef Michael Pelton heads up the Frog Pond dining room (don't worry, no frog legs on the menu). Start with a spiced Vermont quail, served with hand-rolled pappardelle and a wild mushroom ragout. Entrees include a Moroccan-spiced rack of lamb. There's a notably large wine list. A four-course prix fixe is $50. ⊠*311 Lawrence Dr.,*

West Townshend ☎802/874–4080 ⚠Reservations essential ▭AE, D, MC, V.

WHERE TO STAY

¢–$ **Boardman House.** This handsome Greek-revival home on the town green combines modern comfort with the relaxed charm of a 19th century farmhouse. It also happens to be one of the cheapest stays in Vermont. The uncluttered guest rooms are furnished with Shaker-style furniture, colorful duvets, and paintings. Both the breakfast room and front hall have trompe l'oeil floors. **Pros:** cheap, perfect town green location. **Cons:** no phone and cell-phone reception is bad. ✉*On the green ☎802/365–4086 ⇨4 rooms, 1 suite ♨In-room: no phone, no TV, Wi-Fi. In-hotel: no elevator, public Wi-Fi, no kids under 5, no-smoking rooms ▭No credit cards* ꟾ◎ꟾ*BP.*

$$–$$$ ★ **Four Columns Inn.** Rooms and suites in this white-columned, 1834 Greek-revival mansion were designed for luxurious romantic getaways. The inn is right in the heart of town on the lovely Newfane green, giving you the quintessential Vermont village experience. Some of the suites have cathedral ceilings; all have gas fireplaces and double whirlpool baths, and one has a 12-head spa shower. The elegant restaurant ($$$–$$$$; closed Tuesday) serves new American cuisine. Come here for a serene getaway, as tiny Newfane is adorable, but quiet. **Pros:** great rooms, heart-of-town location. **Cons:** little area entertainment. ✉*On the green, 6 mi southeast of Townshend, Newfane* 📫*Box 278, 05345 ☎802/365–7713 or 800/787–6633 🌐www.fourcolumnsinn.com ⇨6 rooms, 9 suites ♨In-room: no TV (some), Wi-Fi. In-hotel: restaurant, bar, pool, no elevator, laundry service, public Internet, public Wi-Fi, some pets allowed, no-smoking rooms ▭AE, DC, MC, V* ꟾ◎ꟾ*BP.*

$$–$$$ ★ **Windham Hill Inn.** Since there's not too much to do nearby, you might find yourself sitting by a fire or swimming in the outdoor pool at this calm, quiet retreat. And that's a good thing. The 165 hillside acres have magnificent views of the West River valley and are perfect for real relaxing. Period antiques, Oriental carpets, and locally made furniture are hallmarks of the 1825 brick farmhouse. The white barn annex has a great rough-hewn parlor that leads to the rooms, most of which have fireplaces. The Marion Goodfollow room has a staircase up to a cozy private cupola with 360-degree views. **Pros:** quiet getaway, good food, lovely setting. **Cons:** little by way of entertainment. ✉*311 Lawrence Dr., West Townshend ☎802/874–4080 or 800/944–4080 🌐www.windhamhill.com ⇨21 rooms ♨In-hotel: restaurant, bar, tennis court, pool, no elevator, laundry service, public Internet, no kids under 12, no-smoking rooms ▭AE, D, MC, V* ꟾ◎ꟾ*BP.*

CENTRAL VERMONT

Central Vermont's economy once centered on marble quarrying and mills. But today, as in much of the rest of the state, tourism drives the economic engine. The center of the dynamo is Killington, the East's largest downhill resort. However, central Vermont has more to discover than high-speed chairlifts and slope-side condos. The old mills of Quechee and Middlebury are now home to restaurants and shops, giving wonderful views of the waterfalls that once powered the mill turbines. Woodstock has upscale shops and America's newest national historic park. Away from these settlements, the protected (except for occasional logging) lands of the Green Mountain National Forest are laced with hiking trails.

Our coverage of towns begins with Norwich, on U.S. 5 near Interstate 91 at the state's eastern edge; winds westward toward U.S. 7; then continues north to Middlebury before heading over the spine of the Green Mountains to Waitsfield.

NORWICH

6 mi north of White River Junction.

On the shores of the Connecticut River, Norwich boasts beautifully maintained 18th- and 19th-century homes set about a handsome green.

WHAT TO SEE

☼ **Montshire Museum of Science.** Numerous hands-on exhibits here explore
Fodor'sChoice nature and technology. Kids can make giant bubbles, watch fish and
★ turtles swim in giant aquariums, explore wind, and wander a maze of outdoor trails by the river. An ideal destination for a rainy day, this is one of the finest museums in New England. ⊠*1 Montshire Rd.* ☎*802/649–2200* ⊕*www.montshire.org* ⊠*$9* ☉*Daily 10–5.*

SHOPPING

★ Are you a baker? **King Arthur Flour Baker's Store** (⊠*135 Rte. 5 S* ☎*802/ 649–3881 or 800/827–6836*) is a must-see for those who love bread. The shelves are stocked with all the ingredients and tools in the company's *Baker's Catalogue,* including flours, mixes, and local jams and syrups. The bakery has a viewing area where you can watch products being made.

QUECHEE

11 mi southwest of Norwich, 6 mi west of White River Junction.

A historic mill town, Quechee sits just upriver from its namesake gorge, an impressive 165-foot-deep canyon cut by the Ottauquechee River. Most people view the gorge from U.S. 4. To escape the crowds, hike along the gorge or scramble down one of several trails to the river.

WHAT TO SEE

Simon Pearce. The main attraction in the village is this glassblowing factory, which an Irish glassmaker by the same name set up in 1981 in a restored woolen mill by a waterfall. Water power still drives the factory's furnace. Visitors may take a free self-guided tour of the factory floor and see the glassblowers at work. The store in the mill sells contemporary glass and ceramic tableware and home furnishings, such as glass lamps and clocks. Seconds and discontinued items are reduced

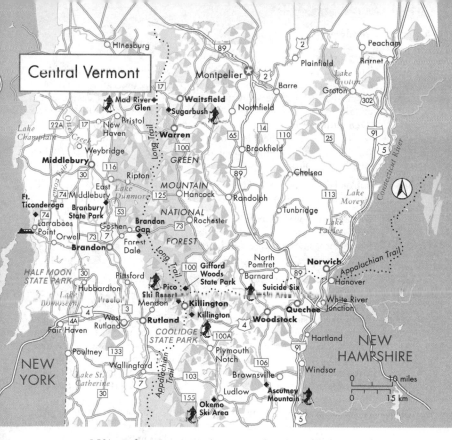

Central Vermont

25%. A fine restaurant here uses the Simon Pearce glassware and is justly popular. ⊠*The Mill, 1760 Main St.* ☎*802/295–2711* ⊕*www.simonpearce.com* ✆*Store daily 9–9; glassblowing Tues.–Sat. 9–9, Sun. and Mon. 9–5.*

☘ **Vermont Institute of Natural Science (VINS) Nature Center.** Next to Quechee Gorge, this science center has 17 raptor exhibits, including bald eagles, peregrine falcons, and a variety of owls. All the caged birds have been found injured and are unable to survive in the wild. Predators of the Sky, a 30-minute-long live bird program, starts daily at 11, 1, and 3:30. ⊠*Rte. 4* ☎*802/359–5000* ⊕*www.vinsweb.org* ✆*$8* ✆*May–Oct., daily 10–5; Nov.–Apr., daily 10–4.*

SPORTS & THE OUTDOORS

FISHING   The **Vermont Fly Fishing School/Wilderness Trails** (⊠*1119 Main St.* ☎*802/295–7620*) leads workshops, rents fishing gear and mountain bikes, and arranges canoe and kayak trips. In winter, the company conducts cross-country and snowshoe treks.

POLO   **Quechee Polo Club** (⊠*Dewey's Mill Rd., ½ mi north of U.S. 4* ☎*802/295–7152*) draws hundreds of spectators on summer Saturdays to its matches near the Quechee Gorge. Admission is $8 per carload.

SHOPPING

ANTIQUES &
CRAFTS

The 40 dealers at the **Hartland Antiques Center** (⊠ *U.S. 4* ☎*802/457–4745*) stock furniture, paper items, china, glass, and collectibles. More than 350 dealers sell their wares at the **Quechee Gorge Village** (⊠*573 Woodstock Rd., off U.S. 4* ☎*802/295–1550 or 800/438–5565* ⊕*www.quecheegorge.com*), an antiques and crafts mall in an immense reconstructed barn that also houses a country store and a classic diner. A merry-go-round and a small-scale working railroad operate when weather permits.

CLOTHING &
MORE

Scotland by the Yard (⊠ *U.S. 4* ☎*802/295–5351 or 800/295–5351*) sells all things Scottish, from kilts to Harris tweed jackets and tartan ties.

WINE

Ottauquechee Valley Winery (⊠*5967 Woodstock Rd. [U.S. 4]* ☎*802/295–9463*), in a historic 1870s barn complex, has a tasting room and sells fruit wines, such as apple and blueberry.

WHERE TO EAT & STAY

$$-$$$
Fodor'sChoice
★
AMERICAN

✕ **Simon Pearce.** Candlelight, sparkling glassware from the studio downstairs, exposed brick, and large windows overlooking the falls of the roaring Ottauquechee River create an ideal setting for contemporary American cuisine. The food is widely considered to be worthy of a pilgrimage. Sesame-seared tuna with noodle cakes and wasabi as well as roast duck with mango chutney sauce are house specialties; the wine cellar holds several hundred vintages. The lunch menu might include a roasted duck quesadilla or Mediterranean lamb burger. ⊠*The Mill, 1760 Main St.* ☎*802/295–1470* ▤*AE, D, DC, MC, V* ⚘*Reservations not accepted.*

$$-$$$

▥ **Parker House.** This beautiful house on the National Historic Register was once home to the mill owner who ran the textile mill next door (which is now Simon Pearce). Rooms are bright and clean with queen and king beds. Walter and Joseph are the names of the two cute rooms that face the river in back. Downstairs is an attractive bar area and a good French restaurant with a nightly changing menu. **Pros:** in-town; riverfront location; spacious, cute rooms. **Cons:** no yard. ⊠*1792 Main St.* ☎*802/295–6077* ⊕*www.theparkerhouseinn.com* ⇖*7 rooms, 1 suite* ⚴*In-room: no TV, Wi-Fi. In-hotel: restaurant, room service, bar, no elevator, laundry service, public Internet, public Wi-Fi, some pets allowed, no-smoking rooms* ▤*AE, MC, V* ⓞ*BP.*

$-$$

▥ **Quechee Inn at Marshland Farm.** Each room in this handsomely restored 1793 country home has Queen Anne–style furnishings and period antiques. From the old barn, the inn runs bike and canoe rentals, a fly-fishing school, and kayak and canoe trips. Eleven miles of cross-country and hiking trails are on property. Guests also have privileges at the Quechee Club, a private golf, tennis, and ski club. The dining room's ($$–$$$) creative entrées include shellfish bouillabaisse and rack of lamb with green peppercorn pesto. **Pros:** historic, spacious property. **Cons:** bathrooms are clean but out-of-date. ⊠*Main St.,* ☎*802/295–3133 or 800/235–3133* ⊕*www.quecheeinn.com* ⇖*22 rooms, 3 suites* ⚴*In-room: Wi-Fi. In-hotel: restaurant, bar, water sports, bicycles, no elevator, public Wi-Fi, no-smoking rooms* ▤*AE, D, DC, MC, V* ⓞ*BP.*

WOODSTOCK

★ *4 mi west of Quechee.*

Woodstock is a Currier & Ives print come to life. Well-maintained Federal-style houses surround the tree-lined village green, which is not far from a covered bridge. The town owes much of its pristine appearance to the Rockefeller family's interest in historic preservation and land conservation, and to town native George Perkins Marsh, a congressman, diplomat, and conservationist who wrote the pioneering book *Man and Nature* in 1864 about man's use and abuse of the land. Only busy U.S. 4 detracts from the town's quaintness.

WHAT TO SEE

⟳ **Billings Farm and Museum.** Founded by Frederick Billings in 1871 as a model dairy farm, this is one of the oldest dairy farms in the country and sits on the property that was the childhood home of George Perkins Marsh. Concerned about the loss of New England's forests to overgrazing, Billings planted thousands of trees and put into practice Marsh's conservationist farming ideas. Exhibits in the reconstructed Queen Anne farmhouse, school, general store, workshop, and former Marsh homestead demonstrate the lives and skills of early Vermont settlers. ⊠ *Rte. 12, ½ mi north of Woodstock* ☎ *802/457-2355* ⊕ *www.billingsfarm.org* 🖃 *$9.50* ◷ *May–late Oct., daily 10–5; call for winter holiday and weekend schedules.*

Marsh-Billings-Rockefeller National Historical Park. This 500-acre park is Vermont's only national park and the nation's first to focus on natural resource conservation and stewardship. The park encompasses the forest lands planned by Frederick Billings according to Marsh's principles, as well as Frederick Billings's mansion, gardens, and carriage roads. The entire property was the gift of Laurance S. Rockefeller, who lived here with his late wife, Mary, Billings's granddaughter. The residential complex is accessible by guided tour only, but you can explore the extensive network of carriage roads and trails on your own. ⊠ *Rte. 12* ☎ *802/457-3368* 🖃 *Tour $6* ◷ *May–Oct., mansion and garden tours 10–5; grounds daily dawn–dusk.*

OFF THE BEATEN PATH

Plymouth Notch Historic District. U.S. president Calvin Coolidge was born and buried in Plymouth Notch, a town that shares his character: low-key and quiet. The perfectly preserved 19th-century buildings resemble nothing so much as a Vermont town frozen in time. In addition to the homestead—where "Silent Cal" was sworn in as president at 2:47 AM on August 3, 1923, after the sudden death of President Harding—there is a visitor center, a general store once run by Coolidge's father (a room above it was once used as the summer White House), a cheese factory, two large barns displaying agricultural equipment, and a one-room schoolhouse. Coolidge's grave is in the cemetery across Route 100A. ⊠ *Rte. 100A, 6 mi south of U.S. 4, 1 mi east of Rte. 100* ☎ *802/672-3773* ⊕ *www.historicvermont.org/coolidge* ◷ *Late May–mid-Oct., daily 9:30–5.*

SPORTS & THE OUTDOORS

BIKING **Biscuit Hill Bike and Outdoor Shop** (⊠*490 Woodstock Rd.* ☎*802/457–3377*) rents, sells, and services bikes and also distributes a free touring map of local rides.

GOLF Robert Trent Jones Sr. designed the 18-hole, par-70 course at **Woodstock Country Club** (⊠*14 The Green* ☎*802/457–1100*), which is run by the Woodstock Inn. Green fees are $67 weekdays, $85 weekends; cart rentals are $18.

HORSEBACK RIDING **Kedron Valley Stables** (⊠*Rte. 106, South Woodstock* ☎*802/457–1480 or 800/225–6301*) conducts one-hour guided trail rides and horse-drawn sleigh and wagon rides.

SHOPPING

ARTWORK In downtown Woodstock, **Stephen Huneck Studio** (⊠*49 Central St.* ☎*802/457–3206*) invites canines and humans to visit the artist's gallery, filled with whimsical animal carvings, prints, and furniture.

CLOTHING ★ **Who Is Sylvia?** (⊠*26 Central St.* ☎*802/457–1110*), in the old firehouse, sells vintage clothing and antique linens, lace, and jewelry.

FOOD The **Woodstock Farmer's Market** (⊠*468 Woodstock Rd., U.S. 4* ☎*802/457–3658*) is a year-round buffet of local produce, fresh fish, and excellent sandwiches and pastries. The maple-walnut scones go fast every morning except Monday, when the market is closed. Near Taftsville, **Sugarbush Farm Inc.** (⊠*591 Sugarbush Farm Rd.* ☎*802/457–1757 or 800/281–1757*) demonstrates how maple sugar is made. The farm also makes excellent cheeses. In winter and spring, the road can be messy, so call ahead for road conditions. East of town, the **Taftsville Country Store** (⊠*U.S. 4, Taftsville* ☎*802/457–1135 or 800/854–0013*) sells a wide selection of Vermont cheeses, moderately priced wines, and Vermont specialty foods.

WHERE TO EAT

$-$$ ★ ECLECTIC ✕**Barnard Inn.** The dining room in this 1796 brick farmhouse breathes 18th century, but the food is decidedly 21st century. Former San Francisco restaurant chef-owners Will Dodson and Ruth Schimmelpfennig create inventive four-course prix-fixe menus with delicacies such as beef carpaccio and pan-seared escolar in lemon-and-caper herb butter. In the back is a local favorite, Max's Tavern, which serves upscale pub fare such as beef with Gorgonzola mashed potatoes and panfried trout with almond *beurre noisette* (browned butter). ⊠*5518 Rte. 12, 8 mi north of Woodstock, Barnard* ☎*802/234–9961* ☐*AE, MC, V* ☺*Closed Sun. and Mon. No lunch* ⚭*Reservations essential.*

$-$$ CAFE ✕**Keeper's Café.** Creative, moderately priced fare draws customers from all over the region to this café. Chef Eli Morse's menus include such light fare as pancetta salad and fresh corn soup as well as such elaborate entrées as herb garlic roast chicken with a sherry caper sauce. Blackboard specials change daily. Housed inside a former general store, the small dining room feels relaxed, with locals table-hopping to chat with friends. ⊠*Rte. 106, 12 mi south of Woodstock, Reading* ☎*802/484–9090* ☐*AE, MC, V* ☺*Closed Sun. and Mon. No lunch.*

$$ ✕ **Pane e Saluto.** One of the most exciting little restaurants in Vermont
Fodor'sChoice is run by the young couple Deirdre Heekin and Caleb Barker. Hip con-
★ temporary decor, an intimately small space, and Deirdre's discretely
ITALIAN passionate front-of-house direction all come together to complement
the chef's slow-food-inspired passion for flavorful, local and farm-
raised dishes. Try *ragu d'agnello e maiale*, spaghetti with an abruzzese
ragu from roasted pork and lamb, followed by *cotechino e lenticche*,
a garlic sausage with lentils. You might expect such a gem in Berkeley
or Brooklyn—here this *osteria* seems to pump life into the blood of old
Woodstock. Ask about the culinary tours the team leads each year in
Italy. ⊠*61 Central Woodstock, upstairs* ☎*802/457–4882* ▭*AE, MC,
V* ⊘*No lunch. Closed Tues. and Wed. and Apr. and Nov.*

$-$$ ✕ **Prince & the Pauper.** Modern French and American fare with a Ver-
★ mont accent is the focus of this candlelit Colonial restaurant off the
FRENCH Woodstock green. The grilled duck breast might have an Asian five-
spice sauce; lamb and pork sausage in puff pastry comes with a honey-
mustard sauce. A three-course prix-fixe menu is available for $46; a
less-expensive bistro menu is available in the lounge. ⊠*24 Elm St.*
☎*802/457–1818* ▭*AE, D, MC, V* ⊘*No lunch.*

WHERE TO STAY

$$-$$$ ☷ **Fan House.** Do you have an elusive dream, one that hankers for an
★ authentic home in the heart of a very small, quaint Vermont town?
Take the one-minute walk from the perfect general store in Barnard to
this 1840 white colonial: and here it is. The three rooms put together
by Sara Widness—who happens to be an expert on luxury travel—are
cozy, comfortable, and avoid romantic clichés. The rooms are simply
adorned with tapestries, antique rugs, claw-foot tubs, comfy sofas, and
old bed frames guarding soft linens and a mountain of pillows. The
living room hearth, the old wood stove in the kitchen, and the library
nook create a real sense of home. **Pros:** center of old town, homey comforts, good library. **Cons:** upstairs rooms can be cool in winter. ⊠*Rte.
12 N* ⊞*Box 294, 05031* ☎*802/234–6704* ⊕*www.thefanhouse.com*
↻*3 rooms* ⚹*In room: no TV, no phone. In hotel: no elevator, public Internet, no kids under 12, no-smoking rooms* ▭*No credit cards*
⊘*Closed Apr.* ⫚*BP.*

$$-$$$ ☷ **Kedron Valley Inn.** Two 19th-century buildings and a 1968 log lodge
make up this inn on 15 acres. Many of the rooms have a fireplace or
a Franklin stove, and some have private decks or terraces. The motel
units in the log lodge boast country antiques and reproductions. A big
spring-fed pond has a white sand beach with toys for kids. In the res-
taurant ($$–$$$$), the chef creates French masterpieces such as fillet
of Norwegian salmon stuffed with herb seafood mousse in puff pastry.
Pros: good food, quiet setting, beach. **Cons:** 5 mi south of Woodstock.
⊠*Rte. 106* ☎*802/457–1473 or 800/836–1193* ⊕*www.kedronvalley
inn.com* ↻*21 rooms, 6 suites* ⚹*In-room: no a/c (some), no phone. In-
hotel: restaurant, bar, no elevator, public Internet, some pets allowed,
no-smoking rooms* ▭*AE, MC, V* ⊘*Closed Apr.* ⫚*BP.*

$$$ ☷ **Maple Leaf Inn.** Nancy and Mike Boyle operate this traditional B&B
set back far from the main road on 16 wooded acres near the center of
little Barnard. The house was built in 1994 and has modern features

like radiant floor heat. Victorian appointments make it feel like its been here quite a while—while still maintaining a spotless order. The light and airy rooms have king-size beds and big whirlpool or soaking tubs. Most rooms have wood-burning fireplaces and sitting areas. The inn includes a pillow library, where you can "check out" pillows of varying firmness. **Pros:** clean, quaint rooms; great front porch. **Cons:** a 10-minute drive from Woodstock, doesn't feel rustic. ⊠*Rte. 12, 8 mi north of Woodstock, Barnard* ☏*802/234–5342 or 800/516–2753* ⊕*www. mapleleafinn.com* ☞*7 rooms* &*In-room: VCR, Wi-Fi. In-hotel: bicycles, no elevator, public Internet, public Wi-Fi, no kids under 14, no-smoking rooms* ☰*AE, D, MC, V* ⊚*BP.*

$$ ⊞**Shire Riverview Motel.** Some rooms in this immaculate motel have decks—and almost all have views—overlooking the Ottauquechee River. Rooms are simple, a step above usual motel fare, with four-poster beds and wing chairs; two rooms have hot tubs and the suite has a full kitchen. Complimentary coffee is served each morning; in summer take it on the riverfront veranda. The real key here is walking distance to the green and all shops. **Pros:** inexpensive access to the heart of Woodstock, views. **Cons:** dull rooms. ⊠*46 Pleasant St.* ☏*802/457–2211* ⊕*www.shiremotel.com* ☞*42 rooms, 1 suite* &*In-room: kitchen (some), refrigerator, no-smoking rooms* ☰*AE, D, MC, V.*

$$$$ ⊞**Twin Farms.** Let's just get out with it: Twin Farms is the best lodg-
Fodor'sChoice ing choice in Vermont. (Some even say it's the best small property in
★ America.) And if you can afford it—stays begin at well over $1,000 a night—you'll want to experience it. Three rooms are in the beautiful main building, which was once home to writer Sinclair Lewis. The rest are individual cottages, secluded among 300 acres. Each incredible room and cottage is furnished with a blend of high art (Jasper Johns, Milton Avery, Cy Twombly), gorgeous folk art, and furniture that goes beyond comfortable sophistication. The food may be the best in Vermont. The service—suave, relaxed—definitely is. Prices include all meals, alcohol and activities—there's a good spa, a pub within a big game room, and a private ski hill. **Pros:** impeccable service; stunning rooms; sensational meals. **Cons:** astronomical prices. ⊠*Royalton Turnpike, Barnard* ☏*802/234–9999* ⊕*www.twinfarms.com* ☞*3 rooms, 10 cottages* &*In room: DVD, Wi-Fi. In-hotel: restaurant, room service, bars, tennis courts, pool(s), gym, spa, water sports, bicycles, no elevator, laundry service, public Internet, public Wi-Fi, no kids under 12, no-smoking rooms* ☰*AE, D, DC, MC, V* ⊙*Closed Apr.* ⊚*AI.*

$$$ ⊞**Woodstock Inn and Resort.** If this is your first time in Woodstock and
Fodor'sChoice you want to feel like you're in the middle of it all, stay here. Set back
★ far from the main road but still on the town's gorgeous green, the Inn is the town's beating heart. You'll feel that right away when looking at the main fireplace, set immediately through the front doors, which burns impressive three-foot-long logs. Rooms are contemporary and luxurious, with huge flat screen TVs, sleek furniture and great bathrooms done in clean-looking subway tiles. The resort also owns and gives you access to Suicide Six ski mountain and the Woodstock Golf Club. **Pros:** exciting, big property; contemporary furnishings; professionally run **Cons:** can lack intimacy. ⊠*14 The Green, U.S. 4* ☏*802/457–1100*

or 800/448-7900 ⊕*www.woodstockinn.com* ↪*135 rooms, 7 suites*
♿ *In-room: safe, refrigerator, Ethernet (some), Wi-Fi (some). In-hotel:*
2 restaurants, room service, bar, golf course, tennis courts, pools, gym,
bicycles, laundry service, concierge, public Internet, no-smoking rooms
�'t*AE, D, MC, V.*

KILLINGTON

15 mi east of Rutland.

With only a gas station, post office, motel, and a few shops at the intersection of Routes 4 and 100, it's difficult to tell that the East's largest
ski resort is nearby. The village of Killington is characterized by unfor-
tunate strip development along the access road to the ski resort. But
the 360-degree views atop Killington Peak, accessible by the resort's
gondola, make it worth the drive.

SPORTS & THE OUTDOORS

BIKING **True Wheels Bike Shop** (✉*Killington Rd.* ☎*802/422-3234*) sells and
rents bicycles and has information on local mountain and bicycle
routes.

FISHING Kent Pond in **Gifford Woods State Park** (✉*Rte. 100, ½ mi north of U.S.
4* ☎*802/775-5354*) is a terrific fishing spot.

GOLF At its namesake resort, **Killington Golf Course** (✉*4763 Killington Rd.*
☎*802/422-6700*) has a challenging 18-hole course. Green fees are $52
midweek and $57 weekends; carts run for $17.

SKI AREA "Megamountain," "Beast of the East," and plain "huge" are apt descrip-
★ tions of **Killington** (✉*4763 Killington Rd.* ☎*802/422-6200, 802/422-
3261 snow conditions, 800/621-6867 lodging* ⊕*www.killington.
com*). The American Skiing Company operates Killington and its neighbor, **Pico**, and over the past several years has improved lifts and snowmaking capabilities. Thanks to its extensive snowmaking system, the
resort typically opens in October and the lifts often run into May.
Killington's après-ski activities are plentiful and have been rated the
best in the East by national ski magazines. With a single call to Killington's hotline or a visit to its Web site, skiers can plan an entire vacation: choose accommodations, book air or railroad transportation, and
arrange for rental equipment and ski lessons. Killington ticket holders
can also ski at Pico: a shuttle connects the two areas.

The Killington–Pico complex has a host of activities, including an
alpine slide, a golf course, two waterslides, a skateboard park, and a
swimming pool. The resort rents mountain bikes and advises hikers.
The K-1 Express Gondola takes you up the mountain, Vermont's sec-
ond-highest summit.

In terms of downhill skiing, it would probably take several weeks to test
all 200 trails on the seven mountains of the Killington complex, even
though all except Pico interconnect. About 70% of the 1,182 acres of
skiing terrain can be covered with machine-made snow. Transporting
skiers to the peaks of this complex are 32 lifts, including 2 gondolas,

5

12 quads (including 6 high-speed express quads), 6 triples, and a Magic Carpet. The K-1 Express Gondola goes to the area's highest elevation, 4,241-foot Killington Peak. The Skyeship Gondola starts on U.S. 4, far below Killington's main base lodge, and savvy skiers park here to avoid the more crowded access road. After picking up more passengers at a mid-station, the Skyeship tops out on Skye Peak. Although Killington has a vertical drop of 3,050 feet, only gentle trails—Juggernaut and Great Eastern—go from top to bottom. The skiing includes everything from Outer Limits, one of the East's steepest and most challenging mogul trails, to 6½-mi Great Eastern. In the Fusion Zones, underbrush and low branches have been cleared away to provide tree skiing. Killington's Superpipe is one of the best rated in the East. Instruction programs are available for youngsters ages 3–8; those from 6 to 12 can join an all-day program.

Mountain Top Inn and Resort (⊠ *195 Mountaintop Rd., Chittenden* ☎ *802/483–6089 or 800/445–2100* ⊕ *www.mountaintopinn.com*) has 50 mi of hilly trails groomed for nordic skiing, 37 mi of which can be used for skate skiing. You can also enjoy snowshoeing, dogsledding, ice skating, and snowmobile and sleigh rides. In the summer there's horseback riding, fishing, hiking, biking, and water sports.

NIGHTLIFE & THE ARTS
On weekends, listen to live music and sip draft Guinness at the **Inn at Long Trail** (⊠ *U.S. 4* ☎ *802/775–7181*). The **Nightspot Outback** (⊠ *Killington Rd.* ☎ *802/422–9885*) serves all-you-can-eat pizza on Monday nights in winter, and $2 Long Trail pints on Sunday. It's open year-round. During ski season, the **Pickle Barrel Night Club** (⊠ *Killington Rd.* ☎ *802/422–3035*) has a band every happy hour on Friday and Saturday. After 8, the crowd moves downstairs for dancing, sometimes to big-name bands. Twentysomethings prefer to dance at the **Wobbly Barn** (⊠ *Killington Rd.* ☎ *802/422–3392*), open only during ski season.

WHERE TO EAT & STAY
$$$$
★
CONTINENTAL
✕ **Hemingway's.** With a national reputation, Hemingway's is as good as dining gets. Among the house specialties are the cream of garlic soup and a seasonal kaleidoscope of dishes created by chef-owner Ted Fondulas. Native baby pheasant with local chanterelles or seared scallops with truffles and caramelized onions are just two entrées that might appear on the menu. Diners can opt for the prix-fixe, three- to six-course menu or the wine-tasting menu. Request seating in either the formal vaulted dining room, the intimate wine cellar, or the garden room. ⊠ *4988 U.S. 4* ☎ *802/422–3886* ⌖ *Reservations essential* ▬ *AE, D, DC, MC, V* ⊙ *Closed Mon. and Tues., early Nov., and mid-Apr.–mid-May. No lunch.*

$$
🛏 **Birch Ridge Inn.** A slate-covered carriageway leads uphill to one of Killington's newest inns, a former executive retreat in two renovated A-frames. Rooms range in style from Colonial and Shaker to Mission, and all have a sitting area with a TV hidden behind artwork (in one room, a dollhouse rotates up to reveal the TV). Six rooms have gas fireplaces, and four have whirlpool baths. In the intimate slate-floored dining room ($$–$$$$; closed Monday and Tuesday), choose either a four-

course prix-fixe dinner or order à la carte. **Pros:** quirky. **Cons:** oddly furnished, slightly older rooms. ⊠*37 Butler Rd.* ☎*802/422–4293 or 800/435 8566* ⊕*www.birchridge.com* ➾*10 rooms* ⚲*In-room: no a/c (some), Wi-Fi. In hotel: restaurant, bar, no elevator, public Wi-Fi, no kids under 12, no smoking rooms* ☐*AE, D, MC, V* ☉*Closed May* ⚭*BP, MAP.*

$$$$ ⚏**Woods Resort & Spa.** These clustered upscale two- and three-bed-room town houses stand in wooded lots along a winding road leading to the spa. Most units have master baths with saunas and two-person whirlpool tubs. Vaulted ceilings in the living rooms give an open, airy feel. The resort has a private shuttle to the ski area. **Pros:** contemporary facility; clean, spacious rooms; lots of room choices. **Cons:** lacks traditional Vermont feeling. ⊠*53 Woods La.* ☎*802/422–3139 or 800/642–1147* ⊕*www.woodsresortandspa.com* ➾*107 units* ⚲*In-room: no a/c, kitchen, VCR, Wi-Fi. In hotel: tennis courts, pool, gym, spa, no elevator, laundry facilities, some pets allowed, no-smoking rooms* ☰*AE, MC, V.*

5

RUTLAND

15 mi southwest of Killington, 32 mi south of Middlebury.

On and around U.S. 7 in Rutland are strips of shopping centers and a seemingly endless row of traffic lights. Two blocks west, however, stand the mansions of the marble magnates. Preservation work has uncovered white and verde marble facades; the stonework harkens back to the days when marble ruled what was once Vermont's second-largest city.

WHAT TO SEE

Paramount Theatre. The highlight of downtown is this 700-seat, turn-of-the-20th-century gilded playhouse. ⊠*30 Center St.* ☎*802/775–0570* ⊕*www.paramountvt.org.*

Chaffee Art Center. The former mansion of the local Paramount Theatre's founder, this arts center exhibits the work of more than 200 Vermont artists. ⊠*16 S. Main St.* ☎*802/775–0356* ⊕*www.chaffeeartcenter.org* ⛶*Free* ☉*Tues. Sat. 10–5, Sun. noon–4.*

Vermont Marble Exhibit. North of Rutland, this monument to marble highlights one of the main industries in this region, and illustrates marble's many industrial and artistic applications. The hall of presidents has a carved bust of each U.S. president, and in the marble chapel is a replica of Leonardo da Vinci's *Last Supper.* Elsewhere you can watch a sculptor-in-residence shape the stone into finished works of art, compare marbles from around the world, and also check out the Vermont Marble Company's original "stone library." Factory seconds and foreign and domestic marble items are for sale. A short walk away is the original marble quarry in Proctor. Marble from here became part of the U.S. Supreme Court building and the New York Public Library. ⊠*52 Main St., 4 mi north of Rutland, off Rte. 3, Proctor* ☎*802/459–2300* *or 800/427–1396* ⊕*www.vermont-marble.com* ⊠*$7* ⊙*Mid-May–Oct., daily 9–5:30.*

Wilson Castle. This 32-room mansion built in 1875 comes complete with 84 stained-glass windows (one inset with 32 Australian opals), hand-painted Italian frescos, and 13 fireplaces. It's magnificently furnished with European and Asian objets d'art. ⊠ *W. Proctor Rd., Proctor* ☎*802/773–3284* ⊕*www.wilsoncastle.com* ⊠*$8.50* ⊙*Late May–mid-Oct., daily 9–5:30.*

SPORTS & THE OUTDOORS

BOATING   Rent pontoon boats, speedboats, waterskiing boats, Wave Runners, and water toys at **Lake Bomoseen Marina** (⊠*145 Creek Rd., off Rte. 4A, 1½ mi west of Castleton* ☎*802/265–4611*).

HIKING   **Deer's Leap** (⊠*Starts at the Inn at Long Trail on Rte. 4 west of Rutland*) is a 3-mi round-trip hike to a great view overlooking Sherburne Gap and Pico Peak. **Mountain Travelers** (⊠*147 Rte. 4 E* ☎*802/775–0814*) sells hiking maps and guidebooks, and gives advice on local hikes.

NIGHTLIFE & THE ARTS

Crossroads Arts Council (⊠*39 E. Center St.* ☎*802/775–5413*) presents films, music, opera, dance, jazz, and theater year-round at venues throughout the region.

WHERE TO EAT & STAY

¢–$ ✕ **Little Harry's.** Locals have packed this restaurant ever since chef-own-
ECLECTIC   ers Trip (Harry) Pearce and Jack Mangan brought Vermont cheddar-cheese ravioli and lamb lo mein to downtown Rutland in 1997. The 17 tabletops are adorned with laminated photos of the regulars. For big appetites on small budgets, the Pad Thai and burrito are huge meals for under $8. ⊠*121 West St.* ☎*802/747–4848* ⊟*MC, V* ⊙*No lunch.*

$$ 🏠 **Inn at Rutland.** If you love B&Bs and are tired of Rutland's chain motels this stately 1889 Victorian mansion on Main Street is a welcome sight. Large plate-glass windows illuminate the entryway, library, and sitting room. A large table dominates the dining room, which has hand-tooled leather wainscoting. Upstairs, the rooms have antiques; two rooms have private porches and whirlpool tubs. **Pros:** solid, non-motel choice. **Cons:** unexciting rooms. ⊠*70 N. Main St.* ☎*802/773–0575 or 800/808–0575* ⊕*www.innatrutland.com* ⟳*8 rooms* &*In-room: Wi-Fi. In-hotel: restaurant, no elevator, public Internet, public Wi-Fi, no-smoking rooms* ⊟*AE, D, MC, V.*

BRANDON

15 mi northwest of Rutland.

Thanks to an active artists' guild, Brandon is making a name for itself. In 2003 the Brandon Artists Guild, led by American folk artist Warren Kimble, auctioned 40 life-size fiberglass pigs painted by local artists. The "Really Really Pig Show" raised money for the guild (as well as other organizations) and brought fame to this once overlooked community. Since then themes have been birdhouses, rocking chairs, artist palettes, cats and dogs, and in 2008, "Thinking Outside the Box." The works are spread throughout town.

WHAT TO SEE

New England Maple Museum and Gift Shop. Maple syrup is Vermont's signature product and this museum south of Brandon explains the history and process of turning maple sap into syrup with murals, exhibits, and a slide show. ⊠*U.S. 7, Pittsford, 9 mi south of Brandon* ☎*802/483–9414* ◲*Museum $2.50* ⊘*Late May–Oct., daily 8:30–5:30; Nov., Dec., and mid-Mar.–late May, daily 10–4.*

SPORTS & THE OUTDOORS

The **Moosalamoo Association** (☎*800/448–0707*) manages, protects, and provides stewardship for more than 20,000 acres of the Green Mountain National Forest, just northeast of Brandon. More than 60 mi of trails take hikers, mountain bikers, and cross-country skiers through some of Vermont's most gorgeous mountain terrain. Attractions include Branbury State Park, on the shores of Lake Dunmore; secluded Silver Lake; and sections of both the Long Trail and Catamount Trail (the latter is a Massachusetts-to-Quebec ski trail).

GOLF **Neshobe Golf Club** (⊠*Rte. 73 east of Brandon* ☎*802/247–3611*) has 18 holes of par-72 golf on a bent-grass course totaling nearly 6,500 yards. The Green Mountain views are terrific.

HIKING For great views from a vertigo-inducing cliff, hike up the Long Trail to **Mt. Horrid.** The steep, hour-long hike starts at the top of Brandon Gap (about 8 mi east of Brandon on Route 73). A large turnout on Route 53 marks a moderate trail to the **Falls of Lana.** West of Brandon, four trails—two short ones of less than 1 mi each and two longer ones—lead to the old abandoned Revolutionary War fortifications at **Mt. Independence.** To reach them, take the first left turn off Route 73 west of Orwell and go right at the fork. The road will turn to gravel and once again will fork; take a sharp left-hand turn toward a small marina. The parking lot is on the left at the top of the hill.

WHERE TO EAT & STAY

$-$$ ✕**Café Provence.** One story above the main street, this large, high-ceil-
CAFE inged café with hints of Provence (flowered seat cushions and dried-flower window valences) specializes in eclectic farm-fresh dishes. Goat-cheese cake with mesclun greens, braised veal cheeks and caramelized endive, and a portobello pizza from the restaurant's hearth oven are just a few of the choices. Breakfast offerings include buttery pastries, eggs Benedict, and breakfast pizza. Umbrellas shade outdoor seating. ⊠*11 Center St.* ☎*802/247–9997* ⊟*MC, V.*

$$-$$$ ◲**Blueberry Hill Inn.** In the Green Mountain National Forest, 5½ mi off
★ a mountain pass on a dirt road, you'll find this secluded inn with its lush gardens and a pond with a wood-fired sauna on its bank. Many rooms have views of the mountains; all are furnished with antiques and quilts. The restaurant prepares a four-course prix-fixe ($$$$) menu nightly, with dishes such as venison fillet with cherry sauce. This is a very popular place for weddings–the grounds are gorgeous and there's lots to do if you're into nature: biking, hiking, and a cross-country ski

center with 43 mi of trails. **Pros:** peaceful setting witin the national forest; terrific property with lots to do; great food. **Cons:** forest setting not right for those who want to be near town. ✉ *1307 Goshen–Ripton Rd., Goshen* ☎ *802/247–6735 or 800/448–0707* ⊕ *www.blueberry hillinn.com* ➷ *12 rooms* ♿ *In-room: no a/c, no phone, no TV, Wi-Fi. In-hotel: restaurant, bicycles, no elevator, public Internet, public Wi-Fi, some pets allowed, no-smoking rooms* ▭ *AE, MC, V* ⑪ *MAP.*

$$-$$$ ⊞ **Brandon Inn.** Built in 1786, this large hotel exudes an aura of elegance from centuries past. The foyer has marble flooring, and this theme continues throughout the three-story inn. The Victorian-furnished common rooms and multipillared dining room, used only for special groups, are expansive (and underutilized). In the main lobby, the state's oldest elevator (circa 1901) leads to two upper floors with comfortable and spacious guest rooms. **Pros:** in-town location. **Cons:** unexciting rooms. ✉ *20 Park St.* ☎ *800/639–8685* ⊕ *www.historicbrandoninn. com* ➷ *39 rooms* ♿ *In-room: no TV. In-hotel: restaurant, pool, no-smoking rooms* ▭ *AE, D, MC, V* ⑪ *BP.*

$$-$$$ ⊞ **Lilac Inn.** This Greek-revival mansion's spacious common areas are filled with lovely antiques. The rooms, all furnished with claw-foot tubs and handheld European showerheads, are charming, and the grand suite has a pewter canopy bed, whirlpool bath for two, and fireplace. Overlooking the gardens, the elegant dining room ($$) serves unique creations such as fig-mango pork short ribs. **Pros:** big manor house, walking distance to town. **Cons:** busy in summer with weddings. ✉ *53 Park St. (Rte. 73)* ☎ *802/247–5463 or 800/221–0720* ⊕ *www.lilacinn. com* ➷ *9 rooms* ♿ *In-room: no a/c. In-hotel: restaurant, public Inter-net, public Wi-Fi, no kids under 12, some pets allowed, no-smoking rooms* ▭ *AE, MC, V* ⑪ *BP.*

MIDDLEBURY

★ *17 mi north of Brandon, 34 mi south of Burlington.*

In the late 1800s Middlebury was the largest Vermont community west of the Green Mountains, an industrial center of river-powered wool and grain mills. This is Robert Frost country: Vermont's late poet laureate spent 23 summers at a farm east of Middlebury. Still a cultural and economic hub amid the Champlain Valley's serene pastoral patchwork, the town and countryside invite a day of exploration.

WHAT TO SEE

Middlebury College. Founded in 1800, Middlebury College was conceived as a more godly alternative to the worldly University of Vermont. The college has no religious affiliation today, however. Set in the middle of town, the early-19th-century stone buildings contrast provocatively with the postmodern architecture of the Center for the Arts and the sports center. Music, theater, and dance performances take place throughout the year at the **Wright Memorial Theatre** and **Center for the Arts** (☎ *802/443–5000).*

Vermont Folklife Center. Located in the Masonic Hall, exhibits include photography, antiques, folk paintings, manuscripts, and other artifacts and contemporary works that examine facets of Vermont life. ⊠*3 Court St.* ☎*802/388–4964* ❦*Donations accepted* ☉*Gallery May–Dec., Tues.–Sat. 11–4.*

Vermont State Craft Center/Frog Hollow. More than a crafts store, this arts center mounts changing exhibitions and displays exquisite works in wood, glass, metal, clay, and fiber by more than 250 Vermont artisans. The center, which overlooks Otter Creek, sponsors classes taught by some of those artists. Burlington and Manchester also have centers. ⊠*1 Mill St.* ☎*802/388–3177* ⊕*www.froghollow.org* ☉*Call for hrs.*

☾ **UVM Morgan Horse Farm.** The Morgan horse—Vermont's official state animal—has an even temper, stamina, and slightly truncated legs in proportion to its body. The University of Vermont's Morgan Horse Farm, about 2½ mi west of Middlebury, is a breeding and training center where in summer you can tour the stables and paddocks. ⊠*74 Battell Dr., off Morgan Horse Farm Rd. (follow signs off Rte. 23), Weybridge* ☎*802/388–2011* ❦*$4* ☉*May–Oct., daily 9–4.*

Robert Frost Interpretive Trail. About 10 mi east of town on Route 125 (1 mi west of Middlebury College's Bread Loaf campus), this easy ¾-mi trail winds through quiet woodland. Plaques along the way bear quotations from Frost's poems. A picnic area is across the road from the trailhead.

Fort Ticonderoga Ferry. Established in 1759, the Fort Ti cable ferry crosses Lake Champlain between Shoreham and Fort Ticonderoga, New York, at one of the oldest ferry crossings in North America. The trip takes seven minutes. ⊠*4675 Rte. 74 W, 18 mi southwest of Middlebury, 9 mi south of Brandon, Shoreham* ☎*802/897–7999* ❦*Cars, pickups, and vans with driver and passenger $8; bicycles $2; pedestrians $1* ☉*May–last Sun. of Oct., daily 8–5:45.*

SHOPPING

ARTWORK **Historic Marble Works** (⊠*Maple St.* ☎*802/388–3701*), a renovated marble manufacturing facility, is a collection of unique shops set amid quarrying equipment and factory buildings. One of them, **Danforth Pewter** (☎*802/388–0098*), sells handcrafted pewter vases, lamps, and tableware.

WHERE TO EAT & STAY

¢–$ ✕**American Flatbread.** On weekends this is the most happening spot
★ in town, and no wonder: the pizza is extraordinary and the attitude
PIZZA is pure Vermont. Wood-fired clay domes create masterful crusts from organically grown wheats. Besides the innovative, delicious pizzas, try an organic mesclun salad tossed in a house raspberry-ginger vinaigrette. During the week, when the restaurant is closed, the space is used to manufacture pizzas for gourmet stores across the country—but if you pop in at any time you can buy whatever is in the oven for a flat $10. (And whatever is in the oven is sure to be delicious.) ⊠*137 Maple St., at the Marble Works* ☎*802/388–3300* ❦*Reservations not accepted* ▤*MC, V* ☉*Closed Sun.–Thurs. No lunch.*

$$-$$$ **✕Mary's at Baldwin Creek.** People drive from the far reaches of Vermont
Fodor'sChoice to eat at this restaurant in Bristol, 13 mi northeast of Middlebury. Chef-
★ owner Douglas Mack founded the Vermont Fresh Network; member-
ECLECTIC ship in this group, which facilitates farm-fresh ingredients, is now a
hallmark of the state's best restaurants. The innovative fare includes
a superb garlic soup and entrées with whimsical names like Swimming with Noodles (shrimp, shiitake mushrooms, roasted tomato, and
asparagus sautéed in garlic white wine and served over fettuccine),
and What's Eating Gilbert Crepe (sesame-and-ginger-marinated tofu
in a crepe). A café menu is also available. ⊠*1869 Rte. 116, Bristol*
☎*802/453–2432* ▤*MC, V* ⊙*Closed Mon. and Tues. No lunch.*

$$-$$$ **✕Storm Café.** Locals rave about the eclectic ever-changing menu at this
ECLECTIC small restaurant in the old Frog Hollow Mill overlooking the Otter
Creek Falls. Chef-owner John Goettelmann's creations include stormy
Thai stew, Jamaican jerk-seasoned pork tenderloin, and melt-in-your-
mouth desserts like an apricot soufflé. Outdoor seating by the river
is available in nice weather. ⊠*3 Mill St.* ☎*802/388–1063* ▤*MC, V*
⊙*No lunch Sun.*

$-$$ **⊡Swift House Inn.** The 1824 Georgian home of a 19th-century governor
showcases white-panel wainscoting, mahogany furnishings, and marble
fireplaces. The stellar rooms—most with Oriental rugs and nine with
fireplaces—have period reproductions such as canopy beds, curtains
with swags, and claw-foot tubs. Some bathrooms have double whirlpool tubs. Rooms in the attractive Gatehouse suffer from street noise
but are charming and a solid value. The seven-room carriage house has
more expensive rooms with wood fireplaces and king-size beds. **Pros:**
attractive, spacious, well-kept rooms; professionally run. **Cons:** near,
but not quite in the heart of town. ⊠*25 Stewart La.* ☎*802/388–9925*
⊕*www.swifthouseinn.com* ⇆*20 rooms* ⚭*In-room: DVD (some),
VCR (some), Wi-Fi. In-hotel: restaurant, room service, bar, laundry
service, public Wi-Fi, some pets allowed, no-smoking rooms* ▤*AE,
D, DC, MC, V* ⎸◎⎹*BP.*

WAITSFIELD & WARREN

32 mi northeast (Waitsfield) and 25 mi east (Warren) of Middlebury.

Skiers discovered the high peaks overlooking the pastoral Mad River
valley in the 1940s. Now the valley and its two towns, Waitsfield and
Warren, attract the hip, the adventurous, and the low-key. Warren is
tiny and adorable, with a general store that attracts tour buses. The
gently carved ridges cradling the valley and the swell of pastures and
fields lining the river seem to keep notions of ski-resort sprawl at bay.
With a map from the Sugarbush Chamber of Commerce you can inves-
tigate back roads off Route 100 that have exhilarating valley views.

SPORTS & THE OUTDOORS

OUTFITTER **Clearwater Sports** (⊠*4147 Main St. [Rte. 100]* ☎*802/496–2708*) rents
canoes, kayaks, and camping equipment and leads guided river trips
and white-water instruction in the warm months; in winter, the store

leads snowshoe and backcountry ski tours and rents telemark equipment, snowshoes, and one-person Mad River Rocket sleds.

GOLF Great views and challenging play are the trademarks of the Robert Trent Jones–designed 18-hole mountain course at **Sugarbush Resort** (✉ *Golf Course Rd.* ☎ *802/583–6725*). The green fees run from $48 to $58; a cart (sometimes mandatory) costs $18 per person.

SLEIGH RIDES **Mountain Valley Farm** (✉ *1719 Common Rd.* ☎ *802/496–9255*) offers in horse-drawn carriage and sleigh rides. Reservations are required.

SKI AREAS **Blueberry Lake Cross-Country Ski Area** (✉ *Plunkton Rd.*, *Warren* ☎ *802/496–6687*) has 18 mi of trails through thickly wooded glades.

The hundreds of shareholders who own **Mad River Glen** (✉ *Rte. 17* ☎ *802/496–3551, 802/496–2001 snow conditions, 800/850–6742 cooperative office* ⊕ *www.madriverglen.com*) are dedicated, knowledgeable skiers devoted to keeping skiing what it used to be—a pristine alpine experience. Mad River's unkempt aura attracts rugged individualists looking for less-polished terrain: the area was developed in the late 1940s and has changed relatively little since then. It remains one of only three resorts in the country that ban snowboarding.

Mad River is steep, with natural slopes that follow the mountain's fall lines. The terrain changes constantly on the 45 interconnected trails, of which 30% are beginner, 30% are intermediate, and 40% are expert. Intermediate and novice terrain is regularly groomed. Five lifts—including the world's last surviving single chairlift—service the mountain's 2,037-foot vertical drop. Most of Mad River's trails are covered only by natural snow. The kids ski school runs classes for little ones ages 4 to 12.

Known as the "Mecca of Free-Heel Skiing," Mad River Glen sponsors telemark programs throughout the season. Every March, the North America Telemark Organization (NATO) Festival attracts up to 1,400. Snowshoeing is also an option. There is a $5 fee to use the snowshoe trails, and rentals are available.

Sugarbush (✉ *Sugarbush Access Rd., accessible from Rtes. 100 or 17* ☎ *Box 350, Warren 05674* ☎ *802/583–6300, 802/583–7669 snow conditions, 800/537–8427 lodging* ⊕ *www.sugarbush.com*) has remade itself as a true skier's mountain, with steep, natural snow glades and fall-line drops. Not as rough around the edges as Mad River Glen, Sugarbush also has well-groomed intermediate and beginner terrain. A computer-controlled system for snowmaking has increased coverage to nearly 70%. At the base of the mountain are condominiums, restaurants, shops, bars, and a sports center.

Sugarbush is two distinct, connected mountain complexes connected by the Slide Brook Express quad. Lincoln Peak, with a vertical of 2,400 feet, is known for formidable steeps, especially on Castlerock. Mount Ellen has more beginner runs near the bottom, with steep fall-line pitches on the upper half of the 2,650 vertical feet. There are 115 trails in all: 23% beginner, 48% intermediate, 29% expert. The resort has

18 lifts: seven quads (including four high-speed versions), three triples, four doubles, and four surface lifts. There's half- and full-day instruction available for children ages 4–12, ski/day care for 3-year-olds, and supervised ski and ride programs for teens. Sugarbear Forest, a terrain garden, has fun bumps and jumps.

SHOPPING

All Things Bright and Beautiful (⊠*Bridge St.* ☎*802/496–3997*) is a 12-room Victorian house jammed to the rafters with stuffed animals of all shapes, sizes, and colors as well as folk art, prints, and collectibles. One of the rooms is a coffee and ice-cream shop. **Cabin Fever Quilts** (⊠*4276 Main St. No. 1 [Rte. 100]* ☎*802/496–2287*), inside a converted old church, sells fine handmade quilts.

NIGHTLIFE & THE ARTS

NIGHTLIFE **Chez Henri** (⊠*Lincoln Peak base area, Sugarbush Village, Warren* ☎*802/583–2600*) is the place to go après-ski. Live bands play most weekends at **Purple Moon Pub** (⊠*Rte. 100* ☎*802/496–3422*).

★ In the basement of the Pitcher Inn, **Tracks** (⊠*275 Main St. Warren* ☎*802/493–6350*) is a public bar run by the Relais & Châteaux property. It has billiards, darts, and a really fun game like shuffle board played on a long table with sawdust. There's a full tavern menu and a giant moose head.

ARTS The **Green Mountain Cultural Center** (⊠*Inn at the Round Barn Farm, 1661 E. Warren Rd.* ☎*802/496–7722*) hosts concerts, art exhibits, and educational workshops. The **Valley Players** (⊠*Rte. 100, Waitsfield* ☎*802/496–9612*) present musicals, dramas, follies, and more.

WHERE TO EAT

$$–$$$ ✕ **1824 House.** Much like the Common Man up the hill closer to Sug-
AMERICAN arbush, this reconverted barn is floor-to-ceiling wood. The 1870 post-and-beam construction is hung with chandeliers and is an enticing setting for a fancy meal cooked up by owner John Lumbra. A specialty is the French onion soup made with Tarentaise, an excellent cheese made only in Vermont. Entrées might include lobster pancakes, filet mignon stuffed with blue cheese and wrapped in bacon, and a lemon sabayon–pine-nut tart. ⊠*2150 Main St., Waitsfield* ☎*802/496–7555* or *800/426–3986* ▤*AE, MC, V* ☉*No lunch. Dec.–Feb. closed Mon. and Tues.; June–Aug. closed Tues. and Wed.*

¢–$ ✕ **American Flatbread.** Is this the best pizza experience in the world? It
FodorśChoice just may be. In summer, dining takes place outside around fire pits in
★ the beautiful valley, a setting and meal not to be forgotten. The secret is
PIZZA in the love, of course, but some clues to the magic are in the organically grown flour and vegetables and the wood-fired clay ovens. The "new Vermont sausage" is Waitsfield pork in a maple-fennel sausage baked with sundried tomatoes, caramelized onions, cheese, and herbs; it's a dream, as are the more traditional pizzas. This is the original American Flatbread location, and the retail bakery is open Monday–Thursday 7:30 AM–8 PM; if you're here during that time anything in the oven is yours for $10. As a restaurant, it's open only Friday and Saturday evenings. Plan your trip around it. ⊠*46 Lareau Rd., off Rte. 100,*

Waitsfield ☎*802/496-8856* ⚒*Reservations not accepted* ▭*MC, V* ☉*Closed Sun.*

$$$-$$$$
ECLECTIC

✗**Common Man.** A local institution since 1972, this restaurant is in a big 1800s barn with hand-hewn rafters and crystal chandeliers hanging from the beams. That's the Common Man for you: fancy and après-ski at once. Bottles of Moët & Chandon signed by the customers who ordered them sit atop the beams. The eclectic New American cuisine highlights locally grown produce and meats. The menu might include an appetizer of sautéed sweetbreads and apples, a salad of organic field greens, and entrées ranging from fish stew in tomato and saffron broth to grilled venison or sautéed and confited rabbit. Dinner is served by candlelight. Couples sit by the big fireplace. ✉*3209 German Flats Rd., Warren* ☎*802/583-2800* ▭*AE, DC, MC, V* ☉*Closed Mon. mid-Apr.–mid-Dec. No lunch.*

¢-$
CAFE

✗**The Green Cup.** You can count on products and ingredients from the community at this local favorite. Chef-owner Jason Galiano is famed for his egg specialties, making this the best place around for breakfast (served every day except Wednesday); or just to hang out with a cup of coffee (there's free Wi-Fi). Jason's sister Sarina works front of house and preps orders. Egg specials, soups, and pastries are all made form scratch. Dinner is served Sunday and Monday nights, filling a void in the area. Dinner plates are designed to be shared. ✉*40 Bridge St., Waitsfield* ☎*802/496-4963* ▭*MC, V* ☉*No dinner Tues.–Sat.*

5

WHERE TO STAY

$$

🔲**1824 House.** Not to be confused with Manchester's 1811 House, this 10-gable farmhouse north of Waitsfield is a traditional Vermont farmhouse converted into an elegant inn with cozy rooms and featherbeds. There are just two room types: queen rooms are simple and cute; king rooms have larger sitting areas. Innkeepers Trae Greene and John Lumbra (the chef) take their dining seriously. The renovated rustic barn is home to good, and expensive, prix-fixe dinners. **Pros:** clean, cheery rooms in a historic inn. **Cons:** on Route 100, slightly outside of town. ✉*2150 Main St. (Rte. 100), Waitsfield* ☎*802/496-7555 or 800/426-3986* ⊕*www.1824house.com* ⇱*8 rooms* ⚲*In-room: no a/ c, no TV, Wi-Fi. In-hotel: restaurant, bar, no elevator, public Internet, public Wi-Fi, some pets allowed, no kids under 7, no-smoking rooms* ▭*AE, MC, V* ⦿*BP, MAP.*

$$
★

🔲**Inn at the Round Barn Farm.** A Shaker-style round barn (one of only five in Vermont) is the physical hallmark of this B&B, but what you'll remember when you leave is how comfortable a stay here is. In winter, you toss your shoes under a bench when you come in and put on a pair of slippers from a big basket. There's magic in that gesture, breaking down barriers between guests and giving you permission to really kick back. You'll feel like a kid in the downstairs rec room with its TV, games, and billiard table. The guest rooms, inside the 1806 farmhouse, have eyelet-trimmed sheets, elaborate four-poster beds, rich-color wallpapers, and brass wall lamps for easy bedtime reading. Many have fireplaces and whirlpool tubs. Cooper, the inn dog, is your guide—literally—as you snowshow or hike the miles of trails on this beautiful property filled with gardens and sculpture. Plan a winter trip around one of the moonlit snowshoe walks, which terminate with hot chocolate in an old cabin. **Pros:** great trails, gardens, and rooms; nice breakfast. **Cons:** no restaurant. ✉*1661 E. Warren Rd., Waitsfield* ☎*802/496–2276* ⊕*www.theroundbarn.com* ⤶*11 rooms, 1 suite* ♿*In-room: no TV, Wi-Fi. In-hotel: pool, no elevator, public Internet, public Wi-Fi, no kids under 15, no-smoking rooms* ⊟*AE, D, MC, V* ⦿|*BP.*

$$$$ 📷**Pitcher Inn.** Across from the justly famous Warren General Store is
Fodor'sChoice the elegant Pitcher Inn, Vermont's only Relais & Châteaux property.
★   Ari Sadri, the hands-on manager, exudes an easygoing sophistication that makes staying here a delight. Each comfortable room has its own unusual and elaborate motif—which you'll either love or hate. The Mountain Room, for instance, is designed as a replica of a fire tower in the Green Mountains, with murals on some walls and others covered in stone and glass to resemble a mountain cliff. All the bathrooms, however, are uniformly wonderful, with rain showerheads and Anchini linens and superb toiletries. **Pros:** exceptional service, great bathrooms, fun pub, great location. **Cons:** many rooms can be considered kitschy or downright silly. ✉*275 Main St., Warren* ☎*802/496–6350 or 888/867–4824* ⊕*www.pitcherinn.com* ⤶*9 rooms, 2 suites* ♿*In-room: refrigerator (some), VCR, Wi-Fi. In-hotel: restaurant, bar, spa, water sports, bicycles, public Internet, public Wi-Fi, no-smoking rooms* ⊟*AE, MC, V* ⦿|*BP.*

NORTHERN VERMONT

Vermont's northernmost region reveals the state's greatest contrasts. To the west, Burlington and its suburbs have grown so rapidly that rural wags now say that Burlington's greatest advantage is that it's "close to Vermont." The north country also harbors Vermont's tiny capital, Montpelier, and its highest mountain, Mt. Mansfield, site of the famous Stowe ski resort. To the northeast of Montpelier is a sparsely populated and heavily wooded territory that former Senator George Aiken dubbed the "Northeast Kingdom." It's the domain of loggers, farmers, and avid outdoors enthusiasts.

Our coverage of towns begins in the state capital, Montpelier; moves west toward Stowe and Burlington; then goes north through the Lake Champlain Islands, east along the boundary with Canada toward Jay Peak, and south into the heart of the Northeast Kingdom.

MONTPELIER

38 mi southeast of Burlington, 115 mi north of Brattleboro.

With only about 8,000 residents, Montpelier is the country's smallest capital city. The well-preserved downtown bustles with state and city workers walking to meetings or down the street for coffee or lunch.

CLOSE UP

Slopes Less Traveled

Since America's first ski tow opened in a farmer's pasture near Woodstock in January 1934, skiers have flocked to Vermont in winter. The Green Mountains are dotted with 18 ski resorts, from Mt. Snow in the south to Jay Peak near the Canadian border. They range in size from Killington, in central Vermont, with its 200 trails and 31 lifts, to the Bear Creek Mountain Club, also in central Vermont, with only 15 trails and one chairlift. On weekends and holidays, the bigger resorts—Mt. Snow, Stratton, and Okemo in southern Vermont; Killington, Sugarbush, and Mad River Glen in the central part of the state; and Stowe, Smugglers' Notch, and Jay Peak in the north—attract most of the skiers and snowboarders. To escape the crowds, try these smaller ski resorts.

SOUTHERN VERMONT

Near Stratton, **Bromley** (✉ *Rte. 11, Peru* ☎ *802/824–5522 or 800/865–4786* ⊕ *www.bromley.com*) is a favorite with families. The 43 trails are evenly divided between beginner, intermediate, and expert. The resort runs a child care center, for kids ages 6 weeks to 4 years, and hosts children's programs, for ages 3–12. An added bonus: the trails face south, making for glorious spring skiing and warm winter days.

CENTRAL VERMONT

Once only a faint blip on skiers' radar, **Ascutney** (✉ *Rte. 44, Brownsville* ☎ *802/484–7711 or 800/243–0011* ⊕ *www.ascutney.com*) has remade itself into a bona-fide destination. The 56 trails on an 1,800-foot vertical drop are served by six lifts, including a high-speed quad chairlift accessing double-diamond terrain near the summit. Day care is available for children

ages 6 weeks to 6 years, with learn-to-ski programs for toddlers and up. On Saturday from 5–8 PM, children ages 4–12 can join Cheddar's Happy Hour and movie night. When weekend hordes hit Killington, the locals head to **Pico** (✉ *Rte. 4, Killington* ☎ *802/422–6200 or 866/667–7426* ⊕ *www.picomountain.com*). One of Killington's "seven peaks," Pico is physically separated from its parent resort. The 50 trails range from elevator-shaft steeps to challenging intermediate trails near the summit, with easier terrain near the bottom of the mountain's 2,000-foot vertical. The learning slope is separated from the upper mountain, so hotshots won't bomb through it. The lower express quad can get crowded, but the upper one rarely has a line.

NORTHERN VERMONT

About an hour's drive from Montpelier is **Burke Mountain** (✉ *Mountain Rd., East Burke* ☎ *802/626–3322* ⊕ *www.skiburke.com*). Racers stick to the Training Slope, served by its own poma lift. The other 44 trails and glades are a quiet playground. Near Burlington, **Bolton Valley Resort** (✉ *4302 Bolton Valley Access Rd., Bolton* ☎ *802/434–3444 or 877/926–5866* ⊕ *www.boltonvalley.com*) is a family favorite. In addition to 61 downhill ski trails (over half rated for intermediates), Bolton has night skiing Wednesday–Saturday, 62 mi of cross-country and snowshoe trails, and a sports center.

For skiing information, contact **Ski Vermont/Vermont Ski Areas Association** (✉ *26 State St., Box 368, Montpelier* ☎ *802/223–2439* ⊕ *www.skivermont.com*). ⇨ *Skiing chart at the end of this chapter for information about the larger ski areas of Vermont.*

5

WHAT TO SEE

Vermont State House. With a gleaming gold dome and columns of Barre granite 6 feet in diameter, the state house is home to the oldest legislative chambers in their original condition in the United States. The goddess of agriculture tops the gilded dome. Interior paintings and exhibits make much of Vermont's sterling Civil War record. ⊠*115 State St.* ☎*802/828–2228* ✉*Donations accepted* ⏱*Weekdays 8–4; tours July–mid-Oct., weekdays every ½ hr 10–3:30 (last tour at 3:30), Sat. 11–3 (last tour at 2:30).*

Vermont Museum. Next door to the capitol, in the Pavilion building, this museum preserves all things Vermont, from a catamount to Ethan Allen's shoe buckles. ⊠*109 State St.* ☎*802/828–2291* ⊕*www.state. vt.us/vhs* ✉*$5* ⏱*May–Oct., Tues.–Sat. 10–4, Sun. noon–4.*

OFF THE BEATEN PATH

Rock of Ages Granite Quarry. The attractions here range from the awe-inspiring (the quarry resembles the Grand Canyon in miniature) to the mildly ghoulish (you can consult a directory of tombstone dealers throughout the country) to the whimsical (an outdoor granite bowling alley). You might recognize the sheer walls of the quarry from *Batman and Robin*, the film starring George Clooney and Arnold Schwarzenegger. At the crafts center, skilled artisans sculpt monuments; at the quarries themselves, 25-ton blocks of stone are cut from sheer 475-foot walls by workers who clearly earn their pay. ⊠*Exit 6 off I–89, follow Rte. 63, 7 mi southeast of Montpelier, Barre* ☎*802/476–3119* ✉*Tour of active quarry $4, craftsman center and self-guided tour free* ⏱*Visitor center May–Oct., Mon.–Sat. 8:30–5, Sun. 10–5; narrated tour on Sat. (call for times).*

Cabot Creamery. The major cheese producer in the state, midway between Barre and St. Johnsbury, has a visitor center with an audiovisual presentation about the dairy and cheese industry. You can taste samples, purchase cheese and other Vermont products, and tour the plant. ⊠*2870 Main St. (Rte. 215), 3 mi north of U.S. 2, Cabot* ☎*800/837–4261* ✉*$2* ⏱*June–Oct., daily 9–5; Nov., Dec., and Feb.–May, Mon.–Sat. 9–4; Jan., Mon.–Sat. 10–4; call ahead to check cheese-making days.*

SHOPPING

Unique shops attract locals and tourists alike to Montpelier. For hip children's clothing made-in-Vermont, head to **Zutano** (⊠*79 Main St.* ☎*802/223–2229*).

WHERE TO EAT

$-$$$
Fodor's Choice
★
ECLECTIC

✕**Ariel's.** Well off the beaten path, this small restaurant overlooking a lake is worth the drive down a dirt road. Chef Lee Duberman prepares eclectic treats such as scallop, lobster, and shrimp ravioli in a ginger shiitake broth. Her husband and sommelier Ricard Fink recommends selections from the wine cellar. The full menu is offered Friday and Saturday; a pub menu ($-$$) is served Wednesday, Thursday, and Sunday. ⊠*29 Stone Hill Rd., 8 mi south of Montpelier, Brookfield* ☎*802/276–3939* ⊟*DC, MC, V* ⏱*Closed Nov. and Apr.; Mon. and Tues. May–Oct.; Mon.–Thurs. Dec.–Mar.*

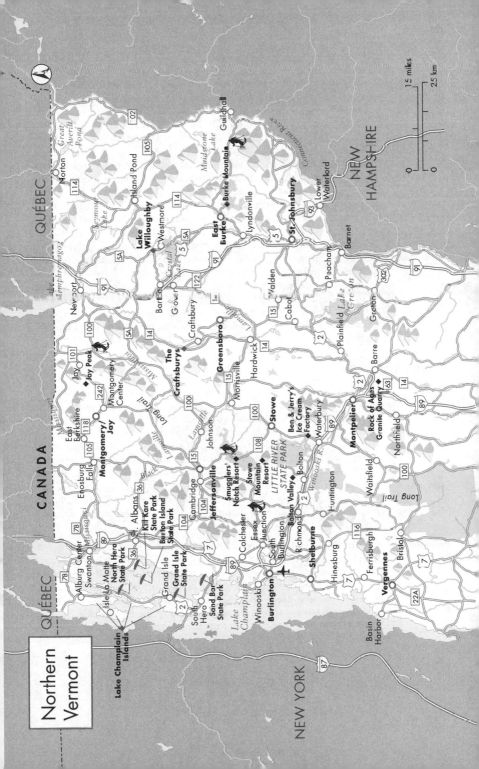

Northern Vermont

QUÉBEC

CANADA

QUÉBEC

NEW YORK

NEW HAMPSHIRE

Lake Champlain Islands

Great Averill Pond
Morton
Island Pond
Westmore
Lake Willoughby
Guildhall
Maidstone Lake
Burke Mountain
East Burke
Lyndonville
St. Johnsbury
Lower Waterford
Barnet
Peacham
Groton
Plainfield Lake Groton
Barre
Walden
Cabot
Hardwick
Greensboro
The Craffsburys
Craftsbury
Barton
Newport
Jay Peak
Jay
Montgomery Center
Montgomery/ Jay
East Berkshire
Enosburg Falls
Alburg Center
Swanton
Isle La Motte
North Hero State Park
Grand Isle State Park
South Hero
Sand Bar State Park
St. Albans
Kill Kare State Park
Burton Island State Park
Cambridge
Jeffersonville
Smugglers' Notch Resort
Johnson
Morrisville
Stowe
Stowe Mountain Resort
Ben & Jerry's Ice Cream Factory
Waterbury
Bolton
Bolton Valley
LITTLE RIVER STATE PARK
Montpelier
Rock of Ages Granite Quarry
Northfield
Waitsfield
Huntington
Richmond
South Burlington
Burlington
Winooski
Essex Junction
Colchester
Shelburne
Hinesburg
Ferrisburgh
Bristol
Vergennes
Basin Harbor

Connecticut River
Lamoille River
Missisquoi
Long Trail
Winooski R.
Lake Champlain

15 miles
25 km

$$ ✕**Chef's Table.** Nearly everyone working here is a student at the New
★ England Culinary Institute. Although this is a training ground, the
AMERICAN quality and inventiveness are anything but beginner's luck. The menu
changes daily. Dining is more formal than at the sister operation down-
stairs, the Main Street Bar and Grill (open daily for lunch and dinner).
A 15% gratuity is added to the bill. ⊠*118 Main St.* ☎*802/229–9202,*
802/223–3188 grill ☐*AE, D, DC, MC, V* ⊘*Closed Sun. and Mon.*
No lunch.

$–$$ ✕**River Run Restaurant.** Mississippi-raised chef Jimmy Kennedy has
SOUTHERN brought outstanding Southern fare to northern Vermont. Fried catfish,
hush puppies, collard greens, and whiskey cake are just a few of the
surprises awaiting diners at this rustic, hip eatery. Try the buttermilk
biscuits at breakfast. There is a full bar. ⊠*Main St., 10 mi east of Montpelier, Plainfield* ☎*802/454–1246* ☐*No credit cards* ⊘*Closed Mon.*

¢–$ ✕**Sarducci's.** Legislative lunches have been a lot more leisurely since
ITALIAN Sarducci's came along to fill the trattoria void in Vermont's capital.
These bright, cheerful rooms alongside the Winooski River are a great
spot for pizza fresh from wood-fired ovens, wonderfully textured
homemade Italian breads, and imaginative pasta dishes such as pasta
pugliese, which marries penne with basil, black olives, roasted eggplant, portobello mushrooms, and sun-dried tomatoes. ⊠*3 Main St.*
☎*802/223–0229* ☐*AE, MC, V* ⊘*No lunch Sun.*

WHERE TO STAY

$–$$ ☷**Inn at Montpelier.** This inn consists of side-by-side homes built in
the early 1800s. The architectural detailing, antique four-poster beds,
Windsor chairs, and classical guitar on the stereo attract the leisure
trade as well as those heading to the capital on business. The formal
sitting room has a wide wraparound Colonial-revival porch, perfect
for reading a book or watching the townsfolk stroll by. The rooms are
small and can be chilly on cool summer days. **Pros:** beautiful home,
relaxed setting. **Cons:** small rooms ⊠*147 Main St.* ☎*802/223–2727*
⊕*www.innatmontpelier.com* ⤴*19 rooms* ♿*In-room: Wi-Fi. In-hotel:
bar, laundry service, no elevator, no-smoking rooms* ☐*AE, D, DC,
MC, V* ⊙*CP.*

EN
ROUTE On your way to Stowe from Interstate 89, be sure to stop at **Ben &
Jerry's Ice Cream Factory,** the Valhalla for ice-cream lovers. Ben and Jerry
began selling ice cream from a renovated gas station in Burlington in
the 1970s. The tour only skims the surface of the behind-the-scenes
goings-on at the plant—a flaw forgiven when the free samples are
dished out. ⊠*Rte. 100, 1 mi north of I–89, Waterbury* ☎*802/846–
1500* ⊕*www.benjerry.com* ▣*Tour $3* ⊙*Late Oct.–June, daily 10–6;
July–mid-Aug., daily 9–9; mid-Aug.–late Oct., daily 9–7. Tours run
every half hour.*

STOWE

Fodor'sChoice
★ *22 mi northwest of Montpelier, 36 mi east of Burlington.*

Long before skiing came to Stowe in the 1930s, the rolling hills and valleys beneath Vermont's highest peak, the 4,395-foot Mt. Mansfield, attracted summer tourists looking for a reprieve from city heat. Most stayed at one of two inns in the village of Stowe. When skiing made the town a winter destination, the arriving skiers outnumbered the hotel beds, so locals took them in. This spirit of hospitality continues, and many of these homes are now lovely country inns. The village itself is tiny, just a few blocks of shops and restaurants clustered around a picture-perfect white church with a lofty steeple, but it serves as the anchor for Mountain Road, which leads north past restaurants, lodges, and shops on its way to Stowe's fabled slopes.

WHAT TO SEE

Mt. Mansfield. With its elongated summit ridge resembling the profile of a recumbent man's face, Mt. Mansfield has long attracted the adventurous. The mountain is ribboned with hiking and ski trails.

Gondola. Mt. Mansfield's "Chin" area is accessible by the eight-seat gondola. At the gondola's summit station is the **Cliff House Restaurant** (☎802/253–3558 Ext. 237), where lunch is served daily 11–3. ⊠*Mountain Rd., 8 mi off Rte. 100* ☎802/253–3000 ☜*Gondola $14* ☉*Mid-June–mid-Oct., daily 10–5; early Dec.–late Apr., daily 8–4.*

Trapp Family Lodge. Built by the von Trapp family, of *Sound of Music* fame, this Tyrolean lodge and its surrounding pastureland are the site of a popular outdoor music series in summer and an extensive cross-country ski-trail network in winter. A tea house serves food and drinks. ⊠*Luce Hill Rd.* ☎802/253–8511 or 800/826–7000.

Vermont Ski Museum. The state's skiing history is documented here with myriad exhibits. ☎802/253–9911.

SPORTS & THE OUTDOORS

CANOEING & KAYAKING **Umiak Outdoor Outfitters** (⊠*849 S. Main St. [Rte. 100], just south of Stowe Village* ☎802/253–2317) rents canoes and kayaks for day trips and leads overnight excursions. The store also operates a rental outpost at Lake Elmore State Park in Elmore, on the Winooski River off Route 2 in Waterbury, at North Beach in Burlington, and on the Lamoille River in Jeffersonville.

FISHING The **Fly Rod Shop** (⊠*Rte. 100, 1½ mi south of Stowe* ☎802/253–7346 or 800/535–9763) provides a guiding service; gives fly-tying, casting, and rod-building classes in winter; rents fly tackle; and sells equipment, including classic and collectible firearms.

GOLF **Stowe Country Club** (⊠*Mountain Rd.* ☎802/253–4893) has a scenic 18-hole, par-72 course; a driving range; and a putting green. Green fees are $45–$75; cart rental is $18.

HIKING Ascending **Mt. Mansfield** makes for a scenic day hike. Trails lead from Route 108 (Mountain Road) to the summit ridge, where they meet

Spa Vacations

Vermont's destination spas have come a long way since the days its *au natural* mineral springs attracted affluent 19th-century city dwellers looking to escape the heat, but the overall principle remains the same. The state remains a natural place to restore mind and body.

Stowe has two destination spas. The largest spa in New England, **Spa at Stoweflake** (⊠ *1746 Mountain Rd. [Rte. 108], Stowe* ☎ *802/760–1083 or 800/253–2232* ⊕ *www.stoweflake. com*) features a massaging hydrotherapeutic waterfall, a Hungarian mineral pool, 30 treatment rooms, a hair and nail salon, and 120 services, such as the Bingham Falls Renewal, named after a local waterfall. This treatment begins with a seasonal body scrub (e.g., immune builder in winter) that's rinsed in a Vichy shower, followed by an aromatherapy oil massage. The spacious men's and women's sanctuaries and locker rooms have saunas, steamrooms, and Jacuzzis.

Opened in early 2005, the **Spa at Topnotch** (⊠ *4000 Mountain Rd. [Rte. 108], Stowe* ☎ *802/253–8585* ⊕ *www.topnotchresort.com*) provides an aura of calm, with its birch wood doors and accents, hardwood floors, natural light, chrome fixtures, and cool colors. Signature services include a Vermont wildflower or woodspice treatment, which includes a warm herb wrap, exfoliation, and massage. Locker areas are spacious, with saunas, steam rooms, and Jacuzzis. The spa also has a full-service salon.

Next door to the swank Pitcher Inn, the **Alta Day Spa** (⊠ *247 Main St., Warren* ☎ *802/496–2582* ⊕ *www. altadayspa.com*) is an Aveda concept spa offering massage, masques,

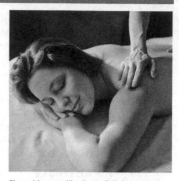

Slopeside spas like Stoweflake's can soothe muscles weary from skiing.

wraps, and facials in four light, airy treatment rooms in a renovated 19th-century house. A two-night spa package through the inn might include daily manicures and hydrating pedicures, facials, and massages, plus lodging and breakfast.

At Killington, the **Woods Resort and Spa** (⊠ *53 Woods La., Killington* ☎ *802/422–3139* ⊕ *www.woodsresortandspa.com*) is a European spa within an upscale condo complex. At the resort's clubhouse, the spa has a 75-foot indoor pool, a sauna, steamroom, and weight room. Spa services include massages, hot stone therapies, facials, salt scrubs, maple-sugar polishes, and mud treatments.

Okemo's ski area has a very similar spa facility to Killington's at the **Jackson Gore Resort** (⊠ *Okemo Ridge Rd., off Rte. 103, Ludlow* ☎ *802/228–1400* ⊕ *www.okemo.com*), with a slopeside outdoor heated pool, hot tubs, a sauna, steam rooms, a fitness center, and massages like Swedish, deep tissue, and hot stone.

the north-to-south Long Trail. Views from the summit take in New Hampshire's White Mountains, New York's Adirondacks across Lake Champlain, and southern Quebec. The Green Mountain Club publishes a trail guide.

ICE-SKATING **Jackson Arena** (✉*Park St.* ☎*802/253–6148*) is a public ice-skating rink, with skate rentals available.

SKI AREA To be precise, the name of the village is Stowe and the name of the
★ mountain is Mt. Mansfield, but to generations of skiers, the area, the complex, and the region are just plain Stowe. **Stowe Mountain Resort** (✉*5781 Mountain Rd.* ☎*802/253–3000, 802/253–3600 snow conditions, 800/253–4754 lodging* ⊕*www.stowe.com*) is a classic that dates from the 1930s. Even today, the area's mystique attracts as many serious skiers as social skiers. Improved snowmaking, new lifts, and free shuttle buses that gather skiers from lodges, inns, and motels along Mountain Road have added convenience to the Stowe experience. Yet the traditions remain: the Winter Carnival in January, the Sugar Slalom in April, ski weeks all winter. Three base lodges provide the essentials, including two on-mountain restaurants. In 2004 the resort broke ground on its 10-year expansion plan at the Spruce Peak base area. Plans are to include new base lodges and lifts, a hotel, retail shops, and a golf course.

The resort provides hiking, in-line skating, an alpine slide, gondola rides, and an 18-hole golf course. It also has 22 mi of groomed cross-country trails and 24 mi of backcountry trails. Four interconnecting cross-country ski areas have more than 90 mi of groomed trails within the town of Stowe.

Mt. Mansfield, with an elevation of 4,395 feet and a vertical drop of 2,360 feet, is one of the giants among eastern ski mountains. The mountain's symmetrical shape allows skiers of all abilities long, satisfying runs from the summit. The famous Front Four (National, Liftline, Starr, and Goat) are the intimidating centerpieces for tough, expert runs, yet there is plenty of mellow intermediate skiing, with 59% of the runs rated at that level. One long beginner trail, the Toll Road Trail, is 3½ mi. Mansfield's satellite sector is a network of intermediate trails and one expert trail off a basin served by a gondola. Spruce Peak, separate from the main mountain, is a teaching hill and a pleasant experience for intermediates and beginners. In addition to the high-speed, eight-passenger gondola, Stowe has 11 lifts, including two quads, two triples, and five double chairlifts, plus one handle tow, to service its 48 trails. Night-skiing trails are accessed by the gondola. The resort has 73% snowmaking coverage. Snowboard facilities include a half-pipe and two terrain parks—one for beginners, at Spruce Peak, and one for experts, on the Mt. Mansfield side. Children's programs are headquartered at Spruce Peak., with ski-school programs for ages 4 to 12.

SHOPPING

In Stowe, Mountain Road is lined with shops from town up toward the ski area. North of Stowe, shops line Route 100 from Interstate 89. Watch apples pressed into cider at the **Cold Hollow Cider Mill** (✉*Rte. 100,*

3 mi north of I–89 ☎*802/244–8771 or 800/327–7537*), a very popular tourist attraction. The on-site store sells cider, baked goods, Vermont produce, and specialty foods. On Route 100 south toward Waterbury, between the cider mill and Ben & Jerry's, you can visit the **Cabot Cheese Annex Store** (⊠*Rte. 100, 2½ mi north of I–89* ☎*802/244–6334*). South of Waterbury, don't miss the freshly baked, maple-glazed sticky buns at the **Red Hen Baking Company** (⊠*Rte. 100* ☎*802/244–0966*).

NIGHTLIFE & THE ARTS

NIGHTLIFE   The **Matterhorn Night Club** (⊠*4969 Mountain Rd.* ☎*802/253–8198*) hosts live music and dancing Thursday–Saturday nights and has a separate martini bar. The **Rusty Nail** (⊠*1190 Mountain Rd.* ☎*802/253–6245*) rocks to live music on weekends.

THE ARTS   **Stowe Performing Arts** (☎*802/253–7792*) sponsors a series of classical and jazz concerts in July in the Trapp Family Lodge meadow. **Stowe Theater Guild** (⊠*Town Hall Theater, Main St.* ☎*802/253–3961 summer only*) performs musicals in summer and performs plays in September.

WHERE TO EAT

$$–$$$ ✕**Mes Amis.** At this small bistro, locals queue up for house specialties
FRENCH   such as fresh oysters, lobster bisque, braised lamb shanks, roast duck (secret recipe), and bananas Foster. You can dine in the candlelit dining room or outside on the patio, especially appealing on a warm summer's night. ⊠*311 Mountain Rd.* ☎*802/253–8669* ☐*AE, D, MC, V* ☺*Closed Mon.*

$$–$$$ ✕**Michael's on the Hill.** Swiss-born chef Michael Kloeti trained in Europe
CONTINENTAL   and New York before opening this dining establishment in a 19th-century farmhouse outside Stowe. In addition to a la carte options, Milchael's four-course prix-fixe menus ($60) highlight European cuisine such as roasted rabbit with mirepoix or ravioli with braised autumn vegetables. There's live piano music weekends. ⊠*4182 Stowe-Waterbury Rd. (Rte. 100), 6 mi south of Stowe, Waterbury Center* ☎*802/244–7476* ☐*AE, DC, MC, V* ☺*Closed Tues. No lunch.*

$–$$ ✕**Red Basil.** Stowe's new "in" dinner spot enhances its traditional Thai
THAI   entrées with fresh cilantro, Kaffir lime leaves, lemongrass, and ginger. The Panang curry (sauteed meat in spicy Panang curry paste, coconut milk, bell peppers, and fresh basil leaves) is smooth, just a bit hot, and delicious; you can also order from the sushi bar. The martini bar has 18 varieties of James Bond's favorite libation. ⊠*294 Mountain Rd.* ☎*802/253–4478* ☐*AE, MC, V* ☺*No lunch weekends.*

WHERE TO STAY

$$–$$$ ▦**Green Mountain Inn.** Welcoming guests since 1833, this classic red-brick inn is across from the landmark Community Church and gives you access to the buzz of downtown. Rooms in the main building and annex still feel like a country inn, with Early American furnishings. Newer buildings have luxury rooms and suites. The Whip Bar & Grill ($$–$$$) puts an interesting twist on comfort food, as in cheddar-cheese-and-apple-stuffed chicken; and the outdoor heated pool is open year-round. **Pros:** fun location, lively tavern. **Cons:** farther from skiing than other area hotels. ⊠*18 Main St.* ☎*802/253–7301 or 800/253–7302* ⊕*www.*

greenmountaininn.com ⇌*105 rooms* ♿*In-room: kitchen (some), refrigerator (some), DVD (some), Wi-Fi. In-hotel: restaurant, bar, pool, gym, laundry service, public Internet, public Wi-Fi, no-smoking rooms* ▭*AE, D, MC, V.*

$$$$ 🏨 **Stone Hill Inn.** This is a contemporary B&B—built in 1998—where classical music plays in the halls. Each soundproof guest room has a king-size bed. Squeaky-clean bathrooms have two-sink vanities and two-person whirlpools in front of two-sided fireplaces. (Can you tell it's for couples?) A pantry is stocked with complimentary snacks and drinks. Common areas include a sitting room and a game room, and the 10 acres of grounds are beautifully landscaped with gardens and waterfalls. The inn is high up Mountain Road not far from the ski resort. **Pros:** clean and new, very comfortable. **Cons:** very expensive, a bit stiff. ⊠*89 Houston Farm Rd.* ☏*802/253-6282* ⊕*www.stonehillinn.com* ⇌*9 rooms* ♿*In-room: no phone, safe, DVD, VCR, Wi-Fi. In-hotel: no elevator, laundry facilities, public Internet, public Wi-Fi, no kids under 18, no-smoking rooms* ▭*AE, D, DC, MC, V* ⊙*BP.*

$ 🏨 **Stowe Motel & Snowdrift.** This family-owned motel sits on 16 acres across the river from the Stowe recreation path. Accommodations range from one-room studios with small kitchenettes to modern two-bedroom fireplace suites. Late-model mountain bikes, kids' bikes, tricycles, bike trailers, and helmets are available to guests. A game room has Ping-Pong and a pool table. The motel is owned by Peter Ruschp, whose father Sepp founded the Mt. Mansfield ski school in 1936. **Pros:** cheap, complimentary bikes and games. **Cons:** basic, motel-style accommodations. ⊠*2043 Mountain Rd. (Rte. 108)* ☏*802/253-7629 or 800/829-7629* ⊕*www.stowemotel.com* ⇌*52 rooms, 4 suites* ♿*In-room: kitchen (some), refrigerator. In-hotel: tennis court, pools, bicycles, no elevator, public Internet, public Wi-Fi, some pets allowed, no-smoking rooms* ▭*AE, D, MC, V* ⊙*CP.*

$$$ 🏨 **Stoweflake Mountain Resort and Spa.** Stoweflake has a lot in common with Topnotch; these two properties have the best and biggest spas in the state, and a contemporary, serious approach to rooms and service. Stoweflake probably has a slightly better spa, perhaps due to the fun of the Bingham hydrotherapy waterfall, a nice 12-foot rock formation cascading into a hot tub. Accommodations range from standard hotel rooms to luxurious suites with fireplaces, refrigerators, double sinks, and whirlpool tubs. One- to three-bedroom town houses sit on the resort's perimeter. The spa overlooks an herb and flower labyrinth and is connected to the fitness center via a faux covered bridge. Stoweflake also hosts Stowe's annual Hot Air Balloon Festival. **Pros:** great spa, excellent service. **Cons:** urban-style resort. ⊠*1746 Mountain Rd., Box 369* ☏*802/253-7355* ⊕*www.stoweflake.com* ⇌*94 rooms, 30 town houses* ♿*In-room: kitchen (some), refrigerator, DVD, VCR, Ethernet (some), Wi-Fi (some). In-hotel: 2 restaurants, room service, bar,*

golf course, tennis courts, pools, gym, spa, bicycles, laundry service, concierge, public Internet, public Wi-Fi, no-smoking rooms ⊟*AE, D, DC, MC, V.*

$$$$ ⚏**Topnotch at Stowe Resort and Spa.** One of the state's poshest resorts occupies 120 acres overlooking Mt. Mansfield. Floor-to-ceiling windows, a freestanding metal fireplace, and heavy stone walls distinguish the lobby. Topnotch is almost a twin to its main competitor, Stoweflakem but it tops it in country-chic, spacious rooms with plush beds, Anichini linens, and other accents like painted barn-board walls. Norma's restaurant ($$–$$$) serves contemporary Continental cuisine in a romantic setting surrounded by torches. Service throughout the resort is impeccable. The tennis center has marvelous indoor and outdoor courts (easily the best facilities in Vermont) and a world-class instructional staff. **Pros:** near the mountain; world-class tennis center; good dining; top spa. **Cons:** the urban look and feel may not be for everyone. ⊠*4000 Mountain Rd.* ☎*802/253–8585 or 800/451–8686* ⊕*www. topnotch-resort.com* ⇝*71 rooms, 9 suites, 14 town houses* ⌂*In-room: safe, Wi-Fi. In-hotel: 2 restaurants, bar, tennis courts, pools, spa, public Internet, public Wi-Fi, no-smoking rooms* ⊟*AE, D, DC, MC, V* ⦿*BP, FAP, MAP.*

THE CRAFTSBURYS

27 mi northeast of Stowe.

The three villages of the Craftsburys—Craftsbury Common, Craftsbury, and East Craftsbury—are among Vermont's finest and oldest towns. Handsome white houses and barns, the requisite common, and terrific views make them well worth the drive. Craftsbury General Store in Craftsbury Village is a great place to stock up on picnic supplies and local information. The rolling farmland hints at the way Vermont used to be: the area's sheer distance from civilization and its rugged weather have kept most of the state's development farther south.

WHERE TO STAY

$$ ⚏**Craftsbury Outdoor Center.** If you think simplicity is bliss and love the outdoors, give this place a try. In winter it's a mecca for cross-country skiing (50 mi of groomed trails). In summer there's a giant lake for swimming and boating (sculling and running camps are held here). Two two-story simple lodges have rooms with communal TV/library areas. Many share baths. The simplest rooms have two twin beds and a wooden peg to hang a towel. Meals are served buffet-style. Cabin D is a paradisiacal setup, a simple three-bedroom cabin right on the edge of the lake. **Pros:** outdoor heaven, activities galore. **Cons:** many rooms have a shared bath, many are sparely furnished. ⊠*535 Lost Nation Rd., Craftsbury Common* ☎*802/586–7767 or 800/729–7751* ⊕*www.craftsbury.com* ⇝*49 rooms, 10 with bath; 4 cabins; 2 suites* ⌂*In-room: no a/c, no phone, kitchen (some), refrigerator (some) no TV, Wi-Fi (some). In-hotel: restaurant, tennis court, gym, water sports, bicycles, no elevator, laundry facilities, public Internet, public Wi-Fi, some pets allowed, no-smoking rooms* ⊟*MC, V* ⦿*MAP.*

$$ ⊡ **Inn on the Common.** All guest rooms at these three renovated Federal-style homes are appointed with antiques and hand-stitched quilts and have sitting areas. Some rooms have fireplaces or woodstoves. The Trellis Restaurant ($$–$$$), which serves excellent "innovative country" cuisine, has indoor and outdoor seating overlooking the gardens. Pros: beautiful setting, simple rooms. Cons: breakfast ends at 9 AM. ⊠ *1162 N. Craftsbury Rd., Craftsbury Common* ☎ *802/586–9619 or 800/521–2233* ⊕ *www.innonthecommon.com* ⊅ *14 rooms, 2 suites* ⅋ *In-room: no a/c, no TV. In-hotel: restaurant, no-smoking rooms* ⊟ *AE, D, DC, MC, V* Ⓞ│ *BP, MAP.*

GREENSBORO

10 mi southeast of Craftsbury Common.

Tucked along the southern shore of Caspian Lake, Greensboro has been a summer resort for literati, academics, and old-money types for more than a century. Yet it exudes an unpretentious, genteel character where most of the people running about on errands seem to know each other. A town beach is right off the main street.

SHOPPING
The **Miller's Thumb** (⊠ *Main St.* ☎ *802/533–2960 or 800/680–7886*) sells Italian pottery, Vermont furniture, crafts and antiques, and April Cornell clothing and linens. **Willey's Store** (⊠ *Main St.* ☎ *802/533–2621*) is a classic general store of the "if-we-don't-have-it-you-don't-need it" kind.

WHERE TO STAY
$$$$ ⊡ **Highland Lodge.** Tranquillity reigns at this 1860 house overlooking a pristine lake. The lodge's 120 acres of rambling woods and pastures are laced with hiking and skiing trails (ski rentals available). Comfortable guest rooms have Early American–style furnishings; most have views of the lake. The one- to three-bedroom cottages are more private (four with gas stoves stay open in winter). The lodge has canoes, kayaks, Sunfish, and paddleboats. There's also a game room with foosball, Ping-Pong, puzzles, and books. In winter there's a complete cross-country touring center; 31 mi of groomed trails connect to the Craftsbuty Outdoor Center. The traditional dinner menu might include such entrées as roast leg of lamb. Pros: across from lake, lots of activities, private beach. Cons: remote, expensive. ⊠ *1608 Craftsbury Rd.* ☎ *802/533–2647* ⊕ *www.highlandlodge.com* ⊅ *8 rooms, 11 cottages* ⅋ *In-room: no a/c, no phone, kitchen, refrigerator, Wi-Fi (some). In-hotel: restaurant, tennis court, water sports, bicycles, no elevator, laundry service, public Internet, public Wi-Fi, no-smoking rooms* ⊟ *D, MC, V* ⓧ *Closed mid-Mar.–late May and mid-Oct.–mid-Dec.* Ⓞ│ *BP, MAP.*

JEFFERSONVILLE

36 mi west of Greensboro, 18 mi north of Stowe.

Jeffersonville is just over Smugglers' Notch from Stowe but miles away in feel and attitude. In summer, you can drive over the notch road as it curves precipitously around boulders that have fallen from the cliffs above, then pass open meadows and old farmhouses and sugar shacks on the way down to town. Below the notch, Smugglers' Notch Ski Resort is the hub of much activity year-round. Downtown Jeffersonville, once home to an artist colony, is quiet but has excellent dining and sophisticated art galleries.

WHAT TO SEE

Boyden Valley Winery. West of town, this winery conducts tours and tastings and showcases an excellent selection of Vermont specialty products and local handicrafts, including fine furniture. The winery is closed Monday, June–December, and Monday–Thursday, January–May. ⊠*Junction of Rtes. 15 and 104, Cambridge* ☎*802/644–8151.*

SPORTS & THE OUTDOORS

KAYAKING **Green River Canoe & Kayak** (☎*802/644–8336 or 802/644–8714*), at the junction of routes 15 and 108 behind Jana's Restaurant, rents canoes and kayaks on the Lamoille River and leads guided canoe trips to Boyden Valley Winery.

LLAMA RIDES **Applecheek Farm** (⊠*567 McFarlane Rd., Hyde Park* ☎*802/888–4482*) runs daytime and evening (by lantern) hay and sleigh rides, llama treks, and farm tours. **Northern Vermont Llamas** (⊠*766 Lapland Rd., Waterville* ☎*802/644–2257*) conducts half- and full-day treks from May through October along the cross-country ski trails of Smugglers' Notch. The llamas carry everything, including snacks and lunches. Advance reservations are essential.

SKI AREA **Smugglers' Notch Resort** (⊠*Rte. 108* ☎*802/644–8851 or 800/451–8752*
☾★ ⊕*www.smuggs.com*) consistently wins accolades for its family programs. Its children's ski school is one of the best in the country—possibly *the* best. But skiers of all levels come here (Smugglers' was the first ski area in the East to designate a triple-black-diamond run—the Black Hole). All the essentials are available in the village at the base of the Morse Mountain lifts, including lodgings, restaurants, and several shops. Smugglers' has a full roster of summertime programs, including pools, complete with waterfalls and waterslides; the Giant Rapid River Ride (the longest water ride in the state); lawn games; mountain biking and hiking programs; and craft workshops for adults.

The self-contained village has outdoor ice-skating and sleigh rides. The numerous snowshoeing programs include family walks and backcountry trips. SmuggsCentral has an indoor pool, hot tub, Funzone playground with slides and miniature golf, and a teen center, open from 5 PM until midnight. In terms of nordic skiing, the area has 18 mi of groomed and tracked trails and 12 mi of snowshoe trails.

For downhill skiing, Smugglers' has three mountains. The highest, Madonna, with a vertical drop of 2,610 feet, is in the center and connects with a trail network to Sterling (1,500 feet vertical). The third mountain, Morse (1,150 feet vertical), is adjacent to Smugglers' "village" of shops, restaurants, and condos; it's connected to the other peaks by trails and a shuttle bus. The wild, craggy landscape lends a pristine wilderness feel to the skiing experience on the two higher mountains. The tops of each of the mountains have expert terrain—a couple of double-black diamonds (and the only triple-black diamond trail in the east) make Madonna memorable. Intermediate trails fill the lower sections. Morse has many beginner and advanced beginner trails. Smugglers' 70 trails are served by eight lifts, including six chairs and two surface lifts. Top-to-bottom snowmaking on all three mountains allows for 62% coverage. There are four progression terrain parks, including one for early beginners. Night skiing and snowboarding classes are given at the new Learning and Fun Park.

Ski camps for kids ages 3–17 provide excellent instruction, plus movies, games, and other activities. Wednesday, Thursday, and Saturday are kids' nights at Treasures, with dinner and supervised activities for children ages 3–11.

SHOPPING

ANTIQUES The **Green Apple Antique Center** (⊠*60 Main St.* ☎*802/644–2989*) has a good bakery in the back of the store. **Smugglers' Notch Antique Center** (⊠*906 Rte. 108* ☎*802/644–8321*) sells antiques and collectibles of 60 dealers in a rambling barn.

CLOTHING **Johnson Woolen Mills** (⊠*Main St., 9 mi east of Jeffersonville, Johnson*
Fodor'sChoice ☎*802/635–2271*) is an authentic factory store with deals on woolen
★ blankets, yard goods, and the famous Johnson outerwear.

CRAFTS **Vermont Rug Makers** (⊠*Rte. 100C, 10 mi east of Jeffersonville, East Johnson* ☎*802/635–2434*) weaves imaginative rugs and tapestries from fabrics, wools, and exotic materials. Its International Gallery displays rugs and tapestries from around the world.

WHERE TO EAT & STAY

$-$$ ✕**158 Main.** As soon as this restaurant opened in January 2004, locals
AMERICAN were lining up at the door. Its menu selections range from sesame-seared yellowfin tuna with jasmine rice and wasabi to the locals' favorite breakfast: eggs, homemade toast, and home fries for $2.58. Portions are big, prices are not. Sunday brunch is served 8 AM–2 PM. ⊠*158 Main St.* ☎*802/644–8100* ⚑*Reservations not accepted* ⊟AE, DC, MC, V ⊘*Closed Mon. No dinner Sun.*

$$$$ 🏨**Smugglers' Notch Resort.** From watercolor workshops to giant water
☾ parks to weeklong camps for kids, this family resort has a plethora
Fodor'sChoice of activities. In winter, the main activity is skiing, but children's pro-
★ grams abound. Lodging is in clustered condominium complexes, with the condos set away from the resort center. Rates are packages for three, five, and seven nights and can include use of all resort amenities and lift tickets and ski lessons in season. **Pros:** great place for families and to learn to ski. **Cons:** with so many kids around, it's not right for

couples. ✉4232 Rte. 108 S05464 ☎802/644–8851 or 800/451–8752
⊕www.smuggs.com ⇆550 condominiums &In-room: no a/c (some).
In-hotel: 4 restaurants, bar, tennis courts, pools, children's programs
(ages 3–17), no-smoking rooms ☰AE, DC, MC, V.

BURLINGTON

Fodor'sChoice 31 mi southwest of Jeffersonville, 76 mi south of Montreal, 349 mi
★ north of New York City, 223 mi northwest of Boston.

As you drive along Main Street toward downtown Burlington, it's easy
to see why the city is so often called one of America's most livable small
cities. Downtown is filled with hip restaurants and nightclubs, art galleries, and the Church Street Marketplace—a bustling pedestrian mall with
trendy shops, craft vendors, street performers, and sidewalk cafés. Just
beyond, Lake Champlain shimmers beneath the towering Adirondacks
on the New York shore. On the shores of the lake, Burlington's revitalized waterfront teems with outdoors enthusiasts who stroll along its recreation path and ply the waters in sailboats and motor craft in summer.

WHAT TO SEE

♻★ **ECHO Leahy Center for Lake Champlain.** Part of the waterfront's revitalization, this aquarium and science center gives kids a chance to check
out 100 hands-on, interactive wind and water exhibits and a sunken
shipwreck. ✉1 College St. ☎802/864–1848 ⊕www.echovermont.org
🎟$9 ⊙Daily 10–5, Thurs. until 8.

Ethan Allen Homestead. One of the earliest residents of the Intervale was
Ethan Allen, Vermont's Revolutionary-era guerrilla fighter, who remains
a captivating figure. Exhibits at the on-site visitor center answer questions about his flamboyant life. The house holds such frontier hall-
marks as rough saw-cut boards and an open hearth for cooking. A
re-created Colonial kitchen garden resembles the one the Allens would
have had. After the tour and multimedia presentation, you can stretch
your legs on scenic trails along the Winooski River. ✉North Ave.,
off Rte. 127, north of Burlington ☎802/865–4556 ⊕www.ethanallen
homestead.org 🎟$5 ⊙May–Oct., Mon.–Sat. 10–4, Sun. 1–4.

University of Vermont. Crowning the hilltop above Burlington is the campus of the University of Vermont, known simply as UVM for the abbre-
viation of its Latin name, Universitas Viridis Montis—the University
of the Green Mountains. With more than 10,000 students, UVM is the
state's principal institution of higher learning. The most architecturally
interesting buildings face the green, which has a statue of UVM founder
Ira Allen, Ethan's brother. ☎802/656–3131.

SPORTS & THE OUTDOORS

BEACHES The **North Beaches** (✉North Beach Park off North Ave. ☎802/864–
0123 ✉Leddy Beach, Leddy Park Rd. off North Ave.) are on the northern edge of Burlington. Leddy Beach is a good spot for sailboarding.

BIKING Burlington's 10-mi Cycle the City loop runs along the waterfront, connecting several city parks and beaches. It also passes the Community

Boathouse and runs within several blocks of downtown restaurants and shops. **North Star Cyclery** (⊠*100 Main St.* ☎*802/863–3832*) rents bicycles and provides maps of bicycle routes. **Ski Rack** (⊠*85 Main St.* ☎*802/658–3313 or 800/882–4530*) rents and services bikes and provides maps.

BOATING **Burlington Community Boathouse** (⊠*Foot of College St., Burlington Harbor* ☎*802/865–3377*) rents 19-foot sailboats. **Shoreline Cruise's** *Spirit of Ethan Allen III.* This 500-passenger, three-level cruise vessel has narrated cruises and dinner and sunset sailings with awesome views of the Adirondacks and Green Mountains. ⊠*Burlington Boat House, College and Battery Sts.* ☎*802/862–8300* ⊕*www.soea.com* ⊠*$12* ⊗*Cruises late May–mid-Oct., daily 10–9.*

Waterfront Boat Rentals (⊠*Foot of Maple St. on Perkins Pier, Burlington Harbor* ☎*802/864–4858*) rents kayaks, canoes, rowboats, skiffs, and Boston whalers. Affordable sailing lessons are available.

OFF THE
BEATEN
PATH
Green Mountain Audubon Nature Center. This is a wonderful place to discover Vermont's outdoor wonders. The center's 300 acres of diverse habitats are a sanctuary for all things wild, and the 5 mi of trails provide an opportunity to explore the workings of differing natural communities. Events include dusk walks, wildflower and birding rambles, nature workshops, and educational activities for children and adults. The center is 18 mi southeast of Burlington. ⊠*255 Sherman Hollow Rd., Huntington* ☎*802/434–3068* ⊠*Donations accepted* ⊗*Grounds daily dawn–dusk, center Mon.–Sat. 8–4.*

SHOPPING

CRAFTS In addition to its popular pottery, **Bennington Potters North** (⊠*127 College St.* ☎*802/863–2221 or 800/205–8033*) stocks interesting gifts, glassware, furniture, and other housewares. **Vermont State Craft Center/ Frog Hollow** (⊠*85 Church St.* ☎*802/863–6458*) is a nonprofit collective that sells contemporary and traditional crafts by more than 200 Vermont artisans.

MARKETS **Church Street Marketplace** (⊠*Main St. to Pearl St.* ☎*802/863–1648*), a pedestrian thoroughfare, is lined with boutiques, cafés, and street vendors. Look for bargains at the rapidly growing **Essex Outlet Fair** (⊠*Junction of Rtes. 15 and 289, Essex* ☎*802/878–2851*), with such outlets as BCBG, Brooks Brothers, Polo Ralph Lauren, and Levi's, among others.

NIGHTLIFE & THE ARTS

NIGHTLIFE The music at **Club Metronome** (⊠*188 Main St.* ☎*802/865–4563*) ranges from cutting-edge sounds to funk, blues, and reggae. National and local musicians come to **Higher Ground** (⊠*1214 Williston Rd., South Burlington* ☎*802/265–0777*). The band Phish got its start at **Nectar's** (⊠*188 Main St.* ☎*802/658–4771*). This place is always jumping to the sounds of local bands and never charges a cover. **Ri Ra** (⊠*123 Church St.* ☎*802/860–9401*) hosts live entertainment with an Irish flair. **Vermont Pub and Brewery** (⊠*144 College St.* ☎*802/865–0500*) makes its own beer and fruit seltzers and is arguably the most popular spot in town. Folk musicians play here regularly.

THE ARTS

The **Fire House Art Gallery** (⊠*135 Church St.* ☎*802/865–7165*) exhibits works by local artists. **Flynn Theatre for the Performing Arts** (⊠*153 Main St.* ☎*802/652–4500 information, 802/863–5966 tickets* ⊕*www.flynncenter.org*), a grandiose old structure, is the cultural heart of Burlington; it schedules the Vermont Symphony Orchestra, theater, dance, big-name musicians, and lectures. **St. Michael's Playhouse** (⊠*St. Michael's College, Rte. 15, Colchester* ☎*802/654–2281 box office, 802/654–2617 administrative office*) stages performances in the McCarthy Arts Center. The **Vermont Symphony Orchestra** (☎*802/864–5741*) performs throughout the state year-round and at the Flynn from October through May.

WHERE TO EAT

¢-$

Fodor's Choice

★

PIZZA

✕ **American Flatbread–Burlington Hearth.** It might be worth going to college in Burlington just to be able to gather with friends at this wildly popular and delicious, organic pizza place. On weekends, it's standing room only (seating is first-come, first-served) as kids bustle for housemade brews. The wood-fired clay dome oven combines with all organic ingredients to create masterful results, like the Punctuated Equilibrium, which has kalamata olives, roasted red peppers, local goat's cheese, fresh rosemary, red onions, mozzarella, and garlic. Here's to the college life! ⊠*115 St. Paul St.* ☎*802/861–2999* ▭*MC, V.*

$$$-$$$$

Fodor's Choice

★

AMERICAN

✕ **Butler's Restaurant.** This formal restaurant is run by instructors and second-year students at the New England Culinary Institute, one of America's best. It's a joy to sample the menu and even the wine selection pulses with enthusiam and vigor. Dishes can be hit or miss, but the high notes can be among the highest in the state. Service is taken very seriously. Adjacent to Butler's is The Tavern, run by the same kitchen, which has a grilled flatbread pizza of the day and a bounty of local draft beers. Expect only local ingredients at both restaurants. ⊠*70 Essex Way, Essex Junction* ☎*802/878–1100* ▭*AE, D, DC, MC, V* ⊘*No dinner Sun. in winter.*

$-$$

ITALIAN

✕ **Cannon's.** Don't let the shopping center location deter you. This family-style Italian restaurant has more than just spaghetti on the menu. Pasta selections are diverse and include such items as fettuccine with sautéed chicken strips and snow peas, and noodle-less eggplant lasagna. Entrées range from traditional Italian (shrimp scampi) to American (sirloin steak). ⊠*1127 North Ave.* ☎*802/652–5151* ▭*DC, MC, V* ⊘*No lunch Sat.*

$-$$

IRISH

✕ **Ri Ra.** Brought to Burlington from Ireland in pieces and reassembled on-site, this Irish pub serves classic fare such as bangers-and-mash and fish-and-chips, along with burgers and fish. ⊠*123 Church St.* ☎*802/860–9401* ▭*AE, MC, V.*

$-$$

CHINESE

✕ **A Single Pebble.** The creative, authentic Asian selections served in the first floor of this residential rowhouse include traditional clay-pot dishes as well as wok specialties, such as sesame catfish and kung pao chicken. The dry-fried green beans (sautéed with flecks of pork, black beans, preserved vegetables, and garlic) are a house specialty. All dishes can be made without meat. ⊠*133-135 Bank St.* ☎*802/865–5200* ⚖*Reservations essential* ▭*AE, D, MC, V* ⊘*No lunch weekends.*

$-$$ ✕**Trattoria Delia.** Didn't manage to rent that villa in Umbria this year?
★ The next best thing, if your travels bring you to Burlington, is this
ITALIAN superb Italian country eatery just around the corner from City Hall
Park. Game and fresh produce are the stars, as in wild boar braised in
red wine, tomatoes, rosemary, and sage served on soft polenta. Wood-
grilled items are a specialty. ⌖*152 St. Paul St.* ☎*802/864-5253* ☰*AE,
D, DC, MC, V* ☉*No lunch.*

WHERE TO STAY

¢ ☷**G.G.T. Tibet Inn.** This motel probably has the cheapest rates in all of
Vermont—$49 for two people in winter, and $59 to $69 in summer. But
that's not the main attraction. The lure here is the friendly face and evident care of the motel's Tibetan owner, whose name is Kalsang G.G.T.
(Yes, G.G.T. really is his real last name.) Bhuddist prayer flags flap
from the exterior. All rooms have a microwave and a refrigerator, and
basic motel furnishings with a big TV. Kalsang's smile at check-in will
bring you back. **Pros:** great price, locally owned. **Cons:** no high-speed
Internet. ⌖*1860 Shelburne Rd., South Burlington* ☎*802/863-7110*
⊕*www.ggtibetinn.com* ⇆*21 rooms* ⚭*In room: dial-up. In-hotel:
pool, no elevator, no-smoking rooms* ☰*AE, D, MC, V.*

$$ ☷**Inn at Essex.** "Vermont's Culinary Resort" is a hotel and conference
center about 10 mi from downtown Burlington, with two good restau-
rants run by the New England Culinary Institute. The best part of a
stay here is access to cooking classes offered each day in professional
test kitchens on site. Very comfortable Susan Sargent–designed rooms
are adorned with her vibrant colors in everything from the wall paint to
the pillow covers; 30 rooms have fireplaces. A 19,000-square-foot spa
is slated to open in fall 2008, along with an Orvis-endorsed fly-fishing
pond. **Pros:** daily cooking classes, colorful rooms, free airport shuttle.
Cons: odd location in suburb of Burlington. ⌖*70 Essex Way, off Rte.
289, Essex Junction* ☎*802/878-1100 or 800/727-4295* ⊕*www.vt
culinaryresort.com* ⇆*60 rooms, 60 suites* ⚭*In-room: Wi-Fi. In-hotel:
2 restaurants, bar, golf course, tennis courts, pool, no-smoking rooms*
☰*AE, D, MC, V.*

$ ☷**Willard Street Inn.** High in the historic hill section of Burlington, this
★ ivy-covered grand house with an exterior marble staircase and English
gardens incorporates elements of Queen Anne and Colonial–Georgian-
revival styles. The stately foyer, paneled in cherry, leads to a more for-
mal sitting room with velvet drapes. The solarium is bright and sunny
with marble floors, many plants, and big velvet couches for contem-
plating views of Lake Champlain. All the rooms have down comforters
and phones; some have lake views and canopied beds. Orange French
toast is among the breakfast favorites. **Pros:** lovely old mansion loaded
with character and details; friendly attention; common room snacks.
Cons: walk to downtown. ⌖*349 S. Willard St.* ☎*802/651-8710 or
800/577-8712* ⊕*www.willardstreetinn.com* ⇆*14 rooms* ⚭*In-room:
Wi-Fi. In-hotel: no elevator, public Internet, public Wi-Fi, no kids
under 12, no-smoking rooms* ☰*AE, D, MC, V* ☉❘*BP.*

5

SHELBURNE

5 mi south of Burlington.

A few miles south of Burlington, the Champlain Valley gives way to fertile farmland, affording stunning views of the rugged Adirondacks across the lake. In the middle of this farmland is the village of Shelburne, chartered in the mid-18th century and now largely a bedroom community for Burlington.

WHAT TO SEE

Shelburne Farms. Founded in the 1880s as a private estate, this 1,400-acre farm is an educational and cultural resource center with, among other things, a working dairy farm, a Children's Farmyard, and a spot for watching the farm's famous cheddar cheese being made. Frederick Law Olmsted, co-creator of New York's Central Park, designed the magnificent grounds overlooking Lake Champlain. For an additional charge of $3, you can tour the 1891 breeding barn. ⊠ *West of U.S. 7 at Harbor and Bay Rds.* ☏ *802/985–8686* ⊕ *www.shelburnefarms.org* ☞ *Day pass $6, tour an additional $5* ☉ *Visitor center and shop daily 10–5; tours mid-May–mid-Oct. (last tour at 3:30); walking trails daily 10–4, weather permitting.*

Fodor's Choice
★

Shelburne Museum. You can trace much of New England's history simply by wandering through the 45 acres and 37 buildings of this museum. The outstanding 80,000-object collection of Americana consists of 18th- and 19th-century period homes and furniture, fine and folk art, farm tools, more than 200 carriages and sleighs, Audubon prints, an old-fashioned jail, and even a private railroad car from the days of steam. The museum also has an assortment of duck decoys, an old stone cottage, a display of early toys, and the *Ticonderoga*, a side-wheel steamship, grounded amid lawn and trees. ⊠ *U.S. 7* ☏ *802/985–3346* ⊕ *www.shelburnemuseum.org* ☞ *$18* ☉ *May–Oct., daily 10–5.*

Vermont Teddy Bear Company. On the 25-minute tour of this fun-filled factory you'll hear more puns than you ever thought possible and learn how a few homemade bears, sold from a cart on Church Street, have turned into a multimillion-dollar business. A children's play tent is set up outdoors in summer, and you can wander the beautiful 57-acre property. ⊠ *6655 Shelburne Rd.* ☏ *802/985–3001* ☞ *Tour $2* ☉ *Tours Mon.–Sat. 9:30–5, Sun. 10:30–4; store daily 9–6.*

SHOPPING

When you enter the **Shelburne Country Store** (⊠ *Village Green off U.S. 7* ☏ *802/985–3657*) you'll step back in time. Walk past the potbellied stove and take in the aroma emanating from the fudge neatly piled behind huge antique glass cases. The store specializes in candles, weather vanes, glassware, and local foods.

WHERE TO EAT & STAY

$$-$$$
★
FRENCH

✕ **Café Shelburne.** This popular restaurant serves creative French bistro cuisine. Specialties include sweetbreads with a port wine and mushroom sauce in puff pastry, and homemade fettuccine with Vermont goat cheese. Desserts such as the sweet chocolate layered terrine and maple-syrup mousse with orange terrine are fabulous. ⊠*U.S. 7* ☎*802/985–3939* ⊟*AE, MC, V* ⊘*Closed Sun. and Mon. No lunch.*

$$-$$$ ⌨**Inn at Shelburne Farms.** This turn-of-the-20th-century Tudor-style inn,
Fodor's Choice once the home of William Seward and Lila Vanderbilt Webb, overlooks
★ Lake Champlain, the distant Adirondacks, and the sea of pastures that make up this 1,400-acre working farm. Each room is different, from the wallpaper to the period antiques. The dining room ($$–$$$) defines elegance, and Sunday brunch (not served in May) is one of the area's best. Breakfast is served Monday–Saturday. Pros: unbeatable setting within the Shelburne Farms property. Cons: some may miss not having a TV in the room. ⊠*Harbor Rd.* ☎*802/985–8498* ⊕*www.shelburne farms.org* ⟿*24 rooms, 17 with bath; 2 cottages* ⟨*In-room: no a/c, no TV. In-hotel: restaurant, tennis court, no-smoking rooms* ⊟*D, DC, MC, V* ⊘*Closed mid-Oct.–mid-May.*

VERGENNES

12 mi south of Shelburne

Vermont's oldest city, founded in 1788, is also the third oldest in New England. The downtown area is a compact district of Victorian homes and public buildings. Main Street slopes down to Otter Creek Falls, where cannonballs were made during the War of 1812. The statue of Thomas MacDonough on the green immortalizes the victor of the Battle of Plattsburgh in 1814.

**OFF THE
BEATEN
PATH**

Lake Champlain Maritime Museum. This museum documents centuries of activity on the historically significant lake. Climb aboard a replica of Benedict Arnold's Revolutionary War gunboat moored in the lake, learn about shipwrecks, and watch craftsmen work at traditional boatbuilding and blacksmithing. Among the exhibits are a nautical archaeology center, a conservation laboratory, and a restaurant. ⊠*Basin Harbor Rd., 7 mi west of Vergennes, Basin Harbor* ☎*802/475–2022* ☞*$9* ⊘*May–mid-Oct., daily 10–5.*

SHOPPING

Dakin Farm (⊠*Rte. 7, 5 mi north of Vergennes* ☎*800/993–2546*) sells cob-smoked ham, aged cheddar cheese, and other specialty foods.

WHERE TO EAT & STAY

$-$$ ✕**Starry Night Café.** This chic restaurant is one of the hottest spots
ECLECTIC around and it's increased in size to meet growing demand. Appetizers include house specials such as honey-chili glazed shrimp and gazpacho. Among the French-meets-Asian entrées are lobster-stuffed sole, pan-seared scallops, and grilled New York steak. ⊠*5371 Rte. 7, 5 mi north of Vergennes, Ferrisburg* ☎*802/877–6316* ⊕*www.starrynight cafe.com* ⊟*MC, V* ⊘*Closed Mon. and Tues. No lunch.*

☾ $$$$ ⌨**Basin Harbor Club.** On 700 acres overlooking Lake Champlain, this
Fodor's Choice ultimate family resort provides luxurious accommodations and a full
★ roster of amenities, including an 18-hole golf course, boating (with a 40-foot tour boat), a 3,200-foot grass airstrip, and daylong children's programs. Some rooms in the guesthouses have fireplaces, decks, or

porches. The cottages are charming and have one to three bedrooms. The restaurant menu ($–$$$) is classic American, the wine list excellent. Jackets and ties are required in common areas after 6 PM from late-June through Labor Day. **Pros:** gorgeous lakeside property; activities galore. **Cons:** open only half the year. ⊠ *48 Basin Harbor Rd.* ☎ *802/475–2311 or 800/622–4000* ⊕ *www.basinharbor.com* ♺*36 rooms, 2 suites in 3 guesthouses, 77 cottages* ♿ *In-room: no a/c, no TV. In-hotel: 3 restaurants, golf course, tennis courts, pool, gym, bicycles, children's programs (ages 3–15), some pets allowed, no-smoking rooms* ▤*MC, V* ☉*Closed mid-Oct.–mid-May* ❍|*BP.*

LAKE CHAMPLAIN ISLANDS

43 mi north of Vergennes, 20 mi northwest of Shelburne, 15 mi northwest of Burlington.

Lake Champlain, which stretches more than 100 mi southward from the Canadian border, forms the northern part of the boundary between New York and Vermont. Within it is an elongated archipelago composed of several islands—Isle La Motte, North Hero, Grand Isle, South Hero—and the Alburg Peninsula. With a temperate climate, the islands hold several apple orchards and are a center of water recreation in summer and ice fishing in winter. A scenic drive through the islands on U.S. 2 begins at Interstate 89 and travels north to Alburg Center; Route 78 takes you back to the mainland.

WHAT TO SEE

Herrmann's Royal Lipizzan Stallions. These beautiful stallions, cousins of the noble white horses bred in Austria since the 16th century, perform intricate dressage maneuvers for delighted spectators for a brief period each summer on North Hero. These acrobatic horses are descendants of animals rescued from the turmoil of World War II by General George Patton and members of the Herrmann family. ⊠*U.S. 2, North Hero* ☎*802/372–5683* ⊠*Barn visits free between performances, shows $17* ☉*Early July–late Aug., Thurs. and Fri. at 6 PM, weekends at 2:30 PM.*

Snow Farm Vineyard and Winery. Take a self-guided tour, sip some samples in the tasting room, and listen to music at the free concerts on the lawn Thursday evenings, mid-June through Labor Day. ⊠*190 W. Shore Rd., South Hero* ☎*802/372–9463* ⊠*Free* ☉*May–Dec., daily 10–5; tours May–Oct. at 11 and 2.*

St. Anne's Shrine. This shrine marks the site where French soldiers and Jesuits put ashore in 1665 and built a fort, creating Vermont's first European settlement. The state's first Roman Catholic Mass was celebrated here on July 26, 1666. ⊠*W. Shore Rd., Isle La Motte* ☎*802/928– 3362* ⊠*Free* ☉*Mid-May–mid-Oct., daily 9–4.*

SPORTS & THE OUTDOORS

On the mainland east of the Alburg Peninsula, **Missisquoi National Wildlife Refuge** (⊠*Tabor Rd., 36 mi north of Burlington, Swanton* ☎*802/868–4781*) consists of 6,642 acres of federally protected wetlands, meadows, and woods. It's a beautiful area for bird-watching, canoeing, or walking nature trails. **Sand Bar State Park** (☒ *U.S. 2, South Hero* ☏ *802/893-2825* ☑ *$3.50* ⊙ *Mid-May–Labor Day, daily dawn-dusk*) has one of Vermont's best swimming beaches.

BOATING   **Apple Island Resort** (☒ *U.S. 2, South Hero* ☏ *802/372-5398*) rents sailboats, rowboats, canoes, kayaks, and motorboats. **Hero's Welcome** (☒ *U.S. 2, North Hero* ☏ *802/372-4161 or 800/372-4376*) rents bikes, canoes, kayaks, and paddleboats.

WHERE TO STAY

$-$$ ⚏ **North Hero House Inn and Restaurant.** This inn has four buildings right on Lake Champlain, including the 1891 Colonial-revival main house with nine guest rooms, the restaurant, a pub room, library, and sitting room. Many rooms have water views, and each possesses country furnishings and antiques. The beach is a popular spot for lake swimming in summer, and there are boat rentals nearby. The Homestead, Southwind, and Cove House have adjoining rooms that are good for families. Dinner ($$–$$$) is served in the informal glass greenhouse or Colonial-style dining room. **Pros:** relaxed vacation complex; superb lakefront setting. **Cons:** open just May to November. ☒ *U.S. 2, North Hero* ☏ *802/372-4732 or 888/525-3644* ⊕ *www.northherohouse. com* ⟲ *26 rooms* ♿ *In-room: no a/c (some). In-hotel: restaurant, bar, no-smoking rooms* ☰ *AE, MC, V* ⊙❘*CP* ⊙ *Closed Dec.—Apr.*

$ ⚏ **Ruthcliffe Lodge.** Good food and splendid scenery make this off-the-beaten-path motel directly on Lake Champlain a great value. If you're looking for a cheap, DIY summer place to take in the scenery, canoe the lake, or bicycle, this will do quite nicely. The lodge is on Isle La Motte—a rarely-visited island. Rooms are very clean and simple: bed, dresser, night table, and stenciled wall border. Owner-chef Mark Infante specializes in Italian pasta, fish, and meat dishes; there's al fresco seating that overlooks a lawn leading to the lakeshore. A full breakfast is included as well. **Pros:** inexpensive; serene setting; laid-back. **Cons:** rooms simple, not luxurious. ☒ *1002 Quarry Rd., Isle La Motte* ☏ *802/928-3200* ⊕ *www.ruthcliffe.com* ⟲ *7 rooms* ♿ *In-hotel: restaurant, bicycles, boating, no-smoking rooms* ☰ *MC, V* ⊙❘*BP* ⊙ *Closed Columbus Day–mid-May.*

MONTGOMERY/JAY

32 mi east of St. Albans, 51 mi northeast of Burlington.

Montgomery is a small village near the Canadian border and Jay Peak ski resort. Amid the surrounding countryside are seven covered bridges.

Trout River Store (☒ *Main St., Montgomery Center* ☏ *802/326-3058*), an old-time country store with an antique soda fountain, is a great place to stock up on picnic supplies, eat a hearty bowl of soup and an overstuffed sandwich, and check out local crafts.

OFF THE
BEATEN
PATH
Lake Memphremagog. Vermont's second-largest lake, Lake Memphremagog extends from Newport 33 mi north into Canada. Prouty Beach in Newport has camping facilities, tennis courts, and paddleboat and canoe rentals. Watch the sun set from the deck of the **East Side Restaurant**

(✉ *Lake St., Newport* ☎ *802/334–2340*), which serves excellent burgers and prime rib. ✉ *Veterans Ave.* ☎ *802/334–7951.*

SPORTS & THE OUTDOORS

SKI AREA **Hazen's Notch Cross Country Ski Center and B&B** (✉ *Rte. 58* ☎ *802/326–4799*), delightfully remote at any time of the year, has 40 mi of marked and groomed trails and rents equipment and snowshoes.

★ Sticking up out of the flat farmland, **Jay Peak** (✉ *Rte. 242, Jay* ☎ *802/988–2611, 800/451–4449 outside VT* ⊕ *www.jaypeakresort. com*) averages 355 inches of snow a year—more than any other Vermont ski area. Its proximity to Quebec attracts Montrealers and discourages eastern seaboarders; hence, the prices are moderate and the lift lines shorter than at other resorts. The area is renowned for its glade skiing and powder.

Off season, Jay Peak runs tram rides to the summit from mid-June through Labor Day, and mid-September through Columbus Day ($10). In the winter, snowshoes can be rented, and guided walks are led by a naturalist. Telemark rentals and instruction are available.

In terms of its downhill-skiing options, Jay Peak has two interconnected mountains, the highest reaching nearly 4,000 feet with a vertical drop of 2,153 feet. The smaller mountain has straight-fall-line, expert terrain that eases mid-mountain into an intermediate pitch. The main peak is served by Vermont's only tramway and transports skiers to meandering but challenging intermediate trails. Beginners should stick near the bottom on trails off the Metro lift. Weekdays at 9:30 AM and 1:30 PM, mountain ambassadors conduct a free tour. The area's 76 trails, including 21 glades and two chutes, are served by eight lifts, including the tram and the longest detachable quad in the East. The area also has two quads, a triple, and a double chairlift; one T-bar; and a moving carpet. Jay has 80% snowmaking coverage. The area also has four terrain parks, each rated for different abilities. There are ski-school programs for children ages 3–18.

WHERE TO STAY

$$$$ ⊞ **Hotel Jay & Jay Peak Condominiums.** Centrally located in the ski resort's base area, the hotel and its simply furnished rooms are a favorite for families. Kids 13 and under stay and eat free, and during non-holiday times, they can ski free, too. Farther afield (but still mostly slope-side) are studio to five-bedroom condominiums and town houses, with fireplaces, modern kitchens, and washer/dryers. Complimentary child care is provided to hotel and condo guests 9 AM–4 PM for kids ages two to seven. **Pros:** great for skiers and summer mountain adverturers. **Cons:** not an intimate, traditional Vermont stay. ✉ *Rte. 242* ☎ *802/988–2611, 800/451–4449 outside VT* ⊕ *www.jaypeakresort. com* ⏎ *48 rooms, 94 condominiums* ♿ *In-room: no a/c. In-hotel: restaurant, bar, tennis courts, pool, no-smoking rooms* ▭ *AE, D, DC, MC, V* ⦿ *MAP.*

$ ⊞ **Inn on Trout River.** Guest rooms at this 100-year-old riverside inn sport a country-cottage style, and all have down quilts and flannel sheets in winter. Lemoine's Restaurant ($–$$) specializes in American and continental fare. Try the raviolini stuffed with Vermont cheddar cheese and walnuts topped with pesto, and the medallions of pork tenderloin in a maple syrup demi-glace sauce. Hobo's Café, also at the inn, serves simpler fare. **Pros:** traditional B&B. **Cons:** rooms heavy on the florals. ✉ *Main St., Montgomery Center* ☎ *802/326–4391 or 800/338–7049* ⊕ *www.troutinn.com* ➪ *9 rooms, 1 suite* ⅃ *In-room: no a/c, no TV. In-hotel: restaurant, bar, no-smoking rooms* ☰ *AE, DC, MC, V* ⊙ *BP, MAP.*

EN ROUTE	Routes 14, 5, 58, and 100 make a scenic drive around the **Northeast Kingdom,** named for the remoteness and stalwart independence that have helped preserve its rural nature. You can extend the loop and head east on Route 105 to the city of Newport on Lake Memphremagog. You will encounter some of the most unspoiled areas in all Vermont on the drive south from Newport on either U.S. 5 or Interstate 91 (Interstate 91 is faster, but U.S. 5 is prettier).

LAKE WILLOUGHBY

30 mi southeast of Montgomery (summer route; 50 mi by winter route), 28 mi north of St. Johnsbury.

The cliffs of Mt. Pisgah and Mt. Hor drop to the edge of Lake Willoughby on opposite shores, giving this beautiful, deep, glacially carved lake a striking resemblance to a Norwegian fjord. The trails to the top of Mt. Pisgah reward hikers with glorious views.

WHAT TO SEE

☾ ★ **Bread and Puppet Museum.** This ramshackle barn houses a surrealistic collection of props used by the world-renowned Bread and Puppet Theater. The troupe has been performing social and political commentary with the towering (they're supported by people on stilts), eerily expressive puppets for about 30 years. They perform at the museum every Sunday June–August at 3 PM. ✉ *753 Heights Rd. (Rte. 122), 1 mi east of Rte. 16, Glover* ☎ *802/525–3031* 🎫 *Donations accepted* ⊙ *June–Oct., daily 10–6.*

EAST BURKE

17 mi south of Lake Willoughby.

Once a sleepy village, East Burke is now the Northeast Kingdom's outdoor-activity hub. The Kingdom Trails attract thousands of mountain bikers in summer and fall. In winter, many trails are groomed for cross-country skiing. Contact the **Kingdom Trails Association** (📮 *Box 204, East Burke 05832* ☎ *802/626–0737* ⊕ *www.kingdomtrails.org*) for details and maps.

SPORTS & THE OUTDOORS

East Burke Sports (✉ *Rte. 114, East Burke* ☎ *802/626–3215*) rents mountain bikes, kayaks, and skis, and provides guides for cycling, hiking, paddling, skiing, and snowshoeing. **Village Sport Shop** (✉ *511*

Broad St., Lyndonville ☎*802/626–8448) rents bikes, canoes, kayaks, paddleboats, rollerblades, skis, and snowshoes.

⇨ "Slopes Less Traveled" box on page 395 for information on Burke Mountain ski area.

WHERE TO EAT & STAY

$-$$ ✗**River Garden Café.** You can eat lunch, dinner, or brunch outdoors on
AMERICAN the enclosed porch, on the patio amid perennial gardens, or inside this bright and cheerful café. The excellent fare includes lamb tenderloin, warm artichoke dip, bruschetta, pastas, and fresh fish, and the popular salad dressing is bottled for sale. ⊠*Rte. 114, East Burke* ☎*802/626–3514* ☰*AE, D, MC, V* ⊗*Closed Mon. and Tues. Nov.–Apr.*

$$ ▦**Wildflower Inn.** The hilltop views are breathtaking at this rambling,
☼ family-oriented complex of old farm buildings on 570 acres. Guest rooms in the restored Federal-style main house and three other buildings are furnished with reproductions and contemporary furnishings. In summer, supervised day and evening programs engage the kids, allowing parents to explore the many nature trails on their own. You can play with farm animals at the petting barn, go biking, and play tennis and volleyball. In winter sleigh rides, snowshoeing, and cross country skiing are popular. Junipers ($–$$; closed Sunday) serves comfort food such as meat loaf and lemon herb chicken, and offers a kids' menu. **Pros:** mega kid-friendly nature resort; best of the Northeast Kingdom's expansiveness; relaxed. **Cons:** most rooms are simply firnished. ⊠*2059 Darling Hill Rd., 5 mi west of East Burke, Lyndonville* ☎*802/626–8310 or 800/627–8310* ⊕*www.wildflowerinn.com* ⇗*10 rooms, 13 suites, 1 cottage* ⚒*In-room: no a/c (some), kitchen (some), no TV. In-hotel: restaurant, tennis court, pool, children's programs (infant–age 17), no-smoking rooms* ☰*MC, V* ⊗*Closed Apr. and Nov.* ⦾*BP.*

ST. JOHNSBURY

16 mi south of East Burke, 39 mi northeast of Montpelier.

St. Johnsbury, the southern gateway to the Northeast Kingdom, was chartered in 1786. But its identity was established after 1830, when Thaddeus Fairbanks invented the platform scale, a device that revolutionized weighing methods. The Fairbanks family's philanthropic efforts gave the city a strong cultural and architectural imprint.

WHAT TO SEE

☼ **Maple Grove Museum and Factory.** East of downtown, this is the world's oldest and largest maple candy factory. On a tour, watch how maple candy is made, then sample some in the gift shop. ⊠*1052 Portland St. (Rte. 2)* ☎*802/748–5141* ⊕*www.maplegrove.com* ▭*Tour $1* ⊗*May–Dec., weekdays 8–2.*

FodorśChoice **St. Johnsbury Athenaeum.** With its dark rich paneling, polished Victo-
★ rian woodwork, and ornate circular staircases, this building is both the town library and one of the oldest art galleries in the country, housing over 100 original works mainly of the Hudson River School. Albert Bierstadt's enormous *Domes of Yosemite* dominates the gallery.

✉ *1171 Main St.* ☎ *802/748–8291* ⊕ *www.stjathenaeum.org* 🎫 *Free* ⏰ *Mon. and Wed. 10–8; Tues., Thurs., and Fri. 10–5:30; Sat. 9:30–4.*

■ OFF THE
BEATEN
PATH

Peacham. Tiny Peacham, 10 mi southwest of St. Johnsbury, is on almost every tour group's list of "must-sees." With views extending to the White Mountains of New Hampshire and a white-steeple church, Peacham is perhaps the most photographed town in New England. *Ethan Frome*, starring Liam Neeson, was filmed here. One of the town's gathering spots, the **Peacham Store** (✉ *Main St.* ☎ *802/592–3310*), sells gourmet soups and stews. Next door, the **Peacham Corner Guild** sells local handcrafts.

WHERE TO STAY

$$$
★

☷ **Rabbit Hill Inn.** Few inns in New England have the word-of-mouth buzz that Rabbit Hill seems to earn from satisfied guests. Most of the spacious, elegant rooms have fireplaces, two-person whirlpool tubs, and views of the Connecticut River and New Hampshire's White Mountains. The grounds have 10 acres of walking trails. The intimate candlelit dining room serves a three- or five-course prix-fixe dinner ($$$$) featuring contemporary new American and regional dishes such as grilled venison loin with cranberry-juniper orange glaze. Afternoon tea in the parlor, horseshoes, garden strolls: this inn is great for small pleasures. **Pros:** attractive, spacious rooms; lovely grounds; good food. **Cons:** might be too quiet a setting for some. ✉ *Rte. 18, 11 mi south of St. Johnsbury, Lower Waterford,* ☎ *802/748–5168 or 800/762–8669* ⊕ *www.rabbithillinn.com* ➾ *19 rooms* ⚭ *In-room: no TV. In-hotel: restaurant, bar, no kids under 14, no-smoking rooms* ▭ *AE, D, MC, V* ⏰ *Closed 1st 3 wks in Apr., 1st 2 wks in Nov.* ⏺ *BP, MAP.*

VERMONT ESSENTIALS

Research prices, get travel advice, and book your trip at fodors.com.

TRANSPORTATION

BY AIR

Continental, Delta, JetBlue, United, and US Airways fly into **Burlington International Airport (BTV)** (✉ *1200 Airport Dr., 4 mi east of Burlington off U.S. 2* ☎ *802/863–1889* ⊕ *www.burlingtonintlairport.com*). **Rutland State Airport (RUT)** (✉ *1004 Airport Rd., North Clarendon* ☎ *802/773–3348*) has daily service to and from Boston on US Airways Express. West of Bennington and convenient to southern Vermont, **Albany International Airport (ALB)** (✉ *737 Albany Shaker Rd., Albany* ☎ *518/242–2200* ⊕ *www.albanyairport.com*) in New York State is served by 10 major U.S. carriers.

BY BIKE

Vermont is a popular destination for cyclists, who find villages and towns—with their inns, B&Bs, and restaurants—spaced closely enough for comfortable traveling. **Vermont Bicycle Touring** (✉ *Monkton Rd.,*

SPORTS & OUTDOORS IN VERMONT

BIKING

Vermont, especially the often deserted roads of the Northeast Kingdom, is great bicycle-touring country. Many companies lead weekend tours and weeklong trips throughout the state. If you'd like to go it on your own, most chambers of commerce have brochures highlighting good cycling routes in their area.

P.O.M.G. Bike Tours of Vermont (*Richmond Box 1080, 05477* 802/434-2270 or 888/635-2453 *www.pomgbike.com*) leads weekend and five-day bike tours.

FISHING

Central Vermont is the heart of the state's warm-water lake and pond fishing area. Harriman and Somerset reservoirs have both warm- and cold-water species; Harriman has a greater variety. Rainbow trout pulled out of Lake Dunmore have set state records; Lakes Bomoseen and St. Catherine are good for rainbows and largemouth bass. In the east, Lakes Fairlee and Morey hold bass, perch, and chain pickerel, while the lower part of the Connecticut River bursts with smallmouth bass, walleye, and perch; shad are returning via the fish ladders at Vernon and Bellows Falls.

In northern Vermont, rainbow and brown trout inhabit the Missisquoi, Lamoille, Winooski, and Willoughby rivers. Lakes Seymour, Willoughby, and Memphremagog and Great Averill Pond in the Northeast Kingdom are good for salmon and lake trout. The Dog River near Montpelier has one of the best wild populations of brown trout in the state, and landlocked Atlantic salmon are returning to the Clyde River following removal of a controversial dam.

Lake Champlain, stocked annually with salmon and lake trout, has become the state's ice-fishing capital; walleye, bass, pike, and channel catfish are also taken. Ice fishing is also popular on Lake Memphremagog. For information about fishing, including licenses, call the **Vermont Fish and Wildlife Department** (802/241-3700 *www.vtfishand wildlife.com*).

HIKING

Vermont is an ideal state for hiking—80 percent of the state is forest, and trails are everywhere. The Appalachian Trail runs the length of the state. In fact, it was the first portion of the trail to be completed, and in Vermont it is called the Long Trail. All bookstores in the state have numerous volumes dedicated to local hiking.

The **Green Mountain Club** (*4711 Waterbury-Stowe Rd. (Rte. 100), Waterbury Center* 802/244-7037 *www.greenmountainclub.org*) publishes hiking maps and guides. The club also manages the Long Trail, the north–south trail that traverses the entire state.

SPORT TOURS

Country Inns Along the Trail (*Box 59, Montgomery 05470* 802/326-2072 or 800/838-3301 *www.inntoinn.com*) arranges self-guided hiking, skiing, and biking trips from inn to inn in Vermont.

VERMONT SKI AREAS

This list is composed of ski areas in Vermont with at least 150 skiable acres.

Ski Area	Vertical Drop (in feet)	Skiable Acres	# of Lifts	Terrain Type*	Boarding Options
Ascutney Mountain	1,800	150	6	30% B 40% I 30% A	Terrain Park
Bolton Valley	1,704	165	6	27% B 47% I 26% A	Terrain Park and Half-pipe
Bromley	1,334	177	10	35% B 34% I 31% A	Terrain Park
Burke Mountain	2,011	250	4	25% B 45% I 30% A	Terrain Park
Jay Peak	2,153	385	8	20% B 40% I 40% A	Terrain Park
Killington	3,050	1,001	26	29% B 29% I 42% A	Terrain Park, Half-pipe
Mount Snow	1,700	590	19	14% B 73% I 13% A	Terrain Park, Half-pipe
Okemo	2,200	624	19	32% B 36% I 32% A	Terrain Park, Half-pipe
Pico Mountain	1,967	214	6	20% B 48% I 32% A	No Terrain Park
Smugglers' Notch	2,610	310	8	19% B 56% I 25% A	Terrain Park, Half-pipe
Stowe	2,360	485	13	16% B 59% I 25% A	Terrain Park, Half-pipe
Stratton	2,003	600	16	42% B 31% I 27% A	Terrain Park, Half-pipe
Sugarbush	2,600	508	16	20% B 45% I 35% A	Terrain Park, Half-pipe

* B = Beginner, I = Intermediate, A = Advanced

5

Bristol ☎*802/453–4811 or 800/245–3868*) leads numerous tours in the state.

BY BOAT

Lake Champlain Ferries (☎*802/864–9804* ⊕*www.lakechamplainferries.com*) operates three ferry crossing routes between the lake's Vermont and New York shores: Grand Isle–Plattsburgh, NY; Burlington–Port Kent, NY; and Charlotte–Essex, NY. Two of the routes are in operation year-round, through thick lake ice in winter; the Burlington–Port Kent route functions from late May to mid-October. This is a convenient means of getting to and from New York State, as well as a pleasant way to spend an afternoon.

BY BUS

Vermont Transit (☎*800/552–8737* ⊕*www.greyhound.com*), operated by Greyhound, connects Bennington, Brattleboro, Burlington, Manchester, Montpelier, Rutland, Waterbury, and many other Vermont cities and towns with Albany, Boston, Springfield, Newport, New York, Montreal, and cities in New Hampshire. Local service in Burlington and surrounding communities is provided by **Chittenden Country Transportation Authority** (☎*802/864–0211*).

BY CAR

Interstate 91, which stretches from Connecticut and Massachusetts in the south to Quebec in the north, serves most points along Vermont's eastern border (as does U.S. 5). Interstate 89, from New Hampshire to the east and Quebec to the north, crosses central Vermont from White River Junction to Burlington. North of Interstate 89, Routes 104 and 15 provide a major east–west transverse. From Barton, near Lake Willoughby, U.S. 5 and Route 122 south are beautiful drives. Strip-mall drudge bogs down the section of U.S. 5 around Lyndonville.

Southwestern Vermont can be reached by U.S. 7 from Massachusetts and U.S. 4 from New York. U.S. 7 and Route 30 are the north–south highways in the west (the more scenic drive is Route 7A). Interstate 89 links White River Junction with Montpelier to the north. U.S. 4, the major east–west route, stretches from White River Junction in the east to Fair Haven in the west. Traffic can be slow through Woodstock. Route 100 is the scenic route. It splits the region in half along the eastern edge of the Green Mountains. In the south the principal east–west highway is twisty Route 9, the Molly Stark Trail, from Brattleboro to Bennington.

The *Vermont Atlas and Gazetteer,* sold in many bookstores, shows nearly every road in the state and is great for driving on the back roads.

For current road conditions, call 800/429-7623.

BY TRAIN

Amtrak (☎*800/872–7245* ⊕*www.amtrak.com*) has daytime service linking Washington, D.C., with Brattleboro, Bellows Falls, White River Junction, Montpelier, Waterbury, Essex Junction, and St. Albans via its Vermonter line. Amtrak's Adirondack, which runs from New York City to Montreal, serves Albany, Ft. Edward (near Glens Falls), Ft.

Ticonderoga, and Plattsburgh, allowing relatively convenient access to western Vermont. The Ethan Allen Express (also Amtrak) connects New York City with Fair Haven and Rutland.

CONTACTS & RESOURCES

VISITOR INFORMATION

State Contacts Vermont Department of Tourism and Marketing (⊠ *6 Baldwin St., Drawer 33, Montpelier* ☎ *802/828-3676 or 800/837-6668* ⊕ *www.vermont vacation.com).* The **Foliage and Snow Hot Line** (☎ *802/828-3239)* has tips on peak foliage viewing locations and times, up-to-date snow conditions, and events in Vermont.

Regional Contacts Lake Champlain Regional Chamber of Commerce (⊠ *60 Main St., Suite 100, Burlington* ☎ *802/863-3489 or 877/686 5253* ⊕ *www. vermont.org).* **Northeast Kingdom Travel and Tourism Association** (⌂ *Box 465, Barton* ☎ *802/525-4386 or 800/884-8001* ⊕ *www.travelthekingdom.com).* **Vermont North Country Chamber of Commerce** (⊠ *246 The Causeway, Newport* ☎ *802/334-7782 or 800/635-4643* ⊕ *www.vtnorthcountry.org).*

Local Contacts Addison County Chamber of Commerce (⊠ *2 Court St., Middlebury* ☎ *802/388-7951 or 800/733-8376* ⊕ *www.midvermont.com).* **Bennington Area Chamber of Commerce** (⊠ *Veterans Memorial Dr., Bennington* ☎ *802/447-3311 or 800/229-0252* ⊕ *www.bennington.com).* **Brattleboro Area Chamber of Commerce** (⊠ *180 Main St., Brattleboro* ☎ *802/254-4565 or 877/254-4565* ⊕ *www.brattleborochamber.org).* **Chamber of Commerce, Manchester and the Mountains** (⊠ *5046 Main St., Manchester* ☎ *802/362-2100 or 800/362-4144* ⊕ *www.manchestervermont.net)* **Lake Champlain Islands Chamber of Commerce** (⊠ *3537 Rte. 2, Suite 100, North Hero* ☎ *802/372-8400 or 800/262-5226* ⊕ *www.champlainislands.com).* **Mt. Snow Valley Chamber of Commerce** (⊠ *W. Main St.* ⌂ *Box 3, Wilmington* ☎ *802/464-8092 or 877/887-6884* ⊕ *www.visit vermont.com).* **Quechee Chamber of Commerce** (⊠ *1789 Quechee St.* ⌂ *Box 106, Quechee* ☎ *802/295-7900 or 800/295-5451* ⊕ *www.quechee.com).* **Stowe Area Association** (⊠ *Main St., Box 1320, Stowe* ☎ *802/253-7321 or 877/467-8693* ⊕ *www.gostowe.com).* **Sugarbush Chamber of Commerce** (⊠ *Rte. 100* ⌂ *Box 173, Waitsfield* ☎ *802/496-3409 or 800/828-4748* ⊕ *www.madrivervalley. com).* **Woodstock Area Chamber of Commerce** (⊠ *18 Central St.* ⌂ *Box 486, Woodstock* ☎ *802/457-3555 or 888/496-6378* ⊕ *www.woodstockvt.com).*

New Hampshire

WORD OF MOUTH

"If you are looking for sights, the cog railway trip up Mt. Washington is fun, and the Mt. Washington Hotel in Crawford Notch is lovely. It's one of the few remaining grand old hotels. A gorgeous drive from there would be taking Rt. 302 through North Conway to Rt. 112 (Kancamagus Highway) to Lincoln, then back up Rt. 3 to Bretton Woods . . . Lots to see along the way. It's slow going, but worth the time."

—colbeck

By Michael de Zayas

CRUSTY, AUTONOMOUS NEW HAMPSHIRE IS often defined more by what it is not than by what it is. It lacks Vermont's folksy charm, and its coast isn't nearly as grand as that of Maine. However, it has a strong political history: it was the first colony to declare independence from Great Britain, the first to adopt a state constitution, and the first to require that constitution be referred to the people for approval.

From the start, New Hampshire residents took their hard-won freedoms seriously. Twenty years after the Revolutionary War's Battle of Bennington, New Hampshire native General John Stark, who led the troops to that crucial victory, wrote a letter to be read at the reunion he was too ill to attend. In it, he reminded his men, "Live free or die; death is not the worst of evils." The first half of that sentiment is now the Granite State's motto.

New Hampshire's independent spirit, mountain peaks, clear air, and sparkling lakes have attracted trailblazers and artists for centuries. Ralph Waldo Emerson, Henry David Thoreau, Nathaniel Hawthorne, and Louisa May Alcott all visited and wrote about the state, sparking a strong literary tradition that continues today. Filmmaker Ken Burns, writer J. D. Salinger, and poet Donald Hall all make their homes here.

The state's diverse terrain makes it popular with everyone from avid adventurers to young families looking for easy access to nature. You can hike, climb, ski, snowboard, snowshoe, and fish as well as explore on snowmobiles, sailboats, and mountain bikes. Natives have no objection to others enjoying the state's beauty as long as they leave some money behind. New Hampshire has long resisted both sales and income taxes, so tourism brings in much-needed revenue.

With a few of its cities consistently rated among the most livable in the nation, New Hampshire has seen considerable growth over the past decade or two. Longtime residents worry that the state will soon take on two personalities: one of rapidly growing cities to the southeast and the other of quiet villages to the west and north. Although the influx of newcomers has brought change, the independent nature of the people and the state's natural beauty remain constant.

EXPLORING NEW HAMPSHIRE

Generally speaking, New Hampshire has four geographic areas: the coast, the central Lakes Region, the White Mountains in the north, and Merrimack Valley and the southwest. The main attractions of southern New Hampshire's coast are historical Portsmouth and bustling Hampton Beach; several somewhat quieter communities such as Durham and Exeter are a bit farther inland. The Lakes Region has good hiking trails, antiques shops, and, of course, water sports. For winter activities, there's no match for the mighty White Mountains, where you can experience the state's best hiking and skiing. The southwest is hemmed in to the east by the central Merrimack Valley, which has a string of fast-growing communities along Interstate 93 and U.S. 3 but for the most part retains its quiet, small-town life.

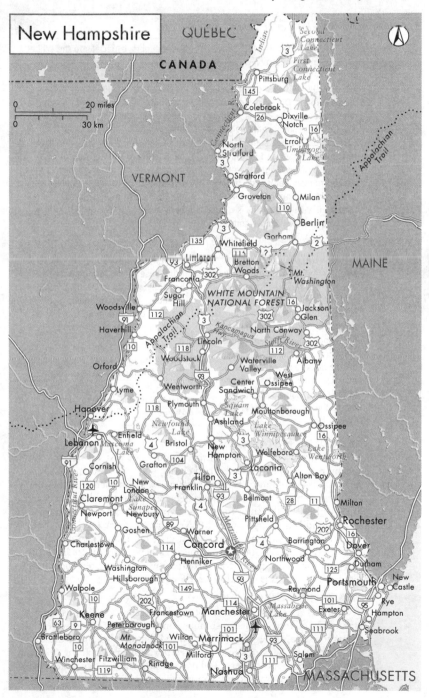

New Hampshire

PLANNING YOUR TRIP

BUDGETING YOUR TIME

Some people come to New Hampshire to hike or ski the mountains, fish and sail the lakes, or cycle along the back roads. Others prefer to drive through scenic towns, visiting museums and shops. Although New Hampshire is a small state, roads curve around lakes and mountains, making distances longer than they appear. You can get a taste of the coast, lake, and mountain areas in three to five days; eight days gives you time to make a more comprehensive loop.

WHEN TO GO

Summer and fall are the best times to visit most New Hampshire. Winter is a great time to visit the White Mountains, but most other tourist sites in the state, including the Portsmouth museums and the Lake attractions, are closed. In summer, people flock to seaside beaches, mountain trails, and lake boat ramps. In the cities, festivals showcase music, theater, and crafts. Fall brings leaf-peepers, especially to the White Mountains and along the Kancamagus Highway (Route 112). Skiers take to the slopes in winter, when Christmas lights and carnivals brighten the long, dark nights. Spring's unpredictable weather—along with April's mud and late May's black flies—tends to deter visitors. Still, the season has its joys, not the least of which is the appearance of the state flower, the purple lilac, from mid-May to early June.

GETTING THERE & AROUND

New Hampshire is an easy drive north from Boston, and serves as a good base for exploring northern New England. Its major destinations are easily located off major highways, so getting around by car is a great way to go in the state.

Though Boston's Logan Airport is nearby, it's easy to reach the state by air directly as well. Manchester Airport is the state's largest airport and has nonstop service to more than 20 cities.

ABOUT THE RESTAURANTS

New Hampshire prides itself on seafood—not just lobster but also salmon pie, steamed mussels, fried clams, and seared tuna. Across the state you'll find country taverns with upscale continental and American menus, many of them embracing regional ingredients. A dearth of agriculture in the state means that you won't find an emphasis on local ingredients like you might in Vermont, and the level of culinary sophistication is lacking. Alongside a growing number of contemporary eateries are such state traditions as greasy-spoon diners, pizzerias, and pubs that serve hearty comfort fare. Reservations are almost never required, and dress is casual in nearly every eatery.

ABOUT THE HOTELS

In the mid-19th century, wealthy Bostonians retreated to imposing New Hampshire country homes in summer months. Grand hotels were built across the state, especially in the White Mountains, when the area was competing with Saratoga Springs, Newport, and Bar Harbor to draw the nation's elite vacationers. Today a handful survive, with their large cooking staffs and tradition of top-notch service. Many of the vacation

NEW HAMPSHIRE TOP 5

■ **The White Mountains:** Great for hiking and skiing, these rugged, dramatic peaks and notches are unforgettable.

■ **Lake Winnipesaukee:** Water parks, arcades, boat cruises, and classic summer camps make for a family fun extravaganza.

■ **Fall Foliage:** Head to the Kancamagus Highway in the fall for one of America's best drives.

■ **Portsmouth:** Less than an hour from the state capital, this great American city has coastline allure, cute and colorful colonial architecture, and a real small-city energy.

■ **Pristine Towns:** Jaffrey Center, Walpole, Tamworth, Center Sandwich, and Jackson are among the most charming tiny villages in New England.

houses have been converted into inns. The smallest have only a couple of rooms and are typically done in period style. The largest contain 30 or more rooms and have in-room fireplaces and even hot tubs. Amenities increase each year at some of these inns, which, along with bed-and-breakfasts, dominate New Hampshire's lodging scene. You'll also find a great many well-kept, often family-owned motor lodges—particularly in the White Mountains and Lakes regions. In the ski areas expect the usual ski condos and lodges. In the Merrimack River valley, as well as along major highways, chain hotels and motels prevail.

WHAT IT COSTS					
	¢	$	$$	$$$	$$$$
RESTAU-RANTS	under $10	$10–$16	$17–$24	$25–$35	over $35
HOTELS	under $100	$100–$149	$150–$199	$200–$250	over $250

Prices are per person, for a main course at dinner. Prices are for a standard double room during peak season and not including tax or gratuities. Some inns add a 15%–18% service charge.

THE COAST

New Hampshire's 18-mi stretch of coastline packs in a wealth of scenery and diversions. The honky-tonk of Hampton Beach gets plenty of attention, good and bad, but first-timers are often surprised by the significant chunk of shoreline that remains pristine—especially through the town of Rye. This section begins in the regional hub, Portsmouth; cuts down the coast to the beaches; branches inland to the quintessential prep-school town of Exeter; and then runs back up north through Dover, Durham (home of the University of New Hampshire), and Rochester. From here it's a short drive to the Lakes Region.

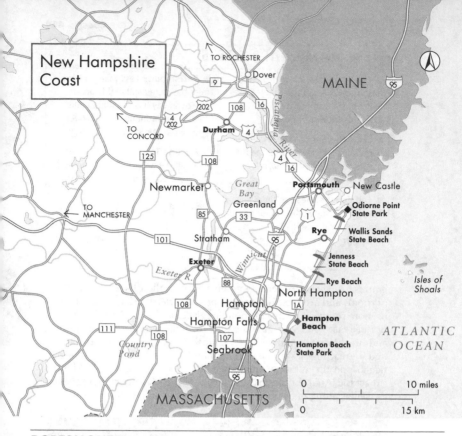

New Hampshire Coast

PORTSMOUTH

★ *47 mi southeast of Concord; 50 mi southwest of Portland, Maine; 56 mi north of Boston.*

Settled in 1623 as Strawbery Banke, Portsmouth became a prosperous port before the Revolutionary War, and like similarly wealthy Newport, Rhode Island, it harbored many Tory sympathizers throughout the campaign. Filled with grand residential architecture spanning the 18th through early 20th century, this city of 23,000 has numerous house museums, including the collection of 40-plus buildings that make up the Strawbery Banke Museum. With hip eateries, quirky shops, swank cocktail bars, respected theaters, and jumping live-music venues, this sheltered harbor city is a hot destination. Downtown, especially around elegant Market Square, buzzes with conviviality.

WHAT TO SEE

John Paul Jones House. The yellow, hip-roof home was a boardinghouse when the Revolutionary War hero lived here while supervising shipbuilding for the Continental Navy. The 1758 structure, now the headquarters of the Portsmouth Historical Society, contains furniture, costumes, glass, guns, portraits, and documents from the late

SIGHTSEEING TRAILS & TROLLEYS

TRAILS

One of the best ways to learn about town history is on the guided tour along the **Portsmouth Harbour Trail** (✉ *Downtown through the South End and along State and Congress Sts.* ☎ *603/427–2020 for guided tour* ⊕ *www.seacoastnh. com/harbourtrail* ⛟ *$8 for guided tour* ☉ *Highlights tour Thurs.–Sat., Mon. 10:30* AM, *Sun. 1:30* PM. *Twilight tour Thurs.–Sat. and Mon. 5:30* PM). You can purchase a tour map ($2.50) at the information kiosk in Market Square, at the chamber of commerce, and at several house museums. Guided walks are conducted late spring to early fall.

Sites important to African-American history in Portsmouth are along the self-guided walk on the **Portsmouth Black Heritage Trail** (✉ *Downtown, starting at Prescott Park wharf* ☎ *603/431–2768* ⊕ *www.seacoastnh.com/blackhistory*). Included are the **New Hampshire Gazette Printing Office,** where skilled slave Primus Fowle operated the paper's printing press for some 50 years

beginning in 1756, and the city's 1866 **Election Hall,** outside of which the city's black citizens held annual celebrations of the Emancipation Proclamation.

TROLLEYS

On the **Seacoast Trolley** (✉ *Departs from Market Sq. or from 14 locations en route* ☎ *603/431–6975* ⊕ *www.locallink.com/seacoasttrolley* ⛟ *$5*) guides conduct narrated tours of Portsmouth, Rye, and New Castle, with views of the New Hampshire coastline and area beaches. The 17-mi round-trip, which you can hop on and off at several stops, runs from mid-June through Labor Day

Portsmouth is also served by the **Downtown Loop Coastal Trolley** (✉ *Departs from Market Sq. every half hour* ☎ *603/743–5777* ⊕ *www.coastbus.org/downtown. html* ⛟ *50¢*). Running from late June to early September, the tours are narrated 90-minute round-trips through downtown and around the waterfront. You can hop on and off at numerous stops.

6

18th century. ✉ *43 Middle St.* ☎ *603/436–8420* ⛟ *$5* ☉ *June–Oct., daily 10–5.*

Moffatt-Ladd House. The period interior of this 1763 home tells the story of Portsmouth's merchant class through portraits, letters, and fine furnishings. The Colonial-revival garden includes a horse chestnut tree planted by General William Whipple when he returned home after signing the Declaration of Independence in 1776. ✉ *154 Market St.* ☎ *603/436–8221* ⛟ *$6, garden and house tour $1* ☉ *Mid-June–mid-Oct., Mon.–Sat. 11–5, Sun. 1–5.*

■ NEED A BREAK? Drop by Annabelle's Natural Ice Cream (✉ *49 Ceres St.* ☎ *603/436–3400*) for a dish of Ghirardelli chocolate chip or Almond Joy ice cream. Breaking New Grounds (✉ *14 Market Sq.* ☎ *603/436–9555*) is a big hangout in town and serves coffee, pastries, and gelato.

Port of Portsmouth Maritime Museum. The USS *Albacore,* built here in 1953, is docked at this museum in Albacore Park. You can board the prototype submarine, which was a floating laboratory assigned to test an innovative hull design, dive brakes, and sonar systems for the Navy. The nearby Memorial Garden and its reflecting pool are dedicated to those who have lost their lives in submarine service. ⊠ *600 Market St.* ☎ *603/436–3680* ✉ *$5* ☼ *Daily 9:30–5.*

Redhook Ale Brewery. Tours here end with a beer tasting. If you don't have time to tour, stop in the Cataqua Public House to sample the fresh ales and have a bite to eat (open daily for lunch and dinner). The building is visible from the Spaulding Turnpike. ⊠ *Pease International Tradeport, 35 Corporate Dr.* ☎ *603/430–8600* ⊕ *www.redhook.com* ✉ *$1* ☼ *Tours weekdays at 2, weekends at 2 and 4; additional tours at noon, 1, and 3 summer weekends.*

Fodor's Choice ★ **Strawbery Banke Museum.** The first English settlers named the area around today's Portsmouth for the wild strawberries abundant along the shores of the Piscataqua River. The name survives in this 10-acre neighborhood, continuously occupied for more than 300 years and now doing duty as an outdoor history museum, one of the largest in New England. The compound has 46 buildings dating from 1695 to 1820—some restored and furnished to a particular period, some used for exhibits, and some viewed from the outside only—as well as restored or re-created period gardens. Half the interior of the Drisco House, built in 1795, depicts its use as a dry-goods store in Colonial times, whereas the living room and kitchen are decorated as they were in the 1950s, showing how buildings were adapted over time. The Shapiro House has been restored to reflect the life of the Russian Jewish immigrant family who lived in the home in the early 1900s. Perhaps the most opulent house, done in decadent Victorian style, is the 1860 Goodwin Mansion, former home of Governor Ichabod Goodwin. ⊠ *Marcy St.* ☎ *603/433–1100* ⊕ *www.strawberybanke.org* ✉ *$15* ☼ *May–Oct., daily 10–5; Feb.–Apr., Nov., and Dec., Wed.–Sat. 10–2.*

Wentworth-Coolidge Mansion Historic Site. A National Historic Landmark now part of Little Harbor State Park, this home site was originally the residence of Benning Wentworth, New Hampshire's first royal governor (1753–70). Notable among its period furnishings is the carved pine mantelpiece in the council chamber. Wentworth's imported lilac trees bloom each May. The visitor center stages lectures and exhibits and contains a gallery with changing exhibits. ⊠ *375 Little Harbor Rd., near South Street Cemetery* ☎ *603/436–6607* ✉ *$3* ☼ *Grounds daily; mansion mid-May–Aug., Wed.–Sat. 10–3, Sun. 1–5; Sept.–mid-May, by appointment.*

OFF THE BEATEN PATH

Though it consists of a single square mile of land, the small island of **New Castle,** 3 mi southeast from downtown via Route 1B, was once known as Great Island. The narrow roads and coastal lanes are lined with prerevolutionary houses making for a beautiful drive or stroll. **Wentworth-by-the-Sea,** the last of the state's great seaside resorts, towers over the southern end of New Castle on Route 1B. It was the site of the signing of the Russo-Japanese Treaty in 1905, when Russian and Japanese delegates stayed at the resort and signed an agreement ending the Russo-Japanese War. President Theodore Roosevelt won a Nobel Peace Prize for bringing this about. The property was vacant for 20 years before reopened as a luxury resort in 2003. Also on New Castle Island, **Ft. Constitution** (✉ *Wentworth St. off Rte. 1B, at the Coast Guard Station* ☎ *603/436–1552* ⊕ *www.nhstateparks.com/fortconstitution. html* 🎫 *Free* ☉ *Daily 9–4*) was built in 1631 and then rebuilt in 1666 as Ft. William and Mary, a British stronghold overlooking Portsmouth Harbor. The fort earned fame in 1774, when patriots raided it in one of revolutionary America's first overtly defiant acts against King George III. The rebels later used the captured munitions against the British at the Battle of Bunker Hill. Panels explain its history. Park at the dock and walk into the Coast Guard installation to the fort.

OFF THE BEATEN PATH

Isles of Shoals. Many of these nine small, rocky islands (eight at high tide) retain the earthy names—Hog and Smuttynose, to cite but two—given them by transient 17th-century fishermen. A history of piracy, murder, and ghosts surrounds the archipelago, long populated by an independent lot who, according to one writer, hadn't the sense to winter on the mainland. Not all the islands lie within the state's border: after an ownership dispute, five went to Maine and four to New Hampshire.

6

Celia Thaxter, a native islander, romanticized these islands with her poetry in *Among the Isles of Shoals* (1873) and celebrated her garden in *An Island Garden* (1894; now reissued with the original color illustrations by Childe Hassam). In the late 19th century, **Appledore Island** became an offshore retreat for Thaxter's coterie of writers, musicians, and artists. The island is now used by the Marine Laboratory of Cornell University. **Star Island** contains a nondenominational conference center and is open to those on guided tours.

From late May to late October you can cruise of the Isles of Shoals or take a ferry to Star Island with **Isles of Shoals Steamship Company** (✉ *315 Market St.* ☎ *800/441–4620 or 603/431–5500* ⊕ *www.islesofshoals.com*).

SPORTS & THE OUTDOORS

Great Bay Estuarine Research Reserve. Just inland from Portsmouth is one of southeastern New Hampshire's most precious assets. Amid its 4,471 acres of tidal waters, mudflats, and about 48 mi of inland shoreline, you can spot blue herons, ospreys, and snowy egrets, particularly during spring and fall migrations. Winter eagles also live here. The best public access is via the **Sandy Point Discovery Center** (✉ *89 Depot Rd., off Rte. 33, Stratham* ☎ *603/778–0015* ⊕ *www.greatbay. org* ☉ *May–Sept., Wed.–Sun. 10–4; Oct., weekends 10–4*). The facility has year-round interpretive programs, indoor and outdoor exhibits, a library and bookshop, and a 1,700-foot boardwalk as well as other trails through mudflats and upland forest. The center, about 15 mi southeast of Durham and 6 mi west of Exit 3 from Interstate 95 in Portsmouth, also distributes maps and information. ⓘ *Information: New Hampshire Fish & Game Dept., 225 Main St., Durham 03824* ☎ *603/868–1095* 🎫 *Free* ☉ *Daily dawn–dusk.*

Prescott Park. Picnicking is popular at this waterfront park. A large formal garden with fountains is perfect for whiling away an afternoon.

SPORTS & OUTDOORS IN NEW HAMPSHIRE

BIKE TOURS

Bike the Whites (☎877/854–6535 ⊕ www.bikethewhites.com) organizes bike tours in New Hampshire and Vermont. **New England Hiking Holidays** (☎603/356–9696 or 800/869–0949 ⊕ www.nehikingholidays.com) arranges bicycling trips in the region.

BIRD-WATCHING

Audubon Society of New Hampshire (✉3 Silk Farm Rd., Concord ☎603/224–9909 ⊕ www.nhaudubon.org) schedules monthly field trips throughout the state and a fall bird-watching tour to Star Isle and other parts of the Isles of Shoals.

CAMPING

New Hampshire Campground Owners Association (✆ Box 320, Twin Mountain, 03595 ☎603/846–5511 or 800/822–6764 ⊕ www.ucampnh.com) publishes a guide to private, state, and national-forest campgrounds. **White Mountain National Forest** (✉U.S. Forest Service, 719 N. Main St., Laconia ☎603/528–8721 or 877/444–6777 ⊕ www.fs.fed.us/r9/forests/white_mountain) campground reservations has 20 campgrounds with more than 900 campsites spread across the region; only some take reservations. All sites have a 14-day limit.

FISHING

Many companies along the coast offer rentals and charters for deep-sea fishing and cruises. Inland, for trout and salmon fishing, try the Connecticut Lakes, though any clear White Mountain stream (there are 650 mi of them in the national forest alone) will do. Many streams are stocked. Conway Lake—the largest of the area's 45 lakes and ponds—is noted for smallmouth bass and, early and late in the season, good salmon fishing. For information about fishing and licenses, call the **New Hampshire Fish and Game Department** (☎603/271–3211 ⊕ www.wildlife.state.nh.us).

HIKING

Among the 86 major peaks in the White Mountains, hiking possibilities are endless. Innkeepers can usually point you toward the better nearby trails; some inns schedule guided day trips for guests. The **White Mountain National Forest** (✉U.S. Forest Service, 719 Main St., Laconia ☎603/528–8721 ⊕ www.fs.fed.us/r9/forests/white_mountain) office has information on hiking as well as on the parking passes ($5) that are required in the national forest. **New England Hiking Holidays** (☎603/356–9696 or 800/869–0949 ⊕ www.nehikingholidays.com) conducts hikes in the White Mountains with lodging in country inns for two to eight nights. Hikes, each with two guides, allow for different levels of ability and cover between 5 and 10 mi per day. The **New Hampshire Parks Department** (☎603/271–3556 ⊕ www.nhparks.state.nh.us) also general hiking information.

SKIING

Contacts Ski New Hampshire (✆ Box 10, North Woodstock, 03262 ☎603/745–9396 or 800/887–5464 ⊕ www.skinh.com).

The park also contains Point of Graves, Portsmouth's oldest burial ground, and two 17th-century warehouses. ✉*Between Strawbery Banke Museum and the Piscataqua River.*

Water Country. New Hampshire's largest water park has a river tube ride, large wave pool, white-water rapids, and 12 large waterslides. ✉*Rte. 1, 3 mi south of downtown Portsmouth* ☎603/427–1112 💲$29 ☉*Mid-June–Labor Day, daily 10–6; until 7:30 in July and early Aug.*

BOAT TOURS **Granite State Whale Watch** (✉*Rye Harbor State Marina, Rte. 1A, Rye* ☎603/964–5545 *or* 800/964–5545 ⊕*www.whales-rye.com*) conducts naturalist-led whale-watching tours aboard the 150-passenger MV *Granite State* out of Rye Harbor State Marina from May to early October, and narrated Isles of Shoals cruises in July and August.

From May to October, **Portsmouth Harbor Cruises** (✉*Ceres Street Dock* ☎603/436–8084 *or* 800/776–0915 ⊕*www.portsmouthharbor.com*) operates tours of Portsmouth Harbor, foliage trips on the Cocheco River, and sunset cruises aboard the MV *Heritage.*

The **Isles of Shoals Steamship Co.** (✉*Barker Wharf, 315 Market St.* ☎603/ 431–5500 *or* 800/441–4620 ⊕*www.islesofshoals.com*) runs a three-hour Isles of Shoals, lighthouses, and Portsmouth Harbor cruise out of Portsmouth aboard the *Thomas Laighton,* a replica of a Victorian steamship, from April through December (twice daily in summer). Lunch and light snacks are available on board or you can bring your own. There are also fall foliage cruises, narrated sunset cruises visiting five local lighthouses, and special holiday cruises.

One of the questions visitors to Portsmouth ask most frequently is whether they can tour the familiar red tugboats plying the waters of Piscataqua River and Portsmouth Harbor. Unfortunately, the answer is no, but you can get a firsthand look at Portsmouth's working waterfront aboard the **Tug Alley Too** (✉*2 Ceres St.* ☎603/430–9556 ⊕*www. tugboatalley.com*), a six-passenger replica. The 90-minute tours pass lighthouses, the Portsmouth Naval Shipyard, and Wentworth Marina. Tours are conducted daily from July through September, Monday through Saturday.

Explore the waters, sites, and sea life of the Piscataqua River Basin and the New Hampshire coastline on a guided kayak tour with **Portsmouth Kayak Adventure** (✉*185 Wentworth Rd.* ☎603/559–1000). Beginners are welcome (instruction is included). Tours are run daily from June through mid-October, at 10 and 2. Sunset tours take off at 6. They also run a kids camp. If you'd rather pedal than drive, stop by **Portsmouth Rent & Ride** (✉*37 Hanover St.* ☎603/433–6777) for equipment, maps, and suggested bike routes to Portsmouth sites, area beaches, and attractions. Guided two-hour tours of the seacoast area are also offered.

SHOPPING

Market Square, in the center of town, has gift and clothing boutiques, book and card shops, and exquisite crafts stores. **Nahcotta** (✉*110 Congress St.* ☎ *603/433–1705*) is a wonderful contemporary art gallery, and has a well-chosen selection of contemporary housewares, artist-crafted jewelry, and glassware. **Byrne & Carlson** (⊠*121 State St.* ☎*888/559–9778*) produces handmade chocolates in the finest European tradition. **N. W. Barrett** (⊠*53 Market St.* ☎*603/431–4262*) specializes in leather, jewelry, pottery, and other arts and crafts. It also sells furniture, including affordable steam-bent oak pieces and one-of-a-kind lamps and rocking chairs.

NIGHTLIFE & THE ARTS

MUSIC Fans of the local music scene should discover **The Red Door** (⊠*401 State St.* ☎*603/431–5202* ⊕*www.reddoorportsmouth.com*), which has a bar and different music series and DJs nightly. Indie music fans shouldn't miss Monday nights at 8 for the acclaimed live acts curated by the Hush Hush Sweet Harlot series. The **Portsmouth Gas Light Co.** (⊠*64 Market St.* ☎*603/430–9122*), a brick-oven pizzeria and restaurant, hosts local rock bands in its lounge, courtyard, and slick upstairs space. People come from as far away as Boston and Portland to hang out at the **Press Room** (⊠*77 Daniel St.* ☎*603/431–5186*), which showcases folk, jazz, blues, and bluegrass performers.

BARS The town's newest bar and its only martini bar is at little **Two Ceres Street** (⊠*2 Ceres St.* ☎*603/431–5967*). If vodka is your thing you'll do no better than the book-lined English oak bar **The Library** (⊠*401 State St.* ☎*603/431–5202*), which has more than 100 brands.

THE ARTS Five galleries participate in the Art 'Round Town Reception, a gallery walk that takes place the second Friday of each month. Check out ⊕*www.artroundtown.org* for more information. Beloved for its acoustics, the 1878 **Music Hall** (⊠*28 Chestnut St.* ☎*603/436–2400, 603/436–9900 film line* ⊕*www.themusichall.org*) brings the best touring events to the seacoast—from classical and pop concerts to dance and theater. The hall also hosts art-house film series. The **Prescott Park Arts Festival** (⊠*105 Marcy St.* ☎*603/436–2848* ⊕*www.prescottpark. org*) presents theater, dance, and musical events outdoors from June through August.

WHERE TO EAT

$$ ✕**Blue Mermaid Island Grill.** This is a fun, colorful place for great fish,
ECLECTIC sandwiches and quesadillas, as well as house-cut sweet-potato chips. Specialties include plantain-encrusted grouper topped with grilled mango vinaigrette and served with black-eyed pea–sweet potato hash; and wood-grilled flat-iron steak with a cilantro-hoisin glaze, cucumber-citrus relish, and noodles. In summer you can eat on a deck that overlooks the adorable Colonial homes of the Hill neighborhood. Entertainers perform (outdoors in summer) on Wednesday through Saturday. ⊠*409 The Hill* ☎*603/427–2583* ▭*AE, D, DC, MC, V.*

$–$$ ✕**Chiangmai Thai.** Portsmouth's first authentic Thai restaurant remains
THAI one of its favorites among locals and visitors. The dining room is small, but the menu lists an extensive array of creative Thai dishes. Duck is a specialty (try it roasted, then lightly fried in egg batter; topped with ginger, scallions, and a spicy red-chili sauce; and served over crispy noodles and roasted pine nuts). Or you can create your own dish with

an assortment of sauces and curries. ⊠*128 Penhallow St.* ☏*603/433–1289* ▭*AE, D, MC, V* ☻*Closed Mon. and Feb.*

☺ ¢–$ ✕**Friendly Toast.** The biggest and best breakfast in town (as well as lunch
★ and dinner) is served at this funky, wildly colorful diner-style restau-
AMERICAN rant loaded with bric-a-brac. Almond Joy cakes (buttermilk pancakes,
chocolate chips, coconut, and almonds), orange French toast, and hefty
omelets (lots of combinations) are favorites. The homemade breads
and muffins are a hit, too. A late-night crowd gathers in the wee hours
after the bars close, since the restaurant is open 24 hours on weekends.
⊠*121 Congress St.* ☏*603/430–2154* ▭*AE, D, MC, V.*

$$ ✕**Jumpin' Jay's.** A wildly popular spot downtown, this offbeat, dim-
SEAFOOD lighted eatery presents a changing menu of world-beat seafood, and
nary a red-meat platter is served. Try the steamed Prince Edward Island
mussels with a spicy lemongrass and saffron sauce, Jonah crab–and-
vegetable lasagna, or the Chilean sea bass with a ginger-orange mari-
nade. Singles often gather at the central bar for dinner and schmoozing.
⊠*150 Congress St.* ☏*603/766–3474* ▭*MC, V* ☻*No lunch.*

$$–$$$ ✕**The Library.** Have an insatiable appetite for words? Don't miss having
★ a cocktail or a fine meal this steak house in a former luxury hotel where
STEAKHOUSE there are bookcases on every wall, and the check arrives between the
pages of a vintage best-seller. The 12-foot hand-painted dining room
ceiling was constructed by the Pullman Car Woodworkers in 1889.
There is hand-carved Spanish mahogany paneling, and original light-
ing fixtures inlaid with semiprecious stones. Although the kitchen
churns out such light dishes as pan-roasted salmon with basmati rice,
the mainstays are thick-cut steaks and chops. Order a vodka in the
English-style pub—there are more than 100 to choose from. Also, Sun-
day brunch is a big to-do. ⊠*401 State St.* ☏*603/431–5202* ▭*AE, D,
DC, MC, V.*

$ ✕**Muddy River Smokehouse.** A wall of red barn shingles, fake trees, and
SOUTHERN a ceiling painted with stars evoke an outdoor summer barbecue joint
at this fun BBQ place. Roll up your sleeves and dig into corn bread and
molasses baked beans as well as blackened catfish or a burger. Devotees
swear by the Pig City platter of grilled ribs, smoked sweet sausage, and
pulled pork. There's a big bar, and downstairs, live music on weekends.
⊠*21 Congress St.* ☏*603/430–9582* ▭*AE, MC, V.*

$$–$$$ ✕**Pesce Blue.** Sleek, modern, and hip, this restaurant specializes in fresh
★ seafood blended with simple Italian flavors. You pass a wall of flicker-
SEAFOOD ing votives before entering the main dining room, which has an indus-
trial feel: cinder-block walls, black industrial grid ceiling, wood and
chrome accents, and mosaic blue tiles. The menu changes daily but may
include grilled Greek sardines, fried anchovies, grilled jumbo prawns
with sweet garlic custard, and a selection of local catches. There's patio
dining in summer. ⊠*103 Congress St.* ☏*603/430–7766* ⊕*www.pesce
blue.com* ▭*AE, D, MC, V* ☻*No lunch Sat.*

$–$$ ✕**Poco's.** Sure, Poco's boisterous downstairs bar and spacious outside
★ deck have earned it a reputation as a local hangout, but the upstairs
LATIN dining room turns out exceptional Southwest and pan-Latin cuisine—
AMERICAN and at great prices. Avocado-wrapped fried oysters with chipotle tar-
tar sauce, fried calamari, and lobster quesadilla are among the better

6

choices. Most tables have great views of the Piscataqua River. ☒*37 Bow St.* ☎*603/431–5967* ▬*AE, D, MC, V.*

WHERE TO STAY

$$$

Fodor'sChoice

★

⊞**Governor's House.** Of Portsmouth's inns and small hotels, the Governor stands apart. Small, plush, and quiet, this four-room inn, a couple blocks from the historic downtown area, is the perfect place for discerning couples. It was the home of Charles Dale, formerly the governor of New Hampshire, from 1930 to 1964. Frette linens, down comforters, in-room Bose CD stereos with 300 CDs to choose from, high-speed wireless, a guest computer, in-room massages, complimentary wine, a private tennis court, as well as DVDs that include collection featuring the last 55 Academy Award winners are among the extras at this 1917 Georgian Colonial house turned bed-and-breakfast. Innkeeper Bob Chaffee is a discerning host. Ask him to tell the history of the hand-painted bathroom tiles. **Pros:** great rooms and home, free bicycle rental, great location. **Cons:** king beds, most showers are small. ☒*32 Miller Ave.* ☎*603/427–5140 or 866/427–5140* ⊕*www. governors-house.com* ⌨*4 rooms* ⌂*In-room: DVD, refrigerator, Wi-Fi. In-hotel: tennis court, bicycles, no elevator, laundry service, public Internet, public Wi-Fi, no kids under 15, no-smoking rooms* ▬*D, MC, V* ⏅*CP.*

$

⊞**Martin Hill Inn.** Once you see it from the street you may fall in love with this adorable yellow 1815 house surrounded by gardens. It's a 10- to 15-minute walk from the historic district and the waterfront. The quiet rooms are furnished with antiques and decorated in formal Colonial or country-Victorian styles. The Greenhouse Suite has a solarium. You'll get to know your fellow travelers at a communal breakfast served at 8:30 each morning at a common table. **Pros:** very clean, real antiques, communal breakfast. **Cons:** not inside historic district, no common spaces, early breakfast. ☒*404 Islington St.* ☎*603/436–2287* ⊕*www.martinhillinn.com* ⌨*4 rooms, 3 suites* ⌂*In-room: no phone, no TV, Wi-Fi. In-hotel: no elevator, public Wi-Fi, no kids under 14, no-smoking rooms* ▬*MC, V* ⏅*BP.*

$$$

Fodor'sChoice

★

⊞**Wentworth by the Sea.** What's not to love about this white colossus overlooking the sea on New Castle island? The closest thing New Hampshire has to a Ritz-Carlton, Wentworth by the Sea has luxurious rooms that are lushly carpeted, come with gas fireplaces, and have modern and opulent amenities. There's has a good spa and an attractive indoor heated pool. The coastline and island location are superb. The luxury property was built in 1874 as a summer resort for East Coast socialites, wealthy patrons, and former presidents. It reopened in spring 2003 after literally being rebuilt. All of the bright airy rooms have ocean and harbor views—the huge sunny suites occupy a new building right on the water, facing the marina. **Pros:** great spa and restaurants, sense of history, oceanfront perch. **Cons:** not in downtown Portsmouth. ☒*588 Wentworth Rd. New Castle* ☎*603/422–7322 or 866/240–6313* ⊕*www.wentworth.com* ⌨*127 rooms, 34 suites* ⌂*In-room: DVD, Wi-Fi. In-hotel: 3 restaurants, room service, bar, golf course, tennis courts, pools, gym, spa, concierge, laundry service, no-smoking rooms* ▬*AE, D, DC, MC, V.*

RYE

8 mi south of Portsmouth.

On Route 1A as it winds south through Rye, you'll pass a group of late-19th- and early-20th-century mansions known as **Millionaires' Row.** Because of the way the road curves, the drive south along this route is especially breathtaking. In 1623 the first Europeans established a settlement at Odiorne Point in what is now the largely undeveloped and picturesque town of Rye, making it the birthplace of New Hampshire. Today the area's main draws are a lovely state park, oceanfront beaches, and the views from Route 1A. Strict town laws have prohibited commercial development in Rye, creating a dramatic contrast with its frenetic neighbor Hampton Beach.

SPORTS & THE OUTDOORS

☉ **Odiorne Point State Park.** This site encompasses more than 330 acres of
★ protected land, on the site where David Thompson established the first permanent European site in what is now New Hampshire. Stroll several nature trails with interpretive panels describing the park's military history or simply enjoy the vistas of the nearby Isles of Shoals. The rocky shore's tidal pools shelter crabs, periwinkles, and sea anemones. Throughout the year, the **Seacoast Science Center** conducts guided walks and interpretive programs and has exhibits on the area's natural history. Displays trace the social history of Odiorne Point back to the Ice Age, and the tidal-pool touch tank and 1,000-gallon Gulf of Maine deepwater aquarium are popular with kids. Day camp is offered for grades K–8 throughout summer and during school vacations. Popular music concerts are held here on Thursday evenings in summer. ✉ *570 Ocean Blvd. (Rte. 1A), north of Wallis Sands, Rye State Beach* ☎ *603/436–8043 science center, 603/436–1552 park* ⊕ *www.seacentr. org* ✆ *$3* ☉ *Science center daily 10–5 (closed Sun. Nov.–Mar.), park daily 8 AM–dusk.*

☉ **Rye Airfield.** If you've got active kids with you, consider spending the day at this extreme-sports park with an indoor in-line-skate and skateboard arena and two BMX tracks. ✉ *U.S. 1* ☎ *603/964–2800.*

BEACHES Good for swimming and sunning, **Jenness State Beach** (✉ *Route 1A* ☎ *603/436–1552*) is a favorite with locals. The facilities include a bathhouse, lifeguards, and metered parking. **Wallis Sands State Beach** (✉ *Route 1A* ☎ *603/436–9404* ✆ *$10*) is a swimmers' beach with bright white sands and a bathhouse. There's plenty of parking.

FISHING For a full- or half-day deep-sea angling charter, try **Atlantic Fishing and Whale Watch Fleet** (✉ *Rye Harbor* ☎ *603/964–5220 or 800/ 942–5364*).

WHERE TO EAT & STAY

$$–$$$ ✗ **The Carriage House.** Walk across scenic Ocean Boulevard from Jenness
★ Beach to this elegant cottage eatery that serves innovative dishes with
AMERICAN a continental flair. Standouts include crab cakes served with a spicy jalepeño sauce, a penne *alla vodka* teeming with fresh seafood, creative Madras curries, and a delectable steak au poivre. Upstairs is a rough-

6

hewn-wood-paneled tavern serving lighter fare. Savor a hot fudge–ice cream croissant or an indulgent tiramisu for dessert while enjoying the ocean views. ⊠*2263 Ocean Blvd.* ☎*603/964–8251* ⊟*AE, MC, V* ☾*No lunch.*

$$ ☷**Rock Ledge Manor.** You can avoid the crowds of Hampton but still enjoy the beach at this three-room B&B. Built out on a point, this mid-19th-century gambrel-roof house with a wraparound porch once anchored a resort colony. Rooms are quite small, with little bathrooms; they do have partial water views. The real joy is sitting out on the porch overlooking the ocean. Owners Karen and Noel Rix serve breakfast in the sunny dining room. **Pros:** great views, quiet, very clean. **Cons:** small rooms and baths, continental breakfast only. ⊠*1413 Ocean Blvd.* ☎*603/431–1413* ⊕*www.rockledgemanor.com* ⤳*3 rooms* ♿*In-room: no phone, Wi-Fi. In-hotel: no elevator, public Wi-Fi, no kids under 11, no-smoking rooms* ⊟*AE, MC, V* ⧼◎⧽*CP.*

HAMPTON BEACH

✿ *8 mi south of Rye.*

Hampton Beach, from Route 27 to where Route 1A crosses the causeway, is an authentic seaside amusement center—the domain of frieddough stands, loud music, arcade games, palm readers, parasailing, and bronzed bodies. An estimated 150,000 people visit the town and its free public beach on the Fourth of July, and it draws plenty of people until late September, when things close up. The 3-mi boardwalk, where kids can play games and see how saltwater taffy is made, looks like a leftover from the 1940s; in fact, the whole community remains remarkably free of modern franchises. Free outdoor concerts are held on many a summer evening, and once a week there's a fireworks display. Talent shows and karaoke performances take place in the Seashell Stage, right on the beach. Each August, locals hold a children's festival, and they celebrate the end of the season with a huge seafood feast on the weekend after Labor Day.

SPORTS & THE OUTDOORS

BEACHES   **Hampton Beach State Park** (⊠*Rte. 1A* ☎*603/926–3784*) is a quiet stretch of sand on the southwestern edge of town at the mouth of the Hampton River. It has picnic tables, a store (seasonal), parking ($8 on summer weekends, $5 weekdays in summer, free Nov.–Apr.), and a bathhouse.

FISHING   Several companies conduct whale-watching excursions as well as half-
& WHALE-   day, full-day, and nighttime cruises. Most leave from the Hampton
WATCHING   State Pier on Route 1A. **Al Gauron Deep Sea Fishing** (☎*603/926–2469*) maintains a fleet of three boats for whale-watching cruises and fishing charters. **Eastman Fishing Fleet** (⊠*Seabrook* ☎*603/474–3461*) offers whale-watching and fishing cruises, with evening and morning charters. **Smith & Gilmore Deep Sea** (☎*603/926–3503 or 877/272–4005*) conducts deep-sea fishing expeditions and whale-watching trips.

NIGHTLIFE

Despite its name, the **Hampton Beach Casino Ballroom** (⊠*169 Ocean Blvd.* ☎*603/929–4100*) isn't a gambling establishment but rather a late-19th-century, 2,000-seat performance venue that has hosted everyone from Janis Joplin to Jerry Seinfeld, George Carlin, and B. B. King. Performances are scheduled weekly from April through October.

WHERE TO EAT & STAY

$$–$$$ ✕**Ron's Landing at Rocky Bend.** Amid the motels lining Ocean Boule-
AMERICAN vard is this casually elegant restaurant. Pan-seared ahi over mixed greens with a Thai peanut dressing makes a tempting starter. For an entrée, try the oven-roasted salmon with a hoisin (soybeans, garlic, and chili peppers) glaze, a Frangelico cream sauce, slivered almonds, and sliced apple or the baked haddock stuffed with scallops and lobster and served with lemon-dill butter. From many tables you can enjoy a sweeping Atlantic view. Brunch is served on Sunday. ⊠*379 Ocean Blvd.* ☎*603/929–2122* ⊟*AE, D, DC, MC, V* ⊘*No lunch.*

$ ☐**Ashworth by the Sea.** You'll be surprised how contemporary this center-of-the-action, across from the beach hotel is, especially after you see its classic old neon sign outside. From the cheery modern lobby to rooms with new carpeting and furniture, this Hampton Beach classic hotel is clean and up-to-the-minute. Most rooms have decks, but request a beachside room for an ocean view; otherwise you'll look out onto the pool or street. The Sand Bar, on the roof deck between the hotel's two buildings, is a great place to watch the town's fireworks each Wednesday, and have food and drinks. **Pros:** center-of-town location and across from beach, open all year. **Cons:** breakfast not included, very busy. ⊠*295 Ocean Blvd.* ☎*603/926–6762 or 800/345–6736* ⊕*www.ashworthhotel.com* ⇥*105 rooms* ⚭*In-room: Wi-Fi. In-hotel: 3 restaurants, room service, pool, laundry service, public Wi-Fi, no-smoking rooms* ⊟*AE, D, DC, MC, V.*

▌EN
ROUTE

At the 400-acre **Applecrest Farm Orchards** you can pick your own apples and berries or buy fresh fruit pies and cookies. Fall brings cider pressing, hay rides, pumpkins, and music on weekends. In winter a cross-country ski trail traverses the orchard. Author John Irving worked here as a teenager, his experiences inspiring the book *The Cider House Rules.* ⊠*133 Rte. 88, Hampton Falls* ☎*603/926–3721* ⊕*www.applecrest.com* ⊘*Daily 9–5.*

EXETER

★ *9 mi northwest of Hampton, 52 mi north of Boston, 47 mi southeast of Concord.*

In the center of Exeter, contemporary shops mix well the esteemed Phillips Exeter Academy, which opened in 1783.

During the Revolutionary War, Exeter was the state capital, and it was here amid intense patriotic fervor that the first state constitution and the first Declaration of Independence from Great Britain were put to paper. These days Exeter shares more in appearance and personality

6

with Boston's blue-blooded satellite communities than the rest of New Hampshire—indeed, plenty of locals commute to Beantown. There are a handful of cheerful cafés and coffeehouses in the center of town, making it a nice spot for a snack break.

WHAT TO SEE

American Independence Museum. Adjacent to Phillips Exeter Academy in the Ladd-Gilman House, this museum celebrates the birth of the nation. The story unfolds during the course of a guided tour focusing on the Gilman family, who lived in the house during the Revolutionary era. See drafts of the U.S. Constitution and the first Purple Heart as well as letters and documents written by George Washington and the household furnishings of John Taylor Gilman, one of New Hampshire's early governors. In July the museum hosts the American Independence Festival. ⊠1 Governor's La. ☎603/772–2622 ⊕www.independence museum.org ☜$5 ⊘ Mid-May–Oct., Wed.–Sat. 10–4 (last tour at 3).

Phillips Exeter Academy. Above all else, the town is energized by the faculty and 1,000 high school students of the Phillips Exeter Academy. The grounds of the Academy's 129 buildings, open to the public, resemble an elite Ivy League university campus. In fact, with over 619 acres, it's bigger than most Ivy schools. The Louis Kahn–designed library contains the largest seconday school book collection in the world. ⊠20 Main St. ☎603/772–4311.

SHOPPING

A Picture's Worth a Thousand Words (⊠65 Water St. ☎603/778–1991) stocks antique and contemporary prints, old maps, town histories, and rare books. Prestigious **Exeter Fine Crafts** (⊠61 Water St. ☎603/778–8282) shows an impressive selection of juried pottery, paintings, jewelry, textiles, glassware, and other fine creations by some of northern New England's top artists.

WHERE TO EAT

¢
Fodor'sChoice
★
AMERICAN

✕**Loaf and Ladle.** There are three components to this extraordinary place: quality, price, and location. The name refers to homemade bread—there are over 30 kinds—and soup—there are over 100 varieties. A bowl of soup, which is a full meal, is $5. It's hard to spend more than that here. Choose a chunk of bread to go with your soup, and take your meal to one of the two decks that hover over the Exeter River, or one of the cafeteria-style tables, and enjoy. It's simplicity. It's a masterpiece. ⊠9 Water St. ☎ 603/778–8955 ⚓Reservations not accepted ⊟AE, D, DC, MC, V.

$$–$$$
AMERICAN

✕**Tavern at River's Edge.** A convivial downtown gathering spot on the Exeter River, this downstairs tavern pulls in parents of prep-school kids, University of New Hampshire (UNH) students, and suburban yuppies. It may be informal, but the kitchen turns out surprisingly sophisticated chow. You might start with sautéed ragout of portobello and shiitake mushrooms, sun-dried tomatoes, roasted shallots, garlic, and Asiago cheese. Move on to New Zealand rack of lamb with rosemary-port demi-glace and minted risotto. In the bar, lighter fare is served daily 3–10. ✉ *163 Water St.* ☎ *603/772-7393* ⊟ *AE, D, DC, MC, V* ☯ *No lunch.*

WHERE TO STAY

$$ ⚏ **The Exeter Inn.** This elegant brick Georgian-style inn on the Phillips
★ Exeter Academy campus has been the choice of visiting parents since it opened in the 1930s. After a complete overhaul, completed in the spring of 2008, the place looks better than ever. Rooms have a clubby Ralph Lauren design, with striped wallpapers, 10-inch pillowtop mattresses, and flat-screen TVs. There's a good lounge and restaurant serving three meals a day. **Pros:** contemporary, well-designed, clean rooms; near Academy. **Cons:** not close to town shops. ✉ *90 Front St.* ☎ *603/772-5901 or 800/782-8444* ⊕ *www.theexeterinn.com* ⛽ *41 rooms, 5 suites* ⚲ *In-room: Wi-Fi. In-hotel: restaurant, room service, bar, gym, laundry service, public Wi-Fi, no-smoking rooms* ⊟ *AE, D, DC, MC, V.*

$$ ⚏ **Inn by the Bandstand.** If you're visiting someone at the academy and
★ want to stay in a B&B, you're bound to love this place smack dab in the heart of town. Rooms are individually furnished—in the extreme. One might be floral Victorian. Another might be the Lakeheath Lodge, which takes a rustic outdoorsy approach, with exposed ceiling beams and antlers over the brick fireplace and pine strung over the headboard. Pillows are piled in profusion atop the Ralph Lauren sheets. Character and comfort continue in all rooms, with crystal decanters of sherry. It's one of the best B&Bs in the state. Note that breakfast is served at one set time: 8:30. **Pros:** perfect location in town, richly furnished rooms. **Cons:** early breakfast. ✉ *4 Front St.* ☎ *603/772-6352 or 877/239-3837* ⊕ *www.innbythebandstand.com* ⛽ *7 rooms, 2 suites* ⚲ *In-room: refrigerator, Wi-Fi. In-hotel: room service, no elevator, public Wi-Fi, no-smoking rooms* ⊟ *AE, D, MC, V* ⚆ *BP.*

DURHAM

12 mi north of Exeter, 11 mi northwest of Portsmouth.

Settled in 1635 and the home of General John Sullivan, a Revolutionary War hero and three-time New Hampshire governor, Durham was where Sullivan and his band of rebel patriots stored the gunpowder they captured from Ft. William and Mary in New Castle. Easy access to Great Bay via the Oyster River made Durham a maritime hub in the 19th century. Among the lures today are the water, farms that welcome visitors, and the University of New Hampshire (UNH), which occupies much of the town's center.

WHAT TO SEE

Little Bay Buffalo Company. Visitors cannot roam the range here, but the several dozen American bison ranging here are visible from an observation area and the parking lot. The store on the property sells bison-related gifts and top-quality bison meat. ✉ *50 Langley Rd.* ☎ *603/868-3300* ☯ *Store Tues.–Sun. 10–5.*

SPORTS & THE OUTDOORS

You can hike several trails or picnic at 130-acre **Wagon Hill Farm** (⊠ *U. S. 4 across from Emery Farm* ☎ *No phone*), overlooking the Oyster River. The old farm wagon on the top of a hill is one of the most-photographed sights in New England. Park next to the farmhouse and follow walking trails to the wagon and through the woods to the picnic area by the water. Sledding and cross-country skiing are winter activities.

SHOPPING

Emery Farm. In the same family for 11 generations, Emery Farm sells fruits and vegetables in summer (including pick-your-own raspberries, strawberries, and blueberries), pumpkins in fall, and Christmas trees in December. The farm shop carries breads, pies, and local crafts. Children can pet the resident goats and sheep and attend the storytelling events that are often held on Tuesday mornings in July and August. ⊠ *U.S. 4, 1.5 mi east of Rte. 108* ☎ *603/742–8495* ⊙ *Late Apr.–Dec., daily 9–6.*

NIGHTLIFE & THE ARTS

NIGHTLIFE   Students and local yupsters head to the **Stone Church** (⊠ *5 Granite St., Newmarket* ☎ *603/659–6321*)—in an authentic 1835 former Methodist church—to listen to live rock, jazz, blues, and folk. The restaurant on the premises serves dinner Wednesday through Sunday.

THE ARTS   The **Celebrity Series** (☎ *603/862–2290* ⊕ *www.unh.edu/celebrity*) at UNH brings music, theater, and dance to several venues. The **UNH Department of Theater and Dance** (⊠ *Paul Creative Arts Center, 30 College Rd.* ☎ *603/862–2919*) produces a variety of shows. UNH's **Whittemore Center Arena** (⊠ *128 Main St.* ☎ *603/862–4000* ⊕ *www. whittemorecenter.com*) hosts everything from Boston Pops concerts to home shows, plus college sports.

WHERE TO EAT & STAY

$$-$$$ ✕ **ffrost Sawyer Tavern.** That's not a typo, but an attempt to duplicate a
★   quirk in obsolete spelling (the way capital letters used to be designated)
SEAFOOD/   of an old resident of this hilltop house. The eccentric stone basement
AMERICAN   tavern of this hilltop house has its original beams, from which hang collections of mugs, hats and—no way around it—bedpans. There's a terrific old bar. Choose from fine fare like grilled sea scallops or salmon and lobster seared in a tomato, lime, and coconut curry sauce; or lighter items like burgers, pizza, and fish-and-chips. ⊠ *17 Newmarket Rd.* ☎ *603/868–7800* ☰ *AE, D, MC, V* ⊙ *No lunch.*

$$$ 🛏 **Three Chimneys Inn.** This stately yellow structure has graced a hill overlooking the Oyster River since 1649. Rooms in the house and the 1795 barn are named after plants from the gardens and filled with Georgian- and Federal-style antiques and reproductions, canopy or four-poster beds with Edwardian drapes, and Oriental rugs; half have fireplaces. There are two restaurants here: a formal dining room, and the ffrost Sawyer, quirky as the name implies. There's an afternoon wine and cheese social. **Pros:** intimate inn experience. **Cons:** have to walk or drive into town. ⊠ *17 Newmarket Rd.* ☎ *603/868–7800 or 888/399–9777* ⊕ *www. threechimneysinn.com* ⟿ *23 rooms* ⟨ *In-room: Wi-Fi. In-hotel: 2 res-*

taurants, room service, bar, no elevator, public Wi-Fi, some pets allowed, no-smoking rooms ■*AE, D, MC, V* ⋈*BP.*

LAKES REGION

Lake Winnipesaukee, an American Indian name for "smile of the great spirit," is the largest of the dozens of lakes scattered across the eastern half of central New Hampshire. With about 240 mi of shoreline full of inlets and coves, it's the largest in the state. Some claim Winnipesaukee has an island for each day of the year—the total, though impressive, falls well short: 274.

In contrast to Winnipesaukee, which bustles all summer long, is the more secluded Squam Lake. Its tranquillity is what no doubt attracted the producers of *On Golden Pond*; several scenes of the Oscar-winning film were shot here. Nearby Lake Wentworth is named for the state's first royal governor, who, in building his country manor here, established North America's first summer resort.

Well-preserved Colonial and 19th-century villages are among the region's many landmarks, and you'll find hiking trails, good antiques shops, and myriad water-oriented activities. This section begins at Wolfeboro, and more or less circles Lake Winnipesaukee clockwise, with several side trips.

WOLFEBORO

40 mi northeast of Concord, 49 mi northwest of Portsmouth.

Quietly upscale and decidedly preppy Wolfeboro has been a resort since Royal Governor John Wentworth built his summer home on the shores of Lake Wentworth in 1768. The town bills itself as the oldest summer resort in America. The town center, bursting with tony boutiques, fringes Lake Winnipesaukee and sees about a tenfold population increase each summer. In 2007 French President Nicolas Sarkozy summered here. Mitt Romney is another summer resident. The century-old, white clapboard buildings of the Brewster Academy prep school bracket the town's southern end. Wolfeboro marches to a steady, relaxed beat, comfortable for all ages.

WHAT TO SEE

New Hampshire Boat Museum. Two miles northeast of downtown, this museum celebrates the Lakes Region's boating legacy with displays of vintage Chris-Crafts, Jersey Speed Skiffs, three-point hydroplanes, and other fine watercraft, along with model boats, antique engines, racing photography and trophies, and old-time signs from marinas. ⊠*397 Center St.* ☎*603/569–4554* ⊕*www.nhbm.org* ⋈*$5* ⊙*Memorial Day–Columbus Day, Mon.–Sat. 10–4, Sun. noon–4.*

Wright Museum. Uniforms, vehicles, and other artifacts at this museum illustrate the contributions of those on the home front to America's World War II effort. ⊠*77 Center St.* ☎*603/569–1212* ⊕*www.wright*

New Hampshire Lakes Region

museum.org 🖂 *$6* 🕐 *May–Oct., Mon.–Sat. 10–4, Sun. noon–4; Apr. and Nov., Sat. 10–4, Sun. noon–4.*

<table>
<tr><td>NEED A
BREAK?</td><td>Brewster Academy students and summer folk converge upon groovy little Lydia's (🖂 30 N. Main St. ☎ 603/569–3991) for espressos, hearty sandwiches, homemade soups, bagels, and desserts. Picking up pastries, cookies, freshly baked breads, and other sweets in the Yum Yum Shop (🖂 16 N. Main St. ☎ 603/569–1919) has been a tradition in these parts since 1948—the butter-crunch cookies are highly addictive.</td></tr>
</table>

SPORTS & THE OUTDOORS

BEACHES   **Wentworth State Beach** (🖂 *Rte. 109* ☎ *603/569–3699* 🖂 *$3*) has good swimming, fishing, picnicking areas, ball fields, and a bathhouse.

HIKING   A short (¼-mi) hike to the 100-foot post-and-beam **Abenaki Tower,** followed by a more rigorous climb to the top, rewards you with a vast view of Lake Winnipesaukee and the Ossipee mountain range. The trailhead is a few miles north of town on Route 109.

WATER SPORTS   Scuba divers can explore a 130-foot-long cruise ship that sank in 30 feet of water off Glendale in 1895. **Dive Winnipesaukee Corp** (🖂 *4 N.*

Main St. ☎*603/569–8080*) runs charters out to wrecks and offers rentals, repairs, scuba sales, and lessons in waterskiing.

SHOPPING

American Home Gallery (✉*49 Center St., Wolfeboro Falls* ☎*603/569–8989*) mixes an amazing array of antiques and housewares in with its architectural elements. You'll find an excellent regional-history section and plenty of children's titles at **Country Bookseller** (✉*23A N. Main St.* ☎*603/569–6030*), Wolfeboro's fine general-interest bookstore. The artisans at **Hampshire Pewter Company** (✉*43 Mill St.* ☎*603/569–4911 or 800/639–7704* ⊕*www.hampshirepewter.com*) use 16th-century techniques to make pewter tableware and accessories. Come to shop or tour: free tours are given Memorial Day through Columbus Day at 9:30, 11, 1:30 and 3 most days and by appointment.

WHERE TO EAT

$-$$

ASIAN

✕ **East of Suez.** Set in a countrified lodge on the south side of town, this warm and friendly restaurant serves creative Pan-Asian cuisine, with an emphasis on Philippine fare, such as *lumpia* (pork-and-shrimp spring rolls with a sweet-and-sour fruit sauce) and Philippine *pancit canton* (panfried egg noodles with sautéed shrimp and pork and Asian vegetables with a sweet oyster sauce). You can also sample Thai red curries, Japanese tempura, and Korean-style flank steak. ✉*775 S. Main St.* ☎*603/569–1648* ▤*AE, MC, V* ⊘*Closed Oct.–mid-May.*

$-$$

★

SEAFOOD

✕ **Wolfetrap Grill and Raw Bar.** The seafood at this festive shanty on Lake Winnipesaukee comes right from the adjacent fish market. You'll find all your favorites here, including a renowned clam boil for one that includes steamers, corn on the cob, onions, baked potatoes, sweet potatoes, sausage, and a hot dog. The raw bar has oysters and clams on the half shell. ✉*19 Bay St.* ☎*603/569–1047* ▤*AE, D, MC, V* ⊘*Closed Labor Day–Memorial Day.*

WHERE TO STAY

$$

★

🛏 **Topsides B & B.** At this stylish retreat, refined rooms subtly convey the allure of a particular region, from coastal France to Martha's Vineyard to Virginia fox-hunting country. Lavish, custom bedding, Persian rugs, marble dressers, and fresh flowers lend an eclectic sophistication to this pale-gray clapboard inn that's steps from downtown shops and restaurants. High-speed wireless, homemade bath amenities, and highly personalized attention complete the experience. **Pros:** great location, clean simple rooms. **Cons:** just continental breakfast. ✉*209 S. Main St.* ☎*603/569–3834* ⊕*www.topsidesbb.com* ⊟*5 rooms* ⚬*In-room: Wi-Fi. In-hotel: no elevator, public Internet, public Wi-Fi, no kids under 12, no-smoking rooms* ▤*D, MC, V* ⊚*CP.*

$$$

★

🛏 **Wolfeboro Inn.** This inn with a great lakefront location opened in 1812 and has been a perennial favorite. In the second part of 2008 it is poised to take a radical step forward, to become, in fact, the freshest and most stylish hotel in the lake region. Call to find out if the rooms have been renovated yet; if so, and you like a contemporary luxurious boutique look, stay here—there will be nothing like it in the state outside of the stylish hotels the same owners have created from classic old properties in Exeter and Concord. **Pros:** lakefront setting, interesting pub, slated for massive renovation. **Cons:** pre-renovation property is tired. ⊠*90 N. Main St.* ☎*603/569–3016 or 800/451–2389* ⊕*www. wolfeboroinn.com* ⬅*41 rooms, 3 suites, 1 apartment* ⏴*In-room: Wi-Fi. In-hotel: 2 restaurants, bar, public Internet, public Wi-Fi, no-smoking rooms* ⊟*AE, D, MC, V* ⫯OI*CP.*

ALTON BAY

10 mi southwest of Wolfeboro.

Lake Winnipesaukee's southern shore is alive with visitors from the moment the first flower blooms until the last maple sheds its leaves. Two mountain ridges hold 7 mi of the lake in Alton Bay, which is the name of both the inlet and the town at its tip. Cruise boats dock here, and small planes land here year-round, on both the water and the ice. There's a dance pavilion, along with miniature golf, a public beach, and a Victorian-style bandstand. Mt. Major, 5 mi north of Alton Bay on Route 11, has a 2.5-mi trail with views of Lake Winnipesaukee..

WHERE TO EAT

$$$$
★
AMERICAN

✕**Crystal Quail.** This 12-table restaurant, inside an 18th-century farmhouse, is worth the drive for the sumptuous meals prepared by longtime proprietors Harold and Cynthia Huckaby, who use free-range meats and mostly organic produce and herbs in their cooking. The prix-fixe contemporary menu changes daily but might include saffron-garlic soup, a house pâté, quenelle-stuffed sole, or goose confit with apples and onions. ⊠*202 Pitman Rd., 12 mi south of Alton Bay, Center Barnstead* ☎*603/269–4151* ⊕*www.crystalquail.com* ⏴*Reservations essential* ⊟*No credit cards* ☞*BYOB* ☉*Closed Mon. and Tues. No lunch.*

WEIRS BEACH

☙ *17 mi northwest of Alton Bay.*

Weirs Beach is Lake Winnipesaukee's center for arcade activity. Anyone who loves souvenir shops, fireworks, waterslides, and hordes of children will feel right at home. Cruise boats also depart from here.

WHAT TO SEE

☙ **Funspot.** The mother ship of Lake Winnipesaukee's several giddy family-oriented amusement parks, Funspot claims to be the second-largest arcade in the country, but it's much more than just a video-game room. Here you can work your way through a miniature golf course, a golf driving range, an indoor golf simulator, 20 lanes of bowling, cash bingo, and more than 500 video games. Some outdoor attractions are closed in winter months. ⊠*Rte. 3, Weirs Beach* ☎*603/366–4377* ⊕*www. funspotnh.com* ✉*Entry free; fee for each activity* ☉*Mid-June–early Sept., daily 9 AM–midnight; early Sept.–mid-June, Sun.–Thurs. 10–10, Fri. and Sat. 10 AM–11 PM.*

☙ **Surf Coaster.** The lake's ultimate water park, Surf Coaster has seven waterslides, a wave pool, and the Barefoot Action Lagoon, a large area for young children. Teams of six can also duke it out in a massive inflatable maze for a game of water tag. ✉*1085 White Oaks Rd., Weirs Beach* ☎*603/366-5600* ⊕*www.surfcoasterusa.com* 🖙*$25* ☉*Late June–early Sept., daily 10–6.*

☺ **MS Mount Washington.** This 230-foot boat makes two-and-a-half-hour
Fodors Choice scenic cruises of Lake Winnipesaukee from Weirs Beach from mid-May
★ to late October, with stops in Wolfeboro, Alton Bay, Center Harbor, and Meredith (you can board at any of these stops). The cruise is a lake tradition. Evening cruises include live music and a buffet dinner. There are nightly music themes, check ahead for your favorites. The same company operates the MV *Sophie C.,* which has been the area's floating post office for more than a century. The boat departs from Weirs Beach with mail and passengers. Since the boat is delivering mail to homes along the shore, you can see areas of the lake not accessible by larger ships. Additionally, you can ride the MV *Doris E.* on one- and two-hour scenic cruises of Meredith Bay and the lake islands throughout summer. ☎*603/366-5531 or 888/843-6686* ⊕*www.cruisenh.com* 🖙*$25* ☉*Day cruises, departures daily every few hours mid-June–Labor Day. Special cruises, departure times vary.*

★ **Winnipesaukee Scenic Railroad.** The period cars of this railroad carry you along the lakeshore on one- or two-hour rides; boarding is at Weirs Beach or Meredith. Special trips that include dinner are also available, as are foliage trains in fall and special Santa trains in December. ✉*U. S. 3, Weirs Beach* ☎*603/279-5253 or 603/745-2135* ⊕*www.hoborr. com* 🖙*$9–$71* ☉*July–mid-Sept., daily; Memorial Day–late June and mid-Sept.–mid-Oct., weekends only. Call for hours.*

SPORTS & THE OUTDOORS

BEACH & **Ellacoya State Beach** (✉*Rte. 11* ☎*603/293-7821*) covers just 600
BOATING feet along the southwestern shore of Lake Winnipesaukee. In season, there's a bathhouse, picnic tables, and a fee ($3 from mid-May to Labor Day) for parking. **Thurston's Marina** (✉*U.S. 3 at the bridge, Weirs Beach* ☎*603/366-4811*) rents watercraft such as pontoon boats and powerboats.

GOLF **Pheasant Ridge Golf Club** (✉*140 Country Club Rd.* ☎*603/524-7808*) has an 18-hole layout with great mountain views. Green fees range from $31 to $40.

SKI AREAS **Gunstock USA.** High above Lake Winnipesaukee, this all-purpose area dates from the 1930s. It once had the country's longest rope tow lift—an advantage that helped local downhill skier and Olympic silver medalist Penny Pitou perfect her craft. Thrill Hill, a snow-tubing park, has 10 runs, multipassenger tubes, and lift service. Clever trail cutting along with grooming and surface sculpting three times daily has made this otherwise pedestrian mountain good for intermediates. That's how most of the 44 trails are rated, with a few more challenging runs as well as designated sections for slow skiers and learners. It's the state's largest night-skiing facility. Gunstock has 30 mi of trails for cross-country skiing and snowshoeing. In summer you'll find a swimming pool, a playground, hiking trails, mountain-bike rentals and trails, a skateboarding-blading park, guided horseback rides, pedal boats, and a campground. ⊠*Rte. 11A* ⌂*Box 1307, Laconia 03247* ☎*603/293–4341 or 800/486–7862* ⊕*www.gunstock.com.*

SHOPPING

Pepi Herrmann Crystal (⊠*3 Waterford Pl.* ☎*603/528–1020*) sells hand-cut crystal chandeliers and stemware. Take a tour and watch artists at work.

NIGHTLIFE & THE ARTS

The **New Hampshire Music Festival** (☎*603/279–3300* ⊕*www.nhmf.org*) presents award-winning orchestras from early July to mid-August; concerts occur at the Festival House on Symphony Lane in Center Harbor or at the Silver Cultural Arts Center on Main Street in Plymouth.

LACONIA

4 mi west of Gilford, 27 mi north of Concord.

The arrival in Laconia—then called Meredith Bridge—of the railroad in 1848 turned the once-sleepy hamlet into the Lakes Region's chief manufacturing hub. It acts today as the area's supply depot, a perfect role given its accessibility to both Winnisquam and Winnipesaukee lakes as well as Interstate 93. Come here when you need to find a chain superstore or fast-food restaurant.

WHAT TO SEE

Belknap Mill. The oldest unaltered, brick-built textile mill in the United States (1823), Belknap Mill contains a knitting museum devoted to the textile industry and a year-round cultural center that sponsors concerts, workshops, exhibits, and a lecture series. ⊠*Mill Plaza, 25 Beacon St. E* ☎*603/524–8813* ⊕*www.belknapmill.org* ▭*Free* ☉*Weekdays 9–5.*

OFF THE BEATEN PATH

Canterbury Shaker Village. Shaker furniture and inventions are well regarded, and this National Historic Landmark helps illuminate the world of the people who created them. Established as a religious community in 1792, the village flourished in the 1800s and practiced equality of the sexes and races, common ownership, celibacy, and pacifism. The last member of the community passed away in 1992. Shakers invented such household items as the clothespin and the flat broom and were known for the simplicity and integrity of their designs. Engaging 90-minute tours pass through some of the 694-acre property's more than 25 restored buildings, many of them still with original Shaker furnishings, and crafts demonstrations take place daily. The Shaker Table restaurant ($$–$$$$) serves lunch daily and candlelight dinners Thursday–Sunday (reservations essential); the food blends contemporary and traditional Shaker recipes to delicious effect. A large shop sells fine Shaker reproductions. ⊠*288 Shaker Rd., 15 mi south of Laconia via Rte. 106, Canterbury* ☎*603/783–9511 or 866/783–9511* ⊕*www.shakers.org* ▭*$15, good for 2 consecutive days* ☉*Mid-May–Oct., daily 10–5; Apr., Nov., and Dec., weekends 10–4.*

SPORTS & THE OUTDOORS

Bartlett Beach (✉ *Winnisquam Ave.*) has a playground and picnic area. **Opechee Park** (✉ *N. Main St.*) has dressing rooms, a baseball field, tennis courts, and picnic areas.

SHOPPING

The more than 50 stores at the **Tanger Outlet Center** (✉ *120 Laconia Rd., I–93 Exit 20, Tilton* ☎ *603/286–7880*) include Brooks Brothers, Eddie Bauer, Coach, and Mikasa.

WHERE TO STAY

$ ⌂ **Ferry Point House.** Four miles southwest of Laconia, this home across the street from Lake Winnisquam gives you a quiet retreat with easy access to a private boat house, row boat, dock and a small beach. Built in the 1800s as a summer retreat for the Pillsbury family of baking fame, this red Victorian farmhouse has superb views of the lake. White wicker furniture and hanging baskets of flowers grace the 60-foot veranda, and the gazebo by the water's edge is a pleasant place to lounge and listen for loons. The pretty rooms have Victorian-style wallpaper. A parlor rooms has decantered sherry. **Pros:** affordable, lovely setting. **Cons:** have to cross street to lake, best for relaxed do-it-yourselfers. ✉ *100 Lower Bay Rd., Sanbornton* ☎ *603/524–0087* ⊕ *www.ferrypointhouse.com* ⬩ *9 rooms* ⬩ *In-room: no a/c (some), no phone, no TV, Wi-Fi. In-hotel: water sports, no elevator, public Wi-Fi, no kids under 11, no-smoking rooms* ⊟ *No credit cards* ⊘ *Closed Dec. and Jan.* ⦿ *BP.*

6

MEREDITH

11 mi north of Laconia.

Meredith, a onetime workaday mill town on U.S. 3 at Lake Winnipesaukee's western end, has watched its fortunes change for the better over the past decade or so. The opening of the Inns at Mills Falls has attracted hundreds of visitors, and crafts shops and art galleries have sprung up. You can pick up area information at a kiosk across from the town docks.

SPORTS & THE OUTDOORS

Red Hill, a hiking trail on Bean Road off Route 25, northeast of Center Harbor and about 7 mi northeast of Meredith, really does turn red in autumn. The reward at the end of the route is a view of Squam Lake and the mountains.

BOATING   Meredith is near the quaint village of Center Harbor, another boating hub that's in the middle of three bays at the northern end of Lake Winnipesaukee. **Meredith Marina and Boating Center** (✉ *2 Bayshore Dr.* ☎ *603/279–7921*) rents powerboats. **Wild Meadow Canoes & Kayaks** (✉ *Rte. 25, between Center Harbor and Moultonboro* ☎ *603/253–7536 or 800/427–7536*) has canoes and kayaks for rent.

SHOPPING

Annalee's Outlet Store (⊠ *Annalee Pl., off Rte. 104* ☎ *603/707–5388* ⊕ *www.annalee.com* ⊘ *Daily 10–6*) sells, at a discount, the seasonal decorations and dolls of the Annalee company, famous for its felt dolls that Annalee Davis Thorndike began making here in 1933. The former museum is now closed. About 170 dealers operate out of the three-floor **Burlwood Antique Center** (⊠ *U.S. 3* ☎ *603/279–6387*), open May–October. **Keepsake Quilting & Country Pleasures** (⊠ *Senter's Marketplace, Rte. 25B, Center Harbor, 5 mi northeast of Meredith* ☎ *603/253–4026 or 800/965–9456*), reputedly America's largest quilt shop, contains 5,000 bolts of fabric, hundreds of quilting books, and countless supplies, as well as handmade quilts.

★ The **Meredith League of New Hampshire Craftsmen** (⊠ *279 U.S. 3, ½ mi north of Rte. 104* ☎ *603/279–7920*) sells works by area artisans. It's next to Church Landing. **Mill Falls Marketplace** (⊠ *U.S. 3 at Rte. 25* ☎ *603/279–7006*), part of the Inns at Mills Falls, contains shops with clothing, gifts, and books set around the old falls that run through it. The **Old Print Barn** (⊠ *343 Winona Rd., New Hampton* ☎ *603/279–6479*) carries rare prints—Currier & Ives, antique botanicals, and more—from around the world.

THE ARTS

The **Lakes Region Summer Theatre** (⊠ *Interlakes Auditorium, Rte. 25* ☎ *603/279–9933*) presents Broadway musicals during its 10-week season of summer stock.

WHERE TO EAT & STAY

$$-$$$
AMERICAN
✕ **Lakehouse Grille.** With perhaps the best lake views of any restaurant in the region, this restaurant might be forgiven for ambitious dishes that fall short of being really good. Come here to be near the lake, especially in the convivial bar area, and you'll leave home quite happy. The setting is an upscale lodge, at Church Landing, within one of the Mill Falls hotels. The best dishes are old reliables like steak, ribs, and little pizzas. Breakfast is served daily. ⊠ *Church Landing* ☎ *603/279–5221* ⊟ *AE, D, MC, V.*

$$-$$$
AMERICAN
✕ **Mame's.** This 1820s tavern, once the home of the village doctor, now contains a warren of convivial dining rooms with exposed-brick walls, wooden beams, and wide-plank floors. Expect mostly American standbys of the fish, steak, veal, and chicken variety, including very good seafood Diane (shrimp, scallops, and salmon sautéed in butter and white wine); the mud pie is highly recommended. A tavern upstairs serves a cheaper menu. ⊠ *8 Plymouth St.* ☎ *603/279–4631* ⊟ *AE, D, MC, V.*

$$
Fodor'sChoice
★ ◫ **Inns and Spa at Mill Falls.** There are four separate hotels here—two new properties on the shore Lake Winnipesaukee, and two connected to a 19th-century mill (now a lively shopping area) and its roaring fall. Combined, the inns have all the amenities of a full resort as well as warmth and personality. The central-most Inn at Mills Falls, which adjoins an 18-shop market, has a pool and 54 spacious rooms. The lakefront Inn at Bay Point has 24 rooms—most with balconies, some with fireplaces. The 23 rooms at the lake-view Chase House at Mill Falls all have fireplaces; some have balconies. The star of the show is

camp-posh Church Landing, a dramatic lakefront lodge where most rooms have expansive decks with terrific water views. The Cascade Spa is one of the poshest in the state. A great heated pool crosses from indoors to outdoors. Pros: many lodging choices and prices, lakefront rooms available, fun environment. Cons: expensive; two buildings are not on lakefront. ⊠*312 Daniel Webster Hwy (Rte 3), at Rte 25* ☎*603/279–7006 or 800/622–6455* ⊕*www.millfalls.com* ⇨*148 rooms, 8 suites* ⚒*In-hotel: 5 restaurants, room service, bar, pools, gym, spa, water sports, laundry service, public Internet, public Wi-Fi, no-smoking rooms* ⊟*AE, D, DC, MC, V* ⋈*CP.*

HOLDERNESS

8 mi southeast of Plymouth, 8 mi northwest of Meredith.

Routes 25B and 25 lead to the small prim town of Holderness, between Squam and Little Squam lakes. *On Golden Pond,* starring Katharine Hepburn and Henry Fonda, was filmed on Squam, whose quiet beauty attracts nature lovers.

WHAT TO SEE

Ⓒ **Squam Lakes Natural Science Center.** Trails on this 200-acre property include a ¾-mi path that passes black bears, bobcats, otters, and other native wildlife in trailside enclosures. Educational events such as the "Up Close to Animals" series in July and August also allow you to study a species in an intimate setting. The Gordon Children's Activity Center has interactive exhibits. A ride on a 28-foot pontoon boat is the best way to tour the lake: naturalists explain the science of the lake and describe the animals that make their home here. You'll learn a ton, too, about loon behavior and communication. ⊠*Rte. 113* ☎*603/968–7194* ⊕*www.nhnature.org* ⋈*Center $13. Boat tour $20. Combination ticket $30* ⊙*May–Oct., daily 9:30–4:30 (last entry at 3:30).*

Fodor's Choice
★

WHERE TO EAT

$$$
AMERICAN

✕**Manor on Golden Pond.** Leaded glass panes and wood paneling set the decidedly romantic and warm tone at this wonderful small dining room on a hill overlooking Squam Lake. The main dining room is in the manor's original billiard room and features the 1902 woodwork. An amuse-bouche of salmon tartare might start things off. A New Hampshire gumbo of duck breast and wild boar sausage in a spicy Cajun broth is unexpected and delicious, and quail and monkfish are very well prepared. A fabulous seven-course tasting menu is $75. ⊠*U. S. 3 and Shepard Hill Rd.* ☎*603/968–3348* ⚒*Reservations required* ⊟*AE, D, MC, V.*

$-$$
AMERICAN

✕**Walter's Basin.** A former bowling alley in the heart of Holderness makes an unlikely but charming setting for meals overlooking gentle Little Squam Lake—local boaters dock right beneath the dining room. Among the specialties on this seafood-intensive menu are crostini topped with lobster and fontina cheese, and almond-crusted rainbow trout with hazelnut beurre blanc. Burgers and sandwiches are served in the adjoining tavern. ⊠*15 Main St. (U.S. 3)* ☎*603/968–4412* ⊟*AE, D, MC, V* ⊙*Closed Mon. and Tues.*

6

WHERE TO STAY

$$ ⊞ **Glynn House Inn.** Jim and Gay Dunlop run this swank, three-story, 1890s Queen Anne–style Victorian with a turret and wraparound porch and, next door, a handsome 1920s carriage house. Expect the best in New England B&B comforts: plush beds, flat-screen TVs, free wine and cheese, and attentive service. Twelve of the 13 rooms have fireplaces; the bi-level Honeymoon Suite has a whirlpool tub and fireplace downstairs and a four-poster bed and skylights above. Breakfast usually includes freshly baked strudel. Squam Lake is minutes away. **Pros:** luxurious, well run B&B; clean, well-equipped; social atmosphere. **Cons:** not much to do in town of Ashland (though the charm in these parts is really the lake and outdoor activities). ⊠ *59 Highland St., Ashland 03217* ☎*603/968–3775 or 800/637–9599* ⊕*www.glynnhouse. com* ⇔*5 rooms, 8 suites* &*In-room: DVD, Wi-Fi. In-hotel: no-smoking rooms, public Internet, public Wi-Fi, some pets allowed, no kids under 12, no-smoking rooms* ⊟*MC, V* ⦿*BP.*

$$ ⊞ **Inn on Golden Pond.** Sweet-as-pie Bill and Bonnie Webb run this comfortable and informal B&B at a slight walk from the lake. Your hosts will provide walking trail maps to the private corners of the lake. In the living room you'll see maps pinned with the origin of guests, who come from all over (especially New York City and Boston). Rooms have hardwood floors, braided rugs, comfortable reading chairs, and country quilt bedspreads and curtains. The homemade jam at breakfast is made from rhubarb grown on the property. **Pros:** friendly innkeepers, very clean rooms and common spaces. **Cons:** 5-minute walk to access lake, not luxurious. ⊠*Rte. 3* ☎*603/968–7269* ⊕*www.innongolden pond.com* ⇔*6 rooms, 2 suites* &*In-room: no phone, no TV, Wi-Fi. In-hotel: no elevator, public Internet, public Wi-Fi, no kids under 12, no-smoking rooms* ⊟*AE, D, MC, V* ⦿*BP.*

$$$ ⊞ **The Manor on Golden Pond.** A name like that is a lot to live up to.
Fodor's Choice   Happily, the Manor is the most charming inn in the Lakes Region.
★   Stroll down to the sandy private beach for a dip in the lake or to paddle their canoe for a bit—this is the only inn with private access to Squam Lake, though you'll need to walk a few minutes to get it. Back in the stately stucco-and-shingle inn, innkeeper and owners Brian and Mary Ellen Shields make sure you're comfortable. The house sits on a slight rise overlooking Squam Lake, on 15 acres of towering pines and hardwood trees. You can sit on the lawn in one of the Adirondack chairs, gazing out at the lake. Rooms in this house carry out a British country theme, most with wood-burning fireplaces and more than half with double whirlpool tubs. Canopy beds, vintage blanket chests, and tartan fabrics fill the sumptuous bedchambers. The restaurant is terrific, and the Three Cock Pub is endearing. There's a small spa, and afternoon tea is served in the library. **Pros:** wood fireplaces, private boathouse with free canoes and paddleboats, private lake access, great food, great hosts. **Cons:** expensive. ⊠*U.S. 3 and Shepard Hill Rd. 03245* ☎*603/968–3348 or 800/545–2141* ⊕*www.manorongoldenpond.com* ⇔*22 rooms, 2 suites, 1 cottage* &*In-room: VCR, Wi-Fi. In-hotel: 2 restaurants, room service, bar, tennis court, pool, spa, water sports, no*

elevator, laundry service, public Internet, public Wi-Fi, no kids under 12, no-smoking rooms ⊟*AE, D, MC, V* ⦿|*BP.*

CENTER SANDWICH

★ *12 mi northeast of Holderness.*

With Squam Lake to the west and the Sandwich Mountains to the north, Center Sandwich claims one of the prettiest settings of any Lakes Region community. So appealing are the town and its views that John Greenleaf Whittier used the Bearcamp River as the inspiration for his poem "Sunset on the Bearcamp." The town attracts artisans—crafts shops abound among its clutch of charming 18th- and 19th-century buildings.

WHAT TO SEE
Castle in the Clouds. This wonderful mountaintop estate was built in 1913–1914 without nails. The elaborate mansion has 16 rooms, eight bathrooms, and doors made of lead. Construction began in 1911 and continued for three years. Owner Thomas Gustave Plant spent $7 million, the bulk of his fortune, on this project and died penniless in 1946. A tour includes the mansion and the Castle Springs springwater facility on this 5,200-acre property overlooking Lake Winnepesaukee; there's also hiking and pony and horseback rides. ⊠*Rte. 171, Moultonborough* ☎*603/476–2352 or 800/729–2468* ⊕*www.castleintheclouds. org* ⊠*$10* ⊗*Weekends mid-May–early June; early June to mid-Oct., daily 10–4:30.*

SPORTS & THE OUTDOORS
The **Loon Center** at the **Frederick and Paula Anna Markus Wildlife Sanctuary** is the headquarters of the Loon Preservation Committee, an Audubon Society project. The loon, recognizable for its eerie calls and striking black-and-white coloring, resides on many New Hampshire lakes but is threatened by boat traffic, poor water quality, and habitat loss. Besides the changing exhibits about the birds, two trails wind through the 200-acre property: vantage points on the Loon Nest Trail overlook the spot resident loons sometimes occupy in late spring and summer. ⊠*Lee's Mills Rd.* ☎*603/476–5666* ⊕*www.loon.org* ⊠*Free* ⊗*Mon.–Sat. 9–5 early Oct.–June; daily 9–5 July–Columbus Day.*

SHOPPING
The **Old Country Store and Museum** (⊠*Moultonborough Corner, 5 mi south of Center Sandwich* ☎*603/476–5750*) has been selling maple products, cheeses aged on site, penny candy, and other items since 1781. Much of the equipment still used in the store is antique, and the museum (free) displays old farming and forging tools.

WHERE TO EAT
$-$$ ✕**Corner House Inn.** This restaurant, in a converted barn adorned with
AMERICAN local arts and crafts, serves classic American fare. Before you get to the white-chocolate cheesecake with key-lime filling, try the chef's lobster-and-mushroom bisque or tasty garlic-and-horseradish-crusted rack

of lamb. There's storytelling Thursday evening. ⊠ *Rtes. 109 and 113* ☎ *603/284–6219* ⊟ *AE, MC, V* ⊘ *No lunch Nov.–May.*

$$-$$$ ✕**The Woodshed.** Farm implements and antiques hang on the walls of this enchanting, romantic 1860 barn. The fare is mostly traditional New England—sea scallops baked in butter and lamb chops with mint sauce—but with some occasional surprises, such as Cajun-blackened pork tenderloin. Either way, the exceptionally fresh ingredients are sure to please. ⊠ *128 Lee Rd., Moultonborough* ☎ *603/476–2311* ⊟ *AE, D, DC, MC, V* ⊘ *Closed Mon. No lunch.*

TAMWORTH

13 mi east of Center Sandwich, 20 mi southwest of North Conway.

President Grover Cleveland summered in what remains a village of almost unreal quaintness—it's equally photogenic in verdant summer, during the fall foliage season, or under a blanket of winter snow. Cleveland's son, Francis, returned to stay and founded the acclaimed Barnstormers Theatre in 1931, one of America's first summer theaters, and one that continues to this day. Tamworth has a clutch of villages within its borders. At one of them—Chocorua—the view through the birches of Chocorua Lake has been so often photographed that you may experience déjà vu.

WHAT TO SEE

☾ **Remick Country Doctor Museum and Farm.** For 99 years—from 1894 to 1993), Dr. Edwin Crafts Remick and his father provided medical services to the Tamworth area and operated a family farm. After he died, these two houses were turned into the Remick Country Doctor Museum and Farm. The exhibits focus on the life of a country doctor and on the activities of the still-working farm. You can tour the farm daily from July to October; during those months there's a daily historic activity, like candle making, at 12:30. The second floor of the house has been kept as it was when Remnick died about 15 years ago—and it's a great way to peer in to the life of a true Tamworth townsman. ⊠ *58 Cleveland Hill Rd.* ☎ *603/323–7591 or 800/686–6117* ⊕ *www. remickmuseum.org* ⊠ *$3* ⊘ *Nov.–June, weekdays 10–4; July–Oct., Mon.–Sat. 10–4.*

SPORTS & THE OUTDOORS

PARK **White Lake State Park.** The 72-acre stand of native pitch pine here is a National Natural Landmark. The park has hiking trails, a sandy beach, trout fishing, canoe rentals, two camping areas, a picnic area, and swimming. ⊠ *Rte. 16, Tamworth* ☎ *603/323–7350.*

SHOPPING

The many rooms with themes—Christmas, bridal, and children's, among them—at the **Chocorua Dam Ice Cream & Gift Shop** (⊠ *Rte. 16, Chocorua* ☎ *603/323–8745*) contain handcrafted items. When you've finished shopping, try the ice cream, coffee, or tea and scones.

NIGHTLIFE & THE ARTS

The **Arts Council of Tamworth** (☎*603/323–8104* 🌐*www.artstamworth.org*) produces concerts—soloists, string quartets, revues, children's programs—from September through June and an arts show in late July. **Barnstormers Summer Theatre** (✉*Main St.* ☎*603/323–8500* 🌐*www.barnstormerstheatre.com*) has performances in July and August. The box office opens in June.

WHERE TO EAT & STAY

¢–$ SEAFOOD ✕ **Jake's Seafood.** Oars and nautical trappings adorn the wood-paneled walls at this stop between West and Center Ossipee, about 8 mi southeast of Tamworth. The kitchen serves some of eastern New Hampshire's freshest and tastiest seafood, notably lobster pie, fried clams, and seafood casserole; other choices include steak, ribs, and chicken dishes. ✉*2055 Rte. 16* ☎*603/539–2805* ▭*D, MC, V* ⊙*Closed Mon.–Wed.*

¢–$ ★ SOUTHERN ✕ **Yankee Smokehouse.** Need a rib fix? This down-home barbecue joint's logo depicting two happy pigs foreshadows the gleeful enthusiasm with which patrons dive into the hefty sandwiches of sliced pork and smoked chicken and immense platters of baby back ribs and smoked sliced beef. Ample sides of slaw, beans, fries, and garlic toast complement the hearty fare. Born-and-bred Southerners have been known to come away impressed. ✉*Rtes. 16 and 25, about 5 mi southeast of Tamworth* ☎*603/539–7427* ▭*MC, V.*

$ ★ **Lazy Dog Inn.** If you travel with your dog, you've just found your new favorite hotel. What began as a stagecoach stop has been operating as an inn almost continuously since 1845. And when Laura and Steven Sousa took over earlier this decade, they converted the inn to a über-doggie friendly B&B. The barn became a "doggie lodge" with a number of runs, a canine lullaby CD plays, and the innkeepers care for the dogs during the day while guests explore the Lakes Region or the White Mountains. It's an exceptional niche, but it's not done at the expense of the rooms, which are the cleanest and best furnished within miles. The lodging rate includes dog care. **Pros:** mega pet friendly, super clean. **Cons:** some rooms share bath. ✉*Rte. 16, Box 395, Chocorua 03817* ☎*603/323–8350 or 888/323–8350* 🌐*www.lazydoginn.com* *6 rooms, 3 with bath* *In-room: no phone, VCR, Wi-Fi. In-hotel: gym, no elevator, public Wi-Fi, some pets allowed, no kids under 14, no-smoking rooms* ▭*D, MC, V* *BP.*

THE WHITE MOUNTAINS

Sailors approaching East Coast harbors frequently mistake the pale peaks of the White Mountains—the highest range in the northeastern United States—for clouds. It was 1642 when explorer Darby Field could no longer contain his curiosity about one mountain in particular. He set off from his Exeter homestead and became the first man to climb what would eventually be called Mt. Washington. The 6,288-foot peak must have presented Field with formidable obstacles—its summit claims the highest wind velocity ever recorded and can see snow every month of the year.

Since Field's climb, curiosity about the mountains has not abated. Today an auto road and a cog railway lead to the top of Mt. Washington, and people come here by the tens of thousands to hike and climb, to photograph the vistas, and to ski. The peak is part of the Presidential Range, whose other peaks are also named after early presidents, and part of the White Mountain National Forest, whose roughly 770,000 acres extend from northern New Hampshire into southwestern Maine. Among the forest's scenic notches (deep mountain passes) are Pinkham, Kinsman, Franconia, and Crawford.

This section begins in Waterville Valley, off Interstate 93, and continues to North Woodstock. It then follows portions of the White Mountains Trail, a 100-mi loop designated as a National Scenic & Cultural Byway.

WATERVILLE VALLEY

60 mi north of Concord.

The first visitors began arriving in Waterville Valley in 1835. A 10-mi-long cul-de-sac cut by one of New England's several Mad rivers and circled by mountains, the valley was first a summer resort and then more of a ski area. Although it's now a year-round getaway, it still has a small-town charm. There are inns, condos, restaurants, shops, conference facilities, a grocery store, and a post office.

SPORTS & THE OUTDOORS

The **White Mountain Athletic Club** (⊠ *Rte. 49* ☎ *603/236–8303*) has tennis, racquetball, and squash as well as a 25-meter indoor pool, a jogging track, exercise equipment, whirlpools, saunas, steam rooms, and a games room. The club is free to guests of many area lodgings.

SKI AREAS   **Waterville Valley.** Former U.S. ski-team star Tom Corcoran designed this family-oriented resort. The lodgings and various amenities are about 1 mi from the slopes, but a shuttle renders a car unnecessary. This ski area has hosted more World Cup races than any other in the East, so most advanced skiers will be challenged. Most of the 52 trails are intermediate: straight down the fall line, wide, and agreeably long. A 7-acre tree-skiing area adds variety. Snowmaking coverage of 100% ensures good skiing even when nature doesn't cooperate. The Waterville Valley cross-country network, with the ski center in the town square, has 65 mi of trails. About two-thirds of them are groomed; the rest are backcountry. ⊠ *1 Ski Area Rd.* ☎ *603/236–8311, 603/236–4144 snow conditions, 800/468–2553 lodging* ⊕ *www.waterville.com.*

WHERE TO STAY

$$–$$$ ⚟ **Black Bear Lodge.** This family-oriented property has one-bedroom suites that sleep up to six and have full kitchens. Each unit is individually owned and decorated. Children's movies are shown at night in season, and there's bus service to the slopes. Guests can use the

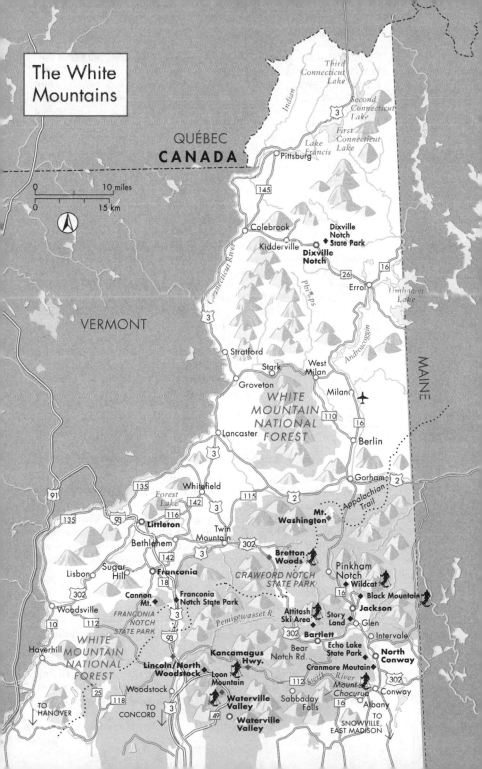

White Mountain Athletic Club. There's a small heated pool and hot tub. **Pros:** affordable. **Cons:** basic in its decor and services. ⊠*3 Village Rd* ☎*603/236–4501 or 800/349–2327* ⊕*www.black-bear-lodge.com* ⟐*107 suites* ⌂*In-room: no a/c (some), kitchen. In-hotel: pool, gym, public Internet, no-smoking rooms* ☰*AE, D, MC, V.*

$$$$ ⊡ **Golden Eagle Lodge.** Waterville's premier condominium property— with its steep roof punctuated by dozens of gabled dormers—recalls the grand hotels of an earlier era. Rooms, however, are contemporary with upscale light-wood furniture and well-equipped kitchens; many have views of the surrounding peaks. The full-service complex has a two-story lobby and a capable front-desk staff. Guests have access to the White Mountain Athletic Club. **Pros:** most reliable accommodation in town. **Cons:** somewhat bland architecture and decor. ⊠*6 Snow's Brook Rd., Box 495, 03215* ☎*603/236–4600 or 888/703–2453* ⊕*www.goldeneaglelodge.com* ⟐*139 condominiums* ⌂*In-room: kitchen, Wi-Fi. In-hotel: pool, public Internet, public Wi-Fi, laundry service, laundry facilities, no-smoking rooms* ☰*AE, D, DC, MC, V.*

$-$$ ⊡ **Snowy Owl Inn.** You're treated to afternoon wine and cheese in the atrium lobby, which has a three-story fieldstone fireplace and many prints and watercolors of snowy owls. The fourth-floor bunk-bed lofts are ideal for families; first-floor rooms are suitable for couples seeking a quiet getaway. Four restaurants are within walking distance. Guests have access to the White Mountain Athletic Club. **Pros:** affordable. **Cons:** bland. ⊠*4 Village Rd., Box 407, 03215* ☎*603/236–8383 or 800/766–9969* ⊕*www.snowyowlinn.com* ⟐*85 rooms* ⌂*In-room: kitchen (some), VCR (some), Wi-Fi. In-hotel: pools, gym, public Internet, public Wi-Fi, no-smoking rooms* ☰*AE, D, DC, MC, V* ⑩*BP.*

LINCOLN/NORTH WOODSTOCK

14 mi northwest of Waterville Valley, 63 mi north of Concord.

These two neighboring towns at the southwestern end of the White Mountains National Forest and one end of the Kancamagus Highway (Route 112), are a lively resort area, especially for Bostonian families who can make an easy day trip straight up Interstate 93 to Exit 32. Festivals, such as the New Hampshire Scottish Highland Games in mid-September, keep Lincoln swarming with people year-round. The town itself is not much of an attraction. Tiny North Woodstock maintains more of a village feel.

WHAT TO SEE

ⓒ **Clarke's Trading Post.** It's undeniably hokey, but is a sure kids' favorite. It consists of a bear show, half-hour train rides over a 1904 covered bridge, a museum of Americana set inside an 1880s firehouse, a restored gas station filled with antique cars, and a replica of the Old Man of the Mountain that you can climb on. Tour guides tell tall tales and vendors sell popcorn, ice cream, pizza, and other snacks. There's also a mammoth gift shop, penny-candy store, and several other places to buy silly keepsakes. ⊠*U.S. 3, off I–93 (Exit 33), North Lincoln*

☏ *603/745–8913* ⊕*www.clarkstradingpost.com* ✉*$12* ⊙*Memorial Day–Columbus Day daily 9–5 (and until 9 PM Sat. July 5–Aug. 16.*

FUN TOUR

A ride on the Hobo Railroad yields scenic views of the Pemigewasset River and the White Mountain National Forest. The narrated excursions take 80 minutes. ☒*Kancamagus Hwy (Rte. 112), Lincoln* ☏*603/745-2135* ⊕*www. hoborr.com* ✉*$10* ⊙*Late June–early Sept., daily; May–late June and early Sept.–Oct., weekends; call for schedule.*

SPORTS & THE OUTDOORS

☾ At **Whale's Tale Waterpark** (☒*U.S. 3, I-93 Exit 33, North Lincoln* ☏*603/745–8810* ⊕*www.whalestalewaterpark.net* ✉*$25* ⊙*Mid-June–Labor Day, daily 10–6*) you can float on an inner tube along a gentle river, careen down one of five water slides, take a trip in a multipassenger tube, or body-surf in the large wave pool. Whale Harbor and Orca Park Play Island contain water activities for small children and toddlers.

☾ At **Lost River Gorge in Kinsman Notch** (☒*Kancamagus Hwy. [Rte. 112], 6 mi west of North Woodstock* ☏*603/745–8720 or 800/346-3687* ⊕*www.findlostriver.com*) you can hike along the sheer granite river gorge and view such geological wonders as the Guillotine Rock and the Lemon Squeezer or pan for gemstones. A cafeteria, garden, and gift shop round out the amenities. It's open daily from mid-May to mid-October; admission is $10.

Pemi Valley Excursions (☒*Main St., off I-93 (Exit 32), Lincoln* ☏*603/ 745-2744* ⊕*www.i93.com/pvsr*) offers a variety of recreational and scenic tours throughout the year. It's one of the best snowmobile outfitters in the region, offering one- to two-hour guided tours and half- and full-day snowmobile rentals. Spring through summer, you can ride horseback along wooded trails and along the Pemigewasset River, enjoy horse-drawn-carriage rides, and embark on moose-watching bus tours into the northernmost White Mountains.

SKI AREA **Loon Mountain.** Wide, straight, and consistent intermediate trails prevail at Loon, a modern resort on the western edge of the Kancamagus Highway (Route 112) and the Pemigewasset River. Beginner trails and slopes are set apart. In winter 2007–08 Loon opened up the new South Peak, with new trails and an express quad. The most advanced among the 47 runs are grouped on the North Peak section farther from the main mountain. Snowboarders have a half-pipe and their own park; an alpine garden with bumps and jumps provides thrills for skiers. The vertical is 2,100 feet. In the base lodge and around the mountain are many food-service and lounge facilities. There's day and nighttime lift-served snow tubing on the lower slopes. The touring center at Loon Mountain has 22 mi of cross-country trails. There's also ice skating. ☒*Kancamagus Hwy. (Rte. 112), Lincoln* ☏*603/745–8111, 603/745– 8100 snow conditions, 800/227–4191 lodging* ⊕*www.loonmtn.com.*

6

NIGHTLIFE & THE ARTS

Skiers head to the **Black Diamond Lounge** (⊠ *Kancamagus Hwy. [Rte. 112]* ☎ *603/745–2244* ⊕ *www.mtnclub.com*) in the Mountain Club at the Loon Mountain resort. The **Olde Timbermill** (⊠ *Mill at Loon Mountain, Kancamagus Hwy. [Rte. 112]* ☎ *603/745–3603*) has live dance music on weekends. The **North Country Center for the Arts** (⊠ *Papermill Theatre, Kancamagus Hwy. [Rte. 112], Lincoln* ☎ *603/745–6032, 603/745–2141 box office* ⊕ *www.papermilltheatre.org*) presents theater for children and adults and art exhibitions in July and August. The draws at the **Thunderbird Lounge** (⊠ *Indian Head Resort, 664 U.S. 3, North Lincoln* ☎ *603/745–8000*) are nightly entertainment year-round and a large dance floor.

WHERE TO EAT & STAY

$ ✕ **Woodstock Station.** If you like eateries loaded with character, don't
AMERICAN   miss this restaurant, sited in the former Lincoln Railroad Station of the late 1800s. Down the hall is a great brewery and pub that serves 13 handcrafted brews and is decorated with old maps and memorabilia. You come here as much to mix with locals and feel part of the town as to eat. The menu is what you might find at a Bennigan's: pizza, quesadilla, wings, chicken, and seafood. The lunch specials are a great value. ⊠ *U.S. 3, North Woodstock* ☎ *603/745–3951* ▤ *AE, D, MC, V.*

☾ $ 🏨 **Indian Head Resort.** When you see the totem pole, you know you've found this fun family resort. Views across the 180 acres of this motel's property, near the Loon and Cannon Mountain ski areas, are of Indian Head Rock Profile and the Franconia Mountains. Cross-country ski trails and a mountain-bike trail from the resort connect to the Franconia Notch trail system. The Profile Room restaurant serves standard American fare. **Pros:** best place for kids around. **Cons:** not directly in town, farther from skiing. ⊠ *U.S. 3, 5 mi north of North Woodstock* ⊕ *R.R. 1, Box 99, North Lincoln 03251* ☎ *603/745–8000 or 800/343–8000* ⊕ *www.indianheadresort.com* ⇆ *100 rooms, 40 cottages* ⚡ *In-room: refrigerator, Wi-Fi. In-hotel: restaurant, room service, bar, tennis court, pools, gym, no elevator, public Internet, public Wi-Fi, no-smoking rooms* ▤ *AE, D, DC, MC, V.*

$$$ 🏨 **Mountain Club on Loon.** If you want ski-in, ski-out on Loon Mountain, this is your best—and only—option. A typical 1990s ski lodge with a stone fireplace in the lobby, a heated outdoor pool with hot tubs, and a small room with Ping-Pong and air hockey for kids, the Club isn't thrilling, but it's clean and modern. There are suites that sleep as many as eight, studios with Murphy beds, and many units with kitchens. All rooms are within walking distance of the lifts, and condominiums are on or near the slopes. Entertainers perform in the lounge on most winter weekends. **Pros:** easy skiing, clean basic rooms, easy access to national forest. **Cons:** unexciting decor. ⊠ *Kancamagus Hwy. (Rte. 112), Lincoln* ☎ *603/745–2244 or 800/229–7829* ⊕ *www. mtnclub.com* ⇆ *234 units* ⚡ *In-room: kitchen (some). In-hotel: restaurant, bar, tennis courts, pool, gym, spa, laundry facilities, public Wi-Fi, no-smoking rooms* ▤ *AE, D, MC, V.*

FRANCONIA

16 mi northwest of Lincoln/North Woodstock.

Travelers have long passed through the White Mountains via Franconia Notch, and in the late 18th century a town evolved just to the north. It and the region's jagged rock formations and heavy coat of evergreens have stirred the imaginations of Washington Irving, Henry Wadsworth Longfellow, and Nathaniel Hawthorne, who penned a short story about the Old Man of the Mountain. There is almost no town proper to speak of here, just a handful of stores, touched though it is by Interstate 93 (aka the Franconia Notch Parkway).

Four miles west of Franconia, Sugar Hill is a town of about 500 people. It's famous for its spectacular sunsets and views of the Franconia Mountains, best seen from Sunset Hill, where formerly a row of grand hotels and mansions once stood.

WHAT TO SEE

Flume. This 800-foot-long chasm has narrow walls that give the gorge's running water an eerie echo. The route through it has been built up with a series of boardwalks and stairways. The visitor center has exhibits on the region's history. ⊠ *Franconia Notch Pkwy. Exit 34A* ☎ *603/745–8391* ⊕ *www.nhstateparks.com/franconia.html* ⧉ *$8* ⊙ *Early May–late Oct., daily 9–5.*

Frost Place. His full-time home from 1915 to 1920 and also his summer home for 19 years, this is where Robert Frost soaked up the spirit of New England, which was the essence of his poetry. This place is imbued with the spirit of that work, down to the rusted mailbox in front that's painted R. FROST in simple lettering. Two rooms host occasional readings and contain memorabilia and signed editions of his books. Out back, you can follow short trails marked with lines from his poetry. A visit here will slow you down, and remind you of the intense beauty of the surrounding countryside. ⊠ *Ridge Rd. off Rte. 116* ☎ *603/823–5510* ⊕ *www.frostplace.org* ⧉ *$5* ⊙ *Memorial Day–early Oct., Wed.–Mon. 1–5.*

Old Man of the Mountain. A famous New Hampshire's geological site is this naturally formed profile in the rock high above Franconia Notch, crumbled unexpectedly on May 3, 2003, from the strains of natural erosion. The iconic image had defined New Hampshire, and the Old Man's "death" stunned and saddened residents. You can still stop at the posted turnouts from Interstate 93 north- or southbound. In Franconia Notch State Park on the northbound side of the highway there is a pull-off and on the southbound side take Exit 34B and follow signs. Another option is to go along the shore of Profile Lake for the best views of the mountain face. There's a small, free Old Man of the Mountain Museum administered by Franconia Notch State Park at the southbound viewing area (by the Cannon Mountain tram parking area); it's open daily 9–5.

6

SPORTS & THE OUTDOORS

SKI AREAS **Cannon Mountain.** This was one of the nation's first ski areas, and the staff at this state-run facility in Franconia Notch State Park is attentive to skier services, family programs, snowmaking, and grooming. All this makes Cannon a very sound value. Cannon's 42 trails present challenges rarely found in New Hampshire—for instance the narrow, steep pitches off the peak of a 2,146-foot vertical rise. There are also two glade-skiing trails—Turnpike and Banshee—and a tubing park with lift service. Nordic skiing is on an 8-mi multiuse recreational path. In summer, for $10 round-trip, the Cannon Mountain Aerial Tramway can transport you up 2,022 feet. It's an eight-minute ride to the top, where marked trails lead to an observation platform. The tram runs daily from mid-May through late October.

The **New England Ski Museum** (☎603/823–7177 ⊕*www.skimuseum. org*) sits at the base of the tramway and traces the history of the sport with displays of early gear as well as photos, books, and videos. Admission is free, and the museum is open daily 10–5 from late December through March and from late May through mid-October. ✉*Franconia Notch State Park, I–93 Exit 34B 03580* ☎*603/823–8800, 603/823–7771 snow conditions, 800/237–9007 lodging* ⊙*Late May–mid-Oct. and late Dec.–Mar., daily 10–5.*

Franconia Village Cross-Country Ski Center. The cross-country ski center at the Franconia Inn has 39 mi of groomed trails and 24 mi of backcountry trails. One popular route leads to Bridal Veil Falls, a great spot for a picnic lunch. There are horse-drawn sleigh rides and ice-skating on a lighted rink. ✉*1300 Easton Rd. 03580* ☎*603/823–5542 or 800/473–5299* ⊕*www.franconiainn.com.*

WHERE TO EAT

¢-$ ✕ **Polly's Pancake Parlor.** Originally a carriage shed built in 1830, this
★ local institution was converted to a tearoom during the Depression,
AMERICAN when the Dexters began serving all-you-can-eat pancakes, waffles, and French toast for 50¢. The prices have gone up, but the descendants of the Dexters continue to serve pancakes and waffles made from grains ground on the property, their own country sausage, and pure maple syrup. The oatmeal-buttermilk pancakes with coconut, blueberries, or walnuts are other favorites. You can purchase home mixes and syrup at the adjoining store. ✉*Rte. 117* ☎*603/823–5575* ▤*AE, D, MC, V* ⊙*Closed mid-Oct.–mid-May. No dinner.*

$$-$$$ ✕ **Sugar Hill Inn.** This 1789 farmhouse is the fine-dining option in these
AMERICAN neck of the woods. Chef Val Fortin serves such haute American fare as peppercorn-crusted sirloin steak with grilled mushrooms and truffle oil; the homemade desserts are always delicious. A four-course prix-fixe meal is $48. ✉*116 Rte. 117* ☎*603/823–5621* ⚞*Reservations required* ▤*AE, MC, V* ⊙*Closed Tues. and Wed. No lunch.*

WHERE TO STAY

$ ▥ **Franconia Inn.** At this 107-acre, family-friendly resort, you can play tennis on four clay courts, swim in the outdoor heated pool or hot tub, and hike. The cross-country ski barn doubles as a horseback-riding center in the warmer months. The white, three-story inn has unfussy country furnishings—you'll find canopy beds and country quilts in the rooms, most of which have period-style wallpapering or wood-paneling; many have working fireplaces. A sunny, plant-filled restaurant serves contemporary continental fare. Pros: good for kids, amazing views, outdoor heated pool, Cons: may be too remote for those who like town access. ⊠*1300 Easton Rd. 03580* ☎*603/823–5542 or 800/473–5299* ⊕*www.franconiainn.com* ⌁*34 rooms, 3 suites, 2 2-bedroom cottages* &*In-room: no phone, no TV, Wi-Fi. In-hotel: restaurant, bar, tennis courts, pool, bicycles, no elevator, public Wi-Fi, no-smoking rooms* ⊟*AE, MC, V* ⊘*Closed May 1–15.*

$$–$$$ 🏨 **Sugar Hill Inn.** Hands down the nicest place in Franconia for a roman-
★ tic retreat is the Sugar Hill Inn. The lawn's old carriage and the wrap-around porch's wicker chairs put you in a nostalgic mood before you even enter this converted 1789 farmhouse. Antique-filled guest quarters are in the main house or one of three cottages. Many rooms and suites have hand-stenciled walls and views of the Franconia Mountains; some have fireplaces. Bette Davis visited friends in this house—the room with the best vistas is named after her. Pros: romantic, classic B&B; fine dinners. Cons: expensive. ⊠*116 Rte. 117 03586* ☎*603/823–5621 or 800/548–4748* ⊕*www.sugarhillinn.com* ⌁*13 rooms, 1 cottage* &*In-room: no phone, DVD (some), no TV (some), Wi-Fi. In-hotel: restaurant, room service, bar, pool, spa, no elevator, public Internet, public Wi-Fi, no-smoking rooms* ⊟*AE, MC, V* ⓞ|*BP, MAP.*

LITTLETON

9 mi northeast of Sugar Hill, 7 mi north of Franconia, 86 mi north of Concord.

One of northern New Hampshire's largest towns (this isn't saying much, mind you) is on a granite shelf along the Ammonoosuc River, whose swift current and drop of 235 feet enabled the community to flourish as a mill center in its early days. Later, the railroad came through, and Littleton grew into the region's commerce hub. In the minds of many, it's more a place to stock up on supplies than a bona fide destination, but few communities have worked harder at revitalization. Today, intriguing shops and eateries line the adorable main street, whose tidy 19th- and early-20th-century buildings suggest a set in a Jimmy Stewart movie.

WHAT TO SEE

Littleton Grist Mill. Stop by this restored 1798 mill just off Main Street of bustling Littleton. On the Ammonoosuc River, it contains a small shop selling stone-ground flour products, and a museum downstairs show-casing the original mill equipment. ⊠*18 Mill St.* ☎*603/444–7478 or 888/284–7478* ⊕*www.littletongristmill.com* ⊘*July–Dec., 10–5; June–Apr., Wed.–Sat., 10–5.*

OFF THE BEATEN PATH

Whitefield. Like Dixville Notch and Bretton Woods, Whitefield, 11 mi northeast of Littleton, became a prominent summer resort in the late 19th century, when wealthy industrialists flocked to the small village in a rolling valley between two precipitous promontories to golf, ski, play

6

polo, and hobnob with each other. The sprawling, yellow clapboard Mountain View hotel, which was established in 1865 and had grown to grand hotel status by the early 20th century, only to succumb to changing tourist habits and close by the 1980s, has been fully refurbished and is now open again as one of New England's grandest resort hotels. It's worth driving through the courtly Colonial center of town—Whitefield was settled in the early 1800s—and up Route 116 just beyond to see this magnificent structure atop a bluff overlooking the Presidentials.

Lancaster. About 8 mi north of Whitefield via U.S. 3, the affable seat of Coos County sits at the confluence of the Connecticut and Israel rivers, surrounded by low serrated peaks. Before becoming prosperous through commerce, Lancaster was an agricultural stronghold; at one time the only acceptable currency was the bushel of wheat. It's still an intimate mountain town. Like Littleton, though, it has restored much of its main street, which now has a dapper mix of Victorian homes, funky artisan and antiques shops, and prim churches and civic buildings.

SHOPPING

The **Village Book Store** (⊠*81 Main St.* ☎*603/444–5263*) has comprehensive selections of both nonfiction and fiction titles. **Potato Barn Antiques Center** (⊠*U.S. 3, 6 mi north of Lancaster, Northumberland* ☎*603/636–2611*) has several dealers under one roof—specialties include vintage farm tools, clothing, and costume jewelry.

NEED A BREAK? Beside the Littleton Grist Mill, Miller's Café & Bakery (⊠ *16 Mill St.* ☎ *603/444– 2146* ⊕ *www.millerscafeandbakery.com* ⊘ *Closed Sun. and Mon.*) serves coffees, microbrews and wines, baked goods, sandwiches, and salads.

WHERE TO EAT

$$–$$$ ★ AMERICAN ✕ **Tim-bir Alley.** This is a rare find in New Hampshire: an independent restaurant in a contemporary setting that's been around a long time (since 1983) and yet still takes its food seriously. If you're in town, don't miss it. Tim Carr's menu changes weekly and uses regional American ingredients in creative ways. Main dishes might include rosemary-and-garlic lamb chops with spinach, feta, and pine nuts, or sunflower-encrusted salmon with a smoked-tomato puree. Save room for such desserts as white chocolate–coconut cheesecake. ⊠*7 Main St.* ☎*603/444–6142* ☐*No credit cards* ⊘ *Closed Tues. and Wed. No lunch.*

WHERE TO STAY

$$ ★ ⌂ **Adair Country Inn.** An air of yestertyear refinement infuses Adair, a three-story Georgian-revival home that attorney Frank Hogan built as a wedding present for his daughter, Dorothy Adair, in 1927. Dorothy's hats adorn the place, as do books and old photos form the era. This is a luxurious, well-run country inn, with walking paths that wind through 200 acres of gardens designed by the Olmstead brothers. Rooms are furnished with period antiques and reproductions; many have fireplaces. Two more pluses: A generous afternoon tea is served in the elegant living room, and a great basement rec room has a 1929 billiards table and a 42-inch flat-screen with a big movie collection. **Pros:** clean, cozy rooms; refined book-filled spaces; good dinners. **Cons:** removed

from town. ⊠*80 Guider La., just off I–93 Exit 40* ☎*603/444–2600 or 888/444–2600* ⊕*www.adairinn.com* 📞*9 rooms, 1 cottage* ৬*In room: no phone, no TV, Wi-Fi. In-hotel: restaurant, tennis court, no elevator, public Wi-Fi, no kids under 12, no-smoking rooms* ▤*AE, D, MC, V* ⊺⊚*|BP.*

$$ 🎭 **Mountain View Grand Resort and Spa.** One of New England's most
ᗺ complete resorts, the Mountain View gives families and couples a seem-
★ ingly endless array of things to do. For instance: horseback riding, a
9-hole golf course, four clay tennis courts, ice skating, tubing, snow-
mobiling, and cross country skiing. Built in 1865 and for decades one
of New England's grandest of the grande dames, the Mountain View
reopened to great fanfare in summer 2002. Nearly all the rooms afford
vast vistas of the mountains or golf course, and all are outfitted with
plush Colonial-style mahogany furniture and floral-print bedspreads.
The main restaurant, Juliet's, serves creative regional New England
cuisine. The state-of-the-art Tower Spa provides myriad treatments.
Pros: full-service resort in the grand tradition, full range of activities,
free shuttle to Cannon. **Cons:** breakfast not included. ⊠*120 Moun-
tain View Rd., Whitefield* ☎*603/837–2100 or 800/438–3017* ⊕*www.
mountainviewgrand.com* 📞*115 rooms, 30 suites* ৬*In-room: Wi-Fi.
In-hotel: 4 restaurants, room service, bar, golf course, tennis courts,
pools, gym, spa, bicycles, children's programs (ages 4–16), laundry ser-
vice, conciere, public Internet, public Wi-Fi, no-smoking rooms* ▤*AE,
D, MC, V.*

ᗺ 🎭 **Thayers Inn.** This stately 1843 Greek-revival hotel is the essence of
Fodor's Choice Littleton. It's not a luxury hotel. Thayers doesn't need to try to impress
★ anyone. The well-kept rooms retain a quaintly old-fashioned look, with
creaky floorboards, exposed pipes, vintage steam radiators, high ceil-
ings, and comfy wing chairs. But if you're traveling on a budget, or just
want an authentic northern town experience, history seems to radiate
from this place. There's no elevator—good to know if you planned to
book an upper-floor room. The Bailiwicks restaurant and bar down-
stairs is a typical delight: you'd never expect it as you head down the
steps, but it's a charmer. **Pros:** one of the best values in New England.
Cons: continental breakfast only. ⊠*111 Main St. 03561* ☎*603/444–
6469 or 800/634–8179* ⊕*www.thayersinn.com* 📞*22 rooms, 13 suites*
৬*In-room: VCR, Wi-Fi. In-hotel: restaurant, bar, no elevator, public
Internet, public Wi-Fi, some pets allowed, no-smoking rooms* ▤*AE,
D, MC, V* ⊺⊚*|CP.*

BRETTON WOODS

14 mi southeast of Bethlehem, 28 mi northeast of Lincoln/Woodstock.

In the early 1900s private railcars brought the elite from New York
and Philadelphia to the Mount Washington Hotel, the jewel of the
White Mountains. A visit to the hotel is not to be missed. The hotel
was the site, in 1944, of a famous United Nations conference that cre-
ated the International Monetary Fund and the International Bank for
Reconstruction and Development and whose decisions governed inter-

national monetary and financial policy until the early 1970s. The area is also known for its cog railway and Bretton Woods ski resort.

WHAT TO SEE

Fodor'sChoice
★

In 1858 Sylvester Marsh petitioned the state legislature for permission to build a steam railway up Mt. Washington. A politico retorted that he'd have better luck building a railroad to the moon. Just 11 years later, the **Mt. Washington Cog Railway** chugged its way along a 3-mi track up the west side of the mountain to the summit, and it is today one of the state's most beloved attractions—a thrill in either direction. In winter the train goes 4,100 feet up, an hour-long roundtrip ($31) with trains departing at 10 AM and 1 PM. The rest of the year the full trip ($59) is three hours, with 20 minutes at the summit; trains depart at 11 AM and 2 PM. *⊠U.S. 302, 6 mi northeast of Bretton Woods* ☎*603/278–5404 or 800/922–8825* ⊕*www.thecog.com* ⊡*$59* ⊗*Two daily departures (hours vary).*

SPORTS & THE OUTDOORS

SKI AREA
Fodor'sChoice
★

Bretton Woods. Skiing with your family? New Hampshire's largest ski area is considered one of the best family ski resorts in the country. It's also probably the best place in New England to learn to ski. (If it's your first time, get started at the free area reached by the Learning Center Quad chairlift.) The views of Mt. Washington alone are worth the visit to Bretton Woods; the scenery is especially beautiful from the **Top of Quad restaurant,** which is open during ski season.

Trails will appeal mostly to novice and intermediate skiers, including two magic carpets lifts for beginners. There are, however, some steeper pitches near the top of the 1,500-foot vertical and glade skiing will satisfy experts. There's night skiing and snowboarding on weekends and holidays. Four terrain parks, including an all-natural Wild West park, will make snowboarders happy. Theres also a half-pipe.

The large, full-service cross-country ski center has 62 mi (100 km) of groomed and double-track trails, many of them lift-serviced. The Nordic ski center, which doubles as the golf clubhouse in summer, is near the hotel.

Options for kids are plentiful. The Hobbit Ski and Snowboard School for ages 4–12 have full- and half-day instruction. Hobbit Ski and Snowplay program ages three to five is an introduction to skiing and fun on the snow. There are also organized instructor activities in the nursery. The complimentary Kinderwoods Winter Playground has a sled carousel, igloos, and a zip line. Parents can buy an innovative innovative interchangeable family ticket that allows parents to take turns skiing while the other watches the kids—both passes come for the price of one. *⊠U.S. 302, 03575* ☎*603/278–3320, 603/278–3333 weather conditions, 800/232–2972 information, 800/258–0330 lodging* ⊕*www.brettonwoods.com.*

WHERE TO EAT

$$$
AMERICAN

✕ **The Bretton Arms Dining Room.** You're likely to have the best meal in the area at the this intimate setting. Though the same executive chef oversees the Mount Washington Hotel dining room, the latter is immense, and the Bretton Arms tiny; you seem to get more chef focus here. Three small interconnected rooms, separated by fireplaces, are private and romantic. Entrées include Maine lobster tossed with fresh pasta and free-range Long Island duck breast. ⌧*U.S. 302* ☎*603/278–1000* ▤*AE, D, MC, V* ⊙*No lunch.*

$$$
★
AMERICAN

✕ **The Dining Room.** Wow. You'd be hard-pressed to find a larger or grander dining room in New Hampshire (only the Balsams can compare). The Mount Washington Hotel's huge octagonal dining room, built in 1902 is adorned with Currier & Ives reproductions, Tiffany glass, chandeliers galore, massive windows that open to the Presidential Range, and a nightly musical trio. Besides the Balsams, this is the only restaurant in the state that requires a jacket—if you forgot yours, fear not, they have about 30 you can borrow. Try seasonal dishes like seared haddock and shrimp fricassee; lemon lobster ravioli with shrimp and scallops; or roast pork with onions and mushrooms. ⌧*In Mount Washington Hotel, U.S. 302* ☎*603/278–1000 Jacket required* ▤*AE, D, MC, V.*

$–$$

✕ **Fabyan's Station.** In 1890, three score of tourist trains a day passed through this station, now a casual restaurant. If you're looking for an easygoing meal in the area, hop on over. Half the restaurant is a tavern with a long bar, and the other half serves sandwiches, fish, and steaks. There's a kids menu too. A model train circles above the dining room. ⌧*Rte. 302, 1 mi north of Bretton Woods ski area* ☎*603/278–2222* ⌔*Reservations not accepted* ▤*AE, D, MC, V.*

WHERE TO STAY

¢
★

▦ **The Lodge.** A stay at this inexpensive roadside motel run by Bretton Woods gives you free access to all of the resort facilities at Mount Washington Hotel, including the pools, gym, and arcade. That makes it a great deal. You can also use the free shuttle to the hotel and the ski area. Even without all that rooms would be a great value: they're very clean and have private balconies that overlook the Presidential range. There's a pizzeria on site, a small arcade, a great indoor pool, and a cute hearthside common area. **Pros:** cheap, free access to Mount Washington amenities, free ski shuttle. **Cons:** across street from resort amenities, continental breakfast only. ⌧*U.S. 302, 03575* ☎*603/278–1000 or 800/258–0330* ⊕*www.mtwashington.com* ⌔*50 rooms* ⌖*In-room: Wi-Fi. In-hotel: restaurant, golf courses, tennis courts, pool, bicycles, children's programs (ages 4–12), laundry facilities, laundry service, public Wi-Fi, no-smoking rooms* ▤*AE, D, MC, V* ▢*CP.*

$$
⟳
Fodor's Choice
★

▦ **The Mount Washington Hotel.** The two most memorable sights in the White Mountains would have to be (a) Mount Washington and (b) the Mount Washington Hotel. Its grand scale and exquisite setting foregrounded with the Presidentials is astonishing. This 1902 resort has a 900-foot-long veranda, stately public rooms, and, after a brilliant renovation, glimmers anew with an early-20th-century formality. It would take a full week to exhaust the recreational activities here: in winter

6

there's tubing, ice skating, a great cross-country facility, a terrific down-hill skiing complex, and sleigh rides; in summer, horseback riding, carriage rides, fly fishing, golf, mountain biking, etc. The adventure desk is a concierge area designed to keep you busy. The Cave provides nightly entertainment in a former 1930s speakeasy. Kids love to run around this huge hotel (so big it has its own post office), and there's an arcade, a sweet shop, playground, as well as kids club with themed day and evening programs. A 25,000-square-foot spa and a renovated 18-hole Donald Ross course (designed in 1915) are set to debut in fall 2008. Rooms aren't as lavish as the public spaces, but they have high ceilings and are comfortable. **Pros:** beuatiful grand resort, loads of activities, free shuttle to skiing and activities. **Cons:** kids love to run around the hotel, big hotel, rooms not as luxurious as rest of property. ⊠*U.S. 302, 03575* ☎*603/278–1000 or 800/258–0330* ⊕*www.mtwashington.com* ⇆*177 rooms, 23 suites* ♿*In-room: Ethernet, Wi-Fi. In-hotel: 3 restaurants, room service, bars, golf courses, tennis courts, pool, gym, spa, bicycles, children's programs (ages 4–12), laundry service, concierge, public Internet, public Wi-Fi, no-smoking rooms* ⊟*AE, D, MC, V* ⏏⏐*EP, BP, MAP.*

$$
Fodor'sChoice
★
🏨 **The Notchland Inn.** To see this house is to believe in fairy tales. Built in 1862 by Sam Bemis, America's grandfather of landscape photography, the house conveys mountain charm on a scale unmatched in New England. It's simply a legenday setting, in Crawford Notch, in the middle of the forest surrounded by the mountains: perhaps drop any cute house here and you couldn't but fall in love. But to their credit, innkeepers Les Schoof and Ed Butler have left wood-burning fireplaces in every room (17 in total in the house) and do everything else you'd hope for, like having a big library, leaving puzzles around, serving five-course meals, and giving range of the place to Abby and Crawford, the immense Bernese Mountain inn dogs. **Pros:** middle-of-the-forest setting, marvelous house and common rooms, original fireplaces, good dinner. **Cons:** will be too isolated for some, rooms could be better equipped (better bedding needed, for example). ⊠*Rte. 302, Hart's Location* ☎*603/374–6131* ⊕*www.notchland.com* ⇆*8 rooms, 5 suites, 3 cottages* ♿*In-room: no phone, Wi-Fi. In-hotel: restaurant, no elevator, public Wi-Fi, some pets allowed, no kids under 12, no-smoking rooms* ⊟*D, MC, V* ⏏⏐*BP.*

EN ROUTE
Scenic U.S. 302 winds through the steep, wooded mountains on either side of spectacular Crawford Notch, southeast of Bretton Woods, and passes through **Crawford Notch State Park** (⊠*U.S. 302, Harts Location* ☎*603/374–2272*), where you can picnic and take a short hike to Arethusa Falls or the Silver and Flume cascades. The visitor center has a gift shop and a cafeteria; there's also a **campground.** ☎*603/271–3628 reservations.*

BARTLETT

18 mi southeast of Bretton Woods.

With Bear Mountain to its south, Mt. Parker to its north, Mt. Cardigan to its west, and the Saco River to its east, Bartlett, incorporated in 1790, has an unforgettable setting. Lovely Bear Notch Road (closed in winter) has the only midpoint access to the Kancamagus Highway (Route 112). There isn't much town here (dining options are just over in Glen). It's best known for the Attitash ski area.

SPORTS & THE OUTDOORS

SKI AREA **Attitash Ski Area.** Enhanced with massive snowmaking (98%), the trails number 75 on two peaks—Attitash (with a vertical drop of 1,760 feet) and Attitash Bear Peak (with a 1,450-foot vertical)—both with full-service base lodges. The bulk of the skiing and boarding is geared to intermediates and experts, with some steep pitches and glades. At 500 feet, the Ground Zero half pipe is New England's longest. The Attitash Adventure Center has a rental shop, lessons desk, and children's programs. ☒ *U.S. 302* ☎ *603/374–2368, 877/677–7609 snow conditions, 800/223–7669 lodging* ⊕ *www.attitash.com.*

WHERE TO EAT

$$–$$$ ✕ **Bernerhof Inn.** There are several options for dining at this inn. The
ECLECTIC dining room is the area's fine dining choice, preparing traditional Swiss specialties such as fondue and Wiener schnitzel as well as contemporary dishes—Asian duck breast or venison filet, for instance. The Black Bear pub pours microbrews and serves sandwiches and burgers, as well as shepherds' pie and other dishes. The CyBear Lounge serves afternoon appetizers you can snack on while checking your e-mail. ☒ *U.S. 302, Glen* ☎ *603/383–9132 or 800/548–8007* ⊕ *www.bernerhofinn. com* ☐ *AE, D, MC, V.*

$–$$ ✕ **Margarita Grill.** Après-ski and hiking types congregate here—in
SOUTHWESTERN the dining room in cold weather and on the covered patio when it's warm—for homemade salsas, wood-fired steaks, ribs, burgers, and a smattering of Tex-Mex and Cajun specialties. Unwind at the tequila bar after a day on the mountains. ☒ *U.S. 302, Glen* ☎ *603/383–6556* ☐ *D, MC, V* ☻ *No lunch weekdays.*

$–$$ ✕ **Red Parka Pub.** Practically an institution, this downtown Glen pub
AMERICAN has been here for more than two decades. The menu has everything a family could want, from an all-you-can-eat salad bar to scallop pie. The barbecued ribs are favorites, as are hand-carved steaks of every type, from aged New York sirloin to prime rib. ☒ *U.S. 302, Glen* ☎ *603/383–4344* ☖ *Reservations not accepted* ☐ *AE, D, MC, V.*

WHERE TO STAY

$$ ▦ **Attitash Mountain Village.** This place across the street form the entrance to Attitash is deceptively large. You can't see the cluster of units form the road because they're in the pine trees (there are also a few slope-side condos). But they're there, along with hiking trails, a playground, a clay tennis courts, two heated pools, an arcade, and free bike rentals. All in all it's a good deal for families on a budget and who want to ski across the street. The look is a no-frills fun, family-style place.

6

There's a restaurant and a loose, sports-style pub. **Pros:** simple, no-frills family place; playground. **Cons:** a bit run-down. ⊠ *U.S. 302 03812* ☎ *603/374–6501 or 800/862–1600* ⊕ *www.attitashmtvillage.com* ⇄ *350 units* ♿ *In-room: no a/c (some), kitchen, refrigerator (some), DVD, Wi-Fi. In-hotel: restaurant, bar, tennis courts, pools, gym, bicycles, laundry facilities, laundry service, public Internet, public Wi-Fi, some pets allowed, no-smoking rooms* ▤ *AE, D, MC, V.*

$$ 🏨 **Grand Summit Hotel & Conference Center.** The contemporary ski hotel at the base of Attitash Bear Peak is the choice for skiers who want ski-in, ski-out convenience. Attractive contemporary-style rooms have kitchenettes, video game TVs, and stereos. Standard rooms have balconies. The main dining room serves passable American fare; dishes at Crawford's Pub and Grill are lighter. **Pros:** ski-in ski-out, nice pool and hot tubs, cheaper with ski package. **Cons:** gerneally bland accommodations. ⊠ *U.S. 302 03812* ☎ *603/374–1900 or 888/554–1900* ⊕ *www. attitash.com* ⇄ *143 rooms* ♿ *In-room: kitchen (some), Wi-Fi. In-hotel: 2 restaurants, room service, bars, pool, gym, children's programs (ages 2–14), laundry facilities, laundry service, concierge, public Internet, public Wi-Fi, no-smoking rooms* ▤ *AE, D, MC, V.*

JACKSON

★ *5 mi north of Glen.*

Just off Route 16 via a red covered bridge, Jackson has retained its storybook New England character. Art and antiques shopping, tennis, golf, fishing, and hiking to waterfalls are among the draws. When the snow falls, Jackson becomes the state's cross-country skiing capital. Four downhill ski areas are nearby.

WHAT TO SEE

☾ **Story Land.** That cluster of fluorescent buildings along Route 16 is a

Fodor'sChoice theme park with life-size storybook and nursery-rhyme characters. The

★ 20 rides and five shows include a flume ride, Victorian-theme river-raft ride, farm tractor–inspired kiddie ride, pumpkin coach, variety show (presented in a new theater, which opened in 2004), and swan boats. In early spring, only parts of the park are open and admission is reduced to $16. ⊠ *Rte. 16* ☎ *603/383–4186* ⊕ *www.storylandnh.com* 💳 *$21* ⊙ *Mid-June–Labor Day, daily 9–6; Memorial Day–mid-June and Labor Day–Columbus Day, weekends 10–5.*

SPORTS & THE OUTDOORS

Nestlenook Farm (⊠ *Dinsmore Rd.* ☎ *603/383–9443*) maintains an outdoor ice-skating rink with rentals, music, and a bonfire. Going snowshoeing or taking a sleigh ride are other winter options; in summer you can fly-fish or ride in a horse-drawn carriage.

SKI AREAS   **Black Mountain.** Friendly, informal, Black Mountain has a warming southern exposure. The Family Passport, which allows two adults and two juniors to ski at discounted rates, is a good value. Midweek rates here ($29) are usually the lowest in Mt. Washington Valley. The 40 trails and glades on the 1,100-vertical-foot mountain are evenly divided among beginner, intermediate, and expert. There's a nursery for kids six months and up. ⊠*Rte. 16B* ☎*603/383–4490, 800/475–4669 snow conditions* ⊕*www.blackmt.com.*

★ **Jackson Ski Touring Foundation.** One of the nation's top four cross-country skiing areas has 97 mi of trails. About 60 mi are track groomed, and 53 mi are skate groomed. There are roughly 39 mi of marked backcountry trails. You can arrange lessons and rentals at the lodge, in the center of Jackson Village. ⊠*153 Main St., Jackson* ☎*603/383–9355* ⊕*www.jacksonxc.org.*

WHERE TO EAT

$ ✕**Red Fox Bar & Grille.** Some say this big family restaurant overlooking
AMERICAN the Wentworth Golf Club gets its name from a wily fox with a penchant for stealing golf balls off the fairway. The wide-ranging menu has barbecued ribs, wood-fired pizzas, and blue-cheese-and-bacon burgers as well as more substantial dishes such as seared sea scallops with Grand Marnier sauce. The Sunday jazz breakfast buffet draws raves. ⊠*49 Rte. 16* ☎*603/383–4949* ⊟*AE, D, MC, V* ⊘*No lunch weekdays.*

$$-$$$ ✕**Thompson House Eatery.** One of the most innovative restaurants in
★ generally staid northern New Hampshire, this romantic eatery inside a
AMERICAN rambling red farmhouse serves such world-beat fare as skewered applewood-smoked shrimp over baby greens with fresh melon and balsamic vinegar. The entrée of grilled lamb chops with cucumber-tomato relish over Israeli couscous, Greek olives, and pancetta wins raves all around. ⊠*193 Main St.* ☎*603/383–9341* ⊟*AE, D, MC, V* ⊘*Closed Apr.–early May. No lunch Mon.–Wed. late May–early Oct., no lunch Thurs. early Oct.–Mar.*

$$$ ✕**Thorn Hill.** The dining room at the famous inn serves up one of New
Fodor'sChoice England's most memorable meals. In warm months dine on the decid-
★ edly romantic porch, which is lined with hanging candles and over-
AMERICAN looks the Presidential mountain range. The wine list is the state's most lauded, with 1,900 labels. It's also fun: the three 2-ounce-glass tasting is affordable and the glasses come with identification tags near the stems. The curated "Top 50" list of changing reasonably priced bottles is a sure guide. Chef John Russ brings subtle and flavorful dishes. A roasted poussin, an organic free-range game hen with grilled bacon and jus, is served with a wonderful Jerusalem artichoke salad. ⊠*42 Thorn Hill Rd.* ☎*603/383–4242 or 800/289–8990* ⚖*Reservations essential* ⊟*AE, D, MC, V* ⊘*No lunch.*

WHERE TO STAY

$ ⌂**Christmas Farm Inn and Spa.** Despite its wintery name, this 1778 inn is an all-season retreat. Rooms in the main building and the saltbox next door have Laura Ashley and Ralph Lauren prints. Other rooms are set in a delightful old barn, in a sugarhouse, and in a few cottages set about the wooded grounds. In the main inn parlor, a Christmas tree is up all year, and there's a great fireplace. The inn's gardens are spectacular. The twelve suites in the contemporary carriage house have two-person whirlpool tubs and gas fireplaces. **Pros:** kids welcome, nice pools. **Cons:** saltbox rooms could use improvement. ⊠*Rte. 16B, Box CC 03846* ☎*603/383–4313 or 800/443–5837* ⊕*www.christmasfarminn.*

com ⮌22 rooms, 15 suites, 5 2-bedroom cottages &In-room: Wi-Fi. In-hotel: restaurant, bar, pool, gym, spa, no elevator, public Wi-Fi, no-smoking rooms ⊟AE, MC, V ⎮O⎮BP.

$ **Inn at Jackson.** This B&B is impeccably maintained, charmingly fur-
Fodor'sChoice   nished, and bright: the pride of ownership shines through. The beautiful
★   inn, a 1902 Victorian designed by Stanford White for the Baldwin family of piano fame, overlooks the village. The foyer's staircase is grand,
but there's a remarkable relaxed and unpretentious ambience and a
great value. The airy guest rooms have oversize windows; eight have
fireplaces. The exceptional full breakfast may include anything from
egg soufflé casserole to blueberry pancakes. **Pros:** super-clean rooms,
great value, peaceful setting. **Cons:** third-floor rooms lack fireplaces.
⊠Thorn Hill Rd., Box 822 03846 ☎603/383–4321 or 800/289–8860
⊕www.innatjackson.com ⮌14 rooms &In-room: DVD, Wi-Fi. In-
hotel: no elevator, public Internet, public Wi-Fi, no kids under 7, no-
smoking rooms ⊟AE, D, MC, V ⎮O⎮BP.

$ **Inn at Thorn Hill.** You won't find a more subtle sophistication any-
Fodor'sChoice   where in New Hampshire than the total experience at Thorn Hill: the
★   dining (considered to be among the country's top hotel meals), service,
and relaxed elegance here are unrivaled. Besides the setting and the
great house (modeled after the Stanford White Victorian that burned
down a decade ago), the brilliance stems from owner/innkeepers James
and Ibby Cooper, wonderful hosts who run the place with aplomb.
Much of the staff are young British interns, who add life and profes-
sionalism to the inn and the dining. All of the rooms abound with cushy
amenities: two-person Jacuzzis, fireplaces, and TVs with DVDs. The
top units have steam showers, wet bars, and refrigerators. Cottages
and rooms in the carriage house are less thrilling. A full spa provides
a full range of beauty treatments and massages. Afternoon tea and a
substantial full breakfast and dinner are included: it's a great value, too.
Pros: great meals; great service; romantic setting. **Cons:** fee for wireless Internet. ⊠42 Thorn Hill Rd., Box A 03846 ☎603/383–4242
or 800/289–8990 ⊕www.innatthornhill.com ⮌15 rooms, 7 suites, 3
cottages &In-room: refrigerator (some), DVD (some), no TV (some),
Wi-Fi. In-hotel: restaurant, room service, bar, pool, gym, spa, laundry
service, public Wi-Fi, no kids under 12, no-smoking rooms ⊟AE, D,
MC, V ⎮O⎮MAP.

MT. WASHINGTON

★   *20 mi northwest of Jackson.*

In summer you can drive to the top of Mt. Washington, the highest
peak (6,288 feet) in the northeastern United States and the site of a
weather station that recorded the world's highest winds, 231 mi per
hour, in 1934. (⇨ Bretton Woods for information on the Mt. Wash-
ingtown Cog Railway.)

WHAT TO SEE
Mt. Washington Auto Road. Opened in 1861, this route begins at the Glen
House, a gift shop and rest stop 15 mi north of Glen on Route 16, and
winds its way up the east side of the mountain, ending at the top, an 8-

mi and approximately half-hour drive later. At the summit is the Sherman Adams Summit Building, built in 1979 and containing a visitor center and a museum focusing on the mountain's geology and extreme weather conditions; you can stand in the glassed-in viewing area to hear the wind roar. The Mt. Washington Observatory is at the building's western end. There are rules limiting what cars may use the road. For instance, cars with automatic transmission must be able to shift down into first gear. It is also possible to reach the top along several rough hiking trails; those who hoof it can make the return trip via shuttle, tickets for which are sold at the Stage Office, at the summit at the end of the cog railway trestle. Remember that the temperature atop Mt. Washington will be much colder than down below—the average year-round is below freezing and the average wind velocity is 35 mph. ⊠ *Rte. 16, Pinkham Notch* ☎ *603/466–3988* ⊕ *www.mountwashington autoroad.com* ⚞ *Car and driver $20, each additional adult passenger $7* ⊙ *Mid-June–early Sept., daily 7:30–6; May–mid-June and early Sept.–late Oct., daily 8–4, 8–5, or 8–5:30; call for specifics.*

SnowCoaches. In winter, when the road is closed to private vehicles, you can opt to reach the top of Mt. Washington via a guided tour in one of the four-wheel-drive vehicles that leave from Great Glen Trails Outdoor Center, just south of Gorham, on a first-come, first-served basis. Great Glen's nine-passenger vans are refitted with snowmobile-like treads and can travel to just above the tree line. You have the option of cross-country skiing, tubing, or snowshoeing down. ⊠ *Rte. 16, Pinkham Notch* ☎ *603/466–2333* ⊕ *www.greatglentrails.com* ⚞ *$40 (includes all-day trail pass)* ⊙ *Dec.–Mar., snow necessary, most days, beginning at 9:15.*

SPORTS & THE OUTDOORS

Although not a town per se, scenic **Pinkham Notch** covers Mt. Washington's eastern side and includes several ravines, including Tuckerman Ravine, famous for spring skiing. The Appalachian Mountain Club maintains a large visitor center here on Route 16 that provides information to hikers and travelers and has guided hikes, outdoor skills workshops, a cafeteria, lodging, regional topography displays, and an outdoors shop.

HIKING The **Appalachian Mountain Club Pinkham Notch Visitor Center** (⊠ *Rte. 16, Box 298, Gorham 03581* ☎ *603/466–2721, 603/466–2727 reservations* ⊕ *www.outdoors.org*) has lectures, workshops, slide shows, and outdoor skills instruction year-round. Accommodations include the adjacent Joe Dodge Lodge, the Highland Center at Crawford Notch with 100-plus beds and a 16-bed bunkhouse next to it, as well as the club's eight high-mountain huts spaced one day's hike from each other in the White Mountain National Forest portion of the Appalachian Trail. The huts provide meals and dorm-style lodging from June to late September or early October; the rest of the year they are self-service.

SKI AREAS **Great Glen Trails Outdoor Center.** Amenities at this fabulous new lodge at the base of Mt. Washington include a huge ski-gear and sports shop, food court, climbing wall, observation deck, and fieldstone fireplace. In winter it's renowned for its dramatic 24-mi cross-country trail system. Some trails have snowmaking, and there's access to more than 1,100 acres of backcountry. It's even possible to ski or snowshoe the lower half of the Mt. Washington Auto Road. Trees shelter most of the trails, so Mt. Washington's infamous weather isn't a concern. In summer it's the base from which hikers, mountain bikers, and trail runners can explore Mt. Washington. The center also has programs in canoeing, kayaking, and fly-fishing. ⊠ *Rte. 16, Pinkham Notch* ☎ *603/466-2333* ⊕ *www.greatglentrails.com.*

Wildcat. Glade skiers favor Wildcat, with 28 acres of official tree skiing. The 47 runs include some stunning double-black-diamond trails. Skiers who can hold a wedge should check out the 2½-mi-long Polecat. Experts can zip down the Lynx. Views of Mt. Washington and Tuckerman Ravine are superb. The trails are classic New England— narrow and winding. Wildcat's expert runs deserve their designations and then some. Intermediates have mid-mountain–to-base trails, and beginners will find gentle terrain and a broad teaching slope. Snowboarders have several terrain parks and the run of the mountain. In summer you can ride to the top on the four-passenger gondola ($10) and hike the many well-kept trails. ⊠ *Rte. 16, Pinkham Notch, Jackson* ☎ *603/466-3326, 888/754-9453 snow conditions, 800/255-6439 lodging* ⊕ *www.skiwildcat.com.*

DIXVILLE NOTCH

63 mi north of Mt. Washington, 66 mi northeast of Littleton, 149 mi north of Concord.

Just 12 mi from the Canadian border, this tiny community is known for two things. One is the Balsams, one of New Hampshire's oldest and most celebrated resorts. The other is the fact that Dixville Notch and another New Hampshire community, Hart's Location, are the first election districts in the nation to vote in presidential general elections. When the 30 or so Dixville Notch voters file into the little Balsams meeting room on the eve of election day and cast their ballots at the stroke of midnight, they invariably make national news.

One of the favorite pastimes in this area is spotting moose, those large, ungainly, yet elusive members of the deer family. Although you may catch sight of one or more yourself, **Northern Forest Moose Tours** (☎ *603/466-3103 or 800/992-7480*) conducts bus tours of the region that have a 97% success rate for spotting moose.

OFF THE BEATEN PATH

Pittsburg. Well north of the White Mountains, in the Great North Woods, Pittsburg contains the four Connecticut Lakes and the springs that form the Connecticut River. The state's northern tip—a chunk of about 250 square mi—lies within the town's borders, the result of a dispute between the United States and Canada that began in 1832 and was resolved in 1842, when the international boundary was fixed.

Remote though it is, this frontier town teems with hunters, boaters, fishermen, hikers, and photographers from early summer through winter. Especially in the colder months, moose sightings are common. The town has more than a dozen lodges and several informal eateries. It's about a 90-minute drive from Littleton and 40-minute drive from Dixville Notch; add another 30 minutes to reach Fourth Connecticut Lake, nearly at the Canadian border. On your way, you pass the village of Stewartson, exactly midway between the Equator and the North Pole.

SPORTS & THE OUTDOORS

Dixville Notch State Park (⊠ *Rte. 26* ☎ *603/538–6707*), in the northernmost notch of the White Mountains, has picnic areas, a waterfall, two mountain brooks, and hiking trails.

SKI AREAS **Balsams.** Skiing was originally provided as an amenity for hotel guests at the Balsams, but the area has become popular with day-trippers as well. Slopes with such names as Sanguinary, Umbagog, and Magalloway may sound tough, but they're only moderately difficult, leaning toward intermediate. There are 16 trails and four glades for every skill level from the top of the 1,000-foot vertical. The Balsams has 59 mi of cross-country skiing, tracked and groomed for skating. Natural-history markers annotate some trails; you can also try telemark and backcountry skiing, and there are 21 mi of snowshoeing trails. ⊠ *Rte. 26* ☎ *603/255–3400, 603/255–3951 snow conditions, 800/255–0600, 800/255–0800 in New Hampshire* ⊕ *www.thebalsams.com.*

WHERE TO EAT

Fodor'sChoice **Le Rendez Vous.** You might not expect to find an authentic French bakery and pastry shop in the small workaday village of Colebrook, 10 mi west of Dixville Notch, but Le Rendez Vous serves simply fabulous tarts and treats—the owners came here directly from Paris. Drop in to this quaint café furnished with several tables and armchairs for coffee, hand-dipped Belgian chocolates, croissants, a tremendous variety of fresh-baked breads, and all sorts of gourmet foods, from dried fruits and nuts to lentils, olive oils, and balsamic vinegar. ⊠ *146 Main St., Colebrook* ☎ *603/237–5150.*
★
FRENCH

WHERE TO STAY

$-$$ **The Balsams.** Nestled in the pine groves of the North Woods, this lavish grande dame has been rolling out the red carpet since 1866. The Balsams encompasses some 15,000 wooded acres—an area roughly the size of the New York City borough of Manhattan. Even when the resort is filled to capacity (figure about 400 guests and another 400 employees), it's still a remarkably solitary place. It draws families, golf enthusiasts, skiers, and others for a varied slate of activities—from dancing to cooking demonstrations. Rooms here are spacious, with large cedar-lined closets and ample dressers. Floral-print wallpaper, modern bathrooms, full-length mirrors, and reproduction antiques impart a dignified old-world grace. Most rooms have views overlooking the lake, gardens, and mountains; still, always inquire about the view when booking, as a handful afford less-promising vistas (the parking area, for example). In the dining room ($$$$; jacket and tie), you might sample a chilled strawberry soup spiked with Grand Marnier, followed
★

by broiled swordfish with white beans and lemon coulis. Rates include breakfast and dinner and unlimited use of the facilities. Pros: splendid grand resort; activities galore. Cons: grand scale limits intimacy. ⊠*Rte. 26 03576* ☎*603/255–3400, 800/255–0600, 800/255–0800 in NH* ⊕*www.thebalsams.com* ⇋*184 rooms, 20 suites* ⚫*In-room: no TV (some). In-hotel: 3 restaurants, room service, bar, golf course, tennis courts, pool, gym, bicycles, children's programs (ages 1–12), laundry service, no-smoking rooms* ⊟*AE, D, MC, V* ⑩*FAP, MAP.*

$–$$ ⊞ **The Glen.** This rustic lodge with stick furniture, fieldstone, and cedar sits amid 180 pristine acres on First Connecticut Lake and is surrounded by log cabins, seven of which are right on the water. The cabins have efficiency kitchens and mini-refrigerators—not that you'll need either, because rates include hearty meals, served family-style, in the lodge restaurant. Pros: rustic, remote setting; charming lodge; loads of character. Cons: remote; not luxurious. ⊠*118 Glen Rd., 1 mi off U.S. 3, Pittsburg* ☎*603/538–6500 or 800/445–4536* ⊕*www.theglen. org* ⇋*6 rooms, 9 cabins* ⚫*In-room: no phone, kitchen, no TV. In-hotel: restaurant, no-smoking rooms* ⊟*No credit cards* ⊘*Closed mid-Oct.–mid-May* ⑩*FAP.*

NORTH CONWAY

76 mi south of Dixville Notch, 7 mi south of Glen, 41 mi east of Lincoln/North Woodstock.

Before the arrival of the outlet stores, the town drew visitors for its inspiring scenery, ski resorts, and access to White Mountain National Forest. Today, however, the feeling of natural splendor is gone. Shopping is the big sport, and businesses line Route 16 for several miles. You'll get a close look at them because traffic slows to a crawl here. You can take scenic West Side Road from Conway to Intervale to circumvent the traffic and take in splendid views.

Ⓒ   The **Conway Scenic Railroad** operates trips aboard vintage trains from historic North Conway Station. The Notch Train, through Crawford Notch to Crawford Depot (a 5-hour round trip) or Fabyan Station (5½ hours), offers wonderful scenic views from the domed observation coach. The Valley Train provides views of Mt. Washington countryside on a 55-minute round trip to Conway or a 1¾-hour trip to Bartlett—lunch and dinner are served on some departures. The 1874 station displays lanterns, old tickets and timetables, and other railroad artifacts. Reserve early during foliage season for the dining excursions. ⊠*Rte. 16 (U.S. 302), 38 Norcross Circle* ☎*603/356–5251 or 800/232–5251* ⊕*www.conwayscenic. com* ⊠*$12–$60* ⊘*Mid-Apr.–mid Dec; call for times.*

WHAT TO SEE

Ⓒ   **Hartmann Model Railroad Museum.** This building houses about 2,000 engines, more than 5,000 cars and coaches, and 14 operating layouts (from G to Z scales), in addition to a café, a crafts store, a hobby shop, and an outdoor miniature trains that you can sit on and ride. ⊠ *15 Town Hall Rd. at Rte. 16 (U.S. 302), Intervale* ☎*603/356–9922* ⊕*www.hartmannrr.com* ⊠*$6* ⊘*Daily 10–5.*

Weather Discovery Center. The hands-on exhibits at this meteorological educational facility teach how weather is monitored and how it affects us. The center is a collaboration between the National and Atmospheric Administration Forecast Systems lab and the Mt. Washington Observatory at the summit of Mt. Washington. ⊠ *Rte. 16 (U.S. 302), 1/5 mi south of rail tracks* ☎ *603/356–2137* ⊕ *www.mountwashington.org* ⊠ *$5* ⊙ *May–Oct., daily 10–5; Nov.–Apr., Sat.–Mon. 10–5 (also open daily during school vacation from mid-Feb. to early Mar.).*

SPORTS & THE OUTDOORS

Echo Lake State Park. You needn't be a rock climber to catch views from the 700-foot White Horse and Cathedral ledges in From the top you'll see the entire valley, in which Echo Lake shines like a diamond. An unmarked trailhead another .7 mi on West Side Road leads to Diana's Baths, a series of waterfalls. ⊠ *Off U.S 302* ☎ *603/271–3556* ⊠ *$3* ⊙ *Late May–mid-June, weekends dawn–dusk; mid-June–early Sept., daily dawn–dusk.*

CANOEING & KAYAKING
River outfitter **Saco Bound Canoe & Kayak** (⊠ *Rte. 16 [U.S. 302], Conway* ☎ *603/447–2177* ⊕ *www.sacobound.com*) leads gentle canoeing expeditions, guided kayak trips, and white-water rafting on seven rivers and provides lessons, equipment, and transportation.

FISHING
North Country Angler (⊠ *2888 White Mountain Hwy.* ☎ *603/356–6000* ⊕ *www.northcountryangler.com*) schedules intensive guided fly-fishing weekends throughout the region. It's one of the best tackle shops in the state.

SKI AREAS
Cranmore Mountain Resort. This downhill ski area has been a favorite of families since it began operating in 1938. Five glades have opened more skiable terrain. The 39 trails are well laid out and fun to ski. Most runs are naturally formed intermediates that weave in and out of glades. Beginners have several slopes and routes from the summit; experts must be content with a few short, steep pitches. In addition to the trails, snowboarders have a terrain park and a half-pipe. Night skiing is offered Thursday–Saturday and holidays. ⊠ *1 Skimobile Rd., North Conway 03860* ☎ *603/356–5543, 603/356–8516 snow conditions, 800/786–6754 lodging* ⊕ *www.cranmore.com.*

King Pine Ski Area at Purity Spring Resort. Some 9 mi south of Conway, this family-run ski area has been going strong since the late 19th century. Some ski-and-stay packages include free skiing for midweek resort guests. Among the facilities and activities are an indoor pool and fitness complex, and ice-skating. King Pine's 16 gentle trails are ideal for beginner and intermediate skiers; experts won't be challenged except for a brief pitch on the Pitch Pine trail. There's tubing on weekend afternoons and night skiing and tubing on Friday and Saturday. There are 9 mi of cross-country skiing. An indoor fitness center is open year-round. In summer this lively place is a big hit for waterskiing, kayaking, loon-watching, tennis, hiking, and other activities; lodging packages are available. ⊠ *Rte. 153, East Madison* ☎ *603/367–8896 or 800/373–3754* ⊕ *www.purityspring.com.*

6

Forty miles of groomed cross-country trails weave through North Conway and the countryside along the **Mt. Washington Valley Ski Touring Association Network** (⊠*Rte. 16, Intervale* ☎*603/356–9920 or 800/282–5220* ⊕*www.crosscountryskinh.com*).

SHOPPING

ANTIQUES **Richard Plusch Antiques** (⊠*Rte. 16 [U.S. 302]* ☎603/356–3333) deals in period furniture and accessories, including glass, sterling silver, Oriental porcelains, rugs, and paintings.

CRAFTS **Handcrafters Barn** (⊠*Main St.* ☎603/356–8996) stocks the work of 350 area artists and artisans. The **League of New Hampshire Craftsmen** (⊠*2526 Main St.* ☎603/356–2441) carries the creations of the state's best artisans. **Zeb's General Store** (⊠*2675 Main St.* ☎603/356–9294 or 800/676–9294) looks just like an old-fashioned country store; it sells food items, crafts, and other products made in New England.

CLOTHES More than 150 factory outlets—including L.L. Bean, Timberland, Pfaltzgraff, London Fog, Polo, Nike, Anne Klein, and Woolrich—line Route 16. A top pick for skiwear is **Joe Jones** (⊠*2709 Main St.* ☎603/356–9411).

NIGHTLIFE & THE ARTS

Horsefeather's (⊠*Main St.* ☎603/356–6862), a restaurant and bar, often has rock, blues, and folk music, especially on weekends.

WHERE TO EAT

$-$$ ✕**Delaney's Hole in the Wall.** This casual sports tavern has eclectic memorabilia such as autographed baseballs and an early photo of skiing at Tuckerman Ravine hanging over the fireplace. Entrées range from fish-and-chips to fajitas to mussels and scallops sautéed with spiced sausage and Louisiana seasonings. There's live music most nights. ⊠*Rte. 16, ¼ mi north of North Conway Village* ☎603/356–7776 ☐*AE, D, MC, V.*

AMERICAN

¢-$ ✕**Muddy Moose.** This family place is inviting and rustic thanks to its fieldstone walls, exposed wood, and understated lighting. Dig into a Greek salad, grilled chicken Caesar wrap, char-grilled pork chops with a maple-cider glaze, or muddy moose pie, the signature ice cream, fudge and crumbled Oreo dessert. ⊠*Rte. 16 just south of North Conway* ☎603/356–7696 ☐*AE, D, MC, V* ⚬*No reservations accepted.*

AMERICAN

WHERE TO STAY

$ ▦**Buttonwood Inn.** A tranquil 17-acre oasis in this busy resort area, the Buttonwood is on Mt. Surprise, 2 mi northeast of North Conway Village. Staying here you can have a peaceful retreat and avoid the noise of downtown but still have access to area restaurants and shopping. Rooms in the 1820s farmhouse are furnished in Shaker style. Wide pine floors, quilts, and period stenciling add warmth. Two rooms have gas fireplaces. Downstairs is the Mt. Surprise room which has a self-serve bar, library, board games, and DVD library. **Pros:** good bedding and amenities, tranquil, clean. **Cons:** unexciting for those not wanting a remote getaway. ⊠*Mt. Surprise Rd* ☎603/356–2625 or 800/258–2625 ⊕*www.buttonwoodinn.com* ⚲*8 rooms, 2 suites* ⚬*In-room:*

DVD (some), no TV. In-hotel: pool, no elevator, public Internet, public Wi-Fi, no-smoking rooms ☰*AE, MC, V* ⏸*BP.*

$ 📷**Darby Field Inn.** After a day of activity in the White Mountains, warm up by this inn's fieldstone fireplace or by the bar's woodstove. Most rooms in this unpretentious 1826 farmhouse have mountain views; several have fireplaces. There are 10 mi of cross-countrry and hiking trails, as well as carriage rides and sleigh rides. The inn's dining room prepares such haute regional American fare. **Pros:** clean, romantic, remote. **Cons:** best for couples. ✉*185 Chase Hill, Albany* ☎*603/447–2181 or 800/426–4147* ⊕*www.darbyfield.com* ✎*9 rooms, 4 suites* ♿*In-room: no a/c (some), no phone, DVD (some), VCR (some), no TV (some), Wi-Fi. In-hotel: restaurant, bar, pool, no elevator, public Wi-Fi, no kids under 8, no-smoking rooms* ☰*AE, MC, V* ⊙*Closed Apr.* ⏸*BP.*

$$–$$$ 📷**Snowvillage Inn.** Journalist Frank Simonds built the gambrel-roofed ★ main house in 1916. To complement the tome-jammed bookshelves, guest rooms are named for famous authors; many have fireplaces. The nicest of the rooms, with 12 windows that look out over the Presidential Range, is a tribute to Robert Frost. Two additional buildings—the carriage house and the chimney house—also have libraries. The menu in the candlelit dining room ($$–$$$$; reservations essential) might include roasted rack of lamb with minted onion marmalade, pistachio-encrusted salmon, or a medley of young duckling prepared three ways. The inn is also home to the White Mountain Cooking School, and overnight packages with cooking classes are available. You can hike easily up to beautiful Foss Mountain, directly from the inn. **Pros:** adorable property; fine dining. **Cons:** on the pricier side. ✉*Stewart Rd., 6 mi southeast of Conway, Snowville 03832* ☎*603/447–2818 or 800/447–4345* ⊕*www.snowvillageinn.com* ✎*18 rooms* ♿*In-room: no TV. In-hotel: restaurant, no kids under 6, no-smoking rooms, no-smoking rooms* ☰*AE, D, MC, V* ⏸*BP, MAP.*

$$$ 📷**White Mountain Hotel and Resort.** West of the traffic of North Conway, the scenery becomes splendid. Rooms in this hotel at the base of Whitehorse Ledge have mountain views. Proximity to the White Mountain National Forest and Echo Lake State Park makes you feel farther away from the outlet malls than you actually are. There's a 9-hole golf course and this is a great area for biking. Three meals a day are available at the at Ledges dining room; there's also a tavern. Kids 18 and under stay free. **Pros:** scenic setting that's close to shopping; lots of activities. **Cons:** two-night minimum summer weekends. ✉*West Side Rd., 03860* ☎*800/533–6301* ☎🖶*603/356–7100* ⊕*www.whitemountain hotel.com* ✎*80 rooms, 13 suites* ♿*In-room: DVD, VCR, Wi-Fi. In-hotel: 2 restaurants, room service, bar, golf course, tennis court, pool, gym, public Internet, public Wi-Fi, no-smoking rooms* ☰*AE, D, MC, V* ⏸*BP, MAP.*

EN ROUTE A great place to settle in to the White Mountains, take in one of the greatest panoramas of the muntains, and get visitor info is at the **Intervale Scenic Vista.** The stop, off Route 16 a few miles north of North Conway, is run by the DOT, has a helpful volunteer staff, and features a wonderful large topographical map and terrific bathrooms.

KANCAMAGUS HIGHWAY

★ *36 mi between Conway and Lincoln/North Woodstock.*

Interstate 93 is the fastest way to the White Mountains, but it's hardly the most appealing. The section of Route 112 known as the Kancamagus Highway passes through some of the state's most unspoiled mountain scenery—it was one of the first roads in the nation to be designated a National Scenic Byway. The Kanc, as it's called by locals, is punctuated by overlooks and picnic areas, erupts into fiery color each fall, when photo-snapping drivers can really slow things down. There are campgrounds off the highway. In bad weather, check with the White Mountains Visitors Bureau for road conditions.

SPORTS & THE OUTDOORS

A couple of short hiking trails off the Kancamagus Highway (Route 112) yield great rewards for relatively little effort. The **Lincoln Woods Trail** starts from the large parking lot of the Lincoln Woods Visitor Center, 4 mi east of Lincoln. You can purchase the recreation pass ($5 per vehicle, good for seven consecutive days) needed to park in any of the White Mountain National Forest lots or overlooks here; stopping briefly to take photos or to use the restrooms at the visitor center is permitted without a pass. The trail crosses a suspension bridge over the Pemigewasset River and follows an old railroad bed for 3 mi along the river. The parking and picnic area for **Sabbaday Falls,** about 15 mi west of Conway, is the trailhead for an easy ½-mi route to a multilevel cascade that plunges through two potholes and a flume.

DARTMOUTH–LAKE SUNAPEE

In the west-central part of the state, the towns around prestigious Dartmouth College and rippling Lake Sunapee vary from sleepy, old-fashioned outposts that haven't changed much in decades to bustling, sophisticated towns rife with cafés, art galleries, and boutiques. Among the latter, Hanover and New London are the area's main hubs, both of them becoming increasingly popular as vacation destinations and with telecommuters seeking a quieter, more economical home base. Although distinct from the Lakes Region, greater Lake Sunapee looks like a miniature Lake Winnipesaukee, albeit with far less commercial development. For a great drive, follow the Lake Sunapee Scenic & Cultural Byway, which runs for about 25 mi from Georges Mills (a bit northwest of New London) down into Warner, tracing much of the Lake Sunapee shoreline. When you've tired of climbing and swimming and visiting the past, look for small studios of area artists. This part of the state, along with the even quieter Monadnocks area to the south, has long been an informal artists' colony where people come to write, paint, and weave in solitude.

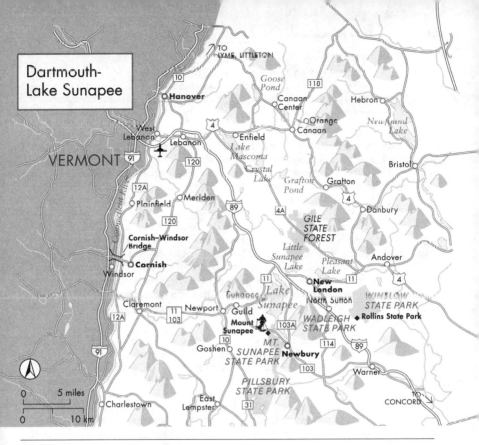

NEW LONDON

16 mi northwest of Warner, 25 mi west of Tilton.

New London, the home of Colby-Sawyer College (1837), is a good base for exploring the Lake Sunapee region. A campus of stately Colonial-style buildings fronts the vibrant commercial district, where you'll find several cafés and boutiques.

SPORTS & THE OUTDOORS

A 3½-mi scenic auto road at **Rollins State Park** (⊠ *Off Rte. 103, Main St., Warner* ☎603/456–3808 ☞*$3*) snakes up the southern slope of Mt. Kearsarge, where you can hike a ½-mi trail to the summit. The road is closed mid-November through mid-June.

SHOPPING

Artisan's Workshop (⊠ *Peter Christian's Tavern, 196 Main St.* ☎603/526–4227) carries jewelry, glass, and other local handicrafts. Near New London in the tiny village of Elkins, **Mesa Home Factory Store** (⊠ *Elkins Bus. Loop* ☎603/526–4497) carries striking hand-painted dinnerware, handblown glassware, wrought-iron decorative arts, and other housewares at bargain prices.

THE ARTS

The **New London Barn Playhouse** (✉ *84 Main St.* ☎ *603/526–6710 or 800/633–2276* ⊕ *www.nlbarn.com*) presents Broadway-style and children's plays every summer in New Hampshire's oldest continuously operating theater.

WHERE TO EAT

$-$$ | ✗ **Four Corners Grille and Flying Goose Brew Pub.** South of downtown, this
AMERICAN | inviting restaurant and adjoining pub is known for massive burgers, pit-barbecued meats, calamari in basil pesto, great ales, and exceptional views of Mt. Kearsarge. More substantial victuals include jambalaya with shrimp, scallops, mussels, and sausage, and char-grilled teriyaki steaks. There's live folk and light rock music many nights. ✉ *40 Andover Rd., Rtes. 11 and 114* ☎ *603/526–6899* ▤ *AE, D, MC, V.*

$ | ✗ **Jack's Coffee.** Nominally a coffeehouse, Jack's is actually much more,
CAFE | presenting a nice range of bountiful salads (try the lemon Caesar) and designer sandwiches. It also has a great breakfast. The restaurant occupies a stately Greek-revival house in the heart of downtown, and a tree-shaded patio out front overlooks the pedestrian action. ✉ *207 Main St.* ☎ *603/526–8003* ▤ *D, MC, V* ☺ *No dinner.*

WHERE TO STAY

$-$$ | 🏠 **Inn at Pleasant Lake.** This 1790s inn lies just across Pleasant Lake
★ | from majestic Mt. Kearsarge. Its spacious rooms have country antiques and modern bathrooms. The restaurant ($$$$; reservations essential) presents a nightly changing prix-fixe menu that draws raves for such entrées as roast tenderloin of Angus beef with a Calvados demi-glace and watercress pesto and such desserts as white-chocolate mousse with a trio of sauces. Afternoon tea and full breakfast are included. **Pros:** lakefront with a small beach; boating. **Cons:** away from town activities. ✉ *853 Pleasant St., 03257* ☎ *603/526–6271 or 800/626–4907* ⊕ *www.innatpleasantlake.com* ⇗ *10 rooms* ♿ *In-room: no phone, no TV. In-hotel: restaurant, gym, beachfront, no-smoking rooms* ▤ *MC, V* ❢ *BP.*

$-$$ | 🏠 **Follansbee Inn.** Built in 1840, this quintessential country inn on the shore of Kezar Lake is a perfect fit in the 19th-century village of North Sutton, about 4 mi south of New London. The common rooms and bedrooms are loaded with collectibles—a traveling trunk here, a wooden school desk there. Each of the 18 rooms is filled with soft country quilts, and several of them overlook the water. In winter, you can ice-fish, borrow the inn's snowshoes, or ski across the lake; in summer you can swim or boat from the inn's pier. A 3-mi walking trail circles the lake. **Pros:** relaxed lakefront setting; clean rooms. **Cons:** young children aren't allowed. ✉ *Rte. 114, North Sutton* ☎ *603/927–4221 or 800/626–4221* ⊕ *www.follansbeeinn.com* ⇗ *18 rooms* ♿ *In-room: no phone, no TV. In-hotel: water sports, bicycles, no kids under 10, no-smoking rooms* ▤ *MC, V* ❢ *BP.*

EN ROUTE About midway between New London and Newbury on the west side of the lake **Sunapee Harbor** is an old-fashioned, all-American summer resort community that feels a bit like a miniature version of Wolfeboro, with a large marina, a handful of restaurants and shops on the water, a tidy village green with a gazebo, and a small museum run by the historical society set in a Victorian stable. A plaque outside Wild Goose Country Store details some of Lake Sunapee's attributes—that it's one of the highest lakes in New Hampshire, at 1,091 feet above sea level, and that it's also one of the least polluted. An interpretive path runs along a short span of the Sugar River, the only outflow from Lake Sunapee, which winds for 18 mi to the Connecticut River.

NEWBURY

8 mi southwest of New London.

Newbury is on the edge of Mt. Sunapee State Park. The mountain, which rises to an elevation of nearly 3,000 feet, and the sparkling lake are the region's outdoor recreation centers. The popular League of New Hampshire Craftsmen's Fair, the nation's oldest crafts fair, is held at the base of Mt. Sunapee each August.

WHAT TO SEE

Fells. John M. Hay, who served as private secretary to Abraham Lincoln and secretary of state for Presidents McKinley and Roosevelt, built the Fells on Lake Sunapee as a summer home in 1890. House tours focus on his life in Newbury and Washington. Hay's son was responsible for the extensive gardens, a mix of formal and informal styles that include a 75-foot perennial border and a hillside planted with heather. More than 800 acres of the former estate are open for hiking and picnicking. ⊠ *Rte. 103A* ☎ *603/763–4789* ⊕ *www.thefells.org* ⊠ *$8* ⊙ *Labor Day–Columbus Day, daily 10–5; grounds daily dawn–dusk.*

SPORTS & THE OUTDOORS

BEACHES & FISHING
Sunapee State Beach has picnic areas, a beach, and a bathhouse. You can rent canoes here, too. ⊠ *Rte. 103* ☎ *603/763–5561* ⊠ *$3* ⊙ *Daily dawn–dusk.* **Lake Sunapee** has brook and lake trout, salmon, smallmouth bass, and pickerel.

BOAT TOURS
Narrated cruises aboard the **MV Mt. Sunapee II** (⊠ *Main St., Sunapee* ☎ *603/938–6465* ⊕ *www.sunapeecruises.com*) provide a closer look at Lake Sunapee's history and mountain scenery; they run from late May through mid-October, daily in summer and on weekends in spring and fall; the cost is $18. Dinner cruises are held on the **MV Kearsarge** (☎ *603/938–6465* ⊕ *www.mvkearsarge.com*); cruises leave from the dock at Sunapee Harbor, June through mid-October, Tuesday–Sunday evenings; the cost is $36, which includes a buffet dinner.

SKI AREA
Mount Sunapee. Although the resort is state-owned, it's managed by Vermont's Okemo Mountain Resort (in Ludlow) known for being family friendly. The agreement has allowed the influx of capital necessary for operating extensive lifts, snowmaking (97% coverage), and trail grooming. This mountain is 1,510 vertical feet and has 60 trails, mostly intermediate. Experts can take to a dozen slopes, including three nice double-black diamonds. Boarders have a 420-foot-long half pipe and a terrain park with music. In summer, the Sunapee Express Quad zooms you to the summit. From here, it's just under a mile hike to Lake Soli-

Maple Sugaring

It's the quintessential condiment of New England breakfasts, the core ingredient of cutely shaped candies, and one of New Hampshire's legendary exports: maple syrup. In fact, the Granite State produces about 90,000 gallons of this sweet elixir every year. And throughout the state, particularly in the Monadnock and Sunapee regions, a number of private sugarhouses open their doors to the public—you can visit to watch maple-sugaring demonstrations, or just to buy fresh syrup. A few sugarhouses even hold parties and festivals.

Stop at a sugar shack to watch maple sap become maple syrup.

The season generally runs from about mid-February through mid-April, depending on weather conditions. Sap runs best when daytime temperatures rise above freezing. Once collected in buckets from the trees, sap is taken to the sugarhouses, where it's boiled down and ultimately reduced to pure maple syrup. You need to boil down about 40 gallons of raw sap to get just a gallon of refined syrup. It's a time-consuming and rather painstaking process, which in part accounts for the relative high cost of pure maple syrup versus the treacly imitation variety sold in many grocery stores.

Make a note on your calendar to attend the state's foremost sugar-ing event, New Hampshire Maple Weekend, held in mid- to late March, when some 50 sugarhouses open their doors to guests, host pancake breakfasts, and show off their often impressive sugaring operations. For a list of syrup producers throughout the state, contact **New Hampshire Maple Producers** (☎ *603/225–3757* ⊕ *www.nhmapleproducers.com*). The organization also produces a cookbook containing some 200 maple recipes; you can order this book from the Web site for $14, which includes shipping and handling.

—Andrew Collins

tude. Mountain bikers can use the lift to many trails, and an in-line skate park has beginner and advanced sections (plus equipment rentals). ⊠*Rte. 103, 03772* ☎*603/763–2356, 603/763–4020 snow conditions, 877/687–8627 lodging* ⊕*www.mtsunapee.com.*

SHOPPING

Overlooking Lake Sunapee's southern tip, **Outspokin' Bicycle and Sport** (⊠*Rtes. 103 and 103A, at the harbor* ☎*603/763–9500*) has a tremendous selection of biking, hiking, skateboarding, waterskiing, skiing, and snowboarding clothing and equipment. Right on the harbor in Sunapee village, on the marina, **Wild Goose Country Store** (⊠*77 Main St.* ☎*603/763–5516*) carries quirky gifts, teddy bears, penny candy, pottery, and other engaging odds and ends.

WHERE TO STAY

$$$ ⭐ 🏨 **Sunapee Harbor Cottages.** A luxurious take on the classic cottage compounds that dot the Sunapee and Lakes regions, this particular collection of six contemporary shingle bungalows tumbles down a gentle hillside just steps from Sunapee Harbor's marina and restaurants. Each light and airy unit sleeps from five to eight people, making this a good deal for larger groups and a bit of a splurge for couples—all have kitchens, gas fireplaces, porches, and a well-chosen mix of antiques and newer furnishings. Nice touches include grocery-delivery service, in-room massage, and even catered meals prepared by the nearby Millstone Restaurant. Pros: clean, contemporary, spacious units. Cons: units are close to each other. ⌂ *4 Lake Ave., Sunapee Harbor* ☎ *603/763–5052 or 866/763–5052* ⊕ *www.sunapeeharborcottages. com* ⋈ *6 cottages* ♿ *In-room: kitchen, DVD, Wi-Fi, no elevator, no-smoking rooms* 🟰 *MC, V.*

HANOVER

12 mi northwest of Enfield, 62 mi northwest of Concord.

6

Eleazer Wheelock founded Hanover's Dartmouth College in 1769 to educate the Abenaki "and other youth." When he arrived, the town consisted of about 20 families. The college and the town grew symbiotically, with Dartmouth becoming the northernmost Ivy League school. Hanover is still synonymous with Dartmouth, but it's also a respected medical and cultural center for the upper Connecticut River valley.

WHAT TO SEE

⭐ **Dartmouth College.** Robert Frost spent part of a brooding freshman semester at this Ivy League school before giving up college altogether. The buildings that cluster around the green include the **Baker Memorial Library,** which houses such literary treasures as 17th-century editions of Shakespeare's works. The library is also well known for the 3,000-square-foot murals by Mexican artist José Clemente Orozco that depict the story of civilization on the American continents. If the towering arcade at the entrance to the **Hopkins Center** (☎ *603/646–2422*) appears familiar, it's probably because it resembles the project that architect Wallace K. Harrison completed just after designing it: New York City's Metropolitan Opera House at Lincoln Center. The complex includes a 900-seat theater for film showings and concerts, a 400-seat theater for plays, and a black-box theater for new plays. The Dartmouth Symphony Orchestra performs here, as does the Big Apple Circus. In addition to African, Peruvian, Oceanic, Asian, European, and American art, the **Hood Museum of Art** (⌂ *Wheelock St.* ☎ *603/646–2808* ⊕ *www.dartmouth.edu/hood* 🎟 *Free* ⊙ *Tues. and Thurs.–Sat. 10–5, Wed. 10–9, Sun. noon–5*) owns the Picasso painting *Guitar on a Table,* silver by Paul Revere, and a set of Assyrian reliefs from the 9th century BC. The range of contemporary works, including pieces by John Sloan, William Glackens, Mark Rothko, Fernand Léger, and Joan Miró, is particularly notable. Rivaling the collection is the museum's architecture: a series of austere, copper-roofed, redbrick buildings arranged around a courtyard. Free campus tours are available on request. ⊠*N. Main and Wentworth Sts.* ☎*603/646–1110.*

NEED A BREAK?

Take a respite from museum-hopping with a cup of espresso, a ham-and-cheese scone, or a freshly baked brownie at the Dirt Cowboy (⊠*7 S. Main St.* ☎*603/643–1323*), a café across from the green and beside a used-book store. A local branch of a small Boston chain, The Wrap (⊠*35 S. Main St.* ☎*603/643–0202*), occupies a slick basement space with comfy sofas and has a small patio to the side. Drop by for healthful burritos, wraps, soups (try the carrot-ginger), and smoothies and energy drinks.

★ **Enfield Shaker Museum.** In 1782, two Shaker brothers from Mount Lebanon, New York, arrived on Lake Mascoma's northeastern side, about 12 mi southeast of Hanover. Eventually, they formed Enfield, the 9th of 18 Shaker communities in this country, and moved it to the lake's southern shore, where they erected more than 200 buildings. The Enfield Shaker Museum preserves the legacy of the Shakers, who numbered 330 members at the village's peak. By 1923, interest in the society had dwindled, and the last 10 members joined the Canterbury community, south of Laconia. A self-guided walking tour takes you through 13 of the remaining buildings, among them the Great Stone Dwelling (which served until recently as a hotel, the Shaker Inn) and an 1849 stone mill. Demonstrations of Shaker crafts techniques and numerous special events take place year-round. ⊠*24 Caleb Dyer La., Enfield* ☎*603/632–4346* ⊕*www.shakermuseum.org* ☜*$7* ⊙*Late May–late Oct., Mon.–Sat. 10–5, Sun. noon–5; late Oct.–late May, Sat. 10–4, Sun. noon–4.*

OFF THE BEATEN PATH

Upper Valley. From Hanover, you can make a 60-mi drive up Route 10 all the way to Littleton for a highly scenic tour of the upper Connecticut River valley. You'll have views of the river and Vermont's Green Mountains from many points. The road passes through groves of evergreens, over leafy ridges, and through delightful hamlets. Grab gourmet picnic provisions at the general store on Lyme's village common—probably the most pristine of any in the state—and stop at the bluff-top village green in historical Haverhill (28 mi north of Hanover) for a picnic amid the panorama of classic Georgian- and Federal-style mansions and faraway farmsteads. You can follow this scenic route all the way to the White Mountains region, or loop back south from Haverhill—along Route 25 to Route 118 to U.S. 4 west—to Enfield, a drive of about 45 mi (75 minutes).

WHERE TO EAT

$$-$$$
AMERICAN

✕**Canoe Club.** This festive spot decked with canoes, paddles, classic Dartmouth paraphernalia presents live jazz and folk music many nights. The mood may be casual, but the kitchen presents rather fancy and imaginative food, including a memorable starter of shrimp, prosciutto, and almonds wrapped in bok choy with sweet-and-sour sauce. Among the main courses, roasted lamb sirloin with white beans, asparagus, and roasted garlic ragout stands out. There's also a lighter, late-night menu. ⊠*27 S. Main St.* ☎*603/643–9660* ▭*AE, D, DC, MC, V.*

$-$$ ✕**Lui Lui.** The creatively topped thin-crust pizzas and huge pasta por
ITALIAN tions are only part of the draw at this chatter-filled eatery. It also has a
dramatic setting inside a former power station on the Mascoma River.
Pizza picks include the Tuscan (mozzarella on the bottom, tomato,
and roasted garlic) and the grilled chicken with barbecue sauce. Pasta
fans should dive into a bowl of linguine with prosciutto, spinach, and
mushrooms. The owners also run Molly's Restaurant and Jesse's Tavern, which are both nearby. ✉*Adjacent to Powerhouse Mall, off Rte.
12A, West Lebanon* ☎*603/298–7070* ▭*AE, MC, V.*

¢ ✕**Lou's.** This is the only place in town where students and locals really
★ mix. After all, it's hard to resist. A Hanover tradition since 1948, this
AMERICAN diner-cum-café-cum-bakery serves possibly the best breakfast in the
valley—a plate of *migas* (eggs, cheddar, salsa, and guacamole mixed
with tortilla chips) can fill you up for the better part of the day; blue-
berry-cranberry buttermilk pancakes also satisfy. Or grab a seat at the
old-fashioned soda fountain and order an ice-cream sundae. ✉*30 S.
Main St.* ☎*603/643–3321* ▭*AE, MC, V* ◎*No dinner.*

$$-$$$ ✕**Murphy's.** Students, visiting alums, and locals regularly descend upon
ECLECTIC this wildly popular pub, whose walls are lined with shelves of old
books. The varied menu of consistently tasty chow lists both familiar and innovative fare: blackened-chicken wraps, char-grilled Black
Angus steaks, Szechuan yellowfin tuna with red curry sauce and ginger
cakes, lobster ravioli, and fajitas. Check out the extensive beer list.
✉*11 S. Main St.* ☎*603/643–4075* ▭*AE, D, DC, MC, V.*

6

WHERE TO STAY

$$$$ 🏨**Hanover Inn.** If you're in town for a Dartmouth event, there's no
★ competition: you'll want to stay here on the town, and the college's,
main square. You'll pay for the location, too. Owned by Dartmouth,
this sprawling, Georgian-style brick structure rises four white-trimmed
stories. The original building was converted to a tavern in 1780, and
this expertly run inn, now greatly enlarged, has been operating ever
since. Rooms have Colonial reproductions, Audubon prints, large sitting areas, and marble-accented bathrooms. The swank Zins Wine
Bistro ($–$$) prepares lighter but highly innovative fare. **Pros:** cen-
ter of campus and town location, well managed. **Cons:** breakfast not
included, overpriced. ✉*The Green, Main and Wheelock Sts., Box
151, 03755* ☎*603/643–4300 or 800/443–7024* ⊕*www.hanoverinn.
com* ↪*92 rooms, 23 suites* ⚄*In-room: Wi-Fi. In-hotel: 2 restaurants,
room service, bar, public Internet, public Wi-Fi, no-smoking rooms*
▭*AE, D, DC, MC, V.*

$$-$$$ 🏨**Trumbull House.** The sunny guest rooms of this white Colonial-style
house—on 16 acres in Hanover's outskirts—have king- or queen-size
beds, window seats, writing desks, feather pillows, and other comfortable touches, as well as wireless Internet. There is also a romantic
guesthouse, complete with a private deck, whirlpool tub, refrigerator,
and wet bar. Breakfast, with a choice of entrées, is served in the formal
dining room or in front of the living room fireplace. Rates include use
of a nearby health club. **Pros:** quiet setting, lovely home, big breakfast.
Cons: 5 mi east of town. ✉*40 Etna Rd., 03755* ☎*603/643–2370 or
800/651–5141* ⊕*www.trumbullhouse.com* ↪*4 rooms, 1 suite, 1 cot-*

tage &*In-room: VCR, Wi-Fi. In-hotel: restaurant, no-smoking rooms* ⊟*AE, D, DC, MC, V* ⓞⅠ*BP.*

CORNISH

22 mi south of Hanover.

Today Cornish is best known for its four covered bridges and for being the home of reclusive author J. D. Salinger, but at the turn of the 20th century the village was known primarily as the home of the country's then most popular novelist, Winston Churchill (no relation to the British prime minister). His novel *Richard Carvell* sold more than a million copies. Churchill was such a celebrity that he hosted Teddy Roosevelt during the president's 1902 visit. At that time Cornish was an enclave of artistic talent. Painter Maxfield Parrish lived and worked here, and sculptor Augustus Saint-Gaudens set up his studio and created the heroic bronzes for which he is known.

WHAT TO SEE

Cornish-Windsor Bridge. This 460-foot bridge, 1½ mi south of the Saint-Gaudens National Historic Site, connects New Hampshire to Vermont across the Connecticut River. It dates from 1866 and is the longest covered bridge in the United States. The notice on the bridge reads: WALK YOUR HORSES OR PAY TWO DOLLAR FINE.

Fodor'sChoice   **Saint-Gaudens National Historic Site.** Just south of Plainfield, where River
★   Road rejoins Route 12A, a small lane leads to this historic site, where you can tour sculptor Augustus Saint-Gaudens's house, studio, gallery, and 150 acres of grounds and gardens. Scattered throughout are full-size casts of his works. The property has two hiking trails, the longer of which is the Blow-Me-Down Trail. Concerts are held every Sunday afternoon in July and August. ⊠ *Off Rte. 12A* ☏ *603/675–2175* ⊕ *www.sgnhs.org* ⊠ *$5* ⊙ *Buildings June–Oct., daily 9–4:30; grounds daily dawn–dusk.*

THE MONADNOCKS & MERRIMACK VALLEY

Southwestern and south-central New Hampshire mix village charm with city hustle across two distinct regions. The Merrimack River valley has the state's largest and fastest-growing cities: Nashua, Manchester, and Concord. To the west, in the state's sleepy southwestern corner, is the Monadnock region, one of New Hampshire's least-developed and most naturally stunning parts. Here you'll find plenty of hiking trails as well as peaceful hilltop hamlets that appear barely changed in the past two centuries. Mt. Monadnock, southern New Hampshire's largest peak, stands guard over the Monadnock region, which has more than 200 lakes and ponds. Rainbow trout, smallmouth and largemouth bass, and some northern pike swim in Chesterfield's Spofford Lake. Goose Pond in West Canaan, just north of Keene, holds smallmouth bass and white perch.

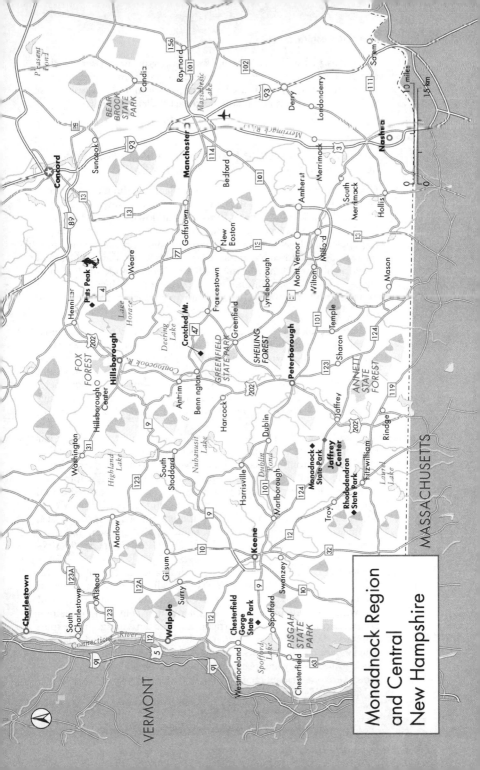

Monadnock Region and Central New Hampshire

The towns are listed in counterclockwise order, beginning with Nashua and heading north to Manchester and Concord; then west to Henniker and Hillsborough and Charleston; south to Walpole; southwest to Keene and Jaffrey; and finally northeast to Peterborough.

NASHUA

98 mi south of Lincoln/North Woodstock, 48 mi northwest of Boston, 36 mi south of Concord, 50 mi southeast of Keene.

Once a prosperous manufacturing town that drew thousands of immigrant workers in the late 1800s and early 1900s, Nashua declined following World War II, as many factories shut down or moved to where labor was cheaper. Since the 1970s, however, the metro area has jumped in population, developing into a charming, old-fashioned community. Its low-key downtown has classic redbrick buildings along the Nashua River, a tributary of the Merrimack River. Though not visited by tourists as much as other communities in the region, Nashua (population 90,000) has some good restaurants and an engaging museum.

WHERE TO EAT

$
AMERICAN

✕**Martha's Exchange.** A casual spot with copper brewing vats, original marble floors, and booth seating, Martha's appeals both to the afterwork set and office workers on lunch breaks. Burgers and sandwiches, maple-stout-barbecued chicken and ribs, Mexican fare, seafood and steak grills, and salads—all in large portions—are your options here. There's also a sweets shop attached, and you can buy half-gallon jugs of house-brewed beers to go. ✉*185 Main St.* ☎*603/883–8781* ▤*AE, DC, MC, V.*

$$–$$$
Fodor's Choice
★
BISTRO

✕**Michael Timothy's Urban Bistro.** Part hip bistro, part jazzy wine bar (with live music many nights), Michael Timothy's is so popular that even foodies from Massachusetts drive here. The regularly changing menu might include stuffed pheasant with foie gras risotto and cranberry-clove jus, or wood-grilled venison loin with port reduction, herb spaetzle, creamed morel mushrooms, and stewed lentils. Wood-fired pizzas are also a specialty—try the one topped with sirloin tips, caramelized onions, mushrooms, salami, sautéed spinach, and three cheeses. Sunday brunch is a big hit here. ✉*212 Main St.* ☎*603/595–9334* ▤*AE, D, MC, V* ⊘*No lunch Sat.*

$–$$
ITALIAN

✕**Villa Banca.** On the ground floor of a dramatic, turreted office building, this airy spot with high ceilings and tall windows specializes in both traditional and contemporary Italian cooking. Get a little taste of everything by ordering a starter sampler platter consisting of seafood risotto cakes, lobster-stuffed artichokes, chicken sausage, fried spinach-and-artichoke ravioli, chicken in phyllo dough, and fried calamari. Then move on to the delicious pastas and grills, including gnocchi with wood-grilled turkey and prosciutto, and chicken-and-sausage lasagna. Note the exotic-martini menu—a big draw at happy hour. ✉*194 Main St.* ☎*603/598–0500* ▤*AE, D, DC, MC, V* ⊘*No lunch weekends.*

MANCHESTER

18 mi north of Nashua, 53 mi north of Boston.

Manchester, with 108,000-plus residents, is New Hampshire's largest city. The town grew up around the Amoskeag Falls on the Merrimack River, which fueled small textile mills through the 1700s. By 1828, Boston investors had bought the rights to the Merrimack's water power and built the Amoskeag Mills, which became a testament to New England's manufacturing capabilities. In 1906 the mills employed 17,000 people and weekly churned out more than 4 million yards of cloth. This vast enterprise served as Manchester's entire economic base; when it closed in 1936, the town was devastated.

Today Manchester is mainly a banking and business center. The old mill buildings have been converted into warehouses, classrooms, restaurants, museums, and office space. The city has the state's major airport, as well as the Verizon Wireless Arena, which hosts minor-league hockey matches, concerts, and conventions.

WHAT TO SEE

Fodor's Choice ★ **Amoskeag Mills.** Miles of brick buildings comprise this mill. To get a sense of what they are and what they meant to Manchester, there are two key museums. The **SEE Science Center** (☎ 603/669-0400 ⊕ *www. see-sciencecenter.org* ☜ *$5* ☉ *Weekdays 10–4, weekends 10–5*) is a hands-on science lab and children's museum with more than 70 exhibits. If you're in Manchester, child or adult, don't miss this. The world's largest permanent LEGO instillation of regular sized LEGOs is here, depicting the city's Amskeag Millyard and the ciy of Manchester as it was in 1915. This is a mind-blowing exhibit, making you awe at the craftsmanship of three million LEGOs across 2,000 square feet. Yes, you'll be awed. But more importantly, the exhibit directly conveys the massive size and importance of the mills, which ran a mile on each side of the Merrimack. It's an eye opener. Upstairs in the same building the **Millyard Museum** (☎ 603/625-2821 ⊕ *www.manchesterhistoric.org* ☜ *$6* ☉ *Tues.–Sat. 10–4*) contains state-of-the-art exhibits depicting the region's history, from when Native Americans lived alongside and fished the Merrimack River to the heyday of Amoskeag Mills. The interactive Discovery Gallery is geared toward kids; there's also a lecture–concert hall and a large museum shop. ⊠ *Mill No. 3, 200 Bedford St. (entrance at 255 Commercial St.)* ☎ 603/625-2821.

Fodor's Choice ★ **Currier Museum of Art.** New England's only Frank Lloyd Wright–designed residence open to the public reopened in spring 2008 after a two-year, $20 million renovation that doubled gallery space, and created new shop, visitor entrance, café, and a winter garden with a Sol LeWitt mural that faces the original 1929 Italianate entrance. There's a permanent collection of European and American paintings, sculpture, and decorative arts from the 13th to the 20th century, including works by Monet, Picasso, Hopper, Wyeth, and O'Keeffe. Also part of the museum is the Frank Lloyd Wright–designed Zimmerman House, built in 1950. Wright called this sparse, utterly functional living space "Usonian," an invented term used to describe fifty such middle-income homes he built

6

with a vision of distinctly American architecture. ⊠*201 Myrtle Way* ☎*603/669–6144, 603/626–4158 Zimmerman House tours* ⊕*www. currier.org* ✉*$7, free Sat. 10–1; Zimmerman House $11 (reservations essential)* ⊙*Sun., Mon., Wed., and Fri. 11–5; Thurs. 11–8; Sat. 10–5; call for Zimmerman House tour hrs.*

NIGHTLIFE & THE ARTS

NIGHTLIFE **Club 313** (⊠*93 S. Maple St.* ☎*603/628–6813*) is New Hampshire's most popular disco for lesbians and gays. It's open Wednesday–Sunday. Revelers come from all over to drink at the **Yard** (⊠*1211 S. Mammoth Rd.* ☎*603/623–3545*), which is also a steak and seafood restaurant.

THE ARTS The **Palace Theatre** (⊠*80 Hanover St.* ☎*603/668–5588 theater, 603/647– 6476 philharmonic, 603/669–3559 symphony, 603/647–6564 opera* ⊕*www.palacetheatre.org*) presents musicals and plays throughout the year. It also hosts the state's philharmonic and symphony orchestras and the Opera League of New Hampshire.

WHERE TO EAT

$–$$ ✕**Cotton.** Mod lighting and furnishings and an arbored patio set a ★ swanky tone at this restaurant inside one of the old Amoskeag Mills AMERICAN buildings. (You might recognize the neon sign that reads FOOD). The kitchen churns out updated comfort food. Start with pan-seared crab cakes or the lemongrass-chicken salad. Stellar entrée picks include possibly the best steaks in the state, including a huge 20-ounce porterhouse, as well as superb grilled pork "mignon" with sweet-potato hash and a spicy honey-chipotle aioli. The same owners run the excellent and similarly hip seafood restaurant, Starfish Grill, at 33 South Commercial Street. ⊠*75 Arms Park Dr.* ☎*603/622–5488* ▭*AE, D, DC, MC, V* ⊙*No lunch weekends.*

¢–$ ✕**Red Arrow Diner.** This tiny diner is ground zero for presidential hope-
Fodor'sChoice fuls in New Hampshire come primary season. The rest of the time,
★ a mix of hipsters and oldsters, including comedian and Manchester
AMERICAN native Adam Sandler, favor this neon-streaked, 24-hour greasy spoon, which has been going strong since 1922. Filling fare—platters of kielbasa, French toast, liver and onions, chicken Parmesan with spaghetti, and the diner's famous panfries—keeps patrons happy. ⊠*61 Lowell St.* ☎*603/626–1118* ▭*D, MC, V.*

$$–$$$ ✕**Richard's Bistro.** Whether you want to celebrate a special occasion or
BISTRO just crave first-rate regional American cuisine, head to this romantic downtown bistro. The kitchen uses traditional New England ingredients in worldly preparations: try the char-broiled filet mignon with Gorgonzola, baked-stuffed potato, and strawberries or the broiled haddock topped with shrimp and scallops on an herb-risotto cake with a honey-peach sauce. ⊠*36 Lowell St.* ☎*603/644–1180* ▭*AE, D, MC, V* ⊙*No lunch Sun.*

WHERE TO STAY

$$ ▦**Ash Street Inn.** Because it's in an attractive residential neighborhood of striking Victorian homes, staying in this bright and clean, five-room B&B will make you appreciate Manchester more. Every room in the historic sage-green 1885 house, run by Darlene and Eric Johnston,

is painted a different warm color, and you can be safe knowing that other details are equally well thought-out. There are good linens, and there's decantered brandy in the sitting room, which has the house's original stained glass. In the summer, a wraparound porch is a nice place to sit on benches and enjoy a cooked-to-order breakfast, served on a flexible schedule. **Pros:** spotless newly decorated rooms, residential location appeal. **Cons:** not a full-service hotel. ⌧ *118 Ash St., 03104* ☎ *603/668–9908* ⊕ *www.ashstreetinn.com* 🛏 *5 rooms* ♿ *In-room: Wi-Fi. In-hotel: no elevator, public Wi-Fi, no kids under 12* ⊟ *AE, MC, V* ⦿ *BP.*

$$$–$$$$ ⊡ **Bedford Village Inn.** If you can trade direct downtown access for a
★ lovely manor outside of town, you'll be rewarded by the comforts of this beautiful and well-run property. The hayloft and milking rooms of this 1810 Federal farmstead, just a few miles southwest of Manchester, contain lavish suites with king-size four-poster beds, plus such modern perks as two phones and high-speed wireless. The restaurant ($$–$$$$)—a warren of elegant dining rooms with fireplaces and wide-pine floors—presents contemporary fare that might include a starter of baked stuffed black mission figs with Gorgonzola, prosciutto, walnuts, and arugula, followed by pan-roasted sea bass with braised fennel and carrots, saffron-whipped potatoes, and rock-shrimp vinaigrette. There's also a casual tavern ($–$$$), where you might sample an herb-grilled steak Cobb salad or tortellini filled with whipped mascarpone cheese and pumpkin. **Pros:** relaxing property just outside Manchester, exceptional grounds, great restaurant. **Cons:** outside of town. ⌧ *2 Olde Bedford Way, Bedford* ☎ *603/472–2001 or 800/852–1166* ⊕ *www. bedfordvillageinn.com* 🛏 *14 suites, 2 apartments* ♿ *In-room: DVD, Wi-Fi. In-hotel: restaurant, room service, bar, laundry service, public Internet, public Wi-Fi, no-smoking rooms* ⊟ *AE, D, DC, MC, V.*

$$ ⊡ **Radisson Manchester.** Of Manchester's many chain properties, the 12-story Radisson has the most central location—a short walk from Amoskeag Mills and great dining along Elm Street. Rooms are simple and clean, perfect for business travelers. Next door is the Center of New Hampshire conference center. Because of it's busy location, this is the only hotel in the state where you have to pay for parking. **Pros:** central downtown location. **Cons:** fee for parking, unexciting chain hotel. ⌧ *700 Elm St., 03101* ☎ *603/625–1000 or 800/333–3333* ⊕ *www. radisson.com/manchesternh* 🛏 *244 rooms, 6 suites* ♿ *In-room: Wi-Fi. In-hotel: 2 restaurants, room service, bar, pool, gym, laundry service, public Internet, public Wi-Fi, parking (fee), some pets allowed, no-smoking rooms* ⊟ *AE, D, DC, MC, V.*

CONCORD

20 mi northwest of Manchester, 67 mi northwest of Boston, 46 mi northwest of Portsmouth.

New Hampshire's capital (population 42,000) is a quiet town that tends to the state's business but little else—the sidewalks roll up promptly at 6. The **Concord on Foot** walking trail winds through the historic district. Maps for the walk can be picked up at the **Chamber of Commerce** (⌧ *40*

Commercial St. ☎*603/224–2508* ⊕*www.concordnhchamber.com*) or stores along the trail.

WHAT TO SEE

Ⓒ **Christa McAuliffe Planetarium.** Shows on the solar system, constellations, and space exploration that incorporate computer graphics, sound, and special effects are presented here in a 40-foot dome theater. Children love seeing the tornado tubes, magnetic marbles, and other hands-on exhibits. Outside, explore the scale-model planet walk and the human sundial. The planetarium was named for the Concord teacher who was selected among 11,000 applicants for NASA's Teacher in Space Project and was killed in the Space Shuttle *Challenger* explosion in 1986. ✉*New Hampshire Technical Institute campus, 2 Institute Dr.* ☎*603/271–7831* ⊕*www.starhop.com* ✉*Exhibit area free, shows $8* ☉*Tues.–Thurs. 9–5, Fri. 9–7, weekends 10–5; call for show times and reservations.*

Pierce Manse. Franklin Pierce lived is this Greek-revival home before he moved to Washington to become the 14th U.S. president. He's buried nearby. ✉*14 Horseshoe Pond La.* ☎*603/225–4555* ✉*$5* ☉*Mid-June–early Oct., Tues.–Sat. 11–3.*

Fodor'sChoice
★ **State House.** A self-guided tour of the neoclassical, gilt-domed state house, built in 1819, is a real treat. You get total access to the building, and can even take a photo with the governor. This is the oldest capitol building in the nation in which the legislature uses its original chambers. In January and June you can watch the assemblies in action once week: the 24 senators of the New Hampshire Senate (the fourth-smallest American lawmaking body) meet Thursdays. In a wild inversion, the state's representatives number 400—one representative per 3,000 residents, a world record. You can see them all when they meet one day a week in January and June (that day varies year to year). Grab a self-guided tour brochure at the visitor center, which has great dioramas and paraphenilia from decades of presidential primaries. Portaits of all New Hampshires governors line the halls. ✉*107 N. Main St.* ☎*603/271–2154* ⊕*www.ci.concord.nh.us/tourdest/statehs* ✉*Free* ☉ *Weekdays 8–4:30.*

SPORTS & THE OUTDOORS

Hannah's Paddles (✉*15 Hannah Dustin Dr.* ☎*603/753–6695*) rents canoes for use on the Merrimack River, which runs through Concord.

NIGHTLIFE & THE ARTS

The **Capitol Center for the Arts** (✉*44 S. Main St.* ☎*603/225–1111* ⊕*www.ccanh.com*) has been restored to reflect its Roaring '20s origins. It hosts touring Broadway shows, dance companies, and musical acts. The lounge at **Hermanos Cocina Mexicana** (✉*11 Hills Ave.* ☎*603/224–5669*) stages live jazz Sunday through Thursday nights.

SHOPPING

Capitol Craftsman Jewelers (✉*16 N. Main St.* ☎*603/224–6166*) sells fine jewelry and handicrafts. The **League of New Hampshire Craftsmen** (✉*36 N. Main St.* ☎*603/228–8171*) exhibits crafts in many media.

Mark Knipe Goldsmiths (⊠ *2 Capitol Plaza, Main St.* ☎ *603/224–2920*) sets antique stones in rings, earrings, and pendants.

WHERE TO EAT

¢-$
AMERICAN

✕**Barley House.** A lively, old-fashioned tavern practically across from the capitol building and usually buzzing with a mix of politicos, business folks, and tourists, the Barley House serves dependable American chow: chorizo-sausage pizzas, burgers smothered with peppercorn-whisky sauce and blue cheese, chicken potpies, Cuban sandwiches, beer braised bratwurst, jambalaya, and Mediterranean chicken salad—it's an impressively comprehensive menu. The convivial bar turns out dozens of interesting beers, on tap and by the bottle, and there's also a decent wine list. It's open till 1 AM. ⊠ *132 N. Main St.* ☎ *603/228–6363* ⊟ *AE, D, DC, MC, V* ☉ *Closed Sun.*

¢-$
★
PIZZA

✕**Foodee's.** A local chain with additional parlors in Keene, Dover, Tilton, Milford, and Wolfeboro, Foodee's serves creative pizzas with especially delicious crusts (sourdough, six-grain, deep-dish). The capital branch is in the heart of downtown and serves such pies as the Polish (with kielbasa, sauerkraut, and three cheeses) and the El Greco (with sweet onions, sliced tomatoes, olive oil, and feta). You can also order pastas, salads, and calzones. The all-you-can-eat buffet, Tuesday through Friday for lunch and dinner, is a great bargain. ⊠ *2 S. Main St.* ☎ *603/225–3834* ⊟ *MC, V.*

¢-$
THAI

✕**Siam Orchid.** This dark, attractive Thai restaurant with a colorful rickshaw gracing its dining room serves spicy and reasonably authentic Thai food. It draws a crowd from the capitol each day for lunch. Try the fiery broiled swordfish with shrimp curry sauce or the pinenut chicken in an aromatic ginger sauce. There's a second location in Manchester. ⊠ *158 N. Main St.* ☎ *603/228–3633* ⊟ *AE, D, DC, MC, V* ☉ *No lunch weekends.*

WHERE TO STAY

$

🏨**The Centennial.** This is the most contemporary hotel in New Hampshire, and it's home to Granite, the state's most contemporary restaurant and bar, making it a draw for the state's politicians and those doing business here. The modernity is unexpected, since this imposing brick-and-stone building was constructed in 1892 for widows of Civil War veterans—but a head-to-toe renovation remade the interior. Boutique furniture and contemporary art sets the immediate tone in the lobby. Rooms have luxury linens, sleek carpet and furniture, and flat-screen TVs. Bathrooms have tumbled stone floors, granite countertops, and stand-alone showers. It's the state's first foray into a boutiquish, well-designed hotel, and it's a huge success. **Pros:** super contemporary and sleek hotel, very comfortable and clean rooms, great bar and restuarant. **Cons:** busy hotel. ⊠ *96 Pleasant St., 03301* ☎ *603/225–7102 or 800/360–4839* ⊕ *www.centennialhotel.com* ↦ *27 rooms, 5 suites* ⌂ *In-room: refrigerator, DVD, VCR, Wi-Fi. In-hotel: restaurant, room service, bar, gym, public Internet, public Wi-Fi, no-smoking rooms* ⊟ *AE, D, DC, MC, V.*

HENNIKER

16 mi southwest of Concord.

Governor Wentworth, New Hampshire's first Royal Governor, named this town in honor of his friend John Henniker, a London merchant and member of the British Parliament (residents delight in their town's status as "the only Henniker in the world"). Once a mill town producing bicycle rims and other light-industrial items, Henniker reinvented itself after the factories were damaged, first by spring floods in 1936 and then by the hurricane and flood of 1938. New England College was established in the following decade, adding life to this town of about 4,000. One of the area's covered bridges is on the NEC campus.

SPORTS & THE OUTDOORS

SKI AREAS **Pats Peak.** A quick trip up Interstate 93 from the Massachusetts border, Pats Peak is geared to families. Base facilities are rustic, and friendly personal attention is the rule. Despite Pats Peak's short 710-vertical-foot rise, the 21 trails and slopes have something for everyone, and the resort has some of the best snowmaking capacity in the state. New skiers and snowboarders can take advantage of a wide slope and several short trails; intermediates have wider trails from the top; and experts have a couple of real thrillers. Night skiing, snowboarding, and tubing take place in January and February. ⊠ *686 Flanders Rd., Rte. 114, 03242* ☎*603/428–3245 information, 888/728–7732 snow conditions* ⊕*www.patspeak.com.*

WHERE TO STAY

$ ⚜ **Colby Hill Inn.** Owner and innkeeper Mason Cobb, greets you with a
★ sincerity and kind inflection that you might expect from someone with the genuine name of Mason Cobb. This is a welcoming place—the old-style bar is in the lobby—and there are cookies and tea for guests all day by the parlor fireplace. You can stroll through the gardens and meadows, or play badminton out back. Rooms in the main house have comfortable four-poster and canopy beds with Colonial-style furnishings, and lace curtains. Bathrooms are on the small side, but are clean and new. The carriage house has four newly renovated suites, a step up in contemporary luxury from the main house; two have two-person whirlpool baths and backyard decks. **Pros:** comfortable, clean rooms, good dining. **Cons:** slightly out of the tourist loop; little by way of town life. ⊠*3 The Oaks, Box 779, 03242* ☎*603/428–3281 or 800/531–0330* ⊕*www.colbyhillinn.com* ⃗*14 rooms, 2 suites* ⚑*In-room: refrigerator (some), VCR (some), no TV (some), Wi-Fi. In-hotel: restaurant, bar, pool, no elevator, public Wi-Fi, no kids under 7, no-smoking rooms* ⊟*AE, D, DC, MC, V* ⦿*BP.*

HILLSBOROUGH

8 mi southwest of Henniker.

Hillsborough comprises four villages, the most prominent of which lies along the Contoocook River and grew up around a thriving woolen and hosiery industry in the mid-1800s. This section, which is really considered Hillsborough proper, is what you'll see as you roll through town on Route 9 (U.S. 202).

Turn north from downtown up School Street, and continue 3 mi past Fox State Forest to reach one of the state's best-preserved historic districts, Hillsborough Center, where 18th-century houses surround a green. Continue north 6 mi through the similarly quaint village of East Washington, and another 6 mi to reach the Colonial town center of Washington. One of the highest villages in New Hampshire, this picturesque arrangement of white clapboard buildings made the cover of *National Geographic* several years back. You can loop back to Hillsborough proper via Route 31 south.

The nation's 14th president, Franklin Pierce, was born in Hillsborough and lived here until he married. He is, alas, one of the least-appreciated presidents ever to serve.

WHAT TO SEE

Franklin Pierce Homestead. Operated by the Hillsborough Historical Society, the house is much as it was during Pierce's life. Guided tours are offered. ⊠ *Rte. 31 just north of Rte. 9* ☎ 603/478–3165 ⊕ *www. franklinpierce.ws/homestead* 🖾 *$3* ⊙ *June and Sept., Sat. 10–4, Sun. 1–4; July and Aug., Mon.–Sat. 10–4, Sun. 1–4.*

SHOPPING

At **Gibson Pewter** (⊠ *18 E. Washington Rd., Hillsborough Center* ☎ 603/464–3410 ⊕ *www.gibsonpewter.com*), Raymond Gibson and his son Jonathan create and sell museum quality pewter pieces. It's open Monday–Saturday 10–4. Next door to the Franklin Pierce Homestead, **Richard Withington Antiques Auction** (⊠ *590 Center Rd., Hillsborough Center* ☎ 603/464–3232 ⊕ *www.withingtonauction.com*) hosts some of the best antiques auctions in New England and stocks an impressive selection of fine pieces for general sale.

CHARLESTOWN

40 mi northwest of Hillsborough, 20 mi south of Cornish.

Charlestown has the state's largest historic district. About 60 homes, handsome examples of Federal, Greek-revival, and Gothic-revival architecture, are clustered about the town center; 10 of them were built before 1800. Several merchants on the main street distribute brochures that describe an interesting walking tour of the district.

WHAT TO SEE

© **Fort at No. 4.** In 1747, this fort was an outpost on the periphery of Colonial civilization. That year fewer than 50 militiamen at the fort withstood an attack by 400 French soldiers, ensuring that northern New England remained under British rule. Today, costumed interpreters at this living-history museum cook dinner over an open hearth and demonstrate weaving, gardening, and candle making. Each year the museum holds reenactments of militia musters and battles of the French and Indian War. ⊠ *Rte. 11, ½ mi north of Charlestown* ☎ 603/826–

5700 or 888/367–8284 ⊕*www.fortat4.org* ⊠*$8* ⊙*Early June–Oct., Wed.–Sun. 10–4:30.*

SPORTS & THE OUTDOORS

On a bright, breezy day you might want to detour to the **Morningside Flight Park** (⊠*357 Morningside La., off Rte. 12/11, 5 mi north of Charlestown* ☎*603/542–4416* ⊕*www.flymorningside.com*), considered to be among the best flying areas in the country. Watch the bright colors of gliders as they take off from the 450-foot peak, or take hang-gliding lessons yourself.

WALPOLE

13 mi south of Charlestown.

Walpole possesses one of the state's most perfect town greens. This one, bordered by Elm and Washington streets, is surrounded by homes built about 1790, when the townsfolk constructed a canal around the Great Falls of the Connecticut River and brought commerce and wealth to the area. The town now has 3,200 inhabitants, more than a dozen of whom are millionaires.

OFF THE BEATEN PATH

Sugarhouses. Maple-sugar season occurs about the first week in March when days become warmer but nights are still frigid. A drive along maple-lined back roads reveals thousands of taps and buckets catching the labored flow of unrefined sap. Plumes of smoke rise from nearby sugarhouses, where sugaring off, the process of boiling down this precious liquid, takes place. Many sugarhouses are open to the public; after a tour and demonstration, you can sample the syrup. You can also buy them online. **Bascom Maple Farm** (⊠*56 Sugarhouse Rd., Alstead* ☎*603/835–6361* ⊕*www.bascommaple.com*) has been family run since 1853 and produces more maple than anyone in New England. Visit the 2,200-acre farm and get maple pecan pie and maple milk shakes. **Stuart & John's Sugar House & Pancake Restaurant** (⊠*Rtes. 12 and 63, Westmoreland* ☎*603/399–4486* ⊕*www.stuartandjohns sugarhouse.com*) conducts a tour and sells syrup and maple gifs in a roadside barn. It also serves a memorable pancake breakfast weekends mid-February–April and mid-September–November.

SHOPPING

★ At **Boggy Meadow Farm** (⊠*13 Boggy Meadow La.* ☎*603/756–3300 or 877/541–3953*) you can watch the cheese process unfold, from the 200 cows being milked to the finer process of cheese-making. The farmstead raw-milk cheeses can be sampled and purchased in the store. It's worth it just to see the beautiful 400-acre farm.

WHERE TO EAT

$-$$
Fodor'sChoice
★
FRENCH

✕**The Restaurant at L. A. Burdick Chocolate.** Famous candy maker Larry Burdick, who sells his artful hand-filled and hand-cut chocolates to top restaurants around the Northeast, is a Walpole resident. This restaurant has the easygoing sophistication of a Parisian café and may tempt you to linger over an incredibly rich hot chocolate. The Mediterranean-inspired menu utilizes fresh, often local ingredients and changes daily. Of course, dessert is a big treat here, featuring Burdick's tempting chocolates and pastries. For dinner, you might start with a selection of artisanal cheeses or the confit of duck with grilled plums and a red wine reduction, followed by striped bass with eggplant, tomatoes, and capers, or roasted chicken with garlic-mashed potato cake and fresh tarragon. ✉47 Main St. ☎603/756-2882 ═AE, D, MC, V ⊗No dinner Sun. and Mon.

KEENE

17 mi southeast of Walpole; 20 mi northeast of Brattleboro, Vermont; 56 mi southwest of Manchester.

Keene is the largest city in the state's southwest corner. Its rapidly gentrifying main street, with several engaging boutiques and cafés, is America's widest (132 feet). Each year, on the Saturday before Halloween, locals use the street to hold a Pumpkin Festival, where they seek to retain their place in the record books for the most carved, lighted jack o' lanterns—more than 25,000 some years.

WHAT TO SEE

Keene State College. This hub of the local arts community is on the tree-lined main street and has a worthwhile art gallery and theater with select showings. The **Thorne-Sagendorph Art Gallery** (☎603/358-2720 ⊕www.keene.edu/tsag) houses George Ridci's *Landscape* and presents traveling exhibitions. The **Putnam Theater** (☎603/358-2160) shows foreign and art films.

OFF THE BEATEN PATH

Chesterfield's Route 63. If you're in the mood for a country drive or bike ride, head west from Keene along Route 9 to Route 63 (about 11 mi), and turn left toward the hilltop town of Chesterfield. This is an especially rewarding journey at sunset, as from many points along the road you can see west out over the Connecticut River valley and into Vermont. The village center consists of little more than a handful of dignified granite buildings and a small general store. You can loop back to Keene via Route 119 east in Hinsdale and then Route 10 north—the entire journey is about 40 mi.

NIGHTLIFE & THE ARTS

Elm City Brewing Co. (✉222 West St. ☎603/355-3335), at the Colony Mill, serves light food and draws a mix of college students and young professionals. At Keene State College, the **Redfern Arts Center at Brickyard Pond** (✉229 Main St. ☎603/358-2168) has year-round music, theater, and dance performances in two theaters and a recital hall.

SHOPPING

★ **Colony Mill Marketplace** (✉222 West St. ☎603/357-1240), an old mill building, holds 30-plus stores and boutiques such as the Toadstool Bookshop, which carries many children's and regional travel and history books, and Ye Goodie Shoppe, whose specialty is handmade confections. Also popular is Antiques at Colony Mill, which sells the wares of more than 200 dealers. There's a food court, too.

6

WHERE TO EAT & STAY

$$ ✕**Luca's.** A deceptively simple storefront bistro overlooking Keene's
Fodor'sChoice graceful town square, Luca's dazzles with knowledgeable and help-
★ ful staff and some of the most deftly prepared cooking in this part
MEDITERRANEAN of the state. Pastas and grills reveal Italian, French, Greek, Spanish,
and North African influences—consider salmon tagine in a sundried-
tomato-and-whole-grain-mustard cream sauce, or shrimp and scallops
El Greco, with plum tomatoes, feta, and baby spinach over linguine.
Dine in the intimate art-filled dining room or at one of the sidewalk
tables in summer. ⊠*10 Central Sq.* 🕾*603/358–3335* 🚍*AE, MC, V*
⊙*No lunch weekends Nov.–Mar.*

$$–$$$ 🔝**Chesterfield Inn.** Surrounded by gardens, the Chesterfield sits above
★ Route 9, the main road between Keene and Brattleboro, Vermont. Fine
antiques and Colonial-style fabrics adorn the spacious guest quarters;
10 have fireplaces, and several have private decks or terraces that face
the stunning perennial gardens and verdant Vermont hills. In the res-
taurant ($$–$$$$) rosemary- and walnut-crusted rack of lamb and
grilled blue-corn-and-smoked-cheddar polenta with black bean rata-
touille are among the highlights. **Pros:** meticulously clean rooms, attrac-
trive gardens, good food. **Cons:** breakfast ends early. ⊠*Rte. 9* 🖃*Box
155, Chesterfield 03443* 🕾*603/256–3211 or 800/365–5515* ⊕*www.
chesterfieldinn.com* ⬿*13 rooms, 2 suites* ♿*In-room: refrigerator, Wi-
Fi. In-hotel: restaurant, no elevator, public Wi-Fi, some pets allowed,
no-smoking rooms.* 🚍*AE, D, MC, V* ⊚*BP.*

$ 🔝**E. F. Lane Hotel.** You can get a rare touch of urbanity in the sleepy
Monadnocks in this upscale redbrick hotel is in the middle of Main
Street. The hotel was retrofitted in 2000 from the former Goodnow
department store, a Keene landmark for over 100 years. That accounts
for some interesting room features, like a wall of exposed brick and
12-foot ceilings. Spacious rooms are furnished individually with reproduction Victorian antiques. "Chairman" suites have stairs that lead to
an upper level, and come with two bathrooms. Ask for your free movie
tickets and popcorn vouchers for the Colonial Theater across the street.
Pros: Spacious, interesting, comfortable rooms; center-of-town location; free movie tickets. **Cons:** no restaurant or gym. ⊠*30 Main St.,
03431* 🕾*603/357–7070 or 888/300–5056* ⊕*www.eflane.com* ⬿*32
rooms, 7 suites* ♿*In-room: refrigerator (some), Wi-Fi. In-hotel: bar,
public Internet, public Wi-Fi, some pets allowed, no-smoking rooms*
🚍*AE, D, MC, V* ⊚*CP.*

$$ 🔝**Inn at East Hill Farm.** If you have kids, and they like animals, meet bliss:
♻ a family resort on a 170-acre 1830 farm overlooking Mt. Monadnock
with daylong kids' programs. Kids can start at 9 AM with cow milking.
Other activities include collecting chicken eggs, horseback- and pony
riding, arts and crafts, storytelling, hiking, sledding, hay rides in sum-
mer and horse-drawn sleigh rides in winter. You can feed sheep, don-
keys, cows, rabbits, horses, chickens, goats, ducks, and play with Chloe
the farm dog. Twice weekly in summer, trips are scheduled to a nearby
lake for boating, waterskiing, and fishing. Rates include most activi-
ties and three meals in a camplike dining hall. Rooms are comfortable,
not fancy. The inn is 10 mi southeast of Keene off Rte 124. **Pros:** rare

agri-tourism and family resort, activities galore, beautiful setting. **Cons:** remote, rural location; noisy mess hall dining. ✉ *460 Monadnock St., Troy* ☎ *603/242–6495 or 800/242–6495* 🌐 *www.east-hill-farm.com* *70 rooms* *In-room: no a/c (some), no phone, refrigerator, no TV (some), Wi-Fi. In-hotel: restaurant, tennis court, pools, no elevator, children's programs (ages 2–18), laundry facilities, public Wi-Fi, some pets allowed, no-smoking rooms* ▭ *D, MC, V* 🍽 *FAP.*

JAFFREY CENTER

16 mi southeast of Keene.

Novelist Willa Cather came to Jaffrey Center in 1919 and stayed in the Shattuck Inn, which now stands empty on Old Meeting House Road. Not far from here, she pitched the tent in which she wrote several chapters of *My Ántonia*. She returned nearly every summer thereafter until her death and was buried in the Old Burying Ground.

WHAT TO SEE

Cathedral of the Pines. This outdoor memorial pays tribute to Americans who have sacrificed their lives in service to their country. There's an inspiring view of Mt. Monadnock and Mt. Kearsarge from the Altar of the Nation, which is composed of rock from every U.S. state and territory. All faiths are welcome to hold services here; organ music for meditation is played at midday from Tuesday through Thursday in July and August. The Memorial Bell Tower, with a carillon of bells from around the world, is built of native stone. Norman Rockwell designed the bronze tablets over the four arches. Flower gardens, an indoor chapel, and a museum of military memorabilia share the hilltop. It's 8 mi southeast of Jaffrey Center. ✉ *10 Hale Hill Rd., off Rte. 119, Rindge* ☎ *603/899–3300 or 866/229–4520* 🌐 *www.cathedralpines.com* *Donations accepted* ⏲ *May–Oct., daily 9–5.*

SPORTS & THE OUTDOORS

★ **Monadnock State Park.** The oft-quoted statistic about Mt. Monadnock is that it's America's most-climbed mountain—second in the world to Japan's Mt. Fuji. Whether this is true or not, locals agree that it's never lonely at the top. Some days more than 400 people crowd its bald peak. Monadnock rises to 3,165 feet, and on a clear day the hazy Boston skyline is visible from its summit. The park maintains picnic grounds and a small campground (RVs welcome, but no hookups) with 28 sites. Five trailheads branch into more than two dozen trails of varying difficulty that wend their way to the top. Allow between three and four hours for any round-trip hike. A visitor center has free trail maps as well as exhibits documenting the mountain's history. In winter, you can cross-country ski along roughly 12 mi of groomed trails on the lower elevations of the mountain. ✉ *Off Rte. 124, 2½ mi north of Jaffrey Center,* ☎ *603/532–8862* *$3* ⏲ *Daily dawn–dusk* ☞ *No pets.*

Rhododendron State Park. More than 16 acres of wild rhododendrons bloom in mid-July at Fitzwilliam's park, which has the largest concentration of *Rhododendron maximum* north of the Allegheny Mountains. Bring a picnic lunch and sit in a nearby pine grove, or follow the marked footpaths through the flowers. On your way here, be sure to pass through Fitzwilliam's well-preserved historic district of Colonial and Federal-style houses, which have appeared on thousands of postcards. ⊠ *Rte. 119 W, off Rte. 12, 10 mi southwest of Jaffrey Center, Fitzwilliam* ☎ *603/239–8153* ⊠ *$3 weekends and holidays, free at other times* ⊗ *Daily 8–sunset.*

SHOPPING

You'll find about 35 dealers at **Bloomin' Antiques** (⊠ *Rte. 12, 3 mi south of Rte. 119, Fitzwilliam* ☎ *603/585–6688*). Meanwhile, **Fitzwilliam Antiques Centre** (⊠ *Rtes. 12 and 119, Fitzwilliam* ☎ *603/585–9092*) sells the wares of some 40 dealers.

THE ARTS

Amos Fortune Forum, near the Old Burying Ground, brings nationally known speakers to the 1773 meetinghouse on summer evenings.

WHERE TO EAT & STAY

$-$$ ✕**Lilly's on the Pond.** An appealing choice either for lunch or dinner, this
AMERICAN rustic-timbered dining room overlooks a small mill pond in Rindge, about 8 mi south of Jaffrey Center. The extensive menu of mostly American fare includes chicken sautéed with lime and tequila, shrimp scampi, and burgers. ⊠ *U.S. 202, Rindge* ☎ *603/899–3322* ▤ *D, MC, V* ⊗ *Closed Mon.*

$-$$ ▦**Benjamin Prescott Inn.** Thanks to the working dairy farm surrounding this 1853 Colonial house—with its stenciling and wide pine floors— you feel as though you're miles out in the country rather than just minutes from Jaffrey Center. A full breakfast of Welsh miner's cakes and baked French toast with fruit and maple syrup prepares you for a day of antiquing or hiking. **Pros:** inexpensive. **Cons:** 2 mi east of town, outdated furnishings. ⊠ *433 Turnpike Rd. (Rt. 124E), 03452* ☎ *603/532–6637 or 888/950–6637* ⊕ *www.benjaminprescottinn. com* ➥ *10 rooms, 3 suites* ⌂ *In-room: no phone, no TV, Wi-Fi. In-hotel: no kids under 10, public Wi-Fi, no-smoking rooms* ▤ *AE, MC, V* ¶⊙*BP.*

$ ▦**Inn at Jaffrey Center.** Rooms in this beautiful home are painted in lively lavenders, yellows, or peaches, a cheery presence in the heart of pristine Jaffrey Center. Although full of period furnishings, they have a hip sensibility as well as high-thread-count bedding, fluffy towels, and fine toiletries. Rocking chairs set out on the front porch overlook the town and the golf course across the street. There's a good restaurant here with an impressive Sunday brunch. **Pros:** located in right in town, across from golf, good food. **Cons:** limited amentities. ⊠ *379 Main St., 03452* ☎ *603/532–7800 or 877/510–7019* ⊕ *www.theinnat jaffreycenter.com* ➥ *9 rooms, 2 suites* ⌂ *In-room: no a/c, no phone, DVD (some), VCR (some), no TV (some), Wi-Fi. In-hotel: restaurant, bar, public Wi-Fi, no elevator, no-smoking rooms* ▤ *AE, D, DC, MC, V* ¶⊙*CP.*

$$-$$$ ▦**Woodbound Inn.** A favorite with families and outdoors enthusiasts, this 1819 farmhouse became an inn in 1892. It occupies 200 acres on the shores of Contoocook Lake. Accommodations are functional

but clean and cheerful; they range from quirky rooms in the main inn to modern hotel-style rooms in the Edgewood building to cabins by the water. There's a nine-hole, par-3 golf course, and of course lots of boating and fishing. **Pros:** relaxed, lakefront resort; new owners in 2008 bring focus on food. **Cons:** older, simple furnishings. ⊠*247 Woodbound Rd., Rindge* ☎*603/532-8341 or 800/688-7770* ⊕*www. woodboundinn.com* ⇆*44 rooms, 39 with bath; 11 cottages* &*In-room: refrigerator (some), no TV (some). In-hotel: restaurant, bar, golf course, tennis court, no-smoking rooms* ☰*AE, MC, V* |◎|*BP, MAP.*

PETERBOROUGH

9 mi northeast of Jaffrey Center, 30 mi northwest of Nashua.

Do you remember Thorton Wilder's play *Our Town?* It's based on Peterborough. The nation's first free public library opened here in 1833. The town, which was the first in the region to be incorporated (1760), is still a commercial and cultural hub.

WHAT TO SEE

⟳ **Mariposa Museum.** You can play instruments from around the world, try on costumes from around the world, and indulge your cultural curiosity at this non-profit museum dedicated to hands-on exploration of international folklore and folk art. The three-floor museum is inside a historic redbrick Baptist church, across the Universalist church in the heart of town. The museum hosts a number of workshops and presentations on dance and arts and crafts. There's also a children's reading nook and a library. ⊠*26 Main St.* ☎*603/924-4555* ⊕*www.mariposa museum.org* ▧*$5* ⊙*July and Aug., daily noon–4; Sept.–May, week-days 3–5; live music performances year-round, Sun. at 3.*

SPORTS & THE OUTDOORS

PARKS **Miller State Park.** About 3 mi east of town, an auto road takes you almost 2,300 feet up Pack Monadnock Mountain. The road is closed mid-November through mid-April. ⊠*Rte. 101* ☎*603/924-3672* ▧*$3.*

GOLF At the Donald Ross–designed **Crotched Mountain Golf Club** (⊠*Off Rte. 47 near Bennington town line, Francestown* ☎*603/588-2923*), you'll find a hilly, rolling 18-hole layout with nice view of the Monadnocks. Greens fee are $30–$38.

SKI AREA **Crotched Mountain.** New Hampshire's southernmost skiing and snow-boarding facility opened in 2004 with 17 trails, half of them interme-diate, and the rest divided pretty evenly between beginner and expert. There's an 875-foot vertical drop. The slopes have ample snowmaking capacity, ensuring good skiing all winter long. Other facilities include a 40,000-square-foot lodge with a couple of restaurants, a ski school, and a snow camp for youngsters. ⊠*615 Francestown Rd. (Rte. 47), Bennington* ☎*603/588-3668* ⊕*www.crotchedmountain.com.*

SHOPPING

The corporate headquarters and retail outlet of **Eastern Mountain Sports** (✉*1 Vose Farm Rd.* ☎*603/924–7231*) sells everything from tents to skis to hiking boots, offers hiking and camping classes, and conducts kayaking and canoeing demonstrations. **Harrisville Designs** (✉*Mill Alley, Harrisville* ☎*603/827–3333*) sells hand-spun and hand-dyed yarn as well as looms. The shop also conducts classes in knitting and weaving. **Sharon Arts Fine Crafts Store** (✉*Depot Sq.* ☎*603/924–2787*) exhibits locally made pottery, fabric, and woodwork and other crafts.

THE ARTS

From early July to late August, **Monadnock Music** (✉*2A Concord St.* ☎*603/924–7610 or 800/868–9613* ⊕*www.monadnockmusic.org*) produces a series of solo recitals, chamber music concerts, and orchestra and opera performances by renowned musicians. Events take place throughout the area on Wednesday through Saturday evenings at 8 and on Sunday at 4; many are free. In winter, the **Peterborough Folk Music Society** (☎*603/827–2905* ⊕*http://pfmsconcerts.org*) presents folk music concerts. The **Peterborough Players** (✉*Stearns Farm off Middle Hancock Rd.* ☎*603/924–7585* ⊕*www.peterboroughplayers.org*) have performed since 1933. Productions are staged in a converted barn.

WHERE TO EAT & STAY

$-$$
★
BISTRO

✕Acqua Bistro. Locals love to come to Peterborough's best restaurant for riverfront patio dining in warm weather. Start at the long bar for an aperitif before settling in for thin-crust pizza or an entrée of wild Arctic char with roasted vegetable-dill couscous and basil-walnut pesto. Save room for the bittersweet chocolate soufflé. ✉*9 School St.* ☎*603/924–9905* ⊟*MC, V* ⊘*Closed Mon. No lunch.*

$
★

Hancock Inn. This Federal-style 1789 inn is the real Colonial deal—the oldest in the state, and the pride of this idyllic town, 8 mi north of Peterborough. Common areas possess the warmth of a tavern, with fireplaces, big wing chairs, couches, dark-wood paneling. In fact, it happens to have a special tavern of its own, painted with Rufus Porter murals from 1825. Colonial rooms have antique four-poster beds over original wood floors. Because the inn is in the heart of Hancock, just over from the green, you're smack dab in the middle of a perfect hamlet. You don't need to go very far to eat—the restaurant here serves an excellent Shaker cranberry pot roast; and across the street is the town market and a very popular café—so you can put away your car keys and relax. **Pros:** quintessential Colonial inn in a perfect New England town, cozy rooms. **Cons:** remote location. ✉*33 Main St., Hancock 03449* ☎*603/525–3318 or 800/525–1789* ⊕*www.hancockinn.com* ⮐*15 rooms* ⌂*In-room: DVD (some), Wi-Fi. In-hotel: restaurant, bar, no elevator, public Internet, public Wi-Fi, some pets allowed, no-smoking rooms* ⊟*AE, D, DC, MC, V* ⦿|*BP.*

¢-$

Inn at Crotched Mountain. Three of the nine fireplaces in this 1822 inn are in Colonial-style guest rooms. The property, with stunning views of the Monadnocks, was once a stop on the Underground Railroad. At the inn's restaurant ($$), where Singapore native Rose Perry is at the helm, you can sample both American and Asian-inspired fare, such as cranberry-port pot roast and Indonesian charbroiled swordfish with a sauce of ginger, green pepper, onion, and lemon. Weekend rates include breakfast and dinner. Pros: spectacular country setting. Cons: might be too remote for some. ✉ *534 Mountain Rd., 12 mi northeast of Peterborough, Francestown* ☎ *603/588–6840* ✑ *13 rooms* ♿ *In-hotel: restaurant, bar, tennis courts, pool, some pets allowed (fee), no-smoking rooms* ⊟ *No credit cards* ⊘ *Closed Apr. and Nov.* ⦾ *BP, MAP.*

$ ★ ⌂ **Jack Daniels Motor Inn.** With so many dowdy motels in southwestern New Hampshire, it's a pleasure to find one as bright and clean as the Jack Daniels, just ½ mi north of downtown Peterborough. The rooms are large and furnished with attractive cherrywood reproduction antiques. Try to get one of two rooms looking out on the Contoocook River; otherwise, second-floor rooms have chairs on the hallway overlooking the river. Pros: afforable and clean rooms, low-key atmosphere. Cons: basic motel-style rooms, have to drive or walk into town. ✉ *80 Concord St. (U.S. 202), 03458* ☎ *603/924–7548* ⊕ *www.jackdaniels motorinn.com* ✑ *17 rooms* ♿ *In-room: refrigerator (some), DVD (some), VCR (some), Wi-Fi. In-hotel: no elevator, public Wi-Fi, some pets allowed* ⊟ *AE, D, DC, MC, V.*

NEW HAMPSHIRE ESSENTIALS

Research prices, get travel advice, and book your trip at fodors.com

TRANSPORATION

BY AIR

Manchester Airport (✉ *1 Airport Rd., Manchester* ☎ *603/624–6539* ⊕ *www.flymanchester.com*), the state's largest airport, has rapidly become a cost-effective, hassle-free alternative to Boston's airport. It has nonstop service to more than 20 cities. **Lebanon Municipal Airport** (✉ *5 Airpark Rd., West Lebanon* ☎ *603/298–8878*), near Dartmouth College, is served by US Airways Express from New York.

BY BUS

C&J Trailways (☎ *603/430–1100 or 800/258–7111* ⊕ *www.cjtrailways. com*) serves the seacoast area of New Hampshire from Boston, with stops in Portsmouth, Durham and Dover. **Concord Coach Lines** (☎ *603/228–3300 or 800/639–3317, 603/448–2800 or 800/637–0123 Dartmouth Coach* ⊕ *www.concordcoachlines.com*) links Boston's South Station and Logan International Airport with points all along Interstate 93 as far north as Littleton and, around Lake Winnipesaukee and the eastern White Mountains, along Route 16. Operated by Concord Coach Lines, the Dartmouth Coach connects Boston's South Station and Logan International Airport with Hanover, Lebanon, and New London. **Greyhound** (☎ *800/231–2222 or 214/849–8100* ⊕ *www. greyhound.com*) has service from Boston to Vermont that stops in southern and western New Hampshire.

BY CAR

Interstate 93, running north from Massachusetts to Québec and passing through Manchester and Concord, is the principal south–north route through central New Hampshire. To the west, Interstate 91 traces the Vermont–New Hampshire border. To the east, Interstate 95, which is a toll road, passes through southern New Hampshire's coastal area on its way from Massachusetts to Maine. Interstate 89 travels from Concord to Montpelier and Burlington, Vermont.

BY TRAIN

Amtrak (☎ *800/872–7245* ⊕ *www.amtrak.com*) runs its Downeaster service from Boston to Portland, Maine. It stops along the seacoast in Exeter, Durham, and Dover, New Hampshire.

CONTACTS & RESOURCES

VISITOR INFORMATION

State Contacts **New Hampshire Fall Foliage hotline** (☎ *800/258–3608*). **New Hampshire Office of Travel and Tourism Development** (✉ *172 Pembroke Rd., Concord* ☎ *603/271–2665, 800/386–4664 free vacation guide* ⊕ *www.visitnh. gov*).

Regional Contacts **Lakes Region Association** (✉ *Rte. 104 off I–93 Exit 23, New Hampton* ☎ *603/744–8664 or 800/605–2537* ⊕ *www.lakesregion.org*). **Lake Sunapee Region Chamber of Commerce** (✉ *Box 532, Sunapee03782* ☎ *603/526–6575 or 877/526–6575* ⊕ *www.sunapeevacations.com*). **North Country Chamber of Commerce** (✉ *Box 1, Colebrook* ☎ *603/237–8939 or 800/698–8939* ⊕ *www.northcountrychamber.org*). **White Mountains Visitors Bureau** (✉ *Kancamagus Hwy. (Rte. 112) at I–93* ✉ *Box 10, North Woodstock* ☎ *603/745–8720 or 800/346–3687* ⊕ *www.whitemtn.org*).

Local Contacts **Concord Chamber of Commerce** (✉ *40 Commercial St., Concord* ☎ *603/224–2508* ⊕ *www.concordnhchamber.com*). **Exeter Area Chamber of Commerce** (✉ *120 Water St., Exeter* ☎ *603/772–2411* ⊕ *www.exeterarea.org*). **Greater Portsmouth Chamber of Commerce** (✉ *500 Market St., Portsmouth* ☎ *603/436–3988* ⊕ *www.portcity.org*). **Hanover Area Chamber of Commerce** (✉ *216 Main St., Hanover* ☎ *603/643–3115* ⊕ *www.hanoverchamber.org*). **Keene Chamber of Commerce** (✉ *48 Central Sq., Keene* ☎ *603/352–1303* ⊕ *www. keenechamber.com*). **Manchester Area Convention & Visitors Bureau** (✉ *889 Elm St., Manchester* ☎ *603/666–6600* ⊕ *www.manchestercvb.com*). **Monadnock Travel Council** (✉ *Box 358, Keene 03431* ☎ *800/432–7864* ⊕ *www.monadnocktravel. com*). **Seacoast New Hampshire Web site** (⊕ *www.seacoastnh.com*).

Maine

WORD OF MOUTH

"Getting up into Maine, the beach towns of York, Ogunquit, and Kennebunkport are wonderful. There are lighthouses, wide sandy beaches, and scenic rocky coastlines."

—zootsi

"Acadia National Park is one of Maine's jewels. You can drive around the Loop Road—about 20 miles or so—and stop at the various overlooks."

—massteacher

AS YOUR DRIVE ACROSS THE boarder into Maine, a sign plainly announces the state's philosophy: THE WAY LIFE SHOULD BE. Romantics luxuriate in the feeling of a down comforter on a yellow pine bed or in the sensation of the wind and salt spray on their faces while cruising in a historic windjammer. Families love the unspoiled beaches and safe inlets dotting the shoreline and the clear inland lakes. Hikers are revived by the exalting and exhausting climb to the top of Mt. Katahdin. Adventure seekers raft the Kennebec and Penobscot rivers or kayak along the coast, and skiers head for the snow-covered slopes of western and northern Maine.

There is an expansiveness to Maine, a sense of distance between places that hardly exists elsewhere in New England and, along with the sheer size and spread of the place, a variety of terrain. People speak of "coastal" Maine and "inland" Maine as though the state could be summed up under the twin emblems of lobsters and pine trees. Yet the topography and character in this state are a good deal more complicated.

Even the coast is several places in one. Rapidly gentrifying Portland may be Maine's largest metropolitan area, but its attitude is decidedly more big town than small city. South of Portland, Ogunquit, Kennebunkport, Old Orchard Beach, and other resort towns predominate along a reasonably smooth shoreline. North of Portland and Casco Bay, secondary roads turn south off U.S. 1 onto so many oddly chiseled peninsulas that it's possible to drive for days without retracing your route. Slow down to explore the museums, galleries, and shops in the larger towns and the antiques and curio shops and harborside lobster shacks in the smaller fishing villages on the peninsulas. Freeport is an entity unto itself, a place where numerous name-brand outlets and specialty stores have sprung up around the retail outpost of famous outfitter L. L. Bean. And no description of the coast would be complete without mention of popular Acadia National Park, with its majestic mountains that are often shrouded in mist.

Inland Maine likewise defies easy characterization. The terrain may be hilly or mountainous, heavily wooded or sprinkled with farms and villages. Much of the North Woods is virtually uninhabited. This is the land Henry David Thoreau wrote about in his evocative mid-19th-century portrait, *The Maine Woods*; in some ways it hasn't changed since the writer passed through.

If you come to Maine seeking an untouched fishing village with locals gathered around a potbellied stove in the general store, you'll likely come away disappointed; that innocent age has passed in all but the most remote spots like Way Down East or in the North Woods. Tourism has supplanted fishing, logging, and potato farming as Maine's number-one industry, and most areas are well equipped to receive the annual onslaught of visitors. But whether you are stepping outside a cabin for a walk in the woods or watching a boat rock at its anchor, you can sense the infinity of the natural world. Wilderness is always nearby, growing to the edges of the most urbanized spots.

MAINE TOP 5

■ **Freeport.** Main Street is like one giant mall—anchored by the L.L. Bean mother ship—except zoning laws ensure that the character and architecture of the street are maintained (witness, for example, the McDonald's located in a Victorian house, with a diminished logo and without a drive-thru).

■ **Portland Head Light.** The most familiar of Maine's 60-plus remaining lighthouses, it's accessible, photogenic, and historic. Watch tugboats head out to sea to escort large ships into Portland Harbor.

■ **Acadia National Park.** Maine has only one national park, and it's regularly one of the most visited in the United States. The scenic Loop Road leads all the way to the top of Cadil-lac Mountain, with 360-degree views of the surrounding coast. To head deeper into the park, walk along the carriage roads, built by John D. Rockefeller Jr.

■ **Seafood.** You should be sure to get some lobster while you're here, but you can also feast on clams, mussels, crabmeat, shrimp, scallops, halibut—the list goes on and on. You really can't go wrong, though—Maine seafood is about as fresh as it gets.

■ **Sailing.** No visit to the Maine Coast is complete without an ocean excursion, even if you don't leave the nearest bay. Take a ferry for an island tour, ride on a whale-watching boat, or sail aboard a grand old multimasted schooner from Maine's storied past.

7

EXPLORING MAINE

Maine is a large state that offers many different experiences. The York County Coast, in the southern portion of the state, is easily accessible and has long sand beaches, historic homes, and good restaurants. The coastal geography changes in Portland, the economic and cultural center of southern Maine. North of the city, long fingers of land jut into the sea, sheltering fishing villages. Penobscot Bay is famed for its rockbound coast, sailing, and numerous islands. Mount Desert Island lures crowds of people to Acadia National Park, which is filled with stunning natural beauty. Way Down East, beyond Acadia, the tempo changes; fast-food joints and trinket shops all but disappear, replaced by family-style restaurants and artisans' shops. Inland, the western lakes and mountains provide an entirely different experience. Summer camps, ski areas, and small villages populate this region. People head to Maine's North Woods to escape the crowds and to enjoy the great outdoors by hiking, rafting, camping, or canoeing.

ABOUT THE RESTAURANTS

Lobster and Maine are synonymous. As a general rule, the closer you are to a working harbor, the fresher your lobster will be. Aficionados eschew ordering lobster in restaurants, preferring to eat them "in the rough" at classic lobster pounds, where you select your dinner out of a pool and enjoy it at a waterside picnic table. Shrimp, scallops, clams, mussels, and crabs are also caught in the cold waters off Maine. Restaurants in Portland and in resort towns prepare shellfish in creative

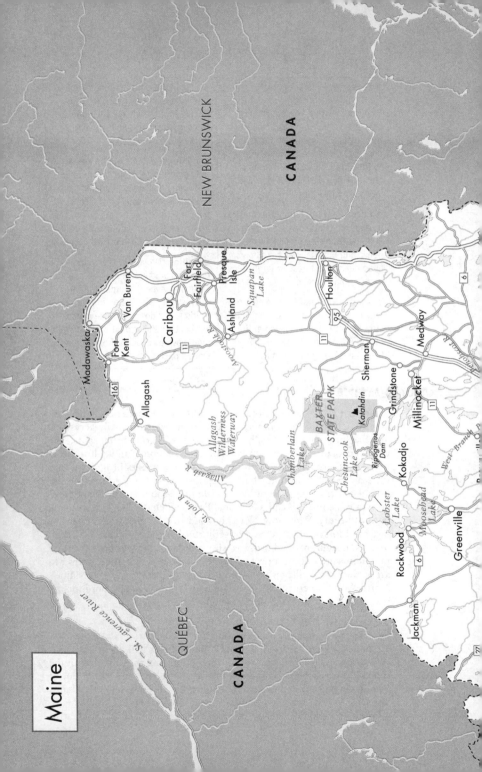

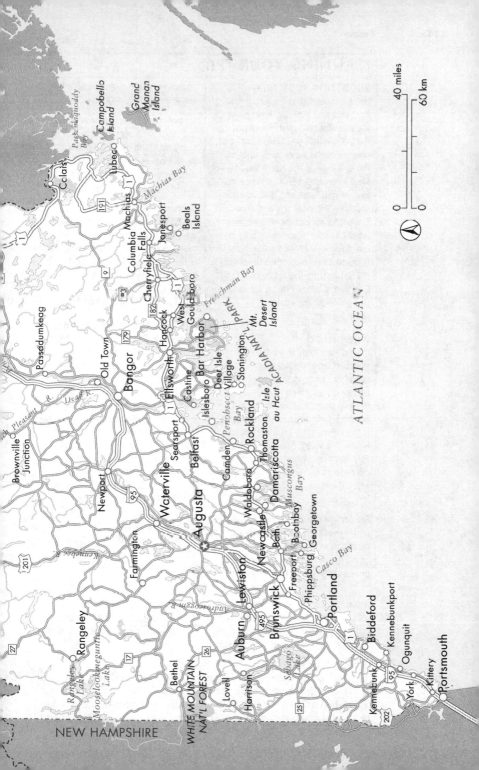

PLANNING YOUR TRIP

BUDGETING YOUR TRIP

You can spend days exploring just the coast of Maine, as these itineraries indicate, so plan ahead and decide whether you want to ski and dogsled in the western mountains, raft or canoe in the North Woods, or simply meander up the coast, stopping at museums and historic sites, shopping for local arts and crafts, and exploring coastal villages and lobster shacks. If you have only a few days, visit either Portland and Freeport or go farther north to Acadia National Park and Camden (and Rockport, if time). Whichever way you go, by all means try some lobster.

WHEN TO GO

In warm weather, the arteries along the coast and lakeside communities inland are clogged with out-of-state license plates, campgrounds are filled to capacity, and hotel rates are high. Even so, July to September is the choice time for a vacation in Maine. The weather is warmest in July and August, so throngs of people head to the beaches. September, when the days are still sunny, is far less crowded.

Fall foliage can be brilliant in Maine and is made even more so by its reflection in inland lakes or streams or off the ocean. Late September is peak season in the north country.

Elsewhere the prime viewing dates are in early or mid-October.

In winter, only a few places along the coast stay open for those who enjoy the solitude of the winter landscape. Maine's largest ski areas usually open in mid-November and provide good skiing often into April.

Springtime is mud season here, followed by spring flowers and the start of wildflowers in roadside meadows. Mid-May to mid-June is the main season for black flies, especially inland. It's best to schedule a trip after mid-June if possible, though this is prime canoeing time.

GETTING THERE & AROUND

Because Maine is large and rural, car transportation is essential, though buses operate in the larger cities. Interstate 95 is the Maine Turnpike, a toll road, from the New Hampshire border through Portland to Augusta. From there the interstate continues to Bangor and its terminus in Houlton at a Canadian border crossing. U.S. 1 winds through coastal regions, linking with peninsular routes. There are few public roads in Maine's North Woods, though private logging roads there are often open to the public (sometimes by permit only). ⇨ *See Maine Essentials at the end of this chapter for airport, train, and bus information.*

combinations with lobster, haddock, salmon, and swordfish. Blueberries are grown commercially in Maine, and local cooks use them generously in pancakes, muffins, jams, pies, and cobblers. Maine prohibits smoking in restaurants and bars.

ABOUT THE HOTELS

The beach communities in the south beckon with their weathered look. Stately digs can be found in the classic inns along the York County Coast. Bed-and-breakfasts and Victorian inns furnished with lace, chintz, and mahogany have joined the family-oriented motels of Ogunquit, Boothbay Harbor, Bar Harbor, and the Camden-Rockport region. Although accommodations tend to be less luxurious away from the coast, Bethel, Carrabassett Valley, and Rangeley have sophisticated hotels and inns. Greenville has the largest selection of restaurants and accommodations in the North Woods region. Lakeside sporting camps, from the primitive to the upscale, are popular around Rangeley and the North Woods. Many have cozy cabins heated with woodstoves and serve three hearty meals a day. At some of Maine's larger hotels and inns with restaurants, rates may include breakfast and dinner during the peak seasons.

WHAT IT COSTS					
	¢	$	$$	$$$	$$$$
RESTAU-RANTS	under $8	$8–$12	$13–$20	$21–$28	over $28
HOTELS	under $80	$80–$120	$121–$170	$171–$220	over $200
CAMPING	under $10	$10–$17	$18–$35	$36–$49	over $50

Restaurant prices are per person, for a main course at dinner. Hotel prices are for a standard double room during peak season and not including tax or gratuities. Some inns add a 15% service charge.

WESTERN LAKES & MOUNTAINS

By Mary Ruoff   Less than 20 mi northwest of Portland and the coast, the sparsely populated lake and mountain areas of western Maine stretch north along the New Hampshire border to Quebec. In winter this is ski country; in summer the woods and waters draw vacationers.

The Sebago–Long Lake region bustles with activity in summer. Harrison and the Waterfords are quieter, Center Lovell is a dreamy escape, and Kezar Lake, tucked away in a fold of the White Mountains, has long been a hideaway of the wealthy. Bethel, in the valley of the Androscoggin River, is a classic New England town, its town common lined with historic homes. The more rural Rangeley Lake area brings long stretches of pine, beech, spruce, and sky—and stylish inns and B&Bs with access to golf, boating, fishing, and hiking. Snow sports, especially snowmobiling, are popular winter pastimes. Carrabassett Valley, just north of Kingfield, is home to Sugarloaf, a major ski resort with a challenging golf course.

SEBAGO LAKE

17 mi northwest of Portland.

Sebago Lake, which provides all the drinking water for Greater Portland, is Maine's best-known lake after Moosehead (⇨ see The North Woods). Many camps and year-round homes surround Sebago, which is popular with watersports enthusiasts.

WHAT TO SEE

Sabbathday Lake Shaker Museum. Established in the late 18th century, this is the last active Shaker community in the United States, with fewer than 10 members. Open for guided tours are four buildings with rooms of Shaker furniture, folk art, tools, farm implements, and crafts from the 18th to the early 20th century: the 1794 Meetinghouse, the 1839 Ministry's Shop, where the elders and eldresses lived until the early 1900s, the 1821 Sister's Shop, where household goods and candies were made for sale and still are on a smaller scale, and the 1816 Spinhouse, where changing exhibits are housed. A store sells herbs and goods handcrafted by the Shakers. ✉ *707 Shaker Rd. (Hwy. 26, 20 mi north of Portland, 12 mi east of Naples, 8 mi west of Lewiston), New Gloucester* ☎ *207/926–4597* ⊕ *www.shaker.lib.me.us* 🎫 *Tour $6.50* ☉ *Late May–Columbus Day, Mon.–Sat. 10–4:30; first Sat. in Dec. for Christmas Fair.*

SPORTS & THE OUTDOORS

Sebago Lake State Park. This 1,300-acre park on the north shore of the lake, provides swimming, picnicking, camping (250 sites), boating, and fishing (salmon and togue). ✉ *11 Park Access Rd., Casco* ☎ *207/693–6613 May–mid-Oct. only, 207/693–6231* ⊕ *www.maine. gov/doc/parks* 🎫 *$4.50 mid-May–mid-Oct., $1.50 mid-Oct.–mid-May* ☉ *Daily 9–sunset.*

NAPLES

32 mi northwest of Portland.

Naples occupies an enviable location between Long and Sebago lakes. On clear days, the view down Long Lake takes in the Presidential Range of the White Mountains, highlighted by often-snowcapped Mt. Washington. The Causeway, which divides Long Lake from Brandy Pond, pulses with activity. Cruise and rental boats sail and motor on the lakes, open-air cafés overflow, and throngs of families parade along the sidewalk edging Long Lake. The town swells with seasonal residents and visitors in summer and all but shuts tight for winter.

ひ *Songo River Queen II,* a 92-foot stern-wheeler, takes passengers on hour-long cruises on Long Lake and longer voyages down the Songo River and through Songo Lock. ✉ *U.S. 302, Naples Causeway* ☎ *207/ 693–6861* ⊕ *www.songoriverqueen.net* 🎫 *Long Lake cruise $8, Songo River ride $15* ☉ *July–Labor Day, 5 cruises daily.*

WHERE TO STAY

$$$$ 🏨 **Migis Lodge.** The pine-paneled cottages scattered along the half mile
ひ of shorefront at this 125-acre resort have fieldstone fireplaces and are handsomely furnished with braided rugs and handmade quilts. A warm, woodsy feeling pervades the main lodge. The long front porch has views—marvelous at sunset—of Sebago Lake. All kinds of outdoor and indoor activities are included in the room rate, and canoes, kayaks, water-skiing and sailboats are available. Three fancy meals are served daily in the dining room. **Pros:** private island, waiters serve drinks at

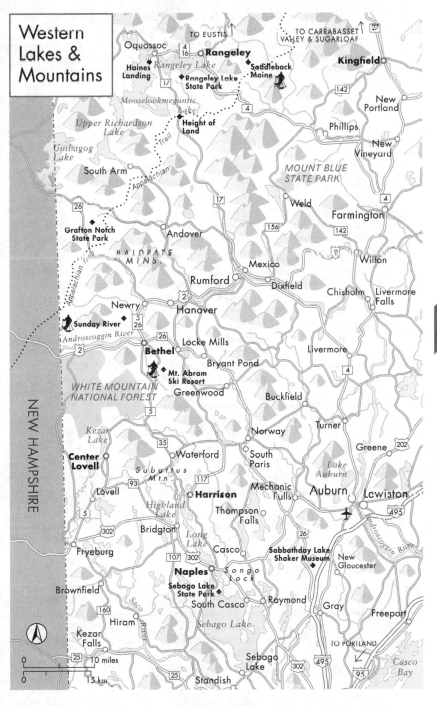

Western Lakes & Mountains

TO EUSTIS ↑

TO CARRABASSET
VALLEY & SUGARLOAF

27

Oquossoc

4
16

Rangeley

Rangeley Lake

♦ Saddleback
Maine

Kingfield

Haines
Landing

♦ Rangeley Lake
State Park

17

*Mooselookmeguntic
Lake*

142

New
Portland

*Upper Richardson
Lake*

♦ Height of
Land

4

Phillips

New
Vineyard

*Umbagog
Lake*

South Arm

Appalachian Trail

**MOUNT BLUE
STATE PARK**

4

26

Weld

Farmington

Grafton Notch
State Park

17

156

142

Wilton

BALDPATE
MTNS.

Andover

Mexico

Dixfield

Chisholm

Livermore
Falls

Appalachian Trail

Rumford

2

Livermore

Newry

Hanover

5
26

4

Sunday River

Androscoggin River

26

Locke Mills

Bethel

Bryant Pond

♦ Mt. Abram
Ski Resort

Buckfield

**WHITE MOUNTAIN
NATIONAL FOREST**

Greenwood

Turner

5

Norway

Greene

202

*Kezar
Lake*

35

*Lake
Auburn*

**Center
Lovell**

Waterford

South
Paris

*Subattus
Mtn.*

117

Mechanic
Falls

Auburn

Lewiston

Lovell

93

495

*Highland
Lake*

Harrison

Thompson
Falls

Androscoggin River

5

Bridgton

*Long
Lake*

26

Fryeburg

Casco

Sabbathday Lake
Shaker Museum ♦

New
Gloucester

107

302

Naples

*Songo
Lock*

Brownfield

Sebago Lake
State Park ♦

Raymond

Gray

Freeport

160

Hiram

Saco River

South Casco

Sebago Lake

Kezar
Falls

TO PORTLAND

*Casco
Bay*

25

0 ___ 10 miles

0 ___ 15 km

Sebago
Lake

302

495

95

25

Standish

NEW HAMPSHIRE

7

cocktail hour, fresh flowers from the gardens in lodgings. **Con:** week minimum in July and August (unless shorter openings occur). ⊠*30 Migis Lodge Rd., off U.S. 302, South Casco* ☎*207/655–4524* ⊕*www. migis.com* ⇆*35 cottages, 6 rooms* ⚷*In-room: no a/c (some), refrigerator, Wi-Fi (some). In-hotel: restaurant, tennis courts, gym, spa, beachfront, water sports, bicycles, children's programs ages 0–12, public Internet, public Wi-Fi, airport shuttle (fee), no-smoking rooms* ⊟*No credit cards* ⊗*Closed mid-Oct.–mid-June* ⦿*FAP.*

HARRISON

10 mi north of Naples, 25 mi south of Bethel.

Harrison anchors the northern end of Long Lake but is less commercial than Naples. The combination of woods, lakes, and views makes it a good choice for leaf-peepers. The nearby towns of North Waterford, South Waterford, and tiny Waterford, a National Historic District, are ideal for outdoors lovers who prefer to get away from the crowds.

WHERE TO STAY

$$-$$$$ 🏠**Bear Mountain Inn.** This rambling farmhouse inn has been meticu-
★   lously decorated in a woodsy theme. The luxurious Great Grizzly room has mesmerizing views and, like the other larger rooms, a fireplace, whirlpool bath for two, and wet bar. Cozy Sugar Bear Cottage is a romantic retreat, and the two-bedroom suites attract families. Breakfast is served in the dining room, which has a fieldstone fireplace and lake views. **Pros:** large lake-view deck with grill, benches and hammocks along riverside trail, "convenience area" with everything from beach bags to wine glasses to snacks. **Con:** one suite is considerably smaller. ⊠*Hwy. 35, Waterford, 04088* ☎*207/583–4404* ⊕*www.bear mtninn.com* ⇆*9 rooms, 2 suites, 1 cabin* ⚷*In-room: no a/c (some), no phone, DVD (some), VCR (some), no TV (some), Wi-Fi. In-hotel: beachfront, no elevator, water sports, public Internet, public Wi-Fi, some pets allowed (cabin only), no-smoking rooms* ⊟*MC, V* ⦿*BP.*

CENTER LOVELL

17 mi northwest of Harrison, 28 mi south of Bethel.

At Center Lovell you can glimpse the secluded Kezar Lake to the west, the retreat of wealthy and very private people. Sabattus Mountain, which rises behind Center Lovell, has a public hiking trail and stupendous views of the Presidential Range from the summit.

SPORTS & THE OUTDOORS

BOATING &   Next to a town boat launch with a small beach, **Kezar Lake Marina** (⊠*219*
FISHING   *W. Lovell Rd., at the Narrows, Lovell* ☎*207/925–3000* ⊕*www. kezarlake.com*) rents boats and watersports equipment. A store sells T-shirts and snacks as well as fishing supplies and water skis. Dine indoors or on the decks at the lakeside restaurant, The Loon's Nest, open mid-June to Labor Day. The marina operates from mid-April to October.

WHERE TO STAY

$ ⌕ **Center Lovell Inn.** The eclectic furnishings blend mid-19th and mid-20th centuries in a pleasing, homey style. In summer the best tables for dining at the on-site restaurant ($$–$$$$) are on the wraparound porch, which has sunset views over Kezar Lake and the White Mountains. Entrées may include pan-seared Muscovy duck, fillet of bison, or fresh swordfish. Breakfast is by reservation only (no lunch). Rooms are upstairs and in the adjacent Harmon House. **Pros:** suite has apartment feel. **Con:** no common TV. ✉ *1107 Main St. (Hwy. 5), 04016* ☎ *207/925 1575 or 800/777–2698* ⊕ *www.centerlovellinn.com* ⌒ *8 rooms, 6 with bath; 1 suite* ⌂ *In-room: no a/c, no phone, no TV (some). In-hotel: restaurant, no elevator, no-smoking rooms* ▬ *D, MC, V* ⊙ *Closed Nov.–late Dec. and Apr.–mid-May.*

$$$$ ⌕ **Quisisana.** This delightful cottage resort on Kezar Lake makes music
☾ a main focus. The staff—students and graduates of the country's finer music schools—perform everything from Broadway tunes to concert-piano pieces throughout your stay. Most of the white clapboard cottages have screened porches, pine-paneled living areas, fireplaces, and simple wicker and country furnishings. **Pros:** Tuesday cocktail party, dinner-hour children's program. **Con:** one-week minimum in peak season (unless shorter openings occur). ✉ *42 Quisisana Dr., off Pleasant Point Rd., 04016* ☎ *207/925–3500* ⊕ *www.quisisanaresort.com* ⌒ *11 rooms in 2 lodges, 32 cottages* ⌂ *In-room: no a/c, no phone, no TV. In-hotel: restaurant, bar, tennis courts, beachfront, water sports, no elevator, public Internet, public Wi-Fi, airport shuttle, no-smoking rooms* ▬ *No credit cards* ⊙ *Closed Sept.–mid-June* ⎪⎢⎥ *FAP.*

BETHEL

28 mi north of Lovell, 66 mi north of Portland.

Bethel is pure New England, a town with white clapboard houses and white-steeple churches and a mountain vista at the end of every street. In winter, this is ski country: Sunday River ski area in Newry is only a few miles north.

WHAT TO SEE

Regional History Center. A stroll in Bethel should begin at this history center at the Bethel Historical Society. The center's campus comprises two buildings, the 1821 O'Neil Robinson House and the 1813 Dr. Moses Mason House; both are listed on the National Register of Historic Places. The Robinson House has exhibits pertaining to the region's history; the Moses Mason House has nine period rooms and a front hall and stairway wall decorated with murals by folk artist Rufus Porter. Pick up materials for a walking tour of Bethel Hill Village. ✉ *10–14 Broad St.* ☎ *207/824–2908 or 800/824–2910* ⊕ *www.bethelhistorical. org* 🎫 *$3* ⊙ *O'Neil Robinson House: Tues.–Fri. 10–noon and 1–4; July–Aug. also Sat.–Sun. 1–4; Dr. Moses Mason House: July–Labor Day, Tues.–Sun. 1–4, and by appointment year-round.*

SPORTS & THE OUTDOORS

Grafton Notch State Park. At this park 14 mi north of Bethel, you can take an easy nature walk to Mother Walker Falls or Moose Cave and see the spectacular Screw Auger Falls, or you can hike to the summit of Old Speck Mountain, the state's third-highest peak. If you have the stamina and the equipment, you can pick up the Appalachian Trail here, hike over Saddleback Mountain, and continue on to Mt. Katahdin. The **Maine Appalachian Trail Club** (☐ *Box 283, Augusta 04330* ⊕ *www.matc. org*) publishes a map and trail guide. ⊠ *Hwy. 26* ☎ *207/824–2912 mid-May–mid-Oct., 207/624–6080* ▤ *Mid-May–mid-Oct. $2, mid-Oct.–mid-May $1.50* ⊙ *Daily 9–sunset.*

White Mountain National Forest. This forest straddles New Hampshire and Maine, with the highest peaks on the New Hampshire side. The Maine section, however, has magnificent rugged terrain, camping and picnic areas, and hiking from hour-long nature loops to a day hike up Speckled Mountain. Highway 113 through the forest is closed in the winter. ⊠ *Evans Notch Visitor Center, 18 Mayville Rd. (U.S. 2)* ☎ *207/824–2134* ⊕ *www.fs.fed.us/r9/white* ▤ *Day pass $3, week pass $5* ⊙ *Forest daily, 24 hours. Center Fri. and Sat. 8–4:30.*

CANOEING **Bethel Outdoor Adventure and Campground** (⊠ *121 Mayville Rd.* ☎ *207/ 824–4224 or 800/533–3607* ⊕ *www.betheloutdooradventure.com*) rents canoes, kayaks, and bikes, guides fishing, kayak, and canoe trips, and operates a hostel and riverside campground.

DOGSLEDDING **Mahoosuc Guide Service** (⊠ *1513 Bear River Rd., Newry* ☎ *207/824– 2073* ⊕ *www.mahoosuc.com*) leads day and multiday dogsledding expeditions on the Maine–New Hampshire border, as well as canoeing trips. Its **Mahoosic Mountain Lodge** (⊕ *www.mahoosucmountainlodge. com*) has dorm and bed-and-breakfast lodging.

HORSEBACK **Sparrowhawk Mountain Ranch** (⊠ *120 Fleming Rd.* ☎ *207/836–2528*
RIDING ⊕ *www.sparrowhawkmountainranch.com*) leads one-hour to daylong trail rides and also has an indoor arena. Parties of up to 10 can rent the guest house for overnight stays.

SKI AREAS **Bethel Inn Nordic Ski and Snowshoe Center** (⊠ *Village Common* ☎ *207/ 824–6276* ⊕ *www.bethelinn.com*) has 25 mi of cross-country trails, 5 mi of packed snowshoe trails, and provides ski and snowshoe rentals as well as lessons. It is located at the Bethel Inn Resort, which has a hotel and townhouse rentals. **Carter's Cross-Country Ski Center** (⊠ *786 Intervale Rd.* ☎ *207/824–3880 or 207/539–4848* ⊕ *www.cartersxcski. com*) has 33 mi of trails for all levels of skiers; lessons and snowshoe, ski, and sled (to pull children) rentals are provided. It also rents lodging rooms and ski-in cabins.

What was once a sleepy little ski area with minimal facilities has evolved into a sprawling resort that attracts skiers from as far away as Europe. Spread throughout the valley at **Sunday River** (⊠ *15 S. Ridge Rd., Turn on Sunday River Rd. from U.S. 2, Newry* ☎ *207/824–3000 main number, 207/824–5200 snow conditions, 800/543–2754 reservations* ⊕ *www.sundayriver.com*) are three base areas, two condominium hotels, trailside condominiums, town houses, and a ski dorm. Sunday River is home to the Maine Handicapped Skiing program, which provides lessons and services for skiers with disabilities. There's plenty else to do, including cross-country skiing, ice-skating, tubing, hiking, and mountain biking. Family-friendly **Mt. Abram Ski Resort** (Box 240, Greenwood 04255) 207/875 5000 www.skimtabram.com), south of Bethel, has night skiing.

SNOW-MOBILING **Sun Valley Sports** (129 Sunday River Rd. 207/824–7533 or 877/851–7533 www.sunvalleysports.com) gives guided snowmobile tours (rentals provided). It also operates fly-fishing trips, canoe and kayak rentals, guided ATV tours, and moose and wildlife safaris.

WHERE TO STAY

$-$$ **Victoria Inn.** It's hard to miss this turreted inn, with its teal-, mauve-, and beige-painted exterior and attached carriage house topped with a cupola. Inside, Victorian details include ceiling rosettes, stained-glass windows, elaborate fireplace mantels, and gleaming oak trim. Guest rooms vary in size (suites sleep three to eight); most are furnished with reproductions of antiques. The restaurant ($$–$$$$) is open most days for dinner, lunch, and (with 24-hour notice) afternoon tea. Choose from entrées like rack of lamb with basil and mint pesto, and duck with pomegranate sauce. **Pros:** lots of breakfast choices, homemade cookies in your room. **Con:** lofts in suites lack decor. 32 Main St. 207/824–8060 or 888/774–1235 www.thevictoria-inn.com 10 rooms, 4 suites In-room: Wi-Fi (some). In-hotel: restaurant, no elevator, Wi-Fi, no-smoking rooms AE, D, MC, V BP.

EN ROUTE The routes north from Bethel to the Rangeley district are all scenic, particularly in autumn when the maples are aflame with color. In the town of Newry, make a short detour to the **Artist's Bridge** (turn off Highway 26 onto Sunday River Road and drive about 4 mi), the most painted and photographed of Maine's eight covered bridges. Highway 26 continues north to the gorges and waterfalls of **Grafton Notch State Park.** Past the park, Highway 26 continues to Errol, New Hampshire, where Highway 16 will return you east around the north shore of Moosclookmeguntic Lake, through Oquossoc, and into Rangeley.

RANGELEY

67 mi north of Bethel.

Rangeley, on the north side of Rangeley Lake on Highways 4 and 16, has long lured anglers and winter-sports enthusiasts to its more than 40 lakes and ponds and 450 square mi of woodlands. Equally popular in summer or winter, Rangeley has a rough, wilderness feel to it. Lodgings are in the woods, around the lake, and along the golf course.

SPORTS & THE OUTDOORS

Rangeley Lake State Park. On the south shore of Rangeley Lake, this park has superb lakeside scenery, swimming, picnic tables, a boat ramp, showers, and 50 campsites. S. Shore Dr., off Hwy. 17 or Hwy. 4

☎*207/864–3858 May 15–Oct. 1 only, 207/624–6080* ⊕*www.state. me.us/doc/parks* ⌨*$3* ⊙*May 15–Oct. 1.*

BOATING & FISHING Rangeley and Mooselookmeguntic lakes are good for canoeing, sailing, and motorboating. Fishing for brook trout and salmon is at its best in May, June, and September; the Rangeley area is especially popular with fly-fishers.

SKI AREAS **Rangeley Lakes Trail Center** (✉ *524 Saddleback Mountain Rd.* ☎*207/864– 4309* ⊕*www.xcskirangeley.com*) rents cross-country skis and snow-shoes and has about 30 mi of groomed trails surrounding Saddleback Mountain.

A family atmosphere prevails at **Saddleback Maine** (✉*976 Saddle-back Mountain Rd., follow signs from Hwy. 4* ☎*207/864–5671 or 866/918–2225, 207/864–5441 or 877/864–5441 reservations* ⊕*www. saddlebackmaine.com*), where the quiet, lack of crowds, and spectacu-larly wide valley views draw return visitors. The 60 trails, accessed by five lifts, are about evenly divided between novice, intermediate, and advanced. On-site is also a day-care center, ski school, rental and retail shop, and trailside condominium lodging. Hiking (the Appalachian Trail crosses Saddleback's summit ridge), mountain biking, canoeing, fly-fishing, and birding are big draws in warm weather.

WHERE TO EAT & STAY

$$-$$$ ✗**Gingerbread House Restaurant.** A big fieldstone fireplace, well-spaced
AMERICAN tables, and an antique marble soda fountain, all with views of the woods beyond, make for comfortable surroundings at this gingerbread-trim establishment, which is open for breakfast, lunch, and dinner. Soups, salads, and sandwiches at lunch give way to entrées such as Maine crab cakes and barbequed ribs with blueberry chipotle sauce and maple syrup. ✉*55 Carry Rd. (Hwy. 4), Oquossoc* ☎*207/864– 3602* ☰*AE, D, MC, V* ⊙*Closed Nov. and Apr.; and Mon. and Tues., Dec.–Mar. No lunch or dinner Sun., Dec.–Mar. and May–mid-June.*

$-$$ ⌂**Country Club Inn.** Built in 1920 as the country club for the adjacent
ⓒ Mingo Springs Golf Course, this secluded hilltop retreat has sweeping lake and mountain views. Fieldstone fireplaces anchor both ends of the lodge-like common room. Rooms downstairs in the main build-ing and in the adjacent 1950s motel are cheerfully, if minimally, deco-rated. Inside the glassed-in dining room ($$-$$$$)—open to nonguests by reservation only—you can dine on such entrées as veal Gruyère and roast duck Montmorency. **Pros:** loads of lawn and board games, lots of photos of Rangeley's long-gone resorts. **Con:** smallish rooms in main building. ✉*56 Country Club Rd.* ☎*207/864–3831* ⊕*www. countryclubinnrangeley.com* ⇦*19 rooms* ⌕*In-room: no a/c (some), no TV, refrigerators (some). In-hotel: restaurant, bar, pool, no elevator, public Internet, some pets allowed, no-smoking rooms* ☰*AE, MC, V* ⊙*Closed Nov. and Apr.* ⊣⊙*BP, MAP.*

¢-$ ⌂**Rangeley Inn and Motor Lodge.** From Main Street you see only the large three-story blue inn, built in the early 1900s for wealthy urbanites on vacation. Behind it is a motel wing with decks on most rooms and views of Haley Pond, a lawn, and a garden. Some of the inn's sizable rooms have iron-and-brass beds. Some baths are marble, some have claw-foot tubs, others have whirlpool tubs. **Pros:** historic hotel last of its kind the region. **Con:** elegant dining room closed at this writing. ✉*2443 Main St., 04970* ☎*207/864–3341 or 800/666–3687* ⊕*www.rangeleyinn.com* ⌕*35 inn rooms, 15 motel rooms (including 1 suite)* ⅃*In-room: no a/c (some), kitchen (some). In-hotel: restaurant, some pets allowed (fee)* ▤*AE, D, MC, V* ⊘*Closed Apr.–May and Nov.–Dec.*

KINGFIELD

33 mi east of Rangeley, 15 mi west of Phillips.

In the shadows of Mt. Abram and Sugarloaf Mountain, Kingfield has everything a "real" New England town should have: a general store, historic inns, and white clapboard churches. Sugarloaf has golf and tennis in summer.

SPORTS & THE OUTDOORS

SKI AREAS Abundant natural snow, a huge mountain, and the only above-tree-
🜊 line lift-service skiing in the East have made **Sugarloaf** (✉*5092 Access Rd., Carrabassett Valley* ☎*207/237–2000, 207/237–6808 snow conditions, 800/843–5623 reservations* ⊕*www.sugarloaf.com)* one of Maine's best-known ski areas. Two slope-side hotels and hundreds of slope-side condominiums provide ski-in, ski-out access, and the base village has restaurants and shops. The Outdoor Center has more than 60 mi of cross-country ski trails as well as snowshoeing, snow tubing, and ice-skating activities. There's also plenty for the kids, from day care to special events. Once you are here, a car is unnecessary—a shuttle connects all mountain operations. Summer is much quieter than winter, but you can bike, fish, and hike, plus golf at the superb 18-hole, Robert Trent Jones Jr.–designed golf course.

THE NORTH WOODS

By Mary Ruoff   Maine's North Woods, the vast area in the north-central section of the state, is best experienced by canoe or raft, on a hiking, snowshoe or snowmobile trip, or on a fishing trip. Some great theaters for these activities are Moosehead Lake, Baxter State Park, and the Allagash Wilderness Waterway—as well as the summer resort town of Greenville. Maine's largest lake, Moosehead supplies more in the way of rustic camps, guides, and outfitters than any other northern locale. Its 420 mi of shorefront, three-quarters of which is owned by paper manufacturers, is virtually uninhabited.

GREENVILLE

160 mi northeast of Portland, 71 mi northwest of Bangor.

Greenville, the largest town on Moosehead Lake, is an outdoors lover's paradise. Boating, fishing, and hiking are popular in summer, while snowmobiling, skiing, and ice fishing reign in winter. The town also has

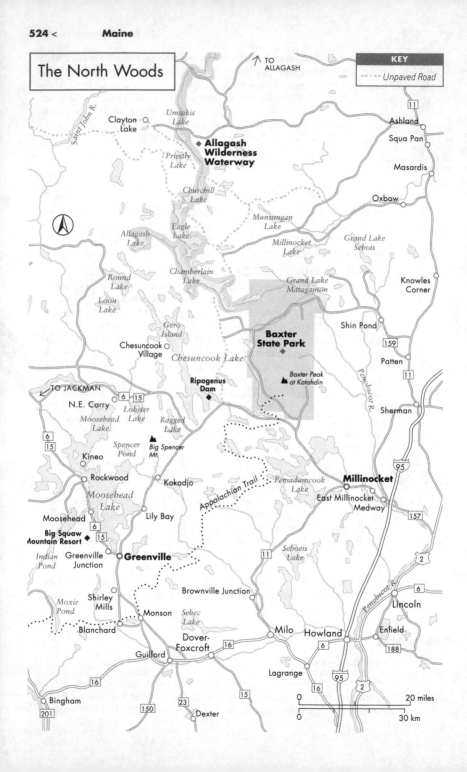

The North Woods

KEY
- - - - *Unpaved Road*

↑ TO ALLAGASH

Saint John R.

Clayton Lake

Umsakis Lake

Ashland

Squa Pan

Masardis

Allagash Wilderness Waterway

Priestly Lake

Churchill Lake

Oxbow

Munsungan Lake

Millinocket Lake

Grand Lake Seboeis

Eagle Lake

Allagash Lake

Knowles Corner

Round Lake

Chamberlain Lake

Grand Lake Matagamon

Loon Lake

Gero Island

Shin Pond

Baxter State Park

159

Chesuncook Village

Chesuncook Lake

Patten

11

←TO JACKMAN

Ripogenus Dam

Baxter Peak at Katahdin

Penobscot R.

Sherman

N.E. Carry

6 15

Lobster Lake

Moosehead Lake

Ragged Lake

Big Spencer Mt.

95

Spencer Pond

6 15

Kineo

Rockwood

Kokadjo

Millinocket

Appalachian Trail

Pemadumcook Lake

East Millinocket

Medway

157

Moosehead Lake

Lily Bay

Moosehead

Big Squaw Mountain Resort

6

15

Seboeis Lake

Indian Pond

Greenville Junction

Greenville

11

Moxie Pond

Shirley Mills

Brownville Junction

2

6

Lincoln

Monson

Sebec Lake

Enfield

Blanchard

Dover-Foxcroft

16

Milo

Howland

188

Lagrange

Guilford

6

95

16

Bingham

16

2

201

150

23

15

Dexter

0   20 miles

0   30 km

the greatest selection of shops, restaurants, and inns in the region—note that some of these, however, are closed mid October to mid June.

WHAT TO SEE

Moosehead Historical Society. The historical society leads guided tours of the Eveleth-Crafts-Sheridan House, a late-19th-century Victorian mansion filled with period antiques, most original to the home. Special exhibits and displays change annually. A small lumberman's museum and a fine exhibit of American Indian artifacts dating from 9,000 BC to the 1700s are in the Carriage House. ☎444 Pritham Ave. ☎207/695–2909 ⊕www.mooseheadhistory.org ☎$4 ☉Eveleth-Crafts-Sheridan House mid-June–Sept., Wed.–Fri. 1–4. Carriage House Tues.–Fri. 9–4 or by appointment.

OFF THE BEATEN PATH

Mt. Kineo. Once a thriving summer resort for the wealthy, the Mount Kineo Hotel (the original was built in 1830, its last successor torn down in the 1940s) was accessed primarily by steamship. Today Kineo makes a pleasant day trip. You can take the Kineo Shuttle, which departs from the State Dock in **Rockwood**, or rent a motorboat in Rockwood and make the journey across the lake in about 15 minutes. It's an easy hike to Kineo's summit for awesome views down the lake. A map is available at the Moosehead Lake Region Chamber of Commerce.

SPORTS & THE OUTDOORS

Lily Bay State Park. Eight miles northeast of Greenville on Moosehead Lake, this park has a good swimming beach, two boat-launching ramps, and two campgrounds with 91 sites. ☎13 Myrle's Way, off Lily Bay Rd. ☎207/695–2700 May 15–Oct. 15 only, 207/941–4014 ⊕www.state.me.us/doc/parks ☎$3 ☉May 15–Oct. 15, daily 9–sunset.

BIKING Mountain biking is popular in the Greenville area, but bikes are not allowed on some logging roads. Expect to pay about $20 per day for a rental bicycle. **Northwoods Outfitters** (☎5 Lily Bay Rd., Greenville ☎207/695–3288 ⊕www.maineoutfitter.com) rents mountain bikes, kids bikes, and more.

FISHING Togue (lake trout), landlocked salmon, small mouth bass, and brook trout lure thousands of anglers to the region from ice-out in mid-May until September; the hardiest return in winter to ice fish.

RAFTING The Kennebec and Dead rivers and the west branch of the Penobscot River provide thrilling white-water rafting (guides are strongly recommended). These rivers are dam-controlled, so trips run rain or shine daily from mid-April to mid-October (day and multiday trips are conducted). Many rafting outfitters operate resort facilities in their base towns. **Raft Maine** (☎800/723–8633 ⊕www.raftmaine.com) has lodging and rafting packages and information about outfitters.

SKIING **Big Squaw Mountain Resort.** This remote but pretty resort overlooking Moosehead Lake is open weekends, holidays, and Maine school-vacation weeks. The chairlift to the black diamond trails has been shut down since a 2004 accident, and the hotel is closed, but with downright cheap prices, families still come here to ski. There are plans to expand the resort and fully reopen. ✉ *Hwys. 6/15* ☎ *207/695–1000 or 800/754–6246* ⊕ *www.bigsquawmountain.com.*

TOURS
★

Katahdin. The Moosehead Marine Museum runs three- and five-hour trips on Moosehead Lake (eight-hour foliage cruise in late fall) aboard the *Katahdin,* a 115-foot 1914 steamship (now diesel). Also called *The Kate,* the ship carried passengers to Mt. Kineo until 1933 and then was used in the logging industry until 1975. The trips range in price from $30 to $35. The boat and the shore-side museum have displays about the steamships that transported people and cargo on the lake more than 100 years ago. ✉ *12 Lily Bay Rd.* ☞ *(board on shoreline by museum)* ☎ *207/695–2716* ⊕ *www.katahdincruises.com* ⊙ *Memorial Day weekend–Columbus Day.*

OFF THE
BEATEN
PATH

Gulf Hagas. From the site of the old Katahdin Iron Works, a hiking trail leads over fairly rugged terrain to Gulf Hagas, a National Natural Landmark with natural chasms, cliffs, a 5.2-mi gorge, waterfalls, pools, exotic flora, and rock formations. Access is on land managed by **North Maine Woods** (☎ *207/435–6213* ⊕ *www.northmainewoods.org*) for public use. From Greenville, take Pleasant Street east (road becomes gravel) about 19 mi, follow signs to gulf. From Millinocket, take Hwy. 11 south about 32 mi to the Katahdin Iron Works Checkpoint, continue 7 mi on dirt road, follow signs.

WHERE TO EAT & STAY

$-$$
ITALIAN

✕ **Villa Banca.** On the ground floor of a dramatic, turreted office building, this airy spot with high ceilings and tall windows specializes in both traditional and contemporary Italian cooking. Get a little taste of everything by ordering a starter sampler platter consisting of seafood risotto cakes, lobster-stuffed artichokes, chicken sausage, fried spinach-and-artichoke ravioli, chicken in phyllo dough, and fried calamari. Then move on to the delicious pastas and grills, including gnocchi with wood-grilled turkey and prosciutto, and chicken-and-sausage lasagna. Note the exotic-martini menu—a big draw at happy hour. ✉ *194 Main St.* ☎ *603/598–0500* ▤ *AE, D, DC, MC, V* ⊙ *No lunch weekends.*

$$$$
★

▦ **Blair Hill Inn.** Beautiful gardens and a hilltop location with marvelous views over the lake distinguish this 1891 estate. So do fine antiques, plush bedding, and elegant baths, some with oversized or footed tubs. Guest rooms are spacious; all have sitting areas and four have fireplaces. A restaurant (reservations required) serves a prix-fixe five-course dinner ($$$$) from mid-June to mid-October on Friday and Saturday nights. Arrive early to enjoy cocktails on the wraparound porch. The inn hosts a music series in July and August. **Pros:** third-floor deck the length of the inn; 15 acres with stone paths, wooded picnic area, and trout pond, flowers from gardens in rooms. **Con:** steep driveway. ✉ *351 Lily Bay Rd. 04441* ☎ *207/695–0224* ⊕ *www.blairhill. com* ➳ *7 rooms, 1 suite* ⚭ *In-room: no a/c (some), no phone. In-hotel: restaurant, no elevator, public Internet, no-smoking rooms* ▤ *D, MC, V* ⊙ *Closed Apr. and Nov.* ❧❘*BP.*

$$$$

▦ **Little Lyford Pond Camps.** When you want to get away from everything—including electricity, plumbing, and phones—head to this remote, rustic wilderness retreat, part of the Appalachian Mountain

NORTH WOODS OUTFITTERS

BOATING

Allagash Canoe Trips (✉ 8 Bigelow, Carrabassett Valley ☎ 207/237–3077 ⊕ www.allagash canoetrips.com) operates guided trips on the Allagash Waterway, plus the Moose, Penobscot, and St. John rivers. **Beaver Cove Marina** (☎ 207/695–3526 ⊕ www.beavercovemarina.com) rents boats. **Katahdin Outfitters** (✉ Less than ¼ mi outside Millinocket on Baxter State Park Rd. ☎ 207/723–5700 or 800/862–2663 ⊕ www.katahdinoutfitters.com) outfits canoeing and kayaking expeditions. **North Woods Ways** (✉ 2293 Elliotsville Rd., Willimantic ☎ 207/997–3723 ⊕ www.northwoodsways.com) leads overnight canoe and snowshoe trips (gear is hauled on toboggans).

If requested, most canoe-rental operations will also arrange transportation, help plan your route, and provide a guide. Transportation to wilderness lakes can be handled through various regional flying services (⇨ By Air in Maine Essentials).

MULTI-SPORT

Moose Country Safaris (☎ 207/876–4907 ⊕ www. moosecountrysafaris.com) leads moose safaris and canoe, kayak, Jeep, snowshoe, and hiking trips. **New England Outdoor Center** (☎ 207/723–5438 or 800/766–7238 ⊕ www.neoc.com) rents snowmobiles and canoes and offers guided snowmobile, whitewater rafting, fishing, canoe, hiking, and moose-watching trips. It also has campgrounds and rents cabins. **Northwoods Outfitters** (✉ 5 Lilly Bay Rd ☎ 207/695–3288 ⊕ www. maineoutfitter.com) outfits for moose watching, biking, skiing, snowmobiling, snowboarding, canoeing, kayaking, and fishing; leads trips for many of these activities; and rents canoes, kayaks, bikes, snowmobiles, snowshoes and more. Shop, get trail advice, and kick back in the Internet café at its downtown outfitters store.

RAFTING

Raft Maine (☎ 800/723–8633 ⊕ www.raftmaine.com) is an association of white-water outfitters licensed to lead trips down the Kennebec and Dead rivers and the west branch of the Penobscot River. Rafting season begins in mid-April and continues through mid-October.

Club lodging network. Gulf Hagas is a 2-mi hike away, moose abundantly populate the area, and the fly-fishing, snowshoeing, and backcountry skiing are excellent. Cabins boast woodstoves and gas and kerosene lanterns. The home-cooked fare is served family style in the main lodge. **Pros:** family adventure camps in summer; cedar sauna in winter. **Con:** winter access is by cross-country ski or snowmobile transport (for a fee). ✉ About 10 mi east of Greenville, access via logging roads ☎ 603/466–2727 ⊕ www.outdoors.org/lodging ➥ 7 cabins, 12-bed bunkhouse ⚒ In-room: no a/c, no phone, no TV. In-hotel: restaurant, water sports, no-smoking rooms ▤ AE, MC, V ⊙ Closed Apr.–mid-May and Nov.–late Dec. ⦿ FAP.

SCENIC DRIVE

For a scenic backwoods trip, travel the Golden Road from the Greenville area east toward Baxter State Park and Millinocket. The road is named for the amount of money it took the Great Northern Paper Company to build it.

From downtown Greenville, take Lily Bay Road north to Kokadjo and follow the dirt Sias Hill/Greenville Road to its end, then turn right on the Golden Road (it soon becomes paved). Note: keep to the right, as logging trucks have the right of way. Turn left on Rip Dam Road to drive across Ripogenus Dam, at the head of Ripogenus Lake (east of Chesuncook Lake) and granite-walled Ripogenus Gorge. It is about 20 mi northeast of Kokadjo, and 16 mi southeast of Chesuncook Village by floatplane.

The turnaround north of the dam has the best gorge views. The Penobscot River drops more than 70 feet per mile through the gorge, giving white-water rafters a hold-on-for-your-life ride. The best spot to watch the rafters is from the overlook at the rock-choked Crib Works Rapid (a Class V rapid). To get there, continue on the Golden Road and turn left on Telos Road. The parking area is just after the single-lane bridge (don't loiter on bridge).

Returning to the Golden Road, take photos of Mt. Katahdin from the foot-bridge alongside one-lane Abol Bridge (park well off the road)—this view is famed. Turn left at North Woods Trading Post to connect with Highway 157; turn left again for Baxter State Park or right for Millinocket.

MILLINOCKET

67 mi north of Bangor, 88 mi northwest of Greenville via Hwys. 6 and 11.

Millinocket, a paper-mill town with a population of 5,000, is a gate-way to Baxter State Park and Maine's North Woods. Although it has a smattering of motels and restaurants, Millinocket is the place to stock up on supplies, fill your gas tank, or grab a hot meal or shower before heading into the wilderness. Numerous rafting and canoeing outfitters and guides are based here.

SPORTS & THE OUTDOORS

★ **Allagash Wilderness Waterway.** A spectacular 92-mi corridor of lakes and rivers, the waterway cuts across 170,000 acres of wilderness, beginning at the northwest corner of Baxter State Park and running north to the town of Allagash, 10 mi from the Canadian border. From mid-May to October, this is prime canoeing (and camping) country, but it should not be undertaken lightly. On the lakes, strong winds can halt your progress for days; on the river, conditions vary greatly with the depth and volume of water, and although the Allagash rapids are ranked Class I and Class II (very easy and easy, respectively), the river is not a piece of cake. The complete 92-mi course requires seven to 10 days. The best bet for a novice is to go with a guide; a good outfitter will help plan your route and provide your craft and transportation. ⊠ *Maine Bureau of Parks and Lands, 106 Hogan Rd., Bangor* ☎ *207/941–4014* ⊕ *www.maine.gov/doc/parks.*

Fodor'sChoice **Baxter State Park.** A gift from Governor Percival Baxter, this is the jewel ★ in the crown of northern Maine, a 209,501-acre wilderness area that surrounds **Mt. Katahdin,** Maine's highest mountain (5,267 feet at Baxter Peak) and the terminus of the Appalachian Trail. Katahdin draws thousands of hikers every year for the daylong climb to the summit and the stunning views of woods, mountains, and lakes. Three trailheads lead to its peak; some routes include the hair-raising Knife Edge Ridge. The crowds climbing Katahdin can be formidable on clear summer days, so if you crave solitude, tackle one of the 45 other mountains in the park, 17 of which exceed an elevation of 3,000 feet and all of which are accessible from an extensive network of trails. South Turner can be climbed in a morning (if you're fit), and its summit has a great view of Katahdin across the valley. On the way you'll pass Sandy Stream Pond, where moose are often seen at dusk. The Owl, the Brothers, and Doubletop Mountain are good day hikes.

Day-use parking areas fill quickly in season at Baxter; it's best to arrive early, between 5 and 6 AM (limited parking held until 8 AM for Maine residents by reservation). No pets, domestic animals, oversize vehicles, radios, all-terrain vehicles, motorboats, or motorcycles are allowed in the park, and there are no pay phones, gas stations, stores, running water, or electricity. The camping is primitive, and sites typically fill up well ahead for peak season. The visitor center is at the southern entrance outside Millinocket. You can also get information about Baxter in town at park headquarters. ⊠*64 Balsam Dr., Millinocket* ⊹ *Togue Pond Gate (southern entrance): Hwy. 157, 18 mi northwest of Millinocket; Matagamon Gate (northern entrance): Grand Lake Rd., 26 mi northwest of Patten via Hwy. 159 and Grand Lake Rd.* ☏*207/723 5140* ⊕*www.baxterstateparkauthority.com* ⊠*$13 per vehicle (free to Maine residents)* ⊙*Daily, sunrise to sunset.*

WHERE TO STAY

CAMPING   ⚠**Baxter State Park Authority.** Camping spaces at the park's 10 primitive campgrounds (no electricity or running water) must be reserved by mail or in person (check or cash) within four months of your trip, or by phone (MC or V only) two weeks prior. Phones reservations are much harder to come by for July, August, and fall weekends, but cancellations do open up spots. There are also primitive backcountry sites. **Pro:** cabins at Daicey Pond and Kidney Pond campgrounds. **Con:** winter access is by ski or snowshoe. ⊠*64 Balsam Dr., Millinocket* ⊹ *Togue Pond Gate (southern entrance): Hwy. 157, 18 mi northwest of Millinocket; Matagamon Gate (northern entrance): Grand Lake Rd., 26 mi northwest of Patten via Hwy. 159 and Grand Lake Rd.* ☏*207/723–5140* ⊕*www.baxterstateparkauthority.com* ⚠ *22 cabins, 4 bunkhouses, 57 lean-tos, 75 tent sites, 13 group tent sites* ⚭*Pit toilets, fire grates, fire rings, picnic tables, ranger stations, swimming (pond, lake, stream)* ▤*MC, V* ⊙*Closed mid-Oct.–Nov. and Apr.–mid-May.*

THE SOUTHERN COAST

By Laura V. Scheel

Maine's southernmost coastal towns—Kittery, the Yorks, Ogunquit, the Kennebunks, and the Old Orchard Beach area—reveal a few of the stunning faces of the state's coast, from the miles and miles of inviting

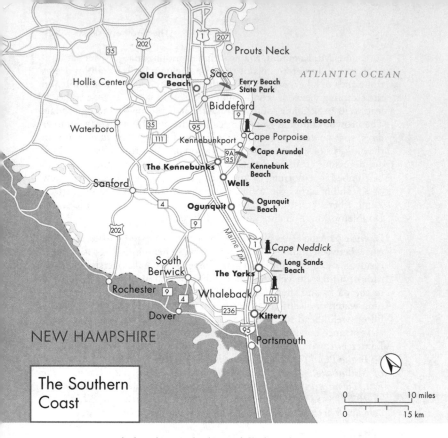

The Southern Coast

sandy beaches to the beautifully kept historic towns and carnival-like attractions. There is something for every taste, whether you seek solitude in a kayak or prefer being caught up in the infectious spirit of fellow vacationers. The Southern Coast is best explored on a leisurely holiday of two days—more if you require a fix of solid beach time.

North of Kittery, long stretches of hard-packed white-sand beach are closely crowded by nearly unbroken ranks of beach cottages, motels, and oceanfront restaurants. The summer colonies of York Beach and Wells brim with crowds and ticky-tacky shorefront overdevelopment, but nearby, quiet wildlife refuges and land reserves promise an easy escape. York evokes yesteryear sentiment with its acclaimed historic district, while upscale Ogunquit tantalizes stylish and sporty visitors with its array of shops and a cliff-side walk.

The Kennebunks—and especially Kennebunkport—provide the complete Maine Coast experience: classic townscapes where white clapboard houses rise from manicured lawns and gardens; rocky shorelines punctuated by sandy beaches; quaint downtown districts packed with gift shops, ice-cream stands, and visitors; harbors with lobster boats bobbing alongside yachts; rustic, picnic-tabled restaurants specializing in lobster and fried seafood (aka lobster pounds in Maine lingo); and well-appointed dining rooms. As you continue north, the scents of french fries, pizza, and cotton candy hover in the air above Maine's version of Coney Island, Old Orchard Beach.

KITTERY

55 mi north of Boston; 5 mi north of Portsmouth, New Hampshire

One of the earliest settlements in the state of Maine, Kittery suffered its share of British, French, and American Indian attacks throughout the 17th and 18th centuries, yet rose to prominence as a vital shipbuilding center. The tradition continues; despite its New Hampshire name, the Portsmouth Naval Shipyard is part of Maine and has been one of the leading researchers and builders of U.S. submarines since its inception in 1800. The shipyard has the distinction of being the oldest naval shipyard continuously operated by the U.S. government and is a major source of local employment. It's not open to the public.

Kittery has come to more recent light as a major shopping destination thanks to its complex of factory outlets. Flanked on either side of U.S. 1 are more than 120 stores, which attract hordes of shoppers year-round. For something a little less commercial, head east on Route 103 to the hidden Kittery most people miss: the lands around **Kittery Point.** Here you can find hiking and biking trails and, best of all, great views of the water.

SHOPPING

Kittery has more than 120 outlet stores. Along a several-mile stretch of U.S. 1 you can find just about anything, from hardware to underwear. Among the stores are Crate & Barrel, Eddie Bauer, Jones New York, Esprit, Waterford/Wedgwood, Lenox, Ralph Lauren, and J. Crew.

WHERE TO EAT

$$-$$$
SEAFOOD
✗**Warren's Lobster House.** A local institution, this waterfront restaurant specializes in seafood and has a huge salad bar. The pine-sided dining room leaves the impression that little has changed since Warren's opened in 1940. Dine outside overlooking the water when the weather is nice. ✉ *U.S. 1 and Water St.* ☎ *207/439-1630* ▭ *AE, MC, V.*

$-$$$
★
SEAFOOD
✗**Chauncey Creek Lobster Pound.** From the road you can barely see this restaurant's red roof hovering below the trees, but chances are you can see the cars parked at this popular spot amid the high banks of the tidal river. The menu has lots of fresh lobster items and a raw bar with locally harvested offerings like clams and oysters. Bring your own beer or wine if you desire alcohol. In season, it's open daily for lunch and dinner. ✉ *Chauncey Creek Rd., Kittery Point* ☎ *207/439-1030* ▭ *MC, V* ⊗ *Closed Nov.–Apr.*

THE YORKS

Beginning about 6 mi north of Kittery on Highway 103 or U.S. 1A.

The Yorks—York Village, York Harbor, York Beach, and Cape Neddick—are typical of small-town coastal communities in New England

and are smaller than most. Many of their nooks and crannies can be explored in a few hours. The beaches are the big attraction here.

Not unlike siblings in most families, the towns within this region reveal vastly different personalities. York Village and York Harbor, 3 mi farther north, abound with old money, picturesque mansions, impeccably manicured lawns, and gardens and shops that cater to a more staid and wealthy clientele. Continue 6 mi north along U.S. 1A to York Beach and soon all the pretense falls away like autumn leaves in a storm—it's family vacation time (and party time), with scores of T-shirt shops, ice-cream and fried-seafood joints, arcades and bowling, and motor court–style motels. Left from earlier days are a number of trailer and RV parks spread across the road from the beach—in prime real estate that must have developers and moneyed old-timers in pure agony. About 4 mi north of York Beach, Cape Neddick blends back into more peaceful and gentle terrain.

WHAT TO SEE

Mount Agamenticus Park. Maintained by the York Parks and Recreation Department, this humble summit of 692 feet above sea level is said to be the highest peak along the Atlantic seaboard. That may not seem like much, but if you choose to hike to the top, you will be rewarded with incredible views that span all the way to the White Mountains in New Hampshire. If you don't want to hoof it (though it's not very steep), there is parking at the top. The Nature Conservancy has chosen the site as very significant owing to the variety of unusual natural flora and fauna. To get here, take Mountain Road just off U.S. 1 in Cape Neddick (just after Flo's Steamed Hot Dogs) and follow the signs. The area is open daily, with no charge. It's a popular place for equestrians and cyclists as well as families and hikers. ⬧ *York Parks and Recreation Department, 200 U.S. Rte. 1 S, York 03909* ☎*207/363–1040.*

Nubble Light. Head out a couple of miles on the peninsula to see one of the most photographed lighthouses on the globe. Set out on a hill of rocks, the lighthouse is still in use. Direct access is prohibited, but an informational center shares the 1879 light's history. Find parking at Sohier Park, at the end of Nubble Road, as well as restrooms and plenty of benches. ✉*End of Nubble Rd., York Beach, off U.S. 1A.*

SHOPPING

Home furnishings with an antique feel are the specialty of **Jeremiah Campbell & Company** (✉*1537 U.S. 1, Cape Neddick* ☎*207/363–8499*). Everything here is handcrafted, from rugs, decoys, furniture, and lighting to glassware. The shop is closed Wednesday. Quilt and fabric lovers will delight in a visit to **Knight's Quilt Shop** (✉*1901 U.S. 1, Cape Neddick* ☎*207/361–2500*), where quilts and everything needed to make them—including instructional classes—can be found.

NIGHTLIFE & THE ARTS

Inn on the Blues (✉*7 Ocean Ave., York Beach* ☎*207/351–3221*) is a hopping blues club that attracts national bands.

WHERE TO EAT

¢
★
AMERICAN
✗**Flo's Steamed Hot Dogs.** Yes, it seems crazy to highlight a hot dog stand, but this is no ordinary place. Who would guess that a hot dog could make it into *Saveur* and *Gourmet* magazines? But there is something grand about this shabby, red-shingle shack that has been dealing dogs since 1959. The line is out the door most days but the operation is so efficient that the wait is not long at all. Flo has passed but her granddaughter keeps the business going, selling countless thousands of hot dogs each year. Be sure to ask for the special sauce—consisting of, among other things, hot sauce and mayo (you can take a bottle of the sauce home, and you'll want to). ⊠*1359 U.S. 1, Cape Neddick* 🕾*No phone* ⊟*No credit cards* ⊘*Closed Wed.*

$$$
SEAFOOD
✗**Foster's Downeast Clambake.** Save your appetite for this one. Specializing in the traditional Maine clambake—a feast consisting of rich clam chowder, a pile of mussels and steamers, Maine lobster, corn on the cob, roasted potatoes and onions, bread, butter, and Maine blueberry crumb cake (phew!)—this massive complex provides entertainment as well as belly-busting meals. You can also opt to have clambake fixings shipped to your home or have a special event catered. ⊠*5 Axholme Rd., York Village* 🕾*207/363–3255 or 800/552–0242* ⊟*AE, MC, V.*

¢-$
AMERICAN
✗**The Goldenrod.** If you wanted to—and you are on vacation—you could eat nothing but the famous taffy here, made just about the same way today as it was back in 1896. The famous Goldenrod Kisses, made to the tune of 65 tons per year, are a great attraction and people line the windows to watch the process. Aside from the famous taffy, this eating place is family oriented, very reasonably priced, and a great place to get ice cream from the old-fashioned soda fountain. Breakfast is served all day while the simple lunch menu doubles as dinner; choose from sandwiches and burgers. There is even penny candy for sale for, yes, a penny apiece. ⊠*Railroad Ave., York Beach* 🕾*207/363–2621* ⊟*AE, MC, V* ⊘*Closed Columbus Day–late May.*

WHERE TO STAY

$$$-$$$$
Fodor's Choice
★
▦**Chapman Cottage.** Set proudly atop a grassy lawn is this impeccably restored inn, named for the woman who had it built as her summer cottage in 1899. The luxurious bedspreads, fresh flowers, antiques, and beautiful rugs only hint at the indulgence found here. Innkeepers Donna and Paul Archibald spoil their guests with sumptuous breakfasts, afternoon hors d'oeuvres, port, sherry, and homemade chocolate truffles, all prepared by Paul, a professionally trained chef. Most rooms have fireplaces and whirlpool tubs; all are spacious, bright, and airy. It's a five-minute walk to either York Village or the harbor, but you may never wish to leave. What used to be an off-season hobby is now a year-round, ambitious little restaurant that serves dinner Wednesday–Sunday ($$–$$$), as well as offers a tasty tapas menu; a great accompaniment to the wine/martini bar. **Pros:** beautifully restored historic lodging, luxury appointments, and attention to detail. **Con:** no water views, most rooms located on upper floors (and no elevator). ⊠*370 York St., York Harbor* 🕾*207/363–2059 or 877/363–2059* ⊕*www. chapmancottagebandb.com* ⇔*6 rooms* ⌂*In-room: no phone, Wi-Fi.*

7

In-hotel: restaurant, bar, no elevator, no kids under 12, no-smoking rooms ▤*AE, D, MC, V* ❑|*BP.*

$$-$$$$ ❐ **York Harbor Inn.** A mid-17th-century fishing cabin with dark timbers
★ and a fieldstone fireplace forms the heart of this inn, while several wings and outbuildings have been added over the years, making for quite a complex with a great variety of styles and appointments. The rooms are furnished with antiques and country pieces; many have decks overlooking the water, and some have whirlpool tubs or fireplaces. The nicest rooms are in two adjacent buildings, Harbor Cliffs and Harbor Hill. The dining room ($$$–$$$$; no lunch off-season) has great ocean views. For dinner, start with Maine crab cakes and then try the lobster-stuffed chicken breast, or the scallops Dijon. Ask about various packages and Internet specials. **Pros:** many rooms have harbor views, close to beaches and scenic walking trails, some luxury appointments. **Cons:** rooms vary greatly in style and appeal, many rooms accessed via stairways (no elevator). ⊠*Rte. 1A, York Harbor 03911* ☎*207/363–5119 or 800/343–3869* ⊕*www.yorkharborinn.com* ⇥*54 rooms, 2 suites* ⌂*In-room: Wi-Fi. In-hotel: restaurants, bar, no elevator, executive floor, no-smoking rooms* ▤*AE, DC, MC, V* ❑|*CP.*

OGUNQUIT

10 mi north of the Yorks via Rte. 1A and 1 or Shore Rd.

A resort-village in the 1880s, stylish Ogunquit gained fame as an artists' colony. Today it has become a mini Provincetown, with a gay population that swells in summer. Many inns and small clubs cater to a primarily gay and lesbian clientele. For a scenic drive, take Shore Road through downtown toward the 100-foot Bald Head Cliff; you'll be treated to views up and down the coast. On a stormy day the surf can be quite wild here.

The **Ogunquit Trolley** is one of the best things that happened to this area. Parking in the village is troublesome and expensive, beach parking is costly and often limited, and so it's often just easier to leave your car parked at the hotel. The trolley begins operation in May and stays in service until Columbus Day. The fare is $1.50 (at each boarding) and kids under 10 ride free with an adult. Stops are numerous along the route that begins at Perkins Cove and follows Shore Road through town, down to Ogunquit Beach, and out along U.S. 1 up to Wells (where a connecting Wells trolley takes over for northern travel). Maps are available wherever you find brochures and at the chamber of commerce Welcome Center on U.S. 1, just as you enter Ogunquit from the south. ☎*Box 2368, Ogunquit 03907* ☎*207/646–1411.*

WHAT TO SEE

★ **Perkins Cove.** A neck of land connected to the mainland by Oarweed Road and a pedestrian drawbridge, Perkins Cove has a jumble of sea-beaten fish houses. These have largely been transformed by the tide of tourism to shops and restaurants. When you've had your fill of browsing and jostling the crowds, stroll out along the **Marginal Way,** a mile-long footpath between Ogunquit and Perkins Cove that hugs the shore of a rocky promontory known as Israel's Head. Benches along the route give walkers an opportunity to stop and appreciate the open sea vistas, flowering bushes, and million-dollar homes.

NIGHTLIFE & THE ARTS

Much of the nightlife in Ogunquit revolves around the precincts of Ogunquit Square and Perkins Cove, where people stroll, often enjoying an after-dinner ice-cream cone or espresso. Ogunquit is popular with gay and lesbian visitors, and its club scene reflects this.

One of America's oldest summer theaters, the **Ogunquit Playhouse** (⊠ *U.S. 1* ☎ *207/646–5511* ⊕ *www.ogunquitplayhouse.org*) mounts plays and musicals with well-known actors of stage and screen from late June to Labor Day.

WHERE TO EAT & STAY

¢-$
★
AMERICAN

✕**Amore Breakfast.** One could hardly find a more-satisfying, full-bodied breakfast than at this smart and busy joint between Ogunquit and Perkins Cove. Amid a lighthearted mix of enamel-topped tables and retro advertising design touches, breakfast is a sophisticated affair. You won't find tired standards here—the only pancakes are German potato—rather, you'll have a hard time choosing among the options. The Oscar Madison omelet combines crabmeat with asparagus and Swiss, topped with a dill hollandaise. For a real decadent start, opt for the Banana Foster: pecan-coated, cream cheese–stuffed French toast with a side of sautéed bananas in rum syrup. The offers of a half-, three-quarter-, or full order give an indication of this item's richness. If you're especially lucky, you'll catch the sometimes special of corned beef hash—this version is made from hearty pieces of the briny beef rather than the often-seen, through-the-blender kind of hash. To ease the wait for a morning table, a self-serve coffee bar is available. ⊠ *178 Shore Rd.* ☎ *207/646–6661* ▭ *D, MC, V* ☉ *Closed Christmas–Mar., and Wed. and Thurs. in spring and fall. No lunch.*

$$$$
Fodor'sChoice
★
ECLECTIC

✕**Arrows.** Elegant simplicity is the hallmark of this restaurant in an 18th-century farmhouse, 2 mi up a back road. Grilled salmon and radicchio with marinated fennel and baked polenta, and Chinese-style duck glazed with molasses are typical entrées on the daily-changing menu—much of what appears is dependent on what is ready for harvest in the restaurant's abundant 1-acre garden. The Maine crabmeat mousse and lobster risotto appetizers, and desserts such as strawberry shortcake with Chantilly cream, are also beautifully executed. The accolades are continual: *Gourmet* magazine rated this small-town restaurant 14th of the 50 best restaurants in the country. ⊠ *41 Berwick Rd.* ☎ *207/361-1100* ⚖ *Reservations essential* ▭ *MC, V* ☉ *Closed Mon. and mid-Dec.–mid-Apr. No lunch.*

$$$–$$$$
Fodor'sChoice
★

⊡**Black Boar Inn.** The original part of this inn dates to 1674, an era that is reflected in the beauty of the wide-pine floors and the fireplaces in every room. A sense of absolute luxury pervades here. The interior is exquisite, with bead board, richly colored rugs and comforters, William Morris–like wallpaper, tiled bathrooms, and many antiques. Although the manager wasn't sure where the "wild boar" name originated, evidence of the beast abounds in art and sculpture throughout. Wine and

7

hors d'ouevres are served on weekend afternoons and can be enjoyed on the front terrace, overlooking the massive gardens and the world of Main Street beyond. Cottages are rented by the week and are notable for their exposed wood, vaulted ceilings, and full kitchens. **Pros:** gracious, historic lodging; most rooms have fireplaces; quiet retreat in the center of town. **Cons:** most rooms accessed via steep stairs; due to home's age, rooms are on the smaller (though uncrowded) side. ⊠277 *Main St.* ☎207/646–2112 ⊕*www.blackboarinn.com* ⇋6 rooms, 3 cottages ⚷In-room: no phone, Wi-Fi. In-hotel: no elevator, no-smoking rooms ⊟MC, V ⊙Closed Nov.–late May ⍥BP.

WELLS

5 mi north of Ogunquit on U.S. 1.

Lacking any kind of noticeable village center, Wells could be easily overlooked as nothing more than a commercial stretch on U.S. 1 between Ogunquit and the Kennebunks. But look more closely—this is a place where people come to enjoy some of the best beaches on the coast. Part of Ogunquit until 1980, this family-oriented beach community has 7 mi of densely populated shoreline, along with nature preserves where you can explore salt marshes and tidal pools, and see birds and waterfowl.

Leave your car at your hotel and take the **Wells Trolley** to the beach or to the shops on U.S. 1. The seasonal trolley makes pickups at the Wells Transportation Center when the *Downeaster* (the Amtrak train with service from Boston to Portland) pulls in. If you want to continue south toward Ogunquit, the two town trolleys meet at the Wells Chamber of Commerce on U.S. 1; get a route map here. Fare is $2. ☎207/646–2451 ⊕*www.wellschamber.org*.

NEED A BREAK?

How would you like a doughnut ... a really superior one that the same family has been making since 1955? The doughnuts from Congdon's (⊠*U.S. 1* ☎*207/646–4219*) easily rival (many say there is no contest) some of those other famous places we won't mention here. Choose from about 30 different varieties, though the plain really gives you an idea of just how good these doughnuts are. There's a drive-through window so you don't have to get out of the car; or you can take a seat inside and have breakfast or lunch.

SPORTS & THE OUTDOORS

Rachel Carson National Wildlife Refuge. Spot migrating birds and waterfowl of many varieties in a white-pine forest that borders the mile-long loop nature trail through a salt marsh and along the Little River. ⊠*Hwy. 9* ☎*207/646–9226*

BEACHES   With its thousands of acres of marsh and preserved land, Wells is a great place to spend a lot of time outdoors. Nearly 7 mi of sand stretch along the boundaries of Wells, making beach going a prime occupation. Tidal pools sheltered by rocks are filled with all manner of creatures awaiting discovery. Parking is available for a fee (take the trolley!) at **Crescent Beach,** along Webhannet Drive; **Wells Beach** (at the end of Mile

Road off U.S. 1) has public restrooms and two parking areas. There is another lot at the far end of Wells Beach, at the end of Atlantic Avenue. Across the jetty from Wells Harbor is **Drakes Island Beach** (end of Drakes Island Road off U.S. 1), which also has parking and public restrooms. Lifeguards are on hand at all the beaches.

WHERE TO EAT & STAY

$-$$
SEAFOOD

✕ **Billy's Chowder House.** Locals head to this simple restaurant in a salt marsh for the generous lobster rolls, haddock sandwiches, and chowders. Big windows in the bright dining rooms overlook the marsh. ⊠ *216 Mile Rd.* ☎ *207/646-7558* ⊟ *AE, D, MC, V* ⊘ *Closed mid-Dec.–mid-Jan.*

$-$$
AMERICAN

✕ **Maine Diner.** It's the real thing here—one look at the nostalgic (and authentic 1953) exterior and you start craving good diner food. You'll get a little more here…how many greasy spoons make an award-winning lobster pie? That's the house favorite, as well as a heavenly seafood chowder. There's plenty of fried seafood in addition to the usual diner fare, and breakfast is served all day, just as it should be. Be sure to check out the adjacent gift shop, Remember the Maine. ⊠ *2265 U.S. 1* ☎ *207/646-4441* ⊟ *D, MC, V* ⊘ *Closed 1 wk in Jan.*

$$-$$$$
Fodor's Choice
★

⊡ **Haven by the Sea.** Once the summer mission of St. Martha's Church in Kennebunkport, this stunning, exquisite inn has retained many of the original details from its former life as a seaside church. The cathedral ceilings and stained-glass windows remain, all gathering and spreading the grand surrounding light. The guest rooms are spacious, some with serene marsh views. Four common areas, including one with a fireplace, are perfect spots for afternoon refreshments. The inn is one block from the beach. **Pros:** unusual structure with elegant appointments, nightly happy hour, walk to beach. **Cons:** some rooms upstairs, not an in-town location. ⊠ *59 Church St.* ☎ *207/646-4194* ⊕ *www. havenbythesea.com* ⊷ *6 rooms, 2 suites, 1 apartment* ⊘ *In-room: Wi-Fi. In-hotel: no elevator, no kids under 12, no-smoking rooms* ⊟ *AE, MC, V* ⊙ *BP.*

THE KENNEBUNKS

6 mi north of Wells via U.S. 1; 23 mi south of Portland via Maine Tpke.

The Kennebunks encompass Kennebunk, Kennebunk Beach, Goose Rocks Beach, Kennebunkport, Cape Porpoise, and Arundel. This cluster of seaside and inland villages provides a little bit of everything— salt marshes, sand beaches, jumbled fishing shacks, and architectural gems.

Handsome white clapboard homes with shutters give Kennebunk, an early-19th-century shipbuilding center, a quintessential New England look. The many boutiques and galleries surrounding Dock Square draw visitors to Kennebunkport. People flock to Kennebunkport mostly in summer, but some come in early December when the Christmas Prelude is celebrated on two weekends. Santa arrives by fishing boat, and the Christmas trees are lighted as carolers stroll the sidewalks.

In Kennebunkport, get a good overview of the sights with an **Intown Trolley** tour. The narrated 45-minute jaunts leave every hour starting at 10 AM at the designated stop on Ocean Avenue, around the corner of Dock Square. The fare is valid for the day so you can hop on and off at your leisure. ⊠ *Ocean Ave., Kennebunkport* ☎*207/967–3686* ⊕*www.intowntrolley.com* ⌦*$13 all-day fare* ☉ *Late May–mid-Oct., daily 10–5.*

WHAT TO SEE

★ **Seashore Trolley Museum.** This museum displays streetcars built from 1872 to 1972 and includes trolleys from major metropolitan areas and world capitals—Boston to Budapest, New York to Nagasaki, San Francisco to Sydney—all beautifully restored. Best of all, you can take a trolley ride for nearly 4 mi over the tracks of the former Atlantic Shoreline trolley line, with a stop along the way at the museum restoration shop, where trolleys are transformed from junk into gems. Both guided and self-guided tours are available. ⊠ *195 Log Cabin Rd., Kennebunkport* ☎*207/967–2800* ⊕*www.trolleymuseum.org* ⌦*$8.50* ☉ *Early May–mid-Oct., daily 10–4:30; reduced hrs in spring and fall, call ahead.*

SPORTS & THE OUTDOORS

Kennebunk Beach has three parts: Gooch's Beach, Mother's Beach, and Kennebunk Beach. Beach Road, with its cottages and old Victorian boardinghouses, runs right behind them. Gooch's and Kennebunk attract teenagers; Mother's Beach, which has a small playground and tidal puddles for splashing, is popular with families.

BOATING & FISHING — Find and catch fish with **Cast Away Fishing Charters** (⊡ *Box 245, Kennebunkport 04046* ☎*207/284–1740* ⊕*www.castawayfishingcharters. com*). **First Chance** (⊠*4-A Western Ave., Kennebunk* ☎*207/967–5507 or 800/767–2628*) leads whale-watching cruises and guarantees sightings in season. Daily scenic lobster cruises are also offered aboard *Kylie's Chance.* For half- or full-day fishing trips as well as discovery trips for kids, book some time with **Lady J Sportfishing Charters** (⊠ *Arundel Wharf, Ocean Ave.* ☎*207/985–7304* ⊕*www.ladyjcharters.com*).

SHOPPING

The **Gallery on Chase Hill** (⊠*10 Chase Hill Rd., Kennebunk* ☎*207/967–0049*) presents original artwork by Maine and New England artists. **Mast Cove Galleries** (⊠*Mast Cove La., Kennebunkport* ☎*207/967–3453*) sells graphics, paintings, and sculpture by 105 artists. **Tom's of Maine Natural Living Store** (⊠*52 Main St., Kennebunk* ☎*207/985–6331*) sells all-natural personal-care products.

WHERE TO EAT

$$-$$$$ — ✕**Grissini.** This popular trattoria draws high praise for its northern Italian cuisine. Dine by the stone hearth on inclement days or on the patio
ITALIAN — when the weather's fine. You can mix and match appetizers, pizzas, salads, pastas, and entrées from the menu to suit your hunger and budget. ⊠*27 Western Ave., Kennebunk* ☎*207/967–2211* ⊟*AE, MC, V.*

$$$$
★
AMERICAN

✗**White Barn Inn.** Formally attired waiters, meticulous service, and exquisite food have earned this restaurant accolades as one of the best in New England. Regional New England fare is served in a rustic but elegant dining room. The three-course, prix-fixe menu ($90), which changes weekly, might include steamed Maine lobster nestled on fresh fettuccine with carrots, ginger, and snow peas. ⊠*37 Beach Ave., Kennebunk* ☎*207/967–2321* ⚠*Reservations essential Jacket required* ⊟*AE, MC, V* ⊘*Closed 3 wks in Jan. No lunch.*

WHERE TO STAY

$$$$
Fodor'sChoice
★

🏠**Captain Lord Mansion.** Of all the mansions in Kennebunkport's historic district that have been converted to inns, the 1812 Captain Lord Mansion is the most stately and sumptuously appointed. Distinctive architecture, including a suspended elliptical staircase, gas fireplaces in all rooms, and near-museum-quality accoutrements, make for a formal but not stuffy setting. Six rooms have whirlpool tubs. The extravagant suite has two fireplaces, a double whirlpool, a hydro-massage body spa, a TV/DVD and stereo system, and a king-size canopy bed. Day-spa services are available for added luxury. **Pros:** elegant and luxurious historic lodging, in-town location, beautiful landscaped grounds and gardens. **Cons:** not for those on a tight budget, not a beachfront location. ⊠*Pleasant and Green Sts., Box 800, Kennebunkport 04046* ☎*207/967–3141* ⊕*www.captainlord.com* ⇆*15 rooms, 1 suite* ⚐*In-room: no TV, Wi-Fi. In-hotel: bicycles, no elevator, public Internet, no kids under 12, no-smoking rooms* ⊟*D, MC, V* ⦿*BP.*

$$$–$$$$
Fodor'sChoice
★

🏠**The Colony.** You can't miss this place—it's grand, white, and incredibly large, set majestically atop a rise overlooking the ocean. The hotel was built in 1914 (after its predecessor caught fire in 1898), and much of the splendid glamour of this earlier era remains. Many of the rooms in the main hotel (there are two other outbuildings) have breezy ocean views from private or semiprivate balconies. All are outfitted with antiques and hardwood floors; the bright white bed linens nicely offset the colors of the Waverly wallpaper. The restaurant ($$–$$$$) features New England fare, with plenty of seafood, steaks, and other favorites. **Pros:** lodging in the tradition of grand old hotels, many ocean views, plenty of activities and entertainment for all ages. **Cons:** not for those looking for more intimate or peaceful lodging, rooms with ocean views come at steep prices. ⊠*Ocean Ave.* ☎*207/967–3331 or 800/552–2363* ⊕*www.thecolonyhotel.com/maine* ⇆*124 rooms* ⚐*In-room: no a/c (some), no TV (some), Wi-Fi. In-hotel: restaurant, room service, bar, pool, beachfront, bicycles, no-smoking rooms, some pets allowed* ⊟*AE, MC, V* ⊘*Closed Nov.–mid-May* ⦿*BP.*

$$$$
♻

🏠**The Seaside.** This handsome seaside property has been in the hands of the Severance family since 1667. The modern hotel units, all with sliding-glass doors that open onto private decks or patios (half with ocean views), are appropriate for families; so are the cottages with one to four bedrooms. You can't get much closer to Kennebunk Beach. **Pros:** ideal beachfront location, lawn games available, great ocean views from upper-floor rooms. **Cons:** rooms are hotel standard and a little outdated (but fairly sized), not an in-town location. ⊠*80 Beach Ave., Kennebunk* ☎*207/967–4461 or 866/300–6750* ⊕*www.kennebunk*

7

beachmaine.com ↩*22 rooms, 11 cottages* ⚴*In-room: refrigerator, Wi-Fi. In-hotel: beachfront, no elevator, laundry service, public Internet, no-smoking rooms* ▭*AE, MC, V* ☽*Cottages closed Nov.–May* ⦿*CP.*

$$$$ 🛏**White Barn Inn.** For a romantic overnight stay, you need look no
★ further than the exclusive White Barn Inn, known for its attentive, pampering service. No detail has been overlooked in the meticulously appointed rooms, from plush bedding and reading lamps to robes and slippers. Rooms are in the main inn and adjacent buildings. Some have fireplaces, hot tubs, and luxurious baths with steam showers. The inn is within walking distance (10–15 minutes) of Dock Square and the beach. **Pros:** elegant, luxurious lodging; full-service; in a historic building. **Cons:** no water views or beachfront, overly steep lodging prices, not in town. ✉*37 Beach Ave., Kennebunk* ☎*207/967–2321* ⊕*www. whitebarninn.com* ↩*16 rooms, 9 suites* ⚴*In-room: VCR, DVD, Wi-Fi. In-hotel: restaurant, bar, pool, spa, bicycles, no elevator, concierge, laundry service, public Internet, no kids under 12, no-smoking rooms* ▭*AE, MC, V* ⦿*CP.*

OLD ORCHARD BEACH AREA

15 mi north of Kennebunkport, 18 mi south of Portland.

Back in the late 19th century, Old Orchard Beach was a classic, upscale, place-to-be-seen resort area. The railroad brought wealthy families who were looking for entertainment and the benefits of the fresh sea air. Although a good bit of this aristocratic hue has dulled in more-modern times—admittedly, the place is more than a little pleasantly tacky these days—Old Orchard Beach remains a good place for those looking for entertainment and thrills by the sea.

The center of the action is a 7-mi strip of sand beach and its accompanying amusement park, which resembles a small Coney Island. Despite the summertime crowds and fried-food odors, the atmosphere can be captivating. During the 1940s and '50s, in the heyday of the Big Band era, the pier had a dance hall where stars of the time performed. Fire claimed the end of the pier—at one time it jutted out nearly 1,800 feet into the sea—but booths with games and candy concessions still line both sides. In summer the town sponsors fireworks (on Thursday night). Places to stay run the gamut from cheap motels to cottage colonies to full-service seasonal hotels. You won't find free parking in town, but there are ample lots. Amtrak has a seasonal stop here.

WHAT TO SEE

Ocean Park. A world away from the beach scene, Ocean Park lies on the southwestern edge of town. Locals and visitors like to keep the separation distinct, touting their area as a more peaceful and wholesome family-style village. This vacation community was founded in 1881 by Free Will Baptist leaders as an interdenominational retreat with both religious and educational purposes, following the example of Chautauqua, New York. Today the community still hosts an impressive variety of cultural happenings, including movies, concerts, recreation, work-

All About Lobsters

Judging from the current price of a lobster dinner, it's hard to believe that lobsters were once so plentiful that servants in rich households would have contracts stating they could be served lobster "no more than two times a week."

The going price for lobsters in the 1840s was three cents per lobster—not per pound, per lobster. Today, Maine is nearly synonymous with lobsters, the fishery being one of Maine's primary industries. Well over 60 million pounds of lobster are landed a year in the state, making Maine, by far, the biggest supplier in the nation.

Because of the size restrictions, most of the lobsters you find in restaurants weigh 1¼ to 1½ pounds. However, lobsters can actually grow much larger and live to a ripe old age. The largest lobster ever caught off the coast of Maine weighed in at nearly 45 pounds and was more than 50 years old!

For an authentic, Maine-style lobster dinner, you must go to a lobster pound, and they're not hard to find. Generally, these places are rustic and simple—they look more like fish-packing plants than restaurants. Hundreds of freshly caught lobsters of varying sizes are kept in pens, waiting for customers. Service is simple in the extreme. You usually sit at a wooden picnic table, and eat off a thick paper plate. A classic "Downeast" feast includes lobster—boiled or steamed—with clam chowder, steamers, potato, and corn on the cob—and, of course, a large bib tied around your neck.

—Stephen Allen

shops, and religious services. Most are presented in the Temple, which is on the National Register of Historic Places. Although the religious nature of the place is apparent in its worship schedule and some of its cultural offerings, visitors need not be a member of any denomination; all are welcome. There's even a public shuffleboard area for those not interested in the neon carnival attractions several miles up the road. Get an old-fashioned raspberry-lime rickey at the Ocean Park Soda Fountain (near the library, at Furber Park); it's also a good place for breakfast or a light lunch. ⊠*Southwestern edge of town* ☎*207/934–9068 Ocean Park Association* ⊕*www.oceanpark.org.* .

SPORTS & THE OUTDOORS

Not far from Old Orchard Beach is the Maine Audubon–run **Scarborough Marsh Nature Center,** where you can rent a canoe and explore on your own, or sign up with a guided trip. The salt marsh is Maine's largest and is an excellent place for bird-watching and peaceful paddling amid its winding ways. The Nature Center has a discovery room for kids, programs for all ages ranging from basket making to astronomy, birding and canoe tours, and a good gift shop. ⊠*Pine Point Rd. (Rte. 9), Scarborough* ☎*207/883–5100* ⊕*www.maineaudubon.org* ⊠Free, guided tours begin at $5 ⊙*Memorial Day–Sept. daily, 9:30–4*

WHERE TO EAT

$-$$
AMERICAN

✗**DennyMike's.** In Old Orchard Beach, you can't help but notice the heavenly smells of briskets and ribs wafting down the street from this bold and authentic barbecue joint. If you've had your fill of lobster and fried seafood, bring your appetite here. Owner DennyMike is no Texan, but that's where he learned the secret of his craft. Portions are very generous; dinner feasts come with a choice of two sides—absolutely get the beans. There's also a good selection of giant burgers, specialty barbecue sandwiches, and hand-cut fries that rival any sold on the pier. It just might be the best barbecue in New England. Takeout and delivery are available. ⊠*27 W. Grand Ave., Old Orchard Beach* ☎*207/934-2207* ⊟*MC, V* ☯*Closed mid-Oct.–mid-May.*

$$-$$$
★
ECLECTIC

✗**The Landmark.** This restaurant almost feels as if it doesn't belong here, at least not in this modern transformation of Old Orchard Beach. Tables are set either on the glassed-in porch or within high, tin-ceiling rooms. Candles and a collection of giant fringed art-nouveau lamps provide a warm, gentle light. The menu has a good selection of seafood and meats, many treated with either Asian or Mediterranean flavors; the mahimahi might be seared and served with a coconut cream sauce. It's the kind of menu that encourages you to try new things and you definitely won't be disappointed. The tiramisu is divine. Reservations are recommended. ⊠*25 E. Grand Ave., Old Orchard Beach* ☎*207/934-0156* ⊟*AE, D, MC, V* ☯*Closed early Jan.–late Mar.*

PORTLAND & ENVIRONS

By John
Blodgett

Maine's largest city is considered small by national standards—its population is just 64,000—but its character, spirit, and appeal make it feel much larger. In fact, it is a cultural and economic center for a metro area of 230,000 residents—one-quarter of Maine's entire population. Portland and its environs are well worth a day or two of exploration.

North of Portland, Freeport was made famous by its L.L. Bean store, whose success led to the opening of scores of other outlets. Meanwhile, the Boothbays attract hordes of vacationing families and flotillas of pleasure craft.

PORTLAND

Several distinct neighborhoods reveal the many faces of a city that embraces its history as well as its art, music, and multicultural scenes.

The most visited section, the restored **Old Port** features a real working waterfront where emblematic lobster boats share ports with modern cruise ships, ferries, and vintage sailing yachts, and renovated redbrick warehouses. Nightlife thrives here, with numerous clubs, taverns, and bars pouring out the sounds of live music and lively patrons. Exceptional restaurants, shops, and galleries, many featuring locally produced goods, abound here as well.

Downtown Portland has emerged from a years-long on-again, off-again funk, during which much retail commerce was lost to shopping malls in the outlying suburbs. Its burgeoning Arts District—which starts at the top of Exchange Street (near the upper end of the Old Port) and extends up past the Portland Museum of Art. Much of Portland's economic heart is here, including several large banking firms. The district's central artery, revitalized Congress Street, is peppered with shops, restaurants, numerous performing arts venues, and excellent museums.

Just beyond the Arts District is the **Western Promenade**, an area of extensive architectural wealth. Predominantly residential, the neighborhood is filled with stunning examples of both the city's historical and economic prominence and its emphasis on preserving this past. A handful of historic homes are open to tours.

Portland is wonderfully walkable; an able-bodied explorer can easily take in the Old Port, the Downtown/Arts District, and the Western Promenade. In fact, in much of the city it's best to park your car and explore on foot. You can park at the city garage on Fore Street (between Exchange and Union streets) or opposite the U.S. Customs House at the corner of Fore and Pearl streets. A helpful hint: Look for the PARK & SHOP sign on garages and parking lots and get one hour of free parking for each stamp collected at participating shops.

Greater Portland's Metro runs seven bus routes in Portland, South Portland, and Westbrook. The fare is $1.25; exact change is required. Buses run from 5:30 AM to 11:45 PM. The **Portland Explorer** (☎207/774–9891 or 207/774–0351 ⊕www.transportme.org) has express shuttle service to the Old Port from the Portland Jetport, the **Portland Transportation Center** (☎207/828–1151), and other downtown locations. The shuttle runs hourly, seven days a week, from noon to 7 PM. Fare is $2. For service around Portland, there's the Metro and shuttle bus service.

If you want a taxi, your best bet is to call ahead (try **ABC Taxi,** ☎207/772–8685; **Elite Cab,** ☎207/871–7667; or **South Portland Taxi,** ☎207/767–5200). However, the small size is an advantage in getting around, for many destinations in downtown are in close proximity. There is even a water taxi (**Portland Express Water Taxi,** ☎207/415–8493) to get to and from the islands of Casco Bay. Meter rates are $1.40 for the first 1/9 mi, 25¢ for each additional 1/9 mi throughout Portland.

Numbers in the margin correspond to numbers on the Portland map.

WHAT TO SEE

2 **Children's Museum of Maine.** Touching is okay at Portland's relatively small but fun Children's Museum, where kids can pretend they are lobster fishermen, shopkeepers, or computer experts. The majority of the museum's exhibits, many of which have a Maine theme, are best for children 10 and younger. Camera Obscura, an exhibit about optics, provides fascinating panoramic views of the city. The museum's newest addition, L. L. Bear's Discovery Woods, takes imagination to the great outdoors, with explorations below the sea, up a tree, on top of Maine's tallest mountain, and within a flowing stream. ⊠*142 Free St.* ☎*207/828–1234* ⊕*www.*

childrensmuseumofme.org ☜*Museum (including Camera Obscura) $6,*
Camera Obscura (without museum) $3 ⊙*Memorial Day–Labor Day,*
Mon.–Sat. 10–5, Sun. noon–5; day after Labor Day–day before Memo-
rial Day, Tues.–Sat. 10–5, Sun. noon–5.

❶ **The Old Port.** A major international port and a working harbor since
Fodor'sChoice the early 17th century, the Old Port bridges the gap between the city's
★ historical commercial activities and those of today. It is home to fishing boats docked alongside whale-watching charters, luxury yachts,
cruise ships, and oil tankers from throughout the globe. Busy Commercial Street parallels the water and is lined with brick buildings and
warehouses that were built following the Great Fire of 1866, and were
intended to last for ages. In the 19th century, candle makers and sail
stitchers plied their trades here; today, specialty shops, art galleries,
and restaurants have taken up residence. While in Old Port, visit the
Harbor Fish Market (⊠*9 Custom House Wharf* ☎*207/775–0251 or*
800/370–1790 ⊕*www.harborfish.com*). A Portland favorite for more
than 30 years, this freshest of the fresh seafood markets now ships
lobsters and other Maine seafood delectables anywhere in the country
from its waterfront location on a working wharf. A bright-red facade
opens into a bustling space with bubbling lobster pens, clams, and
other shellfish on ice, and employees as skilled with a fillet knife as
a sushi chef. For a lively and sensory-filled (you may want to hold
your nose) glimpse into the Old Port's active fish business, take a
free tour of the **Portland Fish Exchange** (⊠*6 Portland Fish Pier, Old*
Port ☎*207/773–0017* ⊕*www.pfex.org*). Watch as the fishing boats
unload their daily haul, the catch gets weighed in, and prices are settled
through an auction process. It's a great behind-the-scenes view of this
dynamic market. Auctions take place Sunday at 11 AM and Monday
through Thursday at noon.

❸ **Portland Museum of Art.** Maine's largest public art institution has a num-
★ ber of strong collections, including fine seascapes and landscapes by
Winslow Homer, John Marin, Andrew Wyeth, Edward Hopper, Mars-
den Hartley, and other painters. Homer's *Pulling the Dory* and *Weath-*
erbeaten, two quintessential Maine Coast images, are here; the museum
owns and displays more than 20 other works by Homer. The Joan
Whitney Payson Collection of impressionist and postimpressionist art
includes works by Monet, Picasso, and Renoir. Harry N. Cobb, an
associate of I. M. Pei, designed the strikingly modern Charles Shipman
Payson building. The nearby and entirely renovated McLellan House
contains additional galleries housing the museum's 19th-century collection and decorative art as well as interactive educational stations.
⊠*7 Congress Sq.* ☎*207/775–6148* ⊕*www.portlandmuseum.org*
☜*$10, free Fri. 5–9* ⊙*Memorial Day–Columbus Day, Mon.–Thurs.*
and weekends 10–5, Fri. 10–9; day after Columbus Day–day before
Memorial Day, Tues.–Thurs. and weekends 10–5, Fri. 10–9.

❹ **Victoria Mansion.** This Italianate-style mansion was built between 1858
★ and 1860 and is widely regarded as the most sumptuously ornamented
dwelling of its period remaining in the country. Architect Henry Aus-
tin designed the house for hotelier Ruggles Morse and his wife, Olive.

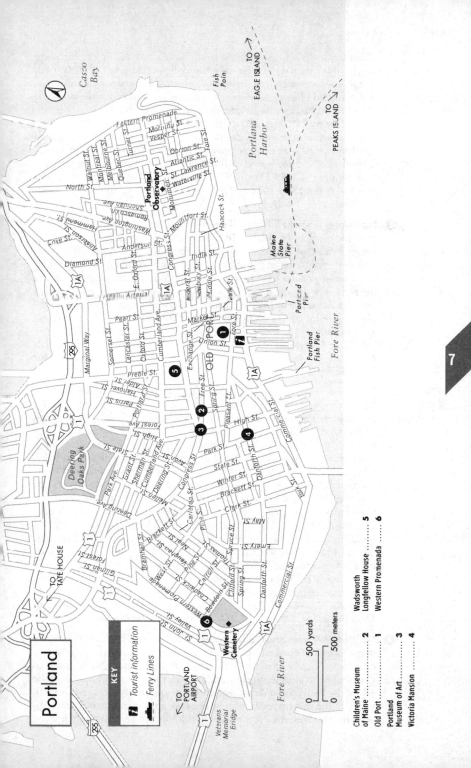

Portland

KEY

🄵 Tourist information

⚓ Ferry Lines

Children's Museum
of Maine **2**

Old Port **1**

Portland
Museum of Art **3**

Victoria Mansion **4**

Wadsworth
Longfellow House **5**

Western Promenada **6**

0 500 yards

0 500 meters

Casco Bay

Portland Harbor

Portland Pier

Fore River

TO
EAGLE ISLAND ➔

TO
PEAKS ISLAND ➔

TO
TATE HOUSE ➔

TO
PORTLAND
AIRPORT ➔

Veterans
Memorial
Bridge

Deering
Oaks Park

**Western
Cemetery**

Portland
Fish Pier

Fore River

Maine
State
Pier

Fish
Point

**Portland
Observatory**

Eastern Promenade

The interior design—everything from the plasterwork to the furniture (much of it original)—is the only surviving commission of New York designer Gustave Herter. Inside the elegant brownstone exterior of this National Historic Landmark are colorful frescoed walls and ceilings, ornate marble mantelpieces, gilded gas chandeliers, a magnificent 6-foot by 25-foot stained-glass ceiling window, and a freestanding mahogany staircase; guided tours, running about 45 minutes, cover all the details. The mansion reopens during the Christmas season, richly ornamented and decorated to reveal the opulence and elegance of the Victorian era. ⊠*109 Danforth St.* ☎*207/772–4841* ⊕*www.victoria mansion.org* ⊠*$10* ☉*May–Oct., Mon.–Sat. 10–4, Sun. 1–5; Christmas tours Nov. 24–Dec. 31.*

❺ Wadsworth Longfellow House. The boyhood home of the poet—which was the first brick house in Portland—is particularly interesting because most of the furnishings are original to the house. The late-Colonial-style structure, built in 1785, sits back from the street and has a small portico over its entrance and four chimneys surmounting the roof. The house is part of the Center for Maine History, which includes the adjacent Maine History Gallery and a research library; the gift shop has a good selection of books about Maine. ⊠*489 Congress St.* ☎*207/774–1822* ⊕*www.mainehistory.org* ⊠ *House $7, Center for Maine History $4* ☉*House and Maine History Gallery May–Oct., Mon.–Sat. 10–5, Sun. noon–5 (last tour at 4); Nov. and Dec., call for hrs. Library Tues.–Sat. 10–3.*

OFF THE BEATEN PATH

Tate House. This magnificent house fully conjures up the style—even high style—of Colonial Maine. Built astride rose granite steps and a period herb garden overlooking the Stroudwater River on the outskirts of Portland, the 1755 house was built by Captain George Tate. Tate had been commissioned by the English Crown to organize "the King's Broad Arrow"—the marking and cutting down of gigantic forest trees, which were transported overland to water and sent to England to be fashioned as masts for English fighting frigates. The house has several period rooms, including a sitting room with some fine English Restoration chairs. With its clapboard still gloriously unpainted, its impressive Palladian doorway, dogleg stairway, unusual clerestory, and gambrel roof, this house will delight all lovers of Early American decorative arts. Guided tours of the gardens are held each Wednesday from mid-June to mid-September, with tea and refreshments served afterward. House tours are offered daily in-season except Monday. Call or visit the Web site for special holiday programs during December. ⊠*1270 Westbrook St.* ☎*207/774–6177* ⊕*www.tatehouse.org* ⊠*$5* ☉*Mid-June–Mid-Oct., Tues.–Sat. 10–4, Sun. 1–4 (1st Sun. each month only).*

❻ The Western Promenade. On the National Register of Historic Places, the neighborhood reveals an extraordinary display of architectural splendor, from High Victorian Gothic to lush Italianate, Queen Anne to Colonial Revival. A leisurely walk through the area should begin at the top of the Downtown/Arts District. From the Old Port, take Danforth Street all the way up to Vaughn Street; take a right and then an immediate left onto Western Promenade. In addition to seeing stately homes, you pass by the Western Cemetery, Portland's second official burial ground laid out in 1829 (inside is the ancestral plot of famous poet Henry Wadsworth Longfellow).

NIGHTLIFE & THE ARTS

NIGHTLIFE Portland has a nicely varied nightlife, with a great emphasis on local, live music and pubs serving award-winning local microbrews. Big, raucous dance clubs are few, but darkened taverns and lively bars (smoke-free by law) pulse with the sounds of rock, blues, alternative, and folk tunes. Several hip wine bars have cropped up, serving appetizers along with a full array of specialty wines and whimsical cocktails. It's a fairly youthful scene in Portland, in some spots even rowdy and rough-around-the-edges, but there are plenty of places where you don't have to shout over the din to be heard.

TAKE A TOUR
Greater Portland Landmarks (⊠ *165 State St.* ☎ *207/774–5561* 🖼*$7*) conducts 1½-hour walking tours of the city from July through September. **Working Waterfront** (☎*207/415–0765* ⊠ *Meet at Union Wharf Market on Commercial St.* 🖼*$10*) walking tours are led by local Angela Clark, who shares a good deal of uncommon history about the docks and alleys of the Old Port. The hour-long tours run weekdays at 11 AM and 2 PM; Saturday at 9 AM and 11 AM. The cost is $10 per person.

Brian Boru (⊠ *57 Center St.* ☎*207/780–1506*) is an Irish pub with occasional entertainment, ranging from Celtic to reggae, and an outside deck. For nightly themed brew specials, plenty of Guinness, and live entertainment, head to **Bull Feeney's** (⊠*375 Fore St.* ☎*207/773–7210*), a lively two-story Irish pub and restaurant. **Gritty McDuff's** (⊠*396 Fore St.* ☎*207/772–2739*) brews fine ales and serves British pub fare and seafood dishes.

THE ARTS Art galleries and studios have spread throughout the city; many are concentrated along the Congress Street downtown corridor; others are hidden amid the boutiques and restaurants of the Old Port and the East End. A great way to get acquainted with the city's artists is to participate in the **First Friday Art Walk** (⊕*www.firstfridayartwalk.com*), a self-guided, free tour of galleries, museums, and alternative art venues happening, you guessed it, on the first Friday of each month, from May to December. **Portland Stage Company** (⊠*25-A Forest Ave.* ☎*207/774–0465*) mounts productions year-round on its two stages.

SPORTS & THE OUTDOORS

Portland has quite a bit of green space in its several parks; in the heat of summer these places make for cool retreats with refreshing fountains and plenty of shade. Local sports teams are the Portland Sea Dogs (baseball) and the Portland Pirates (hockey).

BOAT TRIPS **Casco Bay Lines** (⊠*Maine State Pier, 56 Commercial St.* ☎*207/774–7871* ⊕*www.cascobaylines.com*) provides narrated cruises and transportation to Casco Bay Islands.

SHOPPING

Trendy Exchange Street is great for arts and crafts browsing, while Commercial Street caters to the souvenir hound—gift shops are eager to sell Maine moose, nautical items, and lobster emblems emblazoned on everything from T-shirts to shot glasses.

Several art galleries bring many alternatives to the ubiquitous New England seaside painting. Modern art, photography, sculpture, pottery, and artful woodwork now fill the shelves of many shops, revealing the sophisticated and avant-garde faces of the city's art scene.

ART & ANTIQUES
Abacus (⊠44 Exchange St. ☎800/206–2166 ⊕www.abacusgallery.com), an appealing crafts gallery, has unusual gift items in glass, wood, and textiles, plus fine modern jewelry. **F.O. Bailey Antiquarians** (⊠35 Depot Rd., Falmouth ☎207/781–8001 ⊕www.fobailey.com), carries antique and reproduction furniture and jewelry, paintings, rugs, and china. The **Institute for Contemporary Art** (⊠522 Congress St. ☎207/775–3052), at the Maine College of Art, showcases contemporary artwork from around the world.

BOOKS
Longfellow Books (⊠1 Monument Way ☎207/772–4045) is a grand success story of the independent bookstore triumphing over the massive presence of the large chains. Longfellow's is known for its good service and very thoughtful literary selection. Author readings are scheduled regularly.

CLOTHING
Family-owned **Casco Bay Wool Works** (⊠10 Moulton St. ☎207/879–9665 or 888/222–9665 ⊕www.cascobaywoolworks.com) sells beautiful, handcrafted wool capes, shawls, blankets, and scarves.

WHERE TO EAT

$$$-$$$$
Fodor'sChoice
★
AMERICAN
✕**Fore Street.** Two of Maine's best chefs, Sam Hayward and Dana Street, opened this restaurant in a renovated, airy warehouse on the edge of the Old Port (heating-oil delivery trucks once were parked here—honest). The menu changes daily to reflect the freshest local ingredients available. Every copper-top table in the two-level main dining room has a view of the enormous brick oven and hearth and the open kitchen, where sous-chefs seem to dance as they create entrées such as three cuts of Maine island lamb, Atlantic monkfish fillet, and breast of Moulad duckling. Desserts include artisanal cheeses. ⊠288 Fore St. ☎207/775–2717 ▤AE, MC, V ⊘No lunch.

$$
★
SEAFOOD
✕**Gilbert's Chowder House.** This is the real deal, as quintessential as Maine dining can be. Clam rakes, nautical charts, and a giant plastic marlin hang from the walls of this unpretentious waterfront diner. The flavors are from the depths of the North Atlantic, prepared and presented simply: fish, clam, and corn chowders; fried shrimp, haddock, clam strips, and extraordinary clam cakes. A chalkboard of daily specials is a must-read, and often features steamed mussels, oysters, and peel-and-eat shrimp. But don't miss out on the lobster roll—a toasted hot dog roll bursting with claw and tail meat unadulterated by mayo or other ingredients. It sits on a leaf of lettuce, but who needs more? It's classic Maine, fuss-free and presented on a paper plate. ⊠92 Commercial St. ☎207/871–5636 ▤AE, MC, V.

$$$$ ✗**Hugo's.** Chef-owner Rob Evans has turned Hugo's into one of the
★ city's best restaurants. The warmly lighted dining room is small and
ECLECTIC open, yet you can hold a conversation without raising your voice. The
four-course prix-fixe menu changes weekly, but a pub menu is available to mix and match downsized items for $10 to $20 a dish. These
could include herb-crusted Maine wolffish, Maine diver scallops with
beef tartare, and risotto steeped deep red by beets. Few other restaurants in downtown are so devoted to preparing and serving the freshest
local organic foods. ⊠*88 Middle St.* ☎*207/774–8538* ▭*AE, MC, V*
☉*Closed Sun. and Mon. No lunch.*

$$-$$$ ✗**Ri-Ra.** Whether you're in the mood for a pint of beer and corned beef
IRISH and cabbage, or a crock of mussels and whole roasted rainbow trout,
Ri-Ra delivers. Settle into a comfy couch in the downstairs pub or take
a table in the upstairs dining room, where walls of windows overlook
the busy ferry terminal. After dinner every Thursday, Friday, and Saturday, the lower level gets loud with live local bands playing until closing
time. ⊠*72 Commercial St.* ☎*207/761–4446* ▭*AE, MC, V.*

$$-$$$ ✗**Street and Co.** Fish and seafood are the specialties in this Old Port
SEAFOOD basement establishment. You enter through the bustling kitchen and
dine amid dried herbs and shelves of staples, at one of the copper-top
tables (so your waiter can place a skillet of sizzling seafood directly in
front of you). The daily specials are usually a good bet, and pasta dishes
are popular (garlic and olive oil lovers rejoice; they're loaded with
both). Listen to your server—chances are your plate is very hot indeed.
⊠*33 Wharf St.* ☎*207/775–0887* ▭*AE, MC, V* ☉*No lunch.*

$$-$$$ ✗**Walter's Cafe.** Capturing the 19th-century spirit of the Old Port, with
AMERICAN its brick walls and wood floors, this casual, busy place in the heart
of the Old Port's shopping area manages a good balance of local seafood and meats with Asian and more eclectic flavors. Begin with lobster bisque or deep-fried lemongrass shrimp sticks; then move on to
a shrimp and andouille bake. ⊠*15 Exchange St.* ☎*207/871–9258*
▭*AE, MC, V* ☉*No lunch Sun.*

WHERE TO STAY

$$-$$$ ⌂**Inn on Carleton.** After a day of exploring Portland's museums and
shops, you can find a quiet retreat at this elegant brick town house on
the city's Western Promenade. Built in 1869, it is furnished throughout with period antiques as well as artwork by contemporary Maine
artists. A trompe l'oeil painting by Maine artist Charles Schumacher,
known for the technique, greets you at the entryway, and more fine
examples of his work in this style are either on display or in the process of being uncovered and restored. Pros: European-style elegance,
English garden, Western Promenade location. Con: it's a long walk to
the Old Port. ⊠*46 Carleton St.* ☎*207/775–1910 or 800/639–1779*
⊕*www.innoncarleton.com* ⇔*6 rooms* ⌂*In-room: no phone, no TV.*
In-hotel: no elevator, public Wi-Fi, no kids under 9, no-smoking rooms
▭*D, MC, V* ⏐◑⏐*BP.*

$$$-$$$$ ⌂**Pomegranate Inn.** The classic architecture of this handsome inn in
Fodor'sChoice the architecturally rich Western Promenade area gives no hint of the
★ surprises within. Vivid hand-painted walls, floors, and woodwork combine with contemporary artwork, and the result is both stimulating and

7

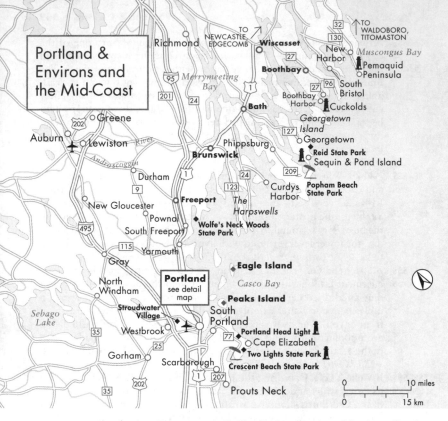

Portland & Environs and the Mid-Coast

comforting. Rooms are individually decorated, and five have fireplaces. Room 8, in the carriage house, has a private garden terrace. **Pros:** near Western Promenade. **Con:** not within reasonable walking distance of Old Port and waterfront. ⊠*49 Neal St.* ☎*207/772–1006 or 800/356–0408* ⊕*www.pomegranateinn.com* ↪*8 rooms* ⌂*In-room: Wi-Fi. In-hotel: no elevator, no kids under 16, no-smoking rooms* ⊟*AE, D, DC, MC, V* †⊙*BP.*

$$$$ ⌗**Portland Harbor Hotel.** Making luxury its primary focus, the Harbor Hotel has become a favorite with business travelers seeking meetings on a more-intimate scale, and vacationing guests who want high-quality service and amenities. In season, eat on the enclosed peaceful garden patio. **Pros:** luxurious amenities, amid the action of the Old Port and waterfront. **Con:** not for the quaint of heart. ⊠*468 Fore St.* ☎*207/775–9090 or 888/798–9090* ⊕*www.portlandharborhotel. com* ↪*85 rooms, 12 suites* ⌂*In-room: Wi-Fi. In-hotel: restaurant, laundry service, concierge, public Internet, no-smoking rooms* ⊟*AE, D, DC, MC, V.*

$$$$ ⌗**Portland Regency Hotel and Spa.** One of the few major hotels in the center of the Old Port, the brick Regency building was Portland's armory in the late 19th century. Most rooms have four-poster beds,

tall standing mirrors, floral curtains, and love seats. The spa features a licensed massage therapist, pedicures and manicures, and even its own healthy cuisine, such as yogurt, salads, and sandwiches. Pros: convenient to shops, restaurants, and museums; has all the extras you'd want. Con: more luxurious than charming. ⊠*20 Milk St.* ☎*207/774–4200 or 800/727–3436* ⊕*www.theregency.com* ⇆*87 rooms, 8 suites* ⚐*In-room: refrigerator, Ethernet, Wi-Fi. In-hotel: restaurant, gym, spa, laundry service, public Wi-Fi, no-smoking rooms* ▤*AE, D, DC, MC, V.*

ISLANDS OF CASCO BAY

The islands of Casco Bay are also known as the Calendar Islands because an early explorer mistakenly thought there was one for each day of the year (in reality there are only 140). Some islands are uninhabited; others support year-round communities as well as stores and restaurants. Nearest to Portland (and in fact considered a suburb of it), **Peaks Island** is the most developed of the Calendar Islands. A trip here allows you to commune with the wind and sea, explore an old fort, and ramble along the alternately rocky and sandy shore without having to venture too far away. A bit farther out, 17-acre **Eagle Island** contains the 1904 home of Admiral Robert E. Peary, the American explorer of the North Pole. It also has a rocky beach and myriad trails.

GETTING
THERE
The brightly painted ferries of **Casco Bay Lines** (☎*207/774–7871* ⊕*www.cascobaylines.com*) are the islands' lifeline. A ride on the bay is a great way to experience the dramatic shape of the Maine Coast while offering a glimpse of some of its hundreds of islands.

CAPE ELIZABETH TO PROUTS NECK

WHAT TO SEE

Fodor'sChoice
★
Portland Head Light. Familiar to many from photographs and Edward Hopper's painting *Portland Head-Light (1927)*, this historic lighthouse was commissioned by George Washington in 1790. The towering white stone lighthouse stands over the keeper's house, a white home with a blazing red roof. Besides a harbor view, its park has walking paths and picnic facilities. The keeper's house is now the Museum at Portland Head Light. The lighthouse is in Fort Williams Park, about 2 mi from the town center. *Museum* ⊠*1000 Shore Rd., Cape Elizabeth* ☎*207/799-2661* ⊕*www.portlandheadlight.com* ☜*$2* ☉*Memorial Day–mid-Oct., daily 10–4; Apr., May, Nov., and Dec., weekends 10–4.*

★ **Two Lights State Park.** On just over 40 acres of Maine's quintessential rocky shoreline, this park is named for the two lighthouses atop the hill (one is now privately owned, the other still in use since 1828). The park has ample beach access, picnic facilities, and great views of the activities of Portland Harbor. ⊠*Rte. 77, Cape Elizabeth* ☎*207/799-5871* ☜*$1.50* ☉*Daily 9 AM–sunset.*

WHERE TO EAT

$$–$$$ ✕ **Joe's Boathouse.** The two small dining rooms of this establishment
SEAFOOD are simple, clean, and finished in sea-foam green, with large windows
looking out to a marina. The ocean motif extends to a lobster boat on
a mantle and a bar that houses an aquarium. Dinner specials include
tuna steak and lemon tarragon sea scallops; for lunch try the Red Riot,
a sandwich featuring spicy sausage, capicola, and red peppers. In summer diners can enjoy the flavors and the scenery from the vantage of
a patio. Altogether, it is low-key, casual, and a hit with the locals. ⊠*1
Spring Point Dr.* ☎*207/741–2780* ▤*AE, MC, V.*

¢–$$ ✕ **Lobster Shack.** You can't beat the location—right on the water, below
SEAFOOD the lighthouse pair that gives Two Lights State Park its name—and
the food's not bad either. Just as the name implies, fresh lobster is the
watchword here, and you can choose your meal right from the tank.
Other menu must-haves include chowder, fried clams, and fish and
chips. It's been a classic spot since the 1920s. Eat inside or out. ⊠*225
Two Lights Rd.* ☎*207/799–1677* ▤*MC, V* ⊙ *Closed Nov.–late Mar.*

WHERE TO STAY

$$$$ 🏨 **Black Point Inn.** Toward the tip of the peninsula that juts into the
ocean at Prouts Neck stands this stylish, tastefully updated historic
resort with spectacular views up and down the coast. The extensive
grounds contain beaches, trails, and sports facilities—including use of
the tennis courts and golf course at the nearby country club. Finer
touches abound, such as nightly turndown service and in-room terry
robes. The Cliff Walk, a pebbled path that wanders past Winslow Hom-
er's former studio, runs along the Atlantic headlands that Homer often
painted. The inn is 12 mi south of Portland and about 10 mi north of
Old Orchard Beach. **Pros:** stunning water views, set amid scenery that
inspired Winslow Homer. **Con:** driving required to get to area attrac-
tions. ⊠*510 Black Point Rd., Scarborough* ☎*207/883–2500* ⊕*www.
blackpointinn.com* ⇋*25 rooms* ⌂*In-room: DVD (some), Wi-Fi. In-
hotel: restaurant, bar, pools, bicycles* ▤*AE, D, MC, V* ⊚*MAP.*

$$$–$$$$ 🏨 **Inn by the Sea.** Every unit in this all-suites inn includes a kitchen and a
view of the Atlantic. It's a short walk down a private boardwalk to sandy
Crescent Beach, a popular family spot. Dogs are welcomed with a room-
service pet menu, evening turndown treats, and oversize beach towels.
The Audubon dining room ($$$–$$$$), open to nonguests, serves fine
seafood and regional dishes. The shingle-style design, typical of turn-of-
the-20th-century New England shorefront cottages and hotels, includes
a varied roofline punctuated by turretlike features and gables, balco-
nies, a covered porch supported by columns, an open deck, and large
windows. **Pros:** on Crescent Beach and a short drive to Two Lights,
Portland Head, and Portland. **Con:** a bit large to be considered charm-
ing. ⊠*40 Bowery Beach Rd., Cape Elizabeth (7 mi south of Portland)*
☎*207/799–3134 or 800/888–4287* ⊕*www.innbythesea.com* ⇋*43
suites* ⌂*In-room: kitchen, refrigerator, VCR, dial-up. In-hotel: restau-
rant, bar, tennis court, pool, laundry service, public Internet, some pets
allowed* ▤*AE, D, MC, V.*

FREEPORT

17 mi northeast of Portland.

Many who come to the area do so simply to shop—L.L. Bean is the store that put Freeport on the map, and plenty of outlets and some specialty stores have settled here. But those who flock straight to L.L. Bean and see nothing else of Freeport are missing out on some real New England beauty. Beyond the shops are charming back streets lined with historic buildings and old clapboard houses, a pretty little harbor on the south side of the Harraseeket River, and bucolic nature preserves with miles of walking trails.

SPORTS & THE OUTDOORS

It shouldn't come as a surprise that one of the world's largest outdoor clothing and supply outfitters also provides its customers with instructional adventures to go with their products. L.L. Bean's year-round **Outdoor Discovery Schools** (☎ *888/552–3261* ⊕ *www.llbean.com/ods*) include half- and one-day classes, as well as longer trips that teach canoeing, shooting, photography, kayaking, fly-fishing, cross-country skiing, and other sports. Classes are for all skill levels; it's best to sign up several months in advance. Check their schedule for special activities held regularly during the summer months.

SHOPPING

The *Freeport Visitors Guide* (☎ *207/865–1212, 800/865–1994 for a copy*) lists the more than 100 shops and factory outlet stores that can be found on Main Street, Bow Street, and elsewhere, including such big-name designers as Coach, Brooks Brothers, Polo Ralph Lauren, and Cole-Haan. Don't overlook the specialty stores and crafts galleries. **Thos. Moser Cabinetmakers** (⊠ *149 Main St.* ☎ *207/865–4519*) sells high-quality handmade furniture with clean, classic lines.

Fodor's Choice Founded in 1912 as a mail-order merchandiser of products for hunters,
★ guides, and anglers, **L.L. Bean** (⊠ *95 Main St. [U.S. 1]* ☎ *800/341–4341*) attracts 3.5 million shoppers a year to its giant store (open 24 hours a day) in the heart of Freeport's shopping district. You can still find the original hunting boots, along with cotton, wool, and silk sweaters; camping and ski equipment; comforters; and hundreds of other items for the home, car, boat, and campsite. The **L.L. Bean Factory Store** (⊠ *Depot St.* ☎ *800/341–4341*) has seconds and discontinued merchandise at discount prices. **L.L. Bean Kids** (⊠ *8 Nathan Nye St.* ☎ *800/341–4341*) specializes in children's merchandise and has a climbing wall and other activities that appeal to kids.

NIGHTLIFE & THE ARTS

Once a week in July and August, sit outside under the stars for the **L.L. Bean Summer Concert Series** (⊠ *Morse St.* ☎ *800/559–0747 Ext. 37222* ⊕ *www.llbean.com*). The free concerts start at 7:30 PM in downtown Freeport at L.L. Bean's Discovery Park. The entertainment ranges from folk, jazz, and country to rock and includes some pretty big names. Bring a blanket and refreshments. Look for special Sunday concert events in late fall and in the winter holiday season. Previous summer

7

acts have included Livingston Taylor, zydeco and bluegrass musicians, and the Don Campbell Band.

WHERE TO EAT & STAY

$$–$$$$

Fodor's Choice

★

AMERICAN

✗**Broad Arrow Tavern.** On the main floor of the Harraseeket Inn, this dark-paneled tavern with mounted moose heads, decoys, snowshoes, and other outdoor sporty decor is known for both its casual nature and its sumptuous menu. The chefs use only organically grown food, with a nearly exclusive emphasis on Maine products, to create treats such as steaks and seafood wood-grilled in a large brick hearth. About the only non-Maine ingredient is the farm-raised South Dakota buffalo, though the burger it makes is a real favorite. For lunch, choose from the ample menu or graze on the well-stocked buffet. Lunch and dinner are served daily from 11 AM. ⊠*162 Main St.* ☎*207/865–9377* ⚑*Reservations not accepted* ▤*AE, D, DC, MC, V.*

$–$$

SEAFOOD

✗**Harraseeket Lunch & Lobster Co.** Seafood baskets and lobster dinners are the focus at this bare-bones place beside the town landing in South Freeport. Order at the counter and find a seat inside or out, depending on the weather. ⊠*On pier, end of Main St.* ☎*207/865–4888* ⚑*Reservations not accepted* ▤*No credit cards* ☉*Closed mid-Oct.–Apr.*

$$$$

Fodor's Choice

★

☵**Harraseeket Inn.** Despite modern appointments such as elevators and whirlpool baths in some rooms, this 1850 Greek Revival home provides a pleasantly old-fashioned, country-inn experience just a few minutes' walk from L.L. Bean. Guest rooms have print fabrics and reproductions of Federal quarter-canopy beds. Ask for a second-floor, garden-facing room. The formal Maine Dining Room ($$$–$$$$) specializes in contemporary American regional (and organic) cuisine such as pan-roasted lobster and all-natural filet mignon. **Pros:** excellent on-site dining, walk to shopping district, afternoon tea. **Con:** building updates over the years have diminished some authenticity. ⊠*162 Main St.* ☎*207/865–9377 or 800/342–6423* ⊕*www.harraseeketinn. com* ⚑*84 rooms* ♿*In-room: refrigerator (some), dial-up. In-hotel: 2 restaurants, pool, no-smoking rooms* ▤*AE, D, DC, MC, V* ☺*BP.*

THE MID-COAST REGION

By Sherry
Hanson

Lighthouses dot the headlands of Maine's Mid-Coast region, where thousands of miles of coastline wait to be explored. Defined by chiseled peninsulas stretching south from U.S. 1, this area has everything from the sandy beaches and sandbars of Popham Beach to the jutting cliffs of Monhegan Island. If you are intent on hooking a trophy-size fish or catching a glimpse of a whale, there are plenty of cruises available. If you want to explore deserted beaches and secluded coves, kayaks are your best bet.

The charming towns, too, each have their array of attractions. Brunswick has rows of historic wood and clapboard homes, while Bath is known for its maritime heritage. Wiscasset Harbor has docks where you can stroll and waterfront seafood restaurants where you can enjoy the catch of the day—Damariscotta, too, is worth a stop for its seafood restaurants. Boothbay has lots of little stores that are perfect for window shopping, while Thomaston and environs offer scenic drives through fishing villages surrounded by water on all sides.

BRUNSWICK & THE HARPSWELLS

10 mi north of Freeport, 30 mi northeast of Portland.

Lovely brick-and-clapboard buildings are the highlight of Brunswick's Federal Street Historic District, which includes Federal Street and Park Row and the stately campus of Bowdoin College. From the intersection of Pleasant and Maine streets, in the center of town, you can walk in any direction and discover an impressive array of restaurants. Plus, from pushcart vendors on the shady town green, known as the Mall, you can sample finger foods such as hamburgers, clam rolls, and that old Maine favorite, steamed hot dogs.

From Brunswick, Routes 123 and 24 take you to the peninsulas and islands known collectively as the Harpswells. Small coves along Harpswell Neck shelter lobster boats, and summer cottages are tucked away amid birch and spruce trees. On your way down to Land's End at the end of Route 24, stop at Mackerel Cove to see a real fishing harbor; there are a few parking spaces where you can stop and picnic and look for beach glass, or put in your kayaks.

NEED A BREAK? The scent of freshly baked scones and breads may draw you into the Wild Oats Bakery (⊠ *149 Maine St., Brunswick* ☎ *207/725-6287* ▭ *D, MC, V*), inside the Tontine Mall downtown. There are also hot soups and chowders or made-to-order sandwiches and salads.

SPORTS & THE OUTDOORS
The coast near Brunswick is full of hidden nooks and crannies waiting to be explored. By kayak you can seek out secluded beaches and tucked-away coves along the shore, and watch gulls and cormorants diving for fish. **H2Outfitters** (⊠ *Rte. 24, Orr's Island* ☎ *207/833–5257 or 800/205–2925* ⊕ *www.h2outfitters.com*) provides top-notch kayaking instruction and gear for people of all skill levels.

WHERE TO EAT
$$–$$$
Fodor'sChoice
★
SEAFOOD
✕ **Cook's Lobster House.** Inhale the salt breeze as you cross the world's only cribstone bridge (designed so that water flows freely through gaps between the granite blocks) on your way south on Route 24 from Cook's Corner in Brunswick to this famous seafood restaurant 15 mi away, which began as a lobster shack on Bailey Island. Try the lobster casserole, or the delectable haddock sandwich. Several specialties come in smaller portions. Lobster dishes are in the $$$$ price range. Whether you choose inside or deck seating, you can watch the activity on the water: men checking lobster pots on the water and kayakers fanning across the bay. ⊠ *68 Garrison Cove Rd., Bailey Island* ☎ *207/833–2818* ⚠ *Reservations not accepted* ▭ *D, MC, V* ⊗ *Closed New Year's Day–mid-Feb.*

7

BATH

11 mi northeast of Brunswick, 38 mi northeast of Portland.

Bath has been a shipbuilding center since 1607. The venerable Bath Iron Works completed its first passenger ship in 1890 and is still building ships today, turning out frigates for the U.S. Navy. Along Front and Centre streets, in the heart of Bath's historic district are some charming 19th-century Victorian homes. Among them are the 1820 Federal-style Pryor House, at 360 Front Street; the 1810 Greek Revival–style mansion at 969 Washington Street, covered with gleaming white clapboards; and the Victorian gem at 1009 Washington Street, painted a distinctive shade of raspberry. All three operate as inns. **It's a good idea to avoid U.S. 1 on weekdays from 3:15 to 4:30 pm, when a major shift change at the factory takes place.**

WHAT TO SEE

FodorśChoice ★ **Reid State Park.** This park on Georgetown Island has 1½ mi of sand split between two beaches. From the top of rocky Griffith Head, you can spot the lighthouses on Seguin Island, the Cuckolds, and Hendricks Head. In summer, parking lots fill by 11 AM on weekends and holidays. If swimming, be aware of the possibility of an undertow. During a storm, this is a great place to observe the ferocity of the waves crashing onto the shore. ⊠*Rte. 127* ☎*207/371–2303*

OFF THE BEATEN PATH **Popham Beach State Park** (⊠*Rte. 209, Phippsburg* ☎*207/389–1335*) has bathhouses and picnic tables. There are no restaurants at this end of the beach, so pack a picnic or get takeout from Spinney's Restaurant near the Civil War–era Fort Popham or Percy's Store behind Spinney's, at 6 Sea Street, phone number 207/389–2010. At low tide you can walk miles of tidal flats and also out to a nearby island, where you can explore tide pools or fish off the ledges. Drive past the entrance to the park and on the right you can see a vista often described as "Million Dollar View." The confluence of the Kennebec and Morse rivers creates an ever-shifting pattern of sandbars.

WHERE TO EAT

$-$$
BARBECUE
✕**Beale Street Barbecue.** Ribs are the thing at this barbecue joint. For hearty eaters, ask for one of the platters piled high with pulled pork, pulled chicken, or shredded beef. If you can't decide, there's always the massive barbecue sampler. Jalapeño popovers and chili served with corn bread are terrific appetizers. Enjoy a beer at the bar while waiting for your table. ⊠*215 Water St.* ☎*207/442–9514* ▤*MC, V.*

$$
AMERICAN
✕**Mae's Café & Bakery.** Some of the region's tastiest pies, pastries, and cakes are baked in this restaurant, a local favorite since 1977. Rotating selections of works by local artists hang in the two turn-of-the-20th-century houses joined together. Dine inside or on the front deck, where you can gaze down at the "City of Ships." The satisfying contemporary cuisine includes savory omelets and seafood quiche as well as seafood specials and traditional chicken, beef, and pasta dishes. Meals also can be packed to go. ⊠*160 Centre St.* ☎*207/442–8577* ▤*D, MC, V.*

$$$-$$$$
Fodor's Choice
★
AMERICAN

✕ **Robinhood Free Meetinghouse.** Though owned by acclaimed chef and owner Michael Gagné—whose 72-layer cream-cheese biscuits are shipped all over the country—this 1855 Greek Revival–style meetinghouse serves meals that are primarily made by chef de cuisine Troy Mains. The menu changes daily but always has a variety of seafood, vegetables, and dairy products purchased locally. You might begin with the lobster and crab cakes, then move on to grilled fillet of beef stuffed with crab or the confit of duck. Finish up with the signature Obsession in Three Chocolates. The wine list offers an array of choices to accompany Mains's creations. The service is excellent. The dining room evokes its meetinghouse past with cream-color walls, pine floorboards, and cherry Shaker-style chairs. Crisp linens add an elegant touch. ⊠ *210 Robinhood Rd., Georgetown* ☎*207/371–2188* ⊟*AE, D, MC, V* ⊘*No lunch.*

WHERE TO STAY

$$$-$$$$
☾
Fodor's Choice
★

☷ **Sebasco Harbor Resort.** This destination family resort, spread across 575 acres at the foot of the Phippsburg Peninsula, has an exceptional range of accommodations and services, to which it continues to add. Comfortable guest rooms in the clapboard-covered main building have antique furnishings and new bathrooms, while rooms in a building designed to resemble a lighthouse have wicker furniture, paintings by local artists, and rooftop access. The Fairwinds, a luxury waterfront spa, was added in 2007; prices for room-and-treatment packages hover around $400. Also added in 2007 was the Harbor Village Suites, set into exquisitely landscaped grounds and featuring 18 spacious and air-conditioned rooms. These units rent for around the same rate, though sometimes a bit lower. The resort's Pilot House restaurant ($$-$$$) is known for its innovative take on classic dishes. Entrées include haddock stuffed with a trio of scallops, shrimp, and vegetables. **Pros:** ocean location, excellent food and service. **Con:** pricey. ⊠*Rte. 217* ⌂*Box 75, Sebasco Estates 04565* ☎*207/389–1161 or 800/225–3819* ⊕*www.sebasco.com* ⤳*115 rooms, 23 cottages* ⚷*In-room: no a/c (some), Wi-Fi (some). In-hotel: 3 restaurants, bar, golf course, tennis courts, pool, gym, bicycles, public Wi-Fi, airport shuttle, no-smoking rooms* ⊟*AE, D, MC, V* ⊘*Closed Nov.–mid-May* ☉*MAP.*

7

WISCASSET

10 mi north of Bath, 46 mi northeast of Portland.

Settled in 1663, Wiscasset sits on the banks of the Sheepscot River. It bills itself "Maine's Prettiest Village," and it's easy to see why: it has graceful churches, old cemeteries, and elegant sea captains' homes (many converted into antiques shops or galleries). U.S. 1 becomes Main Street, and traffic often slows to a crawl. If you park in town, you can walk to most galleries, shops, restaurants, and other attractions. **Try to arrive early in the morning to find a parking space—you'll likely have success if you try to park on Water Street rather than Main.**

SHOPPING

Not to be missed is **Edgecomb Potters** (⊠ *727 Boothbay Rd., Edgecomb* ☎ *207/882–9493* ⊕ *www.edgecombpotters.com*), which specializes in pricey exquisitely glazed porcelain. Open year-round, the shop has one of the best selections in the area and also carries jewelry. **Sheepscot River Pottery** (⊠ *34 U.S. 1, Edgecomb* ☎ *207/882–9410* ⊕ *www.sheepscot. com*) boasts beautifully glazed kitchen tiles as well as kitchenware and home accessories. A second store is located in Damariscotta.

OFF THE BEATEN PATH

When Portlanders want a break from city life, many come north to the **Boothbay region**, which is made up of Boothbay proper, East Boothbay, and Boothbay Harbor. This part of the shoreline is a craggy stretch of inlets where pleasure craft anchor alongside trawlers and lobster boats. Commercial Street, Wharf Street, Townsend Avenue, and the By-Way are lined with shops and ice-cream parlors. You can browse for hours in the trinket shops, crafts galleries, clothing stores, and boutiques around the harbor, or take a walk through the 248-acre **Coastal Maine Botanical Garden** (⊠ *Barters Island Rd.* ☎ *207/633–4333*).

Excursion boats leave from the piers off Commercial Street; some allow you to see the two lighthouses standing at attention near Boothbay Harbor: **Burnt Island Light** and **Cuckolds Light**. Boats to Monhegan Island are also available. Drive out to Ocean Point in East Boothbay for some incredible scenery, or rent a kayak and explore from a lower perspective. You can also catch a ride on a lobster boat and help haul the traps. Boothbay is 13 mi southeast of Wiscasset via U.S. 1 to ME-27.

NEWCASTLE

18 mi north of Boothbay Harbor via Rte. 27 and U.S. 1.

Between the Sheepscot and the Damariscotta rivers, the town of Newcastle was settled in the early 1600s. The earliest inhabitants planted apple trees, but the town later became an industrial center, home to several shipyards and a couple of mills. The oldest Catholic church in New England, St. Patrick's, is here, and the church still rings its original Paul Revere bell to call parishioners to worship.

WHERE TO EAT & STAY

$$$–$$$$ SEAFOOD

✕🏨 **Newcastle Inn.** A riverside location and an excellent dining room make this country inn a classic. All the guest rooms are filled with antiques and decorated with sumptuous fabrics; some rooms have fireplaces and whirlpool baths. On pleasant mornings, breakfast is served on the back deck overlooking the river. The dining room ($$$$), which is open to the public by reservation, serves six-course meals and is open Tuesday through Saturday in season. The emphasis is on local seafood. **Pros:** innkeepers' reception evenings with cocktails and hors d'oeuvres. **Con:** away from town. ⊠ *60 River Rd.* ☎ *207/563–5685 or 800/832–8669* ⊕ *www.newcastleinn.com* ⊅ *14 rooms, 3 suites* ⌂ *In-room: no phone, no TV (some). In-hotel: restaurant, bar, no elevator, no kids under 12, no-smoking rooms* ⊟ *AE, MC, V* ⌷ *BP*.

OFF THE BEATEN PATH

Six miles east of Newcastle, the Damariscotta region comprises several communities along the rocky coast. The town of **Damariscotta,** which sits on the water, is filled with attractive shops and several good restaurants. **Bremen,** which encompasses more than a dozen islands and countless rocky outcrops, offers numerous sporting activities. **Nobleboro** was settled in the 1720s by Colonel David Dunbar, sent by the British to build the fort at Pemaquid. Neighboring **Waldoboro** is situated on the Medomak River and was settled largely by Germans in the early 1770s. You can still visit the old German Meeting House, built in 1772. The peninsula stretches south to include Bristol, Round Pond, South Bristol, New Harbor, and Pemaquid.

PEMAQUID POINT

17 mi south of Damariscotta via U.S. 1 to Rte. 129 to Rte. 130.

Route 130 brings you to Pemaquid Point, home of the famous lighthouse and its attendant fog bell and tiny museum. New Harbor is about 4 mi away, and Round Pond is 6 mi beyond that. To reach those towns, take a left onto Route 32 where it intersects Route 130 just before Pemaquid Point.

WHAT TO SEE

🕲 **Pemaquid Point Light.** Route 130 terminates at this lighthouse that looks
★ as though it sprouted from the ragged, tilted chunk of granite that it commands. The former lighthouse keeper's cottage is now the Fishermen's Museum, which displays historic photographs, scale models, and artifacts that explore commercial fishing in Maine. Also here is the original fog bell and bell house built in 1897 for the two original Shipman engines. Pemaquid Art Gallery, on-site, mounts exhibitions by area artists in July and August, and admission to the gallery, once you have paid your fee to be on the lighthouse property, is free. Restrooms, picnic tables, and barbecue grills are all available on this site. Next door to this property is the Sea Gull Shop, with a dining room, gift shop, and ice-cream parlor. ✉ *Rte. 130 (Bristol Rd.), Pemaquid* ☎ *207/677–2494* 🖙 *$2,* 🕑 *Memorial Day–Columbus Day, Mon.–Sat. 10–5, Sun. 11–5.*

SPORTS & THE OUTDOORS

CRUISES   You can take a cruise to Monhegan with **Hardy Boat Cruises** (✉ *Shaw's Wharf, New Harbor* ☎ *207/677–6026*). On the sightseeing cruises you can spot seals and puffins.

SHOPPING

The **Granite Hall Store** (✉ *9 Back Shore Rd., Round Pond* ☎ *207/529–5864*) has penny candy, wicker baskets, and cards on the first floor and antiques and books on the second. Order ice-cream cones through a window on the side. It's open May to mid-October.

WHERE TO STAY

$$ 🏨 **Unique Yankee Bed & Breakfast.** Spectacular views of the Gulf of Maine,
Fodor'sChoice   John's Bay, and Monhegan Island and the sound of crashing surf greet
★   you at this hilltop B&B. The facility is at Christmas Cove, named

7

when explorer Captain John Smith anchored here one Christmas Eve in the early 1600s. Since that time the cove has been a snug harbor for watercraft of all kinds. If you are looking for an oasis away from the crowds, you will enjoy the 11 gorgeous perennial gardens and the fact that this 2.3-acre property is surrounded by a 2-acre greenbelt. The owners' artwork from all over the world adorns the walls. Extensive libraries of books, videos, and DVDs wind around the staircases going up to the cupola towers, and you will even find a couple of

---

STATE BEVERAGE

It's difficult to get very far in Maine without running into Moxie—the nation's oldest soft drink, invented by Dr. Augustin Thompson of Union, Maine, in 1884. You'll recognize it by its bright orange label. It comes in bottles and cans and is sold in just about every supermarket and convenience store in Maine. A word of warning, however; you gotta get past that first taste!

---

pieces of exercise equipment tucked in a corner on the way. The hosts offer afternoon snacks and a selection of wines every evening. If you are looking for the experience of a lifetime, take that glass of wine up two or three floors to the tower, inside or on the outdoor decks. You can see all the way to Monhegan Island. Each of the guest rooms has a four-season electric fireplace, microwave, coffee pot, and two-person jetted bath (plus separate shower). The inn accepts kids and pets—in fact, pets have their own outdoor courtyard. **Pros:** amenities, view, grounds, hosts. **Con:** dogs on premises. ⊠*53 Coveside Rd., South Bristol* ☎*207/644–1502 or 866/644–1502* ⊕*www.uniqueyankeeofmaine. com* ⋈*4 rooms* ⌂*In-room: refrigerator, DVD, Wi-Fi. In-hotel: no elevator, some pets allowed, no-smoking rooms* ▤*MC, V* ⏀*BP.*

WALDOBORO

10 mi northeast of Damariscotta.

Veer off U.S. 1 onto Main Street or down Route 220 or 32, and you can discover a seafaring town with a proud shipbuilding past. Waldoboro's Main Street is lined with houses representing numerous architectural styles: Cape Cod, Queen Anne, Stick, Greek Revival, and Italianate.

WHAT TO SEE

Old German Church. One of the oldest churches in Maine, the Old German Church was built in 1772. It originally sat on the eastern side of the Medomak River, then was moved across the ice to its present site in 1794. Inside you can find box pews and a 9-foot-tall chalice pulpit. ⊠*Rte. 32* ☎*No phone* ⊙*July and Aug., daily 1–3.*

Olson House. Between 1893 and 1968, Andrew Wyeth painted his famous Christina pictures in the Olson House. Reproductions of many of these enigmatic portraits are hung throughout this historic house, now part of the Farnsworth Museum. ⊠*384 Hathorn Point Rd., Cushing* ☎*207/354–0102* ⊕ *www.farnsworthmuseum.org* ▧*$4* ⊙*Memorial Day–Columbus Day, daily 11–4.*

SHOPPING

The **Waldoboro 5 & 10** (✉*17 Friendship St.* ☏*207/832 1624*) is the oldest continually operated five-and-ten in the country. It offers deli-type sandwiches, soups, and ice cream, plus it sells a nice selection of toys. There's also a penny-candy counter popular with kids.

PENOBSCOT BAY

By Stephen and Neva Allen

Few could deny that Penobscot Bay is one of Maine's most dramatically beautiful regions. Its 1,000-mi-long coastline is made up of rocky granite boulders, wild and often undeveloped shore, a sprinkling of colorful towns, and views of the sea and shore that are a photographer's dream. It is home to hundreds of islands.

Initially, shipbuilding was the primary moneymaker here. In the 1800s, during the days of the great tall ships, or Down Easters as they were often called, more wooden ships were built along Penobscot Bay than in any other place in America. This golden age of billowing sails and wooden sailing ships did not last long, however. It came to an end with the development of the steam engine. Ships propelled by steam-fed pistons were faster, safer, more reliable, and could hold more cargo. By 1900, sailing ships were no longer a viable commercial venture in Maine. However, as you will see when traveling the coast, the tall ships have not disappeared—they have simply been revived as recreational boats, known as windjammers.

If you're driving at night, be wary of moose crossing the road.

THOMASTON

10 mi northeast of Waldoboro, 72 mi northeast of Portland.

Dotted with antiques and specialty shops, the seaside town of Thomaston is a delightful town known for the clapboard houses lining its streets. A National Historic District encompasses parts of High, Main, and Knox streets.

WHERE TO EAT

$$-$$$ ✕**Thomaston Café & Bakery.** A changing selection of works by local artists adorns the walls of this small café, and you are next door to an independent bookstore. You might actually run into a writer or an artist or two here, since this is a popular meeting place for locals. Entrées, prepared with locally grown ingredients, include seared fresh tuna on soba noodles, lobster ravioli with lobster sauce, and filet mignon with béarnaise sauce. Soups and sandwiches are delicious. ✉*154 Main St.* ☏*207/354–8589* ▤*MC, V* ☻*No dinner Sun.–Thurs.*

AMERICAN

Lighting the Way

Ever wonder what makes Maine's more than five dozen lighthouses so bright? It has to do with the lens; you need the right kind of lens to magnify the light. Resembling giant beehives, the original Fresnel lenses used in these lighthouses were made of prisms that redirected light from a lamp into a concentrated beam.

The first Fresnel lens was made in France in 1822 by French physicist Augustine Fresnel. Most lenses that were placed in lighthouses along the coasts of Europe and North America were handmade and shipped unassembled from France. The largest of these lenses, called a first-order lens, could be as much as 12 feet tall. Rings of glass prisms arranged above and below the center drum were intended to bend the light beam. Later designs incorporated a bull's eye into the center of the lens, which acted like a magnifying glass to make the beam even more powerful.

You can see some of the smaller original lenses in museums in Maine, but you can also see a first-order lens in the Mid-Coast area in the lighthouse on Seguin Island, 10 mi from shore, accessible by boat from the Maine Maritime Museum. The Seguin Light is the only first-order lens in Maine, and one of only two remaining lenses still in use north of Virginia. The lens shines with 282 prisms.

The Seguin Island Light was commissioned by George Washington in 1795, and is one of the oldest lighthouses in the United States. Most of the original lenses used in lighthouses in this part of the country were mounted on mercury bases that were designed to rotate; these lenses were later replaced because of the danger of mercury poisoning. The lens at Seguin is a fixed light, meaning that it does not rotate. It used no mercury, so it could be kept in place. Ships can see this beacon 20 mi out to sea. Today the lens reflects the light of a 1,000-watt bulb. Before electricity, incandescent oil vapor was used.

Early Fresnel lenses were fairly standard in size and shape, but that posed problems as more and more lighthouses were built along the coasts. The captain of a ship could not tell one light from another in the dark and stormy night, so he didn't know what headland or ledge he was approaching. The lenses eventually were designed to have different "personalities" that made them easily identifiable. Many lights became known for their distinctive flash patterns. Seguin Island Light is a fixed white light, whereas the Pemaquid Point Light is a white light that flashes every 6 seconds. Monhegan Island Light, visible from Port Clyde, has a white light that flashes for 2.8 seconds every 30 seconds. In Phippsburg, Pond Island Light shines a white beam with 6-second intervals of white and dark.

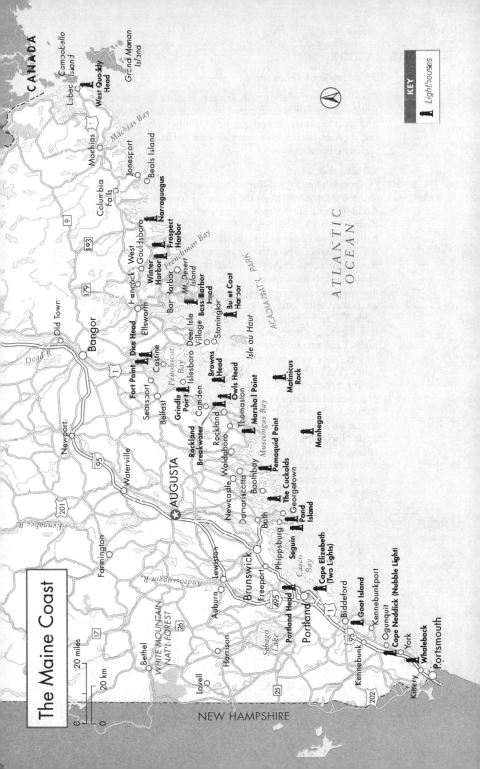

The Maine Coast

CANADA

Campobello Island

Lubec Island

West Quoddy Head

Grand Manan Island

Machias Bay

Machias

Jonesport

Beals Island

Columbia Falls

Narraguagus

West Gouldsboro

Prospect Harbor

Hancock

Winter Harbor

Ellsworth

Bar Harbor

Frenchman Bay

Mt. Desert Island

Bass Harbor Head

Burnt Coat Harbor

ACADIA NAT'L PARK

Deer Isle Village

Stonington

Isle au Haut

ATLANTIC OCEAN

Old Town

Bangor

9

193

179

Dead R.

Fort Point

Dice Head

Castine

Penobscot Bay

Searsport

Islesboro

Grindle Point

Browns Head

Belfast

Camden

Owls Head

Marshal Point

Matinicus Rock

Rockland

Rockland Breakwater

Thomaston

1

Newport

Waterville

95

Waldoboro

Muscongus Bay

Pemaquid Point

Manhegan

AUGUSTA

Newcastle

Damariscotta

Boothbay

The Cuckolds

Georgetown

201

Farmington

Bath

Phippsburg

Seguin

Pond Island

Kennebec R.

Lewiston

Brunswick

Casco Bay

Cape Elizabeth (Two Lights)

Auburn

Freeport

Portland Head

Biddeford

Goat Island

Kennebunkport

17

26

Harrison

Androscoggin R.

Portland

1

Kennebunk

Ogunquit

Cape Neddick (Nubble Light)

Bethel

WHITE MOUNTAIN NAT'L FOREST

Sebago Lake

York

Wholeback

Lovell

495

25

Kittery

Portsmouth

202

NEW HAMPSHIRE

20 miles

20 km

0

0

TENANTS HARBOR

13 mi south of Thomaston.

On a rocky part of the coast, Tenants Harbor is a quintessential coastal town—its harbor is dominated by lobster boats, its shores are slippery, and its downtown streets are lined with clapboard houses, a church, and a general store. It's a favorite with artists, and galleries and studios welcome browsers.

WHERE TO STAY

$$-$$$
Fodor's Choice
★

⊞Craignair Inn. From Route 1 just east of Thomaston, take Route 131 south 6 mi, then turn left on Route 73 for a mile, right at Clark Island Road 1½ mi, all the way to the end of the road to find this lodging dating from 1928. Sitting on four acres right on the water, it was originally built to house granite workers from nearby quarries. The annex was the chapel where the stonecutters and their families worshiped. Rooms are comfortably furnished with antique furniture, and the beds are piled high with colorful quilts. Most rooms have views of the water, and the semi-suite rents for $200 a night. A recent addition here is an apartment with kitchen, gas fireplace, washer and dryer, ceiling fans, cable TV and phone, as well as a private deck, water access, and two kayaks for use by apartment guests. The apartment rents for $200 a night. Chef extraordinaire Chris Seiler, most recently from the Samoset Resort, wins awards for his creative cuisine served in the inn's dining room ($$$). You might want to start with the Caribbean jerk grilled shrimp brochettes, or steamed great eastern mussels, and move on to pecan-crusted salmon, bacon-wrapped tenderloin, or baked stuffed haddock. The dessert menu might feature pastry chef Meg Joseph's lemon pudding cake, key lime square, or a mini crème brûleé. **Pros:** stellar food, some air-conditioned rooms. **Con:** pets allowed in some rooms. ⊠*5 3rd St., Spruce Head* ☎*207/594–7644 or 800/320–9997* ⊕*www.craignair.com* ⬩*21 rooms, 13 with bath* ⬩*In-room: no a/ c. In-hotel: public Wi-Fi, no elevator, some pets allowed, no-smoking rooms* ⊟*D, MC, V* ⦿*BP.*

PORT CLYDE

2 mi south of Tenants Harbor via Rte. 131.

Port Clyde, a fishing village at the end of the St. George Peninsula, is the jumping-off point to Monhegan Island. Shipbuilding was the first commercial enterprise here, and later the catching and canning of seafood. You can still buy Port Clyde sardines. Port Clyde's boat landing is home to the *Laura B*, the mail boat that serves nearby Monhegan Island. It's operated by the **Monhegan Boat Line** (☎*207/372–8848*). Several artists make their homes in Port Clyde, so check to see if their studios are open while you are visiting. From here you also can visit Owls Head Light and the Marshall Point Lighthouse, the latter of which has inspired artists like Jamie Wyeth.

MONHEGAN ISLAND

East of Pemaquid Peninsula, 10 mi south of Port Clyde.

Remote Monhegan Island, with its high cliffs fronting the sea, was known to Basque, Portuguese, and Breton fishermen well before Columbus discovered America. About a century ago, Monhegan was discovered again by some of America's finest painters, including Rockwell Kent, Robert Henri, A. J. Hammond, and Edward Hopper, who sailed out to paint its open meadows, savage cliffs, wild ocean views, and fishermen's shacks. Tourists followed, and today three excursion boats dock here *(at the end of this chapter)*. The village bustles with activity in summer, when many artists open their studios. You can escape the crowds on the island's 17 mi of hiking trails, which lead to the lighthouse and to the cliffs.

Enjoy the silence and serenity of Cathedral Woods on your way to or from the high cliffs at White Head, Black Head, and Burnt Head. Bring drinking water or plan to purchase same, as there is no potable drinking water except in restaurants, inns, and private cottages. You might consider bringing a picnic if you're visiting during the day, or eat at one of the island's restaurants, though they are busy at lunch. If you are planning on hiking, bring sunblock and insect repellant, as well as a hat, and a jacket for the boat trip, which will be an hour or longer, depending on where your boat originates. Plan to pack out whatever trash you generate while you are out and about, as there are few trash receptacles in public places. All trash on Monhegan Island has to be taken off the island by boat. Use the toilet on your boat before you come ashore; the only public toilets on the island are located behind the old Monhegan House, and these are privately maintained and the owners appreciate a small donation. All that being said, if you love the rocky cliffs, this is your place. And if you happen to be an artist you might never leave. Studios and galleries are all over the island and all schedule certain days to be open. Several shops are available for browsers. Bring your camera!

ROCKLAND

4 mi northeast of Thomaston, 14 mi northeast of Tenants Harbor.

The name "Rockland" defines this area's history. If you set fishing aside, rock cutting—specifically granite and limestone—was once the area's principal occupation. In fact, numerous government buildings across the United States were built using granite blocks from Rockland and other nearby quarries. Just outside the town of Rockland, a large cement factory on U.S. 1 serves as a reminder of this rocky past.

Though once merely a place to pass through on the way to tonier ports like Camden, Rockland now attracts attention on its own, thanks to this trio of attractions: the renowned Farnsworth Museum, the increasingly popular summer Lobster Festival, and the lively North Atlantic Blues Festival. Its Main Street Historic District, with its Italianate, Mansard, Greek Revival, and Colonial Revival buildings, is on the

National Register of Historic Places. Specialty shops and galleries line the main street, and at least one of the restaurants, Primo, has become nationally famous. The town has a growing popularity as a summer destination, but it is still a large fishing port and the commercial hub of this coastal area. You can find plenty of working boats moored alongside the yachts.

Rockland Harbor is the berth of more windjammer ships than any other port in the United States. The best place in Rockland to view these beautiful vessels as they sail in and out of the harbor is the mile-long granite breakwater, which bisects the outer portion of Rockland Harbor. To get there, go north on U.S. 1, turn right on Waldo Avenue, and right again on Samoset Road; go to the end of this short road.

WHAT TO SEE

Fodor's Choice   **Farnsworth Art Museum.** This is one of the most important small museums
★ in the country. The **Wyeth Center** is devoted to Maine-related works of the famous Wyeth family: N. C. Wyeth, an accomplished illustrator whose works were featured in many turn-of-the-20th-century books; his son Andrew, one of America's best-known painters; and Andrew's son James, also an accomplished painter who lives nearby on an island. Some works from the personal collection of Andrew and Betsy Wyeth include *The Patriot, Adrift, Maiden Hair, Dr. Syn, The Clearing,* and *Watch Cap.* Also on display are works by Fitz Hugh Lane, George Bellows, Frank W. Benson, Edward Hopper (his paintings of old Rockland are a highlight), Louise Nevelson, and Fairfield Porter. Works by living Maine artists are shown in the **Jamien Morehouse Wing.** The **Farnsworth Homestead,** a handsome circa-1852 Greek Revival dwelling that is part of the museum, retains its original lavish Victorian furnishings. There is a museum store next to the Morehouse Wing (⇨ *Shopping*). In Cushing, a tiny town a few miles south of Thomaston, on the St. George River, the museum also operates the **Olsen House** (⊠*Hathorn Point Rd., Cushing*), which is depicted in Andrew Wyeth's famous painting *Christina's World.* ⊠*16 Museum St., Rockland* ☎*207/596–6457* ⊕*www.farnsworthmuseum.org* ⊠*Museum and Olsen House $10, Olsen House alone $4* ⊙*Daily 10–5.*

☾ **Maine Lighthouse Museum.** The museum displays the largest collection of
★ the famed Fresnel lighthouse lenses to be found anywhere in the world. It also displays a collection of lighthouse artifacts and Coast Guard memorabilia. Sharing the same building is the Penobscot Bay Regional Chamber of Commerce, where tourists and visitors can pick up maps and area information. ⊠*1 Park Dr.* ☎*207/594–3301* ⊕*www.maine lighthousemuseum.com* ⊠*$5* ⊙ *Weekdays 9–5, weekends 10–4.*

SHOPPING

ART GALLERIES   The **Caldbeck Gallery** (⊠*12 Elm St.* ☎*207/594–5935* ⊕*www.caldbeck. com*) displays contemporary Maine works. The **Gallery at 357 Main** (⊠*357 Main St.* ☎*207/596–0084*) specializes in marine paintings.

BOOKS & TOYS   The motto at **Planet Inc.** (⊠*318 Main St.* ☎*207/596–5976*), Maine's largest toy store, is "You're never too old to play." Planet Inc. also has a store in Camden. **Rock City Books & Coffee** (⊠*328 Main St.* ☎*207/594–*

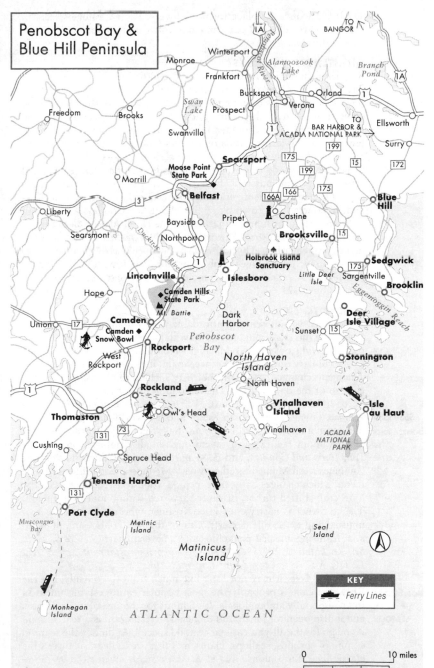

Penobscot Bay & Blue Hill Peninsula

Monroe
Winterport
TO BANGOR
Alantoosook Lake
Branch Pond
1A
Frankfort
Bucksport
Orland
1
Freedom
Brooks
Swan Lake
Prospect
Verona
TO BAR HARBOR & ACADIA NATIONAL PARK →
Ellsworth
Swanville
Surry
Searsport
199
175
15
172
Morrill
Moose Point State Park
199
Belfast
166A 166
175
Blue Hill
Liberty
3
Bayside
Pripet
Castine
Searsmont
Northport
Brooksville
15
Holbrook Island Sanctuary
Sedgwick
175
Lincolnville
Islesboro
Little Deer Isle
Sargentville
Brooklin
Hope
Camden Hills State Park
Eggemoggin Reach
Union
17
Mt. Battie
Dark Harbor
Deer Isle Village
Camden
Camden Snow Bowl
Penobscot Bay
Sunset
15
West Rockport
Rockport
North Haven Island
Stonington
1
Rockland
North Haven
Isle au Haut
Thomaston
Owl's Head
Vinalhaven Island
ACADIA NATIONAL PARK
Cushing
131
73
Vinalhaven
Spruce Head
Tenants Harbor
131
Port Clyde
Metinic Island
Seal Island
Muscongus Bay
Matinicus Island

Monhegan Island

ATLANTIC OCEAN

KEY
Ferry Lines

0   10 miles
0   15 km

7

4123) is a wonderful place for book lovers. There's a huge selection, the staff is friendly, and you can enjoy coffee and a homemade pastry while browsing.

NIGHTLIFE & THE ARTS

FESTIVALS
✪
★

Rockland's annual **Maine Lobster Festival** (☎*207/596–0376 or 800/562– 2529* ⊕*www.mainelobsterfestival.com*), in early August, is more than 60 years old and has become the biggest local event of the year. People come from all over the country to sample lobster in every possible form: steamed, fried, chowder, lobster rolls—you name it. During the few days of the festival, tons of lobsters (about 10 tons, to be exact) are steamed in the world's largest lobster cooker—you have to see it to believe it. In addition, there's shrimp in its many forms, steamed clams, and Maine mussels. The festival, held in Harbor Park, includes a parade, entertainment, craft and marine exhibits, food booths— and, of course, the crowning of the Maine Sea Goddess. More than a dozen well-known artists gather for the **North Atlantic Blues Festival** (☎*207/593–1189* ⊕*www.northatlanticbluesfestival.com*), a two- night affair each July. The show officially takes place at Harbor Park, but it also includes a Blues Club Crawl through downtown Rockland, which gives this staid old Maine town the atmosphere of New Orleans. Admission is $25.

WHERE TO EAT

$$
★
MEDITERRANEAN

✕**Amalfi.** A well-chosen and affordable wine list and excellent service have made this storefront bistro a hit with locals and visitors alike. Chef- owner David Cooke serves delicious Mediterranean cuisine, influenced by the culinary traditions of France, Spain, Italy, Greece, and Morocco. The menu changes seasonally but may include the house paella with chorizo or the duck risotto. The seafood is always fresh. ⊠*421 Main St.* ☎*207/596–0012* ▤*AE, MC, V* ⊘*Closed Mon. No lunch.*

$$$–$$$$
Fodor'sChoice
★
CONTINENTAL

✕**Primo.** Owner-chef Melissa Kelley and her world-class gourmet res- taurant in a restored Victorian home has won many awards and been written about favorably in several high-quality publications, *Vanity Fair, Town and Country,* and *Food and Wine* among them. The cuisine combines fresh Maine ingredients with Mediterranean influences. The menu, which changes daily, may include wood-roasted black sea bass, local crab-stuffed turbot, or diver-harvested-scallop and basil ravioli. The co-owner is pastry chef Price Kushner, who offers a number of unusual and delectable desserts. One of the best is his Cannoli Sicili- ana, featuring crushed pistachios and amarena cherries. ⊠*2 S. Main St., Rockland* ☎*207/596–0770* ⊕*www.primorestaurant.com* ▤*AE, D, DC, MC, V* ⊘*Closed mid-Jan.–mid-Apr.*

$–$$
Fodor'sChoice
★
SEAFOOD

✕**Rockland Cafe.** It may not look like much from the outside, but the Rockland Café is probably the most popular eating establishment in town, especially among locals. It's famous for the size of its breakfasts and is also open for lunch and dinner. The restaurant is a real bargain if you go for the all-you-can-eat seafood special. At dinner, the seafood combo of shrimps, scallops, clams, and fish is excellent, or there's the classic liver and onions. ⊠*441 S. Main St., Rockland* ☎*207/596– 7556* ⊕*www.rocklandcafe.com* ▤*AE, DC, MC, V.*

Windjammer Excursion

Nothing defines the Maine coastal experience more than a sailing trip on a windjammer. Windjammers were built throughout the East Coast in the 19th and early 20th centuries. Designed to carry cargo primarily, these iron- or steel-hulled beauties have a rich past—the *Nathaniel Bowditch* served in World War II, for example, while others plied the waters in the lumbering and oystering trades. They vary in size, but could be as small as 40 feet and hold six passengers (plus a couple of crew members), or more than 130 feet and hold 40 passengers and 10 crew members. During a windjammer excursion, not only do passengers have the opportunity to ride on a historical vessel, but in most cases they are able to participate in the navigation, be it hoisting a sail or playing captain at the wheel.

The majority of windjammers are berthed in Rockland, Rockport, or Camden. You can get information on the fleets by contacting one of two windjammer organizations: The Maine Windjammer Association (☎ 800/807-9463 ⊕ www.sail-mainecoast.com) or Maine Windjammer Cruises (☎ 207/236-2938 or 888/692-7245 ⊕ www.mainewindjammercruises.com). Cruises can be anywhere from one day or one overnight to up to eight days. The price, ranging from nearly $200 to $900, depending on length of trip, includes all meals. Trips leave from Camden, Rockland, and Rockport.

Here is a selection of some of the best windjammer cruises in the area.

CAMDEN-ROCKPORT *Angelique,* Yankee Packet Co., 207/236-8873. *Appledore,* which can take you out for just a day sail, 207/236-8353. *Mary Day,* Coastal Cruises, 207/236-2750. *Olad,* Downeast Windjammer Packet Co., 207/236-2323. *Yacht Heron,* 207/236-8605 or 800/599-8605.

ROCKLAND *American Eagle* and *Schooner Heritage,* North End Shipyard, 207/594-8007. *Nathanial Bowditch,* 207/273-4062. *Summertime,* 800/562-8290. *Victory Chimes,* 207/265-5651. *Wendameen,* 207/594-1751.

WHERE TO STAY

$$$-$$$$
★ **Berry Manor Inn.** Originally the residence of prominent Rockland merchant Charles H. Berry, this 1898 inn is in a historic residential neighborhood. The large guest rooms are elegantly furnished with antiques and reproduction pieces. All rooms have fireplaces; TVs are available upon request, and some rooms have whirlpools. A guest pantry is stocked with sweets. **Pros:** in a nice, quiet neighborhood, within walking distance of downtown and the harbor. **Con:** not handicap accessible. ⊠ *81 Talbot Ave.* ☎ *207/596-7696 or 800/774-5692* ⊕ *www.berrymanorinn.com* ⌖ *12 rooms* ⌂ *In room: no TV, Wi-Fi. In-hotel: public Wi-Fi, no-smoking rooms* ▤ *AE, MC, V* ⍧ *BP.*

$$-$$$
★ **Limerock Inn.** This inn is in the center of town, so you can easily walk to the Farnsworth Museum or any of the other downtown attractions and restaurants. The house is built in the Queen Anne–Victorian style, and among the meticulously decorated rooms is one called Island Cottage, which features a whirlpool tub and doors that open onto a private deck overlooking a garden. The Grand Manan room has a fireplace, a

whirlpool tub, and a four-poster king-size bed. Room TVs are available upon request. **Pro:** free Wi-Fi. **Con:** no dinner options within walking distance. ⊠*96 Limerock St.* ☎*207/594–2257 or 800/546–3762* ⊕*www.limerockinn.com* ↝*8 rooms* ⌂*In-room: no phone, no TV, Wi-Fi. In-hotel: no-smoking rooms* ▭*AE, DC, MC, V* ❙○❙*BP.*

ROCKPORT

4 mi north of Rockland on U.S. 1.

Heading north on U.S. 1, you come to Rockport before you reach the tourist mecca of Camden. The most interesting part of Rockport—the harbor—is not right on U.S. 1, so many people drive by without realizing it's here. You can get there by following the first ROCKPORT sign you see off U.S. 1 at Pascal Road. The cutting and burning of limestone was once a major industry in this area. The stone was cut in nearby quarries and then burned in hot kilns. The resulting lime powder was used to create mortar. Some of the massive kilns are still here.

WHERE TO EAT & STAY

$$$–$$$$

Fodor'sChoice

★

FRENCH

✕**Marcel's.** If you're a serious gourmet and only have time to sample one dining experience in the Rockport-Rockland-Camden area, this lavish restaurant in the big Samoset Resort ought to be the one. Marcel's offers a fine array of Continental cuisine. Enjoy table-side preparation of a classic rack of lamb, châteaubriand, or Steak Diane while admiring the bay view. The menu includes a variety of Maine seafood and a fine wine list. The Sunday brunch buffet, with some of the finest seafood along the coast, is famous and draws a crowd. ⊠*220 Warrenton St., off U.S. 1* ☎*207/594–2511* ⌁*Reservations essential Jacket required* ▭*AE, D, DC, MC, V* ⊘*No lunch.*

$$–$$$$

Fodor'sChoice

★

▦ **Samoset Resort.** This 230-acre, all-encompassing, ocean-side resort on the Rockland-Rockport town line offers luxurious rooms and suites, all with a private balcony or patio, and an ocean or garden view. The spacious rooms are decorated in deep green and burgundy tones. The resort has three dining options: the Breakwater Cafe, the Clubhouse Grille, and the flagship restaurant, Marcel's (⇨ Where to Eat). For a less-formal affair, try the Breakwater Cafe, featuring basic New England fare, such as homemade chowder and lobster rolls; there's outdoor seating when the weather is nice. The Clubhouse Grille, catering to the golf crowd, serves casual food, which you can enjoy inside or on the porch. *Golf Digest* called the resort's 18-hole championship golf course the "Top Ranked Resort Course in New England," and the "Seventh Most Beautiful Course in America." **Pro:** this is a resort property that seems to meet every need. **Con:** not within walking distance of Rockland or Camden shops. ⊠*220 Warrenton St.* ☎*207/594–2511 or 800/341–1650* ⊕*www.samoset.com* ↝*156 rooms, 22 suites* ⌂*In-room: dial-up, Wi-Fi. In-hotel: 3 restaurants, bar, golf course, tennis courts, pools, gym, children's programs (ages 3–12), laundry service, concierge, public Internet, airport shuttle, no-smoking rooms* ▭*AE, D, DC, MC, V* ❙○❙*CP.*

THE PRETTIEST WALK IN THE WORLD

A few years ago, *Yankee*, the quintessential magazine of New England, did a cover story on what it called "the prettiest walk in the world." The two-lane paved road, which winds up and down, with occasional views of the ocean, connects Rockport to Camden. To judge the merits of this approximately 2-mi journey for yourself, you can travel by foot or by car. Begin at the intersection of U.S. 1 and Pascal Road. Take a right off U.S. 1 toward Rockport harbor, then cross the bridge and go up the hill. On your left is Russell Avenue. Take that all the way to Camden. Lining the way are some of the most beautiful homes in Maine, surrounded by an abundance of flora and fauna. Keep an eye out for a farm with Belted Galloway cows, as well as views of the sparkling ocean—for those who may not know, these rare white cows get their name from the foot-wide black "belt" around their middles. The walk or drive is beautiful at any time of the year, but in fall it's breathtaking. Like the rest of New England, the coast of Maine gets a large number of fall foliage "leaf peepers," and the reds and golds of the chestnut, birch, and elm trees along this winding route are especially beautiful.

CAMDEN

2 mi north of Rockport, 5 mi south of Lincolnville.

★ More than any other town along Penobscot Bay, Camden is the perfect picture-postcard of a Maine coastal village. It is one of the most popular destinations on the Maine Coast, so June through September the town is crowded with visitors—but don't let that scare you away; Camden is worth it. Just come prepared for busy traffic on the town's Main Street (U.S. 1), and make lodging reservations well in advance. You'll also want to make restaurant reservations whenever possible.

"The Jewel of the Maine Coast" is the publicity slogan for Camden-Rockport-Lincolnville, and it is an apt description. Camden is famous not only for its geography but also for its large fleet of windjammers—relics and replicas from the age of sailing—with their romantic histories and great billowing sails. At just about any hour during the warm months, you're likely to see at least one windjammer tied up in the harbor. The excursions, whether for an afternoon or a week, are best from June through September.

The town's compact size makes it perfect for exploring on foot: shops, restaurants, and galleries line Main Street (U.S. 1), as well as side streets and alleys around the harbor. Especially worth inclusion on your walking tour is Camden's residential area. It is quite charming and filled with many fascinating old period houses from the time when Federal, Greek Revival, and Victorian architecture were the rage among the wealthy. Many of them now are B&Bs. The chamber of commerce, at the Public Landing, can provide you with a walking map.

★ One of the biggest and most colorful events of the year in Camden is **Windjammer Weekend** (☎*207/374–2993 or 800/807–9463* ⊕*www.*

windjammerweekend.com), which usually takes place at the beginning of September and includes the single largest gathering of windjammer ships in the world, plus lots of good eats.

SPORTS & THE OUTDOORS

Although their height may not be much more than 1,000 feet, the hills in **Camden Hills State Park** (✉ *U.S. 1 just north of Camden* ☎ *207/236–3109*) are lovely landmarks for miles along the low, rolling reaches of the Maine Coast. The 5,500-acre park contains 25 mi of hiking trails, including the easy nature trail up Mt. Battie. Hike or drive to the top for a magnificent view over Camden and island-studded Penobscot Bay. There also is a campground here.

SAILING For the voyage of a lifetime, you and your family should think seriously about a **windjammer trip**—which can be as little as a couple of hours or as much as a week. The following day-sailer windjammers leave from Camden Harbor; most are of the schooner type: **Lazy Jack** (☎ *207/230–0602* ⊕ *www.schoonerlazyjack.com*); **Olad** (☎ *207/236–2323* ⊕ *www.maineschooners.com*); **Shantih II** (☎ *207/236–8605* or *800/599–8605* ⊕ *www.woodenboatco.com*); and **Windjammer Surprise** (☎ *207/236–4687* ⊕ *www.camdenmainesailing.com*). Prices range from $395 to $875, with all meals included—and often that means a lobster bake on a deserted island beach.

SKIING The Maine Coast isn't known for skiing, but the **Camden Snow Bowl** (✉ *Hosmer Pond Rd.* ☎ *207/236–3438, 207/236–4418 snow phone* ⊕ *www.camdensnowbowl.com*) has a 950-foot-vertical mountain with 11 trails accessed by one double chair and two T-bars. The complex also includes a small lodge with a cafeteria, and ski and toboggan rentals. Activities include skiing, night skiing, snowboarding, tubing, tobogganing, and ice-skating—plus magnificent views over Penobscot Bay. The North American Tobogganing Championships, a tongue-in-cheek event open to anyone, is held annually in early February. At **Camden Hills State Park** (✉ *U.S. 1 just north of downtown Camden* ☎ *207/236–0849*), there are 10 mi of cross-country skiing trails.

SHOPPING

Camden has some of the best shopping in the region. The downtown area is a shopper's paradise with lots of interesting places to spend money. Most of the shops and galleries are along Camden's main drag, U.S. 1, so you can easily complete a shopping tour on foot. Start at the Camden Harbor, turn right on Bay View, and walk to Main/High Street. **U.S. 1 has three different names within the town limits—it starts as Elm Street, changes to Main Street, then becomes High Street. So don't let the addresses listed below throw you off.**

Bayview Gallery (✉ *33 Bay View St.* ☎ *207/236–4534* ⊕ *www.bayviewgallery.com*) specializes in original art, prints, and posters, most with Maine themes. **Maine Gold** (✉ *12 Bay View St.* ☎ *702/236–2717*) sells authentic Maine maple syrup. **Planet Toys** (✉ *10 Main St.* ☎ *207/236–4410*) has unusual gifts—including books, toys, and clothing—from Maine and other parts of the world.

NIGHTLIFE

Offering live music, dancing, pub food, and local brews, **Gilbert's Public House** (⊠*12 Bay View St., underneath Peter Ott's pub* ☎*207/236–4320*) is the favorite drinking place of the windjammer crowd.

WHERE TO EAT

$–$$
★
SEAFOOD

✕**Cappy's Chowder House.** Cappy's has been around for so long (more than two decades) it's become somewhat of a Camden institution. As you would expect from the name, Cappy's "chowdah" is the thing to order here—it's been written up in the *New York Times* and in *Bon Appétit* magazine—but there are plenty of other seafood specials on the menu, too. Don't be afraid to bring the kids—this place has many bargain meals. ⊠*1 Main St.* ☎*207/236–2254* ⇗*Reservations not accepted* ☐*MC, V.*

$$–$$$
FRENCH

✕**Natalie's.** Fine dining with a French-American menu is the name of the game here. There's also a prix-fixe meal and a Grand Lobster dish. The lounge is a perfect place for a cocktail in front of the big fireplace. ⊠*83 Bay View St.* ☎*207/236–7008* ☐*AE, DC, MC, V.*

WHERE TO STAY

$$–$$$$
★

Hartstone Inn. This downtown 1835 mansard-roofed Victorian home has been turned into an elegant and sophisticated retreat and a fine culinary destination. No detail has been overlooked, from soft robes, down comforters, and chocolate truffles in the guest rooms to china, crystal, and silver in the elegantly decorated dining room. The inn hosts seasonal food festivals. **Pro:** on-site restaurant is excellent. **Con:** not handicapped accessible. ⊠*41 Elm St. (U.S. 1)* ☎*207/236–4259 or 800/788–4823* ⊕*www.hartstoneinn.com* ⇗*6 rooms, 6 suites* ⬙*In-room: dial-up. In-hotel: restaurant, no-smoking rooms* ☐*MC, V* ⬤*BP.*

$$$$
★

Inn at Sunrise Point. Guests are offered a spectacular setting in this luxury inn. (The Irish manager prides himself on having the highest rates of any Camden inn.) The main house and cottages are right on the ocean, resulting in beautiful ocean views from nearly all rooms. Amenities such as plush robes and oversize tubs and showers are standard; some rooms include romantic wood-burning fireplaces and Jacuzzis. One of the cottages is accessible for people with disabilities. All rooms have flat-screen TVs with DVD players. **Pros:** spectacular views, a delightful Irish manager. **Cons:** pricey, no restaurants nearby. ⊠*U.S. 1* ☎*207/236–7716* ⊕*www.sunrisepoint.com* ⇗*3 rooms, 4 cottages, 2 suites* ⬙*In-room: no a/c, Wi-Fi. In-hotel: no elevator, no-smoking rooms* ☐*MC, V* ⬤*BP.*

$$$–$$$$
★

Lord Camden Inn. The Lord Camden Inn is an excellent location if you want to be in the very center of town near the harbor. The exterior of the building is red brick with bright blue-and-white awnings. The colorful interior is furnished with restored antiques and paintings by local artists. Despite being downtown, the inn offers plenty of ocean views from the upstairs rooms, and some of the rooms have lovely old-fashioned, four-poster beds. There's no on-site restaurant but you can find plenty of dining options within walking distance. Two of the rooms are handicapped accessible, including the bathrooms. All of the rooms are no-smoking, but the hotel is pet-friendly. An elevator goes to the upper floors. **Pro:** the most centrally located accommodation in Camden. **Con:** U.S. 1 traffic may keep you awake in the front rooms. ✉*24 Main St. (U.S. 1)* ☎*207/236–4325 or 800/336–4325* ⊕*www.lordcamdeninn.com* ⊷*37 rooms* ⚲*In-room: refrigerator (some), dial-up. In-hotel: no-smoking rooms* ▭*AE, MC, V* ⦿|*BP.*

$$$–$$$$
Fodor'sChoice
★
▦**Norumbega.** The Norumbega is probably the most unusual-looking B&B you'll ever see. When you see this ivy-coated, gray stone castle, from the outside you may think, "*Wow, Count Dracula would feel right at home here.*" But inside it's cheerier, and elegant, with many of the antique-filled rooms offering fireplaces and private balconies overlooking the bay. The inn was built in 1886 by local businessman and inventor (of duplex telegraphy) Joseph Stearns. Before erecting his home, he spent a year visiting the castles of Europe and adapting the best ideas he found. He named the castle after the original 17th-century name for what is now Maine, "Norumbega." The home was converted into a B&B in 1984 and has been named by the *Maine Times* as the most-photographed piece of real estate in the state. There are no ground-floor guest rooms, and no elevator. Pets are not allowed. **Pro:** you will never again stay in a place this dramatic looking. **Con:** while this is an unusually beautiful property, guests with mobility problems or who have difficulty climbing stairs will not find it comfortable. ✉*63 High St. (U.S. 1), just a little north of downtown Camden* ☎*207/236–4646 or 877/363–4646* ⊕*www.norumbegainn.com* ⊷*13 rooms* ⚲*In-room: no a/c, dial-up, Wi-Fi. In-hotel: no elevator, no-smoking rooms* ▭*AE, DC, MC, V* ⦿|*BP.*

$$–$$$
★
▦**Whitehall Inn.** One of Camden's best-known inns, the Whitehall is an 1834 white clapboard sea captain's home just north of town. The Millay Room, off the lobby, preserves memorabilia of the poet Edna St. Vincent Millay, who grew up in the area and read her poetry here. The inn is a delightful blend of the old and the new. The telephones are antiques, but the electronics are brand new. The rooms, remodeled in 2007, have dark-wood bedsteads, white bedspreads, and claw-foot tubs. The dining room serves traditional and creative American cuisine as well as many seafood specialties, and the popular prix-fixe dinner is $36 a person. One room is handicapped accessible. **Pro:** Edna St. Vincent Millay—wow! **Con:** no air-conditioning, but usually it's fine without it. ✉*52 High St.* ☎*207/236–3391 or 800/789–6565* ⊕*www.whitehall-inn.com* ⊷*50 rooms, 45 with bath* ⚲*In-room: no a/c, no phone (some), Wi-Fi. In-hotel: restaurant, tennis court, public Internet, no-smoking rooms* ▭*AE, MC, V* ☉*Closed mid-Oct.–mid-May* ⦿|*BP.*

LINCOLNVILLE

6 mi north of Camden via U.S. 1.

Looking at a map, you may notice there are two parts to Lincolnville: Lincolnville Beach on U.S. 1 and the town of Lincolnville Center a little inland on Route 73. The area of most interest—where you can find the restaurants and the ferry to Islesboro—is Lincolnville Beach. This is a tiny area; you could be through it in less than a minute. Still, it has a history going back to the Revolution, and you can see a few small cannons on the beach that were intended to repel the British in the War of 1812 (they were never used). Lincolnville is close to Camden, so it's a great place to stay if rooms in Camden are full—or if you just want someplace a little quieter.

WHERE TO EAT & STAY

¢ ¢¢ ✕**Lobster Pound Restaurant.** If you're looking for an authentic place to
Fodor's Choice have your Maine lobster dinner, this is it. This simple restaurant looks
★ more like a cannery than a restaurant, with rustic wooden picnic tables
SEAFOOD and hundreds of live lobsters swimming in tanks—you can pick out (if you want) your own lobster. It'll be served to you with clam chowder and corn. Forget about ordering a predinner cocktail or wine with dinner; have an ice tea instead. On U.S. 1, right on the edge of the sea, the Lobster Pound provides beautiful views from both its indoor and outdoor seating. On the menu here you will see the classic "Shore Dinner," which consists of lobster stew or fish chowder, steamed or fried clams, 1½-pound lobster, potato, and dessert. Lobster and seafood are, of course, the reason to come here, though turkey and steak are also available. This restaurant has seating for nearly 300, so even if it's a busy time, you won't have to wait long. There's also a 70-seat picnic area if you want to take your food to go. ⊠2521 *Atlantic Hwy. (U.S. 1)* ☎207/789–5550 ▤*AE, DC, MC, V* ⊘*Closed Nov.–Apr.*

$$$$ ▦**Inn at Ocean's Edge.** This beautiful white inn on 22 acres has one of
Fodor's Choice the loveliest settings in the area, with heavy forest on one side and the
★ ocean on the other. The inn looks as if it has been here for decades, but the original building was only built in 1999, with the upper building following in 2001. The rooms are styled simply but with old-fashioned New England elegance: a lot of quilts and throws and Colonial-style furniture. Every room has a king-size bed, an ocean view, a fireplace, and a whirlpool for two. One room is handicapped accessible; and there is an elevator for the upper floors. The elevator is small and unobtrusive, not affecting the basic look of the hotel. The inn also includes a fine restaurant, the Edge, with oceanfront dining. **Pro:** it would be tough to find an accommodation in a more beautiful setting than this. **Cons:** abundant shopping and dining options not within walking distance, lodging is pricey. ⊠*20 Stone Coast Rd. (U.S. 1), Lincolnville* ⌁ ☎207/236–0945 ⊕*www.innatoceansedge.com* ⇆*29 rooms, 3 suites* ♨*In-room: VCR, DVD, dial-up, Wi-Fi. In-hotel: bar, gym, pool, restaurant, no-smoking rooms* ▤*AE, DC, MC, V* ⦿*BP.*

ISLESBORO

★ *3 mi east of Lincolnville via Islesboro Ferry (terminal on U.S. 1).*

If you would like to visit one of Maine's area islands but don't have much time, Islesboro is the best choice. The island is only a 20-minute ferry ride off the mainland. You can take your car with you. The drive from one end of the island to the other (on the island's only road) is lovely. It takes you through Warren State Park, a nice place to stop for a picnic and the only public camping area on the island. There are two stores on the island where you can buy supplies for your picnic: the Island Market is a short distance from the ferry terminal on the main road; and Durkee's General Store is 5 mi farther north at 863 Main Road. Next to the island's ferry terminal are the Sailor's Memorial Museum and the Grindle Point Lighthouse, both worth a brief look.

The permanent year-round population of Islesboro is about 625, but it swells to around 3,000 in summer. Most of the people who live on the island full time earn their living in one way or another from the sea. Some of them work at the three boatyards on the island, others are fishermen, and still others run small businesses. Seasonal residents may include some familiar faces: John Travolta and his wife, Kelly Preston, have a home here, as does Kirstie Alley.

The **Islesboro Ferry,** operated by the Maine State Ferry Service, departs from Lincolnville Harbor, a few hundred feet from the Lobster Pound Restaurant. Try to head out on one of the early ferries so you have enough time to drive around and get back. If you miss the last ferry, you'll have to stay on the island overnight. The ferry runs back and forth nine times a day from April through October and seven times a day from November through March. There are fewer runs on Sunday. The round-trip cost for a vehicle and one passenger is $22.25, slightly more with additional passengers, less if you leave the vehicle behind. Call for schedules. ☎207/789–5611.

BELFAST

10 mi north of Lincolnville.

The farther you get up the coast and away from Camden, the less touristy the area becomes and the more you see of the real Maine. Traffic jams and crowded restaurants give way to a more-relaxed and casual atmosphere, and locals start to treat you like a potential neighbor.

A number of Maine coastal towns, such as Wiscasset and Damariscotta, like to think of themselves as the prettiest little town in Maine, but Belfast may be the true winner of this title. It has a full variety of charms: a beautiful waterfront; an old and interesting main street climbing up from the harbor; a delightful array of B&Bs, restaurants, and shops; and a friendly population. The downtown even has old-fashioned street lamps, which set the streets aglow at night. If you like looking at old houses, many of which go all the way back to the Revolution, just drive up and down some of the side streets. In 2007, Belfast was called "one of the top 10 culturally cool towns in the country" by *USA Today.* The biggest employer in town is Bank of America.

WHAT TO SEE

In the mid-1800s, Belfast was home to a number of wealthy business magnates. Their mansions still stand along High Street, offering some excellent examples of Greek Revival and Federal architecture. **The Belfast Chamber of Commerce Visitor Center** (✉*17 Main St., at harbor* ☎*207/338–5900*) can provide you with a free walking tour brochure that describes the various historic homes and buildings, as well as the old business section in the harbor area.

As you walk around Belfast, you will see a number of cream-color signs labeled THE MUSEUM IN THE STREETS. Be sure to read them. They will tell you in easy-to-access fashion everything that you'd want to know about the history of Belfast. They are written in both English and French, for the benefit of Maine's neighbors to the north.

SHOPPING

Colburn Shoe Store (⊠*79 Main St.* ☎*207/338–1934 or 877/338–1934*) is worth a visit simply because it's the oldest shoe store in America. At one time, the making of shoes was a major industry in Belfast. The **Shamrock, Thistle & Rose** (⊠*39 Main St.* ☎*207/338–1864* ⊕*www. shamrockthistlerose.com*) sells clothing, jewelry, art, and music from Ireland, Scotland, and England.

NEED A BREAK? If you're looking for a quick and easy place to have lunch, Alexia's (☎*207/338-9676*), at the main corner of Main and High streets, serves the best pizza in town, plus sandwiches and Italian food.

NIGHTLIFE & THE ARTS

NIGHTLIFE
★ **Rollie's Bar & Grill** (⊠*37 Main St.* ☎*207/338-4502* ⊟*MC, V*) looks like it's been here 100 years, but actually it's been here only since 1972. The tavern is right in the heart of Main Street, and at first glance it might look like a bikers bar. It is that—and a lot more. If you recognize the interior, it's because it was used as a setting in the Stephen King film *Thinner*. The vintage bar is from an 1800s sailing ship. Rollie's is the most popular watering spot in town with the locals, and it just may serve the best cheeseburger in the state of Maine.

WHERE TO EAT & STAY

$-$$
★
CONTINENTAL
✕**Darby's Restaurant and Pub.** Darby's, a charming old-fashioned restaurant and bar, is probably the most popular restaurant in town with the locals. The building, with pressed-tin ceilings, was constructed in 1865 and has been a bar or a restaurant ever since. The antique bar is an original and has been there since 1865. The first Darby is long gone, but his name remains. Artwork on the walls is by local artists and may be purchased. A lot of the regular items on the menu, such as the pad thai and the seafood à la grecque, are quite unusual for a small-town restaurant. It also has hearty homemade soups and sandwiches, as well as dishes with an international flavor. ⊠*155 High St.* ☎*207/338-2339* ⊟*AE, DC, MC, V.*

$$
Fodor'sChoice
★
SEAFOOD
✕**Young's Lobster Pound.** The place looks more like a corrugated steel fish cannery than a restaurant, but this is one of the places to have an authentic Maine lobster dinner. Young's sits right on the edge of the water, across the river from Belfast Harbor (cross Veterans Bridge to get here and turn right on Mitchell Avenue). When you first walk in, you'll see tanks and tanks and tanks of live lobsters of varying size. The traditional meal here is the Shore Dinner: fish or clam chowder; steamed clams or mussels; a 1½-pound boiled lobster; corn on the cob; and rolls and butter. Order your dinner at the counter then find a table inside or on the deck. ■TIP➔ If you are enjoying your lobster at one of the outside tables, don't leave the table with no one to man it. Seagulls are notori-

ous thieves—and they LOVE lobster. ✉ *2 Fairview St.* ☎ *207/338–1160* 🗎 *AE, DC, MC, V* ⊘ *Closed Labor Day–Easter.*

$–$$
Fodor's Choice
★

🏨 **Penobscot Bay Inn.** Formerly the Belfast Bay Meadows Inn, this lovely accommodation is on five meadowed acres overlooking Penobscot Bay and is owned and managed by Kristina and Valentinas Kurapka. The rooms are bright and airy and decorated in pastel shades, with old-fashioned New England quilts on the beds. Some of the rooms even have their own fireplaces. The inn's Continental gourmet restaurant ($$–$$$$) is one of the best in the area. **Pro:** you don't have to go out for dinner. **Con:** if you want to explore Belfast's colorful downtown, you will have to drive. ✉ *192 Northport Ave.* ☎ *207/338–5715 or 800/335–2370* ⊕ *www.penobscotbayinn.com* ⮑ *19 rooms* ⬧ *In-hotel: restaurant, no elevator, no-smoking rooms* 🗎 *AE, DC, MC, V* ⦿ *BP.*

SEARSPORT

6 mi northeast of Belfast.

Searsport is well known as the antique and flea market capital of Maine, and with good reason: the Antique Mall alone, on U.S. 1 just north of town, contains the offerings of 70 dealers, and flea markets during the visitor season line both sides of U.S. 1. But antiques are not the town's only point of interest; Searsport also has a rich history of shipbuilding and seafaring. In the early to mid-1800s, there were 10 shipbuilding facilities in Searsport and the town was home to more than 200 sailing ship captains.

WHAT TO SEE

Fodor's Choice
★
♻

Penobscot Marine Museum. This museum is dedicated to the history of Penobscot Bay and the maritime history of Maine. The exhibits, artifacts, souvenirs, and paintings are displayed in a unique setting of seven historic buildings, including two sea captains' houses, and five other buildings in an original seaside village. The various exhibits provide fascinating documentation of the region's seafaring way of life. The museum's outstanding collection of marine art includes the largest gathering in the country of works by Thomas and James Buttersworth. Also of note are photos of local sea captains; a collection of China-trade merchandise; artifacts of life at sea (including lots of scrimshaw); navigational instruments; tools from the area's history of logging, granite cutting, fishing, and ice cutting; treasures collected by seafarers from around the globe; and models of famous ships. The museum also has a rotating exhibit every year on a different theme. Two recent themes have been "Pirates!" and "Lobstahs!" Next to the museum, you can find the Penobscot Marine Museum Store, where you can buy anything nautical. ✉ *5 E. Main St. (US. 1)* ☎ *207/548–2529* ⊕ *www.penobscotmarinemuseum.org* 🎟 *$8* ⊘ *Memorial Day–mid-Oct., Mon.–Sat. 10–5, Sun. noon–5.*

**▮ OFF THE
BEATEN
PATH**

The 2,120-foot-long **Penobscot Narrows Bridge** ✉ *711 Ft. Knox Rd., at U.S. 104416),* about 9 mi north of Searsport, has been declared an engineering marvel. It is certainly beautiful to look at or to drive over (no toll). Spanning the Penobscot River at Bucksport, the bridge replaced the old Waldo-Hancock bridge, built in 1931. The best part of it is the three story observation tower at the top of the western pilon. This was the first bridge observation tower built in America and, at 420 feet above the river, it's the highest bridge observation tower in the world. An elevator shoots you to the top. The cost is $5. Don't miss it—the view, which encompasses the river, the bay, and the sea beyond, is breathtaking.

SHOPPING

ANTIQUES In Searsport, shopping usually implies antiques or flea markets. Both stretch along both sides of U.S. 1 a mile or so north of downtown. **All Small Antiques** (⊠357 W. Main St. ☎207/338–1613) has just what the name implies. In the very heart of town, **Captain Tinkham's Emporium** (⊠34 E. Main St. ☎207/548–6465) offers antiques, collectibles, old books, magazines, records, paintings, and prints. The biggest collection of antiques is in the **Searsport Antique Mall** (⊠149 E. Main St. [U.S. 1] ☎207/548–2640), which has more than 70 dealers.

BANGOR

133 mi northeast of Portland, 20 mi northwest of Bucksport, 46 mi west of Bar Harbor.

The second-largest city in the state (Portland being the first), Bangor is about 20 mi from the coast and is the unofficial capital of northern Maine. Back in the 19th century its most important product and export in the "Queen City" was lumber from the state's vast North Woods. Bangor's location on the Penobscot River helped make it the world's largest lumber port. A 31-foot-tall statue of legendary lumberman Paul Bunyan stands in front of the Bangor Auditorium.

Lumber is no longer at the heart of its economy, but Bangor has thrived in other ways. Because of its airport, Bangor has become a gateway to Mount Desert Island, Bar Harbor, and Acadia National Park. The city is also home to author Stephen King, who lives in an old Victorian house on West Broadway notable for its bat-winged iron gate.

Bangor has a very good bus system the **BAT Community Connector** (☎207/ 992–4670 ⊕www.bgrme.org), which goes in a number of directions and as far away as Hampden to the south.

WHAT TO SEE

🅲 **Maine Discovery Museum.** The the largest children's museum north of Boston, the Maine Discovery Museum has three floors with more than 60 interactive exhibits. Kids can explore Maine's ecosystem in Nature Trails, travel to foreign countries in Passport to the World, and walk through Maine's literary classics in Booktown. ⊠74 Main St. ☎207/262–7200 ⊕www.mainediscoverymuseum.org ☜$5.50 ⊗Tues.–Thurs. and Sat. 9:30–5, Fri. 9:30–8, Sun. 11–5.

NIGHTLIFE & THE ARTS

The **Penobscot Theatre Company** (✉*131 Main St.* ☎*207/942–3333*) stages live classic and contemporary plays from October to May. From mid-July to mid-August, the company hosts the **Maine Shakespeare Festival** on the riverfront. Admission to the festival is $17.

WHERE TO STAY

$-$$

Fodor'sChoice

★

Lucerne Inn. This is one of the most famous and respected inns in New England. Nestled in the mountains, the Lucerne overlooks beautiful Phillips Lake. The inn was established in 1814, and in keeping with that history, every room is furnished with antiques. The rooms all have a view of the lake, gas-burning fireplaces, and a whirlpool tub; some have wet bars, refrigerators, and balconies as well. There's a golf course directly across the street. The inn's restaurant ($$–$$$$) is nearly as famous as the inn and draws many of the local people for its lavish Sunday brunch buffet. The traditional dinner among guests is the boiled Maine lobster. The inn is about 15 mi from Bangor. Several rooms are available for smokers; two rooms are handicapped accessible. **Pros:** some of the rooms have lovely views of Phillips Lake (you can request one), and the Sunday brunch is famous—but be sure to make a reservation for it. **Con:** the inn, while famous, has been around for awhile, and some of the rooms are a little on the shabby side. ✉*2517 Main St. (Rte. 1A), Dedham* ☎*207/843–5123 or 800/325–5123* ⊕*www.lucerneinn. com* ⟿*31 rooms, 4 suites* &*In-room: Wi-Fi. In-hotel: restaurant, bar, pool, no-smoking rooms* ⊟*AE, DC, MC, V* ⊚*CP.*

BLUE HILL PENINSULA & ENVIRONS

By Lelah Cole
Updated
by George
Semler

If you want to see unspoiled Down East Maine land- and seascapes, explore art galleries, savor exquisite meals, or simply enjoy life at a relaxed and unhurried pace, you should be quite content on the Blue Hill Peninsula. The area is not at all like its coastal neighbors, as very little of it has been developed. There aren't any must-see attractions, so you are left to investigate the area on your own terms, seeking out the villages, hikes, artists, restaurants, or views that interest you most. Blue Hill and Castine are the area's primary business hubs.

The peninsula, approximately 16 mi wide and 20 mi long, juts out into Penobscot Bay. Not far from the mainland are the islands of Deer Isle, Little Deer Isle, and the picturesque fishing town of Stonington. It lacks the mountains, lakes, ponds, and vast network of trails of neighboring Mount Desert Island. Instead, a twisting labyrinth of roads rolls over fields and around coves, linking the towns of Blue Hill, Brooksville, Sedgwick, and Brooklin. This is a place to meander for views of open fields reaching to the water's edge or, around the next bend, a tree-shaded farmhouse with an old stone wall marking the property line.

Painters, photographers, sculptors, and other artists are drawn to the area. You can find more than 20 galleries on Deer Isle and Stonington, and at least half as many on the mainland. And with its small inns, charming bed-and-breakfasts, and outstanding restaurants scattered across the area, the Blue Hill Peninsula may just persuade you to leave the rest of the coastline to the tourists.

CASTINE

30 mi southeast of Searsport.

A summer destination for more than 100 years, Castine is a well-preserved seaside village rich in history. Although a few different American Indian tribes inhabited the area before the 1600s, French explorer Samuel de Champlain was the first European to record its location on a map. The French established a trading post here in 1613, naming the area Pentagoet. A year later, Captain John Smith claimed the area for the British. The French regained control of the peninsula with the 1667 Breda Treaty, and Jean Vincent d'Abbadie de St. Castin obtained a land grant in the Pentagoet area, which would later have his name. Castine's strategic position on Penobscot Bay and its importance as a trading post meant there were many battles for control until 1815. The Dutch claimed the area in 1674 and 1676, and England made it a stronghold during the Revolutionary War. In the 19th century, Castine was an important port for trading ships and fishing vessels. The Civil War and the advent of train travel brought its prominence as a port to an end, but by the late 1800s, some of the nation's wealthier citizens discovered Castine as a pleasant summer retreat.

WHAT TO SEE

Federal- and Greek Revival–style architecture, spectacular views of Penobscot Bay, and a peaceful setting make Castine an ideal spot to spend a day or two. Well worth exploring are its lively harbor front, two small museums, and the ruins of a British fort. For a nice stroll, park your car at the landing and walk up Main Street toward the white Trinitarian Federated Church. Among the white clapboard buildings ringing the town common are the Ives House (once the summer home of poet Robert Lowell), the Abbott School, and the Unitarian Church, capped by a whimsical belfry.

SPORTS & THE OUTDOORS

At Dennett's Wharf, **Castine Kayak Adventures** (⊠ *15 Sea St.* ☎ *207/326–9045*) operates tours with a registered Maine guide. Walk through the restaurant to the deck, where you can sign up for a half day of kayaking along the shore, or a full day of kayaking by shipwrecks, reversing falls, and islands in Penobscot Bay. The steam launch **Laurie Ellen** (⊠ *Dennett's Wharf* ☎ *207/326–9045 or 207/266–2841*) is the only wood-fired, steam-powered passenger steam launch in the country. Climb aboard for a trip around Castine Harbor and up the Bagaduce River.

WHERE TO EAT

$-$$$ ✕ **Dennett's Wharf.** Originally built as a sail rigging loft in the early
AMERICAN   1800s, this longtime favorite is a good place for fresh seafood. The waterfront restaurant also serves burgers, sandwiches, and other light fare. There are several microbrews on tap, including the tasty Dennett's

Wharf Rat Ale. Eat in the dining room or outside on the deck. ⊠*15 Sea St.* ☎*207/326–9045* ▤*MC, V* ⊘*Closed Columbus Day–May.*

BLUE HILL

19 mi east of Castine.

Snuggled between 943-foot Blue Hill mountain and Blue Hill bay, the village of Blue Hill is perched dramatically over the harbor. Originally known for its granite quarries, copper mines, and shipbuilding, today the town charms with its pottery, and a plethora of galleries, shops, and studios line its streets. Blue Hill is also a good spot for shopping, as there are numerous bookstores and antiques shops. The Blue Hill Fair (⊕*www.bluehillfair.com*), held Labor Day weekend, is a tradition in these parts, with agricultural exhibits, food, rides, and entertainment.

SHOPPING

ART GALLERIES
★

Blue Hill Bay Gallery (⊠*11 Tenny Hill* ☎*207/374–5773* ⊕*www.bluehill baygallery.com* ⊘*Daily, Memorial Day–Labor Day; weekends mid-May–Memorial Day and Labor Day–mid-Oct.*) sells oil and watercolor paintings of the local landscape. Bird carvings and other items are also available. **Leighton Gallery** (⊠*24 Parker Point Rd.* ☎*207/374–5001* ⊕*www.leightongallery.com*) shows oil paintings, lithographs, watercolors, and other contemporary art. Many pieces are abstract. Outside, granite, bronze, and wood sculptures are displayed in a gardenlike setting under apple trees and white pines.

POTTERY

Rackliffe Pottery (⊠*126 Ellsworth Rd., Blue Hill* ☎*207/374–2297*) sells colorful pottery made with lead-free glazes. You can choose among water pitchers, tea-and-coffee sets, and sets of canisters. **Rowantrees Pottery** (⊠*9 Union St.* ☎*207/374–5535*) has an extensive selection of dinnerware, tea sets, vases, and decorative items. The shop makes many of the same pieces it did 60 years ago, so if you break a favorite item, you can find a replacement.

WINE

In what was once a barn out behind one of Blue Hill's earliest houses, the **Blue Hill Wine Shop** (⊠*138 Main St.* ✛*Halfway between intersection of Rtes. 172 and 176 and Rte. 15 in center of town* ☎*207/374–2161*) carries more than 1,000 carefully selected wines. Wine tastings are held on the last Saturday of every month.

WHERE TO EAT & STAY

$$–$$$
Fodor'sChoice
★
CONTINENTAL

✕**Arborvine.** Glowing (albeit ersatz) fireplaces, period antiques, exposed beams, and hardwood floors covered with Oriental rugs create an elegant and comforting atmosphere in each of the four candlelit dining rooms in this renovated Cape Cod–style house. You might begin with a salad of mixed greens, sliced beets, and pears with blue cheese crumbled on top. For your entrée, choose from among dishes such as medallions of beef and goat cheese with shoelace potatoes, or pork tenderloin with sweet cherries in a port-wine reduction. The specials and fresh fish dishes are superb, as are the crab cakes. Be sure to save room for a dessert, such as lemon mousse or wonderfully creamy cheesecake. A take-out lunch menu is available at the adjacent Moveable Feasts deli, where the Vinery serves drinks and tapas in the evening. ⊠*33 Tenney Hill* ☎*207/374–2119* ☐*AE, DC, MC, V* ⊘*Closed Mon. and Tues. Sept.–June. No lunch.*

$$$–$$$$
★
⊡ **Blue Hill Inn.** This rambling inn dating from 1830 is a comfortable place to relax after climbing Blue Hill mountain or exploring nearby shops and galleries. Original pumpkin pine and painted floors set the tone for the mix of Empire and early-Victorian pieces that fill the two parlors and guest rooms, several of which have working fireplaces. One of the nicest rooms is No. 8, which has exposures on three sides and views of the flower gardens and apple trees. Two rooms have antique claw-foot tubs perfect for soaking. The spacious Cape House Suite (available after the rest of the inn has closed for the season) has a bed as well as two pullout sofas, a full kitchen, and a private deck. The inn has a bar offering an ample selection of wines and whiskies. Here you can enjoy appetizers before you head out to dinner or try specialty coffees and liqueurs when you return. **Pro:** the bedroom fireplaces and the antique floorboards make you want to stay here forever. **Cons:** rooms are on the small side, and the walls are thin. ⊠*40 Union St.,* ☎*207/374–2844 or 800/826–7415* ⊕*www.bluehillinn.com* ☞*11 rooms, 1 suite* &*In-room: no phone, no TV. In-hotel: bar, no elevator, public Internet, no-smoking rooms* ☐*AE, MC, V* ⊚*BP.*

EN ROUTE Offering kayakers surfable currents when the tide is running full force, **Blue Hill falls** is a reversing falls on Route 175 between Blue Hill and Brooklin. Water flowing in and out of the salt pond from Blue Hill bay roars in and out under the Stevens Bridge. See it by foot or by kayak (use extreme caution, especially with children, on the bridge itself as the hydraulic roar drowns out the sound of oncoming motorists). ⊠*Rte. 175 south of Blue Hill.*

SEDGWICK, BROOKLIN & BROOKSVILLE

Winding through the hills, the roads leading to the villages of Sedgwick, Brooklin, and Brooksville take you past rambling farmhouses, beautiful ocean coves, and blueberry fields with the occasional mass of granite. It's a perfect leisurely drive, ideal for a Sunday afternoon.

Incorporated in 1798, **Sedgwick** runs along much of Eggemoggin Reach, the body of water that separates the mainland from Deer Isle, Little Deer Island, and Stonington. The village of **Brooklin,** originally part of Sedgwick, established itself as an independent town in 1849. Today, it is home to the world-famous Wooden Boat School, a 64-acre oceanfront campus offering courses in woodworking, boatbuilding, and seamanship. The town of **Brooksville,** incorporated in 1817, is almost completely surrounded by water, with Eggemoggin Reach, Walker Pond, and the Bagaduce River marking its boundaries.

WHAT TO SEE
Blue Poppy Garden. Gardens filled with brightly colored poppies, as well as lovely perennials, are the attraction here. A nature trail winds through the woods past native plants identified by small signs. There's a dining room that serves lunch and afternoon tea in July and August.

At the gift shop you can purchase blue poppy plants and seeds. ✉ *1000 Reach Rd., Sedgwick* ☎ *207/359–8392* ⊕ *www.bluepoppygarden.com* ☞ *Free* ⊙ *Mid-May–mid-Oct.*

SHOPPING

The **Gallery at Caterpillar Hill** (✉ *328 Caterpillar Hill Rd.* ☎ *207/359–4600*) is a spectacular refuge for looking at landscape paintings and other artifacts competing, sometimes successfully, with the Penobscot Bay panorama out the window. On Rte. 15 just north of Caterpillar Hill, **Old Cove Antiques** (✉ *106 Caterpillar Hill Rd.* ☎ *207/359–8585*) specializes in antique furniture, quilts, wood carvings and more.

WHERE TO EAT & STAY

$$
FodorsChoice
★
AMERICAN

✕ **Buck's.** Popular among cruisers mooring in Buck's Harbor, this fine dining gem is behind **Buck's Harbor Market**, itself a key food destination for its wines, cheeses, olive oils, and sandwiches. Jonathan Chase, formerly of the Pilgrim's Inn in Deer Isle Village, has put together a superlative and constantly changing market-based menu strong in local ingredients, starring fresh fish, scallops, duck, and lamb. The seared duck breast with cranberries, beer, and maple barbecue sauce is a favorite, as are the sautéed sea scallops. The restaurant has a reasonably priced, carefully selected wine list and a deck for outdoor dining in summer. ✉ *6 Cornfield Hill Rd., at Rte. 176, South Brooksville* ☎ *207/326–8683* ▭ *MC, V* ⊙ *Closed Sun.–Tues. Sept.–June.*

$-$$
★

🏠 **Brooklin Inn.** A comfortable yet elegant atmosphere distinguishes this B&B in downtown Brooklin. There are plenty of homey touches like hardwood floors and an upstairs deck. The sunny rooms have attractive bureaus and beds piled with cozy quilts. The restaurant ($$–$$$$) specializes in fresh fish and locally raised beef, poultry, and lamb. It also has fine soups, salads, and desserts worth saving room for. In summer you can dine on the enclosed porch. An Irish pub downstairs showcases local musicians most Saturday nights. **Pro:** bedroom fireplaces and the antique floorboards make you want to stay here forever. **Cons:** rooms are small, walls are paper thin. ✉ *Rte. 175, Brooklin* ☎ *207/359–2777* ⊕ *www.brooklininn.com* ⟿ *5 rooms, 3 with bath* ⚒ *In-room: no a/c, no phone, no TV. In-hotel: restaurant, no elevator, no-smoking rooms* ▭ *AE, D, DC, MC, V* ⊙ *BP.*

DEER ISLE VILLAGE

16 mi south of Blue Hill.

Around Deer Isle Village, thick woods give way to tidal coves. Stacks of lobster traps populate the backyards of shingled houses, and dirt roads lead to secluded summer cottages. This region is prized by artists, and studios and galleries are plentiful.

WHAT TO SEE

Haystack Mountain School of Crafts. People of all skill levels can sign up for two- and three-week-long courses in crafts such as blacksmithing, basketry, printmaking, and weaving. Artisans from around the world present evening lectures throughout summer (*see Blue Heron Gallery in*

Shopping to learn about buying their work). You can take a free tour of the facility at 1 PM on Wednesday, June through September. In autumn, shorter courses are available to New England residents. The school is 6 mi from Deer Isle Village, off Route 15. ✉ *89 Haystack School Dr., Deer Isle* ☎ *207/348–2306* ⊕ *www.haystack-mtn.org.*

SPORTS & THE OUTDOORS

While enjoying miles of woodland and shore trails at the **Edgar M. Tennis Preserve** (✉ *Tennis Rd. off Sunshine Rd., Deer Isle* ☎ *No phone* ✆ *Free* ⊙ *Daily dawn–dusk*), you can look for hawks, eagles, and ospreys, and wander among old apple trees and fields of wildflowers.

SHOPPING

Purchase a handmade quilt from **Dockside Quilt Gallery** (✉ *33 Church St.* ☎ *207/348–2849 or 207/348–2531* ⊕ *www.docksidequiltgallery. com*). If you don't see anything you like, you can commission a custom-designed quilt. **Nervous Nellie's Jams and Jellies** (✉ *598 Sunshine Rd.* ☎ *207/348–6182 or 800/777–6825* ⊕ *www.nervousnellies.com*) sells jams and jellies, operates the Mountain View café, and has a sculpture garden with work by Peter Beerits.

STONINGTON

7 mi south of Deer Isle.

Stonington is rather isolated, which has helped retain its small-town flavor. The boutiques and galleries lining Main Street cater mostly to out-of-towners, but the town remains a fishing community at heart. The principal activity is at the waterfront, where boats arrive overflowing with the day's catch. The sloped island that rises to the south is Isle au Haut, which contains a remote section of Acadia National Park; it's accessible by mail boat from Stonington.

WHAT TO SEE

Deer Isle Granite Museum. This tiny museum documents Stonington's quarrying tradition. The centerpiece is an 8- by 15-foot working model of quarrying operations on Crotch Island and the town of Stonington at the turn of the last century. ✉ *51 Main St.* ☎ *207/367–6331* ✆ *Free* ⊙ *Memorial Day–Labor Day, Mon.–Sat. 10–5, Sun. 1–5.*

SPORTS & THE OUTDOORS

Old Quarry Ocean Adventures (✉ *130 Settlement Rd.* ☎ *207/367–8977* ⊕ *www.oldquarry.com*) rents bicycles, canoes, and kayaks, and offers guided tours of the bay. Captain Bill Baker's three-hour boat tours take you past Stonington Harbor on the way to the outer islands. You can see Crotch Island, which has the area's only active stone quarry, and Green Island, where you can take a dip in a water-filled quarry. Tours cover the region's natural history, the history of Stonington, and the history of the granite industry. Sunset cruises are also available.

WHERE TO EAT & STAY

$-$$
★
AMERICAN
✕**Lily's.** Homemade baked goods, delicious sandwiches, and fresh salads are on the menu at this friendly café. Try the Italian turkey sandwich, which has slices of oven-roasted turkey and Jack cheese on homemade sourdough bread. The dining room's glass-top tables reveal the seashells and various treasures inside. A produce stand behind the restaurant sells some of the same organic foods used by the chefs here. ⊠*Corner of Rte. 15 and Airport Rd.* ☎*207/367–5936* ▤*MC, V.*

CAMPING
$$-$$$
▲**Old Quarry Campground.** This oceanfront campground offers both open and wooded campsites with raised platforms for tents, table, chairs, and fire rings. Carts are available to tote your gear to your site. Another property, Sunshine Campground, is on Deer Isle. **Pro:** campsites on the water with spectacular views. **Con:** somewhat uproarious in the height of summer when fully booked. ⊠*130 Settlement Rd., off Oceanville Rd.* ☎*207/367–8977* ⊕*www.oldquarry.com* ▲*10 tent sites* ⌂*Flush toilets, drinking water, guest laundry, showers, public telephone, general store, swimming* ▤*MC, V* ◷*Closed Nov.–Apr.*

ISLE AU HAUT

14 mi south of Stonington.

Isle au Haut thrusts its steeply ridged back out of the sea south of Stonington. French explorer Samuel D. Champlain discovered Isle au Haut—or "High Island"—in 1604, but heaps of shells suggest that native populations lived on or visited the island prior to his arrival. The island is accessible only by mail boat, but the 45-minute journey is well worth the effort. As you pass between the tiny islands of Merchants Row, you might see terns, guillemots, and harbor seals. The ferry makes two trips a day between Stonington and the Town Landing from Monday to Saturday, and adds a Sunday trip from mid-May to mid-September. From mid-June to mid-September, the ferry also stops at Duck Harbor, located within Acadia National Park. The ferry will not unload bicycles, kayaks, or canoes at Duck Harbor, however.

Except for a grocery store and a natural-foods store, Isle au Haut does not have any opportunities for shopping. The island is ideal for day-trippers intent on exploring its miles of trails, or those seeking a night or two of low-key accommodations and delicious homemade meals.

WHERE TO STAY

$$$$
▢**Inn at Isle au Haut.** This sea captain's home from 1897 retains its architectural charm. On the eastern side of the island, the seaside inn has views of sheep roaming around distant York Island and Cadillac Mountain. Comfortable wicker furniture is scattered around the porch, where appetizers are served when the weather is good. Downstairs, the

dining room has original oil lamps and a model of the sea captain's boat (which sank just offshore). Breakfast includes granola and a hot dish like a spinach, tomato, and cheese frittata. Dinner is an elaborate five-course meal usually incorporating local seafood. One night a week the inn has a lobster bake on the shore. The first-floor Captain's Quarters, the only room with a private bath, has an ocean view, as do two of the three upstairs rooms. All have colorful quilts and frilly canopies. **Pros:** nonpareil views and first-class dining. **Cons:** shared baths, thin walls. ⊠*78 Atlantic Ave.,* ☎*207/335–5141* ⊕*www.innatisleauhaut. com* ⤶*4 rooms, 1 with bath* &*In-room: no a/c, no phone, no TV. In-hotel: bicycles, no elevator, no-smoking rooms* ⊟*No credit cards* ⊘*Closed Oct.–May* ⍟*FAP.*

MOUNT DESERT ISLAND & ACADIA NATIONAL PARK

By Stephen and Neva Allen

With some of the most dramatic and varied scenery on the Maine Coast, and home to Maine's one and only national park, Mount Desert (pronounced "Mount Dessert" by locals) Island, it's no wonder this is Maine's most popular tourist destination, attracting more than 2 million visitors a year. Much of the approximately 12-mi-long by 9-mi-wide island belongs to Acadia National Park. The rocky coastline rises starkly from the ocean, appreciable along the scenic drives. Trails for hikers of all skill levels lead to the rounded tops of the mountains, providing views of Frenchman and Blue Hill bays, and beyond. Ponds and lakes beckon you to swim, fish, or boat. Ferries and charter boats provide a different perspective on the island and a chance to explore the outer islands, all of which are a part of Maine but not a part of Mount Desert. A network of old carriage roads lets you explore Acadia's wooded interior, filled with birds and other wildlife.

Mount Desert Island has four different townships, each with its own personality. The town of Bar Harbor is on the northeastern corner of the island, and includes Bar Harbor and the little villages of Hulls Cove, Salisbury Cove, and Town Hill. The town of Mount Desert comprises the southeastern corner of the island and parts of the western edge, and includes Mount Desert and the little villages of Somesville, Hall Quarry, Beech Hill, Pretty Marsh, Northeast Harbor, Seal Harbor, and Otter Creek. As its name suggests, the town of Southwest Harbor is on the southwestern corner of the island, although the town of Tremont is at the southernmost tip of the west side. This area includes the villages of Southwest Harbor, Manset, Bass Harbor, Bernard, and Seal Cove. The island's major tourist destination is Bar Harbor, which has plenty of accommodations, restaurants, and shops. Less congested are the smaller communities of Northeast Harbor, Southwest Harbor, and Bass Harbor. Mount Desert Island is a place with three personalities: the hustling, bustling tourist mecca of Bar Harbor, the "quiet side" of the island composed of the little villages, and the vast natural expanse that is Acadia National Park.

Acadia's Park Loop Road provides an excellent overview of the island, but to get a feel for the island's natural beauty, you must leave your car behind. Instead, seek as many opportunities as you can for hiking, biking, and boating. And while Bar Harbor is the best-known town on Mount Desert Island, there's plenty to see and do around the entire island. Take a scenic drive along Sargent Drive for spectacular views of Somes Sound—the only fjord on the East Coast. Visit the villages of Northeast Harbor, Somesville, and Southwest Harbor, each with its own unique character. The west side of the island—also known as the "back side" or the "quiet side"—has its own restaurants and accommodations. To get a unique perspective of the island, take a cruise. Away from the crowds and traffic, you'll have plenty of time to discover some of the island's less-obvious charms.

In Mount Desert Island, the free **Island Explorer (Downeast Transportation)** (☎ *207/667–5796* ⊕ *www.exploreacadia.com*) shuttle service circles the island from the end of May to September, with limited service continuing through mid-October. Buses, which are equipped with racks for bicycles, service the major campgrounds, Acadia National Park, and Trenton's Hancock County–Bar Harbor Airport. They also run from Bar Harbor to Ellsworth.

BAR HARBOR

160 mi northeast of Portland, 22 mi southeast of Ellsworth.

★ A resort town since the 19th century, Bar Harbor is the artistic, culinary, and social center of Mount Desert Island. It also serves visitors to Acadia National Park with inns, motels, and restaurants. The island's unique topography was shaped by the glaciers of the most recent Ice Age. Around the turn of the last century—before the days of air-conditioning—the island was known as the summer haven of the very rich because of its cool breezes; lavish mansions were built throughout the island. Many of them were destroyed in a great fire that devastated the island in 1947, but many of those that survived have been converted into businesses. Shops are clustered along Main, Mount Desert, and Cottage streets. Take a stroll down West Street, a National Historic District, where you can see some fine old houses.

The island and its surrounding Gulf of Maine are home to a great variety of wildlife: whales, seals, eagles, falcons, ospreys, puffins (probably the most unusual-looking birds in the world), and denizens of the forest, such as moose, deer, foxes, coyotes, and black bears.

WHAT TO SEE

♻ **Bar Harbor Whale Museum.** Learn about the history of whaling, the anatomy of whales, and how biologists are working to gain more information about these massive creatures at this interesting museum. All proceeds from the gift shop benefit Allied Whale, a nonprofit organization that conducts marine mammal research. ⊠ *52 West St.* ☎ *207/288–0288* ⊕ *www.barharborwhalemuseum.org* ▨ *Free* ☺ *June, daily 10 am–8 pm; July and Aug., daily 9–9; Sept. and Oct., 10 am–8 pm.*

SPORTS & THE OUTDOORS

AIR TOURS

★

There are few places in America as beautiful to see from the air as the Mount Desert Island and Acadia National Park areas. **Scenic Biplane & Glider Rides Over Bar Harbor** (✉*968 Bar Harbor Rd. [Rt. 3], Trenton* ☎*207/667–7627* ⊕*www.acadiaair tours.com*) is a part of Acadia Air Tours and provides exactly what the name suggests: biplane and glider rides over Bar Harbor and Acadia National Park. It also offers helicopter tours.

BICYCLING

Acadia Bike Rentals (✉*48 Cottage St.* ☎*207/288–9605 or 800/526–8615*) rents mountain bikes good for negotiating the trails in Acadia National Park. The **Bar Harbor Bicycle Shop** (✉*141 Cottage St.* ☎*207/288–3886 or 800/824–2453*) rents bikes by the half- or full day. **Caution:** Riding a bike around Bar Harbor is fun, but be careful; the town is full of gawking tourists, and many of the streets are narrow.

BOATING

☺

Fodor'sChoice

★

Surely, the best boat excursions…must be the rides on **The CAT** (✉*12 Eden St.* ☎*888/249–7245* ⊕*www.catferry.com*), North America's fastest international ferry. This is a high-speed (55 mph) catamaran that, in season, jets from Bar Harbor across the Gulf of Maine to Yarmouth, Nova Scotia, and back. You can do it all in one day, or you can take one of the one- or two-night package trips that include tours. The CAT can whisk you to Nova Scotia in a mere 2¾ hours. You can have lunch at a waterside restaurant, do a little shopping, and come back the same day. On board, you will find a café for food, a bar for drinks, and a duty-free gift shop. The morning departure is around 7:45, and the returns are at 1 and 8:30 PM.

☺

★

The big 151-foot four-masted schooner **Margaret Todd** (✉*Bar Harbor Inn Pier* ☎*207/288–4585* ⊕*www.downeastwindjammer.com*) operates 1½- to 2-hour trips three times a day among the islands of Frenchman's Bay from mid-May to October. The sunset sail is the most popular. The schooner **Rachel B. Jackson** (✉*Harborside Hotel & Marina* ☎*207/288–2216*) offers three-day cruises and sunset cruises.

☺

If you are curious about what's lurking in the deep, set sail on **The Seal** (✉*Bar Harbor Inn Pier* ☎*207/288–3483* ⊕*www.divered.com*). While "Diver Ed" is exploring the sea bottom with his underwater video camera, you can see what he finds by watching an LCD screen on the boat; also get an up-close look at the creatures he brings back.

WHALE-WATCHING

There are two truly unique experiences you can have at Bar Harbor, and both of them are ideal for family outings. One is a trip on the fast CAT boat to Nova Scotia. The other, also at sea, is whale-watching.

FUN THINGS TO DO ON MOUNT DESERT ISLAND

■ Take the circle drive through Acadia National Park.

■ Hike—or drive—to the 1,532-foot top of Cadillac Mountain for a spectacular view.

■ Climb down the rocks to the edge of the ocean to shoot the most photographed lighthouse in Maine, Bass Harbor Head Light.

■ Hop a ride on The CAT (high-speed catamaran) from Bar Harbor to Nova Scotia, Canada.

7

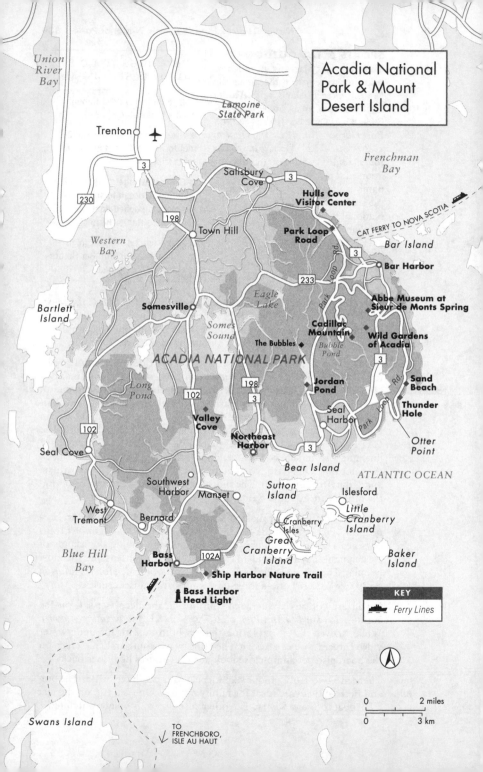

Union
River
Bay

Trenton ✈

Lamoine
State Park

Salisbury
Cove 3

230

198 Town Hill

Western
Bay

Hulls Cove
Visitor Center

Frenchman
Bay

Park Loop
Road

CAT FERRY TO NOVA SCOTIA

Bar Island

Bar Harbor

Somesville

Eagle
Lake

Somes
Sound

233

Abbe Museum at
Sieur de Monts Spring

Bartlett
Island

ACADIA NATIONAL PARK

The Bubbles

Cadillac
Mountain

Bubble
Pond

Wild Gardens
of Acadia

3

Long
Pond

102

198

3

Jordan
Pond

Sand
Beach

Thunder
Hole

102

Valley
Cove

Northeast
Harbor

Seal
Harbor

Otter
Point

Seal Cove

3

West
Tremont

Southwest
Harbor

Manset

Bernard

Bear Island

Sutton
Island

Islesford

ATLANTIC OCEAN

Little
Cranberry
Island

Blue Hill
Bay

Bass
Harbor

102A

Cranberry
Isles

Great
Cranberry
Island

Baker
Island

Ship Harbor Nature Trail

Bass Harbor
Head Light

KEY

Ferry Lines

Acadia National
Park & Mount
Desert Island

TO FRENCHBORO,
ISLE AU HAUT

Swans Island

0   2 miles
0   3 km

★ **Bar Harbor Whale Watch Co.** (✉*1 West St.* ☎*207/288–2386 or 800/ WHALES–4 (800/942–5374)* ⊕ *www.whalesrus.com*) merged with the Acadian Whale Watcher to make one big company with four boats, one of them a 138-foot jet-propelled catamaran with spacious decks. In season, the outfit also offers a lobster-fishing and seal-watching cruise, a nature cruise, and a puffin-watching cruise. How likely are you to actually see a whale? Very. In fact, the company can practically guarantee it—they apparently have some sort of arrangement with the whales.

SHOPPING

★ Bar Harbor is a shoppers paradise, but not necessarily for bargains. Tourism shoppers not only come from the land, they also come from the sea, since some cruise ships, including very large ones like the *Queen Elizabeth,* have made this a destination. (Imagine how delighted the store owners are to see her arrive, with thousands of passengers!)

ARTWORK **FodorsChoice** ★ Paint your own pottery or piece together a mosaic at **All Fired Up** (✉*101 Cottage St.* ☎*207/288–3130* ⊕*www.acadiaallfiredup.com*). The gallery also sells glass sculptures, pendants, paintings, and pottery. The **Alone Moose Fine Crafts** (✉*78 West St.* ☎*207/288–4229*) is the oldest made-in-Maine gallery on the island. It offers bronze wildlife sculpture, jewelry, pottery, and watercolors. The **Eclipse Gallery** (✉*12 Mount Desert St.* ☎*207/288–9048*) carries handblown glass, ceramics, and wood furniture. **Island Artisans** (✉*99 Main St.* ☎*207/288–4214*) sells basketry, pottery, fiber work, and jewelry created by more than 100 of Maine's artisans. The gallery is a co-op owned and operated by the artists. **Native Arts Gallery** (✉*99 Main St.* ☎*207/288–4474* ⊕*www. nativeartsgallery.com*) sells American Indian silver and gold jewelry.

SPORTING GOODS One of the best sporting-goods stores in the state, **Cadillac Mountain Sports** (✉*28 Cottage St.* ☎*207/288–4532* ⊕*www.cadillacmountainsports.com*), has developed a following of locals and visitors alike. You can find top-quality climbing, hiking, and camping equipment. In winter you can rent cross-country skis, ice skates, and snowshoes. **Michael H. Graves Antiques** (✉*10 Albert Meadow* ☎*207/288–3830*) specializes in maps and books focusing on Mount Desert Island.

TREATS **Ben and Bill's Chocolate Emporium** (✉*66 Main St.* ☎*207/288–3281*) is a chocolate lover's nirvana. It also has more than 20 flavors of ice cream, including the popular KGB (Kahlua, Grand Marnier, and Bailey's).

NIGHTLIFE & THE ARTS

★ The **Bar Harbor Music Festival** (✉*59 Cottage St.* ☎*207/288–5744*) hosts jazz, classical, and pop concerts by young professionals from July to early August at the Criterion Theater. It has recently started including one opera every season and has done *La Bohème* and *La Traviata.*

WHERE TO EAT & STAY

$$–$$$ SEAFOOD ✗**Quarterdeck.** If you would like to dine while enjoying a view of the colorful harbor, head here. The majority of menu items are seafood—a good choice is the baked stuffed lobster. If you like your seafood uncooked, take a look at the raw bar, which overflows with oysters. ✉*1 Main St.* ☎*207/288–1161* ⊟*AE, DC, MC, V.*

7

$$$-$$$$
Fodor'sChoice
★
CONTINENTAL
✕**Reading Room at the Bar Harbor Inn & Spa.** This elegant waterfront restaurant serves mostly Continental fare. Look for Maine specialties such as lobster pie and Indian pudding. There's live music nightly. When the weather is nice, what could be more romantic than dining out under the stars at the inn's Terrace Grille with the ships of beautiful Bar Harbor right at your feet? The natural thing to order here would be the Maine lobster bake with all the fixings. For something different, you might try the lobster stew, which is served in a bread bowl. The restaurant is also famous for its Sunday brunch, 11:30–2:30. ⊠*Newport Dr.* ☎*207/288–3351 or 800/248–3351* ⚐*Reservations essential* ⊟*AE, DC, MC, V* ✆*Closed late Nov.–late Mar.*

> ## ACADIA LEAF PEEPING
>
> The fall foliage in Maine can be spectacular. Because of the moisture, the fall foliage comes later along the coast than it does in the interior of the state. In the interior, it's usually the last week of September, whereas along the coast, it's usually around the middle of October. The best way to catch the colors along the coast is travel on the Acadia National Park Loop Road. In fall 2007, the National Park Service placed Acadia National Park on its fall foliage list of "The 10 Best Places in the U.S. to Take Photographs." For up-to-date information, go online to www.mainefoliage.com.

$$$-$$$$
Fodor'sChoice
★
🛏**Bar Harbor Inn & Spa.** Originally established in the late 1800s as a men's social club, this waterfront inn has rooms spread out over three buildings on well-landscaped grounds. Most rooms have gas fireplaces and balconies with great views. Rooms in the Oceanfront Lodge have private decks overlooking the ocean. Many rooms in the main inn have balconies overlooking the harbor. Should you need more room, there are also some two-level suites. A relatively new addition to the inn is a luxury spa, which offers everything from massages and mud wraps to aroma therapy and facials. The inn is a short walk from town, so you're close to all the sights, and a terrific restaurant, the Reading Room, is on-site (⇨ *Where to Eat*). **Pros:** this is one of those resort hotels that truly seems to meet every need, plus it's right at the harbor. **Con:** not as close to Acadia National Park as some other Bar Harbor properties, though still just a short drive. ⊠*Newport Dr.* ☎*207/288–3351 or 800/248–3351* ⊕*www.barharborinn.com* 🛏*138 rooms, 15 suites* ⚘*In-room: safe, refrigerator, DVD. In-hotel: 2 restaurants, pool, gym, no-smoking rooms* ⊟*AE, DC, MC, V* ✆*Closed late Nov.–late Mar.* ⌽*CP.*

ACADIA NATIONAL PARK

4 mi northwest of Bar Harbor.

Fodor'sChoice
★
With more than 30,000 acres of protected forests, beaches, mountains, and rocky coastline, Acadia National Park is the second-most-visited national park in America (the first is the Great Smoky Mountains National Park). According to the national park service, more than 2.2 million people visit Acadia each year. The park holds some of the most spectacular scenery on the eastern seaboard: a rugged coastline of surf-pounded granite, and an interior graced by sculpted mountains,

quiet ponds, and lush deciduous forests. Cadillac Mountain (named after an American Indian, not the car), the highest point of land on the Eastern Coast, dominates the park. Although it's rugged, Acadia National Park also has graceful stone bridges, horse-drawn carriages, and the elegant Jordan Pond House restaurant.

The 27-mi Park Loop Road provides an excellent introduction, but to truly appreciate the park, you must get off the main road and experience it by walking, biking, sea kayaking, or taking a carriage ride. If you get off the beaten path, you can find places you can have practically to yourself. Mount Desert Island was once the site of summer homes for the very rich (still is for some), and, because of this, Acadia is the only national park in America that was largely created by the donations of private land. A small part of the park is on the Isle au Haut, which is out in the ocean and more than 10 mi away.

PARK ESSENTIALS

Admission Fee. A user fee is required if you are anywhere in the park. The fee is $20 per vehicle for a seven-consecutive-day pass. Or use your National Park America the Beautiful Pass, which allows entrance to any national park in the United States. See www.nps.gov for details.

Admission Hours. The park is open 24 hours a day, year-round, though the roads often are closed in winter because of snow. Operating hours are 8 AM–4:30 PM April 15–October and until 6 PM in July and August.

Camping. There are more than 500 campsites in the park. Ask for a guide at the Hulls Cove Visitor Center. Blackwoods Campground has 16 wheelchair-accessible sites. There are no hook-ups, though some sites can fit RVs.

Pets. Pets are allowed at all park locations, but they must be on leashes no longer than six feet.

Visitor Information. ⌂*Acadia National Park, Box 177, Bar Harbor 04609* ☎*207/288–3338* ⊕*www.nps.gov/acad.*

WHAT TO SEE

HISTORIC SITES & MUSEUMS

★ **Bass Harbor Head Light.** Originally built in 1858, this lighthouse is one of the most photographed in Maine. The light, now automated, marks the entrance to Blue Hill Bay. The grounds and residence are Coast Guard property, but two trails around the facility provide excellent views. ■TIP➔**The best place to take a picture of this small but beautiful lighthouse is from the rocks below—but watch your step, they can be slippery.** ⌂*Rte. 102, halfway between Tremont and Manset Bass Harbor* ⌗*Free* ☉*Daily 9–sunset.*

SCENIC DRIVES & STOPS

★ **Cadillac Mountain.** At 1,532 feet, this is the first place in America to see the sun's rays at break of day. It is the highest mountain on the eastern seaboard north of Brazil. Dozens of visitors make the trek to see the sunrise or, for those less inclined to get up so early, sunset. From the smooth summit you have an awesome 360-degree view of the jagged coastline that runs around the island. Decades ago a train took visitors to a hotel at the summit. Today a small gift shop and some rest rooms are the only structures at the top. The road up the mountain is generally closed from the end of October through March because of snow.

> **BOOK A CARRIAGE RIDE**
>
> If you would like to take a horse-drawn carriage ride down one of these roads, from mid-June to mid-October, you can do so by making a reservation with Wildwood Stables (☎207/276–3622). Two of their carriages can accommodate two wheelchairs each.

Ⓒ ★ **Park Loop Road.** This 27-mi road provides a perfect introduction to the park. You can do it in an hour, but allow at least half a day or more for the drive so that you can explore the many sites along the way. Traveling south on Park Loop Road toward Sand Beach, you'll reach a small ticket booth, where, if you haven't already, you will need to pay the park's good-for-seven-consecutive-days $20 entrance fee (the fee is not charged from November through April). Traffic is one-way from the Route 233 entrance to the Stanley Brook Road entrance south of the Jordan Pond House. The section known as Ocean Drive is open year-round.

VISITOR CENTER

Ⓒ At the Hulls Cove entrance to Acadia National Park, northwest of Bar Harbor on Route 3, the **Hulls Cove Visitor Center,** operated by the National Park Service, is a great spot to get your bearings. A large relief map of Mount Desert Island gives you the lay of the land, and you can watch a free 15-minute video about everything the park has to offer. Pick up guidebooks, maps of hiking trails and carriage roads, schedules for naturalist-led tours, and recordings for drive-it-yourself tours. Don't forget the *Acadia Beaver Log,* the park's free newspaper detailing guided hikes and other ranger-led events. Junior-ranger programs for kids, nature hikes, photography walks, tide-pool explorations, and evening talks are all popular. The visitor center is off Route 3 at Park Loop Road. ⊠*Park Loop Rd., Hulls Cove* ☎*207/288–3338* ⊕*www.nps.gov/acad* ☉ *Mid-June–Aug., daily 8–6; mid-Apr.–mid-June, Sept., and Oct., daily 8–4:30.*

The **Acadia National Park Headquarters** is on Route 233 in the park not far from the north end of Eagle Lake. It serves as the park's visitor center during the off-season.

SPORTS & THE OUTDOORS

The best way to see Acadia National Park is to get out of your vehicle and explore by foot, bicycle, or boat. There are more than 40 mi of carriage roads that are perfect for walking and biking in the warmer months, and cross-country skiing and snowshoeing in winter. There are more than 115 mi for hiking, numerous ponds and lakes for canoeing or kayaking, two beaches for swimming, and steep cliffs for rock climbing.

HIKING Acadia National Park maintains more than 120 mi of hiking paths, from easy strolls around lakes and ponds to rigorous treks with climbs up rock faces and scrambles along cliffs. Although most hiking trails are on the east side of the island, the west side also has some scenic trails. For those wishing for a long climb, try the trails leading up Cadillac Mountain or Dorr Mountain. Another option is to climb Parkman, Sargeant, and Penobscot mountains. Most of the hiking is done from mid-May to mid-October. Snow falls early in Maine, so from late October to the end of March, cross-country skiing and snowshoeing replace hiking.

■ TIP→ **The Hulls Cove Visitor Center and area bookstores have trail guides and maps and will help you match a trail with your interests and abilities. You can park at one end of any trail and use the free shuttle bus to get back to your starting point**

★ **Ocean Patch Trail.** This 3.6-mi, easily accessible trail runs parallel to the Loop Road from Sand Beach to Otter Point. It has some of the best scenery in Maine: the cliffs and boulders of pink granite at the ocean's edge, the twisted branches of the dwarf jack pines, and ocean views that stretch to the horizon. ⊠ *Sand Beach or Otter Point parking area.*

★ The **Acadia Mountain Trail** is the king of the trails. The 2½-mi round-trip climb up Acadia Mountain is steep and strenuous—but the payoff is grand: views of Somes Sound and Southwest Harbor. If you want a guided trip, look into the ranger-led hikes for this trail. ⊠ *Acadia Mountain parking area, on Rte. 102.*

SKIING When the snow falls on Mount Desert Island, the more than 40 mi of carriage roads used for biking and hiking during the rest of the year are transformed into a cross-country skiing paradise. With so few visitors on the island at this time of year, you can ski or snowshoe for miles without seeing anyone else. Be sure to bring a carriage road map with you. Snowshoe tracks are usually to the right of or between the ski trails.

SWIMMING The park has two beaches that are perfect for swimming, Sand Beach and Echo Lake Beach. Sand Beach, along Park Loop Road, has changing rooms, restrooms, and a lifeguard on duty from Memorial Day to Labor Day. The water temperature here rarely reaches above 55°F. Echo Lake Beach, on the western side of the island just north of Southwest Harbor, has much warmer water. There are changing rooms, restrooms, and a lifeguard on duty throughout summer.

WHERE TO STAY
Acadia National Park does not have its own hotel, and there are no cabins or lodges. But 500 campgrounds within the park for RVers and tenters are available. There are also five primitive sites on the part of

the park on the Isle au Haut, out to sea 10 mi away. Visitors with RVs do need to be warned, however, that facilities at both of the Acadia National Park campgrounds are deliberately kept minimal. There are no hookups. So if you are used to and like a lot of facilities, you may wish to opt for campgrounds outside the park. Both campgrounds within the park are wooded, and both are within a 10-minute walk of the ocean, but neither is located right on the ocean.

> **THE EARLY BIRD GETS THE SUN**
>
> During your visit to Mount Desert, pick a day when you are willing to get up very early, around 4:30 or 5 AM. Drive with a friend to the top of Cadillac Mountain in Acadia National Park. Stand on the highest rock you can find there and wait for the sun to come up. When it does, have your friend take a photo of you looking at it from behind. Then you can label the photo something like: "The first person in America to see the sun come up on June 1, 2008."

CAMPING
$$

⚠ **Blackwoods Campground.** One of only two campgrounds located inside inland Acadia National Park, Blackwoods is open throughout the year (though restrictions apply for winter camping; call ahead for details). Reservations are handled by the National Recreation Reservation Service ☎877/444–6777, not by the park. Reservations for high season (May–October) can be made up to six months in advance. During the off-season, a limited number of campsites are available for primitive camping, and a camping permit must be obtained from the park headquarters. Rates drop by 50% for the shoulder season (April and November). **Pros:** shuttle bus. **Cons:** no hookups or utilities. ⊠*Rte. 3, 5 mi south of Bar Harbor, Otter Creek* ☎*207/288–3274 or 800/365–2267* ⚠*35 RV sites; 198 tent sites* ♿ *Flush toilets, running water, showers, fire pits, picnic tables* ▤*DC, MC, V.*

$–$$
⚠ **Seawall Campground.** On the "quiet side" of the island, this campground does not accept reservations, but offers space on a first-come, first-served basis, starting at 8 AM. Seawall is open from late May to late September. Walk-in tent sites are $14 per night, while drive-in sites for tents and RVs are $20. **Pros:** quiet. **Cons:** no hookups or utilities. ⊠*Rte. 102A, 4 mi south of Southwest Harbor, Manset* ☎*207/244–3600* ⚠*42 RV sites; 163 tent sites* ♿ *Flush toilets, showers, picnic tables, fire pits* ▤*MC, V* ☼*Closed late Sept.–late May.*

NORTHEAST HARBOR

12 mi south of Bar Harbor via Rtes. 3 and 198 or Rtes. 233 and 198.

The summer community for some of the nation's wealthiest families, Northeast Harbor is a quiet place to stay. The village has one of the best harbors on the coast, and fills with yachts and powerboats during peak season. It's a great place to sign up for a cruise around Somes Sound or to the Cranberry Islands. Other than that, there isn't much to hold your attention for long. There's a handful of restaurants, boutiques, and art galleries on the downtown streets.

SOMESVILLE

7 mi northwest of Northeast Harbor via Rtes. 198 and 102.

Most visitors pass through Somesville on their way to Southwest Harbor, but this well-preserved village, the oldest on the island, is more than a stop along the way. Originally settled by Abraham Somes in 1763, this was once a bustling commercial center with shingle, lumber, and wool mills; a tannery; a varnish factory; and a dye shop. Today, Route 102, which passes through the center of town, takes you past a row of white clapboard houses with black shutters and well-manicured lawns. Designated a historic district in 1975, Somesville has one of the most-photographed spots on the island: a small house with a foot-bridge that crosses an old mill pond. Get out your camera. In spring, summer, or fall, this scene will remind you of a Thomas Kinkade painting. Maybe even in winter, too.

WHERE TO STAY

CAMPING
$$-$$$
Mount Desert Campground. Near the village of Somesville, this campground has one of the best locations imaginable. It lies at the head of Somes Sound, the only fjord on the East Coast. The campground prefers tents, so vehicles longer than 20 feet are not allowed. Many sites are along the waterfront, and all are tucked into the woods for a sense of privacy. Restrooms and showers are placed sensibly throughout the campground and are kept meticulously clean. Canoes and kayaks are available for rent, and there's a dock with access to the ocean. The Gathering Place has baked goods in the morning, and ice cream and coffee in the evening. **Pro:** a lovely location for sightseeing. **Con:** fills up quickly during peak season. ⊠*516 Sound Dr., Mount Desert* ☎*207/244–3710* ⊕*www.mountdesertcampground.com* ⚠*150 sites* ⚑*Flush toilets, drinking water, showers, fire pits, food service, swimming (ocean)* ▤*MC, V* ⊙*Closed mid-Sept.–mid-June.*

BASS HARBOR

4 mi south of Southwest Harbor via Rte. 102 or Rte. 102A

Bass Harbor is a tiny lobstering village with a relaxed atmosphere and a few accommodations and restaurants. If you're looking to get away from the crowds, consider using this hardworking community as your base. Although Bass Harbor does not draw as many tourists as other villages, the Bass Harbor Head Light in Acadia National Park is one of the region's most popular attractions and is undoubtedly the most-photographed lighthouse in Maine. (The best picture is taken from the rocks below, but be careful: they can be slippery.) From Bass Harbor you can hike on the Ship Harbor Nature Trail or take a ferry to Frenchboro.

WHERE TO EAT

¢–$$
SEAFOOD
✕**Thurston's Lobster Pound.** On the peninsula across from Bass Harbor, Thurston's is easy to spot because of its bright yellow awning. You can buy fresh lobsters to go or sit at outdoor tables. Order everything from a grilled cheese sandwich to a boiled lobster served with clams or

mussels. ⊠*1 Thurston Rd., at Steamboat Wharf, Bernard* ☎*207/244–7600* ▤*MC, V* ⊘*Closed Columbus Day–Memorial Day.*

WAY DOWN EAST

By Mary Ruoff   Way Down East covers roughly a fourth of the state's coast, at least as the crow flies. The raw, mostly undeveloped coast in this remote region is more accessible than it is farther south. Pleasure craft don't crowd out lobster boats and draggers in small harbor towns the way they do in other coastal towns. Even in summer here you're likely to have rocky beaches and shady hiking trails to yourself. The slower pace is as calming as a sea breeze.

The region's offerings include national wildlife refuges, state parks, historic sites and preserves, and increasingly, conservancy-owned public land. Cutler's Bold Coast, with its dramatic granite headlands, is protected from development. Waters near Eastport have some of the world's highest tides. Lakes perfect for canoeing and kayaking are sprinkled inland. Rivers snake through marshland as they near the many bays. Boulders are strewn on blueberry barrens. Rare plants thrive in coastal bogs and heaths. Dark-purple-and-pink lupines line the roads in late June.

SCHOODIC PENINSULA

16 mi southeast of Hancock via U.S. 1 and Rte. 186, 25 mi east of Ellsworth.

The landscape of Schoodic Peninsula makes it easy to understand why the overflow from Bar Harbor's wealthy summer population settled in Winter Harbor. The craggy coastline, the towering evergreens, and views over Frenchman Bay are breathtaking year-round. A drive through the well-to-do summer community of Grindstone Neck shows what Bar Harbor might have been like before so many mansions there were destroyed in the Great Fire of 1947. Artists and artisans have opened galleries in and around Winter Harbor. Anchored at the foot of the peninsula, Winter Harbor was once part of Gouldsboro, which wraps around it.

WHAT TO SEE

Within Gouldsboro on the Schoodic Peninsula are several small coastal villages. You drive through **Wonsqueak** and **Birch Harbor** after leaving the Schoodic section of Acadia National Park. Near Birch Harbor you can find **Prospect Harbor,** a small fishing village nearly untouched by tourism. There's also **Corea,** where there's little to do besides watch the fishermen at work, wander along stone beaches, or gaze out to sea—and that's what makes it so special.

Fodor's Choice   The only section of **Acadia National Park** that sits on the mainland is
★   at the southern side of the Schoodic Peninsula. A few miles east of Winter Harbor, the park has a scenic 6-mi one-way loop that edges along the coast and yields views of Grindstone Neck, Winter Harbor,

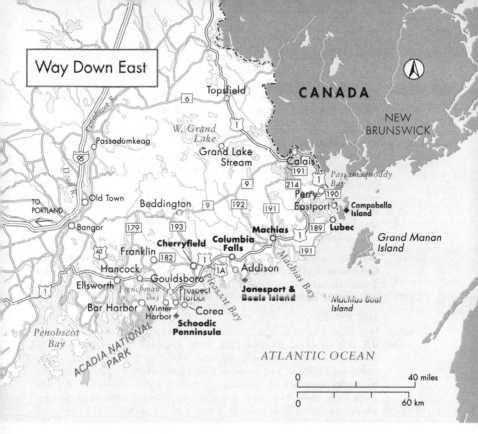

and Winter Harbor Lighthouse. At the tip of the point, huge slabs of pink granite lie jumbled along the shore, thrashed unmercifully by the crashing surf (stay away from water's edge), and jack pines cling to life amid the rocks. Fraser Point at the beginning of the loop is an ideal place for a picnic. Work off lunch with a hike up Schoodic Head for the panoramic views up and down the coast. A free bus called the Island Explorer (☎207/288–4573 [late June–Columbus Day] or 207/667–5796 ⊕www.exploreacadia.com) takes passengers from Prospect Harbor, Birch Harbor, and Winter Harbor and drops them off anywhere in the park. In Winter Harbor you can get off at the ferry to Bar Harbor. The $10 park admission fee is generally not charged when you're just visiting Schoodic. ⊠Rte. 186, Winter Harbor ☎207/288–3338 ⊕www.nps.gov/acad 🖃$10 ⊘ Year-round, 24/7.

NIGHTLIFE & THE ARTS

FESTIVALS Afternoon and evening musical, poetry, puppet, magic and theater performances, and speakers are part of the **Schoodic Arts Festival** (☎207/963–2569 ⊕www.schoodicarts.org), which takes place at venues throughout the peninsula during the first two weeks of August. Schoodic Steel, a community steel pan band, drums up a lot of excitement at its evening performance on the last weekend of the festival. An art show is held on the second Saturday, and you can take workshops in everything from dance to writing. Lobster boats from up and down the Maine Coast race in the **Winter Harbor Lobster Festival** (☎207/963–7658 ⊕*www.acadia-schoodic.org*) on the second Saturday of August. The free event also includes a parade, an arts-and-crafts fair, an art show, a pancake breakfast, and a lobster dinner that draws hundreds.

SPORTS & THE OUTDOORS

KAYAKING   Registered Master Maine Guides lead all-day, half-day, and overnight sea kayaking and hiking trips to the region's less visited islands and trails for **Ardea EcoExpeditions** (✉*242 S. Gouldsboro Rd., Goulds-boro [Rte. 186]* ☎*207/460–9731* ⊕*www.ardea-ecoexpeditions.com*). Learning is part of the fun on these ecotourism adventures. The company also offers sunrise birding and sunset kayaking tours, expeditions that lend a hand to ecological research and conservation projects, and cross-country skiing and snowshoeing trips.

GOLFING   You can see the ocean from every green at the 9-hole **Grindstone Neck Golf Course** (✉*106 Grindstone Ave., Winter Harbor* ☎*207/963–7760* ⊕*www.grindstonegolf.com*), one of Maine's oldest courses. Greens fees are $20 to $45.

SHOPPING

ANTIQUES &   Hand-cast bronze doorbells and wind bells are among the items sold at
MORE   **U.S. Bells** (✉*56 W. Bay Rd. (Rte. 186), Prospect Harbor* ☎*207/963–7184* ⊕*www.usbells.com*). You can also buy finely crafted quilts, wood-fired pottery, and wood and bronze outdoor furniture, all made by family members of the foundry owner. Tours of the foundry are given frequently. The shop is open June through December and by appointment. Children appear in many of the watercolor, pastel, and Asian ink paintings of Down East landscapes by Wendilee Heath O'Brien, the friendly artist-owner of **whopaints** (✉*316 Main St., Winter Harbor* ☎*207/963–2076* ⊕*www.whopaints.com*); the artist's studio-gallery is beside her home. You're welcome to listen in if she's teaching a class. Open year-round. Step back in time at **Winter Harbor 5 & 10** (✉*349 Main St., Winter Harbor* ☎*207/963–7927* ⊕*www.winter harbor5and10.com*), a tried-and-true dime store with a big selection of local T-shirts and sweatshirts. Open year-round.

ART GALLERIES   Handcrafts by area artisans, including jewelry and wool items, and the owner's colorful hooked rugs with animal and nature themes are sold in an old school at **Chapter Two** (✉*611 Corea Rd. [Rte. 195], Corea* ☎*207/963–7269*) You can enjoy a cup of tea, and you might catch a hooking group or class in action. Art of the Schoodic Peninsula is sold in the house-turned-gallery next door, and the garage is stocked with used books. Glass wildlife sculptures, flowers, goblets, and beads are for sale at **Gypsy Moose Glass Co.** (✉*20 Williamsbrook Rd., off Rte. 186, Gouldsboro* ☎*207/963–2674* ⊕*www.gypsymoose.com*), whose owner gives glassblowing demonstrations. It's open March to December.

FOOD & WINE   The wines sold at **Bartlett Maine Estate Winery** (✉*175 Chicken Mill Rd., off U.S. 1, Gouldsboro* ☎*207/546–2408* ⊕*www.bartlettwinery.com*) are produced from locally grown apples, pears, blueberries, and other fruit. Ask the vintners what foods to pair them with while sampling different wines in the tasting room. It's open late May through mid-October and by appointment. Along with mostly organic local produce, **Winter Harbor Farmers' Market** (✉ *10 Main St. [Rte. 186], Winter Harbor* ☎ *207/963–2984*) sells goat cheese, beef and chicken, hand-spun yarn, knitted items, and maple syrup, chutney, and preserves. The market operates on Tuesday mornings from late June to early September.

WHERE TO EAT

$$$–$$$$ ✗ **Bunker's Wharf.** On a narrow harbor that is home to an 18-boat
SEAFOOD   lobster fleet and opens onto the ocean, this restaurant sits near Acadia National Park. Enjoy the views from the stone patio or from the large windows in the blond-wood dining room. Some seats in the bar face the water. The setting—quintessential Maine—isn't all that keeps locals coming back. Lobster (served with roasted corn-bread pudding) is bought off boats in the harbor. The restaurant is also known for generous portions and scrumptious fare, from fried clams on a baguette at lunch to baked haddock with focaccia-bread stuffing at dinner. ✉ *260 E. Schoodic Dr., Birch Harbor* ☎ *207/963–2244* ▢ *MC, V* ⊙ *Closed some days Sept.–June; call for hours.*

$–$$ ✗ **J. M. Gerrish Provisions.** The store that opened here in the early 1900s
CAFE   was where locals and visitors alike went for ice cream. The name remains and part of the old marble counter, but this is now a deli and café where folks bustle in for fudge and coffee and linger at tables inside and on the porch. A simple menu has soups, salads, and savory sandwiches such as turkey and Jarlsberg cheese topped with peach salsa. The deli case offers salads and dishes such as scallops with roasted tomatoes. Baked goods crowd the counter, a building out back that's to open in 2008 will sell wine and beer, and, yes, you can still buy an ice cream. ✉ *352 Main St., Winter Harbor* ☎ *207/963–2727* ▭ *MC, V* ⊙ *Closed mid-Oct.–mid-May.*

WHERE TO STAY

$–$$ ⌂ **Bluff House Inn.** Combining the service of a hotel with the ambi-
☾   ence of a cozy lodge, this modern two-story inn on a secluded hillside
★   has expansive views of Frenchman Bay. You can see the bay's granite shores from the inn's partially screened wraparound porches. There's a picnic area with grill (a lobster pot is available for those who want to boil their own dinner). A stone fireplace warms one of the knotty-pine lounge areas. The individually decorated guest rooms have furnishings from around the state. **Pros:** close to things but secluded, apartment has two bedrooms. **Con:** hill to water a bit steep. ✉ *57 Bluff House Rd., off Rte. 186, Gouldsboro* ☎ *207/963–7805* ⊕ *www.bluffinn.com* ➷ *8 rooms, 1 apartment* ⌂ *In-room: no a/c, no TV (some), kitchen (some), DVD (some). In-hotel: no elevator, no-smoking rooms* ▭ *AE, MC, V* ⦿*CP.*

$$–$$$ ⌂ **Oceanside Meadows Inn.** This place is a must for nature lovers. Trail
☾   maps guide you through a 200-acre preserve dotted with woods,
FodorsChoice   streams, salt marshes, and ponds. Inspired by the moose, eagles, and
★   other wildlife that thrive here, the innkeepers created the Oceanside Meadows Innstitute for the Arts & Sciences, which holds lectures,

7

musical performances, art exhibits, and other events in the restored barn. Furnished with antiques, country pieces, and family treasures, and scented with flowers from the gardens, the inn has sunny, inviting living rooms with fireplaces and a separate guest kitchen. Guest rooms are spread between two white clapboard buildings fronting a private beach shaded by granite ledges. Breakfast is an extravagant multicourse affair that includes chilled fruit soup. **Pros:** one of the region's few sand beaches, many spacious rooms, handicapped-accessible room with water view. **Con:** need to cross road to beach. ⊠*202 Corea Rd. (Rte. 195), Prospect Harbor* ☏*207/963–5557* ⊕*www.oceaninn.com* ⬃*12 rooms, 3 suites* ⚲*In-room: no a/c, no TV, Wi-Fi. In-hotel: beachfront, no elevator, public Internet, public Wi-Fi, no-smoking rooms, some pets allowed* ☰*AE, D, DC, MC, V* ⊘*Closed Nov.–Apr.* ⭾*BP.*

EN ROUTE Visitors are welcome at **Petit Manan National Wildlife Refuge,** a 2,166-acre sanctuary of fields, forests, and rocky shorefront near Millbridge (35 mi east of Ellsworth). The wildlife viewing and bird-watching are renowned. In August the park is a popular spot for picking wild blueberries. You can explore the refuge on two walking trails; the shore trail looks out on sand-color Petit Manan Lighthouse, Maine's second-tallest light. ⊠*Pigeon Hill Rd.* ☏*207/546–2124* ⊕*www.fws.gov/north east/mainecoastal* ⛝*Free* ⊘*Daily, sunrise–sunset.*

CHERRYFIELD

6 mi north of Milbridge via U.S. 1.

In the 1800s, the Narraguagus River was lined with lumber mills, and Cherryfield was a lumbering center. Now this stretch is a lovely waterway (with native salmon) overlooked by a gazebo in a small town park. The industry's legacy remains in the surprising number of ornate Victorian homes, unusual for a small New England village. The town has 52 buildings on the National Historic Register in such styles as Colonial Revival, Greek Revival, Italianate, and Queen Anne. The historic district runs along U.S. 1 and the handful of side streets.

Cherryfield is also known as the "Blueberry Capital of the World." Maine's two largest blueberry plants sit side by side on Route 193. To see the area's wild blueberry barrens, head north past the factories and take a right onto Ridge Road.

OFF THE BEATEN PATH In nearby Millbridge the largest annual event is the **Milbridge Days Celebration** (☏*207/546–2422* ⊕*www.milbridgedays.com*), held each year on the last weekend of July. There's a blueberry-pancake breakfast, clam-and-lobster bake, parade, crafts show, and most famously, a codfish relay race. There's only one screen at **Milbridge Theatre** (⊠*26 Main St.* ☏*207/546–2038*), but it's a large one and the price is right—$4.50. The owner of the only movie theater between Ellsworth and Calais is likely to greet you in the little lobby—he hasn't missed a show since opening the place in 1978. If you're lucky, you'll catch one of the player-piano performances. The theater is open daily Memorial Day through early January and weekends in April and May.

COLUMBIA FALLS

11 mi northeast of Cherryfield via U.S. 1.

Founded in the late 18th century, Columbia Falls is a pretty village along the Pleasant River. True to its name, a waterfall tumbles into the river in the center of town. Once a prosperous shipbuilding center, Columbia Falls still has a number of stately homes dating from that era. U.S. 1 used to pass through the center of town, but now it passes to the west. It's worth driving through even if you don't have time to stop.

WHAT TO SEE

★ **Ruggles House.** Judge Thomas Ruggles, a wealthy lumber dealer, store owner, postmaster, and justice of the Court of Sessions, built this home about 1820. The house's distinctive Federal architecture, flying staircase, Palladian window, and intricate woodwork were crafted over three years by Massachusetts wood-carver Alvah Peterson. ⊠*146 Main St.* ☎*207/483–4637* ⊕*www.ruggleshouse.org* 🖾*$5* ☉*June–mid-Oct., Mon.–Sat. 9:30–4:30, Sun. 11–4:30.*

SHOPPING

Next door to historic Ruggles House, **Columbia Falls Pottery** (⊠*150 Main St.* ☎*207/483–4075* ⊕*www.columbiafallspottery.com*) carries owner April Adams's hand-thrown earthernware pottery. Her work is decorated with local flora (blueberry, columbine, and bunchberry are popular), ships, and lighthouses. It's open June through October and by appointment.

WHERE TO STAY

¢-$ **Pleasant Bay Bed & Breakfast.** This Cape Cod–style inn takes advantage
☾ of its riverfront location. Stroll the nature paths on the 110-acre prop-
★ erty, which winds around a peninsula and out to Pleasant Bay—you can even take one of the inn's llamas along for company. A screened porch and deck overlook the Pleasant River, and the suite has a private deck. The country-style rooms, all with water views, are decorated with antiques, as are the roomy common areas. A library with a fireplace is tucked away from the family room. **Pros:** fireplace at one of three waterfront picnic areas, river mooring, extra bed or pullout couch in most quarters. **Con:** just a Continental breakfast for late risers. ⊠*386 West Side Rd., Box 222, Addison* ☎*207/483–4490* ⇖*3 rooms, 1 with bath; 1 suite* ♿*In-room: no a/c, no phone (some), kitchen (some), TV (some), Wi-Fi. In-hotel: no elevator, public Wi-Fi, no-smoking rooms* ▭*MC, V* ❙⃝❙*BP.*

JONESPORT & BEALS ISLAND

12 mi northeast of Columbia Falls via U.S. 1 and Rte. 187, 20 mi southwest of Machias.

The birding is superb around Jonesport and Beals Island, a pair of fishing communities joined by a bridge over the harbor. A handful of stately homes is tucked away on Jonesport's Sawyer Square, where Sawyer Memorial Congregational Church's exquisite stained-glass

Wild for Blueberries

There's no need to inquire about the cheesecake topping if you dine out in August when the wild blueberry crop comes in. Anything but blueberries would be unthinkable.

Way Down East, wild blueberries have long been a favorite food—and a key ingredient in cultural and economic life. Maine produces about a third of the commercial harvest, which totals about 70 million pounds annually, with Canada supplying virtually all the rest. Washington County yields 65% of Maine's total crop, which is why the state's largest blueberry processors are here: Cherryfield Foods' predecessor and Jasper Wyman & Son were founded shortly after the Civil War.

Wild blueberries, which bear fruit every other year, thrive in the region's cold climate and sandy, acidic soil. Undulating blueberry barrens stretch for miles in Deblois and Cherryfield—"the Blueberry Capital of the World"—and are scattered throughout Washington County. Look for tufts among low-lying plants along the roadways. In spring, fields shimmer as the small-leaf plants turn myriad shades of mauve, honey orange, and lemon yellow. White flowers appear in June. Fall transforms the barrens into a sea of red.

Amid Cherryfield's barrens, a plaque on a boulder lauds the late J. Burleigh Crane for helping advance an industry that's not as wild as it used to be. Honeybees have been brought in to supplement native pollinators. Fields are irrigated. Barrens are burned and mowed to rid plants of disease and insects, reducing the need for pesticides. Most fields are owned by the large blueberry processors.

About 80% of Maine's crop is now harvested with machinery. That requires moving boulders, so the rest continues to be harvested by hand with blueberry rakes, which resemble large forks and pull the berries off their stems. Years ago, year-round residents did the work. Today migrant workers make up two-thirds of this seasonal labor force.

Blueberries get their dark color from anthocyanins, believed to provide their antioxidant power. Wild blueberries have more of these antiaging, anticancer compounds than their cultivated cousins. Smaller and more flavorful than cultivated blueberries, wild ones are mostly used in packaged foods. Less than 1% of the state's crop—about 500,000 pints—is consumed fresh, mostly in Maine. Look for fresh berries (sometimes starting in late July and lasting until early September) at roadside stands, farmers' markets, and supermarkets.

Wild Blueberry Land in Columbia Falls sells everything blueberry, from muffins and ice cream to socks and books. Find farm stores, stands, and markets statewide, many selling blueberries and blueberry jams and syrups, at www.getrealgetmaine.com, a Maine Department of Agriculture site that promotes Maine foods.

—Mary Ruoff

windows are illuminated at night. But the towns are less geared to travelers than those on the Schoodic Peninsula. Lobster traps are still piled in the yards, and lobster-boat races near Moosabec Reach are the highlight of the community's annual Independence Day celebration.

SPORTS & THE OUTDOORS

In business since 1940, **Norton of Jonesport** (☎207/497–5933 ⊕*www. machiassealisland.com*) takes passengers on day trips to Machias Seal Island, where thousands of puffins nest. Arctic terns, razorbill auks, common murres, and many other seabirds also nest on the rocky island. Trips, which cost $100 per person, are offered from late May through August.

WHERE TO EAT

$-$$$ ✕ **Tall Barney's.** Salty accents add plenty of flavor at this down-home
SEAFOOD   restaurant, which serves breakfast, lunch, and dinner (some nights). Reserved for fishermen, the "liar's table" near the entrance is about as legendary as the namesake. The breakfast menu tells of Tall Barney, a brawny fisherman who left truly tall tales in his wake. Your server may be among his multitudinous descendants. The menu includes five types of seafood stew, grilled as well as fried seafood, and oversize desserts such as molasses cookies, a local favorite. ✉*52 Main St.* ☎*207/497–2403* ▤*MC, V* ⊗*Closed Feb. Closed Sun.–Tues. late Oct.–Jan. and Mar. and Apr. No dinner Sun.–Tues. May–mid-Oct.*

MACHIAS

20 mi northeast of Jonesport.

The Machias area—Machiasport, East Machias, and Machias, the Washington County seat—lays claim to being the site of the first naval battle of the Revolutionary War, which took place in what is now Machiasport. Despite being outnumbered and outarmed, a small group of Machias men under the leadership of Jeremiah O'Brien captured the armed British schooner *Margaretta*. That battle, fought on June 12, 1775, is now known as the "Lexington of the Sea." The Margaretta Days Festival on the second weekend in June commemorates the event with a Colonial dinner, period reenactors, and a parade. The town's other claim to fame is wild blueberries. On the third weekend in August, the annual Machias Wild Blueberry Festival is a community celebration complete with parade, crafts fair, concerts, and plenty of blueberry dishes.

WHAT TO SEE

★ The **Burnham Tavern Museum,** housed in a building dating from 1770, details the colorful history of Job Burnham and other early residents of the area. It was in this tavern that the men of Machias laid the plans that culminated in the capture of the *Margaretta* in 1775. Period furnishings show what life was like in Colonial times. ✉*98 Main St. (Rte. 192 section)* ☎*207/255–6930* ⊕*www.burnhamtavern.com* ▤*$5* ⊗*Early June–Fri. before Labor Day, weekdays 9–5, or by appointment.*

7

PEEP AT PUFFINS

Set sail from Jonesport on a cruise to Machias Seal Island, the state's largest puffin colony. Many people come Way Down East just to visit this treeless, rocky isle 10 mi off the coast, a summer home puffins share with scores of other seabirds, including razorbills, common terns, arctic terns, common murres, black guillemots, and common eiders. With clownish ways and a "stuffed toy" look—white breasts beneath jet-black coats, goggle-like eyes, and blue bands on red-orange beaks—thousands of puffins steal the show. Canada and the United States dispute ownership of the migratory bird sanctuary, but tour operators cooperate with the Canadian Wildlife Service to control access. Weather can prevent boat landings, as there is no pier, but if you go ashore, you can walk on boardwalks and grassy paths to closetlike blinds where four people can stand comfortably as puffins court, clatter, and nuzzle. Bring layers: temperatures in July and August can drop to 50°F.

WHERE TO EAT & STAY

$ ★ AMERICAN X⌂**Riverside Inn & Restaurant.** A bright yellow exterior invites a stop at this delightful inn perched on the banks of the Machias River. Inside you can find hammered-tin ceilings and lots of hand-carved wood. The spacious guest rooms have antique furnishings and colorful quilts. The upstairs suite in the coach house has a private balcony overlooking the river. The restaurant ($$$–$$$$) has maintained its excellent reputation. The chef brings a special flair to traditional dishes such as pork served with a pistachio crust. His signature dish is salmon stuffed with crabmeat and shrimp. In summer the menu includes an updated take on the chef salad. Try pairing it with standout appetizers like hake cakes and red tuna wontons. Ask for a table in the intimate sunroom. **Pros:** suites a good value, garden overlooks river, walk to riverside park. **Con:** small grounds. ⊠ *608 Main St. (U.S. 1)* ⌂ *Box 373, East Machias 04630* ☎ *207/255–4134 or 888/255–4344* ⊕ *www. riversideinn-maine.com* ⇆ *2 rooms, 2 suites* ⌂ *In-room: no a/c (some), no phone, kitchen (some), refrigerator (some). In-hotel: no elevator, restaurant, no-smoking rooms* ⊟ *AE, MC, V* ⊗ *Closed Jan.–early Feb. Restaurant closed Mon.–Wed. mid-Feb.–May and Nov. and Dec. No lunch* ⥾ *BP.*

LUBEC

28 mi northeast of Machias via U.S. 1 and Rte. 189.

Lubec is the first town in the United States to see the sunrise. A popular destination for outdoor enthusiasts, there are plenty of opportunities for hiking and biking, and the birding is renowned. It's a good base for day trips to New Brunswick's Campobello Island, reached by a bridge—the only one to the island—from downtown Lubec. The village is perched at the end of a narrow strip of land, so you often can see water in three directions.

FUN TOUR

On educational tours by Tours of Lubec and Cobscook (⊠24 Water St. 🕾207/733-2997 or 888/347-9302 ⊕www.toursoflubecandcobscook.com) you can visit historic locales and lighthouses, walk the shoreline to learn about the area's high tides and tide pools, tour a ninth-generation farm on Cobscook Bay, explore a bog, and visit artist galleries.

SPORTS & THE OUTDOORS

★ The easternmost point of land in the United States, **Quoddy Head State Park**, is marked by candy-striped West Quoddy Head Light. In 1806 President Thomas Jefferson signed an order authorizing construction of a lighthouse on this site. You can't climb the tower, but the former light keeper's house has a museum with a video showing the interior. The museum also has displays on Lubec's maritime past and the region's marine life. A gallery displays lighthouse art by locals. A mystical 2-mi path along the cliffs here, one of four trails, yields magnificent views of Canada's cliff-clad Grand Manan island. Whales can often be sighted offshore. The 540-acre park has a picnic area. ⊠S. Lubec Rd., off Rte. 189 🕾207/733-0911 or 207/941-4014 ⊕www.state.me.us/doc/parks 🖅$2 ☉May 15–Oct. 15, 9–sunset.

WHERE TO EAT & STAY

$-$$$ ✕**Uncle Kippy's Restaurant.** There isn't much of a view from the picture
SEAFOOD windows, but locals don't mind—they come here for the satisfying seafood. There's one large dining room with a bar beside the main entrance. The menu includes seafood dinners and combo platters, and the fresh dough pizza is popular. A take-out window and ice-cream bar are open spring through fall. ⊠170 Main St. 🕾207/733-2400 ▤MC, V ☉Generally closed Mon. Sept. and Oct.; Mon. and Tues. Apr.–June, Nov., and Dec.; and Mon.–Wed. Jan.–Mar.

$-$$ 🏨**Peacock House.** Five generations of the Peacock family lived in this
★ white clapboard house before it was converted into an inn. With a large foyer, library, and living room, the 1860 sea captain's home has plenty of places where you can relax. Minglers are drawn to the sunroom, which opens to the deck and has a handsome bar with glasses for your wine or spirits. The best of the rooms has a separate sitting area and a wet bar and gas fireplace. **Pros:** piano in library, lovely garden off deck, handicapped accessible suite. **Con:** only one off-street parking space. ⊠27 Summer St. 🕾207/733-2403 or 888/305-0036 ⊕www.peacockhouse.com ◖5 rooms, 2 suites ♿In-room: no a/c, no phone, refrigerator (some), VCR (some), no TV (some), Wi-Fi. In-hotel: no elevator, public Wi-Fi, no-smoking rooms ▤MC, V ☉Closed Nov.–Apr. ℣◎BP.

OFF THE BEATEN PATH

A popular excursion from Lubec, New Brunswick's Campobello Island has two fishing villages, Welshpool and Wilson's Beach; it's also home to the **Roosevelt Campobello International Park,** a joint project of the American and the Canadian governments. The only bridge to Campobello Island is from Lubec, but in summer a car ferry shuttles passengers from Campobello Island to Deer Island, where you can continue on to the Canadian mainland. U.S. citizens need a passport or other federal government–approved ID when traveling to Canada.

7

Stop at the information center (open mid-May to mid-October) after passing customs for an update on tides—specifically, when you will be able to walk to **East Quoddy Head Lighthouse** (⊠*East end of Rte. 774, Wilson's Beach*). On a tiny island off the eastern end of Campobello, this distinctive lighthouse is marked with a large red cross and is accessible only at and around low tide, but it's worth a look no matter the sea level. You may spot whales in the island-dotted waters off the small park on the rock-clad headland across from the light.

Spot whales and other creatures from a 20-passenger lobster boat operated by **Island Cruises** (⊠*1 Head Harbour Wharf Rd., Wilson's Beach* ☎*506/752–1107 or 888/249–4400*). It operates daily from July to September. Cruises cost $48 and depart from Head Harbour Wharf.

MAINE ESSENTIALS

Research prices, get travel advice, and book your trip at fodors.com.

TRANSPORTATION

BY AIR

Two primary airports serve Maine: Portland International and Bangor International. Logan International in Boston (about 65 mi from Maine's southern end) is also an option. Additionally, Manchester Boston Regional Airport, in New Hampshire, is only some 45 mi from the beginning of the Maine Coast and a number of discount airlines fly there. Trenton's Hancock County–Bar Harbor Airport offers the closest airport to the Mount Desert Island region, including Acadia National Park; however, only one commuter airline, Colgan Air (operated by US Airways Express), services the airport. Most people going to Mount Desert Island, as well as the Blue Hill peninsula and Penobscot Bay, prefer Bangor International Airport, an hour's drive from the island, though there can be frequent cancellations at this small airport.

Regional flying services, operating from regional and municipal airports, provide access to remote lakes and wilderness areas as well as to Penobscot Bay islands. For visiting the North Woods, Katahdin Air Service offers charter flights by seaplane from points throughout Maine to smaller towns and remote lake and forest areas. It can help you find a guide and also does scenic flights over the Katahdin area. Currier's Flying Service offers sightseeing flights over the Moosehead Lake region. In the mountains and lakes region, Lake Region Air provides access to remote areas, scenic flights, and charter-fishing trips.

Airport Information Bangor International (BGR) (⊠*287 Godfrey Blvd., Bangor* ☎*207/992–4600 or 207/947–0384* ⊕*www.flybangor.com*). **Hancock County–Bar Harbor Airport** (⊠*E Rte. 3, Trenton* ☎*207/667–7329* ⊕*www.bhbairport.com*). **Logan International (BOS)** (⊠*1 Harborside Dr., East Boston, MA* ☎*800/235–6426* ⊕*www.massport.com/logan*). **Manchester Boston Regional Airport (MHT)** (⊠*1 Airport Rd., Manchester, NH* ☎*603/624–6539* ⊕*www.flymanchester.com*). **Portland International Jetport (PWM)** (⊠*1001 Westbrook St., off Rte. 9, Portland*

SPORTS & OUTDOORS IN MAINE

BIRDING

The **Maine Audubon Society** (✉ *20 Gilsland Farm Rd., Falmouth* 🕾 *207/781 6180* 🌐 *www.maine audubon.org*) provides information on birding in Maine and hosts field trips for novice to expert birders.

CAMPING

Reservations for state park campsites (excluding Baxter State Park) can be made through the **Bureau of Parks and Lands** (✉ *State House Station 22, Augusta* 🕾 *207/287-3821, 800/332-1501 in Maine* 🌐 *www. maine.gov/doc/parks*), which also can tell you if you need a camping permit and where to obtain one. The **Maine Campground Owners Association** (✉ *10 Falcon Rd., Lewiston* 🕾 *207/782-5874* 🌐 *www. campmaine.com*) publishes a helpful annual directory of its members.

FISHING

For information about fishing and licenses, contact the **Maine Department of Inland Fisheries and Wildlife** (✉ *284 State St., Augusta* 🕾 *207/287-8000* 🌐 *www.mefish- wildlife.com*). Guides are available through most wilderness camps, sporting goods stores, and canoe outfitters. For assistance in finding a fishing guide, contact the **Maine Professional Guides Association** (✉ *Box 336, Augusta 04332* 🕾 *No phone* 🌐 *www.maineguides. org*), which maintains and mails out listings of its members and their specialties.

HORSEBACK RIDING

Owned by registered Maine guides Judy Cross-Strehlke and Bob Strehlke, **Northern Maine Riding Adventures** (✉ *186 Garland Line Rd., Dover-Foxcroft* 🕾 *207/564-3451*

🌐 *www.mainetrailrides.com*) conducts one-day and two-day trips through parts of Piscataquis County. Or take day rides during a weeklong stay at a wilderness cabin.

KAYAKING & RAFTING

Maine Professional Guides Association (✉ *Box 336, Augusta 04332* 🕾 *No phone* 🌐 *www.maineguides. org*) represents kayaking guides. **Raft Maine** (✉ *Box 78, West Forks 04985* 🕾 *800/723-8633* 🌐 *www. raftmaine.com*) provides information on white-water rafting on the Kennebec, Penobscot, and Dead rivers.

SKIING

Weather patterns that create snow cover for Maine ski areas may come from the Atlantic or from Canada, and Maine may have snow when other New England states do not—and vice versa. Sunday River in Carrabassett Valley and Sugarloaf outside Bethel in Newry are the state's largest ski areas. It's worth the effort to get to Sugarloaf, which provides the only above-tree-line lift-service skiing in New England.

For information on alpine and cross-country skiing, contact **Ski Maine** (✉ *Box 7566, Portland 04112* 🕾 *207/773-7669, 888/624-6345 snow conditions* 🌐 *www.skimaine. com*).

SNOWMOBILING

The **Maine Snowmobile Association** (✉ *Box 80, Augusta 04332* 🕾 *207/622-6983* 🌐 *www.mesnow. com*) distributes an excellent statewide trail map of about 3,500 mi of trails.

7

✆ *207/774-7301* ⊕ *www.portlandjetport.org*).

Regional Flying Services Currier's Flying Service (✉ *Greenville Junction* ✆ *207/695-2778* ⊕ *www.curriersflyingservice.com*). **Katahdin Air Service** (✉ *Millinocket* ✆ *207/723-8378* ⊕ *www.katahdinair.com*). **Lake Region Air** (✉ *Rangeley* ✆ *207/864-5307*).

BY BUS

Concord Coach Lines (✆ *207/945–4000 or 800/639–3317* ⊕ *www.concord coachlines.com*) operates a luxury bus service (including snacks, drinks, and an "in-flight" movie) that travels the length of the coast from Orono (not far from Bangor) to Logan International Airport in Boston, stopping in every major town along the way. **Greyhound** (✆ *800/552–8737 or 800/642–3133* ⊕ *www.greyhound.com*) services towns throughout Maine and northern New England.

BY CAR

A car is helpful when visiting the Maine Coast, and is essential to tour Maine's western lakes and mountains and to negotiate the vast North Woods region—though it may not be useful to someone spending a vacation entirely at a wilderness camp. Interstate 95 is the fastest route to and through the state from coastal New Hampshire and points south; it turns inland at Portland and goes on to Bangor and the Canadian border. U.S. 1, more leisurely and scenic, is the principal coastal highway from New Hampshire to Canada.

Interstate 95 also provides the quickest access to the North Woods, linking with Highway 15, the road to Greenville, in Bangor, and with Highway 11 near Millinocket. U.S. 201 is the major route to Jackman and to Quebec. Highway 15 connects Jackman to Greenville and Bangor. The Golden Road is a private logging company–operated road that links the Greenville area and Millinocket. Be sure to have a full tank of gas before heading onto the many private roads in the region.

Travelers visiting the Mid-Coast region in summer and early fall may encounter fog, especially on the peninsulas and points of land. It's best to leave headlights on. Fog may stay around all day, or it may burn off by late morning. Winter driving in Maine can be challenging when snow and ice coat the roads. "Black ice" is a special hazard along the coast, as the road may appear clear but is actually covered by a nearly invisible coating of ice. Four-wheel-drive vehicles are recommended for driving in winter. Always carry warm clothing and blankets, as well as food and drinking water in case of an emergency.

Public roads in the North Woods are scarce, but lumber companies maintain private roads that are often open to the public (sometimes by permit only). When driving on a logging road, always give lumber-company trucks the right of way. Be aware that loggers must drive in the middle of the road and often can't move over or slow down for cars.

BY TRAIN
Amtrak (☎800/872-7245 ⊕www.amtrak.com) connects Portland with Boston. The train makes five runs to and from Boston each day and makes eight stops along the way, with stops in Wells and Saco and a seasonal stop in Old Orchard Beach.

CONTACTS & RESOURCES

VISITOR INFORMATION

State Tourism Contacts **Maine Tourism Association** (✉ 327 Water St., Hallowell ☎ 207/623-0363 or 800/767-8709 ⊕ www.mainetourism.com).

Local Tourism Contacts **Bar Harbor Chamber of Commerce** (✉ 93 Cottage St. ⌂ Box 158, Bar Harbor 04609 ☎ 207/288-3393, 207/288-5103, or 800/288-5103 ⊕ www.barharborinfo.com). **Camden-Rockport-Lincolnville Chamber of Commerce** (✉ 2 Public Landing, Camden 04843 ☎ 207/236-4404 or 800/223-5459 ⊕ www.visitcamden.com). **Boothbay Harbor Region Chamber of Commerce** (⌂ Box 356, 04538 ☎ 207/633-2353 ⊕ www.boothbayharbor.com). **Convention and Visitors Bureau of Greater Portland** (☎ 207/772-5800 ⊕ www.visitportland. com). **Deer Isle-Stonington Chamber of Commerce** (✉ Rte. 15, Deer Isle 04627 ☎ 207/348-6124 ⊕ www.deerisle.com). **Searsport Chamber of Commerce** (✉ 1 Union St., Searsport 04974 ☎ 207/548-0173 ⊕ www.searsportme.com).

Regional Tourism Contacts **Blue Hill Peninsula Chamber of Commerce** (✉ 28 Water St., Blue Hill ☎ 207/374-3242 ⊕ www.bluehillpeninsula.org). **Mount Desert Chamber of Commerce** (✉ Sea St., Northeast Harbor 04662 ☎ 207/276-5040 ⊕ www.mountdesertchamber.org). **Penobscot Regional Chamber of Commerce** (✉ 1 Park Dr., Rockland ☎ 207/596-0376 or 800/562-2529 ⊕ www. therealmaine.com).

New England Essentials

PLANNING TOOLS, EXPERT INSIGHT,
GREAT CONTACTS

There are planners and there are those who, excuse the pun, fly by the seat of their pants. We happily place ourselves among the planners. Our writers and editors try to anticipate all the issues you may face before and during any journey, and then they do their research. This section is the product of their efforts. Use it to get excited about your trip to New England, to inform your travel planning, or to guide you on the road should the seat of your pants start to feel threadbare.

GETTING STARTED

We're really proud of our Web site: Fodors.com is a great place to begin any journey. Scan Travel Wire for suggested itineraries, travel deals, restaurant and hotel openings, and other up-to-the-minute info. Check out Booking to research prices and book plane tickets, hotel rooms, rental cars, and vacation packages. Head to Talk for on-the-ground pointers from travelers who frequent our message boards. You can also link to loads of other travel-related resources.

▌ RESOURCES

ONLINE TRAVEL TOOLS

Check out the official home page of each New England state for information on state government, as well as for links to state agencies with information on doing business, working, studying, living, and traveling in these areas. Gorp.com is a terrific general resource for just about every kind of recreational activity; just click on the state link under "Destinations," and you'll be flooded with links to myriad topics, from wildlife refuges to ski trips to backpacking advice.

All About New England Begun as a media company to cover Mystic, Connecticut, **www.visitnewengland.com** is now a New England-wide information resource. New England's premier regional magazine also publishes an informative travel Web site at **www.yankeemagazine.com/travel**. Another great Web resource is **www.visitingnewengland.com**.

Connecticut Produced in conjunction with several of the state's leading news sources, **www.ctnow.com** has dining reviews, information on culture and attractions, and other helpful data. The **Connecticut Art Trail** (⊕www.arttrail.org) lists 14 Connecticut museums containing the work of Connecticut's artists, the landscapes that inspired them, and other related sites. The **Connecticut Wine Trail** (⊕www.ctwine.com) celebrates 18 statewide

wineries. Download a trail map from the Web site and start your wine-tasting adventure.

Maine **MaineToday.com** (⊕www.travel.mainetoday.com), produced by the state's largest newspaper chain, provides travel information and is an excellent resource for arts, entertainment, and more. Maine's **Nordic Ski Club** (⊕www.mainenordic.com) provides cross-country info. The **Ski Maine Association** (⊕www.skimaine.com) Web site has information about alpine snow sports.

Massachusetts The home of the Boston Globe online, **www.boston.com,** has news and feature articles, ample travel information, and links to towns throughout Massachusetts. The Boston Phoenix (⊕www.bostonphoenix.com), an arts and entertainment weekly, has nightlife, movie, restaurant, and fine- and performing-arts listings. At its site, the **Cape Cod Times** (⊕www.capecodonline.com) carries news and events information and has town directories with weather, sightseeing, lodging, and dining entries.

New Hampshire Look to **www.nh.com** for features and anecdotes on New Hampshire, as well as advice on accommodations, dining, recreation, and other aspects of New Hampshire. For information on downhill and cross-country skiing, check out **Ski New Hampshire** (⊕www.skinh.com).

Rhode Island The site of The Providence Journal (⊕www.projo.com) contains loads of great information on what to see and do throughout the state.

Vermont The **Vermont Ski Areas Association** (⊕www.skivermont.com) covers the downhill scene. Online **foliage reports** (⊕www.foliage-vermont.com) will keep you up to date; the site also posts information on driving tours, accommodations, and attractions.

BOOKING YOUR TRIP

Have you ever wondered just what the differences are between an online travel agent (a Web site through which you make reservations instead of going directly to the airline, hotel, or car-rental company), a discounter (a firm that does a high volume of business with a hotel chain or airline and accordingly gets good prices), a wholesaler (one that makes cheap reservations in bulk and then re-sells them to people like you), and an aggregator (one that compares all the offerings so you don't have to)? Is it truly better to book directly on an airline or hotel Web site? And when does a real live travel agent come in handy?

▌ ONLINE

You really have to shop around. A travel wholesaler such as Hotels.com or HotelClub.net can be a source of good rates, as can discounters such as Hotwire or Priceline, particularly if you can bid for your hotel room or airfare. Indeed, such sites sometimes have deals that are unavailable elsewhere. They do, however, tend to work only with hotel chains (which makes them just plain useless for getting hotel reservations outside of major cities) or big airlines (so that often leaves out upstarts like JetBlue and some foreign carriers like Air India).

Also, with discounters and wholesalers you must generally prepay, and everything is nonrefundable. And before you fork over the dough, be sure to check the terms and conditions, so you know what a given company will do for you if there's a problem and what you'll have to deal with on your own.

To be absolutely sure everything was processed correctly, confirm reservations made through online travel agents, discounters, and wholesalers directly with your hotel before leaving home.

Booking engines like Expedia, Travelocity, and Orbitz are actually travel agents, albeit high-volume, online ones. And airline travel packagers like American Airlines Vacations and Virgin Vacations—well, they're travel agents, too. But they may still not work with all the world's hotels.

An aggregator site will search many sites and pull the best prices for airfares, hotels, and rental cars from them. Most aggregators compare the major travel-booking sites such as Expedia, Travelocity, and Orbitz; some also look at airline Web sites, though rarely the sites of smaller budget airlines. Some aggregators also compare other travel products, including complex packages—a good thing, as you can sometimes get the best overall deal by booking an air-and-hotel package.

▌ WITH A TRAVEL AGENT

If you use an agent—brick-and-mortar or virtual—you'll pay a fee for the service. And know that the service you get from some online agents isn't comprehensive. For example Expedia and Travelocity don't search for prices on budget airlines like JetBlue, Southwest, or small foreign carriers. That said, some agents (online or not) do have access to fares that are difficult to find otherwise, and the savings can more than make up for any surcharge.

A knowledgeable brick-and-mortar travel agent can be a godsend if you're booking a cruise, a package trip that's not available to you directly, an air pass, or a complicated itinerary including several flights. What's more, travel agents that specialize in a destination may have exclusive access to certain deals and insider information on things such as charter flights. Agents who specialize in types of travelers or types of trips can also be invaluable.

Remember that Expedia, Travelocity, and Orbitz are travel agents, not just booking engines. To resolve any problems with a reservation made through these companies, contact them first.

Most hotels and other lodgings require you to give your credit-card details before they will confirm your reservation. If you don't feel comfortable e-mailing this information, ask if you can fax it (some places even prefer faxes). However you book, get confirmation in writing and have a copy of it handy when you check in.

Be sure you understand the hotel's cancellation policy. Some places allow you to cancel without any kind of penalty—even if you prepaid to secure a discounted rate—if you cancel at least 24 hours in advance. Others require you to cancel a week in advance or penalize you the cost of one night. Small inns and B&Bs are most likely to require you to cancel far in advance. Most hotels allow children under a certain age to stay in their parents' room at no extra charge, but others charge for them as extra adults; find out the cutoff age for discounts.

Assume that hotels operate on the European Plan (EP, no meals) unless we specify that they use the Breakfast Plan (BP, with full breakfast), Continental Plan (CP, Continental breakfast), Full American Plan (FAP, all meals), Modified American Plan (MAP, breakfast and dinner) or are all-inclusive (AI, all meals and most activities).

BED & BREAKFASTS

Historic bed-and-breakfasts and inns proliferate throughout New England. In many rural or less-touristy areas, B&Bs offer an affordable alternative to chain properties, but in tourism-dependent communities (i.e., most of the major towns in this region), you can expect to pay about the same or more for a historic inn as for a full-service hotel. Many of the state's finest restaurants are also found in country inns. Although many B&Bs and smaller establishments continue to offer a

low-key, homey experience without TVs or numerous amenities, in recent years, especially in upscale resort areas, many such properties have begun to cater to business and luxury leisure travelers with high-speed Internet, voice mail, whirlpool tubs, and VCRs. Quite a few inns and B&Bs serve substantial full breakfasts—the kind that may keep your appetite in check for the better part of the day.

HOME EXCHANGES

With a direct home exchange you stay in someone else's home while they stay in yours. Some outfits also deal with vacation homes, so you're not actually staying in someone's full-time residence, just their vacant weekend place.

Exchange Clubs Home Exchange.com (☎ 800/877–8723 ⊕ www.homeexchange. com); $59.95 for a 1-year online listing. **HomeLink International** (☎ 800/638–3841 ⊕ www.homelink.org); $90 yearly for Web-only membership; $140 includes Web access and two catalogs. **Intervac U.S.** (☎ 800/756–4663 ⊕ www.intervacus.com); $78.88 for Web-only membership; $126 includes Web access and a catalog.

HOTELS

All hotels listed have private bath unless otherwise noted.

Hotel and motel chains are amply represented in New England. Some of the large chains, such as Hilton, Holiday Inn, Hyatt, Marriott, and Ramada, operate all-suites, budget, business-oriented, or luxury resorts, often variations on the parent corporation's name (Courtyard by Marriott, for example). Though some chain hotels and motels may have a standardized look to them, this "cookie-cutter" approach also means that you can rely on the same level of comfort and efficiency at all properties in a chain, and at a chain's premier properties—its so-called flagship hotels—the decor and services may be outstanding.

New England is liberally supplied with small, independent motels, which run the

Online Booking Resources

Aggregators

Kayak	www.kayak.com	looks at cruises and vacation packages.
Mobissimo	www.mobissimo.com	examines airfare, hotels, cars, and tons of activities.
Qixo	www.qixo.com	compares cruises, vacation packages, and even travel insurance.
Sidestep	www.sidestep.com	compares vacation packages and lists travel deals and some activities.
Travelgrove	www.travelgrove.com	compares cruises and vacation packages and lets you search by themes.

Booking Engines

Cheap Tickets	www.cheaptickets.com	discounter.
Expedia	www.expedia.com	large online agency that charges a booking fee for airline tickets.
Hotwire	www.hotwire.com	discounter.
lastminute.com	www.lastminute.com	specializes in last-minute travel; the main site is for the U.K., but it has a link to a U.S. site.
Luxury Link	www.luxurylink.com	has auctions (surprisingly good deals) as well as offers on the high-end side of travel.
Onetravel.com	www.onetravel.com	discounter for hotels, car rentals, airfares, and packages.
Orbitz	www.orbitz.com	charges a booking fee for airline tickets, but gives a clear breakdown of fees and taxes before you book.
Priceline.com	www.priceline.com	discounter that also allows bidding.
Travel.com	www.travel.com	allows you to compare its rates with those of other booking engines.
Travelocity	www.travelocity.com	charges a booking fee for airline tickets, but promises good problem resolution.

Online Accommodations

Hotelbook.com	www.hotelbook.com	focuses on independent hotels worldwide.
Hotel Club	www.hotelclub.net	good for major cities and some resort areas.
Hotels.com	www.hotels.com	big Expedia-owned wholesaler that offers rooms in hotels all over the world.
Quikbook	www.quikbook.com	offers "pay when you stay" reservations that allow you to settle your bill when you check out, not when you book; best for trips to U.S. and Canadian cities.

Other Resources

Bidding For Travel	www.biddingfortravel.com	good place to figure out what you can get and for how much before you start bidding on, say, Priceline.

gamut from the tired to the tidy. Don't overlook these mom-and-pop operations; they frequently offer cheerful, convenient accommodations at lower rates than the chains.

Reservations are always a good idea, and they are particularly recommended in summer and in winter resort areas; in college towns in September and at graduation time in spring; and at areas renowned for autumn foliage.

Most hotels and motels will hold your reservation until 6 PM; call ahead if you plan to arrive late. All will hold a late reservation for you if you guarantee your reservation with a credit-card number.

When you call to make a reservation, ask all the necessary questions up front. If you are arriving with a car, ask if there is a parking lot or covered garage and whether there is an extra fee for parking. If you like to eat your meals in, ask if the hotel has a restaurant or whether it has room service (most do, but not necessarily 24 hours a day—and be forewarned that it can be expensive). Most hotels and motels have in-room TVs, often with cable movies, but verify this if you like to watch TV. If you want an in-room crib for your child, there will probably be an additional charge.

Note that in Massachussetts, by state law, all hotels are no-smoking. Also, in Maine, hotels and inns (unless they have 5 or fewer rooms) are not allowed (again, by state law), to put age restrictions on children who can stay there with their parents.

■ AIRLINE TICKETS

The least expensive airfares to New England are priced for round-trip travel. Airlines generally allow you to change your return date for a fee; most low-fare tickets, however, are nonrefundable. Airlines often post discounted "cyberfares" on their Web sites. The best bargains are on unsold seats on upcoming flights. If your plans are flexible, you can often save 60% to 70% by booking online. Discount travel Web sites such as Travelocity.com and Priceline.com also offer reduced fares. (*See Transporation section for more airline information.*)

■ RENTAL CARS

When you reserve a car, ask about cancellation penalties, taxes, drop-off charges (if you're planning to pick up the car in one city and leave it in another), and surcharges (for being under or over a certain age, for additional drivers, or for driving across state or country borders or beyond a specific distance from your point of rental). All these things can add substantially to your costs. Request car seats and extras such as GPS when you book. As a rule, all vehicles feature automatic transmissions and air conditioning and generally are low mileage.

Make sure that a confirmed reservation guarantees you a car. Agencies sometimes overbook, particularly for busy weekends and holiday periods.

Because a car is the most practical way to get around New England, it's wise to rent one if you're not bringing your own. The major airports serving the region all have on-site car-rental agencies. If you're traveling to the area by bus or train, you might consider renting a car once you arrive. A few train or bus stations have one or two major car-rental agencies on site.

Rates at the area's major airport, Boston's Logan Airport, begin at around $50 a day and $250 a week for an economy car with air-conditioning, automatic transmission, and unlimited mileage. The same car might go for around $45 a day and $200 a week at a smaller airport such as Portland International Jetport. These rates do not include state tax on car rentals, which varies depending on the airport but generally runs 12% to 15%. Generally, it costs less to rent a car outside of an

Car Rental Resources

Alamo	800/462-5266	www.alamo.com.
Avis	800/331-1212	www.avis.com.
Budget	800/527-0700	www.budget.com.
Hertz	800/654-3131	www.hertz.com.
National Car Rental	800/227-7368	www.nationalcar.com.

airport, but factor into the value whether it is easy or difficult to get there with all your luggage.

Most agencies won't rent to you if you're under the age of 21. When picking up a rental car, non-U.S. residents need a voucher for any prepaid reservations that were made in their home country, a passport, a driver's license, and a travel policy that covers each driver. Boston's Logan Airport is large, spread out, and usually congested, so if you will be returning a rental vehicle there make sure to allow plenty of time to take care of it before heading for your flight.

CAR-RENTAL INSURANCE

Everyone who rents a car wonders if the insurance that the rental companies offer is worth the expense. No one—including us—has a simple answer. It all depends on how much regular insurance you have, how comfortable you are with risk, and whether or not money is an issue.

If you own a car and carry comprehensive car insurance for both collision and liability, your personal auto insurance will probably cover a rental, but read your policy's fine print to be sure. If you don't have auto insurance, then you should probably buy the collision- or loss-damage waiver (CDW or LDW) from the rental company. This eliminates your liability for damage to the car.

Some credit cards offer CDW coverage, but it's usually supplemental to your own insurance and rarely covers SUVs, minivans, luxury models, and the like. If your coverage is secondary, you may still be liable for loss-of-use costs from

the car-rental company (again, read the fine print). But no credit-card insurance is valid unless you use that card for *all* transactions, from reserving to paying the final bill.

You may also be offered supplemental liability coverage; the car-rental company is required to carry a minimal level of liability coverage insuring all renters, but it's rarely enough to cover claims in a really serious accident if you're at fault. Your own auto-insurance policy will protect you if you own a car; if you don't, you have to decide whether you are willing to take the risk.

U.S. rental companies sell CDWs and LDWs for about $15 to $25 a day; supplemental liability is usually more than $10 a day. The car-rental company may offer you all sorts of other policies, but they're rarely worth the cost. Personal accident insurance, which is basic hospitalization coverage, is an especially egregious rip-off if you already have health insurance.

You can decline the insurance from the rental company and purchase it through a third-party provider such as Travel Guard (www.travelguard.com)—$9 per day for $35,000 of coverage. That's sometimes just under half the price of the CDW offered by some car-rental companies.

In Massachusetts the car-rental agency's insurance is primary; therefore, the company must pay for damage to third parties up to a preset legal limit, beyond which your own liability insurance kicks in.

TRANSPORTATION

■ BY AIR

AIRPORTS

The main gateway to New England is Boston's Logan International Airport (BOS), the region's largest. Bradley International Airport (BDL), in Windsor Locks, Connecticut, 12 mi north of Hartford, is convenient to western Massachusetts and all of Connecticut. T. F. Green Airport (PVD), just outside Providence, Rhode Island, is another major airport. Additional New England airports served by major carriers include Manchester Boston Regional Airport (MHT) in New Hampshire (a rapidly growing, lower-cost alternative to Boston—it's about 50 mi north of Boston); Portland International Jetport (PWM) in Maine; and Burlington International Airport (BTV) in Vermont. Other airports are in Bangor, Maine, and Hyannis, Massachusetts (Barnstable Municipal).

FLIGHTS

Numerous airlines, large and small, fly to and from Boston; additionally, the discount carrier Southwest Airlines (along with other airlines) flies to Albany, Hartford/Springfield (Bradley International Airport), Providence, and Manchester, New Hampshire. Smaller or discount airlines serving Boston include AirTran, Cape Air, and JetBlue. Cape Air also provides service from Cape Cod and the islands to Providence and New Bedford. You can fly to Burlington from New York City on JetBlue, and you can fly to Providence from Fort Myers and Fort Lauderdale on Spirit Airlines.

Airline Contacts AirTran Airways (☎800/247–8726 ⊕www.airtran.com). **American Airlines** (☎800/433–7300 ⊕www.aa.com). **Cape Air** (☎800/352–0714 ⊕www.flycapeair.com). **Continental Airlines** (☎800/523–3273 for U.S. and Mexico reservations, 800/231–0856 for international reservations ⊕www.continental.com). **Delta**

Airlines (☎800/221–1212 for U.S. reservations, 800/241–4141 for international reservations ⊕www.delta.com). **JetBlue** (☎800/538–2583 ⊕www.jetblue.com). **New England Airlines** (☎800/243–2460 ⊕www.block-island.com/nea). **Northwest Airlines** (☎800/225–2525 ⊕www.nwa.com). **Southwest Airlines** (☎800/435–9792 ⊕www.southwest.com). **Spirit Airlines** (☎800/772–7117 or 586/791–7300 ⊕www.spiritair.com). **United Airlines** (☎800/864–8331 for U.S. reservations, 800/538–2929 for international reservations ⊕www.united.com). **USAirways** (☎800/428–4322 for U.S. and Canada reservations, 800/622–1015 for international reservations ⊕www.usairways.com).

■ BY BOAT

Principal ferry routes in New England connect New Bedford on the mainland and Cape Cod with Martha's Vineyard and Nantucket, Boston with Provincetown, southern Rhode Island with Block Island, and Connecticut with New York's Long Island and Block Island. Other routes provide access to many islands off the Maine coast. In addition, ferries cross Lake Champlain between Vermont and upstate New York. International service between Portland and Bar Harbor, Maine, and Yarmouth, Nova Scotia, is also available. With the exception of the Lake Champlain ferries, which are first-come, first-served, car reservations are always advisable. *See the Essentials sections in each chapter for specific information on ferry companies, fares, and schedules.*

■ BY BUS

Regional bus service is relatively plentiful throughout New England. It can be a handy and somewhat affordable means of getting around, as buses travel many routes that trains do not; however, this style of travel prevents the sort of sponta-

TRAVEL TIMES FROM BOSTON TO	BY AIR	BY CAR	BY BUS	BY TRAIN
Hartford, Conn.	no direct flight	1¾ hours	2–2¾ hours	2¼ hours
New York City	½ hour	4 hours	4¼ hours	3½–4¼ hours
Burlington, Vt.	no direct flight	3½ hours	4¼–5 hours	7¾ hours
Portland, Maine	½ hour	2 hours	2 hours	2½ hours
Acadia National Park	1 hour	5 hours	5–7 hours	not applicable
Providence, R.I.	no direct flight	1 hour	1 hour	½–¾ hour
Provincetown, MA	½ hour	2½ hours	1 hour	not applicable
Quebec City	¾ hour	6½ hours	10–11 hours	16–18 hours

neity and freedom to explore that you're afforded if traveling by car. Also, it's often a good idea to compare travel times and costs between bus and train routes to and within New England; in some cases, it's faster to take the train. Reservations are not required on buses serving the region, but they're a good idea for just about any bus trip.

Bus Information Greyhound Lines Inc. (☎800/231–2222 ⊕www.greyhound.com). **Peter Pan Bus Lines** (☎800/343–9999 ⊕www.peterpanbus.com).

▌BY CAR

New England is best explored by car. Areas in the interior are largely without heavy traffic and congestion, and parking is consistently easy to find, even in cities like Hartford and Springfield. Coastal New England is considerably more congested, and parking can be hard to find or expensive in Boston, Providence, and the many smaller resort towns along the coast. Still, a car is typically the best way to get around even on the coast, though you may want to park it at your hotel in Boston or on Cape Cod and use it as little as possible, exploring on foot, on

a bike, or by local transit and cabs once you arrive. In the interior, especially western Massachusetts, Vermont, New Hampshire, and Maine, public transportation options are more limited and a car is almost necessary. Morning and evening rush-hour traffic isn't usually much of a problem, except in larger cities and along the coast. Note that I–95 is a toll highway throughout New England. If you rent a car at Logan International Airport, allow plenty of time to return it—as much as 60 minutes to be comfortable.

GASOLINE

Gas stations are easy to find along major highways and in most communities throughout the region. At this writing, the average price of a gallon of regular unleaded gas in New England is $3.94. However, prices vary from station to station within any city. The majority of stations are self-serve with pumps that accept credit cards, though you may find a holdout full-service station on occasion. Tipping is not expected at these.

PARKING

Parking in New England is a familiar situation. In Boston and other large cities, finding a spot on the street can be time-

and quarter-consuming. The best bet is to park in a garage, which can cost upward of $20 a day. In smaller cities, street parking is usually simpler, though parking garages are always convenient and less expensive than their big-city counterparts. Enforcement varies; in Portland, ME, meter readers might sooner give a warning (a friendly reminder, really) than a ticket.

RULES OF THE ROAD
On city streets the speed limit is 30 mph unless otherwise posted; on rural roads, the speed limit ranges from 40 to 50 mph unless otherwise posted. Interstate speeds range from 50 to 65 mph, depending on how densely populated the area. Throughout the region, you're permitted to make a right turn on red except where posted. Be alert for one-way streets in some of the more congested communities, such as Boston and Providence.

State law requires that front-seat passengers wear seat belts at all times. Children under 16 must wear seat belts in both the front and back seats. Always strap children under age 5 into approved childsafety seats.

▌BY TRAIN
State-run and national train service are options in New England: the Massachusetts Bay Transportation Authority (MBTA) connects Boston with outlying areas on the north and south shores of the state; Amtrak offers frequent daily service along its Northeast Corridor route from Washington and New York to Boston. Amtrak's high-speed *Acela* trains link Boston and Washington, with a stop at Penn Station in New York and other communities along the way. The *Downeaster* connects Boston with Portland, Maine, with stops in coastal New Hampshire.

Other Amtrak services include the *Vermonter* between Washington, D.C., and St. Albans, Vermont; the *Ethan Allen Express* between New York and Rut-

land, Vermont; and the *Lake Shore Limited* between Boston and Chicago, with stops at Pittsfield, Springfield, Worcester, and Framingham, Massachusetts. These trains run on a daily basis. To avoid last-minute confusion, allow 15 to 30 minutes to make train connections.

Private rail lines have scenic train trips throughout New England, particularly during fall foliage season. Several use vintage steam equipment; the most notable is the Cog Railway to Mt. Washington in New Hampshire.

Information **Amtrak** (☎800/872–7245 ⊕www.amtrak.com). **Mount Washington Cog Railway** (☎603/278–5404 or 800/922–8825 ⊕www.thecog.com) **Massachusetts Bay Transportation Authority** (MBTA ☎617/222–3200, 800/392–6100 ⊕www.mbta.com).

ON THE GROUND

CHILDREN IN NEW ENGLAND

New England is an enjoyable part of the country for family road trips, and it's also relatively affordable, excepting some of the fancier resort towns and also Boston. Throughout New England, however, you'll have no problem finding comparatively inexpensive child-friendly hotels and family-style restaurants—as well as some top children's museums, beaches, parks, planetariums, and lighthouses. Just keep in mind that a number of fine, antiques-filled B&Bs and inns punctuate the landscape, and these places are not always suitable for kids—many flat-out refuse to accommodate children. Also, some of the quieter and more rural areas—although exuding history—lack child-oriented attractions.

Favorite destinations for family vacations in New England include Boston, Cape Cod, the White Mountains, Mystic and southeastern Connecticut, and coastal Maine, but in general, the entire region has plenty to offer families. *Fodor's Around Boston with Kids* (available in bookstores everywhere) can help you plan your days together. For general advice about traveling with children, consult *Fodor's FYI: Travel with Your Baby* (available in bookstores everywhere).

FLYING

If your children are two or older, ask about children's airfares. As a general rule, infants under two not occupying a seat fly at greatly reduced fares or even for free. But if you want to guarantee a seat for an infant, you have to pay full fare. Consider flying during off-peak days and times; most airlines will grant an infant a seat without a ticket if there are available seats.

When booking, confirm carry-on allowances if you're traveling with infants. In general, for babies charged 10% to 50% of the adult fare you are allowed one carry-on bag and a collapsible stroller; if the flight is full, the stroller may have to be checked or you may be limited to less.

Experts agree that it's a good idea to use safety seats aloft for children weighing less than 40 pounds. Airlines set their own policies: if you use a safety seat, U.S. carriers usually require that the child be ticketed, even if he or she is young enough to ride free, because the seats must be strapped into regular seats. And even if you pay the full adult fare for the seat, it may be worth it, especially on longer trips. **Do check your airline's policy about using safety seats during takeoff and landing.** Safety seats are not allowed everywhere in the plane, so get your seat assignments as early as possible.

When reserving, request children's meals or a freestanding bassinet (not available at all airlines) if you need them. But note that bulkhead seats, where you must sit to use the bassinet, may lack an overhead bin or storage space on the floor.

LODGING

Chain hotels and motels welcome children, and New England has many family-oriented resorts with lively children's programs. You'll also find farms that accept guests and can be lots of fun for children. Rental houses and apartments abound, particularly around ski areas; off-season, these can be economical as well as comfortable touring bases. Some country inns, especially those with a quiet, romantic atmosphere and those furnished with antiques, are less enthusiastic about little ones, so **be up front about your traveling companions** when you reserve. Many larger resorts and hotels will provide a babysitter at an additional cost. Others will provide a list of sitters in the area.

Most hotels in New England allow children under a certain age to stay in their parents' room at no extra charge, but others charge for them as extra adults; be sure to find out the cutoff age for children's discounts.

Most lodgings that welcome infants and small children will provide a crib or cot, but **be sure to give advance notice** so that one will be available for you. Many family resorts make special accommodations for small children during meals. Be sure to ask in advance.

Most hotels in New England allow children under a certain age to stay in their parents' room at no extra charge, but others charge for them as extra adults; be sure to find out the cutoff age for children's discounts. (Note that in Maine, by state law, hotels and inns (unless they have 5 or fewer rooms) cannot put age restrictions on children that can stay with adults.)

SIGHTS & ATTRACTIONS
Places that are especially appealing to children are indicated by a rubber-duckie icon (🐤) in the margin.

TRANSPORTATION
Each New England state has specific requirements regarding age and weight requirements for children in car seats. If you're renting a car, **be sure to ask about the state(s) you're planning to drive in.** If you will need a car seat, make sure the agency you select provides them and **reserve well in advance.**

▌ HEALTH

Lyme disease, so named for its having been first reported in the town of Lyme, Connecticut, is a potentially debilitating disease carried by deer ticks, which thrive in dry, brush-covered areas, particularly on the coast. Always use insect repellent; outbreaks of Lyme disease all over the East Coast make it imperative that you protect yourself from ticks from early spring through summer. To prevent bites, wear light-color clothing and tuck pant legs into socks. Look for black ticks about the size of a pinhead around hairlines and the warmest parts of the body. If you have been bitten, consult a physician, especially if you see the telltale bull's-eye bite pattern. Influenza-like symptoms often accompany a Lyme infection. Early treatment is imperative.

New England's two greatest insect pests are black flies and mosquitoes. The former are a phenomenon of late spring and early summer and are generally a problem only in the densely wooded areas of the far north. Mosquitoes, however, can be a nuisance just about everywhere in summer—they're at their worst following snowy winters and wet springs. The best protection against both pests is repellent containing DEET; if you're camping in the woods during black fly season, you'll also want to use fine mesh screening in eating and sleeping areas, and even wear mesh headgear. A particular pest of coastal areas, especially salt marshes, is the greenhead fly. Their bite is nasty, and they are best repelled by a liberal application of Avon Skin So Soft.

Coastal waters attract seafood lovers who enjoy harvesting their own clams, mussels, and even lobsters; permits are required, and casual harvesting of lobsters is strictly forbidden. Amateur clammers should be aware that New England shellfish beds are periodically visited by red tides, during which microorganisms can render shellfish poisonous. To keep abreast of the situation, inquire when you apply for a license (usually at town halls or police stations) and pay attention to red tide postings as you travel.

▌ HOURS OF OPERATION

Hours in New England differ little from those in other parts of the United States. Within the region, shops and other businesses tend to keep slightly later hours in larger cities and along the coast, which is generally more populated than interior New England.

Most major museums and attractions are open daily or six days a week (with Monday being the most likely day of closing). Hours are often shorter on Saturday and especially Sunday, and some prominent museums stay open late one or two nights a week, usually Tuesday, Thursday, or Friday. New England also has quite a few smaller museums—historical societies, small art galleries, highly specialized collections—that open only a few days a week, and sometimes only by appointment in winter or slow periods.

∎ MONEY

It costs a bit more to travel in most of New England than it does in the rest of the country, with the most costly areas being Boston and the coastal resort areas. There are also a fair number of somewhat posh inns and restaurants in the Berkshires, northwestern Connecticut, and parts of Vermont and New Hampshire. ATMs are plentiful, and larger denomination bills (as well as credit cards) are readily accepted in tourist destinations during the high season.

Prices throughout this guide are given for adults. Substantially reduced fees are almost always available for children, students, and senior citizens.

CREDIT CARDS

Throughout this guide, the following abbreviations are used: **AE**, American Express; **D**, Discover; **DC**, Diners Club; **MC**, MasterCard; and **V**, Visa.

Major credit cards are readily accepted throughout New England, though in rural areas you may encounter difficulties or the acceptance of only MasterCard of Visa (also note that if you'll be making an excursion into Canada, many outlets there accept Visa but not MasterCard).

Reporting Lost Cards American Express (☏800/528–4800 in the U.S. or 336/393–

1111 collect from abroad ⊕www.american express.com). **Diners Club** (☏800/234–6377 in the U.S. or 303/799–1504 collect from abroad ⊕www.dinersclub.com). **Discover** (☏800/347–2683 in the U.S. or 801/902–3100 collect from abroad ⊕www.discovercard. com). **MasterCard** (☏800/627–8372 in the U.S. or 636/722–7111 collect from abroad ⊕www.mastercard.com). **Visa** (☏800/847–2911 in the U.S. or 410/581–9994 collect from abroad ⊕www.visa.com).

∎ SAFETY

Rural New England is one of the country's safest regions, so much so that residents often leave their doors unlocked. In the cities, particularly in Boston, observe the usual precautions; it's worth noting, however, that crime rates have been dropping in metropolitan areas. You should avoid out-of-the-way or poorly lighted areas at night; clutch handbags close to your body and don't let them out of your sight; and be on your guard in subways, not only during the deserted wee hours but in crowded rush hours, when pickpockets are at work. Keep your valuables in hotel safes. Try to use ATMs in busy, well-lighted places such as bank lobbies.

If your vehicle breaks down in a rural area, pull as far off the road as possible, tie a handkerchief to your radio antenna (or use flares at night—check if your rental agency can provide them), and stay in your car with the doors locked until help arrives. Don't pick up hitchhikers. If you're planning to leave a car overnight to make use of off-road trails or camping facilities, make arrangements for a supervised parking area if at all possible. Cars left at trailhead parking lots are subject to theft and vandalism.

The universal telephone number for crime and other emergencies throughout New England is 911.

TAXES

See Restaurant and Hotel charts at the beginning of each chapter for information about taxes on restaurant meals and accommodations. Sales taxes in New England are as follows: Connecticut 6%; Maine 5%; Massachusetts 5%; Rhode Island 7%; Vermont 6%. No sales tax is charged in New Hampshire. Some states and municipalities levy an additional tax (from 1% to 10%) on lodging or restaurant meals. Alcoholic beverages are sometimes taxed at a higher rate than that applied to meals.

TIME

New England operates on Eastern Standard Time and follows daylight saving time. When it is noon in Boston it is 9 AM in Los Angeles, 11 AM in Chicago, 5 PM in London, and 3 AM the following day in Sydney. When taking a ferry to Nova Scotia, remember that the province operates on Atlantic Standard Time and therefore is an hour ahead.

TIPPING

In New England, the customary tipping rate for taxi drivers is 15%–20%, with a minimum of $2; bellhops are usually given $2 per bag in luxury hotels, $1 per bag elsewhere. Hotel maids should be tipped $2 per day of your stay. A doorman who hails or helps you into a cab can be tipped $1–$2. You should also tip your hotel concierge for services rendered; the size of the tip depends on the difficulty of your request, as well as the quality of the concierge's work. For an ordinary dinner reservation or tour arrangements, $3–$5 should do; if the concierge scores seats at a popular restaurant or show or performs unusual services (getting your laptop repaired, finding a good pet-sitter, etc.), $10 or more is appropriate.

Waiters should be tipped 15%–20%, though at higher-end restaurants, a solid 20% is more the norm. Many restaurants add a gratuity to the bill for parties of six or more. Ask what the percentage is if the menu or bill doesn't state it. Tip $1 per drink you order at the bar, though if at an upscale establishment, those $15 martinis might warrant a $2 tip.

TIPPING GUIDELINES FOR NEW ENGLAND	
Bartender	$1 to $5 per round of drinks, depending on the number of drinks
Bellhop	$1 to $5 per bag, depending on the level of the hotel
Hotel Concierge	$5 or more, if he or she performs a service for you
Hotel Doorman	$1–$2 if he helps you get a cab
Hotel Maid	1$–$3 a day (either daily or at the end of your stay, in cash)
Hotel Room-Service Waiter	$1 to $2 per delivery, even if a service charge has been added
Porter at Airport or Train Station	$1 per bag
Skycap at Airport	$1 to $3 per bag checked
Taxi Driver	15%–20%, but round up the fare to the next dollar amount
Tour Guide	10% of the cost of the tour
Valet Parking Attendant	$1–$2, but only when you get your car
Waiter	15%–20%, with 20% being the norm at high-end restaurants; nothing additional if a service charge is added to the bill
	Restroom attendants in more expensive restaurants expect some small change or $1. Tip coat-check personnel at least $1–$2 per item checked unless there is a fee, then nothing.

INDEX

ABOUT OUR WRITERS

Maine-based **Stephen and Neva Allen** have written extensively about travel for many newspapers and magazines as well chapters for Fodor's. They moved to coastal Maine in 2000 and are devoted to the beautiful area they've come to call home.

Travel writers **Diane Bair and Pamela Wright** spend much of their days hiking, biking, paddling, climbing, and snorkeling on the job, so they know the value of a perfect, cushy bed at the end of the day. This hard-working, hard-playing duo writes for *Yankee Magazine, FamilyFun, Diversion,* and several other publications.

Though based in Salt Lake City, Utah, **John Blodgett** still goes home to Maine—the place he spent much of his first 22 years. The lobster roll at Gilbert's Chowder House in Portland's Old Port alone is worth the airfare, but he also misses sitting next to the booming foghorn at Two Lights State Park and listening to the clang of buoys bobbing in Casco Bay.

Elisabeth Coen and **Jo Kadlecek** live and work in Beverly, Massachusetts, one of Washington's first naval towns and a hidden gem in Boston's North Shore area. Both have traveled and written throughout their lives, but consider the beaches, woods, and cities of the East Coast a constant source of inspiration for stories and real-life adventures.

Former Fodor's staff editor and New England native **Andrew Collins** has contributed to publications such as *Fodor's New Mexico, Travel + Leisure, Sunset,* and *New Mexico Magazine.* He also teaches a course on travel writing for New York City's Gotham Writers' Workshop.

A Maine Coast resident since the early 1990s, **Sherry Hanson** covers everything from the Civil War to how to kayak with a dog and brew beer at home. Her poetry has appeared in many journals as well as her own poetry book, a collection titled *A Cab to Stonehenge,* published in 2006.

When she's not traveling on assignment for Fodor's and assorted other publications, freelance writer **Susan MacCallum-Whitcomb** makes her home in Halifax, Nova Scotia. She remains proud of her New England roots and she returns to Boston as often as possible to visit two of her relatives—Anne Hutchinson and Mary Dyer—both of whom are immortalized in bronze outside the State House.

Nantucket resident **Sandy MacDonald** is a seasoned travel writer who has written several New England guidebooks and contributed to others. She has also written about the Massachusetts islands for publications such as *Boston Magazine* and *New England Travel & Life.*

A contributor to *Bon Appetit Travel + Leisure, Boston Magazine,* and *Continental* magazine, **Erin Byers Murray** enjoys discovering trends as much as she does celebrating old favorites. She and her husband live in Brighton.

As a travel writer who has kids, **Lisa Oppenheimer** has sampled chicken nuggets in 32 states and 3 countries. Lisa also occasionally ventures out solo, where she once in a while gets to enjoy and review attractions devoid of height requirements and joysticks. In addition to authoring books on Boston and Los Angeles, Lisa has contributed to *Family Fun, Parenting, Parents,* and *Nick Jr. Magazines.*

Sarah Pascarella has been a Bostonian for the past seven years. She edits for the Boston-based online travel magazine SmarterTravel.com, and writes for such publications as *Travelers' Tales,* Fodors. com, and *USA Today.*

Andrew Rimas has worked as a staff writer at *The Improper Bostonian* and *Boston Magazine,* and was an associate editor at *Boston Magazine* before becoming a contributing editor.

A graduate of the University of Missouri School of Journalism, Maine-based writer **Mary Ruoff** has enjoyed writing articles about Maine travel, among other topics. She is married to a Mainer, Michael Hodsdon. Along with their son Dmitry ("Dima"), they spend as much time as they can at their family land "Way Down East," where Michael's grandfather was a fisherman.

Laura V. Scheel has spent a good portion of her years in Maine driving and exploring the state's numerous back roads and small towns. She has written frequently for Fodor's, contributing to titles such as Fodor's Maine Coast and Fodor's The Thirteen Colonies.

George Semler has been coming to Maine's Blue Hill Peninsula since the summer before he was born. A frequent writer for Fodor's (France, Spain, Cuba, Morocco, Andalusia, Barcelona-to-Bilbao, and Barcelona) as well as for Saveur, Sky, Forbes, and other publications, Semler writes about the outdoors, food, travel, and culture.

New York City–based **Michael de Zayas** has written about hotels on five continents, including covering them for Fodor's guides to Miami, Spain, the Caribbean, Chile, and New York City.